Perl

HOW TO PROGRAM

Deitel™
Books, Cyber Classrooms and Complete Training Courses
published by
Prentice Hall

***How to Program* Series**
Perl How to Program
XML How to Program
e-Business and e-Commerce How to Program
Internet and World Wide Web How to Program
Java™ How to Program, 3/E
C How to Program, 3/E
C++ How to Program, 3/E
Visual Basic® 6 How to Program

***Multimedia Cyber Classroom* Series**
Perl Multimedia Cyber Classroom
XML Multimedia Cyber Classroom
e-Business and e-Commerce Multimedia Cyber Classroom
Internet and World Wide Web Multimedia Cyber Classroom
Java™ Multimedia Cyber Classroom, 3/E
C++ Multimedia Cyber Classroom, 3/E
Visual Basic® 6 Multimedia Cyber Classroom

***The Complete Training Course* Series**
The Complete XML Training Course
The Complete Perl Training Course
The Complete e-Business and e-Commerce Programming Training Course
The Complete Internet and World Wide Web Programming Training Course
The Complete Java™ 2 Training Course, 3/E
The Complete C++ Training Course, 3/E
The Complete Visual Basic® 6 Training Course

***For Managers* Series**
e-Business and e-Commerce for Managers

Visual Studio® Series
Getting Started with Microsoft® Visual C++™ 6 with an Introduction to MFC
Visual Basic® 6 How to Program
Getting Started with Microsoft® Visual J++® 1.1

For continuing updates on Prentice Hall and Deitel & Associates, Inc. publications visit the Prentice Hall Web site

> `www.prenhall.com/deitel`

To communicate with the authors, send email to:

> `deitel@deitel.com`

For information on corporate on-site seminars and public seminars offered by Deitel & Associates, Inc. worldwide, visit:

> `www.deitel.com`

Perl
HOW TO PROGRAM

H. M. Deitel
Deitel & Associates, Inc.

P. J. Deitel
Deitel & Associates, Inc.

T. R. Nieto
Deitel & Associates, Inc.

D. C. McPhie

PRENTICE HALL
Upper Saddle River,
New Jersey 07458

Library of Congress Cataloging-in-Publication Data
Perl: how to program / H.M. Deitel ... [et al.].
            p. cm. -- (How to program series)
        Includes bibliographical references and index.
        ISBN 0-13-028418-1
            1. Perl (Computer program language) 2. Internet programming
        I. Deitel, Harvey M. II. Series

        QA76.73.P22 P477 2000
        005.2'762--dc21

Vice President and Editorial Director, ECS: *Marcia Horton*
Acquisitions Editor: *Petra J. Recter*
Assistant Editor: *Sarah Burrows*
Project Manager: *Crissy Statuto*
Editorial Assistant: *Karen Schultz*
Vice President of Production and Manufacturing, ESM: *David W. Riccardi*
Executive Managing Editor: *Vince O'Brien*
Managing Editor: *David A. George*
Senior Production Editor: *Camille Trentacoste*
Production Editor: *Penny Cox*
Multimedia Project Manager: *Robert Engelhardt*
Director of Creative Services: *Paul Belfanti*
Creative Director: *Carole Anson*
Art Director: *Heather Scott*
Chapter Opener and Cover Designer: *Tamara Newnam Cavallo*
Manufacturing Manager: *Trudy Pisciotti*
Manufacturing Buyer: *Pat Brown*
Marketing Manager: *Jennie Burger*

© 2001 by Prentice-Hall, Inc.
Upper Saddle River, New Jersey 07458

Printed in the United States of America

10 9 8 7 6 5 4 3 2 1

ISBN 0-13-028418-1

Prentice-Hall International (UK) Limited, *London*
Prentice-Hall of Australia Pty. Limited, *Sydney*
Prentice-Hall Canada Inc., *Toronto*
Prentice-Hall Hispanoamericana, S.A., *Mexico*
Prentice-Hall of India Private Limited, *New Delhi*
Prentice-Hall of Japan, Inc., *Tokyo*
Pearson Education Asia Pte. Ltd., *Singapore*
Editora Prentice-Hall do Brasil, Ltda., *Rio de Janeiro*

To Mark Taub
Editor-in-Chief of Multimedia and Distance Learning at Pearson Technology Group:

For your commitment and dedication to leadership and excellence in education technology. It has been a privilege working with you on the development of our interactive-multimedia Cyber Classroom products.

We sincerely look forward to working with you on the development of our e-learning suites of e-book, e-matter and Web-based training products.

Thank you for being our mentor and our friend.

Harvey, Barbara, Paul and Abbey Deitel

To Clarence Harris, whose friendship I will never forget.
Tem R. Nieto

To my precious daughter, Emily,
and my darling sweetheart, Erin.
David C. McPhie

Contents

3 Control Structures: Part I   60

4 Arrays and Hashes   94

Illustrations

4   Arrays and Hashes

5   Control Structures: Part II

6   Subroutines and Functions

7   Introduction to the Common Gateway Interface (CGI)

8   Regular Expressions

9   String Manipulation

10 File Processing

11 File and Directory Manipulation

12 Formatting

13   References

14   Objects and Modules

15   Databases: SQL and Perl Database Interface (DBI)

16   Session Tracking and Cookies

17 Web Automation and Networking

18 Process Management

19 Security

20 Data Structures

21 Graphics/Tk

22 Extensible Markup Language (XML)

27   Bonus: Introduction to Python Programming

Preface

Welcome to Perl! This book is by an old guy and three young guys. The old guy (HMD; Massachusetts Institute of Technology 1967) has been programming and/or teaching programming for 40 years. The three young guys (PJD; MIT 1991, TRN; MIT 1992 and DCM Harvard 2000) have each been programming and/or teaching programming for many years. The old guy programs and teaches from experience; the young guys do so from an inexhaustible reserve of energy. The old guy wants clarity; the young guys want performance. The old guy seeks elegance and beauty; the young guys want results. We got together to produce a book we hope you will find informative, challenging and entertaining.

Why We Wrote Perl How to Program

Dr. Harvey M. Deitel taught introductory programming courses in universities for 20 years with an emphasis on developing clearly written, well-designed programs. Much of what is taught in these courses is the basic principles of programming with an emphasis on the effective use of data types, control structures, arrays and functionalization. Our experience has been that students handle the material in this book in about the same manner as they handle it in introductory Pascal or C courses. There is one noticeable difference though: students are highly motivated by the fact that they are learning a leading-edge programming language and a leading-edge programming paradigm (object-based programming) that will be immediately useful to them as they leave the university environment and head into a world of e-business and e-commerce in which the Internet and the World Wide Web have a massive prominence.

Our goal was clear: produce a textbook for introductory university-level courses in programming for students with little or no programming experience, yet offer the depth and the rigorous treatment of theory and practice demanded by traditional, upper-level programming courses to satisfy professionals' needs. To meet this goal, we produced a comprehensive book that patiently teaches the principles of control structures, object-based programming and Internet and World Wide Web programming in Perl. After mastering the material in this book, students will be well prepared to take advantage of the Internet and the Web as they take upper-level courses and venture into the rapidly changing business world.

Perl How to Program is the ninth book in the Deitel/Prentice Hall *How to Program* series. The key focus of this book is Web-based applications development. Our audiences want to build real-world, industrial-strength, Web-based applications. These audiences care about good looking Web pages. But they also care about client/server systems, databases and distributed computing.

Many books about the Web are reference manuals with exhaustive listings of features. That is not our style. We concentrate on creating real applications. We provide the live-code™ examples on the CD accompanying this book so that you can run the applications and see the outputs.

We are excited about the enormous range of possibilities the Internet and the Web offer. We performed extensive research for this book and located many Internet and Web resources (which we provide as live links on the CD-ROM that accompanies this book) to help you learn about Perl. These links include general information, tutorials and demonstrations.

We have worked hard to create hundreds of useful live-code™ examples to help you master Perl programming quickly and effectively. All of the code examples are on the accompanying disk and are available for free download from our Web sites:

> www.deitel.com
> www.prenhall.com/deitel

The book's exercises range from simple recall questions to lengthy programming problems to major projects. Instructors requiring substantial term projects will find many appropriate problems listed in the exercises, especially in the later chapters. We have put a great deal of effort into the exercises to enhance the value of this book.

Teaching Approach

Perl How to Program contains a rich collection of examples and exercises that provide the student with a chance to solve interesting real-world problems. The book concentrates on the principles of good software engineering and stresses program clarity. We avoid arcane terminology and syntax specifications in favor of teaching by example. The book is written by educators who spend most of their time writing about and teaching edge-of-the-practice programming topics in industry classrooms worldwide for Deitel & Associates, Inc. The text emphasizes good pedagogy.

Live-Code™ Teaching Approach

The book is loaded with hundreds of live-code™ examples. This is the focus of the way we teach and write about programming, and the focus of each of our multimedia *Cyber Classrooms* as well. Each new concept is presented in the context of a complete, working program immediately followed by one or more windows showing the program's input/output dialog. We call this style of teaching and writing our *live-code™ approach*. We use complete, working programs to teach programming languages. Reading these programs is much like entering and running them on a computer.

Perl How to Program explains cutting-edge technologies for building powerful Web-based applications. There is great stuff to be done in Perl, so let's get right to it! Web programming is not trivial by any means, but it is fun and students can see immediate results. Students can get graphical, database-intensive, network-based programs running quickly through "reusable components." They can implement impressive projects. They can be incredibly creative and productive in a one- or two-semester courses.

World Wide Web Access
All of the code for *Perl How to Program* (and our other publications) is on the CD that accompanies the book and on the Internet free for download at **www.deitel.com** and **www.prenhall.com/deitel**. Please run each program as you read the text. Make changes to the code examples and examine the effects of those changes. This is a great way to learn programming. [*Note:* You must respect the fact that these programs are copyrighted material. Feel free to use them as you study, but you may not republish any portion of them in any form without explicit permission from Prentice Hall and the authors.]

Objectives
Each chapter begins with a statement of objectives. This tells the student what to expect and gives the student an opportunity, after reading the chapter, to determine if they have met these objectives. It is a confidence builder and a source of positive reinforcement.

Quotations
The learning objectives are followed by a series of quotations. Some are humorous, some are philosophical and some offer interesting insights. Our students enjoy relating the quotations to the chapter material. You may appreciate some of the quotations more *after* reading the chapters.

Outline
The chapter outline helps the student approach the material in top-down fashion. This, too, helps students anticipate what is to come and set a comfortable and effective learning pace.

Sections
Each chapter is organized into small sections that address key Perl topics.

12922 Lines of Syntax-Highlighted Code in 271 Example Programs (with Outputs)
We present Perl features in the context of complete, working programs; each program is immediately followed by a window containing the outputs produced when the program is run—we call this our live-code™ approach. This enables the student to confirm that the programs run as expected. Relating outputs back to the program statements that produce those outputs is an excellent way to learn and to reinforce concepts. Our programs exercise the diverse features of Perl. Reading the book carefully is much like entering and running these programs on a computer. The code is "syntax highlighted" with keywords appearing in the second color of the book, comments appearing in a lighter shade of that color and the rest of each program appearing in black. This makes it much easier to read the code—students will especially appreciate the syntax highlighting when they read the many more substantial programs we present.

475 Illustrations/Figures
An abundance of colorized charts and line drawings is included. The discussions of control structures in Chapters 3 through 5 feature carefully drawn flowcharts. [*Note*: We do not teach the use of flowcharting as a program development tool, but we do use a brief

flowchart-oriented presentation to specify the precise operation of Perl's control structures.] Chapter 20, "Data Structures," uses line drawings to illustrate the creation and maintenance of linked lists, queues, stacks and binary trees. The remainder of the book is abundantly illustrated.

324 Programming Tips

We have included seven design elements to help students focus on important aspects of program development, testing and debugging, performance and portability. We highlight hundreds of these tips in the form of *Good Programming Practices*, *Common Programming Errors*, *Look-and-Feel Observations*, *Performance Tips*, *Portability Tips*, *Software Engineering Observations* and *Testing and Debugging Tips*. These tips and practices represent the best we have been able to glean from almost six decades (combined) of programming and teaching experience. One of our students—a mathematics major—told us recently that she feels this approach is somewhat like the highlighting of axioms, theorems and corollaries in mathematics books; it provides a basis on which to build good software.

72 Good Programming Practices

Good Programming Practices are highlighted in the text. They call the student's attention to techniques that help produce better programs. When we teach introductory courses to non-programmers, we state that the "buzzword" of each course is "clarity," and we tell the students that we will highlight (in these Good Programming Practices) techniques for writing programs that are clearer, more understandable and more maintainable.

107 Common Programming Errors

Students learning a language—especially in their first programming course—tend to make certain kinds of errors frequently. Focusing on these Common Programming Errors helps students avoid making the same errors. It also helps reduce long lines outside instructors' offices during office hours!

32 Performance Tips

In our experience, teaching students to write clear and understandable programs is by far the most important goal for a first programming course. But students want to write the programs that run the fastest, use the least memory, require the smallest number of keystrokes, or dazzle in other nifty ways. Students really care about performance. They want to know what they can do to "turbo charge" their programs. So we have included Performance Tips to highlight opportunities for improving program performance.

18 Portability Tips

Software development is a complex and expensive activity. Organizations that develop software must often produce versions customized to a variety of computers and operating systems. So there is a strong emphasis today on portability, i.e., on producing software that will run on a variety of computer systems with few, if any, changes.

66 Software Engineering Observations

The Software Engineering Observations highlight techniques, architectural issues and design issues, etc. that affect the architecture and construction of software systems, especially large-scale systems. Much of what the student learns here will be useful in upper-level courses and in industry as the student begins to work with large, complex real-world systems.

24 Testing and Debugging Tips

This "tip type" may be misnamed. When we decided to incorporate Testing and Debugging Tips into this book, we thought these tips would be suggestions for testing programs to expose bugs and suggestions for removing those bugs. In fact, most of these tips tend to be observations about capabilities and features of Perl that prevent bugs from getting into programs in the first place.

5 Look-and-Feel Observations

We provide Look-and-Feel Observations to highlight graphical user interface conventions. These observations help students design their own graphical user interfaces to conform with industry norms.

Summary

Each chapter ends with additional pedagogical devices. We present an extensive, bullet-list-style *Summary* in every chapter. This helps the student review and reinforce key concepts. There is an average of 48 summary bullets per chapter.

Terminology

We include a *Terminology* section with an alphabetized list of the important terms defined in the chapter—again, further reinforcement. There is an average of 84 terms per chapter.

614 Self-Review Exercises and Answers (Count Includes Separate Parts)

Extensive *Self-Review Exercises* and *Answers to Self-Review Exercises* are included for self study. This gives the student a chance to build confidence with the material and prepare to attempt the regular exercises.

210 Exercises (Count Includes Separate Parts)

Each chapter concludes with a set of exercises including simple recall of important terminology and concepts, writing individual program statements, writing small portions of functions and writing complete functions and programs. The large number of exercises enables instructors to tailor their courses to the unique needs of their audiences and to vary course assignments each semester. Instructors can use these exercises to form homework assignments, short quizzes and major examinations.

Instructor's Manual with Solutions to the Exercises

The solutions for the exercises are included on the *Instructor's Resource CD* and are *available only to instructors* through their Prentice Hall representatives. [*NOTE*: **Please do not write to us requesting the instructor's manual. Distribution of this publication is strictly limited to college professors teaching from the book. Instructors may obtain the solutions manual only from their regular Prentice Hall representatives**. We regret that we **cannot provide the solutions to professionals**.]

3500 Index Entries (Total of 4800 Counting Multiple References)

We have included an extensive *Index* at the back of the book. This helps the student find any term or concept by keyword. The *Index* is useful to people reading the book for the first time and is especially useful to practicing programmers who use the book as a reference. Most of the terms in the *Terminology* sections appear in the *Index* (along with many more index items from each chapter). Thus, the student can use the *Index* in conjunction with the *Terminology* sections to be sure they have covered the key material of each chapter.

Bibliography

An extensive bibliography of books, articles and online documentation is included to encourage further reading.

Software Included with Perl How to Program

The CD-ROM at the end of this book contains a variety of software, including ActiveState ActivePerl 5.6, Perl 5.6.0, MySQL 3.223.x and Apache 1.3.12. The CD also contains the book's code examples and an HTML Web page with links to the Deitel & Associates, Inc. Web site, the Prentice Hall Web site and the many Web sites listed in the Web resources sections of the chapters. If you have access to the Internet, the Web page on the CD can be loaded into your World Wide Web browser to give you quick access to all the resources.

If you have any questions about using this software, please read the introductory documentation on the CD-ROM. Additional information is available at our Web site: **www.deitel.com**. [*NOTE*: **We do not provide technical support for the software application programs. However, if you have any technical questions about the installation of the CD, please e-mail media.support@pearsoned.com. They will respond promptly.**]

Perl How to Program Ancillary Package

We have worked hard to produce a textbook and ancillaries that we hope instructors and students will find valuable. We would like to thank ActiveState, Apache and MySQL AB for providing the products included on the CD-ROM in the back of this textbook. The following ancillary resources are available:

- *Perl How to Program's 271 program examples* are included on the CD in the back of the textbook and are also available for download at **www.deitel.com** and **www.prenhall.com/deitel**. This helps instructors prepare lectures faster and helps students master Perl. When extracting the source code from the ZIP file, you must use a ZIP-file reader such as WinZip (**www.winzip.com**) or PKZIP (**www.pkware.com**) that understands directories. The file should be extracted into a separate directory (e.g., **perlhtp1_examples**). Students should execute each program they study in the text.

- *The Instructor's Manual* on CD contains answers to most of the exercises in the textbook. The programs are separated into directories by chapter and exercise number. [*NOTE*: **Please do not write to us requesting the instructor's manual. Distribution of this publication is strictly limited to college professors teaching from the book. Instructors may obtain the Instructor's Manual only from their regular Prentice Hall representatives. We regret that we cannot provide the solutions to professionals.**]

- *Companion Web Site* (**www.prenhall.com/deitel**) provides instructor and student resources. Instructor resources include textbook appendices and a syllabus manager for lesson planning. Student resources include chapter objectives, true/false review questions with answers, chapter highlights, reference materials and a message board.

- Customizable *PowerPoint*® *Instructor Lecture Notes*, including source code and key discussion points for each program and major illustration. These lecture notes

are available for instructors and students at no charge at our **www.deitel.com**
Web site. Although instructors may modify these notes and use them in class presentations, please be aware that these notes are copyrighted by Prentice Hall and
may not be used without the express written permission of Prentice Hall.

- *Deitel & Associates, Inc. Web site* (**www.deitel.com**) provides a variety of resources, including various installation instructions for the software used in this
book and the examples from the book. Please visit this site to keep apprised of the
latest Deitel & Associates, Inc. publications and news.

Perl Multimedia Cyber Classroom and *The Complete Perl Training Course*

We have prepared an optional interactive, CD-ROM-based, software version of *Perl How
to Program* called the *Perl Multimedia Cyber Classroom*. It is loaded with features for
learning and reference. The *Cyber Classroom* is wrapped with the textbook at a discount in
The Complete Perl Training Course. If you already have the book and would like to purchase the *Perl Multimedia Cyber Classroom* separately, please call 1-800-811-0912 and
ask for ISBN# 0-13-089553-9.

The CD has an introduction with the authors overviewing the *Cyber Classroom*'s features. The live-code™ examples in the textbook truly "come alive" in the *Cyber Classroom*. With many of the examples, you can simply click the lightning bolt icon and the
program will be executed. You will immediately see the program's outputs. If you want to
modify a program and see the effects of your changes, simply click the floppy-disk icon
that causes the source code to be "lifted off" the CD and "dropped into" one of your own
directories so that you can edit the program and try out your new version. Click the speaker
icon for an audio that talks about the program and walks you through the code.

The *Cyber Classroom* also provides navigational aids including extensive hyperlinking.
The *Cyber Classroom* remembers in a "history list" recent sections you have visited and
allows you to move forward or backward in that history list. The thousands of index entries
are hyperlinked to their text occurrences. You can key in a term using the "find" feature and
the *Cyber Classroom* will locate occurrences of that term throughout the text. The *Table of
Contents* entries are "hot," so clicking a chapter name takes you to that chapter.

Students like the solved problems from the textbook that are included with the *Cyber
Classroom*. Studying and running these extra programs is a nice way for students to
enhance their learning experience.

Students and professional users of our *Cyber Classrooms* tell us they like the interactivity and that the *Cyber Classroom* is an effective reference because of the extensive
hyperlinking and other navigational features. We recently had an e-mail from a person who
said that he lives "in the boonies" and cannot take a live course at a university, so the *Cyber
Classroom* was a good solution to his educational needs.

Professors tell us that their students enjoy using the *Cyber Classroom*, spend more time
on the course and master more of the material than in textbook-only courses. Also, the
Cyber Classroom helps shrink lines outside professors' offices during office hours. We
have also published the *C++ Multimedia Cyber Classroom (3/e)*, the *Visual Basic 6 Multimedia Cyber Classroom*, the *Java 2 Multimedia Cyber Classroom (3/e)*, the *Internet and
World Wide Web Programming Multimedia Cyber Classroom*, *e-Business and e-Commerce Multimedia Cyber Classroom* and *the XML Multimedia Cyber Classroom*. Each of

these *Cyber Classrooms* is available in a *Complete Training Course* boxed product that contains the corresponding *How to Program Series* textbook.

Acknowledgements

One of the great pleasures of writing a textbook is acknowledging the efforts of the many people whose names may not appear on the cover, but whose hard work, cooperation, friendship and understanding were crucial to the production of the book.

Many other people at Deitel & Associates, Inc. devoted long hours to this project.

- Barbara Deitel managed the preparation of the manuscript and coordinated with Prentice Hall all the efforts related to the review effort and the production of the book. She did all this in parallel with handling her extensive financial and administrative responsibilities at Deitel & Associates, Inc.

- Abbey Deitel, President of Deitel & Associates, Inc., co-authored Chapter 19, Security.

- Cheryl Yaeger, a graduate of Boston University with a major in Computer Science, performed finishing and polishing work on every chapter of the book.

- Kate Steinbuhler co-authored Appendix F and handled the publication permissions for the book.

- Matthew Kowalewski performed the vast majority of indexing for the book, created the Perl 6 resources appendix and researched the copyrights for the modules used in this book.

- Peter Brandano, a graduate of Boston College with a major in Computer Science, co-authored Chapter 23, "Accessibility."

The Deitel & Associates, Inc. *College Internship Program* offers a limited number of paid positions to Boston-area college students majoring in Computer Science, Information Technology, Marketing or English. Students work at our corporate headquarters in Sudbury, Massachusetts full-time in the summers and/or part-time during the academic year. Full-time positions are available to college graduates. For more information about this competitive program, please contact Abbey Deitel at **deitel@deitel.com** and check our Web site, **www.deitel.com**. Deitel & Associates, Inc. student interns who worked on this book include:

- Andrew Jones, a senior at Dartmouth College, wrote major portions of Chapters 4, 12, 13, 18–20 and 22. He also contributed to Chapter 15.

- Jeff Listfield, a junior at Harvard, wrote major portions of Chapters 6, 8, 10, 14, 16, 17 and 21. He also contributed to Chapters 11 and 13.

- Justin Gordon, a junior at Brandeis University, wrote major portions of Chapters 2, 3, 5, 9 and 11. He also contributed to Chapter 21.

- Rudolf Faust, a Freshman at Stanford University, helped develop and refine the Preface and Chapter 1.

- Chris Poirer, a senior at the University of Rhode Island, co-authored Chapter 15.

- Melissa Jordan, a senior majoring in graphic design at Boston University, created most of the illustrations.

- Jeni Jefferson, a graduate of Boston College, researched the quotes, created the bibliography and helped with the final Preface.

- Christina Carney, a senior at Framingham State, researched the quotes.

- Rioa MacMaster, a graduate of Tufts University with a major in computer science, contributed to the Web resources.

- Gary Grinev, a senior at Framingham High School, contributed to the bibliography and Web resources.

We would also like to acknowledge contributions related to the book's bonus chapters:

- Jacob Ellis—a freshman at the University of Pennsylvania, and David Gusovsky—a freshman at Berkeley, co-authored Chapters 2, 3 and 4 in our *Internet and World Wide Web How to Program* book. It is from these chapters that our Chapters 24, 25 and 26 evolved. We would also like to thank Sean Santry of Deitel and Associates, Inc. for his contributions to these chapters.

- Ben Wiedermann, a senior majoring in computer science at Boston University, co-authored Chapter 27, "Introduction to Python Programming."

We are fortunate to have been able to work on this project with the talented and dedicated team of publishing professionals at Prentice Hall. We especially appreciate the extraordinary efforts of our computer science editor, Petra Recter, our project manager, Crissy Statuto, our assistant editor, Sarah Burrows, and their boss—our mentor in publishing—Marcia Horton, Editor-in-Chief of Prentice-Hall's Engineering and Computer Science Division. Vince O'Brien and Camille Trentacoste did a marvelous job managing production.

The *Perl Multimedia Cyber Classroom* was developed in parallel with *Perl How to Program*. We sincerely appreciate the new-media insight, savvy and technical expertise of our multimedia, computer-based training and Web-based training editors, Mark Taub and Karen McLean. They did a remarkable job bringing the *Perl Multimedia Cyber Classroom* to publication under a tight schedule.

We owe thanks to Tamara Newnam Cavallo (**smart-art@earthlink.net**) who did the art work for our programming tips icons and the cover. She created the delightful creature who shares with you the book's programming tips.

We wish to acknowledge the efforts of our reviewers and to give a special note of thanks to Crissy Statuto of Prentice Hall who managed this extraordinary review effort:

- Jasmine Merced (PerlArchive.com)

- Stephen Potter (Information Control Corporation)

- Simon North (Synopsys)

- Varghese John (University of Rochester)

- Peter Salus (author of "Casting the Net")

- Jeremy Kurtz (Stark State College of Technology)

- Steven Wynn (Carnegie Mellon)

- Rosie Jones (doctoral student in computer science at Carnegie Mellon University)

- Brian D. Foy (Smith Renaud, Inc., Director of Technology)

- Avi Finkel (WhizBang! Labs)

- Scott Walters (illogics.org)

- Nathan Siemers (Bristol-Myers Squibb Pharmaceutical Research Institute)
- Pete Krawczyk (Absolute Performance)
- Thomas Moore (Vice President of Development, RaceSearch.com)
- John Garrett (Garrett-Sigel International)
- Dan Moore (XOR, Inc.)
- Chicheng Zhang (MobileSys, Inc.)
- Jay Di Silvestri (SoftQuad)
- Evelyn Mitchell (tummy.com, ltd.)
- Fred L. Drake, Jr. (Python Labs)
- Cameron Laird (Phaseit, Inc.)
- Jonathan R. Earl (Technical Training and Consulting)
- Phyllis Reuther (Knowledge Management Systems)
- Jim Kurtz (Pragma Systems Corp.)
- Doug Wilson (Racesearch.com, Inc.)
- Steve Latif
- Ed Wright

Under tight deadlines, they scrutinized every aspect of the text and made countless suggestions for improving the accuracy and completeness of the presentation.

The nature of Perl is that members of the Perl community create additions to the language called modules. Like Perl, many of these modules are created as open source and are available for anyone to use in their Perl programs. Here, we present a list of the modules used in this book with acknowledgements to the creator(s). We would also like to thank Jeff Olmstead of ActiveState Tool Corporation for providing copyright information for several modules.

Modules and their Copyrights

- **Benchmark**—Authors: Jarkko Hietaniemi, Tim Bunce.
- **CGI**—© Copyright 1995-1998, Lincoln D. Stein. All Rights Reserved.
- **CGI::Carp**—© Copyright 1995-1998, Lincoln D. Stein. All Rights Reserved.
- **CGI::Pretty**—© Copyright 1999, Brian Paulsen. All Rights Reserved.
- **Chart::Bars**—Author: Peter Clark.
- **Chart::Lines**—Author: Peter Clark.
- **Chart::Points**—Author: Peter Clark.
- **Data::Dumper**—© Copyright 1996-98 Gurusamy Sarathy. All Rights Reserved.
- **DBD::mysql**—© Copyright 1997-1999 Jochen Wiedmann, with code portions © Copyright 1994-1997 their original authors.
- **DBD::ODBC**—© Copyright 1994,1995,1996,1997,1998 Tim Bunce. Portions © Copyright 1997,1998 Jeff Urlwin. Portions © Copyright 1997 Thomas K. Wenrich.
- **DBI**—© Copyright 1994-2000 Tim Bunce. England. All Rights Reserved.

- **Digest::MD5**—© Copyright 1998-2000 Gisle Aas. © Copyright 1995-1996 Neil Winton. © Copyright 1991-2, RSA Data Security, Inc. Created 1991. All Rights Reserved. (This module is derived from the RSA Data Security, Inc. MD5 Message-Digest Algorithm.)
- **Gadfly**—Created by: Chordate Systems. Maintained by: Aaron Watters.
- **GD**—© Copyright 1995-1999, Lincoln D. Stein.
- **HTML::TokeParser**—© Copyright 1998-1999 Gisle Aas.
- **IO::Select**—© Copyright 1997-8 Graham Barr. All Rights Reserved.
- **IO::Socket**—© Copyright 1997-8 Graham Barr. All Rights Reserved.
- **IO::Socket::INET**—© Copyright 1996-8 Graham Barr. All Rights Reserved.
- **LWP::Simple**—Author: Gisle Aas.
- **LWP::UserAgent**—© Copyright 1995-2000 Gisle Aas.
- **Mail::POP3Client**—Based loosely on **News::NNTPClient** by Rodger Anderson.
- **MySQLdb**—Author: Andy Dustman.
- **Net::SMTP**—Author: Graham Barr.
- **Pmw**—© Copyright 1997, 1998 by Telstra Corporation Limited, Australia.
- **Tk**—Author: Nick Ing-Simmons.
- **Win32::OLE**—© Copyright 1995 Microsoft Corporation. All Rights Reserved.
- **odbc** (bundled with win32all module)—© Copyright 1994-2000, Mark Hammon.
- **WWW::Search**—© Copyright 1996 University of Southern California. All Rights Reserved.
- **XML::DOM**—Authors: Enno Derksen and Clark Cooper.
- **XML::Parser**—Author: Larry Wall wrote version 1.0.

We would sincerely appreciate your comments, criticisms, corrections and suggestions for improving the text. Please address all correspondence to:

deitel@deitel.com

We will respond immediately. We sincerely hope you enjoy learning with this book. Our best wishes to you.

Dr. Harvey M. Deitel
Paul J. Deitel
Tem R. Nieto
David C. McPhie

About the Authors

Dr. Harvey M. Deitel, CEO of Deitel & Associates, Inc., has 40 years in the computing field including extensive industry and academic experience. He is one of the world's leading computer science instructors and seminar presenters. Dr. Deitel earned B.S. and M.S. degrees from the Massachusetts Institute of Technology and a Ph.D. from Boston University. He has 20 years of college teaching experience including earning tenure and serving as the Chairman of the Computer Science Department at Boston College before founding Deitel & Associates, Inc. with his son Paul J. Deitel. He is author or co-author of several dozen books and multimedia packages and is currently writing many more. With translations published in Japanese, Russian, Spanish, Elementary Chinese, Advanced Chinese, Korean, French, Polish and Portuguese, Dr. Deitel's texts have earned international recognition. Dr. Deitel has delivered professional seminars internationally to major corporations, government organizations and various branches of the military.

Paul J. Deitel, Executive Vice President of Deitel & Associates, Inc., is a graduate of the Massachusetts Institute of Technology's Sloan School of Management where he studied Information Technology. Through Deitel & Associates, Inc. he has delivered Internet and World Wide Web courses and programming language classes for industry clients including Compaq, Sun Microsystems, White Sands Missile Range, Rogue Wave Software, Computervision, Stratus, Fidelity, Cambridge Technology Partners, Lucent Technologies, Adra Systems, Entergy, CableData Systems, NASA at the Kennedy Space Center, the National Severe Storm Laboratory, IBM and many other organizations. He has lectured on for the Boston Chapter of the Association for Computing Machinery, and has taught satellite-based courses through a cooperative venture of Deitel & Associates, Inc., Prentice Hall and the Technology Education Network. He and his father, Dr. Harvey M. Deitel, are the world's best-selling Computer Science textbook authors.

Tem R. Nieto, Director of Product Development with Deitel & Associates, Inc., is a graduate of the Massachusetts Institute of Technology where he studied engineering and computing. Through Deitel & Associates, Inc. he has delivered courses for industry clients including Sun Microsystems, Compaq, EMC, Stratus, Fidelity, Art Technology, Progress Software, Toys "R" Us, Operational Support Facility of the National Oceanographic and Atmospheric Administration, Jet Propulsion Laboratory, Nynex, Motorola, Federal Reserve Bank of Chicago, Banyan, Schlumberger, University of Notre Dame, NASA, various military installations and many others. He has co-authored several books and multimedia packages with the Deitels and has contributed to virtually every Deitel & Associates, Inc. publication.

David Craig McPhie recently graduated from Harvard College *magna cum laude* with a B.A. in Physics, having completed extensive computer science course work in C, C++, Java and Lisp. His course work included a final project using CGI to implement an online word game ("Elggob") that won accolades from his instructors and peers. Prior to collaborating on *Perl How to Program*, David programmed a Monte Carlo electron path modeling application for AlliedSignal, Electron Vision Group in San Diego. His other computing experience includes software test script writing and implementation with Silk-Test at Cakewalk Software, and debugging courtroom simulation software code at the Education Technology Department of Harvard Law School. David has now changed venues and is studying law at Harvard Law School. He maintains an interest in technology law, and continues to use Perl in Web programming for student organizations. He and his wife Erin and daughter Emily live in Cambridge, MA.

The Deitels are co-authors of the best-selling introductory college computer-science programming language textbooks, *C++ How to Program: Third Edition, Java How to*

Program: Third Edition, Visual Basic 6 How to Program (co-authored with Tem R.
Nieto), *Internet and World Wide Web How to Program* (co-authored with Tem R. Nieto),
e-Business and e-Commerce How to Program (co-authored with Tem R. Nieto) and *XML
How to Program* (co-authored with Tem R. Nieto, Ted M. Lin and Praveen Sadhu). The
Deitels are also co-authors of the *C++ Multimedia Cyber Classroom: Third Edition* (the
first edition of this was Prentice Hall's first multimedia-based textbook), *The Java 2 Mul-
timedia Cyber Classroom: Third Edition, The Visual Basic 6 Multimedia Cyber Class-
room, The Internet and World Wide Web Programming Multimedia Cyber Classroom,
The e-Business and e-Commerce Programming Multimedia Cyber Classroom* and *The
XML Multimedia Cyber Classroom*. The Deitels are also co-authors of *The Complete
C++ Training Course: Third Edition, The Complete Visual Basic 6 Training Course,
The Complete Java 2 Training Course: Third Edition, The Complete Internet and World
Wide Web Programming Training Course, The Complete e-Business and e-Commerce
Programming Training Course* and the *Complete XML Training Course*—these products
each contain the corresponding *How to Program Series* textbook and the corresponding
Multimedia Cyber Classroom.

About Deitel & Associates, Inc.

Deitel & Associates, Inc. is an internationally recognized corporate training and content
creation organization specializing in Internet/World Wide Web software technology, e-
business/e-commerce software technology and computer programming languages education. Deitel & Associates, Inc. is a member of the World Wide Web Consortium. The company provides courses on Internet and World Wide Web programming, e-business and e-
commerce programming, Object Technology and major programming languages. The prin-
cipals of Deitel & Associates, Inc. are Dr. Harvey M. Deitel and Paul J. Deitel. The company's clients include many of the world's largest computer companies, government
agencies, branches of the military and business organizations. Through its publishing part-
nership with Prentice Hall, Deitel & Associates, Inc. publishes leading-edge programming
textbooks, professional books, interactive CD-ROM-based multimedia *Cyber Classrooms*,
satellite courses and Web-based training courses. Deitel & Associates, Inc. and the authors
can be reached via e-mail at

`deitel@deitel.com`

To learn more about Deitel & Associates, Inc., its publications and its worldwide corporate
on-site curriculum, see the last few pages of this book and visit:

`www.deitel.com`

Individuals wishing to purchase Deitel books, Cyber Classrooms, Complete Training
Courses and Web-based training courses can do so through

`www.deitel.com`

Bulk orders by corporations and academic institutions should be placed directly with Prentice Hall. See the last few pages of this book for worldwide ordering details.

The World Wide Web Consortium (W3C)

W3C ®Deitel & Associates, Inc. is a member of the *World Wide Web Consortium (W3C)*. The W3C was founded in 1994 "to develop common protocols for the evolution of the World Wide Web." As a W3C member, we hold a seat

MEMBER on the W3C Advisory Committee (our Advisory Committee representative is our Chief Technology Officer, Paul Deitel). Advisory Committee members help provide "strategic direction" to the W3C through meetings around the world (the Spring 2000 meeting was held in Amsterdam). Member organizations also help develop standards recommendations for Web technologies (such as HTML, XML and many others) through participation in W3C activities and groups. Membership in the W3C is intended for companies and large organizations. For information on becoming a member of the W3C visit **www.w3.org/Consortium/Prospectus/Joining**.

1

Introduction to Computers, the Internet and the World Wide Web

Objectives

- To understand basic computer concepts.
- To become familiar with different types of programming languages.
- To become familiar with the history of the Perl programming language.
- To become familiar with the Perl library.

Things are always at their best in their beginning.
Blaise Pascal

High thoughts must have high language.
Aristophanes

Our life is frittered away by detail … Simplify, simplify.
Henry Thoreau

1.1 Introduction

Welcome to Perl! We have worked hard to create what we sincerely hope will be an informative and entertaining learning experience for you. This book is unique among Perl textbooks for many reasons. We introduce the use of Perl with the Common Gateway Interface (CGI) for programming Web-based applications early in the text so that the remainder of the book can cover a variety of dynamic, Web-based applications. The book discusses many topics, including object-oriented programming, the Perl database interface (DBI), graphics, the Extensible Markup Language (XML), security, an introduction to the Python programming language and a complete chapter on Web accessibility that addresses programming and technologies relevant to people with disabilities. This book is not only appropriate for technically oriented people with little or no programming experience, but also for experienced programmers who want a rigorous treatment of the language.

How can one book appeal to both groups? The answer is that the common core of the book emphasizes achieving program *clarity* through the proven techniques of *structured programming* and *object-based programming*. Non-programmers learn programming the right way from the beginning. We have attempted to write in a clear and straightforward manner, with abundant illustrations. Perhaps most importantly, the book presents hundreds of complete working Perl programs and shows the outputs produced when those programs are run on a computer. We call this our *live-code*™ *approach*. Every example program in this book is provided on the CD that accompanies the book. You may also download these examples from our Web site, **www.deitel.com**.

Many experienced programmers have told us that they value our approach to structured programming. Often they have been programming in a structured language like Pascal or C, but because they were never formally introduced to structured programming, they are not writing the best possible code. As they learn Perl with this book, they are able to improve their programming style. So whether you are a novice or an experienced programmer, there is much here to inform, entertain and challenge you.

Most people are at least somewhat familiar with the exciting tasks computers do. Using this textbook, you will learn how to command computers to do those tasks. It is *software* (i.e., the instructions you write to command the computer to perform *actions* and make *decisions*) that controls computers (often referred to as *hardware*).

The use of computers is increasing in almost every field. In an era of steadily rising costs, computing costs have been decreasing dramatically because of the rapid developments in both hardware and software technology. Computers that filled large rooms and cost millions of dollars 25 to 30 years ago are now inscribed on the surfaces of silicon chips smaller than a fingernail and cost perhaps a few dollars each. Ironically, silicon is one of the most abundant materials on the earth—it is an ingredient as common as sand. Silicon-chip technology has made computing so economical that hundreds of millions of general-purpose computers are in use worldwide. These computers help people in business, industry, government and their personal lives. That number could easily double in a few years.

You are about to start on a challenging and rewarding path. As you proceed, if you would like to communicate with us, please send us email at **deitel@deitel.com** or browse our World Wide Web site at **www.deitel.com**. We hope you enjoy learning Perl with *Perl How to Program*.

1.2 What Is a Computer?

A *computer* is a device capable of performing computations and making logical decisions at speeds millions and even billions of times faster than human beings can. For example, many of today's personal computers can perform hundreds of millions of additions per second. A person operating a desk calculator might require decades to complete the same number of calculations that a powerful personal computer can perform in one second. (Points to ponder: How would you know whether the person added the numbers correctly? How would you know whether the computer added the numbers correctly?) Today's fastest *supercomputers* can perform hundreds of billions of additions per second—about as many calculations as hundreds of thousands of people could perform in one year! Moreover, trillion-instruction-per-second computers are already functioning in research laboratories!

Computers process *data* under the control of sets of instructions called *computer programs*. These programs guide the computer through orderly sets of actions specified by people called *computer programmers*.

A computer is comprised of various devices (such as the keyboard, screen, "mouse," disks, memory, CD-ROM and processing units) that are referred to as hardware. The computer programs that run on a computer are referred to as software. Hardware costs have been declining dramatically in recent years, to the point that personal computers have become a commodity. Unfortunately, software development costs have been rising steadily as programmers develop ever more powerful and complex applications without significantly improved technology for software development. In this book you will learn proven software development methods that can reduce software development costs—structured programming, top-down stepwise refinement, functionalization, object-based programming, object-oriented programming and event-driven programming.

1.3 Computer Organization

Regardless of differences in physical appearance, virtually every computer may be envisioned as being divided into six *logical units*, or sections. These are:

1. *Input unit.* This is the "receiving" section of the computer. It obtains information (data and computer programs) from various *input devices* and places this information at the disposal of the other units so that the information may be processed. Most information is entered into computers today through keyboards and mouse devices. Other input devices include microphones for speaking into your computer, scanners for scanning images and digital cameras for taking photographs and making videos.

2. *Output unit.* This is the "shipping" section of the computer. It takes information that has been processed by the computer and places it on various *output devices* to make the information available for use outside the computer. Most output from computers today is displayed on screens, printed on paper or used to control other devices.

3. *Memory unit.* This is the rapid access, relatively low-capacity "warehouse" section of the computer which provides temporary storage for data. It retains information that has been entered through the input unit so that it may be made immediately available for processing when it is needed. The memory unit also retains processed information until that information can be placed on output devices by the output unit. The memory unit is often called either *memory* or *primary memory.*

4. *Arithmetic and logic unit (ALU).* This is the "manufacturing" section of the computer. It is responsible for performing calculations such as addition, subtraction, multiplication and division. It contains decision mechanisms that allow the computer to complete tasks such as comparing two items from the memory unit to determine whether or not they are equal.

5. *Central processing unit (CPU).* This is the "administrative" section of the computer. It is the computer's coordinator and is responsible for supervising the operation of the other sections. The CPU tells the input unit when information should be read into the memory unit, tells the ALU when information from the memory unit should be used in calculations and tells the output unit when to send information from the memory unit to certain output devices.

6. *Secondary storage unit.* This is the long-term, high-capacity "warehousing" section of the computer. Programs or data not actively being used by the other units are normally placed on secondary storage devices (such as disks) until they are again needed, possibly hours, days, months, or even years later. Information in secondary storage takes much longer to access than information in primary memory. The cost per unit of secondary storage is much less than the cost per unit of primary memory.

1.4 Evolution of Operating Systems

Early computers were capable of performing only one *job* or *task* at a time. This form of computer operation is often called single-user *batch processing*. The computer runs a single program at a time while processing data in groups or *batches*. In these early systems, users generally submitted their jobs to a computer center on decks of punched cards. Users often had to wait hours or even days before printouts were returned to their desks.

Software systems called *operating systems* were developed to help make it more convenient to use computers. Early operating systems managed the transition between jobs. This minimized the time it took for computer operators to switch between jobs and hence increased the amount of work, or *throughput*, computers could process.

As computers became more powerful, it became evident that single-user batch processing rarely utilized the computer's resources efficiently because most of the time was spent waiting for slow input/output devices to complete their tasks. Instead, it was thought that many jobs or tasks could be made to *share* the resources of the computer to achieve better utilization. This is called *multiprogramming,* which involves the "simultaneous" operation of many jobs on the computer—the computer shares its resources among jobs. However with early multiprogramming operating systems, users still submitted jobs on decks of punched cards and waited hours or days for results.

In the 1960s, several groups in the industry and universities pioneered *timesharing* operating systems. Timesharing is a special case of multiprogramming in which users access the computer through *terminals*, typically devices with keyboards and screens. In a typical timesharing computer system, there may be dozens or even hundreds of users sharing the computer at once. The computer does not actually run all the users simultaneously. Rather, it runs a small portion of one user's job and then moves on to service the next user. The computer does this so quickly that it may provide service to each user several times per second. Thus the users' programs *appear* to be running simultaneously. An advantage of timesharing is that the user receives almost immediate responses to requests rather than having to wait long periods for results as with previous modes of computing.

The UNIX operating system, which is now widely used for advanced computing, originated as an experimental timesharing operating system. Dennis Ritchie and Ken Thompson developed UNIX at Bell Laboratories beginning in the late 1960's and developed C as the language in which they wrote it. They created UNIX as *open-source* software, freely distributing the source code to other programmers who wanted to use, modify and extend it. A community of UNIX users quickly grew, and the language grew with them as it incorporated their improvements and their new tools. Through a collaborative effort between numerous researchers and developers, UNIX became a powerful and flexible operating system able to handle almost any type of task that a user required.

1.5 Personal Computing, Distributed Computing and Client/ Server Computing

In 1977, Apple Computer popularized the phenomenon of *personal computing*. Initially, it was a hobbyist's dream. Soon, however, computers became economical enough for people to buy them for their own personal or business use. In 1981, IBM, the world's largest computer vendor, introduced the IBM Personal Computer. Literally overnight, personal computing became legitimate in business, industry and government organizations.

These computers were "stand-alone" units—people did their work on their own machines and then transported disks back and forth to share information (often called "sneak-ernet"). Although early personal computers were not powerful enough to timeshare several users, these machines could be linked together in computer networks, sometimes over telephone lines and sometimes in *local area networks (LANs)* within an organization. This led to the phenomenon of *distributed computing,* in which an organization's computing, instead of being performed strictly at a central computer installation, is distributed over networks to the sites at which the work of the organization is performed. Personal computers were powerful enough to handle the computing requirements of individual users and to handle the basic communications tasks of passing information back and forth electronically.

Today's most powerful personal computers are as powerful as the million dollar machines of just a decade ago. The most powerful desktop machines—called *worksta-tions*—provide individual users with enormous capabilities. Information is easily shared across computer networks, where computers called *file servers* offer a common store of programs and data that may be used by *client* computers distributed throughout the network, hence the term *client/server computing.* C and C++ have become the programming languages of choice for writing software for operating systems, computer networking and distributed client/server applications.

1.6 Machine Languages, Assembly Languages and High-level Languages

Programmers write instructions in various programming languages, some directly understandable by the computer and others that require intermediate *translation* steps. Hundreds of computer languages are in use today. These may be divided into three general types:

1. Machine languages

2. Assembly languages

3. High-level languages.

Any computer can directly understand only its own *machine language.* Machine language is the "natural language" of a particular computer. It is defined by the hardware design of that computer. Machine languages generally consist of strings of numbers (ultimately reduced to 1s and 0s) that instruct computers to perform their most elementary operations one at a time. Machine languages are *machine-dependent,* i.e., a particular machine language can be used on only one type of computer. Machine languages are cumbersome for humans, as can be seen by the following section of a machine language program that adds overtime pay to base pay and stores the result in gross pay.

```
+1300042774
+1400593419
+1200274027
```

As computers became more popular, it became apparent that machine language programming was too slow, tedious and error prone. Instead of using the strings of numbers that computers could directly understand, programmers began using English-like abbreviations to represent the elementary operations of the computer. These abbreviations formed the basis of *assembly languages. Translator programs* called *assemblers* were developed to convert assembly language programs to machine language at computer speeds. The following section of an assembly language program also adds overtime pay to base pay and stores the result in gross pay, but does it more clearly than its machine language equivalent:

```
LOAD    BASEPAY
ADD     OVERPAY
STORE   GROSSPAY
```

Although such code is clearer to humans, it is incomprehensible to computers until translated to machine language.

Computer usage increased rapidly with the advent of assembly languages, but these still required many instructions to accomplish even the simplest tasks. To speed the programming process, *high-level languages*, in which single statements accomplish substantial tasks, were developed. Translator programs called *compilers* convert high-level language programs into machine language. High-level languages allow programmers to write instructions that look almost like everyday English and contain commonly used mathematical notations. A payroll program written in a high-level language might contain a statement such as:

```
grossPay = basePay + overTimePay
```

Obviously, high-level languages are much more desirable from the programmer's standpoint than either machine languages or assembly languages. C, C++, Java and Perl are among the most powerful and most widely used high-level languages.

The process of compiling a high-level language program into machine language can take a considerable amount of computer time. This problem was solved by the development of *interpreter* programs that can directly execute high-level language programs without needing to compile them into machine language. Although compiled programs execute faster than interpreted programs, interpreters are popular in program development environments in which programs are changed frequently as new features are added and errors are corrected. Once a program is developed, a compiled version can be produced to run most efficiently.

Hundreds of high-level languages have been developed, but only a few have achieved broad acceptance. *FORTRAN* (FORmula TRANslator) was developed by IBM Corporation between 1954 and 1957 to be used for scientific and engineering applications that require complex mathematical computations. FORTRAN is still widely used, especially in engineering applications.

COBOL (COmmon Business Oriented Language) was developed in 1959 by computer manufacturers, government and industrial computer users. COBOL is used primarily for commercial applications that require precise and efficient manipulation of large amounts of data. Today, more than half of all business software is still programmed in COBOL.

We will introduce other high-level programming languages in our discussions of structured and object-oriented programming.

1.7 Structured Programming

During the 1960s, many large software development efforts encountered severe difficulties. Software schedules were typically late, costs greatly exceeded budgets and the finished products were unreliable. People began to realize that software development was a far more complex activity than they had imagined. Research activity in the 1960s resulted in the evolution of *structured programming*—a disciplined approach to writing programs that are clear, demonstrably correct and easy to modify.

One of the more tangible results of this research was the development of the *Pascal* programming language by Professor Nicklaus Wirth in 1971. Pascal, named after the seventeenth-century mathematician and philosopher Blaise Pascal, was designed for teaching structured programming in academic environments and rapidly became the preferred introductory programming language in most universities. Unfortunately, the language lacks many features needed to make it useful in commercial, industrial and government applications, so it was not widely accepted in these environments. C, which also arose from research on structured programming, did not have the limitations of Pascal, and therefore became adopted by programmers everywhere.

C evolved from two previous languages, *BCPL* and *B*. BCPL was developed in 1967 by Martin Richards as a language for writing operating systems software and compilers. Ken Thompson modeled many features in his language B after their counterparts in BCPL and used B in 1970 to create early versions of the UNIX operating system at Bell Laboratories on a DEC PDP-7 computer. Both BCPL and B were "typeless" languages—every data item occupied one "word" in memory and the burden of typing variables fell on the shoulders of the programmer. The *C* language was evolved from B by Dennis Ritchie at Bell Laboratories and was originally implemented on a DEC PDP-11 computer in 1972. C uses many of the important concepts of BCPL and B while adding data typing and other powerful features. By the late 1970s, C had evolved into what is now referred to as "traditional C." The publication in 1978 of Kernighan and Ritchie's book, *The C Programming Language,* brought wide attention to the language.

The *Ada* programming language was developed under the sponsorship of the United States Department of Defense (DOD) during the 1970s and early 1980s. Hundreds of separate languages were being used to produce DOD's massive command and control software systems. DOD wanted a single language that would meet its needs. Pascal was chosen as a base, but the final Ada language is quite different from Pascal. The language was named after Lady Ada Lovelace, daughter of the poet Lord Byron. Lady Lovelace is generally credited with writing the world's first computer program in the early 1800s (for the Analytical Engine Mechanical Computing device designed by Charles Babbage). One important capability of Ada is called *multitasking*; this allows programmers to specify that many activities are to occur in parallel. Other widely used high-level languages we discuss—including C and C++—allow the programmer to write programs that perform only one activity at a time.

1.8 Object-Oriented Programming

One of the key problems with procedural programming is that the program units programmers create do not easily mirror real-world entities effectively. Therefore, they are not particularly reusable. It is not unusual for programmers to "start fresh" on each new project and wind up writing very similar software "from scratch." This wastes precious time and money resources as people repeatedly "reinvent the wheel."

Building software quickly, correctly and economically remains an elusive goal, and this at a time when demands for new and more powerful software are soaring. *Objects* are essentially reusable software *components* that model items in the real world. Software developers are discovering that using a modular, object-oriented design and implementation approach can make software development groups much more productive than is possible with previous popular programming techniques, such as structured programming. Object-oriented programs are often easier to understand, correct and modify.

Some organizations report that software reuse is not, in fact, the key benefit they receive from object-oriented programming. Rather, they indicate that object-oriented programming tends to produce software that is more understandable, better organized and easier to maintain, modify and debug. This can be significant because it has been estimated that as much as 80% of software costs are not associated with the original efforts to develop the software, but with the continued evolution and maintenance of that software throughout its lifetime.

Whatever the perceived benefits of object-orientation are, it is clear that object-oriented programming will be the key programming methodology for the next several decades.

Object technology dates back at least to the mid 1960s. The C++ programming language, developed at AT&T by Bjarne Stroustrup in the early 1980s, is based on two languages—C, which was initially developed at AT&T to implement the UNIX operating system in the early 1970s, and *Simula 67*, a simulation programming language developed in Europe and released in 1967. C++ absorbed the capabilities of C and added Simula's capabilities for creating and manipulating objects. Neither C nor C++ was intended for wide use beyond the AT&T research laboratories, but grass-roots support rapidly developed for each.

In the early 1990's, researchers at Sun Microsystems developed a completely object-oriented language called Java. Sun formally announced Java at a trade show in May 1995. Ordinarily, an event like this would not have generated much attention. However, Java generated immediate interest in the business community because of the phenomenal interest in the World Wide Web. Java is now used to create Web pages with dynamic and interactive content, develop large-scale enterprise applications, enhance the functionality of Web servers (the computers that provide the content we see in our Web browsers), and provide applications for consumer devices (such as cell phones, pagers and personal digital assistants), among many other things.

1.9 Hardware Trends

The programming community thrives on a continuing stream of dramatic improvements in hardware, software and communications technologies. Every year, people generally expect to pay at least a little more for most products and services. The opposite has been the case in the computer and communications fields, especially with regard to the hardware costs of supporting these technologies. For many decades, and with no change in the foreseeable future, hardware costs have fallen rapidly, if not precipitously. This is a phenomenon of technology, another driving force powering the current economic boom. Every year or two, the capacities of computers, especially the amount of memory they have in which to execute programs, the amount of secondary storage (such as disk storage) they have to hold programs and data over the longer term, and their processor speeds—the speed at which computers execute their programs (i.e., do their work)—each tend to approximately double. The same growth has occurred in the communications field, with costs plummeting, especially in recent years as the enormous demand for communications bandwidth has attracted tremendous competition. We know of no other fields in which technology moves so quickly and costs fall so rapidly.

When computer use exploded in the sixties and seventies, there was talk of huge improvements in human productivity that computing and communications would bring about. However, these improvements did not materialize. Organizations were spending vast sums of capital on computers and certainly employing them effectively, but without realizing the productivity gains that had been expected. It was the invention of microprocessor chip technology, and its wide deployment in the late 1970s and 1980s, that laid the groundwork for the productivity improvements of the 1990s that have been so crucial to economic prosperity.

1.10 History of the Internet

In the late 1960s, one of the authors (HMD) was a graduate student at MIT. His research at MIT's Project Mac (now the Laboratory for Computer Science—the home of the World Wide Web Consortium) was funded by ARPA—the Advanced Research Projects Agency of the Department of Defense. ARPA sponsored a conference at which several dozen ARPA-funded graduate students were brought together at the University of Illinois at Urbana-Champaign to meet and share ideas. During this conference, ARPA rolled out the blueprints for networking the main computer systems of about a dozen ARPA-funded universities and research institutions. They were to be connected with communications lines operating at a then-stunning 56KB (i.e., 56,000 bits per second), at a time when most people (of the few who could) were connecting over telephone lines to computers at a rate of 110 bits per second. HMD vividly recalls the excitement at that conference. Researchers at Harvard in Massachusetts talked about communication with the Univac 1108 "supercomputer" across the country at the University of Utah to handle calculations related to their computer graphics research. Many other intriguing possibilities were raised. Academic research was about to take a giant leap forward. Shortly after this conference, ARPA proceeded to implement what quickly became called the *ARPAnet*, the grandparent of today's *Internet*.

Things worked out differently than originally planned. Although the ARPAnet did enable researchers to share each others' computers, its chief benefit proved to be its capability of quick and easy communication via what came to be known as *electronic mail (e-mail)*. This is true even today on the Internet, with e-mail facilitating communications of all kinds among hundreds of millions of people worldwide.

One of ARPA's primary goals for the network was to allow multiple users to send and receive information at the same time over the same communications paths (such as phone lines). The network operated with a technique called *packet switching* in which digital data was sent in small packages called *packets*. The packets contained data, address information, error-control information and sequencing information. The address information was used to route the packets of data to their destination. The sequencing information was used to help reassemble the packets (which—because of complex routing mechanisms—could actually arrive out of order) into their original order for presentation to the recipient. Packets of many people were intermixed on the same lines. This packet-switching technique greatly reduced transmission costs as compared to those of dedicated communications lines.

The network was designed to operate without centralized control. This meant that if a portion of the network should fail, the remaining working portions would still be able to route packets from senders to receivers over alternate paths.

The protocol for communicating over the ARPAnet became known as *TCP—the Transmission Control Protocol*. TCP ensured that messages were properly routed from sender to receiver and that those messages arrived intact.

In parallel with the early evolution of the Internet, organizations worldwide were implementing their own networks for both intra-organization (i.e., within the organization) and inter-organization (i.e., between organizations) communication. A huge variety of networking hardware and software appeared. One challenge was to get these to intercommunicate. ARPA accomplished this with the development of *IP*—the *Internetworking*

Protocol, truly creating a "network of networks," the current architecture of the Internet. The combined set of protocols is now commonly called *TCP/IP*.

Initially, use of the Internet was limited to universities and research institutions. Then, the military became a big user. Eventually, the government decided to allow access to the Internet for commercial purposes. Initially, there was resentment among the research and military communities—it was felt that response times would become poor as "the net" became saturated with so many users.

In fact, the exact opposite has occurred. Businesses rapidly realized that, by making effective use of the Internet, they could tune their operations and offer new and better services to their clients. They started spending vasts amounts of money to develop and enhance the Internet. This generated fierce competition among the communications carriers and the hardware and software suppliers to meet this demand. The result is that *bandwidth* (i.e., the information carrying capacity of communications lines) on the Internet has increased tremendously and costs have plummeted. It is widely believed that the Internet has played a significant role in the economic prosperity that the United States and many other industrialized nations have enjoyed over the last decade and are likely to continue enjoying for many years.

1.11 History of the World Wide Web

The *World Wide Web* allows computer users to locate and view, over the Internet, multi-media-based documents (i.e., documents with text, graphics, animations, audios and/or videos) on almost any subject. Even though the Internet was developed more than three decades ago, the introduction of the *World Wide Web* was a relatively recent event. In 1990, *Tim Berners-Lee* of CERN (the European Laboratory for Particle Physics) developed the World Wide Web and several communication protocols that form its backbone.

The Internet and the World Wide Web will surely be listed among the most important and profound creations of humankind. In the past, most computer applications ran on "stand-alone" computers, i.e., computers that were not connected to one another. Today's applications can be written to communicate among the world's hundreds of millions of computers.

The Internet mixes computing and communications technologies. It makes our work easier. It makes information instantly and conveniently accessible worldwide. It makes it possible for individuals and small businesses to get worldwide exposure. It is changing the way business is done. People can search for the best prices on virtually any product or service. Special-interest communities can stay in touch with one another. Researchers can be made instantly aware of the latest breakthroughs worldwide.

We have written two books for academic courses that convey fundamental principles of computing in the context of Internet and World Wide Web programming—*Internet and World Wide Web How to Program* and *e-Business and e-Commerce How to Program*.

1.12 History of Perl

In 1986, Larry Wall was a systems programmer for the National Security Agency's secret (and now defunct) "Blacker" project, delegating the responsibility of building a control and management system with the capability to produce reports for a wide-area network of UNIX computers. Dissatisfied with the available tools for the job, he invented a new language. It aimed to integrate features of the UNIX languages *awk* and *sed* with the framework provided by *shell* (the UNIX command-line scripting language). Awk is a language with powerful string manipulation and regular expressions that facilitate the generation of reports. Sed is a stream editing and filtering tool that complements awk. Wall wanted to find the perfect mix of "manipulexity and whipuptitude." He wanted the language to be powerful and flexible enough to directly manipulate the computer's capabilities, like C, but simple enough that programs could be prototyped quickly. He was also inspired by his background in linguistics to make it a *natural language*, such as human language, which uses redundancy and context to enable the expression of ideas in different ways. The guiding principle was simply to make "the easy things easy and the hard things possible." In 1987, Wall posted version 0 of his new language, the *Practical Extraction and Report Language (PERL)*, to Usenet. He chose to release Perl as open-source (distributing the complete source code for free and allowing users to modify and extend it.)

A flexible, portable and efficient language, Perl began to gain support among the open-source community as it found use in more and more applications. Successive versions of Perl incorporated user suggestions for fixes and expansions, and it grew beyond its original text processing capabilities. Users of Perl created many modular extensions to Perl, some of which were later integrated into the basic source code. From the beginning up to Perl 4, the language was continuously being updated yet remained so stable that developers programmed entire projects using development versions.

Perl 3 adopted the GNU General Public License and Perl 4 adopted an Artistic License to attract more users. Both licenses protect Perl's free, open-source nature, but the Artistic License allows Perl to be embedded in proprietary products under certain conditions.

Perl 5 was a major reorganization that fixed many of the language's limitations, making it more powerful, more readable and more extensible. It had grown from a text-processing tool to a general-purpose programming language with its own complete software development environment. By that time, it could no longer be managed predominantly by Wall. Consequently, he delegated the development and documentation of Perl to people throughout the open-source community, and also to some in the business community, letting the language freely expand in all directions.

Perl's usability, speed, flexibility and portability made it ideal for the World Wide Web. A language based on text processing, it is adaptable for manipulating the text-based medium of the Web. Perl is particularly effective in use with the Common Gateway Interface protocol, which allows Web servers to interact with other applications and pass their output to client applications in the form of dynamic content. The advent of the CGI protocol almost single-handedly transformed Perl from an obscure systems administration tool to the most widely used server-side Internet programming language.

Through the 1990's, Perl and other open-source projects, including its fellow open-source pioneers Linux and Apache, have come together to form an open-source movement. Their aim is to build a cohesive, efficient, functional open-source community that will spread its ideas and innovations throughout the world.

On July 18, 2000, Larry Wall announced the beginning of the development of Perl 6, a complete rewrite of the internals and externals of Perl. Perl 6 will correct two major problems with Perl 5: convoluted internals and backward compatibility. Perl 6 will be more extensible, with features such as threading, signal handling and Unicode®—a standard character set that can represent the majority of the world's spoken language. Perl 6 will not be backwards-compatible with Perl 5. However, Perl 6 is expected to still "feel" like Perl 5. Perl 6, in Larry Wall's words, "should make easy things stay easy, hard things easier, and impossible things hard." See Appendix G, "Perl 6 Web Resources" which contains a brief discussion of Perl 6. This appendix also provides several resources related to Perl 6.

1.13 Perl Library

Perl is a modularly extensible language, so myriads of different *modules* (reusable pieces of software) have been written by Perl developers around the world. Perl modules are defined in library files ending in **.pm**. The primary distribution center for Perl source code, modules and documentation is the *Comprehensive Perl Archive Network (CPAN)*— **www.cpan.org**, which is mirrored by Web sites worldwide. Subdirectories under the main directory include those that contain software indexed by author, documentation, modules, ports to operating systems not supported in the standard distribution, scripts and the source code itself, which can be downloaded with anonymous FTP. Users of ActivePerl— an implementation of Perl for Windows created by ActiveState Tool Corporation—can use the *Perl Package Manager (PPM)* to find and install modules.

1.14 General Notes About Perl and This Book

The Perl approach to programming is best described by two slogans popular in the Perl community. The first states that the qualities of a good programmer are "laziness, impatience and hubris." This motto may seem nonsensical, but it can be explained. Lazy programmers do not like to reinvent the wheel, so they will write code that is reusable and applicable in as many places as possible. Impatient programmers do not want to do manually what they could have a computer do automatically. Therefore, they write code to perform these tasks, making programs more functional. Lastly, programmers must have hubris so that they will show off their code to their friends. For their friends to understand it, however, they must write it clearly. Consequently, a programmer with these characteristics will write reusable, complete and readable code.

The second slogan, "There's more than one way to do it," reflects the Perl community's love of freedom as well as the natural language philosophy of Perl. There is no "right way" to write a Perl program, for just as one can express the same idea in different ways using natural language, one can write the same program in different ways using Perl. Perl programs can be optimized for whatever quality one desires, such as speed, clarity, usability or flexibility.

Perl is one of the most highly portable programming languages in existence. It was originally implemented on UNIX, but has since spread to many other platforms. A Perl program can often be ported from one operating system to another without any changes, and still function properly. Ports are available on CPAN for operating systems not supported in the standard distribution.

1.15 A Tour of the Book

In this section, we take a tour of the subjects you will study in *Perl How to Program*. Many of the chapters end with an Internet and World Wide Web Resources section that provides a listing of resources through which you can enhance your knowledge of Perl programming.

Chapter 1—Introduction to Computers, the Internet and the World Wide Web
In this chapter, we discuss what computers are, how they work and how they are programmed. It introduces the notion of structured programming and explains why this set of

techniques has fostered a revolution in the way programs are written. The chapter gives a brief history of the development of programming languages from machine languages, to assembly languages, to high-level languages. The origin of the Perl programming language is discussed. We present some historical information about computers and computer programming and introductory information about the Internet and the World Wide Web. We also overview the concepts you will learn in the remaining chapters of the book.

Chapter 2—Introduction to Programming in Perl

This chapter includes an introduction to a typical Perl programming environment and provides a concise introduction to writing Perl programs. We discuss scalar variable types, and introduce arithmetic, assignment, increment, decrement, equality, relational and string operators. A detailed treatment of decision making and arithmetic operations in Perl is presented. The chapter ends with a discussion of how Perl interprets numeric and string variables based on their context. We have introduced a new, more open, easier to read "look and feel" for our Perl source programs, most notably using syntax coloring to highlight keywords, comments and regular program text. This helps to make programs more readable. After studying this chapter, the student will understand how to write simple but complete Perl programs.

Chapter 3—Control Structures: Part I

Chapter 3 introduces the notion of algorithms (procedures) for solving problems. It explains the importance of using control structures effectively in producing programs that are understandable, debuggable, maintainable and more likely to work properly on the first try. It introduces the sequence structure, selection structures (**if** and **if/else**) and repetition structures (**while**, **do/while**, **until** and **do/until**). It examines repetition in detail and compares counter-controlled loops and sentinel-controlled loops. It explains the technique of top-down, stepwise refinement that is critical to the production of properly structured programs, and presents the popular program design aid, pseudocode. The techniques presented in Chapter 3 are applicable for effective use of control structures in any programming language, not just Perl. This chapter helps the student develop good programming habits in preparation for dealing with the more substantial programming tasks in the remainder of the text.

Chapter 4—Arrays and Hashes

This chapter discusses lists, and the array and hash data types, which provide programmers with the ability to structure related data items. It is widely recognized that structuring data properly is just as important as using control structures effectively in the development of properly structured programs. Examples in the chapter demonstrate various common array and hash manipulations using an extensive collection of hash and array functions. A feature of this chapter is the discussion of elementary searching techniques.

Chapter 5—Control Structures: Part II

In this chapter, we introduce the remaining control structures in Perl that were not covered in Chapters 2, 3 or 4. The **foreach** repetition structure is introduced with examples. We discuss Perl's special variable **$_** that can be used as a default argument to many functions—an efficient programming shortcut. The functions **grep** and **map**, which are used in place of common loop structures, are demonstrated. The loop controls **next**, **last** and **redo** are also discussed. A case study then integrates many program control elements to demonstrate computing the mean, median and mode using arrays. Block labels, which enable program control to jump between control structures, are covered, as are bare blocks.

In addition, the chapter shows the workings of the logical operators **&&** (and), **||** (or) and **!** (not), as well as **or** and **not**. We also demonstrate mechanisms to deal with errors using the **die** and **warn** error functions that cause the program to terminate or output a warning, respectively. The chapter concludes with a summary of structured programming.

Chapter 6—Subroutines and Functions

Chapter 6 discusses the design and construction of functions. Perl's function-related capabilities include built-in functions, programmer-defined subroutines and recursion. The techniques presented in Chapter 6 are essential to the production of properly structured programs, especially the kinds of larger programs and software that system programmers and application programmers are likely to develop in real-world applications. The "divide and conquer" strategy is presented as an effective means for solving complex problems by dividing them into simpler interacting components. Students enjoy the treatment of random numbers and simulation, and they appreciate the discussion of the dice game of craps which makes elegant use of control structures. The chapter offers a solid introduction to recursion. Scope rules are also discussed. This chapter demonstrates how to create and use packages and modules, which enable programmers to import reusable software components (such as functions) and use those components as if they were originally defined in the program. The chapter concludes with a description of the **strict** and **warnings** pragmas, which respectively force the programmer to follow certain programming guidelines and warn of possible errors in a program. These help Perl programmers write more robust and reusable programs.

Chapter 7—Introduction to the Common Gateway Interface (CGI)

The Common Gateway Interface is a protocol for interactions between applications (CGI programs) and Web servers. The chapter introduces the Hypertext Transfer Protocol (HTTP), which is a fundamental component in the communication of data between a Web server and a Web browser. The most common data sent from a Web server to a Web browser is a Web page—a document that is typically formatted with HyperText Markup Language (HTML). The chapter also discusses how Web pages are sent to a Web browser for display. We learn how to create a simple CGI script. The chapter demonstrates several functions from **CGI.pm**, a module containing reusable functions and shortcuts that simplify CGI script writing. We show how to send user input from a browser to a CGI script and send user input to a CGI script with HTML forms. We also show how to use the functions of **CGI.pm** to create forms for display in the user's browser. The chapter also contains descriptions of various HTTP headers used with CGI. The chapter concludes by integrating the previous CGI material into a case study of a Web portal.

Chapter 8—Regular Expressions

Text manipulation in Perl is usually done with *regular expressions*, which are patterns of text used to search text files and databases. Perl's rich regular expression functionality gives it powerful text processing capabilities. The *match operator*, **m//**, matches text patterns in a string and can be modified to perform different types of matching. In addition to matching, Perl can also substitute expressions with the *substitution operator*, **s///**. We discuss how to incorporate special characters or classes of characters, such as the digits 0-9, into a regular expression. Then we show how the alternation operator can be used similarly to search for a pattern in a list. Next, we examine *quantifiers*, which can be used to match any number of instances at one time, and controlling quantifier "greediness" with **?**. Assertions—zero-width matching constructs that function similarly to special characters—

are discussed. We demonstrate *backreferencing*, which allows regular expressions to use previously matched values. We cover additional regular expression modifiers, including the **/g** modifier, which is used for global searching, then conclude the chapter with an example application that verifies data sent to a CGI program through an HTML form.

Chapter 9—String Manipulation

Strings form the basis of most Perl output. In this chapter, we explore in depth the functions used to manipulate string appearance, order and contents. First, we discuss single and double-quoted strings, their escape sequences and their quote operators, which simplify writing code containing many strings. We present using *here* documents to create strings over many lines of code. We begin our discussion of string processing functions with the basic functions for returning substrings, capitalizing letters and calculating string size. Next, we examine several other powerful string manipulation functions. Functions **chop** and **chomp** trim and return characters from the ends of strings. Functions **index** and **rindex** search a string for a substring. Function **join** concatenates all the strings in a given list into one string. Function **split** breaks a string into a list of strings. The *translation operator*, **tr///**, substitutes specific characters for those found in a string. Functions **printf** and **sprintf** create formatted output. Towards the end of the chapter we discuss function **eval**, which evaluates a string or block as Perl code.

Chapter 10—File Processing

This chapter discusses the techniques for processing sequential-access and random-access text files. The chapter overviews the data hierarchy from bits, to bytes, to fields, to records, to files. Next, Perl's simple view of files and filehandles is presented. Sequential-access files are discussed using programs that show how to open and close files, how to store data sequentially in a file and how to read data sequentially from a file. Random-access files are discussed using programs that show how to sequentially create a file for random access, how to read and write data to a file with random access and how to read data sequentially from a randomly accessed file. The exercises ask the student to implement a variety of programs that build and process both sequential-access files and random-access files.

Chapter 11—File and Directory Manipulation

In this chapter, we present more advanced ways to manipulate files and directories. We show how to conduct file tests; how to change file permissions, timestamps and ownership; and how to rename, delete and copy files using Perl. In addition, the chapter explains how to create hard and symbolic links, which can be used to provide alternate names for a file on some computer platforms. File globbing, a method of searching for all files with a certain name or name format, is also discussed. We cover directory manipulation, explaining how to create, delete and change directories. At the end of the chapter, we put much of the material together into a program that reads recursively through a directory structure and produces a recent update page for a Web site.

Chapter 12—Formatting

Perl's *formats* are used for defining templates which specify how data should be output. They allow you to code your output the way it should appear when printed, specifying fields that will be filled in when the format is executed. We show how to create formatted reports and manipulate fields to customize them. The chapter demonstrates several techniques for creating and using multiple-line fields. It also discusses format variables and their use in customizing formats. The chapter ends with two case studies. In the first, we write a program that outputs the contents of a database in a specific format. In the second, we create a script that analyzes the access logs of a Web server.

Chapter 13—References

This chapter introduces variables that refer to other locations in memory—called *references,* and how they can be used and manipulated. Next, we demonstrate the creation of references to different variable types, to subroutines and to other references. We show how to create anonymous structures and subroutines, which are not associated with any specific variable. Closures in anonymous subroutines are also discussed. One of the most important uses of references is to pass data structures to subroutines, because certain data structures themselves cannot be passed. This particular use of references is covered in detail. The creation and manipulation of nested data structures, such as multidimensional arrays, is also explained. The chapter then examines symbolic references and their specialized uses. Before references were added to Perl, constructs called *typeglobs* were used to perform certain functions that can now be implemented with references. However, typeglobs are still necessary to implement other Perl features such as filehandles. Chapter 13 concludes with examples of programming tasks that are made easier by the use of references, including the use of certain HTML shortcuts in **CGI.pm**.

Chapter 14—Objects and Modules

Perl was not originally designed for object-oriented programming, but object functionality has been added to it. We show how to use and create classes, attributes and methods. Throughout the chapter, we stress the separation of the interface and implementation of a class. We discuss inheritance, a form of software reusability in which new classes are developed quickly and easily by absorbing the capabilities of existing classes and adding appropriate new capabilities. The chapter also explains how to overload methods so that they can manipulate new types of objects. It presents multiple inheritance and composition, two other ways to reuse and expand upon classes. Because Perl does not have a private keyword, it has to encapsulate data in other ways. We demonstrate one of the most common methods for doing so, the *closure method*, which uses scoping rules to privatize variables. Then, we examine implicit subroutines, which Perl, unlike other languages, allows programmers to alter. In particular, we explore the many uses of the **AUTOLOAD** subroutine and the **TIE** subroutine, which attaches a variable to an object

Chapter 15—Databases: SQL and Perl Database Interface (DBI)

Most powerful business and Web applications are driven by data that is stored in database management systems. In this chapter, we show how to make inquiries and manipulate database data with the *structured query language* (SQL) for relational databases. We present basic SQL queries using a database containing employee data. The most popular interface used by Perl programmers to access data in a database is the DBI, which is a database-independent interface that can be used to manipulate one or more databases. We use it to demonstrate SQL and its interactions with an employee database. Discussion of Microsoft Access and the commercial, relational database management system, MySQL, are also provided in this chapter.

Chapter 16—Session Tracking and Cookies

Many Web sites track their users and customers so that they can offer a more personalized and convenient experience. Such tracking is typically performed with session tracking or cookies. First, we discuss methods of storing information about users and using hidden fields to collect information. Then, we demonstrate *cookies*—small text files that contain user information. The chapter also explains how to generate unique user identifiers and use them with files in session tracking. We then discuss Perl modules for dealing with cookies and session tracking. The chapter concludes with a case study of an online shopping cart.

Chapter 17—Web Automation and Networking
Perl has adapted well to the Web world. In addition to CGI applications, Perl can be used with an amazing number of pre-written modules to interact with networks and over the Web. These two features of the language have combined to allow Perl to automate many internet tasks. We introduce the object-oriented library for the World Wide Web in Perl (LWP)—a bundle of useful, WWW-related modules—and cover the most important objects and commands in the LWP. **LWP::Simple**, which provides a procedural interface for simpler networking-related tasks, is also covered. Then, we show how to use the HTML parsing module to process text from a Web page. The chapter continues with a discussion of client-server networking and network protocols. We build TCP client and server programs, two CGI programs for checking e-mail on a POP server, an SMTP application that shows how to send e-mail and a CGI program that performs a search of the Web by retrieving information from several search engines.

Chapter 18—Process Management
Most programming languages provide a simple set of control structures that enable programmers to perform one action at a time and proceed to the next action after the previous one is finished. Such control structures do not allow most programming languages to perform concurrent actions. The kind of concurrency that computers perform today is normally implemented as operating systems "primitives" available only to highly experienced "systems programmers." Perl makes concurrency primitives available to application programmers. This capability, called *multitasking,* gives the Perl programmer powerful capabilities not available in some other languages like C and C++.

We show how to use the **fork** command, which creates a new process, and the **exec** and **system** commands, which execute separate programs. One use of processes is to have one process execute an outside program while another process acts as an interpreter for the input and output to that program. In this chapter, techniques of input and output control are demonstrated and explained. Methods of communication between processes, including signal sending and handling, are also discussed. The chapter concludes with an example of process control using Perl scripts with Microsoft OLE Automation.

Chapter 19—Security
Web programming allows the rapid creation of powerful applications, but it also exposes your computer to outside attack. In this chapter, we begin by discussing security issues in Web programming. We illustrate the mantra of secure programming—never trust anything coming from the user. Then, we focus on defensive programming techniques that help the programmer prevent security problems through the use of certain techniques and tools. One of those tools is Perl's taint mode, which treats any data coming from outside of a script as insecure, forcing the programmer to verify its security. Another is encryption, which can be used in many forms. Chapter 19 examines the systems and technologies–including Public Key Cryptography, Secure Socket Layer (SSL), Secure Electronic Transfer (SET), digital signatures, digital certificates, digital steganography and the cutting-edge technology

of biometrics—used to meet these requirements. Other types of network security such as firewalls and antivirus programs are also covered, and common security threats such as cryptanalytic attacks, viruses, worms and Trojan Horses are discussed.

Chapter 20—Data Structures

Chapter 20 discusses the techniques used to create and manipulate dynamic data structures. The chapter begins with a discussions of self-referential structures and proceeds with a discussion of how to create and maintain various dynamic data structures including linked lists, queues (or waiting lines), stacks and trees. For each type of data structure, we present complete, working programs and show sample outputs. We also look into the inner workings of the hash data type—a data structure called a hash table.

Chapter 21—Graphics/Tk

Perl does not have any built-in graphics manipulating functions, but many modules have been designed and developed to automate certain graphical features. We look at three of the most common modules in this chapter. The first is the **GD** module, which has capabilities similar to those of many graphics programs on the market. With **GD**, we demonstrate how to create shapes and manipulate images. Then, we examine the **Chart** module, which allows us to make custom charts and graphs. Both of these modules require the programmer to use text commands to create their graphics. The third module, **Tk**, is designed to implement Graphical User Interfaces (GUIs). We show how to implement **Tk** and use *components* (i.e., buttons, labels, etc.), then build a calculator as a GUI application.

Chapter 22—Extensible Markup Language (XML)

Perl is well known for its powerful text-processing capabilities, which make it a likely candidate for XML processing. Unlike HTML, which formats information for display, XML structures information. It does not have a fixed set of tags as HTML does, but instead enables the document author to create new ones. A brief overview of *parsers*—programs that process XML documents and their data—is given, as are the requirements for a *well-formed document* (i.e., a document that is syntactically correct). We present *Namespaces*—which differentiate elements with the same name, and *Document Type Definition (DTD)* files and *Schema* files—which provide a structural definition for an XML document by specifying the type, order, number and attributes of the elements in an XML document. By defining an XML document's structure, a DTD or Schema reduces the validation and error-checking work of the application using the document.

The W3C *Document Object Model (DOM)*—an Application Programming Interface (API) for XML that is platform and language neutral—is also presented. The DOM API provides a standard set of interfaces (i.e., methods, objects, etc.) for manipulating an XML document's contents. Because XML documents are hierarchically structured, they are represented in the DOM as a tree structure. Using DOM, scripts and programs can dynamically modify the content, structure and formatting of documents. We also present an alternative to DOM called the Simple API for XML (SAX). Unlike DOM, which builds a tree structure in memory, SAX calls specific methods when a start tag, end tag, attribute, etc., are encountered in a document. For this reason, SAX is often referred to as an *event-based API*.

Chapter 22 also provides an introduction to an XML-related technology—called the Extensible Stylesheet Language (XSL)—for transforming XML documents into other documents such as HTML.

Support for XML is provided through many XML modules which are freely available. In this chapter, we focus on the two most mature Perl/XML modules: **XML::Parser** and **XML::DOM**. We use these modules to create a set of CGI scripts which implement a Web-based message-forums application. The master forum list is an XML document formatted by an XSL stylesheet. We use **XML::DOM**, which works in accordance with the World Wide Web Consortium (W3C) Document Object Model (DOM), to create new forums and messages. We also include alterations to the forum for browsers that do not support XSL.

Chapter 23—Accessibility
Currently, the World Wide Web can present a challenge to those who are impaired in one or more of their senses. Multimedia-rich Web sites often present difficulty to text readers and other programs designed to help the vision impaired, and the increasing amount of audio on the Web is inaccessible to the deaf. To rectify this situation, the World Wide Web Consortium started the Web Accessibility Initiative (WAI), which provides guidelines describing how to make a site accessible to the disabled. This chapter provides a description of these methods, such as use of the **<headers>** tag to make tables more accessible to page readers, use of the **alt** attribute of the **<img>** tag to describe images, and proper use of HTML and related technologies to ensure that a page can be viewed on any type of display or reader. We include a complete example of a Perl/CGI script which facilitates the addition of **alt** information to a Web page. VoiceXML can also be used to increase accessibility with speech synthesis and recognition. In the future, easy navigation of Web sites by all users with all types of hardware and software will be mandated.

Chapter 24—Bonus: Introduction to HyperText Markup Language 4: Part I
This bonus chapter introduces *HTML*—the *Hypertext Markup Language*—to support the programs that use HTML throughout the book. HTML is a *markup language* for describing the elements of an HTML document (Web page) so that a browser, such as Microsoft's Internet Explorer or Netscape's Communicator, can render (i.e., display) that page.

We discuss creating Web pages in HTML using our live-code™ approach. Like in the Perl chapters, every concept is presented in the context of a complete working HTML document (or Web page) that is immediately followed by the screen output produced when that HTML document is rendered by Internet Explorer. We write many simple Web pages. The next chapter introduces more sophisticated HTML techniques, such as tables, which are particularly useful for presenting and manipulating information from databases.

We introduce basic HTML *tags* and *attributes*. A key issue when using HTML is the separation of the *presentation of a document* (i.e., how the document is rendered on the screen by a browser) from the *structure of that document*. This chapter begins our in-depth discussion of this issue. As the book proceeds, you will be able to create increasingly appealing and powerful Web pages.

Some key topics covered in this chapter include: incorporating text and images in an HTML document, linking to other HTML documents on the Web, incorporating special characters (such as copyright and trademark symbols) into an HTML document and separating parts of an HTML document with horizontal lines (called *horizontal rules*).

Chapter 25—Bonus: Introduction to HyperText Markup Language 4: Part II
This bonus chapter continues our HTML discussions with more substantial HTML elements and features. We demonstrate how to present information in *lists* and *tables*. We dis-

cuss how to collect information from people browsing a site. We explain how to use *internal linking* and *image maps* to make Web pages easier to navigate. We also discuss how to use *frames* to make attractive Web sites. By the end of this chapter, we will have covered most commonly used HTML tags and features and will then be able to create more complex and visually appealing Web sites.

Chapter 26—Bonus: Cascading Style Sheets™ (CSS)
In earlier versions of HTML, Web browsers controlled the appearance (i.e., the rendering) of every Web page. For example, if a document author placed an **h1** (i.e., a large heading) element in a document, the browser rendered the element in its own manner. With the advent of Cascading Style Sheets, the document author can specify the way the browser renders the page. Applying Cascading Style Sheets to Web pages can give major portions of a Web site (or the entire Web site for that matter) a distinctive look and feel. CSS technology allows document authors to specify the style of their page elements (spacing, margins, etc.) separately from the structure of their document (section headers, body text, links, etc.). This *separation of structure from content* allows greater manageability and makes changing the style of the document easier and faster.

Chapter 27—Bonus: Introduction to Python Programming
In this chapter, we introduce Python, an interpreted, cross-platform, object-oriented, general-purpose programming language. Like Perl, Python is open source and has a large selection of modules that expand its capabilities. We begin by presenting the basic syntax, data types, control structures and functions of the language, then cover tuples (i.e., immutable lists), lists and dictionaries, which are high-level data structures. The essentials of string processing and regular expressions in Python are demonstrated, as is exception handling, which provides a structured mechanism for dealing with run-time errors. Having covered the fundamentals of Python, we discuss CGI programming and the modules available to facilitate it. We implement an HTML registration form and then show how to use cookies in Python/CGI programming. In addition, we overview Python's database interface (DBI) and object-oriented programming capabilities. The chapter concludes with a case study that creates a GUI for a local database, illustrating how Python can be used to rapidly develop an application for efficient presentation, use and manipulation of data.

Appendix A—HTML Special Characters
A table shows many commonly used HTML special characters, called *character entity references* by the World Wide Web Consortium (W3C).

Appendix B—HTML Colors
An explanation of how to create any color using either color names or hexadecimal RGB value is provided, along with a table that matches colors to values.

Appendix C—ASCII Character Set
This appendix contains a table of the 128 ASCII alphanumeric symbols.

Appendix D—Operator Precedence Chart
This appendix contains the operator precedence chart for Perl.

Appendix E—Number Systems
This appendix explains the binary, octal, decimal and hexadecimal number systems. It explains how to convert between bases and perform mathematical operations in each base.

Appendix F—Career Resources
This appendix provides resources related to careers in Perl and its related technologies.

Appendix G—Perl 6 Web Resources
This appendix provides a listing of URLs and other resources related to Perl 6.

Resources On Our Web Site
Our Web site, **www.deitel.com**, provides a number of Perl-related resources to help you with installation and configuration of Perl on your Windows or UNIX/Linux systems. The resources include *Installing the Apache Web Server with* **mod_perl**, *Installing ActiveState Perl*, *Installing the Perl Database Interface (DBI)* and *Registering an ODBC Data Source*. Also, for the bonus Chapter 27, *Introduction to Python Programming*, we provide resources for downloading and installing Python.

Well, there you have it! We have worked hard to create this book and its optional interactive multimedia *Cyber Classroom* version. The book is loaded with hundreds of working, live-code examples, programming tips, self-review exercises and answers, challenging exercises and projects and numerous study aids to help you master the material. The technologies we introduce will help you write Web-based applications quickly and effectively. As you read the book, if something is not clear, or if you find an error, please write to us at **deitel@deitel.com**. We will respond promptly, and we will post corrections and clarifications on our Web site

        www.deitel.com

Prentice Hall maintains **www.prenhall.com/deitel**—a Web site dedicated to our Prentice Hall textbooks, multimedia packages and Web-based training products. The site contains "Companion Web Sites" for each of our books that include frequently asked questions (FAQs), downloads, errata, updates, self-test questions and other resources.

You are about to start on a challenging and rewarding path. We hope you enjoy learning with *Perl How to Program* as much as we enjoyed writing it!

1.16 Internet and World Wide Web Resources

www.perl.com
Perl.com is the first place to look for information about Perl. The home page provides up-to-date news on Perl, answers to common questions about Perl, and an impressive collection of links to Perl resources of all kinds on the Internet. It includes sites for Perl software, tutorials, user groups and demos.

www.perl.com/CPAN/README.html
The "Comprehensive Perl Archive Network" is exactly what the name suggests. Here you will find an extensive listing of Perl related information.

www.pm.org
This is the home page of Perl Mongers, a group dedicated to supporting the Perl community. This site is helpful in finding others in the Perl community to converse with; Perl Mongers has established Perl user groups around the globe.

www.perlmonth.com
Perlmonth is a monthly online periodical devoted to Perl, with featured articles from professional programmers. This is a good source for those who use Perl frequently and wish to keep up on the latest developments involving Perl.

www.itknowledge.com/tpj
The *Perl Journal* is a large magazine dedicated to Perl. Subscribers are provided with up-to-date Perl news and articles, on the Internet as well as in printed form.

perl.about.com/compute/perl
Perl site provided by **About.com**. This site contains many Perl related articles, downloads and links such as discussion groups and tutorials.

www.devdaily.com/perl
This is the Developer's Daily Perl center. Here you can find articles on Perl as well as tutorials and other Perl-related resources.

www.perlarchive.com
This site contains articles, current Perl news, Perl forms and a Perl programming guide.

SUMMARY

[Because this chapter is primarily a summary of the rest of the book we have not provided a summary section. The remaining chapters provide detailed summaries of their contents.]

TERMINOLOGY

Ada	machine independent
ALU	machine language
arithmetic and logic unit (ALU)	memory
assembler	memory unit
assembly language	multiprocessor
batch processing	multiprogramming
C	multitasking
C++	natural language
central processing unit (CPU)	object-oriented programming
clarity	output unit
client	Pascal
client/server computing	Perl
COBOL	personal computer
computer	portability
computer program	primary memory
computer programmer	programming language
data	run a program
distributed computing	screen
file server	software
FORTRAN	software reusability
function	stored program
functionalization	structured programming
hardware	supercomputer
hardware platform	task
high-level language	terminal
input unit	timesharing
input/output (I/O)	top-down, stepwise refinement
interpreter	translator program
Java	UNIX
logical units	workstation
machine dependent	

SELF-REVIEW EXERCISES

1.1   Fill in the blanks in each of the following:

a) The company that brought the phenomenon of personal computing to the world was _____.

b) The computer that made personal computing legitimate in business and industry was the _____.

c) Computers process data under the control of sets of instructions called computer _____.

d) The six key logical units of the computer are the _____, _____, _____, _____, _____ and the _____.

e) _____ is a special case of multiprogramming in which users access the computer through devices called terminals.

f) The three classes of languages discussed in the chapter are _____, _____ and _____.

g) The programs that translate high-level language programs into machine language are called _____.

h) C is widely known as the development language of the _____ operating system.

i) The _____ language was developed by Wirth for teaching structured programming in universities.

j) The Department of Defense developed the Ada language with a capability called _____ which allows programmers to specify activities that can proceed in parallel.

ANSWERS TO SELF-REVIEW EXERCISES

1.1   a) Apple. b) IBM Personal Computer. c) programs. d) input unit, output unit, memory unit, arithmetic and logic unit (ALU), central processing unit (CPU), secondary storage unit. e) timesharing. f) machine languages, assembly languages, high-level languages. g) compilers. h) UNIX. i) Pascal. j) multitasking.

EXERCISES

1.2   Categorize each of the following items as either hardware or software:

a) CPU

b) ALU

c) input unit

d) a word processor program

e) Perl modules

1.3   Why might you want to write a program in a machine-independent language instead of a machine-dependent language? Why might a machine-dependent language be more appropriate for writing certain types of programs?

1.4   Translator programs such as assemblers and compilers convert programs from one language (referred to as the *source* language) to another language (referred to as the *object* language). Determine which of the following statements are *true* and which are *false*:

a) A compiler translates high-level language programs into object language.

b) An assembler translates source language programs into machine language programs.

c) A compiler converts source language programs into object language programs.

d) High-level languages are generally machine-dependent.

e) A machine language program requires translation before it can be run on a computer.

1.5 Fill in the blanks in each of the following statements:

a) Devices from which users access timesharing computer systems are usually called _____.

b) A computer program that converts assembly language programs to machine language programs is called _____.

c) The logical unit of the computer that receives information from outside the computer for use by the computer is called _____.

d) The process of instructing the computer to solve specific problems is called _____.

e) What type of computer language uses English-like abbreviations for machine language instructions? _____.

f) What are the six logical units of the computer? _____.

g) Which logical unit of the computer sends information that has already been processed by the computer to various devices so that the information may be used outside the computer? _____.

h) The general name for a program that converts programs written in a certain computer language into machine language is _____.

i) Which logical unit of the computer retains information? _____.

j) Which logical unit of the computer performs calculations? _____.

k) Which logical unit of the computer makes logical decisions? _____.

l) The commonly used abbreviation for the computer's control unit is _____.

m) The level of computer language most convenient to the programmer for writing programs quickly and easily is _____.

n) The most common business-oriented language in wide use today is _____.

o) The only language that a computer can directly understand is called that computer's _____.

p) Which logical unit of the computer coordinates the activities of all the other logical units? _____.

1.6 State whether each of the following is *true* or *false*. If *false*, explain your answer.

a) Machine languages are generally machine dependent.

b) Timesharing truly runs several users simultaneously on a computer.

c) Like other high-level languages, Perl is generally considered to be machine-independent.

Introduction to Programming in Perl

Objectives

- To be able to write simple computer programs in Perl.
- To be able to use simple input and output statements.
- To become familiar with fundamental data types.
- To be able to use arithmetic operators.
- To understand the precedence of arithmetic operators.
- To be able to write simple decision-making statements.
- To be able to use assignment operators.
- To be able to use increment and decrement operators.

What's in a name? That which we call a rose
By any other name would smell as sweet.
William Shakespeare, *Romeo and Juliet*

Precedents deliberately established by wise men are entitled to great weight.
Henry Clay

Outline

2.1 Introduction[1]

The Perl programming language facilitates a simple, structured and disciplined approach to computer program design. We now introduce Perl programming and present several examples that illustrate important features of Perl. We analyze each example one line at a time. Chapters 3 through 6 present a detailed treatment of program development, program control and structured programming in Perl.

2.2 Simple Programs that Display Lines of Text

Perl uses notations that may appear strange to nonprogrammers. Learning these notations will help you create well-written Perl programs that are readable and straightforward to understand. The next few examples will help you begin to learn Perl notation.

2.2.1 A Simple Program: Printing a Line of Text

We begin by considering a simple program that displays a line of text. The program and its screen output are shown in Fig. 2.1. You should type this program into a *text editor program* (such as emacs or vi on UNIX, or Notepad on Windows) and save the file as **fig02_01.pl**. When we complete the discussion of this first program, we will demonstrate how to execute the program so you can confirm its results.

---

1. Most of the content in this chapter is intended for people learning to program for the first time. Experienced programmers learning Perl can scan this chapter quickly.

```
1   #!/usr/bin/perl
2   # Fig. 2.1: fig02_01.pl
3   # A first program in Perl
4
5   print "Welcome to Perl!\n";    # print greeting
```

```
Welcome to Perl!
```

Fig. 2.1   Displaying a line of text.

This program illustrates several important features of the Perl language. We consider each line of the program in detail. Lines 1 through 3

```
#!/usr/bin/perl
# Fig. 2.1: fig02_01.pl
# A first program in Perl
```

use the Perl *comment character* (**#**) to indicate that everything on the current line following the **#** is a *comment*. Programmers insert comments to document programs and improve program readability. Comments also help other people read and understand your program. Comments are ignored by Perl, so they do not cause the computer to perform any action when the program is executed. The exception to this rule is the *shebang construct* (**#!**) on line 1. On Unix and Linux systems, this line indicates the normal *path* to the Perl interpreter (such as **#!/usr/bin/perl**); that is, the path refers to the location on the computer where the Perl interpreter resides. On other platforms, this line should be changed to indicate the location of the Perl interpreter on that computer. For example, if Perl is installed in the **c:\perl\bin** directory on a Microsoft Windows system, the shebang construct line would be **#!c:\perl\bin\perl.exe**.

Software Engineering Observation 2.1

*Every program should begin with the "shebang" construct path line **#!/usr/bin/perl** on UNIX and Linux platforms. If you are using another platform, you will need to change this line accordingly.*

Good Programming Practice 2.1

Every program should begin with a comment describing the purpose of the program.

Line 5

```
print "Welcome to Perl!\n";    # print greeting
```

instructs the computer to perform an action, namely to print the string of characters enclosed by the quotation marks to the standard output device, which is normally the screen. Strings of characters are sometimes called *character strings*, *string literals* or simply *strings*. We refer to strings of characters generically as *strings*. In this example, the string is the *argument* to the Perl *built-in function* **print**, which outputs its argument (the text) to the screen. Functions are program building blocks that perform actions. Functions receive arguments to help them perform their actions. A Perl programmer typically uses built-in functions, user-defined functions (see Chapter 6) and other statements to define a program's task. Line 5 *calls* (or *invokes*) function **print** to perform the task of displaying the text contained within the double quotes on the screen.

The characters normally print exactly as they appear between the double quotes following the **print** statement. Notice, however, that the characters **\n** are not printed on the screen. The backslash (****) is called an *escape character*. It indicates that a "special" character is to be output. When a backslash is encountered in a string of characters, the next character is combined with the backslash to form an *escape sequence*. The escape sequence **\n** represents *newline*. It causes the *cursor* (i.e., the current screen-position indicator) to move to the beginning of the next line on the screen—the blank line beneath the text **Welcome to Perl!** in the output window. Some other common escape sequences are listed in Fig. 2.2. Notice that each of the last three is used to output a specific character. As we will see, **$**, ****, **"** and **'** have specific uses. To display these characters, we need the backslash to appear before the character. For instance, we use the character "****" as the escape sequence. But what if we just want to print that symbol? Then we need to use the **** before it, or the interpreter will be expecting some other valid entry, such as **\n** (newline). The first three escape sequences are called *special actions*, because they do not display anything to the screen, but do cause the **print** statement to perform a special action such as move to a different position on the screen before displaying the next character in the string.

The entire line, including **print**, its argument (i.e., the character string being printed) and the *semicolon (;)* make up a single Perl *statement*. Note that semicolons (**;**) separate Perl statements. Also, the descriptive comment from the **#** symbol to the end of line 5 is ignored by Perl, like the other comments we discussed at the beginning of the program.

2.2.2 Executing the Program

We are now ready to execute our program. First, open a command window (a *command shell* on UNIX, an *MS-DOS prompt* on Windows 95/98 or a command prompt on Windows NT/2000). Next, change directories to the location where you saved the program, and type

```
perl fig02_01.pl
```

The **perl** command loads the program into memory and checks it for syntax errors. If the program contains no syntax errors, the program executes, producing the output in Fig. 2.1.

Escape Sequence	Description
\n	Newline. Position the screen cursor at the beginning of the next line.
\t	Horizontal tab. Move the screen cursor to the next tab stop.
\r	Carriage return. Position the screen cursor at the beginning of the current line; do not advance to the next line.
\$	Dollar sign. Used to insert a dollar-sign character in a string.
\\	Backslash. Used to insert a backslash character in a string.
\"	Double quote. Inserts a double-quote character in a double-quoted string.
\'	Single quote. Inserts a single-quote character in a single-quoted string.

Fig. 2.2   Some common escape sequences.

Good Programming Practice 2.2

*All Perl programs should be stored in files ending with the **.pl** extension.*

Testing and Debugging Tip 2.1

*One way to learn how to fix syntax errors is to "break" working programs. This process enables you to see error messages for common typos. For example, take the program of Fig. 2.1 and remove the "**r**" from "**print**." Then, save the program and try to execute it. An error message will be reported, and **perl** will indicate that it is terminating the program's execution, due to compilation errors (i.e., syntax errors).*

Testing and Debugging Tip 2.2

*To compile a program and check for syntax errors, add the **-c** command-line option to the **perl** command (as in **perl -c fileName.pl**).*

When you launch a program with the **perl** command, the program goes through two key phases. The first phase is *compilation*. The *compiler* translates the Perl program (also known as the *source code*) into Perl *opcodes* (also called *operation codes* or *PP codes*)— the language understood by the *Perl interpreter*. If the program compiles correctly, the opcodes will be interpreted during the *execution phase*. In this phase, the computer, under the control of its CPU and with the help of the Perl interpreter, interprets the program one opcode at a time, thus performing the actions specified by the program.

Programs may not work on the first try. The preceding phases can fail because of various errors that we will discuss in this text. For example, an executing program might attempt to divide by zero (an illegal operation in Perl, just as it is in arithmetic). This situation would cause the program to print an error message. The programmer would then edit the program, make the necessary corrections and run the program again to determine if the corrections work properly.

Common Programming Error 2.1

Errors such as division-by-zero errors occur as a program runs, so these errors are called run-time errors, *or* execution-time errors. *Fatal run-time errors* cause programs to terminate immediately without having successfully performed their jobs. *Nonfatal run-time errors* allow programs to run to completion, often producing incorrect results.*

2.2.3 A Simple Program: Printing Several Lines of Text

In Chapter 1, we mentioned the Perl motto, "There's More than One Way to Do It." [In fact, some use the acronym "TMTOWTDI" (pronounced "timtoady") for this saying.] Figure 2.3 shows this motto in action, illustrating the flexible nature of Perl syntax. The program in the figure demonstrates five different ways to accomplish the task of displaying the string "**Welcome to Perl!**" from the previous example.

Upon inspection of this program, we can learn a few things about Perl syntax and how Perl reads your source code. Line 5 shows that the arguments to built-in functions like **print** can be placed in parentheses. In some cases, this technique helps make Perl programs more readable. Line 6 shows that *whitespace characters* (such as spaces, tabs and newlines) are ignored by Perl. Careful use of whitespace nevertheless makes code clearer and more readable for humans.

```
1   #!/usr/bin/perl
2   # Fig. 2.3: fig02_03.pl
3   # Prints a welcome statement in a variety of ways
4
5   print ( "1. Welcome to Perl!\n" );
6   print      "2. Welcome to Perl!\n"         ;
7   print "3. Welcome ", "to ", "Perl!\n";
8   print "4. Welcome ";
9   print "to Perl!\n";
10  print "5. Welcome to Perl!\n";
11  print "6. Welcome\n   to\n\n    Perl!\n";
```

```
1. Welcome to Perl!
2. Welcome to Perl!
3. Welcome to Perl!
4. Welcome to Perl!
5. Welcome to Perl!
6. Welcome
   to

   Perl!
```

Fig. 2.3   Displaying a character string using several different methods.

Line 7 demonstrates **print** with more than one argument. The three arguments are separated by commas, and function **print** outputs each string in order from left to right. The effect is the same as using separate **print** statements for each string to display as shown in lines 8 and 9. Notice that although the statements on lines 8 and 9 are on separate lines, the string **Welcome to Perl!** is displayed on one line. Each **print** command continues printing where the previous **print** completed. Line 8 prints **Welcome** followed by a space, and line 9 begins printing on the same output line immediately following the space. You can also print multiple lines of text using one line of code. For example, line 11

```
print "6. Welcome\n   to\n\n    Perl!\n";
```

uses **\n** (newline) characters to output **Welcome to Perl!** spread over four lines.

Though we have shown more than one way to print a message to the screen, you generally would not want to use them all in a single program. On the contrary, it is good programming style to decide on certain conventions and remain consistent throughout your code. For example, when we need to use **print** command in this book, we generally use the simple syntax in Fig. 2.1.

Common Programming Error 2.2

Omitting the semicolon at the end of a statement is usually a syntax error. *A syntax error is caused when the compiler cannot recognize a statement, so the compiler normally issues an error message to help the programmer locate and fix the incorrect statement. Syntax errors are violations of the language. Syntax errors are also called* compile errors, *compile-time errors* and *compilation errors,* because they appear during the compilation phase.

Common Programming Error 2.3

Leaving out the last semicolon in a program is allowed, but doing so can become an error if more statements are added beyond the end of that program. Always terminate every Perl statement with a semicolon.

Good Programming Practice 2.3

*Many programmers make the last character printed from a program a newline (**\n**). This practice ensures that the cursor will be positioned at the beginning of a new line.*

Good Programming Practice 2.4

Set a convention for the size of indent you prefer, then uniformly apply that convention. The tab key can be used to create indents, but tab stops can vary. We recommend you use either π-inch tab stops or (preferably) three spaces to form a level of indent.

2.3 Another Simple Program: Adding Two Integers

Our next program obtains two numbers typed by a user at the keyboard, computes the sum of these values and prints the result using the **print** statement. The program and sample output are shown in Fig. 2.4.

The program begins by printing a message to the user (line 6). This message is called a *prompt*, because it tells the user to take a specific action, namely to enter a number. Line 7

```
$number1 = <STDIN>;
```

```perl
1   #!/usr/bin/perl
2   # Fig. 2.4: fig02_04.pl
3   # A simple addition program
4
5   # prompt user for first number
6   print "Please enter first number:\n";
7   $number1 = <STDIN>;
8   chomp $number1;            # remove "\n" from input
9
10  print "Please enter second number:\n";
11  $number2 = <STDIN>;
12  chomp $number2;            # remove "\n" from input
13
14  $sum = $number1 + $number2;
15
16  print "The sum is $sum.\n";
```

```
Please enter first number:
45
Please enter second number:
72
The sum is 117.
```

Fig. 2.4   Addition program.

contains our first *variable* (**$number1**). A variable refers to a location in the computer's memory where a value can be stored for later use by a program. In Perl, variable names always begin with a prefix called a *type identifier*. The type identifier **$** specifies that the variable **$number1** is a *scalar variable*. We discuss the term "scalar" in more detail in Section 2.7. For now, think of a scalar variable as a variable that holds a single piece of data, like a number or a string (such as a person's first name).

Common Programming Error 2.4

Forgetting to add the type identifier on a variable name is a syntax error.

In line 7 we use the *assignment operator* **=** to store a value in variable **$number1**. This operator is called a *binary operator*, because it takes two *operands* (in this case, **$number1** and **<STDIN>**). The whole statement is called an *assignment statement,* because the value on the right of the **=** is assigned to (stored in) the variable on the left. For example, the statement

```
$number1 = 12;
```

stores the number 12 in variable **$number1**.

In line 7, the expression **<STDIN>** determines the value assigned to **$number1**. The name **STDIN** is an abbreviation for *standard input*, which usually refers to the keyboard (the standard mechanism that allows a user to provide input to a computer program). The expression **<STDIN>** causes program execution to pause while the computer waits for the user to enter data. When the user types a value (such as 45) and presses the *Enter* key, the line of text entered (including, as we will see, the **\n** newline character the user inputs by pressing the *Enter* key) is assigned to variable **$number1**. [*Note:* Chapter 10 provides a more detailed discussion of the use of **<STDIN>**.]

If the user enters the number **45** (as we do in Fig. 2.4), variable **$number1** will contain the value "**45\n**", because **<STDIN>** returns the newline character as part of the line of text. Often when dealing with strings we want to eliminate this newline. On line 8, *chomp* examines its argument and removes the trailing newline. Otherwise, the value remains unchanged. Remember that you can enclose the arguments to built-in functions in parentheses, so **chomp** can also be invoked with the statement

```
chomp( $number1 );
```

Lines 10 through 12 repeat this procedure for a second number, whose value is assigned to variable **$number2**. The assignment statement in line 14

```
$sum = $number1 + $number2;
```

calculates the sum of the variables **$number1** and **$number2** and assigns the result to variable **$sum** by using the assignment operator **=**. So, if the user types 45 and 72 as the values for **$number1** and **$number2**, respectively, the value of **$sum** will be 117. The statement is read as, "**$sum** gets the value of **$number1** plus **$number2**." Most calculations are performed in assignment statements. Note that because the **+** operator takes two operands, it, like the assignment operator, is also a binary operator.

Good Programming Practice 2.5

Place spaces on either side of a binary operator. This makes the operator stand out and makes the program more readable.

Line 16

```
print "The sum is $sum.\n";
```

uses **print** to output the results of the calculation. Notice the variable name **$sum** in the string to be printed. When a scalar variable name appears in a double-quoted string, Perl *interpolates* the scalar. In other words, Perl inserts the scalar variable's value where the variable name appears in the string. Thus, if **$sum** contains the value 117, the argument to the **print** command is interpreted as **"The sum is 117."**.

2.4 Memory Concepts

In Perl, the values of variables are stored in the *symbol table*, which we discuss in detail later in the book. Here, we present some basic memory concepts to help you understand how a program stores, accesses and updates the values of variables. Variable names, such as **$number1**, **$number2** and **$sum**, actually correspond to *locations* in the computer's memory. Every variable has a *name,* a *type* and a *value.*

In the addition program of Fig. 2.4, when the statement

```
$number1 = <STDIN>;
```

executes, the program places the input value (i.e., the string of characters typed by the user) into the memory location to which Perl assigned the variable named **$number1**. Suppose the user enters the number **45** as the value for **$number1**. The program places the value "**45\n**" in the memory location for variable **$number1**, as shown in Fig. 2.5. Remember, when the user presses the *Enter* key, a **\n** (newline character) is appended to the end of the input string.

Whenever a value is placed in a memory location, that value replaces the previous value in the location. The previous value is lost. Thus, when **chomp $number1;** executes, it replaces the previous value of **$number1** (which was "**45\n**") with the new value "**45**" (see Fig. 2.6).

Now, suppose the user enters the value **72** (followed by the *Enter* key) in response to the statement

```
$number2 = <STDIN>;
```

$number1	45\n

Fig. 2.5   Memory location showing the name and value of a variable.

$number1	45

Fig. 2.6   Memory location of the variable after **chomp** is called.

The statement places the value **"72\n"** into memory location **$number2**. After function **chomp** is called with this value as its argument, the memory appears as in Fig. 2.7. Note that the locations are not necessarily adjacent to one another in the memory.

Next, the program adds the values of **$number1** and **$number2** and places the result in variable **$sum**. The statement

```
$sum = $number1 + $number2;
```

which performs the addition, also replaces the previous value of **$sum**; the previous value is lost. After **$sum** is calculated, the memory appears as in Fig. 2.8. Note that the values of **$number1** and **$number2** appear exactly as they did before they were used in the calculation of **$sum**. These values are used, but not destroyed, as the computer performs the calculation. Thus, when a value is read out of a memory location, the process is nondestructive.

2.5 Scalar Values and Scalar Variables

Now let us examine *scalar values* and *scalar variables*. The term *scalar*, when used in a scientific or mathematical context, refers to a simple or singular value that cannot be broken down into smaller components. Similarly, scalar values in Perl are the simplest building blocks for data in Perl.

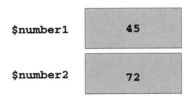

Fig. 2.7   Memory locations after the values for the two variables have been input and **chomp**ed.

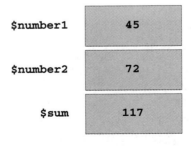

Fig. 2.8   Memory locations after the calculation.

Scalar values in Perl are generally classified as either numbers or strings. (Perl also has *references* that are scalars. References are discussed in Chapter 13.) A numeric scalar value can be an *integer* (such as 12 or -2), a *floating-point number* (i.e., a number with a decimal point, like 9.98, 682.000 and 0.82575), or a number in *scientific notation* (such as 3e8 and 6.62E-27, which are equivalent to 3 times 10^8 and 6.62 times 10^{-27}, respectively). Numbers may also be in binary, octal or hexidecimal formats (see the Number Systems appendix for more information on these number types.).

String scalar values can also be classified further as either *single quoted* (enclosed in **'** characters) or *double quoted* (enclosed in **"** characters). The strings we have seen up to this point have been double-quoted strings. When Perl encounters a double-quoted string, it interpolates variables (such as **$sum**) and escape sequences (such as **\n**) in the string. When Perl encounters a single-quoted string, it interpolates only the escape sequences **\'** and ****, for inserting single-quote characters and backslash characters in the string. The following statement would output the string exactly as it appears between the single quotes:

```
print 'The sum is $sum.\nThank you.';
```

A scalar variable is named as such because it contains a scalar value. As mentioned earlier, scalar-variable names always begin with a dollar sign (**$**). The dollar sign—a fancy "S"—reminds the programmer that the variable refers to a scalar value.

The dollar sign must be followed by a valid *identifier*. An identifier is a series of characters consisting of letters, digits or underscores (**_**) that does not begin with a digit. Perl is *case sensitive*—that is, it handles uppercase and lowercase letters as different characters—so **$sum** and **$Sum** are different identifiers.

Good Programming Practice 2.6

Choosing meaningful variable names helps a program to be "self-documenting," i.e., it is easier to understand the program simply by reading it, rather than having to read manuals or use excessive number of comments.

2.6 Arithmetic Operators

Many programs perform arithmetic calculations on scalars. The *arithmetic operators* are summarized in Fig. 2.9. All the operators shown are binary operators. Note the use of various special symbols not used in algebra, including the *asterisk* (*****), for multiplication, and the double-asterisk (******), for exponentiation.

In addition, the *percent sign* (**%**) is used in Perl as the *modulus operator*. The expression **$x % $y** yields the remainder after the value in **$x** is divided by the value in **$y**. Thus, **7 % 4** yields **3**, and **17 % 5** yields **2**. The operands of the modulus operator must be integers (i.e., whole numbers). If **%** is used with floating-point numbers, any fractional part is simply discarded (or *truncated*) before the operation is performed; no rounding occurs. So **9.8 % 5** is **4**, not **0**, because **9.8** is truncated to **9** before the modulus operation is performed. In later chapters, we discuss some interesting applications of the modulus operator, such as using it to determine if one number is a multiple of another. (A special case of this application is to determine if a number is odd or even.)

Arithmetic expressions in Perl must be entered into a computer in *straight-line form*. Thus, expressions such as "**$c** divided by **$d**" must be written as **$c / $d**. The algebraic notation

Operation	Arithmetic operator	Algebraic expression	Perl expression
Addition	+	$x + y$	`$x + $y`
Subtraction	–	$x - y$	`$x - $y`
Multiplication	*	xy	`$x * $y`
Division	/	x / y or $\dfrac{x}{y}$ or $x \div y$	`$x / $y`
Modulus	%	$x\ mod\ y$	`$x % $y`
Exponentiation	**	x^y	`$x ** $y`

Fig. 2.9   Arithmetic operators.

$$\frac{c}{d}$$

is generally not acceptable in computer programming languages, although some special-purpose software packages exist that support more natural notation for complex mathematical expressions.

Parentheses are used in Perl expressions in much the same manner as in algebraic expressions. For example, to multiply **$x** by the quantity **$y + $z**, we write

```
$x * ( $y + $z )
```

Perl applies the operators in arithmetic expressions in a precise sequence determined by the following *rules of operator precedence*, which are generally the same as those followed in algebra:

1. Operators in expressions contained within pairs of parentheses are evaluated first. Thus, *parentheses may be used to force the order of evaluation to occur in any sequence desired by the programmer.* Parentheses are said to be at the highest level of precedence. In cases of *nested*, or *embedded*, parentheses, the operators in the innermost pair of parentheses are applied first.

2. Next, any exponentiation operators are applied. If there are multiple exponentiation operators in a row, they are applied from right to left.

3. Multiplication, division and modulus operations are applied next. If an expression contains several multiplication, division and modulus operations, these operators are applied from left to right. Multiplication, division and modulus operations are said to be on the same level of precedence.

4. Addition and subtraction operations are applied last. If an expression contains several addition and subtraction operations, these operators are applied from left to right. Addition and subtraction operations also have the same level of precedence.

The rules of operator precedence enable Perl to apply operators in the correct order. When we say that certain operators are applied from left to right, we are referring to the *associativity* of the operators. For example, in the expression

```
$x + $y + $z
```

the addition operators (+) associate from left to right. We will see that some operators associate from right to left. Figure 2.10 summarizes the rules of operator precedence used in Perl. The table in the figure will be expanded as additional Perl operators are introduced. A complete precedence chart is included in the appendices.

Now let us consider several expressions in light of the rules of operator precedence. Each example lists an algebraic expression and its Perl equivalent.

The following is an example of an arithmetic mean (average) of five terms:

Algebra: $m = \dfrac{c + d + e + f + g}{5}$

Perl: `$m = ( $c + $d + $e + $f + $g ) / 5;`

The parentheses are required, because division has higher precedence than addition. The entire quantity **($c + $d + $e + $f + $g)** is to be divided by **5**. If the parentheses are erroneously omitted, we obtain **$c + $d + $e + $f + $g / 5** which evaluates incorrectly as

$$c + d + e + f + \frac{g}{5}$$

The following is the equation of a straight line:

Algebra: $y = mx + b$

Perl: `$y = $m * $x + $b;`

No parentheses are required. The multiplication is applied first, because multiplication has a higher precedence than addition.

Operator(s)	Operation(s)	Order of evaluation (precedence)
( )	Parentheses	Evaluated first. If the parentheses are nested, the expression in the innermost pair is evaluated first. If there are several pairs of parentheses "on the same level" (i.e., not nested), they are evaluated left to right.
**	Exponentiation	Evaluated second. If there is more than one, the operators are evaluated from right to left.
*, / or %	Multiplication Division Modulus	Evaluated third. If there is more than one, the operators are evaluated from left to right.
+ or −	Addition Subtraction	Evaluated last. If there is more than one, the operators are evaluated from left to right.

Fig. 2.10 Precedence of arithmetic operators.

The following example contains modulus (**%**), multiplication, division, addition and subtraction operations:

Algebra: $z = pr\%q + w/x - y$

Perl: **$z   = $p   * $r   % $q   + $w   / $x   - $y;**

⑥   ①   ②   ④   ③   ⑤

The circled numbers under the statement indicate the order in which Perl applies the operators. The multiplication, modulus and division operators are evaluated first in left-to-right order (i.e., they associate from left to right), because they have higher precedence than addition and subtraction operators. The addition and subtraction operators are applied next. These are also applied left to right. The assignment operator is applied last.

When parentheses are used to force evaluation order, the innermost set of nested parentheses is handled first. For example, in the expression **3 * (4 + (5 % 3))**, the modulus operation is calculated first, giving us the expression **3 * (4 + 2)**. The addition is performed next, resulting in **3 * 6**. Finally the multiplication is performed last, to produce the final value, **18**.

Not all expressions with several pairs of parentheses contain nested parentheses. For example, the expression

$j * ($k + $l) + $l * ($m + $n)

does not contain nested parentheses. These parentheses are said to be "on the same level."

To develop a better understanding of the rules of operator precedence, consider how a second-degree polynomial is evaluated:

Algebra: $y = ax^2 + bx + c$

Perl: **$y   = $a   * $x   **   2   + $b   * $x   + $c;**

⑥   ②   ①   ④   ③   ⑤

The circled numbers under the statement indicate the order in which Perl applies the operators. Suppose **$a** is **2**, **$b** is **3**, **$c** is **7** and **$x** is **5**. Figure 2.11 illustrates the order in which the operators are applied in the preceding second-degree polynomial using the foregoing values.

The preceding assignment statement can be parenthesized unnecessarily, for clarity as

$y = ($a * ($x ** 2)) + ($b * $x) + $c;

Good Programming Practice 2.7

As in algebra, it is acceptable to place unnecessary parentheses in an expression to make the expression clearer. These parentheses are called redundant parentheses. *Redundant parentheses are commonly used to group subexpressions in a large expression to make the expression clearer. Breaking a large statement into a sequence of shorter, simpler statements can also promote clarity.*

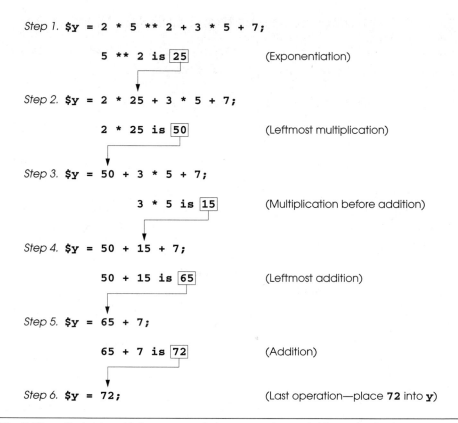

Step 1. `$y = 2 * 5 ** 2 + 3 * 5 + 7;`

        `5 ** 2 is 25`   (Exponentiation)

Step 2. `$y = 2 * 25 + 3 * 5 + 7;`

        `2 * 25 is 50`   (Leftmost multiplication)

Step 3. `$y = 50 + 3 * 5 + 7;`

        `3 * 5 is 15`   (Multiplication before addition)

Step 4. `$y = 50 + 15 + 7;`

        `50 + 15 is 65`   (Leftmost addition)

Step 5. `$y = 65 + 7;`

        `65 + 7 is 72`   (Addition)

Step 6. `$y = 72;`   (Last operation—place **72** into **y**)

Fig. 2.11   Order in which a second-degree polynomial is evaluated.

2.7 Assignment Operators

Perl provides several assignment operators for abbreviating arithmetic operations in assignment expressions. For example, the statement

    `$c = $c + 3;`

can be abbreviated with the *addition assignment operator* **+=** as

    `$c += 3;`

The **+=** operator adds the value of the expression on the right of the operator to the value of the variable on the left of the operator and stores the result in the variable on the left of the operator. Any statement of the form

    variable **=** *variable operator expression***;**

where *operator* is one of the binary operators **+**, **−**, *****, **/** and **%** (or others we will discuss later in the text), can be written in the form

    *variable operator***=** *expression***;**

Thus the assignment **$c += 3** adds **3** to **$c**. Figure 2.12 shows the arithmetic assignment operators, sample expressions using the operators and explanations.

Assignment operator	Sample expression	Explanation	Assigns
Assume that: $c = 3, $d = 5, $e = 4, $f = 6, $g = 12 and $h = 5.			
+=	$c += 7	$c = $c + 7	10 to $c
-=	$d -= 4	$d = $d - 4	1 to $d
*=	$e *= 5	$e = $e * 5	20 to $e
/=	$f /= 3	$f = $f / 3	2 to $f
%=	$g %= 9	$g = $g % 9	3 to $g
**=	$h **= 2	$h = $h ** 2	25 to $h

Fig. 2.12 Arithmetic assignment operators.

2.8 Increment and Decrement Operators

Perl also provides the **++** unary *increment operator* and the **--** unary *decrement operator*, which are summarized in Fig. 2.13. Note that a *unary operator* takes only one operand. If a variable **$c** needs to be incremented by 1, the increment operator **++** can be used to do so, rather than the expressions **$c = $c + 1** or **$c += 1**. If an increment or decrement operator is placed before a variable name, it is referred to as the *preincrement* or *predecrement operator*, respectively. If an increment or decrement operator is placed after a variable name, it is referred to as the *postincrement* or *postdecrement operator*, respectively. Preincrementing/predecrementing a variable causes the variable to be incremented/decremented by 1; then the new value of the variable is used in the expression in which the variable appears. Postincrementing/postdecrementing a variable causes the current value of the variable to be used in the expression in which the variable appears; then the value of the variable is incremented/decremented by 1.

Operator	Name	Sample expression	Explanation
++	preincrement	++$c	Increment $c by 1, then use the new value of $c in the expression in which $c resides.
++	postincrement	$c++	Use the current value of $c in the expression in which $c resides, then increment $c by 1.
--	predecrement	--$d	Decrement $d by 1, then use the new value of $d in the expression in which $d resides.
--	postdecrement	$d--	Use the current value of $d in the expression in which $d resides, then decrement $d by 1.

Fig. 2.13 Increment and decrement operators.

The program in Fig. 2.14 demonstrates the difference between the preincrementing version and the postincrementing version of the **++** operator. Postincrementing the variable **$c** causes it to be incremented after it is used in the output statement. Preincrementing the variable **$d** causes it to be incremented before it is used in the output statement. The decrement operator (**--**) works similarly.

Good Programming Practice 2.8

Unary operators should be placed next to their operands, with no intervening spaces. For example, we should enter **variableName++***, not* **variableName ++***.*

The statement

```
$counter = $counter + 1;
```

can be written more concisely with an assignment operator as

```
$counter += 1;
```

with a preincrement operator as

```
++$counter;
```

and with a postincrement operator as

```
$counter++;
```

Note that, when incrementing or decrementing a variable in a statement by itself, the preincrement and postincrement forms have the same effect, and the predecrement and postdecrement forms have the same effect. It is only when a variable appears in the context of a larger expression that preincrementing the variable and postincrementing the variable have different effects (and similarly for predecrementing and postdecrementing). Also, preincrement and predecrement operate slightly faster than postincrement and postdecrement.

```
1   #!/usr/bin/perl
2   # Fig. 2.14: fig02_14.pl
3   # Demonstrates the difference between pre- and postincrement
4
5   $c = 5;
6   $d = 5;
7
8   print $c,    " ";          # print 5
9   print $c++,  " ";          # print 5 then postincrement
10  print $c,    "\n";         # print 6
11
12  print $d,    " ";          # print 5
13  print ++$d,  " ";          # preincrement then print 6
14  print $d,    "\n";         # print 6
```

```
5 5 6
5 6 6
```

Fig. 2.14   Preincrementing vs. postincrementing.

For now, only a simple variable name may be used as the operand of an increment or decrement operator.

Common Programming Error 2.5

Attempting to use the increment or decrement operator on an expression other than a simple variable name—e.g., entering **++ ($x + 1)**—*is a syntax error.*

Figure 2.15 shows the precedence and associativity of the operators introduced up to this point. The operators are shown from top to bottom in decreasing order of precedence. The second column describes the associativity of the operators at each level of precedence. Notice that exponentiation operators and the assignment operators **=, +=, -=, *=, /=** and **%=** associate from right to left. All other operators in the operator precedence chart of Fig. 2.15 associate from left to right, except for the increment and decrement operators, which have no associativity. The third column provides the names of the various groups of operators. An example of associativity is that addition is left associative. So, an expression like **$x + $y + $z** is evaluated as if it had been written **($x + $y) + $z**. Another example is that the assignment operator **=** associates from right to left. So, an expression like **$x = $y = 0** is evaluated as if it had been written **$x = ($y = 0)**, which, as we will soon see, first assigns **0** to **$y**, then assigns the result of that assignment (i.e., **0**) to **$x**.

2.9 Decision Making: Equality and Relational Operators

This section introduces a simple version of Perl's *if* *structure* that enables a program to make a decision based on the truth or falsity of some *condition*. If the condition is met, i.e., the condition is *true*, the statement in the body of the **if** structure is executed. If the condition is not met, i.e., the condition is *false*, the statement is not executed. We will see an example shortly.

Conditions in **if** structures can be formed by using the *equality operators* and *relational operators* summarized in Fig. 2.16. The relational operators all have the same level of precedence. The equality operators both have the same level of precedence, which is lower than the precedence of the relational operators.

Operator(s)	Associativity	Called
( )	left to right	parentheses
++ or --	none	increment and decrement
**	right to left	exponentiation
*, / or %	left to right	multiplicative
+ or -	left to right	additive
=, +=, -=, *=, /=, %= or **=	right to left	assignment

Fig. 2.15   Precedence and associativity of operators discussed so far.

Standard algebraic equality operator or relational operator	Perl equality or relational operator	Example of Perl condition	Meaning of Perl condition
Relational operators			
>	>	`$x > $y`	`$x` is greater than `$y`
<	<	`$x < $y`	`$x` is less than `$y`
≥	>=	`$x >= $y`	`$x` is greater than or equal to `$y`
≤	<=	`$x <= $y`	`$x` is less than or equal to `$y`
Equality operators			
=	==	`$x == $y`	`$x` is equal to `$y`
≠	!=	`$x != $y`	`$x` is not equal to `$y`

Fig. 2.16   Equality and relational operators.

Common Programming Error 2.6

A syntax error occurs if any of the operators ==, !=, >= and <= appear with spaces between its pair of symbols (such as < = instead of <=).

Common Programming Error 2.7

Reversing the order of the pair of operators in any of the operators !=, >= and <= (by writing them as =!, => and =<, respectively) is normally a syntax error. In some cases, writing != as =! will not be a syntax error, but will almost certainly be a logic error.

Common Programming Error 2.8

Do not confuse the equality operator, ==, with the assignment operator =. The equality operator should be read as "is equal to," and the assignment operator should be read as "gets," "gets the value of," or "is assigned the value of." Some people prefer to read the equality operator as "double equals." As we will soon see, confusing these operators may not necessarily cause an easy-to-recognize syntax error, but may cause subtle logic errors.

The example in Fig. 2.17 uses six **if** structures to compare two numbers input by the user. If the condition in any of these **if** structures is satisfied, the output statement associated with that **if** executes. The program and the input/output dialogs of three sample executions are shown in Fig. 2.17.

```
1   #!/usr/bin/perl
2   # Fig. 2.17: fig02_17.pl
3   # Using if statements with relational and equality operators
4
5   print "Please enter first integer: ";
6   $number1 = <STDIN>;
7   chomp $number1;
```

Fig. 2.17   Using equality and relational operators (part 1 of 2).

```
8
9    print "Please enter second integer: ";
10   $number2 = <STDIN>;
11   chomp $number2;
12
13   print "The integers satisfy these relationships:\n";
14
15   if ( $number1 == $number2 ) {
16       print "$number1 is equal to $number2.\n";
17   }
18
19   if ( $number1 != $number2 ) {
20       print "$number1 is not equal to $number2.\n";
21   }
22
23   if ( $number1 < $number2 ) {
24       print "$number1 is less than $number2.\n";
25   }
26
27   if ( $number1 > $number2 ) {
28       print "$number1 is greater than $number2.\n";
29   }
30
31   if ( $number1 <= $number2 ) {
32       print "$number1 is less than or equal to $number2.\n";
33   }
34
35   if ( $number1 >= $number2 ) {
36       print "$number1 is greater than or equal to $number2.\n";
37   }
```

```
Please enter first integer: 3
Please enter second integer: 7
The integers satisfy these relationships:
3 is not equal to 7.
3 is less than 7.
3 is less than or equal to 7.
```

```
Please enter first integer: 22
Please enter second integer: 12
The integers satisfy these relationships:
22 is not equal to 12.
22 is greater than 12.
22 is greater than or equal to 12.
```

```
Please enter first integer: 7
Please enter second integer: 7
The integers satisfy these relationships:
7 is equal to 7.
7 is less than or equal to 7.
7 is greater than or equal to 7.
```

Fig. 2.17   Using equality and relational operators (part 2 of 2).

Lines 5 through 11 prompt the user to input two numbers, read in the numbers and remove the newline characters with **chomp**. The **if** structure in lines 15–17

```perl
if ( $number1 == $number2 ) {
   print "$number1 is equal to $number2.\n";
}
```

compares the values of variable **$number1** and variable **$number2** to test for equality. [*Note*: that **$number1** and **$number2** must be numbers. If they are strings, this test should be handled differently, as we will see later.] If the values are equal, then the condition **$number1 == $number2** is true, and the statement in line 16 displays a line of text indicating that the numbers are equal. Otherwise, the test is false and line 16 is skipped— i.e., the message is not printed. Similarly, if the conditions in one or more of the remaining **if** structures in lines 19, 23, 27, 31 and 35 are true, the corresponding **print** statements display appropriate messages.

Notice that each **if** structure in Fig. 2.17 has a *body* that is enclosed by a pair of braces (**{ }**), which is required syntax. The code in the body of the **if** structure is indented to enhance program readability.

Common Programming Error 2.9

*Forgetting to type in the braces ({}) that delimit the body of an **if** structure is a syntax error.*

Good Programming Practice 2.9

*Indent the statement in the body of an **if** structure to make the body of the structure stand out and to enhance program readability.*

Good Programming Practice 2.10

There should be no more than one statement per line in a program—even though Perl allows each line to contain more than one statement.

Notice the use of spacing in Fig. 2.17. Remember that whitespace characters, such as tabs, newlines and spaces, are normally ignored by the compiler. So, statements may be split over several lines and may be spaced according to the programmer's preferences. However, it is incorrect to split identifiers, strings or other scalar literals (such as the number **1000**); in these cases, whitespace matters and is referred to as *significant whitespace.*

Common Programming Error 2.10

*It is a syntax error to split an identifier by inserting whitespace characters into it (e.g., writing **print** as **pr int**).*

Good Programming Practice 2.11

A lengthy statement may be spread over several lines. If a single statement must be split across lines, choose breaking points that make sense such as after a comma in a comma-separated list or after an operator in a lengthy expression. If a statement is split across two or more lines, indent all lines of the statement after the first.

Figure 2.18 shows the precedence of the operators introduced in this chapter. The operators are shown from top to bottom in decreasing order of precedence. The last two columns specify the associativity of the operators and the type of each operator.

Operators						Associativity	Type
( )						left to right	parentheses
++	--					none	increment and decrement
**						right to left	exponential
*	/	%				left to right	multiplicative
+	-					left to right	additive
<	<=	>	>=			none	relational
==	!=					none	equality
=	+=	-=	*=	/=	%= **=	right to left	assignment

Fig. 2.18   Precedence and associativity of operators discussed so far.

Good Programming Practice 2.12

*Refer to the operator precedence chart when writing expressions containing many operators. Confirm that the operators in the expression are performed in the order you expect. If you are uncertain about the order of evaluation in a complex expression, break the expression into smaller statements or use parentheses to force the order, exactly as you would do in an algebraic expression. Be sure to observe that some operators such, as assignment (**=**), associate from right to left, rather than from left to right.*

2.10 Confusing Equality (==) and Assignment (=) Operators

There is one type of error that Perl programmers, no matter how experienced, tend to make so frequently that we felt it was worthy of a separate section. That error is accidentally swapping the operators **==** (equality) and **=** (assignment). What makes these swaps so damaging is the fact that they do not cause syntax errors. Rather, programs with these errors compile correctly and run to completion, probably generating incorrect results through runtime logic errors.

There are two aspects of Perl that cause these problems. First, any expression that produces a value can be used in the condition portion of an **if** structure (or any other control structure, as we will see in Chapter 3). If the expression evaluates to **0**, **"0"**, **""** or **undef** (the value for variables that are not yet defined), the condition is considered to be *false*. Any other value is treated as *true*.

Common Programming Error 2.11

*An expression is false if it evaluates to **0**, **"0"**, **""** or **undef**. Any expression that evaluates to some equivalent of zero is also false (e.g., **0.0**). For a string to be considered false, the string must have the value **"0"**, **""** or **undef**. Any other string value is considered to be true, including the string **"0.0"**.*

Second, Perl assignments produce a value, namely the value assigned to the variable on the left side of the assignment operator. For example, suppose we intend to write

```
if ( $paycode == 4 ) {
   print "You get a bonus!\n";
}
```

but we accidentally write

```
if ( $paycode = 4 ) {
    print "You get a bonus!\n";
}
```

The first **if** structure properly awards a bonus to the person whose **$paycode** is equal to 4. The second **if** structure—the one with the error—evaluates the assignment expression in the **if** condition to the constant **4**—a true value. The condition in this **if** structure is *always* true, so the person receives a bonus regardless of their actual paycode! Even worse, the paycode has been modified when it was only supposed to be examined!

Common Programming Error 2.12

*Using the operator **==** for assignment and the operator **=** for equality are logic errors, but not syntax errors.*

Testing and Debugging Tip 2.3

*Programmers normally write conditions such as **$x == 7** with the variable name on the left and the constant on the right. By reversing these so that the constant is on the left and the variable name is on the right, as in **7 == $x**, the programmer who accidentally replaces the **==** operator with **=** will be protected by the compiler. The compiler will treat this as a syntax error, because a constant cannot be placed on the left-hand side of an assignment statement. At least this will prevent the potential devastation of a run-time logic error.*

Variable names are said to be *lvalues* (for "left-hand values"), because they can be used on the left side of an assignment operator. Constants are said to be *rvalues* (for "right-hand values"), because they can be used only on the right side of an assignment operator. Note that *lvalues* can also be used as *rvalues*, but not vice versa.

Accidentally using **==** where **=** was intended can be equally unpleasant. Suppose the programmer wants to assign a value to a variable with a simple statement like

```
$x = 1;
```

but instead writes

```
$x == 1;
```

This expression is not a syntax error. The compiler simply evaluates the conditional expression. If **$x** is equal to **1**, the condition is true. If **$x** is not equal to **1**, the condition is false. Regardless of the expression's value, there is no assignment operator, so the value is simply discarded, and the value of **$x** remains unaltered, probably causing an run-time logic error. Such an error can be tricky to find, unless you run your programs using **perl** with the **-w** command-line option, as in

```
perl -w filename
```

This command requests that **perl** report additional *warning messages*. In the case of the accidental use of **==**, **perl** will likely catch the error and return a message like

```
Useless use of numeric eq (==) in void context
```

with the line number of the expression that contains the problem.

Testing and Debugging Tip 2.4

When running a Perl program, use **perl***'s* **-w** *command-line option to enable reporting of warning messages. Such messages may help you identify logic errors in your code.*

Testing and Debugging Tip 2.5

Many Perl programmers simply add the **-w** *option to the end of the shebang construct, as in* **#!/usr/bin/perl -w**. *On UNIX and Linux systems, this command forces the program always to execute with warnings enabled.*

2.11 String Operators

Just as Perl has a collection of arithmetic, equality, and relational operators for use with numeric scalars, Perl also has a set of operators for string scalars, some of which have numeric counterparts that perform analogous functions. For example, the **eq** ("equals") and **ne** ("not equals") operators test for the equality or inequality of strings, just as the **==** and **!=** do for numbers. String comparisons are case sensitive, so **"august"** does not equal **"August"**. Also, whitespace is significant in string comparisons, so neither of the previous two strings equals **"Aug ust"**.

Likewise, operators **lt** ("less than"), **gt** ("greater than"), **le** ("less than or equal"), and **ge** ("greater than or equal") correspond to numeric operators **<**, **>**, **<=** and **>=**, respectively. Roughly speaking, these string-comparison operators compare strings alphabetically, with the letters later in the alphabet having "greater" value. Thus, Perl considers **"rabbit"** to be greater than **"dragon"** and **"trombone"** to be less than **"trumpet"**. The following **if** conditions would both return true:

```
if ( "rabbit" gt "dragon" )
if ( "trombone" lt "trumpet" )
```

String comparisons are performed using the *ASCII value* of each character. The *ASCII* (*American Standard Code for Information Interchange*) *character set* defines a numeric code for a certain set of 128 characters, including the letters **A** through **Z** (capital and lowercase), the digits **0** through **9** and special characters like the newline. The ASCII value of the letter **r** (114) is greater than that of the letter **d** (100), so a word beginning with **r** is considered greater than one beginning with **d**. A word beginning with **A** (65) is "less than" a word beginning with **a** (97).

These comparisons are performed one character at a time, beginning at the first character of each string and proceeding through both strings until the first inequality is found. This system can lead to strange results, such as in the comparison of **"100"** with **"2"**, because the ASCII value of **1** (49) is less than that of **2** (50), the string **"100"** is considered to be the lesser of the two.

Finally, in the special case where one string is the prefix of another (e.g., **"dog"** and **"doghouse"**), the string relational operators regard the longer string as greater than the other. So **"doghouse" gt "dog"** is true.

Perl also has special operators for "adding" and "multiplying" strings—the *concatenation operator*, **.**, and the *string repetition operator*, **x**. The concatenation operator simply joins (concatenates) two or more strings together. So, after execution of the code

```
$name = "Emily";
$greeting = "Hello, " . $name . "!";
```

the variable **$greeting** contains the string **Hello, Emily!**.

Common Programming Error 2.13

Using a comma instead of the concatenation operator (.) when trying to join two strings together is a logic error and will produce incorrect results.

The string repetition operator (**x**) takes a numeric operand on its right-hand side and concatenates together that many copies of the string on its left-hand side. So,

```
$lamp = "wish" x 3;
```

assigns the string **"wishwishwish"** to **$lamp**. If the numeric operand is less than 1, the empty string, **""** , is returned.

The **++** operator also functions on strings, performing postincrementation or preincrementation depending on its placement relative to the variable. For example, a variable with a value of **"a"** becomes **"b"** after incrementation, and **"David"** becomes **"Davie"**. These increments also "carry," so incrementing a variable with value **"z"** yields **"aa"**, and incrementing **"29"** yields **"30"**.

2.12 Numeric and String Contexts

You might be wondering if there are other operators that work with both strings and numbers, like the operator **++**. Before we answer this question, you need a basic understanding of how Perl distinguishes between strings and numbers.

In many other programming languages (such as C++ and Java), variables must be declared to contain a particular data type before they can be used in a program. For example, the statement

```
int counter;
```

in C++ declares a variable named **counter** as an integer variable (i.e., a location where whole numbers such as 7 and -32 can be stored). After the variable **counter** is designated to hold an integer, **counter** cannot be used to store any noninteger value. Because data types are strongly controlled in these languages, we say that C++ and Java are *strongly typed languages*.

By contrast, Perl scalar variables are more flexible, in that they can refer to either a string or a number, there is no need to predeclare the variable as one type or the other. The variable's value converts to a number or a string automatically, depending on the *context* in which it is used. For this reason, it is crucial when programming in Perl to be aware at all times of the context in which a scalar variable is used.

Testing and Debugging Tip 2.6

*In some cases, using **perl** with the **-w** option displays warning messages when a value is used in an improper context.*

For example, when we read input from a user with the statement

```
$number1 = <STDIN>;
```

the value assigned to **$number1** contains a string (**"43\n"**, for example). After we **chomp** off the newline, the variable's contents more closely resemble a number (**"43"**). In fact, when we add a value to **$number1** with the statement

```
        $sum = $number1 + $number2;
```

then its value (**43**) is certainly acting as a number. But we just as easily could have used **$number1** at this point in the program in a string context instead:

```
        $message = $number1 . " is the first number you typed.";
```

In this case, **$number1** is acting as a string (**"43"**) in a string concatenation expression.

Figure 2.19 shows a simple program that illustrates the rules Perl uses for conversion between strings and numbers. Line 9 applies the binary addition operator, **+**, to a number (**10.0**) and a string (**"Top 10"**). The string is evaluated in a numeric context, so Perl scans the string starting at the beginning and, finding nothing it can interpret as numeric, returns **0** instead. Thus, **$add** gets the value 10 + 0, or 10.

Line 12 uses the concatenation operator, so **$number** is evaluated in a string context. The value of **$number** is converted to a string, in this case **"10"**, which is concatenated with **"Top 10"** to form the string **"10Top 10"**.

```
1   #!/usr/bin/perl
2   # Fig. 2.19: fig02_19.pl
3   # Program to illustrate numeric and string context, and undef
4
5   $string = "Top 10";
6   $number = 10.0;
7   print "Number is 10.0 and string is 'Top 10'\n\n";
8
9   $add = $number + $string;           # 10 (not 20)
10  print "Adding a number and a string:         $add\n";
11
12  $concatenate = $number . $string;   # '10Top 10'
13                                      # (not '10.0Top 10')
14  print "Concatenating a number and a string: $concatenate\n";
15
16  $add2 = $concatenate + $add;        # 20 (not 30, not 1020)
17  print "Adding the previous two results:      $add2\n\n";
18
19  $undefAdd = 10 + $undefNumber;
20  print "Adding 10 to an undefined variable:  $undefAdd\n";
21
22  print "Printing an undefined variable:       $undefVariable(end)\n";
```

```
Number is 10.0 and string is 'Top 10'

Adding a number and a string:         10
Concatenating a number and a string: 10Top 10
Adding the previous two results:      20

Adding 10 to an undefined variable:   10
Printing an undefined variable:       (end)
```

Fig. 2.19   Illustrating context.

Line 13 adds the results of the previous two operations. This time, using **"10Top 10"** in a numeric context, the first two characters are recognized as a number and translated as the value **10**. Note that though other numeric characters are present (at the end of the string), Perl stops conversion at the first character that cannot be used in a numeric context. Thus, when performing arithmetic operations, we do not need to **chomp** input values.

 Good Programming Practice 2.13

> *Use **chomp** to eliminate newline characters from the end of numeric input values to help pre-vent misinterpretation of those values based on the context of their use.*

In Perl, uninitialized or undefined variables (i.e., variables that are used in a program before being assigned a value) have the special value **undef**, which evaluates differently depending on its context. This fact is illustrated in lines 19 through 22. When **undef** is found in a numeric context (e.g., **$undefNumber** in line 19), it evaluates to **0**. In contrast, when it is interpreted in a string context (such as **$undefVariable** in line 22), **undef** evaluates to the empty string (**""**). The value **undef** produces warnings when perl's **-w** flag is used.

We have introduced many important features of Perl, including displaying data on the screen, inputting data from the keyboard, performing calculations and making decisions. In Chapter 3, we build on these techniques as we introduce *structured programming*. We will study how to specify and vary the order in which statements are executed; this order is called *flow of control*.

2.13 Internet and World Wide Web Resources

www.geeksalad.org/business/training/perl
This is a tutorial that covers the basics of Perl. This tutorial assumes that the reader has had some pre-vious programming experience.

perl.about.com/compute/perl/msub3.htm
About.com's list of Perl tutorials.

www.geocities.com/SiliconValley/7331/ten_perl.html
The Take 10 Minutes to Learn Perl page. Teaches Perl basics by breaking down code segments. The examples are technical, and the explanations assume the reader has some programming knowledge.

agora.leeds.ac.uk/Perl/start.html
A quick and compact tutorial that covers the basics of Perl. The tutorial contains exercises and as-sumes a basic knowledge of UNIX.

www.astentech.com/tutorials/Perl.html
Astentech—"if you want to learn something for free." This site contains links to Perl/CGI tutorials (as well as tutorials for 50 other programming languages). The tutorials listed on this site are rated based on the level of the material covered in the tutorial (basic to advanced topics) and ease of use (provided by previous users).

www.effectiveperl.com/toc.html
Effective Perl Programming is an online book. The first couple of chapters contain the basics for learn-ing Perl.

home.bluemarble.net/~scotty/Perl/index.html
This is a "superbasic" tutorial that was designed for people with no programming experience who are working on the UNIX platform.

www.troubleshooters.com/codecorn/littperl/index.htm
Steve Litt's PERLs of Wisdom main page provides an introduction to Perl, as well as tips and pro-gramming pointers.

SUMMARY

- The Perl programming language facilitates a simple, structured and disciplined approach to computer program design.

- You can create a program by typing it into a text editor program.

- The Perl comment character (**#**) indicates that everything on the current line following the **#** is a comment and will be ignored when the program is run.

- Programmers insert comments to document programs and improve program readability.

- The shebang construct indicates the path to the Perl interpreter. The path refers to the location on the computer where the Perl interpreter resides.

- Every program should begin with a comment describing the purpose of the program.

- Function **print** instructs the computer to perform an action, namely to print the string of characters enclosed by the quotation marks to the standard output device, which is normally the screen.

- Strings of characters are sometimes called character strings, string literals or simply strings.

- Functions are program building blocks that perform actions. A Perl programmer typically uses built-in functions, user-defined functions and other statements to define a program's task.

- The backslash (****) is the escape character. It indicates that a "special" character is to be output. When a backslash is encountered in a string of characters, the next character is combined with the backslash to form an escape sequence.

- Some escape sequences are called special actions, because they do not display anything to the screen, but instead cause the **print** statement to perform a special action, such as move to a different position on the screen before displaying the next character in a string.

- Semicolons (**;**) separate Perl statements.

- The **perl** command loads a program into memory and checks it for syntax errors. If the program contains no syntax errors, the program executes.

- All Perl programs should be stored in files ending with the **.pl** extension.

- When you launch a program with the **perl** command, the program goes through compilation and execution phases. The compiler translates the Perl program into Perl opcodes (also called operation codes or PP codes)—the language understood by the Perl interpreter. If the program compiles correctly, the interpreter executes the opcodes during the execution phase. In this phase, the computer, under the control of its CPU and with the help of the Perl interpreter, interprets the program one opcode at a time, thus performing the actions specified by the program.

- Errors such as division-by-zero errors occur as a program runs, so these errors are called run-time errors, or execution-time errors. Fatal run-time errors cause programs to terminate immediately without having successfully performed their jobs. Nonfatal run-time errors allow programs to run to completion, often producing incorrect results.

- Whitespace characters (such as spaces, tabs and newlines) are ignored by Perl.

- A syntax error occurs when the compiler cannot recognize a statement, so the compiler normally issues an error message to help the programmer locate and fix the incorrect statement. Syntax errors are violations of the language. Syntax errors are also called compile errors, compile-time errors, and compilation errors, because they appear during the compilation phase.

- Set a convention for the size of indent you prefer, then uniformly apply that convention. We recommend using three spaces to form a level of indent.

- A prompt tells the user to take a specific action.

- A variable refers to a location in the computer's memory where a value can be stored for later use by a program.

- In Perl, variable names always begin with a prefix called a type identifier. The type identifier **$** specifies that a variable is a scalar variable.
- The assignment operator, **=**, stores a value in a variable.
- A binary operator is an operator that takes two operands.
- The name **STDIN** is an abbreviation for standard input, which usually refers to the keyboard (the standard mechanism that allows a user to provide input to a computer program).
- Function **chomp** examines its argument and removes the trailing newline.
- In Perl, the values of variables are stored in the symbol table.
- Every variable has a name, a type and a value.
- Scalar values are the simplest building blocks for data in Perl and are generally classified as either numbers or strings.
- Strings are either enclosed in **'** characters or in **"** characters.
- Perl interpolates variables and escape sequences in a double-quoted string.
- In a single-quoted string, Perl interpolates only the escape sequences **\'** and ****, for inserting single-quote characters and backslash characters, respectively.
- An identifier is a series of characters consisting of letters, digits or underscores that does not begin with a digit.
- Perl is case sensitive, so **$sum** and **$Sum** are different identifiers.
- Choosing meaningful variable names helps a program to be "self-documenting," i.e., it is easier to understand the program simply by reading it, rather than having to read manuals or use excessive numbers of comments.
- Arithmetic expressions in Perl must be entered into a computer in straight-linc form.
- Perl applies the operators in arithmetic expressions in a precise sequence determined by the rules of operator precedence.
- Parentheses are evaluated first, so they may be used to force the order of evaluation to occur in any sequence desired by the programmer. In cases of nested parentheses, the operators in the innermost pair of parentheses are applied first.
- When we say that certain operators are applied from left to right, we are referring to the associativity of the operators.
- The arithmetic assignment operators (**+=**, **-=**, ***=**, **/=** and **%=**) abbreviate arithmetic operations in assignment expressions.
- The **++** unary increment and **--** unary decrement operator add or subtract 1 from a variable.
- A unary operator takes only one operand.
- If an increment or decrement operator is placed before a variable name, it is referred to as the preincrement or predecrement operator, respectively. If the operator is placed after a variable name, it is referred to as the postincrement or postdecrement operator, respectively.
- Preincrementing/predecrementing a variable causes the variable to be incremented/decremented by 1, then the new value of the variable is used in the expression in which the variable appears. Postincrementing/postdecrementing modifies the variable after its original value is used in the expression.
- The **if** structure enables a program to make a decision based on the truth or falsehood of some condition. If the condition is true, the statement in the body of the **if** structure executes. If the condition is false, the statement does not execute.
- The body of the **if** structure is enclosed by a pair of braces (**{ }**), which is required syntax.

- If you are uncertain about the order of evaluation in a complex expression, break the expression into smaller statements or use parentheses to force the order.

- In a condition, if an expression evaluates to **0**, **"0"**, **""** or **undef**, the condition is considered to be false. Any other value is treated as true.

- Variable names are said to be lvalues, because they can be used on the left side of an assignment operator. Constants are said to be rvalues, because they can be used only on the right side of an assignment operator.

- When running a Perl program, use **perl**'s **-w** command-line option to enable reporting of warning messages. Such messages may help you identify logic errors in your code.

- The **eq** and **ne** operators test for the equality and inequality of strings.

- The string operators **lt**, **gt**, **le** and **ge** correspond to numeric operators **<**, **>**, **<=** and **>=**.

- String comparisons are performed using the ASCII value of each character.

- The ASCII character set defines a numeric code for a certain set of 128 characters, including the letters of the alphabet, the digits **0**–**9** and special characters, like the newline.

- The concatenation operator, **.**, simply joins (concatenates) two or more strings together.

- The string repetition operator, **x**, takes a numeric operand on its right-hand side and concatenates together that many copies of the string (or expression that produces a string) on its left-hand side.

- When programming in Perl, be aware at all times of the context in which a scalar variable is used.

- Uninitialized or undefined variables (variables that are used in a program before being assigned a value) have the special value **undef**, which evaluates differently depending on its context.

TERMINOLOGY

-- unary decrement operator
$ scalar variable
++ unary increment operator
<STDIN>
addition assignment operator **(+=)**
addition operator **(+)**
arguments
arithmetic mean (average)
arithmetic operators
ASCII
assignment operator **(=)**
assignment statement
associativity of operators
backslash escape sequence **(\\)**
binary operator
body
built-in function **print**
-c command-line option (compile)
carriage return escape sequence **(\r)**
case sensitive
character set
chomp
comment
comment character **(#)**
compilation errors

compilation phase
compile error
compiler
compile-time error
concatenation operator **(.)**
condition
context
cursor
data types
division operator **(/)**
dollar sign escape sequence **(\$)**
double quote escape sequence **(\")**
double-quoted string
embedded parentheses
eq ("equals") operator
equality operators **(==, !=)**
escape character **(\)**
escape sequence
exponentiation **(**)**
false
filename extension **(.pl)**
flags
flow of control
ge ("greater than or equal") operator
gt ("greater than") operator

horizontal tab escape sequence (`\t`)	runtime
`if` structure	runtime error
interpolate	runtime logic error
interpret a script	rvalues
interpretation phase	scalar values
`le` ("less than or equal") operator	script
locations in the computer's memory	self-documenting code
logic error	semicolon (`;`)
`lt` ("less than") operator	"shebang" construct (`#!`)
lvalues	single-quoted string
modulus operator (`%`)	standard input
multiplication operator (`*`)	statement
`ne` ("not equals") operator	straight-line form
nested parentheses	string repetition operator (`x`)
newline (`\n`)	structured programming
opcode	subtraction operator (`-`)
operand	syntax error
operator	true
order of evaluation	truncate
parentheses	type identifier
Perl	`undef` value
`perl` executable	valid identifier
postdecrement operator	variable
postincrement operator	variable name
predecrement operator	variable type
preincrement operator	variable value
prompt	`-w` command-line option to `perl`
relational operators (`<`, `<=`, `>`, `>=`)	whitespace
rules of operator precedence	

SELF-REVIEW EXERCISES

2.1   Fill in the blanks in each of the following statements:

a)   Many Perl programs begin with the _____.

b)   Perl statements are separated by a _____.

c)   The _____ function displays information on the screen.

d)   The escape sequence `\n` represents the _____ character, which causes the cursor to position itself at the beginning of the next line on the screen.

e)   _____ is used to obtain data from the keyboard.

f)   The type identifier _____ as the first character of the variable name shows that the variable is scalar.

g)   The _____ structure is used to make decisions.

2.2   State whether each of the following is *true* or *false*. If *false*, explain why.

a)   When the `print` function is called, it always begins printing at the beginning of a new line.

b)   Comments cause the computer to print the text after `#` on the screen when the program is executed.

c)   The escape sequence `\n` when used in a `print` statement causes the cursor to position itself at the beginning of the next line on the screen.

d)   Perl considers the strings `"number"` and `"NuMbEr"` to be identical.

e) The modulus operator (**%**) calculates the remainder when the first operand is divided by the second operand.

f) The arithmetic operators *****, **/**, **%**, **+** and **-** all have the same level of precedence.

g) A Perl program that prints three lines of output must contain three **print** statements.

h) A unary operator takes only one operand.

2.3   Write a single Perl statement to accomplish each of the following:

a) Prompt the user to enter an integer. End your prompting message with a colon (**:**) followed by a space, and leave the cursor positioned after the space.

b) Read an integer from the keyboard, and store the value entered in integer variable **$d**.

c) If the variable **$number** is not equal to **7**, print **"The variable $number is not equal to 7."**

d) Print the message **"This is a Perl program."** on one line.

e) Print the message **"This is a Perl program."** on two lines, where the first line ends with **Perl**.

f) Print the message **"This is a Perl program."** with each word on a separate line.

g) Print the message **"This is a Perl program."** with each word separated by tabs.

2.4   Write statements (or comments) to accomplish each of the following:

a) State that a program will calculate the product of three integers.

b) Prompt the user to input three integers from the keyboard.

c) Compute the product of the three integers contained in variables **$x**, **$y** and **$z**, and assign the result to the variable **$result**.

d) Print **"The product is"**, followed by the value of the variable **$result**.

2.5   Using the statements you wrote in Exercise 2.4, write a complete program that calculates the product of three integers.

2.6   Identify and correct the errors in each of the following statements:

```
a) print "The value is $number.\n;
b) if (  $c = 7 ) {
      print "c is equal to 7\n";
   }
c) if ( $c < 7 ); {
      print "c is less than 7\n";
   }
d) if ( $c => 7 ) {
      print "c is equal to or less than 7\n";
   }
```

ANSWERS TO SELF-REVIEW EXERCISES

2.1   a) shebang construct. b) semicolon. c) **print**. d) newline. e) **<STDIN>**. f) **$**. g) **if**.

2.2   a) False. Function **print** always begins printing where the cursor is positioned, and this location may be anywhere on a line of the screen.

b) False. Comments do not cause any action to be performed when the program is executed. They are used to document programs and improve their readability.

c) True.

d) False. Perl is case sensitive. Uppercase and lowercase letters as different characters.

e) True.

f) False. The operators *****, **/** and **%** are on the same level of precedence, and the operators **+** and **-** are on a lower level of precedence.

g) False. A **print** statement with multiple **\n** escape sequences can print several lines.

h) True.

2.3   a) `print "Enter an integer: ";`
    b) `$d = <STDIN>;`
    c) `if (   $number != 7   ) {`
           `print "The variable number is not equal to 7.\n" );`
        `}`
    d) `print "This is a Perl program.\n";`
    e) `print "This is a Perl\nprogram.\n";`
    f) `print "This\nis\na\nPerl\nprogram.\n";`
    g) `print "This\tis\ta\tPerl\tprogram.\n";`

2.4   a) `# Calculating the product of three integers`
    b) `print "Enter an integer: ";`
       `$x = <STDIN>;`
       `print "Enter an integer: ";`
       `$y = <STDIN>;`
       `print "Enter an integer: ";`
       `$z = <STDIN>;`
    c) `$result = $x * $y * $z;`
    d) `print "The product is $result\n";`

2.5   See the following code.

```perl
1   #!/usr/bin/perl
2   # Exercise 2.5: Ex02_05.pl
3   # Calculating the product of three integers
4
5   print "Enter an integer: ";
6   $x = <STDIN>;
7   print "Enter an integer: ";
8   $y = <STDIN>;
9   print "Enter an integer: ";
10  $z = <STDIN>;
11
12  $result = $x * $y * $z;
13  print "The product is $result\n";
```

```
Enter an integer: 3
Enter an integer: 4
Enter an integer: 5
The product is 60
```

2.6   a) Error: Double quotes (") are missing at the end of the statement.
       Correction: Add the quotes after the **\n**.
    b) Error: Incorrect use of **=**. We want to test for equality, not assign a value.
       Correction: Replace **=** with **==**.
    c) Error: Semicolon after the right parenthesis of the condition in the **if** statement.
       Correction: Remove the semicolon after the right parenthesis.
    d) Error: The relational operator **=>** has its characters reversed.
       Correction: Change **=>** to **>=**.

EXERCISES

2.7   Write a program that asks the user to enter two numbers and prints the sum, product, difference and quotient of the two numbers.

2.8   Write a program that asks the user to input the radius of a circle and prints the circle's diameter, circumference and area. Use the value 3.14159 for π. Use the following formulas (r is the radius): diameter = 2r, circumference = 2πr, area = πr^2.

2.9   Write a program that asks the user to input one number consisting of five digits, separates the number into its individual digits and prints the fifth digit five times, the fourth digit four times, the third digit three times and so forth.

2.10   Write a program that reads in two integers and determines if either is a multiple of the other.

2.11   Write a program that reads two strings input by the user and prints them in alphabetical order, separated by a space. If the two strings are equal, they should be printed on separate lines.

2.12   One interesting application of computers is drawing graphs and bar charts (sometimes called "histograms"). Write a program that reads five numbers (each between 1 and 30) from user input. For each number read, your program should print a line containing that number of adjacent asterisks. For example, if your program reads the number 7, it should print *******.

2.13   Write a program that asks the user to input an integer, then prints a hollow square of asterisks. For example, if the user inputs 5, the output should be as follows:

```
*****
*   *
*   *
*   *
*****
```

3

Control Structures: Part I

Objectives

- To understand basic problem-solving techniques.
- To be able to develop algorithms through the process of top-down, stepwise refinement.
- To be able to use the **if**, **if/else** and **if/elsif/ else** selection structures to choose among alternative actions.
- To be able to use the **while**, **until**, **do/while** and **do/until** repetition structures to execute statements in a program repeatedly.
- To understand counter-controlled repetition and sentinel-controlled repetition.

Let's all move one place on.
Lewis Carroll

The wheel is come full circle.
William Shakespeare, *King Lear*

How many apples fell on Newton's head before he took the hint!
Robert Frost, *Comment*

3.1 Introduction[1]

Before writing a program to solve a particular problem, it is essential to have a thorough understanding of the problem and a carefully planned approach to solving the problem. When writing a program, it is equally essential to understand the types of building blocks that are available and to employ proven program-construction principles. In this chapter, we discuss all of these issues through our presentation of the theory and principles of structured programming. The techniques that you will learn here are applicable to most high-level languages, including Perl.

3.2 Algorithms

Any computing problem can be solved by executing a series of actions in a specific order. A *procedure* for solving a problem in terms of

1. the *actions* to be executed and

2. the *order* in which the actions are to be executed

is called an *algorithm*. The following example demonstrates the importance of correctly specifying the order in which the actions are to be executed.

Consider the "rise-and-shine algorithm" followed by one junior executive for getting out of bed and going to work: (1) Get out of bed, (2) take off pajamas, (3) take a shower, (4) get dressed, (5) eat breakfast, (6) carpool to work.

---

1. Most of the content in this chapter is intended for people learning to program. Experienced programmers learning Perl can scan the chapter quickly.

This routine gets the executive to work well prepared to make critical decisions. Suppose that the same steps are performed in a slightly different order: (1) Get out of bed, (2) take off pajamas, (3) get dressed, (4) take a shower, (5) eat breakfast, (6) carpool to work. In this case, our junior executive shows up for work soaking wet. Specifying the order in which statements are to be executed in a computer program is called *program control*. In this chapter, we begin to investigate the program-control capabilities of Perl.

3.3 Pseudocode

Pseudocode is an artificial and informal language that looks like English and helps programmers develop algorithms. The pseudocode we present here is useful for developing algorithms that will be converted to structured Perl programs. Pseudocode is similar to everyday English; it is convenient and user friendly, but it is not an actual computer programming language.

Pseudocode programs are not actually executed on computers. Rather, they help the programmer "think out" a program before attempting to write it in a programming language, such as Perl. In this chapter, we give several examples of how pseudocode can be used effectively to develop structured Perl programs.

The style of pseudocode we present consists purely of characters, so programmers can conveniently type pseudocode programs using an editor program. The computer can display a fresh copy of a pseudocode program on demand. A carefully prepared pseudocode program can be converted easily to a corresponding Perl program. This conversion is done in many cases (as we will see in this chapter's examples) by replacing pseudocode statements with their Perl equivalents.

3.4 Control Structures

Normally, statements in a program are executed one after the other in the order in which they are written. This system is called *sequential execution*. Various Perl statements we will soon discuss enable the programmer to specify that the next statement to be executed may be a statement other than the next one in sequence. This is called *transfer of control*.

During the 1960s, it became clear that the indiscriminate use of transfers of control was the root of much difficulty experienced by software-development groups. The finger of blame was pointed at the **goto** *statement*, which allows the programmer to specify a transfer of control to one of a wide range of possible destinations in a program. The notion of so-called *structured programming* became almost synonymous with "*goto elimination*."

The research of Bohm and Jacopini[2] has demonstrated that programs can be written without any **goto** statements. The challenge of the era became for programmers to shift their styles to "**goto**-less programming." It was not until the 1970s that programmers started taking structured programming seriously. The results have been impressive, as software development groups have reported reduced development times, more frequent on-time delivery of systems and more frequent within-budget completion of software projects. The key to these successes is that structured programs are clearer, easier to debug and modify and more likely to be bug free in the first place. In this book, we also discuss object-

---

2. Bohm, C. and G. Jacopini, "Flow Diagrams, Turing Machines, and Languages with Only Two Formation Rules," *Communications of the ACM*, Vol. 9, No. 5, May 1966, pp. 336–371.

oriented programming—a technology also rooted in the 1960s that has greatly improved the software-development process.

Bohm and Jacopini's work demonstrated that all programs could be written in terms of only three *control structures*, namely the *sequence structure*, the *selection structure* and the *repetition structure*. The sequence structure is built into Perl. Unless directed otherwise, the computer executes Perl statements one after the other in the order in which they are written. The *flowchart* segment in Fig. 3.1 illustrates a typical sequence structure in which two calculations are performed in order.

A flowchart is a graphical representation of an algorithm or of a portion of an algorithm. Flowcharts are drawn using certain special-purpose symbols, such as rectangles, diamonds, ovals and small circles; these symbols are connected by arrows called *flowlines*.

Like pseudocode, flowcharts are useful for developing and representing algorithms, although pseudocode is preferred by most programmers. Flowcharts clearly show how control structures operate; that is all we use them for in this text.

Consider the flowchart segment for the sequence structure in Fig. 3.1. We use the *rectangle symbol*, also called the *action symbol*, to indicate any type of action, including a calculation or an input/output operation. The flowlines in the figure indicate the order in which the actions are to be performed: First, **$grade** is to be added to **$total**, and then **1** is to be added to **$counter**. Perl allows us to have as many actions as we want in a sequence structure. As we will soon see, anywhere a single action may be placed in a Perl program, we can place several actions in sequence.

When drawing a flowchart that represents a *complete* algorithm, an *oval symbol* containing the word "Begin" is the first symbol used in the flowchart; an oval symbol containing the word "End" is the last symbol used. When drawing only a portion of an algorithm, as in Fig. 3.1, the oval symbols are omitted in favor of using *small circle symbols*, also called *connector symbols*.

Perhaps the most important flowcharting symbol is the *diamond symbol*, also called the *decision symbol*, which indicates a decision is to be made. We will discuss the diamond symbol in the next section.

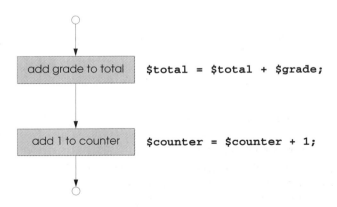

| add grade to total | `$total = $total + $grade;` |
| add 1 to counter | `$counter = $counter + 1;` |

Fig. 3.1   Flowcharting Perl's sequence structure.

Perl provides four types of selection structures. The **if** selection structure either performs (selects) an action if a condition (predicate) is true or skips the action if the condition is false. The **unless** *selection structure* is the opposite of the **if** selection structure: It either performs an action if a condition is false or skips the action if the condition is true. The **if/else** *selection structure* performs an action if a condition is true and performs a different action if the condition is false. We call the **if** selection structure a *single-selection structure*: It selects or ignores a single action. The **if/else** selection structure—a *double-selection structure*—selects between two different actions. Perl also provides the **if/elsif/else** *selection structure—multiple-selection structure*—which selects the action to be performed from many different actions.

Perl provides six types of repetition structures—**while, until, do/while, do/until, for** and **foreach**—some of which will be discussed in Chapter 5. Each of the words **if, else, elsif, unless, while, until, do, for** and **foreach** is a Perl *keyword*. These words are reserved by the language to implement various features, such as Perl's control structures.

Well, that is all there is. Perl has only 11 control structures: the sequence structure, four types of selection structures and six types of repetition structures. Each Perl program is formed by combining as many of each type of control structure as is appropriate for the algorithm the program implements. As with the sequence structure in Fig. 3.1, we will see that each control structure is depicted in a flowchart with two small circle symbols, one at the entry point to the control structure and one at the exit point. These *single-entry/single-exit control structures* make it easy to build programs; the control structures are attached to one another by connecting the exit point of one control structure to the entry point of the next. This method of program building is similar to the way a child stacks building blocks, so we call it *control-structure stacking*. We will learn that there is only one other way to connect control structures, called *control-structure nesting*.

Software Engineering Observation 3.1

Any Perl program we will ever build can be constructed from only 11 different types of control structures (sequence, if, unless, if/else, if/elsif/else, while, until, do/while, do/until, for and foreach) combined in only two ways (control-structure stacking and control-structure nesting).

3.5 `if` and `unless` Selection Structures

A selection structure is used to choose among alternative courses of action. For example, suppose a computer salesperson must sell 50 computers each month to meet a quota. The pseudocode statement

> *If computer sales are greater than or equal to 50*
> > *Print "Earned bonus!"*

determines if the condition "computer sales are greater than or equal to 50" is true or false. If the condition is true, then "Earned Bonus" is printed, and the next pseudocode statement in order is "performed" (remember that pseudocode is not a real programming language). If the condition is false, the print statement is ignored, and the next pseudocode statement in order is performed. Note that the second line of this selection structure is indented. Such indentation is optional, but it is highly recommended, because it emphasizes the inherent structure of structured programs. When you convert your pseudocode into Perl code, the

Perl compiler ignores *whitespace characters*, like blanks, tabs and newlines, used for indentation and vertical spacing, so the whitespace characters are strictly for the benefit of the programmer.

Good Programming Practice 3.1

Consistently applying reasonable indentation conventions throughout your programs greatly improves program readability. We suggest a fixed-size tab of about π inch, or three blanks, per indent.

The preceding pseudocode *if* statement can be written in Perl as

```
if ( $sales >= 50 ) {
    print "Earned bonus!\n";
}
```

Notice that the Perl code corresponds closely to the pseudocode. This correspondence is one of the properties of pseudocode that makes it such a useful program development tool. Notice that a set of curly braces (**{ }**) surrounds the body of code executed if the condition is met. The body of every control structure in Perl must be enclosed by curly braces; this is not the case in the C, C++ and Java programming languages. (There is actually one exception to this rule, and it is described later.) Also, note that there is no semicolon after the closing curly brace (**}**). Each control structure in Perl follows this syntax.

Good Programming Practice 3.2

Pseudocode is often used to "think out" a program during the program-design process. Then the pseudocode program is converted to Perl.

Common Programming Error 3.1

Forgetting to enter one or both of the braces surrounding the body of a control structure will lead to syntax errors in a program.

Good Programming Practice 3.3

Some programmers prefer to type the beginning and ending braces of compound statements before typing the individual statements within the braces. This practice helps avoid omitting one or both of the braces.

Perl offers some flexibility in writing control structures. If only one task is to be completed when a condition is met, such as in a **print** statement, Perl allows the code to be written as follows:

```
print "Earned bonus\n" if $sales >= 50;
```

This code is identical to the previous **if** structure, but is easier to understand, because it reads more like a sentence. Also, note that the parentheses around the test condition, **$sales >= 50**, are optional when this syntax is used and that curly braces are not necessary. This situation is the exception previously mentioned.

Continuing with the previous example, suppose the sales position is competitive and that the computer salesperson should not receive a bonus if they do not meet the quota. The pseudocode statement

Unless computer sales are greater than or equal to 50
    Print "You did not earn your bonus."

analyzes the same condition as the **if** statement, but has the opposite effect. If the condition "computer sales are greater than or equal to 50" is true, the print statement is ignored, and the program performs the next statement. If the condition is false, **"You did not earn your bonus."** is printed, and the next pseudocode statement in order is performed. The preceding pseudocode *unless* statement can be written in Perl as

```
unless ( $sales >= 50 ) {
    print "You did not earn your bonus.\n";
}
```

or alternatively as

```
print "You did not earn your bonus.\n" unless $sales >= 50;
```

The flowcharts in Fig. 3.2 illustrate the single-selection **if** and **unless** control structures. The flowcharts contain what is perhaps the most important flowcharting symbol: The *diamond symbol*, also called the *decision symbol*, which indicates that a decision is to be made. The decision symbol contains an expression, such as a condition, that can be either true or false. The decision symbol has two flowlines emerging from it. One indicates the direction to be taken when the expression in the symbol is true; the other indicates the direction to be taken when the expression is false.

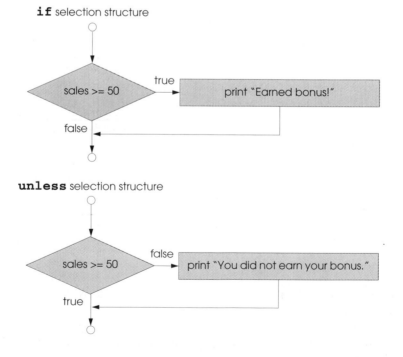

if selection structure

sales >= 50 — true → print "Earned bonus!"

false

unless selection structure

sales >= 50 — false → print "You did not earn your bonus."

true

Fig. 3.2   Flowcharting the single-selection **if** (top) and **unless** (bottom) control structures.

Note that the **if** and **unless** structures are single-entry/single-exit control structures. We will soon learn that the flowcharts for the remaining control structures also contain (besides small circle symbols and flowlines) only rectangle symbols, to indicate the actions to be performed, and diamond symbols, to indicate the decisions to be made. This system is the *action/decision model of programming* we have been emphasizing.

We can envision 11 bins, each containing only control structures of one of the 11 types. These control structures are empty. Nothing is written in the rectangles or in the diamonds. The programmer's task, then, is to assemble a program from as many of each type of control structure as the algorithm demands, combining those control structures in only two possible ways (stacking or nesting) and then filling in the actions and decisions in a manner appropriate for the algorithm. We will discuss the variety of ways in which actions and decisions may be written.

3.6 `if/else` and `if/elsif/else` Selection Structures

The **if** selection structure performs an indicated action only when the condition is true; otherwise, the action is skipped. The **if/else** selection structure allows the programmer to specify that a different action is to be performed when the condition is true than when the condition is false. For example, the pseudocode statement

> *If computer sales are greater than or equal to 50*
> > *Print "Earned bonus!"*
> *Else*
> > *Print "You did not earn your bonus."*

prints *"Earned bonus!"* if the employee's sales are greater than or equal to 50 and prints *"You did not earn your bonus."* if the employee's sales are less than 50. In either case, after printing occurs, the next pseudocode statement in sequence is "performed." Note that in pseudocode, the body of the *Else* is also indented (by convention).

Good Programming Practice 3.4

*Indent each statement in the body of **if/else** and **if/elsif/else** control structures.*

Whatever indentation convention you choose should be applied carefully throughout your programs. It is difficult to read programs that do not obey uniform spacing conventions.

Good Programming Practice 3.5

If there are several levels of indentation, each level should be indented by the same additional amount of space.

The preceding pseudocode **if/else** structure can be written in Perl as

```perl
if ( $sales >= 50 ) {
   print "Earned bonus!\n";
}
else {
   print "You did not earn your bonus.\n";
}
```

The flowchart in Fig. 3.3 nicely illustrates the flow of control in the **if/else** structure. Once again, note that besides small circles and arrows, the only symbols in the flowchart are rectangles (for actions) and a diamond (for a decision). We continue to emphasize this action/decision model of programming. Again, imagine a deep bin containing as many empty double-selection structures as might be needed to build any Perl program. The programmer's job is to assemble these double-selection structures (by stacking and nesting) with any other control structures required by the algorithm, and to fill in the empty rectangles and empty diamonds with actions and decisions appropriate to the algorithm being implemented.

Perl provides the *conditional operator* (**?:**), which is closely related to the **if/else** structure. The conditional operator is Perl's only *ternary operator*; it takes three operands. The operands, together with the conditional operator, form a *conditional expression*. The first operand is a condition, the second operand is the value for the entire conditional expression if the condition is true and the third operand is the value for the entire conditional expression if the condition is false. For example, the output statement

```
print ( $sales >= 50 ? "Earned bonus!\n" :
                       "You did not earn your bonus.\n" );
```

contains a conditional expression that evaluates to the string **"Earned bonus!\n"** if the condition **$sales >= 50** is true and evaluates to the string **"You did not earn your bonus.\n"** if the condition is false. Thus, the statement with the conditional operator performs essentially the same function as the preceding **if/else** statement. As we will see, the precedence of the conditional operator is low, so we suggest you use parentheses in a situation such as this one, although it is not required here.

The values in a conditional expression can also be actions to execute. For example, the conditional expression

```
$sales >= 50 ? print "Earned bonus\n" :
               print "You did not earn your bonus.\n";
```

is read, "If sales are greater than or equal to **50**, then **print "Earned bonus\n"**; otherwise, **print "You did not earn your bonus.\n"**." This expression, too, is comparable to the preceding **if/else** structure. We will see later that conditional operators can be used in some situations where **if/else** statements cannot be used.

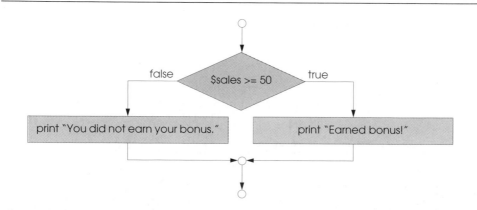

Fig. 3.3   Flowcharting the double-selection **if/else** control structure.

The *if/elsif/else* structure tests for multiple cases. For example, the following pseudocode statement prints **$1500 bonus!** for sales greater than or equal to 100, **$600 bonus!** for sales in the range 70 to 99, **$200 bonus!** for sales in the range 50 to 69 and **You did not earn your bonus.** for sales in the range 0 to 49.

> *If salesperson's sales are greater than or equal to 100*
> > *Print "$1500 bonus!"*
>
> *Else*
> > *If salesperson's sales are greater than or equal to 70*
> > > *Print "$600 bonus!"*
> >
> > *Else*
> > > *If salesperson's sales are greater than or equal to 50*
> > > > *Print "$200 bonus!"*
> > >
> > > *Else*
> > > > *Print "You did not earn your bonus."*

This pseudocode can be written in Perl as

```perl
if ( $sales >= 100 ) {
    print "\$1500 bonus!\n";
}
elsif ( $sales >= 70 ) {
    print "\$600 bonus!\n";
}
elsif ( $sales >= 50 ) {
    print "\$200 bonus!\n";
}
else {
    print "You did not earn your bonus.\n";
}
```

If **$sales** is greater than or equal to 100, the first three conditions are true, but only the **print** after the first test executes. After that **print** executes, each subsequent case is skipped. (Note that in the preceding **if/elsif/else** that we use the backslash **** to escape the dollar sign character so it is not interpreted as the beginning of a scalar variable name.)

The order of the conditions is important. For example, if the condition **$sales >= 50** were to appear before the condition **$sales >= 70**, the preceding structure would never give a $600 bonus. This would occur because every value greater than or equal to 50 would result in a $200 bonus, then the control structure would terminate.

Common Programming Error 3.2

*Spelling **elsif** as **elseif** is a syntax error.*

Performance Tip 3.1

*An **if/elsif/else** structure can be much faster than a series of single-selection **if** structures, because of the possibility of early exit after one of the conditions is satisfied.*

Performance Tip 3.2

*In an **if/elsif/else** structure, test the conditions that are more likely to be true at the beginning of the nested **if/elsif/else** structure. This will enable the **if/elsif/else** structure to exit earlier, and hence run faster, than if infrequently occurring cases are tested first.*

The **if**, **if/else** and **if/elsif/else** selection structures accept multiple statements in their bodies. To include several statements in the body, simply list one statement after another within the pair of curly braces (**{}**). A set of statements contained within a pair of braces is called a *compound statement*.

Software Engineering Observation 3.2

A compound statement can be placed anywhere in a program that a single statement can be placed.

The following example shows a compound statement in the **else** part of an **if/else** structure:

```
if ( $sales >= 50 ) {
    print "Earned bonus!\n";
}
else {
    print "You did not earn your bonus.\n";
    print "Try harder in the next sales period.\n";
}
```

In this case, if **$sales** is less than 50, the program executes both statements in the body of the **else** and prints

```
You did not earn your bonus.
Try harder in the next sales period.
```

Software Engineering Observation 3.3

Just as a compound statement can be placed anywhere a single statement can be placed, it is also possible to have no statement at all, i.e., the empty statement. The empty statement is represented by placing a semicolon (;) where a statement would normally be.

3.7 **while** and **until** Repetition Structures

A *repetition structure* allows the programmer to specify that an action is to be repeated while some condition remains true (or remains false). The pseudocode statement

> *While there are more items on my shopping list*
> *Purchase next item and cross it off my list*

describes the repetition that occurs during a shopping trip. The condition "there are more items on my shopping list" is either true or false. If it is true, then the action "Purchase next item and cross it off my list" is performed. This action will be performed repeatedly while the condition remains true. The statement(s) contained in the *while* repetition structure constitute the body of the *while*. The body of the *while* structure can be a single statement or a compound statement. Eventually, the condition will become false (when the last item on the shopping list has been purchased and crossed off the list). At this point, the repetition terminates, and the first pseudocode statement after the repetition structure is performed.

As an example of an actual **while** loop, consider a program segment designed to find the first power of 2 larger than 1000. Suppose the scalar variable **$product** has been initialized (set) to 2. When the following **while** repetition structure finishes executing, **$product** will contain the desired answer (and can be printed if we wish):

```
$product = 2;

while ( $product <= 1000 ) {
    $product = 2 * $product;
}
```

The flowchart in Fig. 3.4 illustrates the flow of control in the preceding **while** structure. Once again, note that the flowchart contains only a rectangle symbol and a diamond symbol (besides small circles and arrows). Imagine a deep bin of empty **while** structures that can be stacked and nested with other control structures to form a structured implementation of an algorithm's flow of control. The empty rectangles and diamonds are then filled in with appropriate actions and decisions. The flowchart clearly shows the repetition. The flowline emerging from the rectangle wraps back to the decision that is tested each time through the loop until the decision becomes false. Then, the **while** structure exits, and control passes to the next statement in the program.

When control enters the **while** structure, the value of **$product** is 2. The variable **$product** is repeatedly multiplied by 2, taking on the values 4, 8, 16, 32, 64, 128, 256, 512 and 1024 successively. When **$product** becomes 1024, the **while** structure condition, **$product <= 1000**, becomes false. This terminates the repetition; the final value of **$product** is 1024. Program execution continues with the next statement after the **while**.

Common Programming Error 3.3

*Spelling the keyword **while** with an uppercase **W**, as in **While** is a syntax error. (Remember that Perl is a case-sensitive language.) All of Perl's reserved keywords, such as **while**, **if**, **elsif** and **else**, contain only lowercase letters.*

Common Programming Error 3.4

*In the body of a **while** structure, not providing an action that eventually causes the condition in the **while** to become false normally results in an error called an "infinite loop," in which the repetition structure never terminates.*

The ***until*** *repetition structure* acts in an opposite fashion to the **while** repetition structure. The body of **until** repeats while its condition is false (i.e., until its condition becomes true). The repetition ceases when the condition is true. An example is as follows:

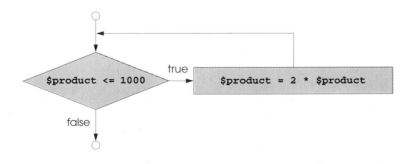

Fig. 3.4   Flowcharting the **while** repetition structure.

```
    $product = 2;

    until ( $product > 1000 ) {
        $product = 2 * $product;
    }
```

In this code, **$product** is repeatedly doubled until the condition, **$product > 1000**, becomes true. This code yields the same final value of **$product** as the preceding **while** version of the code.

3.8 do/while and do/until Repetition Structures

The *do/while* and *do/until* repetition structures are similar to the **while** and **until** structures. In both the **while** and **until** structures, the loop-continuation condition is tested at the beginning of the loop, before the body of the loop is performed. The **do/while** and **do/until** structures test the loop-continuation condition *after* the body of the loop is performed; therefore, the body of the loop will be executed at least once. When a **do/while** or **do/until** terminates, execution continues with the statement after the **while** or **until** clause. As with every Perl control structure, curly braces ({}) must enclose the body of the loop. For example,

```
    do {
        statement(s)
    } while ( condition );
```

or

```
    do {
        statement(s)
    } until ( condition );
```

Common Programming Error 3.5

Infinite loops are caused when the loop-continuation condition in a **while**, *for or* **do/while** *structure never becomes false. To prevent this situation from occurring, make sure the value of the condition does change somewhere in the header or body of the loop, so the condition can eventually become false.*

Common Programming Error 3.6

Infinite loops are likewise caused when the loop-continuation condition in an **until** *or* **do/until** *structure never becomes true. To prevent this situation from occurring, make sure the value of the condition does change somewhere in the header or body of the loop, so the condition can eventually become true.*

Figure 3.5 uses a **do/while** repetition structure to print the numbers from 1 to 10. Note that the control variable **$counter** is preincremented in the loop-continuation test.

```
1   #!/usr/bin/perl
2   # Fig. 3.5: fig03_05.pl
3   # Using the do/while repetition structure
4
```

Fig. 3.5   Using the **do/while** structure (part 1 of 2).

```
5    $counter = 1;
6
7    do {
8        print "$counter ";
9    } while ( ++$counter <= 10 );
10
11   print "\n";
```

```
1 2 3 4 5 6 7 8 9 10
```

Fig. 3.5   Using the **do/while** structure (part 2 of 2).

The program in Fig. 3.6 uses a **do/until** repetition structure to count down and print the integers from 10 to 1.

The **do/while** and **do/until** structures—as demonstrated in Fig. 3.5 and Fig. 3.6—are flowcharted in Fig. 3.7 and Fig. 3.8, respectively.

```
1    #!/usr/bin/perl
2    # Fig. 3.6: fig03_06.pl
3    # Using the do/until repetition structure
4
5    $counter = 10;
6
7    do {
8        print "$counter ";
9    } until ( --$counter == 0 );
10
11   print "\n";
```

```
10 9 8 7 6 5 4 3 2 1
```

Fig. 3.6   Using the **do/until** structure.

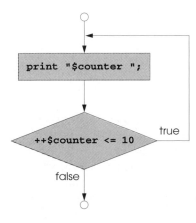

Fig. 3.7   Flowcharting the **do/while** repetition structure.

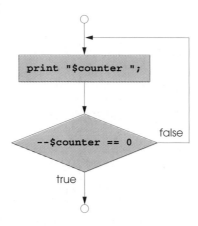

Fig. 3.8   Flowcharting the **do/until** repetition structure.

Each flowchart makes it clear that the loop-continuation condition is not executed until after the action is performed—in each case, once. Again, note that each flowchart contains only a rectangle symbol and a diamond symbol (besides small circles and arrows). Imagine, again, that the programmer has access to a deep bin of empty **do/while** and **do/until** structures—as many as the programmer might need to stack and nest with other control structures to form a structured implementation of an algorithm's flow of control. And again, the rectangles and diamonds are then filled with actions and decisions appropriate to the algorithm being implemented.

3.9 Formulating Algorithms: Case Study 1 (Counter-controlled Repetition)

To illustrate how algorithms are developed, we solve several variations of a sales-averaging problem. Consider the following problem statement:

Determine the average number of computers sold per week in a 10-week interval.

The sales average is equal to the sum of the weekly sales total divided by the number of weeks. The algorithm for solving this problem on a computer must take as input the number of computers sold each week, count the number of weeks, total the sales figures, perform the averaging calculation and print the result.

Let us use pseudocode to list the actions to be executed in the program and specify the order in which these actions should be executed. We use *counter-controlled repetition* to input the sales totals one at a time. This technique uses a variable called a *counter* to control the number of times a set of statements will execute. In this example, repetition terminates when the counter exceeds 10. In this section, we present a completed pseudocode algorithm (Fig. 3.9) and the corresponding program (Fig. 3.10). In the next section, we show the process of developing pseudocode algorithms. Counter-controlled repetition is often called *definite repetition*, because the number of repetitions is known before the loop begins executing.

Set total to zero
Set week counter to one

While week counter is less than or equal to 10
    Input the next sales amount
    Add the sales amount to the total
    Add one to the week counter

Set the sales average to the total divided by 10
Print the sales average

Fig. 3.9   Pseudocode algorithm that uses counter-controlled repetition to solve the average-sales problem.

```perl
1   #!/usr/bin/perl
2   # Fig. 3.10: fig03_10.pl
3   # Average-sales problem with counter-controlled repetition
4
5   # initialization phase
6   $total = 0;                    # clear total
7   $weekCounter = 1;              # prepare to loop
8
9   # processing phase
10  while ( $weekCounter <= 10 ) {    # loop 10 times
11
12      # prompt for input and input a sales value
13      print "Enter sales for week $weekCounter: ";
14      chomp( $sales = <STDIN> );
15
16      $total += $sales;          # add sales to total
17      ++$weekCounter;            # increment counter
18  }
19
20  $average = $total / 10;        # divide to find average
21  print "\nSales averaged $average computers per week\n";
```

```
Enter sales for week 1: 56
Enter sales for week 2: 52
Enter sales for week 3: 64
Enter sales for week 4: 72
Enter sales for week 5: 56
Enter sales for week 6: 58
Enter sales for week 7: 62
Enter sales for week 8: 63
Enter sales for week 9: 48
Enter sales for week 10: 52

Sales averaged 58.3 computers per week
```

Fig. 3.10   Average-sales problem with counter-controlled repetition.

Note the references in the algorithm to a total and a counter. A *total* is a variable used to accumulate the sum of a series of values. A counter is a variable used to count—in this case, to count the number of weekly sales figures entered. Variables used to store totals should normally be initialized to zero before being used in a program; otherwise, the sum will include the previous value stored in the total's memory location. We know that in Perl, unlike in many other popular programming languages, such as C and C++, undefined scalar variables will automatically be interpreted as zero in a numeric context; nevertheless, we explicitly initialize our variables here for clarity.

Lines 6 and 7

```
$total = 0;                      # clear total
$weekCounter = 1;                # prepare to loop
```

initialize **$total** to **0** and **$weekCounter** to **1**.

Note that variables **$total** and **$weekCounter** are initialized before they are used in calculations. Counter variables are normally initialized to zero or one, depending on their use (we will present examples showing each of these uses). An uninitialized variable has the value **undef**, which is treated as the value zero when used in a mathematical context.

Common Programming Error 3.7

If a counter or total that is supposed to be initialized is not initialized explicitly, Perl will set it to zero, probably causing your program to produce an incorrect result. This situation is an example of a logic error.

Good Programming Practice 3.6

Initialize counters and totals explicitly.

Line 10

```
while ( $weekCounter <= 10 ) {    # loop 10 times
```

indicates that the **while** structure should continue as long as **weekCounter**'s value is less than or equal to 10.

Lines 12–14

```
# prompt for input and input a sales value
print "Enter sales for week $weekCounter: ";
chomp( $sales = <STDIN> );
```

correspond to the pseudocode statement "*Input the next sales amount.*" The **print** statement (line 13) displays the prompt "**Enter sales for week** *week number*" on the screen. Line 14 asks the user to input the sales value, places the input into **$sales** and immediately **chomp**s off the newline character (**\n**) from the input value.

Common Programming Error 3.8

Forgetting to print a prompting message prior to waiting to receive input from the user can cause the user to think that the computer is "hung up" and will cause confusion. This situation can lead to serious program errors.

Next, the program updates **$total** with the new **$sales** value entered by the user. Line 16

```
$total += $sales;              # add sales to total
```

adds **$sales** to the previous value of **$total** and assigns the result to **$total**.

The program is now ready to increment the variable **$weekCounter** to indicate that a sales value has been processed and to then read the next sales value from the user. Line 17

```
++$weekCounter;                # increment counter
```

adds **1** to **$weekCounter**, so the condition in the **while** structure will eventually become false and terminate the loop after sales figures have been entered.

Line 20

```
$average = $total / 10;        # divide to find average
```

assigns the results of the averaging calculation to variable **average**. Line 21

```
print "Sales averaged $average computers per week\n";
```

displays the final results of the sales-average program.

Note that the averaging calculation in the program produced a floating-point result. There is no need to specify a specific number type when printing a scalar variable. We will discuss in Chapter 12 how to format output to specific styles and lengths.

Common Programming Error 3.9

When a counter-controlled loop completes, because the loop counter (when counting up by one each time through the loop) is one higher than its last legitimate value (i.e., 11 in the case of counting from 1 to 10), using the counter value in a calculation after the loop often causes an off-by-one logic error.

In Fig. 3.10, if line 20 used **$weekCounter** (which is 11 at this point) rather than 10 for the calculation, the output for this program would display an incorrect value of 53.

3.10 Formulating Algorithms with Top-down, Stepwise Refinement: Case Study 2 (Sentinel-controlled Repetition)

Let us generalize the average-sales problem. Consider the following problem:

Develop a sales-averaging program that will process sales totals for an arbitrary number of weeks each time the program is run.

In the first average-sales example, the number of weeks (10) was known in advance. In this example, no indication is given of how many weeks' sales data are to be entered. The program must process an arbitrary number of weeks. How can the program determine when to stop the input of weekly sales figures? How will it know when to calculate and print the sales average?

One way to solve this problem is to use a special value called a *sentinel value* (also called a *signal value*, a *dummy value* or a *flag value*) to indicate the end of data entry. The user types weekly sales figures in until all legitimate weekly totals have been entered. The user then types in the special sentinel value to indicate that no more sales figures are to be entered. Sentinel-controlled repetition is often called *indefinite repetition*, because the number of repetitions is not known before the loop begins executing.

Clearly, the sentinel value must be chosen so that it cannot be confused with an acceptable input value. Because Perl sees both numeric values and strings as scalar data, the sentinel value can be the simple string **quit**. Thus, a run of the average-sales program might process a stream of inputs such as 57, 86, 58, 48 and **quit**. The program would then compute and print the average for the sales values 57, 86, 58 and 48. (**quit** is the sentinel value, so it should not enter into the averaging calculation.)

Common Programming Error 3.10

Choosing a sentinel value that is also a legitimate data value is a logic error.

We approach the sales-average program with a technique called *top-down, stepwise refinement*, a technique that is essential to the development of well-structured programs. We begin with a pseudocode representation of the *top*:

> *Determine the average sales for the company*

The top is a single statement that conveys the overall function of the program. As such, the top is, in effect, a "complete" representation of a program. Unfortunately, the top (as in this case) rarely conveys a sufficient amount of detail from which to write the Perl program. So we now begin the refinement process. We divide the top into a series of smaller tasks and list the tasks in the order in which they need to be performed. This process results in the following *first refinement*:

> *Initialize variables*
> *Input, sum and count the weekly sales figures*
> *Calculate and print the weekly sales average*

Here, only the sequence structure has been used; the steps listed are to be executed in order, one after the other.

Software Engineering Observation 3.4

Each refinement, as well as the top itself, is a complete specification of the algorithm; only the level of detail varies.

Software Engineering Observation 3.5

Many programs can be divided logically into three phases: an initialization phase that initializes variables; a processing phase that inputs data values and adjusts program variables accordingly and a termination phase that calculates and prints the final results.

The preceding Software Engineering Observation is often all you need for the first refinement in the top-down process. To proceed to the next level of refinement, i.e., the *second refinement*, we commit to specific variables. We need a running total of the sales figures, a count of how many sales figures have been processed, a variable to receive each sales figure as it is input and a variable to hold the calculated average. The pseudocode statement

> *Initialize variables*

can be refined as follows:

> *Initialize total to zero*
> *Initialize week counter to zero*

Notice that only the scalar variables **$total** and **$weekCounter** need to be initialized before they are used; variables **$average** and **$sales** (the calculated average and the user input, respectively) need not be initialized, because their values will be written over as they are calculated or input. (Perl will nevertheless initialize all numeric variables to zero.)

The pseudocode statement

> *Input, sum and count the weekly sales figures*

requires a repetition structure (i.e., a loop) that successively inputs each sales figure. Because we do not know in advance how many weekly sales figures are to be processed, we will use sentinel-controlled repetition. The user will type legitimate weekly sales figures in one at a time. After the last legitimate sales figure is entered, the user will enter the sentinel value. The program will test for the sentinel value after each sales figure is input and will terminate the loop when the sentinel value is entered by the user. The second refinement of the preceding pseudocode statement is then

> *Input the weekly sales total (possibly the sentinel)*
> *Until the user has entered the sentinel*
> > *Add this week's total to the running total*
> > *Add one to the week counter*
> > *Input the next weekly sales total (possibly the sentinel)*

Notice that, in pseudocode, we do not use braces around the set of statements that form the body of the *Until* structure. We simply indent the statements under the *Until* to show that they belong to the *Until*. Again, pseudocode is only an informal program-development aid. We will indeed use curly braces to group the body statements of each control structure in actual Perl code.

The pseudocode statement

> *Calculate and print the weekly sales average*

can be refined as follows:

> *If the week counter is not equal to zero*
> > *Set the average to the total divided by the counter*
> *Else*
> > *Set the average to zero*
>
> *Print "Sales averaged* average *computers per week"*

Notice that we are being careful here to test for the possibility of division by zero—a *fatal logic error* that, if undetected, would cause the program to fail (often called "*bombing*" or "*crashing*"). The complete second refinement of the pseudocode for the sales-average problem is shown in Fig. 3.11.

Common Programming Error 3.11

An attempt to divide by zero causes a fatal error.

Good Programming Practice 3.7

When performing division by an expression whose value could be zero, explicitly test for this case and handle it appropriately in your program (such as by printing an error message), rather than allowing the fatal error to occur.

Figures 3.9 and 3.11 include some blank lines in the pseudocode to make it more readable. The blank lines separate the programs into their various phases.

Initialize total to zero
Initialize week counter to zero

Input the weekly sales total (possibly the sentinel)
Until the user has entered the sentinel
    Add this week's total to the running total
    Add one to the week counter
    Input the next weekly sales total (possibly the sentinel)

If the week counter is not equal to zero
    Set the average to the total divided by the counter
Else
    Set the average to zero

Print "Sales averaged average *computers per week"*

Fig. 3.11   Pseudocode algorithm that uses sentinel-controlled repetition to solve the average-sales problem.

The pseudocode algorithm in Fig. 3.11 solves the more general average-sales problem. This algorithm was developed after only two levels of refinement. Sometimes more levels are necessary.

Software Engineering Observation 3.6

Terminate the top-down, stepwise refinement process when the pseudocode algorithm is specified in sufficient detail for you to convert the pseudocode easily to Perl. Implementing the Perl program is then normally straightforward.

In this example, we see that control structures can be stacked on top of one another (in sequence) just as a child stacks building blocks. In the program in Fig. 3.12, the **until** structure (lines 11 through 16) is immediately followed by an **if/else** structure (lines 18 through 24) in sequence. Some of the code in this program is similar to the code in Fig. 3.10, so we concentrate in this example on the new features and issues.

```
1   #!/usr/bin/perl
2   # Fig. 3.12: fig03_12.pl
3   # Average-sales problem with sentinel-controlled repetition
4
5   $total = 0;
6   $weekCounter = 0;
7
8   print "Enter sales for week or enter quit: ";
9   chomp( $sales = <STDIN> );
10
11  until ( $sales eq 'quit' ) {
12      $weekCounter++;
13      $total += $sales;
14      print "Enter sales for week or enter quit: ";
15      chomp( $sales = <STDIN> );
16  }
```

Fig. 3.12   Average-sales problem with sentinel-controlled repetition (part 1 of 2).

```
17
18   if ( $weekCounter != 0 ) {
19       $average = $total / $weekCounter;
20       print "\nSales averaged $average computers per week.\n";
21   }
22   else {
23       print "\nNo sales figures were entered.\n";
24   }
```

```
Enter sales for week or enter quit: 57
Enter sales for week or enter quit: 86
Enter sales for week or enter quit: 52
Enter sales for week or enter quit: 48
Enter sales for week or enter quit: quit

Sales averaged 60.75 computers per week
```

Fig. 3.12   Average-sales problem with sentinel-controlled repetition (part 2 of 2).

Line 6 initializes the variable **$weekCounter** to **0**, because no weekly sales figures have been entered yet. Remember that this program uses sentinel-controlled repetition. To keep an accurate record of the number of weekly sales figures entered, variable **$week-Counter** is incremented only when a valid weekly sales figure is entered.

Notice that both input statements (lines 9 and 15)

```
chomp( $sales = <STDIN> );
```

are preceded by an output statement that prompts the user for input. This procedure is a good way to make the program easy to use.

Good Programming Practice 3.8

Prompt the user for each keyboard input. The prompt should indicate the form of the input and any special input values (such as the sentinel value that terminates a loop).

Good Programming Practice 3.9

In a sentinel-controlled loop, each prompt requesting data entry should explicitly remind the user what the sentinel value is.

Study the differences between the program logic for sentinel-controlled repetition in Fig. 3.12 that for the counter-controlled repetition in Fig. 3.10. In counter-controlled repetition, we read a value from the user during each pass of the **while** structure for the specified number of passes. In sentinel-controlled repetition, we read in one value (line 9 of Fig. 3.12) before the program reaches the **until** structure. This value is used to determine if the program's flow of control should enter the body of the **until** structure. If the **until** structure's condition is true (i.e., the user has already typed in the sentinel), the body of the **until** structure does not execute (i.e., no weekly totals were entered). If, on the other hand, the condition is false, the body begins execution and the sales figure entered by the user is processed (added to the **$total** in this example). After the value is processed, the next value is input from the user before the end of the **until** structure's body. As the closing right brace (**}**) of the body is reached at line 16, execution continues with the next test of the **until** structure's condition, using the new sales figure just entered by the user to determine if the **until** structure's body should execute again. Notice that the next sales figure is always input from the user immediately before the **until** structure's condition is evaluated. This allows us to determine if the value just entered by the user is the sentinel value *before* that value is processed (i.e., added to the **$total**). If the value entered is the sentinel value, the **until** structure terminates and the value is not added to the **$total**.

Lines 18–24 use an **if/else** structure to determine whether any weekly sales figures have been entered. As mentioned in our pseudocode, we must test for division by zero. Division by zero will lead to a *fatal error*. If **$weekCounter** is not **0** after the **until** structure, line 19 calculates the average and line 20 displays the results. Otherwise, if **$week-Counter** is **0** (false), then a string is output indicating that no weekly sales were entered.

As in our previous average-sales program, Perl prints **$average** as either an integer or a floating-point number, depending only on whether the numerator is evenly divisible by the denominator. Remember that both integers and floating-point numbers are scalar data and can be stored in any scalar variable, such as **$average**.

3.11 Formulating Algorithms with Top-down, Stepwise Refinement: Case Study 3 (Nested Control Structures)

Let us work through another complete problem. We will once again formulate an algorithm by using pseudocode and top-down, stepwise refinement and write a corresponding Perl program. We have seen that control structures can be stacked on top of one another (in sequence) just as a child stacks building blocks. In this case study, we will see the only other way in which control structures can be connected in Perl: through *nesting* of one control structure inside another.

Consider the following problem statement:

> *Naturally, the owner of our computer company wants to know how well his employees are selling computers. You have been asked to write a program to summarize the results. You have been given a list of the 10 salespeople. Next to each name is written "yes" if the salesperson has met his or her quota and "no" if the salesperson has not.*
>
> *Your program should analyze the summary as follows:*
>
> 1. *Receive as input each quota result (i.e., yes or no). Display the message "Enter quota result" on the screen each time the program requests another test result.*
>
> 2. *Count the number of quota results of each type, i.e., the number of "yes" responses and the number of "no" responses.*
>
> 3. *Display a summary of the quota results indicating the number of salespeople who have met their quota and the number of salespeople who have not.*
>
> 4. *If more than 8 salespeople have met their quota, print the message "Raise holiday bonuses!"*

After reading the problem statement carefully, we make the following observations:

1. The program must process 10 results. A counter-controlled loop will be used.

2. Each test result is a string—either "yes" or "no." Each time the program reads a result, the program must determine if the string is "yes" or "no." We test for "yes" in our algorithm. If the result is not "yes," we assume it is "no." (The reader should reflect on the consequences of this assumption. Normally, such assumptions are

not a good idea. We make the assumption here to simplify the code. Note that if the user of the program inputs "yed" by accident when he or she meant to input "yes", the result would be incorrectly evaluated as "no.")

3. Two counters are used: one to count the number of salespeople who met their quota and one to count the number of salespeople who have not.

4. After the program has processed all the results, it must decide if more than eight sales people have met their quota.

Let us proceed with top-down, stepwise refinement. We begin with a pseudocode representation of the top:

> *Analyze sales results and decide if holiday bonuses should be raised*

Once again, it is important to emphasize that the top is a complete representation of the program, but several refinements may be needed before the pseudocode can be evolved easily into a Perl program. Our first refinement is

> *Initialize variables*
> *Input the 10 quota results and count "yes" responses and "no" responses*
> *Print a summary of the results and decide if holiday bonuses should be raised*

Here, too, even though we have a complete representation of the entire program, further refinement is necessary. We now commit to specific variables. Counters are needed to record the number of "yes" responses and "no" responses; a counter will be used to control the looping process and a variable is needed to store the user input. The pseudocode statement

> *Initialize variables*

can be refined as follows:

> *Initialize metQuota to zero*
> *Initialize didNotMeetQuota to zero*
> *Initialize employee counter to one*

Notice that only the counters and totals are initialized. The pseudocode statement

> *Input the 10 quota results and count "yes" responses and "no" responses*

requires a loop that successively inputs each result. Here it is known in advance that there are precisely 10 results, so counter-controlled looping is appropriate. Inside the loop (i.e., *nested* within the loop), a conditional operator will determine whether each quota result is met and will increment the appropriate counter accordingly. The refinement of the preceding pseudocode statement is then

> *While employee counter is less than or equal to 10*
> > *Input the next quota result*
> >
> > *If the employee met quota*
> > > *Add one to metQuota*
> >
> > *Else*
> > > *Add one to didNotMeetQuota*
> >
> > *Add one to employee counter*

The pseudocode statement

Print a summary of the results and decide if holiday bonuses should be raised

can be refined as follows:

Print the number of people who met quota
Print the number of people who did not meet quota

If more than 8 employees met quota
    Print "Raise holiday bonuses!"

The complete second refinement appears in Fig. 3.13. Notice that blank lines are once again used to set off each of the control structures for program readability.

This pseudocode is now sufficiently refined for conversion to Perl. The Perl program and one sample execution are shown in Fig. 3.14.

Initialize metQuota to zero
Initialize didNotMeetQuota to zero
Initialize employee counter to one

While employee counter is less than or equal to 10
    Input the next quota result

    If the employee met quota
        Add one to metQuota
    Else
        Add one to didNotMeetQuota

    Add one to employee counter

Print the number of employees that met their quota
Print the number of employees that did not meet their quota

If more than 8 employees met quota
    Print "Raise holiday bonuses!"

Fig. 3.13   Pseudocode for quota-results problem.

```
1   #!/usr/bin/perl
2   # Fig. 3.14: fig03_14.pl
3   # Analysis of sales results
4
5   # initialize loop variables
6   $metQuota = 0;              # employees who met quota
7   $didNotMeetQuota = 0;       # employees who did not meet quota
8   $employeeCounter = 1;       # employee counter
9
```

Fig. 3.14   Quota-results problem (part 1 of 2).

```
10   # process 10 employees; counter-controlled loop
11   while ( $employeeCounter <= 10 ) {
12      print "Enter quota result, (yes or no): ";
13      chomp( $result = <STDIN> );
14
15      # conditional operator nested in while
16      $result eq 'yes' ? ++$metQuota : ++$didNotMeetQuota;
17
18      $employeeCounter++;
19   }
20
21   # termination phase
22   print "\nMet quota: $metQuota\n";
23   print "Failed to meet quota: $didNotMeetQuota\n";
24
25   if ( $metQuota > 8 ) {
26      print "Raise holiday bonuses!\n";
27   }
```

```
Enter quota result, (yes or no): yes
Enter quota result, (yes or no): yes
Enter quota result, (yes or no): no
Enter quota result, (yes or no): yes
Enter quota result, (yes or no): yes
Enter quota result, (yes or no): yes
Enter quota result, (yes or no): yes
Enter quota result, (yes or no): yes
Enter quota result, (yes or no): yes
Enter quota result, (yes or no): yes

Met quota: 9
Failed to meet quota: 1
Raise holiday bonuses!
```

```
Enter quota result, (yes or no): no
Enter quota result, (yes or no): no
Enter quota result, (yes or no): no
Enter quota result, (yes or no): no
Enter quota result, (yes or no): yes
Enter quota result, (yes or no): yes
Enter quota result, (yes or no): no
Enter quota result, (yes or no): no
Enter quota result, (yes or no): yes
Enter quota result, (yes or no): no

Met quota: 3
Failed to meet quota: 7
```

Fig. 3.14   Quota-results problem (part 2 of 2).

Lines 6 through 8

```
$metQuota = 0;          # employees who met quota
$didNotMeetQuota = 0;   # employees who did not meet quota
$employeeCounter = 1;   # employee counter
```

assign initial values to our total and counter variables. (**$metQuota** is assigned **0**, **$did-NotMeetQuota** is assigned **0** and **$employeeCounter** is assigned **1**.)

Software Engineering Observation 3.7

Experience has shown that the most difficult part of solving a problem on a computer is developing the algorithm for the solution. Once a correct algorithm has been specified, the process of producing a working Perl program from the algorithm is normally straightforward.

Software Engineering Observation 3.8

Many experienced programmers write programs without ever using program-development tools like pseudocode. These programmers feel that their ultimate goal is to solve the problem on a computer and that writing pseudocode merely delays the production of final outputs. Although this method may work for simple and familiar problems, it can lead to serious errors and delays on large, complex projects.

3.12 Internet and World Wide Web Resources

larc.ee.nthu.edu.tw/~cthuang/perl/03_control_structure.html
This site gives a basic overview of Perl control structures.

perl.about.com/compute/perl/library/weekly/aa112899.htm
This is a tutorial on control structures found on **about.com**.

www.cs.rpi.edu/~hollingd/eiw/5-Perl/control.html
This site presents Perl control structures and compares them with those in C.

agora.scs.leeds.ac.uk/Perl/control.html
This Web page is the portion of a Perl tutorial on control structures. It assumes the user has some previous programming experience. It compares Perl control structures to those found in C and Pascal.

home.bluemarble.net/~scotty/Perl/control.html
This is the section on control structures of a tutorial for people with no previous programming experience who are working off UNIX. It contains a brief explanation of the control structures found in Perl, including examples.

www.gamehendge.org/Marvin/Perl/ Teach_Yourself_Perl_in_21_Days/ ch8.htm
This site contains the chapter on control structures of an online book entitled *Teach Yourself Perl in 21 Days*.

www.internetz.com/programming/perl/control.html
This site is a good quick reference for the experienced programmer.

SUMMARY

- Any computing problem can be solved by executing a series of actions in a specific order.
- A procedure for solving a problem in terms of actions to be executed and the order in which the actions are executed is called an algorithm.
- Specifying the order in which statements execute in a computer program is called program control.

- Pseudocode is an artificial and informal language that looks like English and helps programmers develop algorithms. It helps the programmer "think out" a program before attempting to write it in a programming language, such as Perl.

- A carefully prepared pseudocode program converts easily to a corresponding Perl program.

- A program executes statements one after the other in the order in which they are written, unless otherwise specified. This system is called sequential execution.

- Various Perl statements enable the programmer to specify that the next statement to be executed may be a statement other than the next one in sequence. This process is called transfer of control.

- All programs can be written in terms of three control structures: the sequence structure, the selection structure and the repetition structure.

- A flowchart is a graphical representation of an algorithm or a portion of an algorithm. Like pseudocode, flowcharts are useful for developing and representing algorithms.

- Anywhere a single action may be placed in a program, several actions can be placed in sequence.

- The **if** selection structure either performs (selects) an action if a condition (predicate) is true or skips the action if the condition is false.

- The **unless** selection structure either performs an action if a condition is false or skips the action if the condition is true.

- The **if/else** selection structure performs an action if a condition is true and performs a different action if the condition is false.

- The **if** selection structure is a single-selection structure: It selects or ignores a single action.

- The **if/else** double-selection structure selects between two different actions.

- Perl provides the **if/elsif/else** multiple-selection structure, which selects the action to be performed from many different actions.

- The six Perl repetition structures are **while**, **until**, **do/while**, **do/until**, **for** and **foreach**.

- Each of the words **if**, **else**, **elsif**, **unless**, **while**, **until**, **do**, **for** and **foreach** is a Perl keyword. These words are reserved by the language to implement various features, such as Perl's control structures.

- Each Perl program is formed by combining as many of each type of control structure as is appropriate for the algorithm the program implements.

- Single-entry/single-exit control structures are attached to one another by connecting the exit point of one control structure to the entry point of the next.

- There are only two ways to connect control structures: control-structure stacking and control-structure nesting. Control-structure stacking refers to placing control structures one after another in sequence, while control-structure nesting refers to placing one or more control structures in the body of a control structure.

- Any Perl program we will ever build can be constructed from only 11 different control structures (sequence, **if**, **unless**, **if/else**, **if/elsif/else**, **while**, **until**, **do/while**, **do/until**, **for** and **foreach**) combined in only two ways (stacking and nesting).

- In Perl code, the compiler ignores whitespace characters, like blanks, tabs and newlines, used for indentation and vertical spacing.

- Consistently applying reasonable indentation conventions throughout your programs greatly improves program readability. We suggest three blanks per indent.

- Perl offers some flexibility in writing control structures. If only one task is to be completed when a condition is met, Perl allows the code to be written as *statement* **if** *condition***;**

- Perl provides the conditional operator **?:**, that is closely related to the **if/else** structure. The conditional operator is Perl's only ternary operator; it takes three operands.

- A set of statements contained within a pair of curly braces (**{}**) is called a compound statement. A compound statement can be placed anywhere in a program that a single statement can be placed.

- A repetition structure allows the programmer to specify that an action is to be repeated while some condition remains true or while some condition remains false (depending on the control structure).

- The body of **until** repeats while its condition is false (i.e., until its condition becomes true). The repetition ceases when the condition is true.

- In both the **while** and **until** structures, the loop-continuation condition is tested at the beginning of the loop, before the body of the loop is performed.

- The **do/while** and **do/until** structures test the loop-continuation condition after the body of the loop is performed; therefore, the body of the loop always will be executed at least once.

- Counter-controlled repetition is a technique that uses a variable called a counter to control the number of times a set of statements executes.

- Counter-controlled repetition is often called definite repetition because the number of repetitions is known before the loop begins executing.

- In Perl, undefined scalar variables are interpreted as zero in a numeric context.

- When a counter-controlled loop completes, because the loop counter (when counting up by one each time through the loop) is one higher than its last legitimate value, using the counter value in a calculation after the loop often causes an off-by-one logic error.

- We can use a special value called a sentinel value (also called a signal value, a dummy value or a flag value) to indicate the end of data entry. This procedure helps avoid off-by-one errors.

- Sentinel-controlled repetition is often called indefinite repetition, because the number of repetitions is not known before the loop begins executing.

- Top-down, stepwise refinement is a technique by which a problem is continuously broken down into smaller and smaller steps in order to solve the problem efficiently.

- Many programs can be divided logically into three phases: an initialization phase that initializes the program variables; a processing phase that inputs data values and adjusts program variables accordingly; and a termination phase that calculates and prints the final results.

- The programmer terminates the top-down, stepwise refinement process when the pseudocode algorithm is specified in sufficient detail for the programmer to be able to convert the pseudocode easily to Perl. Implementing the Perl program is then normally straightforward.

TERMINOLOGY

action symbol	connector symbol
action/decision model of programming	control structure
actions	control-structure nesting
algorithm	control-structure stacking
arrow	counter-controlled repetition
assignment statement	crashing
bombing	decision symbol
calculations	definite repetition
compound statement	diamond symbol
condition	**do/until** repetition structure
conditional expression	**do/while** repetition structure
conditional operator (**?:**)	double-selection structure

dummy value	multiple-selection structure
editor program	order
empty statement	oval symbol
end of data entry	procedure
expression	processing phase
false	program control
fatal logic error	pseudocode
first refinement	rectangle symbol
flag value	refinement process
flow of control	repetition structure
flowchart	rise-and-shine algorithm
flowline	second refinement
for repetition structure	selection structure
foreach repetition structure	sentinel value
goto elimination	sentinel-controlled loop
goto statement	sequence structure
goto-less programming	sequential execution
graphical representation of an algorithm	signal value
high-level language	single-entry/single-exit control structure
if selection structure	single-selection structure
if/else selection structure	small circle symbol
if/elsif/else selection structure	structured programming
increment	syntax errors
indefinite repetition	termination phase
infinite loop	ternary operator
initialization phase	top-down, stepwise refinement
initialize	transfer of control
input/output operation	true
keyword	**unless** selection structure
logic error	**until** repetition structure
loop body	**while** repetition structure
loop-continuation condition	whitespace characters
memory location	

SELF-REVIEW EXERCISES

3.1   Fill in the blanks in each of the following statements:
   a) All programs can be written in terms of three types of control structures: _____, _____ and _____.
   b) The _____ selection structure is used to execute one action when a condition is true and another action when that condition is false.
   c) Repeating a set of instructions a specific number of times is called _____ repetition.
   d) When it is not known in advance how many times a set of statements will be repeated, a _____ value can be used to terminate the repetition.

3.2   Write four different Perl statements that each add 1 to integer variable **$x**.

3.3   Write Perl statements to accomplish each of the following:
   a) Assign the sum of **$x** and **$y** to **$z**, and increment the value of **$x** by 1 after the calculation.
   b) Test if the value of the variable **$count** is greater than 10. If it is, print "**Count is greater than 10.**"

   c) Decrement the variable **$x** by 1, and then subtract it from the variable **$total** and store the result in **total**.

   d) Calculate the remainder when the value of variable **$value** is divided by the value of variable **$divisor**, and assign the result to **$value**. Write this statement in two different ways.

3.4   Write a Perl statement to accomplish each of the following tasks:

   a) Initialize variable **$x** to **1**.

   b) Initialize variable **$sum** to **0**.

   c) Add variable **$x** to variable **$sum**, and assign the result to variable **$sum**.

   d) Print **"The sum is: "**, followed by the value of variable **$sum**.

3.5   Use the statements you wrote in Exercise 3.4 and your current knowledge of Perl to create a program that prints the sum of the integers from 1 to 10. Use the **while** structure to loop through the calculation and increment statements. The loop should terminate when the value of **$x** becomes 11.

3.6   Write single Perl statements that do the following:

   a) Input integer variable **$x** with **<STDIN>**.

   b) Input integer variable **$y** with **<STDIN>**.

   c) Initialize integer variable **$i** to **1**.

   d) Initialize integer variable **$power** to **1**.

   e) Multiply variable **$power** by **$x**, and assign the result to **$power**.

   f) Increment variable **$y** by **1**.

   g) Test **$i** to see if it is less than or equal to **$y**.

   h) Output integer variable **$power** with **print**.

3.7   Write a program that uses the statements in Exercise 3.6 to calculate **x** raised to the **y** power. The program should have a **while** repetition control structure.

3.8   Identify and correct the errors in each of the following:

   a)
```
until ( $c <= 5 ) {
    $product *= $c;
    ++$c;
```

   b)
```
<STDIN> = $value;
```

   c)
```
if ( $size eq 'small' ) {
    print "Small\n";
}
elsif {
    print "Large\n";
}
```

3.9   What is wrong with the following **while** repetition structure?

```
while ( $integer >= 0 ) {
    $sum += $integer;
}
```

ANSWERS TO SELF-REVIEW EXERCISES

3.1   a) sequence, selection and repetition. b) **if/else**. c) counter-controlled or definite. d) sentinel, signal, flag or dummy.

3.2
```
$x = $x + 1;
$x += 1;
++$x;
$x++;
```

3.3   a) `$z = $x++ + $y;`
       b) `if ( $count > 10 ) {`
              `print "Count is greater than 10."`
           `}`
       c) `$total -= --$x;` or
          `$total = $total - --$x;`
       d) `$value = $value % $divisor;`
          `$value %= $divisor;`

3.4   a) `$x = 1;`
       b) `$sum = 0;`
       c) `$sum = $sum + $x;` or
          `$sum += $x;`
       d) `print "The sum is: $sum.";`

3.5   See the following code:

```perl
1    #!/usr/bin/perl
2    # Ex. 3.5: Ex03_05.pl
3
4
5    $x = 1;
6    $sum = 0;
7
8    while ( $x <= 10 ) {
9        $sum += $x;
10       ++$x;
11   }
12
13   print "The sum is $sum.";
```

```
The sum is 55.
```

3.6   a) `chomp ( $x = <STDIN> );`
       b) `chomp ( $y = <STDIN> );`
       c) `$i = 1;`
       d) `$power = 1;`
       e) `$power *= $x;`
       f) `++$y;`
       g) `$i <= $y`
       h) `print "$power";`

3.7   See below.

```perl
1    #!/usr/bin/perl
2    # Ex. 3.7: Ex03_07.pl
3
4
5    $i = 1;
6    $power = 1;
7    print "Input a number: ";
```

```
8   chomp( $x = <STDIN> );
9   print "Input the value you want the number raised to: ";
10  chomp( $y = <STDIN> );
11
12  while ( $i <= $y ) {
13      $power *= $x;
14      ++$i;
15  }
16
17  print "The result is $power.";
```

```
Input a number: 2
Input the value you want the number raised to: 3
The result is 8.
```

3.8   a) Error: Missing the closing right brace of the **until** body.
           Correction: Add the closing right brace after the statement **++$c;**.
       b) Error: The values are backwards in the assignment statement. This statement will cause
           a fatal error, because **<STDIN>** cannot have values assigned to it.
           Correction: Rearrange the values: **$value = <STDIN>;**
       c) Error: The word **elsif** is used instead of **else**. This statement will cause a fatal error.
           Correction: Replace the word **elsif** with **else**.

3.9   The value of **$integer** is never changed in the **while** structure. Therefore, an infinite
loop is created. To prevent the infinite loop from being created, **$integer** must be decremented so
that it eventually becomes **0**.

EXERCISES

3.10   Drivers are concerned with the gas mileage obtained by their automobiles. One driver has
kept track of several tankfuls of gasoline by recording the miles driven and gallons used for each tankful. Develop a program that will receive as input the miles driven and gallons used for each tankful.
The program should calculate and display the miles per gallon obtained for each tankful. After processing all input information, the program should calculate and print the combined miles per gallon
obtained for all tankfuls. Sample output of the program is as follows:

```
Enter the gallons used (-1 to end): 12.8
Enter the miles driven: 287
The miles / gallon for this tank was 22.421875

Enter the gallons used (-1 to end): 10.3
Enter the miles driven: 200
The miles / gallon for this tank was 19.417475

Enter the gallons used (-1 to end): 5
Enter the miles driven: 120
The miles / gallon for this tank was 24.000000

Enter the gallons used (-1 to end): -1

The overall average miles/gallon was 21.601423
```

3.11   Write a program that receives as input a series of numbers. At the end of the input list, the program should output the total number of numbers input, the largest number, the smallest number, and the average of all the numbers.

3.12   A palindrome is a number or a text phrase that reads the same backwards as forwards. For example, each of the following five-digit integers is a palindrome: 12321, 55555, 45554 and 11611. Write a program that reads in a number of arbitrary length and checks if it is a palindrome. [*Hint:* Use the division and modulus operators to separate the number into its individual digits. Note that when you divide by 10, the remainder from this division will result in the last digit of the original number. For instance, 12345 divided by 10 results in a remainder of 5, and 789 divided by 10 results in a remainder of 9.]

3.13   Receive as input an integer containing only 0s and 1s (i.e., a "binary" integer), and print its decimal equivalent. [*Hint:* Use the modulus and division operators to pick off the "binary" number's digits one at a time from right to left. Just as in the decimal-number system, where the rightmost digit has a positional value of 1, the next digit to the left has a positional value of 10, then 100, then 1000, etc., in the binary-number system, the rightmost digit has a positional value of 1, the next digit to the left has a positional value of 2, then 4, then 8, etc. Thus the decimal number 234 can be interpreted as 4 * 1 + 3 * 10 + 2 * 100. The decimal equivalent of binary 1101 is 1 * 1 + 0 * 2 + 1 * 4 + 1 * 8 or 1 + 0 + 4 + 8, or 13.]

3.14   The factorial of a nonnegative integer n is written as $n!$ (pronounced "n factorial") and is defined as follows:

$$n! = n \cdot (n - 1) \cdot (n - 2) \cdot \ldots \cdot 1 \quad \text{(for values of } n \text{ greater than or equal to 1)}$$

and

$$n! = 1 \quad \text{(for } n = 0\text{).}$$

For example, $5! = 5 \cdot 4 \cdot 3 \cdot 2 \cdot 1$, which is 120.

    a) Write a program that reads a nonnegative integer and computes and prints its factorial.

    b) Write a program that estimates the value of the mathematical constant e by using the following formula: (One way to do this is to have the program print the result after each term is added, so you can see what value e comes close to. Prompt the user for the number of terms they wish to have calculated, to ensure that the program does not go on forever.)

$$e = 1 + \frac{1}{1!} + \frac{1}{2!} + \frac{1}{3!} + \ldots$$

    c) Write a program that computes the value of e^x by using the following formula (again, have the program print after each iteration, stopping after a specified number of terms) and prints the current value after each iteration:

$$e^x = 1 + \frac{x}{1!} + \frac{x^2}{2!} + \frac{x^3}{3!} + \ldots$$

    d) Write a program to calculate the value of π from the following infinite series (once again, print after each term is added, stopping after a specified number of terms) and prints the current value after each iteration:

$$\pi = 4 - \frac{4}{3} + \frac{4}{5} - \frac{4}{7} + \frac{4}{9} - \frac{4}{11} + \ldots$$

4

Arrays and Hashes

Objectives

- To introduce lists of values.
- To introduce the array data structure.
- To be able to initialize an array and refer to individual elements of an array.
- To be able to use the functions for manipulating lists and arrays.
- To introduce the hash data structure.
- To be able to initialize a hash and refer to individual elements of a hash.
- To be able to use the functions for manipulating hashes.

With sobs and tears he sorted out
Those of the largest size …
Lewis Carroll

Attempt the end, and never stand to doubt;
Nothing's so hard, but search will find it out.
Robert Herrick

Now go, write it before them in a table,
and note it in a book.
Isaiah 30:8

'Tis in my memory lock'd,
And you yourself shall keep the key of it.
William Shakespeare

Outline

4.1 Introduction

Until now, our Perl programs have used only scalar data. This chapter introduces the important topic of *data structures*—aggregations of related data items. Here, we introduce the two other fundamental Perl data types: *arrays* and *hashes* (also called *associative arrays*). Arrays are data structures consisting of related data items. Hashes are sets of *key-value pairs* wherein each *key* has a corresponding *value*. In this chapter, we discuss how to create and manipulate variables of each of these two data types. In Chapter 20, we introduce other popular data structures, such as linked lists, stacks, queues and binary trees.

4.2 Additional Data Types

As you know, scalar data can store only one value at a time. What if we have a set of related values? It would be useful to be able to store them all together. We cannot do so with scalars. Perl does, however, provide two fundamental data types that can indeed hold multiple values. These data types are the *array* and the *hash*. As mentioned in Chapter 2, every variable must be prefixed with a type-identifier symbol. Array variables are prefixed with the **@** *type identifier symbol*, and hash variables are prefixed with the **%** *type identifier symbol*.

4.3 Lists and List Context

Before we discuss these new data types, we first consider *lists*. A list in Perl is a collection of values. To create a list, separate a series of values with commas and enclose the list in parentheses, `( )`. The following is an example of a list of strings:

```
( "dog", "cat", "horse" )
```

As always, it is important to know the context in which a variable will be used. *List context* is a region of a Perl program in which a list is required for the program to complete its task. A region of a Perl program in which only a single value is expected is said to be *scalar context*. The operation being performed on a variable helps determine its context. For example, a scalar variable on the left side of an assignment operator gives scalar context to what is on the right side, so a value can be assigned to the variable on the left side of the assignment operator. Similarly, when a list appears on the left side of the assignment operator, the right side is interpreted in list context.

We have already seen functions, such as **print**, that use lists as arguments. For example, the statement

```
print "1 + 7 = ", 1 + 7, "\n";
```

calls **print** with a list containing the string **"1 + 7 = "**, the expression **1 + 7** (which evaluates to **8**) and the newline character. Note that the parentheses are not required for a list that is passed to function **print**.

When a list is evaluated, each element in the list is evaluated, and all sublists are *flattened*. For example, the list

```
( 1, 4 + 6, ( 'hi' , 2, ( 4 , 1 ) , 1 + 6 ), 'c' )
```

evaluates to

```
( 1, 10, 'hi', 2, 4, 1, 7, 'c' )
```

4.4 Arrays

An array variable stores a list of scalars. Each array can hold 0 or more individual scalars. Each individual array element has a *position number* (or *index*), which is used to access (or refer to) that element. The primary difference between a list and an array is that an array is a named variable, whereas a list is considered to be a constant.

Figure 4.1 shows an array called **@c**. This array contains 12 *elements*, each of which is a scalar. Elements are accessed by giving the name of the array (preceded by **$**, not **@**), followed by the position number of the particular element in *square brackets ([])*. The first element in every array is the *zeroth element.* Thus, the first element of array **@c** is referred to as **$c[0]**; the second element of array **@c** is referred to as **$c[1]**; the seventh element of array **@c** is referred to as **$c[6]** and, in general, the *i*th element of array **@c** is referred to as **$c[i - 1]**. Again, array elements are preceded by the **$** symbol (not the **@** symbol), because the individual array elements are scalars. The array name indicates which array to access, and the position number in brackets after the array name indicates which scalar element within the array to access.

Name of array. (Note that all
elements of this array have the
same name, **c**.)

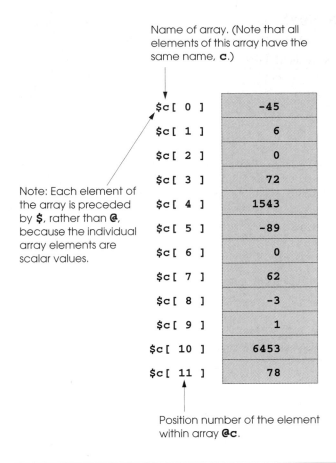

Note: Each element of
the array is preceded
by **$**, rather than **@**,
because the individual
array elements are
scalar values.

Position number of the element
within array **@c**.

Fig. 4.1   A 12-element array.

Common Programming Error 4.1

*When referring to an individual array element, using **@** rather than **$** before the array name
may result in a logic error. Using **perl** with the **-w** flag to run the program generates warning messages in this case.*

Common Programming Error 4.2

*When initializing an array with a list, accidentally using **$** rather than **@** before the array
name may result in a logic error. Using **perl** with the **-w** flag to run the program generates
warning messages in this case.*

The position number contained within square brackets is more formally called a *subscript*. A subscript should be an integer or an integer expression. If a program uses an
expression as a subscript, then the expression is evaluated to determine the subscript. For
example, if we assume that variable **$number1** is equal to **5** and that variable **$number2**
is equal to **6**, then the statement

```
$c[ $number1 + $number2 ] += 2;
```

adds 2 to array element $c[11]. Note that a subscripted array name is an *lvalue*; it can be used on the left side of an assignment to store a new value in that location of the array.

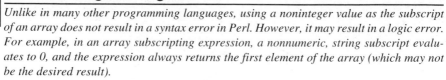
Common Programming Error 4.3

Unlike in many other programming languages, using a noninteger value as the subscript of an array does not result in a syntax error in Perl. However, it may result in a logic error. For example, in an array subscripting expression, a nonnumeric, string subscript evaluates to 0, and the expression always returns the first element of the array (which may not be the desired result).

Let us examine array **@c** in Fig. 4.1 more closely. The *name* of the entire array is **@c**. Its 12 elements are named $c[0], $c[1], $c[2], ..., $c[11]. The *value* of $c[0] is **-45**; the value of $c[1] is **6**; the value of $c[2] is **0**; the value of $c[7] is **62** and the value of $c[11] is **78**. To print the sum of the values contained in the first three elements of array **c**, we would write

```
print $c[ 0 ] + $c[ 1 ] + $c[ 2 ], "\n";
```

To divide the value of the seventh element of array **@c** by **2** and assign the result to the variable **$result**, we would write

```
$result = $c[ 6 ] / 2;
```

Common Programming Error 4.4

It is important to note the difference between the "seventh element of the array" and "array element seven." Because array subscripts begin at 0, the "seventh element of the array" has a subscript of 6, while "array element seven" has a subscript of 7 and is actually the eighth element of the array. Unfortunately, this distinction is a source of "off-by-one" errors.

The brackets, **[]**, that enclose the subscript of an array are actually an operator in Perl. This operator can be applied to lists as well as arrays. For example, to access the second element of the list

```
( "dog", "cat", "horse" )
```

you can write

```
( "dog", "cat", "horse" )[ 1 ]
```

However, this notation obscures the clarity of your program and should not be used.

It is legal in Perl to have an array and a scalar with the same name, because different type identifiers are used to specify if a variable is a scalar (**$**) or an array (**@**). For example, the statement **$c = 5;** creates scalar variable **$c**, which would not be related to array **@c**.

Good Programming Practice 4.1

Avoid using the same name for a scalar and an array. This practice helps make programs more readable and easier to debug and maintain.

It is not required that all the elements of an array be of the same type (e.g., integers, floating-point numbers or strings). However, it is required that all the elements of an array be scalars. Thus, an array that contains integers also may contain strings and floating-point numbers.

4.5 Creating and Manipulating an Array

There are several ways to create an array in Perl. The most straightforward is to assign a list of values to an array variable (Fig. 4.2). This process creates an array whose elements contain the individual list items.

Line 5 in Fig. 4.2

```
@array = ( "Hello", 283, "there", 16.439 );
```

creates the array **@array** by assigning it a list of values. Each value in the list is assigned to a new array element, so the statement creates **@array** with four elements having subscripts from 0 through 3. After this statement, **$array[0]** contains **"Hello"**; **$array[1]** contains **283**; **$array[2]** contains **"there"** and **$array[3]** contains **16.439**.

Lines 8–13 use a **while** structure to display the subscript of each element and its corresponding value. Line 8 declares counter **$i** and initializes it to 0—the first subscript in the array. Line 10 begins the **while** structure and specifies that the loop should continue executing while **$i** is less than 4—the number of elements in the array. During each iteration of the loop, line 11

```
print "$i    $array[ $i ]\n";
```

displays the subscript and value of the array element at index **$i**. Line 12

```
++$i;
```

increments the counter-control variable **$i**. Eventually, **$i** will contain 4, and the loop will terminate.

```
1   #!/usr/bin/perl
2   # Fig. 4.2: fig04_02.pl
3   # Creating and initializing an array with list assignment.
4
5   @array = ( "Hello", 283, "there", 16.439 );
6
7   # display every element of the array
8   $i = 0;
9
10  while ( $i < 4 ) {
11      print "$i    $array[ $i ]\n";
12      ++$i;
13  }
```

```
0    Hello
1    283
2    there
3    16.439
```

Fig. 4.2   Creating and initializing an array with list assignment.

4.6 Repetition with the **for** Structure

Perl provides two other repetition structures—*for* and *foreach*—that are more appropriate than the **while** repetition structure for looping through an array of elements. For the remainder of this chapter, we will use the **for** repetition structure. In Chapter 5, we introduce the **foreach** repetition structure.

The **for** repetition structure handles all the details of counter-controlled repetition. To illustrate the power of the **for** structure, let us rewrite the program in Fig. 4.2. The result is shown in Fig. 4.3.

When the **for** structure (line 8) begins executing, the control variable **$i** is created and initialized to 0. Then, the loop-continuation condition **$i < 4** is tested. If the loop-continuation condition is satisfied (i.e., **$i**'s value is less than **4**), the body statement (line 9) displays the subscript and the value of the array element at index **$i**. (**0** and **Hello** are displayed during the first iteration of the loop.) Next, control variable **$i** is incremented in the expression **++$i**, and execution proceeds with the next evaluation of the loop-continuation test. Counter **$i** is now 1, so the body executes again. This entire process continues until the loop-continuation test evaluates to false (when **$i** becomes 4). When this occurs, repetition terminates, and the program continues executing with the next statement after the closing brace, **}**, of the **for** structure; in this example, the program simply terminates.

Figure 4.4 takes a closer look at the **for** structure in Fig. 4.3. Notice that the **for** structure "does it all": It specifies each of the items needed for counter-controlled repetition with a control variable. Also note that, as with other control structures we have seen, curly braces (**{}**) must enclose the body of the loop.

Notice that Fig. 4.3 uses the loop-continuation condition **$i < 4**. If the programmer incorrectly wrote **$i <= 4**, then the loop would be executed 5 times, rather than 4. This is a common logic error called an *off-by-one error*.

Common Programming Error 4.5

Using an incorrect relational operator or using an incorrect final value of a loop counter in the condition of a repetition structure can cause off-by-one errors.

```
1   #!/usr/bin/perl
2   # Fig. 4.3: fig04_03.pl
3   # Looping through an array with the for repetition structure.
4
5   @array = ( "Hello", 283, "there", 16.439 );
6
7   # display every element of the array
8   for ( $i = 0; $i < 4; ++$i ) {
9      print "$i   $array[ $i ]\n";
10  }
```

```
0    Hello
1    283
2    there
3    16.439
```

Fig. 4.3   Using the **for** structure to print an array.

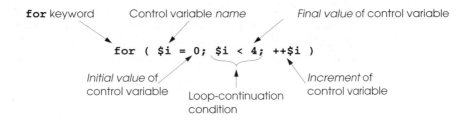

Fig. 4.4   Components of a typical **for** header.

Many programmers prefer so-called *zero-based counting*, in which, to count 10 times through the loop, the counter variable (**$i**, for example) would be initialized to zero and the loop-continuation test would be **$i < 10**. Zero-based counting works well for arrays, because array subscripts start at 0.

The general format of the **for** structure is

```
for ( initialization; loopContinuationTest; increment ) {
    statements
}
```

where the *initialization* expression initializes the loop's control variable, *loopContinuationTest* is the loop-continuation condition (containing the final value of the control variable for which the condition is true) and *increment* increments the control variable. In most cases, the **for** structure can be represented by an equivalent **while** structure, as follows:

```
initialization;

while ( loopContinuationTest ) {
    statements
    increment;
}
```

There is an exception to this rule, which we discuss in Section 5.6.

Sometimes, the *initialization* and *increment* expressions are comma-separated lists of expressions. The *comma operator*, as used in this context, guarantees that lists of expressions evaluate from left to right. In other words, this operator evaluates the expression on its left-hand side (ignoring the value of that expression), then evaluates the expression on the right-hand side (returning that value). This is why an expression like

```
$a = ( 1, 3 )
```

sets **$a** to 3. The comma operator is one of the lowest precedence operators in Perl.

Good Programming Practice 4.2

*Place only expressions involving the control variables in the initialization and increment sections of a **for** structure. Manipulations of other variables should appear either before the loop (if they execute only once, like initialization statements) or in the loop body (if they execute once per repetition, like incrementing or decrementing statements).*

The three expressions in the **for** structure are optional. If the *loopContinuationTest* is omitted, Perl assumes that the loop-continuation condition is true, thus creating an infinite loop. One might omit the *initialization* expression if the control variable is initialized elsewhere in the program. One might omit the *increment* expression if the increment is calculated by statements in the body of the **for** structure or if no increment is needed. The increment expression in the **for** structure acts like a stand-alone statement at the end of the body of the **for**. Therefore, the expressions

```
$i = $i + 1
$i += 1
++$i
$i++
```

are all equivalent in the incrementing portion of the **for** structure. Many programmers prefer the form **$i++**, because the incrementing occurs after the loop body is executed. The postincrementing form therefore seems more natural. Preincrementing and postincrementing have the same effect, because the variable being incremented here appears by itself and not in a larger expression. However, using preincrementation is more efficient. The two semicolons in the **for** structure are required.

Common Programming Error 4.6

*Using commas instead of the two required semicolons in a **for** header is a syntax error.*

The initialization, loop-continuation condition and increment portions of a **for** structure can contain arithmetic expressions. For example, assume that **$x = 2** and **$y = 4**. If **$x** and **$y** are not modified in the loop body, the statement

```
for ( $i = $x; $i <= 5 * $x * $y; $i += $y / $x )
```

is equivalent to the statement

```
for ( $i = 2; $i <= 40; $i += 2 )
```

The "increment" of a **for** structure can be negative (in which case it is really a decrement, and the loop actually counts downwards). For example,

```
for ( $i = 10; $i > 0; --$i )
```

counts down from 10 to 1 and terminates when **$i** is 0.

Common Programming Error 4.7

*Using a **<** or **<=** operator in the condition of a loop that counts downwards is a logic error. When creating such a loop, the condition should normally use a **>** or **>=** operator. Otherwise, the condition will most likely be false as program control enters the loop, and the body of the loop will never execute.*

If the loop-continuation condition is initially false when control enters the **for** structure, the body of the **for** structure is not performed. Instead, execution proceeds with the statement after the **for** structure.

The control variable is frequently printed or used in calculations in the body of a **for** structure, but it does not have to be. It is common to use the control variable for controlling repetition while never mentioning it in the body of the **for** structure.

Good Programming Practice 4.3

*Although the value of the control variable can be changed in the body of a **for** loop, avoid doing so, because this practice can lead to subtle logic errors.*

The **for** structure is flowcharted much like the **while** structure. Figure 4.5 shows the flowchart of the **for** statement

```
for ( $i = 0; $i < 10; ++$i ) {
    print "$i\n";
}
```

The flowchart makes it clear that the initialization occurs once and that incrementing occurs each time *after* the body statement executes. Note that—besides small circles and arrows—the flowchart contains only rectangle symbols and a diamond symbol. Imagine, again, that the programmer has a bin of empty **for** structures—as many as needed to stack and nest with other control structures to form a structured implementation of an algorithm. The programmer fills rectangles and diamonds with actions and decisions appropriate to the algorithm.

4.7 Additional Examples of Creating Arrays

Another way to create an array is to assign a value to any element of an array that does not yet exist. The array is automatically created with the appropriate number of elements to allow for the specified subscript value—i.e., if a subscript of 5 is specified, a six-element array is created. Perl creates the array for you. This concept also applies to adding new elements to existing arrays. If an array element did not previously exist, assigning a value to it will create that element (and any other elements between the original last element of the array and the new last element of the array). Accessing an array element for which a value has not been provided returns the undefined value, **undef**. You can check to see if an element has been defined or not by using *function **defined***. Figure 4.6 demonstrates the method of creating arrays by referring to nonexistent elements.

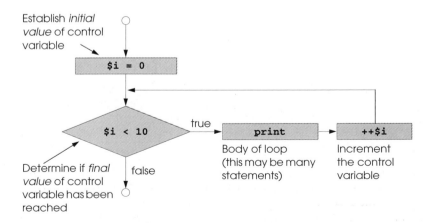

Fig. 4.5   Flowcharting a typical **for** repetition structure.

```perl
1   #!/usr/bin/perl
2   # Fig. 4.6: fig04_06.pl
3   # Create an array by referring to nonexistent elements.
4
5   # Create @array with one element by referring to
6   # nonexistent element 0.
7   $array[ 0 ] = "happy";
8   print "@array\n";
9
10  # Add more elements to @array by referring to
11  # nonexistent element 3. There are now 4 elements
12  # in the array. Elements 1 and 2 have undefined values.
13  $array[ 3 ] = "birthday";
14  print "@array\n\n";
15
16  # Loop through the array and replace every undefined
17  # value with an actual value.
18  for ( $i = 0; $i < 4; ++$i ) {
19
20     # if the element is not defined, assign it a value
21     if ( ! defined( $array[ $i ] ) ) {
22        $array[ $i ] = "happy";
23     }
24  }
25
26  print "@array\n";
27  print @array, "\n";
```

```
happy
happy    birthday

happy happy happy birthday
happyhappyhappybirthday
```

Fig. 4.6   Creating an array by referring to nonexistent elements.

Line 7

```perl
$array[ 0 ] = "happy";
```

assigns **"happy"** to **$array[0]**. Before this statement, **@array** did not exist. Assigning a value to an element of nonexistent array **@array** automatically creates the array. Line 8

```perl
print "@array\n";
```

displays the contents of the array. As you will see when there are more elements in the array, if an array is output as part of a double-quoted string, all the array elements normally are displayed separated by a space character between each element. You can specify the separator string by assigning a string to special variable **$"**. Line 13

```perl
$array[ 3 ] = "birthday";
```

assigns **"birthday"** to **$array[3]**. At this point, **@array** already exists as a result of line 7, but element **$array[3]** does not yet exist. So three new elements are added to the array automatically, and the modified array accommodates the assignment at line 13. Elements **$array[1]** and **$array[2]** are assigned the value **undef**. Line 14 outputs the array as part of a double-quoted string. Notice that the elements are separated by spaces. Remember that the elements with subscripts 1 and 2 are undefined, so they are not displayed. However, we can see that they exist from the extra spaces that were printed.

Testing and Debugging Tip 4.1

*When using Perl with the **-w** flag for warnings, printing an undefined element produces a warning indicating that the element is not initialized.*

Lines 18–24 use a **for** repetition structure to assign values to all the undefined elements. The **if** structure at lines 21–23

```
if ( ! defined( $array[ $i ] ) ) {
    $array[ $i ] = "happy";
}
```

introduces two new features: function **defined** and the *logical negation operator* (**!**). Function **defined** returns a value of true if its argument is defined (i.e., it has been assigned a value); otherwise, it returns a value of false. The logical negation operator (**!**) reverses the value of a condition: If the expression to its right returns true, the logical negation operator makes the value false, and if the expression to its right returns false, the logical negation operator makes the value true. Thus, the preceding **if** structure executes its body only if the argument to function **defined** is not defined. You can read the condition as "if not defined **$array[$i]**," or as "if **$array[$i]** is not defined." In line 22, if an element's value is not defined, we assign it the value **"happy"**.

Lines 26 and 27 each print the elements of **@array**. Line 26 encloses the array name in double quotes, so the elements are displayed separated by spaces. Line 27 does not enclose the array in double quotes. In this case, the elements of the array are displayed as one long string, with the values concatenated.

The automatic memory allocation and manipulation done in Perl are different than in other languages, like C or C++, where you have to declare the exact size of the array before it can be used. These details are taken care of behind the scenes in Perl and simplify programming.

Perl provides operators that help create lists of values. For a list of strings that do not contain spaces, Perl provides *operator* **qw** to simplify list creation. When passed strings separated by spaces, operator **qw** converts the strings into a list of strings. Thus,

```
qw( horse donkey mule )
```

and

```
( 'horse', 'donkey', 'mule' )
```

are equivalent, except that the former is less error prone, because you do not have to type the quotes and commas.

Perl also provides the *range operator* (**..**), for creation of a consecutive range of string or numeric values. For example, the notation

```
( 1 .. 5 )
```

is equivalent to the list

```
( 1, 2, 3, 4, 5 )
```

This operator is especially useful for creating wide ranges of consecutive values. The range operator can also be used for nonnumeric values. For example, ('a' .. 'z') is equivalent to a list containing the 26 lowercase letters of the alphabet. Figure 4.7 demonstrates the **qw** and .. operators.

Line 5 in Fig. 4.7

```
@array = qw( this is an array of strings );
```

uses operator **qw** to create an array with the strings **"this"**, **"is"**, **"an"**, **"array"**, **"of"** and **"strings"**. Using operator **qw** enables us to eliminate the commas and quotes normally used in a list of strings. Line 6 displays the contents of **@array**.

Line 8 uses the range operator to create an array of the numbers 1–5. The **for** structure at lines 11–14 adds each element to variable **$total** and then displays the element and the running total of the elements, separated by a tab character (**\t**) to create two columns of output.

```
1   #!/usr/bin/perl
2   # Fig. 4.7: fig04_07.pl
3   # Demonstrating the qw and .. operators.
4
5   @array = qw( this is an array of strings );
6   print "@array\n\n";
7
8   @array2 = ( 1 .. 5 );
9   print "Value\tRunning Total\n";
10
11  for ( $i = 0; $i < 5; ++$i ) {
12      $total += $array2[ $i ];
13      print( $array2[ $i ], "\t$total\n");
14  }
15
16  @array2 = ( 'a' .. 'z' );
17  print "\n@array2\n";
```

```
this is an array of strings

Value   Running Total
1       1
2       3
3       6
4       10
5       15


a b c d e f g h i j k l m n o p q r s t u v w x y z
```

Fig. 4.7   Demonstrating the **qw** and .. list operators.

Line 16

```
@array2 = ( 'a' .. 'z' );
```

demonstrates the range operator with strings. The range operator increments the starting value in the range repeatedly until it reaches the ending value in the range. Thus, **a** becomes **b**, then **b** becomes **c**, etc. When the range operator supplies strings with more than one letter, it begins by incrementing the letters furthest to the right. During an increment of the string, if the rightmost character is **z**, the rightmost character becomes **a** and the next character to the left is incremented. So, **aa** becomes **ab**, **ab** becomes **ac** and **az** becomes **ba**.

4.8 Array Manipulation

There are a number of other common and powerful array manipulation features. For example, you can determine the length of an array, access elements in an array backwards (i.e., from the highest numbered to the lowest-numbered subscript) and extract or view portions of an array.

In scalar context (i.e., when a single value is expected), an array returns the total number of elements of the array. Lists operate differently; in a scalar context, a list returns the value of the rightmost element of the list. You can force an array to return a scalar result by using *function* **scalar**. Thus, the expression **scalar(@array)** returns the total number of elements in **@array**. To determine the last index number of an array, precede the array name with the *$# prefix*, as in *$#array*.

An interesting feature of **$#array** is that it can be used to change the length of an array. Assigning an integer to **$#array** makes that integer value the new high index number in the array. If this command causes new elements to be added to the array, those elements have undefined values. To remove all the elements from the array **@array**, assign to the array the empty list, **( )**.

Sometimes programmers process an array by iterating backwards through the array. Perl provides a shortcut for this procedure with negative subscript values. For example, the expression **$array[-1]** returns the last element of the array, and **$array[-4]** returns the fourth-to-last element of the array. Figure 4.8 demonstrates the features introduced in this section.

```
1   #!/usr/bin/perl
2   # Fig. 4.8: fig04_08.pl
3   # Manipulating the length of an array.
4
5   @array =
6      qw( zero one two three four five six seven eight nine );
7
8   # output the number of elements and the last index number
9   print "There are ", scalar( @array ),
10        " elements in \@array.\n";
11  print "The last index in \@array is $#array.\n\n";
12
13  # output the last element in the array
14  print "\@array[ $#array ] is $array[ $#array ].\n\n";
```

Fig. 4.8   Manipulating the length of an array (part 1 of 2).

```
15
16   # use negative subscripts to access
17   # elements from the end of the array
18   print "\@array[ -1 ] is $array[ -1 ].\n";
19   print "\@array[ -4 ] is $array[ -4 ].\n\n";
20
21   $#array = 5;          # reduce the number of elements to 6
22   print "@array.\n";
23
24   $#array = 10;         # increase the number of elements to 11
25   print "@array.\n";
26
27   @array = ();          # remove all elements in the array
28   print "@array.\n";
29   print "There are now ", scalar( @array ),
30          " elements in \@array\n";
```

```
There are 10 elements in @array.
The last index in @array is 9.

@array[ 9 ] is nine.

@array[ -1 ] is nine.
@array[ -4 ] is six.

zero one two three four five.
zero one two three four five       .
.
There are now 0 elements in @array
```

Fig. 4.8   Manipulating the length of an array (part 2 of 2).

Lines 5 and 6 create an array in which each element contains the English word for the index number (**"one"**, **"two"**, etc.). Line 9 uses function **scalar** to obtain the number of elements in the **@array**. Line 11 uses the **$#array** notation to determine the last index number.

Line 14 uses **$#array** as the subscript of **@array** to access the value of the last element of the array. Lines 18 and 19 use negative subscripts to access elements of the array from the end of the array. The subscript **-1** accesses the last element of the array (**"nine"**) and the subscript **-4** accesses the element four positions from the end of the array (**"six"**).

Line 21 assigns 5 to **$#array**, thus making the new high subscript number 5 and deleting the elements at index numbers 6–9. Then, line 24 increases the number of elements in the array by making 10 the new high subscript value. Note that when the array is displayed, there are additional spaces between the last original element in the array and the period at the end of the output line. This is because each undefined element still causes a space to be output. Line 27 removes all the elements in the array by assigning the empty list to **@array**. Line 29 outputs the new number of elements in the array.

The bracket operator, **[]**, also can be used to create a list containing the specified set of elements from an array. Thus, **@array[1, 2, 3]** returns a list containing the second, third and fourth elements of **@array**. (Remember that subscripts start from 0 for the first element.) These sections of arrays are called *array slices*. Note that the array is prefixed with the **@** character, rather than the **$** character, when obtaining an array slice. One way to think of an array slice is that it is a list of the individual elements indicated by the specified subscript numbers. Normally, an array slice returns a list of consecutive elements in an existing array, but this is not required. For example, the array slice **@array[1, 3, 5]** creates a list containing the elements with subscripts 1, 3 and 5 from **@array**. In addition, **@array[1]** returns a one-element array slice whose single element is **$array[1]**. So, if **@array** contains the list of values **(0, 3)**, then **@array[1]** returns the list **(3)**, while **$array[1]** returns the value **3**.

Another useful feature of lists, called *list assignment*, enables a list of values to be assigned to a list of scalars. For example, in the assignment

```
( $first, $second ) = ( "first", 2 );
```

the string **"first"** in the list on the right side of the assignment operator is assigned to the variable **$first**. Similarly, the value **2** is assigned to the variable **$second**. This process repeats for each matching pair of list elements on the right and left side of the assignment operator. This procedure is useful for assigning list values directly to a set of scalars. It is also useful for exchanging the values of two variables. For example, assuming the preceding assignment, after the following assignment

```
( $first, $second ) = ( $second, $first );
```

variable **$first** contains **2** and variable **$second** contains **"first"**. Also, array slices can be used on either side of a list assignment.

In general, if there are more variables in the list on the left side of the assignment operator than there are values to assign, the remaining variables have the value **undef**. If an array appears on the left side of a list assignment, Perl allocates enough elements in the array to store all the remaining elements in the list on the right side of the assignment operator. Any other variables after the array on the left-side are assigned the value **undef**. Figure 4.9 demonstrates array slices and list assignment.

```perl
1   #!/usr/bin/perl
2   # Fig. 4.9: fig04_09.pl
3   # Demonstrating array slices and list assignment.
4
5   @array =
6      qw( zero one two three four five six seven eight nine );
7   print "@array\n\n";
8
9   # display slices of @array
10  print "@array[ 1, 3, 5, 7, 9 ]\n";
11  print "@array[ 2 .. 6 ]\n\n";
12
13  # perform list assignments and display results
14  ( $chiquita, $dole ) = ( "banana", "pineapple" );
15  print "\$chiquita = $chiquita\n\$dole = $dole\n";
16  @array[ 1, 3, 5, 7, 9 ] = qw( 1 3 5 7 9 );
17  print "@array\n\n";
```

Fig. 4.9   Array slices and list assignment (part 1 of 2).

```
18
19   # use list assignment to swap the values of two variables
20   ( $chiquita, $dole ) = ( $dole, $chiquita );
21   print "After swapping values:\n";
22   print "\$chiquita = $chiquita\n\$dole = $dole\n\n";
23
24   # show that an array on the left of a list assignment
25   # receives all remaining initializers in the list on the
26   # right side of a list assignment
27   ( $first, @array2, $second ) = ( 1 .. 8 );
28   print "\$first = $first\n";
29   print "\@array2 = @array2\n";
30   print "\$second = $second\n";
```

```
zero one two three four five six seven eight nine

one three five seven nine
two three four five six

$chiquita = banana
$dole = pineapple
zero 1 two 3 four 5 six 7 eight 9

After swapping values:
$chiquita = pineapple
$dole = banana

$first = 1
@array2 = 2 3 4 5 6 7 8
$second =
```

Fig. 4.9   Array slices and list assignment (part 2 of 2).

Lines 5 and 6 create an array in which each element contains the English word for the index number (**"one"**, **"two"**, etc.). Lines 10 and 11 demonstrate array slices. Line 10 displays the slice containing the elements at locations 1, 3, 5, 7 and 9 of **@array**. Line 11 displays the slice containing all the elements at locations 2–6 of **@array**.

Line 14 uses list assignment to assign the string **"banana"** to variable **$chiquita** and the string **"pineapple"** to variable **$dole**, and then line 15 displays the results. Line 16 uses an array slice on the left side of a list assignment to assign new values to the elements at locations 1, 3, 5, 7 and 9 of **@array**, and then line 17 displays the results.

Line 20 demonstrates that list assignment can be used to swap variable values. In the statement, the values of variables **$chiquita** and **$dole** are exchanged, so **$chiquita** now contains **"pineapple"** and **$dole** now contains **"banana"**.

Line 27 demonstrates the use of an array as part of the list on the left side of a list assignment. First, variable **$first** is assigned the value 1 from the list on the right side of the assignment. Next, **@array** is assigned the remaining values (2 through 8) from the list on the right side of the assignment. There are no more values in the list when variable **$second** is reached in the assignment, so **$second** is assigned the value **undef**.

4.9 Array Functions

There are a number of functions designed to simplify array manipulation. These functions modify the contents of an array variable, so they cannot be used with lists.

 Common Programming Error 4.8

Using a list where an array is expected in an array manipulation function is a syntax error.

*Function **push*** receives two arguments: an array and a list of elements to be inserted at the end of the array. For example, the function call **push(@array, $element)** is identical to **$array[@array] = $element**. In this expression, **@array** is used in a scalar context (i.e., the array subscript must be an integer), so the result of the expression is to assign the new value **$element** to the element that is one past the end of the array. (Recall that the number of elements in the array is a value one higher than the last subscript.) The counterpart to function **push** is *function **pop***, which removes the last element from an array, returns that element and reduces the size of the array by one.

Functions ***shift*** and ***unshift*** manipulate elements at the beginning of an array. Function **unshift** inserts an element at the front of an array, and function **shift** removes and returns the first element of an array. Figure 4.10 demonstrates functions **push**, **pop**, **shift** and **unshift**.

Lines 6–9 of Fig. 4.10 use function **push** to add elements with values 1 through 5 to the end of **@array**. During each iteration of the loop, line 8 displays the array's current contents. Note in the output window that the new value always appears at the end of the array. Lines 14–17 use function **pop** to remove the elements from **@array** and add each element to **$firstTotal**. During each iteration of the loop, line 16 displays the array's current contents. Note again that the **pop**ped elements are removed from the end of the array. Also, note that the condition in the **while** loop at line 14 is the array **@array**. In this boolean context (the condition of a loop), **@array** is evaluated as true or false. If there are elements in the array, the condition is true. If the array is empty (i.e., when all elements have been removed from the array), the condition is false, and the loop terminates.

```perl
1   #!/usr/bin/perl
2   # Fig. 4.10: fig04_10.pl
3   # Demonstrating the push, pop, shift and unshift functions.
4
5   # Use push to insert elements at the end of @array.
6   for ( $i = 1; $i <= 5; ++$i ) {
7      push( @array, $i );              # add $i to end of @array
8      print "@array\n";                # display current @array
9   }
10
11  # While there are more elements in @array, pop each element.
12  # Note the use of @array as a condition. When @array is empty,
13  # the condition becomes false; otherwise, it is true.
14  while ( @array ) {
15     $firstTotal += pop( @array );   # remove last element
16     print "@array\n";                # display current @array
17  }
```

Fig. 4.10   Functions **push**, **pop**, **shift** and **unshift** (part 1 of 2).

```
18
19   print "\$firstTotal = $firstTotal\n\n";
20
21   # Use unshift to insert elements at the front of @array.
22   for ( $i = 1; $i <= 5; ++$i ) {
23      unshift( @array, $i );          # add $i to front of @array
24      print "@array\n";               # display current @array
25   }
26
27   # While there are more elements in @array, remove each element
28   # with shift.
29   while ( @array ) {
30      $secondTotal += shift( @array );   # remove first element
31      print "@array\n";                  # display current @array
32   }
33
34   print "\$secondTotal = $secondTotal\n";
```

```
1
1 2
1 2 3
1 2 3 4
1 2 3 4 5
1 2 3 4
1 2 3
1 2
1

$firstTotal = 15

1
2 1
3 2 1
4 3 2 1
5 4 3 2 1
4 3 2 1
3 2 1
2 1
1

$secondTotal = 15
```

Fig. 4.10   Functions **push**, **pop**, **shift** and **unshift** (part 2 of 2).

Common Programming Error 4.9

*If an array element is used as a condition (e.g., **while ($array[0])**), accidentally prefixing the array name with @, rather than $, may result in a logic error. The @ notation will result in an array slice. If that slice contains defined elements, the condition will always be true, which can lead to infinite loops.*

Common Programming Error 4.10

Logic errors may occur if you assume that an array evaluates to false because it contains only false elements.

Lines 22–34 perform the same tasks as lines 6–19, using **unshift** and **shift** rather than **push** and **pop**. Note in the output window that as elements are added to **@array** with **unshift**, each element is placed at the beginning of the array. Similarly, when elements are removed from **@array** with **shift**, the first element in the array is always removed.

Performance Tip 4.1

*Function **unshift** must make room for the new element being inserted at the beginning of an array by adding one element to the array and moving all the other elements to the next higher subscript location (e.g., the element at subscript 0 is moved to subscript 1). Similarly, function **shift** deletes one element from the array and moves all other elements in the array to the next lower subscript location (e.g., the element at subscript 1 is moved to subscript 0). For large arrays, this volume of data movement can result in poor program performance.*

Performance Tip 4.2

*Always use **push** and **pop** instead of **unshift** and **shift** when possible; **push** and **pop** are generally more efficient, especially with large arrays.*

Another function that modifies an array is *function **splice***, which removes or replaces slices of an array. Function **splice** can receive up to four arguments. The first argument is the array to modify. The second is the *offset* into the array—i.e., the index of the first element to modify in the array. The third argument is the length of the slice to modify. The fourth argument is a list to replace the specified slice of the array. If the fourth argument is omitted, the slice is simply removed from the array. If the third and fourth arguments are omitted, the slice from the offset to the end of the array is removed. If only the first argument is supplied, **splice** removes all the array elements. In all cases, **splice** returns one or more of the elements that were removed, or **undef** if no elements were removed. The actual value returned depends on the context. In list context, **splice** returns a list of all the removed elements. In scalar context, **splice** returns only the last element removed. Figure 4.11 demonstrates function **splice**.

Line 6 creates **@array** containing the numbers 0–20, and line 7 creates **@array2** containing the letters A–F. Line 12

```
@replaced = splice( @array, 5, scalar( @array2 ), @array2 );
```

replaces elements in **@array**. Starting from element 5 in **@array**, all six elements of **@array2** replace six elements of **@array**. The list of replaced elements returned from **splice** is stored in **@replaced** for use in the **print** statement at lines 13–15.

```perl
1   #!/usr/bin/perl
2   # Figure 4.11: splice.pl
3   # Demonstrating function splice.
4
5   # create two arrays and display their initial contents
6   @array = ( 0 .. 20 );
7   @array2 = ( A .. F );
8   print "\@array:  @array\n";
9   print "\@array2: @array2\n\n";
10
```

Fig. 4.11   Function **splice** (part 1 of 2).

```
11   # replace part of @array with the elements from @array2
12   @replaced = splice( @array, 5, scalar( @array2 ), @array2 );
13   print "replaced:        @replaced\n",
14         "with:            @array2\n",
15         "resulting in: @array\n\n";
16
17   # remove 3 elements, beginning with element 15 of @array
18   @removed = splice( @array, 15, 3 );
19   print "removed:          @removed\n",
20         "leaving:          @array\n\n";
21
22   # remove all elements from element 8 to the end of @array
23   @chopped = splice( @array, 8 );
24   print "removed:          @chopped\n",
25         "leaving:          @array\n\n";
26
27   # delete all remaining elements
28   splice( @array );
29
30   unless ( @array ) {
31      print "\@array has no elements remaining\n";
32   }
```

```
@array:  0 1 2 3 4 5 6 7 8 9 10 11 12 13 14 15 16 17 18 19 20
@array2: A B C D E F

replaced:        5 6 7 8 9 10
with:            A B C D E F
resulting in: 0 1 2 3 4 A B C D E F 11 12 13 14 15 16 17 18 19 20

removed:         15 16 17
leaving:         0 1 2 3 4 A B C D E F 11 12 13 14 18 19 20

removed:         D E F 11 12 13 14 18 19 20
leaving:         0 1 2 3 4 A B C

@array has no elements remaining
```

Fig. 4.11   Function **splice** (part 2 of 2).

Line 18

```
@removed = splice( @array, 15, 3 );
```

removes elements from **@array** with **splice**. Starting from element 15 in **@array**, three elements are removed, and the returned list is stored in **@removed**. Line 23

```
@chopped = splice( @array, 8 );
```

removes all elements from subscript 8 to the end of **@array** with **splice**. The returned list is stored in **@chopped**.

Line 28

```
splice( @array );
```

simply deletes all remaining elements in **@array**. Note the use of **@array** as the condition in the **unless** structure at line 30. There are no elements in the array at this point, so the condition is false, and the **print** statement executes.

4.10 List Functions

In addition to functions that modify arrays, there are also built-in functions that take lists as arguments and return new lists. Such functions allow complex processing to be specified in relatively simple expressions.

The first list function we discuss is also the simplest. *Function **reverse*** takes a list as an argument and returns a new list with the same contents in reverse order; the original list is left unchanged.

Another function that modifies a copy of a list is *function **sort***. When passed a list, function **sort** returns a copy of the list sorted lexically (i.e., in ASCII order); the original list is left unchanged. The programmer can specify a sorting order that is not based on individual characters as well. To do so, we must supply function **sort** with code that compares two elements in the list to determine their sorting order. This code must compare two elements, called **$a** and **$b**, and return **1** if **$a** is greater than **$b**, **0** if **$a** and **$b** are equal and **-1** if **$a** is less than **$b**.

Common Programming Error 4.11

*When specifying sorting order for function **sort**, the names of the variables that represent the two values being compared for sorting order must be **$a** and **$b**. Otherwise, function **sort** will not sort the values in the list properly, and there will be no indication of error.*

Good Programming Practice 4.4

*Do not use **$a** and **$b** as variables in your Perl programs. These variables are special to function **sort** and should be reserved for use with that function.*

The operators that are most useful for modifying sort order are the operators **cmp** and **<=>**. Operator **cmp** compares its two operands lexically (the default for function **sort**), and operator **<=>** compares its two operands numerically. Both operators return **1**, **0** or **-1**, as discussed previously. Figure 4.12 demonstrates functions **sort** and **reverse**.

Line 7 defines **@array** and initializes the array with values from 0–9. Line 8 uses function **reverse** to reverse the elements and stores the results in **@reversed**, which is output on line 10.

```
1   #!/usr/bin/perl
2   # Fig. 4.12: fig04_12.pl
3   # Reversing the elements of an array and
4   # sorting arrays lexically and numerically.
5
6   # create @array with values from 1-10 and reverse the values
7   @array = ( 0 .. 9 );
8   @reversed = reverse( @array );
9   print "Original:     @array\n";
10  print "Reversed:     @reversed\n\n";
11
```

Fig. 4.12   Functions **reverse** and **sort** (part 1 of 2).

```
12  # create an unsorted array of numbers and sort it
13  @array2 = ( 100, 23, 9, 75, 5, 10, 2, 50, 7, 96, 1, 40 );
14  @sortedLexically = sort @array2;
15  @sortedNumerically = sort { $a <=> $b } @array2;
16  print "Unsorted:    @array2\n";
17  print "Lexically:   @sortedLexically\n";
18  print "Numerically: @sortedNumerically\n";
```

```
Original:     0 1 2 3 4 5 6 7 8 9
Reversed:     9 8 7 6 5 4 3 2 1 0

Unsorted:     100 23 9 75 5 10 2 50 7 96 1 40
Lexically:    1 10 100 2 23 40 5 50 7 75 9 96
Numerically:  1 2 5 7 9 10 23 40 50 75 96 100
```

Fig. 4.12   Functions **reverse** and **sort** (part 2 of 2).

Line 13 defines **@array2** and initializes it with numeric values. Note that three values start with the digit 1, and two values start with each of the digits 2, 5, 7 and 9. (We will see why this observation is important when we sort the array lexically.) Line 14

```
    @sortedLexically = sort @array2;
```

sorts **@array2** lexically (alphabetically). When the results of this statement are output (line 17), note that all the element values starting with the digit 1 appear first, followed by all the element values starting with 2, etc. This occurs because function **sort** does string comparisons by default. In fact, the preceding sort call is equivalent to

```
    @sortedLexically = sort { $a cmp $b } @array2;
```

Line 15

```
    @sortedNumerically = sort { $a <=> $b } @array2;
```

sorts **@array2** numerically by specifying the sorting order with **{ $a <=> $b }**. When the results of this statement are output (line 18), note that the elements appear in numerical sort order from lowest to highest. To sort in descending order, use **{ $b <=> $a }** instead.

4.11 Searching Sorted Arrays

Often, a programmer will be working with large amounts of data stored in arrays. It may be necessary to determine whether an array contains a value that matches a certain *key value*. The process of finding a particular element of an array is called *searching*. In this section, we discuss two searching techniques: the simple *linear search* technique and the more efficient *binary search* technique.

4.11.1 Linear Search

The linear search (Fig. 4.13) compares each element of an array with the *search key*. In a linear search of an unsorted array, it is just as likely that the value will be found in the first element as in the last. Therefore, on average, the program must compare the search key with half the elements of the array to find a value in the array. In the worst-case scenario, the program must compare the search key with every element in the array to determine that a value is not in the array or that the value is in the last element of the array. Note that the program in Fig. 4.13 introduces the **&&** operator (logical AND).

This program introduces several new Perl features in addition to the linear search concept. Lines 6–8 create **@array** and initialize it with the even integers from 0 to 198. Lines 11 and 12 prompt the user to enter a search key.

```perl
1   #!/usr/bin/perl
2   # Fig. 4.13: fig04_13.pl
3   # Linear search of an array.
4
5   # populate @array with the even integers from 0 to 198
6   for ( $i = 0; $i < 100; ++$i ) {
7      $array[ $i ] = 2 * $i;
8   }
9
10  # prompt the user for a search key
11  print "Enter an integer search key: ";
12  chomp( $searchKey = <STDIN> );
13
14  # a boolean value to help determine when to stop searching
15  $found = 0;    # $found is initially false
16
17  # use a loop to access every element of @array
18  for ( $i = 0; $i < @array && !$found; ++$i ) {
19
20      # determine if the current element is the search key
21      if ( $array[ $i ] == $searchKey ) {
22         $index = $i;    # store index where it was found
23         $found = 1;     # indicates we should stop looping
24      }
25  }
26
27  if ( $found ) {        # $found == 1
28     print "Found $searchKey at subscript $index \n";
29  }
30  else {                 # $found == 0
31     print "$searchKey not found \n";
32  }
```

```
Enter an integer search key: 50
Found 50 at subscript 25
```

```
Enter an integer search key: 17
17 not found
```

Fig. 4.13   Linear search of an array.

Line 15 defines variable **$found**, which will be used to help determine if and when the value is found in **@array**. Initially, **$found** is set to 0 (false) to indicate that the value has not been found yet. A variable that is used to represent true/false values is sometimes called a *boolean variable*.

The **for** structure at lines 18 through 25 performs the linear search. Line 18

```
for ( $i = 0; $i < @array && !$found; ++$i ) {
```

first initializes the control variable **$i** to 0. Note the condition. Here we introduce a *compound condition* in which multiple simple conditions are tested. Overall, the condition is testing whether the counter **$i** is less than the number of elements in **@array** *and* (**&&**) if the search key is "not found." (Recall that the operator **!** is the logical negation operator introduced earlier in this chapter.) The new operator **&&** is a *logical operator* called the *logical AND operator*. The logical AND operator combines two conditions to create a more complex condition. In a logical AND expression, the condition on the left of the operator is tested first. If that condition is true, the condition on the right side of the operator is tested next. The entire logical AND expression is considered to be true if and only if both the left-side condition and the right-side condition are true. If either is false, the entire expression is false. Thus, the preceding **for** structure will continue to loop as long as we have not reached the end of the array and as long as the value has not been found. In Chapter 5, we continue our discussion of logical operators **&&** and **!** and introduce a third logical operator, **||**, the logical OR operator.

The **if** structure at lines 21 through 24 determines if the current element of **@array** contains the **$searchKey** value. If so, **$index** is assigned the subscript of the element at which the key was found and **$found** is set to 1 (true) to indicate that the key was found. When the condition at line 18 is evaluated, the logical AND expression will evaluate to false, because **$found** is now 1 (true) and the logical negation operator (**!**) reverses this condition from true to false. If the value is not found during an iteration of the loop, the body of the **if** structure is skipped, the control variable is incremented and the condition is tested. In this case, the condition will fail only if we reach the end of the array.

Linear searching works well for small arrays and for unsorted arrays. However, for large arrays, linear searching is inefficient. If the array is sorted, the high-speed *binary search* technique can be used instead.

4.11.2 Binary Search

The binary search algorithm requires the array to be in sorted order beforehand. This algorithm eliminates from the search one half of the elements in the array being searched after each comparison. The algorithm locates the middle element of the array and compares it with the search key. If they are equal, the search key is found and the array subscript of that element is returned. Otherwise, the problem is reduced to searching one half of the array. If the search key is less than the middle element of the array, the first half of the array is searched; otherwise, the second half of the array is searched. If the search key is not the middle element in the specified subarray (i.e., a piece of the original array), the algorithm is repeated on one quarter of the original array. The search continues until the search key is equal to the middle element of a subarray or until the subarray consists of one element that is not equal to the search key (i.e., the search key is not found).

In the worst-case scenario, searching an array of 1024 elements takes only 10 comparisons using a binary search. Repeatedly dividing 1024 by 2 (because after each comparison, we are able to eliminate half of the array) yields the values 512, 256, 128, 64, 32, 16, 8, 4, 2 and 1. The number 1024 (2^{10}) is divided by 2 only 10 times to get the value 1. Dividing by 2 is equivalent to one comparison in the binary search algorithm. An array of 1048576 (2^{20}) elements takes a maximum of 20 comparisons to find the search key. An array of one billion elements takes a maximum of 30 comparisons to find the search key. This is a tremendous increase in performance over linear searching, which requires comparison of the search key to an average of half the elements in the array. For a one-billion-element array, this is a difference between an average of 500 million comparisons and a maximum of 30 comparisons! The maximum number of comparisons needed for the binary search of any sorted array is determined by finding the first power of 2 greater than the number of elements in the array.

Performance Tip 4.3

The tremendous performance gains of the binary search over the linear search do not come without a price. Sorting an array is an expensive operation compared with searching an entire array once for one item. The overhead of sorting a large array becomes worthwhile when the array will need to be searched with high performance many times.

Figure 4.14 implements the binary search algorithm. We use four main variables: the array to sort (**@array**), the element value we are attempting to locate (**$searchKey**), the low subscript of the subarray being searched (**$lowIndex**) and the high subscript of the subarray being searched (**$high**).

Lines 6–8 create **@array** and initialize it with the even integers from 0 to 28 (a total of 15 elements). Lines 11 and 12 prompt for a search key and input that value from the user.

Lines 17–21 display the header of our program output. In this example, we use a more elaborate output to help you visualize the binary search. During each iteration of the loop that performs the binary search, we display only the subarray that is currently being searched. After the header is displayed, the code for the binary search begins (lines 24–61). Lines 32–46 of the program are specifically for our visual output and are not part of the binary search algorithm.

```perl
1   #!/usr/bin/perl
2   # Fig. 4.14: fig04_14.pl
3   # Binary search of an array.
4
5   # populate @array with the even integers from 0 to 28
6   for ( $i = 0; $i < 15; ++$i ) {
7       $array[ $i ] = 2 * $i;
8   }
9
10  # prompt the user for a search key
11  print "Enter an integer search key: ";
12  chomp( $searchKey = <STDIN> );
13
14  # display header string for output
15  print "\n";                    # output a blank line
16
```

Fig. 4.14   Binary search (part 1 of 3).

```
17   for ( $i = 0; $i < @array; ++$i ) {
18      print $i < 10 ? "   $i " : " $i ";
19   }
20
21   print "\n", "-" x ( 4 * @array ), "\n";
22
23   # perform a binary search
24   $found = 0;                      # search while !$found
25   $lowIndex = 0;                   # start index for search
26   $highIndex = $#array;            # end index for search
27
28   while ( $lowIndex <= $highIndex && !$found ) {
29      $middleIndex = ( $lowIndex + $highIndex ) / 2;
30
31      # lines 32 through 46 are for output purposes only
32      for ( $i = 0; $i < @array; ++$i ) {
33         if ( $i < $lowIndex || $i > $highIndex ) {
34            print "      ";
35         }
36         elsif ( $i == $middleIndex ) {
37            print $array[ $i ] < 10 ? "   $array[ $i ]*" :
38                                      " $array[ $i ]*";
39         }
40         else {
41            print $array[ $i ] < 10 ? "   $array[ $i ] " :
42                                      " $array[ $i ] ";
43         }
44      }
45
46      print "\n";
47      # back to binary searching
48
49      # the following if/elsif/else determines if $searchKey
50      # has been found
51      if ( $searchKey == $array[ $middleIndex ] ) {  # match
52         $index = $middleIndex;
53         $found = 1;
54      }
55      elsif ( $searchKey < $array[ $middleIndex ] ) {
56         $highIndex = $middleIndex - 1;  # search low end of array
57      }
58      else {
59         $lowIndex = $middleIndex + 1;   # search high end of array
60      }
61   }
62
63   # display results
64   if ( $found ) {       # $found == 1
65      print "\nFound $searchKey at subscript $index \n";
66   }
67   else {               # $found == 0
68      print "\n$searchKey not found \n";
69   }
```

Fig. 4.14   Binary search (part 2 of 3).

```
Enter an integer search key: 25

  0   1   2   3   4   5   6   7   8   9  10  11  12  13  14
-----------------------------------------------------------
  0   2   4   6   8  10  12  14* 16  18  20  22  24  26  28
                             16  18  20  22* 24  26  28
                                             24  26* 28
                                             24*

25 not found
```

```
Enter an integer search key: 8

  0   1   2   3   4   5   6   7   8   9  10  11  12  13  14
-----------------------------------------------------------
  0   2   4   6   8  10  12  14* 16  18  20  22  24  26  28
  0   2   4   6*  8  10  12
                  8  10* 12
                  8*

Found 8 at subscript 4
```

```
Enter an integer search key: 6

  0   1   2   3   4   5   6   7   8   9  10  11  12  13  14
-----------------------------------------------------------
  0   2   4   6   8  10  12  14* 16  18  20  22  24  26  28
  0   2   4   6*  8  10  12

Found 6 at subscript 3
```

Fig. 4.14   Binary search (part 3 of 3).

Lines 24–26 define three variables used in the binary search algorithm. Variable $found is set to 0 (false). As in the linear search of Fig. 4.13, this variable helps the program determine when the binary search completes. If $found is set to 1 (true) during the binary search, then the search key was located in the array. Variable $lowIndex is set to 0—the first element's index—and variable $highIndex is set to $#array—the last element's index. These values indicate that the search initially processes the entire array.

The **while** loop at line 28 will iterate while $lowIndex is less than or equal to $highIndex and the value of $found is not true. If $lowIndex becomes greater than $highIndex, the binary search was unable to locate the search key in the array. Line 29 determines the subscript of the middle element and assigns it to $middleIndex. This variable will be used to compare the search key with the value at location $middleIndex in the array.

The **for** structure at lines 32–44 displays the current subarray. If the control variable's value is outside the current subarray's subscript range, then spaces are output. If the control variable's value equals **$middleIndex**, then the middle element of the subarray is output, followed by an asterisk (*****) to highlight that element as the middle element. For all other control variable values, that element of the subarray is displayed. Notice in line 33 the new operator **||**—the *logical OR operator*.

The **if/elsif/else** structure in lines 51–60 performs the most important logic of the binary search. If **$searchKey** equals the middle of the current subarray, the search is complete, so **$index** is assigned **$middleIndex** and **$found** is assigned 1 (true). If **$searchKey** is less than the middle element's value, then the search must continue in the first half of the subarray. So, line 56 adjusts the **$highIndex** by assigning it the index one less than **$middleIndex**. For all other **$searchKey** values, line 59 adjusts the **$lowIndex** by assigning it the index one greater than **$middleIndex**, which enables the search to continue in the second half of the subarray. When the **while** loop at line 28 terminates, lines 64 through 69 display an appropriate message indicating whether or not the **$searchKey** was found.

4.12 Introduction to Hashes

The second multivalued (nonscalar) data type that is fundamental to the Perl language is the *hash*, or *associative array*. A hash is an unordered collection of *key-value pairs*. Rather than accessing a hash element with a subscript like an array, elements in a hash are accessed using a string known as a *key*. Each *key* must be unique. Hashes are sometimes known as associative arrays, because they define associations between keys and their values.

Common Programming Error 4.12

The keys in a hash must be unique. Using the same key more than once in a hash causes the original value for that key to be replaced with a new value; this situation could be a logic error, or it could be a normal update operation.

The special symbol for a hash is **%**. Hashes are implementations of a data structure known as a *hash table*. Chapter 20, "Data Structures," provides more insight into the inner workings of hashes. For now, we simply show you how to use them.

Because each value has an associated key, hashes take up more space than arrays. However, the internal structure of a hash provides fast lookup capabilities through which a value can often be located in one operation.

Performance Tip 4.4

Hashes are particularly useful in situations where extremely fast retrieval of values is required.

Performance Tip 4.5

Hashes require more memory than arrays. Often, there is a delicate balance between the time it takes to locate values and the amount of memory required to maintain the data. These issues are normally categorized as space-time trade-offs.

4.13 Creating and Manipulating a Hash

Like arrays, hashes can be created in two ways: either by assigning a list to the hash variable or by assigning values to single elements. Figure 4.15 shows the creation of a hash and the accessing of its elements; watch for the **=>** operator, which we have not covered yet.

```
1   #!/usr/bin/perl
2   # Fig. 4.15: fig04_15.pl
3   # Creating and accessing hash elements
4
5   # create a hash and output its values
6   %hash = ( width => '300',
7             height => '150' );
8   print "\$hash{ 'width' } = $hash{ 'width' }\n";
9   print "\$hash{ 'height' } = $hash{ 'height' }\n\n";
10
11  # assigning to a new hash element
12  $hash{ 'color' } = 'blue';
13  print "\$hash{ 'width' } = $hash{ 'width' }\n";
14  print "\$hash{ 'height' } = $hash{ 'height' }\n";
15  print "\$hash{ 'color' } = $hash{ 'color' }\n\n";
16
17  # display a hash with print
18  print "%hash\n";       # no interpolation, unlike with arrays
19  print %hash, "\n";     # difficult to read, no spaces
```

```
$hash{ 'width' } = 300
$hash{ 'height' } = 150

$hash{ 'width' } = 300
$hash{ 'height' } = 150
$hash{ 'color' } = blue

%hash
height150width300colorblue
```

Fig. 4.15   Creating and using hashes.

Lines 6 and 7 define a hash by assigning a list to a hash variable (**%hash**). As with arrays, a hash variable can have any valid identifier as a name, including the name **hash**, used here. Here, we introduce the *"corresponds to" operator*, **=>**. This operator is similar to the comma operator, except that it interprets its left-side operand as a string, so no quotes need to be placed around the string. The first value in this list (**width**) is the key of the first element to be created in the hash, and the second value in the list (**'300'**) is the value that corresponds to that key. The list elements are grouped this way into key-value pairs. So, the value **height** is the key for the second element in the hash, and the element's corresponding value is **'150'**. Lines 8 and 9 display the individual hash elements. Note that you can access a key's corresponding value by preceding the hash name with a **$** and enclosing the key in curly braces (**{}**). This expression "looks up" the value that corresponds to the key and returns that value.

Line 12

```
$hash{ 'color' } = 'blue';
```

adds a new element to the existing hash. Assigning a value to a new key in a hash automatically creates a new element in that hash. Individual hash elements are accessed in a similar manner to arrays, except that the subscript is now the key surrounded by curly braces, as shown in line 12. The technique of adding new elements to a hash can be used to create a new hash as well. Note that if a particular key already exists in the hash, assigning a value to that key replaces the old value with the new one. Lines 13–15 display the updated contents of **%hash**.

Lines 18 and 19

```
print "%hash\n";        # no interpolation, as with arrays
print %hash, "\n";      # difficult to read, no spaces
```

attempt to output **%hash** using techniques we demonstrated for arrays earlier in this chapter. Unlike arrays, hashes are not interpolated when enclosed in double quotes. So, line 18 simply displays the string **%hash**. Outputting the hash with **print** (line 19) concatenates all the key-value pairs and outputs them as one long string. Note that the key-value pairs do not appear in a way that indicates the order in which they were added to the hash.

Just as arrays have array slices, hashes have *hash slices* (Fig. 4.16). Providing multiple keys in curly braces (**{}**) returns a list of the corresponding values for those keys. The resulting list is manipulated as an array of values rather than a key-value pairs, so the **@** symbol is used for hash slices as well as array slices.

Common Programming Error 4.13

Using parentheses, ( ), rather than braces, { }, when creating a hash slice is a syntax error.

Lines 5–14 create hash **%romanNumerals**, where the keys are English words representing the numbers from 1 to 10 and the values are the Roman numerals representing these numbers. Note that the keys are not placed in quotes because they appear to the left of the "corresponds to" operator. Lines 16 and 17 display the results of a hash slice containing the values for the keys **'three'**, **'five'** and **'eight'**.

```
1   #!/usr/bin/perl
2   # Fig. 4.16: fig04_16.pl
3   # Demonstrating hash slices.
4
5   %romanNumerals = ( one   => 'I',
6                      two   => 'II',
7                      three => 'III',
8                      four  => 'IV',
9                      five  => 'V',
10                     six   => 'VI',
11                     seven => 'VII',
12                     eight => 'VIII',
13                     nine  => 'IX',
14                     ten   => 'X' );
15
16  print "The Roman numerals for three, five and eight are: ",
17        "@romanNumerals{ 'three', 'five', 'eight' }\n";
```

```
The Roman numerals for three, five and eight are: III V VIII
```

Fig. 4.16   Demonstrating hash slices.

4.14 Hash-related Functions

As with arrays, there are functions for hashes that simplify the processes of accessing and manipulating hashes. *Function* **keys** returns a list of all the keys in a hash. This function can be especially useful for looping through an entire hash table and performing an operation on the value that corresponds to each key. Similarly, *function* **values** returns a list of all the values in a hash.

Another useful function for enumerating elements of a hash is *function* **each**. This function returns one key-value pair at a time as a list in which the first element is the key and the second element is the value. Function **each** keeps track of its location in the hash, so every call to this function returns a new key-value pair. When there are no more pairs, **each** returns **undef**; if you start a new loop at this point, the next call to **each** restarts from the beginning of the hash. Calling either the **keys** or **values** function will reset the **each** function to start from the beginning of the hash when it is next called.

Function **reverse** has an interesting effect when used with hashes. It returns a list of pairs in which the keys and values of the original hash are reversed so the keys are now the values and the values are the keys. When this new list is assigned to a hash, the new hash is reversed from the old one. A hash works correctly with function **reverse** only if all the values in the hash are unique. This is because a hash requires its keys to be unique. Figure 4.17 demonstrates these functions.

```perl
1   #!/usr/bin/perl
2   # Fig. 4.17: fig04_17.pl
3   # Demonstrates hash functions keys, values, each and reverse.
4
5   %presidents = ( George => "Washington",
6                   Abe    => "Lincoln",
7                   Thomas => "Jefferson",
8                   Harry  => "Truman" );
9
10  # obtain the list of keys and display each key-value pair
11  @keys = keys( %presidents );
12
13  while ( $key = pop( @keys ) ) {
14     print "$key => $presidents{ $key }\n";
15  }
16
17  # display the list of values
18  @values = values( %presidents );
19  print "\nThe values of the hash are:\n@values\n\n";
20
21  # reverse the hash and use function each to get each pair
22  print "%presidents with its keys and values reversed\n";
23  %hash = reverse( %presidents );
24
25  while ( ( $key, $value ) = each( %presidents ) ) {
26     print "$key => $value\n";
27  }
```

Fig. 4.17   Hash functions **keys**, **values**, **each** and **reverse** (part 1 of 2).

```
Harry => Truman
Abe => Lincoln
Thomas => Jefferson
George => Washington

The values of the hash are:
Washington Jefferson Lincoln Truman

%presidents with its keys and values reversed
Washington => George
Truman => Harry
Jefferson => Thomas
Lincoln => Abe
```

Fig. 4.17   Hash functions **keys**, **values**, **each** and **reverse** (part 2 of 2).

Lines 5–8 define **%presidents** and initialize it with four key-value pairs. Line 11 uses function **keys** to obtain a list of all the keys in **%presidents** and assign them to array **@keys**. Lines 13–15 use the keys to loop through **%presidents** and display all the key-value pairs. The condition at line 13

```
$key = pop( @keys )
```

first assigns the result of function **pop** to variable **$key**, which is then used as the condition to determine if the loop should continue executing. When the array is empty, this expression evaluates to false.

Line 18 uses function **values** to obtain a list of the values in **%presidents**. Line 19 displays the list of values. Line 23

```
%presidents = reverse( %presidents );
```

uses function **reverse** to obtain a list of key-value pairs in which the keys and values are reversed. The returned list is assigned to **%presidents**. We then use the **each** function in a **while** loop (lines 25–27) to display the reversed key-value pairs. Notice that the condition in the loop

```
( $key, $value ) = each( %presidents )
```

uses list assignment to assign **$key** and **$value** the key-value pair returned by **each**. The condition becomes false when there are no more pairs to return from the hash.

Figure 4.18 demonstrates three functions: *delete*, *exists* and *defined*. Function **delete** removes an element from a hash. Function **exists** and function **defined** help us with an important concept in Perl: the differences between an element that "exists," an element that is "defined," an element with an **undef** value and an element that evaluates to true, respectively. These are confusing concepts. Some people think that if an element is not defined, it must not exist. Similarly, some people think that if an element is false, it must not be defined; these are both incorrect. If an element has never been created, then it does not exist. If an element has been created, but has not been assigned a value, then it is undefined. If a scalar contains a value that is either numeric zero (**0**) or the empty string (**""**), then it is false. To determine if a variable exists, use function **exists**. To determine if a variable has been assigned a value, use function **defined**. Of course, any condition (such as an **if** structure condition) can be used to test a variable's value for truth or falsehood. Figure 4.18 demonstrates these concepts.

```perl
1   #!/usr/bin/perl
2   # Fig. 4.18: fig04_18.pl
3   # Demonstrating functions delete, exists and defined.
4
5   %hash = ( Karl  => 12,
6             Joe   => 43,
7             Shawn => 0,
8             Paul  => 11,
9             Bill  => undef );
10
11
12  @hashKeys = keys( %hash );
13
14  for ( $i = 0; $i < @hashKeys; ++$i ) {
15     print "$hashKeys[ $i ] => $hash{ $hashKeys[ $i ] }\n";
16  }
17
18
19  delete( $hash{ 'Joe' } );
20
21
22
23  while ( $key = pop( @hashKeys ) ) {
24     print "\n";
25
26
27     if ( exists( $hash{ $key } ) ) {
28        print "$key exists in the hash.\n";
29     }
30     else {
31        print "$key doesn't exist in the hash.\n";
32     }
33
34
35     if ( defined( $hash{ $key } ) ) {
36        print "$key is defined as $hash{ $key }.\n";
37     }
38     else {
39        print "$key is undefined.\n";
40     }
41
42
43     if ( $hash{ $key } ) {
44        print "$key is true.\n";
45     }
46     else {
47        print "$key is false.\n";
48     }
49  }
```

Fig. 4.18   Hash functions **delete**, **exists** and **defined** (part 1 of 2).

```
Joe => 43
Bill =>
Karl => 12
Paul => 11
Shawn => 0

Shawn exists in the hash.
Shawn is defined as 0.
Shawn is false.

Paul exists in the hash.
Paul is defined as 11.
Paul is true.

Karl exists in the hash.
Karl is defined as 12.
Karl is true.

Bill exists in the hash.
Bill is undefined.
Bill is false.

Joe doesn't exist in the hash.
Joe is undefined.
Joe is false.
```

Fig. 4.18   Hash functions **delete**, **exists** and **defined** (part 2 of 2).

Lines 5–9 create **%hash**. Line 12 assigns to **@hashKeys** all the keys in **%hash** using function **keys**. Array **@hashKeys** is used in lines 14–16 to display **%hash**'s contents and lines in 23–49 to demonstrate functions **exists** and **defined**.

Line 19

```
delete( $hash{ 'Joe' } );
```

removes the key-value pair for key **'Joe'** from **%hash**. At this point, the key **'Joe'** no longer exists in the hash.

The **while** structure (lines 23–49) iterates over array **@hashKeys** and uses three **if/else** structures to test various conditions. The **if/else** structure in lines 27–32 tests the condition

```
exists( $hash{ $key } )
```

Function **exists** returns true in this context if the key **$key** is in the hash. For all the keys in **@hashKeys** except **'Joe'**, this condition is true.

The **if/else** structure at lines 35–40 tests the condition

```
defined( $hash{ $key } )
```

Function **defined** returns true in this context if the key **$key** is in the hash and its value is defined. Keys **'Shawn'**, **'Paul'** and **'Karl'** each have defined values in the hash. So, for these three keys, the condition evaluates to true. The key **'Bill'** does exist in the hash, but its value was originally specified as **undef**. So, for key **'Bill'**, the condition evaluates to false. Finally, key **'Joe'** does not even exist in the hash, so its value cannot be defined. Therefore, the condition also evaluates to false for key **'Joe'**.

The **if/else** structure at lines 43–48 tests the condition

```
$hash{ $key }
```

to determine if the value for each **$key** is true or false when evaluated in a boolean context. In this case, the condition is false for the undefined keys **'Bill'** and **'Joe'** and for the key **'Shawn'**, which has a value of 0 (false). The other two keys, **'Paul'** and **'Karl'**, are nonzero, so they evaluate to true.

4.15 Internet and World Wide Web Resources

tlc.perlarchive.com/9910/01c.shtml
This site provides a comprehensive overview of hashes.

www.geeksalad.org/business/training/perl/Chapter_HASH.html
This site discusses the syntax, initialization and functions of hashes.

www.devdaily.com/Dir/Perl/Articles_and_Tutorials/Arrays
This site contains links to various tutorials and articles on the subject of arrays and hashes.

tlc.perlarchive.com/9909/01b.shtml
This site provides a comprehensive overview of arrays.

www.cclabs.missouri.edu/things/instruction/perl/
perlcourse.html#elements
This section of a Perl tutorial briefly discusses arrays, associative arrays (hashes) and scalar variables.

docs.rinet.ru/Using_Perl5_in_Web/ch1.htm#DataTypes
This Web page provides an overview of the Perl data types, including scalar variables, arrays and associative arrays (hashes).

SUMMARY

- Arrays are data structures consisting of related data items of the same type.

- Array variables are prefixed with the **@** type identifier symbol.

- A list in Perl is a collection of values. To create a list, separate a series of values with commas and enclose the list in parentheses, **()**.

- List context is when a Perl operation expects a list to complete its task.

- Scalar context is when a Perl operation expects only a single value to complete its task.

- An array variable stores a list of scalars. Each array can hold zero or more scalars.

- Each individual array element has a position number (or index), which is used to access (or refer to) that element. Elements are accessed by giving the name of the array (preceded by **$**, not **@**), followed by the position number of the particular element in square brackets (**[]**). The position number contained within the square brackets is formally called a subscript.

- The primary difference between a list and an array is that an array is a named variable, whereas a list is considered to be a constant. An array stores a list for future use in a program.

- To access an array element, precede the name of the array with the **$** symbol, not the **@** symbol.

- The brackets, **[]**, that enclose the subscript of an array are actually an operator in Perl. This operator can be applied to lists as well as arrays.

- It is not required that all the elements of an array be of the same type (e.g., integers, floating-point numbers and strings). However, it is required that all the elements of an array be scalars.

- There are several ways to create an array in Perl. The most straightforward way is to assign a list of values to an array variable. Another way to create an array is to assign a value to an element of an array that does not yet exist. The array is automatically created with the appropriate number of elements to allow for the specified subscript value.

- Perl provides two repetition structures—**for** and **foreach**—that are useful for looping through an array of elements.

- The general format of the **for** structure is

  ```
  for ( initialization; loopContinuationTest; increment ) {
      statements
  }
  ```

  where the *initialization* expression initializes the loop's control variable, *loopContinuationTest* is the loop-continuation condition (containing the final value of the control variable for which the condition is true) and *increment* increments the control variable.

- The three expressions in the **for** structure are optional; however, the two semicolons in the **for** structure are required.

- The initialization, loop-continuation condition and increment portions of a **for** structure can contain arithmetic expressions.

- The control variable is frequently printed or used in calculations in the body of a **for** structure, but it does not have to be. It is common to use the control variable for controlling repetition while never mentioning it in the body of the **for** structure.

- In a **for** structure, the initialization occurs once and the incrementation occurs each time after the body executes.

- Accessing an array element for which a value has not been provided returns the undefined value, **undef**.

- You can check to see if an element has been defined or not by using function **defined**. Function **defined** returns a value of true if its argument is defined (i.e., it has been assigned a value); otherwise, it returns a value of false.

- If an array is output as part of a double-quoted string, all the array elements are displayed normally, separated by a space character between each element. You can specify the separator string by assigning a string to **$"**.

- The logical negation operator (**!**) reverses the value of a condition: If the expression to its right returns true, the logical negation operator makes the value false, and if the expression to its right returns false, the logical negation operator makes the value true.

- The operator **qw** takes strings separated by spaces as arguments and converts the strings into a list of strings.

- The range operator (**..**) creates a consecutive range of string or numeric values.

- In scalar context, an array returns the total number of elements of the array.

- In a scalar context, a list returns the value of the rightmost element of the list.

- The expression **scalar(@array)** returns the total number of elements in **@array**.

- To determine the last index number of an array, precede the array name with the **$#** prefix.

- The bracket operator, **[]**, can also be used to create a list containing the specified set of elements from an array. These sections of arrays are called array slices.

- List assignment enables a list of values to be assigned to a list of scalars.

- If there are more variables in the list on the left side of the assignment operator than there are values to assign, the remaining variables have the value **undef**. If an array appears on the left side of a list assignment, Perl allocates enough elements in the array to store all the remaining elements in the list on the right side of the assignment operator. Any other variables after the array on the left-side are assigned the value **undef**.

- Function **push** receives two arguments: an array and a list of elements to be inserted at the end of the array. The result of the expression is to assign the new value to the element that is one past the end of the array.

- Function **pop** removes the last element from an array and returns that element.

- Function **unshift** inserts an element at the front of an array.

- Function **shift** removes and returns the first element of an array.

- Function **splice** removes or replaces slices of an array. The function returns one or more of the elements that were removed or **undef** if no elements were removed. The actual value returned depends on the context. In list context, **splice** returns a list of all the removed elements. In scalar context, **splice** returns only the last element removed.

- Function **reverse** takes a list as an argument and returns a new list with the same contents in reverse order; the original list is left unchanged.

- Function **sort** returns a copy of a list sorted lexically, while the original list passed to it is left unchanged.

- Operator **cmp** compares its two operands lexically (the default for function **sort**), and operator **<=>** compares its two operands numerically.

- The process of finding a particular element of an array is called searching.

- The linear search compares each element of an array with the search key.

- The logical AND operator, **&&**, combines two conditions to create a more complex condition. In a logical AND expression, the condition on the left of the operator is tested first. If that condition is true, the condition on the right side of the operator is tested next. The entire logical AND expression is considered to be true only if both the left-side condition and the right-side condition are true. If either is false, the entire expression is false.

- Linear search works well for small arrays and for unsorted arrays. However, for large arrays, linear search is inefficient. If the array is sorted, the high-speed binary search technique can be used.

- The binary search algorithm requires the array to be sorted beforehand. This algorithm eliminates from the search one half of the elements in the array being searched after each comparison.

- A hash, or associative array, is an unordered collection of key-value pairs, where each key has a corresponding value.

- Elements in a hash are accessed using a string known as a key. Each key must be unique.

- Hashes are sometimes known as associative arrays, because they define associations between keys and their values.

- The type identifier symbol for a hash is **%**.

- Because each value has an associated key, hashes take up more space than arrays.

- Hashes are particularly useful in situations where extremely fast retrieval of values is required.

- Hashes can be created in two ways: either by assigning a list to a hash variable or by assigning values to single elements. Individual hash elements are accessed in a similar manner as elements of arrays, except the subscript is a key surrounded by curly braces.

- The "corresponds to" operator, **=>**, is similar to the comma operator, except that it interprets its left-side operand as a string, so no quotes need to be placed around the string.

- Hashes are not interpolated when enclosed in double quotes.
- Just as arrays have array slices, hashes have hash slices. The resulting list is manipulated as an array of values, so the **@** symbol is used for hash slices as well as array slices.
- Function **keys** returns a list of all the keys in a hash.
- Function **values** returns a list of all the values in a hash.
- Function **each** returns one key-value pair at a time as a list in which the first element is the key and the second element is a value.
- Function **reverse** returns a list of pairs in which the keys and values of the original hash are reversed so the keys are now the values and the values are now the keys.
- Function **delete** removes an element from a hash.
- If an element has never been created, then it does not exist.
- If an element has been created, but has not been assigned a value, then it is undefined.
- To determine if a variable exists, use function **exists**.

TERMINOLOGY

$# prefix
% type identifier symbol
&& (logical AND operator)
.. (range operator)
@ type identifier symbol
[] (subscript operator)
|| (logical OR operator)
<=> (numeric comparison operator)
=> ("corresponds to" operator)
array
array in scalar context
array slice
associative array
binary search
body of a loop
boolean variable
cmp operator
collection of values
comma operator (**,**)
comma-separated list
control variable
defined function
delete function
diamond symbol
each function
element of an array
empty list (**()**)
exists function
final value of a control variable
flatten a sublist
for repetition structure
foreach repetition structure
hash

hash element
hash element value
hash slice
hash table
increment a control variable
index
infinite loop
key
key-value pair
keys function
linear search
list
list assignment
list context
list element
logical AND operator (**&&**)
logical operator
logical OR operator (**||**)
loop-continuation condition
lvalue ("left value")
name of an array
negative subscript
off-by-one error
pop function
push function
qw operator
range operator (**..**)
rectangle symbol
relational operator(s)
reverse function
scalar context
scalar function
search an array

search key

shift function

sort function

splice function

sublist

subscript

subscript operator (**[]**)

undef

unshift function

values function

zero-based counting

zeroth element

SELF-REVIEW EXERCISES

4.1   Fill in the blanks in each of the following statements:
a) Lists and tables of values are stored in _____ or _____.
b) The elements of an array are related by the fact that they have the same _____.
c) The number used to refer to a particular element of an array is called its _____.
d) The process of placing the elements of an array in order is called _____ the array.
e) Determining if an array contains a certain key value is called _____ the array.
f) _____ is when a Perl operation expects a list to complete its task.
g) Functions _____ and _____ insert and remove elements at the end of an array.
h) Functions _____ and _____ insert and remove elements at the beginning of an array.
i) A hash stores _____-_____ pairs.
j) The _____ type qualifier precedes a hash variable.
k) The _____ type qualifier precedes an array variable.
l) Operator _____ is used to access the individual elements of an array.
m) When accessing a value for a particular key in a hash, _____ containing the key are placed after the hash name.

4.2   State whether the following are *true* or *false*. If *false*, explain why.
a) An array can store many different types of values.
b) An array subscript can be a floating-point number.
c) If there are fewer initializers in an initializer list than the number of elements in the array, the remaining elements are initialized with **undef**.
d) The expression **$hash[$key]** returns the value associated with **$key** in **%hash**.
e) A binary search of an array is slower than a linear search of an array.
f) A linear search requires that the array elements be in sorted order before searching.
g) If an array is output as part of a double-quoted string, the elements of the array are all displayed as one long string, with no spaces between the elements.
h) The statement **print "%hash\n";** displays **%hash** followed by a newline (i.e., no elements of the hash are displayed).

4.3   Write statements to accomplish the following:
a) Create an array called **numbers**, and set its elements to the integers from 1 to 100.
b) Add a new element containing the value 0 to the beginning of array **numbers**.
c) Print array **numbers** with a space between each element.
d) Repeat part (c) using a **for** loop to output each element.
e) Exchange the values at locations 0 and 1 of array **numbers** using list assignment.
f) Remove the first two elements of the array using function **splice**.

4.4   Find the error in each of the following program segments, and correct the error:
a) `@array[ 3 ];   # obtain the value at location 3`
b) `for ( $i = 0, $i < @numbers, ++$i )`
   `     print "$numbers[ $i ] ";`
c) `@hash[ 'key1', 'key2', 'key3' ];   # create hash slice`

ANSWERS TO SELF-REVIEW EXERCISES

4.1   a)   arrays, hashes. b) name. c) subscript. d) sorting. e) searching. f) List context. g) **push**, **pop**. h) **unshift**, **shift**. i) key, value. j) **%**. k) **@**. l) **[]**. m) **{}**.

4.2   a)   True.
b)   False. An array subscript must be an integer or an integer expression.
c)   True.
d)   False. The expression **$hash{ $key }** returns the value associated with **$key** in **%hash**. The square brackets are used with array elements.
e)   False. Binary searching is faster.
f)   False. Binary searching requires array elements to be in sorted order. For a linear search, the elements can be in any order.
g)   False. Every element is separated by a space.
h)   True.

4.3   a)   `@numbers = ( 1 .. 100 );`
b)   `unshift( @numbers, 0 );`
c)   `print "@numbers";`
d)   `for ( $i = 0; $i < @numbers; ++$i )`
         `print "$numbers[ $i ] ";`
e)   `( $numbers[ 0 ], $numbers[ 1 ] ) = ( $numbers[ 1 ], $numbers[ 0 ] );`
f)   `splice( @numbers, 0, 2 );`

4.4   a)   Error: To access the value of an array element, the array name must be preceded by **$**. In the current form, an array slice containing one element is returned.
Correction: Replace **@** with **$**.
b)   Error: The commas in the **for** structure header result in syntax errors.
Correction: Replace the commas with semicolons.
c)   Error: The square brackets (**[]**) are used when creating array slices, not hash slices.
Correction: Change the square brackets to braces (**{}**).

EXCERCISES

4.5   Create an array containing the values 0 through 9. Then create a hash with the values from 0 through 9 as the keys of the hash. The corresponding values should be the English word for each numeric value. So, the key **'0'** should be associated with **'zero'**, **'1'** with **'one'**, etc. Display the contents of both the array and the hash.

4.6   Create an array with an even number of elements. Assign that array to a hash. Display the keys of the hash, and then display the values of the hash.

4.7   Create a deck of cards using an array (the numbers 1 to 52 will suffice). Now shuffle that deck once such that after the shuffle, the deck contains the values in the order 1, 27, 2, 28, 3, 29, etc.

4.8   Create an array of two-digit positive numbers. Display the size of the array, the sum of the array elements and the average of the array elements. Then, determine and print the five largest values in the array.

4.9   Create an array of values. Use a hash to determine if there are any duplicate values in the array. [*Hint:* For each value in the array, determine if that value is a key in the hash. If it is, the value is a duplicate. Otherwise, insert that value in the hash.]

4.10   Section 4.3 stated that when a list is evaluated, all sublists in the list are "flattened." Write a program that defines a list of values and proves this statement. In that list, include sublists in parentheses and at least one array and one hash.

Control
Structures: Part II

Objectives

- To be able to use the **foreach** repetition structure to use list elements as control variables in repeated statements.
- To be able to use and understand the **next**, **last** and **redo** loop controls.
- To be able to use blocks and block labels.
- To understand Perl's logical operators and their precedence.
- To be able to use the **die** and **warn** functions to test a program for errors.

Who can control his fate?
William Shakespeare, *Othello*

The used key is always bright.
Benjamin Franklin

Intelligence...is the faculty of making artificial objects, especially tools to make tools.
Henri Bergson

Man is a tool-making animal.
Benjamin Franklin

5.1 Introduction

This chapter completes our discussion of control structures. We begin by discussing the **foreach** repetition structure and comparing it with the **for** structure. We focus on using Perl's control structures to help us write clean and effective code. We also introduce logical operators and discuss how they can be used in controlling program flow. We conclude the chapter with a summary of Perl's control structures and of the principles of structured programming; these control structures are the building blocks of Perl program control and constitute the foundations of all structured programming.

5.2 `foreach` Repetition Structure

The **foreach** *repetition structure* allows a programmer to *iterate* over a list of values, accessing and manipulating each element. A benefit of this control structure is that the programmer is not required to maintain a separate counter-control variable to manage the repetition structure. To demonstrate the **foreach** structure, Fig. 5.1 computes the squares of the numbers from 1 to 10 and displays the results.

Testing and Debugging Tip 5.1

*The **foreach** repetition structure eliminates the off-by-one errors that occur when programmers use counter-controlled repetition to iterate over the elements of an array.*

Using the range operator, `..`, in line 5, we store the integers 1 to 10 in **@array**. When the **foreach** structure (line 7) executes, the control variable **$number** is assigned the first element of the list (the value 1). Line 8 uses the exponentiation operator to raise the value of variable **$number** to the second power (i.e., square the value).

```
1   #!/usr/bin/perl
2   # Fig. 5.1: fig05_01.pl
3   # Using foreach to iterate over an array.
4
5   @array = ( 1 .. 10 );              # create array containing 1-10
6
7   foreach $number ( @array ) {       # for each element in @array
8       $number **= 2;                 # square the value
9   }
10
11  print "@array\n";                  # display the results
```

```
1 4 9 16 25 36 49 64 81 100
```

Fig. 5.1   Using **foreach** to iterate over an array.

After the exponentiation is performed, the next iteration of the loop begins, setting **$number** to the second element of the list (the value 2) and squaring it. The loop continues to set **$number** to the next element of the array until every element of **@array** is processed. At that point, the **foreach** structure terminates.

It is important to note that the control variable **$number** represents a particular item in **@array**. Changing the value of the control variable in the body of a **foreach** structure modifies the element in **@array** that the control variable is currently representing. We prove this point in line 11, when the program displays the contents of **@array**. We can see that each time line 8 was executed, the current value of **@array** was modified.

The general format for the **foreach** structure is

```
foreach controlVariable ( list ) {
    statements
}
```

where *list* can be any list, literal or array and *controlVariable* represents one item of *list* during each iteration. Figure 5.2 demonstrates the **foreach** structure.

```
1   #!/usr/bin/perl
2   # Fig. 5.2: fig05_02.pl
3   # Demonstrating different properties of the foreach structure.
4
5   # This structure loops 10 times, not requiring a control variable.
6   foreach ( 1 .. 10 ) {
7       print "*";
8   }
9
10  print "\n";
11
12  # Standard foreach structure. Prints the letters A-G.
13  foreach $letter ( 'A' .. 'G' ) {
14      print "$letter";
15  }
```

Fig. 5.2   Demonstrating different properties of the **foreach** structure (part 1 of 2).

```
16
17   print "\n";
18
19   # Duplicate of the structure above, but with the for keyword.
20   # This structure will behave exactly the same way.
21   for $letter ( 'A' .. 'G' ) {
22       print "$letter";
23   }
24
25   print "\n";
26
27   # Standard for structure.
28   # Loops 5 times, printing the multiples of 5 from 0-20.
29   for ( $number = 0; $number <= 20; $number += 5 ) {
30       print "$number ";
31   }
32
33   print "\n";
34
35   # Duplicate of the structure above with the foreach keyword.
36   # Again, this structure will behave the same as the one above.
37   foreach ( $number = 0; $number <= 20; $number += 5 ) {
38       print "$number ";
39   }
40
41   print "\n";
```

```
**********
ABCDEFG
ABCDEFG
0 5 10 15 20
0 5 10 15 20
```

Fig. 5.2   Demonstrating different properties of the **foreach** structure (part 2 of 2).

Lines 6–8 introduce the first **foreach** structure, which does not have a control variable. This feature is one of the properties of the **foreach** structure that makes it so useful: It can be used as a shorthand replacement for the **for** structure. In the code in Fig. 5.2, we use the **foreach** structure to loop 10 times, printing an asterisk with each iteration. This type of repetition does not need a counter-control variable, test condition or increment statement. As a result, the code is cleaner and more readable.

Lines 13–15

```
foreach $letter ( 'A' .. 'G' ) {
    print "$letter";
}
```

show a standard **foreach** structure in which **$letter** is the control variable, the repetition structure iterates over the letters from A through G and the **print** statement that outputs each letter forms the body of the loop. The **for** repetition structure in lines 21–23 is identical to the **foreach** structure in lines 13–15. This demonstrates that the **foreach** keyword itself is interchangeable with the keyword **for**. Note that when a **for** structure mimics a **foreach** structure, the semicolons that normally separate the initialization, condition and increment of the loop are not required.

Lines 29–31

```
for ( $number = 0; $number <= 20; $number += 5 ) {
   print "$number ";
}
```

show a standard **for** structure. An equivalent **foreach** structure is shown in lines 37–39. Note that when a **foreach** structure mimics a **for** structure, the semicolons separating the initialization, condition and increment of the loop are required.

Good Programming Practice 5.1

*To avoid confusion, always use **for** structures for counter-controlled repetition and always use **foreach** structures for iterating over a list of values.*

5.3 Special Variable $_

The Perl programming language defines a set of *special variables*, which perform a variety of functions. These variables are created by Perl for the programmer's convenience, and frequently they are used as default variables. For example, the **$_** *special variable* is the default argument for many Perl functions and is also the default control variable for many Perl control structures, including the **foreach** structure. Thus, the **$_** special variable will take the place of a missing parameter in a function call or the missing control variable in a **foreach** repetition structure.

To demonstrate use of the **$_** variable, we discuss the fact that the control variable is optional in **foreach**. Thus, the following is a correct use of **foreach**:

```
foreach ( list ) {
   statements
}
```

When no control variable is explicitly stated, special variable **$_** stores the value of the current element of the list during each iteration of the loop.

Figure 5.3 shows a simple example using **$_**. When no control variable is explicitly stated, the special variable **$_** stores the value of the current element of the list during each iteration of the loop. Consider the first two **foreach** structures in Fig. 5.3. The first one (lines 6–8) is the standard way to use the **foreach** repetition structure, with a control variable. This structure uses the control variable to display each value in the list. The **foreach** structure at lines 13–15 leaves out the control variable. In this case, special variable **$_** is used as the control variable, and its current value (i.e., the current element in the list) is displayed during each iteration of the loop. The last **foreach** structure (lines 19–21) uses **$_** both as the control variable for the **foreach** structure and the default argument for the **print** statement. During each iteration of the loop, **print** implicitly uses the variable **$_** to output each name. Note that all the **foreach** structures in this program are equivalent to

```
foreach $_ ( 'Amanda ', 'Jeff ', 'Sarah ', 'David' ) {
```

and all the **print** statements are equivalent to

```
print $_;
```

```perl
1   #!/usr/bin/perl
2   # Fig. 5.3: fig05_03.pl
3   # Using variable $_ with foreach and print.
4
5   # Standard foreach structure, printing the values in a list
6   foreach $name ( 'Amanda ', 'Jeff ', 'Sarah ', 'David ' ) {
7      print "$name";
8   }
9
10  print "\n";
11
12  # $_ takes the place of the control variable
13  foreach ( 'Amanda ', 'Jeff ', 'Sarah ', 'David ' ) {
14     print "$_";
15  }
16
17  print "\n";
18
19  foreach ( 'Amanda ', 'Jeff ', 'Sarah ', 'David ' ) {
20     print;    # print the default variable's ($_) value
21  }
22
23  print "\n";
```

```
Amanda Jeff Sarah David
Amanda Jeff Sarah David
Amanda Jeff Sarah David
```

Fig. 5.3   Explicitly and Implicitly using variable **$_** with **foreach** and **print**.

5.4 Loop Control Shortcuts: grep and map

Certain operations are performed iteratively on a list's elements so frequently that Perl provides built-in functions to simplify the operations. These functions are shortcuts, which allow programmers to simplify the structure and reduce the size of their programs. This, in turn, increases the readability of the program, an extremely important feature when working on large group projects.

Functions *grep* and *map* serve as encapsulated forms of common operations that iterate over lists. Following the fundamentals of the **foreach** repetition structure, both iterate through a given list and assign each list item to the **$_** special character in turn.

Function **grep** is named after the UNIX utility of the same name, which performs searches on text files. Similarly, the Perl function **grep** searches through a list and creates a new list containing only elements that satisfy a specified condition. Function **grep** takes both a conditional expression and a list as parameters, as in

> *newList* = **grep(** *conditionalExpression*, *list* **);**

Function **grep** is essentially a shortcut for

```
foreach ( list ) {
   push( newList, $_ ) if conditionalExpression;
}
```

where every element of *list* that satisfies the *conditionalExpression* is placed in *newList* by function **push**.

Function **map** allows a programmer to create a list reflecting a function applied to each element of a given list. Function **map** is called with two arguments, as follows:

> *newList* = **map(** *function*, *list* **);**

Function **map** returns a new list reflecting the changes. Function **map** is equivalent to

```
foreach ( list ) {
    push( newList, function applied to $_ );
}
```

It is important to note that it is possible for function **map** to modify the elements of the original list by assigning a value to **$_** in the code, where **$_** will apply to every element of the original list.

Performance Tip 5.1

*Functions **grep** and **map** are optimized to perform their tasks more efficiently that corresponding repetition structure implemented by the programmer.*

Figure 5.4 demonstrates functions **grep** and **map** and their equivalent "long form" versions using **foreach** repetition structures. Lines 9–11 are equivalent to the **grep** function call in line 16. The call to **grep** specifies that each element of **@numbers** that is less than 6 should be part of the resulting list (which is assigned to **@smallNumbers2**). Lines 20–22 are equivalent to the **map** function call in line 27. The call to **map** specifies that each element of **@numbers** should be multiplied by 2 and then placed in the resulting list (which is assigned to **@doubledNumbers2**).

```perl
1   #!/usr/bin/perl
2   # Fig. 5.4: fig05_04.pl
3   # Demonstrating map and grep.
4
5   @numbers = ( 1 .. 10 );
6   print "\@numbers: @numbers\n\n";
7
8   # locate all numbers less than 6
9   foreach ( @numbers ) {
10      push( @smallNumbers, $_ ) if $_ < 6;
11  }
12
13  print "Numbers less than 6:\n",
14        "foreach: @smallNumbers\n";
15
16  @smallNumbers2 = grep( $_ < 6, @numbers );
17  print "grep:    @smallNumbers2\n\n";
18
19  # multiply every number by 2
20  foreach ( @numbers ) {
21      push( @doubledNumbers, $_ * 2 );
22  }
23
```

Fig. 5.4   Demonstrating **grep** and **map** (part 1 of 2).

```
24    print "Double each number:\n",
25          "foreach: @doubledNumbers\n";
26
27    @doubledNumbers2 = map( $_ * 2, @numbers );
28    print "map:      @doubledNumbers2\n";
```

```
@numbers: 1 2 3 4 5 6 7 8 9 10

Numbers less than 6:
foreach: 1 2 3 4 5
grep:    1 2 3 4 5

Double each number:
foreach: 2 4 6 8 10 12 14 16 18 20
map:     2 4 6 8 10 12 14 16 18 20
```

Fig. 5.4   Demonstrating **grep** and **map** (part 2 of 2).

5.5 Case Study: Computing Mean, Median and Mode

We now turn to a larger, more practical example to show how the **foreach** control structure can be used with arrays to analyze a set of data. Computers are commonly used to compile and analyze the results of surveys and opinion polls. Figure 5.5 initializes array **@opinions** with 50 responses to a survey (lines 5 through 9). Each response is a number from 1 to 9. The program computes the *mean*, *median* and *mode* of the 50 values and displays the results and a graph containing the frequency of each response.

```
1    #!/usr/bin/perl
2    # Fig. 5.5: fig05_05.pl
3    # Survey data analysis: Determining the mean, median and mode.
4
5    @opinions = ( 8, 9, 4, 7, 8, 5, 6, 4, 9, 9,
6                  7, 8, 9, 5, 4, 8, 7, 8, 7, 7,
7                  6, 6, 8, 9, 1, 9, 8, 7, 8, 7,
8                  7, 8, 9, 8, 9, 4, 9, 6, 8, 4,
9                  6, 7, 3, 4, 8, 7, 9, 8, 9, 2  );
10
11   # determine the mean
12   $total = 0;
13
14   foreach ( @opinions ) {
15       $total += $_;
16   }
17
18   $mean = $total / @opinions;
19   print "Survey mean result:    $mean\n";
20
21   # determine the median
22   @sorted = sort { $a <=> $b } @opinions;
23   $middle = @sorted / 2;       # middle element subscript
```

Fig. 5.5   Survey data analysis program (part 1 of 2).

```
24
25    # for an even number of elements, average the two middle
26    # elements to determine the median; otherwise, use the
27    # middle element
28    if ( @sorted %2 == 0 ) {   # even number of elements
29       $median =
30          ( $sorted[ $middle - 1 ] + $sorted[ $middle ] ) / 2;
31    }
32    else {                     # odd number of elements
33       $median = $sorted[ $middle ];
34    }
35
36    print "Survey median result: $median\n";
37
38    # determine the mode
39    $mode = 0;
40
41    foreach ( @opinions ) {
42       ++$frequency[ $_ ];       # increment the frequency counter
43
44       # if the current frequency is greater than the $mode's
45       # frequency, change $mode to $_
46       if ( $frequency[ $_ ] > $frequency[ $mode ] ) {
47          $mode = $_;
48       }
49    }
50
51    print "Survey mode result:    $mode\n\n";
52
53    # display a frequency graph
54    print "Response\tFrequency\n";
55    print "--------\t---------\n";
56
57    foreach ( 1 .. 9 ) {
58       print "$_\t\t", "*" x $frequency[ $_ ], "\n";
59    }
```

```
Survey mean result:    6.86
Survey median result: 7
Survey mode result:    8

Response          Frequency
--------          ---------
1                 *
2                 *
3                 *
4                 ******
5                 **
6                 *****
7                 *********
8                 ************
9                 **********
```

Fig. 5.5   Survey data analysis program (part 2 of 2).

The mean is the arithmetic average of the 50 values. Lines 12–19 compute and print the mean by totaling the 50 elements (lines 12–16) and dividing the result by **@opinions** (line 18), which returns the array's length (50) in this scalar context.

The median is the "middle value" in the sorted set of responses. Lines 22–36 determine the median. First, line 22 calls Perl's **sort** function with the **<=>** numerical comparison operator to sort the array of responses into ascending numerical order. When there is an even number of elements (as is the case here), the median should be calculated as the mean of the two middle elements. To make this calculation, line 23 divides the number of elements by 2 to determine the latter of the two middle-element subscripts in the array. (In a 50-element array, subscripts 24 and 25 are the two middle-element subscripts.) The **if/else** structure in lines 28–34 determines if the number of elements in the array is even or odd. In this example, lines 29 and 30 execute to calculate the average of the two middle elements. If the array contains an odd number of elements, line 33 would execute and simply determine the value of the middle element of the array.

The mode is the value that occurs most frequently among the 50 responses. Lines 41–49 count the responses and find the mode. Here, we keep track of how many votes each survey response (1 through 9) has received, storing these results in array **@frequency**. The responses 1 through 9 serve as the indices of the array. Note that we do not need to create array **@frequency** before we use it; we simply start adding elements.

Let us examine closely how the counting of responses works. In line 42

```
++$frequency[ $_ ];       # increment the frequency counter
```

the expression **$frequency[$_]** accesses the value in **@frequency** with index **$_** and uses **++** to add 1 to that element's value. We have just started counting results, so if **$frequency[$_]** has never been used, it is created with an undefined value. Incrementing this element means that it will be evaluated in a numeric context, giving it the value of zero before the incrementing takes place. Once the variable is evaluated to zero and the incrementing is performed, its value will be 1. For example, in the first iteration, **$_** is equal to 8 (the first element of **@opinions**). The variable **$frequency[8]** has never been used, and so it is created with an undefined value. Because it is evaluated in a numeric context, its value before the increment becomes zero. Therefore, after the increment, the value of **$frequency[8]** is 1. During the next iteration of the **foreach** loop, **$frequency[9]** will be incremented, followed by **$frequency[4]**, etc.

Each time we count a survey response, we also calculate the current mode. The check is performed by the **if** structure at line 46, which checks if the count for the current response (**$_**) is greater than the count for the current **$mode**. If so, **$_** is the most popular response so far, and **$mode** is assigned **$_**. Note that on the first iteration, **$mode** automatically becomes 8. Variable **$mode** is initially 0, and **$frequency[0]** is undefined. When **$frequency[8]** and **$frequency[0]** are compared, the undefined value of **$frequency[0]** evaluates to 0, which is less than **$frequency[8]** (that is, 1). So the **$mode** becomes 8 at this point. In this example, we do not test for the case of a tie, in which two or more response values have the same frequency.

A **foreach** loop also can iterate over a hash using the keys of the hash returned by function **keys**. Figure 5.6 shows how you might perform the same type of analysis performed in Fig. 5.5 to calculate the frequency of a value in an array where the values are strings, instead of numbers.

```perl
1   #!/usr/bin/perl
2   # Fig. 5.6: fig05_06.pl
3   # Using foreach loops with hashes.
4
5   @opinions = qw( what word is being used most in this array is
6                   what this is used what most is is array what
7                   word used is most is array what is this is array
8                   what is is array this is most );
9
10  foreach ( @opinions ) {
11     ++$hash{ $_ };
12  }
13
14  # display sorted by key in ascending order
15  print "Word\tFrequency\n";
16  print "----\t---------\n";
17
18  foreach ( sort keys( %hash ) ) {
19     print "$_\t", "*" x $hash{ $_ }, "\n";
20  }
21
22  # display sorted by frequency in descending order
23  print "\nWord\tFrequency\n";
24  print "----\t---------\n";
25
26  foreach ( sort { $hash{ $b } <=> $hash{ $a } } keys( %hash ) ) {
27     print "$_\t", "*" x $hash{ $_ }, "\n";
28  }
```

```
Word       Frequency
----       ---------
array      *****
being      *
in         *
is         ***********
most       ****
this       ****
used       ***
what       ******
word       **

Word       Frequency
----       ---------
is         ***********
what       ******
array      *****
most       ****
this       ****
used       ***
word       **
in         *
being      *
```

Fig. 5.6   String data analysis program.

Lines 10–12 count the frequency of each string in the array in a similar manner to that in Fig. 5.5. However, here the counters are elements in a hash. When the **++** operator is applied to the value associated with a particular key (as in line 11), that key's value is incremented and replaces the original value associated with that key in the hash.

After the frequencies of the words are tallied, we display the results, sorted by key in ascending order (lines 15–20) and sorted by frequency in descending order (lines 23–28). The **foreach** structure in line 18 iterates over the list returned by the expression

```
sort keys( %hash )
```

First, function **keys** returns the set of keys in **%hash**. Then, function **sort** orders the keys into lexically ascending order. Function **sort** returns the sorted list that is used in the **foreach** structure. Line 19

```
print "$_\t", "*" x $hash{ $_ }, "\n";
```

prints the current value in the list (**$_**), followed by a tab character to start a new column. Then, a row of asterisks (*****) is displayed to provide a graphical representation of the current value in the list.

The **foreach** structure at line 26 iterates over the list returned by the expression

```
sort { $hash{ $b } <=> $hash{ $a } } keys( %hash )
```

The sorting order **$hash{ $b } <=> $hash{ $a }** specifies that the values in the hash for keys **$b** and **$a** should be compared and sorted in descending numerical order. Remember that function **sort** requires variables called **$a** and **$b** to be used in specifying sort order. Also remember that if **$a** is on the left side of the **<=>** operator (or **cmp** operator for strings) the sort order is ascending; otherwise, the sort order is descending.

5.6 Loop Controls: The next Statement

The next three sections deal with *loop controls*. The loop controls **next**, **last** and **redo** alter the flow of control in a control structure. The **next** *statement*, when executed in a **while**, **until**, **for** or **foreach** repetition structure, skips the remaining statements in the body of that structure and performs the next iteration of the loop. In **while** and **until** structures, the loop-continuation condition is evaluated immediately after the **next** statement executes. In **for** structures, the increment expression executes, and then the loop-continuation test is evaluated. In **foreach** structures, the control variable is set to the next element of the list.

Earlier, we stated that the **while** structure could be used in most cases to represent the **for** structure. The one exception occurs when the increment expression in the **while** structure follows the **next** statement. In this case, the increment does not execute before the test of the loop-continuation condition, and the **while** does not execute in the same manner as the **for**. If the loop does not automatically increment the control variable (as **for** and **foreach** do), further steps should be taken to prevent an infinite loop.

Figure 5.7 shows a simple example using **next**. A **foreach** loop (lines 5–13) prints the numbers 1 through 10, using **$_** as the control variable. If **$_** is equal to 5 (line 7), then line 8 saves the current value of **$_** in variable **$skipped** and executes the **next** statement (line 9). This process skips the **print** statement in line 12 and continues with the next iteration of the **foreach** loop (in which **$_** now has the value 6).

```perl
1   #!/usr/bin/perl
2   # Fig. 5.7: fig05_07.pl
3   # Using the next statement in a foreach structure.
4
5   foreach ( 1 .. 10 ) {
6
7      if ( $_ == 5 ) {
8         $skipped = $_;  # store skipped value
9         next;  # skip remaining code in loop only if $_ is 5
10     }
11
12     print "$_ ";
13  }
14
15  print "\n\nUsed 'next' to skip the value $skipped.\n";
```

```
1 2 3 4 6 7 8 9 10

Used 'next' to skip the value 5.
```

Fig. 5.7   Using the **next** statement in a **foreach** structure.

5.7 Loop Controls: The `last` Statement

The *last statement*, when executed in a **while**, **until**, **for** or **foreach** structure, causes immediate exit from that structure. Program execution continues with the first statement after the structure. The **last** statement is commonly used to escape early from a loop. Figure 5.8 demonstrates the **last** statement in a **foreach** repetition structure. When the **if** structure (line 7) detects that **$_** is 5, **$number** is assigned the current value of **$_** and **last** executes. This command terminates the **foreach** loop, and the program continues with the **print** statement at line 15.

```perl
1   #!/usr/bin/perl
2   # Fig. 5.8: fig05_08.pl
3   # Using the last statement in a foreach structure.
4
5   foreach ( 1 .. 10 ) {
6
7      if ( $_ == 5 ) {
8         $number = $_;  # store current value before loop ends
9         last;          # jump to end of foreach structure
10     }
11
12     print "$_ ";
13  }
14
15  print "\n\nUsed 'last' to terminate loop at $number.\n";
```

Fig. 5.8   Using the **last** statement in a **foreach** structure (part 1 of 2).

```
1 2 3 4

Used 'last' to terminate loop at 5.
```

Fig. 5.8   Using the **last** statement in a **foreach** structure (part 2 of 2).

5.8 Loop Controls: The redo Statement

The **redo** statement, when executed in a **while**, **until**, **for** or **foreach** structure, returns to the first statement in the body of the loop without evaluating the loop-continuation test. This command is useful when it is necessary to repeat a particular iteration of a loop (perhaps because an invalid input value was received).

Figure 5.9 contains a **while** structure (lines 7–14) that is supposed to iterate five times. The **if** structure in lines 9–13 prints **$number**, increments **$number** and executes the **redo** statement as long as **$number** is less than or equal to 10. When **redo** executes, program control continues, starting from the **{** at the end of line 7; the loop-continuation condition is not tested. Thus, once the condition is tested for the first time at line 7, the condition no longer controls the number of iterations in the program. Rather, the **if** structure condition now determines when the loop terminates. When **$number** becomes 11, the body of the **if** structure is skipped, and program control continues with the condition in the **while** loop. At this point, the loop terminates, because the condition is now false. Without the **redo** statement, the loop-continuation condition would stop the iteration when **$number** becomes 6.

Software Engineering Observation 5.1

There is a tension between achieving quality software engineering and achieving the best performing software. Often, one of these goals is achieved at the expense of the other.

```
1    #!/usr/bin/perl
2    # Fig. 5.9: fig05_09.pl
3    # Using the redo statement in a while structure.
4
5    $number = 1;
6
7    while ( $number <= 5 ) {
8
9        if ( $number <= 10 ) {
10           print "$number ";
11           ++$number;
12           redo;  # Continue loop without testing ( $number <= 5 )
13       }
14   }
15
16   print "\nStopped when \$number became $number.\n";
```

```
1 2 3 4 5 6 7 8 9 10
Stopped when $number became 11.
```

Fig. 5.9   Using the **redo** statement in a **while** structure.

5.9 Block Labels

Any loop block except a **do/while** or **do/until** structure can have a *label*. This label, besides acting as a one-word description of the block of code, acts as a target for the loop control commands **next**, **last** and **redo**. These commands may use a block label as an argument to refer to a specific loop block. When these commands execute without any arguments, they operate on the loop in which they appear.

Figure 5.10 shows a **for** structure with a label. When **next** executes, it forces the next iteration of the block labeled **LOOP**. Notice that the label is followed by a colon. Because the label **LOOP** already refers to the repetition block containing **next**, Fig. 5.10 operates the same as if there were no label. However, consider the following:

```
OUTER: repetition block {
    INNER: repetition block {
        next OUTER;
    }
}
```

When **next OUTER** is executed, control jumps out of the **INNER** block and immediately executes the **next** iteration of the **OUTER** block.

Good Programming Practice 5.2

Use only uppercase letters in labels. This practice avoids conflicts between labels and Perl keywords and increases readability.

Figure 5.11 demonstrates the ability to control loop iterations from any repetition block. Notice that we can control loop iterations of repetition structures in which we are not currently operating. When line 11

```
next OUTER;
```

executes, loop control continues with the **OUTER** block, ignoring the remaining iterations of **INNER**.

```
1   #!/usr/bin/perl
2   # Fig. 5.10: fig05_10.pl
3   # Using block labels with next.
4
5   LOOP: for ( $number = 1; $number <= 10; ++$number ) {
6           next LOOP if ( $number % 2 == 0 );
7           print "$number ";   # displays only odd numbers
8       }
```

```
1 3 5 7 9
```

Fig. 5.10   Using block labels.

```
1   #!/usr/bin/perl
2   # Fig. 5.11: fig05_11.pl
3   # Using block labels with next in nested looping structures.
```

Fig. 5.11   Multiple block labels (part 1 of 2).

```
4
5   OUTER: foreach $row ( 1 .. 10 ) {
6
7       INNER: foreach $column ( 1 .. 10 ) {
8
9                   if ( $row < $column ) {
10                      print "\n";
11                      next OUTER;
12                  }
13
14                  print "$column     ";
15              }
16          }
```

```
1
1    2
1    2    3
1    2    3    4
1    2    3    4    5
1    2    3    4    5    6
1    2    3    4    5    6    7
1    2    3    4    5    6    7    8
1    2    3    4    5    6    7    8    9
1    2    3    4    5    6    7    8    9    10
```

Fig. 5.11   Multiple block labels (part 2 of 2).

5.10 Bare Blocks

A *bare block* is a block (zero or more lines) of code enclosed by curly braces, with or without a label, but with no accompanying control-structure keyword. Such a block can be used with loop control statements **last** and **redo**. Note that **next** is equivalent to **last** in a bare-block context.

Figure 5.12 uses bare blocks to demonstrate an alternative to an **if/elsif/else** multiple-selection structure. This keeps with Perl's philosophy of "there is more than one way to do it." Note the use of **last** to exit the block when the **if** structure for a particular guess executes. Also, note the use of **redo** to restart the block after an invalid guess.

```
1   #!/usr/bin/perl
2   # Fig. 5.12: fig05_12.pl
3   # Using bare blocks to form a multiple-selection structure.
4
5   print "Enter your guess (1-3): ";
6   $guess = <STDIN>;
7
8   BLOCK: { # start of bare block
9      if ( $guess == 1 ) {
10        print "Right!\n";
11        last BLOCK;              # jump to end of BLOCK
12     }
```

Fig. 5.12   Demonstrating bare blocks (part 1 of 2).

```
13
14      if ( $guess == 2 ) {
15          print "Close!\n";
16          last BLOCK;           # jump to end of BLOCK
17      }
18
19      if ( $guess == 3 ) {
20          print "Wrong!\n";
21          last BLOCK;           # jump to end of BLOCK
22      }
23
24      # default case; executes only if $guess is not 1, 2 or 3
25      {
26          print "Please re-enter your guess (1-3): ";
27          $guess = <STDIN>;
28          redo BLOCK;           # jump to beginning of BLOCK
29      }
30  } # start of bare block
```

```
Enter your guess (1-3): 1
Right!
```

```
Enter your guess (1-3): 77
Please re-enter your guess (1-3): 22
Please re-enter your guess (1-3): 1
Right!
```

Fig. 5.12   Demonstrating bare blocks (part 2 of 2).

In the **BLOCK** bare block (lines 8–30), there are three **if** structures and a nested bare block. Each of the **if**-structure bodies ends with the statement

```
last BLOCK;         # jump to end of BLOCK
```

which immediately terminates the **BLOCK** bare block when it executes. So, only the body of the first **if** structure with a true condition will execute. If none of the **if**-structure bodies executes, program control continues with the bare block in lines 25–29, which acts as a "default case" in this simulated multiple-selection structure, i.e., code that executes only if the value input is not 1, 2 or 3. The **redo** statement at line 28 returns control to the beginning of the **BLOCK** bare block.

5.11 Logical Operators

So far, most of the conditions we have studied have been *simple conditions*, such as **$number <= 10**, **$total > 1000** and **$string eq 'yes'**. We have expressed these conditions in terms of the numeric relational operators **>**, **<**, **>=** and **<=**, the equality operators **==** and **!=** and the corresponding string operators. Each decision tested precisely one condition. To test multiple conditions while making a decision, we performed these tests in separate statements or in nested **if** or **if/else** structures.

Perl provides *logical operators* that are used to form more complex conditions by combining simple conditions. The logical operators are **&&** (*logical AND*), **||** (*logical OR*) and **!** (*logical NOT*, also called *logical negation*). We consider examples of each of these.

Suppose we wish to ensure that two conditions are *both* true before we choose a certain path of execution. In this case, we can use the logical **&&** operator as follows:

```
if ( $gender eq 'female' && $age >= 65 ) {
    ++$seniorFemales;
}
```

to test two simple conditions. The condition **$gender eq 'female'** is evaluated to determine if a person is a female. The condition **age >= 65** is evaluated to determine if a person is a senior citizen. The simple condition to the left of the **&&** operator is evaluated first. Note that because the precedence of **eq** is higher than the precedence of **&&**, no parentheses are necessary.

If the condition on the left is false, then the entire logical **&&** expression evaluates to false, and the right-side condition is not evaluated.

Performance Tip 5.2

*In expressions using operator **&&**, if the separate conditions are independent of one another, make the condition that is most likely to be false the leftmost condition. This can increase a program's performance and is sometimes referred to as "short-circuit evaluation."*

However, if the condition on the left is true, the simple condition to the right of the **&&** operator is evaluated next.

The complete expression evaluates to truc if and only if both simple conditions are true. If the combined condition is indeed true, then the count of **$seniorFemales** is incremented by **1** in the preceding **if** structure. If either or both of the simple conditions are false, then the program skips the incrementation and proceeds to the statement following the **if** structure. Some programmers find that the preceding combined condition is more readable when redundant parentheses are added to the expression as follows:

```
( $gender eq 'female' ) && ( $age >= 65 )
```

Common Programming Error 5.1

*Although **3 < $x < 7** is a mathematically correct condition, it does not evaluate correctly in Perl. Use **(3 < $x && $x< 7)**.*

Common Programming Error 5.2

*Placing a space between the **&**'s of the **&&** operator (or any operator consisting of two or more characters) is a syntax error.*

The table in Fig. 5.13 summarizes the **&&** operator. The table shows all four possible combinations of false and true values for *expression1* and *expression2*. Such tables are often called *truth tables.* Perl evaluates to false or true all expressions that include relational operators, equality operators and/or logical operators.

Now let us consider the **||** (logical OR) operator. Suppose we wish to ensure at some point in a program that either *or* both of two conditions are true before we choose a certain path of execution in the program. In this case, we use the **||** operator, as in the following program segment:

expression1	expression2	expression1 && expression2
false	false	false
false	true	false
true	false	false
true	true	true

Fig. 5.13   Truth table for the **&&** (logical AND) operator.

```
if ( $semesterAverage >= 90 || $finalExam >= 90 ) {
   print "Student grade is A";
}
```

The preceding condition also contains two simple conditions. The simple condition **$semesterAverage >= 90** is evaluated to determine if the student deserves an "A" in the course because of a solid performance throughout the semester. The simple condition **$finalExam >= 90** is evaluated to determine if the student deserves an "A" in the course because of an outstanding performance on the final exam. The **if** statement then considers the combined condition

```
$semesterAverage >= 90 || $finalExam >= 90
```

and awards the student an "A" if either or both of the simple conditions are true. Note that the message "**Student grade is A**" is printed unless both of the simple conditions are false. Figure 5.14 is a truth table for the logical OR operator (**||**).

The **&&** operator has a slightly higher precedence than the **||** operator. Both operators associate from left to right. As with **&&**, the **||** operator evaluates the left and right conditions only until truth or falsehood is known. Thus, evaluation of the expression

```
$semesterAverage >= 90 || $finalExam >= 90
```

stops immediately if **$semesterAverage** is greater than or equal to 90, because only one side of the OR operator must be true for the logical OR expression to return true. If **$semesterAverage** is less than 90, the right-hand side is evaluated to determine the value of the condition. If the right side is true, the entire expression is true; otherwise, the entire expression is false.

expression1	expression2	expression1 || expression2
false	false	false
false	true	true
true	false	true
true	true	true

Fig. 5.14   Truth table for the **||** (logical OR) operator.

Common Programming Error 5.3

*In expressions using the operator **&&**, it is possible that a condition—we will call this condition the* dependent condition—*might require another condition to be true for it to be meaningful to evaluate the* dependent condition. *In this case, the* dependent condition *should be placed after the other condition, or else an error might occur.*

Performance Tip 5.3

In expressions using the operator | |, *make the condition that is most likely to be true the leftmost condition. This practice is another example of "short-circuit evaluation" and can increase a program's performance.*

Perl provides the **!** (logical negation) operator to reverse the truth or falsity of a condition. Unlike the **&&** and | | operators, which each combine two operands, (and hence are binary operators), the logical negation operator has only a single operand (and hence is a unary operator). The logical negation operator is placed before a condition when we are interested in choosing a path of execution if the original condition (without the logical negation operator) is false, such as in the following program segment:

```
if ( !( $grade eq 'quit' ) ) {
   print "The next grade is $grade\n";
}
```

The parentheses around the condition **$grade eq 'quit'** are needed because the logical negation operator has a higher precedence than the string equality operator. Figure 5.15 is a truth table for the logical negation operator.

Normally, the programmer can avoid using logical negation by expressing the condition differently with an appropriate relational or equality operator. For example, the preceding statement can also be written as follows:

```
if ( $grade ne 'quit' ) {
   print "The next grade is $grade\n";
}
```

Alternatively, the Perl programmer could write

```
unless ( $grade eq 'quit' ) {
   print "The next grade is $grade\n";
}
```

This flexibility can often help a programmer express a condition in a more natural or convenient manner. In the next section, we discuss three other logical operators.

expression	! expression
false	true
true	false

Fig. 5.15   Truth table for operator **!** (logical negation).

5.12 Using Logical Operators for Flow Control

Perl provides three additional logical operators: *and*, *or* and *not*. These operators are particularly useful for combining statements based on the value of the statement on the left side of the operator. The only difference between these logical operators and the logical operators presented in the previous section is that **and**, **or** and **not** have lower precedence than any other operators in Perl. This fact allows these operators to be used in complex expressions containing any other operator without the need to use parentheses to force the order of evaluation.

Another benefit of Perl's logical operators **&&**, **and**, **||** and **or** is that the value of the entire logical expression is the value of the individual expression evaluated last. Thus, in logical AND expressions,

> *expression1* **&&** *expression2*
> *expression1* **and** *expression2*

if *expression1* evaluates to false, the value of the entire logical expression is the value of *expression1*. If *expression1* evaluates to true, *expression2* is then evaluated, and its value becomes the value of the entire logical expression. In other words, if *expression2* is true, then the entire expression is true, and if *expression2* is false, then the entire expression is false. Similarly, in logical OR expressions,

> *expression1* **||** *expression2*
> *expression1* **or** *expression2*

if *expression1* evaluates to true, the value of the entire logical expression is the value of *expression1*. If *expression1* evaluates to false, the value of the entire logical expression is the value of *expression2*.

Perl programmers have developed a style of programming that controls program flow using the properties of the lower precedence logical operators. You will notice that these operators are used in many ways, from testing the control variables of control structures to assigning variable values and executing commands.

The program in Fig. 5.16 allows the user to input two numbers and divides the first number (the numerator) by the second number (the denominator) to produce the result. This program has the potential for a divide-by-zero error. As we mentioned in Chapter 2, division by zero is a fatal run-time error. To prevent division by zero, this example uses the logical operators **and** and **or** and the **redo** statement to have the user reenter the denominator if it is zero.

Lines 5 and 6 input the value of the numerator. The bare block (lines 9–14) inputs the denominator at lines 10 and 11. Then, the statement in lines 12 and 13,

```
$denominator != 0 or
    print "Cannot divide by zero\n" and redo;
```

uses a logical OR expression with operator **or** to determine if the user input 0 for the denominator. If the value of **$denominator** is nonzero, the condition on the left of the **or** evaluates to true, the logical expression short circuits and the remainder of the statement is ignored. On the other hand, if **$denominator** is equal to zero, the condition on the left of the **or** evaluates to false, and Perl evaluates the right side of the **or** operator:

```
print "Error, dividing by zero\n" and redo;
```

```perl
1   #!/usr/bin/perl
2   # Fig. 5.16: fig05_16.pl
3   # Using logical operators in flow control.
4
5   print "Please enter a numerator: ";
6   chomp( $numerator = <STDIN> );
7
8   # bare block; redo continues from beginning of this block
9   {
10     print "Please enter a denominator: ";
11     chomp( $denominator = <STDIN> );
12     $denominator != 0 or
13        print "Cannot divide by zero\n" and redo;
14  }
15
16  print "\nThe result is ", $numerator / $denominator, "\n";
```

```
Please enter a numerator: 7
Please enter a denominator: 3

The result is 2.33333333333333
```

```
Please enter a numerator: 22
Please enter a denominator: 0
Cannot divide by zero
Please enter a denominator: 7

The result is 3.14285714285714
```

Fig. 5.16   Using logical operators in flow control.

Function **print** returns true when it successfully prints. The value returned by **print** is used as the left-side expression for the logical operator **and**. If this value is true, control continues with the expression on the right side of **and**. In this case, the **redo** command restarts the bare block, so the user can reenter the denominator. So, the statement at lines 12 and 13 basically says, "If the denominator is zero, display an error message and have the user reenter the denominator."

Using logical operators as follows can yield code that is easy and natural to read.

```perl
$denominator != 0 ||
    ( print "Cannot divide by zero\n" and redo );

$denominator != 0 ||
    ( print "Cannot divide by zero\n" ) && redo;

$denominator != 0 or
    ( print "Cannot divide by zero\n" ) && redo;
```

Note that if any other combination of logic operators is used on this expression, parentheses must be added to the expression on the right of the logical OR operation to get the same results.

5.13 Error Functions: die and warn

There are times when certain program elements are crucial to a program's continued proper execution. If these elements are not processed or input correctly, the program should not continue. In such cases, the programmer may want to issue a message indicating why or where the program went wrong.

Function **die** allows a programmer to terminate program execution and print a message, assisting in both debugging the program and writing clearer code. Instead of using

```
if ( essential condition ) {
    rest of program
}
else {
    print "Error: Essential condition not met\n";
}
```

You can use the shortcut **die**:

```
unless ( essential condition ) {
    die "Error: Essential condition not met\n";
}
```

The preceding statement can be written as

```
essential condition or die "Error: Essential condition not met\n";
```

In the previous example, the user was given several chances to enter a nonzero denominator to avoid a division-by-zero error. If the programmer does not wish to allow multiple chances, the programmer can use function **die** as shown in line 12 of Fig. 5.17.

```
1   #!/usr/bin/perl
2   # Fig. 5.17: fig05_17.pl
3   # Using function 'die' to terminate a program.
4
5   print "Please enter a numerator: ";
6   chomp( $numerator = <STDIN> );
7
8   print "Please enter a denominator: ";
9   chomp( $denominator = <STDIN> );
10
11  # if condition is false, program prints message and terminates
12  $denominator != 0 or die "Cannot divide by zero";
13
14  # executes only if $denominator is not 0
15  print "\nThe result is ", $numerator / $denominator, "\n";
```

```
Please enter a numerator: 7
Please enter a denominator: 3

The result is 2.33333333333333
```

Fig. 5.17　Using function **die** to display an error message and terminate a program (part 1 of 2).

```
Please enter a numerator: 22
Please enter a denominator: 0
Cannot divide by zero at fig05_17.pl line 12, <STDIN> line 2.
```

Fig. 5.17   Using function **die** to display an error message and terminate a program (part 2 of 2).

When the user inputs 0 for the denominator, additional information consisting of a filename and a line number is output after our error message. The function **die** adds this output to help the programmer debug the program. To prevent function **die** from inserting this additional information, add a newline character to the error-message string supplied to function **die**, as in the following:

```
die "Cannot divide by zero\n"
```

As a convenience, Perl stores the most recent system error message in the *special variable $!*. In this example, no error message is stored, because we do not actually attempt to divide by zero. In Chapter 10, we use **die** and **$!** to find errors in programs that read and write files on your local disk drive.

Function **warn** produces the same output as **die**, but program execution continues. This function allows a programmer to **warn** users of a nonfatal error in a program.

5.14 Summary of Structured Programming

Just as architects design buildings by employing the collective wisdom of their profession, so should programmers design programs. Our field is younger than architecture is, and our collective wisdom is considerably sparser. We have learned that structured programming produces programs that are easier than unstructured programs to understand and hence are easier to test, debug, modify and even prove correct in a mathematical sense.

Figures 5.18 and 5.19 summarize Perl's control structures. Small circles are used in the figures to indicate the single entry point and the single exit point of each structure. Connecting individual flowchart symbols arbitrarily can lead to unstructured programs. Therefore, the programming profession has chosen to combine flowchart symbols to form a limited set of control structures and to build structured programs by properly combining control structures in two simple ways.

For simplicity, only single-entry/single-exit control structures are used; there is only one way to enter and only one way to exit each control structure. Connecting control structures in sequence to form structured programs is simple: The exit point of one control structure is connected to the entry point of the next control structure. That is, the control structures are simply placed one after another in a program; we have called this process's "control structure stacking." The rules for forming structured programs also allow for control structures to be nested.

The table in Fig. 5.20 shows the rules for forming properly structured programs. The rules assume that the rectangle flowchart symbol may be used to indicate any action, including input/output. The rules also assume that we begin with the simplest flowchart (Fig. 5.21).

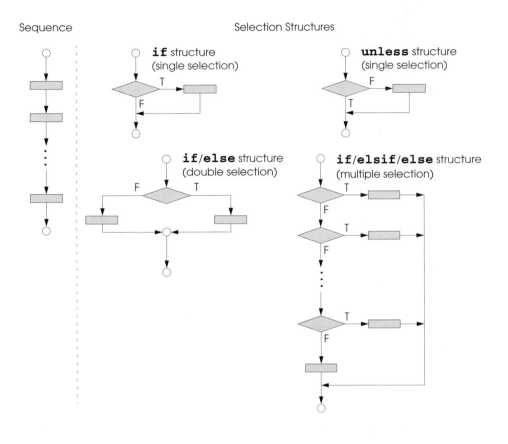

Fig. 5.18   Single-entry/single-exit sequence and selection structures.

Applying the rules of Fig. 5.20 always results in a structured flowchart with a neat, building-block appearance. For example, repeatedly applying rule 2 to the simplest flowchart results in a structured flowchart containing many rectangles in sequence (Fig. 5.22). Notice that rule 2 generates a stack of control structures, so let us call rule 2 the *stacking rule*.

Rule 3 is called the *nesting rule*. Repeatedly applying rule 3 to the simplest flowchart results in a flowchart with neatly nested control structures. For example, in Fig. 5.23, the rectangle in the simplest flowchart is first replaced with a double-selection (**if/else**) structure. Then rule 3 is applied again to both of the rectangles in the double-selection structure, replacing each of the rectangles with double-selection structures. The dashed boxes around each of the double-selection structures represent the rectangle that was replaced in the original simplest flowchart.

Rule 4 generates larger, more involved and more deeply nested structures. The flowcharts that emerge from applying the rules in Fig. 5.20 constitute the set of all possible structured flowcharts and hence the set of all possible structured programs.

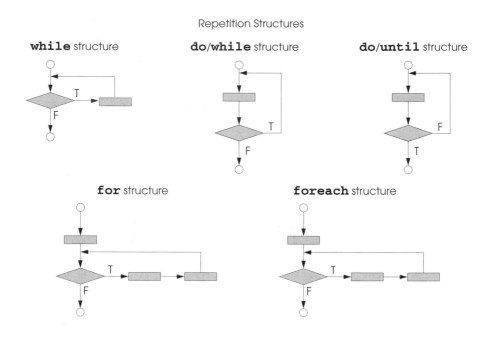

Fig. 5.19   Single-entry/single-exit repetition structures.

Rules for Forming Structured Programs

1)   Begin with the "simplest flowchart" (Fig. 5.21).

2)   Any rectangle (action) can be replaced by two rectangles (actions) in sequence.

3)   Any rectangle (action) can be replaced by any control structure (sequence, **if**, **if/else**, **if/elsif/else**, **while**, **until**, **do/while**, **do/until**, **for** or **foreach**).

4)   Rules 2 and 3 can be applied as often as you like and in any order.

Fig. 5.20   Rules for forming structured programs.

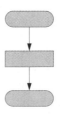

Fig. 5.21   Simplest flowchart.

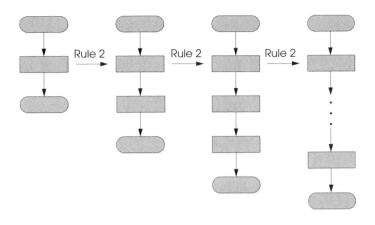

Fig. 5.22   Repeatedly applying rule 2 of Fig. 5.20 to the simplest flowchart.

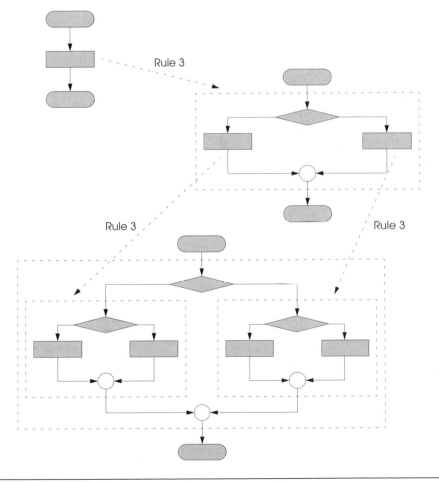

Fig. 5.23   Applying rule 3 of Fig. 5.20 to the simplest flowchart.

The beauty of the structured approach is that we use only 11 simple single-entry/single-exit pieces, and we assemble them in only two simple ways. Figure 5.24 shows the kinds of stacked building blocks that emerge from applying rule 2 and the kinds of nested building blocks that emerge from applying rule 3. The figure also shows the kind of overlapped building blocks that cannot appear in structured flowcharts (because of the elimination of the **goto** statement).

If the rules in Fig. 5.20 are followed, an unstructured flowchart (such as that in Fig. 5.25) cannot be created. If you are uncertain whether a particular flowchart is structured, apply the rules of Fig. 5.20 in reverse to try to reduce the flowchart to the simplest flowchart. If the flowchart is reducible to the simplest flowchart, the original flowchart is structured; otherwise, it is not.

Structured programming promotes simplicity. Bohm and Jacopini have given us the understanding that only three forms of control are needed:

- sequence,

- selection and

- repetition.

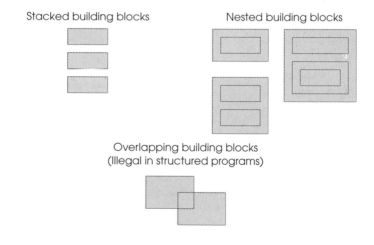

Fig. 5.24   Stacked, nested and overlapped building blocks.

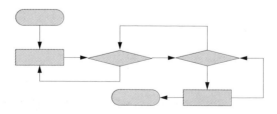

Fig. 5.25   An unstructured flowchart.

Sequence is trivial. Selection is implemented in one of four ways:

- **if** structure (single selection),
- **unless** structure (single selection),
- **if/else** structure (double selection) and
- **if/elsif/else** structure (multiple selection).

In fact, it is straightforward to prove that the simple **if** structure is sufficient to provide any form of selection: Everything that can be done with the **unless** structure, the **if/else** structure and the **if/elsif/else** structure can be implemented with **if** structures (although perhaps not as clearly and efficiently).

Repetition is implemented in one of six ways:

- **while** structure,
- **until** structure,
- **do/while** structure,
- **do/until** structure,
- **for** structure and
- **foreach** structure.

It is straightforward to prove that the **while** structure is sufficient to provide any form of repetition: Everything that can be done with the other looping structures also can be done with the **while** structure (although perhaps not as clearly).

Combining these results illustrates that any form of control ever needed in a Perl program can be expressed in terms of

- sequence,
- **if** structure (selection) and
- **while** structure (repetition)

and that these control structures can be combined in only two ways: stacking and nesting. Indeed, structured programming promotes simplicity.

SUMMARY

- The **foreach** repetition structure allows a programmer to iterate over a list of values, accessing and manipulating each element. A benefit of this control structure is that the programmer is not required to maintain a separate control variable to manage the repetition structure.

- The general format for the **foreach** structure is

```
foreach controlVariable ( list ) {
    statements
}
```

  where *list* can be any list, literal or array and *controlVariable* represents one item of *list* during each iteration.

- The **foreach** repetition structure can be used as a shorthand replacement for the **for** structure.

- Note that when a **for** structure mimics a **foreach** structure, the semicolons that normally separate the initialization, condition and incrementation of the loop are not required. However, when a **foreach** structure mimics a **for** structure, the semicolons separating the initialization, condition and incrementation of the loop are required.

- The **$_** special variable is the default parameter for many Perl functions and the default control variable for many Perl control structures. The **$_** special variable also can take the place of a missing argument in a function call.

- The control variable in a **foreach** structure is optional and defaults to the value of **$_**.

- Perl function **grep** searches through a list and creates a new list containing only elements that satisfy a specified condition.

- Function **map** creates a list reflecting a function applied to each element of a given list.

- A **foreach** loop also can iterate over a hash using the keys of the hash returned by function **keys**.

- Function **sort** orders keys of a hash into lexically ascending order and returns the sorted list that is used in the **foreach** structure.

- The loop controls **next**, **last** and **redo** alter the flow of control in a control structure.

- The **next** statement skips the remaining statements in the body of a loop structure and performs the next iteration of the loop.

- The **last** statement causes immediate exit from a structure. Program execution continues with the first statement after the structure.

- The **redo** statement restarts a loop without evaluating the loop-continuation test.

- Any loop block except a **do/while** or **do/until** structure can have a label.

- A label, besides acting as one-word description for the block of code, acts as a target for the loop control commands **next**, **last** and **redo**. These commands may use a block label as an argument to refer to a specific loop block. When these commands execute without any arguments, they operate on the loop in which they appear.

- A bare block is a block of code enclosed by curly braces, with or without a label, but with no accompanying control structure keyword.

- A block of code is equivalent to a loop that executes only once, making it accessible to loop control statements **last** and **redo**. (**next** is equivalent to **last** in a bare block context.)

- Perl provides logical operators that are used to form more complex conditions by combining simple conditions. The logical operators are **&&** (logical AND), **||** (logical OR) and **!** (logical NOT, also called logical negation).

- Perl evaluates to false or true all expressions that include relational operators, equality operators and/or logical operators.

- The **||** (logical OR) operator ensures that at some point in a program either or both of two conditions are true before we choose a certain path of execution.

- Both the **&&** and **||** operators associate from left to right.

- The logical negation operator (**!**) has only a single condition as an operand (unary operator). The logical negation operator is placed before a condition when we are interested in choosing a path of execution when the original condition (without the logical negation operator) is false.

- Perl provides three additional logical operators: **and**, **or** and **not**. The only difference between these logical operators and the logical operators presented before them is that **and**, **or** and **not** have lower precedence than any other operators in Perl.

- Function **die** allows a programmer to terminate program execution and print a message, assisting in both debugging the program and writing clearer code.

- Perl stores the most recent system error message in the special variable **$!**.

- Function **warn** produces the same output as the **die** function, but allows program execution to continue. This function allows a programmer to **warn** users of a nonfatal error in a program.

- We have learned that structured programming produces programs that are easier to understand and hence are easier to test, debug, modify and even prove correct in a mathematical sense.

- Applying the rules of forming properly structured programs always results in a structured flow-chart with a neat, building-block appearance.

- The beauty of the structured approach is that we use only 11 simple single-entry/single-exit pieces, and we assemble them in only two simple ways.

- If the rules of forming properly structured programs are followed, an unstructured flowchart cannot be created.

- Structured programming promotes simplicity. Only three forms of control are needed: sequence, selection and repetition.

- Selection is implemented in one of four ways: **if** structure (single selection), **unless** structure (single selection), **if/else** structure (double selection) and **if/elsif/else** structure (multiple selection).

- The simple **if** structure is sufficient to provide any form of selection. Everything that can be done with the **unless** structure, the **if/else** structure and the **if/elsif/else** structure can be implemented with **if** structures (although perhaps not as clearly and efficiently).

- Repetition is implemented in one of six ways: **while** structure, **until** structure, **do/while** structure, **do/until** structure, **for** structure and **foreach** structure.

- The **while** structure is sufficient to provide any form of repetition. Everything that can be done with the other looping structures also can be done with the **while** structure (although perhaps not as clearly).

- Any form of control ever needed in a Perl program can be expressed in terms of the following: sequence, **if** structure (selection) and **while** structure (repetition). These control structures can be combined in only two ways: stacking and nesting.

TERMINOLOGY

! (logical negation operator)
$! special variable
$_ special variable
&& (logical AND operator)
|| (logical OR operator)
and (logical AND operator
bare block
block
block label
building-block appearance
complex conditions
control-structure stacking
deeply nested structures
dependent condition
die function
divide-by-zero error
double selection
entry point of a control structure
exit point of a control structure

factorial
foreach repetition structure
goto statement
grep function
if/else selection structure
if/elsif/else selection structure
iterate
last statement
leftmost condition
logical operator
loop block
map function
mean
median
middle value
mode
multiple selection
ne (string equality operator)
nested building block

nested control structure
next statement
not (logical negation operator)
or (logical OR operator)
overlapped building block
redo statement
simple condition
simplest flowchart

single-entry/single-exit control structure
stacked building blocks
structured flowchart
structured program
truth table
unstructured flowchart
warn function
while repetition structure

SELF-REVIEW EXERCISES

5.1   Fill in the blanks in each of the following statements:
a) The special variable _____ is the default parameter for many of the Perl functions and control structures.
b) Function _____ allows a programmer to easily create a list reflecting a function applied to each element of a given list.
c) Function _____ allows a programmer to print a message if a certain event occurs, whereas the function _____ terminates the program after printing an error message.
d) The _____ statement, when executed in a repetition structure, causes the next iteration of the loop to be performed immediately.
e) The _____ statement, when executed in a repetition structure, causes immediate exit from the structure.
f) The logical operator _____ is used to ensure that one of two conditions are true before we choose a certain path of execution.

5.2   State whether the following are *true* or *false*. If the answer is *false*, explain why.
a) Perl stores the most recent system error message in the special variable **$?**.
b) Any loop block, except **do/while** and **do/until** structures, can have a label.
c) The expression **($x > $y || $w < $z)** is true if and only if both **$x > $y** is true and **$w < $z** is true.
d) The **redo** statement, when executed in a **while**, **for** or **foreach** structure, restarts the loop and evaluates the loop-continuation test.

5.3   Write a program to accomplish the following tasks:
a) Create an array called **@array** with the numbers 1 to 99.
b) Use the function **grep** to create a new array, called **@oddArray**, whose elements consist of the odd elements of **@array**.
c) Use a **foreach** structure to sum the integers in **@oddArray**.
d) Print the result.

5.4   Write a program to accomplish the following tasks:
a) Create two **foreach** loops, one labeled **PROMPT** and the other labeled **PRINTING**. Both are **foreach** loops, with the **PRINTING** loop nested inside the **PROMPT** loop. Each structure loops through the numbers 1–10.
b) In the **PROMPT** (outer) loop, prompt the user to enter a value, and store that value in the scalar variable **$stars**.
c) In the **PRINTING foreach** loop, if **$_** is greater than the value of **$stars**, print a newline character and have the program immediately go to the next **PROMPT** loop. Otherwise, print an asterisk followed by a space.
d) After each set of asterisks, have the program print a newline.

5.5 Find the error in each of the following code segments and explain how to correct it:

a) The following code should input a number and a value to divide the number by. The code should calculate the quotient if the denominator is not zero, or prompt the user for new values if the denominator is zero. It should terminate after the user gives valid input.

```
$done = 0;
while ( $done != 1 ) {
    print "Enter numerator: \n";
    chomp( $numerator = <STDIN> );
    print "Enter denominator: \n";
    chomp( $denominator = <STDIN> );

    $denominator != 0 ||
        print "Cannot divide by zero\n" and next;

    $done = 1;
    $result = $numerator/$denominator;
}
```

b)
```
LOOP for ( $number = 1; $number <= 10; ++$number ) {
        print $number, " ";
    }
```

c) The following code should print the values 1 to 10:

```
$number = 1;
while ( $number < 10 ) {
    printf "$number\n";
    $number++;
}
```

ANSWERS TO SELF-REVIEW EXERCISES

5.1 a) **$_**. b) **map**. c) **warn**, **die**. d) **next**. e) **last**. f) **&&** or **or**.

5.2 a) False. Perl stores the most recent system error message in the special variable **$!**.
    b) True.
    c) False. Only one of the relational expressions must be true in order for the entire expression to be true when using the **||** operator.
    d) False. Statement **redo** restarts the loop, but does not evaluate the loop-continuation test.

5.3 See the following code.

```
1   #!/usr/bin/perl
2   # Exercise 5.3: ex05_03.pl
3   # Calculating the sum of the odd integers from 1 to 99
4
5   $total = 0;
6   @array = ( 1 .. 99 );
7   @oddArray = grep( ( $_ % 2 ) == 1, @array );
8
9   foreach ( @oddArray ) {
10      $total += $_;
11  }
12
13  print $total, "\n";
```

2500

5.4   See the following code.

```perl
#!/usr/bin/perl
# Ex. 5.4: ex05_04.pl
# Printing a specified number of asterisks

PROMPT: foreach ( 1 .. 10 ) {

        print "Enter number of stars wanted: ";
        chomp( $stars = <STDIN> );

    PRINTING: foreach ( 1 .. 10 ) {

            if ( $_ > $stars ) {
                print "\n";
                next PROMPT;
            }

            print "* ";
        }

        print "\n";
    }

    print "\n";
```

```
Enter number of stars wanted: 3
* * *
Enter number of stars wanted: 4
* * * *
Enter number of stars wanted: 5
* * * * *
Enter number of stars wanted: 1
*
Enter number of stars wanted: 2
* *
Enter number of stars wanted: 9
* * * * * * * *
Enter number of stars wanted: 8
* * * * * * * *
Enter number of stars wanted: 7
* * * * * * *
Enter number of stars wanted: 6
* * * * * *
Enter number of stars wanted: 5
* * * * *
```

5.5   a) Error: Infinite loop. The precedence of | | is higher than that of **and**, so the | | is eval-
uated with the first two statements before the **and** with the last statement is evaluated.
As a result, the **next** statement is always evaluated.
Correction: Place everything after the | | in parentheses to force the order.

    b) Error: Missing colon (`:`) after the label in the **for** loop.

        Correction: Add the colon so that the loop looks like this:

```
LOOP: for ( $number = 1; $number <= 10; ++$number ) {
          print $number, " ";
      }
```

    c) Error: Improper relational operator used in the **while** repetition-continuation condition.

        Correction: Use `<=` rather than `<`.

EXERCISES

5.6   The factorial of a nonnegative integer n is written $n!$ (pronounced "n factorial") and is defined as follows:

$$n! = n \cdot (n - 1) \cdot (n - 2) \cdot \dots \cdot 1 \quad \text{(for values of } n \text{ greater than or equal to 1)}$$

and

$$n! = 1 \quad \text{(for } n = 0\text{)}.$$

For example, $5! = 5 \cdot 4 \cdot 3 \cdot 2 \cdot 1$, which is 120. Write a program that reads a nonnegative integer and uses a **foreach** structure to compute and print its factorial.

5.7   (*Pythagorean Triples*) A right triangle can have sides that are all integers. The set of three integer values for the sides of a right triangle is called a Pythagorean triple. These three sides must satisfy the relationship that the sum of the squares of two of the sides is equal to the square of the hypotenuse. Find all Pythagorean triples no larger than 500 for **side1**, **side2** and **hypotenuse**. Use a triple-nested **for** loop that tries all possibilities. This method is an example of "brute force" computing. You will learn in more advanced computer science courses that there are many interesting problems for which there is no known algorithmic approach other than using sheer brute force.

5.8   Use a single **foreach** loop to print out the following pattern:

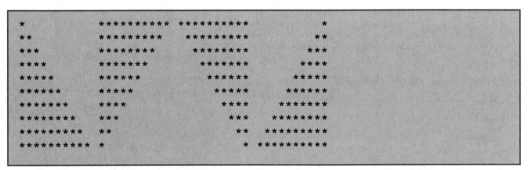

Hints: The asterisks should be printed row by row. Use the **x** string multiplier to print out the correct number of asterisks, then the proper number of spaces, then asterisks, then spaces, etc. You should use a single **foreach** structure containing a **print** statement that prints one row. The **print** statement should contain calculations that determine the proper number of asterisks or spaces to display during each iteration of the loop.

5.9   Read in 10 numbers and store them in an array.

    a) Use a **foreach** loop to print the square of each number if the square is between **100** and **200**.

    b) Use the **map** and **grep** functions to do the same as in (a).

5.10   Modify Exercise 3.10 to use an infinite **for** loop. In addition to the average miles per gallon, the program should print the average miles between tank refills and the average number of gallons per filling. If a negative number is entered for either the number of miles or number of gallons (other than -1 for the number of gallons), use **redo** to obtain new user input.

Subroutines and Functions

Objectives

- To understand how to construct programs modularly from small pieces called subroutines and functions.
- To be able to create new subroutines and functions.
- To understand the mechanisms used to pass information between subroutines.
- To introduce simulation techniques using random number generation.
- To understand how the visibility of identifiers is limited to specific regions of programs.
- To understand how to write and use subroutines that call themselves.

Form ever follows function.
Louis Henri Sullivan

E pluribus unum.
(One composed of many.)
Virgil

O! call back yesterday, bid time return.
William Shakespeare, *Richard II*

Call me Ishmael.
Herman Melville, *Moby Dick*

When you call me that, smile.
Owen Wister

Outline

6.1 Introduction

Most computer programs that solve real-world problems are much larger than the programs presented in the first few chapters (although many powerful Perl programs are compact in size). Experience has shown that the best way to develop and maintain a large program is to construct it from smaller pieces or components, each of which is more manageable than the original program. This technique is called *divide and conquer.* Splitting a program into smaller pieces makes debugging easier. We can isolate a certain section of code and work on that without interference from another portion of the code. This chapter describes many key features of the Perl language that facilitate the design, implementation, operation and maintenance of large programs.

6.2 Subroutines in Perl

User-defined functions in Perl are called *subroutines.* Perl programs are typically written by combining new subroutines the programmer writes with built-in functions available in Perl. In this chapter, we concentrate on user-defined subroutines and provide a brief introduction to packages and modules, which allow us to reuse preexisting subroutines, functions and variables. [*Note*: In this chapter, we use the term "function" when referring to a Perl built-in function and the term "subroutine" when referring to a user-defined function. These terms are actually interchangeable and we use the term function for the rest of the book.]

Perl provides a rich collection of built-in functions (functions that are part of the Perl programming environment) for performing common mathematical calculations, string manipulations, character manipulations, input/output, error checking and many other useful operations. This makes the programmer's job easier, because these functions provide many of the capabilities programmers need. Indeed, you have already encountered several such functions, including **print**, **chomp**, **push** and **sort**. In addition to the Perl built-in functions, there are many libraries of Perl code available for download from the Internet. For example, the *Comprehensive Perl Archive Network (CPAN)*—**www.cpan.org**— provides a searchable archive containing thousands of Perl libraries (called *packages* and *modules*, as we discuss toward the end of this chapter).

Software Engineering Observation 6.1

Avoid reinventing the wheel. When possible, use Perl built-in functions instead of writing new subroutines. This reduces program development time. Familiarize yourself with the rich collection of built-in functions in your Perl implementation's **perlfunc** *documentation page and those available in the extensive Perl library on CPAN. To access the* **perlfunc** *documentation page on UNIX/Linux systems, type* **man perlfunc**. *On many other systems, you can type* **perldoc perlfunc** *or view the online documentation that was distributed with your Windows version of Perl.*

Portability Tip 6.1

Using the Perl built-in functions in standard Perl modules and packages helps make programs more portable.

Performance Tip 6.1

Do not try to rewrite built-in functions to make them more efficient. You usually will not be able to increase the performance of these functions.

The programmer can write subroutines to define specific tasks that could be used at many points in a program. These are known as *user-defined subroutines*. The actual statements defining the subroutine are written only once, and these statements are hidden from other subroutines.

A subroutine is *invoked* (i.e., made to perform its designated task) by a *subroutine call*. The subroutine call specifies the subroutine name and provides information (as *arguments*) that the called subroutine requires to do its job. A common analogy for this is the hierarchical form of management. A boss (the *calling subroutine* or *caller*) asks a worker (the *called subroutine*) to perform a task and *return* (report back) the results when the task is done. The boss subroutine does not know *how* the worker subroutine performs its designated tasks. The worker might call other worker subroutines, and the boss will be unaware of this. We will soon see how this "hiding" of implementation details promotes good software engineering. Figure 6.1 shows a program (the boss) communicating with several worker subroutines in a hierarchical manner. Note that **worker1** acts as a boss subroutine to **worker4** and **worker5**. Relationships among subroutines may be other than the hierarchical structure shown in this figure.

Software Engineering Observation 6.2

In programs containing many subroutines, the program should be implemented in two parts: The first consists mainly of calls to subroutines, and the second would be the subroutines themselves, which perform the bulk of the work.

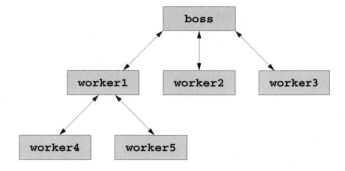

Fig. 6.1   Hierarchical boss–subroutine/worker–subroutine relationship.

There are several motivations for "*functionalizing*" a program (i.e., breaking a program into interacting subroutines). The divide-and-conquer approach makes program development more manageable. Another motivation is *software reusability*—using existing subroutines as building blocks to create new programs. Software reusability is a major factor in *rapid application development (RAD)*. With good subroutine naming and definition, programs can be created from standardized subroutines that accomplish specific tasks, rather than by creating custom code. A third motivation is to avoid repeating code in a program. Packaging code as a subroutine allows the code to be executed from several locations in a program simply by calling the subroutine.

Software Engineering Observation 6.3

Each subroutine should be limited to performing a single, well-defined task, and the subroutine name should express that task effectively. This promotes software reusability.

Software Engineering Observation 6.4

If you cannot choose a concise name that expresses what the subroutine does, your subroutine may be attempting to perform too many diverse tasks. It is usually best to break such a subroutine into several smaller subroutines.

6.3 Built-in Math Functions

The built-in math library functions allow the programmer to perform common mathematical calculations. We use various math library functions here to introduce subroutines and functions in more detail. Later in the book, we discuss many other functions in the Perl libraries. In this section, we generically refer to functions and subroutines as "functions."

Functions are normally called by writing the name of the function, followed by a left parenthesis, followed by the *argument* (or a comma-separated list of arguments) of the function, followed by a right parenthesis. For example, a programmer desiring to calculate the square root of **900** might write

```
$result = sqrt( 900 );
```

When this statement executes, the math function *sqrt* is called to calculate the square root of the number **900** contained in the parentheses. The number **900** is the *argument* of **sqrt**. Function **sqrt** calculates the square root of **900** and *returns* the value 30, which is assigned to **$result**. Function **sqrt** takes a scalar argument and returns a scalar result.

Arguments can be scalars, hashes, arrays or expressions. If **$c = 13**, **$d = 3** and **$e = 4**, then the statement

```
print sqrt( $c + $d * $e );
```

calculates and prints the square root of **13 + 3 * 4 = 25**, namely, **5**. Some math functions are summarized in Fig. 6.2.

Figure 6.3 shows some of these math functions in use. Note in lines 8 and 10 that math functions can use the special variable **$_** as their default argument if no argument is provided in the function call.

6.4 User-defined Subroutines

Previous programs were composed of statements and control structures that called built-in functions to accomplish their tasks. We now consider how programmers write their own customized subroutines.

Function	Description	Example
cos($x)	trigonometric cosine of x (x in radians)	cos(0) is 1
exp($x)	e to the power of x (e^x)	exp(1) is 2.71828 exp(2) is 7.38906
abs($x)	absolute value of x	abs(5.1) is 5.1 abs(0) is 0 abs(-8.76) is 8.76
log($x)	natural logarithm of x (base e)	log(2.718282) is 1 log(7.389056) is 2
sin($x)	trigonometric sine of x (x in radians)	sin(0) is 0
sqrt($x)	square root of x	sqrt(900) is 30 sqrt(9) is 3

Fig. 6.2   Some Perl built-in math functions.

```
1   #!/usr/bin/perl
2   # Fig. 6.3: fig06_03.pl
3   # Demonstrating some math functions.
4
5   $_ = -2;
6   print "Absolute value of 5 is: ", abs( 5 ), "\n",
7          "Absolute value of -5 is: ", abs( -5 ), "\n",
8          "Absolute value of $_: ", abs, "\n\n";
9
10  print "exp( $_ ): ", exp, "\n";
11  print "log( 5 ): ", log( 5 ), "\n";
12  print "sqrt( 16 ): ", sqrt( 16 ), "\n";
```

Fig. 6.3   Demonstrating some math functions (part 1 of 2).

```
Absolute value of 5 is: 5
Absolute value of -5 is: 5
Absolute value of -2: 2

exp( -2 ): 0.135335283236613
log( 5 ): 1.6094379124341
sqrt( 16 ): 4
```

Fig. 6.3   Demonstrating some math functions (part 2 of 2).

Figure 6.4 defines subroutines **subroutine1** and **subroutine2**. Each subroutine takes no arguments and simply displays a message when it is called. [Soon we will discuss subroutines that do take arguments.]

Line 5

```
subroutine1();  # call the subroutine with no arguments
```

calls (or invokes) **subroutine1**. Normally, subroutines are called by following the subroutine name with a set of parentheses. An empty set of parentheses indicates that the subroutine does not receive any arguments.

When a subroutine or function is called, program control continues at the definition of the subroutine or function. In this case, line 5 calls **subroutine1** and program control continues at line 10 (the beginning of the subroutine definition). Next, the body of the subroutine (lines 11–13) executes to perform the subroutine's task (display the string **"called subroutine1\n"**).

```
1   #!/usr/bin/perl
2   # Fig 6.4: fig06_04.pl
3   # User-defined subroutines that take no arguments.
4
5   subroutine1();  # call the subroutine with no arguments
6   subroutine2();  # call the subroutine with no arguments
7
8   # the code after this comment executes only if the program
9   # explicitly calls these subroutines (as in lines 5 and 6).
10  sub subroutine1
11  {
12     print "called subroutine1\n";
13  }
14
15  sub subroutine2
16  {
17     print "called subroutine2\n";
18  }
```

```
called subroutine1
called subroutine2
```

Fig. 6.4   Calling user-defined subroutines that take no arguments.

Note that the subroutine's body is a block of statements enclosed in curly braces (**{ }**). When execution reaches the closing right curly brace (**}**) of the subroutine (line 13), program control returns to the first statement (in this case, line 6) after the point at which the subroutine was called (line 5). Line 6 repeats this process by calling **subroutine2** (lines 15–18), which displays the string **"called subroutine2\n"**. Line 6 of the program is actually the last statement in this program, so, after this line executes, the program terminates. The body of a subroutine executes only in response to a subroutine call.

Common Programming Error 6.1

Assuming that the body of a subroutine executes simply because the subroutine definition is placed between other executable Perl statements can be a logic error. Subroutine definitions can be placed anywhere in a Perl program, but they execute only when they are explicitly called.

The general format of a subroutine definition is

```
sub subroutineName
{
    statements
}
```

Every subroutine definition begins with keyword **sub**. The *subroutineName* can be any valid identifier (conforming to the same rules as scalar, array and hash variable names). The *statements* in braces (**{ }**) form the *subroutine body*. The subroutine body is also referred to as a block of code.

Good Programming Practice 6.1

Place a blank line between adjacent subroutine definitions to separate the subroutines and enhance program readability.

Good Programming Practice 6.2

Choosing meaningful subroutine names makes programs more readable and helps avoid excessive use of comments.

Software Engineering Observation 6.5

A subroutine should fit in an editor window. Regardless of how long a subroutine is, it should perform one task well.

Software Engineering Observation 6.6

Large programs should be written as collections of interacting small subroutines. This makes programs easier to write, debug, maintain and modify.

6.5 Argument Lists

Many prior examples have passed information to functions as arguments, to help functions perform their tasks (e.g., the arguments to function **print**, or the math functions). Subroutines can also receive arguments. The list of arguments passed to a function is stored in the special array variable **@_**. Figure 6.5 demonstrates a user-defined subroutine that receives a list of arguments and displays the value of each argument.

```
1   #!/usr/bin/perl
2   # Fig 6.5: fig06_05.pl
3   # Demonstrating a subroutine that receives arguments.
4
5   displayArguments( "Sam", "Jones", 2, 15, 73, 2.79 );
6
7   # output the subroutine arguments using special variable @_
8   sub displayArguments
9   {
10      # the following statement displays all the arguments
11      print "All arguments: @_\n";
12
13      # the following loop displays each individual argument
14      for ( $i = 0; $i < @_; ++$i ) {
15         print "Argument $i: $_[ $i ]\n";
16      }
17   }
```

```
All arguments: Sam Jones 2 15 73 2.79
Argument 0: Sam
Argument 1: Jones
Argument 2: 2
Argument 3: 15
Argument 4: 73
Argument 5: 2.79
```

Fig. 6.5   Subroutine that receives arguments.

Subroutine **displayArguments** (lines 8–17) can receive any number of arguments. First, the subroutine uses **print** to display the contents of the special array variable **@_**; then it uses a **for** structure to output each individual argument.

Line 5 calls subroutine **displayArguments** with six string and numeric arguments. Program control continues with the subroutine definition at line 8. Line 11 displays the contents of the entire arguments array with each argument separated by a space. The **for** structure at lines 14–15 accesses each argument individually, with the expression **$_[$i]**, and displays the argument value. Note that the expression **$_[$i]** accesses an element of array **@_** and has no relation to special variable **$_**.

Special variable **@_** is interesting in that it *flattens* all arrays and hashes. This means that if you send a subroutine an array value and a scalar value, **@_** will contain one list with all the data from the array and the scalar value. Similarly, a hash is flattened into a list of its key/value pairs (e.g., *key1*, *value1*, *key2*, *value2*, etc.). In the body of a subroutine, if you try to assign the contents of **@_** to an array and a scalar by using the list assignment

```
( @first, $second ) = @_;
```

then **@first** will take all the data in **@_** and **$second** will remain undefined.

Common Programming Error 6.2

Passing arguments in an order that causes unexpected flattening of your data can cause errors in your program. Flattening can be prevented with techniques demonstrated in Chapter 13, References.

6.6 Returning Values

When a subroutine completes its task, data are returned to the subroutine caller via the **return** *keyword*, as shown in Fig. 6.6.

Lines 14–18 define subroutine **square**, which calculates the square of the value the subroutine receives as its argument. The **for** structure at lines 7–9 calls subroutine **square** repeatedly with each of the values from 1 through 10. In each call (line 8), the value of **$_** passed as an argument to **square** is stored in the special array for arguments, **@_**.

Line 16 uses a common Perl idiom to access the argument value in the subroutine. Function **shift**, when used without any arguments, operates on the **@_** special array variable and removes the first element of the array. Thus, the expression **$value = shift** removes the first element of **@_** and assigns it to scalar variable **$value**.

Line 17

```
     return $value ** 2;    # returns the result of $value ** 2
```

evaluates the expression **$value ** 2** (the square of **$value**) and passes the result back to the caller via the **return** keyword. Line 8 displays the squared value followed by a space. Note that the subroutine's execution terminates immediately when the **return** statement executes. Any code in the body of the subroutine that appears after the **return** statement does not execute. Note also that if a subroutine does not contain a **return** statement, the subroutine returns the value of the last statement it executes.

In Perl, the return value from a subroutine can return a scalar, as shown in Fig. 6.6, or it can return a list. A subroutine can even return a list *or* a scalar, depending on the context in which the subroutine is called. To support this functionality, Perl provides function **wantarray**. When called in the body of a subroutine, function **wantarray** returns true if the subroutine was called from a list context and returns *false* if the subroutine was called from a scalar context. Figure 6.7 demonstrates a subroutine that returns either a list or a scalar, depending on the context in which the subroutine is called.

```
1    #!/usr/bin/perl
2    # Fig 6.6: fig06_06.pl
3    # Demonstrating a subroutine that returns a value.
4
5    # for the numbers from 1-10, call subroutine square to
6    # square each value, and display each result
7    for ( 1 .. 10 ) {
8        print square( $_ ), " ";
9    }
10
11   print "\n";
12
13   # subroutine square returns the square of a number
14   sub square
15   {
16       $value = shift();      # use shift to get first argument
17       return $value ** 2;    # returns the result of $value ** 2
18   }
```

Fig. 6.6   Subroutine that returns a value (part 1 of 2).

```
1  4  9  16  25  36  49  64  81  100
```

Fig. 6.6   Subroutine that returns a value (part 2 of 2).

```
1   #!/usr/bin/perl
2   # Fig 6.7: fig06_07.pl
3   # Demonstrating a subroutine that returns a scalar or a list.
4
5   # call scalarOrList() in list context to initialize @array,
6   # then print the list
7   @array = scalarOrList();   # list context to initialize @array
8   $" = "\n";                 # set default separator character
9   print "Returned:\n@array\n";
10
11  # call scalarOrList() in scalar context and concatenate the
12  # result to another string
13  print "\nReturned: " . scalarOrList();  # scalar context
14
15  # use wantarray to return a list or scalar
16  # based on the calling context
17  sub scalarOrList
18  {
19     if ( wantarray() ) {    # if list context
20        return 'this', 'is', 'a', 'list', 'of', 'strings';
21     }
22     else {                  # if scalar context
23        return 'hello';
24     }
25  }
```

```
Returned:
this
is
a
list
of
strings

Returned: hello
```

Fig. 6.7   Subroutine that returns a scalar *or* a list, depending on the return value of
function **wantarray**.

Line 7

```
@array = scalarOrList();  # list context to initialize @array
```

uses the return value of **scalarOrList** (defined at lines 17–25) to initialize **@array**.
An array initializer is in list context. Thus, in the **if** structure at line 19

```
if ( wantarray() ) {    # if list context
```

function **wantarray** returns true and **scalarOrList** returns a list of strings. In line 8, we introduce the **$"** *special variable*. This is the default separator character, which usually holds the value **" "**, or just a blank space. The value in **$"** specifies what will be printed in between the values of an array when an array is printed in double quotes. As a result, when **@array** is printed in line 9, each element is printed on a separate line. Line 13

```
print "\nReturned: " . scalarOrList();   # scalar context
```

uses the return value of **scalarOrList** in a string-concatenation operation. This is a scalar context. In this case, function **wantarray** returns *false*, and **scalarOrList** returns the string **'hello'**.

6.7 Other Ways to Invoke a Subroutine

The last several examples demonstrated that a program can call a subroutine by following the name of the subroutine with parentheses. If the subroutine requires arguments to perform its task, those arguments are placed within the parentheses. Actually, there are several ways to call subroutines. This section describes the syntax of the different types of subroutine calls. Normally, we call subroutines by using the syntax demonstrated in the last several programs.

As we have seen with variable names, Perl uses type identifier characters to distinguish types. Prefixing the type identifier *ampersand* (**&**) to a subroutine name, as in

```
&subroutine1;
```

calls **subroutine1**. When using this syntax for a subroutine call with no arguments or for a subroutine that will receive only the caller's **@_** variable as a default argument, we can omit the parentheses in the subroutine call. Parentheses always are required in this syntax if any explicit arguments are passed to the subroutine.

One other syntax for calling subroutines is the *bareword*. In this case, there are no special symbols around the subroutine name to help Perl determine the purpose of the name in the program. If the subroutine is defined before the bareword appears in the program, the subroutine will be called. If the bareword appears before the subroutine definition, Perl interprets the bareword like a string and does not call the subroutine. For subroutines that do not return values, the only problem here is that the subroutine is not called. However, if the return value is required for use in the program, Perl tries to use this string as the return value.

Common Programming Error 6.3

Using barewords can lead to logic errors.

Good Programming Practice 6.3

For clarity and to prevent logic errors, always use parentheses in a subroutine call.

The program of Fig. 6.8 summarizes the different ways to call a subroutine. For a syntax that is not allowed or causes no action to be taken by the program, we output a line of text stating this fact. Note, in line 36, that parentheses are not required to pass arguments to a subroutine that is defined before it is used in the program.

```perl
1   #!usr/bin/perl
2   # Fig 6.8: fig06_08.pl
3   # Syntax for calling a subroutine.
4
5   # subroutine with no arguments defined before it is used
6   sub definedBeforeWithoutArguments
7   {
8      print "definedBeforeWithoutArguments\n";
9   }
10
11  # subroutine with arguments defined before it is used
12  sub definedBeforeWithArguments
13  {
14     print "definedBeforeWithArguments: @_\n";
15  }
16
17  # calling subroutines that are defined before use
18  print "-----------------------------\n";
19  print "Subroutines defined before use\n";
20  print "-----------------------------\n";
21  print "Using & and ():\n";
22  &definedBeforeWithoutArguments();
23  &definedBeforeWithArguments( 1, 2, 3 );
24
25  print "\nUsing only ():\n";
26  definedBeforeWithoutArguments();
27  definedBeforeWithArguments( 1, 2, 3 );
28
29  print "\nUsing only &:\n";
30  &definedBeforeWithoutArguments;
31  print "\"&definedBeforeWithArguments 1, 2, 3\"",
32        " generates a syntax error\n";
33
34  print "\nUsing bareword:\n";
35  definedBeforeWithoutArguments;
36  definedBeforeWithArguments 1, 2, 3;
37
38  # calling subroutines that are not defined before use
39  print "\n---------------------------\n";
40  print "Subroutines defined after use\n";
41  print "---------------------------\n";
42  print "Using & and ():\n";
43  &definedAfterWithoutArguments();
44  &definedAfterWithArguments( 1, 2, 3 );
45
46  print "\nUsing only ():\n";
47  definedAfterWithoutArguments();
48  definedAfterWithArguments( 1, 2, 3 );
49
50  print "\nUsing only &:\n";
51  &definedAfterWithoutArguments;
52  print "\"&definedAfterWithArguments 1, 2, 3\"",
53        " generates a syntax error\n";
```

Fig. 6.8   Different ways to call subroutines (part 1 of 3).

```
54
55   print "\nUsing bareword:\n";
56   definedAfterWithoutArguments;
57   print "\"definedAfterWithoutArguments\" causes no action\n";
58   print "\"definedAfterWithArguments 1, 2, 3\"",
59        " generates a syntax error\n";
60
61   # subroutine with no arguments defined after it is used
62   sub definedAfterWithoutArguments
63   {
64      print "definedAfterWithoutArguments\n";
65   }
66
67   # subroutine with arguments defined after it is used
68   sub definedAfterWithArguments
69   {
70      print "definedAfterWithArguments: @_\n";
71   }
```

```
------------------------------
Subroutines defined before use
------------------------------
Using & and ():
definedBeforeWithoutArguments
definedBeforeWithArguments: 1 2 3

Using only ():
definedBeforeWithoutArguments
definedBeforeWithArguments: 1 2 3

Using only &:
definedBeforeWithoutArguments
"&definedBeforeWithArguments 1, 2, 3" generates a syntax error

Using bareword:
definedBeforeWithoutArguments
definedBeforeWithArguments: 1 2 3


------------------------------
Subroutines defined after use
------------------------------
Using & and ():
definedAfterWithoutArguments
definedAfterWithArguments: 1 2 3

Using only ():
definedAfterWithoutArguments
definedAfterWithArguments: 1 2 3

Using only &:
definedAfterWithoutArguments
"&definedAfterWithArguments 1, 2, 3" generates a syntax error
```

Fig. 6.8   Different ways to call subroutines (part 2 of 3).

```
Using bareword:
"definedAfterWithoutArguments" causes no action
"definedAfterWithArguments 1, 2, 3" generates a syntax error
```

Fig. 6.8   Different ways to call subroutines (part 3 of 3).

The program begins by creating two subroutines—**definedBeforeWithoutAr-**
guments (lines 6–9) and **definedBeforeWithArguments** (lines 12–15). Each is
called several times to demonstrate the different ways to call subroutines that are defined
before they are used in a program. Lines 22 and 23 call each subroutine with both **&** and
(). Lines 26 and 27 call each subroutine with the common **()** notation. Using each syntax,
the subroutines execute correctly. In lines 29–32, **definedBeforeWithoutArgu-**
ments is called with an **&** but no parentheses. This syntax is not allowed for subroutines
that are passed explicit arguments. So, **definedBeforeWithArguments** is not
explicitly called here, because a syntax error would occur. Lines 35 and 36 call the subroutines again as barewords without **&** or parentheses. This syntax works only because the subroutines are defined before they are called.

The second half of the program performs the same tests, but with the subroutines that
are defined after they are used in the program (hence the names **definedAfterWith-**
outArguments and **definedAfterWithArguments**). Again the subroutines are
invoked correctly when using **&** and **()** or when using just **()**. As discussed previously,
lines 52 and 53 once again show that subroutines with arguments can be called with the **&**
syntax only if parentheses are used also. Finally, lines 55–59 demonstrate an attempt to use
the subroutines as barewords. This worked earlier with the subroutines that were defined
before they were used (lines 34–36). In this case, however, the subroutine without arguments did not cause an action to occur, because there was no context to help Perl determine
the purpose of the identifier. In this part of the program, the subroutine with arguments is
not called, because it would cause a syntax error.

6.8 Random-Number Generation

We now take a brief and, it is hoped, entertaining diversion into a popular programming
application—simulation and game playing. In this section and the next, we will develop a
nicely structured game-playing program that includes multiple subroutines. The program
uses many of the control-structure and subroutine concepts discussed so far in the book.

There is something in the air of a gambling casino that invigorates every type of person
from the high-rollers at the plush mahogany-and-felt craps tables to the quarter-poppers at
the one-armed bandits. It is the *element of chance,* the possibility that luck will convert a
pocketful of money into a mountain of wealth. The element of chance can be introduced
into computer applications by using function ***rand***.

Consider the following statement:

```
$i = rand();
```

The function **rand** generates a floating-point scalar value greater than or equal to 0 and
less than 1. If **rand** truly produces scalars at random, every number in this range has an
equal *chance* (or *probability*) of being chosen each time **rand** is called.

The range of values produced directly by **rand** is often different from that needed in a specific application. For example, a program that simulates coin tossing might require only 0 for "heads" and 1 for "tails." A program that simulates rolling a six-sided die would require random integers in the range from 1 to 6. A program that randomly predicts the next type of spaceship (out of four possibilities) that will fly across the horizon in a video game might require random integers in the range from 1 through 4.

We can manually set the range of values that **rand** returns by passing it a numeric argument. In this case, **rand** returns a random value greater than or equal to 0 and less than the argument. As we mentioned, some applications require random integer values. A floating-point value is truncated to an integer with function *int* (e.g., **int(7.835)** becomes **7**).

Figure 6.9 demonstrates function **rand** with and without arguments. In particular, notice the expression

```
1 + int( rand( 6 ) )
```

in line 20. The call to **rand** in this expression produces a value greater than or equal to 0 and less than 6. That value is truncated with **int** to produce integers in the range from 0 through 5. We then add 1 to the result to produce a value in the range from 1 through 6, which could be used to simulate the rolling of a six-sided die in a game.

Try running this program several times and observe the results of each execution. Notice that a *different* sequence of random numbers is obtained each time the program executes. Now let us look at another program that produces random integers in the range from 1 through 6 (Fig. 6.10).

```perl
1   #!usr/bin/perl
2   # Fig. 6.9: fig06_09.pl
3   # Demonstrating function rand.
4
5   print "Random numbers produced by rand():\n";
6
7   for ( 1 .. 3 ) {
8      print "   ", rand(), "\n";
9   }
10
11  print "\nRandom numbers produced by rand( 100 ):\n";
12
13  for ( 1 .. 3 ) {
14     print "   ", rand( 100 ), "\n";
15  }
16
17  print "\nRandom integers produced by 1 + int( rand( 6 ) ):\n";
18
19  for ( 1 .. 3 ) {
20     print "   ", 1 + int( rand( 6 ) ), "\n";
21  }
```

Fig. 6.9   Using the random number generator (part 1 of 2).

```
Random numbers produced by rand():
   0.76605224609375
   0.387115478515625
   0.648834228515625

Random numbers produced by rand( 100 ):
   32.4371337890625
   90.948486328125
   83.7890625

Random integers produced by 1 + int( rand( 6 ) ):
   6
   4
   1
```

Fig. 6.9   Using the random number generator (part 2 of 2).

```perl
1   #!/usr/bin/perl
2   # Fig. 6.10: fig06_10.pl
3   # Seeding the random number generator.
4
5   # during each iteration, set seed to 1,
6   # then produce three random integers
7   for ( 1 .. 3 ) {
8      print "\n\nSetting seed to 1\n";
9      srand( 1 );
10
11      # produces same three values each time
12      for ( 1 .. 3 ) {
13         print "  ", 1 + int( rand( 6 ) );
14      }
15   }
16
17   print "\n\nResetting seed\n";
18   srand();   # let system determine seed
19
20   for ( 1 .. 3 ) {
21
22      print "\n\nAfter seed has been reset\n";
23
24      for ( 1 .. 3 ) {
25         print "  ", 1 + int( rand( 6 ) );
26      }
27
28   }
29
30   print "\n";
```

Fig. 6.10   Seeding the random number generator (part 1 of 2).

```
Setting seed to 1
   1   4   2

Setting seed to 1
   1   4   2

Setting seed to 1
   1   4   2

Resetting seed


After the seed has been reset
   2   4   6

After the seed has been reset
   5   5   2

After the seed has been reset
   4   5   5
```

Fig. 6.10   Seeding the random number generator (part 2 of 2).

Notice that, during the three iterations of the **for** structure at line 7, the same sequence of values is displayed each time. How can these be random numbers? Ironically, this repeatability is an important characteristic of **rand**. Function **rand** actually generates *pseudorandom numbers*. Calling **rand** repeatedly produces a sequence of numbers that appears to be random. The random numbers produced by **rand** are based on an algorithm that uses the previous random number and a *seed* to create the next random number. These are called pseudorandom numbers because, if you know the value of the seed and the algorithm used, you can determine the next number in the sequence. The sequence of pseudorandom numbers repeats itself each time the seed is set to the same value. Function ***srand*** sets the seed during each iteration of the **for** structure (line 9). Normally, function **srand** takes a different scalar argument and *seeds* the **rand** function to produce a different sequence of random numbers. In this case, we set the same seed three times to demonstrate repeatability.

Testing and Debugging Tip 6.1

*When debugging a program that uses random numbers, seed the random number generator with **srand** to produce the same sequence of values during each execution of the program. This repeatability makes such programs easier to debug by allowing the programmer to confirm the execution of the program before randomizing it (changing the final program so that it uses random values where desired). This way, we can repeat the exact situation that caused an error, and we can work quickly to solve the problem.*

The program changes the seed for function **rand** at line 18:

```
srand();   # let system determine seed
```

This causes the computer to read its system clock to obtain the value for the seed automatically. This is the default behavior for **srand**. In fact, even this is unnecessary. As we showed in Fig. 6.9, using **rand** without setting the seed causes the seed to be set automatically from the system clock. Notice that lines 20 through 28 loop three times and produce different sets of random values each time.

Common Programming Error 6.4

*If function **srand** is used at all, it need only be called once in a program to have the desired seeding effect. Calling it more than once in a program actually has the effect of making the random number generator less random.*

The values produced directly by **rand** are always in the following range:

```
0 ≤ rand( $x ) < $x
```

Previously, we demonstrated how to simulate the rolling of a six-sided die with

```
1 + int( rand( 6 ) )
```

which always produces an integer (at random) in the range from 1 through 6. Note that the width of this range (i.e., the number of consecutive integers in the range) is 6 and the starting number in the range is 1. Referring to the preceding expression, we see that the width of the range is determined by the number passed as an argument to function **rand** and the starting number of the range is equal to the number (i.e., 1) that is added to the result of the expression **int(rand(6))**. We can generalize this result as

```
$number = $shiftValue + int( rand( $scaleFactor ) );
```

where **$shiftValue** is the *shifting value*, which is equal to the first number in the desired range of consecutive integers, and **$scaleFactor** is the *scaling factor*, which is equal to the width of the desired range of consecutive integers.

Common Programming Error 6.5

*Using **srand** in place of **rand** to attempt to generate random numbers is a logic error because **srand** does not return random numbers—it always returns 1.*

6.9 Example: A Game of Chance

One of the most popular games of chance is a dice game known as "craps," which is played in casinos and back alleys throughout the world. The rules of the game are straightforward:

> *A player rolls two dice. Each die has six faces. These faces contain 1, 2, 3, 4, 5 and 6 spots. After the dice have come to rest, the sum of the spots on the two upward faces is calculated. If the sum is 7 or 11 on the first throw, the player wins. If the sum is 2, 3 or 12 on the first throw (called "craps"), the player loses (i.e., the "house" wins). If the sum is 4, 5, 6, 8, 9 or 10 on the first throw, then that sum becomes the player's "point." To win, you must continue rolling the dice until you "make your point." The player loses by rolling a 7 before making the point.*

The program in Fig. 6.11 simulates the game of craps and shows several sample executions. Notice that the player must roll two dice on the first roll and on all subsequent rolls. We define a subroutine **rollDice** (lines 37 through 43) to roll the dice, compute and print their sum and return the sum. Subroutine **rollDice** is defined once, but it is called from two places in the program (lines 5 and 22). Notice the use of list assignment at line 39 to assign values to **$die1** and **$die2**.

```perl
1   #!/usr/bin/perl
2   # Fig. 6.11: fig06_11.pl
3   # The game of Craps.
4
5   $roll = rollDice();              # start the game
6
7   # determine if the game is a win or loss,
8   # or if the game should continue
9   if ( $roll == 7 or $roll == 11 ) {              # won?
10     $status = "WON";
11  }
12  elsif ( $roll == 2 or $roll == 3 or $roll == 12 ) {  # lost?
13     $status = "LOST";
14  }
15  else {                           # game continues
16     $status = "CONTINUE";
17     $myPoint = $roll;             # must roll this before 7 to win
18     print "Point is $myPoint.\n";
19  }
20
21  while ( $status eq "CONTINUE" ) {  # game not won or lost
22     $roll = rollDice();            # roll dice again
23
24     if ( $roll == $myPoint ) {     # won?
25        $status = "WON";
26     }
27     elsif ( $roll == 7 ) {         # lost?
28        $status = "LOST";
29     }
30  }
31
32  print message( $status );  # display message with result
33
34  # subroutines to support the game of craps
35
36  # rollDice rolls two dice and returns the sum of the dice
37  sub rollDice
38  {
39     ( $die1, $die2 ) = ( rollDie(), rollDie() );
40     $sum = $die1 + $die2;
41     print "Player rolled $die1 + $die2 = $sum.\n";
42     return $sum;
43  }
44
45  # rollDie rolls one die and returns its value
46  sub rollDie
47  {
48     return 1 + int( rand( 6 ) );
49  }
50
51  # prints a message based
52  sub message
53  {
```

Fig. 6.11   Game of craps (part 1 of 2).

```
54        $status = shift;   # get argument value
55        return "Sorry, you lost.\n" if $status eq "LOST";
56        return "Congratulations, you won!\n";
57  }
```

```
Player rolled 6 + 5 = 11.
Congratulations, you won!
```

```
Player rolled 1 + 1 = 2.
Sorry, you lost.
```

```
Player rolled 4 + 6 = 10.
Point is 10.
Player rolled 2 + 4 = 6.
Player rolled 6 + 5 = 11.
Player rolled 3 + 3 = 6.
Player rolled 6 + 4 = 10.
Congratulations, you won!
```

```
Player rolled 1 + 3 = 4.
Point is 4.
Player rolled 1 + 4 = 5.
Player rolled 5 + 4 = 9.
Player rolled 4 + 6 = 10.
Player rolled 6 + 3 = 9.
Player rolled 1 + 2 = 3.
Player rolled 5 + 2 = 7.
Sorry, you lost.
```

Fig. 6.11   Game of craps (part 2 of 2).

We define two other subroutines—**rollDie** and **message**. Subroutine **rollDie** is called by **rollDice** to generate a random number from 1 through 6. Subroutine **message** takes a single argument (**WON** or **LOST**) and returns an appropriate message indicating whether the game was won or lost.

The game is reasonably involved. The player could win or lose at any point in the game, after any roll. The variable **$status** keeps track of the current state of the game. We assign the strings **"WON"**, **"LOST"** or **"CONTINUE"** to **$status**, which helps direct program execution (controlled by lines 5 through 32).

The game begins with the roll of the dice at line 5. The **if/elsif/else** structure at lines 9–19 determines the status of the game after the first roll. If the game is over after the first roll (i.e., the sum of the dice is 7, 11, 2, 3 or 12), variable **$status** is set to **"WON"** or **"LOST"** and the body of the **while** structure (lines 21–30) is skipped, because

$status is not equal to **"CONTINUE"**. The program continues at line 32, which calls subroutine **message** with the current **$status**. This value gets passed to **message** in the variable **@_**, and we use the function **shift** to assign the first value of **@_** to **$status**. Subroutine **message** returns **"Sorry, you lost.\n"** if the status is **"LOST"**; otherwise, it returns **"Congratulations, you won!\n"**. Notice that, although we have two **return** statements (lines 55 and 56), the second is ignored if **$status** equals **"LOST"**, because the subroutine terminates when the first **return** statement executes.

If the game is not over after the first roll, **$roll** (i.e., the sum of the two dice) is saved in **$myPoint** (line 17). Execution proceeds with the **while** structure (line 21) because **$status** is equal to **"CONTINUE"**. Each iteration of the **while** calls **rollDice** (line 22) to produce a new **$roll**. If **$roll** matches **$myPoint**, **$status** is set to **"WON"**, the **while** condition fails, the congratulatory message prints and execution terminates. If **$roll** is equal to **7**, **$status** is set to **"LOST"**, the **while** condition fails, the message **"Sorry, you lost."** prints and the program terminates. Try running the program several times to see the random results.

Note the interesting use of the various program control mechanisms we have discussed. The craps program uses the **while** and **if/elsif/else** control structures and three subroutines (**rollDice**, **rollDie** and **message**), one of which (**rollDie**) is called from another (**rollDice**). Lastly, notice that all of our subroutines are at the end of the program. This enhances readability and code reuse.

Good Programming Practice 6.4

Group all your subroutines together at the end of your program rather than interspersing them throughout the program. This makes them faster to find and manipulate.

6.10 Recursion

The programs we have discussed generally are structured as subroutines that call one another in a disciplined, hierarchical manner. For some problems, it is useful to have subroutines call themselves. A *recursive subroutine* is a subroutine that calls itself, either directly or (through another subroutine) indirectly. Recursion is an important topic discussed at length in upper-level computer science courses. In this section and the next, simple examples of recursion are presented.

We first consider recursion conceptually and then examine several programs containing actual "live-code™" recursive subroutines. Recursive problem-solving approaches have a number of elements in common. When a recursive subroutine is called to solve a problem, the subroutine actually knows how to solve only the simplest case(s), or so-called *base case(s)*. If the subroutine is called with a base case, the subroutine simply returns a result. If the subroutine is called with a more complex problem, the subroutine divides the problem into two conceptual pieces—a piece that the subroutine knows how to do and a piece that the subroutine does not know how to do. To make recursion feasible, the latter piece must resemble the original problem, but be a slightly simpler or slightly smaller version of the original problem. Because this new problem looks like the original problem, the subroutine launches a fresh copy of itself (i.e., calls itself) to go to work on the smaller problem—this is referred to as a *recursive call* and is also called the *recursion step*. The recursion step normally includes the keyword **return**, because its result will be combined with the portion of the problem the subroutine knew how to solve to form a result that will be passed back to the original caller—the previous call to the subroutine or possibly the program itself.

The recursion step executes while the original call to the subroutine is still "open," i.e., it has not yet finished executing. The recursion step can result in many more such recursive calls as the subroutine keeps dividing each new subproblem with which the subroutine is called into two conceptual pieces. For the recursion to terminate eventually, each time the subroutine calls itself with a slightly simpler version of the original problem this sequence of smaller and smaller problems must eventually converge on the base case. At that point, the subroutine recognizes the base case and returns a result to the previous call of the subroutine, and a sequence of returns ensues all the way up the line until the original call of the subroutine eventually returns the final result to the program. All of this sounds quite exotic compared to the kind of conventional problem solving we have been using to this point. As an example of these concepts at work, let us write a recursive program to perform a popular mathematical calculation.

The factorial of a nonnegative integer *n,* written *n!* (and pronounced "*n* factorial"), is the product

$$n \cdot (n - 1) \cdot (n - 2) \cdot \ldots \cdot 1$$

with 1! equal to 1, and 0! defined to be 1. For example, 5! is the product $5 \cdot 4 \cdot 3 \cdot 2 \cdot 1$, which is equal to 120.

The factorial of an integer, **$number**, greater than or equal to 0, can be calculated *iteratively* (nonrecursively) by using **foreach** as follows:

```
$factorial = 1;

foreach ( 1 .. $number ) {
   $factorial *= $_;
}
```

The preceding **foreach** structure has a two special cases that should be mentioned. The first is that if **$number** is equal to 1, then the **foreach** structure loops only once, and if **$number** is equal to zero, the structure does not loop at all. To understand this, we should look at the list we will be iterating over. In the first case, we iterate over a list from 1 to 1. This list contains only one number, 1, and so we iterate once. In the second case, the list is 1 to 0. Since we start out by already exceeding 0, the list will have no elements, and so the loop is never executed.

A recursive definition of the factorial subroutine is arrived at by observing the following relationship:

$$n! = n \cdot (n - 1)!$$

For example, 5! is clearly equal to $5 \cdot 4!$, as is shown by the following:

$$5! = 5 \cdot 4 \cdot 3 \cdot 2 \cdot 1$$
$$5! = 5 \cdot (4 \cdot 3 \cdot 2 \cdot 1)$$
$$5! = 5 \cdot (4!)$$

The evaluation of 5! would proceed as shown in Fig. 6.12. Figure 6.12 part (a) shows how the succession of recursive subroutine calls proceeds until 1! is evaluated to be 1, which terminates the recursion. Figure 6.12 part (b) shows the values returned from each recursive call to its caller until the final value is calculated and returned.

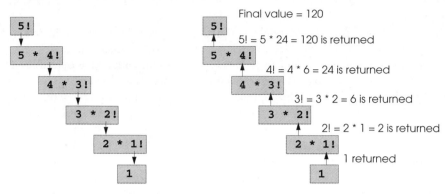

a) Procession of recursive calls.   b) Values returned from each recursive call.

Fig. 6.12   Recursive evaluation of 5!.

The program of Fig. 6.13 uses recursion to calculate and print the factorials of the integers from 0 to 10.

The recursive subroutine **factorial** (lines 13–23) sets the variable **$number** to the first argument it receives. It also uses the keyword **my** to the left of the variable named **$number**. This keyword creates what is called a *lexically scoped variable*. A lexically scoped variable exists only during the block in which it was defined. Every time that block is entered during the execution of the program, the lexically scoped variable is created. Every time that block terminates, the lexically scoped variable is destroyed. This means that each call to subroutine **factorial** has its own copy of the variable **$number**, which cannot be modified by any other call to **factorial**. This is very important—if we were to leave the keyword **my** out, the program would produce incorrect results. Consider the case of **2!**. Without the keyword **my**, **$number** begins by being set to two, as usual. Two is greater than one, so the program makes the recursive call to calculate **$number * factorial($number - 1)**. In the second call, **$number** is equal to one, so the subroutine returns the value one. Here is where we run into a problem. At this point, we want to calculate **$number * factorial($number - 1)** from the first call. The value of **factorial($number - 1)** is one, but the value of **$number** is also one now, because its value was changed in the last recursive call. As a result of this, 2! calculates as 1, which is incorrect. Section 6.13 discusses variable scope and keyword **my** in more detail.

On line 17, the subroutine tests the base case to determine whether a terminating condition is true, i.e., is **$number** less than or equal to 1. If **$number** is indeed less than or equal to 1, **factorial** returns 1, no further recursion is necessary and the subroutine terminates. If **$number** is greater than 1, the recursive step (line 21)

```
return $number * factorial( $number - 1 );
```

expresses the problem as the product of **$number** (an expression that evaluates to a simple numeric value) and a recursive call to **factorial** evaluating the factorial of **$number - 1**. Note that **factorial($number - 1)** is a slightly simpler problem than the original calculation **factorial($number)**.

```perl
1   #!/usr/bin/perl
2   # Fig. 6.13: fig06_13.pl
3   # Recursive factorial subroutine
4
5   # call function factorial for each of the numbers from
6   # 0 through 10 and display the results
7   foreach ( 0 .. 10 ) {
8      print "$_! = " . factorial( $_ ) . "\n";
9   }
10
11  # factorial recursively calculates the factorial of the
12  # argument it receives
13  sub factorial
14  {
15     my $number = shift;    # get the argument
16
17     if ( $number <= 1 ) { # base case
18        return 1;
19     }
20     else {                 # recursive step
21        return $number * factorial( $number - 1 );
22     }
23  }
```

```
0! = 1
1! = 1
2! = 2
3! = 6
4! = 24
5! = 120
6! = 720
7! = 5040
8! = 40320
9! = 362880
10! = 3628800
```

Fig. 6.13   Recursive **factorial** subroutine.

Common Programming Error 6.6

Forgetting to return a value from a recursive subroutine when one is needed can cause errors.

Common Programming Error 6.7

Either omitting the base case or writing the recursion step incorrectly so that it does not converge on the base case will cause "infinite" recursion, eventually exhausting memory. Infinite recursion is analogous to an infinite loop in an iterative (nonrecursive) solution.

6.11 Example Using Recursion: Fibonacci

The Fibonacci series,

0, 1, 1, 2, 3, 5, 8, 13, 21, ...

begins with 0 and 1 and has the property that each subsequent Fibonacci number is the sum of the previous two Fibonacci numbers. The series describes a form of spiral. The ratio of successive Fibonacci numbers converges on the constant value 1.618…. This number repeatedly occurs in nature and has been called the *golden ratio* or the *golden mean.* Humans tend to find the golden mean aesthetically pleasing. Architects often design windows, rooms, and buildings whose length and width are in the ratio of the golden mean. Postcards are often designed with a golden mean length/width ratio.

The Fibonacci series can be defined recursively as follows:

> *fibonacci(0) = 0*
> *fibonacci(1) = 1*
> *fibonacci(n) = fibonacci(n – 1) + fibonacci(n – 2)*

The program of Fig. 6.14 inputs a number *n* from the user and outputs the *n*th Fibonacci number.

The first two calls to **fibonacci** at line 9 are not recursive calls, but all subsequent calls to **fibonacci** are recursive. Each **fibonacci** call immediately tests for the base case—**$number** equal to 0 or 1 (line 18). If this is true, **$number** is returned. Interestingly, if **$number** is greater than 1, the recursion step (lines 23 and 24) generates *two* recursive calls, each of which is a slightly simpler problem than the original call to **fibonacci**. Figure 6.15 shows how subroutine **fibonacci** would evaluate **fibonacci(3)**—we abbreviate **fibonacci** simply as **f** to make the figure more readable.

```perl
1   #!/usr/bin/perl
2   # Fig 6.14: fig06_14.pl
3   # Recursive fibonacci function.
4
5   @sampleValues = (0, 1, 2, 3, 4, 5, 6, 10, 20, 30, 35);
6
7   # Calculate and print the fibonacci value of all the above values
8   foreach ( @sampleValues ) {
9      print "fibonacci( $_ ) = ", fibonacci( $_ ), "\n";
10  }
11
12  # fibonacci recursively calculates the fibonacci number
13  # of its integer argument
14  sub fibonacci
15  {
16     my $number = shift;   # get the first argument
17
18     if ( $number == 0 or $number == 1 ) { # base case
19        return $number;
20     }
21
22     else {                                 # recursive step
23        return fibonacci( $number - 1 ) +
24               fibonacci( $number - 2 );
25     }
26  }
```

Fig. 6.14   Recursive **fibonacci** subroutine (part 1 of 2).

```
fibonacci( 0 ) = 0
fibonacci( 1 ) = 1
fibonacci( 2 ) = 1
fibonacci( 3 ) = 2
fibonacci( 4 ) = 3
fibonacci( 5 ) = 5
fibonacci( 6 ) = 8
fibonacci( 10 ) = 55
fibonacci( 20 ) = 6765
fibonacci( 30 ) = 832040
fibonacci( 35 ) = 9227465
```

Fig. 6.14　Recursive **fibonacci** subroutine (part 2 of 2).

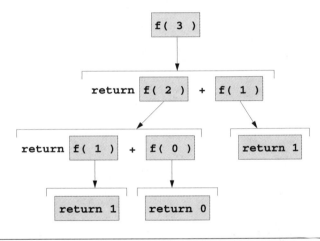

Fig. 6.15　Set of recursive calls to subroutine **fibonacci**.

A word of caution is in order about recursive programs like the one we use here to generate Fibonacci numbers. Each level of recursion in subroutine **fibonacci** has a doubling effect on the number of subroutine calls—the number of recursive calls required to calculate the nth Fibonacci number is on the order of 2^n. This rapidly gets out of hand. Calculating only the 20th Fibonacci number would require on the order of 2^{20} or about a million calls, calculating the 30th Fibonacci number would require on the order of 2^{30} or about a billion calls, and so on. Computer scientists refer to this as *exponential complexity*. Problems of this nature humble even the world's most powerful computers! Complexity issues in general, and exponential complexity in particular, are discussed in detail in the upper-level computer science curriculum course generally called "Algorithms."

Performance Tip 6.2

Avoid fibonacci-style recursive programs that result in an exponential "explosion" of calls.

6.12 Recursion vs. Iteration

In the previous sections, we studied two subroutines that can be implemented either recursively or iteratively. In this section, we compare the two approaches and discuss why the programmer might choose one approach over the other in a particular situation.

Both iteration and recursion are based on control structures—iteration uses a repetition structure; recursion uses a selection structure. Both iteration and recursion involve repetition—iteration explicitly uses a repetition structure; recursion achieves repetition through repeated subroutine calls. Iteration and recursion both involve a termination test—iteration terminates when the loop-continuation condition fails; recursion terminates when a base case is recognized. Iteration with counter-controlled repetition and recursion both gradually approach termination—iteration keeps modifying a counter until the counter assumes a value that makes the loop-continuation condition fail; recursion keeps producing simpler versions of the original problem until the base case is reached. Both iteration and recursion can occur infinitely—an infinite loop occurs with iteration if the loop-continuation test never becomes false; infinite recursion occurs if the recursion step does not reduce the problem each time in a manner that converges on the base case.

Recursion has many negatives. It repeatedly invokes the mechanism, and consequently the overhead, of subroutine calls. This can be expensive in both processor time and memory space. Each recursive call causes another call of the subroutine; this can consume considerable memory. Iteration normally occurs within a single subroutine, so the overhead of repeated subroutine calls and extra memory assignment is avoided. So why choose recursion?

Software Engineering Observation 6.7

Any problem that can be solved recursively can also be solved iteratively (nonrecursively). A recursive approach is normally chosen in preference to an iterative approach when the recursive approach more naturally mirrors the problem and results in a program that is easier to understand and debug. Another reason to choose a recursive solution is that an iterative solution is not apparent.

Performance Tip 6.3

Avoid using recursion in performance situations. Recursive calls take time and consume additional memory.

Common Programming Error 6.8

Accidentally having a nonrecursive subroutine call itself, either directly or indirectly (through another subroutine), is a logic error.

Let us reconsider some observations that we make repeatedly throughout the book. Good software engineering is important. High performance is important. Unfortunately, these goals are often at odds with one another. Good software engineering is key to making more manageable the task of developing and maintaining larger and more complex software systems. High performance in these systems is crucial to realizing the systems of the future that will place ever greater computing demands on hardware. Where do subroutines fit in here?

Software Engineering Observation 6.8

Functionalizing programs in a neat, hierarchical manner promotes good software engineering, but it has a price.

Performance Tip 6.4

A heavily functionalized program with large numbers of subroutine calls consumes execution time and space on a computer's processor(s), but monolithic programs (i.e. "one-piece" programs that are not divided into interacting subroutines) are difficult to program, test, debug, maintain and evolve.

Functionalize your programs judiciously, always keeping in mind the delicate balance between performance and good software engineering.

6.13 Scope Rules: Global, Lexical and Dynamic

An identifier's *scope* is the portion of the program in which the identifier can be referenced. Some identifiers can be referenced throughout a program; others can be referenced from limited portions of a program. This section discusses the scope of identifiers.

The three scopes for an identifier are *global scope, lexical scope* and *dynamic scope*. Most of the variables used in the book to this point are *global variables*. Such variables have global scope, exist throughout the program's execution and can be manipulated anywhere in the program. As we will see, there are keywords that prefix variable definitions for variables with lexical or dynamic scope. Variables defined without any keyword prefix are automatically global variables and have global scope.

A *lexically scoped variable* is a variable that exists only during the block in which it was defined. A *dynamically scoped variable* is one that exists from the time it is created until the end of the block in which it was created. Such variables are accessible both to the block in which they are defined and to any subroutines called from that block. The program in Fig. 6.16 demonstrates scoping issues with global variables, lexical variables and dynamic variables.

```perl
1   #!/usr/bin/perl
2   # Fig. 6.16: fig06_16.pl
3   # Demonstrating variable scope.
4
5   # before global variables are defined, call subroutine1
6   print "Without globals:\n";
7   subroutine1();
8
9   # define global variables
10  our $x = 7;
11  our $y = 17;
12
13  # call subroutine1 to see results with defined global variables
14  print "\nWith globals:";
15  print "\nglobal \$x: $x";
16  print "\nglobal \$y: $y\n";
17  subroutine1();
18  print "\nglobal \$x: $x";
19  print "\nglobal \$y: $y\n";
20
21  # subroutine1 displays its own $x (lexical scope )
22  # and $y (dynamic scope) variables, then calls subroutine2
```

Fig. 6.16 Variable scope (part 1 of 2).

```
23   sub subroutine1
24   {
25      my $x = 10;
26      local $y = 5;
27      print "\$x in subroutine1: $x\t(lexical to subroutine1)\n";
28      print "\$y in subroutine1: $y\t(dynamic to subroutine1)\n";
29      subroutine2();
30   }
31
32   # subroutine2 displays global $x and subroutine1's $y which
33   # has dynamic scope
34   sub subroutine2
35   {
36      print "\$x in subroutine2: $x\t(global)\n";
37      print "\$y in subroutine2: $y\t(dynamic to subroutine1)\n";
38   }
```

```
Without globals:
$x in subroutine1: 10    (lexical to subroutine1)
$y in subroutine1: 5     (dynamic to subroutine1)
$x in subroutine2:       (global)
$y in subroutine2: 5     (dynamic to subroutine1)

With globals:
global $x: 7
global $y: 17
$x in subroutine1: 10    (lexical to subroutine1)
$y in subroutine1: 5     (dynamic to subroutine1)
$x in subroutine2: 7     (global)
$y in subroutine2: 5     (dynamic to subroutine1)

global $x: 7
global $y: 17
```

Fig. 6.16   Variable scope (part 2 of 2).

Keywords *our*, *my* and *local* determine the scope of a variable. Keyword **our** explicitly defines a variable as a global variable. Keyword **my** defines a lexically scoped variable. Keyword **local** defines a dynamically scoped variable. Let us trace the execution of Fig. 6.16 to see how these keywords affect the scope of identifiers.

Line 7 calls **subroutine1** (defined at lines 23–30) before any global variables are defined. This subroutine defines a lexical variable **$x** (using keyword **my** at line 25) and initializes it to 10, and defines a dynamic variable **$y** (using keyword **local** at line 26) and initializes it to 5. Next, **subroutine1** displays the values of both variables. Then, **subroutine1** calls **subroutine2** (defined at lines 34–38).

Line 36 of **subroutine2** displays the value of **$x**. At this point, the only defined variable **$x** is the one that is lexically scoped to **subroutine1**—**subroutine2** cannot "see" **subroutine1**'s lexically scoped variables. So, **subroutine2** attempts to locate a global definition of **$x**. It cannot locate such a definition, so it does not output a value. Line 37 of **subroutine2** displays the value of variable **$y**. This variable was defined in **subroutine1** with dynamic scope. When **subroutine1** calls **subroutine2**, all the dynamically scoped variables in **subroutine1** are accessible to **subroutine2**, so **subroutine2** outputs the value of **subroutine1**'s **$y** variable (5).

When **subroutine1** completes execution, program control continues at line 10, where the program defines global variables **$x** and **$y**, using keyword **our**. Global **$x** is set to 7 and global **$y** is set to 17. Remember that any variable not explicitly preceded by **my** or **local** in its definition is a global variable. From now on, we will use **our**, **my** and **local** to define all variables explicitly as global, lexical or dynamic scope.

Good Programming Practice 6.5

*Explicitly define every variable with **our**, **my** or **local**.*

Portability Tip 6.2

*The **our** keyword exists only in Perl version 5.6 and later.*

Line 17 calls **subroutine1** (its output is the same as the first time it was called). Notice that **subroutine1** uses its own definitions of **$x** and **$y**, rather than the global definitions. Lexical and dynamic variables in a subroutine always "hide" (but do not destroy) global variables that have the same name. However, the output changes when **subroutine1** calls **subroutine2** for the second time. In this case, **subroutine2** now displays the value of the global **$x** and **subroutine1**'s dynamically scoped **$y**.

The **local** keyword applied to **$y** in line 26 actually creates a temporary copy of the global variable. The old value is saved while there is a new value in **$y**. This new value exists until the end of the current block (i.e., **subroutine1**'s body), at which point the old value is restored. Thus, **subroutine2** can "see" the **local $y** declaration from **subroutine1**, because **subroutine1** has not terminated yet. When **subroutine1** does finally terminate, the original value is restored and the remainder of the program can access it. At this point, if the program calls **subroutine2** from a location other than **subroutine1**, **subroutine2** would output the global variable **$y**.

Good Programming Practice 6.6

Avoid variable names that hide names in outer scopes. This can be accomplished by avoiding the use of duplicate identifiers in a program.

Software Engineering Observation 6.9

Variables used only in a particular subroutine should be declared as lexical variables in that subroutine rather than as global variables or dynamic variables.

Software Engineering Observation 6.10

Declaring a variable as global rather than lexically scoped allows unintended side effects to occur when a subroutine that does not need access to the variable accidentally or maliciously modifies it. In general, use of global variables should be avoided except in certain situations with unique performance requirements.

Software Engineering Observation 6.11

*Programmers almost always use the **my** keyword instead of **local**. Such variables are accessible only in that subroutine and cannot be seen or modified by other subroutines in the program.*

Software Engineering Observation 6.12

In general, if a variable from one subroutine is required by another subroutine to complete its task, pass that variable explicitly as an argument to the subroutine instead of declaring it as a global or a dynamic variable.

6.14 Namespaces, Packages and Modules

Perl uses *packages* (or *namespaces*) to determine the accessibility of variables and subroutine identifiers. Packages can also be used to access identifiers that are defined in other files, called *modules*. Most of Perl's scoping rules derive from this package concept.

Each package has its own *symbol table*, which stores all of the package's variables and subroutine names. By default, the global identifiers in a Perl source code file—global variables and subroutines—are part of the **main** *package's* symbol table. In fact, Perl does not actually have truly global variables. Such variables are actually called *package global variables* or *package variables*. We will see shortly that you can specify your own package names.

Lexical variables are special in that they are not inserted in the package's symbol table. Rather, each block of code in which lexical variables are defined has its own temporary storage for lexical variables. This temporary storage is known as a *scratchpad*.

The symbol table for a package is really a hash with identifiers as keys and memory locations as values (for more information on hashes, see Chapter 4, "Arrays and Hashes"). Just as keys in a hash must be unique, variable names for variables of the same type in a package also must be unique. For example, one package cannot have two scalars named **$variable**. However, one package could contain both a scalar named **$variable** and an array named **@variable**, because these are different types.

6.14.1 Defining a Package and Importing it with `require`

Until now, we have dealt only with the default package for a program, i.e., the **main** package. This is the name of the current package (and thus, the namespace) if we have not specified one. If we create identifiers in this file, it will be a part of the **main** package. However, the current package can be changed with a ***package*** statement. Creating a new package causes Perl to create a new, empty symbol table. Normally, there is only one package statement per source code file. If a program contains two or more packages, each package maintains its own unique set of identifiers. Thus, multiple packages can have identically named identifiers without the potential for conflicting names. The next program consists of two source code files (Fig. 6.17 and Fig. 6.18). The main program (Fig. 6.17) uses identifiers defined in its default package (**main**) and in a package from the second source code file (Fig. 6.18).

```
1   #!usr/bin/perl
2   #Fig. 6.17: fig06_17.pl
3   # Demonstrating packages.
4
5   # make FirstPackage.pm available to this program
6   require FirstPackage;
```

Fig. 6.17   Using a package (part 1 of 2).

```
7
8   # define a package global variable in this program
9   our $variable = "happy";
10
11  # display values from the main package
12  print "From main package:\n";
13  print "\$variable = $variable\n";
14  print "\$main::variable = $main::variable\n";
15
16  # display values from FirstPackage
17  print "\nFrom FirstPackage:\n";
18  print "\$FirstPackage::variable = $FirstPackage::variable\n";
19  print "\$FirstPackage::secret = $FirstPackage::secret\n";
20
21  # use a subroutine in FirstPackage to display the
22  # values of the variables in that package
23  FirstPackage::displayFirstPackageVariables();
```

```
From main package:
$variable = happy
$main::variable = happy

From FirstPackage:
$FirstPackage::variable = birthday
$FirstPackage::secret =
$variable in displayFirstPackageVariables = birthday
$secret in displayFirstPackageVariables = new year
```

Fig. 6.17   Using a package (part 2 of 2).

```
24  #!usr/bin/perl
25  # Fig 6.18: FirstPackage.pm
26  # Our first package.
27
28  package FirstPackage;    # name the pacakge/namespace
29
30  # define a package global variable
31  our $variable = "birthday";
32
33  # define a var\iable known only to this package
34  my $secret = "new year";
35
36  # subroutine that displays the values of
37  # the variables in FirstPackage
38  sub displayFirstPackageVariables
39  {
40     print "\$variable in displayFirstPackageVariables = ",
41           $variable, "\n";
42     print "\$secret in displayFirstPackageVariables = ",
43           $secret, "\n";
44  }
```

Fig. 6.18   Defining a package.

In Fig. 6.17, line 6

```
require FirstPackage;
```

uses keyword *require* to tell Perl to locate **FirstPackage.pm** and add it to the program. Perl first looks for this file in the current directory. If the file cannot be found there, Perl searches for directories that are named in the array **@INC**. This special built-in array tells Perl where to locate the built-in Perl libraries on your computer. Whenever you tell Perl to include a file, it will look for that file in the directories specified by this array, unless it was first found in the current directory. The **require** keyword assumes a **.pm** file name extension, which makes it optional (notice we left it out on line 6 in Fig. 6.17). Packages included in a program using **require** are loaded during the program's execution phase.

Line 9 declares a **main** package variable named **$variable** and assigns it the string **"happy"**. Lines 13 and 14 display the value of **$variable**. Line 13 implicitly searches for **$variable** in the current package (i.e., **main**). Line 14

```
print "\$main::variable = $main::variable\n";
```

uses **$variable**'s *fully qualified name*, in which the package and the variable names are joined by the *double colon operator* (**::**). This operator specifies that the identifier to its right is in the package to its left (i.e., **$variable** is in package **main**). This notation helps Perl determine in which symbol table it should look to locate an identifier. Notice that the **$** indicating the variable is a scalar is placed at the beginning of the fully qualified name.

Lines 17–23 use identifiers defined in the file **FirstPackage.pm** (Fig. 6.18). Before we study these lines, look at the package definition (Fig. 6.18). Line 28

```
package FirstPackage;
```

tells Perl that all variable and subroutine definitions for the remainder of that file (or until the next package statement) are in the **FirstPackage** package (or namespace). The package contains three identifiers—package global variable **$variable** (line 31), lexical variable **$secret** (line 34) and subroutine **displayFirstPackageVariables** (lines 38–44).

In the main program, line 18

```
print "\$FirstPackage::variable = $FirstPackage::variable\n";
```

displays the value of **$FirstPackage::variable**. Our program is able to display this variable from a different package because line 6 included the file **FirstPackage.pm**. This allows all the subroutines and nonlexical variables in **FirstPackage.pm** to be used by their fully qualified names in **fig06_17.pl**. Line 19

```
print "\$FirstPackage::secret = $FirstPackage::secret\n";
```

attempts to display the value of the lexical variable **$secret** in **FirstPackage**. Notice that nothing is displayed in this case. Remember, lexical variables can be accessed only in the block or file in which they are originally defined. Line 23

```
FirstPackage::displayFirstPackageVariables();
```

calls subroutine **displayFirstPackageVariables** to display the contents of the variables in **FirstPackage**. Because this subroutine is in the same package as the lexical variable **$secret**, the subroutine is able to output **$secret**'s value.

6.14.2 Modules and the `use` Statement

A *module* is simply a package that provides the programmer more control over how a user of the module can reference the identifiers in that module's package. One benefit of a module is that a programmer can specify that identifiers should always be made available to the module user as if those identifiers were originally defined in the user's program. This allows the identifiers to be used without their fully qualified names.

This section also introduces the **use** statement, which is similar to the **require** statement shown in Fig. 6.17. The primary difference between **use** and **require** is that **use** imports modules and packages at compile time and **require** does so at execution time. Importing at compile time allows Perl to ensure that the package is available before the program reaches execution time. Otherwise, we might not notice that a package is missing until it is first referenced at execution time. The program of Fig. 6.19 and Fig. 6.20 shows an example of creating and using a simple module.

```
1   #!/usr/bin/perl
2   # Fig 6.19: fig06_19.pl
3   # program to use our first module
4
5   use FirstModule;    # import identifiers from another package
6
7   print "Using automatically imported names:\n";
8   print "\@array contains: @array\n";   # @FirstModule::array
9   greeting();                           # FirstModule::greeting
```

```
Using automatically imported names:
@array contains: 1 2 3
Modules are handy!
```

Fig. 6.19　Demonstrating modules.

```
10  #!/usr/bin/perl
11  # Fig 6.20: FirstModule.pm
12  # Our first module.
13
14  package FirstModule;
15
16  # the following two lines allow this module to export its
17  # identifiers for use in other files.
18  use Exporter;                  # use module Exporter
19  our @ISA = qw( Exporter );     # this module "is an" Exporter
20
21  # @array and &greeting are imported automatically into a
22  # file that uses this module
23  our @EXPORT = qw( @array &greeting );
24
25  # define identifiers for use in other files
26  our @array = ( 1, 2, 3 );
27
```

Fig. 6.20　Module **firstmodule.pm** used by **fig06_19.pl** (part 1 of 2).

```
28   sub greeting
29   {
30       print "Modules are handy!";
31   }
32
33   return 1;   # indicate successful import of module
```

Fig. 6.20   Module **firstmodule.pm** used by **fig06_19.pl** (part 2 of 2).

Figure 6.19 is a simple program that imports the module of Fig. 6.20 and uses an array and a subroutine defined in that module. Line 5 imports module **FirstModule** (defined in lines 10 through 33 of Fig. 6.20). Line 8 displays the contents of **@array** from module **FirstModule**. Line 9 calls subroutine **greeting** from module **FirstModule**. Note that in each case the identifier from module **FirstModule** is not preceded by the package name and operator **::**, as was required in Fig. 6.17. This is because the array **@array** and subroutine **greeting** are exported by module **FirstModule** and are automatically imported into the **main** package's namespace by line 5.

Now let us discuss the module, which has a few additional requirements beyond a basic package. First, the file must have a **.pm** extension. Keyword **require** allows you to specify other extensions (such as **.pl**), but **use** does not.

Common Programming Error 6.9

Specifying a file-name extension other than **.pm** *for a module that will be used in a* **use** *statement is an error.*

Perl allows a module programmer to export identifiers from a module for use in another file's namespace. This allows the other file to use the identifiers without fully qualified names. To do this, the module must be set up as an *Exporter module*. This standard Perl module provides the functionality for exporting identifiers for use in other files. Line 18

```
    use Exporter;                    # use module Exporter
```

indicates that the current module uses the **Exporter** module. Line 19

```
    our @ISA = qw( Exporter );    # this module "is an" Exporter
```

indicates that the special built-in array **@ISA** contains **Exporter**. In other words, the current module "is a(n)" **Exporter**; thus, our module has the features of the **Exporter** module that allow names to be exported from a module into other namespaces. This concept is called *inheritance* and is discussed in more detail with the **Exporter** module in Chapter 14, "Objects and Modules." For now, just mimic lines 18 and 19 when you create your own modules.

Now that our module is capable of exporting identifiers, we must specify the identifiers to export. Line 23

```
    our @EXPORT = qw( @array &greeting );
```

adds items to the special built-in array **@EXPORT**. Any program that uses this module will have direct access to the identifiers in this array without using the fully qualified identifier names. In this case, array **@array** and subroutine **&greeting** will be available to any program that uses this module. Following lines 18, 19 and 23 are the definitions of the variables and subroutines that can be imported into another program's namespace.

Software Engineering Observation 6.13

Identifiers that are not explicitly exported from a module are still available for use in other programs, provided that their fully qualified names are used.

Line 33

```
return 1;   # indicate successful import of module
```

is required in modules that are imported with **use**. Such modules are imported during the compilation phase. This line indicates to Perl that the module has been successfully imported. The last executable statement in a module must be a statement that returns a true value.

Common Programming Error 6.10

*Forgetting to **return** a true value from a module will cause a fatal compile-time error.*

6.14.3 Other Features of the **use** Statement

Keyword **use** has several other features. If you follow **use** with a *version number*, as in

```
use v5.6.0;
```

Perl compares the version number specified with the current version number of Perl installed on that system. If the version number specified is greater than the Perl version number under which the program is running, a fatal error occurs and the program terminates.

Software Engineering Observation 6.14

*If a Perl program requires a specific version of Perl or higher to execute correctly, include a **use** statement containing the minimum version number for successful program execution.*

Versioning also can be applied to modules with the **use** *module* feature to allow Perl to check the version number of the module to be imported. For example, if a program requires version 2.0 or higher of module **FirstModule**, the statement

```
use FirstModule 2.0;
```

forces Perl to check that the version of the module is 2.0 or higher before using the module. If the module is a lower version number, a fatal error occurs and the program terminates. This feature of **use** allows you to write version-specific code that will not execute unless the program uses the proper module version numbers. Module versioning requires that the version number be specified in the module file. This is accomplished with the statement

```
our $VERSION = 2.0;
```

where 2.0 should be the actual version number.

In addition to being able to import a whole module, Perl allows you to import pieces of a module. If you provide an argument list for **use**, it will import only those specific items from the module. For example,

```
use FirstModule qw( @array );
```

imports only array **@array**. An attempt to use subroutine **greeting** in Fig. 6.19 without a fully qualified name would result in a compile-time error.

Software Engineering Observation 6.15

Identifiers that are automatically imported from a module can "pollute" a namespace with identifiers that are not required. Specifying a list of names to import allows selective importing of identifiers. To prevent any identifiers from being imported, use an empty list. In both cases, all identifiers from the module are still available via their fully qualified names.

Keyword **use** also has a counterpart—***no***—that allows a program to "unimport" specified items from a namespace. Its syntax is identical to **use**. This allows programmers to define their own subroutines that otherwise might have been imported from a module.

6.15 Pragmas

Perl *pragmas* are statements that the compiler uses to set compiler options. There are two important Perl pragmas in use today that we will include in all of our programs from this point forward, unless explicitly stated otherwise—***use strict*** and ***use warnings***.

The statement **use strict** forces the programmer to declare all variables as package variables or lexically scoped variables. It also forces the programmer to use quotes around all strings and call each subroutine explicitly.

Testing and Debugging Tip 6.2

*The **strict** pragma makes programs easier to debug and maintain.*

We can also pass **strict** special *tag* arguments to let Perl know what it should check. Two of these tags are **'vars'** and **'subs'**.

If you specify

```
use strict 'vars';
```

at the beginning of a program, Perl checks all package variables to ensure that each is fully qualified with its package name. The fully qualified name consists of the package name, followed by two colons, followed by the variable name. For example, a variable named **$variable** declared in the **main** namespace would be **$main::variable**.

There are four ways in which a variable can satisfy **use strict**. First, variables defined with the **my** keyword are lexically scoped and can be referenced with their short name throughout the block in which they are defined. Second, package variables defined with the **our** keyword are placed in the symbol table. Such variables can be accessed with their short names throughout the package in which they are defined. Outside that package, package variables must be accessed with their fully qualified names. Third, variables can be used with their fully qualified names in all instances, including the package in which they are defined. Finally, a program can specify a ***use vars*** statement followed by a list containing the names of variables to use as in

```
use vars qw( variable1 variable2 variable3 );
```

For each name, a package global variable is created that can be accessed with its short name throughout the current package.

If you specify

```
use strict 'subs';
```

Perl refuses to allow the programmer call a subroutine with a *bareword*. A bareword is an identifier that is not preceded by a type identifier character and is not followed by the parentheses that are normally used to invoke a subroutine. Barewords normally are used with subroutine calls and strings.

Common Programming Error 6.11

*When barewords are not allowed, subroutine calls must use either parentheses or ampersand (**&**) character (or both). Similarly, strings must use quotes. Otherwise, Perl does not know whether a bareword is a subroutine call or a string and a fatal error will occur.*

The other important pragma is the **warnings** pragma. This pragma warns the user of possible typos, the use of uninitialized variables and other potential problems in the code. None of these are fatal errors, but messages will be displayed to warn the user that something is ambiguous. For example, if you use **warnings** in your program, the statement

```
use warnings;
print ( 3 + 4 ) * 5;
```

will be flagged and a message (actually two in this case) will be sent to your screen. First, it will output

```
print (...) interpreted as function
```

telling you that the **print** with parentheses was read as a subroutine call. Perl will tell you this every time something was interpreted as a subroutine call if it is possible that the programmer's original intention was not a subroutine call. It will then display the warning

```
Useless use of integer multiplication (*) in void context
```

which indicates that the **return** value of **print** was multiplied by 5, but the result was not stored anywhere. This informs us that a useless calculation was performed by **Perl**.

Portability Tip 6.3

*The pragma **use warnings** is new to version 5.6. To get the same effect on earlier versions of Perl, the program must be run with the **-w** flag set at the command line or added to the shebang construct.*

The programmer can also use the **no** command to turn off **warnings** and **strict**. If you have written a piece of code and you want **strict** to be turned off, just type

```
no strict;
```

inside the block of code where the pragmas should be disabled. Remember that this turns off **strict** until the end of the block, or until you tell the compiler to **use strict** again. You can also send **no strict** tags just like you would for a **use strict** statement.

There are some other pragmas used by Perl programmers. One particularly useful pragma is the **use constant** statement. The statement

```
use constant PI => 3.14159;
```

creates *constant* scalar variable **PI** and assigns to it the value 3.14159. After this statement, you can use **PI** as a *named constant*, but you cannot change it.

Another pragma is **use diagnostics**, which provides more detailed error messages. In fact, it can sometimes provide too much explanation. In general, use this only if

use warnings does not provide enough information for you to debug your program. Diagnostics can be toggled at run time with the **enable()** and **disable()** commands.

The last pragma is **use *integer***. This tells your compiler to perform all arithmetic operations as integer operations. This can be used if you have a long block of code that uses only integers and you do not wish to preface each operation with the **int** keyword.

SUMMARY

- Experience has shown that the best way to develop and maintain a large program is to construct it from smaller pieces or components, each of which is more manageable than the original program. This technique is called *divide and conquer*.

- User-defined functions in Perl are called subroutines.

- Perl provides a rich collection of built-in functions for performing common mathematical calculations, string manipulations, character manipulations, input/output, error checking and many other useful operations.

- In addition to the Perl built-in functions, there are many libraries of Perl code available for download from the Internet. The Comprehensive Perl Archive Network (CPAN)—**www.cpan.org**— provides a searchable archive containing thousands of Perl libraries.

- A subroutine is invoked by a subroutine call. The subroutine call specifies the subroutine name and provides information (as arguments) that the called subroutine requires to do its job.

- There are several motivations for "functionalizing" a program (i.e., breaking a program into subroutines). The divide-and-conquer approach makes program development more manageable. Another motivation is software reusability—using existing subroutines as building blocks to create new programs.

- Software reusability is a major factor in rapid application development.

- With good subroutine naming and definition, programs can be created from standardized subroutines that accomplish specific tasks, rather than by creating custom code.

- The built-in math library functions allow the programmer to perform common mathematical calculations.

- Functions are normally called by writing the name of the function, followed by a left parenthesis, followed by the argument (or a comma-separated list of arguments) of the function, followed by a right parenthesis.

- An empty set of parentheses indicates that the subroutine does not receive any arguments.

- Arguments can be scalars, hashes, arrays or expressions.

- When a subroutine or function is called, program control continues at the definition of the subroutine or function. When execution reaches the closing right curly brace (**}**) of the subroutine, program control returns to the next statement in the program.

- The body of a subroutine executes only in response to a subroutine call.

- The general format of a subroutine definition is

      sub *subroutineName*
      {
          statements
      }

Every subroutine definition begins with keyword **sub**. The *subroutineName* can be any valid identifier (conforming to the same rules as scalar, array and hash variable names). The statements in braces (**{}**) form the subroutine body. The subroutine body is also referred to as a *block of code*.

- The list of arguments passed to a function is stored in the special array variable **@_**.

- Special variable **@_** flattens all arrays and hashes. This means that if you send a subroutine an array value and a scalar value, **@_** will contain one list with all the data from the array and the scalar value. Similarly, a hash is flattened into a list of its key/value pairs.

- Data is returned from a subroutine via the **return** keyword.

- Subroutine execution terminates immediately when the **return** statement executes. Any code in the body of the subroutine that appears after the **return** statement does not execute.

- If a subroutine does not contain a **return** statement, the subroutine returns the value of the last statement it executes.

- Perl can return any value it chooses from a subroutine. It can return a scalar or it can return a list. A single Perl subroutine can even return a list or a scalar, depending on the context in which the subroutine is called. To support this functionality, Perl provides function **wantarray**. When called in the body of a subroutine, function **wantarray** returns true if the subroutine was called from a list context, false if the subroutine was called from a scalar context.

- The type identifier character for a subroutine is **&** (ampersand).

- Function **rand** generates a floating-point scalar value greater than or equal to 0 and less than 1. A larger range can be produced by passing a number to **rand**.

- A floating-point value is truncated to an integer with function **int**.

- Function **rand** actually generates pseudorandom numbers. The random numbers are based on an algorithm that uses the previous random number and a seed to create the next random number. These are called pseudorandom numbers because, if you know the value of the seed and the algorithm used, you can determine the next number in the sequence.

- Function **srand** seeds the **rand** function to produce a different sequence of random numbers.

- A recursive subroutine is a subroutine that calls itself, either directly or (through another subroutine) indirectly.

- When a recursive subroutine is called to solve a problem, the subroutine actually knows how to solve only the simplest case(s), or so-called base case(s). If the subroutine is called with a base case, the subroutine simply returns a result. If the subroutine is called with a more complex problem, the subroutine divides the problem into two conceptual pieces—a piece that the subroutine knows how to do, and a piece that the subroutine does not know how to do. To make recursion feasible, the latter piece must resemble the original problem, but be a slightly simpler or slightly smaller version of the original problem. Because this new problem looks like the original problem, the subroutine launches a fresh copy of itself (i.e., calls itself again) to go to work on the smaller problem—this is referred to as a recursive call and is also called the recursion step.

- The recursion step normally includes the keyword **return**, because its result will be combined with the portion of the problem the subroutine knows how to solve to form a result that will be passed back to the original caller.

- For recursion to terminate eventually, each time the subroutine calls itself with a slightly simpler version of the original problem, this sequence of smaller and smaller problems must eventually converge on the base case.

- The factorial of a nonnegative integer n, written $n!$ (and pronounced "n factorial"), is the product

$$n \cdot (n - 1) \cdot (n - 2) \cdot \ldots \cdot 1$$

with 1! equal to 1, and 0! defined to be 1. A recursive definition of the factorial subroutine is arrived at by observing the following relationship:

$$n! = n \cdot (n - 1)!$$

- Keyword **my** creates a lexically scoped variable, which exists only during the block in which the variable was defined. Every time that block is entered during the execution of the program, the lexically scoped variable is created. Every time that block terminates, the lexically scoped variable is destroyed.

- The Fibonacci series

  0, 1, 1, 2, 3, 5, 8, 13, 21, ...

  begins with 0 and 1 and has the property that each subsequent Fibonacci number is the sum of the previous two Fibonacci numbers. The series describes a form of spiral. The ratio of successive Fibonacci numbers converges on a constant value of 1.618.... This number repeatedly occurs in nature and has been called the golden ratio or the golden mean.

- The Fibonacci series can be defined recursively as follows:

  fibonacci(0) = 0
  fibonacci(1) = 1
  fibonacci(n) = fibonacci(n – 1) + fibonacci(n – 2)

- Both iteration and recursion are based on control structures—iteration uses a repetition structure; recursion uses a selection structure.

- Both iteration and recursion involve repetition—iteration explicitly uses a repetition structure; recursion achieves repetition through repeated subroutine calls.

- Iteration and recursion both involve a termination test—iteration terminates when the loop-continuation condition fails; recursion terminates when a base case is recognized.

- Iteration with counter-controlled repetition and recursion both gradually approach termination—iteration keeps modifying a counter until the counter assumes a value that makes the loop-continuation condition fail; recursion keeps producing simpler versions of the original problem until the base case is reached.

- Both iteration and recursion can occur infinitely—an infinite loop occurs with iteration if the loop-continuation test never becomes false; infinite recursion occurs if the recursion step does not reduce the problem each time in a manner that converges on the base case.

- An identifier's scope is the portion of the program in which the identifier can be referenced. Some identifiers can be referenced throughout a program; others can be referenced from limited portions of a program.

- The three scopes for an identifier are global scope, lexical scope and dynamic scope.

- Variables that have global scope exist throughout the program's execution and can be manipulated anywhere in the program. Such variables are defined with keyword **our**.

- A lexically scoped variable is a variable that exists only during the block in which it was defined.

- A dynamically scoped variable (defined with keyword **local**) is one that exists from the time it is created until the end of the block in which it was created. Such variables are accessible both to the block in which they are defined and to any subroutines called from that block.

- Perl uses packages to determine the variable and subroutine identifiers that are accessible to every piece of code in a program. Packages can also be used to access identifiers that are defined in other files called modules. Most of Perl's scoping rules derive from this package concept.

- Each package has its own symbol table, which stores all of the package's variables and subroutine names. By default, the global identifiers in a Perl source code file—global variables and subroutines—are part of the **main** package's symbol table. Global variables are actually called package global variables or package variables.

- Lexical variables are not inserted in a package's symbol table. Rather, each block of code in which a lexical variable is defined has its own temporary storage for lexical variables. This temporary storage is known as a scratchpad.

- The current package can be changed with a **package** statement. Creating a new package causes Perl to create a new, empty symbol table.

- Keyword **require** tells Perl to locate a module and add it to the program. Perl first looks for this file in the current directory. If it cannot be found there, it searches for directories that are named in the array **@INC**. The **require** keyword assumes a **.pm** file-name extension. Packages included in a program by using **require** are loaded during the program's execution phase.

- Variables and subroutines in a package are accessed through their fully qualified names, in which the package name and the variable or subroutine name are joined by the double colon operator (**::**). This operator specifies that the identifier to its right is in the package to its left. This notation helps Perl determine in which symbol table it should look to locate an identifier.

- A module is simply a package that provides the programmer more control over how a user of the module can reference the identifiers in that module's package. One benefit of a module is that a programmer can specify that identifiers should always be made available to the module user as if those identifiers were originally defined in the user's program. This allows the identifiers to be used without their fully qualified names.

- The primary difference between **use** and **require** is that **use** imports modules and packages at compile time, **require** at execution time. Importing at compile time allows Perl to ensure that the package is available before the program reaches execution time. Otherwise, a missing package would not be noticed until it is first referenced at execution time.

- Perl allows a module programmer to export identifiers from a module for use in another file's namespace. This allows the other file to use the identifiers without fully qualified names. To do this, the module must be set up as an **Exporter** module.

- To specify the identifiers to export from a module, add the identifiers to the special built-in array **@EXPORT**. Any program that uses this module will have direct access to the identifiers in this array without using the fully qualified identifier names.

- Keyword **use** also has a counterpart—**no**—that allows a program to "unimport" specified items from a namespace. Its syntax is identical to **use**. This allows programmers to define their own subroutines that might otherwise have been imported from a module.

- Perl pragmas are statements that are sent to the compiler to set compiler options. Two important pragmas are **use strict** and **use warnings**.

- The **use strict** pragma forces the programmer to declare all variables as package variables or lexically scoped variables. It also forces the programmer to use quotes around all strings and call each subroutine explicitly.

- The **use warnings** pragma warns the user of possible typos, the use of uninitialized variables and other potential problems in the code. None of these are fatal errors, but messages will be displayed to warn the user that something is ambiguous.

- The **use constant** pragma creates a constant scalar variable.

TERMINOLOGY

& type identifier
:: double colon operator
abs function
absolute value
argument

automatically seeding **rand**
bareword
base case
block
body of a subroutine

built-in function
calling a subroutine
comma-separated list of arguments
Comprehensive Perl Archive Network (CPAN)
constant scalar variable
converge on the base case
`cos` function
`diagnostics` pragma
divide and conquer
dynamically scoped variable
dynamic scope
dynamic variable
`exp` function
exponential complexity
`@EXPORT` array
`Exporter` module
factorial
Fibonacci series
fully qualified name
globally scoped variable
global scope
global variable
golden mean
golden ratio
import a module
`@INC` array
infinite recursion
inheritance
`int` function
`integer` pragma
invoke a subroutine
`@ISA` array
lexically scoped variable
lexical scope
lexical variable
`local`
`log` function
`main` package
module
module version number
`my`

namespace
`no`
`our`
`package`
package global variable
package variable
Perl library
`.pm` file name extension
pragma
pseudorandom numbers
`rand` function
random number
recursion
recursion step
recursive call
recursive subroutine
`require`
`return` statement
scope
scope rules
scratchpad
simulation
`sin` function
software reuse
`sqrt` function
`srand` function
`strict` pragma
`sub`
subroutine
subroutine body
subroutine call
subroutine definition
type identifier `&`
`use`
`use strict`
`use vars`
`use warnings`
user-defined subroutine
`warnings` pragma
`www.cpan.org`

SELF-REVIEW EXERCISES

6.1   Fill in the blank in each of the following statements:
   a) User-defined functions in Perl are called _____.
   b) Subroutine definitions begin with keyword _____.
   c) The statements in _____ form the subroutine body.
   d) The list of arguments passed to a function is stored in the special variable _____.
   e) Data is returned from a subroutine via the _____ keyword.

f) When called in the body of a subroutine, function _____ returns *true* if the subroutine was called from a list context, and returns *false* if the subroutine was called from a scalar context.

g) Function _____ generates pseudorandom numbers.

h) Function _____ seeds the random number generator to produce a different sequence of random numbers.

i) When a recursive subroutine is called to solve a problem, the subroutine actually knows how to solve only the _____.

j) Keyword **my** creates a _____ scoped variable.

k) An identifier's _____ is the portion of the program in which the identifier can be referenced.

l) Perl uses _____ (or namespaces) to determine the variable and subroutine identifiers that are accessible to every piece of code in a program.

m) Each package has its own _____, which stores all of the package's variables and subroutine names.

n) By default, the global identifiers in a Perl source code file—global variables and subroutines—are part of the _____ package's symbol table.

o) The current package can be changed with a _____ statement.

p) Variables and subroutines in a package are accessed through their fully qualified names, in which the package name and the variable or subroutine name are joined by the _____ operator.

q) To specify the identifiers to export from a module, add the identifiers to the special built-in array _____. Any program that uses this module will have direct access to the identifiers in this array without using the fully qualified identifier names.

r) Perl _____ are statements that are sent to the compiler to set compiler options.

6.2 State whether the following are *true* or *false*. If *false*, explain why.

a) Functions are normally called by writing the name of the function, followed by a left parenthesis, followed by the argument (or a comma-separated list of arguments) of the function, followed by a right parenthesis.

b) An empty set of curly braces (**{}**) indicates that the subroutine receives no arguments.

c) Arguments to subroutines can be only scalars.

d) When a subroutine or function is called, program control continues at the definition of the subroutine or function.

e) When execution reaches the closing right curly brace (**}**) of a subroutine, the program terminates.

f) The body of a subroutine executes only in response to a subroutine call.

g) Special variable **@_** flattens all arrays but does not flatten hashes.

h) Subroutine execution terminates immediately when the **return** statement executes.

i) Perl can return a scalar or a list from a subroutine.

j) The type identifier character for a subroutine is ampersand (**%**).

k) Function **rand** generates a floating-point scalar value greater than or equal to 1 and less than 32767.

l) A recursive subroutine is a subroutine that calls itself, either directly or indirectly.

m) A lexically scoped variable can be accessed from any point in a program.

n) A dynamically scoped variable (defined with keyword **local**) is accessible both to the block in which it is defined and to any subroutines called from that block.

o) All variables are inserted in a package's symbol table.

p) Creating a new package causes Perl to create a new, empty symbol table.

q) The primary difference between **use** and **require** is that **require** imports modules and packages at compile time and **use** does so at execution time.

r) The **use strict** pragma forces the programmer to use the word **strict** in the name of every variable defined in a program.

s) The **use constant** pragma creates a constant scalar variable.

6.3   Find the error in each of the following code segments and explain how to correct it.

a) `use constant PI --> 3.14159;`

b)
```
subroutine square
{
    my $value = shift( @_ );
    return $value ** 2;
}
```

c) `$value = srand( 100 ); # random number 0 <= $value < 100`

ANSWERS TO SELF-REVIEW EXERCISES

6.1   a) subroutines. b) **sub**. c) braces (**{}**). d) **@_**. e) **return**. f) **wantarray**. g) **rand**. h) **srand**. i) simplest case or base case. j) lexically. k) scope. l) packages. m) symbol table. n) **main**. o) **package**. p) double colon (**::**). q) **@EXPORT**. r) pragmas.

6.2   a) True.

b) False. An empty set of parentheses (**()**) indicates that the subroutine does not receive any arguments.

c) False. Arguments to subroutines can be scalars, hashes, arrays or expressions.

d) True.

e) False. When execution reaches the closing right curly brace **}**) of a subroutine, program control returns to the point at which the subroutine was called and continues with the next statement in the program.

f) True.

g) False. Special variable **@_** flattens all arrays and hashes.

h) True.

i) True.

j) False. The type identifier character for a subroutine is ampersand (**&**).

k) False. Function **rand** generates a floating-point scalar value greater than or equal to 0 and less than 1.

l) True.

m) False. A lexically scoped variable is a variable that exists only during the block in which it was defined.

n) True.

o) False. Lexical variables are not inserted in a package's symbol table.

p) True.

q) False. The primary difference between **use** and **require** is that **use** imports modules and packages at compile time and **require** does so at execution time.

r) False. The **use strict** pragma forces the programmer to declare all variables as package variables or lexically scoped variables.

s) True.

6.3   a) Error: Operator **-->** does not exist in Perl.
Correction: Replace **-->** with **=>**.

b) Error: **subroutine** is not a keyword in Perl.
Correction: Replace **subroutine** with **sub**.

c) Error: Function **srand** does not produce random numbers. Rather, it seeds the random number generator.
Correction: Replace **srand** with **rand**.

EXERCISES

6.4   Write a subroutine that prints the number of arguments passed to it.

6.5   Define a constant called PI with the value 3.14159. Use this constant in a subroutine that receives the radius of a circle and returns the area of the circle if it is called in scalar context but a list containing the area, the diameter and the circumference if called in list context. Use the following formulas (r is the radius): $area = \pi r^2$, $diameter = 2r$, $circumference = 2\pi r$.

6.6   Write a program that simulates the rolling of a die 6000 times and displays in a tabular format the number of occurrences of each side of the die.

6.7   Write two subroutines to calculate the maximum of a set of values passed as arguments. One subroutine should calculate the maximum value iteratively and the other should calculate the maximum value recursively.

6.8   (For readers who know HTML) Write a package that provides subroutines and variables to help a programmer write a Perl program that outputs HTML markup. The package should provide a package variable called **$title** to which the programmer can assign the title of the Web page. The package should also contain the following subroutines:

   a) **startDocument**—This subroutine should return the markup for the **head** section of the Web page and start the **body** section by using the string

```
"<html><head><title>$title</title></head><body>\n"
```

   b) **createParagraph**—This subroutine outputs the markup for a paragraph in the document by returning its argument in a string that starts with **<p>** and ends with **</p>**.

   c) **createHyperlink**—This subroutine outputs the markup for a hyperlink to another Web page. The subroutine should receive two arguments—the text that should be displayed to the user and the location of the other Web page. For example, to create a hyperlink to the Deitel & Associates, Inc. Web page, the subroutine would be called as follows:

```
createHyperlink( "Deitel & Associates, Inc.",
                 "http://www.deitel.com" );
```

The subroutine should return a string containing the markup for the link in the following format:

```
<a href= \"firstArgument\">secondArgument</a>\n
```

   d) **endDocument**—This subroutine should complete the document by returning the string **"</body></html>\n"**.

Write a program that uses this package to create the HTML markup for a simple Web page.

6.9   The program of Fig. 6.7 demonstrated **wantarray**, which allowed a function to return a single value when called from a scalar context and a list of values when called from a list context. Perl's built-in function **localtime** is an example of such a function—it returns a string representing the time when called in scalar context and a list of integers representing parts of the time when called in list context. Write a program that demonstrates these features of **localtime**.

7

Introduction to the Common Gateway Interface (CGI)

Objectives

- To understand the Common Gateway Interface (CGI) protocol.
- To understand the HyperText Transfer Protocol (HTTP) and be able to use HTTP headers.
- To implement a simple CGI script.
- To be able to send input to CGI scripts using HTML forms.
- To be able to use the **CGI.pm** module to generate HTML, create forms and read input.

This is the common air that bathes the globe.
Walt Whitman

The longest part of the journey is said to be the passing of the gate.
Marcus Terentius Varro

Railway termini... are our gates to the glorious and unknown. Through them we pass out into adventure and sunshine, to them, alas! we return.
E. M. Forster

There comes a time in a man's life when to get where he has to go—if there are no doors or windows—he walks through a wall.
Bernard Malamud

Outline

7.1 Introduction

The *Common Gateway Interface* (*CGI*) describes a set of protocols through which applications (commonly called *CGI programs* or *CGI scripts*) interact with Web servers and (indirectly) with clients (e.g., Web browsers). These protocols often are used to generate *dynamic Web content* based on client input. A Web page is dynamic if its content changes without being manually altered by a person responsible for that page on the server side, unlike *static Web content*, which requires alteration by a person. For example, we can use CGI to have a Web page ask you for your zip code, then automatically send you to another Web page that is specifically for people in your area. In this chapter, we introduce the basics of CGI and use Perl to write our first CGI scripts.

The Common Gateway Interface is "common" in the sense that it is not specific to any particular operating system (such as Linux or Windows) or to any one programming language. CGI was designed to be used with virtually any programming or scripting language. Thus, CGI scripts can be written in C, C++, Java or Visual Basic without much difficulty. Yet, from the beginning, Perl has been the language of choice for CGI programming, because of its powerful text-processing capabilities. The advent of CGI was the most important factor that led to Perl's popularity as a programming language, despite the fact that Perl was originally designed as a system administration tool, not for CGI scripting.

The CGI protocol was developed in 1993 by *NCSA* (*National Center for Supercomputing Applications*—**www.ncsa.uiuc.edu**) for use with its popular *HTTPd Web server*. It was built as a simple implementation for dynamic Web page creation. Unlike other Web protocols and languages that have formal specifications, the initial concise description of CGI protocol written by NCSA proved simple enough the CGI was adopted as an unofficial standard worldwide. CGI support was quickly incorporated into other Web servers as well, such as Apache (**www.apache.org**).

7.2 A Simple HTTP Transaction

Before exploring how CGI operates, it is necessary to have a basic understanding of networking and how the World Wide Web works. In this section, we will examine the inner workings of the *HyperText Transfer Protocol* (*HTTP*) and discuss what goes on behind the scenes when a browser displays a Web page. HTTP describes a set of *methods* and *headers* that allows clients and servers to interact and exchange information in a uniform and predictable way.

A Web page in its simplest form is nothing more than an *HTML* (*HyperText Markup Language*) document. This document is just a plain text file containing markings (*markup* or *tags*) that describe to a Web browser how to display and format the information in the document. For example, the HTML

```
<title>My Web Page</title>
```

indicates to the browser that the text between the opening **<title>** tag and the closing **</title>** tag is the title of the Web page. HTML documents can also contain *hypertext* information (usually called *hyperlinks*) that create links to different pages or to other portions of the same page. When the user activates a hyperlink (usually by clicking on it with a mouse), a new Web page (or a different part of the same Web page) is loaded for the user to view. Note that in HTML, tags are not case sensitive, so **<TITLE>** works the same as **<title>**. (For more information on HTML, please refer to Chapters 24 and 25.)

Any HTML file available for viewing over the Web has a *URL* (*Universal Resource Locator*) associated with it—an address of sorts. The URL contains information that directs a browser to the resource (most often a Web page) that the user wishes to access. For example, let us break down the URL

```
http://www.deitel.com/books/downloads.htm
```

into its basic components. The **http://** indicates that the resource is to be obtained using the Hypertext Transfer Protocol.

The middle portion, **www.deitel.com**, is the *hostname* of the server. The hostname is the name of the computer where the resource resides, and likewise, this computer is usually referred to as the *host*, because it houses and maintains the resource. The hostname **www.deitel.com** is translated into an *IP address* (**207.60.134.230**) that identifies the server (just as a telephone number uniquely defines a particular phone line). The translation of the hostname into an IP address is normally performed by a *domain name server* (*DNS*), a computer that maintains a database of hostnames and their corresponding IP addresses. Many people refer to this translation operation as a *DNS lookup*.

The name of the resource being requested, **/books/downloads.htm** (an HTML document), is the remainder of the URL. This portion of the URL specifies both the name of the resource (**downloads.htm**) and its path (**/books**). The path could represent an actual directory in the Web server's file system. However, for security reasons, the path often is a *virtual directory*. In this case, the server translates the path into a real location on the server (or even on another computer), thus hiding the true location of the resource. In fact, it is even possible that the resource is created dynamically and does not reside anywhere on the server computer. Thus, the URL uses the hostname to locate the correct server, and the server uses the path and resource information to locate (or create) the resource to respond to the client's request. As we will see, URLs can also be used to provide input to a program on the server.

Now we consider how a browser, when given a URL, performs a simple HTTP transaction to fetch and display a Web page. Figure 7.1 illustrates the transaction in detail. The transaction is performed between a Web browser application on the client side and a Web server application on the server side.

In step 1 of Fig. 7.1, the browser sends an HTTP request message to the server. The request (in its simplest form) looks something like the following:

```
GET /books/downloads.htm HTTP/1.0
```

The word **GET** is an *HTTP method* (a term for functions in HTTP) indicating that the client wishes to get a resource. The remainder of the request provides the name and path of the resource (an HTML document) and the protocol's name and version number (**HTTP/1.0**).

Any server that understands HTTP (version 1.0) will be able to translate this request and respond appropriately. Part 2 of Fig. 7.1 shows the results of a successful request. The server first responds with a line indicating the HTTP version, followed by a numeric code and a phrase describing the status of the transaction. For example,

```
HTTP/1.0 200 OK
```

indicates success, while

```
HTTP/1.0 404 Not found
```

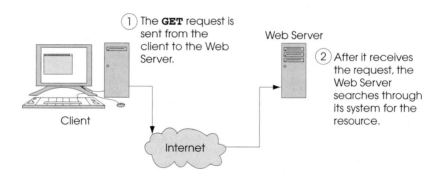

Fig. 7.1   Client interacting with server and Web server. Step 1: The **GET** request, **GET /books/downloads.htm HTTP/1.0** (part 1 of 2).

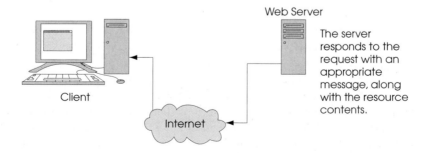

Fig. 7.1   Client interacting with server and Web server. Step 2: The HTTP response, HTTP/1.0 200 OK (part 2 of 2).

informs the client that the requested resource was not found on the server in the specified location.

The server normally then sends one or more *HTTP headers*, which provide additional information about the data being sent. In this case, the server is sending an HTML text document, so the HTTP header reads

```
Content-type: text/html
```

This information is known as the *MIME type* of the content. Each type of data sent from the server has a MIME type that helps the browser determine how to process the data it receives. For example, the MIME type **text/txt** indicates that the data are text that should be displayed without attempting to interpret any of the content as HTML markup. Similarly, the MIME type **image/gif** indicates that the content is a GIF image. When this MIME type is received by the browser, it attempts to display the image.

The header or set of headers is followed by a blank line, which indicates to the client that the server is finished sending HTTP headers. The server then sends the text in the requested HTML document (**downloads.htm**). The connection is terminated when the transfer of the resource is complete. The client-side browser interprets the HTML it receives and displays (or renders) the results.

Common Programming Error 7.1

Forgetting to place a blank line after a header is a logic error.

7.3 A Simple CGI Script

As long as an HTML file on the server remains unchanged, its associated URL will display the same content in clients' browsers each time the file is accessed. For that content to change (e.g., to include new links or the latest company news), someone must alter the file manually on the server, probably with a text editor or Web-page-design software.

This need for manual change is a problem for Web page authors who want to create interesting and dynamic Web pages. To have a person continually alter a Web page is tedious. For example, if you want your Web page always to display the current date or weather, the page would require continuous updating.

It is fairly straightforward to write a Perl script that outputs the current time and date (to the monitor of the local computer). In fact, the main code can be fit into a single line:

```
print scalar( localtime() );
```

Built-in function *localtime*, when evaluated in scalar context, returns a string such as

```
Mon Jul 31 13:10:37 2000
```

which, in this case, is output directly to the screen by **print**.

What if we wish to send the current time to a client's browser window for display (rather than outputting it to the screen)? CGI makes this possible by allowing us to *redirect* the output of a script to the server, which can send the output to a client's browser. Redirection of output allows output (for example, from a **print** statement) to be sent somewhere other than the screen. We can redirect our output to many different places, such as Web browsers or files. (This process is discussed in more detail in Chapter 10.)

Figure 7.2 shows the full program listing for our first CGI script. Note that the main program (lines 8–12) consists entirely of **print** statements. Until now, the output of **print** has always been displayed on the screen. However, technically speaking, the default target for **print** is *standard output*. When a Perl program is executed as a CGI script, the standard output is redirected to the client Web browser. To execute the program, you must place the Perl file in your Web server's **cgi-bin** directory. Assuming that the server is on your local computer, you can execute the program by typing

```
http://localhost/cgi-bin/fig07_02.pl
```

in your browser's **Address** or **Location** field. If you are using a server on a different computer, you will need to replace **localhost** with the server's hostname or IP address.

The notion of standard output is similar to that of standard input, which we have seen frequently referenced with the expression **<STDIN>**. Just as standard input refers to the standard method of input into a program (normally, the keyboard), standard output refers to the standard method of output from a program (normally, the screen). It is possible to redirect (or *pipe*) standard output to another destination. Thus, in our CGI script, when we print an HTTP header (line 8) or HTML tags (lines 9, 11 and 12), the output is sent to the Web server, as opposed to the screen. The server sends that output to the client, which interprets the headers and tags as if they were part of a normal server response to an HTML document request.

Figure 7.3 illustrates this process in more detail. In step 1, the client requests the resource named **fig07_02.pl** from the server, just as it requested **downloads.htm** in the previous example. If the server was not configured to handle CGI scripts, it might just return the Perl code in Fig. 7.2 to the client, as if it were just any other document.

```perl
1   #!/usr/bin/perl
2   # Fig 7.2: fig07_02.pl
3   # Displays the current date and time in a Web browser.
4
5   use warnings;
6   use strict;
7
8   print "Content-type: text/html\n\n";
9   print "<html><head><title>Current date and time</title>";
10  print "</head>\n<body>";
11  print scalar( localtime() );
12  print "</body></html>";
```

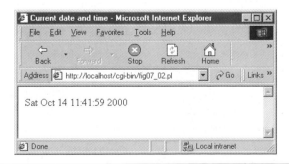

Fig. 7.2   A first CGI script.

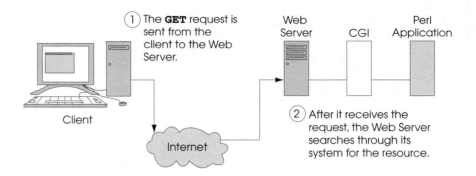

Fig. 7.3   Step 1: The **GET** request, **GET /books/downloads.htm HTTP/ 1.0** (part 1 of 4).

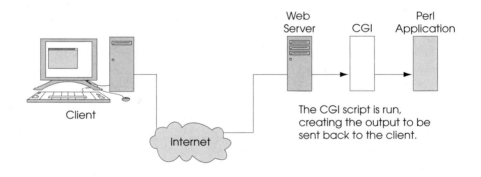

Fig. 7.3   Step 2: The Web server starts the CGI script (part 2 of 4).

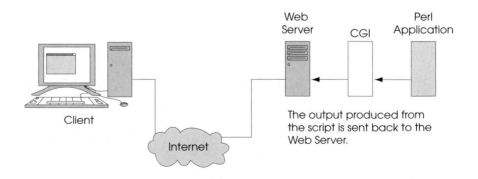

Fig. 7.3   Step 3: The output of the script is sent to the Web server (part 3 of 4).

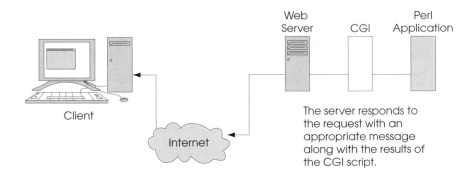

The server responds to the request with an appropriate message along with the results of the CGI script.

Fig. 7.3   Step 4: The HTTP response, **HTTP/1.0 200 OK** (part 4 of 4).

A properly configured Web server, however, will recognize that certain resources are to be handled differently. For example, when the resource is a CGI script, the script must be executed by the Web server. A resource is usually designated as a CGI script in one of two ways: either it has a special filename extension (such as **.cgi** or **.pl**) or it is located in a specific directory (often **/cgi-bin**). In addition, the server administrator must give permission explicitly for remote clients to be able to access and execute CGI scripts. (For more information, you can refer to our Perl Web resources at **www.deitel.com** or consult the ActiveState home page at **www.activestate.com**. If you are using the Apache Web Server and would like more information on configuration, consult the Apache home page at **www.apache.org**.)

In step 2 of Fig. 7.3, the server recognizes that the resource is a Perl script and invokes Perl to compile and execute the script. In step 3, the five print statements (lines 8–12 of Fig. 7.2) are executed, and the text sent to standard output is returned to the Web server. Finally, in step 4, the Web server prints an additional line to the output indicating the status of the HTTP transaction (such as **HTTP/1.0 200 OK**, for success) and sends the whole body of text to the client.

The browser on the client side then interprets the HTML output and displays the results appropriately. It is important to note that the browser is completely oblivious to what has transpired on the server end. In other words, as far as the browser is concerned, it is requesting a resource like any other and receiving a response like any other. It is not even necessary to have a Perl interpreter on the client side, because the entire script operation occurs on the server. The client simply receives and interprets the script's output, just as if it were a simple, static HTML document.

In fact, you can see what that browser receives by simply executing **fig07_02.pl** from the command line, as we would in any of the programs from the previous chapters:

```
Content-type: text/html

<HTML><HEAD><TITLE>Current date and time</TITLE></HEAD>
<BODY>Mon Jul 31 13:49:19 2000</BODY></HTML>
```

Notice that with the CGI script, we must explicitly include the **Content-type** header, whereas for a normal HTML document, the header would be added automatically by the Web server.

The script could be made even shorter if we output plain text instead of HTML. We simply replace lines 8–12 with

```
print "Content-type: text/plain\n\n";
print scalar( localtime() );
```

To review, the CGI protocol for output to be sent to a Web browser consists of printing to standard output the **Content-type** header, a blank line and the data (HTML, plain text, etc.) to be output. We will later see other content types that may be used in this manner, as well as other headers that may be used in place of **Content-type**.

7.4 Using CGI.pm to Generate HTML

In this section, we introduce **CGI.pm**, a popular Perl module that provides a vast arsenal of functions for simplifying the creation of CGI scripts.

Among other things, **CGI.pm** includes a set of functions to aid in dynamic HTML generation. We introduce several of these functions in Fig. 7.4, which is a CGI script that outputs in tabular format the names and values of all available *environment variables* to the browser window. These special global variables contain information about the client and server environment, surroundings or circumstances, such as the type of Web browser being used, the HTTP host or the HTTP connection.

The **use** statement in line 7 directs the Perl interpreter to include a set of functions from the **CGI.pm** module. This standard function set is designated by the import tag **:standard**. Even though there is only one tag name in the list, we use the **qw** operator here to make it easy to add additional tags or functions later.

```
1   #!/usr/bin/perl
2   # Fig. 7.4: fig07_04.pl
3   # Program to display CGI environment variables.
4
5   use warnings;
6   use strict;
7   use CGI qw( :standard );
8
9   print header(), start_html( "Environment Variables" );
10
11  print '<table border = "0" cellspacing = "2">';
12
13  foreach my $variable ( sort( keys %ENV ) ) {
14     print Tr( td( b( "$variable:" ) ),
15              td( i( $ENV{ $variable } ) ) );
16  }
17
18  print '</table>', end_html();
```

Fig. 7.4   Printing environment variables using **CGI.pm** (part 1 of 2).

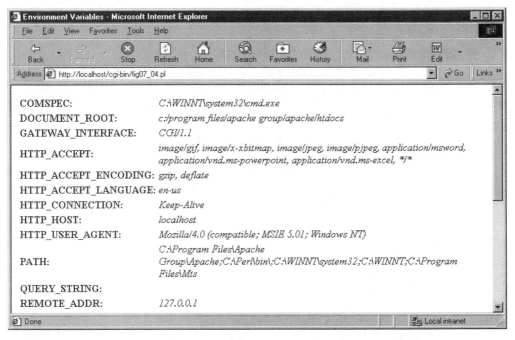

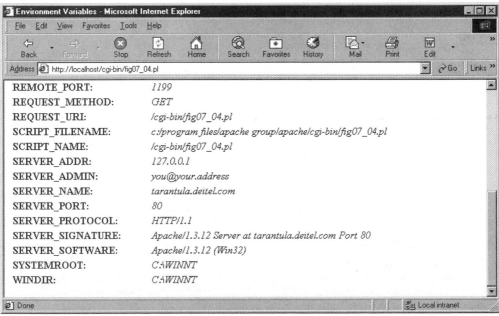

Fig. 7.4   Printing environment variables using **CGI.pm** (part 2 of 2).

Line 9 directs the Perl program to **print** the HTTP header using function *header* from the **CGI** library. If we have imported **header** into our namespace, we can call the function without the use of the ampersand or parentheses. Function **header** returns the string **Content-type: text/html\n\n**, which is then output by function **print**.

Likewise, function **start_html** (line 9) returns a string containing the standard opening tags of an HTML document (**<html>**, **<head>**, **<title>**, etc., up to the opening **<body>** tag). When the function is called with a single argument, the argument is embedded between the **<title>** tags of the returned string to give the Web page a name, which is displayed in the browser's title bar. Line 11 begins the HTML table in which the data will be displayed.

The **%ENV** *hash* (line 13) is a built-in hashtable in Perl that contains the names and values of all the environment variables. The names of the environment variables are the keys used to access the associated values of the environment variables. We use a **foreach** loop to iterate through each of the **keys** of **%ENV**, **sort**ing them lexically first.

Lines 14 and 15 print each row of the table. Let us examine each element of these two lines closely. Function **Tr** returns a string containing the opening **<tr>** (table row) tag and the closing **</tr>** tag to create a table row. (Note that the function name is **Tr**, not **tr**, so as not to conflict with the Perl **tr** operator.)

In this example, function **Tr** takes two arguments, each of which represent one cell in the table row; thus, the table is output with two columns. The first argument,

```
td( b( "$variable:" ) )
```

calls function **td** to generate the opening and closing **<td>** (table data) tags around each cell of the table column. Each cell contains the output of the **b** function, which generates **<b>** (bold) tags around text to be output in bold type. The actual text to be output in the cell is simply the name of the environment variable, followed by a colon (**"$variable:"**).

The second argument to **Tr** is similar to the first:

```
td( i( $ENV{ $variable } ) )
```

We output the value of the environment variable, **$ENV{ $variable }**, italicized (with **<i>** tags generated by function **i** within a table cell (using **td**).

Of course, we could have simply output the HTML directly in the **foreach** loop, using **print** as follows:

```
print "<tr><td><b>$variable:</b></td>";
print "<td><i>$ENV{ $variable }</i></td></tr>";
```

In our two-column table example, the savings from using **CGI.pm**'s shortcuts is small. However, in Chapter 13, we will see how to use a data type in Perl called *references* to output large and complex tables in a concise manner using the **CGI.pm** functions.

We close the table in line 18 and call **end_html** to generate the final **</body>** and **</html>** tags.

Examine the output of **fig07_04.pl** in a browser window. We have already seen that a CGI script sends output to the server via standard output. Environment variables are the second means through which servers interact with CGI scripts. CGI-enabled Web servers set certain environment variables that provide information about both the server's and the client's script execution environment. In fact, nearly all of the environment variables displayed in Fig. 7.4 are set specifically by the server.

A CGI script can gather a significant amount of data by examining environment variables. For example, a script might examine the **HTTP_USER_AGENT** variable to determine what type of browser the client is using and then send a browser-specific Web page based on that information.

7.5 Sending Input to a CGI Script

Though preset environment variables provide a lot of information, we would like to be able to supply any sort of data to our CGI scripts, such as a client's name or a search engine query. The environment variable **QUERY_STRING** provides a mechanism to do just that. The **QUERY_STRING** variable contains extra information that is appended to a URL in a **GET** request, following a question mark (**?**). For example, the URL

www.*somesite*.com/cgi-bin/script.pl?state=California

causes the Web browser to request a resource from **www.*somesite*.com**. The resource uses a CGI script (**cgi-bin/script.pl**) to execute. The information following the **?** (**state=California**) is assigned by the server to the **QUERY_STRING** environment variable. Note that the question mark is not part of the resource requested, nor is it part of the query string. It simply serves as a *delimiter* (or separator) between the two.

Figure 7.5 shows a simple example of a CGI script that reads and reacts to data passed through the **QUERY_STRING**. Note that data in a query string can be structured in a variety of ways, provided that the CGI script reading the string knows how to interpret the formatted data. In the example in Fig.7.5, the query string contains a series of name–value pairs joined with ampersands (**&**), as in

country=USA&state=California&city=Sacramento

Each name–value pair consists of a name (e.g., country) and a value (e.g., USA), connected with an equal sign. The **&** will help us separate one name–value pair from the next.

In line 9 of Fig. 7.5, we place the value of **QUERY_STRING** into variable **$query**. After printing a header, some beginning HTML tags and the title (lines 11–12), we test to see if **$query** is empty (line 14). If so, we print a message instructing the user to add a query string to the URL. We also provide a link to a URL that includes a sample query string. Note that query-string data may be specified as part of a hypertext link in a Web page when encoded in this manner.

```
1   #!/usr/bin/perl
2   # Fig. 7.5: fig07_05.pl
3   # An example of using QUERY_STRING.
4
5   use warnings;
6   use strict;
7   use CGI qw( :standard );
8
9   my $query = $ENV{ "QUERY_STRING" };
10
11  print header(), start_html( "QUERY_STRING example" );
12  print h2( "Name/Value Pairs" );
13
```

Fig. 7.5   Reading input from **QUERY_STRING** (part 1 of 3).

```
14   if ( $query eq "" ) {
15      print 'Please add some name-value pairs to the URL above. ';
16      print 'Or try <a href = "fig07_05.pl?name=Joe&age=29">this</a>.';
17   }
18   else {
19      print i( "The query string is '$query'." ), br();
20
21      my @pairs = split( "&", $query );
22
23      foreach my $pair ( @pairs ) {
24         my ( $name, $value ) = split( "=", $pair );
25         print "You set '$name' to value '$value'.", br();
26      }
27   }
28
29   print end_html();
```

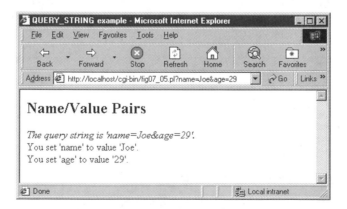

Fig. 7.5   Reading input from **QUERY_STRING** (part 2 of 3).

Fig. 7.5   Reading input from **QUERY_STRING** (part 3 of 3).

To break apart each of these resulting name–value pairs, we use a **foreach** loop that iterates through each **$pair** in turn. In line 24, we call **split** again to break the pair at the equals sign into a **$name** and a **$value**, which we print out in line 25.

7.6 Using HTML Forms to Send Input

Of course, having a client directly enter input into a URL is not a user-friendly approach. Fortunately, HTML provides the ability to include *forms* on Web pages that provide a more intuitive way for users to input information to be sent to a CGI script.

The **<form>** and **</form>** tags surround an HTML form. The **<form>** tag generally takes two attributes. The first attribute is **action**, which specifies the action to take when the user submits the form. For our purposes, the action will usually be to call a CGI script to process the form data. The second attribute used in the **<form>** tag is **method**, which normally is either **GET** or **POST**. In this section, we will show examples using both methods to illustrate them in detail.

An HTML form may contain any number of form elements. Figure 7.6 gives a brief description of several possible elements to include. (If you do not know basic HTML, please refer to Chapters 24 and 25.)

Tag name	**type** attribute (for **input** tags)	Description
<input>	**text**	Provides a single-line text field for text input. This tag is the default input type.
	password	Like **text**, but each character typed by the user appears as an asterisk (*) to hide the input for security.
	checkbox	Displays a checkbox that can be checked (true) or unchecked (false).

Fig. 7.6   HTML form elements (part 1 of 2).

Tag name	type attribute (for input tags)	Description
	radio	Radio buttons are like checkboxes, except that only one radio button in a group of radio buttons can be selected at a time.
	button	A standard push button.
	submit	A push button that submits form data according to the form's **action**.
	image	The same as **submit**, but displays on image rather than a button.
	reset	A button that resets form fields to their default values.
	file	Displays a text field and button that allow the user to specify a file to upload to a Web server. The button displays a file dialog box that allows the user to select the file.
	hidden	Allows hidden form data that can be used by the form handler on the server.
<select>		Drop-down menu or selection box. This tag is used with the <option> tag to specify options to select.
<textarea>		This is a multiline area in which text can be input or displayed.

Fig. 7.6   HTML form elements (part 2 of 2).

Figure 7.7 demonstrates a basic HTML form using the HTTP **GET** method. The form is output in lines 14–17 with the **<form>** tags. Notice that the **method** attribute is **GET** and the action attribute is **fig07_07.pl** (i.e., the script actually calls itself to handle the form data once they are submitted).

The form contains two input fields. The first (line 15) is a single-line text field (**type = "text"**) with the name **word**. The second (line 16) displays a button, labeled **Submit word**, to submit the form data.

The first time the script is executed, there should be no value in **QUERY_STRING** (unless the user has specifically appended the query string to the URL). However, once a word is entered into the **word** field and the **Submit word** button is clicked, the script is called again. This time, the name of the text input field (**word**) and the value entered by the user are put into the **QUERY_STRING** variable automatically. That is, once the word "**panache**" is entered and the **Submit word** button is clicked, **QUERY_STRING** is assigned the value **word=panache** and the query string is appended to the URL in the browser window.

```
1   #!/usr/bin/perl
2   # Fig 7.7: fig07_07.pl
3   # Demonstrates GET method with HTML form.
```

Fig. 7.7   Using **GET** with an HTML form (part 1 of 3).

```
4
5   use warnings;
6   use strict;
7   use CGI qw( :standard );
8
9   our ( $name, $value ) = split( '=', $ENV{ QUERY_STRING } );
10
11  print header(), start_html( 'Using GET with forms' );
12  print p( 'Enter one of your favorite words here: ' );
13
14  print '<form method = "GET" action = "fig07_07.pl">';
15  print '<input type = "text" name = "word">';
16  print '<input type = "submit" value = "Submit word">';
17  print '</form>';
18
19  if ( $name eq 'word' ) {
20      print p( 'Your word is: ', b( $value ) );
21  }
22
23  print end_html();
```

Fig. 7.7   Using **GET** with an HTML form (part 2 of 3).

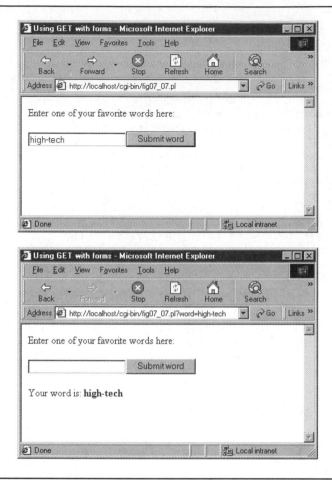

Fig. 7.7   Using **GET** with an HTML form (part 3 of 3).

Thus, during the second execution of the script, when the query string is decoded as in Fig. 7.5, line 9 assigns the value **word** to variable **$name** and assigns the user's favorite word to variable **$value** (line 9). When this happens, the conditional statement in line 19 is true and the word outputs to the screen in line 20.

Using **GET** with an HTML form passes data to the CGI script in the same way that we saw previously—through an environment variable. A third way that CGI scripts interact with servers is via standard input and the **POST** method. For comparison purposes, let us now reimplement the application of Fig. 7.7 using **POST**. Notice that the code in the two figures is virtually identical. The HTML form indicates that we are now using the **POST** method to submit the form data.

The **POST** method sends data to a CGI script via standard input. The data are encoded just as in **QUERY_STRING** (that is, with name–value pairs connected by equals signs and ampersands), but the **QUERY_STRING** environment variable is not set. Instead, the **POST** method sets the environment variable **CONTENT_LENGTH**, to indicate the number of characters of data that were sent (or posted).

The reason that **CONTENT_LENGTH** is set in this manner is so that the CGI script that receiving the data knows exactly how much to read from standard input. Line 11 uses function *read* to read in exactly that many characters from standard input (**STDIN**) and store the characters in the **$data** variable. (Function **read** will be explained in greater detail in Chapter 10.)

```perl
1   #!/usr/bin/perl
2   # Fig 7.8: fig07_08.pl
3   # Demostrates POST method with HTML form.
4
5   use warnings;
6   use strict;
7   use CGI qw( :standard );
8
9   our ( $data, $name, $value );
10
11  read( STDIN, $data, $ENV{ 'CONTENT_LENGTH' } );
12  ( $name, $value ) = split( '=', $data );
13
14  print header(), start_html( 'Using POST with forms' );
15  print p( 'Enter one of your favorite words here: ' );
16
17  print '<form method = "POST" action = "fig07_08.pl">';
18  print '<input type = "text" name = "word">';
19  print '<input type = "submit" value = "Submit word">';
20  print '</form>';
21
22  if ( $name eq 'word' ) {
23     print p( 'Your word is: ', b( $value ) );
24  }
25
26  print end_html();
```

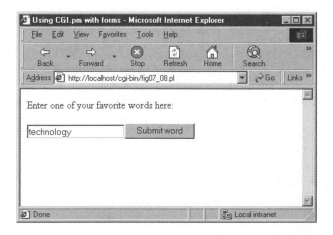

Fig. 7.8   Using POST with an HTML form (part 1 of 2).

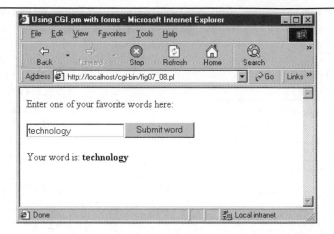

Fig. 7.8   Using POST with an HTML form (part 2 of 2).

In all of our examples thus far, we have read data from standard input using an expression such as

```
$data = <STDIN>;
```

Indeed, the same construction might function in our CGI script as a replacement for the **read** statement. However, remember that in a scalar context, **<STDIN>** reads data from standard input up to and including the next newline character read or **EOF**, whichever comes first. The CGI specification does not require a newline or **EOF** to be appended after the last name–value pair. Although some browsers may append a newline or **EOF**, they are not required to do so. If **<STDIN>** is used with a browser that sends only the name–value pairs, and nothing more (as per the CGI specification), **<STDIN>** will be left waiting for the newline or **EOF** that will never come. In this case, the server eventually terminates the script. Therefore, **read** should be preferred over **<STDIN>** in this situation.

It may seem at this point that not much is different between **GET** and **POST**, so we will provide a little bit of background for you. A **GET** request sends form content as part of the URL. A **POST** request *posts* form contents to the end of an HTTP request.

Another difference lies in how browsers handle the response. Browsers often *cache* (save on disk) Web pages for quick reloading. This process speeds up the user's browsing experience by reducing the amount of data downloaded to view a Web page. Browsers are not allowed to cache the server's response to a **POST** request, however, because the next **POST** request may not contain the same information. For example, several users might request the same Web page to participate in a survey. Each user's response changes the overall results of the survey.

This method of handling responses is different from a **GET** request. When a Web-based search engine is used, a **GET** request normally supplies the search engine with the information specified in the HTML form. The search engine then performs the search and returns the results as a Web page. These pages are often cached in the event that the user performs the same search again.

Unfortunately, the CGI scripts from this section, while useful for explaining how **GET** and **POST** operate, are missing some vital features described in the CGI protocol. For example, if we enter the words **didn't translate** into the form and click the **submit** button, the script informs us that our word is **didn%27t+translate**.

What has happened here? Today's Web browsers automatically *URL encode* the HTML form data they send. This means that spaces are turned into plus signs and certain other symbols (such as the apostrophe) are translated into their ASCII value in hexadecimal format and preceded with a percent sign. URL encoding occurs because certain characters, such as spaces and apostrophes, are not allowed to appear in a URL.

Perl has powerful text-processing capabilities and is well equipped for the task of parsing and decoding URL-encoded data. However, we will now leave alone the low-level details of handling form data and instead turn again to the **CGI.pm** module, which elegantly takes care of these details for us.

7.7 Using CGI.pm to Create Forms and Read Input

Figure 7.9 reimplements the script of Fig. 7.8, making full use of the shortcuts **CGI.pm** offers. Note first the use of function **param** (for parameter) in line 9. Function **param** takes one argument: the name of an HTML form field. If form data containing a name–value pair with the given name (in this case, **word**) were submitted, then the name's associated value would be returned. Otherwise, **param** returns **undef**. No **read**, **split** or URL decoding is required, and the function works with both **GET** and **POST** submissions.

Lines 14 and 15 make use of **CGI.pm** functions to generate HTML tags that create a form. Function ***start_form*** generates the opening **<form>** tag. When no arguments are given, **start_form** defaults to the **POST** method. (Normally, the **<form>** tag defaults to the **GET** method.) Because no action is given explicitly, the script calls itself when the user submits the form. To explicitly declare these options, use the syntax

```
start_form( -method => "POST", -action => "fig07_09.pl" );
```

Note here that **start_form** (like most **CGI.pm** functions) can be used with an optional *named-argument* syntax, in which each attribute and value are paired together with an arrow (**=>**), as in a hash. When the named-argument syntax is used, the order of the arguments does not matter. Also notice that in this syntax, attribute names are preceded with a hyphen (as in **-method**).

```perl
1   #!/usr/bin/perl
2   # Fig 7.9: fig07_09.pl
3   # Demonstrates use of CGI.pm with HTML form.
4
5   use warnings;
6   use strict;
7   use CGI qw( :standard );
8
9   my $word = param( "word" );
10
11  print header(), start_html( 'Using CGI.pm with forms' );
12  print p( 'Enter one of your favorite words here: ' );
13
14  print start_form(), textfield( "word" );
15  print submit( "Submit word" ), end_form();
16
17  print p( 'Your word is: ', b( $word ) ) if $word;
18  print end_html();
```

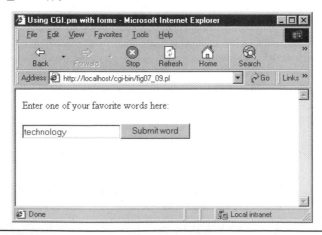

Fig. 7.9   Using **CGI.pm** with an HTML form (part 1 of 2).

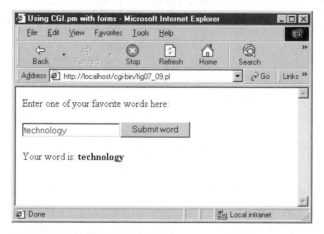

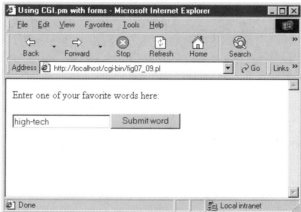

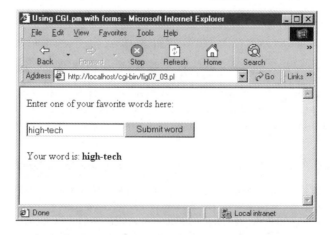

Fig. 7.9   Using **CGI.pm** with an HTML form (part 2 of 2).

Function *textfield* generates HTML to create an **<input>** single-line form element with the name **word**. The corresponding HTML is

```
<input type = "text" name = "word">
```

A value entered into a text field created with function **textfield** becomes "sticky"; that is, when the user submits the form and the server sends back the same form (possibly so the user can correct an error), the value just entered into the text field becomes the default value for the field in the new page. It is often useful to have a page be able to remember the form-field settings from a previous invocation. When the user makes a mistake in one field of a large form, they can simply fix their mistake rather than reenter every piece of information. This behavior can be overridden by setting the *override* attribute to true (**1**), using a named-argument syntax as follows:

```
textfield( -name => "word", -override => 1 );
```

Function *submit* (called at line 15) creates a **submit** button with the given argument (**Submit word**) as a label. Function *end_form* (called at line 15) prints the closing form tag, **</form>**.

In line 17, we use an **if** structure to execute the **print** statement only if **$word** was assigned a value from function **param**. Otherwise, **$word** is **undef** (which evaluates to false) and the **print** statement in line 17 is not executed. We can also use **param** to test whether or not any form data were submitted; when called without any arguments, **param** returns true only if form data were sent to the script.

In this program, note how using **param** and the HTML shortcuts creates a more concise and elegant CGI script. We rely on these features of **CGI.pm** through the remaining CGI examples in this book.

7.8 Other Headers

We mentioned at the close of Section 7.3 that there are alternatives to the standard HTTP header

```
Content-type: text/html
```

Function **header** outputs this header by default, but we can pass arguments to the function to specify different attributes. For example, **header("text/plain")** prints the **Content-type** header with the **text/plain** content type.

A CGI script can supply other HTTP headers in addition to **Content-type**. In most cases, the server passes these extra headers to the client untouched. For example, the following **Refresh** header redirects the client to a new location after a specified amount of time:

```
Refresh: "5; URL = http://www.deitel.com/newpage.html"
```

Five seconds after the Web browser receives this header, the browser requests the resource at the specified URL. Alternatively, the **Refresh** header can omit the URL, in which case it will refresh the current page at the given time interval. Extra headers like **Refresh** can be included in **CGI.pm**'s **header** function, using the named-parameter syntax as follows:

```
header( -Refresh => "5; URL = www.deitel.com/newpage.html" );
```

This produces both the **Refresh** header and the standard **Content-type** header.

The CGI protocol indicates that certain types of headers output by a CGI script are to be handled by the server, rather than be passed directly to the client. The first of these is the **Location** header. Like **Refresh**, **Location** redirects the client to a new location:

> ```
> Location: http://www.deitel.com/newpage.html
> ```

If used with a relative (or virtual) URL (i.e., **Location: /newpage.html**), the **Location** header indicates to the server that the redirection is to be performed on the server side without sending the **Location** header back to the client. In this case, it appears to the user as if they requested that resource originally. With **CGI.pm**, the **Location** header can be output using function *redirect*:

> ```
> redirect( "/newpage.html" );
> ```

In this case, the **Content-type** header is not necessary, because the new resource has its own content type, so the **Content-type** header is not output.

The CGI specification also includes a **Status** header, which tells the server to output a corresponding status header line (such as **HTTP/1.0 200 OK**). Normally, the server will automatically send the appropriate status line to the client (adding, for example, the **200 OK** status line in most cases). However, CGI allows you to change the response status if you so desire. For example, sending a

> ```
> Status: 204 No Response
> ```

header indicates that, although the request was successful, the client should not update the browser window. This header might be useful if you want to allow users to submit forms without moving to a new page. To send this header using function **header**, pass the code and explanation (e.g., **204 No Response**) as the second argument to **header**, or use the named-parameter syntax:

> ```
> header( -status => "204 No Response" );
> ```

We have now covered the fundamentals of the Common Gateway Interface protocol. To review, the CGI protocol allows scripts to interact with servers in three basic ways:

1. through the output of headers and content to the server via standard output;

2. by the server's setting of environment variables (including the URL-encoded **QUERY_STRING**) whose values are available within the script (via **%ENV**) and

3. through **POST**ed, URL-encoded data that the server sends to the script's standard input.

7.9 Example: An Interactive Portal

Figures 7.10 and 7.11 show the implementation of a simple interactive portal for the fictional Deitel Travel Web site. The example queries the client for a name and password, and then displays information based on the data entered. For simplicity, the example does not encrypt the data sent to the server.

Figure 7.10 displays the opening page. It is a static HTML document containing a form that **POST**s data to the **fig07_11.pl** CGI script (lines 9 and 10). The form contains one field each to collect the client's name (line 13) and the member password (line 16). *Note: This HTML document was placed in the root directory of the Web server.*

```html
1   <!DOCTYPE html PUBLIC "-//W3C//DTD HTML 4.0 Transitional//EN">
2   <!-- Fig. 7.10: fig07_10.html -->
3
4   <html><head><title>Enter here</title></head>
5
6   <body>
7   <h1>Welcome to Deitel Travel!</h1>
8
9   <form method = "POST"
10          action = "http://localhost/cgi-bin/fig07_11.pl">
11
12  Please enter your name:<br/>
13  <input type = "text" name = "name"><br/>
14
15  Members, please enter the password:<br/>
16  <input type = "password" name = "password"><br/>
17
18  <font size = "-1">
19  <i>Note that password is not encrypted.</i><br/><br/>
20
21  <input type = "submit">
22  </form>
23
24  </body></html>
```

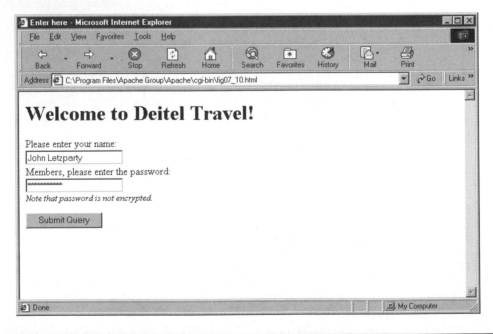

Fig. 7.10   Interactive portal to create a password-protected Web page.

Figure 7.11 is the CGI script that handles the data from the client. First, line 9,

```perl
print redirect( "/fig07_10.html" ) unless param( "name" );
```

checks if any data were posted for the **name** field using function **param**. Unless data have been posted, the client is redirected to the portal page (Fig. 7.10) in the root directory of the Web server (as indicated with the **/** at the beginning of the resource name). Therefore, clients who try to directly access **fig07_11.pl** without going through the login procedure will be blocked automatically and forced to enter through the portal.

In lines 11 and 12, we assign the form-field values to variables **$name** and **$password**. We use **$name** in line 15 to print a personal greeting for the client. The current weekly specials are displayed in lines 17 and 18. (In this simple example, we include this information as part of the script. In Chapters 10 and 15, we learn how to access data in a file or database for inclusion in a Web page.)

```perl
1   #!perl
2   # Fig. 7.11: fig07_11.pl
3   # Handles entry to Deitel Travel
4
5   use warnings;
6   use strict;
7   use CGI qw( :standard );
8
9   print redirect( "/fig07_10.html" ) unless param( "name" );
10
11  my $name = param( "name" );
12  my $password = param( "password" );
13
14  print header(), start_html( "Deitel Travel" ),
15        h1( "Welcome, $name!" );
16
17  print "Here are our weekly specials:", br(),
18        ul( li( "Boston to Taiwan for \$300" ) );
19
20  if ( $password eq "Coast2coast" ) {
21     print hr(), "Current specials just for members:", br(),
22           ul( li( "San Diego to Hong Kong for \$250" ) );
23  }
24  elsif ( $password ne "" ) {
25     print i( "Sorry, you entered the wrong password.",
26              "If you have the correct password, enter",
27              "it to see more specials." );
28  }
29  else {
30     print i( "Become a member today for more great deals!" );
31  }
32
33  print hr(), end_html();
```

Fig. 7.11 Interactive portal handler (part 1 of 3).

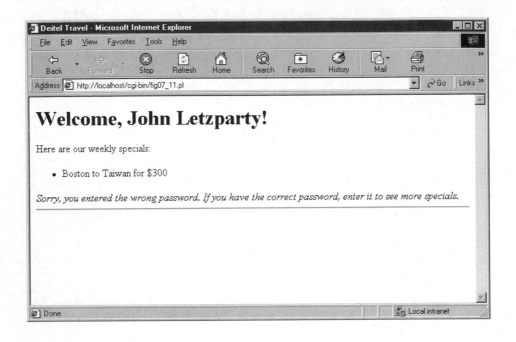

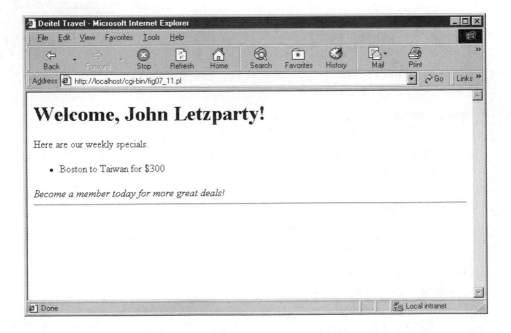

Fig. 7.11   Interactive portal handler (part 2 of 3).

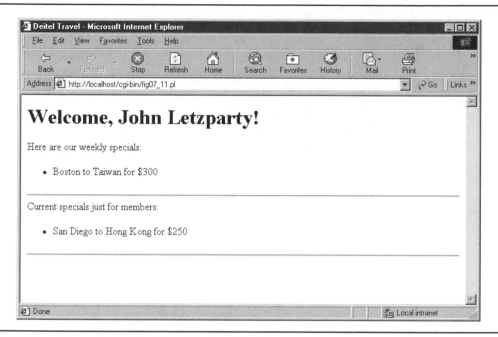

Fig. 7.11   Interactive portal handler (part 3 of 3).

If the member password is correct, additional specials are output (lines 21 and 22). If the password is not correct and the client submitted anything other than the empty string (line 24), the client is informed that the password was invalid. Otherwise, no password was entered, so a message promoting the benefits of membership is output (line 30).

Note that we use a combination of a static Web page and a CGI script here. We could have incorporated the opening HTML form and the processing of the data into a single CGI script, as we did in previous examples in this chapter.

Performance Tip 7.1

It is always much more efficient for the server to provide static content rather than execute a CGI program, because it takes time for the server to execute the program (whereas an HTML file needs only to be sent to the client, not to be executed). It is a good practice to use a mix of static HTML (for content that generally stays the same) and CGI scripting (for mostly dynamic content). This practice allows the Web server to respond to clients more quickly than if only CGI scripting were used.

7.10 Internet and World Wide Web Resources

www.speakeasy.org/~cgires
This is a collection of tutorials and scripts related to CGI.

www.cgi101.com
CGI 101 is a site for those looking to improve their programming ability through familiarity with CGI. The site contains a six-chapter class outlining techniques for CGI programming in the Perl language. The class includes both basic and sophisticated scripts, with working examples. Also included are script libraries and links to other resources.

www.jmarshall.com/easy/cgi
A good, brief explanation of CGI for those with programming experience.

wdvl.internet.com/Authoring/CGI
The Web Developer's Virtual Library provides tutorials for learning both Perl and CGI.

www.w3.org/CGI
The World Wide Web Consortium page on CGI is concerned with security issues involving the Common Gateway Interface. This page provides links concerning CGI specifications, as indicated by the National Center for Supercomputing Applications (NCSA).

hotwired.lycos.com/webmonkey/98/47/index2a.html?tw=programming
An amusing tutorial that introduces Perl and CGI. This tutorial covers the basics of Perl with an introduction to CGI at the end.

SUMMARY

- The Common Gateway Interface (CGI) describes a set of protocols through which applications (commonly called CGI programs or CGI scripts) can interact with Web servers and interact (indirectly) with clients.

- When we say that a page is dynamic, we mean that its content changes without being altered manually by a person on the server side. Static Web content requires alteration by a person responsible for the files containing that Web content on the server.

- The Common Gateway Interface is "common" in the sense that it is not specific to any particular operating system (such as Linux or Windows), or to any one programming language.

- HTTP describes a set of methods and headers that allow clients and servers to interact and exchange information in a uniform and predictable way.

- A Web page in its simplest form is nothing more than an HTML (HyperText Markup Language) document. This document is just a plain text file containing markings (markup or tags) that describe to a Web browser how to display and format the information in the document.

- Hypertext information creates links to different pages or to other portions of the same page.

- Any HTML file available for viewing over the Internet has a URL (Universal Resource Locator) associated with it. The URL contains information that directs a browser to the resource that the user wishes to access.

- The hostname is the name of the computer where the resource resides.

- The hostname is translated into an IP address, which identifies the server on the Internet.

- To request a resource, the browser first sends an HTTP request message to the server. The server responds with a line indicating the HTTP version, followed by a numeric code and a phrase describing the status of the transaction. The server normally then sends one or more HTTP headers, which provide additional information about the data being sent. The header or set of headers is followed by a blank line, which indicates that the server finished sending HTTP headers. Then the server sends the contents of the requested resource, and the connection is terminated. The client-side browser interprets the HTML it receives and displays the results.

- **GET** is an HTTP method that indicates that the client wishes to get a resource.

- The built-in function **localtime**, when evaluated in scalar context, returns a string value such as **Mon Jul 31 13:10:37 2000**.

- Redirecting output refers to when we send our output to somewhere other than standard output, which is normally the screen.

- Just as standard input usually refers to the standard method of input into a program (the keyboard), standard output usually refers to the standard method of output from a program (the screen).

- If the server is not configured to handle CGI scripts, it might just return the Perl code as if it were any other document.

- A properly configured Web server will recognize a CGI script and execute it. A resource is usually designated as a CGI script in one of two ways: either it has a specific filename extension (such as **.cgi** or **.pl**) or it is located in a special directory (often **/cgi-bin**). The server administrator must explicitly give permission for remote clients to be able to access and execute CGI scripts.

- When the server recognizes that the resource requested is a Perl script, the server invokes Perl to compile and execute the script. The Perl program executes and the output is piped to the Web server. Finally, the Web server adds an additional line to the output indicating the status of the HTTP transaction (such as **HTTP/1.0 200 OK**, for success) and sends the whole body of text to the client. The browser on the client side then interprets the output and displays the results appropriately.

- With a CGI script, we must explicitly include the **Content-type** header, whereas with a normal HTML document, the header would be automatically added by the Web server.

- The CGI protocol for output to be sent to a Web browser consists of printing to standard output the **Content-type** header, a blank line and the data (HTML, plain text, etc.) to be output.

- The Perl module **CGI.pm** provides functions that simplify the creation of CGI scripts. Among other things, **CGI.pm** includes a set of functions to aid in dynamic HTML generation.

- Function **header** returns the string **Content-type: text/html\n\n**.

- Function **start_html** returns a string containing the standard opening tags of an HTML document. When the function is called with a single argument, the argument is embedded between the tags **<title>** and **</title>** to give the Web page a name.

- The **%ENV** hash is a built-in hashtable in Perl that contains the names and values of all the environment variables.

- Function **Tr** generates the start and end **<tr>** and **</tr>** (table row) tags to create a table row.

- Function **td** generates the opening and closing **<td>** and **</td>** (table data) tags around each cell of the table column.

- The **b** function generates **<b>** (bold) tags around text to be output in bold type.

- Function **i** generates **<i>** (italics) tags around text to be output in italics.

- Function **end_html** generates the final **</body>** and **</html>** tags.

- CGI-enabled Web servers set environment variables that provide information about both the server's and the client's script execution environment.

- The environment variable **QUERY_STRING** provides a mechanism to that enables us to supply any sort of data we wish to our CGI scripts. The **QUERY_STRING** variable contains extra information that is appended to a URL following a question mark (**?**). The question mark is not part of the resource requested or of the query string. It simply serves as a delimiter between the two.

- Data put into a query string can be structured in a variety of ways, provided that the CGI script that reads the string knows how to interpret the formatted data.

- Function **split** breaks apart a string at the specified delimiter.

- Forms provide another way for users to input information to be sent to a CGI script.

- The **<form>** and **</form>** tags surround an HTML form.

- The **<form>** tag generally takes two attributes. The first attribute is **action**, which specifies the action to take when the user submits the form. The second attribute is **method**, which normally is either **GET** or **POST**.

- Using **GET** with an HTML form causes data to be passed to the CGI script through environment variable **QUERY_STRING**, which is set by the server.

- The **POST** method enables CGI scripts to interact with servers via standard input.

- With **POST**, data are encoded just as with **QUERY_STRING**, but the **QUERY_STRING** environment variable is not set. Instead, the **POST** method sets the environment variable **CONTENT_LENGTH** to indicate the number of characters of data that are being sent or posted, and then function **read** is used with **STDIN** to obtain the data.

- Today's Web browsers automatically URL encode HTML-form data they send. This means that spaces are turned into plus signs, and certain other symbols (such as the apostrophe) are translated into their ASCII value in hexadecimal and preceded with a percent sign.

- Function **param** takes as its argument the name of an HTML form field. If the form data contain a name–value pair with the given name, then the associated value of the name is returned. Otherwise, **param** returns **undef**.

- Function **start_form** generates the opening **<form>** tag. When no arguments are given, **start_form** defaults to the **POST** method. Function **start_form** can be used with an optional named-argument syntax, in which each attribute and value are paired together with an arrow (**=>**), as in a hash. In this syntax, attribute names are preceded with a hyphen.

- Function **textfield** generates HTML to create an **<input>** single-line form element.

- Function **submit** creates a **submit** button with the given argument as a label.

- Function **end_form** prints the closing **</form>** tag.

- Function **header** prints the header **Content-type: text/html** by default, but we can pass arguments to the function to specify different headers.

- A CGI script can supply HTTP headers in addition to **Content-type**. In most cases, the server passes these extra headers to the client untouched.

- The CGI protocol indicates that certain types of headers output by a CGI script are to be handled by the server, rather than be passed directly to the client.

- The **Location** header redirects the client to a new location. If used with a relative URL, the **Location** header indicates to the server that the redirection is to be performed automatically, without sending the **Location** header back to the client.

- With **CGI.pm**, the **Location** header can be output using function **redirect**.

- The CGI specification also includes a Status header, which tells the server to output a corresponding status header line (such as **HTTP/1.0 200 OK**). Normally, the server will automatically add the appropriate status line to the output sent to the client (adding, for example, the **200 OK** status line in most cases). However, CGI allows you to change the response status if you so desire.

TERMINOLOGY

%ENV hash in Perl
.cgi file extension
.pl file extension
/cgi-bin
:standard import tag for CGI.pm
<body> tag
<form> tag
<head> tag
<html> tag
<input> form element

<select> form element
<textarea> form element
<title> tag
action attribute
Apache Web Server
b function from CGI.pm
backslash (\) escape sequence
button type attribute for input tags
CGI (Common Gateway Interface)
CGI programs

CGI protocol
CGI script
CGI.pm module
checkbox type attribute for input tags
CONTENT_LENGTH environment variable
Content-type header
delimiter
dynamic vs. static Web content
dynamic Web content
end_form function in **CGI.pm**
end_html function in **CGI.pm**
EOF
file type attribute for input tags
filepath
forms
GET
hash
header
header function in **CGI.pm**
hidden type attribute for **input** tags
host
hostname
HTML
HTML form element
HTML forms
HTML tag
HTTP
HTTP connection
HTTP header
HTTP host
HTTP method
HTTP transaction
HTTP_USER_AGENT environment variable
HyperText Markup Language (HTML)
Hypertext Transfer Protocol (HTTP)

i function in **CGI.pm**
image type attribute for input tags
IP address
localtime built-in function
markup
method form attribute
newline
override attribute of **textfield**
param function in **CGI.pm**
password type attribute for input tags
pipe
POST
QUERY_STRING environment variable
radio type attribute for input tags
redirect
redirect function in **CGI.pm**
reset type attribute for input tags
select function
split function
standard output
start_form function in **CGI.pm**
start_html function in **CGI.pm**
static Web content
submit function in **CGI.pm**
submit type attribute for input tags
tags
td function in **CGI.pm**
text type attribute for input tags
textfield function in **CGI.pm**
The Common Gateway Interface
Tr function in **CGI.pm**
URL (Universal Resource Locator)
use statement
Web server

SELF-REVIEW EXERCISES

7.1   Fill in the blanks in each of the following statements:

  a) In the URL **http://www.deitel.com/books/downloads.htm**, the part that consists of **www.deitel.com** is the _____ of the server, where a client can find the desired resource.

  b) An _____ document is a text file containing markings that describe to a Web browser how to display and format the information in the document.

  c) The **CGI.pm** function _____ returns a string containing the standard opening tags of an HTML document.

  d) The environment variable _____ provides a mechanism to supply any sort of data to send to our CGI scripts.

  e) A user-friendly approach to reading input from the user is to implement _____.

7.2   State whether each of the following is *true* or *false*. If *false*, explain why.
   a) A dynamic Web page is a Web page that never changes, whereas a static Web page is a Web page that does change.
   b) In **CGI.pm**, the **end_html** function generates the final **</body>** and **</html>** tags.
   c) We put data into a query string using a format that consists of a series of name–value pairs joined with exclamation points (**!**).
   d) It is always more efficient to use a CGI script than an HTML document.

7.3   Write a program that does the following, using **CGI.pm**:
   a) Print the header and opening tags of an HTML file. Make the title "Self-Help Exercise."
   b) Print this question on the screen: "True or false: The default target for **print** is the screen. Enter T for true, F for false." **print** should be in bold.
   c) Create a form that reads in a response.
   d) Print an appropriate message based on the user's response. If the user entered something other than a T or an F, print a message telling the user to try again.
   e) Print the ending tags of the HTML document.

7.4   What is wrong with this code? (Assume that this is the entire program, minus comments.)

```
#!/usr/bin/perl
# Can you find the mistake?
use warnings;
use strict;
use CGI qw( :standard );
print start_html( "Welcome" );
print i( "Hello World!" );
print end_html();
```

ANSWERS TO SELF REVIEW EXERCISES

7.1   a) hostname.
   b) HTML.
   c) **start_html**.
   d) **QUERY_STRING**.
   e) forms.

7.2   a) False. A dynamic Web page is a Web page that changes; a static Web page is a Web page that does not.
   b) True.
   c) False. The pairs are joined with an ampersand (**&**).
   d) False. It is more efficient to use an HTML document, because an HTML document does not need to be executed on the server side before the output is sent to the client.

7.3   See the following code:

```
1   #!/usr/bin/perl
2   # Exercise 7.3: Ex07_03.pl
3   # Prompting the user and analyzing the input, using forms.
4
5   use warnings;
6   use strict;
7   use CGI qw( :standard );
8
9   my $word = param( "word" );
```

```
10
11   print header(), start_html( 'Self Help Exercise' );
12   print p( 'True or False: "The default target for ',
13          b( 'print' ),
14          ' is the screen". Enter T for true, F for false.' );
15
16   print start_form(), textfield( "word" );
17   print submit( "Submit Answer" ), end_form();
18
19   if ( $word ) {
20
21      if ( $word eq "T" ) {
22         print p( i( 'Congratulations! You are correct!' ) );
23      }
24      elsif ( $word eq "F" ) {
25         print p( i( 'Sorry, that answer is incorrect.' ) );
26      }
27      else {
28         print p( i( 'Unable to understand your response.
29                     Please try again.' ) );
30      }
31   }
32
33   print end_html();
```

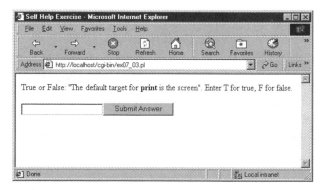

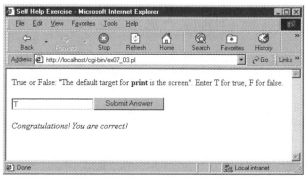

7.4   Error: The required header is missing.
Solution: Above the first `print` statement, enter the following:

```
print header();
```

EXERCISES

7.5   Write a CGI script that prints the squares of the integers from 1 to 10 on separate lines. Do not use the functions of `CGI.pm` to create the HTML markup.

7.6   Modify your solution to Exercise 7.5 to display its output in an HTML table. The left column should be the number, and the right column should be the square of that number. Use the HTML tag-generating functions in the `CGI.pm` module for all tags except the `<table>` and `<\table>` tags.

7.7   Write a CGI script that receives as input three numbers from the client and returns a statement indicating whether the three numbers could represent an equilateral triangle (all three sides are the same length), an isosceles triangle (two sides are the same length) or a right triangle (the square of one side is equal to the sum of the squares of the other two sides.)

7.8   Write a soothsayer program that allows the user to submit a question. When the question is submitted, the server should choose a random response from a list of vague answers and return a new page displaying the answer. Implement this program as a Perl program using **CGI.pm**.

7.9   You are provided with a portal page (see the code and output below) where people can go to buy products. Write the CGI script to enable this interactive portal. The user should be able to specify how many of each item to buy. The total cost of the items purchased should be displayed to the user

```
1   <!DOCTYPE html PUBLIC "-//W3C//DTD HTML 4.0 Transitional//EN">
2   <!-- Ex. 7.9: Ex07_09.html -->
3
4
5
6   <html><head><title>Buy Something</title></head>
7
8   <body>
9   <h1>Clearance!</h1>
10  <p>Please enter how many of each product you would like to order
11     into the box in the right-hand column.</p>
12
13  <form method = "POST" action =
14                  "http://localhost/cgi-bin/ch07sol/Ex7_4.pl">
15
16  <table width = "100%" border = "3">
17     <tr>
18        <th>Product Name</th>
19        <th>Description</th>
20        <th>Price</th>
21        <th>Order</th>
22     </tr>
23     <tr>
24        <td>CD</td>
25        <td>Buy this really cool CD</td>
26        <td>$12.00</td>
27        <td><input type = "text" name = "CD" size = "5"></td>
28     </tr>
29     <tr>
30        <td>Book</td>
31        <td>Buy this really cool book</td>
32        <td>$19.99</td>
33        <td><input type = "text" name = "book" size = "5"></td>
34     </tr>
35     <tr>
36        <td>Airplane</td>
37        <td>Buy this really cool airplane</td>
38        <td>$1,000,000</td>
39        <td><input type = "text" name = "airplane" size = "5"></td>
40     </tr>
41
42  </table>
43        <input type = "submit" value = "submit">
44  </form>
45
46  </body></html>
```

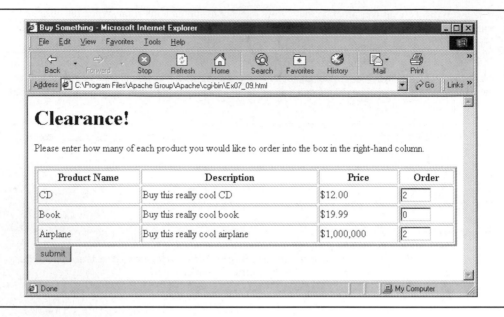

Regular Expressions

Objectives

- To learn the basics of regular expressions.
- To understand the matching and substitution operators.
- To be able to use regular expression modifiers.
- To be able to use alternation.
- To be able to use quantifiers.
- To be able to use assertions.
- To understand the concept of greediness.
- To become familiar with the global modifier.
- To be able to write regular expressions.

There is no substitute for hard work.
Thomas Alva Edison

You ought to be able to show that you can do it a good deal better than anyone else with the regular tools before you have a license to bring in your own improvements.
Ernest Hemingway

I could never make out what those damned dots meant.
Winston Churchill

Outline

8.1 Introduction

Text processing is one of Perl's most powerful capabilities. Text manipulation in Perl is accomplished with *regular expressions*—patterns of characters used to search through text files and databases. Regular expressions allow complex searches to be performed using relatively simple expressions. In this chapter, we explore Perl's rich regular-expression functionality. We finish the chapter with a practical CGI application in which regular expressions are used with HTML form verification.

8.2 Matching Operator m//

We begin our discussion of regular expressions with a simple pattern-matching example (Fig. 8.1).

```
1   #!/usr/bin/perl
2   # Fig. 8.1: fig08_01.pl
3   # Simple matching example.
4
5   use strict;
6   use warnings;
7
8   my $string = 'It is winter and there is snow on the roof.';
9   my $pattern = 'and';
10
11  print "String is: '$string'\n\n";
12
13  print "Found 'snow'\n" if $string =~ m/snow/;
14
```

Fig. 8.1   Matching operator (part 1 of 2).

```
15   print "Found 'SNOW'\n" if $string =~ m/SNOW/;
16
17   print "Found 'on the'\n" if $string =~ m/on the/;
18
19   print "Found '$pattern'\n" if $string =~ m/$pattern/;
20
21   print "Found '$pattern there'\n" if $string =~ m/$pattern there/;
```

```
String is: 'It is winter and there is snow on the roof.'

Found 'snow'
Found 'on the'
Found 'and'
Found 'and there'
```

Fig. 8.1   Matching operator (part 2 of 2).

Let us go through this example step by step. The odd-looking construction in the **if** condition of line 13

    $string =~ m/snow/

uses the *matching operator*, **m//**, to search for the string **snow** inside variable **$string**. The matching operator takes two operands. The first is the regular expression (or *matching pattern*) to search for, which is placed between the slashes of the **m//** operator. In this case, the pattern consists of the literal string **snow**. The second operand is the string in which to search, which is assigned to the match operator using **=~**. This operator is sometimes called the *binding operator*, because it binds whatever is on its left side to a regular-expression operator on its right and thereby allows the matching function to be applied to a string. [*Note:* Regular expressions operate on the value in special variable **$_**, if they are not bound to a specific string.] The string **snow** exists in the string being searched (**$string**), so the matching operator returns true, and the **print** statement in line 13 executes.

By default, regular expressions are case sensitive. Thus, a similar search for the string **SNOW** (line 15) returns false, and the associated **print** statement does not execute. The search in line 17 is successful, because the entire pattern (including the space) is found.

Note that the regular expression can contain more than just literal characters. For example, lines 19 and 21 use variable **$pattern** in the regular expression. Rather than searching for the literal characters "**$pattern**," the matching operator interpolates the value of **$pattern** (the string **and**) into the search pattern.

The syntax of the **m//** operator is flexible. Its forward slashes are not required; any nonalphanumeric, nonwhitespace character can serve as a *delimiter*—the character that separates the parts of the operator. For example, the following are all equivalent:

```
$string =~ m#there#
$string =~ m(there)
$string =~ m{there}
$string =~ m[there]
$string =~ m,there,
$string =~ m.there.
$string =~ m'there'
$string =~ /there/
```

The last case is special. When forward slashes delimit the pattern, the **m** prefix is optional. This form is actually the most popular syntax for the matching operator. Note that Perl will not interpolate variables if the pattern is delimited with single quotes.

In place of the binding operator, we may also use **! ~**, which negates the value returned from **m//**. If **m//** with **=~** would have returned a value of true, **m//** with **! ~** would return a value of false, and vice versa. If the binding operator is omitted, the pattern is applied to the string in variable **$_**. Consider the following example:

```
foreach ( "not here", "nor here", "finally found" ) {
    print if /found/;
}
```

The **foreach** loop iterates through the elements of the given list, assigning each element to **$_**. The binding operator is not used with **/found/**, so the **$_** variable is searched during each iteration. When the matching operator returns a value of true (on the third iteration only), **print** outputs the current value of **$_** (i.e., the string "**finally found**").

8.3 Substitution Operator s ///

In addition to matching patterns, Perl allows pattern *substitutions*, as shown in Fig. 8.2. This script highlights several important points. Line 11 demonstrates the *substitution operator*, **s///**. Place the pattern, denoting the string to be replaced, between the first two slashes. Between the second two slashes, place the *substitution pattern* that will replace the first pattern. Like the matching operator, the substitution operator uses the binding operator to specify the string in which to search. Also, like the matching operator, the substitution operator can use delimiters other than **/** (see line 20). However, the **s** in the substitution operator is required. Line 16 demonstrates the substitution operator using the string currently stored in **$_**.

```
1   #!/usr/bin/perl
2   # Fig. 8.2: fig08_02.pl
3   # Substitution Example
4
5   use strict;
6   use warnings;
7
8   my $string = "Hello to the world";
9
10  print "The original string is: \"$string\"\n";
11  $string =~ s/world/planet/;
12  print "s/world/planet/ changes string: $string \n";
13
14  our $_ = $string;
15  print "The original string is: \"$_\"\n";
16  s/planet/world/;
17  print "s/planet/world/ changes string: $_ \n";
18
19  print "The original string is: \"$_\"\n";
20  s(world)(planet);
21  print "s(world)(planet) changes string: $string \n";
```

Fig. 8.2   Substitution operator (part 1 of 2).

```
22
23   $string = "This planet is our planet.";
24   print "$string\n";
25   my $matches = $string =~ s/planet/world/g;
26   print "$matches occurences of planet were changed to world.\n";
27   print "The new string is: $string\n";
```

```
The original string is: "Hello to the world"
s/world/planet/ changes string: Hello to the planet
The original string is: "Hello to the planet"
s/planet/world/ changes string: Hello to the world
The original string is: "Hello to the world"
s(world)(planet) changes string: Hello to the planet
This planet is our planet.
2 occurences of planet were changed to world.
The new string is: This world is our world.
```

Fig. 8.2   Substitution operator (part 2 of 2).

Line 25 introduces *modifiers*, which change how a regular expression works. The *global modifier*, */g*, at the end of the regular expression causes the substitution operator to replace every occurrence of the first pattern (**planet**) with the second pattern (**world**). Also, there is an assignment operator on line 25. This line provides a good example of the difference between the binding operator and an assignment operator: The binding operator denotes the string in which to search (**$string** in this example), while the assignment operator takes the value returned from the **s///** operator and assigns it to **$matches**. When the substitution operator performs a *global substitution* and the value returned is in scalar context, **s///** returns the number of substitutions. In a list context, **s///** returns the substrings that were changed in the original string.

8.4 Special Characters and Character Classes

Regular-expression patterns can contain more than letters, words and variables. The program in Fig. 8.3 explores some simple *special characters* and *character classes*.

```
1    #!/usr/bin/perl
2    # Fig 8.3: fig08_03.pl
3    # Determine if a string has a digit.
4
5    use strict;
6    use warnings;
7
8    my $string1 = "hello there";
9    my $string2 = "this one has a 2";
10
11   number1( $string1 );
12   number1( $string2 );
13   number2( $string1 );
14   number2( $string2 );
```

Fig. 8.3   Special character **\d** and character classes (part 1 of 2).

```
15
16   sub number1
17   {
18      my $string = shift();
19
20      if ( $string =~ /\d/ ) {
21          print "'$string' has a digit.\n";
22      }
23      else {
24          print "'$string' has no digit.\n";
25      }
26   }
27
28   sub number2
29   {
30      my $string = shift();
31
32      if ( $string =~ /[0-9]/ ) {
33          print "'$string' has a digit.\n";
34      }
35      else {
36          print "'$string' has no digit.\n";
37      }
38   }
```

```
'hello there' has no digit.
'this one has a 2' has a digit.
'hello there' has no digit.
'this one has a 2' has a digit.
```

Fig. 8.3   Special character **\d** and character classes (part 2 of 2).

The first new pattern in this example is **\d** (line 20). This pattern is called a *special character*. It matches any digit. The second new pattern (line 32) is an example of a character class. Brackets (**[]**) enclose the character class to separate it from the surrounding pattern. Inside the brackets, a dash indicates a range. So, **[0-9]** matches any digit, like **\d**. A character class matches only one character, but it matches with anything in the character class. So, **[abc]** will match "**a**" or "**b**" or "**c**." However, it will not match the entire string "**abc**." Similarly, **[hh]** will match the character "**h**" or a space. The repeated characters in a character class are ignored. Figure 8.4 lists the character class shortcuts.

Character	Matches	Character	Matches
\d	any digit	\D	any nondigit
\w	any word	\W	any nonword
\s	any whitespace	\S	any nonwhitespace

Fig. 8.4   Some special characters.

A *word character* is any alphanumeric character or the underscore. A *whitespace* character is a space, a tab, a carriage return, a newline or a form feed. In addition to the special characters in Fig. 8.4, the *dot* special character (**.**) matches everything except a newline.

8.5 Alternation

In this section, we introduce *alternation*. In the previous section, we used character classes to create a pattern that matches one character from a list of characters. Alternation chooses one word or pattern from a list of words or patterns. The alternation symbol is the *vertical bar* (or *pipe symbol*) **|**. Figure 8.5 provides an example that uses the alternation symbol.

The condition in lines 21 and 22 searches **$string** to determine if it contains one of the strings **stop**, **quit** or **end**, and it does not contain **not** or **don't**. If the pattern matches, the condition is true and **alright, we're finished.** is displayed; otherwise, **ok, let's keep going** is displayed.

```perl
1   #!/usr/bin/perl
2   # Fig. 8.5: fig08_05.pl
3   # Using alternation.
4
5   use strict;
6   use warnings;
7
8   my $string1 = "i think we should stop";
9   my $string2 = "lets continue";
10  my $string3 = "i don't want to end";
11
12  finish( $string1 );
13  finish( $string2 );
14  finish( $string3 );
15
16  sub finish
17  {
18     my $string = shift();
19     print "$string\n";
20
21     if ( $string =~ /stop|quit|end/ &&
22          $string !~ /not|don't/ ) {
23        print "alright, we're finished.\n";
24     }
25     else {
26        print "ok, lets keep going.\n";
27     }
28  }
```

```
i think we should stop
alright, we're finished.
lets continue
ok, lets keep going.
i don't want to end
ok, lets keep going.
```

Fig. 8.5   Alternation.

Alternation can be dangerous. The alternation symbol has the lowest precedence of all the symbols. This means that it is performed last. Figure 8.6 highlights one of the dangers of alternation.

In lines 16 through 18, we want to search for "**hello**" or "**hi**," and then "**there**." However, Perl treats the matching pattern as "**hello**" or "**hi there**." Perl interprets the space in the pattern the same as any other character. So, "**hi there**" is considered as one whole string. Thus, it is also considered as one option for the alternation operator. This logic error may cause our pattern to miss positive matches and accept negative matches.

Good Programming Practice 8.1

When using alternation, use parentheses to separate the alternated portion from the rest of the pattern.

```perl
1   #!usr/bin/perl
2   # Fig. 8.6: fig08_06.pl
3   # Showing the dangers of using alternate without parentheses.
4
5   use strict;
6   use warnings;
7
8   my $string1 = "hello";
9   my $string2 = "hello there";
10  my $string3 = "hi there";
11
12  print "$string1\n$string2\n$string3\n";
13
14  print "watch this:\n";
15
16  print "1: how are you?\n" if ( $string1 =~ m/hello|hi there/ );
17  print "2: how are you?\n" if ( $string2 =~ m/hello|hi there/ );
18  print "3: how are you?\n" if ( $string3 =~ m/hello|hi there/ );
19
20  print "now watch this:\n";
21
22  print "1: how are you?\n"
23      if ( $string1 =~ m/(hello|hi) there/ );
24  print "2: how are you?\n"
25      if ( $string2 =~ m/(hello|hi) there/ );
26  print "3: how are you?\n"
27      if ( $string3 =~ m/(hello|hi) there/ );
```

```
hello
hello there
hi there
watch this:
1: how are you?
2: how are you?
3: how are you?
now watch this:
2: how are you?
3: how are you?
```

Fig. 8.6   Dangers of alternation.

In the second part of this example, lines 22 through 27, the alternation expression **hello|hi** is separated from the rest of the pattern with parentheses. This pattern is the one that we wanted to match in the first place.

Testing and Debugging Tip 8.1

When programming in Perl, especially when using regular expressions, always test your code thoroughly. Try to think of any input that might break your code, and make sure that your program deals with it appropriately.

8.6 Quantifiers

Perl regular expressions use special symbols called *quantifiers* to match more than one instance of a pattern at a time. Figure 8.7 demonstrates some quantifiers.

Line 24 introduces the *asterisk (*) quantifier*. This operator tells the regular-expression engine to match *any number of (including zero) matches* of the preceding pattern. In the pattern **s/1\d*1/22/**, **\d*** indicates a pattern containing any number of consecutive digit characters. So, the whole pattern is trying to find a **1**, followed by any number of digits, followed by another **1**. Quantifiers have higher precedence than alternation; they are one of the first parts evaluated in a regular expression. In this case, the quantifier is being applied only to the special character **\d**. It will not be applied to the **1** at the beginning of the pattern. If you want the quantifier to apply to more than one part of the pattern, those parts must be grouped in parentheses.

```
1   #!usr/bin/perl
2   # Fig. 8.7: fig08_07.pl
3   # Some quantifiers.
4
5   use strict;
6   use warnings;
7
8   my $string = "11000";
9
10  change1( $string );
11  change2( $string );
12  change3( $string );
13
14  $string = "1010001";
15
16  change1( $string );
17  change2( $string );
18  change3( $string );
19
20  sub change1
21  {
22      my $string = shift();
23      print "  Original string: $string\n";
```

Fig. 8.7   Quantifiers (part 1 of 2).

```
24        $string =~ s/1\d*1/22/;
25        print "After s/1\\d*1/22/: $string\n\n";
26    }
27
28    sub change2
29    {
30        my $string = shift();
31        print "  Original string: $string\n";
32        $string =~ s/1\d+1/22/;
33        print "After s/1\\d+1/22/: $string\n\n";
34    }
35
36    sub change3
37    {
38        my $string = shift();
39        print "  Original string: $string\n";
40        $string =~ s/1\d?1/22/;
41        print "After s/1\\d?1/22/: $string\n\n";
42    }
```

```
  Original string: 11000
After s/1\d*1/22/: 22000

  Original string: 11000
After s/1\d+1/22/: 11000

  Original string: 11000
After s/1\d?1/22/: 22000

  Original string: 1010001
After s/1\d*1/22/: 22

  Original string: 1010001
After s/1\d+1/22/: 22

  Original string: 1010001
After s/1\d?1/22/: 220001
```

Fig. 8.7   Quantifiers (part 2 of 2).

Line 32 introduces the *plus* (**+**) *quantifier*, which tells the engine to *match one or more instances* of a pattern. In the pattern **s/1\d+1/22/**, **\d+** is equivalent to **\d\d*** (remember that the ***** refers only to the second **\d**).

Line 40 introduces the *question mark* (**?**) *quantifier*, which tells the engine to *match 0 or 1 instances* of a pattern. So line 40 searches for a **1**, followed by 0 or 1 digits, followed by a **1**.

There are other quantifiers. If you use braces around a number, as in **{n}**, Perl will match exactly *n* instances of the pattern. If you put two numbers in the brace, separated by a comma, as in **{n,m}**, Perl will match from *n* to *m*, inclusive, occurrences of the pattern. Figure 8.8 summarizes the quantifiers and what they will match.

Quantifier	Matches
pattern∗	any number of occurrences of *pattern*
pattern+	one or more occurrences of *pattern*
pattern?	zero or one occurrences of *pattern*
pattern{n}	exactly *n* occurrences of *pattern*
pattern{n,m}	from *n* to *m*, inclusive, occurrences of *pattern*

Fig. 8.8　Special characters.

8.7 Quantifier Greediness

Quantifiers are inherently *greedy*. A ∗ or + matches the maximum number of occurrences of a pattern that satisfy the regular expression. The programmer can use the question mark (?) to indicate that quantifiers should be *nongreedy*. If the question mark is placed after another quantifier (even after another question mark), it makes that quantifier nongreedy. This means that the quantifier will match the least number of occurrences of a pattern that still satisfies the regular expression. The program in Fig. 8.9 illustrates this concept.

Lines 13 and 16 perform substitutions. Line 13 tries to match an uppercase **N**, followed by any number of nonnewlines, followed by **here**. The problem with this set of commands is that there are two places where this sequence could match. The **N** matches the first letter of the second sentence. The **here** could match at the end of the second sentence or at the end of the third sentence. When the quantifier is greedy (no ?), the dot will match as many characters as it possibly can, leaving the **here** to match at the end of the third sentence. When the quantifier is not greedy, (.∗?), the period matches as little as possible, leaving the **here** to match at the end of the second sentence.

```perl
1   #!usr/bin/perl
2   # Fig. 8.9: fig08_09.pl
3   # Greedy and non-greedy quantifiers.
4
5   use strict;
6   use warnings;
7
8   my $string1 =
9      "Hello there. Nothing here. There could be something here.";
10  my $string2 = $string1;
11
12  print "$string1\n";
13  $string1 =~ s/N.*here\.//;
14  print "$string1\n";
15  print "$string2\n";
16  $string2 =~ s/N.*?here\.//;
17  print "$string2\n\n";
```

Fig. 8.9　Greedy and nongreedy quantifiers (part 1 of 2).

```
Hello there. Nothing here. There could be something here.
Hello there.
Hello there. Nothing here. There could be something here.
Hello there.  There could be something here.
```

Fig. 8.9   Greedy and nongreedy quantifiers (part 2 of 2).

Any quantifier can be made to be nongreedy, which would match the preceding pattern once only if it were required to make the match succeed. Of course, some quantifiers would not act any differently if they were made to be nongreedy. The pattern **a{2}?** is the same as **a{2}**. Because the **{2}** quantifier matches exactly two instances of "**a**," there is no room to be greedy. So, making the pattern nongreedy does not change anything in that example. Notice that the substitution in line 16 matches only the second sentence and replaces it with nothing (i.e., it removes the sentence).

8.8 Assertions

Assertions are similar to the special characters we saw previously, except they are *zero width*. This means that they do not add any length to your matched string. It also means that they do not change any of the string.

There is a set of assertions that govern case and escaping. The **\u** *assertion* makes the next letter uppercase, while the **\l** *assertion* makes the next letter lowercase. The **\U** and **\L** *assertions* raise or lower the case, respectively, of the rest of the text until a **\E** is found or the end of the regular expression or string is reached. The **\Q** *assertion* escapes all non-alphabetic characters until **\E** or the end of the string or regular expression is reached. These assertions can be used in matching patterns, substitution patterns and even in strings (assignments, print statements, etc.). The assertions are particularly useful when the programmer cannot guarantee that a user will type a string in the appropriate case (e.g., the program requires the user to type "**YES**," but the user types "**Yes**" or "**yes**").

Another set of assertions match the beginning of a string or line and end of a string or line. The *caret* (**^**) and **\A** assertions match at the beginning of a string. The *dollar sign* (**$**) and **\Z** assertions match at the end of a string or right before the newline at the end of a string.

Common Programming Error 8.1

*When using the **$** assertion, characters following the **$** may be interpolated together with the **$** as a scalar variable name and cause a logic error in the program.*

The **\z** assertion matches only at the end of a string. These assertions are generally used to anchor the pattern to either the beginning or the end of a string or line. (For an explanation of the differences between **^** and **\A** and the differences between **$** and **\Z**, see Section 8.10.)

There are two more related assertions known as *word-boundary assertions*. To match a word boundary, use **\b**; to match a nonword boundary, use **\B**. These ensure that a pattern you are matching is a stand-alone word. They can also ensure that you are matching a portion of a word. A word boundary is defined to be a spot in a string where there is a **\w** character on one side and a **\W** character on the other side (these can be in any order).

Another type of assertion is the *look-behind* assertion. This assertion takes the form

(?<=*value1*) *value2*

where we check to see if *value1* occurred right before *value2*. Figure 8.10 demonstrates the look-behind assertion.

Line 20 contains the first look-behind assertion (?<=i). This assertion tests whether the string matched "**i**" right before it matched "**be**." If so, "**be**" is replaced with "**am**." Similar look-ahead assertions are shown in lines 21 and 22. Other assertions include the *look-ahead* assertion, *(?=pattern)*, and the complementary *not look-ahead* and *not look-behind* assertions, *(!=pattern)* and *(!<=pattern)*, respectively.

Common Programming Error 8.2

In many cases, a backslash followed by a lowercase letter matches a certain class of characters, and a backslash followed by an uppercase letter matches everything not in that class. Two important exceptions to this general rule are \a versus \A and \z versus \Z.

```perl
1   #!usr/bin/perl
2   # Fig. 8.10: fig08_10.pl
3   # Testing the look behind assertion.
4
5   use strict;
6   use warnings;
7
8   my $string1 = "i be hungry.";
9   my $string2 = "we be here.";
10  my $string3 = "he be where?";
11
12  conjugate( $string1 );
13  conjugate( $string2 );
14  conjugate( $string3 );
15
16  sub conjugate
17  {
18     my $string = shift;
19     print "$string\n";
20     $string =~ s/(?<=i )be/am/;
21     $string =~ s/(?<=we )be/are/;
22     $string =~ s/(?<=he )be/is/;
23     print "$string\n";
24  }
```

```
i be hungry.
i am hungry.
we be here.
we are here.
he be where?
he is where?
```

Fig. 8.10 Look-behind assertion.

8.9 Backreferences

Perl's regular-expression engine allows you to use values that were previously matched. These values are called *backreferences*. The program in Fig. 8.11 shows how to use backreferences in a pattern.

Consider the regular expression in line 20:

```
$string =~ /(\w)\W*(\w)\W*(\w)\W*(\w)\W*\4\W*\3\W*\2\W*\1/
```

Let's examine this expression piece by piece. We are telling the regular-expression engine to match any word character, followed by any number of nonword characters, followed by any word character, etc. Then we reach **\4**. This expression is called a *backreference*. In regular expressions, parentheses *capture* bits of a string that can be referenced later in a pattern with a ****, followed by a number that indicates the set of parentheses that captured the value. In this example, the character that the first **\w** matches inside the parentheses gets stored as **\1**. The next gets stored as **\2**, the next as **\3** and the last as **\4**. So, when we next ask for **\4\W*\3\W*\2\W*\1**, we are simply asking for the first four letters in reverse order, with any number of nonword characters between them. So, the whole expression is trying to match an eight-letter palindrome. The second part of the **if** statement (after the **or**) tries to find a seven-letter palindrome. Put together, these two statements will find any palindrome seven letters or eight letters long within the given string (this is to handle the even and odd cases for a palindrome). Note that the palindrome might be even longer; however, this program does not check for that case.

```
1   #!usr/bin/perl
2   # Fig. 8.11: fig08_11.pl
3   # Using backreferencing to find palindromes.
4
5   use strict;
6   use warnings;
7
8   my $string1 = "madam im adam";
9   my $string2 = "the motto means something";
10  my $string3 = "no palindrome here";
11
12  findPalindrome( $string1 );
13  findPalindrome( $string2 );
14  findPalindrome( $string3 );
15
16  sub findPalindrome
17  {
18     my $string = shift();
19
20     if ( $string =~
21           /(\w)\W*(\w)\W*(\w)\W*(\w)\W*\4\W*\3\W*\2\W*\1/
22        or $string =~
23           /(\w)\W*(\w)\W*(\w)\W*(\w)\W*\3\W*\2\W*\1/ ) {
24        print "$string - ",
25           "has a palindrome of at least 7 characters.\n";
26     }
```

Fig. 8.11   Backreferences within the matching pattern (part 1 of 2).

```
27      else {
28          print "$string - has no long palindromes.\n";
29      }
30  }
```

```
madam im adam - has a palindrome of at least 7 characters.
the motto means something - has a palindrome of at least 7 characters.
no palindrome here - has no long palindromes.
```

Fig. 8.11 Backreferences within the matching pattern (part 2 of 2).

Within a regular expression, backreferencing is accomplished by using a backslash followed by a number. Each number represents a set of parentheses that occur earlier in the pattern: The backreference `\1` denotes the set of parentheses with the leftmost open parenthesis; the backreference `\2` denotes the set of parentheses with the open parenthesis second from the left, and so on.

You can also backreference substrings outside the actual matching pattern. This is done using the `$n` special variables, where **n** is some number. The program in Fig. 8.12 uses this type of backreferencing.

Line 24 contains a fairly complex regular expression. The first part is as follows:

```
(([.!?]|\A)\s*)
```

```
1   #!usr/bin/perl
2   # Fig. 8.12: fig08_12.pl
3   # Capitalize all sentences.
4
5   use strict;
6   use warnings;
7
8   my $string1 = "lets see. there should be two things capitalized.";
9   my $string2 = "This string is fine.";
10  my $string3 = "this could use some work. what needs to be fixed?";
11  my $string4 = "yes! another string to be capitalized.";
12  my $string5 = "all done? yes.";
13
14  capitalize( $string1 );
15  capitalize( $string2 );
16  capitalize( $string3 );
17  capitalize( $string4 );
18  capitalize( $string5 );
19
20  sub capitalize
21  {
22      my $string = shift();
23      print "$string\n";
24      $string =~ s/(([.!?]|\A)\s*)([a-z])/$1\u$3/g;
25      print "$string\n";
26  }
```

Fig. 8.12 Backreferences after the matching pattern (part 1 of 2).

```
lets see. there should be two things capitalized.
Lets see. There should be two things capitalized.
This string is fine.
This string is fine.
this could use some work. what needs to be fixed?
This could use some work. What needs to be fixed?
yes! another string to be capitalized.
Yes! Another string to be capitalized.
all done? yes.
All done? Yes.
```

Fig. 8.12   Backreferences after the matching pattern (part 2 of 2).

First, we have the character class. This class tells the regular-expression engine to search for a period, an exclamation point or a question mark. The character class is alternated with a **\A**, which matches the beginning of a string. If any of these characters matches, we know that the next letter is the beginning of a sentence, and thus the letter should be capitalized. This character (or **\A**) is captured in the second set of parentheses, which also separates the alternation from the rest of the pattern. The engine next matches any amount of whitespace. It will match spaces after punctuation, a tab at the beginning of a string, etc. Next, we have the character class **[a-z]**, which matches any lowercase letter. So, the whole pattern tells the engine to find a sentence-ending punctuation mark or the start of the string, followed by any amount of whitespace, followed by a lowercase letter. The first part will be captured in **$1** and the second part in **$3** (the punctuation or **\A** will be captured in **$2**, but will also get captured in **$3**).

Now we consider the replacement pattern

    $1\u$3

This pattern tells the engine to replace what we found with **$1** (containing everything up to and including the whitespace), and then **$3** (containing the letter that is to be capitalized). In other words, this regular expression searches for the places where a letter might need to be capitalized (the information that gets captured in **$1**), finds the letter to be capitalized (stored in **$3**) and capitalizes it (using **\u**).

This pattern can be changed to enhance performance and readability. The second set of parentheses in the matching pattern is needed only to split the alternation from the rest of the pattern. We do not use its capturing capabilities, and the regular expression would work a little bit faster if the parentheses did not perform their capturing. In Perl, this capturing can be turned off for a given set of parentheses. This feature is actually considered an assertion, but it does not mean anything until you understand backreferencing, so the explanation has been deferred until now. If, instead of using regular parentheses, as in **(pattern)**, you use these modified parentheses, as in **(?:pattern)**, then the parentheses become noncapturing. So, our substitution from the previous example would now be

    s/((?:[.!?]|\A)\s*)([a-z])/$1\u$2/g

While this expression might not look any better, if you know what the **?:** assertion does, the matching pattern is understandable. Now, the substitution pattern does not skip over **$2**, as the previous statement did. It is now obvious which parentheses we are referring to when we use **$1** and **$2**. This change will also increase performance (although in this small program, that benefit is negligible).

8.10 More Regular-Expression Modifiers

The programmer can change how Perl handles certain regular expressions through regular-expression *modifiers*, which are called as such because they do not explicitly change the pattern, but rather how Perl looks at the pattern, the string or the match. Modifiers are usually placed at the end of a statement after the last **/** (or whatever separator you are using). Modifiers can also be specified within a matching pattern with **(?***modifier***)**. The program of Fig. 8.13 demonstrates the **/x** modifier. Section 8.11 revisits the **/g** modifier.

The regular expression in line 16 uses the **/x** modifier, which allows the programmer to add comments and extra whitespace into a pattern in the program's source code. Notice that the substitution pattern is split over lines 12–17. This format allows a programmer to use comments in the middle of a regular expression to explain complicated matching patterns.

Another regular-expression modifier is the **/i** modifier. When you use this modifier, the engine will match the pattern without considering case sensitivity. So, a lowercase "**a**" will match "**a**" or "**A**." This modifier is often useful with data input by the user, because some users might type capital letters, while others may not.

The next two modifiers—**/s**, the *single-line modifier*, and **/m**, the *multiline modifier*—are related. The **/m** stands for multiline mode. It alters whether the caret (**^**) and dollar sign (**$**) match embedded newlines. The **^** and the **$** are regular-expression assertions. Without the **/m** modifier, **^** and **$** only anchor at the beginning and the end of a string; they do not match embedded newlines. In this mode, they are identical to **\A** and **\Z**. With multiline mode turned on, the caret and dollar sign will match at the beginning and at the end of a string, and right before or after an embedded newline. This modifier allows **^** and **$** to match at the beginning and the end of lines in multiple-line strings.

```
1   #!usr/bin/perl
2   # Fig. 8.13: fig08_13.pl
3   # Using the x modifier.
4
5   use strict;
6   use warnings;
7
8   my $string = "hello there. i am looking for a talking dog.";
9
10  print "$string\n";
11
12  $string =~ s/          # start the pattern
13     talking             # match talking
14     \040                # here is a space
15     dog\.               # and then dog and a period
16     /what?/x;           # replace it with 'what?'
17  print "$string\n";
```

```
hello there. i am looking for a talking dog.
hello there. i am looking for a what?
```

Fig. 8.13   Demonstrating modifier **x**.

The /s stands for single-line mode. It alters whether the period, ., matches newlines. Without the /s modifier, the period does not match newlines. With the /s modifier, the period matches newlines.

8.11 Global Searching and the /g Modifier

We have already seen some uses of the /g modifier in programs. These programs mainly used the basic function of the /g modifier to perform global substitutions (i.e., make as many substitutions as possible in the target string). However, there are more complicated uses of this modifier. This section presents additional uses of the global modifier.

When the /g modifier is used with the match operator in a list context, the match operator returns the values captured by parentheses from all possible matches in the list.

The /g modifier used with the match operator in a scalar context produces different results (Fig. 8.14).

```perl
1   #!usr/bin/perl
2   # Fig 8.14: fig08_14.pl
3   # Search perl code for variables.
4
5   use strict;
6   use warnings;
7
8   my $string = '$one $two @three $four @five $six $seven @eight';
9
10  findScalar( $string );
11  findArray( $string );
12
13  sub findScalar
14  {
15     my $string = shift();
16
17     while ( $string =~ m/\$(\w+)/g ) {
18        print "scalar name: $1\n";
19     }
20
21     print "\n";
22  }
23
24  sub findArray
25  {
26     my $string = shift();
27
28     while ( $string =~ m/@(\w+)/g ) {
29        print "array name: $1\n";
30     }
31
32     print "\n";
33  }
```

Fig. 8.14 Picking out variable names from a string (part 1 of 2).

```
scalar name: one
scalar name: two
scalar name: four
scalar name: six
scalar name: seven

array name: three
array name: five
array name: eight
```

Fig. 8.14 Picking out variable names from a string (part 2 of 2).

The **/g** modifier is first seen in line 17, which includes the regular expression

```
$string =~ m/\$(\w+)/g
```

This regular expression looks for a dollar sign (which needs to be escaped in the pattern) followed by some number of word characters. This search is accomplished in a **while** loop condition. The word characters are stored in **$1** (representing the first set of parentheses in the pattern), and then printed in the body of the loop.

Without the **/g** modifier, this match would start from the beginning of the string at each iteration of the loop. This means that the same match (the first one in the string) would be found each time the loop executes and would cause an infinite loop. The **/g** modifier alters the position of the start of the match. Each time the loop executes, the matching operator finds a different substring that matches. This "**while** loop with **/g** modifier" construct is often seen when iterating through all matches in a string.

The position in a string that the **/g** modifier uses can also be altered manually. The command **pos($string)** returns the current position in *string* at which a **/g** match will start. This means that there is only one position for each string. Therefore, you can use the return value of **pos** from one match to begin the search for another match. (Note that **pos** returns the position just after the match.) You can also use **pos** as an *lvalue*. This means that you can manually set the starting point of a match. Finally, you can **reset** the position of a string. This will make the next match start from the beginning of the string.

There is also a **\G** modifier. This modifier is actually more of an assertion, in that it is inserted into the match pattern and adds zero length to the match, but it cannot be used without the **/g** modifier, so it is usually considered as a modifier. The **\G** modifier is similar to the **\A** assertion, except while the **\A** matches only the beginning of a string, **\G** matches only where the previous **/g** match left off.

Another modifier used with the **/g** modifier is the **/c** modifier, which tells the regular-expression engine not to reset the search position after a failed match.

8.12 Example: Form Verification

Figure 8.15 demonstrates how you can use regular expressions to verify user input from an HTML form. This program consists of an HTML page that displays a form and a CGI script that verifies the form's data and returns the data as a simple Web page.

The HTML document in Fig. 8.15 is fairly straightforward. The page consists of a form with five fields: first name, last name, phone number, date and time. These fields are specified in lines 14–27. Line 12 specifies the form's method as **POST**, and the action is to run the Perl script in Fig. 8.16, a CGI script that processes the information sent from the form to the Web server. Lines 29 and 30 specify a **submit** and **reset** button for the form.

Figure 8.16 presents the CGI script that processes the information entered into the form from **fig08_15.html**.

Lines 9–13 store the parameters from the Web page into variables that are used later in the code to formulate the part of the Web page that will be returned to the client. Lines 15 and 16 begin the document that will be returned to the client. The rest of the program (except for line 52, which ends the document) parses and validates the data entered by the user with regular expressions.

Let us look at each parameter individually. The **if** structure of line 18

```
if ( $firstName =~ /^\w+$/ )
```

uses the regular expression **/^\w+$/**. As mentioned earlier, the **^** assertion matches at the beginning of the string, and the **$** assertion matches at the end of the string. Within these two assertions is the **\w+** pattern, which checks for one or more words. The condition in this **if** structure executes if there are one or more words that make up the entire string (the words must be at the beginning and the end, because of the **^** and **$** assertions). We use the **+** so that we know there is at least one word. If not, the **if** structure's body does not execute. A hello message should be printed only if the Web page's user entered their first name. In this case, a personal greeting will be printed to the user. The **\L** in this statement puts the remaining string in lowercase letters and the **\u** makes the letter right after the string uppercase. Together, these expressions will print the first letter in uppercase and the subsequent letters in lowercase, regardless of what the user entered. Lines 22–24 work similarly to print out a personal greeting with the user's last name.

```
1   <!DOCTYPE html PUBLIC "-//W3C//DTD HTML 4.0 Transitional//EN">
2   <!-- Fig. 8.15: fig08_15.html -->
3
4
5   <html>
6   <head>
7   <title>form page</title>
8   </head>
9
10  <body>
11  <p>here's my test form</p>
12  <form method = "post" action = "/cgi-bin/fig08_16.pl">
13
14  <p>First name:
15  <input name = "firstName" type = "text" size = "20"></p>
16
17  <p>Last name:
18  <input name = "lastName" type = "text" size = "20"></p>
19
20  <p>Phone number:
21  <input name = "phone" type = "text" size = "20"></p>
22
```

Fig. 8.15   HTML to generate a simple form (part 1 of 2).

```
23    <p>Date (MM/DD/YY):
24    <input name = "date" type = "text" size = "20"></p>
25
26    <p>Time (HH:MM:SS):
27    <input name = "time" type = "text" size = "20"></p>
28
29    <input type = "submit" value = "submit">
30    <input type = "reset" value = "reset">
31
32    </form>
33    </body>
34
35    </html>
```

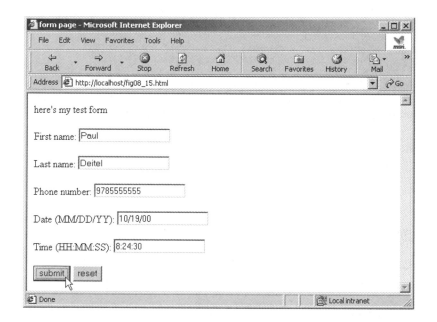

Fig. 8.15   HTML to generate a simple form (part 2 of 2).

Lines 26–42 present a complex regular expression for matching telephone numbers. We discuss the expression in parts. Lines 26 and 39 of the expression are similar to the first part of the program. Using ^ and $, they ensure that the pattern being matched is at the beginning and the end of the string. (In other words, we are parsing the entire string.) The modifier **/x** placed at the end of the regular expression allows us to add easy-to-read comments that explain the expression. The part of the expression on line 27 checks for the 1 that a person might enter before his or her phone number (perhaps to dial long distance). We use **?:** to avoid capturing this value, as it is extraneous. Let us examine the remainder of the expression (lines 28–38) by first seeing it as one line:

```
(?: \(((\d{3})\) | (\d{3})) -? (\d{3}) -? (\d{4})
```

```perl
1   #!/usr/bin/perl
2   # Fig. 8.16: fig08_16.pl
3   # Form processing CGI program.
4
5   use strict;
6   use warnings;
7   use CGI ':standard';
8
9   my $firstName = param( "firstName" );
10  my $lastName = param( "lastName" );
11  my $phone = param( "phone" );
12  my $date = param( "date" );
13  my $time = param( "time" );
14
15  print header();
16  print start_html( -title => "form page" );
17
18  if ( $firstName =~ /^\w+$/ ) {
19     print "<p>Hello there \L\u$firstName.</p>";
20  }
21
22  if ( $lastName =~ /^\w+$/ ) {
23     print "<p>Hello there Mr./Ms. \L\u$lastName.</p>";
24  }
25
26  if ( $phone =~ /^        # beginning of line
27        (?:1-?)?           # optional 1-
28        (?:                # start alternate
29           \(              # left paren
30           (\d{3})         # capture three digits
31           \)              # right paren
32        |                  # or
33           (\d{3})         # capture three digits
34        )                  # end alternate
35        -?                 # optional dash
36        (\d{3})            # capture three more digits
37        -?                 # optional dash
38        (\d{4})            # capture the final four digits
39        $/x )              # end of line, with x modifier
40  {
41     print "<p>Your phone number is ", $1 || $2 , " - $3 - $4.</p>";
42  }
43
44  if ( $date =~ m#^(1[012]|0?[1-9])/([012]?\d|3[01])/(\d\d)$# ) {
45     print "<p>The date is $1 / $2 / $3.</p>";
46  }
47
48  if ( $time =~ m#^(1[012]|[1-9]):([0-5]\d):([0-5]\d)$# ) {
49     print "<p>The time is $1 : $2 : $3.</p>";
50  }
51
52  print end_html();
```

Fig. 8.16 Form-processing script (part 1 of 2).

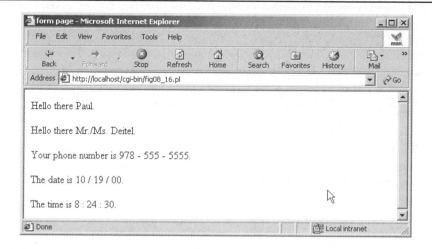

Fig. 8.16   Form-processing script (part 2 of 2).

Once again, we use **?:** (line 28) so that the value in the set of parentheses (lines 28–34) is not captured. The **?:** does not apply to the nested parentheses in lines 30 and 33. These values can be captured. Lines 29–33 use alternation. We are checking for the pattern in lines 29–31 or for the pattern in line 33. The first part captures three digits and stores them in **$1** if the three digits are in parentheses. Otherwise, an attempt is made to match the other case, where the first three digits are captured and stored in **$2**. This alternation accounts for the fact that some people enter their area code surrounded by parentheses and some do not. Either way, this part of the string is parsed and the area code is entered into one of the two variables. Line 35 (and subsequently line 37) checks for a dash, which the user may or may not enter. The **?** after the dash checks for zero or one dash. All that is left are lines 36 and 38, which are very similar to line 33. The first part captures the first three digits of the phone number, and the second part captures the last four digits of the phone number, storing them in **$3** and **$4**, respectively. Line 41 formats and outputs the area code and phone number.

The remainder of the code parses the date and time entered by the user. Both use the matching operator (**m//**), but use **#** delimiters instead of **/** delimiters. If the result of the regular expression (line 44) is found in **$date**, the **print** statement in line 45 executes. The first part is another example of alternation,

```
(1[012]|0?[1-9])
```

which checks for the month. The first half checks for a one followed by one of the digits 0, 1 or 2 (i.e., months 10, 11 and 12). This locates the numbers for the months October, November and December. If one of these numbers is found, its value is stored in **$1**. Otherwise, we check the next half of the alternation. This part first determines if the user input an optional **0** followed by a digit from 1 through 9, denoting the first 9 months of the year. The result is stored in **$1**. After the first slash is another alternation that checks for the day of the month and stores it in **$2**. It checks for any value up to 31. Notice that in this part we have **[012]?\d**. The **?** checks for (at most) one digit in the beginning, this digit being 0, 1 or 2. This may not occur at all, because if the day is under 10, then there will be only one digit, which will be caught by the **\d**. For the year, we store two digits (**\d\d**) in **$3**. Line 45 formats and outputs the date.

Lines 48–50 work similarly to parse the time and format it for output. Here, the slashes are replaced by the expected **:** from the user and we search for values that someone would enter for the time of day, such as 0 to 59 for the minutes or seconds.

8.13 Internet and World Wide Web Resources

mail.csai.com/retran/biblio/perl-re.html
This Web page summarizes regular expression syntax.

www.troubleshooters.com/codecorn/littperl/perlreg.htm
This Web page contains an introduction to regular expressions.

www.perl.com/pub/doc/manual/html/pod/perlre.html
Perl.com's Perl regular expression page.

virtual.park.uga.edu/humcomp/perl/regex2a.html
This Web page provides a tutorial on Perl regular expressions.

www.harefield.nthames.nhs.uk/nhli/protein/perl_re.html
This Web page summarizes the metacharacters used in regular expressions.

www.geocities.com/SiliconValley/Bay/3464/regex.htm#Table
This Web page discusses literal patterns, character sets, etc.

www.softpanorama.org/Scripting/Perl/Ch05_regex/regex_overview.shtml
This Perl tutorial page provides an overview of regular expressions.

SUMMARY

- Perl text manipulation is often accomplished with regular expressions—patterns of characters used to search through text files and databases.
- Regular expressions allow complex searches to be performed using relatively simple expressions.
- Regular expressions are particularly useful when the programmer cannot guarantee that a user will type a string in the expected syntax.
- The matching operator (**m//**) searches for a pattern in a string.
- The binding operator **=~** binds the string on its left to a regular expression operator on its right, allowing the regular expression to be applied to the string.
- Regular expressions operate on the value in special variable **$_** if not bound to a specific string.
- By default, regular expressions are case sensitive.
- A regular expression can contain more than just literal characters.
- The syntax of the **m//** operator is flexible. Its forward slashes are not required; any nonalphanumeric, nonwhitespace character can serve as a delimiter character.
- When forward slashes delimit the matching operator's pattern, the **m** prefix is optional.
- Strings in single quotes are not interpolated.
- We may use **!~** in place of the binding operator to negate the value returned by **m//**.
- When using the substitution operator, **s///**, place the pattern to be replaced between the first two slashes and the substitution pattern between the second two slashes.
- The substitution operator uses the binding operator to specify the string in which to search. The substitution operator can use delimiters other than **/**.

- Modifiers change how a regular expression works.
- The global modifier, **/g** at the end of a regular expression causes the substitution operator to replace every occurrence of the first pattern with the second pattern.
- When the substitution operator performs a global substitution and the value returned is in scalar context, **s///** returns the number of substitutions. In a list context, **s///** returns a list of substrings that were changed in the original string.
- Regular expressions can use special characters and character classes.
- The special character **\d** matches any digit, and **\D** matches any nondigit.
- Brackets (**[]**) enclose a character class to separate it from the surrounding pattern. Inside the brackets, a dash indicates a range. Repeated characters in a character class are ignored.
- A word character is any alphanumeric character or the underscore. The special character **\w** matches any word character, and **\W** matches any nonword character.
- A whitespace character is a space, a tab, a carriage return, a newline or a form feed. The special character **\s** matches any whitespace character, and **\S** matches any nonwhitespace character.
- The dot special character (**.**) matches everything except a newline.
- Alternation chooses one word or pattern from a list of words or patterns.
- The alternation symbol is the vertical bar (or pipe symbol) **|**. The alternation symbol has the lowest precedence of all the symbols. This means that it is performed last.
- Perl regular expressions use special symbols called quantifiers to match more than one instance of a pattern at a time.
- The asterisk (*****) quantifier matches any number of (including zero) the preceding pattern.
- The plus (**+**) quantifier matches one or more occurrences of a pattern.
- The question mark (**?**) matches 0 or 1 occurrences of a pattern.
- Using braces around a number, as in **{n}**, matches exactly *n* occurrences of the pattern.
- Placing two numbers in braces separated by a comma, as in **{n,m}**, matches from *n* to *m*, inclusive, occurrences of the pattern.
- Quantifiers are inherently greedy; a ***** or **+** matches the maximum number of occurrences of a pattern that satisfies the regular expression.
- The question mark (**?**) indicates that quantifiers should be nongreedy. If the question mark is placed after a quantifier, it makes that quantifier nongreedy. This means that the quantifier will match the least number of occurrences of a pattern that still satisfies the regular expression.
- Assertions are similar to the special characters we saw previously, except they are zero width. This means that they do not add any length to the matched string, and they do not change the string.
- Assertions can be used in matching patterns, substitution patterns and even in strings.
- Assertion **\u** makes the next letter uppercase and the **\l** assertion makes the next letter lowercase.
- The **\U** and **\L** assertions raise or lower the case, respectively, of the rest of the text until a **\E** is found or the end of the regular expression or string is reached.
- The **\Q** assertion escapes all nonalphabetic characters until it reaches **\E** or the end of the string or regular expression is reached.
- The caret (**^**) and **\A** assertions match at the beginning of a string.
- The dollar sign (**$**) and **\Z** assertions match at the end of a string or right before the newline at the end of a string.
- The **\z** assertion matches only at the end of a string.

- There are also word-boundary assertions. To match a word boundary, use **\b**. To match a nonword boundary, use **\B**. These assertions ensure that a pattern you are matching is a stand-alone word. A word boundary is defined to be a spot in the string where there is a **\w** character on one side and a **\W** character on the other side (these characters can be on either side).

- Another type of assertion is the look-behind assertion. This assertion takes the form

    (?<=*value1***)** *value2*

    in which it is determined if *value1* occurred right before *value2*.

- Other assertions include the look-ahead assertion, **(?=pattern)**, and the complementary not look-ahead and not look-behind assertions, **(!=pattern)** and **(!<=pattern)**, respectively.

- Perl's regular-expression engine allows you to use values that were previously matched. These are called *backreferences.* Within a regular expression, backreferencing is accomplished with a backslash followed by a number. Each number represents a set of parentheses earlier in the pattern. The backreference **\1** denotes the set of parentheses with the leftmost open parenthesis; the backreference **\2** denotes the set of parentheses with the open parenthesis second from the left, and so on.

- You can also backreference substrings outside the actual matching pattern. This is done using the **$n** special variables, where **n** is some number.

- Capturing can be turned off for a given set of parentheses. If, instead of using regular parentheses, as in **(***pattern***)**, you use modified parentheses, as in **(?:***pattern***)**; then the parentheses become noncapturing.

- Regular-expression modifiers change how Perl handles certain regular expressions. They do not explicitly change the pattern, but rather how Perl looks at the pattern, the string or the match. Modifiers are usually placed at the end of a statement after the last **/** (or whatever separator you are using). Modifiers can also be specified within a matching pattern by using **(?***modifier***)**.

- The **/x** modifier allows the programmer to add comments and extra whitespace into a pattern in the program's source code.

- The **/i** modifier matches a pattern without considering case sensitivity. So a lowercase "**a**" will match "**a**" or "**A**." This modifier is often useful with data input from the user, because some users might type capital letters, and others may not.

- The **/m** stands for multiline mode. It alters whether the caret (**^**) and dollar sign (**$**) match embedded newlines. The **^** and the **$** are regular-expression assertions. Without the **/m** modifier, **^** and **$** anchor only at the beginning and the end of the string; they do not match embedded newlines. In this mode, they are identical to **\A** and **\Z**. With multiline mode turned on, the caret and dollar sign will match at the beginning and the end of a string and right before or after an embedded newline. This allows **^** and **$** to match the beginning and the end of lines in multiple-line strings.

- The **/s** alters whether the period **.** matches newlines. Without the **/s** modifier, the period does not match newlines. With the **/s** modifier, the period matches newlines.

- When the **/g** modifier is used with the match operator in a list context, the match operator returns the values captured by parentheses from all possible matches in the list.

- The **/g** modifier alters the position of the start of a match. Hence, if we loop through a string, the matching operator finds different substrings that match. This "**while** loop with **/g** modifier" construct is often seen when iterating through all matches in a string.

- The position in a string that the **/g** modifier uses can be altered manually. The command **pos(** *$string* **)** returns the current position in the string at which a **/g** match will start. You can also use **pos** as an lvalue. This means that you can manually set the starting point of a match.

- You can also **reset** the position of a string. This will make the next match start from the beginning of the string.

- The **\G** modifier is similar to the **\A** assertion, except while **\A** matches only the beginning of a string, **\G** matches only where the previous **/g** match left off.

- Another modifier used with the **/g** modifier is the **/c** modifier, which tells the regular-expression engine not to reset the search position after a failed match.

TERMINOLOGY

!~ operator	global modifier
$ regular-expression assertion	global modifier, **/g**
$n special variable	global searching
* quantifier	global substitution
/g global modifier	greediness
/g modifier	greedy quantifiers
/m multiline modifier	HTML form verification
/s single-line modifier	instances of a pattern
\a pattern match	look-ahead assertion
\A pattern match	look-behind assertion
\b assertion	**m** prefix
\B assertion	**m//** matching operator
\d	matching operator, **m//**
\G modifier	matching pattern
\l assertion	multiline modifier, **/m**
\o assertion	nongreedy quantifier
\u assertion	operator **!~**
\z pattern match	pattern (**n**) sequential
\Z pattern match	pattern (**n, m**)
^ regular expression assertion	pattern **?**
| alternation symbol	pattern **+**
+ quantifier	quantifier greediness
=~ binding operator	quantifier, *****
alternation	quantifiers
alternation symbol, **|**	regular expression
assertions	regular-expression assertion **$**
backreferences	regular-expression assertion **^**
backreferences	regular-expression modifiers
binding operator, **=~**	**reset** position of a string
capture	**s///** substitution operator
caret, **^**	single-line modifier, **/s**
character classes	special characters
character-class shortcuts	substitution operator, **s///**
delimiter	substitution pattern
dot, **.**	word character
expression modifiers	zero-width assertions
form verification	

SELF REVIEW EXERCISES

8.1   Fill in the blanks in each of the following statements:

a)   A _____ is any alphanumeric character or the underscore.

b) The _____ special character matches everything except the newline.

c) The _____ quantifier tells the regular-expression engine to match one or more instances of a pattern.

d) The _____ takes two patterns: one it will search for, and one that will replace the first pattern.

e) Perl's regular-expression engine allows you to use values that were previously matched. These values are called _____.

f) The _____ modifier allows the programmer to add comments and extra whitespace into a pattern in the program's source code.

g) The _____ and _____ assertions match at the beginning of a string, while the _____ and _____ assertions match at the end of the string (or right before a newline).

h) The alternation symbol is the _____.

8.2   State whether each of the following is *true* or *false*. If *false*, explain why.

a) A question mark after a quantifier means that the quantifier will match the most number of instances in a pattern.

b) The matching operator, **m//**, can use any nonalphanumeric, nonwhitespace character as a delimiter.

c) The **\u** assertion makes the next letter uppercase, and the **\l** makes the next letter lowercase. The **\U** and **\L** assertions raise or lower the case, respectively, of the rest of the text until a **\E** is found or the end of the regular expression or string is reached.

d) The binding operator (**=~**) binds whatever is on its left side to a regular expression on its right and allows the matching function to be applied to this string.

e) With the **/m** multiline modifier, **^** and **$** anchor only at the beginning and the end of the string; they do not match embedded newlines.

8.3   Write a program that does the following, using regular expressions where applicable:

a) Prompt the user for their birthday. They may enter it in either of the following forms:

```
1/2/34
05/06/78
```

b) Take the string the user entered and use a regular expression to determine what month and year the user was were born in.

c) Use the function **localtime** and parse it to find out what month and year we are in.

d) Calculate how many months are left until the user's birthday (roughly).

e) Print this information out for the user.

8.4   Find the error in each of the following regular expressions:

a) `$string =~ ($(\d*)^);`

b) `$string =~ m\[1-9]\;`

c)
```
$string =~ s/    # start the pattern
   (\w+)         # match any number of words
   (\D?)         # match a non-digit
   /no digits/;  # replace with 'what?'
```

d) `$string =~ s/(?=<i )be/am/;`

ANSWERS TO SELF REVIEW EXERCISES

8.1   a) word character. b) dot. c) plus (**+**). d) substitution operator (**s///**). e) backreferences. f) **\x**. g) caret (**^**), **\A**, dollar sign (**$**), **\Z**. h) vertical bar or pipe symbol.

8.2   a) False. If we use the question mark after a quantifier, then the quantifier will match the least number of instances of a pattern that still satisfies the regular expression.

b) True.

c) True.

d) True.

e) False. Without the **/m** modifier, **^** and **$** anchor only at the beginning and the end of the string; they do not match embedded newlines.

8.3 See the following code:

```perl
1   #!/usr/bin/perl
2   # Exercise 8.3: Ex08_03.pl
3   # Comparing months of the year.
4
5   use strict;
6   use warnings;
7
8   my $CurrentMonth;
9   my $totalMonths = 12;
10
11  my $currentDate = scalar( localtime() );
12
13  if ( $currentDate =~ /^(\w{3})(\s{1})(\w{3})/ ) {
14      $CurrentMonth = $3;
15  }
16
17  print "Please enter your birthday: ";
18  chomp( my $birthday = <STDIN> );
19
20  my $birthdayMonth;
21
22  if ( $birthday =~ m#^(1[012]|0?[1-9])/([012]?\d|3[01])/(\d\d)$# ) {
23      $birthdayMonth = $1;
24  }
25
26  if ( $CurrentMonth eq "Jan" ) {
27      $CurrentMonth = 1;
28  }
29  elsif ( $CurrentMonth eq "Feb" ) {
30      $CurrentMonth = 2;
31  }
32  elsif ( $CurrentMonth eq "Mar" ) {
33      $CurrentMonth = 3;
34  }
35  elsif ( $CurrentMonth eq "Apr" ) {
36      $CurrentMonth = 4;
37  }
38  elsif ( $CurrentMonth eq "May" ) {
39      $CurrentMonth = 5;
40  }
41  elsif ( $CurrentMonth eq "Jun" ) {
42      $CurrentMonth = 6;
43  }
44  elsif ( $CurrentMonth eq "Jul" ) {
45      $CurrentMonth = 7;
46  }
```

```
47   elsif ( $CurrentMonth eq "Aug" ) {
48       $CurrentMonth = 8;
49   }
50   elsif ( $CurrentMonth eq "Sep" ) {
51       $CurrentMonth = 9;
52   }
53   elsif ( $CurrentMonth eq "Oct" ) {
54       $CurrentMonth = 10;
55   }
56   elsif ( $CurrentMonth eq "Nov" ) {
57       $CurrentMonth = 11;
58   }
59   else {
60       $CurrentMonth = 12;
61   }
62
63   my $difference;
64
65   if ( $CurrentMonth >= $birthdayMonth ) {
66       $difference = $totalMonths + $birthdayMonth - $CurrentMonth;
67   }
68   else {
69       $difference = $birthdayMonth - $CurrentMonth;
70   }
71
72   print "$difference months until your birthday month!\n";
```

```
Please enter your birthday: 8/8/88
10 months until your birthday month!
```

```
Please enter your birthday: 01/9/89
3 months until your birthday month!
```

8.4   a) Error: The **^** and **$** are out of order.
Correction: Exchange the positions of **^** and **$**.
b) Error: The character **** causes an error when it is used as a delimiter.
Correction: Choose a different delimiter character.
c) Error: Without the **/x** modifier, the additional comments and whitespace in this multiline
regular expression will not be seen as comments by Perl.
Correction: Add the **x** modifier between the **/** and **;** that end the regular-expression statement.
d) Error: The **=** and **?** are out of order.
Correction: Exchange the positions of **=** and **?**.

EXERCISES

8.5   Write a program that will convert the first letter of all words to uppercase. Have it do this for
an arbitrary string input by the user.

8.6   Use a regular expression to count the number of digits, characters, whitespace characters and
words in a string.

8.7   Search through an HTML string and use a regular expression to pick out all valid URLs. A URL is enclosed in quotes and should begin with "`http://`."

8.8   Write a regular expression that will search a string and match a valid number. A number can have any number of digits, but it can have only digits and a decimal point. The decimal point is optional, but if it appears in the number, there must be only one, and it must have digits on its left and its right. There should be whitespace or a beginning or end-of-line character on either side of a valid number. Negative numbers are preceded by a minus sign.

8.9   Write a program that will take HTML as input and will output the number of HTML tags in the string. The program should count the number of tags nested at each level. For example, the HTML:

```
<p><strong>hi</strong></p>
```

has a **p** tag (nesting level 0—i.e., not nested in another tag) and a **strong** tag (nesting level 1).

String Manipulation

Objectives

- To understand the differences between Perl's string types and quote operators.
- To understand how to use "here" documents.
- To be able to use basic string-manipulation functions, such as **substr**, **lc**, **uc**, **index**, **join**, **split** and the **tr///** operator.
- To be able to use **printf** and **sprintf** to format output.
- To be able to use **eval** to interpret strings or blocks of code at runtime.

The chief defect of Henry King
Was chewing little bits of string.
Hilaire Belloc

Vigorous writing is concise. A sentence should contain no unnecessary words, a paragraph no unnecessary sentences.
William Strunk, Jr.

I have made this letter longer than usual, because I lack the time to make it short.
Blaise Pascal

The difference between the almost-right word & the right word is really a large matter—it's the difference between the lightning bug and the lightning.
Mark Twain

Outline

9.1 Introduction

An important part of the solution to any problem is the neat and effective presentation of its results. In this chapter, we discuss the manipulation of strings—our basis for output. The various functions described in this chapter help to manipulate the appearance, order and content of strings.

9.2 Quotes and Quote Operators

As we mentioned in Chapter 2, Perl provides two forms of scalar strings. A *single-quoted string* is any sequence of characters enclosed in single quotes (`'`). You can think of these strings in the most literal sense. Perl views each character enclosed in single quotes as having no special meaning. The only exceptions to this are the escape sequences backslash single quote (`\'`), representing a literal single quote in the string, and backslash backslash (`\\`)—representing a literal backslash. Outside of these exceptions, backslashes have no special meaning in a single-quoted string.

We demonstrate the different cases in which single quotes are used in Fig. 9.1, which mostly consists of **print** statements. Line 8 prints the word **I've**, showing that single quotes recognize the backslash-single-quote escape sequence. The only other escape sequence that is recognized is the backslash backslash escape sequence, as demonstrated on line 15. Other escape sequences print literally, as shown in line 10, which prints **\n** after the word **Days**. A newline may be added by formatting a single-quoted string exactly as it should appear on the screen (lines 19–21).

```perl
1   #!/usr/bin/perl
2   # Fig. 9.1: fig09_01.pl
3   # Demonstrating properties of printing with single quotes.
4
5   use warnings;
6   use strict;
7
8   print 'I\'ve ';          # single quotes interpret "\'"
9   print 'Had Better ';
10  print 'Days. \n';        # single quotes do not interpret "\n"
11
12  print "\n\n";
13
14  # single quotes interpret "\\"
15  print 'Printing a backslash: \\';
16
17  print "\n\n";
18
19  print
20  'La di da
21     di da di';
```

```
I've Had Better Days. \n

Printing a backslash: \

La di da
   di da di
```

Fig. 9.1   Printing with single quotes.

A *double-quoted string* is any sequence of characters enclosed in double quotes (**"**). Double-quoted strings can contain escape sequences such as newline (**\n**), tab (**\t**), or any of a number of other escape-sequence characters. Perl interpolates escape sequences in double-quoted strings. Figure 9.2 contains a table listing escape sequences.

Escape Sequence	Represents
\n	Newline.
\r	Carriage return.
\t	Tab.
\"	Literal double quote (**"**).
\'	Literal single quote (**'**).
\\	Literal backslash (****).
\$	Literal dollar sign (**$**).
\@	Literal commercial at symbol (**@**).

Fig. 9.2   Some of Perl's escape sequences (part 1 of 2).

Escape Sequence	Represents
\%	Literal percent sign (%).
\u	Uppercase next-letter command.
\l	Lowercase next-letter command.
\b	Backspace.

Fig. 9.2   Some of Perl's escape sequences (part 2 of 2).

Perl provides two operators to simplify both the creation and readability of strings. Similar to the **qw** operator, both the **q** and **qq** operators take a series of characters as an argument and create either a single-quoted or a double-quoted string.

The **q** operator surrounds its argument in single quotes. While its function might seem arbitrary, it simplifies the readability of more complex strings. For example,

```
'Don\'t cross the street'
```

which contains an escaped single-quote character, can be replaced by

```
q(Don't cross the street)
```

The **q** operator replaces the opening and closing parentheses with single quotes. Note that an escape sequence is not needed for the nested single quote in the word **Don't**.

The **qq** operator surrounds its argument in double quotes. The resulting string possesses all the features of normal double-quoted strings, including interpolation of escape sequences (see Fig. 9.2) and variables. The double-quoted string

```
"Tim asked, \"What time is it?\""
```

can be replaced by

```
qq(Tim asked, "What time is it?")
```

Note that the nested double quotes do not require an escape sequence.

Operator **qr** creates and compiles a regular expression. This means that the separators used with the **qr** operator can have special meanings (like single quotes and question marks). In addition, modifiers can be specified after the second separator (see Section 8.10). Once a regular expression has been stored in a variable, it can be either interpolated into a matching pattern, or used as the whole match. For example, the statements

```
$string = "snow";
$pattern = qr( snow );
print "matched." if $string =~ $pattern;
```

print the string **"matched."**, because **$string** contains the pattern in **$pattern**.

Although we have chosen to use parentheses with the quote operators in this section, Perl allows programmers to use any delimiter, just as with the regular-expression operators **m//** and **s///**. Thus, the following double-quote operator expressions are each valid:

```
qq(string)
qq/string/
```

qq#string#
qq[string]

Nevertheless, parentheses appear to be the most commonly used delimiters in the Perl community.

Good Programming Practice 9.1

When using quote operators, the delimiters of the string can be included in the string by escaping those characters with \. Rather than escaping the delimiter characters in the string, choose different delimiter characters to make the code more readable.

9.3 "Here" Documents

Perl allows programmers to quote blocks of code. A *here document*, such as

```
<<identifier;
line of text
line of text
identifier
```

enables programmers to create a string over any number of lines of code. A programmer follows the **<<** with a terminating string—that is, an *identifier* followed by the standard semicolon to define the beginning of a here document. Note that there is no space between the **<<** and the *identifier*. Perl quotes the subsequent lines and stops only when the interpreter recognizes the closing *identifier*. For Perl to recognize the *identifier*, it must be both unquoted and at the beginning of an empty line; no other code may be placed on this line, including the *end-of-file marker*, that is, a special marker that ends a file. If the closing *identifier* is on the last line of the program, there must be a carriage return. Note that, while the *identifier* may be quoted, the closing *identifier* may not be.

Common Programming Error 9.1

*A space between the **<<** and the identifier at the beginning a here document causes a logic error. The space causes Perl to cease quoting at the first newline.*

Common Programming Error 9.2

When closing a here document, the identifier must be at the beginning of its own line of code. If there are any other characters on this line, including whitespace, the here document will not be closed.

An optional set of quotes surrounding the *identifier* results in different properties in the here document. Figure 9.3 demonstrates these properties. If the *identifier* is unquoted (line 10) or double quoted, the resulting string inherits the properties of a double-quoted string, including interpolation of escape sequences and variables.

```
1   #!/usr/bin/perl
2   # Fig. 9.3: fig09_03.pl
3   # Demonstration of here documents
4
5   use warnings;
6   use strict;
```

Fig. 9.3 "Here" documents (part 1 of 2).

```
 7
 8   my $notInterpolated = "Interpolated!";
 9
10   print <<DONE;
11   For here documents the type of quotes determines
12   what kind of interpolation is done.  No quotes means
13   double quoted interpolation.  $notInterpolated
14
15   DONE
16
17   print <<'DONE';
18   Single quotes do not allow interpolation.
19   $notInterpolated.
20
21   DONE
22
23   my $variable = <<'DONE';
24   Here documents do not have to be used
25   with the print function.
26
27   DONE
28
29   print $variable;
30
31   ($variable = <<DONE) =~ s/^\s+//gm;
32      All the leading spaces will be
33          ignored so you can indent to
34              your heart's content.
35
36   DONE
37
38   print $variable;
```

```
For here documents the type of quotes determines
what kind of interpolation is done.  No quotes means
double quoted interpolation.  Interpolated!

Single quotes do not allow interpolation.
$notInterpolated.

Here documents do not have to be used
with the print function.

All the leading spaces will be
ignored so you can indent to
your heart's content.
```

Fig. 9.3   "Here" documents (part 2 of 2).

If the *identifier* is single quoted (line 17), the string inherits the properties of a single-quoted string. Lines 23–27 and 31–36 show how the here document does not necessarily have to be used with the **print** function. In this case, a here document is used to assign a multiline string to the scalar **$variable**.

Here documents are often used in CGI scripts as a convenient way to print out large amounts of HTML without making multiple calls to **print**. This format can be used as an alternative to the **CGI.pm** functional shortcuts, thus:

```
print <<HTML;
<html><head><title>Here we are</title></head>
<body>
My web page here. The time is now $time.
</body></html>
HTML
```

9.4 Basic String Functions

Perl provides many useful string functions. Function *substr* returns a substring of a given string. It uses the following syntax:

substr(*string, offset, length, replacement* **)**

Starting from the *offset* number of characters, this function returns *length* number of characters. You can replace the substring with *replacement*, which can be a string or a variable containing a string. To extract characters starting from the beginning of *string*, the *offset* would be zero. If the last argument is omitted, the substring is returned, and *string* remains unchanged.

Both the *offset* and the *length* argument can be either positive or negative values. If the *offset* is negative, the function extracts *offset* number of characters from the end of the *string*. A negative *length* forces the function to extract until *length* characters from the end of the string. Note that the *length* argument is optional. Without a specified *length*, the function extracts from *offset* until the end of *string*.

The *uc* (*uppercase*) and *lc* (*lowercase*) *functions* change the case of each character in an expression and return the resulting string. The **uc** function returns its argument in uppercase. The **lc** function returns its argument in lowercase. If the argument to either function is omitted, the default **$_** is used.

The *ucfirst* and *lcfirst* functions change the case of only the first character in a given expression. The **ucfirst** function returns its expression with the first character in uppercase. The **lcfirst** function returns its expression with the first character in lowercase. If the argument to either function is omitted, the default **$_** is used.

The *length* function returns the length of its expression in characters. Note that **length** returns different values, depending on whether the argument is in double or single quotes. The escape sequences **\n** and **\t** are interpolated as the newline and tab characters only when they appear in double quotes; otherwise, each is considered to be two characters. The argument to **length** must be a scalar value. Specifically, **length(@array)** will not give you the number of elements in **@array**. To find the size of **@array**, simply use **@array** in scalar context. Figure 9.4 demonstrates the functions described in this section.

Lines 12–26 demonstrate the use of the function **substr** with a variety of arguments. We begin by using **substr** with only the first two arguments (line 13). The *string* is **$string**, and the *offset* is 2 (i.e., skip the first two characters), returning everything from the third character to the end of **$string**. The second call (line 15) adds the *length* argument, specifying that the returned substring should skip the first two characters and pick three characters from the string; thus, the substring is **llo**.

```perl
1   #!/usr/bin/perl
2   # Fig. 9.4: fig09_04.pl
3   # Demonstrating basic string functions.
4
5   use warnings;
6   use strict;
7
8   my $string = "hello there\n";
9   print "The original string: ", 'hello there\n', "\n\n";
10
11  # Using substr
12  print "Using substr with the string and the offset (2): ";
13  print substr( $string, 2 );
14  print "Using substr with the string, offset (2) and length (3): ";
15  print substr( $string, 2, 3 ), "\n";
16  print "Using substr with offset (-6), and length (2): ";
17  print substr( $string, -6, 2 ), "\n";
18  print "Using substr with offset (-6) and length (-2): ";
19  print substr( $string, -6, -2 ), "\n\n";
20
21  # replace first 5 characters of $string with "bye"
22  # assign substring that was replaced to $substring
23  my $substring = substr( $string, 0, 5, "Bye" );
24
25  print "The string after the replacement: $string";
26  print "The substring that was replaced: $substring\n\n";
27
28  # convert all letters of $string1 to uppercase
29  $string = uc( $string );
30  print "Uppercase: $string";
31
32  # convert all letters of $string to lowercase
33  $string = lc( $string );
34  print "Lowercase: $string \n";
35
36  # only change first letter to lowercase
37  $string = lcfirst( $string );
38  print "First letter changed to lowercase: $string";
39
40  # only change first letter to uppercase
41  $string = ucfirst( $string );
42  print "First letter changed to uppercase: $string \n";
43
44  # calculating the length of $string
45  my $length = length( 'Bye there\n' );
46  print "The length of \$string without whitespace: $length \n";
47
48  $length = length( "Bye there\n" );
49  print "The length of \$string with whitespace: $length \n";
50
51  $length = length( $string );
52  print "The length of \$string (default) is: $length \n";
```

Fig. 9.4   Basic string functions (part 1 of 2).

```
The original string: hello there\n

Using substr with the string and the offset (2): llo there
Using substr with the string, offset (2) and length (3): llo
Using substr with offset (-6), and length (2): th
Using substr with offset (-6) and length (-2): ther

The string after the replacement: Bye there
The substring that was replaced: hello

Uppercase: BYE THERE
Lowercase: bye there

First letter changed to lowercase: bye there
First letter changed to uppercase: Bye there

The length of $string without whitespace: 11
The length of $string with whitespace: 10
The length of $string (default) is: 10
```

Fig. 9.4   Basic string functions (part 2 of 2).

The next two calls to **substr** (lines 17 and 19) use the first three arguments, but with negative values for the *offset* or *length* of the substring. Line 17 uses an *offset* of -6 and a *length* of 2, printing two letters of this string, starting from the letter **t**, six characters from the end of the string. Note that the escape sequence **\n** is the last character in the string. Line 19 uses the *offset* -6 and the *length* -2, thus printing all of the letters from the **t** six characters from the end of the string up to, but not including, the second-to-last character.

Line 23 uses all of the arguments (*replacement* is set to **"bye"**) with **substr** and assigns the returned value to **$substring**. In this statement, the first five letters of **$string** are replaced with the word **"bye"**, changing **$string** to **"bye there\n"**. The substring that was changed (**"hello"**) is returned and assigned to **$substring**.

Lines 29–30 use operator **uc** to make each letter in **$string** uppercase, and lines 33–34 use operator **lc** to make each letter in **$string** lowercase. Lines 37–38 and 41–42 operate similarly, showing the **ucfirst** and **lcfirst** functions.

The remainder of the program demonstrates the **length** function and how it is used to determine the length of several strings. The first case (line 45) determines the length of the string **'bye there\n'** in single quotes, resulting in the value 11 (remember that the **\n** is not interpolated here). Line 48 determines the length of the same string (**"bye there\n"**), but in double quotes. This case returns the value 10, because **\n** is interpolated as the newline character, rather than as the two characters that compose the escape sequence. When the variable **$string** is passed as the argument to **length** (line 51), the string is interpolated as if it were enclosed in double quotes.

9.5 chop and chomp functions

The **chop** *function* removes the last character from a string and returns that character. While programmers normally use this function to chop off newline characters from the end of user input (**<STDIN>** contains a newline character at the end), **chop** can (and will) remove (and return) any character that is located at the end of a string.

The **chop** function takes a list as an argument (although the list could be a single item). If the argument omitted, the function is applied to **$_** by default. The **chop** function removes the last character of each string in the argument list. Because the function changes its argument, the argument must not be a literal list or a literal string.

Common Programming Error 9.3

*Passing literal lists or strings to function **chop** or **chomp** results in a syntax error.*

The **chomp** *function* "chomps" the last character off the end of a string, if the character matches the contents of the special variable **$/** (*input record separator*). This variable defaults to the newline character, so if the programmer's intention is simply to remove a newline character at the end of a string, **chomp** guarantees that only newlines are removed. The **chomp** only function removes one character from the end of a string, but when provided with a list of strings, **chomp** removes a character from each string in the list (provided that the last character matches **$/**). The **$_** variable is used as the default argument, if no argument is provided. As with the **chop** function, its argument must not be a literal list or a literal string. The **chomp** function returns the scalar number of removed characters.

There is an exception to **chomp**'s behavior. If the **$/** special variable contains an empty string (**""**), then **chomp** removes all of the newline characters at the end of a string. For example, when **chomp** receives the argument **"Hello\n\n\n"**, the resulting string normally would be **"Hello\n\n"**, and the value returned from **chomp** would be 1. However, if **$/** is set to **""**, the resulting string would be **"Hello"**, and **chomp** would return 3. Figure 9.5 highlights the differences between **chop** and **chomp**.

```perl
1   #!/usr/bin/perl
2   # Fig. 9.5: fig09_05.pl
3   # Using the chop and chomp functions
4
5   use warnings;
6   use strict;
7
8   print "Input something and we'll print it: ";
9   my $string = <STDIN>;
10
11  print "\nOur input ( $string ) contains a newline. Remove it:\n";
12  chop( $string );
13
14  print "\nThis is more like it: '$string' without the newline.\n";
15
16  # Removing the last character, regardless of what it is
17  my $character = chop( $string );
18  print "\nOops! We removed $character; now it is '$string.'\n";
19
20  chomp( $string );   # Last character removed only if a newline
21  print "\nAhh. This is safer. Still '$string.'\n";
22
```

Fig. 9.5   Functions **chop** and **chomp** (part 1 of 2).

```
23   my @array = ( "One\n", "Two\n", "Three", "Four", "Five\n" );
24
25   # We can apply chomp to all elements of an array
26   my $newlines = chomp( @array );
27   print "\nWe just removed $newlines newlines from that list!\n";
28   print "\nThe list is now @array.";
```

```
Input something and we'll print it: Hi there

Our input (Hi there
) contains a newline. Remove it:

This is more like it: 'Hi there' without the newline.

Oops! We removed e; now it is 'Hi ther.'

Ahh. This is safer. Still 'Hi ther.'

We just removed 3 newlines from that list!

The list is now One Two Three Four Five.
```

Fig. 9.5   Functions **chop** and **chomp** (part 2 of 2).

Lines 9–14 demonstrate the use of **chop** to remove the newline from our input. When the function is called again in line 17, it causes another character to be removed from the end of the input. Running **chomp** on the current string (line 20) results in no action, because **chomp** removes the last character only if it is a newline (remember that **$/** defaults to **\n**). The last call to **chomp** (line 26) is performed on an array. When this call occurs, **chomp** operates on all of the elements of the array. Because three of the elements in **@array** have trailing newlines, three newlines are removed. Line 28 prints the resulting array on one line, because there are no newline characters remaining.

Figure 9.6 demonstrates several uses of **chomp**. In this program, **$string1** has a trailing **"g"**. When we make the special variable **$/** equal to this value (line 9) and call **chomp** on **$string1** (line 12), the last character is removed. In the second half of the program, we use a string that has three newline characters at its end. Changing **$/** to the empty string causes **chomp** to remove all of the trailing newlines.

```
1    #!/usr/bin/perl
2    # Fig. 9.6: fig09_06.pl
3    # Demonstrating special properties of chomp.
4
5    my $string1 = "This is a string";
6    print "\$string1 is \"$string1\"";
7    print "\n\nChanging \$/ to \"g\" \n\n";
8
9    $/ = "g";
10
```

Fig. 9.6   Properties of **chomp** (part 1 of 2).

```
11   # Removing last character if it is equal to "g"
12   chomp( $string1 );
13   print "The new \$string1 is \"$string1\"\n";
14
15   my $string2 = "This is a string with three newlines\n\n\n";
16
17   print "\n\$string2 now is \"$string2\" <-- Where \$string2 ends.";
18
19   print "\n\nChanging \$/ to \"\" \n\n";
20
21   $/ = "";
22
23   # All trailing newlines are removed
24   my $numberNewlines = chomp( $string2 );
25
26   print "\$string2 was called with chomp.\n";
27   print "It now has no newlines: \"$string2\"";
28
29   # chomp returns the number of characters removed
30   print "\nchomp returned the number $numberNewlines.\n";
```

```
$string1 is "This is a string"

Changing $/ to "g"

The new $string1 is "This is a strin"

$string2 is "This is a string with three newlines


" <-- Where $string2 ends.

Changing $/ to ""

$string2 was called with chomp.
It now has no newlines: "This is a string with three newlines"
chomp returned the number 3.
```

Fig. 9.6   Properties of **chomp** (part 2 of 2).

Testing and Debugging Tip 9.1

*Using **chomp** is a safe method to get rid of a possible newline character. With the **chop** function the possibility of removing an important character from the end of a string remains.*

9.6 `index` and `rindex` Functions

Function ***index*** returns the position of the first occurrence of a given substring within a given string. It uses the following syntax:

> **index(** *string, substring, startPosition* **)**

This function begins searching at the *startPosition* character of the *string* and continues searching until the first occurrence of the *substring* is found in the original string, or until the end of the string is reached. If the substring is not found, the function returns the value **-1**. The *string* can be either literal or scalar. The expression

```
index( 'Perl How To Program', 'How', 0 )
```

returns **5**, because **How** is found at the fifth position (starting from position zero) in the string. The statement

```
index( 'Perl How To Program', 'How', 6 )
```

returns **-1**, because, starting at position six, there are no more occurrences of **How**. Note that *startPosition* is optional. Without this argument, the **index** function starts from the beginning of the string (i.e., position zero).

Figure 9.7 finds and indexes each occurrence of the substring **bab** in a larger string. The **while** condition at line 17

```
while ( ( $foundAt = index( $string, 'bab', $offset ) ) > -1 )
```

searches for **bab** in **$string**, starting from the location **$offset** (which is initialized to zero in line 13). Each time **bab** is found, the location is assigned to variable **$foundAt**, which is compared with **-1**. If **$foundAt** is greater than **-1**, line 18 adds an entry to hash **%positions**, using **$foundAt** as the key. The value associated with the key is a number (stored in **$label**) indicating how many occurrences have been found so far (starting with 1 for the first, 2 for the second, etc.). Line 18 increments the **$label** after placing its value in the hash, and then line 19 adjusts the **$offset** so that the next search will begin one character after the last-found occurrence.

```
1    #!/usr/bin/perl
2    # Fig. 9.7: fig09_07.pl
3    # Demonstration of the index function
4
5    use warnings;
6    use strict;
7
8    my $string = "babaababababbaababbababababaaabblp";
9    print "We're going to number each bab.\n";
10   print $string, "\n";
11
12   my $foundAt = 0;
13   my $offset = 0;
14   my $label = 1;
15   my %positions;
16
17   while ( ( $foundAt = index( $string, 'bab', $offset ) ) > -1 ) {
18      $positions{ $foundAt } = $label++;
19      $offset = $foundAt + 1;
20   }
21
22   foreach ( 0 .. length( $string ) - 1 ) {
23      print $positions{ $_ } ? $positions{ $_ } : " ";
24   }
```

Fig. 9.7   Function **index** (part 1 of 2).

```
We're going to number each bab.
babaababababbaababbbababababaaabblp
1     2 3       4  5 6 7 8
```

Fig. 9.7   Function **index** (part 2 of 2).

When all occurrences have been found, function **index** returns **-1**, and the **while** loop terminates. We then iterate over the **length** of the string, printing out the label if a **bab** was found at that index, and a space otherwise.

The *rindex function* is identical to the **index** function, except that it searches the string in reverse, starting with the last character in the string. For example, the statement

> **rindex('Perl Perl Perl Perl', 'Perl')**

returns **15**—the rightmost occurrence of **'Perl'** in the original string.

9.7 Function **join**

The *join function*

> **join(** *separator,* *list* **)**

joins the individual strings in a given *list* into one string. The returned string contains each string of the *list*, separated by the specified *separator*. The *separator* can be any string, but is normally one containing a comma, a colon or another useful field divider. For example,

> **join(' and ', (1..5))**

takes each entry in the list **(1..5)** and returns a list with each entry separated by the *separator* string **' and '**.

Figure 9.8 **join**s user input into one scalar string. Lines 13 through 16 iterate until the user enters **done**. For each iteration, the input gets **push**ed into **@array**. Line 18

> **$string = join(', ', @array);**

joins each input into one scalar **$string**, separating each input by the separator **', '**.

```
1   #!/usr/bin/perl
2   # Fig. 9.8: fig09_08.pl
3   # The join function
4
5   use warnings;
6   use strict;
7
8   my ( @array, $line, $string );
9
10  print "Input several words on separate ";
11  print "lines, typing \"done\" when finished:\n\n";
12
```

Fig. 9.8   Function **join** (part 1 of 2).

```
13    while ( $line = <STDIN> ) {
14        chomp $line;
15        $line eq 'done' ? last : push ( @array, $line );
16    }
17
18    $string = join( ', ', @array );
19    print "\n$string";
```

Input several words on separate lines, typing "done" when finished:

Now
I
am
one
string
done

Now, I, am, one, string

Fig. 9.8   Function **join** (part 2 of 2).

9.8 Function `split`

The ***split*** *function*

> split(*/RegularExpression/*, *string*, *limit*)

scans a *string* and splits it into separate *fields*. A field is composed of every character between two delimiters (also called *field separators*). Every nonoverlapping match of the regular expression is considered a field separator. The **split** function splits the original string into these fields and returns them as a list, if used in list context. The function returns the number of fields, if used in scalar context. If no matches are found, **split** returns the original string as a single element in a list. The *limit* argument specifies the maximum number of fields into which the function **split**s the string.

All of the arguments to function **split** are optional. The arguments can be omitted from right to left. For example, you cannot omit the *RegularExpression* argument unless both the *limit* and *string* arguments are also omitted. Without the *limit* argument, any fields consisting of empty strings are stripped off of the returned list. If the *string* is also omitted, the **split** function operates on special variable **$_** by default. If all of its arguments are omitted, the function uses the whitespace regular expression **\s+** as a field separator.

Figure 9.9 demonstrates various uses of the **split** function. Line 9 splits on the space character. Line 13 does the same, but only splits the string three ways (because it is given a *limit* argument of **3**). Thus, the substring **be divided up.** stays together. Line 19 gives a character class of delimiters on which to split.

```
1    #!/usr/bin/perl
2    # Fig. 9.9: fig09_09.pl
3    # Demonstrates the split function
```

Fig. 9.9   Function **split** (part 1 of 2).

```
4
5   use warnings;
6   use strict;
7
8   my $string = "I will be divided up.";
9   my @words = split( / /, $string );
10  print "$_\n" foreach ( @words );
11
12  # Divide it into a specific number of fields.
13  @words = split( / /, $string, 3 );
14  print "\n";
15  print "$_\n" foreach ( @words );
16
17  # Divide according to multiple separators
18  $string = "\nI-will:be\@divided-up,*too.";
19  @words = split( /[-:@*]/, $string );
20  print "$_\n" foreach ( @words );
21
22  # Keeping the separators (by having them in parentheses)
23  $string = join( ',', split( /([-:@*])/, $string ) );
24  print "$string\n\n";
25
26  # Defaults to split(' ', $_)
27  $_ = "Separated by whitespace\n";
28  print "$_\n" foreach ( split );
```

```
I
will
be
divided
up.

I
will
be divided up.

I
will
be
divided
up,
too.

I,-,will,:,be,@,divided,-,up,,*,too.

Separated
by
whitespace
```

Fig. 9.9   Function **split** (part 2 of 2).

Line 23

```
$string = join( ',', split( /([-:@*])/, $string ) );
```

splits the **$string**, but keeps the separators. The separators are considered as fields and stored as such. By using parentheses in the matching expression, the **split** function maintains the enclosed separators. These strings are joined together with delimiting commas by using the **join** function.

9.9 `tr///` Translation Operator

Similar to the substitution operator, the *translation operator* substitutes specific characters for ones found in a given string. The *tr operator*

   tr/ *searchCharacters* **/** *replacementCharacters* **/**

uses the binding operator (**=~**) to scan a scalar variable (string) for specific characters listed in the *searchCharacters* and replace them with their corresponding characters in the *replacementCharacters*. If there are more *searchCharacters* than *replacementCharacters*, all of the extra *searchCharacters* are replaced with the last *replacementCharacters*. If the binding operator is not used, the operator searches and modifies variable **$_**. Although the translation operator uses the binding operator, it does not use regular expressions, as do the matching and substitution operators. Instead, the *searchCharacters* and *replacementCharacters* are composed of either individual or logical groups (i.e., 0–9 or A–Z) of characters.

The translation operator allows programmers easily to modify existing strings. For example,

   $existingString =~ tr/a-z/A-Z/;

changes every lowercase alphabetic character in **$existingString** to uppercase. The expression

   $existingString =~ tr/ABC/+-*/;

scans **$existingString** for the letters **A**, **B** and **C**. Every **A** is replaced with a **+** character, every **B** with a **–** character and every **C** with a ***** character. Instead of scanning for a substring, the translation operator scans for individual characters of the set of *searchCharacters* and replaces each with the corresponding character in the *replacementCharacters*.

Figure 9.10 shows the translation operator's effect on two strings. Each letter is changed to its corresponding character, based on the given replacement characters. We use the translation operator for the first time on line 14. The letters **a** to **z**, specified after the first **/**, are translated into the characters following the next **/**. Then, we use the binding operator (**=~**) to assign the translated string to **$string**. In this line, the operator takes each character within the first two backslashes and replaces it with its corresponding character in the last two backslashes. For example, in the string **"lots of letters"**, **"l"** is the 12th element in the first set of characters, so it is replaced with the 12th element in the subsequent set of characters (**,**). The translation operator without the binding operator uses **$_**, as shown in line 15. The translation is performed as before, but it is performed on the string in the special variable **$_**. The string **"hello, cuz"** contains one character that is not in the *searchCharacters* set (**,**) and another character that has no corresponding replacement character (**z**). The comma, like the spaces in each string, is not translated. However, the letter **z** is one of the *searchCharacters*. In this case, it is translated into the last element (**!**) of the *replacementCharacters*. The results are printed in lines 17 and 18.

```
1    #!/usr/bin/perl
2    # Fig. 9.10: fig09_10.pl
3    # Introducing the translation operator
4
5    use warnings;
6    use strict;
7
8    my $string = "lots of letters";
9    $_ = "hello, cuz";
10
11   print "$string\n";
12   print "$_\n\n";
13
14   $string =~ tr/a-z/0123456789.,';)(*&^%#@!/;
15   tr/a-z/0123456789.,';)(*&^%#@!/;
16
17   print "$string\n";
18   print "$_\n";
```

```
lots of letters
hello cuz

,)%^ )5 ,4%%4&^
74,,), 2#!
```

Fig. 9.10   Translation operator.

Figure 9.11 lists the modifiers used with the translation operator. The **/c** modifier scans for the complement of *searchCharacters* (i.e., any characters not in *searchCharacters*), modifying every character not contained in the list. If we look again at the example in Fig. 9.10 and add **/c** to the translations, the program will change the character **'A'**, if it was found, because **'A'** is not in the list **a-z**. The character will be replaced by its translated character in the set of *replacementCharacters*. If the character found is the 14th element of the complement to *searchCharacters*, then it will be replaced by the 14th element of *replacementCharacters*, or **;**. The **/d** modifier deletes characters that are contained in *searchCharacters*, but have no corresponding replacement character in *replacementCharacters*. By default (without **/d**), the translation operator replaces all of these occurrences with the last character in the replacement list.

```
        $example =~ tr/ABCDE/ab/;
```

Modifier	Represents
/c	Replace the complement of *searchCharacters*
/d	Delete characters from *string* that have no corresponding replacement.
/s	Squash duplicate consecutive matches into one replacement

Fig. 9.11   Translation-operator modifiers.

For example, changes each **A** to **a**, each **B** to **b** and, realizing that there are no corresponding values for the remaining search elements, **b** replaces the remaining **C**, **D** and **E**. Using the **/d** modifier on the same expression

```
$example =~ tr/ABCDE/ab/d;
```

replaces every **A** and **B**, but deletes every **C**, **D** and **E** found in **$example**. The **/s** modifier "squashes" duplicate consecutive matches into one replacement, changing **'PPPEERRRLL'** to **'PERL'** with the expression

```
tr/A-Z/A-Z/s;
```

Note that, in the example above, we actually could have written the expression as

```
tr/A-Z//s;
```

because the *searchCharacters* are inserted as the *replacementCharacters*, if the second argument is omitted. Lastly, we can use the **tr///** operator to calculate the number of translations that took place. In the following expression,

```
$numberTranslations = ( $example =~ tr/?/!/ );
```

all of the occurrences of **?** will be replaced with **!** in the string **$example**, and the number of translations made will be assigned to **$numberTranslations**. So, if **$example** is "**Hey there??**", after the expression is evaluated, **$example** will equal "**Hey there!!**" and **$numberTranslations** will be **2**.

9.10 Formatting Outputs with `printf` and `sprintf`

Our outputs to this point have been fairly simple. In general, **print** is powerful enough to output data in almost any manner we could want. However, there are times when you might want more control over your output, desiring *formatted output*. Formatted output allows a programmer to specify output lengths and types, forcing output expressions to be converted into a specific format. The **printf** and **sprintf** functions create precisely formatted outputs.

Every **printf** call contains a *format-control string* that describes the format of the output. The format-control string consists of *literal characters*, *conversion specifiers* and *flags*. Conversion specifiers and flags control *field widths* and *precisions*. Together with the percent sign (**%**), conversion specifiers form the *conversion specifications*. Function **printf** has the following formatting capabilities:

1. *Rounding* floating-point values to an indicated number of decimal places.
2. *Aligning* a column of numbers with decimal points appearing one above the other.
3. *Right justification* and *left justification* of outputs.
4. *Inserting literal characters* at precise locations in a line of output.
5. Representing floating-point numbers in exponential form.
6. Representing unsigned integers in octal and hexadecimal form. See the Appendix, "Number Systems," for more information on octal and hexadecimal values.
7. Displaying all types of scalar data with fixed-size field widths and precisions.

The **printf** function has the following form

> **printf** *format-control-string, other-arguments***;**

The *format-control-string* describes the format of the output, and the *other-arguments*, which are optional, correspond to each conversion specification in the *format-control-string*. Each conversion specification begins with a percent sign and ends with a conversion specifier. There can be many conversion specifications in one *format-control-string*.

A *conversion specification* is a basic output formula. For each conversion specifier, Perl looks for and converts a corresponding argument. The *format-control-string* has the same appearance and rules as every other string we have **print**ed, only with the addition of conversion specifiers. Figure 9.12 lists conversion specifiers and their descriptions.

The program in Fig. 9.13 prints an integer using each of the integer conversion specifiers. Note that negative numbers are displayed with minus signs, but plus signs are suppressed for positive values. Also note that the value -455 is read by **%u** and converted to the unsigned value 4294966841 on a computer with four-byte integers. See your version of Perl's documents for more information on **printf** and **sprintf**.

Conversion specifier	Description
Integers	
%d	Displays a signed decimal integer.
%o	Displays an unsigned octal integer.
%u	Displays an unsigned decimal integer.
%x or **%X**	Displays an unsigned hexadecimal integer. **X** causes the digits **0–9** and the letters **A–F** to be displayed, and **x** causes the digits **0–9** and **a–f** to be displayed.
Floating-point numbers	
%e or **%E**	Display a floating-point value in exponential notation.
%f	Display floating-point values.
%g or **%G**	Display a floating-point value in either the floating-point form **f** or the exponential form **e** (or **E**).
Characters and strings	
%c	Displays a character given an ASCII value.
%s	Displays a string.
%%	Displays a percent sign.

Fig. 9.12   Conversion specifiers.

```
1  #!/usr/bin/perl
2  # Fig. 9.13: fig09_13.pl
3  # Using the integer conversion specifiers
4
```

Fig. 9.13   Integer conversion specifiers (part 1 of 2).

```
 5   use warnings;
 6   use strict;
 7
 8   printf "%d\n", 455.954;
 9   printf "%d\n", +455.34;
10   printf "%d\n", -455;
11   printf "%o\n", 455;
12   printf "%u\n", 455;
13   printf "%u\n", -455;
14   printf "%x\n", 455;
15   printf "%x\n", -455;
```

```
455
455
-455
707
455
4294966841
1c7
fffffe39
```

Fig. 9.13   Integer conversion specifiers (part 2 of 2).

Figure 9.14 demonstrates character and string conversion specifiers. Notice that the *format-control-string* can contain additional conversion specifiers, as shown in line 14

```
printf "%s %s %s %s %s\n", @arrayOfStrings;
```

Because there are only three fields in **@arrayOfStrings**, the function ignores the extra **%s** specifiers.

Function **sprintf** is identical to **printf**, except that it returns, rather than prints, the formatted string. **sprintf** enables you to maintain a formatted string within your program. Figure 9.15 demonstrates **sprintf** returning a formatted string and that string is assigned to **$line**. In the next section, we discuss precision, which is allowing financially related values, such as **$price**, to output exactly two floating digits representing cents.

```
 1   #!/usr/bin/perl
 2   # Fig. 9.14: fig09_14.pl
 3   # Printing formatted characters and strings
 4
 5   use warnings;
 6   use strict;
 7
 8   my $string = "I am a string";
 9   my @arrayOfStrings = ( "An", 'array', "of strings" );
10
11   printf "%c is ASCII value 65 and %c is value 66\n", 65, 66;
12   printf "The string is \"%s\"\n", $string;
13   printf "This string is %s\n", "literal";
14   printf "%s %s %s %s %s\n", @arrayOfStrings;
15   printf "%d%%\n", 45;  # printing a percent sign after 45
```

Fig. 9.14   Printing formatted characters and strings (part 1 of 2).

```
A is ASCII value 65 and B is value 66
The string is "I am a string"
This string is literal
An array of strings
45%
```

Fig. 9.14   Printing formatted characters and strings (part 2 of 2).

```perl
1   #!/usr/bin/perl
2   # Fig. 9.15: fig09_15.pl
3   # Using sprintf
4
5   use warnings;
6   use strict;
7
8   my $product = "sweater";
9   my $price = 39;
10
11  my $line = sprintf "The %s costs \$%d\n.", $product, $price;
12  print $line;
```

```
The sweater costs $39.
```

Fig. 9.15   Function **sprintf**.

9.11 Printing with Field Widths and Precision

The exact size of a field in which data is printed is specified by a *field width*. If the field width is larger than the length of the data being printed, the data normally is right justified in that field and preceded by leading blanks. To format data in a field, an integer representing the field width is inserted between the percent sign (**%**) and the conversion specifier in the conversion specification. The program in Fig. 9.16 **print**s two groups of six numbers each, right justifying the numbers that contain fewer digits than the integer representing the field width. Note that the field width is automatically increased to **print** values wider than the field and that the minus sign for a negative value uses one character in the field width. Field widths can be used with all conversion specifiers.

Common Programming Error 9.4

Not providing a sufficiently large field width to handle a value to be printed can offset other data being printed and can produce confusing output. Know your data!

```perl
1   #!/usr/bin/perl
2   # Fig. 9.16: fig09_16.pl
3   # Printing integers right-justified
4
5   use warnings;
6   use strict;
7
```

Fig. 9.16   Printing integers right justified (part 1 of 2).

```
 8    printf "%4d\n", 1;
 9    printf "%4d\n", 12;
10    printf "%4d\n", 123;
11    printf "%4d\n", 1234;
12    printf "%4d\n", 12345;
13    printf "%4d\n\n", 123456789;
14
15    printf "%4d\n", -1;
16    printf "%4d\n", -12;
17    printf "%4d\n", -123;
18    printf "%4d\n", -1234;
19    printf "%4d\n", -12345;
20    printf "%4d\n", -123456789;
```

```
   1
  12
 123
1234
12345
123456789

  -1
 -12
-123
-1234
-12345
-123456789
```

Fig. 9.16   Printing integers right justified (part 2 of 2).

We can also specify the *precision* with which data is printed. Precision has different meanings for different data types. When used with integer conversion specifiers, precision indicates the minimum number of digits to be printed. If the printed value contains fewer digits than the precision value, zeros are prefixed to the printed value until the total number of digits is equivalent to the precision value. The default precision for integers is **1**. When used with floating-point conversion specifiers **e**, **E** and **f**, the precision is the number of digits to appear after the decimal point. When used with conversion specifiers **g** and **G**, the precision is the maximum number of significant digits to be printed. When used with conversion specifier **s**, the precision is the maximum number of characters to be written from the string. To use precision, place a decimal point (**.**) followed by an integer representing the precision between the percent sign and the conversion specifier. The program in Fig. 9.17 demonstrates the use of precision in format-control strings. Note that, when a floating-point value is printed with a precision smaller than the original number of decimal places in the value, the value is rounded. The program uses the **\t** escape sequence to print tabs.

The field width and the precision can be combined by placing the field width, followed by a decimal point, followed by a precision specification, between the percent sign and the conversion specifier, as in the statement

```
    printf "%9.3f", 123.456789;
```

which displays **123.457** right justified in a nine-digit field, with three digits to the right of the decimal point.

```perl
1    #!/usr/bin/perl
2    # Fig. 9.17: fig09_17.pl
3    # Using precision while printing integers,
4    # floating-point numbers, and strings
5
6    use warnings;
7    use strict;
8
9    my $integer = 873;
10   my $float = 123.94536;
11   my $string = "Happy Birthday";
12
13   printf "Using precision for integers\n";
14   printf "\t%.2d\n\t%.4d\n\t%.9d\n\n", $integer, $integer, $integer;
15
16   printf "Using precision for floating-point numbers\n";
17   printf "\t%.3f\n\t%.3e\n\t%.3g\n\n", $float, $float, $float;
18
19   printf "Using precision for strings\n";
20   printf "\t%.11s\n", $string;
```

```
Using precision for integers
        873
        0873
        000000873

Using precision for floating-point numbers
        123.945
        1.239e+002
        124

Using precision for strings
        Happy Birth
```

Fig. 9.17   Using precisions to display information of several types.

It is possible to specify both the field width and precision by using integer expressions in the argument list following the format-control string. To do so, insert an ***** (asterisk) in place of the field width or precision (or both). The matching argument in the argument list is evaluated and used in place of the asterisk. For example, the statement

```perl
printf "%*.*f", 7, 2, 98.736;
```

uses **7** for the field width, **2** for the precision and outputs the value **98.74**. The value of the argument can be negative for the field width, but must be positive for the precision. A negative value for the field width causes the output to be left justified in the field, as described in the next section.

9.12 Using Flags in the `printf` Format Control String

Functions **printf** and **sprintf** also provide *flags* to supplement their formatting capabilities. Five flags are available for use in format-control strings (see Fig. 9.18).

To use a flag in a format-control string, place the flag immediately to the right of the percent sign. Several flags may be combined in one conversion specification. Figure 9.18 describes the formatting flags.

The program in Fig. 9.19 prints a positive number and a negative number, each with and without the **+** flag. Note that the minus sign is displayed in both cases, but the plus sign is displayed only when the **+** flag is used.

The program in Fig. 9.20 uses the space flag to prefix a space to positive numbers. This flag is useful for aligning positive and negative numbers with the same number of digits.

The program in Fig. 9.21 uses the **#** flag to prefix **0** to the octal value, **0x** and **0X** to the hexadecimal values and to force a decimal point to appear in a value printed with **g**.

Flag	Description
− (minus sign)	Left justify the output within the specified field.
+ (plus sign)	Display a plus sign preceding positive values and a minus sign preceding negative values.
space	Print a space before a positive value not printed with the **+** flag.
#	Prefix **0** to the output value when used with the octal conversion specifier, **o**.
	Prefix **0x** or **0X** to the output value when used with one of the hexadecimal conversion specifiers, **x** and **X** respectively.
	Force a decimal point to be printed in a floating-point number printed with **e**, **E**, **f**, **g** or **G** that does not contain a fractional part. (Normally, the decimal point is printed only if a digit follows it.) For **g** and **G** specifiers, trailing zeros are not eliminated.
0 (zero)	Pad a field with leading zeros.

Fig. 9.18   Flags for format-control strings.

```
1   #!/usr/bin/perl
2   # Fig. 9.19: fig09_19.pl
3   # Printing numbers with and without the + flag
4
5   use warnings;
6   use strict;
7
8   printf "%d\n%d\n", 786, -786;
9   printf "%+d\n%+d\n", 786, -786;
```

```
786
-786
+786
-786
```

Fig. 9.19   Printing positive and negative numbers with and without the **+** flag.

The program in Fig. 9.22 combines the **+** flag and the **0** (zero) flag to print **452** in a 9-space field with a **+** sign and leading zeros, and then prints **452** again using only the **0** flag and a **9**-space field.

```perl
1   #!/usr/bin/perl
2   # Fig. 9.20: fig09_20.pl
3   # Printing a space before signed values
4   # not preceded by + or -
5
6   use warnings;
7   use strict;
8
9   printf "% d\n% d\n", 547, -547;
```

```
547
-547
```

Fig. 9.20   Using the space flag.

```perl
1   #!/usr/bin/perl
2   # Fig. 9.21: fig09_21.pl
3   # Using the # flag with conversion specifiers
4   # o, x, X, and any floating-point specifier
5
6   use warnings;
7   use strict;
8
9   my $integer = 1427;
10  my $float = 1427.0;
11
12  printf( "%#o\n", $integer );
13  printf( "%#x\n", $integer );
14  printf( "%#X\n", $integer );
15  printf( "\n%g\n", $float );
16  printf( "%#g\n", $float );
```

```
02623
0x593
0X593

1427
1427.00
```

Fig. 9.21   Using the **#** flag.

```perl
1   #!usr/bin/perl
2   # Fig. 9.22: fig09_22.pl
3   # Printing with the 0 (zero) flag fills in leading zeros
4
```

Fig. 9.22   Using the **0** (zero) flag (part 1 of 2).

```
5   use warnings;
6   use strict;
7
8   printf( "%+09d\n", 452 );
9   printf( "%09d", 452 );
```

```
+00000452
000000452
```

Fig. 9.22   Using the **0** (zero) flag (part 2 of 2).

9.13 Evaluating Strings as Perl Code

The **eval** *function* takes a single argument (either a string or a block) and evaluates it as Perl code in the body of a program. This function allows for interesting user interactive applications. Consider the following line:

```
eval( $line = <STDIN> );
```

This line will directly execute Perl code input from a keyboard. The **eval** function should be used with extreme caution. For example, a CGI script that lets unknown clients execute arbitrary code on a server would constitute a major security risk. Even the line shown above is a security risk, because the user could input anything, and the program would attempt to execute the code.

The **eval** function returns the value of the last evaluated expression. If a syntax error or other fatal error exists in the block, **eval** returns **undef** and stores the error message in the *special variable $@*. If no error exists, **$@** is set to an empty string. Note that a fatal error in the **eval** block will not prematurely terminate the program. The **eval** function makes the program aware of any problems and stores the resulting message in the **$@** variable. For this reason, Perl programmers use this function to do exception handling.

 Testing and Debugging Tip 9.2

*It is useful when debugging a program to use the **eval** function. This function can be used for exception handling—that is, having the program print a message to the user when certain problems occur, especially if the problem can cause a fatal error. This will aid in finding problems in your code without unexpected program termination.*

Figure 9.23 demonstrates **eval** capturing a normally fatal division-by-zero error.

```
1   #!usr/bin/perl
2   # Fig. 9.23: fig09_23.pl
3   # Capturing fatal errors
4
5   use warnings;
6   use strict;
7
8   my $line = "25 / 0";
9
```

Fig. 9.23   Capturing fatal errors (part 1 of 2).

```
10    eval ( $line; )
11
12    print "There is an error:\n" if $@;
13    print $@;
14    print "Without eval, a fatal error would have ended the program.";
```

```
There is an error:
Illegal division by zero at (eval 1) line 2.
Without eval, a fatal error would have ended the program.
```

Fig. 9.23   Capturing fatal errors (part 2 of 2).

Software Engineering Observation 9.1

*The **eval** function does not provide the user with any safeguards to prevent potential security violations. Using **eval** on user-inputted code should be avoided whenever possible to avoid such security risks.*

Evaluation in the style of **eval** also can be embedded in the substitution operator. The **/e** modifier evaluates the replacement portion of the substitution operator, instead of treating it merely as a string. Figure 9.24 uses the **/e** modifier to evaluate the **uc** function placed in the replacement side of the substitution operator.

The regular expression in line 11

```
(\bw\w+\b)
```

matches a word (surrounded by word boundaries **\b**) beginning with **w** and containing one or more additional letters (**\w+**). The surrounding parentheses cause any matching word to be assigned to **$1**. Variable **$1**, in turn, is used as the argument to the function **uc** in the replacement portion of the substitution operator. The **/e** modifier causes this function to be evaluated after **$1** is interpolated, replacing the found text with an uppercase version of the text.

```
1    #!usr/bin/perl
2    # Fig. 9.24: fig09_24.pl
3    # Using /e modifier to evaluate
4
5    use warnings;
6    use strict;
7
8    my $string = "Let us convert a word to uppercase.";
9
10    print "$string\n";
11    $string =~ s/(\bw\w+\b)/uc($1)/e;
12    print "$string\n";
```

```
Let us convert a word to uppercase.
Let us convert a WORD to uppercase.
```

Fig. 9.24   Modifier **/e**.

SUMMARY

- Perl provides two forms of scalar strings: single-quoted strings and double-quoted strings.

- A single-quoted string is any sequence of characters enclosed in single quotes. Each character enclosed in single quotes has no special meaning, with the exception of \' and \\.

- A double-quoted string is any sequence of characters enclosed in double quotes. Double-quoted strings can use Perl's escape sequences, which are various combinations of the backslash and characters taken by Perl to mean a newline, tab or one of many other control characters.

- The **q** operator surrounds its argument in single quotes.

- The **qq** operator surrounds its argument in double quotes. Such a string supports interpolation.

- The **qr** operator creates and compiles a regular expression.

- A "here" document enables programmers to create a string over any number of lines of code and is formed as follows:

    > <<*identifier;*
    > *line of text*
    > *line of text*
    > *identifier*

   The closing identifier of a "here" document must be at the beginning of its own line of code.

- If the identifier in a here document is unquoted or double quoted, the resulting string inherits the properties of a double-quoted string.

- If the identifier is single quoted, the string inherits the properties of a single-quoted string.

- A "here" document can be used with the **print** function, or it can be used to assign a multiline string to a variable.

- "Here" documents are often used in CGI scripts as an easy way to output large amounts of HTML without making multiple calls to **print** or having to use the **CGI.pm** functional shortcuts.

- Function **substr** returns a substring of a given string. It uses the following syntax:

    substr(*string, offset, length, replacement* **)**

   If the third argument to **substr** is omitted, everything from the offset to the end of the string is returned. If only the fourth argument of **substr** is omitted, the substring is returned, and the original string is unchanged.

- The **uc** (uppercase) and **lc** (lowercase) functions change the case of each character in an expression and return the resulting string. The **uc** function returns its argument in uppercase, while the **lc** function returns its argument in lowercase.

- The **ucfirst** and **lcfirst** functions change the case of only the first character in a given expression. **ucfirst** returns its expression with the first character in uppercase. **lcfirst** returns its expression with the first character in lowercase.

- The **length** function returns the length of its expression in characters. The argument to **length** must be a scalar value.

- The **chop** function removes the last character from a string and returns that character.

- The **chomp** function removes the last character of a string if that character matches the contents of the special variable **$/** (the input-record separator). The function will remove only one character from the end of a string, but when given a list of strings, **chomp** will remove a character from each string in the list, provided that the last character matches **$/**. The function returns the scalar number of removed characters **chomp**ed.

- The special variable **$/** defaults to the newline character, **\n**.

- With both **chop** and **chomp**, the argument must not be a literal list or a literal string, because these functions change their arguments. Both the **chop** and **chomp** functions take a list as an argument. The list can be a single element.

- If the special variable **$/** contains an empty string (**" "**), then **chomp** removes all newline characters at the end of the string.

- Using **chomp** is a safe method of getting rid of a possible newline character. The **chop** function leaves the possibility of chopping an important character off of a string.

- The **index** function returns the position of the first occurrence of a desired substring within a given string. When using **index**, if the substring is not found, the function returns **-1**. The **index** function has the following syntax:

    index(*string, substring, startPosition* **)**

    Without the last argument, the **index** function starts from position zero.

- The **rindex** function is identical to the **index** function, except **rindex** searches in reverse.

- The **join** function joins the individual strings in a given *list* into one string. The returned string contains each string of the *list* separated by a given *separator*. The *separator* can be any string, but is normally one containing a comma, colon or other useful field separator.

- The **split** function scans a given *string* and splits it into separate field, as follows:

    split(*/RegularExpression/, string, limit* **)**

    A field is composed of every character between two delimiters (field separators). Every nonoverlapping match of the regular expression is considered a field separator. The **split** function returns the fields as a list, if used in list context. The function returns the number of fields, if used in scalar context. If no matches are found, **split** returns the original string as a single-element list. The *limit* argument specifies the maximum number of fields into which the string is split. The **split** function's arguments are optional—they can be omitted from right to left.

- Similar to the substitution operator, the translation operator substitutes specific characters for characters found in a given string. The **tr** operator,

    tr/ *searchCharacters* **/** *replacementCharacters* **/**

    uses the binding operator (**=~**) to scan a scalar variable (string) for specific characters listed in the *searchCharacters* and replaces them with the corresponding characters in *replacementCharacters*. If there are more *searchCharacters* than *replacementCharacters*, all of the extra *searchCharacters* are replaced with the last character in *replacementCharacters*. If the binding operator is not used, the operator searches and modifies the variable **$_**. Although the translation operator uses the binding operator, it does not use regular expressions as do the matching and substitution operators.

- The **/c** translation modifier scans for the complement of *searchCharacters* (any characters not in *searchCharacters*), modifying every character not contained in the list.

- The **/d** modifier deletes characters that are contained in *searchCharacters*, but have no corresponding replacement character in *replacementCharacters*.

- The **/s** modifier "squashes" duplicate consecutive matches into one replacement.

- The *searchCharacters* are used as the *replacementCharacters* if the second argument is omitted.

- The **tr///** operator can calculate and return the number of translations that took place.

- The **printf** and **sprintf** functions create precisely formatted outputs. Function **printf** has the form

    printf *format-control-string, other-arguments***;**

The *format-control-string* describes the output format, and (optional) *other-arguments* corresponds to each conversion specification in the *format-control-string*. Each conversion specification begins with a percent sign and ends with a conversion specifier. There can be many conversion specifications in one *format-control-string*. The *format-control-string* consists of literal characters, conversion specifiers and flags.

- A conversion specification is a basic formula for output. For each conversion specifier, Perl looks for and converts a corresponding argument.

- The **sprintf** function is identical to the **printf** function, except that **sprintf** returns, rather than prints, the formatted string.

- The exact size of a field in which data is printed is specified by a field width. If the field width is larger than the length of the data being printed, the data normally will be right justified in that field and preceded by leading blanks. An integer representing the field width is inserted between the percent sign (**%**) and the conversion specifier in the conversion specification. Field widths can be used with all conversion specifiers.

- Functions **printf** and **sprintf** also provide the ability to specify the precision with which data is printed. To specify precision, place a decimal point (**.**) followed by an integer representing the precision between the percent sign and the conversion specifier.

- When used with integer conversion specifiers, precision indicates the minimum number of digits to be printed. If the printed value contains fewer digits than the specified precision value, zeros are prefixed to the printed value until the total number of digits is equivalent to the precision value. The default precision for integers is **1**.

- When used with floating-point conversion specifiers **e**, **E** and **f**, the precision is the number of digits to appear after the decimal point. When used with conversion specifiers **g** and **G**, the precision is the maximum number of significant digits to be printed.

- When used with the conversion specifier **s**, the precision indicates the maximum number of characters to be written from the string.

- When a floating-point value is printed with a precision smaller than the original number of decimal places in the value, the value is rounded.

- The field width and the precision can be combined by placing the field width. followed by a decimal point, followed by a precision, between the percent sign and the conversion specifier.

- It is possible to specify the field width and precision by using integer expressions in the argument list following the format-control string. To do so, insert an ***** (asterisk) in place of the field width or precision (or both). The matching argument in the argument list is evaluated and used in place of the asterisk. The value of the argument can be negative for the field width, but must be positive for the precision. A negative value for the field width causes the output to be left justified in the field.

- Functions **printf** and **sprintf** provide flags to supplement their formatting capabilities. To use a flag in a format-control string, place the flag immediately to the right of the percent sign. Several flags may be combined in one conversion specification.

- The **eval** function takes a single argument and evaluates it as Perl code in the body of a program.

- The **eval** function returns the value of the last evaluated expression. If a syntax error or other fatal error exists in the block, **eval** returns **undef** and stores the error message in the special variable *$@*. If no error exists, *$@* is set to an empty string.

- It is useful when debugging a program to use the **eval** function for exception handling—that is, having the program print a message to the user when certain problems occur. This will aid in finding problems in your code without having the program terminate unexpectedly.

- Evaluation in the style of **eval** can also be embedded in the substitution operator. The **/e** modifier evaluates the replacement portion of the substitution operator, instead of treating it merely as a string.

TERMINOLOGY

%d	format-control string of **printf**
%%	formatted output
– format-control string flag	"here" document
# format-control string flag	**index** function
%c	**join** function
%e	**lc** function
%E	**lcfirst** function
%f	leading zero
%g	left justification
%G	**length**
%o	literal characters
%s	newline
%u	pad a field
%x	precision
%X	**printf** function
/c	**q** operator
/d	**qq** operator
/s	**qr** operator
+ format-control string flag	quote operators
0 format-control string flag	right justification
asterisk as field width	**rindex** function
asterisk as precision	rounding
backspace	**s** translation-operator modifier
c translation-operator modifier	single-quoted string
carriage return	space format-control string flag
chomp function	**split** function
chop function	**sprintf** function
conversion specifiers	**substr** function
d translation-operator modifier	substring
double-quoted string	tab
escape sequence	**tr** operator
eval function	**tr///** function
field-separator translation operator	**uc** function
field width	**ucfirst** function
flag	

SELF-REVIEW EXERCISES

9.1   Fill in the blanks in each of the following statements.
   a) Perl provides two forms of scalar strings: _____ and _____.
   b) The _____ function removes the last character from the string it is given, regardless of what the character is.
   c) The _____ and _____ functions change the case of only the first character in a given expression.
   d) The _____ function returns the position of the first occurrence of a given substring within a given string.

e) The _____ function joins the individual strings in a given list into one string.

f) A _____ enables programmers to create a string over many lines of code.

g) The _____ function returns a substring of a given string.

h) The _____ function is identical to the _____ function, except that it returns, rather than prints, the formatted string.

i) The _____ function takes a single argument and evaluates it as Perl code in the body of the program.

9.2   State whether each of the following is *true* or *false*. If *false*, explain why.

a) When using the **q** operator, double quotes do not need to be escaped; likewise, when using the **qq** operator, single quotes do not need to be escaped.

b) The **chomp** function "chomps" the last character off of the end of a string if that character matches the contents of the special variable **$/**.

c) One can use the **tr///** operator in place of the **uc** and **lc** functions.

d) The **chomp** function will always remove at most one character from a string.

e) The **length** function takes scalars and arrays as an argument.

f) If the last argument of **substr** is removed, the original string is replaced by the substring determined by the function.

g) The **eval** function returns the value of the last evaluated expression.

h) To specify precision in formatted output, place a decimal point (**.**) followed by an integer representing the precision between the percent sign and the conversion specifier.

9.3   Write a Perl statement to accomplish each of the following tasks:

a) Calculate the length of the string **"Hello\n"**. The length should calculate **\n** as one character.

b) Change the string **"Hello"** (in the variable **$string**) so that all of the letters are lowercase. Do this task in three ways, each way with a different function.

c) Use the **substr** function to change the string **"How are you?"** (in the variable **$string**) to **"How are things?"**.

d) Change the string **"Hello\n"** (in the variable **$string**) so that there is no newline at the end. Do this using the function we have stated as the proper one to use in this case.

e) Change the string **"Is it sunny today?"** (in the variable **$string**) into separate strings for each word.

f) Use **printf** to print the value of the variable **$variable** as a hexadecimal number. The letters in the hexadecimal number should be lowercase.

g) Use the **tr///** operator to translate A–Z to a–f, deleting any characters that do not have a corresponding replacement character. Apply this translation to the variable **$string**.

9.4   Write a program to accomplish the following tasks (*Note:* You can use this program to check some of your answers for Exercise 9.3):

a) Prompt the user to enter a Perl string that they want to be evaluated as code. Use a "here" document.

b) Tell the user to enter **"exit"** when they are done.

c) Remove the trailing newline of the string.

d) Use the function **eval** to evaluate the input.

e) Assign the result to the variable **$result**.

f) Print out the solution or error, if there was one.

g) Put parts (c)–(d) in a **while** statement, so that the user can enter as many strings as they want. Do not worry about the program exiting when the user enters **"exit"**; the function **eval** will evaluate this input and end the program.

9.5   State what is wrong with the syntax in each of the following segments of code:

a) **index(0, "hi", "hello");**

b) **chomp 'Is it rainy tomorrow?';**

c) `print <<DONE;`
   `This is text in a Perl`
   `program. DONE`
d) `split( $variable, /[-:@*]/, 5 );`

ANSWERS TO SELF-REVIEW EXERCISES

9.1   a) single-quoted strings, double-quoted strings.   b) **chop**.   c) **ucfirst**, **lcfirst**.
d) **index**. e) **join**. f) here document. g) **substr**. h) **sprintf**, **printf**. i) **eval**.

9.2   a) False. When using the **q** operator, *single* quotes do not need to be escaped, and when using the **qq** operator, *double* quotes do not need an escape sequence.
   b) True.
   c) True.
   d) False. If **$/** is set to the empty string, **chomp** will remove as many trailing newlines as exist in the argument string. Also, if the value of **$/** is not contained in the original string, no characters are removed.
   e) False. The **length** function takes only scalar values as arguments.
   f) False. If the last argument of **substr** is removed, then the substring determined by the function is returned, but the original string is not modified.
   g) True.
   h) True.

9.3   a) `length( "Hello\n" );`
   b) `lc( $string );`
      `lcfirst( $string );`
      `$string =~ tr/A-Z/a-z/;`
   c) `substr( $string, 8, 3, "things" );`
   d) `chomp( $string );`
   e) `@words = split( /[ ?]/, $string );`
   f) `printf "%x\n", $variable;`
   g) `$string =~ tr/A-Z/a-z/d;`

9.4   See the following program.

```
1   #!/usr/bin/perl
2   # Ex. 9.4: ex09_04.pl
3   # Evaluating a user inputted expression.
4
5   print <<prompt;
6   Enter an expression with as many numbers as you want,
7   and we will output the result. Enter "exit" to end.
8   prompt
9
10  while ( <> ) {
11      chomp();
12      $result = eval();
13
14      if ( $@ ) {
15          print "There is an error: \n$@\n";
16      }
17      else {
18          print $result, "\n";
19      }
20  }
```

```
Enter an expression with as many numbers as you want,
and we will output the result. Enter "finished" to end.
25/5
5
25/5*8
40
substr( "Hello There", 6 );
There
uc( "There" );
THERE
finished
```

9.5   a) Error: The arguments of **index** are not in the correct order.
Correction: Swap the first and last arguments.

b) Error: **chomp** cannot accept a literal string as an argument.
Correction: Place the string into a variable, and apply **chomp** to that variable.

c) Error: The "here" document will not execute unless the closing identifier is on a line of its own.
Correction: Move **DONE** to the next line.

d) Error: The arguments of **split** are not in the correct order.
Correction: Switch the first two arguments.

EXERCISES

9.6   Nested **printf** and **sprintf** calls can be useful if you need to format combinations of strings. Write a script that receives as input five numbers from the user. Use a **sprintf** statement as one of the arguments to a **printf** statement in order to print a list of numbers, each with two digits following the decimal point. Each number should be separated by a space, and the list should be right justified in a 35-character-wide field.

9.7   Write a function that takes a list of dollar values separated by commas, converts each number from dollars to pounds (at an exchange rate 0.667 dollars per pound) and prints the results in a comma-separated list. Each converted value should have the £ symbol in front of it. This symbol can be obtained by passing the ASCII value of the symbol **156** to the **chr** function, which returns a string composed of that character. Ambitious programmers can attempt to do the conversion all in one statement.

9.8   Write a program in which the user inputs a sentence. Print the sentence back with the first letter of each word in uppercase. *Hint:* Use **split** and **join**, or use **s///e**.

9.9   One common use of here documents is to print out large amounts of HTML. Rewrite your answer to Exercise 7.9 to use a here document to print out the HTML for the portal page, rather than redirecting the client to a separate file.

10

File Processing

Objectives

- To understand the notion of the data hierarchy.
- To be able to use filehandles to read and write to files.
- To be able to use the **@ARGV** variable.
- To become familiar with sequential-access and random-access file processing.
- To be able to use CGI with file-processing tools.

I can only assume that a "Do Not File" document is filed in a "Do Not File" file.
Senator Frank Church
Senate Intelligence Subcommittee Hearing, 1975

Consciousness ... does not appear to itself chopped up in bits ... A "river" or a "stream" are the metaphors by which it is most naturally described.
William James

Private faces in public places
Are wiser and nicer
Than public faces in private places.
W. H. Auden

It is quite a three-pipe problem.
Sir Arthur Conan Doyle

Outline

Summary • Terminology • Self-Review Exercises • Answers to Self-Review Exercises • Exercises

10.1 Introduction

Storage of data in variables is temporary; all such data are lost when a program terminates. *Files* permanently retain large amounts of data. Computers store files on secondary storage devices, such as disk storage devices. In this chapter, we explain how data files are created, updated and processed by Perl programs. We consider both *sequential-access files* and *random-access files* (also called *direct-access files*).

Perl imposes no structure on a file. Perl thinks of a file as a series of characters. Essentially, all files in Perl can be thought of as text files. Any underlying structure that you wish a file to have must be defined in your program. This means that you could create and use a comma-delimited file, but Perl provides no built-in functions that accomplish this; you would have to program the steps to convert regular output into comma-delimited output and take that comma-delimited output and turn it into useful data. In this chapter, we present techniques to perform such operations.

10.2 Data Hierarchy

Ultimately, all data items processed by a computer are reduced to combinations of zeros and ones. This conversion occurs because it is simple and economical to build electronic devices that can assume two stable states; one of the states represents **0**, and the other represents **1**. It is remarkable that the impressive functions performed by computers involve only the most fundamental manipulations of **0**s and **1**s.

The smallest data item in a computer can assume the value **0** or the value **1**. Such a data item is called a *bit* (short for *binary digit*—a digit that can assume one of two values). Computer circuitry performs such various simple bit manipulations as determining the value of a bit, setting the value of a bit and reversing a bit (from **1** to **0** or from **0** to **1**).

It is cumbersome for programmers to work with data in the low-level form of bits. Instead, programmers prefer to work with data in the form of *decimal digits* (i.e., 0, 1, 2, 3, 4, 5, 6, 7, 8 and 9), *letters* (i.e., A through Z and a through z) and *special symbols* (i.e., $,

@, %, &, *, (,), -, +, ", :, ?, / and many others). Digits, letters and special symbols are referred to as *characters*. The set of all characters that may be used to write programs and represent data items on a particular computer is called that computer's *character set*. Because computers can process only **1**s and **0**s, every character in a computer's character set is represented as a pattern of **1**s and **0**s. This pattern of bits is called a *byte* and on most contemporary computers is typically eight bits long. Programmers create programs and data items as characters. Computers then manipulate and process the characters as patterns of bits. (Note that two-byte data characters are increasingly being used, most notably with the Unicode international character set.)

Just as characters are composed of bits, *fields* are composed of characters. A field is a group of characters that conveys meaning. A field consisting only of decimal digits could represent a number. A field consisting only of letters could represent a string.

Data items processed by computers form a *data hierarchy* in which data items become larger and more complex in structure as we progress from bits to characters (bytes) to fields and so on.

A *record* is composed of several fields. A *file* is a group of related *records*. A company's payroll file might contain one record for each employee. A record might consist of the following fields:

- employee identification number (i.e., social security number)

- name

- address

- hourly salary rate

- number of exemptions claimed

- year-to-date earnings

- amount of federal income taxes withheld, etc.

Thus, a payroll file for a small company might contain only 22 records, whereas a payroll file for a large company might contain 100,000 records. It is not unusual for an organization to have hundreds, or even thousands, of files, with many containing millions, or even billions, of characters of information. Figure 10.1 illustrates the data hierarchy.

To facilitate the retrieval of specific records from a file, at least one field in each record is often chosen as a *record key*. A record key identifies a record as belonging to a particular person or entity. For example, in the payroll file described in this section, the Social Security number would normally be chosen as the record key.

There are many ways of organizing records in a file. The most popular type of organization is called a *sequential file*, in which records are typically stored in order by the record key field. In a payroll file, records are usually placed in order by Social Security number. The first employee record in the file contains the lowest Social Security number, and subsequent records contain increasingly higher Social Security numbers.

Most businesses use many different files to store data. For example, companies may have payroll files, accounts receivable files (listing money due from clients), accounts payable files (listing money due to suppliers), inventory files (listing facts about all the items handled by the business) and many other types of files. A group of related files is sometimes called a *database*. A collection of programs designed to create and manage databases is called a *database management system* (DBMS).

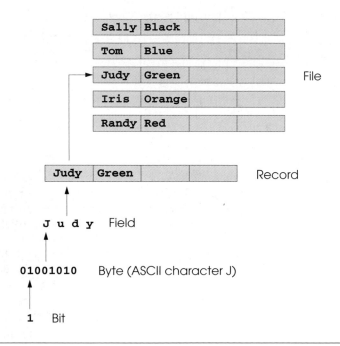

Fig. 10.1   Data hierarchy.

10.3 Filehandles

Perl views every file simply as a sequential stream of characters (Fig. 10.2). Every file ends with an end-of-file marker. When a file is *opened*, a *filehandle* is associated with the file. The filehandle is used to refer to the opened file whenever the programmer wishes to read or write to it. Filehandles are, in a sense, similar to other variables we have seen, except that they are not prefixed by any special character. For this reason, filehandle names usually appear in all uppercase letters, for readability.

Filehandles are not necessarily associated with files on a disk. In fact, three filehandles are opened automatically when program execution begins: **STDIN**, **STDOUT** and **STDERR**. We have seen the first of these (**STDIN**, or *standard input)* used with the syntax **<STDIN>** to get input from the user. We learned in Chapter 7 that function **print** usually outputs to *standard output* (**STDOUT**), though we have not yet seen the filehandle named explicitly. The third, **STDERR**, or *standard error*, indicates a location where a program is to output error messages. (As with standard output, this location is typically the screen).

We will soon see that reading from and writing to files is just as easy as reading from and writing to standard input and standard output.

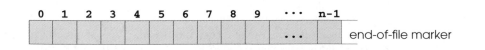

Fig. 10.2   Perl's view of a file of *n* bytes.

10.4 Opening and Closing Filehandles

To use a file in a Perl program, the file must first be opened and associated with a filehandle. This procedure is accomplished with function **open**. An **open** statement normally has the following form:

```
open( HANDLE, 'filename' ) or die( "Cannot open file : $!" );
```

Function **open** receives two arguments. The first is the filehandle name (*HANDLE*), which we use to refer to the file we are opening. The second argument is the *filename* (which is case sensitive in some operating systems). The *filename* can include path information that helps Perl locate the file. Such path information may be operating-system dependent. If the *filename* is specified without path information, Perl assumes that the file is located in the same directory as the program. If the program is able to open the file, then Perl associates the file with the filehandle *HANDLE*. Now, when the program reads from *HANDLE*, it takes input from *filename*. If the program writes to *HANDLE*, it outputs to *filename*.

The second half of the preceding statement handles errors. If the call to function **open** does not succeed, it returns false, and the first part of the **or** statement evaluates to false. This causes the right side of the **or** operator to evaluate, triggering the **die** command, which prints an error message containing the message stored in the **$!** special variable and terminates the program. As we learned in Chapter 5, special variable **$!** holds the latest system-error message (in this case, the one resulting from a failed file **open** operation).

Programs may process zero or more files. Each file used in a program must have a unique filehandle and must be opened with an **open** statement. All subsequent file-processing functions after a file is opened must refer to the file with the appropriate filehandle.

Files may be opened in one of several modes by appending prefixes to the filename (Fig. 10.3). To create a file or to discard the contents of a file before writing data, open the file for writing (**">**filename**"**). To read an existing file, open it for reading (**"<**filename**"**, or simply **"**filename**"**). To add data to the end of an existing file, open the file for appending (**">>**filename**"**). Note that **">>**filename**"** will also create the file if it does not yet exist. To open a file so that it may be written to and read from, open the file for updating in one of the two update modes by using **+<** or **+>**. Mode **+<** opens a file for reading and writing, keeping the existing data. Mode **+>** creates a file for reading and writing; if the file already exists, the file is opened and the current contents of the file are discarded. If you want to read and write to an existing file, you will almost always want to use **+<** rather than **+>**.

Mode	Description
<	Open a file for reading.
>	Create a file for writing. If the file already exists, discard the current contents.
>>	Append. Open or create a file for writing at the end of a file.
+<	Open a file for update (reading and writing).
+>	Create a file for update. If the file already exists, discard the current contents.
+>>	Append. Open or create a file for update. Writing is done at the end of the file.

Fig. 10.3   File open modes.

Common Programming Error 10.1

Opening a nonexistent file for reading is an error.

Common Programming Error 10.2

Opening a file for writing when no disk space is available is an error.

Common Programming Error 10.3

Forgetting to open a file before attempting to use it in a program is an error.

Common Programming Error 10.4

Opening a file with the incorrect file mode can lead to devastating errors. For example, opening a file in write mode (" > ") when it should be opened in update mode ("+<") causes the contents of the file to be discarded.

Good Programming Practice 10.1

Open a file only for reading (and not updating) if the contents of the file should not be modified. This prevents unintentional modification of the file's contents. This is an example of the principle of least privilege, which states that each component of a system should have sufficient rights and privileges to accomplish its designated task, but no additional rights or privileges. This helps prevent accidental and/or malicious errors from occurring to systems.

Portability Tip 10.1

A filename can vary from system to system. Specifically, Unix uses the / character to separate directories, while Windows and DOS use the \ character.

When you open a filehandle in a program, you want to **close** that filehandle explicitly as well. Perl will automatically close any unclosed filehandles once the program exits. However, if any errors occur while these files are being closed, the error messages will be lost. For this reason, you should use a statement such as the following to close a file:

```
close( FILE ) or die( "Cannot close file : $!" );
```

The **or die** construct allows the programmer to trap any errors that occurred while the file was being closed. The errors warn the user that something unexpected has happened.

Good Programming Practice 10.2

*Always capture errors from system commands, such as **open**. This allows you to print a customized error message along with the system-generated error message. It also allow the programmer to fix a problem before a fatal error occurs.*

Good Programming Practice 10.3

Explicitly close each file as soon as it is known that the program will not reference the file again. This helps prevent accidental file corruption.

Performance Tip 10.1

Closing a file can free resources for which other users or programs may be waiting.

Testing and Debugging Tip 10.1

During program development, always print out meaningful error messages, and use the built-in error special variables. This will makes debugging the program easier.

10.5 Using Filehandles

Data are stored in files so that the data may be retrieved for processing when needed. In this section, we discuss how to use filehandles to read and write data sequentially from a file.

To retrieve data sequentially from a file, a program normally starts reading from the beginning of the file and reads all data consecutively until the desired data are found. Earlier, we saw how this reading was done from **STDIN** with the *diamond operator*, **<>** (as in **<STDIN>**). This operator reads in data until it reaches a character that matches the value in **$/**. By default, **$/** stores the value **\n**, so the operator will read in one line of data. A special way to use the diamond operator is in list context. If you use the diamond operator and set a list as its return value, it will read in as many lines from the file as there are items in the list. This operator can also be used to read from other filehandles; simply place the filehandle inside the diamond operator (as with **<STDIN>**). Figure 10.4 presents a simple program that reads information from a file (Fig. 10.5).

The actual reading is done in line 11. Notice that the filehandle is inserted into the diamond operator (**<IN>**). Another thing to realize when we look at the output is the blank line between lines of output. In our **print** statement, we print the string we read from the file, followed by a single newline. So, why do the lines in the program output appear double spaced? Each line in our data file already has a newline character at the end of the line. This newline character is read and stored in **$line**. When the program outputs **$line**, the newline in variable **$line** and the one in the **print** statement are both displayed. When reading data from a file, it is important to remember that the strings have trailing newline characters. If you wish to use these data, it is often useful to **chomp** it first to remove the trailing newline.

```perl
1   #!/usr/bin/perl
2   # Fig. 10.4: fig10_04.pl
3   # Program that reads lines from a file and displays each line.
4
5   use strict;
6   use warnings;
7
8   open( IN, "in.txt" )
9      or die( "Cannot open in.txt for reading: $!" );
10
11  while ( my $line = <IN> ) {
12     print( "file: $line\n" );
13  }
14
15  close( IN ) or die( "Cannot close file: $!" );
```

```
file: This is a sample text file that

file: contains three separate lines of

file: text for demonstration purposes.
```

Fig. 10.4   Program that reads and echoes data from a file.

> This is a sample text file that
> contains three separate lines of
> text for demonstration purposes.

Fig. 10.5   The file **in.txt** read into the program of Fig. 10.4.

Common Programming Error 10.5

*Forgetting that an inputted string has a trailing newline can cause logic errors in your program. It is almost always beneficial to **chomp** each string that is read into the program.*

Of course, programs often output data as well. Figure 10.6 demonstrates writing data to a file. On line 12, we use the **print** function to print to a file designated by a filehandle. We send **print** two arguments. The first argument is a filehandle. The second argument is a string. Function **print** outputs the string from its second argument to the file associated with the filehandle in the second argument. For this to work, the file must be opened for writing (lines 9 and 10) or for appending (lines 22 and 23). When the file is opened for writing, Perl takes an existing file and clears its contents, or creates a new file if the file does not already exist. When the file is opened for appending, Perl opens an existing file and adds lines to the end, or creates a new file if the file does not already exist.

```
1   #!usr/bin/perl
2   # Fig. 10.6: fig10_06.pl
3   # Demonstrating writing to and reading from a file.
4
5   use strict;
6   use warnings;
7
8   print( "Opening file for output\n" );
9   open( OUTFILE, ">file.txt" )
10      or die( "Can't find file.txt : $!" );
11  print( "Outputting to file\n" );
12  print( OUTFILE "There was an old lady\n" );
13  close( OUTFILE ) or die( "Can not close file.txt: $!" );
14
15  print "The file now contains:\n";
16  open( INFILE, "file.txt" )
17      or die( "Can not open file.txt: $!" );
18  print while ( <INFILE> );
19  close( INFILE ) or die( "Can not close file.txt: $!" );
20
21  print( "\nAppend to the end of the file\n" );
22  open( OUTFILE, ">>file.txt" )
23      or die( "Can not open file.txt: $!" );
24  print( OUTFILE "who lived in a shoe.\n" );
25  close( OUTFILE ) or die( "Can not close file.txt: $!" );
26
27  print( "It now reads:\n" );
28  open( INFILE, "file.txt" )
29      or die( "Can not open file.txt: $!" );
```

Fig. 10.6   Program to read from and write to files (part 1 of 2).

```
30   print while ( <INFILE> );
31   close( INFILE ) or die( "Can not close file.txt: $!" );
```

```
Opening file for output
Outputting to file
The file now contains:
There was an old lady

Append to the end of the file
It now reads:
There was an old lady
who lived in a shoe.
```

Fig. 10.6   Program to read from and write to files (part 2 of 2).

```
There was an old lady
who lived in a shoe.
```

Fig. 10.7   The final version of **file.txt** produced by Fig. 10.6.

Common Programming Error 10.6

*Placing a comma after the filehandle argument to a **print** statement is a syntax error.*

Line 18 is a useful construct. It reads through a file sequentially and prints each line of the file using the default value stored in variable **$_**. When the diamond appears by itself in the **while** condition, the input from the file gets assigned to the **$_** special variable. This **while** structure loops until the end-of-file indicator is returned by the diamond operator. With each iteration, a line is stored in **$_** and then output by **print**. Function **print** is not given an argument, so it prints the contents of **$_** by default. This is just one example of how a reasonably complicated action can be stated simply with Perl.

An important note about filehandles is that they cannot be passed as arguments to a function. There are a couple of ways to circumvent this problem. One way is to pass the filename to the function. The function can create a local filehandle, open the file and manipulate the file. This method can cause problems, however, if more than one function in your program requires access to that file. Another mechanism for circumventing this problem is described in the typeglobs section of Chapter 13, References.

Common Programming Error 10.7

Passing a function a filehandle argument will cause a fatal error in your program. For the moment, work around this problem by passing the function the name of the file, and have the function explicitly create a filehandle.

10.6 @ARGV Special Variable

Like other Perl functions and operators we have seen, the diamond operator also exhibits special behavior when used alone. When no filehandle is specified within the diamond operator, **<>**, Perl gets the filename from a special variable called **@ARGV**. This array variable stores all *command-line arguments*—strings supplied to the program at the time it is executed. For example, if you type

```
perl fig10_06.pl in.txt
```

The command-line argument to the program is the item (or list of items) that appears immediately after the program name. In the preceding command, **in.txt** is the only command-line argument. Command-line arguments can include filenames. If the diamond operator is used without a filehandle (**<>**), it uses the filenames specified as command-line arguments (now the values in **@ARGV**). In fact, it will process every filename in the array **@ARGV**. If there are no command-line arguments (i.e., **@ARGV** is empty), **<>** reads from **STDIN**. Figure 10.8 demonstrates the diamond operator using **@ARGV**.

This simple program opens each file the user supplies as a command-line argument and displays its contents. If no command-line arguments are specified, the program will instead echo input from **STDIN**. If input is echoed from **STDIN**, then the user must enter the end-of-file key sequence (*<ctrl>-z* in Windows, and *<ctrl>-d* in UNIX/Linux) to end the program.

10.7 Other Ways to Read from Files

The diamond operator is not the only way to read from files. Just like everything else in Perl, there are many ways to read from a file.

When you read from a file, you will frequently use the diamond operator and read one line at a time. You can also read data in formats other than line by line. For example, the function call ***read(FILE, $input, 80)*** reads 80 bytes from **FILE** and stores them in **$input**. This method is useful if you know exactly how much data you want to read at a given time. You can also read data one character at a time using function ***getc***. Function **getc(FILE)** will get one character from **FILE** and return that character.

So far, we have discussed reading data line by line, character by character and by a certain number of bytes. What if you want to read in the whole file all at once? Perl programmers refer to this task as *slurping a file*. One way to slurp a file is to use the diamond operator in list context. For example, assigning the diamond-operator expression to an array causes the diamond operator to read the entire file and place each line into a cell in the array. Another way to slurp a file is to alter the **$/** special variable.

```
1   #!/usr/bin/perl
2   # Fig. 10.8: fig10_08.pl
3   # Using the diamond operator with @ARGV.
4
5   use strict;
6   use warnings;
7
8   print while ( <> );
```

```
This is a sample text file that
contains three separate lines of
text for demonstration purposes.
```

Fig. 10.8   Displaying the contents of the file supplied as a command-line argument in the command **perl fig10_06.pl in.txt**.

As we mentioned in Chapter 9, **$/** holds the input-line record separator (for which the default separator character is **\n**). So, each time the diamond operator is used to read data, it will read until it finds the character stored in **$/**. Therefore, if you set **$/** to **undef**, the diamond operator will input the whole file and store it in a scalar.

Common Programming Error 10.8

*Changing the default value of a special variable, such as **$/**, to a particular value that helps you complete a task may lead to errors later in your program. Be sure to reset the special variable's default value when you complete your task.*

Good Programming Practice 10.4

*Whenever you alter the value of **$/** or another special variable, use **local** within that block, so that the previous value is restored once the special action has been completed. This will avoid certain hard-to-find errors.*

10.8 Implementing a Random-Access File

Until now, we have been using sequential access files, in which lines of text are written and read in order. Perl also allows you to create *random-access files*. Individual records of a random-access file normally are fixed in length and may be accessed directly (and thus quickly) without searching through other records. This makes random-access files appropriate for airline reservation systems, banking systems, point-of-sale systems and other kinds of *transaction-processing systems* that require rapid access to specific data.

Because every record in a random-access file normally has the same length, the exact location of a record relative to the beginning of the file can be calculated as a function of the record key. We will soon see how this attribute facilitates immediate access to specific records, even in large files.

Software Engineering Observation 10.1

All lines in a random-access file must be of equal length. This allows the programmer to input a byte number to find a specific position in the file.

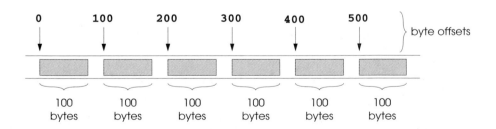

Fig. 10.9   Perl's view of a random-access file.

Data can be inserted in a random-accessed file without destroying other data in the file. Data stored previously can also be updated or deleted without rewriting the entire file. Figure 10.10 illustrates one way to implement a simple random-access file.

```perl
1   #!/usr/bin/perl
2   # Fig. 10.7: fig10_07.pl
3   # random access file
4
5   use strict;
6   use warnings;
7
8   print( "Creating a file with the numbers 0-9\n" );
9   open( FILE, "+>file.txt" )
10      or die( "Unable to open file: $!\n" );
11  print( FILE "0\n1\n2\n3\n4\n5\n6\n7\n8\n9\n" );
12  close( FILE ) or die( "Unable to open file: $!\n" );
13
14  # this part of the code determines the length of a record
15  open( FILE, "<file.txt" )
16      or die( "Unable to open file: $!\n" );
17  <FILE>;
18  my $length = tell( FILE );
19  print( "The length of a record is: $length\n" );
20  close( FILE ) or die( "Unable to open file: $!\n" );
21
22  open( FILE, "+<file.txt" )
23      or die( "Unable to open file: $!\n" );
24  print( "The file contains:\n" );
25  print while ( <FILE> );
26
27  print( "\nSeek to the sixth record\n" );
28  seek( FILE, 5 * $length, 0 );  # move past first five records
29  print( "Truncate file to ", tell( FILE ), " bytes\n" );
30  truncate( FILE, tell( FILE ) )
31      or die( "Unable to truncate: $!\n" );
32  seek( FILE, 0, 0 );            # position to beginning of file
33  print( "The file now contains:\n" );
34  print while ( <FILE> );
35
36  print( "\nSeek to the third record and print its contents: " );
37  seek( FILE, 2 * $length, 0 );  # move past first two records
38  my $in = <FILE>;
39  print( "$in" );
40  print( "The remainder of the file from this point is:\n" );
41  print while ( <FILE> );
42
43  print( "\nUpdating the second item with the value 7\n" );
44  seek( FILE, $length, 0 );      # move past first record
45  print( FILE "7" );
46  seek( FILE, 0, 0 );
47  print( "The file now contains:\n" );
48  print while ( <FILE> );
```

Fig. 10.10   Implementing a random-access file (part 1 of 2).

```
49
50   close( FILE ) or die( "Unable to close file: $!" );
```

```
Creating a file with the numbers 0-9
The length of a record is: 3
The file contains:
0
1
2
3
4
5
6
7
8
9

Seek to the sixth record
Truncate file to 15 bytes
The file now contains:
0
1
2
3
4

Seek to the third record and print its contents: 2
The remainder of the file from this point is:
3
4

Updating the second item.
The file now contains:
0
7
2
3
4
```

Fig. 10.10 Implementing a random-access file (part 2 of 2).

Lines 9 and 10 open the file for reading and writing. Next, line 11 writes records to the file. In this example, each record consists of a single-digit number and a newline; thus, every record is of the same length—an important feature for a random-access file. At this point, we close the file (line 12). Lines 15–20 open the file for reading so that we can determine the length in bytes of a record in the file. Line 17 reads one line from the file. Line 18 uses function **tell** to determine the current position in the file (i.e., the byte following the first record). In this case, the value returned from **tell** is also the length in bytes of a record. For example, if a record is three bytes long, bytes 0, 1 and 2 are read at line 17. So, the current byte position in the file is 3—the length of a record. This is a programmatic way to determine the length of a record. We did this here to support multiple operating systems. The character **\n** in some systems is 1 byte and in others is 2 bytes. Lines 22–25 reopen the file for updating and output the current contents of the file (the numbers 0–9).

If the length of a record is known, function **seek** can be used to find any record in the file. Function **seek** receives three arguments: a filehandle, an *offset* and a *method*. The offset is the number of bytes to move to determine the new current position in the file. This number is typically calculated as the number of records to skip multiplied by the number of bytes in a record. The method indicates the location from which to seek: 0 indicates that the position is to be measured from the beginning of the file, 1 indicates that the position is to be measured from the current position and 2 indicates that the position is to be measured from the end of the file (in this case, the offset is usually negative). Line 28

```
seek( FILE, 5 * $length, 0 );  # move past first five records
```

uses the calculation **5 * $length** and the method **0** to skip the first five records of the file, making the sixth record the current position in the file.

We can truncate a file by using function **truncate** (line 30). Function **truncate** receives the filehandle and a byte position in the file as arguments and removes everything in the file from that position to the end of the file. Lines 32–34 display the contents of the file after truncation.

Lines 36–39 demonstrate seeking to the third record and displaying its contents (2). Then, lines 40 and 41 output the remainder of the file from that point.

We can update specific records in the file by **seek**ing to the appropriate record and writing over it with **print**. Lines 43–45 demonstrate an update of the second record (we seek past the first record). Lines 46–48 display the new contents of the file, showing that the value 1 was replaced with a 7.

Common Programming Error 10.9

When you update a random-access file, you must be certain that the length of a record does not change.

As we have seen, random-access files are similar to sequential-access files. However, the fixed-length records in random-access files enable us to use **seek**, **tell** and **truncate** to facilitate our direct-access file manipulations.

10.9 Example: Web-Page Log Generator

Figure 10.11 presents a CGI program that keeps track of information about the computer and browser used to access a page and returns the log as a Web page to the user.

```
1   #!/usr/bin/perl
2   # Fig. 10.11: fig10_11.pl
3   # Logs visitors to web site.
4
5   use strict;
6   use warnings;
7   use CGI qw( :standard );
8   use Fcntl qw( :flock );
9
10  my @vars =
11      qw( REMOTE_ADDR REMOTE_PORT REQUEST_URI QUERY_STRING );
12  my @stuff = @ENV{ @vars };
```

Fig. 10.11   CGI program that generates a Web-page log (part 1 of 2).

```
13   my $info = join( " | ", @stuff );
14
15   open( FILE, "+>>log.txt" )
16      or die( "Could not open log.txt: $!" );
17   flock( FILE, LOCK_EX )
18      or die( "Could not get exclusive lock: $!" );
19   print( FILE "$info\n\n" );
20   flock( FILE, LOCK_UN ) or die( "Could not unlock file: $!" );
21
22   close( FILE );
23
24   if ( $stuff[3] ne "" ) {
25      print( header( -Refresh=> '5; URL=http://www.deitel.com' ) );
26      print( start_html( "log.txt" ) );
27      print( h1( "Welcome to Deitel & Associates, $stuff[3]!\n" ) );
28      print( p( i( "You will now be redirected to our home page." ) ) );
29   }
30   else {
31      print( header() );
32      print( start_html( "log.txt" ) );
33      print( h1( "Please add a \"?\" and your name to the URL.\n" ) );
34   }
35
36   print( end_html() );
```

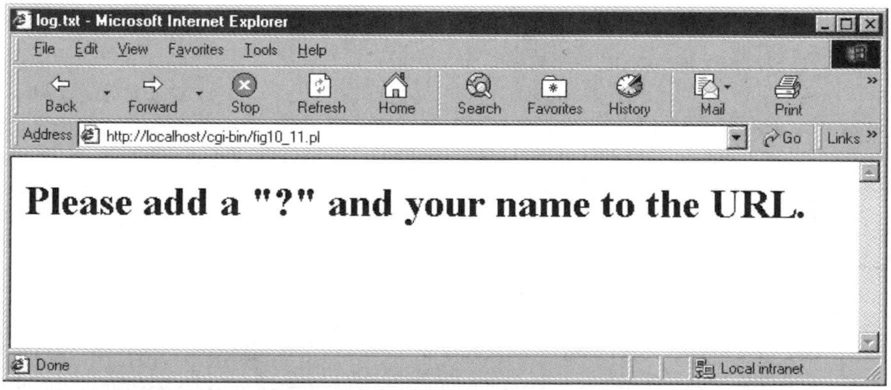

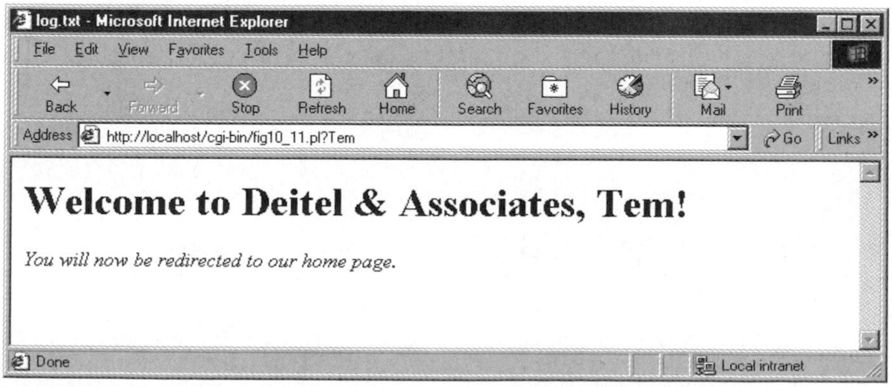

Fig. 10.11 CGI program that generates a Web-page log (part 2 of 2).

Good Programming Practice 10.5

*Whenever there is a chance that more than one program will access a file, use the **flock** function to restrict access to the file. This helps prevent multiple programs from modifying the program at the same time.*

Good Programming Practice 10.6

*When you use **flock** on a file, try to lock it for as little time as possible. That way, when another program needs to use that file, there is less of a chance that the file is unavailable.*

This CGI program redirects the user to the Deitel & Associates, Inc.'s home page after logging some information about the computer and the browser that interacted with the CGI program. In line12, we store the user's **REMOTE_ADDR**, **REMOTE_PORT**, **REQUEST_URI** and **QUERY_STRING** in **@stuff**. All of our file commands start at line 15, where we open our log file for appending. Each new visit to this program places another line in this log file. Then we use function **flock** to *lock* the file to help prevent multiple programs from modifying the program at the same time. Function **flock** takes a filehandle as its first argument and a lock type as its second argument. We use two lock types that are made available via the **Fcntl** module's **:flock** tag: Lock type **LOCK_EX** (**2**) locks the file with an *exclusive lock*, and lock type **LOCK_UN** (**8**) *unlocks* the file. Locking the file with exclusive access prevents other programs from accessing the file while our program uses the file, thus preventing corruption of the data. We then write data into the file, unlock the file and close the file. Its important to keep the file locked for as short a time as possible. If the file is locked for a long time, CGI programs that need to access the log will be delayed from accessing it and may terminate (time out) as a result.

After we log this information, we output a greeting to the user and then redirect the browser to another Web page. Notice that much of the HTML that is generated by this program is contained in an **if/else** structure. If **QUERY_STRING** was not specified, then a message pops up in the browser prompting the user to add a question mark followed by the user's first name to the end of the request. If **QUERY_STRING** was specified, then the program takes this value and uses it as the person's name. Before a greeting is returned to the user, the **Refresh** header (line 25) is sent to the browser with a timeout value of five seconds. The program will print the greeting, and then five seconds later it redirects the user to the **www.deitel.com** Web site. Figure 10.12 shows the data that are written to **log.txt**. In this case, four users have visited the site (**fig10_11.pl**). All of the data from the environment variables captured at the beginning of the program are written to the file, separated by pipe characters. Notice that the last two visitors look almost identical. It is likely that this person first went to the site, but did not enter a value into the **QUERY_STRING** in his or her first attempt to access the program.

```
192.168.1.62 | 1202 | /cgi-bin/fig10_11.pl?Jane | Tem

127.0.0.1 | 1354 | /cgi-bin/fig10_11.pl?Harvey | Harvey

192.168.1.60 | 1090 | /cgi-bin/fig10_11.pl |

192.168.1.60 | 1090 | /cgi-bin/fig10_11.pl?Jeni | Jeni
```

Fig. 10.12 Contents of **log.txt**.

10.10 Example: Guestbook

Figures 10.13 and 10.14 present two CGI programs that work together to implement a common CGI application, *guestbooks*. Figure 10.15 shows the **book.txt** file containing all of the guestbook entries.

```perl
1   #!/usr/bin/perl
2   # Fig. 10.13: fig10_13.pl
3   # A program to implement a guestbook.
4
5   use strict;
6   use warnings;
7   use CGI qw( :standard );
8
9   print( header() );
10  print( start_html( -title => "My guest book." ) );
11
12  print <<FORM;
13  <form method = "post" action = "fig10_14.pl">
14  <p><strong>Name: </strong>
15  <input name = "name" type = "text" size = "25"></p>
16  <p><strong>Please enter your comment here:</strong></p>
17  <p><textarea name = "comment" rows = "4" cols = "36"></textarea></p>
18  <input type = "submit" value = "sign in to guestbook">
19  <input type = "reset" value = "clear entry">
20  </form>
21  FORM
22
23  print( end_html() );
```

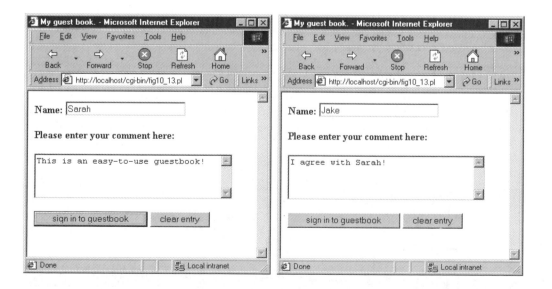

Fig. 10.13 CGI program to read in values for a guestbook.

```perl
1   #!/usr/bin/perl
2   # Fig. 10.14: fig10_14.pl
3   # a program to implement a guestbook.
4
5   use strict;
6   use warnings;
7   use CGI qw( :standard );
8   use Fcntl qw( :flock );
9
10  print( header() );
11  print( start_html( -title => "My guest book." ) );
12  print( p( b( i( "Entries in my guestbook: \n" ) ) ) );
13
14  my $name = param( "name" );
15  my $text = param( "comment" );
16
17  if ( $name ) {
18     open( BOOK, ">>book.txt" ) or die( "Cannot open: $!" );
19     flock( BOOK, LOCK_EX ) or die( "Cannot get exclusive lock: $!" );
20     print( BOOK "$name said: \t" );
21     print( BOOK "$text\n" );
22     flock( BOOK, LOCK_UN ) or die( "Cannot unlock file: $!" );
23     close( BOOK ) or die( "Cannot close guestbook: $!" );
24  }
25
26  open( BOOK, "<book.txt" ) or die( "Cannot open guestbook: $!" );
27  flock( BOOK, LOCK_EX ) or die( "Cannot get exclusive lock: $!" );
28
29  while ( <BOOK> ) {
30     s|\t|<br/>|g;
31     print( p( "$_" ) );
32  }
33
34  close( BOOK ) or die( "Cannot close guestbook: $!" );
35  print( end_html() );
```

Fig. 10.14 CGI program to implement a guestbook.

Sarah said: This is an easy-to-use guestbook!
Jake said: I agree with Sarah!

Fig. 10.15 Contents of **book.txt**.

The program in Fig. 10.13 prints a form for the user to fill out with his or her name and any comments he or she would like to add to the guestbook. The user can insert what he or she entered into the book or clear their entry and start over. The HTML for the form is printed in a straightforward manner using a here document in lines 12–21. Line 13 specifies that the information entered is to be sent to the program in Fig. 10.14.

In Fig. 10.14, if someone signed the guestbook, the condition in the **if** structure in line 17 returns a value of true, and the information is added to the guestbook. Line 18 opens the book for appending and gets an exclusive lock (line 19). The file opened is **book.txt**, and the filehandle is called **BOOK**. Lines 20 and 21 print the values to **book.txt**. Lines 22 and 23 unlock the file and close it. The rest of the program prints the guestbook. At this point, all we need to do is read the file, so we open it in open mode **<**, which prevents the program from accidentally writing to the file. Lines 29–32 provide a **while** structure that loops through every line of the file and prints it for the user. Each entry is printed using a regular expression in which each entry is output with the name first, then a **
** tag, then the comment. If the user hits the "back" button on the browser, he or she can enter a new name and comment. We show the results of two users adding entries to the guestbook in Fig. 10.14. The first output window shows the browser's contents after Sarah adds an entry, and the second output window shows the browser's contents after Jake adds an entry.

10.11 Internet and World Wide Web Resources

www.networkcomputing.com/netdesign/perl1.html
This document provides an introduction to Perl files. This document is an abridged version of a chapter from *Beginning Perl*.

www.perl.com/pub/doc/manual/html/pod/perlfaq5.html
Perl.com's answers to frequently asked questions about file handling and formatting.

media.njit.edu/~asim/perl_tutorial/filehandling.html
This document is part of a Perl tutorial that briefly file processing.

www.codebits.com/p5be/ch09.cfm
This document discusses Perl file processing in detail. It is a chapter from *Perl by Example*.

www.softpanorama.org/Scripting/Perl/ch04_files.shtml
This document contains a detailed discussion of Perl file processing.

www.perlmonks.org/
index.pl?node=File%20Input%20and%20Output&lastnode_id=954
This document contains a brief tutorial on Perl file processing.

SUMMARY

- Files permanently retain large amounts of data.
- Computers store files on secondary storage devices, such as disk storage devices.
- Two file types are sequential-access files and random-access files (also called direct-access files).

- Perl imposes no structure on a file. Perl thinks of a file as a series of characters. Essentially, all files in Perl can be thought of as text files.

- Any underlying structure that you wish to make a file to have must be defined in your program.

- Ultimately, all data items processed by a computer are reduced to combinations of zeros and ones. This conversion occurs because it is simple and economical to build electronic devices that can assume two stable states; one of the states represents **0**, and the other represents **1**.

- The smallest data item in a computer can assume the value **0** or the value **1**. Such a data item is called a bit (short for "binary digit"—a digit that can assume one of two values). Computer circuitry performs such various simple bit manipulations as determining the value of a bit, setting the value of a bit and reversing a bit (from **1** to **0** or from **0** to **1**).

- Programmers work with data in the form of decimal digits (i.e., 0, 1, 2, 3, 4, 5, 6, 7, 8 and 9), letters (i.e., A through Z and a through z) and special symbols (i.e., $, @, %, &, *, (,), -, +, ", :, ?, / and many others). Digits, letters and special symbols are referred to as characters.

- The set of all characters that may be used to write programs and represent data items on a particular computer is called that computer's character set.

- Because computers can process only **1**s and **0**s, every character in a computer's character set is represented as a pattern of **1**s and **0**s. This pattern of bits is called a byte and on most contemporary computers is typically eight bits long. Programmers create programs and data items as characters. Computers then manipulate and process these characters as patterns of bits.

- Just as characters are composed of bits, fields are composed of characters. A field is a group of characters that conveys meaning. A field consisting only of decimal digits could represent a number. A field consisting only of letters could represent a string.

- Data items processed by computers form a data hierarchy in which data items become larger and more complex in structure as we progress from bits to characters (bytes) to fields and so on.

- A record is composed of several fields. A file is a group of related records.

- To facilitate the retrieval of specific records from a file, at least one field in each record is often chosen as a record key.

- A record key identifies a record as belonging to a particular person or entity.

- There are many ways of organizing records in a file. The most popular type of organization is called a sequential file, in which records are typically stored in order by the record-key field.

- A group of related files is sometimes called a database.

- A collection of programs designed to create and manage databases is called a database management system (DBMS).

- Each file ends with an end-of-file marker.

- When a file is opened, a filehandle is associated with the file. This filehandle is used to refer to the opened file whenever the programmer wishes to read or write to it. Filehandles are, in a sense, similar to other variables we have seen, except they are not prefixed by any special character. For this reason, filehandle names usually appear in all uppercase letters, for readability.

- Three filehandles are opened automatically when program execution begins: **STDIN** (standard input), **STDOUT** (standard output) and **STDERR** (standard error).

- To use a file in a Perl program, the file must first be opened and associated with a filehandle. This is accomplished with function **open**.

- An **open** statement normally has the following form:

```
open( HANDLE, 'filename' ) or die( "Cannot open file : $!" );
```

- The filename can include path information that helps Perl locate the file. Such path information may be operating-system dependent. If the filename is specified without path information, Perl assumes that the file is located in the same directory as the program.

- If the program is able to open the file, then Perl associates the file with the filehandle HANDLE. Now, when the program reads from HANDLE, it takes input from *filename*. If the program writes to HANDLE, it outputs to *filename*.

- The **die** function is used for error handling. If the call to function **open** does not succeed, it returns a value of false, and thus the first part of the **or** statement evaluates to false. This causes the right side of the **or** operator to evaluate, triggering the **die** command, which prints an error message containing the message stored in the **$!** special variable and terminates the program.

- Programs may process no files, one file or several files. Each file used in a program must have a unique filehandle and must be opened with an **open** statement. All subsequent file-processing functions after the file is opened must refer to the file with the appropriate filehandle.

- Files may be opened in one of several modes by appending prefixes to the filename.

- To create a file or to discard the contents of a file before writing data, open the file for writing (**">***filename***"**).

- To read an existing file, open it for reading (**"<***filename***"**, or simply **"***filename***"**).

- To add data to the end of an existing file, open the file for appending (**">>***filename***"**). Note that **">>***filename***"** will also create the file if it does not yet exist.

- To open a file so that it may be written to and read from, open the file for updating in one of the two update modes, using **+<** or **+>**. Mode **+<** opens a file for reading and writing, keeping the existing data. Mode **+>** creates a file for reading and writing; if the file already exists, the file is opened, and the current contents of the file are discarded.

- To read and write to an existing file, you will almost always want to use **+<** rather than **+>**.

- The principle of least privilege states that each component of a system should have sufficient rights and privileges to accomplish its designated task, but no additional rights or privileges.

- Explicitly close each file as soon as it is known that the program will not reference the file again. Closing a file can free resources for which other users or programs may be waiting.

- During program development, always print out meaningful error messages, and use the built-in error special variables. This will make debugging the program easier.

- To retrieve data sequentially from a file, a program normally starts reading from the beginning of the file and reads all data consecutively until the desired data are found.

- The diamond operator (**<>**) operator reads in data until it reaches a character that matches the value in **$/**. By default, **$/** stores the value **\n**, so the operator will read in one line of data.

- If you use the diamond operator and set a list as its return value, it will read in as many lines from the file as there are items in the list. This operator can also be used to read from other filehandles. Simply place the filehandle inside the diamond operator.

- When no filehandle is specified within the diamond operator, **<>**, Perl gets the filename from a special variable called **@ARGV**. This array variable stores all command-line arguments—strings supplied to the program at the time it is executed. If there are no command-line arguments (i.e., **@ARGV** is empty), **<>** reads from **STDIN**.

- Function **read** reads the specified number of bytes from a file (specified by the filehandle).

- Function **getc(FILE)** gets one character from **FILE** and returns that character.

- Perl programmers refer to reading an entire file at once as slurping a file. One way to slurp a file is to use the diamond operator in list context.

- Another way to slurp a file is to change special variable **$/** to **undef**.

- Perl also allows you to create random-access files. Individual records of a random-access file normally are fixed in length and may be accessed directly (and thus quickly) without searching through other records. This attribute makes random access files appropriate for transaction-processing systems that require rapid access to specific data.

- Because every record in a random-access file normally has the same length, the exact location of a record relative to the beginning of the file can be calculated as a function of the record key.

- Function **tell** determines the current position in the file (i.e., the byte following the first record).

- If the length of a record is known, function **seek** can be used to locate any record in the file. Function **seek** receives three arguments: a filehandle, an offset and a method. The offset is the number of bytes to move to determine the new current position in the file. This number is typically calculated as the number of records to skip multiplied by the number of bytes in a record. The method indicates the location from which to seek: 0 indicates that the position is to be measured from the beginning of the file, 1 indicates that the position is to be measured from the current position and 2 indicates that the position is to be measured from the end of the file (in this case, the offset is usually negative).

- Function **truncate** receives the filehandle and a byte position in the file as arguments and removes everything in the file from that position to the end of the file.

- Function **flock** locks a file to prevent multiple programs from modifying the file simultaneously.

- Locking a file with exclusive access means that only the current CGI program can access the file. We need to lock the file so that two CGI programs do not try to update the file at the same time and thereby end up deleting one set of input.

- Whenever there is a chance that more than one program will access a file, use the **flock** command to restrict access to the file.

- When you use **flock** on a file, try to lock it for as little time as possible. That way, when another program needs to use that file, there is less of a chance that the file is unavailable.

TERMINOLOGY

$/ special variable
:flock tag
@ARGV special variable
+< update mode
+> update mode
+>> update mode
< read mode
<> diamond operator
<STDERR> standard error filehandle
<STDIN> standard input filehandle
<STDOUT> standard output filehandle
> write mode
>> append mode
appending to a file
binary digit
bit
byte offset
CGI guestbook
character
character set
close command
closing a file
command line
data hierarchy

database
database management system (DBMS)
decimal digits
diamond operator in list context
die command
direct access to a file
disk storage devices
end-of-file marker
exclusive lock
Fcntl module
field
file
file opening modes
filehandles
flock command
getc
guestbook
HTTP_REFERER
letters
LOCK_EX
LOCK_NB
LOCK_SH
LOCK_UN
locking a file

nonblocking access	**seek** command
offset	sending a function a filehandle
open command	sequential-access file
opening a file	shared lock
principle of least privilege	slurping a file
print function	special symbols
random-access file	**tell** command
read command	transaction-processing systems
reading a file	**truncate** command
reading from a file	truncating a file
record	Unicode international character set
record key	unlocking a file
REMOTE_ADDR	Web-page log
REMOTE_HOST	writing to a file
restricting access to a file	

SELF-REVIEW EXERCISES

10.1 Fill in the blanks in each of the following statements:
a) Data items processed by computers form a _____ in which data items become larg-er and more complex in structure as we progress from bits to characters (bytes) to fields and so on.
b) To facilitate the retrieval of specific records from a file, at least one field in each record is often chosen as a _____.
c) When a file is opened, a _____ is associated with the file.
d) Mode _____ opens a file for reading and writing, keeping the existing data, while mode _____ creates a file for reading and writing.
e) The _____ operator reads in data until it reaches a character that matches the value in **$/**.
f) The _____ array variable stores all command-line arguments—strings supplied to the program at the time it is executed.
g) Individual records of a _____ normally are fixed in length and may be accessed di-rectly without searching through other records.

10.2 State whether each of the following is *true* or *false* and if *false*, explain why.
a) A record is a group of related files.
b) Passing a function a filehandle argument will cause a fatal error in your program.
c) Forgetting to open a file before attempting to use it in a program is not an error; Perl will automatically open the file for you if it is not explicitly opened in the code.
d) When no filehandle is specified within the diamond operator, **<>**, Perl uses **STDIN**.
e) Perl will automatically **close** any unclosed filehandles once the program exits.

10.3 Write a program that does the following, using **Fcntl**:
a) Read in one command-line argument from the user. The argument will be used as a file to which the user appends information. Ignore any other command-line arguments.
b) Open this file, using a mode that will allow you to append to a file. Call the filehandle **EXERCISE1**.
c) Prompt the user to enter what he or she wishes to add to the file.
d) Place (c) in a loop where the user enters as much as he or she to add, entering **'quit'** to end.
e) Add these lines to the file. Close the file.
f) Reopen the file. Call the filehandle **EXERCISE2**. Print the new file.
g) Close the file, and end the program.

10.4   What is wrong with this code? (Assume that this code is the entire program, minus comments. Note that there are five errors in the sample code and that some of the errors may not halt the program or necessarily generate error messages.)

```
1   #!/usr/bin/perl
2   # Can you find the mistake(s)?
3   use warnings;
4   use strict;
5   use Fcntl;
6
7   open( FILEHANDLE, >>"file.txt" )
8      or die( "Cannot open file: $!" );
9   seek( FILEHANDLE, 4 * 3, 0 );
10  print( FILEHANDLE, "This is new text.\n" );
11  close( FILEHANDLE ) or die( "Cannot close file: $!" );
```

ANSWERS TO SELF REVIEW EXERCISES

10.1   a) data hierarchy. b) record key. c) filehandle. d) **+<**, **+>**. e) diamond (**<>**). f) **@ARGV**. g) random-access file.

10.2   a) False. A file is a group of related records.
   b) True.
   c) False. Forgetting to open a file before attempting to use it in a program is an error.
   d) False. When no filehandle is specified within the diamond operator, **<>**, Perl gets the filename from a special variable called **@ARGV**.
   e) True.

10.3   See the following code.

```
1   #!/usr/bin/perl
2   # Exercise 10.3: ex10_03.pl
3   # Appending to a file. New text and filename specified by the user.
4
5   use strict;
6   use warnings;
7   use Fcntl qw( :flock );
8
9   my $file = $ARGV[0];
10
11  open( EXERCISE1, ">>$file" ) or die( "Cannot open $file: $!" );
12  flock( EXERCISE1, LOCK_EX ) or die( "Cannot lock $file: $!" );
13
14  my $newLine = "";
15
16  while ( $newLine ne "quit\n" ) {
17     print "Enter what you wish to add, 'quit' to end.";
18     $newLine = <STDIN>;
19     last if ( $newLine eq "quit\n" );
20     print( EXERCISE1 "$newLine" );
21  }
22
23  flock( EXERCISE1, LOCK_UN ) or die( "Cannot unlock file: $!" );
```

```
24   close( EXERCISE1 ) or die ( "Cannot close $file: $!" );
25
26   open( EXERCISE2, "<$file" ) or die( "Cannot open $file: $!" );
27   flock( EXERCISE2, LOCK_EX ) or die( "Cannot lock $file: $!" );
28
29   print( "\n" );
30   print( "The file now contains: \n" );
31   print while( <EXERCISE2> );
32
33   flock( EXERCISE2, LOCK_UN ) or die( "Cannot unlock file: $!" );
34   close( EXERCISE2 ) or die ( "Cannot close $file: $!" );
```

```
>perl Ex10_03.pl text.txt
Enter what you wish to add, 'quit' to end: I want this to be line 1.
Enter what you wish to add, 'quit' to end: I want this to be line 2.
Enter what you wish to add, 'quit' to end: This should be the end.
Enter what you wish to add, 'quit' to end: quit


The file now contains:
I want this to be line 1.
I want this to be line 2.
This should be the end.
```

```
>perl Ex10_03.pl text.txt
Enter what you wish to add, 'quit' to end: No - this is the end!
Enter what you wish to add, 'quit' to end: quit

The file now contains:
I want this to be line 1.
I want this to be line 2.
This should be the end.
No - this is the end!
```

10.4   a)   Double quotes must be placed around the mode and filename during the open command
              (`">>$file"`).
          b)   The file is never locked or unlocked, which could cause severe problems if the file is be-
              ing accessed by many people.
          c)   We opened the file for appending, meaning that we are at the end of the file. The function
              seek is used for updating modes.
          d)   We automatically use 3 as the length argument in **seek**, but we need to first find out this
              length; this program will not run correctly on systems where the length is not 3.
          e)   In the **print** statement, there is no comma after the filehandle.

EXERCISES

10.5   Open a file, and print every third line to another, new file. Start by printing the first line, and
continue by printing the third line after that, and the third after that and so on.

10.6   Open a file, and output its contents in reverse order to a second file.

10.7   Create an HTML indenter. This program will take an HTML file as input, open the file and output the HTML fully indented.

10.8   Create a random-access file holding nine numerical IDs (1–9) and corresponding timestamps. Update some of the timestamps. The result is similar to creating a file to log the most recent time a certain file was accessed.

10.9   Create a program that will open an HTML document and change all relative hyperlinks to absolute hyperlinks.

11

File and Directory Manipulation

Objectives

- To discover information about files by using file tests.
- To explore alternative methods of opening files.
- To understand file permissions.
- To understand hard links and symbolic links.
- To learn how to create, manipulate and use directories and directory handles.
- To be able to create a Web site recent update page.

I read part of it all the way through.
Samuel Goldwyn

Hats off!
The flag is passing by.
Henry Holcomb Bennett

A name pronounced is the recognition of the individual to
whom it belongs. He who can pronounce my name aright, he
can call me, and is entitled to my love and service.
Henry David Thoreau

Outline

11.1 Introduction

We have now learned most of the basic procedures for opening a file, reading from a file, writing to a file, etc. In this chapter, we will learn some more advanced details of using files, such as file permissions and file tests. We will also see how to manipulate directories. The chapter closes with a CGI example that creates a Web page containing recent-update information about the files in a particular directory on a Web server.

11.2 File Tests and sysopen

As we discussed in Chapter 10, opening a file for writing when the file already exists and contains data can be dangerous; the original contents of the file are discarded. What if your program needs to open a new file for writing, but you want to avoid the possibility of accidentally deleting an existing file of the same name? It is possible that the name of the file your program wishes to create already exists and that the file contains important data. We would like to be able to test whether a file exists to avoid such accidental overwriting.

Perl provides *file tests* that enable a program to discover information about a file or directory on disk. For example, the filename test *-e* determines whether a file exists. Using this test would enable the program to prevent an accidental overwrite of an existing file by choosing a new filename. Similarly, *-r* and *-w* determine whether a file has read permission or write permission, respectively. Figure 11.1 lists several file tests.

Test	Meaning	Test	Meaning
-r	Is the file readable?	-w	Is the file writable?
-e	Does the file exist?	-z	File exists and has a size of zero.
-s	File exists and has a nonzero size. The size in bytes is returned.	-f	Is the file a plain file?
-d	File is directory.	-T	Is the file a text file?
-B	File is a binary file.	-M	Age from last time file was modified.

Fig. 11.1   Some file tests (part 1 of 2).

Test	Meaning	Test	Meaning
-A	Age from time file was last accessed.	**-C**	Age since file was created.
-x	Is the file executable?		

Fig. 11.1   Some file tests (part 2 of 2).

File test **-f** file test shows whether or not a file is a *plain file*. Calling a file "plain" means that the file is not a special type of file or listing, such as a directory, symbolic link (to be discussed later in the chapter) or character special file. If a file is nonempty, **-s** returns the size of the file in bytes. File tests **-M**, **-A** and **-C** return the number of days (or fraction thereof) since the file was last modified, last accessed or created, respectively. All other tests simply return 1 for true and 0 for false. If the filename is omitted, these tests default to whatever is stored in special variable **$_**. The program in Fig. 11.2 uses several file tests from Fig. 11.1. There is a comment at the end of each line that uses a file test.

```perl
1   #!/usr/bin/perl
2   # Fig. 11.2: fig11_02.pl
3   # A program that uses file tests
4
5   use strict;
6   use warnings;
7
8   foreach my $file ( @ARGV ) {
9      print( "Checking $file: " );
10
11     if ( -e $file ) {          # does file exist?
12        print( "$file exists!\n" );
13
14        if ( -f $file ) {       # is the file a plain file?
15           print( "The file $file is:" );
16           print( " executable" ) if ( -x $file );  # executable?
17           print( " readable" ) if ( -r $file );    # readable?
18           print( " writable" ) if ( -w $file );    # writable?
19           print( "\n" );
20           print( "It is ", -s $file, " bytes.\n" ); # size
21           my @time = timeconv( -A $file );          # accessed
22           print( "Last accessed at $time[0] days, ",
23                  "$time[1] hours, $time[2] minutes ",
24                  "and $time[3] seconds.\n" );
25           @time = timeconv( -M $file );             # modified
26           print( "Last modified at $time[0] days, ",
27                  "$time[1] hours, $time[2] minutes, ",
28                  "and $time[3] seconds ago.\n" );
29        }
30        elsif ( -d $file ) {   # is it a directory?
31           print( "$file is a directory!\n" );
32        }
33     }
```

Fig. 11.2   Program that uses file tests (part 1 of 2).

```
34      else {
35          print( "$file doesn't exist.\n" );
36      }
37
38      print( "\n" );
39  }
40
41  sub timeconv
42  {
43      my $time = shift();
44      my $days = int( $time );
45      $time = ( $time - $days ) * 24;
46      my $hours = int( $time );
47      $time = ( $time - $hours ) * 60;
48      my $minutes = int( $time );
49      $time = ( $time - $minutes ) * 60;
50      my $seconds = int( $time );
51      return ( $days, $hours, $minutes, $seconds );
52  }
```

```
Checking fig11_02.pl: fig11_02.pl exists!
The file fig11_02.pl is: executable readable writable
It is 1550 bytes.
Last accessed at 0 days, 0 hours, 0 minutes and 0 seconds.
Last modified at 0 days, 0 hours, 2 minutes, and 20 seconds ago.
```

```
Checking /home/pauldeitel: /home/pauldeitel exists!
/home/pauldeitel is a directory!
```

```
Checking file.txt: file.txt exists!
The file file.txt is: readable writable
It is 51 bytes.
Last accessed at 0 days, 2 hours, 40 minutes and 16 seconds.
Last modified at 1 days, 17 hours, 39 minutes, and 28 seconds ago.
```

```
Checking fakefile.txt: fakefile.txt doesn't exist.
```

Fig. 11.2   Program that uses file tests (part 2 of 2).

The file tests listed in Fig. 11.1 and demonstrated in Fig. 11.2 work well in most cases to help prevent accidental overwriting of an existing file. However, what happens when files are being created and destroyed rapidly? What happens if your program tests to determine whether a file exists, determines that the file does not exist at that moment in time and then the file gets created by another program before your program creates the file? The file test and file creation are performed in two separate steps, so it is possible that between the two steps, the file will get created by a different program. Thus, our program would potentially overwrite the other program's file or possibly not be able to create a file at all. To deal with these problems, we can combine the file test and the opening of the file into one command with *function **sysopen***.

Function **sysopen** takes three or four arguments. The first two arguments are a filehandle and a filename. This version of opening a file does not require a file open-mode specification, which is provided as the third argument to function **sysopen**. In general, the third argument consists of several flags that are separated by a vertical bar (|) to specify the open mode. These flags are imported from the **Fcntl** module. The optional fourth argument sets the permissions for the file (permissions are discussed in Section 11.3). The file open-mode flags for **sysopen**'s third argument are shown in Fig. 11.3.

To mimic a call to function open with the **>** file open mode, pass

```
O_WRONLY | O_CREAT | O_TRUNC
```

as the third argument to **sysopen**. This **sysopen** call can be used to create a file for writing (only if it does not exist) all in one step. This way, there is no chance that a preexisting file will accidentally get deleted.

Testing and Debugging Tip 11.1

When you create a file in an existing directory, use a file test to make sure that you do not accidentally overwrite and delete critical data.

Testing and Debugging Tip 11.2

When using filenames input by the user, your program should use file tests to determine the permissions on the specified file, allowing you to trap errors and print proper warnings to the user.

11.3 Permissions

File permissions can be changed with *function **chmod***. Though file permissions are ultimately controlled by your file system, function **chmod** has access to the permissions and is allowed to change the settings. File permissions allow programmers to limit the user's rights to read, write or execute a file.

Flag	Meaning
O_RDONLY	Open for reading only.
O_WRONLY	Open for writing only.
O_RDWR	Open for reading or writing.
O_CREAT	Create the file if it does not exist.
O_EXCL	Do not open the file if it already exists.
O_APPEND	Append to the end of the file.
O_TRUNC	Truncate the file's existing contents.
O_NONBLOCK	Non-blocking access.

Fig. 11.3　Flags for **sysopen** imported from **Fcntl**.

Function **chmod** is called in the following form:

    chmod(*mode*, *fileList*);

The *mode* argument specifies the permissions for each file in the *fileList*, a comma-separated list of filenames.

Ideally, the *mode* should be a four-digit octal number. The first digit of the number should be zero, to indicate that the number is in octal format. The remaining three digits represent a code specifying which permissions will be granted and to whom they will be granted. The second digit represents permissions for the owner of the file. The third digit represents permissions for the *group* to which the file belongs. The fourth digit represents permissions for all other users. Groups are used to bring together multiple users sharing access to the same files. Figure 11.4 lists the possible digits and the permissions each digit grants.

The following are valid uses of **chmod**:

    chmod(0777, myfile.pl); # RWX (owner, group, and other)
    chmod(0751, text.txt); # RWX (owner), RX (group), R (other)
    chmod(0666, myfile.pl); # RW (owner, group, and other)

[*Note*: If you are running Perl on a Windows platform, only the read and write attributes may be changed on a file. Because Windows bases the execution status of a file on its extension (e.g., **.exe** and **.pl**), the execute attribute cannot be changed. Therefore, a Windows user is limited to permissions **4** and **6**.]

11.4 File Manipulation

Programmers can access many basic system commands that allow files to be renamed, deleted and even copied under the control of a Perl program. In this section, we discuss the Perl functions that perform these basic system tasks.

Function **rename**,

    rename(*fileName*, *newFileName*)

renames the file *fileName* to the new name specified by *newFileName*. This function returns **1** if it is successful; otherwise, it returns **0**.

Permission	Allows
0	The user(s) can do nothing.
1	The user(s) can execute.
2	The user(s) can write.
3	The user(s) can execute and write.
4	The user(s) can read.
5	The user(s) can read and execute.
6	The user(s) can read and write.
7	The user(s) can read, write and execute.

Fig. 11.4   Some of Perl's file permissions.

Common Programming Error 11.1

*Be aware that function **rename** will overwrite any existing file with the new filename and that the file's contents will be lost. As a precaution, use a file test to determine if the new filename exists before calling **rename**.*

Figure 11.5 tests whether a file named **file.txt** exists before opening it for writing and hence deleting any currently stored data. If an existing file is found, the program renames it **file.old** (essentially creating a copy) and proceeds to open and write to **file.txt**.

Figure 11.5 deals with the scenario in which **file.txt** already exists. When the user enters **no** at the prompt, the file is renamed as **file.old** (line 11), and **file.txt** now contains only the text

```
A copy of file.txt is saved in file.old.
```

Figures 11.6, 11.7 and 11.8 show the files before and after the execution of the program. If the user had entered **yes** at the prompt, then Fig. 11.8 would not exist.

```perl
1   #!/usr/bin/perl
2   # Fig. 11.5: fig11_05.pl
3   # Renaming a file before accidental deletion
4
5   use warnings;
6   use strict;
7
8   if ( -e 'file.txt' ) {
9       print( "Do you want to write over file.txt? (yes or no): " );
10      chomp( my $response = <STDIN> );
11      rename( 'file.txt', 'file.old' )
12          or die( "Error renaming : $!" )
13              if ( $response eq 'no' );
14  }
15
16  open( FILE, ">file.txt" ) or die( "Error opening: $!" );
17  print( FILE "A copy of file.txt is saved in file.old.\n" );
18  close( FILE ) or die( "Cannot close: $!" );
```

```
Do you want to write over file.txt? (yes or no): no
```

Fig. 11.5   Using **rename** to create a copy of a file.

```
This is the original text from file.txt.
```

Fig. 11.6   Contents of **file.txt** before **fig11_05.pl** executes.

```
A copy of file.txt is saved in file.old.
```

Fig. 11.7   Contents of **file.txt** after **fig11_05.pl** executes.

> **This is the original text from file.txt.**

Fig. 11.8   Contents of **file.old** (after **fig11_05.pl** is executed).

To delete files from a directory, we can use *function **unlink***,

    unlink(*listOfFiles* **)**

which deletes a list of files and returns the number of files successfully deleted. If no file-names are given, the function deletes the file whose name is in special variable **$_** by default. Figure 11.9 asks the user for a file to delete. The program displays a message indicating whether or not the file was deleted.

    *Function **chown*** is used in UNIX to change ownership of a file. The Windows NT and Windows 2000 file systems use ownership properties that cannot be accessed through Perl. [*Note*: The Win32 modules do provide this functionality, but it is not built into Perl.] In UNIX, every user has an ID number, and every group of users has a group ID number. These ID numbers are determined by the system administrator. The **chown** function,

    chown(*userID, groupID, fileList* **);**

gives specific user and group ID numbers to a list of files, changing each file's ownership in the UNIX file system. The ownership properties relate directly with the file permissions, as discussed in Section 11.3.

```
1   #!usr/bin/perl
2   # Fig. 11.9: fig11_09.pl
3   # Deleting a file with unlink
4
5   use strict;
6   use warnings;
7
8   print( "Input a file you want deleted: " );
9   chomp( my $file = <STDIN> );
10
11  if ( -f $file && unlink( $file ) ) {
12     print( "The file was successfully deleted.\n" );
13  }
14  else {
15     print( "It was not deleted: $!" );
16  }
```

```
Input a file you want deleted: file.old
The file was successfully deleted.
```

```
Input a file you want deleted: doesnotexist.txt
It was not deleted: No such file or directory
```

Fig. 11.9   Deleting a file by using the function **unlink**.

To change only one ownership property (user or group), replace the ignored argument with **-1**. The function returns the number of successful changes. Note that the user ID and group ID must be in numeric form. If you are familiar with only your user and group ID's symbolic names, consult the system administrator for their numeric equivalents. The following line changes the ownership properties of **file.txt** on a UNIX system:

```
chown( 55, 100, 'file.txt' ); # User now ID 55, group now 100
```

*Function **utime*** modifies a file's timestamps. Every file contains three timestamps, representing the time at which the file was created, the time at which the file was last modified and the time at which the file was last accessed. By modifying either of the first two, you automatically change the third. Function **utime**,

       utime(*creation,* *lastModified,* *fileList* **);**

modifies the timestamps for a list of files and returns the number of files successfully modified. The *creation* and *lastModified* timestamps should be in *interval time*—i.e., the integer number of seconds past midnight Greenwich Mean Time (GMT), January 1, 1970 (January 1, 1904, for the Mac operating system). As of this book's publication, this number is over 960 million. Programmers normally modify the value of *function **time*** returned when using **utime**. Function **time** takes no arguments and returns the current interval time. To change the creation and last-modification timestamps of a file to three days ago, a programmer would use

```
$newtime = ( time() - ( 3600 * 72 ) );
utime( $newtime, $newtime, 'file' );
```

where **3600 * 72** represents the number of seconds in three full days.

11.5 Hard Links and Symbolic Links

It is possible to have more than one name for a particular file. Alternative names for files can be created, destroyed, renamed, opened, etc., in Perl. This notion of alternative names is called *linking*. There are two types of links: *hard links* and *symbolic links*.

A hard link can be thought of as a name for a file on a disk. Multiple hard links may be used to provide several names for a single file. A hard link appears to the user of the file to be the original filename. The operating system keeps track of the number of hard links to any given file. If the hard-link count for a file becomes zero and the file is closed, the file is deleted from the hard drive. Hard links cannot link to a file on a different file system. Hard links may not be created for directories.

A *symlink* (symbolic link) is a special file that refers to another file. When a symlink is opened, the operating system follows the symlink and opens the file to which the symlink refers. A symlink does not factor into an operating system's link count. Symlinks can refer to files that do not exist as well as to files not on the current file system and directories. Symlinks can even be made to point to other symlinks. Because symlinks do not factor into an operating system's link count, removing all symlinks to a file does not cause the file to be deleted.

In Perl, hard links are created using *function **link***, which takes two arguments: the original filename and the name of the new hard link. Symlinks are created using *function* *symlink*. This function also takes two arguments: the original filename (which does not need to exist and could be a directory name) and the name of the symbolic link. Symbolic links can be followed using *function* **readlink**. *Function* **unlink** removes all existing hard links to a file, causing the file to be deleted.

11.6 File Globbing

What if your program needs to manipulate a set of files? Perhaps you want to process all **.txt** files, or all the files whose name follows a certain format. Most operating systems provide a means to do this and Perl does as well. In Perl, this process is called *globbing* (no relation to typeglobs, a data type to be discussed in Chapter 13) and is done using the *asterisk wildcard character*, *****, or any other *glob character*. Perl can be told that it should perform file globbing two ways. If you enclose the filename in angle brackets, as in **<*.txt>**, Perl expands the wildcard character. In scalar context, Perl returns the first file that matches the pattern (if such a file exists). In list context, Perl returns all files that match the pattern. This can also be done using the built-in **glob** *function*, **glob("*.txt")**. Filenames for globbing can also be specified using variables, so the following code

```
$glob = "*.txt";
@files = glob( $glob );
```

will function properly. Perl programmers usually prefer to use function **glob** over the angle brackets.

11.7 Directory Handles and Manipulation

Files have filehandles, and directories have *directory handles*, which are almost identical to filehandles. They can be opened, closed and read; however, you cannot write information using a directory handle. To open and create a directory handle, pass *function* **opendir** two arguments: the name of the directory handle and the name of the directory. Unlike function **open** for files, you cannot specify modes such as reading, writing, appending, etc. *Function* **closedir** closes directory handles.

Once a directory handle is opened, the program can read from the directory by using *function* **readdir**. This function iterates through the directory, returning all files and directories stored in the directory. *Function* **rewinddir** resets the directory handle to point to the first item in the directory.

Although we cannot use directory handles to write to directories, we can do it in another way. Directories can hold files and other directories. So, to write to a directory, all we have to do is create new files or new directories in the directory. We already know how to create files, so now we consider how to create directories with *function* **mkdir**, which takes two arguments: the name of the new directory and permissions for the directory. What if we wish to change our current directory and create our new directory somewhere else? This is done using *function* **chdir**. Directories can also be deleted using *function* **rmdir**. These functions should provide all of the capabilities you need to manipulate directories.

It is important to remember that Windows and UNIX have different *path separators*—characters that separate the directory names when specifying the location of a file or directory. In UNIX, the path separator character is the forward slash, **/**. In Windows, the path separator character is the backslash, ****. Other operating systems may use different characters. So, how can we write a program that is portable across these platforms? One way to work around this limitation is Perl's **$^O** special variable. This variable contains the name of the operating system under which the program is running. Your program can use this variable with an **if** structure and a regular expression to adapt to the current operating system and use the appropriate path separator character.

Portability Tip 11.1

*When programs require different code for different operating systems, use the **$^O** special variable to determine the operating system and enable you to execute the appropriate operating-system-specific code.*

11.8 Example: Web Site Recent-Update Page

The program in Fig. 11.10 demonstrates many of the features described in this chapter. It recursively searches through a Web site directory and finds all Perl files, HTML files and subdirectories (then searches through the subdirectories) and prints them in an HTML page. Any file or directory updated within the last seven days is designated as "**brand new!**", and anything updated within the last 30 days is designated as "**new!**".

The main portion of this program (lines 5 through 19) is fairly short: most of the work is done by the two functions **search** (line 21) and **printFile** (line 42). This program provides a good example of modularity. The program begins by declaring four variables with the keyword **our**, so that these values can be accessed by the user-defined functions that follow. We declare **$root** (line 10) to hold the value **"I:/Apache/cgi-bin/"** and use **chdir** (line 11) to change the working directory to this value. Lines 14–16 start the HTML page, and lines 18–19 end the page.

Line 17 is a call to the function **search**. Let us focus the rest of our discussion on what occurs as a result of this call to **search**. This function (lines 21–40) begins by assigning the two arguments to **$directory** and **$offset**. In this case, **$directory** is **""**, and **$offset** is **1**. The **$offset** variable helps us indent the output of the program to represent the directory structure. Lines 24 and 25 use **opendir** to create a directory handle for the current directory to search. The **foreach** structure in line 27 iterates through all the file and directory names in the current directory. The variable **$file** (line 28) is assigned the directory in which we started (**$directory**) concatenated with the current value returned from **readdir**. Lines 29 and 30 call the **printFile** function. This function, which will be discussed in detail shortly, displays the name of a file or directory. The first line calls **printFile** if the file is an HTML file, and the second line calls **printFile** if the file is a Perl program file. The second section of the **search** function occurs in the **if** structure of lines 32–38. If the current file is a directory, then we want to iterate through that directory as well. To do this, we use recursion, a concept we introduced in Chapter 6. The directory name is printed by calling **printFile** (line 33), and then line 34 recursively calls **search**. In this call to **search**, we provide the new directory name (**$file**) concatenated with a path separator. This is because in the next call to **search**, we want the files in this subdirectory to be processed. The next line prints the **$indent** in a **for** structure based on **$offset**. The variable **$offset** is incremented based on the current indent level. It begins at 1 when we are in the directory specified by **$root** and increments every time we move to a subdirectory. If we begin processing files in a subdirectory of **"I:/Apache/cgi-bin/"** called **"ch07"**, then **$offset** becomes 2. If we then start looking at files in a subdirectory of **"example1"**, **$offset** will become 3.

When this recursive call eventually returns, we go back to using a value of **$offset** that denotes the current level; each recursive call maintains its own offset value. These recursive calls to **search** iterate through all of the files in a subdirectory (including the files in a subdirectory of the original subdirectory) until there are no more directories through which to iterate. At this point, the original call to **search** returns.

```perl
1   #!perl
2   # Fig. 11.10: fig11_10.pl
3   # Website update-page creator.
4
5   use strict;
6   use warnings;
7   use CGI qw( :standard );
8
9   our $indent = "|" . ( " " x 5 );
10  our $root = "I:/Apache/cgi-bin/";
11  chdir( $root );
12  our @colors = qw( red orange green );
13  our @fileTypes = qw( html perl dir );
14  print( header(), start_html( -title => 'Update Page' ),
15     '<font size = "+1">' );
16  print( "$root:<br/>\n" );
17  search( "", 1 );
18  print( "</font>" );
19  print( end_html() );
20
21  sub search
22  {
23     my ( $directory, $offset ) = @_;
24     opendir( DIR, $root . $directory )
25        or die( "Error opening: $!" );
26
27     foreach ( readdir( DIR ) ) {
28        my $file = $directory . $_;
29        printFile( 0, $file, $_, $offset ) if ( m/\.html/ );
30        printFile( 1, $file, $_, $offset ) if ( m/\.pl/ );
31
32        if ( -d $file && /[A-Za-z]/ ) {
33           printFile( 2, $file, $_ . '/', $offset );
34           search( $file . '/', $offset + 1 );
35           print( "$indent" ) for ( 2 .. $offset );
36           print( br(), "\n" );
37           next;
38        }
39     }
40  }
41
42  sub printFile
43  {
44     my ( $type, $file, $name, $offset ) = @_;
45     my $full = $root . $file;
46     print( "$indent" ) for ( 2 .. $offset );
```

Fig. 11.10 Website update-page generator (part 1 of 2).

```
47      print( "|----" );
48      my $color = $colors[ $type ];
49      my $extension = $fileTypes[ $type ];
50      print( "<font color = \"$color\">$extension: " );
51      print( "$_</font>\n" );
52      print( em( strong( "brand " ) ) ) if ( -M $full < 7 );
53      print( strong( "new!" ), "\n" ) if ( -M $full < 30 );
54      print( br(), "\n" );
55    }
```

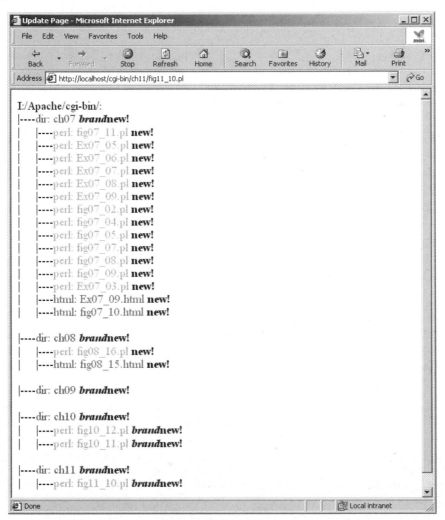

Fig. 11.10 Website update-page generator (part 2 of 2).

Now we examine the user-defined function **printFile** (lines 42–55). This function reads in its arguments (line 44) and uses the filename with the root directory to assign the full path name of **$file** to **$full**. The current color is also determined based on the type of file or directory being printed: red for HTML documents, orange for Perl programs and green for directories. The file **$extension** is also assigned in this way. The remainder of the function outputs HTML. The first line sets the font color based on the previously set value **$color** and prints the type of file to be printed. Then, the filename is printed. The next two lines print only if the file was modified in the last seven days (line 52) and/or the last 30 days (line 53). If the file was modified in the last seven days (and thus also in the last 30 days), both **"brand "** and **"new!"** are printed after the file. If the file was modified in the last 30 days, only the word **"new!"** is printed.

Lastly, this program uses some new HTML concepts. In line 9, **$indent** is set to **"|"** concatenated with five copies of the string ***" "*** (*nonbreaking space*). Every time **$indent** is printed, we will see **"|"** followed by five spaces. Normally, HTML converts several spaces in a row into one space character. The browser is required to render all nonbreaking spaces. There are also two new **CGI.pm** functions in line 52: *em* and ***strong***. These can be thought of as the functions **i** and **b** (to make strings bold and/or italic). The function **em** is used to create emphasized text and normally is rendered as italic text. Function **strong** creates strong text and normally is rendered as bold text.

SUMMARY

- The file test **-e** determines whether a file exists.
- The file test **-r** determines whether a file is readable. The file test **-w** determines whether a file is writable.
- The file test **-z** determines whether a file exists and has zero size. The file test **-s** determines whether a file exists and returns the number of bytes in the file.
- The file test **-f** determines whether a file is a plain file. The file test **-T** determines whether a file is a text file. The file test **-B** file test determines whether a file is a binary file.
- The file test **-d** determines whether a file is a directory.
- The file test **-M** determines the number of days since a file was last modified.
- The file test **-A** determines the number of days since a file was last accessed.
- The file test **-C** determines the number of days since a file was created.
- The file test **-x** determines whether a file is executable.
- File tests **-M**, **-A** and **-C** return a value in number of days.
- Other file tests simply return 1 for true and 0 for false.
- Function **sysopen** combines the two steps of creating a file and testing to see if a file exists. A **sysopen** call can be used to create a file for writing (only if it does not exist) all in one step. This way, there is no chance that a preexisting file will accidentally get deleted.
- Function **sysopen** takes three or four arguments. The first two are a filehandle and a filename. The third argument consists of flags imported from the **Fcntl** module and separated by vertical bars (|). The fourth argument sets the permissions of the file.
- File permissions can be changed with the **chmod** function. File permissions allow programmers to limit the access rights of a file to users. The **chmod** function takes a list of arguments, the first of which is a mode. The permissions granted by the mode are granted on each of the files. The mode should be a four-digit octal number. The first digit of the number should be zero. The remaining three digits represent a code specifying which permissions will be granted and to whom. The second digit represents the owner of the file, the third digit represents the group of users to which the file belongs and the fourth digit represents all other users.
- Groups are used to bring together multiple users sharing access of the same files.

- Programmers can access many basic system commands that enable them to rename files, delete files and even copy files under the control of a Perl program.

- The **rename** function renames the file specified by its first argument to the new name specified by its second argument. This function returns **1** if the function is successful and **0** if not.

- To delete files from a directory, use the **unlink** function, which deletes a list of files and returns the number of files successfully deleted.

- Function **chown** is used in UNIX to change ownership of a file. In UNIX, every user has an ID number, and every group of users has a group ID number. These ID numbers are determined by the system administrator. The **chown** function gives specific user ID (first argument) and group ID (second argument) numbers to a list of files (remaining arguments), changing each file's ownership within a UNIX file system. If you want to change only one ownership property (user or group) replace the ignored argument with **-1**. The function returns the number of successful changes.

- Function **utime** modifies a file's timestamps. Every file contains three timestamps, representing the time of the file's creation, last modification and last access. By modifying either of the first two, you automatically change the third. The **utime** function modifies the timestamps for a list of files and returns the number of files successfully modified.

- Interval time is the integer number of seconds since midnight GMT, January 1, 1970 (January 1, 1904, for the Mac operating system).

- Programmers normally modify the value of the **time** function returned when using **utime**. The **time** function takes no arguments and returns the current interval time.

- It is possible to have more than one name for a particular file. Alternative names for files can be created, destroyed, renamed, opened, etc., in Perl. The notion of alternative names is called *linking*.

- A hard link can be thought of as a name for a file on a disk. Multiple hard links may be used to provide several names for a single file. The operating system keeps track of the number of hard links to any given file, similar to a reference count for variables. If this hard-link count drops to zero and the file is closed, the file is deleted from the hard drive.

- A symlink (symbolic link) is a special type of file that refers to another file. When a symlink is opened, the operating system follows the symlink and opens the file to which the symlink refers. A symlink does not factor into an operating system's link count. Symlinks can refer to files that do not exist, files not on the current file system and directories. Symlinks can even be made to point to other symlinks. Because symlinks do not factor into an operating system's link count, removing all symlinks to a file does not cause the file to be deleted.

- In Perl, hard links are created using function **link**. This function takes two arguments: the original filename and the name of the new hard link.

- Symlinks are created using function **symlink**. This function also takes two arguments: the original filename (may not exist and could be a directory) and the name of the symbolic link.

- Symbolic links can be followed using function **readlink**.

- Function **unlink** removes all existing hard links to a file, effectively deleting it.

- In Perl, allocating multiple files at once is called *globbing* and is done using the asterisk wildcard character, *****, or any other glob character.

- To specify in Perl that you wish something to be globbed, you can do one of two things. If you enclose the filename with angle brackets, as in **<*.txt>**, then Perl will expand the wildcard character. In scalar context, Perl returns the first file that matches the pattern (if it exists) and in list context, it returns all of the files that match. This can also be done using the built-in **glob** function, **glob("*.txt")**. Perl programmers prefer to use function **glob** over the angle brackets.

- Files have filehandles, and directories have directory handles, which are almost identical to filehandles. They can be opened, closed and read.

- To open and create a directory handle, use function **opendir**, which takes two arguments. The first is the directory handle and the second is the name of the directory. Unlike function **open** for files, you cannot specify open modes like reading, writing, appending, etc.

- Function **closedir** closes directory handles.

- Once a directory has been opened, it can be read using function **readdir**. This function iterates through the directory, returning all files and directories stored in the directory.

- Function **rewinddir** will resets the directory handle to point to the first item in the directory.

- Although we cannot write to directories using directory handles, we can do it in another way: Directories can hold files and other directories. So, to write to a directory, all we have to do is create new files or new directories.

- Function **mkdir** takes two arguments. It creates a directory in the current directory whose name is specified by the first argument and whose permissions are specified by the second argument.

- To change the current directory, use function **chdir**.

- Directories can also be deleted with function **rmdir**.

- A way to make programs portable is to use Perl's **$^O** special variable. This variable contains the name of the operating system under which the program is running.

- In HTML, multiple spaces are converted into only one space when printed in browsers. The string **" "** adds a space that will not be ignored.

TERMINOLOGY

$^O special variable	**mkdir** function
$_ special variable	mode
** ** HTML symbol	**O_APPEND** flag for **sysopen**
* asterisk wildcard character	**O_CREAT** flag for **sysopen**
-A file test	**O_EXCL** flag for **sysopen**
-B file test	**O_NONBLOCK** flag for **sysopen**
-C file test	**O_RDONLY** flag for **sysopen**
chdir function	**O_RDWR** flag for **sysopen**
chmod function	**O_TRUNC** flag for **sysopen**
chown function	**O_WRONLY** flag for **sysopen**
closedir function	**open** function
-d file test	**opendir** function
directory handle	path separator
-e file test	Perl file permissions
em function in **CGI.pm**	permission
-f file test	plain file
Fcntl module	**-r** file test
file globbing	**readdir** function
file linking	**readlink** function
file permission	real uid/gid
file test	recursion
glob character	**rename** function
glob function	**rewinddir** function
globbing	**rmdir** function
group	**-s** file test
hard link	**strong** function in **CGI.pm**
link function	symbolic link
-M file test	symlink

symlink function	**unlink** function
sysopen function	**utime** function
-T file test	**-w** file test
time function	**-z** file test

SELF-REVIEW EXERCISES

11.1 Fill in the blanks in each of the following statements:

a) The **-e** file test determines whether a file _____.

b) The **-w** file test determines whether a file is _____.

c) The **-s** file test returns the size of a file in _____.

d) The **sysopen** constants are imported from the _____ module.

e) The _____ constant tells **sysopen** to truncate a file.

f) The three last digits of a permissions mode determine the access rights given to the _____, _____ and _____.

g) The _____ function deletes a file.

h) A file is also known as a _____ link.

i) Choosing all files that have a **.html** extension is one example of _____.

j) The _____ command changes the current working directory.

11.2 Determine whether each statement is *true* or *false*. If *false*, explain why.

a) The **-r** file test checks a file for readability.

b) The **-A** file test returns a value in number of days.

c) Whenever files are created, altered and destroyed rapidly, a **sysopen** command should be used.

d) The largest a permission number can be is 8.

e) Ownership of a file can be changed with function **chmod**.

f) A hard link can point to a directory.

g) A symlink must point to an existing file.

h) Enclosing a statement with an asterisk within angle brackets represents a globbing operation.

i) The function **readdir** returns all of the files in the current directory.

j) All directory handles must be explicitly opened using the **opendir** function.

11.3 Write a program to accomplish the following:

a) Prompt the user to enter a file (in the current directory) that he or she wishes to read.

b) Check to see if the file exists.

c) If the file does not exist, print a message to the user and end the program.

d) If the file does exist, open it for reading. Do so using **sysopen**, in case the file was deleted in the interim. Open the file for reading only, and do not set the permissions: that is, leave out the fourth argument to **sysopen**.

e) Print out the contents of the file.

f) Ask the user what he or she wishes to rename the file as.

g) Rename the file, and end the program. If a file with the new name already exists, do not rename the file.

11.4 Write a line of code to accomplish each of the following:

a) Change the permissions of a file (**file.txt**) so that the owner can read, write and execute the file, the group can read the file and all others can do nothing.

b) Create a symlink to **file.txt** called **symlink.txt**.

c) Create a hard link to **file.txt** called **link.txt**.

d) Delete **file.txt**. (Assume that part (b) has been executed.)

e) Use function **glob** to find all **.pl** files in the current directory.

ANSWERS TO SELF-REVIEW EXERCISES

11.1   a) exists. b) writable. c) bytes. d) **Fcntl**. e) **O_TRUNC**. f) owner, group, all others.
g) **unlink**. h) hard. i) globbing. j) **chdir**.

11.2   a) True.
　　　　　b) True.
　　　　　c) True.
　　　　　d) False. The largest permission value is 7.
　　　　　e) False. Ownership is changed with function **chown**.
　　　　　f) False. Hard links can point only to files.
　　　　　g) False. A symlink can point to any file or directory, whether or not it currently exists.
　　　　　h) True.
　　　　　i) False. It returns the names of all the files and all the directories in the current directory.
　　　　　j) True.

11.3   See the following code.

```
1   #!/usr/bin/perl
2   # Opening a file using sysopen and renaming it.
3
4   use strict;
5   use warnings;
6   use Fcntl;
7
8   print( "Enter a file you wish to read." );
9   chomp( my $file = <STDIN> );
10
11  if ( -e $file ) {
12     sysopen( FILE, $file, O_RDONLY ) or die( "Cannot open: $!" );
13     print while ( <FILE> );
14     close( FILE ) or die( "Cannot close: $!" );
15     print( "Enter new file name: " );
16     chomp( my $newFile = <STDIN> );
17     rename( "$file", "$newFile" ) unless ( -e $newFile );
18  }
19  else {
20     print( "Sorry, that file does not exist.\n" );
21  }
```

11.4   a) **chmod(0740, "file.txt");**
　　　　　b) **symlink("file.txt", "symlink.txt");**
　　　　　c) **link("file.txt", "link.txt");**
　　　　　d) **unlink("file.txt", "link.txt");**
　　　　　e) **glob("*.pl*");**

EXERCISES

11.5   Write a program that receives one filename as input. Use the file tests to determine whether
the file exists; if it exists, determine its size, when it was last accessed, when it was last updated and
what type of file it is.

11.6   Rename all **.txt** files in a certain directory (below the current directory) to have **.text**.

11.7   Create a hard link to a file. Open the new hard link, and update the file. Close the link and delete the link. Open the original file, and that make sure it was changed. As an extra challenge, create the link in another directory.

11.8   Write an archiving script. The script should iterate recursively through some directory and archive any files that are older than 30 days. Archiving could be as simple as renaming the file or could be something more complex, such as creating a new directory and moving all of the old files there. For this example, print the names of the files that would be archived to the screen.

11.9   Write a CGI program(s) that will take as input one filename. It should then print the file's contents into a **textarea** of a form. The user should be allowed to change the file however he or she chooses, and when they press the submit button, the new form data should be stored in the file.

12

Formatting

Objectives

- To understand Perl's formatting capabilities.
- To be able to use the different field types.
- To be able to use top-of-page processing.
- To be able to use multiple-line format fields.
- To be able to use the special format variables.

The chief merit of language is clearness.
Galen

My object all sublime
I shall achieve in time.
W. S. Gilbert

He had a wonderful talent for packing thought close, and
rendering it portable.
Thomas Babington Macaulay

Egad, I think the interpreter is the hardest to be understood
of the two!
Richard Brinsley Sheridan

Outline

12.1 Introduction

Perl's *formats* allow programmers to define templates that specify how data should appear when they are output. The formats enable you to specify fields that will be filled in when the formats execute. Formats are flexible tools that can be used for precise report generation. In this chapter, we discuss how to specify formats and how to use formats to create reports to output data in different ways. We see examples of these tools in action at the end of the chapter, in case studies on outputting a database and creating a Web log analyzer.

12.2 Creating Formatted Reports

A format declaration starts with keyword **format** and takes the following form:

```
format formatName =
text
.
```

The *text* portion of the format definition consists of three types of lines: comments, *picture lines* and *argument lines*. Comments start with a **#** character and are ignored when the format is printed. Picture lines specify the content of the format. Picture lines contain regular (literal) text and *format fields*. The regular text is printed as it is written, with no interpolation. Format fields specify placeholders for values that will be output later in the format. Argument lines specify the content that replaces the fields in the preceding picture line. An argument line contains a comma-separated list in which the first element of the list corresponds to the first field on the preceding line, the second element of the list corresponds to the second field on the preceding line, etc. Fields start with either an **@** or **^** character followed by *justification specifiers* that indicate the field length and how to interpolate the value. Like user-defined functions, formats are not required to be defined before they are used in a program.

Formats are invoked using function **write**. When **write** is called, it writes either to the currently selected filehandle or to the filehandle passed as an argument to the function. The default format that should be used with a particular filehandle has the same name as the filehandle itself. Thus, to specify a default format for use with **STDOUT**, name the format **STDOUT**. Figure 12.1 demonstrates a simple example of the use of formats.

```
1   #!/usr/bin/perl
2   # Fig. 12.1: fig12_01.pl
3   # A simple format example
4
5   use warnings;
6   use strict;
7
8   my $greeting = 'Hello';
9   my $planet = 'world';
10  write();
11
12  $greeting = 'Greetings';
13  $planet = 'Mars';
14  write();
15
16  $greeting = 'Howdy';
17  $planet = 'Pluto';
18  write();
19
20  format STDOUT =
21  I would like to say @<<<<<<<<< @<<<<<<<!
22                          $greeting, $planet
23  .
```

```
I would like to say Hello      world   !
I would like to say Greetings  Mars    !
I would like to say Howdy      Pluto   !
```

Fig. 12.1   A simple example of the use of formats.

A format without a name automatically defaults to **STDOUT**, so in our format declaration (line 20), we can remove the name. The format consists of one picture line (line 21) and one argument line (line 22). The picture line contains the literal text "**I would like to say**," followed by a 10-character field, followed by an 8 character field, and ending with an exclamation point. Looking again at line 21, it seems as though the fields are actually 9 and 7 characters long, because there are 9 **<** characters in the first field and 7 **<** characters in the second field. The character **@**, which introduces the field, is counted as part of the field width. Thus, when **@** is combined with **<** symbols, the fields become 10 characters wide and 8 characters wide, respectively. Line 22 is an argument line which indicates that we would like to have the contents of the variable **$greeting** placed in the first field and the contents of **$planet** placed in the second. When using this format, all we have to do is assign the values that we want to be printed to the variables **$greeting** and **$planet**, as we do in lines 8 and 9, 12 and 13 and 16 and 17. Then we simply call the **write** function, which formats the data as specified (lines 10, 14 and 18).

The characters following the **@** character specify the type of justification to use for that field. The **<** character specifies left justification of a field, the **>** character specifies right justification of a field, and the **|** character specifies that the contents of a field should be centered. The total number of characters in a field, including the **@** character, indicates the field width. Thus in the preceding example, the fields are of fixed width and left justified; Figure 12.2 outputs address labels using the different field justifications.

```perl
1   #!/usr/bin/perl
2   # Fig. 12.2: fig12_02.pl
3   # demonstrates different types of fields
4
5   use warnings;
6   use strict;
7
8   my $name = 'John Doe';
9   my $streetAddress = '12 Nowhere Place';
10  my $town = 'Springfield';
11  my $state = 'OH';
12  my $zip = '11111-1111';
13  write();
14
15  $name = 'Washington Irving';
16  $streetAddress = '12 Kirkland Road';
17  $town = 'Sleepy Hollow';
18  $state = 'NY';
19  $zip = '01942-3234';
20  write();
21
22  $name = 'Tarzan';
23  $streetAddress = 'One Jungle Lane';
24  $town = 'Tarzanville';
25  $state = 'AQ';
26  $zip = '01234-5678';
27  write();
28
29  format STDOUT =
30  @|||||||||||||||||||||||||||
31  $name
32  @|||||||||||||||||||||||||||
33  $streetAddress
34  @<<<<<<<<<<<, @< @>>>>>>>>>
35  $town,        $state, $zip
36
37  .
```

```
        John Doe
     12 Nowhere Place
Springfield , OH 11111-1111

     Washington Irving
     12 Kirkland Road
Sleepy Hollo, NY 01942-3234

         Tarzan
     One Jungle Lane
Tarzanville , AQ 01234-5678
```

Fig. 12.2   Different types of fields.

The format in Fig. 12.2 is defined on lines 29–37. Line 30 of the format prints the contents of **$name** centered in a 27-character field. The next format line (line 32) prints the **$streetAddress** centered in a 27-character field. The final format line (line 34) prints **$town** left justified, followed by a comma, followed by the two characters of **$state**, and then **$zip** right justified in a 10-character field. Lines 8–27 assign values to these variables and **write** them for three different addresses.

You might have noticed in Fig. 12.2 that although we assigned to **$town** the value **Sleepy Hollow** on line 17, it was printed as **Sleepy Hollo**. With this type of field, if the string to be placed in the field is longer than the allotted field length, the string is truncated to fit the field.

Common Programming Error 12.1

Declaring a format where the fields are not wide enough for the values they hold causes the values to be truncated.

A caveat of formats is that any variable used in a format must be in the scope in which the format is declared. Thus, to use **my** variables in a format, the format must be declared after the variables are defined and before the variables go out of scope. This rule can be tricky when you are using a format in a subroutine; you are forced either to declare the format inside the subroutine or to use global variables instead. Variables dynamically scoped with **local** do not have the same problem as lexically scoped variables.

Common Programming Error 12.2

Trying to use a lexically scoped variable in a format that is not declared in the lexical variable's scope causes an error.

Software Engineering Observation 12.1

*Formats do not work well with lexically scoped variables because formats were part of Perl before lexically scoped variables and the **my** keyword were introduced. Formats were not updated when lexically scoped variables were introduced. Placing the functionality of formats into a module is one of the parts of the language that could be implemented in the future.*

12.3 Top-of-Form Processing

A format that prints at the top of every page can be specified. Perl determines when to output the *top-of-page* (or *top-of-form*) *format* based on the number of lines per page, which is stored in the special variable **$=** (**$FORMAT_LINES_PER_PAGE**). At the beginning of the output and every time that number of lines is output, the top-of-page format executes. The default top-of-page format triggered by a **write** function is the name of the current filehandle with **_TOP** appended to it. Figure 12.3 demonstrates this format. Figure 12.3 also introduces the numeric justification symbol, **#**. A decimal point character (**.**) can be used to line up decimal positions in a floating-point number.

```
1    #!/usr/bin/perl
2    # Fig. 12.3: fig12_03.pl
3    # demonstrates top-of-page formatting
```

Fig. 12.3   Top-of-page formatting (part 1 of 2).

```
4
5    use warnings;
6    use strict;
7
8    my $product = 'Sound Card';
9    my $price = 99.00;
10   my $number = '0132';
11   write();
12
13   $product = 'Monitor';
14   $price = 550.34521;
15   $number = '13341522';
16   write();
17
18   $product = 'Mouse';
19   $price = '5';
20   $number = '115136';
21   write();
22
23   format STDOUT_TOP =
24   Product                        Price           ID Number
25   ----------------               ---------       ---------
26   .
27
28   format STDOUT =
29   @<<<<<<<<<<<<<<<<<<<<           $@####.##        @<<<<<<<<
30   $product,                       $price,          $number
31   .
```

```
Product                        Price           ID Number
----------------               ---------       ---------
Sound Card                     $    99.00      0132
Monitor                        $   550.35      13341522
Mouse                          $     5.00      115136
```

Fig. 12.3   Top-of-page formatting (part 2 of 2).

On lines 23–26, we define the top-of-page header, which outputs the specified text each time the total number of lines that have been output equals the value stored in **$=** (in other words, at the beginning of each page). The format we use on lines 28–31 consists of **$product** left justified, **$price** justified with respect to the decimal point and **$number** left justified.

Top-of-form processing is handled automatically by the **write** function. The **write** function looks at the **$-** variable (**$FORMAT_LINES_LEFT**), which specifies the number of lines remaining in the current page, and determines if there is enough room on the current page for what it needs to output. If there is not enough room, **write** outputs the value of the special variable **$^L**, which is **\f** (form feed) by default, but can be changed to any string. The form-feed character starts a new page. Then, the top-of-page format is output.

Testing and Debugging Tip 12.1

*Some platforms display the **\f** character on the screen. So, if you are getting a funny symbol at the start of every page and want to remove it, set **$^L** to an empty string.*

Perl does not provide bottom-of-the-page formatting automatically, as it does top-of-the-page formatting. If you really need a footer, there are a few ways in which to create one. A simple solution is to decrease the lines per page by the number of lines to be in the footer and then put the text of the footer in the **$^L** variable. Because the **$^L** variable is output before a new page starts, the text in it will appear at the bottom of the previous page. If you need to do more than just print text at the bottom of each page, then this solution is not adequate. In this case, you need to monitor the **$-** variable yourself and perform the necessary processing when it reaches the correct value. Section 12.7 show some examples of this.

12.4 Multiple-Line Format Fields

If a value to be output is longer than the field in which it will be placed, the value is truncated to fit the field. What if we know that we have long values and want to be able to have them automatically continue on the next line? Using the formats discussed previously, we would have to break the value into different variables and specify each part of the format separately. Luckily, however, Perl provides several ways to print *multiple-line fields*.

Multiple-line fields are specified with the ^ character, which tells Perl to print as many words from a variable as can fit in a field and then remove whatever was printed from the front of that variable's contents. The next time the variable is referenced in the format, the contents of the variable are output beginning from the point at which the last line of the format ended. We can use this method to extend variables over multiple lines of the format. Unfortunately, this style of format causes function **write** to change the value of the variable. If you intend to use the value after the **write** call, use a temporary variable to hold the value during the **write** call. Figure 12.4 demonstrates multiple-line fields.

```
1   #!/usr/bin/perl
2   # Fig. 12.4: fig12_04.pl
3   # Demonstration of multiline fields.
4
5   use warnings;
6   use strict;
7
8   my $name = 'John Doe';
9   my $letters = 'SWM';
10  my $phone = '(413)223-4445';
11  my $description = <<'DONE';
12  I like long romantic walks along the beach, reading a good book,
13  and stuff like that. Please call me.
14  DONE
15  write();
16
17  $name = 'Robin Hood';
18  $letters = 'SWM';
19  $phone = '(324)596-5678';
20  $description = <<'DONE';
21  Looking for energetic Lady who shares my zeal for politics. I enjoy
22  robbing from the rich and giving to the poor. Must be willing to
23  live in the forest.
24  DONE
```

Fig. 12.4   Multiple-line format fields with the ^ character (part 1 of 2).

```
25   write();
26
27   $name = 'Tarzan';
28   $letters = 'SWM';
29   $phone = '';
30   $description = 'Me Tarzan.';
31   write();
32
33   format STDOUT =
34   Name: @<<<<<<<<<<<<<<<<    Description:   ^<<<<<<<<<<<<<<<<<<<<<<<
35         $name,                              $description
36   letters: @<<<<<                           ^<<<<<<<<<<<<<<<<<<<<<<<<
37           $letters,                         $description
38   phone: @|||||||||||                       ^<<<<<<<<<<<<<<<<<<<<<<<~
39          $phone,                            $description
40   ~                                         ^<<<<<<<<<<<<<<<<<<<<<<<
41                                             $description
42   ~                                         ^<<<<<<<<<<<<<<<<<<<<<<<
43                                             $description
44   ~                                         ^<<<<<<<<<<<<<<<<<<<<<<<...
45                                             $description
46
47   .
```

```
Name: John Doe            Description:   I like long romantic
letters: SWM                             walks along the beach,
phone: (413)223-4445                     reading a good book,  and
                                         stuff like that. Please
                                         call me.

Name: Robin Hood          Description:   Looking for energetic
letters: SWM                             Lady who shares my zeal
phone: (324)596-5678                     for politics. I enjoy
                                         robbing from the rich and
                                         giving to the poor. Must
                                         be willing to  live in...

Name: Tarzan              Description:   Me Tarzan.
letters: SWM
```

Fig. 12.4   Multiple-line format fields with the ^ character (part 2 of 2).

This example uses formats to output hypothetical personal ads. The description category often takes up more than one line, so we use the ^ character to create a multiple-line field (lines 34, 36, 38, 40, 42 and 44). We do not want to waste space outputting lines that would be blank if the person has a short description. In this example, Tarzan has a short description. Rather than printing six lines for such a short description, we can use ~ characters on lines that might be empty in the output (lines 40, 42 and 44, causing those lines to be suppressed when they are empty. In this case, we have a maximum of six lines of output for the description. The three dots (. . .) on the end of the last field (line 44) indicate that the description is actually longer than what can be output. The three dots are printed only if there is overflow. If we did not want a limit on how many lines to output, we could place two tilde characters (~~) on a line, which causes the line to be repeated in the format until the entire contents of the variables are output.

With multiple-line fields, Perl attempts to stop lines at word boundaries by splitting the text after certain characters. These characters are stored in the special variable **$:** (**$FORMAT_LINE_BREAK_CHARACTERS**), which can be changed if you have a special case. By default, **$:** holds a space, a dash (-) and the newline character.

A less flexible option for multiple-line output is the **@*** *field*. This field splits a variable into multiple lines and outputs the variable in its entirety. The **@*** field is best used on a line by itself. Any text or fields on the line before the **@*** field are output once and not repeated for any overflow. The **@*** field breaks the variable into lines of equal length without considering other text on the line, so having text before **@*** causes the line endings to be inconsistent. Putting text after the **@*** is not recommended, as this can have unexpected results. Another difference between the **@*** field and the **^** multiple-line field is that **@*** fields recognize \n and \t characters and will print tabs and newlines, whereas **^** fields translate \n and \t characters into spaces. Figure 12.5 shows how you might use the **@*** field.

```perl
1   #!/usr/bin/perl
2   # Fig. 12.5: fig12_05.pl
3   # Demonstration of the @* field.
4
5   use warnings;
6   use strict;
7
8   my $name = 'John Doe';
9   my $letters = 'SWM';
10  my $phone = '(413)223-4445';
11
12  my $description = <<'DONE';
13  I like long romantic walks along the beach, reading a good book,
14  and stuff like that.
15  Please call me.
16  DONE
17  write();
18
19  $name = 'Robin Hood';
20  $letters = 'SWM';
21  $phone = '(324)596-5678';
22
23  $description = <<'DONE';
24  Looking for energetic Lady who shares my zeal for politics. I enjoy
25  robbing from the rich and giving to the poor. Must be willing to
26  live in the forest.
27  DONE
28  write();
29
30  $name = 'Tarzan';
31  $letters = 'SWM';
32  $phone = '';
33  $description = 'Me Tarzan.';
34  write();
```

Fig. 12.5   Multiple-line format fields with the **@*** character (part 1 of 2).

```
35
36   format STDOUT =
37   Name: @<<<<<<<<<<<<<<<<<<<   letters: @<<<<< phone: @<<<<<<<<<<<<
38         $name,                           $letters,     $phone
39   @*
40   $description
41
42   .
```

```
Name: John Doe              letters: SWM     phone: (413)223-4445
I like long romantic walks along the beach, reading a good book,
and stuff like that.
Please call me.

Name: Robin Hood            letters: SWM     phone: (324)596-5678
Looking for energetic Lady who shares my zeal for politics. I enjoy
robbing from the rich and giving to the poor. Must be willing to
live in the forest.

Name: Tarzan                letters: SWM     phone:
Me Tarzan.
```

Fig. 12.5   Multiple-line format fields with the **@*** character (part 2 of 2).

The format in this example (line 36 through 42) is similar to the one used in the example in Fig. 12.4, except the name, letters and phone number are all on the first line (line 37). The **@*** field in line 39 causes the entire contents of **$description** to be output, on multiple lines if necessary.

12.5 Format Variables

There are a number of special variables that can be used to customize your formats. You have seen some of them in previous sections. Figure 12.6 provides a complete list of the format-specific special variables. For convenience, there is a module that allow us to use more logical-sounding names for these built-in variables: The pragma **use English** allows us to use alternative names. The format variables are specific to each filehandle. To access the variables of a filehandle other than the current one, select the filehandle with the **select** function.

Performance Tip 12.1

Although useful, the **English** *module can decrease efficiency and should not be used if performance is an important issue for the program.*

Name	use English name	Description	Default
$~	$FORMAT_NAME	Current format name	STDOUT
$^	$FORMAT_TOP_NAME	Current top-of-form format name	STDOUT_TOP

Fig. 12.6   Special format variables (part 1 of 2).

Name	use English name	Description	Default
$%	$FORMAT_PAGE_NUMBER	Current page number	0
$=	$FORMAT_LINES_PER_PAGE	Number of lines output per page	60
$-	$FORMAT_LINES_LEFT	Number of lines remaining on the current page	0
$:	$FORMAT_LINE_BREAK_CHARACTERS	Characters at which multiple lines are split	-\n
$^L	$FORMAT_FORMFEED	Text output to start a new page	\f

Fig. 12.6   Special format variables (part 2 of 2).

The example of Fig. 12.7 receives a filename and the number of lines per page as command-line arguments and outputs the file using two different formats. Figure 12.8 shows the contents of the file **sample.txt**, which was used to demonstrate the formatting in Fig. 12.7.

The filename specified on the command line is assigned to **$file** on line 9, and the lines per page is assigned to **$FORMAT_LINES_PER_PAGE** on line 11 (we specified **use English** on line 7 to enable the English names). In this example, the file is **sample.txt** (Fig. 12.8), and we specify eight lines per page. The program opens the file on line 14. Lines 17–19 use a **while** loop to read through the file and output the file using the default-selected formats **STDOUT** (lines 45–50) and **STDOUT_TOP** (lines 38–43). For now, we set the form feed text to **" "** (line 12), so that nothing is output to start a new page.

Line 27 changes the top-of-page format by assigning to **$FORMAT_TOP_NAME** the format **NEW_TOP** (line 27). Also, line 28 changes the regular format by assigning the format **NEWFORMAT** to **$FORMAT_NAME**. Line 29 assigns a new value to variable **$FORMAT_FORMFEED** to demonstrate the text that is output to start a new page. Line 30 reopens the file, and lines 32–34 output the contents of the file using the new formats.

Notice that in line 41, the **STDOUT_TOP** format uses the special variable **$%** (**$FORMAT_PAGE_NUMBER**) to print the page number at the top of each page. Also note that line 47 of the **STDOUT** format uses special variable **$.** (**$INPUT_LINE_NUMBER**) to number each line read from the input file.

We can point out a number of things from this example. First of all, as we mentioned earlier, if a multiple-line **write** cannot fit on a page, the **write** function starts a new page. This situation occurs in the sample program output, because the first "page" printed in this example was only six lines long, instead of the specified eight. If, for some reason, you must have exactly the same number of lines printed per page, you can monitor the **$-** variable and do some extra processing to make this layout work. If the format is of a fixed length each time, you can just check to see if the next **write** will skip any lines and then print out the necessary number of lines before executing the format. Another option, which works when you do not know if the next **write** will need a new page or not, is to make sure that the format form-feed variable, **$^L**, always contains a newline for each remaining line. That way, when the form feed is printed, it will fill in the lines that were skipped.

```perl
1   #!/usr/bin/perl
2   # Fig. 12.7: fig12_07.pl
3   # Demonstrates the special format variables
4
5   use warnings;
6   use strict;
7   use English;
8
9   my $file = $ARGV[ 0 ];
10  # setting the lines per page.
11  $FORMAT_LINES_PER_PAGE = $ARGV[ 1 ];
12  $FORMAT_FORMFEED = "";
13
14  open( FILE, $file ) or die( "Cannot open $file:: $!" );
15  my $line;
16
17  while ( $line = <FILE> ) {
18      write();
19  }
20
21  close( FILE ) or die( "Cannot close: $!" );
22
23  print( "\n", '*' x 60, "\n" );
24  print( "Now we are going to print using the new format" );
25  print( "\n", '*' x 60, "\n\n" );
26
27  $FORMAT_TOP_NAME = 'NEW_TOP';
28  $FORMAT_NAME = 'NEWFORMAT';
29  $FORMAT_FORMFEED = "Form Feed:\n";
30  open( FILE, $file ) or die( "Cannot open $file: $!" );
31
32  while ( $line = <FILE> ) {
33      write();
34  }
35
36  close( FILE ) or die( "Cannot close: $!" );
37
38  format STDOUT_TOP =
39  -------------------------------------------------------------------
40  File: @<<<<<<<<<<<<<<<<<<<<<<                    Page: @|||
41        $file,                                          $%
42  -------------------------------------------------------------------
43  .
44
45  format STDOUT =
46  Line @<<<    ^<<<<<<<<<<<<<<<<<<<<<<<<<<<<<<<<<<<<<<<<<<<<<<<<<<<<<
47       $.,     $line
48  ~~          ^<<<<<<<<<<<<<<<<<<<<<<<<<<<<<<<<<<<<<<<<<<<<<<<<<<<<<
49              $line
50  .
51
52  format NEW_TOP =
53  -------------------------------------------------------------------
```

Fig. 12.7   Special format variables (part 1 of 2).

```
54   Without putting the page or line numbers into @<<<<<<<<<<<<<<<<<<<
55                                                 $file
56   ------------------------------------------------------------------
57   .
58
59   format NEWFORMAT =
60   @<<<<<<<<<<<<<<<<<<<<<<<<<<<<<<<<<<<<<<<<<<<<<<<<<<<<<<<<<<<<<<<<<<<
61   $line
62   .
```

```
----------------------------------------------------------------
File: sample.txt                                    Page:   1
----------------------------------------------------------------
Line 1       This is a sample text file.
Line 2       The ~'s can be anywhere in the line,
Line 3       and show up as a space when printed.
----------------------------------------------------------------
File: sample.txt                                    Page:   2
----------------------------------------------------------------
Line 4       There are a number of special variables which are
             associated with Perl and can be used to further
             customize your formats. You have seen some of them.
Line 5       line was not printed at all.

******************************************************************
Now we are going to print using the new format
******************************************************************

This is a sample text file.
Form Feed:
----------------------------------------------------------------
Without putting the page or line numbers into sample.txt
----------------------------------------------------------------
The ~'s can be anywhere in the line,
and show up as a space when printed.
There are a number of special variables which are associated with
line was not printed at all.
```

Fig. 12.7   Special format variables (part 2 of 2).

```
This is a sample text file.
The ~'s can be anywhere in the line,
and show up as a space when printed.
There are a number of special variables which are associated with Perl
and can be used to further customize your formats. You have seen some
of them.
line was not printed at all.
```

Fig. 12.8   Contents of **sample.txt**.

Also note in Fig. 12.7 that when we changed formats and wrote to the new format, function **write** did not begin by printing the top-of-page format; the first line printed by the new format was "**This is a sample text file**." To force the top-of-page format to output, set the format lines' left variable (**$-**) to zero. The log file analysis case study at the end of the chapter (Section 12.7) contains an example of this procedure.

Testing and Debugging Tip 12.2

*When using **$-**, **print** statements do not automatically decrement **$-**. Variable **$-** is decremented automatically only when you use **write**. If you use **print** and want the **$-** variable to remain accurate, you need to decrement it yourself.*

12.6 Case Study: Outputting a Database

Formats simplify the generation od similar reports for large amounts of data. Ideally, we would like to create a template for outputting a database. Fig. 12.9 presents a simple implementation of such a template.

The "database" (Fig. 12.10) we use here is a text file with each individual record on a separate line and each element in the record separated by two colons. Thus, to read a record, we just read in a line of input, and to access the elements, we use **split(/::/)**. We can assign the elements directly to the variables used by a format and then call **write** to output the variables in the specified format.

Our example data consist of some of the books that are offered by Deitel & Associates, Inc. The file has each category heading on a line by itself, followed by the records that fit under the category. The individual records consist of fields containing the name of a book, the ID number of the book, the year it was published, the price of the book, the number of copies in stock and a short description of the book.

Our program uses one format for the column headers and a different format for the records. The program uses the first command-line argument as the name of the file to be processed. Normally, we should print out all of the records without any top-of-form processing, but if a **-t** flag is the second argument passed to the program, the program will use a top-of-page format. The user can also specify a third argument when using the **-t** argument that sets the number of lines per page, with the default at 24. When the **-t** mode is enabled, the top of the page should always be output after the exact number of lines specified. Also, the year of publication is stored in the file as a number, but when it is printed, it should have a copyright symbol before it. The sample execution of this program that follows the code uses the **-t** command-line argument.

```perl
1   #!/usr/bin/perl
2   # Fig. 12.9: fig12_09.pl
3   # Printing a database using formats
4
5   use warnings;
6   use strict;
7   my $Top;
8
9   if ( defined( $ARGV[ 1 ] ) && $ARGV[ 1 ] eq '-t' ) {
10      $Top = 1;
11      $^ = 'FORMAT_TOP';
12
```

Fig. 12.9   Printing a database using formats (part 1 of 3).

```perl
13      if ( defined( $ARGV[ 2 ] ) &&
14          !( ( $ARGV[ 2 ] <= 0 ) || ( $ARGV [ 2 ] > 1000 ) ) ) {
15          $= = $ARGV[ 2 ];
16      }
17      else {
18          $= = 24;
19      }
20   }
21
22   my ( $name, $id, $year, $price, $num, $description );
23   open( FILE, "<$ARGV[ 0 ]" ) or die( "Cannot open: $!" );
24
25   while ( <FILE> ) {
26      ($name, $id, $year, $price, $num, $description) = split( /::/ );
27
28      if ( !defined( $id ) ) {
29          $~ = "CATEGORY";
30          write();
31          $~ = "STDOUT";
32      }
33      else {
34          write();
35      }
36
37      $^L = "\n" x $- if ( $Top );
38   }
39
40   close( FILE ) or die( "Cannot close: $!" );
41
42   sub copyright {
43      return "(c)".$_[ 0 ];
44   }
45
46   format FORMAT_TOP =
47   Product List:   Deitel & Associates Inc.              Page @|
48                                                              $%
49   --------------------------------------------------------------------
50   .
51
52   format =
53   @|||||||||||||||||||||||||||||||||||||||||||||||||||||||||||||||||||||||||
54   $name
55
56   @|||||||||||||||||||||||||||||||||||||||||||||||||||||||||||||||||||||||||
57   copyright( $year )
58
59   ISBN:   @<<<<<<<<<<<<< ^<<<<<<<<<<<<<<<<<<<<<<<<<<<<<<<<<<<<<<
60                  $id,        $description
61   Cost: $@###.##         ^<<<<<<<<<<<<<<<<<<<<<<<<<<<<<<<<<<<<<
62          $price,         $description
63   Number In Stock: @<<   ^<<<<<<<<<<<<<<<<<<<<<<<<<<<<<<<<<<<<<
64                  $num, $description
```

Fig. 12.9   Printing a database using formats (part 2 of 3).

```
65   ~~                          ^<<<<<<<<<<<<<<<<<<<<<<<<<<<<<<<<<<<<<<
66                              $description
67   ----------------------------------------------------------------
68   .
69
70   format CATEGORY =
71   ================================================================
72   @||||||||||||||||||||||||||||||||||||||||||||||||||||||||||||||||
73   $name
74   ================================================================
75   .
```

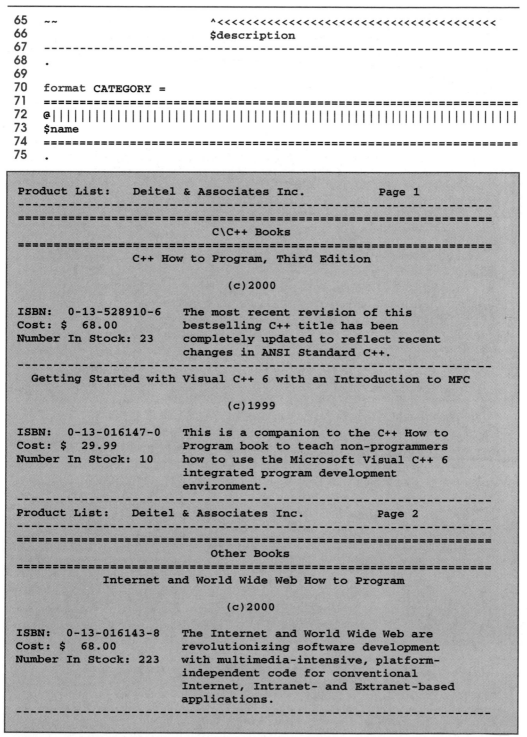

```
Product List:   Deitel & Associates Inc.        Page 1
----------------------------------------------------------------
================================================================
                       C\C++ Books
================================================================
            C++ How to Program, Third Edition


                        (c)2000

ISBN:  0-13-528910-6    The most recent revision of this
Cost: $  68.00          bestselling C++ title has been
Number In Stock: 23     completely updated to reflect recent
                        changes in ANSI Standard C++.
----------------------------------------------------------------
  Getting Started with Visual C++ 6 with an Introduction to MFC


                        (c)1999

ISBN:  0-13-016147-0    This is a companion to the C++ How to
Cost: $  29.99          Program book to teach non-programmers
Number In Stock: 10     how to use the Microsoft Visual C++ 6
                        integrated program development
                        environment.
----------------------------------------------------------------
Product List:   Deitel & Associates Inc.        Page 2
----------------------------------------------------------------
================================================================
                       Other Books
================================================================
        Internet and World Wide Web How to Program


                        (c)2000

ISBN:  0-13-016143-8    The Internet and World Wide Web are
Cost: $  68.00          revolutionizing software development
Number In Stock: 223    with multimedia-intensive, platform-
                        independent code for conventional
                        Internet, Intranet- and Extranet-based
                        applications.
----------------------------------------------------------------
```

Fig. 12.9   Printing a database using formats (part 3 of 3).

```
C\C++ Books
C++ How to Program, Third Edition::0-13-528910-6::2000::68.00::23::The
most recent revision of this bestselling C++ title has been completely
updated to reflect recent changes in ANSI Standard C++.
Getting Started with Visual C++ 6 with an Introduction to MFC::0-13-
016147-0::1999::29.99::10::This is a companion to the C++ How to
Program book to teach non-programmers how to use the Microsoft Visual
C++ 6 integrated program development environment.
Other Books
Internet and World Wide Web How to Program::0-13-016143-
8::2000::68.00::223::The Internet and World Wide Web are
revolutionizing software development with multimedia-intensive,
platform-independent code for conventional Internet, Intranet- and
Extranet-based applications.
```

Fig. 12.10 Contents of `list.txt`.

Lines 9–20 process the command-line arguments, checking to see if the **-t** flag was specified (line 9). If it was, then we set a flag (**$Top**) to indicate that top-of-form processing is being used during this execution of the program, and we set the format-top variable, **$^**, to be **FORMAT_TOP** (line 11). Next, the program determines if there was a third argument and if it is within a reasonable range (lines 13 and 14). If the condition is true, the program sets **$=** (**$FORMAT_LINES_PER_PAGE**) to the value specified from the command line (line 15). Otherwise, the program sets **$=** to the default value of 24 (line 18).

Line 22 declares the variables that will be used in the format, so that they are in scope both when they are being used and when the format is declared. Line 23 opens the file for input, and the **while** loop starting on line 25 processes the file and outputs the results.

In the **while** loop, we **split** the data into individual fields in line 26. We then check if the data input represent a category name or a record. We will be outputting records much more often than categories, so we decided to make the record format the default format. Thus, if we have a category, we must change the format to **CATEGORY**, **write** the category and change the format back (lines 28–32). This way, when we have a record, we can just call the **write** function, without doing anything else. Now, if we are using top-of-page formatting, we want to put into the **$^L** variable the amount of newlines needed (line 37) to keep the tops of the pages consistent, as described in Section 12.5.

We declared our formats on lines 46–75. Instead of worrying about appending the copyright symbol before calling **write**, we defined a subroutine (**copyright**) that does it for us, and we call the function (line 57) to fill that particular field. Values to be placed in fields are not required to be variables.

In this example, formats simplify a job that normally would be fairly complicated and difficult to modify. The format approach makes our program much more flexible and easier to debug, maintain and modify.

12.7 Case Study: Web Log Analyzer

In this case study, we write a script that analyzes the log files created by the Apache Web server. These files contain information about the accessing of the files that are served. First, we analyze the access log. Apache writes to the access log every time a request is received by the server. The access log contains information about which file was requested, when it was requested, who requested it, how it was requested, the result of the request and how many bytes were transferred. From this log, we can generate statistics on issues such as how often each file is accessed and when files are most often accessed. The following is an example of a line from **access.log**:

```
192.168.1.75 - - [12/Jul/2000:15:30:26 -0400]
"GET /cgi-bin/test.pl HTTP/1.0" 500 600
```

Perl is ideal for analyzing log files, because of the power of Perl's regular expressions. We can break a line like this one into separate parts by using just one regular expression. To write this expression we start at the beginning of the line and specify a pattern for each part we want to extract from the log. For example, the first part we want to keep is the IP address, which consists of four numbers separated by periods. Thus, our regular expression will start with **/^(\d+\.\d+\.\d+\.\d+)**. By creating a pattern for each part of the data we wish to extract, we can quickly write a regular expression that extracts the parts we want from a line of text in the access log.

After we have a way to extract the parts from each entry, we can write a format that can be used to output the entries. We can also keep running totals of statistics on different parts of the log and then use formats to print the statistics out. We are going to take advantage of the variable that keeps track of the number of lines remaining on a page to monitor when we are at the end of a page and allow the user to pause until he or she has read the page and wants to continue. Figure 12.11 shows the code for this example.

We set the special format variables before using each one in this example, because different formats are used for each part of the output. Lines 15, 40 and 53 set the variables using list assignment. Variable **$~** is assigned the current format name. Variable **$^** is assigned the top-of-page format name. The lines left (**$-**) and page number (**$%**) are both reset to 0 before we start writing a new list.

We wrote function **parseAccessEntry** (lines 74–90) to split the access-log entries into their components. This function returns a list of the components, which we assign directly to the variables used by the format (line 23) and then we output the data. After outputting the entry, we look at the entry to update the statistics we are keeping—the number of times each document has been accessed and the total bytes transferred per hour of day.

After each **write** call, the lines remaining variable, **$-**, is checked. If there is only one line left, function **prompt** is called to prompt the user to press *Enter* to continue. The function waits for the user to do so. [*Note*: The **PRINTACCESS** format used in this example was compressed to fit on one line of this book. Normally, some of the fields, like the filename, would be longer.]

```
1   #!/usr/bin/perl
2   # Fig. 12.11: fig12_11.pl
3   # Analyzes the Apache access log file.
4
5   use warnings;
6   use strict;
7   use English;
8
9   # System settings changed to make output appear correctly
```

Fig. 12.11 Printing the Apache Web server access log (part 1 of 5).

```perl
10   $FORMAT_LINES_PER_PAGE = 25;
11   $FORMAT_FORMFEED = '';
12   my $access='C:\Program Files\Apache Group\Apache\logs\access.log';
13   my $interval = 3;
14
15   ( $~, $^, $-, $% ) = ( 'PRINTACCESS', 'PRINTACCESS_TOP', 0, 0 );
16   my ( @entry, %most, %hourly );
17
18   # loop that prints each entry and gathers the statistics
19   open( FILE, $access ) or die( "Cannot open $access" );
20
21   while ( <FILE> ) {
22      next if ( $_ eq "\n" );             # skip blank lines
23      @entry = parseAccessEntry( $_ );
24      write();
25
26      prompt() if ( $FORMAT_LINES_LEFT == 1 );
27      $most{ $entry[ 3 ] }++;
28
29      my $hour = ( split( /:/, $entry[ 1 ], 3 ) )[ 1 ];
30      $hourly{ $hour.'requests' }++;
31      $hourly{ $hour.'transferred' } += $entry[ 6 ]
32                    unless ( $entry[ 6 ] eq '-' );
33   }
34
35   close( FILE ) or die( "Cannot close: $!" );
36   print( "\n" x ( $- - 1 ) );
37   prompt();
38
39   # printing most frequently accessed statistics
40   ( $~, $^, $-, $% ) = ( 'MOST', 'MOST_TOP', 0, 0 );
41   my $key;
42
43   foreach $key ( sort { $most{ $b } <=> $most{ $a } }
44              ( keys( %most ) ) ) {
45      write();
46      prompt() if ( $FORMAT_LINES_LEFT == 1 );
47   }
48
49   print( "\n" x ( $- - 1 ) );
50   prompt();
51
52   # printing hourly access rate and bytes transferred.
53   ( $~, $^, $-, $% ) = ( 'TIME', 'TIME_TOP', 0, 0 );
54   my ( $requests, $transferred, $startTime );
55
56   for ( $startTime = 0; $startTime < 24;
57         $startTime += $interval ) {
58      ( $requests, $transferred ) = ( 0, 0 );
59
60      for ( my $hour = $startTime;
61            $hour < $startTime + $interval && $hour < 24;
62            $hour++ ) {
```

Fig. 12.11   Printing the Apache Web server access log (part 2 of 5).

```
63           $requests += $hourly{ $hour.'requests' }
64                      if exists( $hourly{ $hour.'requests' } );
65           $transferred += $hourly{ $hour.'transferred' }
66                      if exists( $hourly{ $hour.'transferred' } );
67        }
68
69        write();
70        prompt() if ( $- == 1 );
71     }
72     print( "\n" x ( $- - 2 ) );
73
74     sub parseAccessEntry
75     {
76        my $entry = shift;
77
78        if ( $entry =~ /^( \d+\.\d+\.\d+.\d+ )\s-\s-\s\[ #IP Address
79                          ( [\d\w:\/]+ )\s-\d{4}\]\s\"    #time
80                          ( \w* )\s                       #Request type
81                          ( [^\s]* )\s                    #File name
82                          ( [^\"]* )\"\s                  #Protocol
83                          ( \d+ )\s                       #Request result
84                          ( \d+|\- )\s*\n$/x ) {          #Total bytes
85           return ( $1, $2, $3, $4, $5, $6, $7 );
86        }
87
88        warn "Not a normal access log entry.\n$entry\n";
89        return undef;
90     }
91
92     sub prompt
93     {
94        print( "--- Press Enter to Continue ---" );
95        <STDIN>;
96        $FORMAT_LINES_LEFT--;
97     }
98
99     # format definitions
100    format PRINTACCESS_TOP =
101    access.log                                                    Page @<<
102                                                                      $%
103    Requester      Date and time            Type File           Size Code
104    -----------    --------------------     ---- ----            ---- ----
105    .
106
107    format PRINTACCESS =
108    @<<<<<<<<<<< @<<<<<<<<<<<<<<<<<<<<< @<<< @<<<<<<<<<<<<<<... @<<<<<@<<
109    $entry[0], $entry[1],    $entry[2], $entry[3], $entry[6], $entry[5]
110    .
111
112    format MOST_TOP =
113    Most Accessed Files                          Page @<<
114                                                    $%
```

Fig. 12.11 Printing the Apache Web server access log (part 3 of 5).

```
115  File                          Requests
116  --------------------          --------
117  .
118
119  format MOST =
120  @<<<<<<<<<<<<<<<<<<<<<<<<<<<<<< @|||||||
121  $key,                         $most{ $key }
122  .
123
124  format TIME_TOP =
125                                                      Page @<<
126                                                          $%
127  Times                    Requests         Total bytes Transferred
128  -----------              --------         ----------------------
129  .
130
131  format TIME =
132  @#:00 - @#:00         @|||||||        @|||||||||||||||||||||||||
133  { hour( $startTime ), hour( $startTime + $interval ),
134                        $requests,        $transferred }
135  .
136
137  sub hour
138  {
139      return ( $_[ 0 ] % 12 == 0 )? 12 : ( $_[ 0 ] % 12 );
140  }
```

```
access.log                                        Page 1
Requester       Date and time        Type File    Size Code
-----------     --------------------  ---- ----    ---- ----
127.0.0.1       21/Sep/2000:10:43:42 GET  /              1396 200
127.0.0.1       21/Sep/2000:10:43:42 GET  /apache_pb.gif 2326 200
127.0.0.1       21/Sep/2000:10:49:40 GET  /cgi-bin/test.pl 613 500
127.0.0.1       21/Sep/2000:10:50:29 GET  /cgi-bin/test.pl 111 200
127.0.0.1       21/Sep/2000:10:51:41 GET  /cgi-bin/test.pl 111 200
127.0.0.1       21/Sep/2000:10:59:08 GET  /cgi-bin/speci... 613 500
127.0.0.1       21/Sep/2000:10:59:20 GET  /cgi-bin/time.pl 111 200
127.0.0.1       21/Sep/2000:11:05:51 GET  /cgi-bin/speci... 304 404
127.0.0.1       21/Sep/2000:11:08:03 GET  /special.shtml 296 404
127.0.0.1       21/Sep/2000:11:13:44 GET  /cgi-bin/test.pl 111 200
127.0.0.1       21/Sep/2000:11:13:53 GET  /cgi-bin/envir... 2181 200
127.0.0.1       21/Sep/2000:11:24:55 GET  /cgi-bin/time.pl 613 500
127.0.0.1       21/Sep/2000:11:26:02 GET  /cgi-bin/time.pl 111 200
127.0.0.1       21/Sep/2000:11:28:53 GET  /cgi-bin/envir... 4358 200
127.0.0.1       21/Sep/2000:11:29:18 GET  /cgi-bin/query.pl 263 200
127.0.0.1       21/Sep/2000:11:29:23 GET  /cgi-bin/query... 278 200
127.0.0.1       21/Sep/2000:11:29:57 GET  /cgi-bin/query... 284 200
127.0.0.1       21/Sep/2000:11:31:00 GET  /cgi-bin/getfo... 310 200
127.0.0.1       21/Sep/2000:11:31:10 GET  /cgi-bin/getFo... 345 200
127.0.0.1       21/Sep/2000:11:31:16 GET  /cgi-bin/getFo... 352 200
127.0.0.1       21/Sep/2000:11:35:17 GET  /cgi-bin/postf... 274 200
--- Press Enter to Continue ---
```

Fig. 12.11 Printing the Apache Web server access log (part 4 of 5).

```
Most Accessed Files              Page 1
File                             Requests
--------------------             --------
/cgi-bin/fig10_11.pl                58
/cgi-bin/cheryl.pl                  54
/cgi-bin/ch07sol/Ex7_4.pl           30
/cgi-bin/fig07_11.pl                28
/cgi-bin/book.pl                    27
/cgi-bin/fig07_02.pl                26
/cgi-bin/ch07sol/Ex7_5.pl           24
/cgi-bin/Ex07_03.pl                 20
/cgi-bin/book2.pl                   19
/cgi-bin/update.pl                  19
/cgi-bin/special.shtml              17
/cgi-bin/ch07sol/ex07_07.pl         17
/cgi-bin/ch07sol/Ex7_3.pl           16
/cgi-bin/solution5b.pl              16
/cgi-bin/fig10_14.pl                15
/cgi-bin/test.pl                    14
/cgi-bin/fig10_12.pl                14
/cgi-bin/fig07_15.pl                13
/cgi-bin/fig07_09.pl                12
/cgi-bin/ex09_04.pl                 12
/cgi-bin/log.pl                     12
--- Press Enter to Continue ---
```

```
                                                  Page 1
Times                      Requests     Total bytes Transferred
-----------                --------     ----------------------
12:00  -    3:00              0                    0
 3:00  -    6:00              0                    0
 6:00  -    9:00              0                    0
 9:00  -  12:00            242               347229
12:00  -    3:00            189                66045
 3:00  -    6:00            186                63578
 6:00  -    9:00             63                31856
 9:00  -  12:00              0                    0
```

Fig. 12.11 Printing the Apache Web server access log (part 5 of 5).

The hash table **%most** keeps a running total of how often each page has been accessed. Each time we read an entry, we increment the value of the hash element with the name of the file as the key (line 27). When the loop completes execution, the hash holds key–value pairs in which the key is the name of a document and the value is the number of times that document has been accessed. To print these key–value pairs in order, from most accessed to least accessed, we first **sort** the keys of **%most** in descending order of value in **%most** (line 43).

Keeping track of hourly statistics is a bit more complicated, because each hour has two running totals associated with it—the number of accesses and the total number of bytes. To compensate for this the hash **%hourly** has two keys for each hour. The number of requests per hour is accessed by appending the string **requests** to the end of the hour number (lines 30 and 63), and the total number of bytes transferred is accessed by appending **transferred** to the end (lines 31 and 65). Adding to the complexity is the fact that function **parseAccessEntry** returns a string containing the day, month, year, minute and second, in addition to the hour. Because the hour is always between the first and second colons of the string, function **split** can be used to divide the string into three parts (line 29), where the second part contains the hour.

Rather than displaying the hourly statistics for each individual hour, we divide the time into larger intervals. The number of hours in each interval is held in the **$interval** variable, so that it can be modified easily. Before printing each interval, we total the statistics for the hours that make up the interval. A **for** structure (lines 56–71) loops through all of the start times, while a nested **for** (lines 60–67) totals the statistics for each interval. After totalling the statistics, function **write** is called to output the statistics. The conversion from 24-hour time to 12-hour time is performed in the format by calling function **hour** (defined in lines 137–140).

Now that we have a script that prints out the access log, we will write a script that prints the error log. The following is a sample line from the error log:

```
[Mon Jul 17 12:43:06 2000] [error] [client 192.168.1.75]
(Missing operator before digest?)
```

A difference between the access log and the error log is that a single request can generate multiple lines in the error log, whereas each line in the access log is from a unique request. Thus, when each error log entry is printed, it is not automatically just one line. This factor makes monitoring the **$-** variable and maintaining uniform pages more of a challenge. To solve this problem, we defined function **paginate**, which receives a string, the number of lines per page and the number of lines left on the current page as arguments and breaks the string into separate strings where the page boundaries would be. That way, each separate page can be output individually, and the user can be prompted to continue after viewing each page.

To write this function, we need a thorough understanding of how lines are broken up into multiple-line formats. The characters at which the format splits lines in a string are held in the **$:** variable (**$FORMAT_LINE_BREAK_CHARACTERS**). The default value for this variable is **" -\n"**. The best way to find out exactly how a format splits lines is to use the format with sample strings, allowing us to test special cases. The tests of special cases show that leading whitespace is ignored and that the last character on a line is either a **-** or any character preceding whitespace. Knowing these rules, we can now write a subroutine that divides a string into different lines. The code for printing the error log is in Fig. 12.12 and an explanation of the code follows.

```perl
1   #!/usr/bin/perl
2   # Fig. 12.12: fig12_12.pl
3   # Analyzes the Apache error log file.
4
5   use warnings;
6   use strict;
7   use English;
8
```

Fig. 12.12 Apache Web server error-log analyzer (part 1 of 5).

```perl
 9    # System settings - change to make output appear correctly
10    $FORMAT_LINES_PER_PAGE = 25;
11    $FORMAT_FORMFEED = '';
12    my $error='C:\Program Files\Apache Group\Apache\logs\error.log';
13
14    # The format and format top are ERROR_LOG_TOP
15    # Number of lines left is set to the amount of lines in a page
16    # Page number is set to 1
17    ( $~, $^, $-, $% ) = ( 'ERROR_LOG_TOP', 'ERROR_LOG_TOP', $=, 1 );
18    write();
19
20    # Change format to ERROR_LOG
21    $~ = 'ERROR_LOG';
22    my @total = ('','');
23
24    open( FILE, $error ) or die( "Cannot open: $!" );
25
26    # Loop that prints each entry and gathers information
27    while ( <FILE> ) {
28       next if ( $_ eq "\n" );          # skip blank lines
29
30       my @entry = parseErrorEntry( $_ );
31
32       # if message has same date, time and client number
33       if ( ( $total[ 0 ] eq $entry[ 0 ] )
34            && ( $total[ 1 ] eq $entry[ 1 ] ) ) {
35          # add new information to the error message
36          $total[2] .= ( ' 'x58 ).$entry[ 2 ];
37       }
38       # if we have a new message to print
39       elsif ( defined( $total[ 2 ] ) ) {
40
41          # paginate analyzes the error message, putting the
42          # information into different pages as necessary
43          my @pages = paginate( $total[ 2 ], 44, $- - 1, $= - 4 );
44
45          foreach my $page ( @pages[ 0 .. $#pages - 1 ] ) {
46             # assign the message to total[2]
47             $total[ 2 ] = $page;
48             # print the error message, date and client
49             write();
50             # prompt the user at the end of the page
51             prompt();
52          }
53
54          $total[ 2 ] = $pages[ $#pages ];
55          write();
56
57          if ( $- < 4 ) {
58             print( "\n" x ( $- - 1 ) );
59             prompt();
60             $- = 0;
61          }
```

Fig. 12.12 Apache Web server error-log analyzer (part 2 of 5).

```perl
62          else {
63              print( "\n" );
64              $---;
65          }
66          @total = @entry;
67      }
68      # otherwise get a new message to print
69      else {
70          @total = @entry;
71      }
72  }
73
74  my @pages = paginate( $total[ 2 ], 44, $- - 1, $= - 4 );
75
76  foreach my $page ( @pages[ 0 .. $#pages - 1 ] ) {
77      $total[ 2 ] = $page;
78      write();
79      prompt();
80  }
81
82  $total[ 2 ] = $pages[ $#pages ];
83  write();
84
85  print( "\n" x ( $- - 2 ) );
86
87  sub parseErrorEntry
88  {
89      my $entry = shift;
90
91      # this line of the regex captures the time and day
92      if ( $entry =~ /^\[(\w{3}\s\w{3}\s\d\d?\s[\d:]+\s\d\d\d\d)\]
93      # this line captures the IP address and error message
94                  \s\[error\]\s\[client\s([\d.]+)\]\s(.*)\n$/x ) {
95
96          # return the time and day, client and message
97          return ( $1, $2, $3 );
98      }
99
100     warn "Not a normal error log entry.\n$entry\n";
101     return undef;
102 }
103
104 sub prompt
105 {
106     print( "--- Press Enter to Continue ---" );
107     <STDIN>;
108     $FORMAT_LINES_LEFT--;
109 }
110
111 sub paginate
112 {
113     my ( $string, $length, $firstPage, $perPage ) = @_ ;
114     my ( $lineStart, $pageStart, $lines, $page ) = (0, 0, 0, 1);
```

Fig. 12.12 Apache Web server error-log analyzer (part 3 of 5).

```perl
115      my @pages = ();
116      my $totalLines = ( $firstPage > 0 )? $firstPage : $perPage;
117
118      # counts how many lines we have gone through so far
119      while ( defined( $lineStart ) ) {
120
121         if ( $lines >= $totalLines ) {
122            my $next = '';
123            $next .= "(page $page of message)" . ' ' x $length
124                                                  if ( $page > 1 );
125            $next .= substr(
126                    $string,$pageStart,$lineStart-$pageStart );
127            push( @pages, $next );
128            $totalLines = $perPage;
129            $lines = 1;
130            $pageStart = $lineStart;
131            $page++;
132         }
133
134         $lineStart = getNextLine( $string, $lineStart, $length );
135         $lines++;
136      }
137      my $next = '';
138
139      # in case a message has run onto another page
140      $next .= "(page $page of message)" . ' ' x $length
141             if ( $page > 1 );
142      $next .= substr( $string, $pageStart );
143      push( @pages, $next );
144      return @pages;
145   }
146
147   # determines where lines will break
148   # returns the index of the beginning of the next line
149   sub getNextLine {
150      my ( $string, $start, $length ) = @_;
151
152      # ignoring whitespace at the front of a line
153      $start++ while ( ( $start < length( $string ) )
154            && ( substr( $string, $start, 1 ) =~ /^[\s\n]$/ ) );
155      return undef if ( length( $string ) < $start + $length );
156
157      if ( substr( $string, $start + $length, 1 ) =~ /^[\n\s]$/ ) {
158         return ( $start + $length + 1 );
159      }
160
161      $length--;
162
163      while ( $length > 0 ) {
164
165         if ( substr( $string, $start + $length, 1 ) =~ /^[\n\-\s]$/ ) {
166            return ( $start + $length + 1 );
167         }
```

Fig. 12.12 Apache Web server error-log analyzer (part 4 of 5).

```
168
169        $length--;
170      }
171      return ( $start + $_[2] );
172 }
173
174 format ERROR_LOG_TOP =
175 error.log                                               Page @<<<
176                                                              $%
177 Time and Client        Error Message
178 ---------------        ---------------------------------------------
179 .
180
181 format ERROR_LOG =
182 @<<<<<<<<<<<<<<<<<<<  ^<<<<<<<<<<<<<<<<<<<<<<<<<<<<<<<<<<<<<<<<<<<<<~
183 $total[0],             $total[2]
184 @<<<<<<<<<<<<<<       ^<<<<<<<<<<<<<<<<<<<<<<<<<<<<<<<<<<<<<<<<<<<<<~
185 $total[1],             $total[2]
186 ~~                    ^<<<<<<<<<<<<<<<<<<<<<<<<<<<<<<<<<<<<<<<<<<<<<
187                        $total[2]
188 .
```

```
error.log                                           Page 1
Time and Client        Error Message
---------------        ---------------------------------------------
Thu Sep 21 10:49:40    (2)No such file or directory: couldn't spawn
127.0.0.1              child process: c:/program files/apache
                       group/apache/cgi-bin/test.pl

Thu Sep 21 10:59:08    Premature end of script headers: c:/program
127.0.0.1              files/apache group/apache/cgi-bin/special.pl
                       syntax error at c:/program files/apache
                       group/apache/cgi-bin/special.pl line 9, near
                       ""Saturday Steak Sandwich" )"
                       Missing right curly or square bracket at
                       c:/program files/apache group/apache/cgi-
                       bin/special.pl line 14, at end of line
                       Execution of c:/program files/apache
                       group/apache/cgi-bin/special.pl aborted due
                       to compilation errors.

Thu Sep 21 11:05:51    (2)No such file or directory: script not
127.0.0.1              found or unable to stat: c:/program
                       files/apache group/apache/cgi-
                       bin/special.shtml

--- Press Enter to Continue ---
```

Fig. 12.12 Apache Web server error-log analyzer (part 5 of 5).

The subroutine that parses the error-log entries—**parseErrorEntry** (lines 87–102)—differs from **parseAccessEntry** in Fig. 12.11 only in the regular expression used to parse the error-log information.

Function **getNextLine** (lines 149–172) predicts where **write** will split the lines. Function **getNextLine** receives the string containing the text to split, the index of the beginning of the line and the field width as arguments and returns the index of the beginning of the next line. This function first loops to skip whitespace at the beginning of the line (lines 153–154). Function **substr** returns the character at each index. We continue increasing the index of the start of the line until a nonwhitespace character is encountered. If no non-whitespace characters are found before the end of the line, we return **undef** in line 155 to indicate that there is no next line. If we find a character that begins a line, we analyze the characters of the string from this starting index through a length that is as wide as the field. If the character after the end of this string is whitespace, then the line broke perfectly, and we can return that index (lines 157–159). Otherwise, we start at the end of the line and move backwards until either a whitespace character or the – character is found, at which point we return the previous index viewed (lines 163–170). If there are no whitespace or – characters, we return the character just beyond the end of the line (line 171).

Function **paginate** uses function **getNextLine** to read each message (line 134) and counts the number of lines (line 135). When the end of a page is reached, **substr** extracts this page from the string and inserts it in an array that holds the pages (lines 125–127). If we are not on the first page, we include a message on the first line saying that this page is a continuation of the message (lines 123–124).

Once the page is added, we reset the line-numbers and lines-per-page variables (lines 128 and 129), set **$pageStart** to the location where the old page ended (line 130) and increment the page count (line 131). When we reach the end of the message, we add the remaining portion that was not part of a previous page to the array as the last page (lines 140–143). We then return the array (line 144).

To output the whole log, we read line by line through the error log. The **@total** array holds the running totals for error messages, and the **@entry** array holds parsed single lines from the log. When we parse a message and assign it to **@entry** (line 30), there are three possible actions to take. If **@entry**'s error message happened at the same time and was requested by the same client as were the messages in **@total**, then we assume it is from the same request and is a continuation of the message in **@total**. Thus, we append the message, on a new line, to the end of the message in **@total** (lines 33–37). Because multiple-line formats do not recognize the **\n** character for newlines, a line of spaces is used instead of the normal newline character. If the line from **@entry** is not part of the same message as **@total**'s message, then we want to print **@total**'s message and start keeping track of this new message (lines 39–67). However, if the new message is the first message, we do not want to print **@total** because **@total** is undefined at this point; we just want to assign **@entry** to **@total** (lines 69–71).

To print the message, we first break the message into pages if necessary, using function **paginate** (line 43). We then go through each of the pages (line 45), assign it to the variable used in the format (line 47) and **write** its, prompting after each page before the last (line 37). When we finish printing a page, we prepare for the next page. If there are fewer than four lines left (one for a new line to separate the messages, one for the prompt and two for the minimum message length), we want to start the next page immediately by printing the necessary blank lines, prompting the user and setting the lines left to zero (lines 49 and 51). If there will be enough room for a new entry, we print a line to separate the messages and decrement the lines remaining to account for this non-**write** printing (lines 57–65).

When the whole log has been read, we print the last message remaining (lines 76–83) and then print the necessary blank lines to align the last page with the top of the screen (line 85).

SUMMARY

- Formats are used to define templates that specify how data should appear when they are output.
- Formats are flexible tools that can be used for precise report generation.
- Formats do not have to be defined before they are used in a program.
- A format declaration starts with keyword **format** and takes the following form:

  > **format** *formatName* **=**
  > *text*
  > .

  The text portion of the format definition consists of three types of lines: comments, picture lines and argument lines.
- Comments start with a **#** character and are ignored when the format is printed.
- Picture lines specify the format. These lines contain regular text and fields. The regular text is printed as it is written, with no interpolation. Fields specify placeholders for values.
- Argument lines specify the content to be placed in the fields of the preceding picture line. An argument line contain a comma-separated list, where the first element in the list corresponds to the first field on the preceding line, the second element in the list corresponds to the second field on the preceding line, etc.
- Fields start with either an **@** or a **^** character. The characters following the **@** or **^** character specify what type of justification is used for that field.
- Formats are invoked by function **write**. When **write** is called, it writes to either the currently selected filehandle or the filehandle passed to it as an argument. The default format for a filehandle has the same name as the filehandle.
- The **<** character is used to left justify a field, the **>** character is used to right justify a field, and the **|** character is used to center the contents of a field.
- The total number of characters in a field, including the **@** or **^** character, indicates the field width.
- Another justification symbol is the **#** characters, which is used for numbers.
- A **.** can be used to line up decimal places.
- Declaring a format where the fields are not long enough for the values they hold causes the values to be truncated.
- Any variable used in the format has to be in the scope in which the format is declared.
- Trying to use a lexically scoped variable in a format that is not declared in the lexical variable's scope causes an error.
- A format that prints at the top of every page can be specified.
- The number of lines per page is held in the **$= ($FORMAT_LINES_PER_PAGE)** variable. Every time that number of lines prints, the top of page format is executed.
- The default top-of-page format triggered by the **write** function is the name of the current filehandle with **_TOP** appended to it.
- Top-of-form processing is handled automatically by the **write** function. The **write** function looks at the **$-** variable (**$FORMAT_LINES_LEFT**) and checks to make sure there is enough room on the current page for what it needs to print. If there is not enough room, **write** outputs the contents of the **$^L** variable, which holds **\f** by default, but can be changed to any string.

- There is no way to do bottom-of-the-page formatting automatically. One way to create one is to decrease the lines per page by the number of lines in the footer and then put the footer text in the **$^L** variable. Otherwise, you can monitor the **$-** variable yourself and perform the necessary processing when it reaches the correct value.

- The field type starting with the **^** character tells Perl to print as many words from a variable as can fit in the field, and then remove whatever was printed off the front. The next time the variable is referenced, it starts where the previous line left off. We can use this procedure to extend variables over multiple lines.

- By truncating the front of the variable (when using **^**), the function **write** changes the value of the variable. If you want to use the value after the **write** call, you need to use a temporary variable to hold the value during the **write** call.

- Putting a **~** character on format lines for which there may be no data suppresses those lines when they have no values to be substituted into their fields.

- To indicate that there should be no limit on the number of lines to be printed, put two tilde characters (**~~**) on a format line, to repeat the line until all the fields have nothing left in them.

- In multiple-line fields, Perl attempts to wrap lines at word boundaries by splitting text after characters stored in the **$:** variable (**$FORMAT_LINE_BREAK_CHARACTERS**). By default, **$:** holds a space, a dash and the newline character.

- A less flexible option for multiple-line output is to use the **@*** field. This field causes the contents of a variable to be split into multiple line and printed out in their entirety. The **@*** field is best used on a line by itself. Any text or fields on the line before the **@*** field are printed once and not repeated for any overflow.

- For convenience, there is a module that allow us to use more logical-sounding names for certain built-in variables. The pragma **use English** allows us to use alternative names.

- The **$~** (**$FORMAT_NAME**) variable contains the name of the current format.

- The **$^** (**$FORMAT_TOP_NAME**) variable contains the name of the current top-of-form format.

- The **$%** (**$FORMAT_PAGE_NUMBER**) variable contains the current page number.

- The **$=** (**$FORMAT_LINES_PER_PAGE**) variable contains the number of lines per page.

- The **$-** (**$FORMAT_LINES_LEFT**) variable contains the number of lines left on the current page.

- The **$:** (**$FORMAT_LINE_BREAK_CHARACTERS**) variable contains the characters at which multiple lines are split.

- The **$^L** (**$FORMAT_FORMFEED**) variable contains what will be output to perform a form feed.

- The format variables are specific to each filehandle. To access the variables of a filehandle other than the current one, select the filehandle by using the **select** function.

- To force the top-of-line format to output, set the number of format lines left (**$-**) to zero.

- Regular **print** statements do not decrement variable **$-** automatically. If you use **print** and want the **$-** variable to remain accurate, you need to decrement it yourself.

TERMINOLOGY

# numeric-justification character	**$^L** special variable
$- special variable	**$~** special variable
$% special variable	**$=** special variable
$. special variable	**.** format character
$: special variable	**@** format character
$^ special variable	**@*** format character

\f form-feed character escape sequence
^ format character
| center-justification character
~ format character
~~ format character
< left-justification character
> right-justification character
argument line
default top-of-page format
English module
field
field length
field type
filehandle
format
format **_TOP**
format argument line
format associated with a filehandle
format character **@***
format character ^
format character ~
format character ~~
format field
$FORMAT_FORMFEED
$FORMAT_LINE_BREAK_CHARACTERS
$FORMAT_LINES_LEFT
$FORMAT_LINES_PER_PAGE
$FORMAT_NAME
$FORMAT_PAGE_NUMBER

format picture line
format scope
$FORMAT_TOP_NAME
format variable
$INPUT_LINE_NUMBER
justification specifier
left justification
multiple-line format field
multiple-line format fields with the **@*** character
multiple-line format fields with the ^ character
numeric-justification character **#**
picture line
right justification
select function
special format variable
special variable **$-**
special variable **$%**
special variable **$.**
special variable **$:**
special variable **$^**
special variable **$^L**
special variable **$~**
special variable **$=**
STDOUT default formatting
the ^ character
top-of-form format
top-of-form processing
top-of-page format
truncating

SELF-REVIEW EXERCISES

12.1 Fill in the blanks in each of the following statements:

a) Formats can be invoked by using function _____.

b) The _____ character is used to left justify a field, the _____, character is used to right justify a field, and _____ is used to center the contents of a field.

c) The number of lines per page is held in the _____ variable.

d) The default top-of-page format triggered by the **write** function is the name of the current filehandle with _____ appended to it.

e) The field type starting with the _____ symbol tells Perl to print as many words from a variable as it can fit in the field and then remove whatever was printed off the front.

f) The **write** function looks at the _____ variable and checks to make sure there is enough room on the current page for what it needs to print.

g) Putting the _____ character on a line in a format causes that line to be suppressed when no value is going into the field.

h) The _____ pragma allows us to use alternative names for certain built-in variables.

i) The **STDOUT_TOP** format uses the _____ variable to print the page number at the top of each page.

j) The **STDOUT** format uses the _____ variable to number each line of the input file.

12.2 State whether the following are *true* or *false*. If *false*, explain why.

a) The first character of a field (**@**, ^) is not considered part of the field width.

b) The **#** justification symbol is used for lining up decimal places.

c) The default format for a filehandle has the same name as the filehandle.

d) Formats must be defined before they can be used in a program.

e) Declaring a format where the fields are not long enough for the values they hold causes the values to be truncated.

f) When we begin a field with the ^ characters, the variable being printed out will be unchanged.

g) Any variable used in a format has to be in the scope in which the format was declared.

h) The **use English** pragma is useful and helps increase efficiency.

12.3   Write a program to accomplish the following:

a) Prompt the user for a filename.

b) Set a top-of-form field to print the page number, filename and a line of dashes above and below these values to separate the header from the file.

c) Allow each page to have only 10 lines, including the header.

d) Print the file, with the header at the beginning of each page.

12.4   Write a few lines of code to accomplish the following:

a) Create a format named **FORMAT1** that prints the value in **$variable** left justified. Print only the first 10 characters of this variable.

b) Create a format named **FORMAT2** that prints the value in **$variable** centered. Print only three lines of the contents of this variable, five characters per line.

c) Modify part (b) so that the value is right justified and if there are lines with no values, they are truncated. Call this format **FORMAT3**.

d) Create a format named **FORMAT4** that prints the value in **$variable**. Print the entire variable.

ANSWERS TO SELF-REVIEW EXERCISES

12.1   a) **write.** b) **<, >, |.** c) **$= ($FORMAT_LINES_PER_PAGE).** d) **_TOP.** e) ^ (caret).
f) **$- ($FORMAT_LINES_LEFT).** g) **~.** h) **use English.** i) **$% ($FORMAT_PAGE_NUMBER).**
j) **$. ($INPUT_LINE_NUMBER).**

12.2   a) False. These characters are considered to be part of the field width.

b) False. The **.** is used to line up decimal places.

c) True.

d) False. Formats do not have to be defined before they can be used in a program.

e) True.

f) False. The value of the variable is changed when **write** is called.

g) True.

h) False. Using the **English** module can actually decrease efficiency.

12.3   See the following code.

```
1   #!/usr/bin/perl
2   # Ex. 12.3: Ex12_03.pl
3   # Printing a formatted file.
4
5   use strict;
6   use warnings;
7   use English;
8
9   print( "Enter which file you want printed: " );
```

```
10    chomp( my $file = <STDIN> );
11    $FORMAT_LINES_PER_PAGE = 10;
12    $FORMAT_FORMFEED = "";
13
14    open( FILE, "<$file" ) or die( "Cannot open: $!" );
15    $/ = undef;
16    my $text = <FILE>;
17    close( FILE ) or die( "Cannot close: $!" );
18
19    write();
20
21    format STDOUT_TOP =
22    --------------------------------------------------------------
23       @<<<<<<<<<<<<<<<<<<<<<<<<<<<        Page:@<<<
24       $file,                                   $%
25    --------------------------------------------------------------
26    .
27
28    format STDOUT =
29    @*
30    $text
31
32    .
```

```
Enter which file you want printed: Ex12_03.txt
--------------------------------------------------------------
    Ex12_03.txt                          Page:1
--------------------------------------------------------------
This
needs
to
be
a
long
file.
--------------------------------------------------------------
    Ex12_03.txt                          Page:2
--------------------------------------------------------------

Longer
than
one
page.


--------------------------------------------------------------
    Ex12_03.txt                          Page:3
--------------------------------------------------------------
Maybe
three
pages
long.
```

12.4 a) `format FORMAT1 =`
            `@<<<<<<<<<`
            `$variable`
            `.`

  b) `format FORMAT2 =`
     `^||||`
     `$variable`
     `^||||`
     `$variable`
     `^||||`
     `$variable`
     `.`

  c) `format FORMAT3 =`
     `~  ^>>>>`
        `$variable`
     `~  ^>>>>`
        `$variable`
     `~  ^>>>>`
        `$variable`
     `.`

  d) `format FORMAT4 =`
     `@*`
     `$variable`
     `.`

EXERCISES

12.5 Calculate the squares of the integers 0–20. Use a format to print each integer and its square in two columns, center justified.

12.6 Write a program that reads data from a file. Each line of the file has three elements: a name, a description and a price. The three elements are separated by the **%** sign. The name should be no longer than 15 characters, the description no longer than 35 characters and the price no longer than 7 characters. The output should have the name and description left justified, and the price should be right justified on the decimal point. The file output and the program should appear as in Figs. 12.13 and 12.14.

```
Cup%A good cup for drinking%5
Window%A good window with two panels%80.99
Computer%A good computer for computing%1299.99
Chair%A good chair for sitting%45.2
```

Fig. 12.13 Contents of **Ex12_06.in**.

```
Name              Description                          Price
-----------       -----------------                    --------
Cup               A good cup for drinking             $    5.00
Window            A good window with two panels       $   80.99
Computer          A good computer for computing       $1299.99
Chair             A good chair for sitting            $   45.20
```

Fig. 12.14 Output of **Ex12_06.pl**.

12.7   Define a format that prints the tags for a row in an HTML table. The table should have three columns. Have the array **@columns** hold the three entries that will be accessed when **write** is called. There should be no limit on the length of the text in the name and description fields. Use the data from the previous example as in the data table.

12.8   Modify the program in Fig. 12.12 so that the user specifies a day and the program prints only messages from that day. Before each new error, the program should also print a header with the time and the client that caused the error. The separate lines of the error should be numbered. You do not have to pause after each page of output. Figure 12.15 shows some sample output from this program.

```
What day was the request made (Ex. Jul 14)? Jul 14
Time: Fri Jul 14 09:21:48 2000        Client: 192.168.1.75
Line 1    File does not exist: c:/program files/apache
          group/apache/htdocs/_vti_inf.html

Line 2    File does not exist: c:/program files/apache
          group/apache/htdocs/_vti_bin/shtml.exe/_vti_rpc

Time: Fri Jul 14 15:29:41 2000        Client: 192.168.1.75
Line 3    Premature end of script headers: c:/program files/apache
          group/apache/cgi-bin/test.pl

Line 4    No comma allowed after filehandle at c:/program files/apache
          group/apache/cgi-bin/test.pl line 5.

Time: Fri Jul 14 16:25:43 2000        Client: 192.168.1.75
Line 5    Premature end of script headers: c:/program files/apache
          group/apache/cgi-bin/bad.pl

Line 6    No comma allowed after filehandle at c:/program files/apache
          group/apache/cgi-bin/bad.pl line 7.
```

Fig. 12.15 Sample output from **Ex12_08.pl**.

13

References

Objectives

- To understand how to create and use references.
- To understand anonymous data structures and be able to create them using composers.
- To understand the principles behind closures.
- To be able to create nested data structures using references.
- To be able to use symbolic references.
- To be able to use typeglobs to create constant variables.
- To be able to use typeglobs to reference filehandles.

Addresses are given to us to conceal our whereabouts
Saki (H. H. Munro)

By indirections find directions out.
William Shakespeare
Hamlet

Many things, having full reference
To one consent, may work contrariously.
William Shakespeare
King Henry V

You will find it a very good practice always to verify your references, sir!
Dr. Routh

Outline

13.1 Introduction

The programs you have seen to this point used scalar and nonscalar variables as well as functions to perform tasks. Those programs manipulated the variables and functions by the names we provided for them in the program or by the names provided by Perl (for variables and functions in the Perl libraries). This chapter introduces a new scalar data type called a *reference* and demonstrates how it can be used and manipulated. References provide indirect access to a variable or function. We will learn how to use references to access other variables, helping us to manipulate many variables at once, and we will demonstrate how references simplify the passing of certain arguments to functions. References are used to create and manipulate *multidimensional (nested) data structures* and anonymous data structures, both shown in this chapter. We also introduce other topics related to references, such as *typeglobs*, which were used before Perl added the reference construct, and closures—a special form of function.

13.2 References

Normal scalars directly contain values. Scalars can also hold a value, which tells them where to find another value in memory. This type of a scalar is called a *reference*. A reference *indirectly* points to a value. Pointing to a value using a reference is called *indirection*.

There are two types of references—*hard references* and *symbolic references*. References do just what their name implies—they refer to other things. Hard references refer directly to a value (not a variable) in memory. The value to which the reference refers is known as the *referent*. Symbolic references, which are sometimes known as *soft references,* hold just the name of the variable to which they refer.

Performance Tip 13.1

Hard references are more efficient than symbolic references and are the typical reference type used by Perl programmers. When you see the term reference, normally you can assume that it is a hard reference. With the exception of Section 13.9, the remainder of this chapter discusses hard references.

Hard references to variables are created by preceding the name of the variable that contains the referent with the *unary backslash operator*, ****. Reference variables are named like other scalars by preceding the name of the variable with a **$**. To get the value to which the reference points, you must *dereference* the reference by using its entire name (including the **$** that precedes it) like a normal variable name. So, if **$reference** refers to a scalar, the value **$reference** refers to can be accessed with **$$reference**. Similarly, you can use **@$reference** and **%$reference** to access the array or hash to which the reference refers. Figure 13.1 demonstrates how to use references.

```
1   #!/usr/bin/perl
2   # Fig. 13.1: fig13_01.pl
3   # Demonstrates creating and dereferencing a reference.
4
5   use strict;
6   use warnings;
7
8   my $variable = 10;
9   my $reference = \$variable;
10
11  print( "\$variable = $variable\n" );
12  print( "\$reference = $reference\n" );
13  print( "\$\$reference = $$reference\n" );
14  $variable++;
15  print( "\$variable = $variable\n" );
16  print( "\$reference = $reference\n" );
17  print( "\$\$reference = $$reference\n" );
18  $$reference++;
19  print( "\$variable = $variable\n" );
20  print( "\$reference = $reference\n" );
21  print( "\$\$reference = $$reference\n" );
```

```
$variable = 10
$reference = SCALAR(0x8a31018)
$$reference = 10
$variable = 11
$reference = SCALAR(0x8a31018)
$$reference = 11
$variable = 12
$reference = SCALAR(0x8a31018)
$$reference = 12
```

Fig. 13.1   Creating and dereferencing references.

Line 9 creates **$reference**—a hard reference to scalar **$variable**. Lines 11–13 print the values of **$variable**, **$reference** and **$$reference** (the value to which **$reference** refers). You can see that printing out a reference without dereferencing it prints out a string with the reference type and the location of the referent (the value of **$variable**) in memory. Although references can be converted to strings, these strings cannot be converted back to references.

Line 14 increments **$variable**, then lines 15–17 print the values of **$variable**, **$reference** and **$$reference**. Notice that the output shows the same value (11) for **$$reference** and **$variable**. This proves that they refer to the same value. Line 18 increments **$variable** using the reference **$reference**. Note that the output once again shows the same value (12) for **$$reference** and **$variable**.

13.3 References to Nonscalars

We can create references to any kind of data structure. Creating a reference to a nonscalar variable follows the same syntax as creating a reference to a scalar—precede the nonscalar variable name with the unary backslash operator. Thus **\@array** returns a reference to array **@array** and **\%hash** returns a reference to the hash **%hash**. Dereferencing these nonscalar references, however, is a little bit different than dereferencing scalars.

There are two ways to dereference an array and access specific elements. The first is to use the reference as you would use the array name to access one of its values. For example, if **$reference** refers to an array, we can access the third element in the array with **$$reference[2]**. The second way to dereference an array reference uses the *arrow operator* (**->**). For example, the preceding dereferencing operation can also be written with arrow notation as **$reference->[2]**. To refer to the entire array, place an **@** type identifier before the reference name as in **@$reference**.

The preceding methods of accessing array elements through a reference can be used with hashes as well (with the appropriate symbols, of course). Thus to access the element with the key **poodle** in the hash pointed to by **$reference**, we can either say **$$reference{ 'poodle' }** or **$reference->{ 'poodle' }**. To refer to the entire hash, place a **%** type identifier before the reference name as in **%$reference**.

If a block of code returns a reference, it can be dereferenced directly using these methods. Thus, the expression **${ ($x > 2) ? $reference1 : $reference2 }** dereferences **$reference1** if $x > 2; otherwise, **$reference2** is dereferenced. Figure 13.2 demonstrates using references to hashes and arrays.

```
1   #!/usr/bin/perl
2   # Fig. 13.2: fig13_02.pl
3   # Demonstrates how to use references to arrays and hashes.
4
5   use strict;
6   use warnings;
7
8   my @array = qw( duck pig horse rooster cow );
9   my %hash = ( duck     => "quack",
10                pig      => "oink",
11               horse    => "neigh",
```

Fig. 13.2   References to arrays and hashes (part 1 of 2).

```
12                        rooster => "cock-a-doodle-doo",
13                        cow     => "moo" );
14
15    my $arrayReference = \@array;
16    my $hashReference = \%hash;
17
18    sub returnReference
19    {
20       return \@array;
21    }
22
23    print( "@$arrayReference\n" );
24
25    print( "\$\$arrayReference[ 1 ] = $$arrayReference[ 1 ]\n" );
26    print( "\$arrayReference->[ 1 ] = $arrayReference->[ 1 ]\n" );
27    print
28      ( "\${returnReference()}[ 1 ] = ${returnReference()}[ 1 ]\n\n" );
29
30    print( "\$\$hashReference{ duck } = $$hashReference{ duck }\n" );
31    print
32      ( "\$hashReference->{ duck } = $hashReference->{ duck }\n\n" );
33
34    foreach ( keys( %$hashReference ) ) {
35       print( "The $_ goes $hashReference->{ $_ }.\n" );
36    }
```

```
duck pig horse rooster cow
$$arrayReference[ 1 ] = pig
$arrayReference->[ 1 ] = pig
${returnReference()}[ 1 ] = pig

$$hashReference{ duck } = quack
$hashReference->{ duck } = quack

The cow goes moo.
The pig goes oink.
The duck goes quack.
The horse goes neigh.
The rooster goes cock-a-doodle-doo.
```

Fig. 13.2   References to arrays and hashes (part 2 of 2).

Line 15 creates a reference to **@array** called **$arrayReference**, and line 16 creates a reference to **%hash** called **$hashReference**. Lines 18–21 define function **returnReference**, which returns a reference to **@array**. We use this function to demonstrate dereferencing a reference as it is returned from a function.

Line 23 dereferences the entire array to which **$arrayReference** refers and returns the contents of the array. Lines 25 and 26 show the different ways to access individual array elements discussed previously. Lines 27 and 28 show that references returned from functions can be dereferenced directly—even without a reference variable name. This statement dereferences the reference returned from function **returnReference** to access an element of **@array**.

Line 30 demonstrates how to access a hash element through a hash reference, and lines 31–32 demonstrate accessing a hash element with arrow notation. Line 34 uses function **keys** and a **foreach** loop to output all the key/value pairs in **%hash** through a dereferenced hash reference.

It is also possible to create a reference to an existing function. References to functions are often used when calling library functions. You can pass a reference to one of your own functions into a library function, which, in turn, will call your function. This concept is known as a *callback*. We use this concept in the examples of Chapter 22, Extensible Markup Language (XML).

To create a reference to a function, use the unary backslash operator with the **&** type identifier for functions. For example, **\&yourFunction** creates a reference to function **yourFunction**. If variable **$functionRef** contains a function reference, the function it refers to can be invoked with **&$functionRef()**. As usual, arguments to the function are placed in parentheses. Like other references, the arrow notation can be used with function references. The preceding function call would be written as **$functionRef->()**. Figure 13.3 demonstrates a reference to a function.

Line 8 creates a reference to **function** (defined at lines 12–15), which is called **$functionReference**. Lines 9 and 10 demonstrate how to call the function through the reference **$functionReference** using an ampersand on line 9 and the arrow notation on line 10.

It is even possible to have references to references, which are known as *nested references*. You can nest references to any depth you want. To dereference these nested references, you just need to dereference the reference pointing to it an extra time. Thus to dereference a reference to a reference to a scalar we would say **$$$name**. To use a reference to a reference to an array to access the fourth element of the array, we can write **$$$name[3]** or **$$name->[3]**. Figure 13.4 demonstrates nested references.

```
1   #!/usr/bin/perl
2   # Fig. 13.3: fig13_03.pl
3   # Using function references
4
5   use strict;
6   use warnings;
7
8   my $functionReference = \&function;
9   &$functionReference( "a", "bunch", "of", "words" );
10  $functionReference->( "some", "other", "words" );
11
12  sub function
13  {
14     print( "I have been called with @_ as arguments.\n" );
15  }
```

```
I have been called with a bunch of words as arguments.
I have been called with some other words as arguments.
```

Fig. 13.3   Using function references.

```
1   #!/usr/bin/perl
2   # Fig. 13.4: fig13_04.pl
3   # References to references
4
5   use warnings;
6   use strict;
7
8   my $variable = 5;
9   my $reference1 = \$variable;
10  print( "$variable, $reference1, $$reference1\n" );
11  my $reference2 = \$reference1;
12  print( "$variable, $reference1, $$reference1, $reference2, ",
13          "$$reference2, $$$reference2\n" );
14  my $reference3 = \\\\$variable;
15  print( "$reference3, $$reference3, $$$reference3,\n",
16          "   $$$$reference3, $$$$$reference3\n" );
```

```
5, SCALAR(0x8a31018), 5
5, SCALAR(0x8a31018), 5, SCALAR(0x8a4a8c0), SCALAR(0x8a31018), 5
SCALAR(0x85d3aac), SCALAR(0x85d3aa0), SCALAR(0x85d3a10),
    SCALAR(0x8a31018), 5
```

Fig. 13.4 References to references.

Line 9 creates a reference to **$variable** called **$reference1**, and line 10 outputs the values of **$variable** and **$reference1** followed by the value of the dereferenced **$reference1**. Note that the values of **$variable** and **$$reference1** are identical.

Line 11 creates a reference to **$reference1** called **$reference2**, thus **$reference2** is a reference to a reference to **$variable**. Lines 12–13 print the values of **$variable**, **$reference1**, **$reference1** dereferenced, **$reference2**, **$reference2** dereferenced and **$reference2** dereferenced twice. Note that **$variable**, **$$reference1** and **$$$reference2** all produce the same value (5). Also note that **$reference1** and **$$reference2** produce the same value (**SCALAR(0x8a31018)**).

Line 14 creates reference **$reference3**. Using four backslashes before **$variable** creates four levels of indirection—a reference to a reference to a reference to a reference to **$variable**. Lines 15 and 16 use various levels of dereferencing to show you the values of the references and **$variable**. When we created **$reference3**, we also created three other references that did not have names. These are called *anonymous structures* and are discussed in the next section.

13.4 Anonymous Structures

Anonymous structures are not associated directly with variable names. In other words, there exists a reference to the data, but no variable name to access the data directly. These can be handy when you do not need to keep a permanent name for the structure as part of your program.

Perl provides several methods for creating anonymous structures. The *anonymous array composer* creates anonymous arrays. To use the anonymous array composer, enclose a list in square brackets ([ ]) rather than parentheses. The value returned is a reference to an unnamed array. The *anonymous hash composer* works the same way except it uses curly braces ({ }) instead of square brackets. An anonymous structure is accessed through a reference like any other structure. Figure 13.5 demonstrates using the anonymous array and hash composers.

Line 8 creates an anonymous array with the anonymous array composer, and Line 9 creates an anonymous hash with the anonymous hash composer. We output the contents of the anonymous structures via their references at lines 12 and 13.

Line 16 shows how to create an anonymous array without the anonymous array composer. The list is assigned to **@$array2**. Initially, **$array2** is not a reference to an array. However, treating **$array2** like an array reference and assigning a list to **@$array2**, creates an anonymous array and enables **$array2** to refer to that array. This automatic creation of variables is known as *autovivification* (to "come alive"). Another example of autovivification occurs when an array is created simply by assigning a value to an element of a nonexistent array.

Adding elements to anonymous arrays or hashes is just like adding elements to any other array or hash through a reference—we just assign to previously undefined elements as demonstrated in lines 17–19.

Portability Tip 13.1

It is important to remember a that hashes by nature are unordered. Also, their implementations may differ across platforms. For this reason, the contents of the hash in the program of Fig. 13.5 appear in a different order when the program is executed on different platforms.

```perl
1   #!/usr/bin/perl
2   # Fig. 13.5: fig13_05.pl
3   # Anonymous arrays and hashes
4
5   use warnings;
6   use strict;
7
8   my $array = [ qw( There was an old lady who lived in a shoe... ) ];
9   my $hash = { "I'm a"  => " little tea cup",
10                " short" => " and stout..." };
11
12  print( "@$array\n" );
13  print( %$hash, "\n" );
14
15  my $array2;
16  @$array2 = ( "Humpty", "Dumpty" );
17  $$array2[ 5 ] = "wall...";
18  $array2->[ 2 ] = "sat";
19  @$array2[ 3 , 4 ] = ( "on", "a" );
20  print( "@$array2\n" );
```

```
There was an old lady who lived in a shoe...
I'm a little tea cup short and stout...
Humpty Dumpty sat on a wall...
```

Fig. 13.5   Anonymous arrays and hashes.

We have demonstrated that references can be created many different ways. It is important to note that line 16

```
@$array2 = ( "Humpty", "Dumpty" );
```

is not equivalent to

```
\( "Humpty", "Dumpty" )
```

The preceding reference expression is actually equivalent to creating a list of references as in the following expression

```
( \"Humpty", \"Dumpty" )
```

Common Programming Error 13.1

Attempting to create a reference to a list by applying the backslash character to a list is a logic error that creates a list of references rather than a reference to a list of values.

Declaring an anonymous function is similar to declaring a regular function, except that the function name is omitted. An anonymous function can be assigned to a reference for later use. Figure 13.6 shows an example of an anonymous function and calling that function through a reference to the function.

```perl
1   #!/usr/bin/perl
2   # Figure 13.6: fig13_06.pl
3   # Anonymous functions
4
5   use warnings;
6   use strict;
7
8   my $productRef = sub
9   {
10      my $product = 1;
11
12      foreach ( @_ ) {
13         $product *= $_;
14      }
15
16      return $product;
17   };
18
19   my $printVal = &$productRef( 1, 2, 3, 4 );
20   print( join( ' * ', 1, 2, 3, 4 ), " = " );
21   print( "$printVal\n" );
22
23   $printVal = $productRef->( 6, 8, -5, 2 );
24   print( join( ' * ', 6, 8, -5, 2 ), " = " );
25   print( "$printVal\n" );
26
27   $printVal = $productRef->( 4, 3, 2, 1 );
28   print( join(' * ', 4, 3, 2, 1 ), " = " );
29   print( "$printVal\n" );
```

Fig. 13.6 Anonymous functions (part 1 of 2).

```
1 * 2 * 3 * 4 = 24
6 * 8 * -5 * 2 = -480
4 * 3 * 2 * 1 = 24
```

Fig. 13.6   Anonymous functions (part 2 of 2).

The anonymous function is defined on lines 8–17 and assigned to the reference **$pro-ductRef**. This function takes a list of numbers as arguments and returns the product of all the numbers in the list. We call the function by dereferencing the reference to the function with an ampersand on line 19 and with arrow notation on lines 23 and 27.

One handy trick that can be done using references and anonymous structures allows us to interpolate the return value of a function into a double-quoted string. Normally if we try to call a function in a double-quoted string, the function call is not interpolated (i.e., the function is not called) and the function call is simply treated as literal text in the string. However, if we create a reference to the return of the function call then dereference that reference, the reference will be interpolated and we will be able to see the results of the function call. Figure 13.7 demonstrates this on line 9. The expression **${ \square(5) }** uses curly braces to create a block of code in which the function square is called. The **** before the function name creates a reference to the value returned by the function. The **$** before the left brace dereferences the reference to the return value. The entire expression is interpolated to display the result of the function call.

13.5 Closures

Anonymous functions come into existence at runtime. The part of the code in which an anonymous function is created has its own lexical context. The values of variables created in the same lexical context as an anonymous function can be used by the anonymous function when it is called later in the program. Anonymous functions save the information about the context in which they were created and execute as if they were still in that context. The anonymous functions act as *closures* with respect to lexical variables.

```
1    #!/usr/bin/perl
2    # Fig. 13.7: fig13_07.pl
3    # Interpolating function returns into a double quoted string.
4
5    use warnings;
6    use strict;
7
8    print( "The number is square( 5 ).\n" );
9    print( "The number is ${ \square( 5 ) }.\n" );
10
11   sub square
12   {
13       my $x = shift();
14       return $x * $x;
15   }
```

Fig. 13.7   Interpolating function returns into a double-quoted string (part 1 of 2).

```
The number is square( 5 ).
The number is 25.
```

Fig. 13.7   Interpolating function returns into a double-quoted string (part 2 of 2).

An example of where this can be useful is when a function returns an anonymous function reference. The function reference will contain the state information pertaining for the lexical context in which it was created. Figure 13.8 demonstrates this concept.

Function **animalInFood** (lines 8–16) returns a reference to an anonymous function (defined at lines 11 through 15). Line 10 creates a lexical variable **$x**, which stores the value passed to function **animalInFood** as an argument. Note that the anonymous function uses the lexical variable **$x** in line 14. Each time the **animalInFood** function is called, a new **$x** is created because it is declared with the **my** keyword. When the anonymous function is created on line 11, the **$x** it refers to is the specific **$x** that exists at the time the function is created, not the value that **$x** holds when the anonymous function is called. This association of the variable **$x** in the closure with the specific instance of **$x**, rather than the name **$x**, is known as *deep binding*. Only lexical variables provide deep binding. If we used the **local** keyword on line 10 instead of **my**, we would not have deep binding and the anonymous function returned would not be a closure.

```
1   #!/usr/bin/perl
2   # Fig. 13.8: fig13_08.pl
3   # A simple closure example
4
5   use warnings;
6   use strict;
7
8   sub animalInFood
9   {
10     my $x = shift();
11     return sub
12     {
13        my $y = shift();
14        print( "There is a $x in my $y!\n" );
15     };
16   }
17
18   my $flyInFood = animalInFood( "fly" );
19   my $frogInFood = animalInFood( "frog" );
20
21   &$flyInFood( "soup" );
22   &$frogInFood( "coffee" );
```

```
There is a fly in my soup!
There is a frog in my coffee!
```

Fig. 13.8   Demonstrating closures.

You can see that **animalInFood** returns closures because when we assign variable **$flyInFood** the closure returned by passing **animalInFood** the word **"fly"**, then call **animalInFood** again with the value **"frog"**. Each closure is stored in a reference. These references are used at lines 21 and 22 to invoke each closure. Note that the closure invoked at line 21 prints a string containing the word **fly**, which was passed to the first call to **animalInFood**. Similarly, the closure invoked at line 22 prints a string containing the word **frog**, which was passed to the second call to **animalInFood**.

13.6 References as Function Arguments

Until now we have had no way to pass anything other than lists of scalars to functions. Remember that the arguments passed to a function are flattened into the special array variable **@_**. One of the primary uses of references is to pass to functions arguments that are not necessarily scalars, such as arrays and hashes. However, with references, a function can receive as an argument anything that can be stored in a reference. Figure 13.9 shows an example of this in which we use references to pass a function two arrays.

```
1    #!/usr/bin/perl
2    # Fig. 13.9: fig13_09.pl
3    # Demonstrates passing arrays to a function
4
5    use warnings;
6    use strict;
7
8    my @array1 = ( 1 .. 8 );
9    my @array2 = ( 'a' .. 'e' );
10   my @mixed = arrayMixer( \@array1, \@array2 );
11   print( "@mixed\n" );
12   my @mixed2 = arrayMixer( [ 'I', 'to', 'park' ], [ 'go', 'the' ] );
13   print( "@mixed2\n" );
14
15   sub arrayMixer
16   {
17      my @firstArray = @{ $_[ 0 ] };
18      my @secondArray = @{ $_[ 1 ] };
19      my ( $first, $second, @array );
20
21      while ( ( $first = shift( @firstArray ) ) &&
22               ( $second = shift ( @secondArray ) ) ) {
23         push( @array, $first, $second );
24      }
25
26      push( @array, $first, @firstArray ) if ( $first );
27      push( @array, @secondArray ) if ( $second );
28
29      return @array;
30   }
```

```
1 a 2 b 3 c 4 d 5 e 6 7 8
I go to the park
```

Fig. 13.9   Passing nonscalars to functions .

Function **arrayMixer** takes two arrays as arguments and mixes them by using function **shift** to extract the first element of each array and using function **push** to add those elements to a new array (the element from the first array is always inserted in the new array first). This process is repeated until one of the array has no more elements, at which point the remaining values from the other array are added to the end of the new array. Then the new array is returned to the caller. Without references, this relatively simple function would have been much more difficult to implement. Originally this required passing the number of elements in each array before passing the arrays so that we could break **@_** into the two arrays. With references this was unnecessary.

References are passed to functions like any other scalar. Line 10 passes references to the arrays **@array1** and **@array2**. These references are accessed in the function as **$_[0]** and **$_[1]**, respectively. To dereference these references and access the arrays, lines 17 and 18 use curly braces to specify what we actually want dereferenced. The braces are required to force the order of evaluation because the precedence of the dereferencing **@** symbol is higher than the square bracket operator. If we remove the curly braces, the **@** in **@$_[0]** would dereference **$_** and the square brackets operator would make an array slice containing the 0th element of this dereferenced array.

Line 12 calls function **arrayMixer** again. In this case, we create two anonymous arrays to pass to the function.

This example showed how to pass arrays to functions, but anything that a reference can point to could be passed in as well. This includes hashes and even functions.

Sometimes we might want to perform a different action depending on what kind of a reference is passed to us. In this case we can use function *ref* to determine the type of the reference. Function **ref** receives a reference argument and returns a string describing the type of reference. For example, an array reference returns the string **ARRAY**. Figure 13.10 shows the different strings the **ref** function returns. Notice that in Fig. 13.10 we did not specify the **use warnings** pragma. We removed the **use warnings** pragma for the purpose of this example because it produces warning messages indicating that we use values only once in the program. This warning is not relevant to the example as we only use each value once so we can demonstrate the string returned by function **ref**.

```
1   #!/usr/bin/perl
2   # Fig. 13.10: fig13_10.pl
3   # Demonstrates the return values of the ref function
4
5   use strict;
6
7   my @array = qw( hello world );
8   my %hash = ( key => "data" );
9
10  print( 'ref(10) = ', ref( 10 ), "\n" );    # undefined
11  print( 'ref(\10) = ', ref( \10 ), "\n" );
12  print( 'ref(\@array) = ', ref( \@array ), "\n" );
13  print( 'ref(\%hash) = ', ref( \%hash ), "\n" );
14  print( 'ref(\&function) = ', ref( \&function ), "\n" );
15  print( 'ref(\\@array) = ', ref( \\@array ), "\n" );
16  print( 'ref(\*hash) = ', ref( \*hash ), "\n" );
```

Fig. 13.10 Function **ref** (part 1 of 2).

```
17
18   sub function
19   {
20       print( "Hello world.\n" );
21   }
```

```
ref(10) =
ref(\10) = SCALAR
ref(\@array) = ARRAY
ref(\%hash) = HASH
ref(\&function) = CODE
ref(\\@array) = REF
ref(\*hash) = GLOB
```

Fig. 13.10 Function **ref** (part 2 of 2).

Figure 13.11 shows an example that uses function **ref** in a function to determine the course of action to pursue based on the reference type passed to the function.

Function **printStructures** is a recursive function that uses function **ref** to determine the type of data structure to which a reference points. It uses a **foreach** loop to iterate through all the arguments passed to the function (line 25). If the element is not a reference, we just print it (lines 27–29). If the element is a reference to a scalar, we dereference and print the element (lines 30–32).

If the element is an array (lines 33–46), we go through each element, printing the array index. If the element is a reference, we call **printStructures** recursively with an increased indent (line 40). Otherwise we just print the element (line 43). If the element is a hash (lines 47–60), we print the key instead of the index and perform the same processing on the values, calling **printStructures** recursively at line 54 if necessary.

If the reference is to a function (lines 61–63), we print out **CODE**. If **ref** returns **GLOB** (lines 64–66), it is a reference to a typeglob (these are discussed in Section 13.10) and we just print **GLOB**.

```
1    #!/usr/bin/perl
2    # Fig. 13.11: fig13_11.pl
3    # Using ref inside a function
4
5    use strict;
6    use warnings;
7
8    my @array1 = ( "This","is","the","first","array." );
9    my @array2 = ( "This","is","the","second","array." );
10   my %hash = ( Tarzan    => "Jane",
11               Superman => "Lois Lane",
12               Batman   => "Catwoman", );
13   my $array3 = [ "anonymous", [ "array", "in", "an", "array" ],
14               { "plus" => "a",
15                 "hash" => "in",
16               },
17               "as", "well" ];
```

Fig. 13.11 Function **ref** inside a function (part 1 of 3).

```
18
19   printStructures( 5, \@array1, \%hash, \@array2, $array3);
20
21   sub printStructures
22   {
23      my $indent = shift();
24
25      foreach my $element ( @_ ) {
26
27         unless ( ref( $element ) ) {
28            print( ' ' x $indent, $element, "\n" );
29         }
30         elsif ( ref( $element ) eq 'SCALAR' ) {
31            print( ' ' x $indent, $element, "\n" );
32         }
33         elsif ( ref( $element ) eq 'ARRAY' ) {
34
35            foreach ( 0 .. $#$element ) {
36               print( ' ' x $indent, "[ $_ ] " );
37
38               if ( ref( $element->[ $_ ] ) ) {
39                  print( "\n" );
40                  printStructures( $indent + 3, $element->[ $_ ] );
41               }
42               else {
43                  print( "$element->[ $_ ]\n" );
44               }
45            }
46         }
47         elsif ( ref( $element ) eq 'HASH' ) {
48
49            foreach my $key ( keys( %$element ) ) {
50               print( ' ' x $indent, $key, ' => ' );
51
52               if ( ref ( $element->{ $key } ) ) {
53                  print( "\n" );
54                  printStructures( $indent + 3, $element->{$key} );
55               }
56               else {
57                  print( "$element->{ $key }\n" );
58               }
59            }
60         }
61         elsif ( ref( $element ) eq 'CODE' ) {
62            print( ' ' x $indent, "CODE\n" );
63         }
64         elsif ( ref( $element ) eq 'GLOB' ) {
65            print( ' ' x $indent, "GLOB\n" );
66         }
67
68         print( "\n" );
69      }
70   }
```

Fig. 13.11 Function **ref** inside a function (part 2 of 3).

```
        [ 0 ]  This
        [ 1 ]  is
        [ 2 ]  the
        [ 3 ]  first
        [ 4 ]  array.

     Batman  =>  Catwoman
     Superman  =>  Lois Lane
     Tarzan  =>  Jane

        [ 0 ]  This
        [ 1 ]  is
        [ 2 ]  the
        [ 3 ]  second
        [ 4 ]  array.

        [ 0 ]  anonymous
        [ 1 ]
           [ 0 ]  array
           [ 1 ]  in
           [ 2 ]  an
           [ 3 ]  array

        [ 2 ]
           hash  =>  in
           plus  =>  a

        [ 3 ]  as
        [ 4 ]  well
```

Fig. 13.11 Function **ref** inside a function (part 3 of 3).

13.7 Nested Data Structures

Arrays and hashes are collections of scalars. Any scalar can be a reference to any other type of variable, enabling us to create complex data structures using the basic Perl data types.

An example of these more complicated data structures is an *array of arrays*. This data structure consists of an array whose elements are references to other arrays. To access an element of this array we need two subscripts, one to determine the location in the first array and one to determine the location in the referenced array. This type of data structure is known as a *two-dimensional array* or a *double-subscripted array*.

Using arrow notation, the element would look like **$array[$i]->[$j]** where **$i** is the index of the first array and **$j** is the index of the second array. When the array elements are actually references to other arrays, you can leave out the arrow operator and reference the array elements with the syntax **$array[$i][$j]**. In this case, the arrow operator is implied between the bracketed subscripts. Figure 13.12 shows an example using a two-dimensional array.

```perl
1   #!/usr/bin/perl
2   # Fig. 13.12: fig13_12.pl
3   # Shows how to use two dimensional arrays.
4
5   use warnings;
6   use strict;
7
8   my @array;
9
10  foreach my $outer ( 0 .. 3 ) {
11
12      foreach my $inner ( 0 .. 3 ) {
13          $array[ $outer ][ $inner ] = $outer * $inner;
14      }
15  }
16
17  foreach ( 0 .. $#array ) {
18      $array[ $_ ]->[ 4 ] = $_ * 4;
19  }
20
21  print( "@array\n" );
22  push( @array, [ 0, 4, 8, 12, 16 ] );
23
24  print( "\$array[ 1 ]->[ 3 ] = $array[ 1 ]->[ 3 ]\n" );
25  print( "\$array[ 2 ][ 3 ] = $array[ 2 ][ 3 ]\n" );
26  print( "\@\$array[ 1 ] = @{$array[ 1 ]}\n\n" );
27
28  my @array2 = (
29      [ 1, 2, 3, 4 ],
30      [ 2, 3, 4, 5 ],
31      [ 3, 4, 5, 6 ],
32      [ 4, 5, 6, 7 ]
33  );
34
35  my $array3 = [
36      [ 1, 2, 3, 4 ],
37      [ 2, 3, 4, 5 ],
38      [ 3, 4, 5, 6 ],
39      [ 4, 5, 6, 7 ]
40  ];
41
42  foreach ( 0 .. $#array ) {
43      print( "@{ $array[ $_ ] }\n" );
44  }
45
46  print( "\n" );
47
48  foreach my $row ( @array2 ) {
49      print( "@$row\n" );
50  }
51
52  print( "\n$array3->[ 2 ][ 2 ]\n" );
```

Fig. 13.12 Two-dimensional array (part 1 of 2).

```
ARRAY(0x85d3ad0) ARRAY(0x85deb24) ARRAY(0x85debb4) ARRAY(0x85dec44)
$array[ 1 ]->[ 3 ] = 3
$array[ 2 ][ 3 ] = 6
@$array[ 1 ] = 0 1 2 3 4

0 0 0 0 0
0 1 2 3 4
0 2 4 6 8
0 3 6 9 12
0 4 8 12 16

1 2 3 4
2 3 4 5
3 4 5 6
4 5 6 7

5
```

Fig. 13.12 Two-dimensional array (part 2 of 2).

Lines 10–15 show the initialization of a multidimensional array using nested **foreach** loops. To compute each individual element of a multidimensional array individually, you can nest two loops where the outer one iterates over the first array subscript and the inside loop iterates over the second subscript. Lines 17–26 show ways to access different parts of the arrays. Lines 17 through 19 add one more element to each of the rows in **@array**. Line 21 outputs the locations of each array to which **@array** refers. Line 22 adds a row to **@array**.

It is important when working with multidimensional arrays to note that what we are looking at is not actually a multidimensional array. We can manipulate the structure and access its elements as if it is a multidimensional array, but in reality we have an array of references. This explains why line 21 of the Fig. 13.12 returns address values.

Lines 28–33 initialize **@array2** with anonymous arrays. The initialization on lines 35–40 uses square brackets instead of parentheses to return a reference to the multidimensional array rather than the array itself. As you can see, anonymous array composers make defining multidimensional arrays straightforward.

Lines 42–50 show two different ways of printing out the arrays. The first (printing out **@array**) uses a **foreach** structure to loop through the index numbers, printing the array for each index number. The second (printing **@array2**) uses a **foreach** loop to assign each reference in **@array2** to **$row**, which is subsequently dereferenced and printed.

Line 52 uses reference **$array3** to access an element of the multidimensional array to which **$array3** refers. Note the use of the arrow operator in this case.

The technique used to create a multidimensional array can be used to create any other type of nested data structure. You can make arrays of hashes, hashes of arrays, hashes of hashes, or mix them in any way you please. You can also nest them as deeply as you like. For example, a three-dimensional array would just be an array of arrays of arrays.

Figure 13.13 demonstrates a hash of arrays. This is useful because it allows you to associate multiple values with a single key. This would be difficult without references, because keys in a hash must be unique. However, by associating each key with an array reference, we solve this problem. To create the hash, we can either assign array references to keys in the hash individually, or we can do it all at once by assigning a list of key/array reference pairs to a hash. Accessing elements is also similar to the multidimensional array, except that the first index is a key.

In this example, we create a hash of arrays by asking the user for input and assigning each element individually to the hash. To create the hash in the program as it existed in the sample execution of Fig. 13.13 (before elements were deleted), we can write:

```
%hash = ( duck  => [ 'Huey', 'Louie', 'Dewey' ],
          horse => [ 'Mr. Ed' ],
          dog   => [ 'Lassie', 'Benji' ]
        );
```

Notice the use of anonymous array composers.

```
1   #!/usr/bin/perl
2   # Fig. 13.13: fig13_13.pl
3   # Demonstrates a hash of arrays
4
5   use warnings;
6   use strict;
7
8   instructions();
9   my $choice = prompt();
10  my %hash;
11
12  while ( $choice ne 'q' ) {
13     addElement() if ( $choice eq 'a' );
14     deleteElement() if ( $choice eq 'd' );
15     deleteKey() if ( $choice eq 'k' );
16     printAll() if ( $choice eq 'p' );
17     instructions() if ( $choice eq 'i' );
18     $choice = prompt();
19  }
20
21  sub instructions
22  {
23  print <<DONE;
24  Enter 'a' to add an element.
25  Enter 'd' to delete an element.
26  Enter 'k' to delete a key.
27  Enter 'p' to print all elements.
28  Enter 'q' to quit.
29  DONE
30  }
31
32  sub prompt
33  {
34     print( "? " );
35     chomp( my $answer = <STDIN> );
36     return $answer;
37  }
```

Fig. 13.13 Hash of arrays (part 1 of 3).

```
38
39   sub addElement
40   {
41      print( "What is the key you would like to add? " );
42      chomp( my $key = <STDIN> );
43      print( "What is the value? " );
44      chomp( my $value = <STDIN> );
45      push @{ $hash{ $key } }, $value;
46   }
47
48   sub deleteElement
49   {
50      print( "What is the key of the element? " );
51      chomp( my $key = <STDIN> );
52      print( "What is the value of the element? " );
53      chomp( my $value = <STDIN> );
54
55      for ( 0 .. $#{ $hash{ $key } } ) {
56
57         if ( $hash{ $key }[ $_ ] eq $value ) {
58            print( "Deleting element $hash{ $key }[ $_ ]\n" );
59            splice( @{ $hash{ $key } }, $_, 1 );
60            return;
61         }
62      }
63   }
64
65   sub deleteKey
66   {
67      print( "What key would you like to delete? " );
68      chomp( my $key = <STDIN> );
69      delete( $hash{ $key } );
70   }
71
72   sub printAll
73   {
74      foreach ( keys( %hash ) ) {
75         print( " $_ => ", join( ', ', @{ $hash{ $_ } } ), "\n" );
76      }
77   }
```

```
Enter 'a' to add an element.
Enter 'd' to delete an element.
Enter 'k' to delete a key.
Enter 'p' to print all elements.
Enter 'q' to quit.
? a
What is the key you would like to add? duck
What is the value? Huey
? a
What is the key you would like to add? duck
What is the value? Louie
```
continued on next page...

Fig. 13.13 Hash of arrays (part 2 of 3).

```
                                              continued from previous page...
?a
What is the key you would like to add? duck
What is the value? Dewey
? a
What is the key you would like to add? horse
What is the value? Mr. Ed
? a
What is the key you would like to add? dog
What is the value? Lassie
? a
What is the key you would like to add? dog
What is the value? Benji
? p
  dog => Lassie, Benji
  duck => Huey, Louie, Dewey
  horse => Mr. Ed
? d
What is the key of the element? duck
What is the value of the element? Huey
Deleting element Huey
? k
What key would you like to delete? dog
? p
  duck => Louie, Dewey
  horse => Mr. Ed
? q
```

Fig. 13.13 Hash of arrays (part 3 of 3).

13.8 Garbage Collection and Circular References

Until now we have not really discussed memory management. When we finish using a data structure, we simply forget about it. Perl will automatically free the memory associated with the structure. The part of Perl that actually frees the memory is known as the *garbage collector*. The garbage collector frees any memory that it is absolutely sure will not be used again in the script. The garbage collector works through a mechanism called *reference counting*. Each block of memory has an internal *reference count*, which indicates how many references contain that address (i.e., how many references are pointing to that block of memory). When this count becomes zero, there are no more references to the block of memory and the memory is freed. For example, if we wrote

```
{
    my $reference;
    {
        my $variable = 5;
        $reference = \$variable;
    }
}
```

when **$variable** is created, the memory allocated for **$variable** has a reference count of 1. We then create a reference to **$variable** and assign it to **$reference**. This increases the reference count for this block of memory to 2. At the end of the inner block,

$variable goes out of scope. At this point, we can no longer refer to this memory through **$variable**, so the reference count is decremented to 1. Variable **$reference** still holds a reference to the block of memory containing 5, therefore the memory allocated cannot be reclaimed by the garbage collector yet. At the end of the outer block, variable **$reference** goes out of scope. At this point, there are no more references to the block of memory containing 5, so the reference count becomes zero and the garbage collector is able to reclaim the memory for later use in the program.

In most cases, you do not actually have to worry about what gets collected and why. However, there is a case where this type of garbage collection will not free memory, even when there is no way to access it from your program. If you have *circular references*, where one reference points to something that eventually points back to the original reference, that memory will never be freed. This is known as a *memory leak*. Here is an example:

```
{
    my $reference1;
    my $reference2 = \$reference1;
    $reference1 = \$reference2;
}
```

Because **$reference1** refers to **$reference2** and **$reference2** refers to **$reference1**, their reference counts will never go to zero, even after the block ends causing **$reference1** and **$reference2** to go out of scope. There is no way to access the memory from the program, but the reference counts stay at 1 because they refer to each other. When you are finished with circular references you need to break the circle explicitly before allowing the variables that are in the circle to go out of scope. This is done by assigning other values to the variables. For example, if we had assigned 5 to **$reference1** before it went out of scope, **$reference2**'s reference count would drop to zero at the end of the block causing it to be garbage collected. That would cause **$reference1**'s count to drop to zero causing it to be garbage collected as well.

Common Programming Error 13.2

Circular references can lead to memory leaks, which, over time, may lead to other problems in your programs such as running out of memory.

13.9 Symbolic References

Symbolic references are scalars that refer to another variable by holding the variable's name. While they are not as efficient as hard references, they can be useful. To declare a symbolic reference we just assign the name of a variable (without the special character) to another variable. Now the second variable can be dereferenced just like a normal reference. Thus if we want to reference the variable **$name** with the variable **$reference**, we would say **$reference = name**, then use **$$reference** to access the value. We could also say **${ $reference }**.

The primary use of symbolic references is for scenarios in which you will not know the variable name to which the reference will refer until runtime. Figure 13.14 demonstrates the former.

This example allows the user to enter the name of a variable to which they want to add 20. The user inputs the name of the variable to be modified, so we have no way to specify the variable name before runtime. This is why we must use symbolic references.

```perl
1   #!/usr/bin/perl
2   # Fig. 13.14: fig13_14.pl
3   # Demonstrates symbolic references
4
5   use warnings;
6   use strict;
7   no strict 'refs';
8
9   my ( $choice, @variables );
10  instructions();
11
12  do {
13     print( "? " );
14     chomp( $choice = <STDIN> );
15
16     if ( $choice eq 'v' ) {
17        print( "What variable would you like to add to? " );
18        chomp( my $name = <STDIN> );
19
20        if ( !( $$name ) ) {
21           push( @variables, $name );
22           $$name = 0;
23        }
24
25        $$name += 20;
26     }
27
28     if ( $choice eq 'p' ) {
29        print( "What variable would you like to print? " );
30        chomp( my $name = <STDIN> );
31        print( "$$name\n" );
32     }
33
34     if ( $choice eq 'a' ) {
35
36        foreach my $name ( @variables ) {
37           print( "\$$name = $$name\n" );
38        }
39     }
40
41     instructions() if ( $choice eq 'i' );
42
43  } while ( $choice ne 'q' );
44
45  sub instructions
46  {
47  print <<DONE;
48  Enter 'v' to add to a variable
49  Enter 'p' to print a variable
50  Enter 'a' to print all the variables
51  Enter 'i' to print the instructions
52  Enter 'q' to quit
```

Fig. 13.14 Symbolic references (part 1 of 2).

```
53   DONE
54   }
```

```
Enter 'v' to add to a variable
Enter 'p' to print a variable
Enter 'a' to print all the variables
Enter 'i' to print the instructions
Enter 'q' to quit
? v
What variable would you like to add to? name1
? v
What variable would you like to add to? name1
? v
What variable would you like to add to? name2
? v
What variable would you like to add to? name1
? v
What variable would you like to add to? name3
? v
What variable would you like to add to? name2
? p
What variable would you like to print? name1
60
? v
What variable would you like to add to? name1
? a
$name1 = 80
$name2 = 40
$name3 = 20
? q
```

Fig. 13.14 Symbolic references (part 2 of 2).

Line 17 prompts the user for the name of the variable to which we will add 20, and line 18 obtains this name from the user. If the name has not been entered previously, lines 20–23 add the name to an array of variable names and initialize the variable to 0. We use the array of variable names to keep track of the variable names; otherwise, we would not know what variable names to print. To add 20 to the variable specified, we dereference the variable like it was any other reference and use the **+=** operator to add 20 to it (line 25).

Although this program shows an example of how symbolic references can be used, it is generally a good idea to avoid symbolic references. What would have happened if we had chosen to overwrite the **$_** variable? One of the problems with symbolic references is that they can overwrite existing variables. This is why the use of symbolic references is generally deprecated. In this previous example, we could have used a hash to keep track of the count for each name. This would have been preferable to using symbolic references because it would remove the risk of incrementing a variable that should not be modified. When the pragma **use strict** is specified, Perl gives a fatal error when symbolic references are used. To prevent the error in this program, we specified

```
no strict 'refs';
```

to disable the **strict** checking of references in this program.

Common Programming Error 13.3

Using symbolic references when the **strict 'refs'** *tag is enabled causes fatal errors.*

13.10 Typeglobs

References are a recent addition to Perl. Before references were added to the language, a construct known as a *typeglob* was used to get the same sort of functionality as references. To understand typeglobs, we must first understand more about the inner workings of Perl.

As we discussed in Chapter 6, all package global variables are stored in a symbol table. Perl uses this table to keep track of variables and their locations in memory. When a variable is used in a program, Perl looks up the name of the variable in the symbol table to determine the variable's location. Each package global variable has an entry in a symbol table, and this entry contains the different variable types for that particular name. The entries in the symbol table are called *typeglobs*.

Each typeglob consists of all the different types to which the name of the typeglob could refer. The type identifier for a typeglob is ***** (like the regular expression character) because it represents all types. The typeglob ***name** consists of the scalar **$name**, the array **@name**, the hash **%name**, the function **&name**, the filehandle **name** and the format **name**.

Typeglobs can be assigned to each other, as in ***newname = *name**. This makes everything named **newname** a synonym for the corresponding type named **name**. Accessing the variable through **newname** is actually faster than if we were dereferencing a reference to **$name** held in **$newname**. This is because **$newname** now is the same as **$name** and dereferencing is not required.

You need to be careful because if we already have a variable **@newname** and assign ***newname = *name** to make **$newname** an alias for **$name**, **@newname** is obliterated and now becomes whatever **@name** was. However, using references, we can do a more explicit typeglob assignment. By assigning a reference to **$name** to ***newname**, we alias **$newname** directly to **$name** without having **@newname** aliased to **@name**. Figure 13.15 demonstrates using typeglobs.

Line 7 turns off the **strict 'vars'** pragma. We want our variable assignments to work with the global symbol table, so we cannot use the **my** keyword. Turning off **strict 'vars'** allows us to work with the global symbol table and not worry about explicitly declaring package names to create our own symbol table in this example.

Lines 9–24 assign values to the different variables associated with the typeglob ***cow** in the normal manner (line 9 is a scalar, line 10 is a hash, line 11 is an array and lines 13–24 are a function). Line 26 assigns the ***cow** typeglob to the ***heifer** typeglob. This causes all the variables in ***heifer** to refer to the variables in ***cow**. This is shown by calling function **printAnimal** (lines 29, 35 and 44) with either ***cow** or ***heifer** as an argument. Function **printAnimal** (lines 46–58) receives the typeglob as ***animal** and uses each of the variables associated with the typeglob received in the function call.

Notice in lines 31 and 32 that we change the values in **@cow** by using **@heifer** and call **printAnimal** to show this on line 35. We then change only the scalar part of ***heifer** by assigning it a reference to a scalar.

You may have noticed that we did not use **my** variables in that last example (Fig. 13.15). This is because **my** variables do not work with typeglobs. Typeglobs belong to the symbol table, while **my** variables are not placed in the symbol table.

```
1   #!/usr/bin/perl
2   # Fig. 13.15: fig13_15.pl
3   # Demonstrates the use of typeglobs
4
5   use warnings;
6   use strict;
7   no strict 'vars';
8
9   $cow = "cow";
10  %cow = ( sound => "mooo" );
11  @cow = ( 'gills', 'brain', 'eyes', '', 'feet', '', 'udders' );
12
13  sub cow
14  {
15  print <<'DONE';

17                          \__/
18       _____/oo\
19      /                  ||
20     /|        _____   /
21    /||   /|||        | |
22     |_|           |_|
23  DONE
24  }
25
26  *heifer = *cow;
27
28  print( "Printing Cow.\n" );
29  printAnimal( *cow );
30
31  $heifer[ 2 ] = 'nostrils';
32  $heifer[ 4 ] = 'stomachs';
33
34  print( "\nPrinting modified cow.\n" );
35  printAnimal( *cow );
36
37  print( "\nChanging the cow's name\n" );
38
39  {
40     my $newname = "heifer";
41     *heifer = \$newname;
42  }
43
44  printAnimal( *heifer );
45
46  sub printAnimal
47  {
48     local *animal = shift();
49     print( "A $animal goes $animal{ sound }!\n" );
50
51     for ( my $i = $#animal; $i >= 0; $i-- ) {
52        print( "A $animal has $i $animal[ $i ]!\n" )
```

Fig. 13.15 Using typeglobs (part 1 of 2).

```
53                    if ( $animal[ $i ] );
54        }
55
56        print( "A $animal looks something like this.\n" );
57        animal();
58    }
```

```
Printing Cow.
A cow goes mooo!
A cow has 6 udders!
A cow has 4 feet!
A cow has 2 eyes!
A cow has 1 brain!
A cow has 0 gills!
A cow looks something like this.

                      \__/
_____/oo\
   /                     ||
  /|          _____    /
 /||   /|||          | |
   |_|              |_|
Printing modified cow.
A cow goes mooo!
A cow has 6 udders!
A cow has 4 stomachs!
A cow has 2 nostrils!
A cow has 1 brain!
A cow has 0 gills!
A cow looks something like this.

                      \__/
_____/oo\
   /                     ||
  /|          _____    /
 /||   /|||          | |
   |_|              |_|
Changing the cow's name
A heifer goes mooo!
A heifer has 6 udders!
A heifer has 4 stomachs!
A heifer has 2 nostrils!
A heifer has 1 brain!
A heifer has 0 gills!
A heifer looks something like this.

                      \__/
_____/oo\
   /                     ||
  /|          _____    /
 /||   /|||          | |
   |_|              |_|
```

Fig. 13.15 Using typeglobs (part 2 of 2).

Common Programming Error 13.4

*Variables declared with the **my** keyword do not exist in the symbol table. Trying to access them through the symbol table could cause fatal errors.*

Typeglobs also provide another way to produce references. Treating a typeglob as a hash with the name of the type of variable you want a reference to will give you a reference to that variable. For example, ***name{ SCALAR }** gives a reference to **$name**. Dereferencing a typeglob with the symbol name of the type you want will give you the value of the type as demonstrated in Fig. 13.16.

```perl
1   #!/usr/bin/perl
2   # Fig. 13.16: fig13_16.pl
3   # Two more ways of using typeglobs
4
5   use warnings;
6   use strict;
7   no strict 'vars';
8
9   $variable = 10;
10  @variable = ( 1, 2, 3, 4, 5 );
11
12  sub variable
13  {
14     print( "green\n" );
15  }
16
17  print( "$variable\n" );
18  print( "@variable\n" );
19  variable();
20
21  $scalarRef = *variable{ SCALAR };
22  $arrayRef = *variable{ ARRAY };
23  $codeRef = *variable{ CODE };
24
25  print( "$$scalarRef\n" );
26  print( "@$arrayRef\n" );
27  &$codeRef();
28
29  print( "${ *variable }\n" );
30  print( "@{ *variable }\n" );
31  &{ *variable };
```

```
10
1 2 3 4 5
green
10
1 2 3 4 5
green
10
1 2 3 4 5
green
```

Fig. 13.16 Two more ways of using typeglobs.

The new syntax for producing references is shown on lines 21–23. We also show that typeglobs can be dereferenced just like a reference. The difference is that references can only refer to a specific type while typeglobs refer to all the types.

Testing and Debugging Tip 13.1

In general, it is best not to use typeglobs unless you absolutely have to and you know exactly what you are doing. This is because it is easy to destroy or overwrite data that you did not mean to destroy or overwrite.

One good use for typeglobs is to create constant scalars. By assigning a reference to something that is not an lvalue to a typeglob, we can make a constant variable. Here is a simple example that shows how to create a read-only variable

```
*PI = \3.14159;
$PI = 3;
```

Note that the second line will cause an error like

Modification of a read-only value attempted

Another use for typeglobs is to name previously anonymous data structures. The following statement demonstrates this:

```
my $anonymous = [ 1, 2, 3, 4 ];
*name = $anonymous;
print "@name\n";
```

This code creates an anonymous array, then assigns it to ***name**. This causes **@name** to refer to the formerly anonymous array. The **print** statement then outputs the array.

13.11 Referencing Filehandles

Another use of typeglobs is referencing filehandles. Filehandles do not have a special character to identify them as filehandles, so you cannot create a reference to a filehandle. However, a typeglob consists of the filehandle with the same name as the typeglob (among other things). Thus a typeglob can act like a reference to a filehandle. We can assign this typeglob to a scalar and then use that scalar anywhere where we would normally use the filehandle. Figure 13.17 demonstartes using typeglobs as references to filehandles. The program reads itself in and outputs itself with line numbers.

```
1   #!/usr/bin/perl
2   # Fig. 13.17: fig13_17.pl
3   # Demonstrates using typeglobs to alias filehandles
4
5   use warnings;
6   use strict;
7
8   open( TEXT, 'fig13_17.pl' ) or
9       die( "File could not be opened : $!" );
10
11  my $filehandle = *TEXT;
12  my $out = *STDOUT;
```

Fig. 13.17 Referencing filehandles (part 1 of 2).

```
13
14   while ( <$filehandle> ) {
15       printf( $out "%-3d %s", $., $_ );
16   }
```

```
1    #!/usr/bin/perl
2    # Figure 13.17: fig13_17.pl
3    # Demonstrates using typeglobs to alias filehandles
4
5    use warnings;
6    use strict;
7
8    open( TEXT, 'fig13_17.pl' ) or
9        die( "File could not be opened : $!" );
10
11   my $filehandle = *TEXT;
12   my $out = *STDOUT;
13
14   while ( <$filehandle> ) {
15       printf( $out "%-3d %s", $., $_ );
16   }
```

Fig. 13.17 Referencing filehandles (part 2 of 2).

Line 11 assigns **$filehandle** the typeglob for **TEXT**. Line 12 assigns **$out** the typeglob for **STDOUT**. These scalars are used like the original filehandles. Line 14 uses the angle bracket operators on **$filehandle**, and line 15 writes to **$out** using **printf**.

Typeglob references can go anywhere a normal reference can. We can pass filehandles into functions in this way, thus solving the problem of not being able to pass filehandles to functions (discussed in Chapter 10). Figure 13.18 demonstrates how to use typeglobs to pass filehandles to functions.

```
1    #!/usr/bin/perl
2    # Fig. 13.18: fig13_18.pl
3    # Passing filehandles to functions
4
5    use warnings;
6    use strict;
7
8    my $file = shift( @ARGV );
9    open( FILE, $file ) or die( "Error opening $file: $!" );
10   my $filehandle = *FILE;
11   readhandle( $filehandle );
12   close( FILE ) or die( "Error closing $file: $!" );
13
14   print( "\n\nNow a 2nd time...\n" );
15   open( FILE, $file ) or die( "Error opening $file: $!" );
16   $filehandle = \*FILE;
17   readhandle( $filehandle );
18   close( FILE ) or die( "Error closing $file: $!" );
```

Fig. 13.18 Passing filehandles to functions (part 1 of 2).

```
19
20   print( "\n\nAnd finally...\n" );
21   readfile( $file );
22
23   sub readhandle
24   {
25      my $fh = shift();
26      print while ( <$fh> );
27   }
28
29   sub readfile
30   {
31      my $file = shift();
32      local *FILE;
33      open( FILE, $file ) or die( "Error opening $file: $!" );
34      print while ( <FILE> );
35   }
```

```
This is a sample text file...

Now a 2nd time...
This is a sample text file...

And finally...
This is a sample text file..
```

Fig. 13.18 Passing filehandles to functions (part 2 of 2).

```
This is a sample text file...
```

Fig. 13.19 Contents of **sample.txt** file used for **$file**.

Lines 10 and 11 demonstrate passing a typeglob to a function. Other ways to pass filehandles into functions include taking a reference to a typeglob and passing the reference, rather than the whole typeglob (lines 16 and 17) or passing the name of a file and opening it inside the function (line 21). To pass the name of the file, we wrote a separate function (**readfile**) that opens the file before using it (lines 29–35). The file **sample.txt** that was used to demonstrate this example is shown in Fig 13.19.

13.12 Uses for References

This section shows examples in which references can make Perl programming simpler. For example, many modules use hash or array references for passing option lists or preference lists into a function. An example of this is from the **CGI.pm** module, which uses references cleverly to provide a syntax for indicating HTML tag attributes (such as alignment in an HTML paragraph). Figure 13.20 demonstrates this concept.

In this example we use the **CGI::Pretty** module. This module is almost identical to the regular **CGI.pm** module except that the HTML, which it outputs (shown in the output window), is indented to make it easier to read. Most of the **CGI::Pretty** module's functions have similar actions. If a tag generating function (like **p()** in this example to create the **<p>** tag) is passed nonreferences (line 11), it joins the arguments, separating them with a space, and outputs them between the beginning and end tags (see the first **<p>** and **</p>** tags in the sample output). If the first argument is a hash reference (line 12), **CGI::Pretty** takes the key/value pairs and creates a tag with the key/value pairs as attributes of the HTML tag. For example, the call to **p** on line 12 created the **<p align="right">** tag. When passed an array reference, the function creates separate tag pairs for each element in the array. The array on line 14 generated three separate **<P>** tags. Lines 13 and 14 show how you can use the hash references with the array references to create tags, which have attributes that are repeated for each element in the array. Note that the output shown for this program is the HTML sent to a browser when this CGI program is invoked.

```perl
1   #!/usr/bin/perl
2   # Fig. 13.20: fig13_20.pl
3   # Demonstrates the reference syntax
4
5   use warnings;
6   use strict;
7   use CGI::Pretty qw( :standard );
8
9   print( header(),
10          start_html( 'Demo' ),
11          p( 'Some', 'random', 'text' ),
12          p( { -align => 'right' }, 'right', 'aligned text' ),
13          p( { -align => 'center' },
14              [ 'on', 'separate', 'lines' ] ),
15          end_html() );
```

```
<!DOCTYPE HTML PUBLIC "-//IETF//DTD HTML//EN">
<HTML><HEAD><TITLE>Demo</TITLE>
</HEAD><BODY>
<P>
        Some random text
</P>
<P ALIGN="right">
        right aligned text
</P>
<P ALIGN="center">
        on
</P>
<P ALIGN="center">
        separate
</P>
<P ALIGN="center">
        lines
</P>
</BODY></HTML>
```

Fig. 13.20 Using references with **CGI.pm**.

Figure 13.21 shows more HTML tag examples in which hash references and array references are used.

Line 12 uses a hash reference to assign attributes to an image tag (**<img>**). Lines 15 and 16 use an array reference to cause individual **li** tags to be created for a list of elements. Lines 19–29 create a table using a combination of hash and array references. The hash reference on line 19 sets the **border** attribute of the table to 2. The **Tr** tag on line 21 sets the **align** attribute to **CENTER** and distributes this attribute across the four rows created on lines 22–27 using an anonymous array. The **td** tag is distributed across a list in this way as well (lines 23–26).

```perl
1   #!/usr/bin/perl
2   # Fig. 13.21: fig13_21.pl
3   # Use of references in CGI.pm
4
5   use strict;
6   use warnings;
7   use CGI::Pretty qw( :standard :html3 );
8
9   my @words = qw( and a few );
10  print header(),
11      start_html( 'Hash and array references with CGI.pm' ),
12      img( { -src => '/images/image.gif', -alt => 'Image' } ),
13      h1( "Here's a list!!!!" ),
14      ol(
15         li( [ 'a', 'bunch', 'of', 'elements'.
16               ul( li( \@words ) ), 'more' ] )
17         ),
18      h2( "Now were going to have a table." ),
19      table( { border => 2 },
20         caption( strong( "Hi, I'm a table" ) ),
21         Tr( { -align => 'CENTER' },
22            [
23               th( [ '', 'Col1', 'Col2', 'Col3' ] ),
24               th( 'Row1' ).td( [ 'val1', 'val2', 'val3' ] ),
25               th( 'Row2' ).td( [ 'val4', 'val5', 'val6' ] ),
26               th( 'Row3' ).td( [ 'val7', 'val8', 'val9' ] )
27            ]
28         )
29      ),
30      start_form( -action => '/cgi-bin/ch13/fig13_21.pl' ),
31         hidden( -name  => 'name',
32                 -value => [ 'val1', 'val2', 'val3' ] ),
33         popup_menu( -name    => 'menu',
34                     -value   => [ 'c1', 'c2', 'c3', 'c4' ],
35                     -default => 'c2' ),
36         radio_group( -name    => 'choices',
37                      -value   => [ 'c1', 'c2', 'c3', 'c4' ],
38                      -default => 'c2' ),
39      end_form(),
40      end_html();
```

Fig. 13.21 Other **CGI.pm** tags that use hash and array references (part 1 of 2).

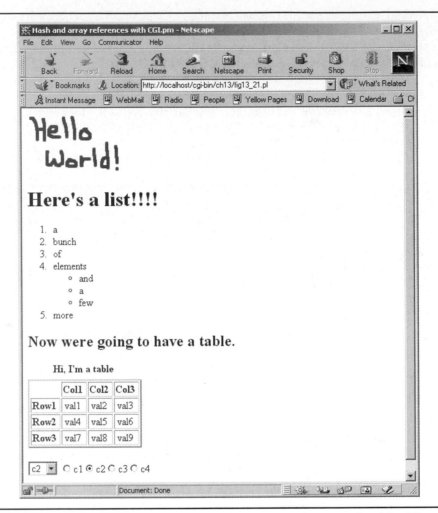

Fig. 13.21 Other **CGI.pm** tags that use hash and array references (part 2 of 2).

Lines 30–38 show how to create an HTML form. Function **start_form** (line 30) starts the form. Function **hidden** (line 31) uses an anonymous array to create three separate hidden tags with those values. Function **popup_menu** (line 33) creates a popup menu with a list of elements specified in an anonymous array. Function **radio_group** (line 36) operates in the same manner as **popup_menu**. Function **end_form** (line 39) ends the form and function **end_html** ends the HTML document.

13.13 Internet and World Wide Web Resources

www.perl.com/CPAN-local/doc/manual/html/pod/perldsc.html
This is the Perl Data Structures cookbook. It contains information on data structures in Perl as well as references.

perl.plover.com/FAQs/references.html
This site provides a brief tutorial on references.

SUMMARY

- Normal scalars directly contain values. Scalars can also hold a value that tells them where to find another value. This type of a scalar is called a reference. References indirectly point to values.
- Pointing to a value using a reference is called indirection.
- There are two types of references—hard references and symbolic references.
- The value to which a hard references refers is known as the referent.
- Symbolic references hold just the name of the variable to which they refer. Symbolic references are sometimes known as soft references.
- Hard references to variables are created by placing the unary backslash operator, \, in front of the name of the variable whose contents should be the referent.
- To obtain the value the reference points to, we must dereference the reference. To dereference a reference, just use it like you would a normal variable name. So to dereference a reference to a scalar, precede the variable with **$** to the front as if the reference were the name of a scalar variable. Another way to dereference a scalar is to use a **$** with curly braces around the variable.
- References can refer to any kind of data structure.
- There are two different ways to dereference array references. The first is to use the square brackets (**[]**) operator like a normal array. To access the third element in the array referred to by **$ref-erence**, we would say **$$reference[2]**. The second involves using the arrow operator (**->**) as in the expression **$reference->[2]**.
- To access the entire array, use **@** before the reference name as in **@$reference**.
- The methods for accessing array elements through a reference can be used with hashes, with curly braces rather than square brackets and with a **%** type identifier when referring to the entire hash.
- If a block of code returns a reference, it can be dereferenced directly.
- To create a reference to a function, use the unary backslash operator with the function type identifier (**&**).
- References to other references are called nested references.
- Data structures that are not associated directly with any variable names are known as anonymous structures.
- The anonymous array composer can be used to create anonymous arrays. To use the anonymous array composer, enclose a list of items in square brackets (**[]**) instead of parentheses. The value returned is a reference to an anonymous array.
- The anonymous hash composer can be used to create anonymous hashes. To use the anonymous hash composer enclose a list of key/value pairs in curly braces (**{}**).
- Applying the backslash character to a list creates a reference to each element in the list.
- The automatic creation of variables that do not exist previously is known as autovivification.
- Adding elements to anonymous arrays or hashes through a reference is like adding elements to any other array or hash—simply assign to previously undefined elements and they are created.
- Declaring an anonymous function is similar to declaring a regular function, except that the function name is omitted. This anonymous function can be assigned to a reference for later use.
- Using references and anonymous structures allows us to interpolate the return value of a function into a double quoted string. Normally a function called in a double-quoted string is not interpolated. However, by creating a reference to the return of the function and dereferencing it, the return value will be interpolated, returning the results of the function call.
- Anonymous functions come into existence at runtime and maintain the lexical context of the lexical scope in which they are created. Lexical variables are said to have deep binding. The functions

that use such lexical variables are known as closures. An example of where this can be useful is when a function is run that returns an anonymous function reference, this function reference will contain the state information pertaining to the point in the program at which it was created.

- References can be used to pass anything to a function. If a reference to a data structure is passed, that data structure will not be flattened into the function's **@_** argument array.

- Sometimes we might want to perform a different action depending on what kind of a reference is passed to a function. We can use function **ref** to determine the type to which a reference points. Function **ref** is passed a reference and returns a string describing the type of reference. For example an array reference will return the string **ARRAY**. For a function, **ref** returns **CODE**. For a typeglob, **ref** returns **GLOB**.

- Arrays and hashes are just collections of scalars, so any scalar can be a reference to any other type of variable. This allows us to create complex data structures from the basic Perl data types.

- An example of these more complicated data structures is an array of arrays. This data structure consists of an array whose elements are references to other arrays. To access an element of this array we need two subscripts, one for the first array and one for the second array. This type of data structure is known as a two-dimensional (or double-subscripted) array.

- Using arrow notation, a two-dimensional array element is accessed as **$array[$i]->[$j]** where **$i** is the index of the first array and **$j** is the index of the second array. You can leave out the arrow, which is implied by this context. Therefore, we could also say **$array[$i][$j]** to access the same element.

- Anonymous array composers make the declaration of a multidimensional array straightforward.

- The technique used to create a multidimensional array can be used to create any other type of nested data structure. You can make arrays of hashes, hashes of arrays, hashes of hashes or mix them in any way you please. You can also nest them as deeply as you like. For example, a three-dimensional array would just be an array of arrays of arrays.

- A hash of arrays allows you to associate multiple values with a single key.

- Perl's garbage collector frees unused memory. The garbage collector frees any memory it is absolutely sure will not be used again in the script. The garbage collector works through a mechanism called reference counting. Each block of memory has an internal reference count, which indicates how many references contain that address (i.e., how many references are referring to that block of memory). When this count becomes zero, the memory can be collected.

- If you have circular references, where one reference points to something that eventually points back to the original reference, that memory will never be freed. This is known as a memory leak.

- Symbolic references are scalars that refer to another variable by holding the variable's name.

- To declare a symbolic reference, assign the name of a variable (without the special character) to another variable. Now the second variable can be dereferenced just like a normal reference.

- When the use strict pragma is enabled, Perl gives a fatal error when symbolic references are used. To prevent such errors, specify **no strict 'refs'** tag.

- References are a recent addition to Perl. Before references, typeglobs were used to get the same sort of functionality as references.

- All package global variables are stored in a symbol table. Perl uses the symbol table to keep track of where each variable is located in memory. When a variable is used, Perl looks up the name of the variable in the symbol table to determine where the variable is located. Each variable name has an entry in this symbol table, and this entry contains all the different variable types for that particular name. The entries in the symbol table are called typeglobs.

- Each typeglob consists of all the different types to which the name of the typeglob could refer. The prefix for a typeglob is *****, because it represents all types.

- Typeglobs can be assigned, as in ***newname = *name**. This makes everything named **newname** a synonym for the corresponding type named **name**. Accessing the variable through **newname** is actually faster than if we were dereferencing a reference to **$name** held in **$newname**. This is because **$newname** now is the same as **$name**, so dereferencing is not required.

- Lexically scoped **my** variables do not work with typeglobs. Typeglobs belong to the symbol table, while **my** variables are not part of the symbol table.

- Typeglobs also give you another way to produce references. Treating a typeglob as a hash with the name of the type of variable you want a reference to will give you a reference to that variable. For example, ***name{ SCALAR }** gives a reference to **$name**. Dereferencing a typeglob with the symbol name of the type you want will give you the value of the type.

- In general, use typeglobs only when necessary.

- One good use for typeglobs is to create constant scalars. By assigning a reference to something that is not an lvalue to a typeglob, we can make a constant variable.

- Another use for typeglobs is for referencing filehandles. Because filehandles do not have a special character to identify them as filehandles, you cannot create a reference to a filehandle. However, a typeglob includes the filehandle with the same name as the typeglob. Thus a typeglob can act like a reference to a filehandle. We can assign this typeglob to a scalar and then use that scalar anywhere we would normally use the filehandle.

- Typeglob references can go anywhere a normal reference can. We can pass filehandles into functions in this way.

TERMINOLOGY

& function symbol
* typeglob symbol
[] anonymous array composer
**** unary backslash operator
{} anonymous array composer
-> arrow operator
a tag in **CGI.pm**
anonymous array
anonymous array composer
anonymous function
anonymous hash
anonymous hash composer
anonymous structure
array of arrays
array of hashes
arrow notation
arrow operator
autovivification
CGI.pm
CGI::Pretty
circular references
closure
constant scalar
creating and dereferencing references
deep binding
dereference

dereferencing a function
dereferencing a reference
dereferencing a scalar
dereferencing an array reference
dereferencing nonscalar references
filehandle
garbage collector
hard reference
hash of arrays
hash of hashes
hidden function in **CGI.pm**
href tag in **CGI.pm**
indirection
interpolation
list of references
memory leak
multidimentional array
nested data structure
nested references
no strict 'refs' pragma
no strict 'vars' pragma
passing filehandles to functions
passing nonscalars to functions
pointing to a value
popup_menu function in **CGI.pm**
radio_group function in **CGI.pm**

SELF-REVIEW EXERCISES

13.1 Fill in the blanks in each of the following questions.
  a) Hard references to variables are created by putting the _____ before the name of the variable you would like to reference.
  b) References to other references are called _____.
  c) _____ are structures not associated directly with a variable name.
  d) The automatic creation of variables that did not previously exist is known as _____.
  e) The _____ function receives a reference and returns a string describing the type of reference.
  f) The part of Perl that frees memory is known as the _____.
  g) Each block of memory has _____, which indicates how many references contain that address.
  h) If you have one reference pointing to something that eventually points back to the original reference your program contains a _____, which may cause a _____.
  i) All package global varibles are stored in a _____.
  j) Each variable name has an entry in this symbol table and this entry contains all the different variable types for that particular name. These entries are called _____.

13.2 State whether each of the following is *true* or *false*. If *false*, explain why.
  a) Hard references are more efficient than symbolic references and are almost always used in favor of symbolic references.
  b) References can be converted to strings and back to references again.
  c) References can refer to any type of data structure.
  d) The anonymous array composer can be used to create anonymous arrays. To use the anonymous array composer, take a list that you want turned into an array and enclose it inside curly braces (**{}**) instead of parentheses.
  e) Taking a reference to a list creates a reference to the entire list.
  f) Using symbolic references when the **strict 'refs'** tag is enabled causes fatal errors.
  g) Each typeglob consists of all the different nonscalar types to which the name of the typeglob could refer.

13.3 Write Perl statements to accomplish each of the following:
  a) Prompt the user to enter a variable name without the **$**, and create a soft reference to this variable.
  b) Create a hard reference from one variable to another.
  c) Create a reference to an array that contains two values, **"true"** and **"false"**. Do this in two different ways.

d) Create a reference to a two-dimensional array of strings with four columns and four rows. Have each entry contain a string with the number of the row, an underscore (_) and then the number of the column. For example, the second element of the first row would contain the string **"1_2"**.

e) Create a typeglob called ***new**. Alias its scalar and hash values to those of ***old**. Do not modify any of ***new**'s other values.

13.4   Determine the four errors in the following program. Note that the error may not stop the program from executing or produce any error messages.

```perl
1   #!/usr/bin/perl
2   # Exercise 13.4
3
4   use warnings;
5   use strict 'refs';
6
7   $variable = 5;
8   @variable = ( "true", "false" );
9   $reference1 = /$variable;
10  print( "Enter a variable name: " );
11  chomp( my $name = <STDIN> );
12  print( "$$name\n" );
13  $variable = \$reference1;
14  @reference2 = \@variable;
15  $reference1 = \$variable;
```

ANSWERS TO SELF-REVIEW EXERCISES

13.1   a) unary backslash operator (\). b) nested references. c) anonymous structures. d) autovivication. e) **ref**. f) garbage collector. g) reference count. h) circular reference, memory leak. i) symbol table. j) typeglobs.

13.2   a) True.

b) False. Although references can be converted to strings, these strings cannot be converted back to references.

c) True.

d) False. To use the anonymous array composer, take a list you want turned into an array and enclose it inside square brackets (**[]**) instead of parentheses.

e) False. Taking a reference to a list creates a reference to each element of the list.

f) True.

g) False. Each typeglob consists of all the different types to which the name of the typeglob could refer.

13.3   a) `print( "Enter variable name: " );`
       `chomp( my $name = <STDIN> );`

b) `$variable1 = \$variable2;`

c) `my @array = ( "true", "false" );`
   `$array = \@array;`
   or
   `my $array = [ "true", "false" ];`

d) `my $array = [`
   `    [ "1_1", "1_2", "1_3", "1_4" ],`
   `    [ "2_1", "2_2", "2_3", "2_4" ],`

```
          [ "3_1", "3_2", "3_3", "3_4" ],
          [ "4_1", "4_2", "4_3", "4_4" ],
      ];
  e) *new = \$old;
     *new = \%old;
```

13.4 a) Using symbolic references and including the **use strict 'refs'** pragma will cause a fatal error.

b) A front slash is used instead of a backslash on line 9.

c) References are scalars. Line 14 creates an array as a reference. All this will do is make the first element of the array the reference, while the following elements will be unde-fined. Other methods must be used if we want to create an array of references where each element is a reference to an element in an array.

d) Lines 13 and 15 will create a circular reference, which causes memory leaks.

EXERCISES

13.5   Write a function, **hashsum**, which takes a hash reference as its first argument and an array reference as its second. The function should take the elements of the array and use them as keys in the hash. The values in the hash corresponding to the keys in the array should be totalled, and the sum should be returned to the user. If a key passed in the array does not exist in the hash, ignore it.

13.6   Write the equivalent of the **map** function. Your function should take a function reference fol-lowed by a list. It should apply the function to each element in the list and return a list of all the return values. If the first argument to your function is not a code reference, your program should call func-tion **die** with an error message stating the correct usage of your function.

13.7   Use closures to make a function-generating function. Create a function that when passed a number will return a reference to a function that will add that number to whatever is passed to it.

13.8   Other languages have a control structure called a switch statement. The switch statement is used as follows:

```
switch( val ) {
    case a:
    case b:
    case c:
}
```

where different code is run depending on the case that **val** matches. Perl has no switch statement, but the functionality can be emulated in a number of different ways. One of them is with a hash of code references. Make a program that has a prompt for the user. The program should print a number, which starts at zero, to the screen after each user input. If the user enters **a**, add one to the number. If the user enters **s**, subtract one from the number. If the user enters **m**, multiply the number by two. And if the user enters **d**, divide the number by two. The program should keep asking for input until the user enters **q**. If the user does not enter one of those choices, print a statement saying what the choices are. Use a hash of code references to perform the different functions on the number.

13.9   Write a game of three-dimensional tic-tac-toe. The board should be kept track of in a three-dimensional array. You need only check for horizontal and vertical wins, not diagonals.

14

Objects and Modules

Objectives

- To be able to create, use and destroy class objects.
- To be able to control access to object data members and member functions.
- To begin to appreciate the value of object orientation.
- To learn about inheritance, composition, using and other relationships among objects.
- To understand data encapsulation.
- To learn about implicit functions, especially **AUTOLOAD** and the group of tie functions.

Is it a world to hide virtues in?
William Shakespeare, *Twelfth Night*

Your public servants serve you right.
Adlai Stevenson

Instead of this absurd division into sexes they ought to class people as static and dynamic.
Evelyn Waugh

This above all: to thine own self be true.
William Shakespeare, Hamlet

Outline

14.1 Introduction

What is *object-oriented programming (OOP)*? OOP is a method of programming that thinks of everything as objects. It stems from the theory that everything in life is an object and can be described in objects terminology.

Let us introduce some key concepts and terminology of object orientation. Object-oriented programming (OOP) *encapsulates* data (attributes) and functions (behavior) into packages called *classes;* the data and functions of a class are intimately tied together. A class is like a blueprint. Out of a blueprint, a builder can build a house; out of a class, a programmer can create an object. One blueprint can be reused many times to make many houses; one class can be reused many times to make many objects of the same class. Classes have the property of *information hiding.* This means that although class objects may "know" how to communicate with one another across well-defined *interfaces,* classes normally are not allowed to "know" how other classes are implemented—implementation details are hidden within the classes themselves. Surely it is possible to drive a car effectively without knowing the details of how engines, transmissions and exhaust systems work internally. We will see why information hiding is so crucial to good software engineering.

This book is an object. It is an object of type book. The type of an object is its *class.* The fact that an object is a book means that it has some inherent properties. It has pages with information on them. It has an author (perhaps more than one). It has a publisher. It has a copyright. It has a subject. In OOP terminology, these are called the object's data or *attributes.* You can also perform specific actions on this book. It can be opened. It can be read. You can turn the pages or go to a specific page. It can also be closed. In OOP terminology these actions are called *methods.* Every object has certain attributes and methods associated with it. By saying that a certain object is of type book, we already know certain things about that object.

The same holds true in object-oriented programming. As an example, we will think of how we might emulate a book in a program. We could use a scalar to hold the title, a list to hold the authors and another scalar to hold the copyright information. We could use an array to hold all the pages in the book, where the page number could be used to access the page in the array. Now we can write methods for using this book class. For example, to read a page, we could use a function that takes the page number as an argument and prints the contents of the array element corresponding to that page number.

Object-oriented programming allows for the creation of interfaces to data that are independent of the implementation of the data. If we have many programs using an object through its methods, we can completely change the way the data is implemented without having to change the programs using the data. For example, if we found a more efficient way to implement our book class, implementing it where the pages are held in a hash instead of an array somehow, as long as we did not change the calls and return values of the methods, someone using our book class would not have to change anything to use this new implementation. In this chapter, we begin our introduction to object orientation in Perl.

Software Engineering Observation 14.1

It is important to write programs that are understandable and easy to maintain. Change is the rule rather than the exception. Programmers should anticipate that their code will be modified. As we will see, classes can facilitate program modifiability.

Software Engineering Observation 14.2

Perl encourages programs to be implementation independent. When the implementation of a class used by implementation-independent code changes, that code need not be modified.

Software Engineering Observation 14.3

A central theme of object-oriented programming is "reuse, reuse, reuse." We will carefully discuss a number of techniques for "polishing" classes to encourage reuse.

14.2 Using a Class

The **FileHandle** module defines a class that provides an object-oriented interface to a filehandle. It offers several advantages over normal filehandles, such as being able to reference them without using typeglobs and being able to alternate between multiple filehandles without using function **select**.

To use this or any other class, we first must make an *instance of the class* (also known as an *object of the class*). This is done using the class' *constructor*. Traditionally, the constructor is called **new**, although Perl allows the constructor name to be different, depending on the class. The constructor returns an instance (object) of the class.

After constructing an object of a class, a program can call the object's methods by using the arrow operator as follows:

   objectName->*method*(*arguments*)

FileHandle objects provide some extra magic, which allow them to be used where any filehandle can be used. For demonstration purposes, the following example Figs. 14.1, 14.2 and 14.3) uses **FileHandle** objects entirely through their object-oriented methods.

```perl
1   #!/usr/bin/perl
2   # Fig. 14.1: fig14_01.pl
3   # Using the FileHandle module
4
5   use warnings;
6   use strict;
7   use FileHandle;
8
9   my $write = new FileHandle;
10  my $read  = new FileHandle;
11
12  $write->open( ">filehandle.txt" ) or
13      die( "Could not open write" );
14  $read->open( "input.txt" ) or
15      die( "Could not open read" );
16
17  $write->autoflush( 1 );
18
19  my $i = 1;
20
21  while ( my $line = $read->getline() ) {
22      $write->print( $i++, " $line" );
23  }
```

Fig. 14.1   Using the **FileHandle** module.

```
This is a sample file.
With some lines for
demonstration purposes.
```

Fig. 14.2   Contents of **input.txt**.

```
1 This is a sample file.
2 With some lines for
3 demonstration purposes.
```

Fig. 14.3   Contents of **filehandle.txt** (after the program has executed).

Lines 9 and 10 in Fig. 14.1 create **FileHandle** objects using the constructor **new**, which returns an object that we assign to a scalar. The files are opened using the **File-Handle**'s **open** method on lines 12 and 14. To demonstrate one of the advantages of the using filehandles in an object-oriented manner, line 17 accesses one of the special variables of the **$write** filehandle without first using function **select** to specify the current file-handle. The loop in lines 21–23 uses the **getline** method to read a line from the **$read** filehandle and the **print** method to output the line using the **$write** filehandle. Notice the use of the arrow notation for each of these method calls. After running this program, view the contents of the file **filehandle.txt** (Fig. 14.3) on your system to see that the program correctly copied the text of the file **input.txt** (Fig. 14.2).

14.3 Creating a Simple Class

The last example demonstrated some *interface methods* of class **FileHandle**. The *interface* of a class consists of the class' methods and the syntax for calling them. The interface defines the user's (or *client's*) view of the class. Now that we have seen the *interface* of a class, let us consider the *implementation* of a class. The *implementation* is the underlying details—how the class is organized as well as what data types and algorithms it uses. One of the principles of good software engineering is to separate interface from implementation, making it easier to modify programs. Changes to the implementation of a class do not affect the client code as long as the interface of the class originally provided to the client remains unchanged. If this is the case, the client code should still be able to call all the interface methods in the same manner and may be provided with new methods as well.

Software Engineering Observation 14.4

Clients of a class use the class without knowing the internal details of how the class is implemented. If the class implementation changes, the class' client code need not change unless the interface of the class changes.

Software Engineering Observation 14.5

Clients can have access to the interface of a class, but should not have access to the implementation of a class.

Figure 14.4 shows a class for manipulating a date. We then use that class in the program of Fig. 14.5.

```
1   #!/usr/bin/perl
2   # Fig. 14.4: Date.pm
3   # A simple Date class
4
5   package Date;
6
7   use strict;
8   use warnings;
9
10  sub new
11  {
12     my $date =    { the_year => 1000,
13                     the_month => 1,
14                     the_day => 1, };
15
16     bless( $date );
17     return $date;
18  }
19
20  sub year
21  {
22     my $self = shift();
23
24     $self->{ the_year } = shift() if ( @_ );
25
```

Fig. 14.4   Implementation of class **Date** (part 1 of 2).

```perl
26      return $self->{ the_year };
27   }
28
29   sub month
30   {
31      my $self = shift();
32
33      $self->{ the_month } = shift() if ( @_ );
34
35      return $self->{ the_month };
36   }
37
38   sub day
39   {
40      my $self = shift();
41
42      $self->{ the_day } = shift() if ( @_ );
43
44      return $self->{ the_day };
45   }
46
47   sub setDate
48   {
49      if ( @_ == 4 ) {
50         my $self = shift();
51         $self->month( $_[ 0 ] );
52         $self->day( $_[ 1 ] );
53         $self->year( $_[ 2 ] );
54      }
55      else {
56         print( "Method setDate requires three arguments.\n" );
57      }
58   }
59
60   sub print
61   {
62      my $self = shift();
63      print( $self->month );
64      print( "/" );
65      print( $self->day );
66      print( "/" );
67      print( $self->year );
68   }
69
70   return 1;
```

Fig. 14.4   Implementation of class **Date** (part 2 of 2).

```perl
1   #!/usr/bin/perl
2   # Fig. 14.5: fig14_05.pl
3   # Using class Date.
4
```

Fig. 14.5   Using class **Date** (part 1 of 2).

```
 5   use Date;
 6   use strict;
 7   use warnings;
 8
 9   my $today = new Date;
10
11   $today->setDate( 7, 14, 2000 );
12   print( $today->month() );
13   print( "\n" );
14   $today->print();
15   print( "\n" );
```

```
7
7/14/2000
```

Fig. 14.5   Using class **Date** (part 2 of 2).

Our implementation of the **Date** class uses a hash to store variables **the_year**, **the_month** and **the_day** for each date. Lines 10–18 define the constructor for this class. In the constructor, we create the hash reference that holds the data for the object, setting the fields to default starting values (lines 12–14). To turn this hash reference into a **Date** object, we use built-in function *bless*, which receives a reference and turns it into an object. [*Note:* In Perl, all objects are references.] The object type defaults to the current package name. However, providing a second argument to **bless** changes the object type to the type specified by the second argument. In this example, **bless** uses the default type **Date**. To use two arguments we could have also blessed the reference with

```
    bless( $date, Date );
```

To demonstrate function **bless**, if we print out the value of **$date** before calling **bless** on it, the output would be something like **HASH(0x8bbf0b0)**, which is the typical string printed for a hash reference. If we print the value of **$date** after the **bless** function is called, we would see **date=HASH(0x8bbf0b0)**, because **$date** has been converted into a **Date** object. After creating the object, **new** returns it on line 17.

We provide the **year**, **month** and **day** methods to allow access to the data associated with each **Date** object. Each method can be used to change the value of **the_year**, **the_month** or **the_day** if an argument is passed to the method. Otherwise, each method can be used to retrieve the value of one of the attributes. In OOP terminology, these are called *get/set methods* or *accessor methods*. We will look at the implementation of the **year** method in detail to illustrate how these methods work.

When a method is called, it works like any other function, except the first element in **@_** is the object for which the method was called. Thus, calling the **year** method on a **date** object called **$birthDate**—as in **$birthDate->year()**—is the same as calling the function using its full package specification and passing **$date** as the first argument—as in **date::year($birthDate)**. The first line of the **year** method's body (line 22) uses **shift** to obtain the first method argument—the object on which the method was called—and assigns it to **$self**. Line 24 checks to see whether there was an argument passed and, if so, assigns the value to **the_year** in the hash. Line 26 returns the value of **the_year**.

The simple *get/set* methods used here were for demonstration purposes. When you are writing your own methods, it is important to validate your data to confirm that the data received by the method is consistent with the use of the object. For example, for attribute **the_month**, method **month** should ensure that the value being set is in the range 1–12.

Software Engineering Observation 14.6

The class designer need not provide set *or* get *functions for each data item; these capabilities should be provided only when appropriate. If the service is useful to the client code, that service should be provided in the interface of the class.*

Testing and Debugging Tip 14.1

Every method (such as a set*) that modifies the data members of an object should ensure that the data remain in a consistent state.*

Method **setDate** allows the user to set all the attributes at once. Line 49 checks that there were enough arguments passed to the method. If so, the **month**, **year** and **day** methods are called to set the individual attributes (lines 51–53). Otherwise, if an incorrect number of arguments is passed, **setDate** prints an error message (line 56).

The **print** method outputs the date in the month/day/year format. The object on which we call **print** is assigned to **$self** on line 62, and the **month**, **day** and **year** methods fetch the attribute values to be output.

After creating the **Date** module, we can use it like any other module, as shown in Fig. 14.5. We include the new **Date.pm** module on line 5. Line 9 uses the constructor to create a new **Date** object and assigns it to the variable **$today**. We set the date on line 11 with the **setDate** method. Line 12 uses the **month** method to access only the **month** attribute, and line 14 uses the **print** method to print the whole date.

Software Engineering Observation 14.7

Object methods are usually shorter than functions in non-object-oriented programs, because the data stored in data members have ideally been validated by object methods that store new data. Because the data are already in the object, the object method calls often have no arguments or at least have fewer arguments than typical function calls in non-object-oriented languages. Thus, the calls and the function definitions are shorter.

Software Engineering Observation 14.8

A phenomenon of object-oriented programming is that once a class is defined, creating and manipulating objects of that class usually involve issuing only a simple sequence of method calls—few control structures are needed. By contrast, it is common to have control structures in the implementation of a class' methods.

14.4 Inheritance

Often, classes will be *derived* from other classes that provide attributes and behaviors the new classes can use. Similarly, classes can include objects of other classes as members. Such *software reuse* can greatly enhance programmer productivity. Deriving new classes from existing classes is called *inheritance*. Including class objects as members of other classes is called *composition* (or *aggregation*).

Returning to the book class we discussed in the first section, classifying something as a book is a rather general class. We might want to implement more specific book types that would have specific attributes or methods for each type. For example, we might want a textbook class that would have an added time-of-the-day attribute or a coloring book class that would provide a draw method. These two classes would still need all the functionality of the book class, so rather than redoing the work we did in making the book class, we can inherit from the book class. The two *subclasses* of the book class would have all the functionality of the book class, plus whatever else we implement. Inheritance allows us more flexibility in reusing code because we can now expand on preexisting classes and objects, taking all of the functionality from them and adding even more.

Figures 14.6 through 14.8 demonstrate inheritance. We will first create *base class* **Employee** (Fig. 14.6), which has attributes and methods common to any type of **Employee**. We will then create and implement a subclass (derived class) of **Employee** called **Hourly** (Fig. 14.7), which has specific attributes and methods applying to workers who are paid hourly. Finally, we use each of these classes in a program (Fig. 14.8).

```perl
1   #!/usr/bin/perl
2   # Fig. 14.6: Employee.pm
3   # Implementation of class Employee.
4   \
5   package Employee;
6
7   use strict;
8   use warnings;
9   use Date;
10
11  sub new
12  {
13     my $type = shift();
14     my $class = ref( $type ) || $type;
15
16     my $hireDay = new Date;
17     my $self = {  firstName => undef,
18                   lastName => undef,
19                   hireDay => $hireDay  };
20
21     bless( $self, $class );
22     return $self;
23  }
24
25  sub firstName
26  {
27     my $self = shift();
28
29     $self->{ firstName } = shift() if ( @_ );
30
31     return $self->{ firstName };
32  }
33
34  sub lastName
35  {
36     my $self = shift();
37
```

Fig. 14.6   Implementation of class **Employee** (part 1 of 2).

```
38        $self->{ lastName } = shift() if ( @_ );
39
40        return $self->{ lastName };
41    }
42
43    sub hireDay
44    {
45        my $self = shift();
46
47        if ( @_ ) {
48            $self->{ hireDay }->setDate( @_ );
49        }
50        else {
51            $self->{ hireDay }->print();
52        }
53    }
54
55    return 1;
```

Fig. 14.6   Implementation of class **Employee** (part 2 of 2).

```
1    #!/usr/bin/perl
2    # Fig. 14.7: Hourly.pm
3    # Implementation of class Hourly.
4
5    package Hourly;
6
7    use strict;
8    use warnings;
9    use Employee;
10   our @ISA = ( "Employee" );
11
12   sub new
13   {
14       my $object = shift();
15       my $class = ref( $object ) || $object;
16
17       my $self = $class->SUPER::new();
18       $self->{ rate } = undef;
19
20       bless( $self, $class );
21       return $self;
22   }
23
24   sub rate
25   {
26       my $self = shift();
27
28       $self->{ rate } = shift() if ( @_ );
29
30       return $self->{ rate };
31   }
```

Fig. 14.7   Implementation of class **Hourly** (part 1 of 2).

```
32
33    return 1;
```

Fig. 14.7   Implementation of class **Hourly** (part 2 of 2).

```perl
1    #!/usr/bin/perl
2    # Fig. 14.8: fig14_08.pl
3    # Using classes Hourly and Employee
4
5    use strict;
6    use warnings;
7    use Employee;
8    use Hourly;
9
10   my $worker = new Hmployee;
11
12   $worker->firstName( "Jason" );
13   $worker->lastName( "Black" );
14   $worker->hireDay( 8, 5, 1995 );
15   print( $worker->firstName(), " ",
16          $worker->lastName(), " was hired on " );
17   $worker->hireDay();
18   print( ".\n\n" );
19
20   my $hour = new Hourly;
21
22   $hour->firstName( "John" );
23   $hour->lastName( "White" );
24   $hour->hireDay( 11, 30, 1999 );
25   $hour->rate( 9.50 );
26   print( $hour->firstName(), " ", $hour->lastName(),
27          " was hired on " );
28   $hour->hireDay();
29   print( ".\n" );
30   printf( "He makes \$%.2f per hour.\n", $hour->rate() );
```

```
Jason Black was hired on 8/5/1995.

John White was hired on 11/30/1999.
He makes $9.50 per hour.
```

Fig. 14.8   Demonstrating inheritance with classes **Employee** and **Hourly**.

Class **Employee** is similar in many ways to our **Date** class in Fig. 14.4. Class **Employee** has attributes and *get/set* methods for those attributes. The only thing we have to do differently when implementing a base class from which we can later inherit is in the constructor **new**. The reason this has to be implemented differently is that **new** may be inherited by other classes that will use it to create objects of their type, not the base-class type. Thus, the first thing we do in the constructor is to determine the type of the object being created. This type is passed to **new** as the first argument, so we use function **shift** to obtain that type on line 13. There are two ways this constructor might have been called: It can be called with the name of the type (*Type*->**new()** or **new** *Type*) or as method of an object that has the same type as the object we would like to create (**$object->new()**). Line 14 sets **$class** to **ref($type) || $type**—either the type of the reference or the type name passed. Now that we know what class we are using to create an object, we create the attributes (data members) of the class and place them in a hash. Class **Employee** contains **firstName**, **lastName** and **hireDay** attributes. The **hireDay** attribute is an object of type **Date** (from Fig. 14.4) and a hash to hold the data. Next, we use the two-argument form of **bless** (line 21) to convert the hash reference into an object of type **$class** (**Employee**). The remainder of the class defines the accessor methods for manipulating the attributes of this class.

Software Engineering Observation 14.9

Always implement a class as if it will be inherited by another class. This enables other programmers to extend any class you create.

Software Engineering Observation 14.10

*Using the two-argument form of **bless** is recommended if the class may be extended in the future with inheritance.*

Common Programming Error 14.1

*When using **bless**, specifying a second argument that evaluates to false is an error.*

Class **Hourly** (Fig. 14.7) inherits from class **Employee**. To specify the base classes (or superclasses) from which class **Hourly** inherits, we use the special **@ISA** array on line 10. The **@ISA** array was first mentioned in our discussion of modules in Chapter 6. The **@ISA** array was used to import variables and methods from other packages. In Chapter 6 we set **@ISA** to inherit from **Exporter**. Our module was actually inheriting certain methods (the **import** method) from the **Exporter** module. Including **Employee** in the **@ISA** array specifies that our new class inherits from **Employee**. Perl automatically sets **$class::SUPER** to **Employee** to specify this. When we call a method that is not defined in the current class, Perl will search the classes in the **@ISA** array to locate a class that contains the method. Literally speaking, an object of class **Hourly** is an **Employee** as well. We call this the "is a" (inheritance) relationship.

Our constructor for the **Hourly** class is the **new** method on lines 12–22. As in the constructor for class **Employee**, line 15 determines the class type for the object being created (in case someone decides to inherit from class **Hourly** later). An object of class **Hourly** is also an **Employee** object, so we need to call the **Employee** constructor to initialize the attributes inherited from class **Employee**. Line 17

```
$class->SUPER::new();
```

explicitly invokes the **new** method (the constructor) in superclass **Employee**. Class **Hourly**'s **new** method will send **Employee**'s **new** method type **Hourly** as its argument. Thus, the **Employee** constructor will **bless** its hash reference into an **Hourly** object, not an **Employee** object. The resulting object is returned to **Hourly**'s constructor. Line 18 adds the **rate** attribute to the object's hash. Then we re**bless** our object and return it to the program that originally created the **Hourly** object.

When we define the *get/set* methods of class **Hourly**, we do not have to redefine the *get/set* methods from class **Employee**. Class **Employee** is in class **Hourly**'s **@ISA** array, so Perl will look in the **Employee** class for unknown methods.

Using classes that inherit from other classes is no different than using any other class.In Fig. 14.8, lines 10–18 create an **Employee** object, set its attributes and print them. Lines 20–30 do the same for an **Hourly** employee. Note that we are able to use all the methods of both the **Employee** and **Hourly** classes in lines 20–30.

14.5 Overriding Methods

The most important concepts in OOP are the reuse of code, the separation of implementation and interface and the ability to change and update your code easily. Let us say that you have created a base class and derived classes and used these throughout some programs. What happens if you want to change one of the methods that a derived class inherits? You could change that method in the base class, but that would also change the method in any other class that inherits from the base class. You could create a method with a different name that either accomplished the task on its own or called the old method with some minor changes, but you would have to change the interface, which could be scattered throughout many programs. Perl provides a simple answer to this problem: *method overriding*. Using method overriding, you can write a method that overrides the base class's implementation.

Inherited methods can be overridden in the class that inherits the method. When you call an object's method, Perl first attempts to locate the method in the class to which the object belongs. If the method cannot be found there, Perl attempts to locate the method in the object's base class(es). This means that if you redefine an inherited method in a derived class, Perl calls the derived-class version instead of the inherited base-class version—the derived-class version supersedes (or overrides) the base-class version.

Figures 14.9 through 14.12 define classes **Employee2**, **Hourly2** and **Boss** to demonstrate method overriding. [*Note:* Class **Employee2** contains one attribute that is an instance of class **Date** from Fig. 14.4.]

```perl
1   #!/usr/bin/perl
2   # Fig. 14.9: Employee2.pm
3   # Implementation of class Employee2.
4
5   package Employee2;
6
7   use strict;
8   use warnings;
9   use Date;
10
11  sub new
12  {
13     my $object = shift();
14     my $class = ref( $object ) || $object;
15
16     my $self = { firstName => shift(),
17                  lastName => shift(), };
18
19     my $hireDay = new Date;
20
21     if ( $_[ 0 ] ) {
22        my ( $month, $day, $year ) = split( /\//, $_[ 0 ] );
```

Fig. 14.9   Implementation of class **Employee2** (part 1 of 2).

```
23              $hireDay->day( $day );
24              $hireDay->month( $month );
25              $hireDay->year( $year );
26          }
27
28          $self->{ hireDay } = $hireDay;
29
30          bless( $self, $class );
31          return $self;
32      }
33
34      sub firstName
35      {
36          my $self = shift();
37
38          $self->{ firstName } = shift() if ( @_ );
39
40          return $self->{ firstName };
41      }
42
43      sub lastName
44      {
45          my $self = shift();
46
47          $self->{ lastName } = shift() if ( @_ );
48
49          return $self->{ lastName };
50      }
51
52      sub hireDay
53      {
54          my $self = shift();
55
56          if ( @_ ) {
57              $self->{ hireDay }->setDate( @_ );
58          }
59          else {
60              $self->{ hireDay }->print();
61          }
62      }
63
64      sub write
65      {
66          my $self = shift();
67
68          print( "Hello, my name is ", $self->firstName, ".\n" );
69          print( "I was hired on " );
70          $self->hireDay();
71          print( ".\n" );
72      }
73
74      return 1;
```

Fig. 14.9   Implementation of class **Employee2** (part 2 of 2).

```perl
1   #!/usr/bin/perl
2   # Fig. 14.10: Hourly2.pm
3   # Implementation of class Hourly2.
4
5   package Hourly2;
6
7   use strict;
8   use warnings;
9   use Employee2;
10  our @ISA = ( "Employee2" );
11
12  sub new
13  {
14     my $object = shift();
15     my $class = ref( $object ) || $object;
16
17     my $self = $class->SUPER::new( @_[ 0 .. 2 ]);
18     $self->{ rate } = $_[ 3 ];
19
20     bless( $self, $class );
21     return $self;
22  }
23
24  sub rate
25  {
26     my $self = shift();
27
28     $self->{ rate } = shift() if ( @_ );
29
30     return $self->{ rate };
31  }
32
33  sub write
34  {
35     my $self = shift();
36     $self->SUPER::write();
37     printf( "I make \$%.2f per hour.\n", $self->rate );
38  }
39
40  return 1;
```

Fig. 14.10   Implementation of class **Hourly2**.

```perl
1   #!/usr/bin/perl
2   # Fig. 14.11: Boss.pm
3   # Implementation of class Boss.
4
5   package Boss;
6
7   use strict;
8   use warnings;
9   use Employee2;
```

Fig. 14.11   Implementation of class **Boss** (part 1 of 2).

```
10   our @ISA = ( "Employee2" );
11
12   sub new
13   {
14      my $object = shift();
15      my $class = ref( $object ) || $object;
16
17      my $self  = $class->SUPER::new( @_[ 0 .. 2 ] );
18
19      $self->{ title } = $_[ 3 ];
20
21      bless( $self, $class );
22      return $self;
23   }
24
25   sub title
26   {
27      my $self = shift();
28
29      $self->{ title } = shift() if ( @_ );
30
31      return $self->{ title };
32   }
33
34   sub write
35   {
36      my $self = shift();
37
38      print( "My name is Mr. ", $self->lastName(), ".\n" );
39      print( "I am the boss and I am a ", $self->title(), ".\n" );
40   }
41
42   return 1;
```

Fig. 14.11 Implementation of class **Boss** (part 2 of 2).

```
1    #!/usr/bin/perl
2    # Fig. 14.12: fig14_12.pl
3    # Overriding base class methods.
4
5    use strict;
6    use warnings;
7    use Employee2;
8    use Hourly2;
9    use Boss;
10
11   my $worker = new Employee2( "Jason", "Black", "8/5/1995" );
12
13   print( $worker->firstName(), " ",
14          $worker->lastName(), " was hired on " );
15   $worker->hireDay();
16   print( ".\n" );
```

Fig. 14.12 Overriding base-class methods (part 1 of 2).

```
17    $worker->write();
18    print( "\n" );
19
20    my $hour = new Hourly2;
21
22    $hour->firstName( "John" );
23    $hour->lastName( "White" );
24    $hour->hireDay( 11, 30, 1999 );
25    $hour->rate( 9.50 );
26    print( $hour->firstName(), " ",
27           $hour->lastName(), " was hired on " );
28    $hour->hireDay();
29    print( ".\n" );
30    printf( "This worker makes \$%.2f per hour.\n", $hour->rate() );
31    $hour->write();
32    print( "\n" );
33
34    my $boss = new Boss;
35
36    $boss->firstName( "George" );
37    $boss->lastName( "Red" );
38    $boss->hireDay( 5, 31, 1979 );
39    $boss->title( "manager" );
40    print( $boss->firstName(), " ",
41           $boss->lastName(), " is the boss.\n" );
42    print( "This worker was hired " );
43    $boss->hireDay();
44    print( " and their title is ", $boss->title(), ".\n" );
45    $boss->write();
46    print( "\n" );
```

```
Jason Black was hired on 8/5/1995.
Hello, my name is Jason.
I was hired on 8/5/1995.

John White was hired on 11/30/1999.
This worker makes $9.50 per hour.
Hello, my name is John.
I was hired on 11/30/1999.
I make $9.50 per hour.

George Red is the boss.
This worker was hired 5/31/1979 and their title is manager.
My name is Mr. Red.
I am the boss and I am a manager.
```

Fig. 14.12 Overriding base-class methods (part 2 of 2).

Our implementation of class **Employee2** is similar to that of class **Employee** in Fig.
14.6, but has several enhancements. The constructor **new** (lines 11–32) was rewritten to
allow it to be called with arguments so that the attributes can be initialized as the object is
created, rather than calling the set methods later. In addition, method **write** (lines 64–72)
was provided for easy printing of the **Employee**'s data.

Class **Hourly2** is similar to class **Hourly** in Fig. 14.7. Like **Employee2**, we have added the option to set the attributes using the constructor. Because **hourly** employees have more information to print, we have overridden the version of method **write** that was inherited from class **Employee2**. In the implementation of method **write** (lines 33–38), we invoke the super class' **write** function with the **$self->SUPER::write** (line 36), and then output the **Hourly2** employee specific data (line 37).

Class **Boss** also inherits from class **Employee2**. It adds the **title** attribute and a corresponding *get/set* method. It also overrides method **write**. In this case, **write** does not call class **Employee2**'s **write** method.

In Fig. 14.12, line 11 shows the new use of **Employee2**'s **new** method with arguments to initialize the object as it is constructed. When you look at the output of this program, notice that each **write** method call (lines 17, 31 and 45) produces output that is specific to the type of **Employee** object on which the method is called.

14.6 Other Class Relationships: Multiple Inheritance, Composition and Containment

We have now seen one of the most common ways to reuse and enhance a class definition, but there are other ways as well. In addition to single inheritance (shown in the previous inheritance examples), we can use *multiple inheritance* by adding more than one class to the derived class' **@ISA** array. Now, when Perl wants to find an inherited method, it will look through your **@ISA** array in a *depth-first search*. Thus, when a method is called on an object, Perl first looks in that object's class for the method. If the method is not found there, Perl looks in the first class specified in the **@ISA** array. If the method is still not found, Perl then continues by looking for the method in that class' **@ISA** array. Perl will search through the entire base-class hierarchy before moving on to the next class in the original **@ISA** array in the derived class.

In addition to single inheritance and multiple inheritance, there is another common way to reuse a class: *composition* (or the "*has a*" relationship). This can also be called a *using relationship*. In this relationship, an object of one class can have one or more attributes that are objects of other classes. In fact, we have seen this in use already: In our **Employee** and **Employee2** classes in the two previous examples, our objects of these classes had a **hireDay** field of type **Date**.

Another relationship between classes is the *containment relationship*, in which an object of a class contains a collection of other objects. Such classes are often called *container classes*. Figures 14.13 and 14.14 demonstrate a container class. An object of class **WorkGroup** can store objects of our **Employee2**, **Hourly2** and **Boss** classes. A **WorkGroup** object consists of an array of **Employee2**s. These employees could be regular employees, hourly workers or boss employees.

```
1   #!/usr/bin/perl
2   # Fig. 14.13: WorkGroup.pm
3   # Implementation of class WorkGroup.
4
5   use strict;
6   use warnings;
```

Fig. 14.13 Implementation of class **WorkGroup** (part 1 of 2).

```perl
7    use Employee2;
8    use Hourly2;
9    use Boss;
10
11   package WorkGroup;
12
13   sub new
14   {
15      my $object = shift();
16      my $class = ref( $object ) || $object;
17
18      my $group = [ @_ ];
19
20      bless( $group, $class );
21      return $group;
22   }
23
24   sub add
25   {
26      my $object = shift();
27
28      foreach my $employee ( @_ ) {
29         push( @$object, $employee );
30      }
31   }
32
33   sub listMembers
34   {
35      my $object = shift();
36
37      foreach my $employee ( @$object ) {
38         $employee->write();
39      }
40   }
41
42   return 1;
```

Fig. 14.13 Implementation of class **WorkGroup** (part 2 of 2).

```perl
1    #!/usr/bin/perl
2    # Fig. 14.14: fig14_14.pl
3    # Demonstrating composition.
4
5    use strict;
6    use warnings;
7    use Employee2;
8    use Hourly2;
9    use Boss;
10   use WorkGroup;
11
12   my $worker = new Employee2( "Jason", "Black", "8/5/1995" );
13   my $hour = new Hourly2( "John", "White", "11/30/1999", 9.50 );
```

Fig. 14.14 Creating a container class (part 1 of 2).

```
14
15   my $group = new WorkGroup( $worker, $hour );
16
17   my $boss = new Boss( "George", "Red", "5/31/1979", "manager" );
18
19   $group->add( $boss );
20
21   $group->listMembers();
```

```
Hello, my name is Jason.
I was hired on 8/5/1995.
Hello, my name is John.
I was hired on 11/30/1999.
I make $9.50 per hour.
My name is Mr. Red.
I am the boss and I am a manager.
```

Fig. 14.14 Creating a container class (part 2 of 2).

Our constructor for class **WorkGroup** (Fig. 14.13) is straightforward. The object uses an array to hold the employees in the group. We create this anonymous array on line 18. Any employees passed to method **new** will be stored in the array. We **bless** this reference on line 20 to convert it to a **WorkGroup** object. Lines 24–31 define method **add**. To add a worker to our group, we simply **push** that worker onto our array (line 29). The **list-Members** method iterates through the array, calling each **Employee2**'s **write** method. Perl makes all this simple to use. We do not need to know what type of **Employee2** each worker is. A **Boss** will call the proper **write** method, just like an **Hourly2** or an **Employee2**. This is known as *polymorphism*. Perl's interpreter and underlying data storage deal with the details of determining each object's actual data type.

Software Engineering Observation 14.11

In a collection of objects whose classes form a class hierarchy, Perl can distinguish the type of each object in the collection and call the correct methods for that object.

14.7 Base Class UNIVERSAL

As you delve into more complicated inheritance hierarchies, it is important to have some means of seeing what classes an object inherits from and what methods are available to an object. These means, or capabilities, are in every class, inherited from the **UNIVERSAL** base class. After Perl has looked through all the other classes to find a method, it automatically looks in the **UNIVERSAL** base class. Thus, if you want to add a function to every class, you can add it to the **UNIVERSAL** class.

The **UNIVERSAL** class currently provides the *isa* and *can* methods. Method **isa** determines whether a class inherits from another class, and method **can** determines whether a class has an implementation for a particular method. Figure 14.15 demonstrates these functions with our **Employee2**, **Hourly2** and **Boss** classes from Figs. 14.9, 14.10 and 14.11, respectively.

```perl
1   #!/usr/bin/perl
2   # Fig. 14.15: fig14_15.pl
3   # Using the UNIVERSAL base class methods.
4
5   use strict;
6   use warnings;
7   use Employee2;
8   use Hourly2;
9   use Boss;
10
11  my %people = ( employee => new Employee2,
12                 hourly   => new Hourly2,
13                 boss     => new Boss );
14
15  foreach my $key ( keys( %people ) ) {
16     my $object = $people{ $key };
17
18     print( "$key is a employee2\n" )
19        if $object->isa( 'Employee2' );
20     print( "$key is a hourly2\n" ) if $object->isa( 'Hourly2' );
21     print( "$key is a boss\n" ) if $object->isa( 'Boss' );
22     print( "$key can write\n" ) if $object->can( 'write' );
23     print( "$key can rate\n" ) if $object->can( 'rate' );
24     print( "$key can title\n" ) if $object->can( 'title' );
25     print( "\n" );
26  }
```

```
employee is a employee2
employee can write

boss is a employee2
boss is a boss
boss can write
boss can title

hourly is a employee2
hourly is a hourly2
hourly can write
hourly can rate
```

Fig. 14.15 UNIVERSAL base-class methods.

14.8 Encapsulation: Public vs. Private

We have mentioned the importance of separating implementation from interface. The goal is to allow clients to interface with an object of a class, without having to know the implementation details behind that object. This means that we can change the implementation without changing the interface. But what if we have a client that did not want to use the interface we provided? For example, accessing attribute **the_month** in class **Date** by typing **$today->{ the_month }** instead of **$today->month()** bypasses the interface by working directly with the implementation details of the attributes. There is no rule in Perl that says this is wrong, but if the implementation changes and the hash element with key **the_month** no longer exists as part of class **Date**, any program that directly accessed the attributes of class **Date** would no longer work. Sometimes we would like to make it impossible for the user of a class to directly access these implementation details. This is called *encapsulation*—the hiding of data.

Software Engineering Observation 14.12

Encapsulation promotes reusability, maintainability, modifiability and debugability.

In other OOP languages—for example, C++ and Java, there are ways to keep attributes and methods private. In fact, both of these languages have the **private** keyword built into them to do just that. Perl, on the other hand, does not explicitly provide a way to do this. Perl prefers to trust that clients will stay out of the implementation of classes and work only through the interface provided for them. If a client refuses to do so, Perl assumes either that the client knows what he or she is doing or that the client accepts whatever consequences might come from this (or both). If you prefer not to trust your client, then there are a couple of ways to force the client to comply.

Our previous examples each use public data in the class definitions. The next few sections present examples of *data hiding*, which allows programmers to prevent others from accessing certain code directly. To do this, we will modify class **Employee2** from previous sections.

14.9 Closure Method

In the discussion of references from Chapter 13, you learned about lexical variables, deep binding and closures. We can use deep bindings and closures to "privatize" data. The *closure method* of data encapsulation uses the fact that the variables in a closure are not available outside the closure. In this next example, we define a new version of our employee class called **EmployeeClosure** with "private" variables.

```
1   #!/usr/bin/perl
2   # Fig. 14.16: EmployeeClosure.pm
3   # Encapsulating data using closures.
4
5   package EmployeeClosure;
6
7   use strict;
8   use warnings;
9   use Date;
10
11  sub new
12  {
13      my $object = shift();
14      my $class = ref( $object ) || $object;
15
16      my $employee =  { firstName => shift(),
17                        lastName => shift(), };
18
19      my $hireDay = new Date;
```

Fig. 14.16 Implementation of class **EmployeeClosure** (part 1 of 3).

```
20
21      if ( $_[ 0 ] ) {
22          my ( $month, $day, $year ) = split( /\//, $_[ 0 ] );
23          $hireDay->day( $day );
24          $hireDay->month( $month );
25          $hireDay->year( $year );
26      }
27
28      $employee->{ hireDay } = $hireDay;
29
30      my $self = sub {
31                    my $field = shift();
32
33                    $employee->{ $field } = shift() if ( @_ );
34                    return $employee->{ $field };
35                };
36
37      bless( $self, $class );
38      return $self;
39  }
40
41  sub firstName
42  {
43      my $self = shift();
44
45      &{ $self }( "firstName", @_ );
46  }
47
48  sub lastName
49  {
50      my $self = shift();
51
52      &{ $self }( "lastName", @_ );
53  }
54
55  sub hireDay
56  {
57      my $self = shift();
58
59      my $date = &{ $self }( "hireDay" );
60
61      $date->setDate( @_ ) if ( @_ );
62
63      return $date;
64  }
65
66  sub write
67  {
68      my $self = shift();
69
70      print( "Hello, my name is ", $self->( 'firstName' ), ".\n" );
71      print( "I was hired on " );
72
```

Fig. 14.16   Implementation of class **EmployeeClosure** (part 2 of 3).

```
73      my $date = $self->( 'hireDay' );
74      $date->print();
75      print( ".\n" );
76   }
77
78   return 1;
```

Fig. 14.16 Implementation of class **EmployeeClosure** (part 3 of 3).

```
1    #!/usr/bin/perl
2    # Fig. 14.17: fig14_17.pl
3    # Using the EmployeeClosure class
4
5    use strict;
6    use warnings;
7    use EmployeeClosure;
8
9    my $first = new EmployeeClosure( "Jason", "Black", "8/5/1995" );
10   my $second = new EmployeeClosure;
11
12   $second->firstName( "John" );
13   $second->lastName( "White" );
14   $second->hireDay( 11, 30, 1999 );
15
16   $first->write();
17   $second->write();
```

```
Hello, my name is Jason.
I was hired on 8/5/1995.
Hello, my name is John.
I was hired on 11/30/1999.
```

Fig. 14.17 Encapsulating data using closures.

The interface of class **EmployeeClosure** (Fig. 14.16) is identical to that of class **Employee2**. If we name this class **Employee2** instead, we can simply replace the old **Employee2** class with this one. The programs that previously used **Employee2** should not have to change. We were able to change the implementation while keeping the interface the same, thus demonstrating the power of object orientation.

The closure method keeps the attributes private to the class. Rather than having the object be a reference to a hash containing the data, it is now a reference to a closure that contains the data. When the constructor is called, it creates the hash reference (lines 16 to 28). The constructor then creates a closure that will return the attributes when passed the correct arguments. This closure is **bless**ed and returned to the program when a new **EmployeeClosure** object is created.

The *get/set* methods access the data through the closure, rather than directly with the hash. To do this, they call the closure by dereferencing the function reference, using the ampersand, and call the closure with the appropriate arguments. Our closure was written like a *get/set* method, so that if it is passed just one argument, it will return the element in the hash whose key was passed. If two arguments are passed to it, the first argument is the key of the element and the second is the new value for the element. Thus in the **first-Name** *get/set* method, we call the closure with the first argument of **firstName** and whatever was passed into the method (line 45).

The program of Fig. 14.17 does not really demonstrate that the data in the class **EmployeeClosure** are truly private data. To prove this, we could write a line that attempts to directly access the data, as in

```
$first->{ "firstName" } = "Paul";
```

which will produce a compiler error when you attempt to execute the program.

14.10 Implicit Functions

All the functions we have seen until now need to be explicitly called in the program. These types of functions are called *explicit functions*. Perl also has *implicit functions*, which it automatically calls. Many languages have these implicit functions, but most languages do not allow the programmer to alter them. In Perl, implicit functions are generally denoted by a name in all uppercase letters.

Common Programming Error 14.2

Using all uppercase letters in a function name implies that it is an implicit function.

BEGIN is an implicit function. It acts like a function—it can be declared and the **sub** that prefaces the function is implied. We never explicitly call **BEGIN** in the program. This is because each time Perl encounters a **BEGIN** block, it executes the block automatically. In fact, calling **BEGIN** in your program is an error. **BEGIN** functions are called in the order they are declared, ignoring all control structures. In general, **BEGIN** functions are used to initialize global variables and import modules and pragmas.

Another implicit function is the **END** function, which executes as the program ends, immediately after the last statement completes execution. **END** functions are executed in the reverse order of **BEGIN** functions, with the last one declared getting executed first. Any housekeeping that needs to be done as the program terminates should be placed in an **END** function. This can be something as simple as a **print** statement or as complex as closing a network connection or closing files.

A third implicit function is function **DESTROY**, which is called when an object is destroyed—either when it goes out of scope or as the program terminates. This function can be used to perform clean-up of an object that uses a resource. For example, this function might be used to close a database or network connection that the object obtained earlier in the program.

Figures 14.18 and 14.19 demonstrate **DESTROY** being called as an object goes out of scope. Note that as each object goes out of scope in Fig. 14.19, a line of text is output from function **DESTROY** to prove that it is called implicitly.

```
1   #!/usr/bin/perl
2   # Fig. 14.18: Circular.pm
3   # Using the DESTROY function to destroy objects.
4
```

Fig. 14.18 Implementation of class **Circular** (part 1 of 2).

```
5    package Circular;
6
7    use strict;
8    use warnings;
9
10   sub new {
11      my $class = shift();
12
13      my $a;
14      my $b = \$a;
15
16      $a = \$b;
17
18      my $self = {};
19
20      $self->{ name } = shift();
21      $self->{ Circle } = \$a;
22
23      bless( $self, $class );
24      return $self;
25   }
26
27   sub sayHi {
28      my $self = shift();
29
30      print( "$self->{ name } says hi.\n" );
31   }
32
33   sub DESTROY {
34      my $self = shift();
35
36      print( "Destroying $self->{ name }.\n" );
37      ${ $self->{ Circle } } = undef;
38   }
39
40   return 1;
```

Fig. 14.18   Implementation of class **Circular** (part 2 of 2).

```
1    #!/usr/bin/perl
2    # Fig. 14.19: 19.pl
3    # Demonstrating the DESTROY function.
4
5    use warnings;
6    use strict;
7    use Circular;
8
9    my $a = new Circular( "Bob" );
10
11   {
12      print( "Entering First Scope.\n" );
13
```

Fig. 14.19   Demonstrating function **DESTROY** (part 1 of 2).

```
14      my $b = new Circular( "Joe" );
15
16      {
17          print( "Entering Second Scope.\n" );
18
19          my $c = new Circular( "Alice" );
20          $c->sayHi();
21          print( "Exiting Second Scope.\n" );
22      }
23
24      $b->sayHi();
25      print( "Exiting First Scope.\n" );
26  }
27
28  $a->sayHi();
29  print( "Exiting program.\n" );
```

```
Entering First Scope.
Entering Second Scope.
Alice says hi.
Exiting Second Scope.
Destroying Alice.
Joe says hi.
Exiting First Scope.
Destroying Joe.
Bob says hi.
Exiting program.
Destroying Bob.
```

Fig. 14.19 Demonstrating function **DESTROY** (part 2 of 2).

14.11 AUTOLOAD Function

One of the more important implicit functions is function **AUTOLOAD**. If a method is called and the interpreter cannot find it in the object's class or in any class from which the object inherits, Perl normally exits with a fatal error. This can be avoided with an **AUTOLOAD** function. When a class method is not found, Perl looks for function **AUTOLOAD** in that class (or its base classes). If **AUTOLOAD** is found, it is called, and the special variable **$AUTO-LOAD** is set to the name of the called method. **AUTOLOAD** can be used to catch what would otherwise be fatal errors. It can also be used to avoid declaring many individual functions that do almost the same thing. You may have noticed from the previous examples that all of the *get/set* methods were almost identical, except for the variable that they accessed. **AU-TOLOAD** can be used to combine these *set/get* methods, as shown in the program of Figs. 14.20 and 14.21.

```
1   #!/usr/bin/perl
2   # Fig. 14.20: Date2.pm
3   # Implementation of autoloaded date2 class.
4
```

Fig. 14.20 Implementating class **Date2** class with function **AUTOLOAD** (part 1 of 3).

```
5   package Date2;
6   use strict;
7   use warnings;
8
9   my @months = ( 0, 31, 28, 31, 30, 31, 30, 31, 31, 30, 31, 30, 31 );
10
11  sub new
12  {
13      my $object = shift();
14      my $class = ref( $object ) || $object;
15
16      my $date = { year => 1000,
17                   month => 1,
18                   day => 1, };
19
20      bless( $date, $class );
21      return $date;
22  }
23
24  sub AUTOLOAD
25  {
26      my $object = shift();
27      my $type = ref( $object ) ||
28          die( "$object is not an object" );
29
30      my $name = $Date2::AUTOLOAD;
31
32      $name =~ s/.*://;
33      exit() if ( $name eq 'DESTROY' );
34
35      unless ( exists( $object->{ $name } ) ) {
36          die( "Cannot access '$name' field of class $type" );
37      }
38
39      if ( @_ ) {
40          return $object->{ $name } = shift();
41      }
42      else {
43          return $object->{ $name };
44      }
45  }
46
47  sub setDate
48  {
49      if ( @_ == 4 ) {
50          my $object = shift();
51
52          $object->year( $_[ 0 ] );
53          $object->month( $_[ 1 ] );
54          $object->day( $_[ 2 ] );
55      }
56      else {
57          print( "the .\n" );
```

Fig. 14.20   Implementating class **Date2** class with function **AUTOLOAD** (part 2 of 3).

```
58       }
59    }
60
61    sub print
62    {
63       my $object = shift();
64       print( $object->month );
65       print( "/" );
66       print( $object->day );
67       print( "/" );
68       print( $object->year );
69    }
70
71    return 1;
```

Fig. 14.20 Implementating class **Date2** class with function **AUTOLOAD** (part 3 of 3).

```
1    #!/usr/bin/perl
2    # Fig. 14.21: fig14_21.pl
3    # Interface with autoloaded date2.pm.
4
5    use Date2;
6    use strict;
7    use warnings;
8
9    my $today = new Date2;
10
11   $today->setDate( 2000, 7, 14 );
12   print $today->month(), "\n";
13   $today->print();
```

```
7
7/14/2000
```

Fig. 14.21 Using **AUTOLOAD**.

The interface for class **Date2** is identical to the interface for the original **Date** class. The only change is in the implementation. Our implementation now has only four methods. Of these, **new**, **print** and **setDate** are the same. But we have replaced our three *get*/*set* functions with one **AUTOLOAD** function.

In our **AUTOLOAD** function, the first thing we do is **shift** to get the object on which the method was called (line 26). To ensure that the method was called correctly, we determine whether the method was called on an object (line 27). We then store the name of the method call in our **$name** variable (line 30) and use a simple substitution of a regular expression to eliminate the package name (line 32). Line 33 ensures that the method called was not **DESTROY**. Remember that **DESTROY** will be called implicitly, so we do not want to capture this call. Our last test determines whether the attribute the user wants to change exists in the class (line 35). Now that we have finished our extensive tests, we can actually write out the *get*/*set* part of **AUTOLOAD**. Line 39 determines whether **AUTOLOAD** received a value. If so, we want to implement a *set* method, changing the current value of the field and returning that value (line 40). If not, we continue to the **else** block (line 42) and simply return the current value of the field (line 43). The hardest part of creating this **AUTOLOAD** function was the initial tests, but they are also important: We do not want our program to die suddenly without giving a proper error message indicating the problem.

14.12 Tied Variables

Other useful implicit functions are those used to *tie* variables to certain classes. These functions also can be used to hide the implementation of a class from the user. When a variable is manipulated by a program, an implicit function is called. For example, when we assign a value to a scalar, the *STORE* function is called on the scalar. By defining our own **STORE** function in a class and using function **tie** to tie a variable to that class, we can override the variable's **STORE** function to provide different functionality for assignments to that scalar. Other implicit functions can be used to change the functionality of the other basic manipulations. (For more information on these functions, type **man perltie** on your UNIX/Linux-based system or **perldoc perltie** on Windows.)

Our next example (Figs. 14.22 and 14.23) shows how we can use implicit functions to make a scalar variable behave like a queue.

Class **Queue** (Fig. 14.22) uses implicit function overrides to convert a scalar into a *queue data structure* in which the first item placed in the queue is the first item removed. A queue also is known as a *first-in, first-out (FIFO) data structure*. Queues are easy to implement in Perl because of the built-in **push** and **shift** array functions (see Chapter 4). Perl also has built-in **pop** and **unshift** array functions that violate the FIFO rules of a queue. Tieing is one way to eliminate this problem. In our class, we defined three implicit functions: *TIESCALAR* (lines 9–16), **STORE** (lines 18–24) and *FETCH* (lines 26–30). **TIESCALAR** (discussed shortly) provides the means by which we tie a scalar to this class. Function **STORE** defines how a value is assigned to an object of the class. Function **FETCH** determines how a value is retrieved from an object of the class.

```perl
1    #!/usr/bin/perl
2    # Fig. 14.22: Queue.pm
3    # Implementation of queue using a tied scalar.
4
5    package Queue;
6    use strict;
7    use warnings;
8
9    sub TIESCALAR
10   {
11       my ( $class ) = shift();
12       my @data = split( ' ', $_[ 0 ] );
13
14       bless( \@data, $class );
15       return \@data;
16   }
17
18   sub STORE
19   {
```

Fig. 14.22 Implementation of a scalar tied to a queue (part 1 of 2).

```
20      my $obj = shift();
21      my $data = shift();
22
23      push( @$obj, $data );
24   }
25
26   sub FETCH
27   {
28      my $obj = shift();
29      return shift( @$obj );
30   }
31
32   return 1;
```

Fig. 14.22 Implementation of a scalar tied to a queue (part 2 of 2).

```
1    #!/usr/bin/perl
2    # Fig. 14.23: fig14_23.pl
3    # Using a queue tied scalar.
4
5    use Queue;
6    use strict;
7    use warnings;
8
9    my $line;
10
11   tie( $line, 'Queue', 'a b c d' );
12
13   print( "$line\n" );
14   print( "$line\n" );
15   $line = 'e';
16   $line = 'f';
17   print( "$line\n" );
18   print( "$line\n" );
19   print( "$line\n" );
```

```
a
b
c
d
e
```

Fig. 14.23 Function **tie**.

Common Programming Error 14.3

*A **TIESCALAR** function must return a scalar, whereas a **TIEARRAY** function must return an array, and so on for the other data types.*

In Fig. 14.23, the most important line when tying a variable to a class is line 11

```
tie( $line, 'queue', 'a b c d' )
```

The **tie** function is similar to the constructor for regular classes, in that it initializes the object for use. The **tie** function requires two arguments. The first is the variable that is to be tied. The second is the class to which the variable is being tied. In this case, the **tie** function takes a third argument to initialize the variable to a starting value.

When the **tie** function receives a scalar as its first argument, it implicitly calls function **TIESCALAR** (Fig. 14.22) and passes as arguments the remaining arguments that were originally passed to **tie**. **TIESCALAR** takes its first argument (the class of our object) and assigns it to variable **$class** (line 11 of Fig. 14.22). This is for use when we **bless** our object. Line 12 creates the array that will be used to hold the values in the queue. This reference is **bless**ed and returned to the calling program.

Our tied scalar **$line** now contains the reference to an array, **bless**ed into our queue class. The next thing we try to do is **print** that tied scalar. The **print** function actually calls class **Queue**'s **FETCH** function (lines 26–30) to get the value of the variable. We have overridden this function so that the interpreter will find our user-defined **FETCH** function. If we look at the function, all it does is **shift** an item off of our queue and **return** it (line 29).

Lines 20 and 21 try to assign a value to our tied scalar. This assignment statement implicitly calls class **Queue**'s **STORE** function (lines 18–24). Again, the interpreter will find our user-defined version of this function, which will **push** an item onto our queue (line 23).

14.13 Internet and World Wide Web Resources

perl.about.com/compute/perl/msub71.htm?terms=Perl%2B+object+ oriented
A list of tutorials about object-oriented programming in Perl found on **About.com**.

docs.rinet.ru/P7/ch19.htm
This is the chapter on object-oriented programming from the online version of the book *Teach Yourself Perl 5 in 21 Days*, by David Till.

www.keller.com/perlweb/chap2/o-o-perl.html
This Web page provides a brief review of object-oriented programming in Perl.

genome-www.stanford.edu/perlOOP
This Web site is dedicated to spreading knowledge about object-oriented programming in Perl. The site contains links to examples and other resources.

www.perl.com/pub/doc/manual/html/pod/perltoot.html
An object-oriented programming tutorial at **www.perl.com**.

SUMMARY

- OOP (object-oriented programming) is a method of programming that treats everything as objects. It stems from the theory that everything in life is, and can be described as, an object.

- The type of an object is known as a class.

- Objects have properties, which are known as data or attributes.

- Actions performed by objects are defined as methods in a program.

- Object-oriented programming allows for the creation of interfaces to data that are independent of the implementation of the data. If we have many programs using an object through its methods, we can completely change the way the data is implemented without having to change the programs using the data.

- It is important to write programs that are understandable and easy to maintain. Change is the rule rather than the exception. Programmers should anticipate that their code will be modified. Classes can facilitate program modifiability.

- When the implementation of a class used by implementation-independent code changes, that code need not be modified.

- The **FileHandle** class provides an object-oriented interface to a filehandle. It offers several advantages over normal filehandles, such as being able to reference them without using typeglobs and being able to alternate between multiple filehandles without using the **select** function.

- To class **FileHandle**, we first must make an instance of the class. This is done using the class's constructor. Traditionally, the constructor is called **new**, although Perl allows the constructor name to be different, depending on the class. The constructor returns an instance of the class.

- Once an instance of a class (i.e., an object) has been constructed, the object's methods can be called. To do this, the arrow operator is used, as in

  objectName->*method*(*arguments*)

- The interface of a class is the class's methods and the syntax for calling them—what the user or client of the class sees. The implementation is the underlying details—how the class is organized, as well as the data it contains and the algorithms it uses.

- One of the principles of good software engineering is to separate interface from implementation, making it easier to modify programs. Changes in a class' implementation do not affect the client, as long as the class' interface originally provided to the client remains unchanged.

- Clients have access to the interface of a class, but should not have access to its implementation.

- Function **bless** converts a reference into an object. In Perl, all objects are based on references. The objects' type will default to the current package name, but providing a second argument to **bless** will cause the type to be changed to the second argument.

- In OOP terminology, there are *get/set*, or accessor, methods. A *get* method will access and return a value, while a *set* method will change a variable, returning a new value.

- When a method of an object is called, it works like any other function, except that the first element in **@_** is the object on which the method was called.

- The class designer need not provide *set* or *get* functions for each data item; these capabilities should be provided only when appropriate.

- Every method (such as a *set*) that modifies the data members of an object should ensure that the data remains in a consistent state.

- Object methods are usually shorter than functions in non-object-oriented programs, because the data stored in data members have ideally been validated by object methods that store new data. Since the data are already in the object, the object method calls often have no arguments or at least have fewer arguments than typical function calls in non-object-oriented languages.

- Once a class is defined, creating and manipulating objects of that class usually involves issuing only a simple sequence of method calls—few control structures are needed. By contrast, it is common to have control structures in the implementation of a class' methods.

- Often, classes may be derived from other classes. Classes can also include objects of other classes as members. Such software reuse can greatly enhance programmer productivity.

- Deriving new classes from existing classes is called inheritance. Including class objects as members of other classes is called composition (or aggregation).

- Subclasses of a class would have all the functionality of the original (or base) class, plus whatever else we implement. Inheritance allows us more flexibility in reusing code, because we can now expand on preexisting classes and objects, taking all of the functionality from them and adding more.

- To specify what classes our subclass will inherit from, we set the **@ISA** array. This array is used to import variables and methods.

- To call a base-class method, we use the **$class::SUPER->method()**. This looks for the method in our class' superclass.

- Perl will look in the class specified by the **@ISA** array for unknown methods.

- Perl provides method overriding so that you can write a method that overrides the base class' implementation.

- In addition to single inheritance, we can use multiple inheritance by adding more than one class to the inheriting class' **@ISA** array.

- The **UNIVERSAL** class provides the **isa** and **can** methods. The **isa** method can be used to determine whether a class inherits from another class, and the **can** method can be used to determine whether a class has an implementation for a particular method.

- Perl does not provide an explicit way to make data private (i.e., encapsulate the data).

- We can use deep bindings and closures to "privatize" data. The closure method of data encapsulation uses the fact that the variables in a closure are not available outside the closure.

- Implicit functions are functions that are automatically called by Perl. In Perl, implicit functions are generally denoted by having a name in all uppercase letters.

- **BEGIN** is an implicit function, which is automatically executed as it is encountered in the program. **BEGIN** functions will be called in the order they are declared, ignoring all control structures.

- Function **END** is executed as the program terminates. **END** functions are executed in the reverse order of **BEGIN** functions, with the last one declared getting executed first. Any cleanup that needs to be done as the script is exiting should be placed in **END** functions.

- Function **DESTROY** is called when an object goes out of scope or as the program ends. This function can be used if you have an object that requires cleanup before it is deallocated.

- Function **AUTOLOAD** is called if Perl cannot find a called method in the object's class or in any class from which the object inherits. If **AUTOLOAD** is found, it is called, and the special variable **$AUTOLOAD** is set to the name of the called method. **AUTOLOAD** can be used to catch what would otherwise be fatal method calls (for nonexistent methods).

- Other useful implicit functions are those used to **tie** variables to certain classes. This technique can also be used to hide the implementation of a class from the user. When a variable is manipulated, an implicit function is being called.

- The **tie** function is similar to the constructor for regular classes, in that it initializes an object for use. The **tie** function requires two arguments. The first is the variable that is to be tied. The second is the class to which the variable is being tied. Additional arguments can be provided to initialize an object

TERMINOLOGY

accessor methods	**bless** function
aggregation	**can** method
attributes	class
AUTOLOAD function	client
base class	closure method
BEGIN function	composition

consistent state	**isa** method
constructor	method
containing relationship	method overriding
control structure	multiple inheritance
data encapsulation	**new**
data hiding	object-oriented programming
derive one class from another	objects
DESTROY function	overriding
encapsulating data by using closures	**private** keyword
encapsulation	**read** function
END function	reuse
explicit functions	**select** function
Exporter	separate interface from implementation
FETCH function	set method
FileHandle module	setting the value of a data item
get method	software reuse
get/set methods	**STORE** function
getline function	**sub** keyword
getting the value of a data item	subclasses
implementation	**SUPER**
implementation independent	**tie** function
implementation of a class	**TIESCALAR** function
implicit functions	**UNIVERSAL** base class
inheritance	using relationship
interface	**write** function
@ISA special array	

SELF-REVIEW EXERCISES

14.1 Fill in the blanks in each of the following statements:
 a) Functions written for manipulating objects are known as _____.
 b) The facilities for using and manipulating an object are its _____, whereas the underlying details are the object's _____.
 c) If a class is derived from another class, it is said to _____ from that class.
 d) Including class objects as data members of other classes is called _____.
 e) Providing a new implementation of a method inherited from a base class is called
  _____.
 f) The _____ array holds the list of classes from which a class is derived.
 g) The _____ class is the base class for every other class.
 h) The **BEGIN**, **END** and **AUTOLOAD** functions are examples of _____.

14.2 State whether each of the following is *true* or *false*. If *false*, explain why.
 a) A class constructor must be named **new**.
 b) A class does not have to have a constructor.
 c) The following statements are identical:

```
$object->method( @arguments );
method( $object, @arguments );
```

 d) The underlying details of a class are its interface.
 e) Including class objects as data members of other classes is known as inheritance.
 f) A class can inherit from at most one other class.
 g) Implicit functions will be called only if specifically called in a program.

h) The **AUTOLOAD** function is called whenever a method is used that is not defined else-where in the class.

i) You can use the **tie** function only with scalars.

14.3   Create a module, **Calculator.pm**, with methods to add, subtract, multiply and divide two numbers. Create the module so that when a new instance of **Calculator** is created, the two numbers are initialized to one. Program each method so that the user may enter the two numbers or simply use the two numbers that are already stored in the object.

14.4   Create a module called **Exponential.pm** that inherits from **Calculator.pm**. The module should use the constructor from **Calculator.pm**, but only to create its new constructor. There should be a method to calculate exponents. Have this method call the **multiply** method in **Calculator.pm**. For this exercise, do not worry about negative exponents.

After doing this, create a small program to use this module. The program should prompt the user for two numbers and calculate the value of the first number to the power of the second number.

ANSWERS TO SELF-REVIEW EXERCISES

14.1   a) methods. b) interface, implementation. c) inherit. d) composition. e) method overriding f) **@ISA**. g) **UNIVERSAL**. h) implicit functions.

14.2   a) False. The constructor can have any valid method name.
b) False. A class must have a constructor.
c) True.
d) False. They are the implementation.
e) False. It is known as composition.
f) False. A class can inherit from multiple classes.
g) False. Implicit subroutines can be invoked without being explicitly called.
h) True.
i) False. The **tie** function can be used to tie other variable types as well.

14.3   See the following program.

```
1   #!/usr/bin/perl
2   # Ex. 14.3: calculator.pm
3   # A simple calculator
4
5   package calculator;
6
7   use strict;
8   use warnings;
9
10  sub new
11  {
12      my $calculator =    { number1 => 1,
13                            number2 => 1, };
14
15      bless( $calculator );
16      return $calculator;
17  }
18
19  sub add
20  {
21      my $self = shift;
22
```

```
23      $self->{ number1 } = shift if ( @_ );
24      $self->{ number2 } = shift if ( @_ );
25
26      return $self->{ number1 } + $self->{ number2 };
27   }
28
29   sub subtract
30   {
31      my $self = shift;
32
33      $self->{ number1 } = shift if ( @_ );
34      $self->{ number2 } = shift if ( @_ );
35
36      return $self->{ number1 } - $self->{ number2 };
37   }
38
39   sub multiply
40   {
41      my $self = shift;
42
43      $self->{ number1 } = shift if ( @_ );
44      $self->{ number2 } = shift if ( @_ );
45
46      return $self->{ number1 } * $self->{ number2 };
47   }
48
49   sub divide
50   {
51      my $self = shift;
52
53      $self->{ number1 } = shift if ( @_ );
54      $self->{ number2 } = shift if ( @_ );
55
56      return $self->{ number1 } / $self->{ number2 };
57   }
58
59   return 1;
```

14.4   See the following programs.

```
1    #!/usr/bin/perl
2    # Ex. 14.4: exponential.pm
3    # A class to calculate exponents
4
5    package exponential;
6
7    use strict;
8    use warnings;
9    use calculator;
10   our @ISA = ( "calculator" );
11
12   sub exponent_new
13   {
```

```perl
14      my $object = shift;
15      my $class = ref( $object ) || $object;
16
17      my $self = $class->SUPER::new();
18
19      bless( $self, $class );
20      return $self;
21   }
22
23   sub exponent
24   {
25      my $self = shift;
26      my $i = 0;
27
28      $self->{ number1 } = shift if ( @_ );
29      $self->{ number2 } = shift if ( @_ );
30
31      my $exponent = $self->{ number2 };
32
33      my $result = $self->{ number1 };
34
35      if ( $exponent <= 0 ) {
36         return 1;
37      }
38
39      for( $i = 1; $i < $exponent; $i++ ) {
40         $result =
41            $self->SUPER::multiply( $self->{ number1 }, $result );
42      }
43
44      return $result;
45
46   }
47
48   return 1;
```

```perl
1    #!/usr/bin/perl
2    # Ex. 14.4: ex14_04.pl
3    # Interface with exponential
4
5    use strict;
6    use warnings;
7    use exponential;
8
9    my $my_calculator = exponential->exponent_new();
10
11   print( "Please enter first value: " );
12   chomp( my $first = <STDIN> );
13
14   print( "Please enter the exponent you want this raised to: " );
15   chomp( my $second = <STDIN> );
16
17   my $value = $my_calculator->exponent( $first, $second );
```

```
18
19   print( $value );
```

```
Please enter first value: 2
Please enter the exponent you want this raised to: 3
8
```

EXERCISES

14.5 Take one of your previous CGI programs that was written in **CGI.pm**'s functional style, and rewrite it to use **CGI.pm**'s object-oriented style. [*Hint*: You create an instance of CGI by saying **$instance = new CGI**. After this, all you need to do is use this instance to call the same functions that you used before.]

14.6 Create a **CEO.pm** module that creates a **CEO** object. This object should inherit from the **Boss** class described in **Boss.pm** (Fig. 14.11).

14.7 Use the **Date** class to create a **Calendar** class.

14.8 Use **AUTOLOAD** to rewrite the **Employee**, **Boss** and **Hourly** classes.

14.9 Using a tied array, implement a string class in which the string is represented as an array of characters.

15

Databases: SQL and Perl Database Interface (DBI)

Objectives

- To understand the relational database model.
- To be able to write database queries using the Structured Query Language (SQL).
- To be able to manipulate a MySQL database and Microsoft Access database from Perl.
- To understand the Perl Database Interface (DBI).
- To be able to retrieve data from a database using DBI.
- To be able to create a database administration tool using DBI and CGI.

It is a capital mistake to theorize before one has data.
Arthur Conan Doyle

Now go, write it before them in a table, and note it in a book, that it may be for the time to come for ever and ever.
The Holy Bible: The Old Testament

Let's look at the record.
Alfred Emanuel Smith

True art selects and paraphrases, but seldom gives a verbatim translation.
Thomas Bailey Aldrich

Get your facts first, and then you can distort them as much as you please.
Mark Twain

I like two kinds of men: domestic and foreign.
Mae West

Outline

15.1 Introduction[1]

A *database* is an integrated collection of data. There are many different strategies for organizing data to facilitate easy access and manipulation of the data. A *database management system (DBMS)* provides mechanisms for storing and organizing data in a manner consistent with the database's format. Database management systems allow for the access and storage of data without worrying about the internal representation of the database.

The most popular database systems in use today are *relational databases*. A language called *Structured Query Language* (*SQL*—pronounced "sequel") is almost universally used with relational database systems to make *queries* (i.e., to request information that satisfies given criteria) and manipulate data. Some popular enterprise-level relational database systems include Microsoft SQL Server, Oracle, Sybase, DB2, Informix and MySQL. In this chapter, we present examples using an *ODBC* database (with Microsoft Access) and a MySQL database. *Open Database Connectivity* (*ODBC*) is a technology developed by Microsoft to allow generic access to disparate database systems on the Windows platform (and some UNIX platforms).

A programming language connects to, and interacts with, relational databases via an *interface*—software that facilitates communications between a database management

---

1. Portions of Sections 15.1 and 15.2 are based on Deitel, H. M., *Operating Systems, 2/E*, pp. 404–409. Reading, MA: Addison-Wesley, Copyright 1990.

system and a program. The most popular interface used by Perl programmers is *Perl Database Interface* (*DBI*)—a database-independent interface that enables Perl to interact with databases. In this chapter, we use DBI to demonstrate SQL and its interactions with an employee database. We also build a *distributed application*—a program composed of several components residing on multiple computers—using DBI and the Common Gateway Interface (CGI). A discussion of a relational database management system, MySQL, is also presented.

Please note that this chapter is geared toward learning about databases and the Perl DBI in general. For the discussions presented here, we use the most easily accessible database systems—Microsoft Access on the Windows platform and MySQL on UNIX/Linux. For other database systems (such as Oracle, Sybase and SQL Server), the codes used in this chapter may require some changes to execute correctly. If you are using one of these systems, you should consult the documentation for that particular system. [*Note:* Please visit our Web site **www.deitel.com** for instructions on setup and configuration of DBI and MySQL on UNIX/Linux and DBI on Windows.]

15.2 Relational Database Model

The *relational database model* is a logical representation of data that allows the relationships between the data to be considered without concerning oneself with the actual physical structure of the data.

A relational database is composed of *tables*. Figure 15.1 illustrates a sample table that might be used in a personnel system. The table name is **Workers** and its primary purpose is to illustrate the attributes of a worker and how they are related to a specific employee. Any particular row of the table is called a *record* (or *row*). This table consists of six records. The **Number** field of each record in the table is used as the *primary key* for referencing data in the table. A *primary key* is a field (or fields) in a database which contains unique data that cannot be contained in other records. This guarantees each record can be identified by a unique value. Good examples of primary fields are a social security number or employee ID. The records of Fig. 15.1 are *ordered* by primary key.

Software Engineering Observation 15.1
Tables in a database normally have primary keys.

Software Engineering Observation 15.2
Primary key fields in a table cannot contain duplicate values.

Common Programming Error 15.1
Inserting a new record with a duplicate primary key in a table is an error.

Each column of the table represents a different *field* (or *column* or *attribute*). Records are normally unique (by primary key) within a table, but particular field values may be duplicated between records. For example, three different records in the **Worker** table's **Department** field contain number 413. The primary key can be composed of more than one column (or field) in the database.

Table: **Workers**

	Number	Name	Department	Salary	Location
	23603	JONES, A.	413	1100	NEW JERSEY
	24568	KERWIN, R.	413	2000	NEW JERSEY
A record	34589	LARSON, P.	642	1800	LOS ANGELES
	35761	MYERS, B.	611	1400	ORLANDO
	47132	NEUMANN, C.	413	9000	NEW JERSEY
	78321	STEPHENS, T.	611	8500	ORLANDO

Primary key   A column

Fig. 15.1   Relational database structure.

Different users of a database are often interested in different data and different relationships among those data. Some users want only certain subsets of the table columns. To obtain table subsets, we use SQL statements to specify the data to *select* from the table. SQL provides a complete set of commands (including **SELECT**) that enable programmers to define complex *queries* that select data from a table. The results of a *query* are commonly called *result sets* (or *record sets*). SQL queries are discussed in Section 15.4.

For example, we might select data from the table in Fig. 15.1 to create a new result set that shows where departments are located. This result set is shown in Fig. 15.2.

15.3 Relational Database Overview: **Employee.mdb**

In this section, we overview the Structured Query Language (SQL) in the context of a sample database (**Employee.mdb**—a Microsoft Access database) we created for this chapter. Before we discuss SQL, we overview the tables of the database. We use this database throughout the chapter to introduce various database concepts, including the use of SQL to obtain information from the database and to manipulate the database. The database is included in with the Chapter 15 examples on the CD that accompanies this book.

The database consists of one table, **Employee**. Typically, databases contain multiple tables. For simplicity, this chapter uses only one table.

The **Employee** table (shown in Fig. 15.3) consists of five fields. They are the employee's unique ID number (primary key) in the database, first name, last name, the year born and their social security number. Figure 15.4 contains the data from the **Employee** table of the **Employee.mdb** database.

Department	Location
413	NEW JERSEY
611	ORLANDO
642	LOS ANGELES

Fig. 15.2   A result set formed by selecting data from a table.

Field	Description
`EmployeeID`	An integer representing the employee's ID number in the database.
`FirstName`	A string representing the employee's first name.
`LastName`	A string representing the employee's last name.
`YearBorn`	A string representing the employee's year of birth.
`SocialSecurity`	A string representing the employee's social security number.

Fig. 15.3   `Employee` table from `Employee.mdb`.

EmployeeID	FirstName	LastName	YearBorn	SocialSecurity
0001	Jim	Blue	1943	999-85-3698
0002	Kate	Green	1977	111-21-7454
0003	Wendy	White	1959	000-84-3196
0004	Michael	Black	1965	222-44-8888

Fig. 15.4   Data from the `Employee` table of `Employee.mdb`.

15.4 Structured Query Language (SQL)

In this section, we provide an overview of *Structured Query Language* (*SQL*) in the context of the `Employee.mdb` sample database we provided for this chapter. SQL queries discussed here can be practiced in the examples shown later in the chapter.

Some SQL commands for querying a database, inserting records into a database and updating existing records in a database are shown in Fig. 15.5 and discussed in the context of complete SQL queries in the next several sections. For more information on SQL, see the resources at the back of the chapter.

SQL commands	Description
SELECT	Select (retrieve) fields from one or more tables.
FROM	Tables from which to get fields. Required in every **SELECT**.
WHERE	Criteria for selection that determine the rows to be retrieved.
ORDER BY	Criteria for ordering (sorting) of records.
INSERT INTO	Insert values into one or more tables. [*Note:* Some database management systems do not require the SQL keyword **INTO**.]
UPDATE	Update existing data in one or more tables.

Fig. 15.5   Some SQL query commands.

15.4.1 Basic SELECT Query

Let us consider several SQL queries that extract information from the **Employee.mdb** database. A typical SQL query selects information from one or more tables in a database. Such selections are performed by ***SELECT*** *queries*. The simplest **SELECT** query form is

> **SELECT** *Fields* **FROM** *TableName*

If we want to select all the fields in the database, the *asterisk* (*****) indicates that all rows and columns (fields) from *TableName* should be selected. For example, to select the entire contents of the **Employee** table (i.e., all the data in Fig. 15.4), use the query

> **SELECT * FROM Employee**

To select specific fields from a table, list the field names separated by commas. For example, to select only the fields **EmployeeID** and **LastName** for all rows in the **Employee** table, use the query

> **SELECT EmployeeID, LastName FROM Employee**

The preceding query selects the data shown in Fig. 15.6. If a field name contains spaces, it must be enclosed in *square brackets* (**[]**) in the query. For example, if the field name is **First Name**, the field name would appear in the query as **[First Name]**.

Software Engineering Observation 15.3

Specifying the actual field names to select from a table (or several tables) guarantees that the fields are always returned in the same order, even if the actual order of the fields in the database table(s) changes. By specifying the field names, we can process the result sets, knowing the order of the fields. Using an asterisk to select all the field names does not always return the fields in the same order due to table changes.

Common Programming Error 15.2

*When performing an SQL statement using the asterisk (*****) to select fields, assuming that the fields in the result set of the query are always returned in the same order may result in incorrect processing of the data in the application receiving the result set. If the order of the fields in the database table(s) changes, the order of the fields in the result set changes accordingly.*

Common Programming Error 15.3

*In a query, forgetting to enclose a field name containing spaces in square brackets (**[]**) is an error.*

EmployeeID	LastName
0001	Blue
0002	Green
0003	White
0004	Black

Fig. 15.6   EmployeeID and **LastName** from the **Employee** table.

Good Programming Practice 15.1

Avoid field names containing spaces when designing database tables.

15.4.2 WHERE Clause

In most cases, it is necessary to locate records in a database that satisfy certain *selection criteria*. Only records that match the selection criteria are selected. SQL uses the optional *WHERE clause* in a **SELECT** query to specify the selection criteria for the query. The simplest form of a **SELECT** query with selection criteria is

SELECT *fieldName1*, *fieldName2*, ... FROM *TableName* WHERE *criteria*

For example, to select the **EmployeeID**, **FirstName**, **LastName** and **YearBorn** fields from the **Employee** table where the employee's **YearBorn** is greater than **1960**, use the query

```
SELECT EmployeeID, FirstName, LastName, YearBorn
FROM Employee
WHERE YearBorn > 1960
```

Our database contains four employees in the **Employee** table. Two of the employees were born after 1960, so only two records are selected by the preceding query (Fig. 15.7).

Performance Tip 15.1

Using selection criteria improves performance by selecting a portion of the database that is normally smaller than the entire database. Working with a smaller portion of the data is easier and faster than working with the entire set of data stored in the database.

The **WHERE** clause condition can contain the **<**, **>**, **<=**, **>=**, **=**, **<>** and **LIKE** operators. The *LIKE operator* is used for *pattern matching* with the wildcard characters *percent* (**%**) and *question mark* (**?**). Pattern matching allows SQL to search for similar strings that "match a pattern." The **%** and **?** characters are used differently in SQL's pattern matching than in Perl's regular expression pattern matching. An *percent character (%)* in the pattern indicates any number of (i.e., zero or more) characters in a row at the percent character's location in the pattern (like the **.** regular expression). [*Note:* Some databases use the ***** *character* in place of the **%** in a **LIKE** expression.] For example, the following query locates the records of all the employees whose last names start with the letter **b**:

```
SELECT EmployeeID, FirstName, LastName, YearBorn,
       SocialSecurity
FROM Employee
WHERE LastName LIKE 'b%'
```

EmployeeID	FirstName	LastName	YearBorn
0002	Kate	Green	1977
0004	Michael	Black	1965

Fig. 15.7   Employees born after 1960 from the **Employee** table.

Notice that the *pattern string* is surrounded by *single-quote characters*. The preceding query selects the two records (Fig. 15.8), because two of the four employees in the database have last names starting with the letter **b** (followed by zero or more characters). The ***** in the **WHERE** clause's **Like** pattern indicates that any number of characters can appear after the letter **b** in the **LastName** field.

A *question mark* (**?**) in the pattern string indicates a single character at that position in the pattern. For example, the following query locates the records of all the employees whose last names start with any character (specified with **?**), followed by the letter **r**, followed by any number of additional characters (specified with *****):

```
SELECT EmployeeID, FirstName, LastName, YearBorn,
       SocialSecurity
FROM Employee
WHERE LastName LIKE '?r*'
```

The preceding query produces one record (Fig. 15.9), because one employee in our database has a last name that contains the letter **r** as its second letter.

A query can be specialized to allow any character in a range of characters in one position of the pattern string. A range of characters can be specified as follows:

[*startValue*–*endValue*]

where *startValue* is the first character in the range and *endValue* is the last value in the range. For example, the following query locates the records of all the employees whose last names start with any letter (specified with the **?**), followed by any letter in the range **q** to **z** (specified with **[q-z]**), followed by any number of additional characters (specified with an *****):

```
SELECT EmployeeID, FirstName, LastName, YearBorn,
       SocialSecurity
FROM Employee
WHERE LastName LIKE '?[q-z]*'
```

[*Note*: Ranges are not supported by some databases such as MySQL.]   ]

EmployeeID	FirstName	LastName	YearBorn	SocialSecurity
0001	Jim	Blue	1943	999-85-3698
0004	Michael	Black	1965	222-44-8888

Fig. 15.8   Employees whose last names start with **b** from the **Employee** table.

EmployeeID	FirstName	LastName	YearBorn	SocialSecurity
0002	Kate	Green	1977	111-21-7454

Fig. 15.9   Employee from the **Employee** table whose last name contains **r** as the second letter.

The preceding query selects only one record (Fig. 15.10) of the **Employee** table (Fig. 15.4), because only one employee in the table has a last name that contains a second letter in the range **q** to **z**.

Portability Tip 15.1
SQL is case sensitive on some database systems. See your database system documentation to determine if SQL is case sensitive on the system and to determine the syntax that should be used for SQL keywords (i.e., all uppercase letters, all lowercase letters or a mixture of upper case and lowercase letters).

Portability Tip 15.2
*Not all database systems support the **LIKE** operator, so be sure to read your database system's documentation carefully. Some databases use other keywords, like **MATCHES** or **CONTAINS**, to provide the **LIKE** operator's functionality.*

Good Programming Practice 15.2
*By convention, SQL keywords should use all uppercase letters (e.g. **SELECT**) and field or table names should have the first letter of each word capitalized (e.g., **LastName**) on systems that are not case sensitive to make the statements more readable.*

15.4.3 ORDER BY Clause

The results of a query can be sorted into ascending or descending order by using the optional ***ORDER BY*** clause. The simplest forms of an **ORDER BY** clause are

```
SELECT fieldNames … FROM TableName ORDER BY fieldName ASC
SELECT fieldNames … FROM TableName ORDER BY fieldName DESC
```

where **ASC** specifies ascending (lowest to highest) order, **DESC** specifies descending (highest to lowest) order and *fieldName* represents the field (the column of the table) that is used for sorting purposes. For example, to obtain the list of employees in ascending order by last name (Fig. 15.11), use the query

```
SELECT EmployeeID, FirstName, LastName, YearBorn,
       SocialSecurity
FROM Employee
ORDER BY LastName ASC
```

Note that the default sorting order is ascending, so **ASC** is optional.

EmployeeID	FirstName	LastName	YearBorn	SocialSecurity
0002	Kate	Green	1977	111-21-7454

Fig. 15.10 Employee from the **Employee** table whose last name contains a second letter in the range **q** to **z**.

EmployeeID	FirstName	LastName	YearBorn	SocialSecurity
0004	Michael	Black	1965	222-44-8888
0001	Jim	Blue	1943	999-85-3698
0002	Kate	Green	1977	111-21-7454
0003	Wendy	White	1959	000-84-3196

Fig. 15.11 Employees from the **Employee** table in ascending order by **LastName**.

To obtain the same list of employees in descending order by last name (Fig. 15.12), use the query

```
SELECT EmployeeID, FirstName, LastName, YearBorn,
       SocialSecurity
FROM Employee
ORDER BY LastName DESC
```

Multiple fields can be used for ordering purposes with an **ORDER BY** clause of the form

    ORDER BY *field1 SortingOrder*, *field2 SortingOrder, ...*

where *SortingOrder* is either **ASC** or **DESC**. Note that the *SortingOrder* does not have to be identical for each field. The query

```
SELECT EmployeeID, FirstName, LastName, YearBorn,
       SocialSecurity
FROM Employee
ORDER BY LastName, FirstName
```

sorts in ascending order all the employees by last name, then by first name. In the set of selected records, the records for employees with the same last name are sorted in ascending order by their first name. Figure 15.13 shows the results of this query. None of the employees in the database have the same last name, so the result is the same as it would have been if we were sorting in ascending order by last name only.

EmployeeID	FirstName	LastName	YearBorn	SocialSecurity
0003	Wendy	White	1959	000-84-3196
0002	Kate	Green	1977	111-21-7454
0001	Jim	Blue	1943	999-85-3698
0004	Michael	Black	1965	222-44-8888

Fig. 15.12 Employees from the **Employee** table in descending order by **LastName**.

EmployeeID	FirstName	LastName	YearBorn	SocialSecurity
0004	Michael	Black	1965	222-44-8888
0001	Jim	Blue	1943	999-85-3698
0002	Kate	Green	1977	111-21-7454
0003	Wendy	White	1959	000-84-3196

Fig. 15.13 Employees from the **Employee** table in ascending order by **LastName**, then by **FirstName**.

The **WHERE** and **ORDER BY** clauses can be combined in one query. The query

```
SELECT EmployeeID, FirstName, LastName, YearBorn,
       SocialSecurity
FROM Employee
WHERE SocialSecurity LIKE '*8'
ORDER BY LastName ASC
```

selects all records that have a **SocialSecurity** number ending with an **8** and orders them in ascending order by **LastName**. The results of the query are shown in Fig. 15.14.

Good Programming Practice 15.3

Spread long SQL statements over multiple lines, using indentation to maximize readability.

15.4.4 Inserting a Record

Often it is necessary to insert data into a table (e.g., add a new record). This is accomplished using an **INSERT INTO** operation. The simplest form for an **INSERT INTO** statement is

```
INSERT INTO TableName ( fieldName1, fieldName2, ..., fieldNameN )
    VALUES ( value1, value2, ..., valueN )
```

where *TableName* is the table into which the record will be inserted. The *TableName* is followed by a comma-separated list of field names in parentheses (this list is not required if the **INSERT INTO** operation fills a complete row in the table). The list of field names is followed by the *SQL keyword* **VALUES** and a comma-separated list of values in parentheses. The values specified here should match the field names specified after the table name in order and type (i.e., if *fieldName1* is supposed to be the **FirstName** field, then *value1* should be a string in single quotes representing the first name). The **INSERT INTO** statement

EmployeeID	FirstName	LastName	YearBorn	SocialSecurity
0004	Michael	Black	1965	222-44-8888
0001	Jim	Blue	1943	999-85-3698

Fig. 15.14 Employees from the **Employee** table whose **SocialSecurity** number ends in an **8**.

```
INSERT INTO Employee ( EmployeeID, FirstName, LastName,
                       YearBorn, SocialSecurity )
VALUES ( 0005, 'Iris', 'Indigo', 1960, '333-66-9999' )
```

inserts a record into the **Employee** table. The statement indicates that values will be inserted for the **EmployeeID**, **FirstName**, **LastName**, **YearBorn** and **SocialSecurity** fields. The corresponding values to insert are **0005**, **'Iris'**, **'Indigo'**, **1960** and **'333-66-9999'**. Figure 15.15 shows the **Employee** table after the **INSERT INTO** operation.

Common Programming Error 15.4

*The single quote (**'**) character is used as a delimiter for strings being inserted in the database. Therefore, to insert a name containing quotes (such as O'Malley) into a database, the name must contain two single quotes in the position where the quote character appears in the name (e.g.,* **'O''Malley'***).*

15.4.5 Updating a Record

Often it is necessary to modify data in a table (e.g., update a record). This is accomplished by using an *UPDATE* operation. The simplest form for an **UPDATE** statement is

```
UPDATE TableName
SET fieldName1 = value1, fieldName2 = value2, ..., fieldNameN = valueN
WHERE criteria
```

where *TableName* is the table in which the record will be updated. The *TableName* is followed by keyword *SET* and a comma-separated list of field name/value pairs in the format *fieldName = value*. The **WHERE** *clause* specifies the criteria used to determine which record(s) to update. The **UPDATE** statement

```
UPDATE Employee
SET YearBorn = '1969'
WHERE LastName = 'Green' AND FirstName = 'Kate'
```

EmployeeID	FirstName	LastName	YearBorn	SocialSecurity
0001	Jim	Blue	1943	999-85-3698
0002	Kate	Green	1977	111-21-7454
0003	Wendy	White	1959	000-84-3196
0004	Michael	Black	1965	222-44-8888
0005	Iris	Indigo	1960	333-66-9999

Fig. 15.15 Employee table after an **INSERT INTO** operation to add a record.

EmployeeID	FirstName	LastName	YearBorn	SocialSecurity
0001	Jim	Blue	1943	999-85-3698
0002	Kate	Green	1969	111-21-7454
0003	Wendy	White	1959	000-84-3196
0004	Michael	Black	1965	222-44-8888
0005	Iris	Indigo	1960	333-66-9999

Fig. 15.16 Employee table after an **INSERT INTO** operation to add a record.

updates a record in the **Employee** table. The statement indicates that the **YearBorn** field will be assigned the value **1969** for the record in which **LastName** is equal to **Green** and **FirstName** is equal to **Kate**. Figure 15.16 shows the **Employee** table after the **UP-DATE** operation.

15.4.6 Deleting a Record

Sometimes you want to remove a record from the table entirely. The **DELETE** operation provides this functionality. The **DELETE** function has the following form:

```
DELETE FROM TableName
WHERE criteria
```

TableName specifies which table to delete from, and the **WHERE** clause specifies what record to delete. The statement

```
DELETE FROM Employee
WHERE EmployeeID = 0005
```

deletes employee number **0005**, **Iris Indigo**, from the table. Figure 15.17 shows the **Employee** table after the **DELETE** operation.

Good Programming Practice 15.4

If possible, use the primary key field to specify which record to update or delete.

EmployeeID	FirstName	LastName	YearBorn	SocialSecurity
0001	Jim	Blue	1943	999-85-3698
0002	Kate	Green	1969	111-21-7454
0003	Wendy	White	1959	000-84-3196
0004	Michael	Black	1965	222-44-8888

Fig. 15.17 Employee table after an **INSERT INTO** operation to add a record.

15.5 Introduction to DBI

Many of today's Web sites provide their users with services such as the ability to purchase items online, store files remotely and access e-mail. These Web sites require databases to authenticate the users that access the sites and to maintain data about those users. Databases have become a crucial part of *distributed applications*. A distributed application is a program that divides the work needed to be done across multiple computer systems. For instance, one computer might be responsible for managing a Web site and another for a database management system. A distributed application uses both computers to perform the task of retrieving a result set from a database and displaying those results on another computer—typically called a client.

The Perl *Database Interface* (*DBI*) provides a means of accessing relational databases from Perl programs. There are many different implementations of relational databases (e.g., MySQL, Microsoft Access, Oracle, etc.). A software program—called a *driver*—helps programs access a database. Each database implementation requires its own driver and each driver can have different syntax for its use in a program. To make using all these different databases easier, an *interface* was created to provide uniform access to all databases. This interface is known as DBI. The database vendors create drivers for their databases that can receive interactions through DBI and process those interactions in a database-specific manner. DBI is database independent, so it allows for easy migration from one DBMS to another. While DBI is not the only interface available for database connectivity in Perl, it is the most widely used.

DBI uses an object-oriented interface. The DBI objects are known as *handles*. There are three different handle types—*driver handles*, *database handles* and *statement handles*. Driver handles encapsulate the driver for the database; they are rarely used in a script. Database handles encapsulate a specific connection to a database. They can be used to send SQL statements to a database. Statement handles encapsulate specific SQL statements and the results returned from them. Any number of database handles can be created with a driver handle and any number of statement handles can be created with a database handle.

 Testing and Debugging Tip 15.1

DBI functions do not use the standard predefined Perl error variables. Generally, when DBI function calls fail they return **undef** *and store the error string in* **$DBI::errstr**. *The error number is stored in* **$DBI::err**. *Each handle also stores its error information, which can be accessed through method calls* **errstr** *and* **err** *on the handle.*

15.6 Working with DBI

In this section, we demonstrate a basic example using DBI. We will be accessing an ODBC database, specifically, a Microsoft Access database, **Employee.mdb**, which contains the data used in the previous sections. Note that this database needs to be registered as a valid ODBC source first. Also, the **DBI.pm** module and the ODBC driver must be installed before the programs that interact with Microsoft Access databases can be executed. The Perl resources posted at our Web site, **www.deitel.com**, include step-by-step instructions on registering a Microsoft Access database as an ODBC data source on a Windows system, installing the **DBI.pm** module and installing the ODBC database driver (**DBD::ODBC**). You can find the resources for all our books by clicking the "Downloads/Resources" link.

In our first DBI program (Fig. 15.18), the contents of the employee database are output. The **use DBI** statement on line 7 loads the DBI module and line 8 loads the database driver, **DBD::ODBC**.

To create a connection to a database, we pass a *data source name* (*DSN*) to method **connect** (line 10). A data source name tells **connect** where to find the database and is constructed in the following format for ODBC databases:

*interface name***:***database driver***:***data source name*

```
1   #!/usr/bin/perl
2   # Fig. 15.18: fig15_18.pl
3   # Program to query a database and display the contents in a table
4
5   use warnings;
6   use strict;
7   use DBI;
8   use DBD::ODBC;
9
10  my $dbh = DBI->connect( "DBI:ODBC:employeeDB", "", "" ) or
11     die( "Could not make connection to database: $DBI::errstr" );
12
13  my $sth = $dbh->prepare( q{ SELECT * FROM employee } ) or
14     die( "Cannot prepare statement: ", $dbh->errstr(), "\n" );
15
16  $sth->execute() or
17     die( "Cannot execute statement: ", $sth->errstr(), "\n" );
18
19  my @array;
20
21  while ( @array = $sth->fetchrow_array() ) {
22     write();
23  }
24
25  # Check to see if fetch terminated early
26  warn( $DBI::errstr ) if $DBI::err;
27  $dbh->disconnect();
28  $sth->finish();
29
30  format STDOUT =
31  @<<<<<<@<<<<<<<<<@<<<<<<<<<<@<<<<<@<<<<<<<<<<<<
32  $array[ 0 ], $array[ 1 ], $array[ 2 ], $array[ 3 ], $array[ 4 ]
33  .
```

```
0004    Michael    Black      1965    222-44-8888
0001    Jim        Blue       1943    999-85-3698
0002    Kate       Green      1977    111-21-7454
0003    Wendy      White      1959    000-84-3196
```

Fig. 15.18 Using DBI to query a database.

In this program, the *interface name* is **DBI**, the *database driver* is **ODBC** and the *data source name* is **employeeDB**. Method **connect** returns a database handle that is assigned to **$dbh**. The second and third arguments to **connect** represent the username and password. We use empty strings here, because the database does not have a username and password. As with every DBI method call, the remainder of the statement (line 11) determines if the connection was successful and prints an error message and terminates the program if not.

Line 13 creates a *statement handle* by calling the database handle's ***prepare*** method. This method prepares the database driver for a statement. which can be executed multiple times later. The SQL query is passed to the **prepare** statement as a string. The SQL in this case is selecting all the fields from the table. The statement handle returned by method **prepare** is assigned to **$sth**.

After a statement has been prepared, and before the results can be processed, the statement must be executed. This is done by calling the statement handle's **execute** method (line16). The result set generated by the query is stored with the statement handle. Each row of the result set is retrieved from the object and placed into an array by calling method **fetchrow_array** (line 21). We use function **write** to print each row using the format defined on lines 30–33. Method **fetchrow_array** returns *false* after all the rows have been read, thus ending the **while** loop. Other functions for extracting the results of a query are shown in Fig. 15.19.

Because **fetchrow_array** returns false when there are no more rows and when there is an error fetching data, we need to check for an error after the end of the loop (line 26). If an error occurs during the fetching of the data, **$DBI::err** is defined. So, we warn the user that an error did occur on line 26. Once we are finished with a database connection, we close it by using method ***disconnect*** (line 27). If you do not need to fetch all the data from a statement handle, you should call method **finish** to indicate when you are done. When all the data of a result set is fetched, method **finish** is called automatically.

Good Programming Practice 15.5

*Perl will close statement and database handles for you when they go out of scope. It is, however, best to close them explicitly by using the **finish** or **disconnect** method when you are done using them.*

Function Name	Return Type	Description
fetchrow_array	array	Returns a single row in an array.
fetchrow_arrayref	array ref	Returns a single row in an array reference.
fetchrow_hashref	hash ref	Returns a single row in a hash reference with field-name value pairs.
fetchall_arrayref	array ref	Returns the whole result set in a reference to an array. The array consists of references to arrays that hold the rows of data.

Fig. 15.19 Functions for extracting the results of a query.

15.7 Manipulating a Database with DBI

In this section we demonstrate how to add, delete and update records in a database by using DBI. We start with an example of inserting a row into the **Employee** table of the database (Fig. 15.20).

```perl
1   #!/usr/bin/perl
2   # Fig. 15.20: fig15_20.pl
3   # Program to insert a new record into the database.
4
5   use warnings;
6   use strict;
7   use DBI;
8   use DBD::ODBC;
9
10  my $dbh = DBI->connect( "dbi:ODBC:employeeDB", "", "",
11                          { RaiseError => 1 } );
12
13  print( "Please enter your employee ID: " );
14  chomp( my $newemploy = <STDIN> );
15  print( "Please enter your first name: " );
16  chomp( my $newfirst = <STDIN> );
17  print( "Please enter your last name: " );
18  chomp( my $newlast = <STDIN> );
19  print( "Please enter your year of birth: " );
20  chomp( my $newbirthyr = <STDIN> );
21  print( "Please enter your social security number: " );
22  chomp( my $newsoc = <STDIN> );
23
24  my $querystring = "INSERT INTO employee VALUES
25          ( '$newemploy','$newfirst','$newlast',
26            '$newbirthyr','$newsoc' );";
27
28  # Execute the statement
29  $dbh->do( $querystring );
30
31  # Now print the updated database
32  my $sth = $dbh->prepare( q{ SELECT * FROM employee  } );
33
34  $sth->execute();
35
36  print( "\n" );
37
38  my @array;
39
40  while ( @array = $sth->fetchrow_array() ) {
41     write();
42  }
43
44  # Clean up
45  warn( $DBI::errstr ) if $DBI::err;
46  $sth->finish();
47  $dbh->disconnect();
```

Fig. 15.20 Inserting records by using DBI (part 1 of 2).

```
48
49   format STDOUT =
50   @<<<<<<@<<<<<<<<<@<<<<<<<<<<<@<<<<<@<<<<<<<<<<<<
51   $array[ 0 ], $array[ 1 ], $array[ 2 ], $array[ 3 ], $array[ 4 ]
52   .
```

```
Please enter your employee ID: 0005
Please enter your first name: Orinthal
Please enter your last name: Orange
Please enter your year of birth: 1947
Please enter your social security number: 999-88-7777

0004    Michael    Black      1965    222-44-8888
0001    Jim        Blue       1943    999-85-3698
0005    Orinthal   Orange     1947    999-88-7777
0002    Kate       Green      1977    111-21-7454
0003    Wendy      White      1959    000-84-3196
```

Fig. 15.20   Inserting records by using DBI (part 2 of 2).

In the previous example, we did all the error checking manually by examining the return value of each method call, which can become tedious. We can have the error checking done for us by passing a hash reference to **connect** as the fourth argument. In the hash, setting **RaiseError** to **1** (lines 10 and 11) causes function **die** to be called with an error message if an error occurs. If we do not want the program to **die** if there is an error, we can set **PrintError** instead. This causes the function to **warn** us if something goes wrong.

In this example, the user is prompted (lines 13–22) to enter information for a new employee record. The user input is stored in variables that are used to create an SQL statement, **$querystring** (lines 24–26).

The insert statement is executed only once and no result set will be returned. So, rather than preparing a statement for later use, we execute the SQL statement immediately by using the database handle's **do** method (line 29). Lines 38–42 output the modified database, as we did in the previous example.

Deleting from a database and updating a database are similar to inserting. Figure 15.21 shows an example that delets a record from the database, and Fig. 15.22 shows an example that updates a record from the database.

```
1   #!/usr/bin/perl
2   # Fig. 15.21: fig15_21.pl
3   # Program to delete a record from the database
4
5   use warnings;
6   use strict;
7   use DBI;
8   use DBD::ODBC;
9
10  my $dbh = DBI->connect( "dbi:ODBC:employeeDB", "", "",
11                          { RaiseError => 1 } );
```

Fig. 15.21   Deleting a record by using DBI (part 1 of 2).

```perl
12
13   print( "Enter the Employee ID number of the record ",
14          "you wish to delete: " );
15   chomp( my $IDdel = <STDIN> );
16   print( "Delete this record: ($IDdel)? (Y/N) " );
17   chomp( my $choice = <STDIN> );
18
19   if ( $choice eq 'Y' || $choice eq 'y' ) {
20      my $query = "DELETE FROM employee " .
21                  "WHERE EmployeeID = '$IDdel'";
22      print( "$query \n\n" );
23      $dbh->do( $query );
24   }
25
26   my $sth = $dbh->prepare( q{ select * FROM employee } );
27
28   $sth->execute();
29
30   my @array;
31
32   while ( @array = $sth->fetchrow_array() ) {
33      write( STDOUT );
34   }
35
36   # Clean up
37   warn( $DBI::errstr ) if $DBI::err;
38   $dbh->disconnect();
39   $sth->finish();
40
41   format STDOUT =
42   @<<<<<<@<<<<<<<<<@<<<<<<<<<<<@<<<<<@<<<<<<<<<<<
43   $array[ 0 ], $array[ 1 ], $array[ 2 ], $array[ 3 ], $array[ 4 ]
44   .
```

```
Enter the Employee ID number of the record you wish to delete: 0005
Delete this record: (0005)? (Y/N) y
DELETE FROM employee WHERE EmployeeID = '0005'

0004    Michael    Black      1965    222-44-8888
0001    Jim        Blue       1943    999-85-3698
0002    Kate       Green      1977    111-21-7454
0003    Wendy      White      1959    000-84-3196
```

Fig. 15.21   Deleting a record by using DBI (part 2 of 2).

```perl
1    #!/usr/bin/perl
2    # Fig. 15.22: fig15_22.pl
3    # Program to update a record in the database.
4
5    use warnings;
6    use strict;
```

Fig. 15.22   Updating a record by using DBI (part 1 of 3).

```perl
7   use DBI;
8   use DBD::ODBC;
9
10  my $dbh = DBI->connect( "dbi:ODBC:employeeDB", "", "",
11                          { RaiseError => 1 } );
12
13  print( "Enter the Employee ID number of the record ",
14         "you wish to change: " );
15
16  chomp( my $ID = <STDIN> );
17
18  print( "Which value would you like to change:\n" );
19  print( "1. Employee Identification. \n" );
20  print( "2. First name.\n" );
21  print( "3. Last name.\n" );
22  print( "4. Year of Birth.\n" );
23  print( "5. Social Security Number.\n" );
24  print( "? " );
25  chomp( my $change = <STDIN> );
26
27  my $field;
28
29  if ( $change == 1 ) {
30     $field = "EmployeeID";
31     print( "Enter the employee's new employee number: " );
32  }
33  elsif ( $change == 2 ) {
34     $field = "FirstName";
35     print( "Enter the employee's new First name: " );
36  }
37  elsif ( $change == 3 ) {
38     $field = "LastName";
39     print( "Enter the employee's new Last name: " );
40  }
41  elsif ( $change == 4 ) {
42     $field = "YearBorn";
43     print( "Enter the employee's new year of birth: " );
44  }
45  elsif ( $change == 5 ) {
46     $field = "SocialSecurity";
47     print( "Enter the employee's new social security number: " );
48  }
49  else {
50     print( "Invalid value.\n" );
51     return;
52  }
53
54  chomp( my $newvalue = <STDIN> );
55  my $query = "UPDATE employee SET $field =
56          '$newvalue' WHERE EmployeeID = '$ID'";
57
58  print( "$query \n" );
59  $dbh->do( $query );
```

Fig. 15.22 Updating a record by using DBI (part 2 of 3).

```
60
61   # Now print the updated database
62   my $sth = $dbh->prepare( q{ SELECT * FROM employee  } );
63
64   $sth->execute();
65
66   print( "\n" );
67   my @array;
68
69   while ( @array = $sth->fetchrow_array() ) {
70      write();
71   }
72
73   # Clean up
74   warn( $DBI::errstr ) if $DBI::err;
75   $dbh->disconnect();
76   $sth->finish();
77
78   format STDOUT =
79   @<<<<<<@<<<<<<<<<@<<<<<<<<<<@<<<<<@<<<<<<<<<<<<
80   $array[ 0 ], $array[ 1 ], $array[ 2 ], $array[ 3 ], $array[ 4 ]
81   .
```

```
Enter the Employee ID number of the record you wish to change: 0004
Which value would you like to change:
1. Employee Identification.
2. First name.
3. Last name.
4. Year of Birth.
5. Social Security Number.
? 2
Enter the employee's new First name: Michelle
UPDATE employee SET FirstName =  'Michelle' WHERE EmployeeID = '0004'

0004   Michelle   Black      1965   222-44-8888
0001   Jim        Blue       1943   999-85-3698
0002   Kate       Green      1977   111-21-7454
0003   Wendy      White      1959   000-84-3196
```

Fig. 15.22 Updating a record by using DBI (part 3 of 3).

Testing and Debugging Tip 15.2

It is helpful to output the query string while programming with DBI. This allows the programmer to verify that the query string is constructed properly and that correct data is being added or retrieved from the database.

15.8 DBI and the Web

Providing a Web interface for a database is just like programming any other CGI script. There are no database-specific issues when programming for the Web. In this section, we present an example that provides all the functionality of the four previous examples, with a Web interface, all in one CGI program (Fig. 15.23).

```perl
1   #!perl
2   # Fig. 15.21: fig15_21.pl
3   # Demonstrates providing a web interface for a database.
4
5   use warnings;
6   use strict;
7   use DBI;
8   use DBD::ODBC;
9   use CGI qw( :standard );
10
11  my $DSN = "dbi:ODBC:employeeDB";
12
13  print header(),
14      start_html( { title => "Working with DBI",
15          background => "http://localhost/images/background.jpg" } );
16
17  unless ( param ) {
18      print h1( "Database Manager" ),
19              start_form(),
20              popup_menu( -name => 'selection',
21                          -value => [ 'View the Database',
22                                      'Insert a Record',
23                                      'Delete a Record',
24                                      'Update a Record' ] ),
25          hidden( { -name => "LAST", -value => "MAIN" } ),
26          br(), br(), br(), br(), br(),
27          submit( -value => "Click to Proceed" ),
28          end_form();
29  }
30  else {
31      my $dbh = DBI->connect( $DSN, "", "", { RaiseError => 1 } );
32
33      if ( param( "LAST" ) eq "MAIN" ) {
34          my $selection = param( "selection" );
35
36          view( $dbh ) if ( $selection eq "View the Database" );
37          displayInsert() if ( $selection eq "Insert a Record" );
38          displayDelete( $dbh ) if ( $selection eq "Delete a Record" );
39          displayUpdate( $dbh ) if ( $selection eq "Update a Record" );
40      }
41      elsif ( param( "LAST" ) eq "INSERT" ) {
42          insertRecord( $dbh );
43          view( $dbh );
44      }
45      elsif ( param( "LAST" ) eq "DELETE" ) {
46          deleteRecord( $dbh );
47          view( $dbh );
48      }
49      elsif ( param( "LAST" ) eq "UPDATE1" ) {
50          updateRecordForm( $dbh );
51      }
52      elsif ( param( "LAST" ) eq "UPDATE2" ) {
53          updateRecord( $dbh );
```

Fig. 15.23 A Web interface for a database (part 1 of 8).

```
54            view( $dbh );
55        }
56        $dbh->disconnect();
57    }
58
59    print end_html();
60
61    sub view
62    {
63        my $dbh = shift();
64
65        my $sth = $dbh->prepare(
66            "SELECT * FROM employee ORDER BY EmployeeID ASC" );
67        $sth->execute();
68
69        my $rows = $sth->fetchall_arrayref();
70        $sth->finish();
71
72        my $tablerows =
73            Tr( th( { -bgcolor => "#dddddd", -align=>'left' },
74                    [ "ID", "First", "Last"] ),
75                th( { -bgcolor => "#dddddd" }, [ "YOB", "SSN" ] ) );
76
77        foreach my $row ( @$rows ) {
78            $tablerows .= Tr( td( { -bgcolor => "#dddddd" }, $row ) );
79        }
80
81        print h1( "Employee Database" ),
82            table( { -border => 0, -cellpadding => 5,
83                    -cellspacing => 0 }, $tablerows ),
84            br(), br(),
85            "Your query yielded ", b( scalar( @$rows ) ),
86            " records.",br(), br(),
87            a( { -href => "/cgi-bin/fig15_23.pl" },
88                "Back to the Main Database Page" );
89    }
90
91    sub displayInsert
92    {
93        print h3( "Add a new employee to the database." ), br(),
94            start_form(),
95                "Employee ID", br(),
96                textfield( -name => 'ID' ), br(),
97                "First Name", br(),
98                textfield( -name => 'FIRST' ), br(),
99                "Last Name", br(),
100               textfield( -name => 'LASTNAME' ), br(),
101               "Year of Birth", br,
102               textfield( -name => 'YEAR' ), br(),
103               "Social Security Number", br(),
104               textfield( -name => 'SSN' ),
105               hidden( { -name => "LAST", -value => "INSERT",
106                       -override => "1" } ),
```

Fig. 15.23 A Web interface for a database (part 2 of 8).

```
107                    br(), br(), submit( -value => "Add New Employee" ),
108               end_form(), br(), br(),
109               a( { -href => "/cgi-bin/fig15_23.pl" },
110                  "Back to the Main Database Page" );
111  }
112
113  sub displayDelete
114  {
115      my $dbh = shift();
116
117      my $sth = $dbh->prepare(
118         "SELECT EmployeeID, FirstName, LastName FROM employee " );
119
120      $sth->execute();
121
122      my ( %names, @ids );
123
124      while ( my @row = $sth->fetchrow_array ) {
125         push( @ids, $row[ 0 ] );
126         $names{ $row[ 0 ] } = join( " ", @row[ 1, 2 ] );
127      }
128
129      $sth->finish;
130
131      print h3( "Delete an employee from the database" ), br(),
132         start_form(),
133            "Select an Employee to delete ",
134            popup_menu( -name => 'DELETE_ID',
135                        -value => \@ids,
136                        -labels => \%names ), br(), br(), br(),
137            hidden( { -name => "LAST", -value => "DELETE",
138                     -override => 1 } ),
139            submit( -value => "Delete a Record" ), br(), br(),
140         end_form(),
141         font( { -color => "red" },
142              "This action removes the record permanently." ),
143         br(), br(), a( { -href => "/cgi-bin/fig15_23.pl" },
144                        "Back to the Main Database Page" );
145  }
146
147  sub displayUpdate
148  {
149      my $dbh = shift();
150
151      my $sth = $dbh->prepare(
152         "SELECT EmployeeID, FirstName, LastName FROM employee " );
153
154      $sth->execute();
155
156      my ( %names, @ids );
157
158      while ( my @row = $sth->fetchrow_array ) {
159         push( @ids, $row[ 0 ] );
```

Fig. 15.23 A Web interface for a database (part 3 of 8).

```
160            $names{ $row[ 0 ] } = join( " ", @row[ 1, 2 ] );
161        }
162
163        $sth->finish;
164
165        print h3( "Update an employee in the database" ), br(),
166            start_form(),
167                "Select an Employee to update ",
168                popup_menu( -name => 'UPDATE_ID',
169                            -value => \@ids,
170                            -labels => \%names ), br(), br(), br(),
171                hidden( { -name => "LAST", -value => "UPDATE1",
172                          -override => 1 } ),
173                submit( -value => "Update a Record" ), br(), br(),
174            end_form(),
175            a( { -href => "/cgi-bin/fig15_23.pl" },
176                "Back to the Main Database Page" );
177    }
178
179    sub updateRecordForm
180    {
181        my $dbh = shift();
182        my $statement = "SELECT * FROM employee " .
183                        "WHERE EmployeeID = '" .
184                        param( 'UPDATE_ID' ) . "'";
185        my $sth = $dbh->prepare( $statement );
186
187        $sth->execute();
188
189        my @values = $sth->fetchrow_array;
190        my @names = ( "", "First Name ", "Last Name ", "Year Born ",
191                    "Social Security Number " );
192        $sth->finish();
193
194        print h3( "Updating the record for employee #$values[ 0 ]." ),
195            br(), br(),
196            start_form(),
197                "@values\n", br(),
198                hidden( { -name => '0', -value => $values[ 0 ] } );
199
200        foreach ( 1 .. 4 ) {
201            print $names[$_], br(),
202                textfield( -name=>$_, -value => $values[ $_ ],
203                           -override => 1 ), br();
204        }
205
206        print submit( -value => "Update the Record" ),
207            hidden( { -name => "LAST", -value => "UPDATE2",
208                      -override => 1 } ),
209            end_form(),
210            a( { -href => "/cgi-bin/fig15_23.pl" },
211                "Back to the Main Database Page" );
212    }
```

Fig. 15.23   A Web interface for a database (part 4 of 8).

```perl
213
214  sub insertRecord
215  {
216     my $dbh = shift();
217     my ( $id, $first, $last, $year, $ssn ) =
218        ( param( 'ID' ), param( 'FIRST' ), param( 'LASTNAME' ),
219           param( 'YEAR' ), param( 'SSN' ) );
220     my $string = "INSERT INTO employee VALUES
221           ( '$id', '$first', '$last', '$year', '$ssn' );";
222
223     $dbh->do( $string );
224  }
225
226  sub deleteRecord
227  {
228     my $dbh = shift();
229     my $string = "DELETE FROM employee ".
230                   "WHERE EmployeeID = '" .
231                   param( 'DELETE_ID' ) . "'";
232
233     $dbh->do( $string );
234     print "Employee #", param( 'DELETE_ID' ),
235           " deleted.", br(), br();
236  }
237
238  sub updateRecord
239  {
240     my $dbh = shift();
241     my ( $id, $first, $last, $year, $ssn ) =
242        ( param( '0' ), param( '1' ), param( '2' ),
243           param( '3' ), param( '4' ) );
244     my $string = "UPDATE employee SET FirstName = '$first', " .
245                   "LastName = '$last', YearBorn = '$year', " .
246                   "SocialSecurity = '$ssn' " .
247                   "WHERE EmployeeID = '$id'";
248
249     $dbh->do( $string );
250  }
```

Fig. 15.23 A Web interface for a database (part 5 of 8).

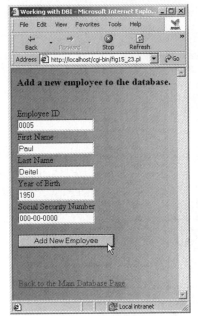

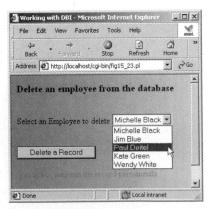

Fig. 15.23   A Web interface for a database (part 6 of 8).

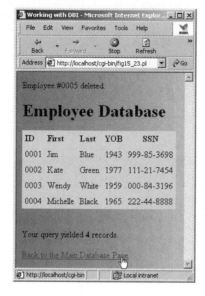

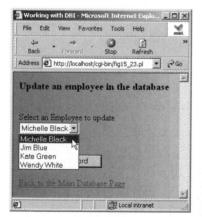

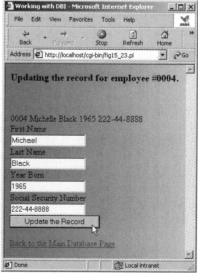

Fig. 15.23   A Web interface for a database (part 7 of 8).

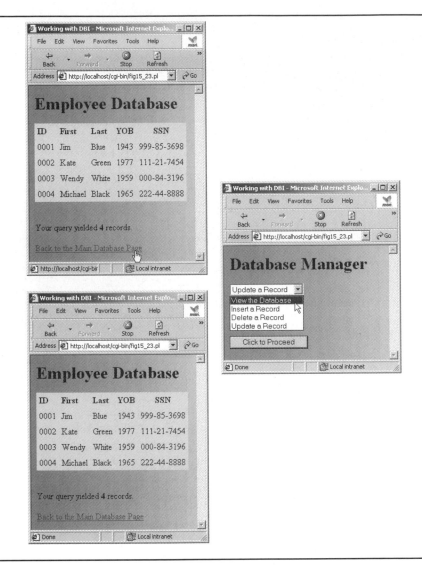

Fig. 15.23 A Web interface for a database (part 8 of 8).

The program uses **if** statements that output different HTML pages to the user, based on the HTML page from which a request is made and based on the options selected by the user. Each request uses a hidden form element named **LAST** to store the page from which the request is made.

If no parameters are passed to the script, then the user is visiting the site for the first time and should be shown a page that allows him or her to choose the task to perform on the database (lines 17–29). Lines 20–24 display a popup menu from which the user chooses to view the database, insert a record into the database, delete a record from the database or update an existing record in the database. We also use a **hidden** form element to set the **LAST** parameter to **MAIN** (for the main page) on line 25. When the user clicks the **submit** button (labeled "**Click to Proceed**") generated on line 27, the program outputs a new page for the selected option.

After the user makes his or her first selection from the **MAIN** page, line 31 calls **connect** to open the database connection. The **if/elsif/else** structure, starting at line 33, determines the page from which the request was made, then calls the appropriate function. For example, when the **LAST** parameter contains **MAIN** after the user makes the first selection, the code in lines 33–40 executes to determine the selected option. The **selection** parameter contains the item selected from the popup menu. Lines 36–39 invoke one of the functions **view** (to view the database contents), **displayInsert** (to allow the user to insert a new record), **displayDelete** (to allow the user to delete a record) and **displayUpdate** (to allow the user to update an existing record), based on that selection.

Function **view** (lines 61–89) prepares and executes an SQL statement that selects the whole database and orders it by ascending **EmployeeID** number (lines 65–67). Line 69 uses method **fetchall_arrayref** to extract the results of the query and return a reference to an array containing the data. Lines 72–88 build and output an HTML table containing the data. Lines 72–75 generate the table header and lines 77–79 generate the table rows with a **foreach** loop. Lines 81–88 output the HTML page.

If the user decided to insert an element, function **displayInsert** (lines 91–111) outputs a form in which the user will enter the information for a new record. Each field in the record is represented with a textfield element. Lines 105 and 106 set the **hidden** form element **LAST** to **INSERT**. Note the use of attribute **override** for the **hidden** form element. By nature, CGI forms are "sticky"—they maintain form field values. Using override allows us to replace the previous value of **hidden** form element **LAST** with the value **INSERT** to ensure that the proper action is taken when we submit insert form contents back to the server.

Once the user submits their form, lines 41–44 invoke function **insertRecord** (lines 214–224). Function **insertRecord** reads the form data on lines 217–219 and creates the SQL statement (lines 220 and 221) to perform the insertion. Line 223 invokes method **do** to execute the SQL statement. When program control returns to line 43, the program calls function **view** to display the updated database.

If the user decided to delete a record, the program calls function **displayDelete** (lines 113–145). This function creates a popup menu from which the user can select the employee he or she wishes to delete. When the user selects the employee, we want the **EmployeeID** of that employee to be set as the value of the popup menu that is sent back to the server when the user submits the form. To make a popup menu with these properties, we query the database to return the first names, last names and ID numbers of all the employees (lines 117–120). We then make an array of all the ID numbers (line 122) and a hash that has the **EmployeeID** as the key and the first and last name of the employee as the value (lines 124–127). The array provides the names of the menu selections, and the hash labels the selections (lines 134–136). The **LAST** parameter is set to **DELETE** (lines 137 and 138).

When the user selects the employee to delete and submits the form, the program calls function **deleteRecord** from line 46. This function (defined at lines 226–236) creates a SQL statement (lines 229–231) to delete the employee with the selected ID and executes the statement (line 233). When **deleteRecord** completes, the program calls function **view** to display the contents of the database (line 47).

If the user decides to update a record, the program calls function **displayUpdate** (lines 147–177). This function creates the same menu used in function **displayDelete** to allow the user to select an employee. After choosing the employee to update, there are two parts to processing the update. First the user must enter the new information, then the update must be performed. We use two different values for the **hidden** form element **LAST**—**UPDATE1**—for this reason. Lines 171 and 172 set **LAST** to **UPDATE1** in this case, so the user will be presented with the form created by function **updateRecordForm**, which allows the user to specify the changes to the record of the data.

Function **updateRecordForm** (lines 179–212) fetches the selected employee's information from the database (lines 182–185). The **EmployeeID** is recorded in a **hidden** form element (line 198), so that we know later what record was updated. The other data can be modified by using the textfields generated on lines 200–204. The values returned from the database are displayed in each textfield to enable the user to see the current information for the record. The **hidden** form element **LAST** is set to **UPDATE2**; hence, the **updateRecord** function can be called to perform the update.

When the user submits the form with the updated data, line 53 calls **updateRecord** (lines 238–250). The function reads the updated information the user submitted on lines 241–243 and constructs a SQL statement (lines 244–247). This statement executes on line 249. After the subroutine finishes, the program calls function **view** to display the updated database contents.

15.9 DBI Utility Functions

DBI provides *utility functions* allowing you to determine the database support provided by the computer running your program. These are function ***available_drivers*** and function ***data_sources***. Function **available_drivers** returns the available database drivers (DBDs) that are installed. Function **data_sources** returns the databases that are registered with the system. For a complete listing of utility functions for DBI, please refer to the manpage for DBI (**man DBI** on UNIX/Linux systems and **perldoc DBI** on Windows).

15.10 MySQL Server

In this section, we present a brief introduction to MySQL—a robust and scalable database management system (DBMS). The focus of this chapter has primarily been on Microsoft Access and ODBC on the Windows platform. Microsoft Access has many limitations because it is a personal database management system. For industrial applications, Microsoft has the more robust SQL Server DBMS. However, the popularity of the Linux operating system in recent years has created a demand for a powerful, enterprise, database management system usable on Linux platforms. MySQL is a multiuser, multithreaded DBMS server allowing multiple connections to a database at one time.

Note that MySQL must be downloaded and installed before executing the examples in this section. Also, the **DBI.pm** module and **DBD::mysql** (the MySQL driver) must be installed. The Perl resources posted at our Web site, **www.deitel.com**, include step-by-step instructions on downloading and installing these components. You can find the resources for all our books by clicking the "Downloads/Resources" link.

Like Linux, MySQL is an open source software (available from **www.mysql.org**), which means that the source code may be obtained and customized to suit the needs of a corporation. The ability to change the source code is crucial to optimizing certain queries, storing proprietary data and the like. MySQL may also be compiled for most popular operating systems, making it portable across different architectures. The source code for Microsoft Access and many other popular DBMSs normally is not available to programmers. The following MySQL examples were written and tested on a computer running Red Hat Linux 6.2 with the Apache Web Server (version 1.3.12 and 1.3.14) and MySQL (version 3.22). Note that MySQL and Apache are also available on Windows. However, the Windows version of MySQL is not available free of charge. The Apache Web server is distributed with most versions of Linux and may be downloaded free from the Apache organization's Web site **www.apache.org**.

To use MySQL with DBI, the **DBD::mysql** database driver is needed—this driver can be found on CPAN (**www.cpan.org**), or can be downloaded from

www.mysql.com/downloads/api-dbi.html

Please refer to the documentation packaged with the driver for installation guidelines.

We now show how to create a database to store information entered by a user to register a product. First, we need to create a database. This can be done by using the program **mysql**, which allows you to interact with the MySQL DBMS. We are going to call our database **USERDB**. It is created by running the following command:

create database USERDB;

You will need the password for the **root** user of the database to create a database, and you need to be logged on to the computer as the super user (at the root level). If you do not have this level of access, speak with your system administrator about creating the database. Once the database has been created, you should exit the **mysql** program by typing **quit**.

Now that the database is created, we need to create a table in this database for our data. Although this can be done with the utilities provided with MySQL, we will need to create it with a Perl program. The SQL statement for creating a table is

> **CREATE TABLE** *TableName* **(**
>   *ColumnName type modifiers*, *ColumnName type modifiers*, **...** **)**

We discuss only the types and modifiers used in our programs. Consult the documentation provided with MySQL for the different data types and modifiers that can be specified.

Before creating a table, we must determine the columns that will be placed in the table. Our examples here are based on a registration database that will include each user's first name, last name, e-mail address, phone number, continent, average hours spent using a product and a rating of the product on a scale of 1 to 5. Figure 15.24 demonstrates creating a table with these columns and the addition of a single row to the table.

```
1   #!/usr/bin/perl
2   # Fig. 15.24: fig15_24.pl
3   # Creating a table.
4
5   use warnings;
6   use strict;
7   use DBI;
8   use DBD::mysql;
```

Fig. 15.24 Creating a table in a MySQL database (part 1 of 2).

```
9
10    my $dbh = DBI->connect( "DBI:mysql:USERDB", "root", "",
11                             { RaiseError => 1 } );
12
13    my $string = "CREATE TABLE Users (
14                    FirstName VARCHAR( 30 ),
15                    LastName  VARCHAR( 30 ),
16                    Email     VARCHAR( 30 ),
17                    Phone     VARCHAR( 30 ),
18                    Continent ENUM( 'North America',
19                                    'South America',
20                                    'Europe',
21                                    'Asia',
22                                    'Africa',
23                                    'Australia',
24                                    'Antarctica' ),
25                    OpSys     ENUM( 'Windows NT',
26                                    'Windows 98',
27                                    'Macintosh',
28                                    'Linux',
29                                    'Other' ),
30                    Hours     INT,
31                    Rating    INT )";
32
33    $dbh->do( $string );
34
35    $dbh->do( "INSERT INTO Users (
36                FirstName, LastName, Email, Phone,
37                Continent, OpSys, Hours, Rating )
38              VALUES ( 'John', 'Doe', 'john\@doe.net',
39                       '(555)555-5555', 'North America',
40                       'Windows 98', 3, 4 )" );
41
42    my $sth = $dbh->prepare( "SELECT * FROM Users" );
43    $sth->execute();
44
45    while ( my @row = $sth->fetchrow_array() ) {
46        print( "@row\n" );
47    }
48
49    warn( $DBI::errstr ) if ( $DBI::err );
50    $dbh->disconnect();
51    $sth->finish();
```

```
John Doe john@doe.net (555)555-5555 North America Windows 98 3 4
```

Fig. 15.24 Creating a table in a MySQL database (part 2 of 2).

Line 8 loads the MySQL driver (**DBD::mysql**), and line 10 connects to the database. Lines 13–31 build the SQL statement to create the table. For the table columns named **FirstName**, **LastName**, **Email** and **Phone**, we use type **VARCHAR**, which specifies that they are variable-length text fields. The number in parentheses following the type specifies the maximum number of characters used to represent each column. We use type **ENUM** for the **Continent** and **OpSys** columns. Type **ENUM** allows us to specify a list of options available for that column. The choices are specified as a comma-separated list in parentheses following the **ENUM** keyword. Finally, we use type **INT** for the columns **Hours** and **Rating**, which restricts them to being integers.

We execute the SQL statement in line 33. Then, lines 35–40 insert a single record into the table. Lines 42–47 query the database and display all the records currently in the table (i.e., the one that was just inserted).

Now that the database exists, Fig. 15.25 defines a CGI program which allows users to register through a Web site and inserts the users' information into a database. [Note that because DBI is database independent, we could easily convert this program (and the previous one) to use a Microsoft Access called **USERDB**—the only changes in the program would be replacing **use DBD::mysql** on line 8 with **use DBD::ODBC** and replacing the data source name **dbi:mysql:USERDB** on line 69 with **dbi:ODBC:USERDB**.]

```perl
1   #!/usr/bin/perl
2   # Fig. 15.25: fig15_25.pl
3   # Using a MySQL database
4
5   use warnings;
6   use strict;
7   use DBI;
8   use DBD::mysql;
9   use CGI qw( :standard );
10
11  print( header(), start_html( "Registration Form" ),
12         h1( "Registration Form" ) );
13
14  if ( param( "No" ) || !param ) {
15     registrationForm();
16  }
17  elsif ( !param( "Yes" ) ) {
18     my $first = param( "FIRST" );
19     my $last  = param( "LAST" );
20     my $email = param( "EMAIL" );
21     my $phone = param( "PHONE" );
22     my $land  = param( "CONTINENT" );
23     my $os    = param( "OS" );
24     my $time  = param( "HOURS" );
25     my $value = param( "RATING" );
26
27     if ( $phone !~ / \( \d{3} \) \d{3} - \d{4} /x ) {
28        print( "Please enter your phone number ",
29               "in the correct format.", br() );
30        registrationForm();
31     }
32     elsif ( ( $time !~ / \d+ /x ) || $time < 0 || $time > 24 ) {
33        print( "Please enter an integer for hours that is ",
34               "between 0 and 24", br() );
35        registrationForm();
36     }
```

Fig. 15.25 Registration form processor (part 1 of 5).

```
37        else {
38            print( h4( "You entered", br(),
39                        "Name:                    $first $last", br(),
40                        "E-mail:                  $email", br(),
41                        "Phone:                   $phone", br(),
42                        "Continent:               $land", br(),
43                        "OS:                      $os", br(),
44                        "Hours using product: $time", br(),
45                        "Rating of product:    $value:" ), br(),
46
47                start_form(),
48                hidden( -name => "FIRST" ), hidden( -name => "LAST" ),
49                hidden( -name => "EMAIL" ), hidden( -name => "PHONE" ),
50                hidden( -name => "CONTINENT" ), hidden( -name => "OS" ),
51                hidden( -name => "HOURS" ), hidden( -name => "RATING" ),
52
53                "Is this information correct? ", br(),
54                submit( -name => "Yes" ), submit( -name => "No" ),
55                end_form() );
56        }
57    }
58    else {
59        my $first = param( "FIRST" );
60        my $last  = param( "LAST" );
61        my $email = param( "EMAIL" );
62        my $phone = param( "PHONE" );
63        my $land  = param( "CONTINENT" );
64        my $os    = param( "OS" );
65        my $time  = param( "HOURS" );
66        my $value = param( "RATING" );
67
68        if ( $phone =~ / \( \d{3} \) \d{3} - \d{4} /x ) {
69            my $dbh = DBI->connect( "DBI:mysql:USERDB", "root", "",
70                                    { RaiseError => 1 } );
71
72            my $statement = "INSERT INTO Users VALUES
73                ( '$first', '$last', '$email', '$phone',
74                  '$land', '$os', '$time', '$value' )";
75
76            $dbh->do( $statement );
77
78            print( "Thank you for completing the ",
79                    "registration form $first", br(),
80                    "The following information has been recorded:",
81                    br(), br(),
82                    table( { -border => 3, -cellspacing => 3 },
83                    Tr( th( [ "Name", "E-mail", "Phone Number",
84                              "Continent", "OS", "Hours",
85                              "Rating" ] )),
86                    Tr( td( { -align => "center" },
87                            [ "$first $last", $email, $phone,
88                              $land, $os, $time, $value ] ) ) ) ) );
89        }
```

Fig. 15.25 Registration form processor (part 2 of 5).

```
90      else {
91          print( "Please enter your phone number in the ",
92                  " correct format.", br() );
93          registration_form();
94      }
95  }
96
97  print end_html();
98
99  sub registrationForm {
100     print(
101         h3( "Please fill in all fields and then click Proceed." ),
102         start_form(),
103         table( { -cellpadding => "3" },
104         Tr( { -valign => "top" },
105             td( { -width => '300' }, strong( "First Name:" ), br(),
106                 textfield( -name => "FIRST", -size => 15 ) ),
107
108             td( strong( "Last Name:" ), br(),
109                 textfield( -name => "LAST", -size => 15 ) ) ),
110
111         Tr( { -valign => "top" },
112             td( strong( "E-mail Address:" ), br(),
113                 textfield( -name => "EMAIL", -size => 25 ) ),
114
115             td( strong( "Phone Number" ), br(),
116                 textfield( -name => "PHONE", -size => 20 ), br(),
117                 "Must be of the form (555)555-5555" ) ) ),
118
119         h4( "What Continent do you live on? " ),
120         popup_menu( -name => "CONTINENT",
121                     -value => [ "North America", "South America",
122                                 "Asia", "Europe", "Australia",
123                                 "Africa", "Antarctica" ] ),
124         br(),
125         h4( "Which Operating System are you currently running?" ),
126         radio_group( -name  => 'OS',
127                     -value => [ "Windows 98", "Windows NT",
128                                 "Macintosh", "Linux", "Other" ] ),
129         br(),
130         h4( "How many hours a day do you use our product? " ,
131         textfield( -name => 'HOURS', -size => 3 ) ),
132
133         h4( "How would you rate our product on a scale of 1 - 5" ),
134         radio_group( -name => "RATING",
135                     -value => [ '1', '2', '3', '4', '5' ] ),
136         br(),
137         submit( "Proceed" ),
138         end_form() );
139 }
```

Fig. 15.25 Registration form processor (part 3 of 5).

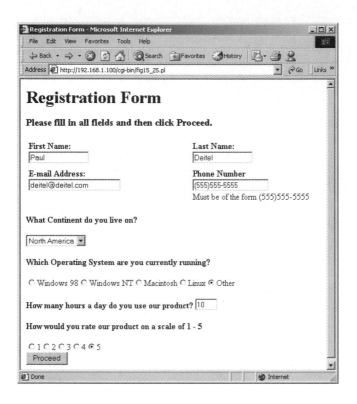

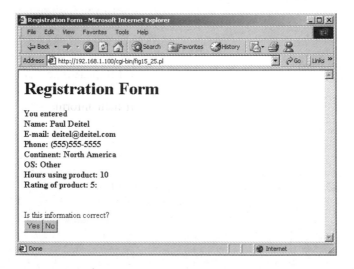

Fig. 15.25   Registration form processor (part 4 of 5).

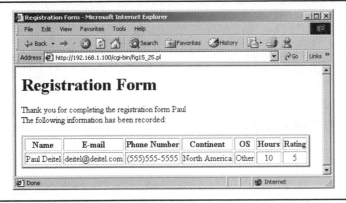

Fig. 15.25 Registration form processor (part 5 of 5).

The form into which the user enters data is output by function **registrationForm** (lines 99–139). The form contains textfields for the first and last names (lines 106 and 109), e-mail address (line 113), phone numbers (line 116) and the number of hours the product is used (line 131). A popup menu (lines 120–123) allows the user to select the continent. Radio buttons allow the user to select the operating system (lines 126–128) being used and the rating for the product (lines 134 and 135).

Line 15 calls function **registrationForm** if the user is arriving at the site for the first time or if the user would like to reenter information. The program also calls this function if the user did not enter the phone number in the correct format (lines 27–31) or if the user did not enter a value for number of hours using the product (lines 32–36). If all the information is entered correctly, the information is printed so that the user can verify that he or she entered the correct information (lines 37–56). Hidden form elements are used to remember the information the user entered.

If the user verifies that the information is correct, then we want to enter this information into the database (lines 58–95). We read the information for the insertoperation by using function **param** on lines 59–66. Lines 69 and 70 connect to the database. Lines 72–74 construct the SQL statement for the insert operation, and line 76 executes the SQL statement with method **do**. After the insert operation, an HTML page is sent to the user to confirm the data that was inserted in the database.

The program of Fig. 15.25 allows users to insert their information in the database. Figure 15.26 summarizes the information in the database. The program generates a Web page that tells us the total number of registered users, the average number of hours the user uses the product, the average rating the user gives it, the percentage of users from each continent and the percentage that use each operating system.

Lines 11 and 12 connect to the database. Lines 14 and 15 prepare a statement to retrieve the columns from which we are going to be generating statistics. Line 16 executes this SQL statement, and line 18 extracts the results using method **fetchall_arrayref**.

The total number of respondents is the total number of rows returned, which is also the size of the array in **$results**. The loop on lines 24–29 totals the hours per day and the ratings of the product. Hashes are used to count the total number of people from each continent and the total number of people using each operating system. Once we have these totals, we can get the averages by simply dividing by the total responses (lines 31 and 32).

```perl
1   #!/usr/bin/perl
2   # Fig. 15.26: fig15_26.pl
3   # Makes a webpage of statistics from the database.
4
5   use warnings;
6   use strict;
7   use DBI;
8   use DBD::mysql;
9   use CGI qw( :standard );
10
11  my $dbh = DBI->connect( "DBI:mysql:USERDB", "root", "",
12                                  { RaiseError => 1 } );
13
14  my $sth = $dbh->prepare( "SELECT Continent, OpSys, Hours, Rating
15                              FROM Users" );
16  $sth->execute();
17
18  my $results = $sth->fetchall_arrayref();
19
20  my $total = scalar( @$results );
21
22  my ( $rating, $hours, %lands, %op );
23
24  foreach my $row ( @$results ) {
25     $lands{ $row->[ 0 ] }++;
26     $op{ $row->[ 1 ] }++;
27     $hours += $row->[ 2 ];
28     $rating += $row->[ 3 ];
29  }
30
31  $hours /= $total;
32  $rating /= $total;
33
34  print header, start_html( "User Stats" ),
35      h1( "User Statistics" );
36
37  printf "You have a total of %d users spending an average of %.2f
38          hours using your product. They rate it an average of
39          %.2f out 5.", $total, $hours, $rating;
40
41  my $landrows = Tr( th( { width => "100" }, "Continent" ),
42                     th( { width => "50" }, "Total Users" ),
43                     th( "Percent Of Users" ) );
44
45  foreach ( sort  { $lands{ $b } <=> $lands{ $a } } keys( %lands ) ) {
46     my $percent = int( $lands{ $_ } * 100 / $total );
47     $landrows .= Tr( td( $_ ), td( $lands{ $_ } ),
48                      td(  table( { -width => "100%" },
49                           Tr( td( { -width => "$percent%",
50                                     -bgcolor => "#0000FF" }, br ),
51                               td( br ) ) )
52                           ) );
53  }
```

Fig. 15.26   Generating statistics from a database (part 1 of 3).

```
54
55   print h3( { -align => "center" }, "Users by Continent" ),
56        table( { -border => 1, -width => "100%" }, $landrows );
57
58   my $oprows = Tr( th( { width => "100" }, "Operating System" ),
59                    th( { width => "50" }, "Total Users" ),
60                    th( "Percent Of Users" ) );
61
62   foreach ( sort { $op{ $b } <=> $op{ $a } } keys( %op ) ) {
63      my $percent = int( $op{ $_ } * 100 / $total );
64      $oprows .= Tr( td( $_ ), td( $op{ $_ } ),
65                     td(   table( { -width => "100%" },
66                        Tr( td( { -width => "$percent%",
67                                  -bgcolor => "#0000FF" }, br ),
68                           td( br )
69                           ) ) ) );
70   }
71
72   print h3( { -align => "center" }, "Operating System statistics" ),
73        table( { -border => 1, -width => "100%" }, $oprows );
74
75   $dbh->disconnect();
```

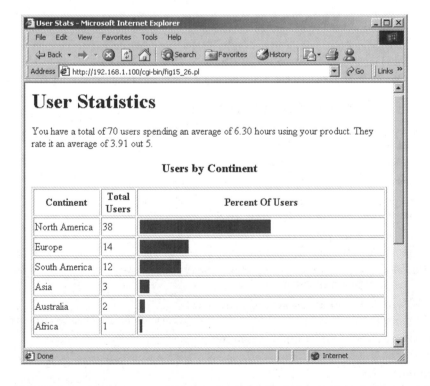

Fig. 15.26 Generating statistics from a database (part 2 of 3).

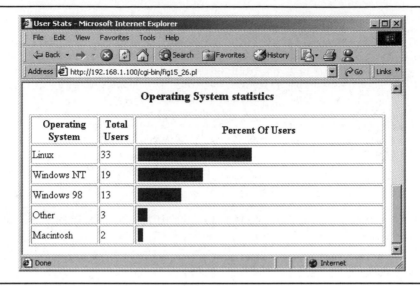

Fig. 15.26 Generating statistics from a database (part 3 of 3).

The program builds an HTML table containing the statistics for each continent by using a **foreach** loop on lines 45–53. Variable **$landrows** stores all the table rows. The percent of users in each continent is calculated by dividing the number of users by the total users and multiplying by 100 (line 46). We create a bar graph showing the percent of each country using a nested table for each continent (lines 48–51). This row has two cells, one of which is colored and one not. The width of the colored cell is based on the percentage of total users that are from that country. Lines 62–70 create the same table for the operating system statistics.

15.11 Internet and World Wide Web Resources

perl.about.com/compute/perl/library/weekly/aa120699a.htm
This site provides an introduction to DBI.

www.inlink.com/~perlguy/sql
This site provides an introduction to SQL databases and Perl.

www.extropia.com/tutorials/sql/dbi%5Fapi.html
This tutorial overviews the methods of the Perl DBI.

www.perl.com/pub/1999/10/DBI.html
This site provides a brief overview of DBI.

www-ee.swan.ac.uk/%7eeechris/Perl:DBI/DBI.html
This site covers all aspects of DBI.

www.cciw.com/content/relationaldb.html
This site provides an overview of relational databases and contains links to other database resources.

perl.about.com/compute/perl/msub68.htm
About.com's list of SQL tutorials.

www.mysql.com
This the MySQL main page. It contains MySQL resources, as well as the latest developments in MySQL. Linux/UNIX users can download MySQL from this site.

SUMMARY

- A database is an integrated collection of data.

- There are many different strategies for the organization of data to facilitate easy access and manipulation of the data.

- A database management system (DBMS) provides mechanisms for storing and organizing data in a manner consistent with the database's format. Database management systems allow for the access and storage of data without worrying about the internal representation of the database.

- The most popular database systems in use today are relational databases.

- A language called Structured Query Language (SQL—pronounced "sequel") is almost universally used with relational database systems to make queries (i.e., to request information that satisfies given criteria) and manipulate data. Some popular enterprise-level relational database systems include Microsoft SQL Server, Oracle, Sybase, DB2, Informix and MySQL.

- Open Database Connectivity (ODBC) is a technology developed by Microsoft to allow generic access to disparate database systems on the Windows platform (and some UNIX platforms).

- The most popular interface used by Perl programmers to connect to databases is the Perl Database Interfac (DBI)—a database-independent interface.

- A distributed application is a program composed of several components that reside on multiple computers connected by a network.

- The relational database model is a logical representation of data that allows data relationships to be considered without concerning oneself with the actual physical structure of the data.

- A relational database is composed of tables.

- Any particular row of the table is called a record (or row).

- Primary key fields in a table cannot contain duplicate values.

- Each table column represents a field (or column, or attribute). Records are normally unique (by primary key) within a table, but particular field values may be duplicated between records.

- The primary key can be composed of more than one column (or field) in the database.

- Different users of a database are often interested in different data and different relationships among those data. Some users want only certain subsets of the table columns. To obtain table subsets, we use SQL statements to specify the data to select from the table. SQL provides a complete set of commands that enable programmers to define complex queries which select data from a table. The results of a query are commonly called result sets (or record sets).

- Typically, databases contain multiple tables.

- A typical SQL query selects information from one or more tables in a database. Such selections are performed by **SELECT** queries.

- The simplest form of a **SELECT** query is

      SELECT *Fields* **FROM** *TableName*

- If we want to select all the fields in the database, the asterisk (*****) indicates that all rows and columns (fields) from *TableName* should be selected.

- To select specific fields from a table, list the field names separated by commas.

- Specifying the actual field names to select from a table (or several tables) guarantees that the fields are always returned in the specified order, even if the actual order of the fields in the database table(s) changes.

- In most cases, it is necessary to locate records in a database that satisfy certain selection criteria. Only records that match the selection criteria are selected. SQL uses the optional **WHERE** clause in a **SELECT** query to specify the selection criteria for the query. The simplest form of a **SELECT** query with selection criteria is

> **SELECT** *fieldName1*, *fieldName2*, ... **FROM** *TableName* **WHERE** *criteria*

- Using selection criteria improves program performance by selecting a portion of the database that is normally smaller than the entire database. Working with a smaller portion of the data is easier and faster than working with the entire set of data stored in the database.

- The **WHERE** clause condition can contain the **<**, **>**, **<=**, **>=**, **=**, **<>** and **LIKE** operators.

- The **LIKE** operator is used for pattern matching with the wildcard characters asterisk (*****) and question mark (**?**).

- Pattern matching allows SQL to search for similar strings that "match a pattern." The **%** and **?** characters are used differently in SQL's pattern matching than in Perl's regular expression pattern matching. A percent (**%**) in the pattern indicates any number of (i.e., zero or more) characters in a row at the percent's location in the pattern (like the **.*** regular expression).

- Notice that the pattern string is surrounded by single-quote characters. The ***** in the **WHERE** clause's **Like** pattern indicates that any number of characters can appear after the letter **b** in the **LastName** field.

- A question mark (**?**) in the pattern string indicates a single character at that position in the pattern.

- A query can be specialized to allow any character in a range of characters in one position of the pattern string. A range of characters can be specified as follows:

> **[** *startValue*–*endValue* **]**

where *startValue* is the first character in the range and *endValue* is the last value in the range.

- SQL is case sensitive on some database systems. See your database system documentation to determine if SQL is case sensitive on your database system and to determine the syntax that should be used for SQL keywords (i.e., all uppercase letters, all lowercase letters or a mixture of upper case and lowercase letters).

- Not all database systems support the **LIKE** operator, so be sure to read your database system's documentation carefully. Some databases use other keywords, such as **MATCHES** or **CONTAINS**, to provide the **LIKE** operator's functionality.

- By convention, SQL keywords should use all uppercase letters (e.g. **SELECT**) and field or table names should have the first letter of each word capitalized (e.g., **LastName**) on systems that are not case sensitive to make the statements more readable.

- The results of a query can be sorted into ascending or descending order by using the optional **OR-DER BY** clause. The simplest forms of an **ORDER BY** clause are

> **SELECT** *fieldNames* ... **FROM** *TableName* **ORDER BY** *fieldName* **ASC**
> **SELECT** *fieldNames* ... **FROM** *TableName* **ORDER BY** *fieldName* **DESC**

where **ASC** specifies ascending order, **DESC** specifies descending order and *fieldName* represents the field (the column of the table) that is used for sorting purposes.

- Note that the default sorting order is ascending, so **ASC** is optional.

- Multiple fields can be used for ordering purposes with an **ORDER BY** clause of the form

> **ORDER BY** *field1 SortingOrder*, *field2 SortingOrder*, ...

where *SortingOrder* is either **ASC** or **DESC**. Note that the *SortingOrder* does not have to be identical for each field.

- The **WHERE** and **ORDER BY** clauses can be combined in one query.

- Spread long SQL statements over multiple lines, using indentation to maximize readability.
- Often it is necessary to insert data into a table (e.g., add a new record). This is accomplished using an **INSERT INTO** operation. The simplest form for an **INSERT INTO** statement is

    > **INSERT INTO** *TableName* **(** *fieldName1, fieldName2, ..., fieldNameN* **)**
    >   **VALUES** **(** *value1, value2, ..., valueN* **)**

  The list of field names is followed by the *SQL keyword* **VALUES** and a comma-separated list of values in parentheses. The values specified in an **INSERT INTO** operation should match the field names specified after the table name in order and type.
- The single quote (**'**) character is used as a delimiter for strings being inserted in the database.
- Often it is necessary to modify data in a table (e.g., update a record). This is accomplished using an **UPDATE** operation. The simplest form for an **UPDATE** statement is

    > **UPDATE** *TableName*
    >   **SET** *fieldName1* **=** *value1,* *fieldName2* **=** *value2, ..., fieldNameN* **=** *valueN*
    >   **WHERE** *criteria*

- Sometimes you want to remove a record from the table entirely. The **DELETE** operation provides this functionality. The **DELETE** function has the following form:

    > **DELETE FROM** *TableName*
    >   **WHERE** *criteria*

- If possible, use the primary key field to specify which record to update or delete.
- A distributed application is a program that divides the work needed to be done over multiple computer systems.
- A software program—called a driver—allows programmatic access to a database.
- Each DBMS requires its own driver.
- DBI uses an object-oriented interface. The DBI objects are known as handles. There are three different types—driver handles, database handles and statement handles.
- Driver handles encapsulate the driver for the database and are rarely used in a script.
- Database handles encapsulate a specific connection to a database. They can be used to execute SQL statements on this database.
- Statement handles encapsulate specific SQL statements and the results returned from them.
- Any number of database handles can be created with a driver handle and any number of statement handles can be created with a database handle.
- DBI functions do not use the standard predefined Perl error variables. Generally, when DBI function calls fail, they return **undef** and store the error string in **$DBI::errstr**. The error number is stored in **$DBI::err**. Each handle also stores its error information, which can be accessed through method calls **errstr** and **err** on the handle.
- A data source name tells the **connect** function where to find the database and is constructed in the following format:

    > *interface name***:***database driver***:***data source name*

- The **connect** function returns a database handle.
- A statement handle is created by calling the database handle's **prepare** method. This method equips the database driver for a statement that can be executed multiple times later. The SQL query is passed to the **prepare** statement as a string.

- After a statement has been prepared, and before the results can be processed, the statement must be executed. This is done by calling the statement handle's **execute** method. The result set generated by the query is stored with the statement handle.

- Each result set row is retrieved from the object and placed into an array by calling method **fetchrow_array**, which returns *false* after all the rows have been read.

- When finished with a database connection, close it using the **disconnect** method. If you do not need to fetch all the data from a statement handle, you should call the **finish** method to indicate when you are done. Because we did fetch all the data, this was not necessary, as it was done for us.

- Perl will close statement and database handles for you when they go out of scope. It is however best to close them explicitly by employing the **finish** or **disconnect** method when you are done using them.

- We can have the error checking done for us by passing a hash reference to **connect** as the fourth argument in which **RaiseError** is set to **1**. With **RaiseError** set, the program will **die** with an error message if an error occurs. To simply print a warning, set **PrintError** instead. This calls **warn** if something goes wrong.

- Deleting from and updating a database is similar to inserting. We just use the **do** method with different SQL statements as the argument.

- DBI provides utility functions allowing you to check on the support for databases on the system running your script. These are the **available_drivers** function and the **data_sources** function. The **available_drivers** function returns the available database drivers (DBDs) that have been installed on the system, and the **data_sources** returns the databases which have been registered with the system.

- Using MySQL with DBI requires the **DBD::mysql** database driver.

- The SQL statement for creating a table is

> **CREATE TABLE** *TableName* **(**
> *ColumnName type modifiers***,** *ColumnName type modifiers***,** **...** **)**

- The **VARCHAR** type specifies that fields are variable-length text. We specify the maximum length they will be with the number in parentheses.

- The **ENUM** type allows us to specify a list of options of what that column can hold. The choices are specified in the comma-separated fields after the **ENUM** keyword.

- Type **INT** restricts the field values to integers.

TERMINOLOGY

$DBI::err
< SQL operator
<= SQL operator
<> SQL operator
= SQL operator
> SQL operator
>= SQL operator
ASC SQL keyword
ascending order
asterisk (*****)
attribute
available_drivers function
column

Common Gateway Interface (CGI)
connect function
CREATE TABLE SQL command
data attribute
data source name (DSN)
data_sources function
database
database handles
Database Independent Interface (DBI)
database management systems (DBMS)
database table
DB2
DELETE SQL command

DESC SQL keyword

descending order

disconnect function

distributed application

do function

driver

driver handles

ENUM SQL field type

execute function

fetchall_arrayref field type

fetchall_arrayref function

fetchrow_array function

fetchrow_arrayref function

fetchrow_hashref function

field

field in a database

finish function

FROM SQL command

handles

Informix

INSERT INTO SQL command

INT field type

interface

LIKE SQL keyword

Microsoft SQL Server

MySQL

ODBC (Open Database Connectivity)

Oracle DBMS

ORDER BY SQL clause

ordered

param function

pattern string

prepare function

primary key

query

querying a database

RaiseError

range of characters in a database query

record

record set

relational database

relational database model

relational database structure

relational database table

result sets

row

select

SELECT SQL command

selecting data from a table

selection criteria

SET SQL command

sorting

sorting order

SQL case sensitive

SQL query keywords

SQL statement

square brackets ([ ])

statement handle

Structured Query Language (SQL)

Structured Query Language (SQL) commands

Sybase

UPDATE SQL command

utility functions for DBI

VALUES SQL keyword

VARCHAR SQL field type

WHERE clause

WHERE clause in a SELECT query

WHERE clause's Like pattern

WHERE SQL clause

WHERE SQL command

wildcard characters

SELF-REVIEW EXERCISES

15.1 Fill in the blanks in each of the following:

   a) The most popular database query language is _____.

   b) A table in a database consists of _____ and _____.

   c) The _____ uniquely identifies each record in a table.

   d) SQL keyword _____ is followed by the selection criteria that specify the records to select in a query.

   e) SQL keyword _____ specifies the order in which records are sorted in a query.

   f) The DBD used in the first four programs is _____.

   g) A _____ is an integrated collection of data that is centrally controlled.

   h) A _____ provides the connection to the database from a Perl script.

   i) Method _____ is used when a statement is not prepared.

15.2   State whether the following are *true* or *false*. If *false*, explain why.
    a)   A data source name is required to connect to a database.
    b)   **DELETE** is not a valid SQL keyword.
    c)   Only one statement handle is allowed per Perl program.
    d)   Microsoft Access is an example of a DBMS that uses ODBC.
    e)   A field name in a query must be in parentheses if it contains a space.
    f)   ODBC stands for Open Database Connectivity.
    g)   DBI is database dependent.
    h)   Tables in a database must have a primary key.
    i)   Statements are never executed when a prepare method is called.

ANSWERS TO SELF-REVIEW EXERCISES

15.1   a) SQL. b) rows, columns. c) primary key. d) **WHERE**. e) **ORDER BY**. f) ODBC. g) database. h) database handle. i) **do**.

15.2   a) True.
    b)   False. **DELETE** is a valid SQL keyword—it is the function used to delete records.
    c)   False. Any number of statement handles can be created with a database handle.
    d)   True.
    e)   False. If a field name contains spaces, it must be enclosed in square brackets (**[]**) in the query.
    f)   True.
    g)   False. DBI is database independent.
    h)   False. Tables in a database normally have primary keys.
    i)   True.

EXERCISES

15.3   Write SQL queries for the **Employee.mdb** database (discussed in Section 15.3) that perform each of the following tasks:
    a)   Select all employees from the **Employee** table.
    b)   Select all social security numbers from the **Employee** table.
    c)   Select all employees who were born before 1970. Order the information alphabetically by last name.

15.4   Write SQL statements for the **Employee.mdb** database (discussed in Section 15.3) that perform the following task:
    a)   Add a new employee to the **Employee** table.
    b)   Sort all employees according to last name in ascending order.
    c)   Select all employees whose Social Security numbers start with a 9.

15.5   Modify the program of Fig. 15.21 to allow a user to delete by using a last name instead of an **EmployeeID**.

15.6   Using the **Employee.mdb** database, write a program that checks the first and last name to ensure that it is unique. If this is not unique, the user should be prompted to try a different name.

15.7   Create a MySQL database that will be used to manage information about students in a university. Possible fields might include date of birth, major, current grade point average, credits earned, etc. Write a Perl program to manage the database. Include the following functionality: sort all students according to GPA (descending), create a display of all students in one particular major and remove all records from the database where the student has the required amount of credits to graduate.

16

Session Tracking and Cookies

Objectives

- To understand the need for gathering data over the Internet and storing them.
- To be able to use the browser to store information—with either query strings or hidden fields.
- To be able to read and write client data using cookies stored on the client computer.
- To understand how to construct programs that interact with server-side files and/or databases.
- To be able to implement a Web shopping cart.

Me want cookie!
The Cookie Monster, Sesame Street

If any man will draw up his case, and put his name at the foot of the first page, I will give him an immediate reply. Where he compels me to turn over the sheet, he must wait my leisure.
Lord Sandwich

A client is to me a mere unit, a factor in a problem.
Sir Arthur Conan Doyle

Rule One: Our client is always right.
Rule Two: If you think our client is wrong, see Rule One.
Anonymous

Outline

16.1 Introduction

A limitation of HTTP is that after the server sends its reply (normally in the form of a Web page), the connection with the client is closed. As a result, during a request/response interaction between the client and the server, the client can send data to the server only once (the request), and the client can receive information from the server only once for each request (the response). To enable multiple interactions, several Web documents must be linked, and each Web document must call the next one in the chain. Because many Web applications are implemented as a series of calls between documents, the ability to store data between calls (also called *maintaining state information*) becomes important. This chapter discusses how *session tracking* and *cookies* are used to maintain state information.

16.2 Uses of Storing Data

Many of today's most popular Web applications are *online stores*. Such stores require the applications to maintain user information, such as the current user and that user's *shopping cart*. There are many other Web-based applications that require similar information to be maintained as well. The growth of *electronic commerce* (*e-commerce*) and Web sites that are customized to each user has led to the need for maintaining user-specific information.

There are other benefits of being able to store information. For example, keeping track of user data can make a Web site more interactive. Say you have a Web page devoted solely to letting the user customize a Web site to his or her specifications; many sites allow users to add and remove features and even customize the colors and graphics shown on the site. Although users enjoy such features they do not want to customize a site each time they return to it. Thus, the Web site must store each user's preferences. Then, when the user returns, the site can appear as the user specified previously.

16.3 Methods of Storing Data

In an HTTP transaction, there are three locations in which state information can be stored: the *client*, the *server* and the *browser*. The *client* refers to the client's computer. When you load a Web site, that Web site has the ability to store small amounts of text, called *cookies*, on your computer. When you load the Web site again, the site's cookies are sent back to the server. The server can use this information to recognize users from one visit to the next. A potential problem with this approach is that the user has the option of disabling the cookies feature. Browsers such as Microsoft Internet Explorer and Netscape Communicator allow users to disable cookies.

Software Engineering Observation 16.1

User information can be stored in cookies only if users have the cookies feature enabled in their Web browsers.

The *server* refers to the server computer and software. CGI programs have the ability to create, edit and save files on the server computer. If such files are given unique names, then, at a later time, a CGI program can use the files that correspond to particular users. This way, a user's information can be stored from one visit to the next. While this method is probably the best way to maintain state, it may require large amounts of storage space on the server computer and may involve extra overhead to store and retrieve unique files.

Performance Tip 16.1

Maintaining individual files with information for each user consumes storage space and processor time to manipulate the files on the server computer.

The *browser* refers to the browsing application. The browser has the ability to store and pass data from one page to another.

Software Engineering Observation 16.2

Programs can mimic a browser's ability to maintain data between pages. This method of preserving state is not robust and can introduce security holes into a program. For this reason, this method is used only when the data is not vital and security issues are unimportant.

The next four sections describe four different methods for storing data, two that use the browsing application's built-in features, one that deals with client-side cookies and one that deals with unique server-side files.

16.4 Query Strings

When a client makes a request to a server, a *query string* can be attached to the request URL. This attachment is actually what occurs when a **get** request is performed. In earlier chapters, we used a question mark appended to the end of a URL, followed by the information we wished to send, in key–value pairs, to specify the query string. Figure 16.1 presents an HTML document and Fig. 16.2 presents a simple Perl program that uses query strings to maintain state information.

```
1   <!DOCTYPE HTML PUBLIC "-//W3C//DTD HTML 4.0 Transitional//EN">
2   <!-- Fig. 16.1: fig16_01.html -->
3   <!-- Web page offering different color options. -->
4
5   <html>
6      <head>
7         <title>Preserving State Through Query Strings</title>
8      </head>
```

Fig. 16.1　HTML document that presents style choices to the user (part 1 of 3).

```
 9
10    <body>
11        <p>Which Style do you Prefer?</p>
12        <table bgcolor = "#ffffff">
13            <tbody>
14                <tr>
15                    <td>
16                        <font color = "#000000">Normal Style</font>
17                    </td>
18                    <td>
19                        <a href = "/cgi-bin/fig16_02.pl?type=normal">
20                        <font color = "#0000ff">Click here</font>
21                    </td>
22                </tr>
23            </tbody>
24        </table>
25        <br/>
26        <table bgcolor = "#dddddd">
27            <tbody>
28                <tr>
29                    <td>
30                        <font color = "#000000">Dark Style</font>
31                    </td>
32                    <td>
33                        <a href = "/cgi-bin/fig16_02.pl?type=dark">
34                        <font color = "#002060">Click here</font>
35                    </td>
36                </tr>
37            </tbody>
38        </table>
39        <br/>
40        <table bgcolor = "#5555ff">
41            <tbody>
42                <tr>
43                    <td>
44                        <font color = "#ee3333">Bright Style</font>
45                    </td>
46                    <td>
47                        <a href = "/cgi-bin/fig16_02.pl?type=bright">
48                        <font color = "#ffff00">Click here</font>
49                    </td>
50                </tr>
51            </tbody>
52        </table>
53        <br/>
54        <table bgcolor = "#ffffc0">
55            <tbody>
56                <tr>
57                    <td>
58                        <font color = "#ee82ee">Another Style</font>
59                    </td>
60                    <td>
61                        <a href = "/cgi-bin/fig16_02.pl?type=another">
```

Fig. 16.1   HTML document that presents style choices to the user (part 2 of 3).

```
62                      <font color = "#3cb371">Click here</font>
63                  </td>
64              </tr>
65          </tbody>
66      </table>
67      <br/>
68  </body>
69 </html>
```

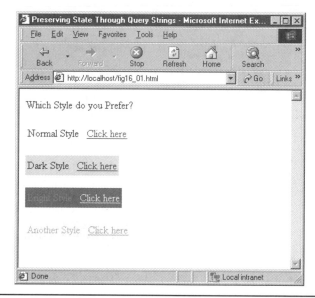

Fig. 16.1　HTML document that presents style choices to the user (part 3 of 3).

```
1  #!/usr/bin/perl
2  # Fig. 16.2: fig16_02.pl
3  # Create a page with a specified style.
4
5  use strict;
6  use warnings;
7  use CGI qw( :standard );
8
9  print( header() );
10
11 my $type = param( "type" );
12
13 my %colors = ( "normal" => [ "#ffffff", "#000000", "#0000ff" ],
14     "dark" => [ "#dddddd", "#000000", "#002060" ],
15     "bright" => [ "#5555ff", "#ee3333", "#ffff00" ],
16     "another" => [ "#ffffc0", "#ee82ee", "#3cb371" ] );
17
18 my $style = $colors{ $type };
19 my @style = @{ $style };
```

Fig. 16.2　Perl CGI program that creates a Web page that uses the style selected by the user in Fig. 16.1 (part 1 of 2).

```
20
21   print <<HTML;
22   <html><head><title>Your Style Page</title></head>
23   <body bgcolor = "$style[ 0 ]" text = "$style[ 1 ]"
24      link = "$style[ 2 ]" vlink = "$style[ 2 ]">
25   <p>This is your style page.</p>
26   <p>You chose the colors.</p>
27   <a href = "/fig16_01.html">Choose a new style.</a>
28   </body></html>
29   HTML
```

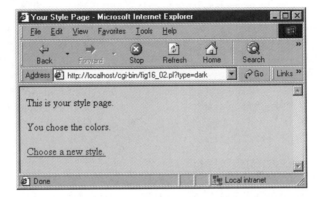

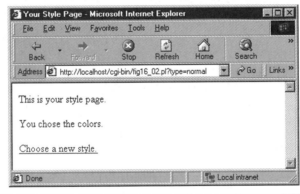

Fig. 16.2   Perl CGI program that creates a Web page that uses the style selected by the user in Fig. 16.1 (part 2 of 2).

Figure 16.1 outputs an HTML page that lists the four styles from which the user can select. The page displays a table that presents a preview of each style. Each style consists of a background color, a text color and a link color. The tables also provide links to the Perl program (**fig16_02.pl**) that outputs a page in the preferred style, such as in line 19:

```
<a href = "/cgi-bin/fig16_02.pl?type=normal">
```

This line is not a simple hyperlink—it includes the preferred style as a query string. Notice that the link refers to our **fig16_02.pl** program. The query string begins with a question mark, followed by **type=** and one of the styles (**normal**, in this case). This query-string format is identical to that used by a form when the form is submitted as part of a **get** request.

Now let us look at the program in Fig. 16.2. The first thing the program does is use **CGI.pm**'s **param** method to retrieve the chosen style (line 11). Our query string was used to mimic a request from an HTML form, so we can use **CGI.pm**'s built-in form-handling subroutines to collect information from the query string. Next, the program creates a hash (lines 13–16) with each style as the key and a reference to an array of colors as the value. We use the style to look up the three colors listed for that style in the Web page stored in the hash—the list is stored in **@style**. The rest of this program uses a "here" document to output the Web page with the styles selected by the user. Lines 23 and 24 use our array to denote the proper colors for the page.

This simple use of query strings to pass information highlights an important security issue. Notice that the style argument we passed to the program in Fig. 16.2 appears as plain text in the URL in the browser window. Anyone who wants to change the style can do so just by altering the URL. This also means that someone could input a nonexistent style. This is one of the security holes that query strings introduce into a CGI program. In this example, there really is not a risk—it does not matter if someone can change our style manually or input an improper style. After all, we are specifying only colors. So, if someone specifies a nonexistent style, they simply receive a blank page, because an error occurs in the program. The point here is that the data can be seen by anyone; therefore, it is not secure. For more details on security issues, see Chapter 19.

Software Engineering Observation 16.3

Query strings should be used only when the information that appears in the query string is of little importance and is not required to be securely transmitted.

Another thing to notice about this program is that we pass the style we want by name, not by the colors associated with the style. We could have passed the three colors in the query string. Had we passed all three colors in the query string, the user could change the colors manually to anything they want. We do not want the user to have that level of flexibility. Again, for this simple example, it is not important to us to protect the style data; users could change the styles as much as they want and still not breach our server's security. In later programs, this ability to change the query string could prove to be more costly.

16.5 Hidden Fields

A second method of maintaining state information through the browser also creates HTML-form capabilities. This method passes data through *hidden fields* that can be a part of any form. Figure 16.3 uses hidden fields to keep track of data input by the user.

Lines 9–11 use **CGI.pm**'s **param** method to retrieve the form-field values that were passed to this program. When we run the program the first time, these statements return nothing. In subsequent executions of the program, the statements will obtain all the data that we posted from the form to the program. Lines 13 and 14 add the new data (sent through the **name** and **value** fields) to the old data, **$data**. The rest of the program outputs a form to enter data. Line 25 uses a hidden field to transfer all of the old data (**$data**) to the next execution of the program. Lines 30–34 format the information in **$data** so that it can be printed to the page in a readable style. Note that the field name can be overwritten; if the user entered **Food** and **Pasta** for the field's name and value, respectively, and then later entered **Food** and **Tacos** (as shown in the screen shots following the program), the earlier value would have been overwritten.

This method of maintaining state information has its own security hole, introduced by using **CGI.pm**'s **param** method. This method is the easiest way to collect data sent to a program with forms. However, the method does not distinguish between **post** data and **get** data; the hidden-field data could be sent to this script through query strings, and the program would not be able to recognize the difference. It is important to note that both the **get** and **post** methods of sending data to the server potentially are insecure.

There are means of determining what method was used for a form. With such a capability, we can ensure that the field values were sent using the **post** method for the form. However, **post**s are easy to mimic. There are just too many ways for a user to access and change this data. For this reason, the hidden-fields method is usually not good for passing important data. In this example, the data is again trivial, so the security issues are not significant.

```perl
1   #!/usr/bin/perl
2   # Fig. 16.3: fig16_03.pl
3   # Use hidden form fields to keep track of data.
4
5   use warnings;
6   use strict;
7   use CGI qw( :standard );
8
9   my $data = param( "HIDDEN" );
10  my $name = param( "NAME" );
11  my $value = param( "VALUE" );
12
13  $data .= "$name ";
14  $data .= "$value ";
15
16  print( header() );
17  print( start_html( -title => 'Using Hidden Fields' ) );
18
19  print <<Form;
20  <form method = "post" action = "fig16_03.pl">
21  <strong>Please enter the fields name: </strong>
22  <input type = "TEXT" name = "NAME"><br>
23  <strong>Please enter the fields value: </strong>
24  <input type = "TEXT" name = "VALUE"><br>
25  <input type = "HIDDEN" name = "HIDDEN" value = "$data">
26  <input type = "SUBMIT" value = "enter your data">
27  </form>
28  Form
29
30  my %values = split( ' ', $data );
31
32  foreach ( keys( %values ) ) {
33     print( p( "$_: $values{ $_ }" ) );
34  }
35
36  print( end_html() );
```

Fig. 16.3   Using hidden form fields to store state information (part 1 of 2).

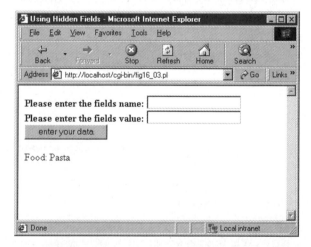

Fig. 16.3   Using hidden form fields to store state information (part 2 of 2).

16.6 Cookies

In the last two sections, we discussed two ways in which information may be passed between programs (or executions of the same program) through a browser. This section concentrates on storing state information on the client computer with *cookies*. Cookies are essentially small text files that a Web server sends to your browser, which then writes the cookie onto your computer. Many Web sites use cookies to track a user's progress through their site (as in a shopping-cart application) or to help customize the site to an individual user. Cookies do not break into your computer, nor do they erase your hard drive. However, they can be used to keep track of how often you visit a site or what you buy at a site. For this reason, cookies are considered to be a security and privacy concern. Popular Web browsers provide support for cookies. These browsers also allow users who are concerned about their privacy and security to disable this support. Most major Web sites use cookies. As a programmer, you should be aware of the possibility that cookies will be disabled by your clients. Figure 16.4, Fig. 16.5 and Fig. 16.6 use cookies to store and manipulate information about a user.

```
1   <!DOCTYPE HTML PUBLIC "-//W3C//DTD HTML 4.0 Transitional//EN">
2   <!-- Fig. 16.4: fig16_04.html -->
3   <!-- Web page to read in some data from the user. -->
4
5   <html>
6      <head>
7         <title>Writing a cookie to the client computer</title>
8      </head>
9
10     <body>
11        <font face = "arial,sans-serif" size = 2>
12
13           <font size = +2>
14              <b>Click Write Cookie to save your cookie data.</b>
15           </font><br>
16
17           <form method = "post" action = "/cgi-bin/fig16_05.pl">
18              <strong>Name:</strong><br>
19              <input type = "text" name = "name"><br>
20
21              <strong>Height:</strong><br>
22              <input type = "text" name = "height"><br>
23
24              <strong>Favorite Color</strong><br>
25              <input type = "text" name = "color"><br>
26
27              <input type = "SUBMIT" value = "Write Cookie">
28           </form>
29
30     </body>
31  </html>
```

Fig. 16.4   HTML document that contains a form to post data to the server (part 1 of 2).

Fig. 16.4   HTML document that contains a form to post data to the server (part 2 of 2).

```perl
1   #!/usr/bin/perl
2   # Fig. 16.5: fig16_05.pl
3   # Program to write a cookie to a client's machine.
4
5   use strict;
6   use warnings;
7   use CGI qw( :standard );
8
9   my $name = param( "name" );
10  my $height = param( "height" );
11  my $color = param( "color" );
12
13  my $expires = "Monday, 11-JUN-01 16:00:00 GMT";
14
15  print( "Set-Cookie: Name=$name; expires=$expires; path=\n" );
16  print( "Set-Cookie: Height=$height; expires=$expires; path=\n" );
17  print( "Set-Cookie: Color=$color; expires=$expires; path=\n" );
18
19  print( header(), start_html( "Cookie Saved" ) );
20
21  print <<End_Data;
22  <font face = "arial,sans-serif" size = 3>
23  The cookie has been set with the following data:<br><br>
24
25  <font color = blue>Name:</font> $name<br>
26  <font color = blue>Height:</font> $height<br>
27  <font color = blue>Favorite Color:</font>
28     <font color = $color> $color<br></font><br>
29
```

Fig. 16.5   Writing cookies (part 1 of 2).

```
30    Click <a href = "fig16_06.pl">here</a>
31       to read saved cookie.
32    End_Data
33
34    print( end_html() );
```

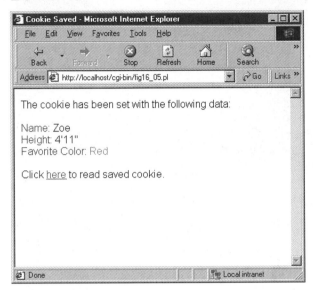

Fig. 16.5   Writing cookies (part 2 of 2).

```
1     #!/usr/bin/perl
2     # Fig. 16.6: fig16_06.pl
3     # Program to read cookies from the client's computer.
4
5     use strict;
6     use warnings;
7     use CGI qw( :standard );
8
9     print( header(), start_html( "Read cookies" ) );
10    print( "<font face = \"arial,sans-serif\" size = 3>" );
11    print( strong( "The following data is saved in a cookie " ) );
12    print( strong( "on your computer." ) );
13    print( br(), br() );
14
15    my %cookies = readCookies();
16
17    print( "<table border = \"5\" cellspacing = \"0\" " );
18    print( "cellpadding = \"10\">" );
19
20    foreach ( "Name", "Height", "Color" ) {
21       print( "<tr>" );
22       print( "   <td bgcolor = #aaaaff>$_</td>" );
23       print( "   <td bgcolor = #aaaaaa>$cookies{ $_ }</td>" );
```

Fig. 16.6   Program to read cookies from the client's computer (part 1 of 2).

```
24        print( "</tr>" );
25     }
26
27     print( "</table>" );
28     print( end_html() );
29
30     sub readCookies
31     {
32        my @cookieArray = split( "; ", $ENV{ 'HTTP_COOKIE' } );
33        my $cookieName;
34        my $cookieValue;
35        my %cookieHash;
36
37        foreach ( @cookieArray ) {
38           ( $cookieName, $cookieValue ) = split( "=", $_ );
39           $cookieHash{ $cookieName } = $cookieValue;
40        }
41
42        return %cookieHash;
43     }
```

Fig. 16.6   Program to read cookies from the client's computer (part 2 of 2).

Figure 16.4 creates an HTML page with a form in which values are to be input. The form posts its information to **fig16_05.pl** (Fig. 16.5). This program uses the **param** method from **CGI.pm** to obtain the data that was sent to it. Line 13 declares and initializes variable **$expires** to contain the expiration date of the cookie. This value can be a string, like the one in this example, or it can be a relative value. For instance, **+30d** sets the cookie to exist for 30 days. The browser deletes a cookie after it expires.

After obtaining the data from the form, the program creates cookies (lines 15–17). In this example, we create cookies by adding a line of text for each cookie containing the cookie's information. The lines must be output before the header is written to the client.

The line of text begins with **Set-Cookie:**, indicating that the browser should store the incoming data in a cookie. We set three attributes for each cookie: a name–value pair containing the data to be stored, a name–value pair containing the expiration data and a name–value pair containing the URL path of the server domain for which the cookie is valid. For this example, **path** is not set to any value, making the cookie readable from any server in the domain of the server that originally wrote the cookie. Lines 19–34 send a Web page indicating that the cookie has been written to the client. Each client Web browser has its own way to store the cookie information. For example, Internet Explorer stores cookies as text files in the **Temporary Internet Files** directory on the client's machine.

Figure 16.6 reads the cookie written in Fig. 16.5 and displays the information in a table. When a request is made from the client Web browser, the Web browser locates any cookies previously written by the server to which the request is being made. These cookies are sent by the browser as part of the request. On the server, the environment variable **'HTTP_COOKIE'** stores the client's cookies sent as part of the request. Line 15 calls function **readCookies** (lines 30–43) and places the returned value into hash **%cookies**. The user-defined function **readCookies** splits the environment variable containing the cookie's information into separate cookies (using **split**) and stores these cookies as distinct elements in **@cookieArray** (line 32). For each cookie in **@cookieArray**, we call **split** again to obtain the original name–value pair, which in turn is stored in the hash **%cookieHash** in line 39. Then the hash is returned to line 15. The **foreach** structure in line 20 then iterates through the hash with the names of the keys, printing the key and value for the data from the cookie in an HTML table.

While cookies are not as troublesome as some people would have you believe, they, too, present a security risk. If an unauthorized person logs onto a person's computer, he or she can look at the local disk and view the cookies stored on that computer.

16.7 Server-side Files

The final mechanism by which to maintain state information is to create *server-side files*. This mechanism is probably the most secure method by which to maintain vital information. In this mechanism, only someone with access and the ability to change files on the server can alter the files. The only possible security hole is that you somehow need to link anonymous clients to their respective files. Fortunately, there are many ways to do this. Figure 16.7 and Fig. 16.8 ask a user for contact information and then store it on the server. The file that is subsequently created is shown in Fig. 16.9.

```
1    <!DOCTYPE HTML PUBLIC "-//W3C//DTD HTML 4.0 Transitional//EN">
2    <!-- Fig. 16.7: fig16_07.html -->
3    <!-- Web page to read in some data that will be -->
4    <!-- entered into a file. -->
5
6    <html>
7       <head>
8          <title>
9             Please enter your contact information.
10         </title>
11      </head>
```

Fig. 16.7   HTML document to read a user's contact information (part 1 of 2).

```
12
13      <body>
14          <p>
15             Please enter your information in the form below:
16          </p>
17          <form method = "post" action = "/cgi-bin/fig16_08.pl">
18              <strong>
19                  <p>
20                      First name:
21                      <input type = "text" name = "first" size = "10">
22                      Last name:
23                      <input type = "text" name = "last" size = "15">
24                  </p>
25                  <p>
26                      Address:
27                      <input type = "text" name = "address" size = "25">
28                      <br/>
29                      Town:
30                      <input type = "text" name = "town" size = "10">
31                      State:
32                      <input type = "text" name = "state" size = "2">
33                      <br/>
34                      Zip Code:
35                      <input type = "text" name = "zip" size = "5">
36                      Country:
37                      <input type = "text" name = "country" size = "10">
38                  </p>
39                  <p>
40                      E-mail Address:
41                      <input type = "text" name = "email">
42                  </p>
43                  <input type = "submit" value = "Enter">
44                  <input type = "reset" value = "Clear">
45          </form>
46      </body>
47  </html>
```

Fig. 16.7   HTML document to read a user's contact information (part 2 of 2).

```perl
1   #!/usr/bin/perl
2   # Fig. 16.8: fig16_08.pl
3   # Program to enter user's contact information into a
4   # server-side file.
5
6   use strict;
7   use warnings;
8   use CGI qw( :standard );
9   use Fcntl;
10
11  my $first = param( 'first' );
12  my $last = param( 'last' );
13  my $address = param( 'address' );
14  my $town = param( 'town' );
15  my $state = param( 'state' );
16  my $zip = param( 'zip' );
17  my $country = param( 'country' );
18  my $email = param( 'email' );
19
20  my $name;
21  my @characters = ( 'a' .. 'z', '0' .. '9' );
22
23  do {
24
25     for ( 1 .. 10 ) {
26        my $number = rand( 36 );
27        $name .= $characters[ $number ];
28     }
29  }
30  until sysopen( FILE, "$name.txt", O_WRONLY | O_EXCL | O_CREAT );
31
32  print( FILE "$first $last\n" );
33  print( FILE "$address\n" );
34  print( FILE "$town $state $country $zip\n" );
35  print( FILE "$email\n" );
36  close( FILE ) or die( "Cannot close file: $!" );
37
38  print( header() );
39  print( start_html( -title => 'Contact Information is entered' ) );
40  print( strong(  "The following information has been stored:\n" ) );
41
42  print( "<table><tbody>" );
43
44  print( Tr( td( "First Name: " ), td( $first ) ) );
45  print( Tr( td( "Last Name: " ), td( $last ) ) );
46  print( Tr( td( "Address: " ), td( $address ) ) );
47  print( Tr( td( "Town: " ), td( $town ) ) );
48  print( Tr( td( "State: " ), td( $state ) ) );
49  print( Tr( td( "Zip Code: " ), td( $zip ) ) );
50  print( Tr( td( "Country: " ), td( $country ) ) );
51  print( Tr( td( "E-mail: " ), td( $email ) ) );
52
53  print( "</tbody></table>" );
```

Fig. 16.8   Creating server-side files to store user data (part 1 of 2).

```
54
55   print( p( "Your ID number is $name" ) );
56
57   print( end_html() );
```

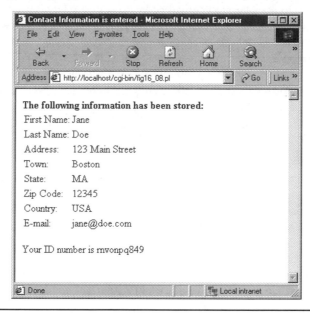

Fig. 16.8   Creating server-side files to store user data (part 2 of 2).

```
Jane Doe
123 Main Street
Boston MA USA 12345
jane@doe.com
```

Fig. 16.9   Contents of **rnvonpq849.txt**.

The HTML document in Fig. 16.7 posts the form data to the CGI program in Fig. 16.8. In the program, lines 11–18 read the parameters that were posted by the client. Lines 23–30 create a 10-character filename by randomly selecting one of the items in the **@characters** array and concatenating it with our filename. Once we have this filename, we use a **sysopen** with the flags **O_WRONLY**, **O_EXCL** and **O_CREAT**. This will open a file for writing, creating the file if it does not exist and failing if it does exist. The filename is created in a **do/until** repetition structure so the program can loop until it creates a filename that does not exist. This way, we will not overwrite anyone else's information. Lines 32–35 output our information to the file, which in this example is called **rnvonpq849.txt** (see Fig. 16.9 for the contents of the file). The rest of the program outputs an HTML document that confirms the user's information. Line 55 prints out the name of the file stored in the **$name** variable, so that the user can find his or her information again later.

There are a few important points that we left out of this program that make this script unusable in the real world. First, we do not perform any validity checking of the data before storing them in a file on the server. Normally, we would check for typos, bad data, incomplete data, etc. Second, we have a simple key to our files. If someone knew that all our ID numbers were randomly created 10-character strings, it would be relatively easy to access someone else's contact information and change it. One way to work around this problem is to send a password to the user at the email address provided. Not only would this method provide a reasonably safe way to send the user a password, but it also would be an indirect way of verifying that the email address is valid.

This script is not ready for use in a real server, but it does provide an example of the use of server-side files to store information. Once the files are stored on the server, users cannot change the files unless they are allowed to do so by the server administrator. Thus, these files are one of the safest ways to store user data. Note that many systems store user information in a password-protected database for higher levels of security.

16.8 Example: Shopping Cart

Many businesses now provide Web sites containing shopping-cart applications, which allow customers to buy items conveniently on the Web. The sites record what the consumer wants to purchase and provide an easy, understandable way to shop online. They do so by using an electronic shopping cart, just as people would use physical shopping carts in retail stores. Users can add or remove items from their shopping carts, and the sites will update the contents automatically. When users "check out," they pay for the items currently in their shopping carts. To see a real-world electronic shopping cart, we suggest going to the online bookstore **Amazon.com** (**www.amazon.com**).

The shopping cart implemented in this example (Fig. 16.10, Fig. 16.11, Fig. 16.12 and Fig. 16.13 provide the functionality of the shopping cart) allows users to purchase books from an online bookstore that sells five books (see Fig. 16.14). This example uses more security features than do our earlier examples, which makes the programs in the example more complex. This example uses four programs, two server-side files and cookies. Figure 16.10 shows the first of these programs, the login page.

```perl
1   #!/usr/bin/perl
2   # Fig. 16.10: fig16_10.pl
3   # Script to login to a Web page.
4
5   use strict;
6   use warnings;
7   use CGI qw( :standard );
8   use Digest::MD5;
9   use Digest::MD5 qw( md5_hex );
10
11  # parameters are read in from the previous Web page
12  my $password = param( "password" );
13  my $user = param( "user" );
14  my $new = param( "new" );
15
16  if ( param( "new" ) ) {
17      my @search1;
18
```

Fig. 16.10 Program that outputs a login page (part 1 of 5).

```perl
19      # Write nothing to the cookie ---
20      # Users just logging in will not have a cart
21      writeCookie();
22
23      # Encryption of password so that it is protected
24      my $encrypt;
25      my $digestObject = Digest::MD5->new();
26      $digestObject->add( "$password" );
27      $encrypt = $digestObject->digest();
28
29      print( header() );
30      print( start_html() );
31
32      open( LOG, "<log.txt" ) or die( "Cannot open: $!" );
33
34      while ( <LOG> ) {
35         @search1 = split( "\t" );
36
37         # If this username is found in the log,
38         # it has already been taken
39         if ( $search1[ 0 ] eq $user ) {
40            print( "This name has already been taken.<br>" );
41            print( "<a href = \"fig16_10.pl\">Try again</a>." );
42            print( end_html() );
43            exit;
44         }
45      }
46      close( LOG ) or die( "Cannot close: $!" );
47
48      # Add new user to the file
49      open( LOG, ">>log.txt" ) or die( "Cannot open: $!" );
50      print( LOG "$user\t$encrypt\n" );
51      close( LOG ) or die( "Cannot close: $!" );
52
53      print( i( "Your information has been processed." ) );
54      print( br() );
55      print( "<a href = \"fig16_11.pl\">Start Shopping!</a>" );
56      print( end_html() );
57   }
58   elsif ( param( "password" ) ) {
59      my $found = 0;
60      my @search2;
61
62      writeCookie();
63      print( header(), start_html() );
64
65      my $digestObject = Digest::MD5->new();
66      $digestObject->add( "$password" );
67      my $encrypt = $digestObject->digest();
68
69      # Search the log for this person
70      open( LOG, "<log.txt" ) or die( "Cannot open: $!" );
71
```

Fig. 16.10   Program that outputs a login page (part 2 of 5).

```
72        while ( <LOG> ) {
73           @search2 = split( "\t" );
74           chomp( $search2[ 1 ] );
75
76           if ( $search2[ 0 ] eq $user ) {
77
78              # The password entered is correct
79              if ( $search2[ 1 ] eq $encrypt ) {
80                 print( "Thank you for returning, $user!" );
81                 print( br() );
82                 print( "<a href = \"fig16_11.pl\">Start Shopping!" );
83                 print( "</a>" );
84                 $found = 1;
85                 last;
86              }
87              else {
88                 print( i( "You have entered an incorrect " ) );
89                 print( i( "password. Please try again." ) );
90                 print( br() );
91                 print( "<a href = \"fig16_10.pl\">Back to login" );
92                 print( "</a>" );
93                 $found = 1;
94                 last;
95              }
96           }
97        }
98        close( LOG );
99
100       # This person is not found in the log
101       # They are new or have entered an incorrect username
102       if ( $found == 0 ) {
103          print( "You are not a registered user.<br>" );
104          print( "<a href = \"fig16_10.pl\">Register</a>" );
105       }
106       print( end_html() );
107 }
108 else {
109       print( header() );
110       print( start_html( -title => 'Please login' ) );
111
112       print <<"    FORM";
113
114       <p>Please login.</p>
115
116       <form method = "post" action = "fig16_10.pl"><p>
117
118       User Name: <input type = "text" name = "user"><br/>
119       Password: <input type = "password" name = "password"><br/>
120       New? <input type = "checkbox" name = "new" value = "1"></p>
121
122       <input type = "submit" value = "login">
123       </form>
124
```

Fig. 16.10 Program that outputs a login page (part 3 of 5).

```
125      FORM
126
127      print( end_html() );
128   }
129
130   # Function writeCookie creates a cookie containing
131   # the array that was passed in during the function call
132   sub writeCookie
133   {
134      my $expires = "Monday, 11-JUN-01 16:00:00 GMT";
135      print( "Set-Cookie: " );
136      print( "CART=", join( "\t", @_ ), "; expires=$expires\n" );
137      return;
138   }
```

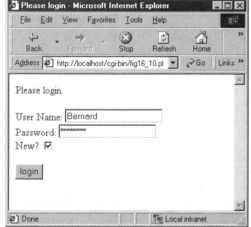

Fig. 16.10 Program that outputs a login page (part 4 of 5).

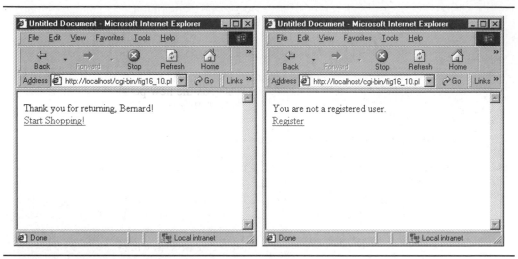

Fig. 16.10 Program that outputs a login page (part 5 of 5).

Figure 16.10 is the most complex of all the programs in this example. The entire program is in one large **if/elsif/else** structure. The first condition checks to see if the **"new"** parameter exists (line 16), and the second condition checks to see if the **"password"** parameter exists (line 58). The first time we run this program neither, of these values will be defined, so we move ahead to the **else** block in the structure, starting at line 108. At this point, the program is reduced to a "here" document that outputs an HTML form for the user, as shown in the first screen capture of Fig. 16.10. When the user fills in the form and clicks on the **login** button, **fig16_10.pl** executes again.

Let us assume that this time the user checked the **New** checkbox on the Web page. If so, the condition on line 16 is true, and lines 16–57 execute. Line 21 calls our function **write-Cookie** (defined on lines 132–138) with no arguments. This function creates a cookie called **CART** and assigns it the values in **@_**, with each element separated by a tab (line 136). This cookie will be used to store the contents of the user's cart. This user is new, so he or she should not have anything in his or her cart. At this moment in time, the cookie has no value.

Lines 24–27 *encrypt* the user's password to make it more secure. Line 25 creates a new *MD5 digest*, and lines 26–27 add the password to the digest and store the resulting value in variable **$encrypt**. The *MD5 encryption algorithm* (imported from the **Digest::MD5** module) encrypts the user's password with *one-way encryption*—we cannot get the original password back from the encrypted string. Topics such as message digests and encryption are discussed in more detail in Chapter 19, Security. For now, keep in mind that encryption helps hide data to ensure the security of the data. Digests use hash functions to achieve this goal, ensuring that only a person who knows the keys in the hash will be able to access the information. Encryption algorithms convert important data (such as passwords) into new strings that are unreadable to someone who might break into the system.

When testing whether a password is valid, we compare it with this encrypted string. This way, if someone managed to get access to our log file, he or she would find only usernames and encrypted passwords. In this example, this information would be enough to access a user's file. However, because the cracker still does not know the original password, other security measures can be implemented to make sure that this person cannot gain access to the user's file. Next, we open **log.txt**—the file that will contain all the usernames and their encrypted passwords. Lines 34–45 search through this file, comparing each username with the name entered. If it is already in the list, a message is printed to the user saying that the name has already been taken, and a link is provided for him or her to fill out the form again. Otherwise, the new user is valid. The file is opened again on line 49, this time for appending. Line 50 adds the new person's information to the log. A resulting line in **log.txt** might look as follows:

```
Bernard   ¿˘V¡àØÓÜ»h"{
```

Lines 53–56 send a hyperlink to the Web browser that allows the user to start buying items (Fig. 16.11).

The last possible case in this program exists for returning users (lines 58–107). This part of the program executes when the user enters a name and password, but does not check the **New** checkbox. In this case, we assume that the user is one who has already has a username and password in **log.txt**. We again use **writeCookie** with no value to clear the **CART** cookie (line 62) and encrypt the entered password (lines 65–67). Lines 72–95 search through **log.txt** for this user. If the username is found in the file (line 76), we proceed to test if the password is valid. Line 79 compares the user's password that is stored in the log to the password entered—both have been encrypted using the same algorithm, so the two strings will be identical if the proper password was entered. If they are identical, the user is granted access to begin shopping. Otherwise, a message is output to the user stating that the password entered is invalid, and a hyperlink is provided to return to the login page and reenter the password. In both cases, the variable **$found** is set to 1. If the username was not found, **$found** remains 0, and line 103 prints a message to the user stating that he or she was not found in the log.

Figure 16.11 also divides the program using an **if/else** structure, this time depending on whether the user is adding an item to the cart or removing an item from the cart. If the person is not removing an item, lines 32–97 execute. This section begins by adding a new book to the cart if the user selected a book to purchase (lines 33 and 36). If the **"newbook"** parameter is not defined, nothing will be added in line 36. Lines 40–43 check to see if the cart is empty. If the cart is empty, the user is redirected to the program in Fig. 16.12, which displays the items the user can buy. If the user has not been redirected, we write the user's cart information (**@cart**) to the **CART** cookie (starting at line 46) and output a table with the cart's contents. The table contains a **form** for each entry in the table (line 69). These forms each include a **submit** button (line 76) and hidden-field data (lines 78–81). We use the **hidden** function from **CGI.pm** to generate the HTML that creates the hidden fields. Submitting any of these **Remove** forms sets the number of the book to remove in the shopping cart (according to **$counter**) and also sets the **remove** field to 1 (true), indicating that a book removal must be performed. The data is posted to this same program to be processed (as specified by the form's **action** at line 70).

To total the price of all books in the cart, one additional step is required. We cannot immediately add all of the prices, because they are preceded with a dollar-sign character. These strings would therefore be evaluated as **undef** in a numeric context. So, we must remove the dollar-sign character. Line 84 uses the substitution pattern-matching operator (**s///**) discussed in Chapter 8 to remove the dollar sign. This value, which is stored in **$book[3]**, is then added to the total price.

```perl
1   #!/usr/bin/perl
2   # Fig. 16.11: fig16_11.pl
3   # Add or remove a book from cart and print cart contents
4
5   use warnings;
6   use strict;
7   use CGI qw( :standard );
8
9   my @cart = readCookie();
10  my $remove = param( "remove" );
11  my @book;
12
13  if ( $remove ) {
14     my $number = param( "number" );
15
16     # The book is removed from the cart array
17     @book = splice( @cart, 4 * ( $number - 1 ), 4 );
18
19     # The new array is written to the cookie
20     writeCookie( @cart );
21     print( header() );
22     print( start_html( "Book removed" ) );
23
24     print <<"   End_Remove";
25     <center><p>The book <i>$book[0]</i> has been removed.</p>
26     <a href = "fig16_11.pl">Return to cart</a>
27     <br>
28     <a href = "fig16_13.pl">Sign Out</a>
29     End_Remove
30
31  }
32  else {
33     @book = param( "newbook" );
34
35     # Add the book the user wants to the cart array
36     push( @cart, @book );
37
38     # If there is nothing in the cart,
39     # simply show the items for sale
40     if ( !@cart ) {
41        print( redirect( "fig16_12.pl" ) );
42        exit;
43     }
44
45     # Change cookie so it has the new entry
46     writeCookie( @cart );
47     print( header() );
48     print( start_html( "Shopping Cart" ) );
49
50     print <<"   End_Add";
51     <center><p>Here is your current order.</p>
52     <table border = "1" cellpadding = "7">
53        <tr>
```

Fig. 16.11 Program to view and update the user's shopping cart (part 1 of 4).

```
54              <th>Item</th>
55              <th>Name</th>
56              <th>Year</th>
57              <th>ISBN</th>
58              <th>Price</th>
59              <th></th>
60          </tr>
61      End_Add
62
63      my $counter = 1;
64      my $total = 0;
65      my @cartCopy = @cart;
66
67      # print out the cart for the user
68      while ( @book = splice( @cartCopy, 0, 4 ) ) {
69          print( "<tr><form method = \"post\"" );
70          print( "action = \"fig16_11.pl\">" );
71          print( "<td>$counter</td>" );
72          print( "<td>$book[ 0 ]</td>" );
73          print( "<td>$book[ 1 ]</td>" );
74          print( "<td>$book[ 2 ]</td>" );
75          print( "<td>$book[ 3 ]</td>" );
76          print( "<td>", submit( "Remove" ), "</td>" );
77
78          param( "remove", 1 );     # set "remove" variable to true
79          param( "number", $counter );   # book number to remove
80          print( hidden( "remove" ) );
81          print( hidden( "number" ) );
82          print( "</form></tr>" );
83
84          $book[ 3 ] =~ s/\$//;              # remove $ sign
85          $total += $book[ 3 ];              # add price
86          $counter++;
87      }
88
89      print( "<tr><th colspan = \"4\">Total Order</th><th>" );
90      printf( "\$%0.2f", $total );         # print the total
91
92      print( "</tr>" );
93      print( "</table><br>" );
94      print( "<a href = \"fig16_12.pl\">Buy more books</a>" );
95      print( br() );
96      print( "<a href = \"fig16_13.pl\">Sign out</a>" );
97  }
98  print( end_html() );
99
100 sub writeCookie
101 {
102     my $expires = "Monday, 11-JUN-01 16:00:00 GMT";
103     print( "Set-Cookie: " );
104     print( "CART=", join( "\t", @_ ), "; expires=$expires\n" );
105     return;
106 }
```

Fig. 16.11 Program to view and update the user's shopping cart (part 2 of 4).

```
107
108  # Read the user's cookies
109  # Return the information from the CART cookie
110  sub readCookie
111  {
112     my @cookieValues = split( "; ", $ENV{ 'HTTP_COOKIE' } );
113     my $name;
114     my $value;
115     my @data;
116
117     foreach ( @cookieValues ) {
118        ( $name, $value ) = split ( "=" );
119
120        if ( $name eq "CART" ) {
121           @data = split( "\t", $value );
122           last;
123        }
124     }
125     return @data;
126  }
```

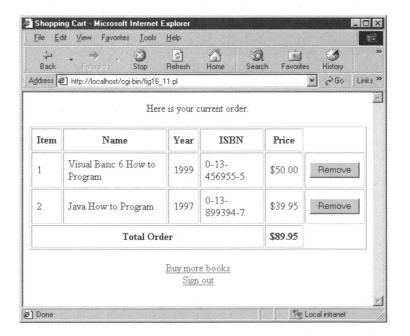

Fig. 16.11 Program to view and update the user's shopping cart (part 3 of 4).

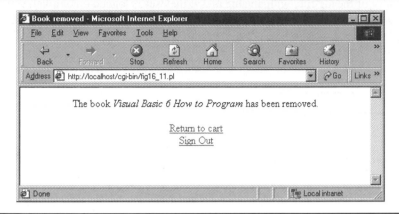

Fig. 16.11 Program to view and update the user's shopping cart (part 4 of 4).

Now let us return to the code that removes a book from the cart, beginning at line 13. First we obtain the number of the book to be removed with **param**. Line 17 uses **splice** to remove the appropriate book from **@cart** by removing four elements, beginning with index **4 * ($number-1)**, and assigning the removed elements to **@book**. Each book in the cart contains four fields, so the data for the first book in the **@cart** array begins at index 0, the second at index 4, and so on.

The new contents of the cart are written to a cookie in line 20, and a message is output informing the user that the book has been removed. The link to **fig16_11.pl** in line 26 runs the script again, but without passing any form data. Thus, when the link is followed, the field **remove** has no value, and the **if** statement in line 13 will return a value of false on the following execution.

Figure 16.12 uses the values in **catalog.txt** (Fig. 16.14) to output the items that the user can purchase. The **while** structure of lines 33–48 outputs a table containing the items. The last column for each row includes a button the user can click on to buy the item. Hidden form fields are specified for each book and its associated information. The **remove** field is specifically set to zero, so the program **fig16_11.pl** skips its **remove** case when the current cart is displayed for the user. Lines 43–45 output the different values for each book (stored in **@data** on line 35), and line 47 outputs the **submit** button the person can click on to buy a new item.

Figure 16.13 allows the user to log out of the shopping-cart application. This program prints a message to the user and calls **writeCookie** with no arguments, thus erasing the current information in the cart.

Figure 16.14 shows the contents of the **catalog.txt** file. This file must reside in the same directory as the CGI programs for the shopping-cart application to work correctly in this example.

The example in Fig. 16.10, Fig. 16.11, Fig. 16.12 and Fig. 16.13 has many steps. There are still some security holes in the example, but it is more secure than the programs shown earlier in the chapter. A remaining security hole in the example is that the user actually is not required to log in. Once he or she knows the URL to see the items and start buying (**fig16_12.pl**), he or she can go right there by pasting this address into the browser. We could prevent this problem in many ways. One straightforward fix would be to add a flag to each entry of the log file, with a value of 1 if the user is logged on or a value of 0 if not. Then, each program can begin by checking the value of this flag. If it is 0, access can be denied to the user, and he or she could be redirected to the login page automatically. For more information on security issues, see Chapter 19, Security.

```perl
1   #!/usr/bin/perl
2   # Fig. 16.12: fig16_12.pl
3   # Reads books from a database and prints them in a table
4
5   use warnings;
6   use strict;
7   use CGI qw( :standard );
8
9   my @data;
10
11  print( header(), start_html( "Book List" ) );
12
13  open( BOOKS, "catalog.txt" ) or
14     die( "The database could not be opened." );
15
16  print <<End_Begin;
17
18  <center>Books available for sale<br>
19
20  <a href = "fig16_13.pl">Sign Out</a><br>
21
22  <table border = "1" cellpadding = "7">
23  <tr>
24     <th>Name</th>
25     <th>Year</th>
26     <th>ISBN</th>
27     <th>Price</th>
28  </tr>
29
30  End_Begin
31
32  # print books the user can buy
33  while ( <BOOKS> ) {
34
35     @data = split( "\t" );            # Variable $_ assumed
36
37     print( "<form method = \"post\" action = \"fig16_11.pl\">" );
38     param( "remove" , 0 );     # The user is not removing a book,
39     param( "newbook", @data );    # They are adding a book
40     print( hidden( "remove" ) );
41     print( hidden( "newbook"), "\n<tr>" );
42
43     foreach ( @data ) {
44        print( "<td>$_</td>" );     # print data item within a cell
45     }
46
```

Fig. 16.12 Program that outputs the catalog of books (part 1 of 2).

```
47      print( "<td>", submit( "Buy" ), "</td></tr></form>\n" );
48  }
49
50  print( "</table>" );
51
52  print( end_html() );
53  close( BOOKS ) or die( "Cannot close: $!" );
```

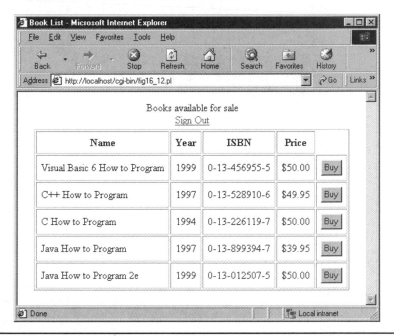

Fig. 16.12 Program that outputs the catalog of books (part 2 of 2).

```
1   #!/usr/bin/perl
2   # Fig. 16.13: fig16_13.pl
3   # Web page used to sign user out.
4
5   use strict;
6   use warnings;
7   use CGI qw( :standard );
8
9   # Erase the user's cart information
10  writeCookie();
11
12  print( header() );
13  print( start_html( -title => 'Logged out' ) );
14  print( "You are now logged out." );
15  print( br(), "You will be billed accordingly." );
16
17  print( br(), "To login again, " );
18  print( "<a href = \"fig16_10.pl\">click here</a>." );
```

Fig. 16.13 Logout program (part 1 of 2).

```
19
20   print( end_html() );
21
22   sub writeCookie
23   {
24      my $expires = "Monday, 11-JUN-01 16:00:00 GMT";
25      print( "Set-Cookie: " );
26      print( "CART=", join( "\t", @_ ), "; expires=$expires\n" );
27      return;
28   }
```

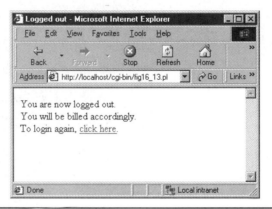

Fig. 16.13 Logout program (part 2 of 2).

```
Visual Basic 6 How to Program    1999      0-13-456955-5    $50.00
C++ How to Program        1997    0-13-528910-6    $49.95
C How to Program          1994    0-13-226119-7    $50.00
Java How to Program       1997    0-13-899394-7    $39.95
Java How to Program 2e    1999    0-13-012507-5    $50.00
```

Fig. 16.14 Contents of `catalog.txt`.

SUMMARY

- A limitation of HTTP is that the connection with the client is closed after the server sends its response. As a result, data can be sent to the server and returned to the client once per request.

- To create a program that interacts with the user multiple times, several Web documents must be linked together, and each Web document must call the next one in the chain.

- The ability to store data (also called *maintaining state information*) is important in Web sites that require interaction between many Web documents.

- User preferences can be stored to customize a Web site to a particular user each time that user visits the site.

- In an HTTP transaction, there are three locations in which to store state information: the client, the server and the browser. The *client* refers to the client's computer. The *server* refers to the server computer. CGI programs have the ability to create, edit and save files on the server computer. If each file is given a unique name, then a later CGI program can find the file that corresponds to a particular user. The *browser* refers to the browsing application. The browser has the ability to store and pass data from one page to another. A limitation with this approach is that if the user visits another site and then returns, the earlier information gets erased or overwritten.

- A query string can be used to pass information between pages. Query strings are used in **get** requests. The information is passed as a part of the URL.

- Query strings have a security problem: The user can enter any query string he or she wishes. For this reason, query strings should be used only when modifications to the query string will not affect the program's execution.

- Another method of maintaining state information through the browser uses hidden fields in HTML forms. Hidden fields also have a security hole, introduced by using **CGI.pm**'s **param** method. This is the easiest way to collect data posted to a CGI program with forms. Note that **param** makes no distinction between **post** data and **get** data.

- There are means of determining what type of method was used for a form. This information can be used to ensure that the form fields were sent to the server using a **post** action. Even so, **post** actions are easy to mimic. There are just too many ways for a user to access and change this data. For this reason, the hidden-fields method is usually not good for passing secure data.

- Another mechanism for storing information is a cookie—text-based data saved on the client's computer. When a browser requests a Web site, that Web site has the ability to store a small file called a *cookie* on your computer. Whenever the browser requests that Web site again, it locates the cookies originally written by the server and sends them back to the server as part of the request. This information can help the server recognize users from one visit to the next. A potential problem is that the user of the browsing application must have cookies enabled.

- Cookies are essentially small text files (Netscape stores them in a single text file) that get stored on your computer when you visit a Web site. They can keep track of how often you visit a site or what you buy at a site (or any other information the server chooses to write in them). Popular browsers provide support for cookies; they also allow the users to disable this support. Most major Web sites use cookies.

- The expiration data of a cookie can be a string, or it can be a relative value. For instance, **+30d** sets the cookie to exist for 30 days. The browser deletes a cookie after it expires.

- A line of text that begins with **Set-Cookie:** indicates that the browser should store the incoming data in a cookie.

- A cookie can contain many fields, such as a name–value pair containing the data to be stored, the expiration date, the URL path of the server domain over which the cookie is valid and the domain on which the server resides.

- If the **path** of a cookie is not set to any value, the cookie becomes readable from anywhere within the server's domain.

- If the client is Internet Explorer, cookies are stored in the **Temporary Internet Files** directory on the client's machine.

- On the server, environment variable **'HTTP_COOKIE'** contains the client's cookies that were sent as part of a request.

- User information can be maintained in server-side files. This method is probably the most secure mechanism for maintaining vital information. The information is stored on the server, so only someone with access to the server and the ability to change files on the server can alter the files.

- Once we have a filename, it is good to use a **sysopen** with the flags **O_WRONLY**, **O_EXCL** and **O_CREAT**. This step will open a file for writing to a file, creating the file if it does not exist and failing if the file does exist.

- To make the method of using server-side files safer, a difficult-to-determine key to the files must be used—something that cannot easily be guessed. Another security measure would be to send a password to the user at an e-mail address provided by the user. Not only would this method provide a reasonably safe way to send the user a password, but it is an indirect way to verify that the e-mail address supplied by the user is valid.

- Many Web applications systems store user information in password-protected databases to make their programs even more secure.

- Many businesses now have online shopping carts. These sites allow customers to buy items conveniently online. The sites record what the consumer wants to purchase and provide an easy, understandable way to shop online. They do so with an electronic shopping cart. Users can add or remove items from their shopping carts, and the site will automatically update the contents. When users "check out," they pay for whatever items are in their shopping carts.

- The MD5 encryption algorithm (imported form the **Digest::MD5** module) can be used to encrypt important information, such as a user's password. This is a one-way encryption algorithm— the original information cannot be obtained from the encrypted string.

- Digests use hash functions to keep important information secure, ensuring that only a person who knows the keys will be able to access the information.

- The **hidden** function in **CGI.pm** generates HTML needed to create the hidden fields.

- Creating a cookie with the same name as another cookie overwrites the original cookie. For instance, we can empty a cookie by creating one with the same name, but no value.

- A cookie can be erased by setting its expiration date to sometime in the past.

TERMINOLOGY

browser	password
client	password-protected database
client-side cookie	**path** attribute in cookies
connection	**post** request
cookie	query string
customized Web pages	**readCookies** function
digest	request
Digest::MD5 module	security
electronic commerce (e-commerce)	security hole
encryption algorithm	server
expires attribute	server-side file
form handling	session tracking
get request	**Set-Cookie:** command in HTML
hidden field	shopping-cart application
HTTP (Hypertext Transfer Protocol)	state information
hyperlink	storage space
maintaining state information	**Temporary Internet Files** directory
MD5 digest	user-specific information
MD5 encryption algorithm	Web application
one-way encryption	Web browser
online store	Web server
param method	

SELF-REVIEW EXERCISES

16.1   Fill in the blanks in each of the following statements:
   a) The three locations where state information in an HTTP transaction can be maintained are _____, _____ and _____.

b) Information is passed via query strings by adding a _____ to the end of the URL.
c) Hidden fields are a type of _____ HTML element.
d) When state information is maintained via the browser and the user leaves the site, the state is _____.
e) Cookies are stored on the _____ computer.
f) In the shopping-cart example, we use the _____ module to encrypt information and create random filenames.

16.2 State whether each of the following is *true* or *false*. If *false*, explain why.
a) Query strings mimic the format of an HTML form for a **get** request.
b) Hidden fields require an HTML form element.
c) Query strings and hidden fields use the same CGI method to read in the passed information.
d) Cookies cannot be disabled by the user.
e) An expiration date for a cookie can be sometime in the past.
f) Server-side files are the best method to use to maintain state information in all cases.
g) One of the problems with server-side files is matching a user to his or her respective file.
h) The shopping-cart example provided in this chapter is completely secure.

ANSWERS TO SELF-REVIEW EXERCISES

16.1   a) browsing application, b) client computer, server computer. b) question mark. c) input. d) reset. e) client. f) **Digest::MD5**.

16.2   a) True.
b) True.
c) True.
d) False. Browsers normally provide a mechanism by which the user can disable cookies.
e) True.
f) False. Different methods should be used to maintain state information based on the situation. Although server-side files are usually the most secure method, it is important to remember that they are not perfect. This method can increase overhead as well as pose security risks, just like the other methods.
g) True.
h) False. The shopping-cart example provided in this chapter is not secure. For instance, the user can get back to the catalog of books and start shopping without even logging in.

EXERCISES

16.3   Use query strings to implement a Web page that presents the user with an HTML form which asks them for their name and favorite animal. Have another program read these values and print an appropriate message to the user. Add a link to another program, which again will read these values using query strings and print another appropriate message to the user.

16.4   Repeat Exercise 16.3 using hidden fields.

16.5   Repeat Exercise 16.3 using cookies.

16.6   Use cookies to implement the following: Create a Web page that presents the user with a set of checkboxes. One should be for sports, one for the news and one for the weather. Then print a customized Web page for the user, showing only what he or she checked off. For instance, if the user checks news and weather, but not sports, he or she should only get an update on the news and the weather.

16.7   Use server-side files and your knowledge of Cascading Style Sheets (see Chapter 26 for a review of CSS) to implement a Web page that presents the user with an HTML form. This form should ask the user to enter a color in hexadecimal format for each attribute mentioned. Have the user enter colors for the background, text, links, viewed links, hover links, strong text and emphasis text. Then enter this data into a **.css** file in the valid format. Finally, output a custom Web page for the user, using the **.css** file. This file should have a random name created in the program.

17

Web Automation and Networking

Objectives

- To learn how to grab Web pages automatically from the Internet.
- To learn how to parse HTML.
- To understand some basic protocols.
- To examine a TCP chat program.
- To learn about SMTP and POP and e-mail applications.
- To learn how to do World Wide Web searches through a Perl program.

If the presence of electricity can be made visible in any part of a circuit, I see no reason why intelligence may not be transmitted instantaneously by electricity.
Samuel F. B. Morse

Mr. Watson, come here, I want you.
Alexander Graham Bell

Science may never come up with a better office-communication system than the coffee break.
Earl Wilson

It's currently a problem of access to gigabits through punybaud.
J. C. R. Licklider

Outline

17.1 Introduction

Perl is an Internet-based language. One of its primary applications is for creating CGI programs. Perl makes it easy to automate many Internet and Web-related tasks. In this chapter, we explore several of Perl's Internet and Web-related modules and demonstrate how to automate certain tasks on the Web. We also show how to implement such popular Internet applications as e-mail, searching and chatting.

17.2 Introduction to LWP

In Chapter 7, we discussed the basic interactions between a client and a server. In most cases, it is the server that sends automated responses to a human using a Web browser on the client computer. Perl has a bundle of modules called **LWP** (*Library for the WWW in Perl*), which allows us to automate client-side Web-related activities. Most of the modules in this bundle provide an object-oriented interface. One of the most common uses of LWP is to mimic a browser request for a Web page. We consider some important object-oriented LWP terminology before using the LWP modules.

A *request object* of class **HTTP::Request** contains the information that describes the client's request to the server. The attributes of an **HTTP::Request** are *method*, *URL*, *headers* and *content*. Attribute **method** is one of *get*, *put*, *post* or *head*. These will be explained later. Attribute **URL** is simply the address of the requested item. Attribute **headers** is a set of key/value pairs that provide additional information about the request. Attribute **content** contains the data sent from the client to the server as part of the request.

When the server receives a request, it creates a *response object* of the class **HTTP::Response** containing the response to the client. The attributes of an **HTTP::Response** are *code*, *message*, *headers* and *content*. Attribute **code** is a status indicator for the outcome of the request. It can represent that the request was success or that an error occurred. Attribute **message** is a string that corresponds to **code**.

Attribute **headers** contains additional information about the response and provides a description of the content that the client uses to determine how to process the response. Attribute **content** is the data associated with the response.

Now that we have discussed a request object and a response object, how do we turn the request object into a response object? This is the basis of LWP and is done with a *user agent* object of class **LWP::UserAgent**. This object acts like the browser in a normal Web interaction—it handles the details of making a request and creating a response object from that request. The response object specifies the response back to the user agent (normally a Web browser). The user agent's primary attributes are *timeout*, *agent*, *from* and *credentials*. Attribute **timeout** specifies how long the user agent should wait for a response before timing out (i.e., cancelling the request). Attribute **agent** specifies the name of your user agent. This name will be used when the user agent talks to the network. Attribute **from** is the e-mail address of the person using the Web browser. The attribute **credentials** contains any user names or passwords needed to get a successful response.

17.3 LWP Commands

The program of Fig. 17.1 demonstrates using **LWP** to interact programmatically between a Perl program and a Web server. The output window shows the resulting **response.txt** file that is created by this program.

On line 13, we create a new user agent object. On line 14, we create a new request object. The argument to the constructor is a key/value pair indicating that the request is a **GET** request and that the URL being requested is **$url ('http://localhost/home.html')**. Line 15 calls the user agent's *request* method to request the document specified in line 14. The result of this call is stored in a new **HTTP::Response** object. Line 17 calls the **HTTP::Response** object's *is_success* method to determine whether the request was successful. If so, line 18 calls the **HTTP::Response** object's *content* method and outputs the response to filehandle **OUT**. If the request was not successful, line 21 calls the **HTTP::Response** object's *status_line* method to output an error message to filehandle **OUT**. This method returns the status code and message from the response object. In general, if the request is successful, it is unnecessary to view this status code and message.

```
1   #!usr/bin/perl
2   # Fig 17.1: fig17_01.pl
3   # Simple LWP commands.
4
5   use strict;
6   use warnings;
7   use LWP::UserAgent;
8
9   my $url = "http://localhost/home.html";
10  open( OUT, ">response.txt" ) or
11     die( "Cannot open OUT file: $!" );
12
13  my $agent = new LWP::UserAgent();
14  my $request = new HTTP::Request( 'GET' => $url );
15  my $response = $agent->request( $request );
16
```

Fig. 17.1   Using **LWP** (part 1 of 2).

```
17   if ( $response->is_success() ) {
18      print( OUT $response->content() );
19   }
20   else {
21      print( OUT "Error: " . $response->status_line() . "\n" );
22   }
23
24   print( OUT "\n----------------------\n" );
25
26   $url = "http://localhost/cgi-bin/fig16_02.pl";
27
28   $request = new HTTP::Request( 'POST', $url );
29   $request->content_type( 'application/x-www-form-urlencoded' );
30   $request->content( 'type=another' );
31   $response = $agent->request( $request );
32
33   print( OUT $response->as_string() );
34   print( OUT "\n" );
35   close( OUT ) or die( "Cannot close out file : $!" );
```

```
<html>
<title>This is my home page.</title>

<body bgcolor = "skyblue">
<h1>This is my home page.</h1>
<b>I enjoy programming, swimming, and dancing.</b>
<br></br>
<b><i>Here are some of my favorite links:</i></b>
<br></br>
<a href = "http://www.C++.com">programming</a>
<br></br>
<a href = "http://www.swimmersworld.com">swimming</a>
<br></br>
<a href = "http://www.abt.org">dancing</a>
<br></br></body>
</html>
----------------------
HTTP/1.1 200 OK
Connection: close
Date: Tue, 21 Nov 2000 15:20:19 GMT
Server: Apache/1.3.12 (Win32)
Content-Type: text/html
Client-Date: Tue, 21 Nov 2000 15:20:19 GMT
Client-Peer: 127.0.0.1:80
Title: Your Style Page

<html><head><title>Your Style Page</title></head>
<body bgcolor = "#ffffc0" text = "#ee82ee"
   link = "#3cb371" vlink = "#3cb371">
<p>This is your style page.</p>
<p>You chose the colors.</p>
<a href = "/fig16_01.html">Choose a new style.</a>
</body></html>
```

Fig. 17.1   Using **LWP** (part 2 of 2).

```
<html>
   <title>This is my home page.</title>

   <body bgcolor = "skyblue">
      <h1>This is my home page.</h1>
      <b>I enjoy programming, swimming, and dancing.</b>
      <br></br>

      <b><i>Here are some of my favorite links:</i></b>
      <br></br>
      <a href = "http://www.C++.com">programming</a>
      <br></br>
      <a href = "http://www.swimmersworld.com">swimming</a>
      <br></br>
      <a href = "http://www.abt.org">dancing</a>
      <br></br>
   </body>
</html>
```

Fig. 17.2   Contents of **home.html**.

Good Programming Practice 17.1

When using LWP to grab a page from the Internet, test the HTTP response code for errors to avoid unexpected errors later in the program.

Next, we try to use a *post* request. This type of request mimics the HTML form element's *post* method. Line 28 creates a new request. The argument to the constructor is a key/value pair indicating that the request is a **POST** request and that the URL being requested is **$url ('http://localhost/cgi-bin/fig16_02.pl')**. The URL specified here is that of a CGI program in Chapter 16 that can handle *post* requests. Line 29 uses the **HTTP::Request** object's *content_type* method to set the content type to **'application/x-www-form-urlencoded'**. This specifies how the HTTP protocol will encode the request.

Line 30 uses the **HTTP::Request** object's **content** method to specify the data that will be posted to the CGI program. This **content** should be a string that we would send to a *post* request (in this case, **"type=another"**). This information helps the CGI program **fig16_02.pl** create a Web page based on the type it receives. Line 31 executes the request. Line 33 outputs the response to filehandle **OUT**. Note the use of the **HTTP::Response** object's **as_string** method, which returns a text representation of the response. This includes some extra information that the **content** method (line 18) does not print.

Another useful request type is a *head* request, which returns only the headers of a request. The headers include information such as the document's type, size and age. This is useful for testing whether a document exists. It is also useful in determining whether the entire document must be downloaded. Web browsers often use such a request to compare the version of a document on the Web server with the version cached on the local computer. If the versions are the same, the Web browser will load the local version for better performance.

Performance Tip 17.1

Using the head *request takes up less time and resources than any of the others. To test whether a page exists, it is almost always better to use a* head *request.*

17.4 The LWP::Simple Module

The previous section presented the full functionality of LWP using objects. This provides the user with access to headers and allows more control of the LWP commands. Simple LWP functionality can be attained by the **LWP::Simple** module, which provides procedural interface to LWP as opposed to the object-oriented approach we saw previously. Figure 17.2 demonstrates **LWP::Simple**.

Good Programming Practice 17.2

*If the object-oriented functionality and control of the regular LWP bundle is not required, it is normally better to use the **LWP::Simple** module.*

Line 10 uses the **LWP::Simple** module's **get** function to retrieve a Web page and store its contents in a scalar, which is output at line 11. Line 12 uses use the **LWP::Simple** module's **getprint** function, which retrieves a Web page and outputs it to **STDOUT**. Function **getprint** returns the HTTP response code. Line 14 uses the **LWP::Simple** module's **getstore** method, which retrieves the Web page and stores it in a file (the second argument). This also returns the HTTP response code. These are the three primary functions of the **LWP::Simple** module. As you can see, they can make coding simpler than the regular LWP modules.

Software Engineering Observation 17.1

*A disadvantage of using module **LWP::Simple** is that it does not provide the ability to perform a post request.*

```perl
1   #!usr/bin/perl
2   # Fig 17.3: fig17_03.pl
3   # A program that uses LWP::Simple.
4
5   use strict;
6   use warnings;
7   use LWP::Simple;
8
9   my $url = "http://localhost/home.html";
10  my $page = get( $url );
11  print( "\n$page\n\n" );
12  my $status = getprint( $url );
13  print( "\n\n$status\n" );
14  $status = getstore( $url, "page.txt" );
15  print( "\n$status\n" );
```

```
<html>
<title>This is my home page.</title>

<body bgcolor = "skyblue">
<h1>This is my home page.</h1>
<b>I enjoy programming, swimming, and dancing.</b>
<br></br>
```
(continued on next page)

Fig. 17.3   Using **LWP::Simple** (part 1 of 2).

```
                          (continued from previous page)
<b><i>Here are some of my favorite links:</i></b>
<br></br>
<a href = "http://www.C++.com">programming</a>
<br></br>
<a href = "http://www.swimmersworld.com">swimming</a>
<br></br>
<a href = "http://www.abt.org">dancing</a>
<br></br>
</body>
</html>

<html>

<title>This is my home page.</title>

<body bgcolor = "skyblue">
<h1>This is my home page.</h1>
<b>I enjoy programming, swimming, and dancing.</b>
<br></br>

<b><i>Here are some of my favorite links:</i></b>
<br></br>
<a href = "http://www.C++.com">programming</a>
<br></br>
<a href = "http://www.swimmersworld.com">swimming</a>
<br></br>
<a href = "http://www.abt.org">dancing</a>
<br></br>
</body>
</html>

200

200
```

Fig. 17.3　Using **LWP::Simple** (part 2 of 2).

17.5 HTML Parsing

We have now retrieved Web pages using LWP. However, the content is in HTML format, making it difficult to read. We could parse through the HTML with regular expressions and other string manipulation capabilities, picking out useful content, but there is another module—***HTML::TokeParser***—that can extract this information for us. Figure 17.3 demonstrates the **HTML::TokeParser** module.

 Good Programming Practice 17.3

Use prewritten modules when possible. Typically, they are more robust and comprehensive than self-written code.

The first part of this program is similar to what we have seen previously. Lines 10–14 retrieve a Web page and store its HTML content in a string (**$document**). Line 16 creates a new **TokeParser** object and passes a reference to the scalar **$document**, which contains the Web page retrieved previously. The **TokeParser** constructor accepts a string, a reference to a string or a filehandle as its argument. If it receives a string, the string is interpreted as the name of a file to be open and read. If it receives a reference to a string, the argument is interpreted as a reference to the data to parse. If it receives a filehandle, the **TokeParser** object will attempt to read from that filehandle.

Line 18 calls the **TokeParser** object's ***get_token*** method, which returns a *token* from the parsed document. The **while** loop (lines 18–25) iterates through the tokens until the end of the HTML file is found. Tokens are array references and have five potential types—*start token*, *end token*, *text token*, *comment token* or *declaration token*. A start token is a starting HTML tag. In the array for a start token, the first element is **"S"**, the next element holds the tag name, the next element is an array of tag variables, the next element is a hash that contains attributes for each tag and the last element is the original text. The array for an *end token* contains three elements—**"E"**, the tag name and the original text. Text tokens, comment tokens and declaration tokens each have two elements in their arrays—a character representing the type and the text in the token. The types for text tokens, comment tokens and declaration tokens are **"T"**, **"C"** and **"D"**, respectively.

```
<html>
<title>This is my home page.</title>

<body bgcolor = "skyblue">
<h1>This is my home page.</h1>
<b>I enjoy programming, swimming, and dancing.</b>
<br></br>

<b><i>Here are some of my favorite links:</i></b>
<br></br>
<a href = "http://www.C++.com">programming</a>
<br></br>
<a href = "http://www.swimmersworld.com">swimming</a>
<br></br>
<a href = "http://www.abt.org">dancing</a>
<br></br>
</body>
</html>
```

Fig. 17.4   Resulting **page.txt** file.

```
1   #!/usr/bin/perl
2   # Fig 17.5: fig17_05.pl
3   # A program to strip tags from an HTML document.
4
5   use strict;
6   use warnings;
7   use LWP::UserAgent;
8   use HTML::TokeParser;
9
10  my $url = "http://localhost/home.html";
11  my $agent = new LWP::UserAgent();
12  my $request = new HTTP::Request( 'GET' => $url );
```

Fig. 17.5   Stripping tags from HTML (part 1 of 2).

```
13   my $response = $agent->request( $request );
14   my $document = $response->content();
15
16   my $page = new HTML::TokeParser( \$document );
17
18   while ( my $token = $page->get_token() ) {
19       my $type = shift( @{ $token } );
20       my $text = shift( @{ $token } );
21
22       if ( $type eq "T" ) {
23           print( "$text" );
24       }
25   }
```

```
This is my home page.


This is my home page.
I enjoy programming, swimming, and dancing.


Here are some of my favorite links:

programming

swimming

dancing
```

Fig. 17.5   Stripping tags from HTML (part 2 of 2).

The **HTML::TokeParser** module combined with LWP is useful for extracting text from Web sites. For example, these modules could be used together to extract and format the most current headlines from a news Web site. Or they could be used to get the local weather. They could even be used to create an automatic Web page link tester that would examine a Web site and pick out any dead links.

17.6 Introduction to Advanced Networking

All network communications are done via *sockets*. Sockets are endpoints of communications. A connection that you can communicate over consists of two sockets. Data can be passed in via *streams* or via *datagrams*. Streams provide a bidirectional, sequenced and reliable means of communication. A datagram connection is much less reliable and is not sequenced. In a datagram connection, information is sent in small packets. While datagrams are not as reliable as streams, datagrams require fewer system resources, because they do not maintain a permanent connection between the two computers communicating.

All connections require two sockets (or endpoints). In general, one socket is maintained by a *server* program and the other is maintained by a *client* program. Normally, a server application is installed on a computer where it listens for connections (as a Web server waits for connections from Web browsers). The client program must know where server it will connect to is located. The client program initiates a connection with the proper server. Then, the client sends the server its request. The server knows how to process certain requests from the client and how to return results to the client. Many such requests can be processed.

An e-mail application is an example of a client program. E-mail resides on a server, which is constantly running. When someone sends you e-mail, it gets directed to this server, which stores the e-mail in your mailbox. When you check your e-mail, you send a request to the server to view all e-mail. If any new e-mail has arrived since you last checked, the e-mail application recognizes this and tells you that new e-mail has arrived. Then, if you wish to reply to a message, you type out the reply and your e-mail application tells your server that it wishes to send an e-mail. Checking and sending e-mail are just two examples of client requests.

17.7 Protocols

Communication between applications would be difficult if each server understood different commands—generalized client programs such as e-mail applications would be almost impossible to create. Each client program would have to know how to talk to each different server. To help standardize conversations between computers over a network, several *protocols* were created. *HTTP* is one such protocol, which we discussed in Chapter 7. Two e-mail protocols are *Post Office Protocol* (*POP*) and *Simple Mail Transfer Protocol* (*SMTP*). Lets us reconsider our e-mail example in the context of protocols.

Usually, an e-mail application deals with two different servers. It talks to a *POP server* to retrieve the user's e-mail and it talks to an *SMTP server* to send e-mail from the user. Each of these servers understands a limited number of commands. Usually this is enough to receive e-mail from an inbox and send e-mail from an outbox. You tell your e-mail application to check for new messages. The e-mail application translates this into a command to be sent to the POP server. This server returns all the messages in your inbox. The e-mail application then compares these messages with the ones it has stored. If any messages are new, it tells the user. The server does not deal with the concept of new e-mail. The e-mail application handles that.

Now assume that you want to reply to a message, so you click the e-mail application's *reply* button. Sending e-mail requires an interface with an SMTP server. The e-mail application cannot tell the server to reply to the message, because the server does not understand that command. However, the server does understand a *send* command. So the e-mail application creates a new message and specifies the original sender's address as the recipient and your address as the sender. This message is sent just like any other e-mail message. The only thing that makes it special is the predefined *recipient* and *from* fields (and often *subject* field).

17.8 Transport Control Protocol (TCP)

The main connection-oriented Internet protocol is called *Transport Control Protocol* (*TCP*). This is the most common and generalized way to talk with remote computers. In this section we will show you how to create a simple *client/server chat application*. Figure 17.6 presents a *TCP client* and Fig. 17.7 presents a *TCP server* application.

```
1   #!/usr/bin/perl
2   # Fig 17.6: fig17_06.pl
3   # TCP chat client.
```

Fig. 17.6   TCP chat client (part 1 of 2).

```
4
5   use strict;
6   use warnings;
7   use IO::Socket;
8
9   my $host = '192.168.1.71';
10  my $port = 5833;
11
12  my $socket = new IO::Socket::INET(
13     PeerAddr => $host,
14     PeerPort => $port,
15     Proto => "tcp",
16     Type => SOCK_STREAM )
17        or die( "Cannot connect to $host:$port : $@\n" );
18
19  local $| = 1;
20  print( $socket "What is your name?\n" );
21  print( "What is your name?\n" );
22
23  my $response = <$socket>;
24  print( "From server: $response" );
25
26  my $input = <STDIN>;
27
28  chomp( $input );
29
30  while ( $input ne "q" ) {
31     print( $socket "$input\n" );
32     $response = <$socket>;
33     print( "From server: $response" );
34
35     $input = <STDIN>;
36     chomp( $input );
37  }
38
39  print( "done\n" );
40  print( $socket "$input\n" );
41
42  close ( $socket ) or die( "Cannot close socket: $!" );
```

Fig. 17.6   TCP chat client (part 2 of 2).

```
1   #!/usr/bin/perl
2   # Fig 17.7: fig17_07.pl
3   # TCP chat server.
4
5   use strict;
6   use warnings;
7   use IO::Socket;
8
9   my $port = 5833;
10
```

Fig. 17.7   TCP chat server (part 1 of 3).

```
11   my $server = new IO::Socket::INET(
12       LocalPort => $port,
13       Type => SOCK_STREAM,
14       Listen => 10 )
15           or die( "Cannot be a server on $port: $@\n" );
16
17   local $| = 1;
18
19   my $client = $server->accept();
20   my $response = <$client>;
21
22   chomp $response;
23   print( "From client: $response\n" );
24
25   while ( $response ne "q" ) {
26       my $input = <STDIN>;
27       print( $client "$input" );
28
29       $response = <$client>;
30       chomp( $response );
31       print( "From client: $response\n" );
32   }
33
34   close ( $server ) or die( "Cannot end connection: $!" );
```

Fig. 17.7   TCP chat server (part 2 of 3).

Fig. 17.7 TCP chat server (part 3 of 3).

The chat client (Fig. 17.6) uses the **IO::Socket** module. Lines 9 and 10 initialize the location of our server. The variable **$host** contains the IP address of the server to which the client will connect and **$port** indicates the *port number* over which this connection will take place. The port number specifies where a server waits for and receives connections from clients. In this case, we have hard coded the server and port number into the program. You will need to change these to run the program on your compute.

Next, we use module **IO::Socket** to create an **IO::Socket::INET** object. This is an **IO::Socket** object that performs an Internet (**INET**) connection. We pass the constructor four arguments—the IP address of the chat server (**PeerAddr**, the port on the remote computer set up for TCP chat (**PeerPort**), the protocol (**Proto**; in this case TCP) and the whether this is a stream connection or a datagram connection (**Type**). In this example, we wish to create a stream connection, so we send the constructor the **SOCK_STREAM** constant which is exported from the **IO::Socket** module.

Now, not only will this constructor create a socket, but it will automatically connect with the chat server (if the chat server is running). This automatic connection could result in many errors. For this reason, we use the "**or die**" construct again to trap errors. Next we set **$|** (the line-buffering special variable) to 1 denoting that buffering should be turned off. Normally, a socket waits until the buffer has filled before sending the data. This can cause problems if the other end of the socket is waiting for information, but the buffer has not filled yet. Now we can start talking with the other end of our connection without worrying about having to wait for the buffer to fill.

The rest of this program deals with the actual chatting. We first ask the person at the server end what their name is. We get a response back and **print** it to **STDOUT**. We alternate between sending and receiving data, similar to a regular conversation (in which only one participant talks at a time). This conversation is much more polite than most conversations—there is no interrupting and each person can only make one statement at a time. The program is set up in such a way that one end of the connection cannot talk when it is supposed to be listening and vice versa. More complicated chat programs can work around these limitations.

Notice that we use the socket like a filehandle. This is another benefit to using an already existing module. All of the interface details of the socket are hidden. The socket looks and acts like a filehandle. We do not really need to know how the socket is implemented; we just need to know how to interact with it.

Our chat functionality is performed in a **while** loop that tests the **$input** variable to determine if the user typed **'q'** on a line by itself. If so, the connection will be closed (line 42).

Figure 17.7, the chat server, is quite similar to the client program. First we set the port value to the same number from the server program. This is important because all client programs must use this number to connect to the server. Next, we create a new **IO::Socket::INET** object. In this case, the arguments are the port the server listens to (**LocalPort**), the type of connection to create (**Type**; again, **SOCK_STREAM**) and the number of clients that can be waiting to interact with the server (**Listen**)—the server prevents additional clients from waiting. **Listen** must be defined for a server. After setting up the server, we use method **accept** in class **IO::Socket::INET** to accept a client connection. This method waits until a client attempts to access the server, at which point the server sets up the connection. The rest of the program implements the details of the chat.

17.9 Simple Mail Transfer Protocol (SMTP)

If you want to send e-mail you need a *Simple Mail Transfer Protocol* (*SMTP*) server. Perl has a module to deal with SMTP transfers. It is the **Net::SMTP** module. Figure 17.8 demonstrates the **Net::SMTP** module.

```
1   #!/usr/bin/perl
2   # Fig. 17.8: fig17_08.pl
3   # Form to send an e-mail message.
4
5   use strict;
6   use warnings;
7   use CGI qw( :standard );
8
9   print( header() );
```

Fig. 17.8   Form to send an e-mail message (part 1 of 2).

```
10   print( start_html( "Send e-mail!" ) );
11
12   print( h1( "The e-mail home page." ) );
13
14   print( start_form( -action => "fig17_09.pl" ) );
15
16   print( "Enter the SMTP server to connect to: " );
17   print( textfield( "server" ), br() );
18
19   print( "Enter what you want to appear in the \"from\" header: " );
20   print( textfield( "from" ), br() );
21
22   print( "Enter where you would like to send this e-mail: " );
23   print( textfield( "address" ), br() );
24
25   print( "Enter what you want to appear in the \"to\" header: " );
26   print( textfield( "to" ), br() );
27
28   print( "Enter what you want to appear in the \"subject\" header: " );
29   print( textfield( "subject" ), br() );
30
31   print( "Enter the message you want to send in the e-mail: " );
32   print( br() );
33   print( textarea( -name => "message", -rows => 5, -columns => 50,
34      -wrap => 1 ), br() );
35
36   print( br(), submit( "submit" ), end_form() );
37
38   print( end_html() );
```

Fig. 17.8   Form to send an e-mail message (part 2 of 2).

```perl
1   #!/usr/bin/perl
2   # Fig 17.9: fig17_09.pl
3   # Send an e-mail message.
4
5   use strict;
6   use warnings;
7   use Net::SMTP;
8   use CGI qw( :standard );
9
10  my $server = param( "server" );
11  my $from = param( "from" );
12  my $address = param( "address" );
13  my $to = param( "to" );
14  my $subject = param( "subject" );
15  my $message = param( "message" );
16  my $my_address = 'my_address.smtp';
17
18  my $smtp = new Net::SMTP( "$server", Hello => "$server" )
19     or die( "Cannot send e-mail: $!" );
20
21  $smtp->mail( "$my_address" );
22  $smtp->to( "$address" );
23
24  $smtp->data();
25  $smtp->datasend( "From: $from\n" );
26  $smtp->datasend( "To: $to\n" );
27  $smtp->datasend( "Subject: $subject\n\n" );
28  $smtp->datasend( "$message\n" );
29  $smtp->dataend();
30  $smtp->quit();
31
32  print( header() );
33  print( start_html( "Send e-mail!" ) );
34  print( h1( "Your e-mail has been sent." ) );
35  print( end_html() );
```

Fig. 17.9   Send an e-mail message.

Figure 17.8 presents a form for the user to fill out. To send the e-mail we need the SMTP server (lines 16–17) and the address to which the e-mail will be sent (lines 22–23). Figure 17.9 analyzes the data and attempts to send the e-mail.

Figure 17.9 begins by importing the **Net::SMTP** module. Line 17 creates an instance of this class. The first argument passed to the constructor must be a valid SMTP server. You can also send as optional arguments the mail domain of the user (**Hello**), a timeout for the connection (**Timeout**) and an indication of whether debugging should be on or off (**Debug**). This constructor creates the object and connects to the server in one step.

We then create a new e-mail message with method *mail*. Line 20 passes as an argument to this method the user's e-mail address (**$address**). This value will be placed in the *from* field of the message. Then we use method *to* (line 21) to specify the recipient of this e-mail.

Method *data* starts the transfer of data for the e-mail message. Once the transfer has started, we can send information using method *datasend*. To complete the message, we use method **dataend**. As with all connections, we should explicitly close, or in this case **quit**, the connection.

17.10 Post Office Protocol (POP)

Post Office Protocol (*POP*) was created to facilitate storage and retrieval of e-mail from a remote server. POP servers allow you to check, read, store and delete e-mail. Figure 17.10 and Fig. 17.11 are CGI programs that will check your e-mail for you using the **Mail::POP3Client** module. Figure 17.10 presents the user with an HTML form that can be used to input your e-mail username and password and the POP server. [*Note:* The password in this example is not encrypted.] Then, the data is posted to Fig. 17.11 and used to check your e-mail. Figure 17.11 returns an HTML document containing five messages at a time. If you have more than five messages, an HTML submit button is provided so you can retrieve the next five.

Figure 17.10 allows the user to log in. It asks for a username, a password and a server (which must be a valid POP server). Figure 17.11 actually does the real work. First, it imports the **Mail::POP3Client** module (line 7). Then, it gets the parameters (lines 10–13) from the form data that was posted—username, password, server and offset (we will see that later). Lines 18 and 19 create a new **Mail::POP3Client** object which is initialized with the username, password and server. The **Mail::POP3Client** object will automatically log in to the server with the specified username and password. Line 22 calls the **Mail::POP3Client** object's *Count* method to determine the number of messages in the mailbox. We then set two offset values, **$offset1** and **$offset2**. When we show the user the messages in the mailbox, we do not want to show all of them at once. Instead, we show only five messages. To allow the user to see the rest of the messages, we provide buttons that allows the user to move forwards and backwards through the messages in the mailbox. The offset values help determine the starting message number. We discuss this again shortly.

After setting these two offset values, we set a **$start** and **$end** number for the mailbox. This is the range of message numbers that we will be showing the user. We then iterate over this range with a **for** loop (lines 29–37). For each message, we output the message number. Then, lines 32–34 iterate through each of the message's headers using method *Head*, which returns all of the messages headers. These contain all the relevant information about the e-mail such as who sent the mail. When the header lines **From:** and **Subject:** are encountered, they are output as part of the resulting Web page.

```perl
1    #!/usr/bin/perl
2    # Fig. 17.10: fig17_10.pl
3
4    use strict;
5    use warnings;
6    use CGI qw( :standard );
7
8    print( header() );
9    print( start_html( -title => 'Please Login' ) );
10
11   print <<FORM;
12   <form action = "fig17_11.pl" method = "post">
13   <p>Username:
14   <input name = "userName" type = "text" size = "20"></p>
15   <p>Password:
16   <input name = "password" type = "password" size = "20"></p>
17   <p>Server:
18   <input name = "server" type = "text" size = "20"></p>
19   <input name = "offset" value = "0" type = "hidden">
20   <input type = "submit" value = "check mail">
21   <input type = "reset" value = "reset">
22   </form>
23   FORM
24
25   print( end_html() );
```

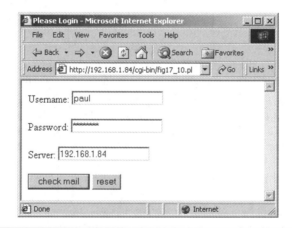

Fig. 17.10 Program to input name, password and server .

```perl
1    #!/usr/bin/perl
2    # Fig. 17.11: fig17_11.pl
3
4    use strict;
5    use warnings;
6    use MD5;
7    use Mail::POP3Client;
```

Fig. 17.11 Program to print from and subject lines from e-mail headers (part 1 of 3).

```perl
8    use CGI qw( :standard );
9
10   my $user = param( "userName" );
11   my $password = param( "password" );
12   my $server = param( "server" );
13   my $offset = param( "offset" );
14
15   print( header() );
16   print( start_html( -title => "Check your mail!" ) );
17
18   my $pop = new Mail::POP3Client( USER => $user,
19      PASSWORD => $password, HOST => $server ) or
20      print( h1( "Cannot connect: $!" ) );
21
22   my $messages = $pop->Count();
23   print( "<p>You have $messages messages in your inbox.</p>" );
24   my $offset1 = $offset - 5;
25   my $offset2 = $offset + 5;
26   my $start = 1 + $offset;
27   my $end = ( $offset2 < $messages ? $offset2 : $messages );
28
29   for ( $start .. $end ) {
30      print( "<p>$_: " );
31
32      foreach ( $pop->Head( $_ ) ) {
33         /^(From|subject):\s+/i and print $_, "<br/>";
34      }
35
36      print( "</p>\n" );
37   }
38
39   print <<FORM1 if ( $offset );
40   <form action = "fig17_11.pl" method = "post">
41   <input name = "userName" value = $user type = "hidden">
42   <input name = "password" value = $password type = "hidden">
43   <input name = "server" value = $server type = "hidden">
44   <input name = "offset" value = $offset1 type = "hidden">
45   <input type = "submit" value = "See previous 5">
46   </form>
47   FORM1
48
49   print <<FORM2 if ( $end != $messages );
50   <form action = "fig17_11.pl" method = "post">
51   <input name = "userName" value = $user type = "hidden">
52   <input name = "password" value = $password type = "hidden">
53   <input name = "server" value = $server type = "hidden">
54   <input name = "offset" value = $offset2 type = "hidden">
55   <input type = "submit" value = "See next 5">
56   </form>
57   FORM2
58
59   print( end_html() );
60
```

Fig. 17.11 Program to print from and subject lines from e-mail headers (part 2 of 3).

61   `$pop->Close();`

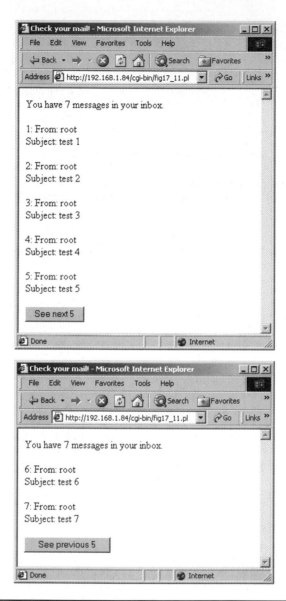

Fig. 17.11 Program to print from and subject lines from e-mail headers (part 3 of 3).

After the message headers are output, the program determines if a form should be displayed to allow the user to navigate their remaining e-mails. If there are fewer than five messages, the form is not displayed. Otherwise, one of two nearly identical HTML **form**s is output. The only difference between the two forms is the offset value that they post to the server. To see the previous five messages, we send a lower offset value. For the next five messages, we send a higher offset value.

17.11 Searching the World Wide Web

A major application of the Internet is searching for information. Perl provides modules to interface with many Internet search engines. Figure 17.12 and Fig. 17.13 mimic a metasearch. The first program enables the user to specify a query and select several search engines to which the query should be submitted. The second program searches one or more of the AltaVista, HotBot, WebCrawler and NorthernLight search engines for the query. The program retrieves up to 50 results from each search engine and displays them for the user.

```perl
1   #!/usr/bin/perl
2   # Fig. 17.12: fig17_12.pl
3   # Program to begin a Web search.
4
5   use strict;
6   use warnings;
7   use CGI qw( :standard );
8
9   print( header(), start_html( "Web Search" ) );
10  print( h1( "Search the Web!" ) );
11
12  print( start_form( -method => "post", -action => "fig17_13.pl" ) );
13
14  print( "Enter query: " );
15  print( textfield( "query" ), br(), br() );
16
17  print( "Enter number of sites you want " );
18  print( br() );
19  print( "from each search engine, 1-50: " );
20  print( textfield( "amount" ), br(), br() );
21
22  print( "<input type = \"checkbox\" " );
23  print( "name = \"AltaVista\" value = \"1\">" );
24  print( "AltaVista", br() );
25
26  print( "<input type = \"checkbox\" " );
27  print( "name = \"HotBot\" value = \"1\">" );
28  print( "HotBot", br() );
29
30  print( "<input type = \"checkbox\" " );
31  print( "name = \"WebCrawler\" value = \"1\">" );
32  print( "WebCrawler", br() );
33
34  print( "<input type = \"checkbox\" " );
35  print( "name = \"NorthernLight\" value = \"1\">" );
36  print( "NorthernLight", br() );
37
38  print( br(), submit( "Search!" ), end_form() );
39
40  print( end_html() );
```

Fig. 17.12 Form to specify a search query and search engines (part 1 of 2).

Fig. 17.12 Form to specify a search query and search engines (part 2 of 2).

```perl
1   #!/usr/bin/perl
2   # Fig 17.13: fig17_13.pl
3   # A program that collects search results.
4
5   use strict;
6   use warnings;
7   use WWW::Search;
8   use CGI qw( :standard );
9
10  my @engines;
11  my $search;
12
13  my $query = param( "query" );
14  my $amount = param( "amount" );
15
16  if ( !$query ) {
17     print( header(), start_html() );
18     print( h1( "Please try again." ) );
19     print( "<a href = \"/cgi-bin/fig17_12.pl\">Go back</a>" );
20     print( end_html() );
21     exit();
22  }
23
24  if ( !$amount || $amount > 50 ) {
25     $amount = 5;
26  }
27
```

Fig. 17.13 Performing a Web search (part 1 of 2).

```
28    my $value;
29
30    push( @engines, "AltaVista" ) if ( param( "AltaVista" ) );
31    push( @engines, "HotBot" ) if ( param( "HotBot" ) );
32    push( @engines, "WebCrawler" ) if ( param( "WebCrawler" ) );
33    push( @engines, "NorthernLight" ) if ( param( "NorthernLight" ) );
34
35    print( header() );
36    print( start_html( "Web Search" ) );
37
38    foreach ( @engines ) {
39       my $search = new WWW::Search( $_ );
40       $search->native_query( WWW::Search::escape_query( $query ) );
41       print( b( i( "Web sites found by $_:" ) ), br() );
42
43       for ( 1 .. $amount ) {
44          my $result = $search->next_result();
45          $value = $result->url();
46          print( "<a href = $value>$value</a>" );
47          print( br() );
48       }
49
50       print( br() );
51    }
52
53    print( end_html() );
```

Fig. 17.13 Performing a Web search (part 2 of 2).

Figure 17.12 simply presents a Web page with options for the user. The first option asks the user what topic they are searching for (lines 14–15). The next field asks the user how many results they want from each search engine and the final option allows the user to specify which of the four engines to use.

Figure 17.13 analyzes the data entered and performs the Web search. Line 7 imports the **WWW::Search** module that provides an interface to a large list of search engines. This module is extended by several modules that enable programmatic interaction with the search engines. For example, to perform a search with the four search engines mentioned in this example, the program requires the **WWW::Search::NorthernLight** module, **WWW::Search::AltaVista** module, **WWW::Search::HotBot** module and the **WWW::Search::WebCrawler** module. If you install the **WWW::Search** module from of CPAN, these modules will be installed as well.

Lines 13 and 14 obtain parameter values for **$query** and **$amount**. Lines 16–22 print a message to the user if they did not enter a query. In lines 24–26, if the number of sites was not specified or the number was larger than 50, **$amount** is set to 5.

After the error handling code, we begin the Web search. Lines 30–33 insert elements in the array **@engines** based on the user's choices in Fig. 17.12. To implement this search, we iterate through the array in a **foreach** structure (lines 38–51). Each time we want to perform a search on a particular engine, we create a new **WWW::Search** object (line 39). To format a query, we pass that query as an argument to the **escape_query** method in the **WWW::Search** module. This converts a simple sentence into an HTML-encoded sentence suitable for the **WWW::Search** module. Then, to perform the search, we call the **native_query** method on the current search object and pass the encoded query as the argument. To get results of the search from a particular search engine, we call method **next_result** (line 44) on that **WWW::Search** object. Method **url** (line 45) reformats the result as a URL value that we can use and read. We use these methods to iterate through the results and display them in a Web page for the user.

SUMMARY

- Perl has a bundle of modules called **LWP** (Library for the WWW in Perl), which allows us to automate client-side Web-related activities.

- A request object of class **HTTP::Request** contains the information that describes the client's request to the server.

- The attributes of an **HTTP::Request** are **method**, **URL**, **headers** and **content**. Attribute **method** is one of get, put, post or head. Attribute **URL** is simply the address of the requested item. Attribute **headers** is a set of key/value pairs that provide additional information about the request.

- Attribute **content** contains the data sent from the client to the server as part of the request.

- When the server receives a request, it creates a response object of the class **HTTP::Response** containing the response to the client.

- The attributes of an **HTTP::Response** are **code**, **message**, **headers** and **content**. Attribute **code** is a status indicator for the outcome of the request. It can represent that the request was success or that an error occurred. Attribute **message** is a string that corresponds to **code**. Attribute **headers** contains additional information about the response and provides a description of the content that the client uses to determine how to process the response. Attribute **content** is the data associated with the response.

- The user agent object of class **LWP::UserAgent** acts like the browser in a normal Web interaction—it handles the details of making a request and creating a response object from that request.

- The response object specifies the response back to the user agent.

- The user agent's primary attributes are **timeout**, **agent**, **from** and **credentials**. Attribute **timeout** specifies how long the user agent should wait for a response before timing out. Attribute **agent** specifies the name of your user agent. This name will be used when the user agent talks to the network. Attribute **from** is the e-mail address of the person using the Web browser. Attribute **credentials** contains any user names or passwords needed to get a successful response.

- The user agent's **request** method is used to request the document specified. The result of this call is stored in a new **HTTP::Response** object.

- The **HTTP::Response**'s **is_success** method is used to determine whether the request was successful. If it was successful, we can call **HTTP::Response**'s **content** method and output the response. If the request was not successful, **HTTP::Response**'s **status_line** method can be called to output an error message. This method returns the status code and message from the response object.

- A post request mimics the HTML form element's *post* method.

- The **HTTP::Request** object's **content_type** method is used to set the content type of the request. This specifies how the HTTP protocol will encode the request.

- The **HTTP::Request** object's **content** method specifies the data that will be posted to the CGI program. This **content** should be a string that we would send to a *post* request.

- The **HTTP::Response**'s **as_string** method returns a text representation of the response.

- The head request returns only the headers of a request. The headers include information such as the document's type, size and age.

- Simple LWP functionality can be attained by the **LWP::Simple** module, which provides procedural interface to LWP as opposed to the object-oriented approach we saw previously.

- The **LWP::Simple** module's **get** function is used to retrieve a Web page and store its contents in a scalar.

- The **LWP::Simple** module's **getprint** function retrieves a Web page and outputs the page to **STDOUT**. Function **getprint** returns the HTTP response code.

- The **LWP::Simple** module's **getstore** method retrieves the Web page and stores it in a file. This also returns the HTTP response code.

- The **HTML::TokeParser** module and LWP are useful for extracting text from Web sites.

- The **TokeParser** constructor accepts a string, a reference to a string or a filehandle as its argument. If it receives string, the string is interpreted as the name of a file to be open and read. If it receives a reference to a string, the argument is interpreted as a reference to the data to parse. If it receives a filehandle, the **TokeParser** object will attempt to read from that filehandle.

- The **TokeParser** object's **get_token** method returns a token from the parsed document.

- Tokens are array references and have five potential types—start token, end token, text token, comment token or declaration token.

- A start token is a starting HTML tag. In the array for a start token, the first element is **"S"**, the next element holds the tag name, the next element is an array of tag variables, the next element is a hash that contains attributes for each tag and the last element is the original text.

- The array for an end token contains three elements—**"E"**, the tag name and the original text.

- Text tokens, comment tokens and declaration tokens each have two elements in their arrays—a character representing the type and the text in the token. The types for text tokens, comment tokens and declaration tokens are **"T"**, **"C"** and **"D"**, respectively.

- Sockets are endpoints of communications. All network communications are done via sockets.

- A connection that you can communicate over consists of two sockets.

- Data can be passed via streams or via datagrams.

- Streams provide a bidirectional, sequenced and reliable means of communication.

- A datagram connection is much less reliable and not sequenced. In a datagram connection, information is sent in small packets.

- While datagrams are not as reliable as streams, datagrams require fewer system resources because they do not maintain a permanent connection between the two computers communicating.

- All connections require two sockets (or endpoints). In general, one socket is maintained by a server program and the other is maintained by a client program.

- Normally, a server application is installed on a computer where it listens for connections. The client program must know where server it will connect to is located.

- To help standardize conversations between computers over a network, several protocols were created. Usually, an e-mail application deals with two different servers. It talks to a POP server to retrieve the user's e-mail and it talks to an SMTP server to send e-mail from the user.

- The main connection-oriented Internet protocol is called TCP.

- We can use the **IO::Socket** module to create a client/server chat application. We can use this module to easily specify the location of our server.

- The port number specifies where a server waits for and receives connections from clients.

- We use the **IO::Socket** module to create an instance of an **IO::Socket::INET** object. This is an **IO::Socket** object that performs an Internet (**INET**) connection.

- We send the constructor for **IO::Socket::INET** four arguments—the **PeerAdress** which is the IP address of the chat server, the **PeerPort** which is the port on the remote computer set up for TCP chat, the **Proto**, which is the protocol, and the **Type**, which denotes whether this is a stream connection or a datagram connection.

- The **$|** (line-buffering) special variable specifies whether buffering should be turned on or off. Normally, a socket waits until the buffer has filled before sending the data.

- The **LocalPort** argument to **IO::Socket::INET** specifies the listening port on the server.

- The **Type** argument is the type of connection we wish to create.

- The **Listen** argument specifies how many clients can be queued up on the server before it starts ignoring new clients. **Listen** must be defined for a server. Once we have the server set up, we have to accept a connection from a client.

- The **accept** method in the **IO::Socket::INET** class waits until a client tries to access the server. Once a client does access the server, the server will set up the connection.

- If you want to send e-mail you need an SMTP server. Perl has a module to deal with SMTP transfers—the **Net::SMTP** module.

- The first argument passed to the constructor of **Net::SMTP** must be a valid SMTP server. This constructor creates the object and connects to the server all in one step.

- You can also send the optional arguments **Hello**, which identifies the mail domain of the user, **Timeout**, which specifies a timeout for the connection and **Debug**, which will turn debugging on and off.

- You can create a new e-mail message with method **mail**, which receives the user's e-mail address as an argument. We use the **to** method in **Net::SMTP** to specify the recipient of this e-mail. The **data** method starts the transfer of data for the e-mail message. Once the transfer has started, we can send information using the **datasend** method and send the full message with the **dataend** method. The **quit** method in **Net::SMTP** closes the connection.

- POP was created to facilitate storage and retrieval of e-mail from a remote server. POP servers allow you to check, read, store and delete e-mail.
- The **Mail::POP3Client** module can be used to check e-mail.
- The **Count** method in **Mail::POP3Client** returns the number of messages in the mailbox.
- The **head** method in **Mail::POP3Client** will return all of the messages headers. These contain all the relevant information about the e-mail.
- The **WWW::Search** module provides an interface to a large list of search engines. This module is extended by several modules that enable using each different engine.
- To specify a query, we send the original query (entered by the user) to the **escape_query** method in the **WWW::Search** module. This converts a simple sentence into an HTML-encoded sentence suitable for the **WWW::Search** module.
- The **native_query** method takes the return value from **escape_query** and starts the search.
- To get results, we call the **next_result** method on a **WWW::Search** object.
- The **url** method in **WWW::Search** serves to reformat the result as a URL value that we can use and read. We use these methods to iterate through the results and print them to the user.

TERMINOLOGY

$| special variable
accept in **IO::Socket::INET**
agent attribute of a user agent
AltaVista
as_string in **LWP::UserAgent**
back end
buffering
chat client
chat server
chatting
client program
client request
client/server chat application
code attribute of a response object
comment token
content attribute of a request object
content attribute of a response object
content in **LWP::UserAgent**
content_type in **LWP::UserAgent**
Count in **Mail::POP3Client**
credentials attribute of a user agent
data in **Net::SMTP**
datagrams
datasend in **Net::SMTP**
Debug for **Net::SMTP**
declaration token
e-mail
e-mail application
end token
escape_query in **WWW::Search**
from attribute of a user agent

from field of an e-mail message
front end
get function in **LWP::Simple**
get request
get_token in **HTML::TokeParser**
getprint in **LWP::Simple**
getstore in **LWP::Simple**
head in **Mail::POP3Client**
head request
headers attribute of a request object
headers attribute of a response object
HotBot
HTML::TokeParser module
HTTP
HTTP response code
HTTP::Request module
HTTP::Response module
InfoSeek
Internet (**INET**) connection
Internet search engines
Internet-and-Web-related modules
Internet-and-Web-related tasks
Internet-based language
IO::Socket module
IO::Socket::INET module
IP address
is_success in **LWP::UserAgent**
Library for the WWW in Perl
line buffering special variable
Listen for **IO::Socket::INET**
LocalPort for **IO::Socket::INET**

LWP   send an e-mail message
LWP module   server program
LWP terminology   Simple Mail Transfer Protocol (SMTP)
LWP::Simple module   SMTP server
LWP::UserAgent module   **SOCK_STREAM** constant
mail function in **Net::SMTP**   socket
Mail::POP3Client module   start token
message attribute of a response object   **status_line** function in **LWP::UserAgent**
method attribute of a request object streams
mimicking a Web search   stripping tags from HTML
native_query function in **WWW::Search**   subject field of an e-mail
Net::SMTP module   TCP chat client
new method in **HTML::TokeParser**   TCP chat server
next_result function in **WWW::Search**   TCP client
PeerAddr for **IO::Socket::INET**   TCP server
PeerPort for **IO::Socket::INET**   text token
POP server   **Timeout** for **Net::SMTP** constructor
Post Office Protocol (POP)   **timeout** attribute of a user agent
post request   to field of an e-mail
prewritten modules   **to** function in **Net::SMTP**
Proto for **IO::Socket::INET**   token
protocol   Transport Control Protocol (TCP)
put request   **Type** for **IO::Socket::INET** constructor
quit function in **Net::SMTP**   **URL** attribute of a request object
receiving e-mail   **url** function in **WWW::Search**
recipient field of an e-mail   user agent
reply   Web server
request function in **LWP::UserAgent**   WebCrawler
request object   **WWW::Search** module
response object   **WWW::Search::AltaVista** module
search engines   **WWW::Search::HotBot** module
searching   **WWW::Search::Infoseek** module
send   **WWW::Search::WebCrawler** module

SELF-REVIEW EXERCISES

17.1   Fill in the blanks in each of the following.
  a) The three objects that are part of a LWP program are _____, _____ and _____.
  b) LWP can be used to mimic the operations of a _____.
  c) **LWP::Simple** uses a _____ interface.
  d) **HTML::TokeParser** splits HTML up into _____.
  e) An item from **HTML::TokeParser** is one of five types: _____, _____, _____, _____ and _____.
  f) Networks require open connections which consist of two _____.
  g) The two main e-mail protocols are _____ and _____.
  h) The _____ method will return the number of messages in a POP mailbox.
  i) SMTP is used to _____ e-mail.
  j) The _____ module mimics a Web-based search.

17.2   State whether each of the following is *true* or *false*. If *false*, explain why.
  a) To grab a Web page using LWP, you call the **request** method of a **userAgent** object.

b) **LWP::Simple** provides simple functionality of LWP, but without an object-oriented interface.

c) **HTML::TokeParser** is the only way to parse HTML.

d) Protocols are standardized means of communicating over a network.

e) The **$|** variable controls the buffering of a filehandle.

f) The **listen** method must be used to create the **IO::Socket::INET** object if it is to be used as a server.

g) We use the **Net::POP** module to perform POP e-mail operations.

h) In **Net::SMTP**, we create a new e-mail message with the **e-mail** method.

i) It is important to use the **escape_query** method on a string before using it in a **WWW::Search** object.

ANSWERS TO SELF-REVIEW EXERCISES

17.1   a) request object, response object, user agent.   b) browser.   c) procedural.   d) tokens.
e) start, end, text, declaration, comment. f) sockets. g) post office protocol, simple mail transfer protocol. h) **Count**. i) send. j) **WWW::Search**.

17.2

a) True.

b) True.

c) False. We can parse through the HTML with regular expressions and other string manipulation capabilities.

d) True.

e) True.

f) True.

g) False. We use the **Mail::POP3Client** module to perform POP operations.

h) False. In **Net::SMTP**, we create a new e-mail message with the **new** method.

i) True.

EXERCISES

17.3   Create a program using **LWP** that will input a link from the user and determine whether the page contains the word "Perl."

17.4   Use **LWP** in combination with **HTML::TokeParser** to access a Web page and determine whether that page contains a form. If so, print the form. This consists of the text from the start form tag to the end form tag.

17.5   Use **LWP** in combination with **HTML::TokeParser** to access a Web page and indent the source code properly. This is similar to Exercise 10.7, but should use **LWP** to grab a Web page from the Internet and should use **HTML::TokeParser** to split up the HTML into tags.

17.6   Write a program that uses the **Mail::POP3Client** module and extends the **getServer.pl** (Fig. 17.6) and **checkMail.pl** (Fig. 17.7) programs and allows you to read the e-mail's contents.

17.7   Write a link checker program. This program should use the **LWP** modules to get an HTML page, use **HTML::TokeParser** to parse the page and find all links from that page. Then use **LWP** again to check those links. Use CGI to output the information in a Web page.

18

Process Management

Objectives

- To understand the notion of separate processes and multithreading.
- To be able to create separate processes using the **fork** command.
- To be able to launch outside programs.
- To be able to communicate between processes.
- To understand the notion of signals.
- To be able to create custom signal handlers.
- To be aware of Microsoft's OLE Automation capabilities.

The spider's touch, how exquisitely fine!
Feels at each thread, and lives along the line.
Alexander Pope

A person with one watch knows what time it is; a person with two watches is never sure.
Proverb

Conversation is but carving!
Give no more to every guest,
Than he's able to digest.
Jonathan Swift

Learn to labor and to wait.
Henry Wadsworth Longfellow

The most general definition of beauty…Multeity in Unity.
Samuel Taylor Coleridge

Outline

18.1 Introduction

It would be nice if we could "do one thing at a time" and "do it well." Often, it is useful to process several tasks at the same time. For example, the human body performs a great variety of operations *in parallel*—or as we will say throughout this chapter, *concurrently*. Respiration, blood circulation and digestion occur concurrently. All of the senses—seeing, touching, smelling, tasting and hearing—can occur concurrently. Computers, too, perform operations concurrently. It is common today for desktop personal computers to be compiling a program, printing a file and receiving electronic mail messages over a network concurrently.

Concurrency is important in our lives. Ironically, though, most programming languages do not enable programmers to specify concurrent activities. Rather, they provide only a simple set of control structures that enable programmers to perform one action at a time, then proceed to the next action after the previous action completes. The kind of concurrency that computers perform today is normally implemented as operating systems *primitives* available only to highly experienced *systems programmers*.

There are two primary ways to implement concurrency. One is to have each task operate in completely separate memory spaces. Each has its own separate section of memory in which to execute. Each of these is known as a *process*. The other way is to have the two executions, also known as *threads of execution*, operating in the same memory space. This is known as *multithreading*. Creating a thread is more efficient than creating a process, because a new virtual memory space does not need to be created. The trade-off is that threads are riskier. Processes protect us from having one process manipulating shared data without the other process knowing about it. This type of a problem is known as a *race condition*. Race conditions depend on the complex timing between threads, so they can be among the most difficult bugs to locate in a program.

One of the main uses of Perl is as a glue language. Perl can take disparate programs that do not fit together well and bridge the gaps between them so they can meaningfully work together. Perl allows us to access the shell to run other programs and grab control of their input or output. To execute the separate programs concurrently, separate processes are required for each.

Some operating systems, like Unix, have the built-in ability to make separate processes. There are system commands that create and manage processes. On systems that directly support processes, Perl uses the basic system commands to implement the process functions. On systems that do not have such system commands, processes are emulated by cloning the interpreter and executing the separate processes in their own instances of the interpreter.

Portability Tip 18.1

Creating separate processes from a program is not available on every operating system. For this reason, processes are one of the least portable Perl features.

Perl's multithreading features currently are labeled as experimental. This means that they are to be used with caution, as they can be buggy. Also, the interface could change in future versions. Threads are being built into Perl 6 and should be more stable there. For this reason, we will cover processes, but not threads, in this chapter.

18.2 The `fork` command

The simplest way to create a new process is to use function **fork**. When **fork** is called, it either calls the system's **fork** function (if there is one) to create a new process or emulates it by cloning the interpreter. The process that calls **fork** is known as the *parent process*. Any process that is forked from this process is known as a *child process*. Each process has a unique *process id* number, or *pid*. When the **fork** function is called, if it succeeds, it creates a new child process that is identical to the parent process. Note that because the child process is identical to the parent, it inherits many values from the parent, such as environment variables. The only difference between the two processes is the return value of the **fork** call. In the **child** process, it returns 0, while in the parent process, the *pid* of the child is returned. If the **fork** call is not successful, it returns **undef**. Thus, you can use **if** statements to determine which process is executing and perform process-specific steps. When the program executes, the separate processes will share processor time. Figure 18.1 shows an example of function **fork**.

Portability Tip 18.2

*Function **fork** is unavailable for Win32 versions of Perl before Perl 5.6.*

```
1   #!/usr/bin/perl
2   # Fig. 18.1: fig18_01.pl
3   # Using fork to create child processes.
4
5   use warnings;
6   use strict;
7
8   my ( $start, $middle, $end, $pid );
9   $| = 1;
10
11  $start = time();
12
13  if ( $pid = fork() ) {
14      sleep( 1 );
15      print( "Parent executing.\n" );
```

Fig. 18.1   Using **fork** to create child processes (part 1 of 2).

```
16      sleep( 2 );
17      print( "Parent finished.\n" );
18   }
19   elsif ( defined( $pid ) ) {
20      sleep( 1 );
21      print( "Child executing.\n" );
22      sleep( 2 );
23      print( "Child finished.\n" );
24      exit();
25   }
26   else {
27      die( "Could not fork" );
28   }
29
30   $middle = time();
31
32   print( "That took " );
33   print( $middle - $start );
34   print( " seconds with fork.\n" );
35
36   sleep( 3 );
37   sleep( 3 );
38   $end = time();
39
40   print( "That took " );
41   print( $end - $middle );
42   print( " seconds without fork.\n" );
43   print( "Total of ", ( $end - $start ), " seconds.\n" );
```

```
Parent executing.
Child executing.
Parent finished.
Child finished.
That took 3 seconds with fork.
That took 6 seconds without fork.
Total of 9 seconds.
```

Fig. 18.1   Using **fork** to create child processes (part 2 of 2).

The **fork** function call in line 13 creates a clone of the current process that has the same variables and code as the original process. The only difference is that the return value from the **fork** function in the cloned process is 0, while in the parent process the return value is the *pid* of the child. If function **fork** returns true, lines 13–18 execute in the parent process. If function **fork** returns false, lines 19–25 execute in the child process. When the child process finishes, we call function **exit** to end the process (line 24). Otherwise, both processes would execute the code after the **if** statements and each **print** statement would execute twice.

One thing to note about the output of Fig. 18.1 is that the output may differ between program executions. In some executions, the child prints first. In other executions, the parent prints first. Sometimes the message **That took 3 seconds** prints before the final child output. Thus, the order in which actions occur in forked processes is not as well defined as if all the actions are performed in one process.

On line 9, we set special variable $| (also known as $OUTPUT_AUTOFLUSH) to 1. If this variable has a nonzero value, the selected output channel will be flushed automatically when a **print** or **write** statement executes. This is important when two or more processes output to the same handle and the output should reflect exactly when each **print** or **write** occurred. With the $| variable set to false, the output of Fig. 18.1 sometimes does not reflect the order in which outputs actually occurred.

In some cases, the parent process needs to wait for a child process to finish before continuing. Function **wait** waits for all the children of a particular process to finish before allowing the parent process to continue its execution. This function returns the *pid* of a finished child, or -1 if there are no more children. Figure 18.2 demonstrates function **wait**.

To create two child processes in Fig. 18.2, we use function **fork** twice (line 11). When the first call to **fork** executes, it creates the first child. When the child process reaches that same function call in the code, **fork** returns zero and prevents the execution of the second call to **fork**. In the first child, $pid is 0 and $pid2 is undefined. In the parent process, the first call to **fork** returns true, causing the second **fork** to be executed. The child created in this process has $pid set to the process id number of the first child and $pid2 equal to zero. Thus the **if** block that executes when both are true (lines 11–15) is executed in the parent's process. If $pid is true, but $pid2 is zero, the second child is executing (lines 16–21). When $pid is zero, the first child is executing (lines 22–26).

```perl
1   #!/usr/bin/perl
2   # Fig. 18.2: fig18_02.pl
3   # Demonstrates the wait function.
4
5   use warnings;
6   use strict;
7
8   my ( $pid, $pid2 );
9   $| = 1;
10
11  if ( ( $pid = fork() ) && ( $pid2 = fork() ) ) {
12     print( "I have to wait for my kids.\n" );
13     my $straggler = wait();
14     print( "Finally $straggler finished, now I can go.\n" );
15  }
16  elsif ( $pid && defined( $pid2 ) ) {
17     sleep( 2 );
18     print( "Kid 2: So is mine...\n" );
19     sleep( 4 );
20     exit();
21  }
22  elsif ( defined( $pid ) ) {
23     sleep( 1 );
24     print( "Kid 1: My parent is patient...\n" );
25     sleep( 2 );
26  }
27  else {
28     die( "Forking problems: " );
29  }
```

Fig. 18.2 Using the **wait** function to wait for all the child processes (part 1 of 2).

```
I have to wait for my kids.
Kid 1: My parent is patient...
Kid 2: So is mine...
Finally 296 finished, now I can go.
```

Fig. 18.2   Using the **wait** function to wait for all the child processes (part 2 of 2).

Common Programming Error 18.1

*Do not use **$PID** (with the letters all in uppercase) as it is a special variable. This is the process number of the running program itself. It is also equivalent to the special variables **$PROCESS_ID** and **$$**. Using these special variables can cause logic errors.*

If you want to wait for a specific process to complete, you can use function **waitpid**, which takes a process id as the first argument. It waits for that process to finish then returns the *pid* of that process. If there is no child for that *pid* or it is already dead, the **waitpid** function returns -1. The exit status of the child process is stored in special variable **$?**. Figure 18.3 is similar to Fig. 18.2, but modified so we only wait for the first child.

```perl
1   #!/usr/bin/perl
2   # Fig. 18.3: fig18_03.pl
3   # Demonstrating the waitpid function.
4
5   use warnings;
6   use strict;
7
8   my ( $pid, $pid2 );
9   $| = 1;
10
11  if ( ( $pid = fork() ) && ( $pid2 = fork() ) ) {
12      print( "I have to wait for my kids.\n" );
13      my $straggler = waitpid( $pid, 0 );
14      print( "Finally $straggler finished, now I can go.\n" );
15  }
16  elsif ( $pid && defined( $pid2 ) ) {
17      sleep( 2 );
18      print( "Kid 2: Mine is not...\n" );
19      sleep( 4 );
20      print( "Kid 2: Hey! Wait for me!!!\n" );
21      exit();
22  }
23  elsif ( defined( $pid ) ) {
24      sleep( 1 );
25      print( "Kid 1: My parent is patient...\n" );
26      sleep( 2 );
27  }
28  else {
29      die( "Forking problems: " );
30  }
```

Fig. 18.3   Using the **waitpid** function to wait for a specific child process (part 1 of 2).

```
I have to wait for my kids.
Kid 1: My parent is patient...
Kid 2: Mine is not...
Finally 269 finished, now I can go.
Kid 2: Hey! Wait for me!!!
```

Fig. 18.3 Using the **waitpid** function to wait for a specific child process (part 2 of 2).

18.3 The `system` and `exec` functions

There are two ways to execute other programs from a program. The simplest is function *exec*, which uses the system's shell to invoke the program specified as an argument, then replaces the current process with the program that was launched. Thus, when the newly launched program terminates, the current process terminates.

Shell processing is performed on the first argument passed to **exec**—all shell wild cards are in effect. Thus, the shell will process wildcard expansion (e.g., **dir *.exe**), piping (e.g., **dir *.exe | more**) or any other operation supported by your system's shell. To prevent shell processing on the arguments to a program, pass to **exec** a list of arguments in which the first element is the command to execute and the remaining elements are the arguments to pass directly to that command without shell processing.

Function *system* is similar to function **exec** in that it can be used to execute shell commands. The difference is that **system** returns back to the original process. It does this by using **fork** to create a separate process and causing the original process to **wait** until the child process is finished. Figure 18.4 shows an example using **system**. Figure 18.5 shows the contents of the **hello.pl** file we created from Figure 18.4.

```perl
1   #!/usr/bin/perl
2   # Fig. 18.4: fig18_04.pl
3   # Uses the system function to clear the screen.
4
5   use warnings;
6   use strict;
7
8   print( "What file would you like to create? " );
9   chomp( my $file = <STDIN> );
10
11  ( $^O =~ /Win/ ) ? system( "cls" ) : system( "clear" );
12
13  print( "Type the text you wish to be in this file.\n" );
14  print( "Type clear on a blank line to start over.\n" );
15  print( "Type quit on a blank line when you are finished.\n" );
16  open( FILE, ">$file" ) or die( "Cannot open: $!" );
17
18  while ( <STDIN> ) {
19      last if ( /quit/ );
20
21      if ( /clear/ ) {
22          ( $^O =~ /Win/ ) ? system( "cls" ) : system( "clear" );
```

Fig. 18.4 Simple example using **system** (part 1 of 2).

```
23            print( "Type the text you wish to be in this file.\n" );
24            print( "Type clear on a blank line to start over.\n" );
25            print( "Type quit on a blank line " );
26            print( "when you are finished.\n" );
27            open( FILE, ">$file" ) or die( "Cannot open: $!" );
28        }
29        else {
30            print( FILE );
31        }
32    }
33
34    close( FILE ) or die( "Cannot close: $!" );
```

```
What file would you like to create? hello.pl
```

```
Type the text you wish to be in this file.
Type clear on a blank line to start over.
Type quit on a blank line when you are finished.
#!/usr/bin/perl
# hello.pl
# Typical "hello world" program.

use warnings;
use strict;

print( "Hello World" );
quit
```

Fig. 18.4   Simple example using **system** (part 2 of 2).

```
#!/usr/bin/perl
# hello.pl
# Typical "hello world" program.

use warnings;
use strict;

print( "Hello World" );
```

Fig. 18.5   Contents of the resulting **hello.pl** file.

Portability Tip 18.3

*Functions **system** and **exec** execute shell commands directly from the shell, so they can make your program less portable.*

Line 11 attempts to make Fig. 18.4 more portable by using special variable **$^O** to determine the operating system on which the program is executing before deciding what command to execute. However, this program will work only on the Windows operating system and any platform that uses the shell command **clear** to empty the text in a command prompt.

Figure 18.6 shows a slightly more complicated text-editing example. The example uses module **LWP** to get a URL passed to it on the command line, then it uses **exec** to start a native editing program to edit this page. [Note that for simplicity, this program only handles URLs that begin with **http://**. The program can be easily modified to handle URL formats.] The outputs for this program demonstrate the **Notepad** text editor on Windows and the **vi** text editor operating in a command window on Linux.

```perl
1   #!/usr/bin/perl
2   # Fig. 18.6: fig18_06.pl
3   # Gets a web page and opens for editing.
4
5   use warnings;
6   use strict;
7   use LWP::Simple;
8
9   my( $URL, $filename ) = @ARGV;
10
11  if ( $URL !~ m#http://# ) {
12      $URL =~ s#^#http://#;
13  }
14
15  if ( is_error( getstore( $URL, $filename ) ) ) {
16      die( "Could not get file: $!" );
17  }
18
19  my $program = ( $^O =~ /Win/ ? "notepad.exe" : "vi" );
20
21  exec( $program, $filename );
```

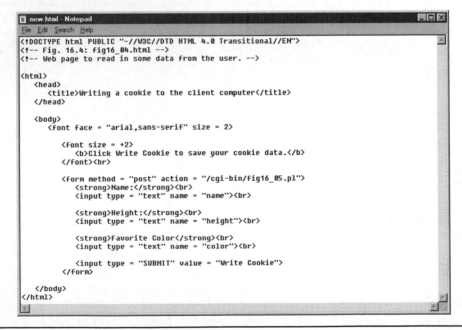

Fig. 18.6 Using function **exec** to transfer control to another program (part 1 of 2).

```
paul@localhost.localdomain: /home/paul
 File  Sessions  Options  Help
<title>Deitel</title>
<style type="text/css">
   BODY { font-family: helvetica, arial, sans-serif }
</style>
<base target="content">
</head>

<frameset framespacing="2" frameborder="0" cols="185,*">
   <frameset frameborder="0" rows="130,*">
      <frame name="uleft" scrolling="no" target="rtop" src="logo.htm" style="font-fami
ly: sans-serif, serif; font-size: 12pt" marginwidth="5" marginheight="5" noresize>
         <frame name="left" scrolling="auto" noresize target="rtop" src="toc.htm" style="
font-family: sans-serif, serif; font-size: 12pt" marginwidth="5" marginheight="5">
   </frameset>
   <frameset frameborder="0" rows="130,*">
      <frame name="banner" target="rbottom" src="frbanner.htm" scrolling="auto" style=
"font-family: sans-serif, serif; font-size: 12pt" marginwidth="5" marginheight="5">
         <frame name="content" scrolling="auto" marginwidth="5" marginheight="5" src="hom
e.htm" target="_self">
   </frameset>
   <noframes>
   <body>
   <table border="1" width="100%" height="147" cellpadding="4">
      <tr>
@
```

Fig. 18.6 Using function **exec** to transfer control to another program (part 2 of 2).

18.4 Controlling the Input and Output of Processes

What if we want to be able to use the output of one program as the input to another? What if we want to manipulate the output of a process before displaying the output to the user? Perl answers these questions by providing multiple options for grabbing the **STDOUT** or **STDIN** from files.

Function **open** lets us emulate the functionality of command-line piping by placing a pipe (|) symbol in the string that specifies the command to execute. If the pipe is placed at the beginning of the string, the input of the program to execute is attached to the specified file handle. If the pipe is at the end of the string, the output of the program to execute is attached to the specified handle. These handles can be treated like any other file handles. To write to the input of a program, print or write to the appropriate handle; the data are piped automatically to the input of the program. To read the output from a program, read from the piped handle just as we would read from any other file handle.

Figure 18.7 shows an example using function **open** to take the output of one command-line function, process it, then feed it as the input to another command.

```
1   #!/usr/bin/perl
2   # Fig. 18.7: fig18_07.pl
3   # Demonstrating using open to connect different processes.
4
5   use warnings;
6   use strict;
7
8   open( DIR, "dir *.* |" ) or die( "Cannot open dir pipe: $!" );
9   open( MORE, "| more" ) or die( "Cannot open more: $!" );
```

Fig. 18.7 Using pipes to connect two processes (part 1 of 2).

```
10
11   while ( <DIR> ) {
12      print( MORE );
13   }
14
15   close( DIR ) or die( "Cannot close DIR: $!" );
16   close( MORE ) or die( "Cannot close MORE: $!" );
```

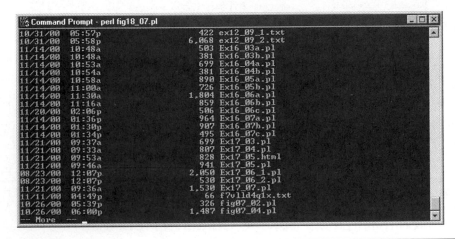

Fig. 18.7   Using pipes to connect two processes (part 2 of 2).

Figure 18.7 is a contrived example, but it does demonstrate how these pipes work. Line 8 executes the shell command **dir *.*** and connects its **STDOUT** to the handle **DIR**. Line 9 connects the handle **MORE** to the **STDIN** of the shell command **more**. Then, we use these handles like any other filehandle. Line 11 reads from the output of the command **dir *.*** and line 12 writes the data as the input to the command **more**. It is important to ensure that you close a pipe to the input of another command as we did on line 15. This tells the process that it will not receive any more input. Otherwise, the process may continue executing and wait for more input.

These pipe capabilities can be useful. In Chapter 12, one of the examples went through a lot of trouble to ensure that the user was prompted after each screen of output. This would have been a lot simpler had we just opened a pipe to the **more** command and wrote to that handle instead. However, not all operating systems have the **more** command (or it may be called by a different name), so that approach was more portable.

Another shorthand way to execute a shell command and capture its output is operator **qx//**, also known as the *quoted execution operator*. As with the other quoting operators, this has special quoting characters—called *backquotes*, or *backticks* ` `. The backticks interpolate any variables that appear in the string, then pass the result to the shell for execution. In scalar context, the result of a backtick expression is a single string containing the complete output of the executed command. In list context, the result is a list of values in which each line is returned as a separate element. Note that newline characters are not removed for you in either case. If necessary, you should **chomp** the results to remove the newlines. Figure 18.8 gives an example using backticks. Lines 12 and 13 execute Windows commands, and lines 16 and 17 execute Linux commands.

Performance Tip 18.1

*Using **open** to get a pipe to a command is more efficient than using backticks because all the results from a backtick expression are loaded into memory at the same time.*

Function **open** does not provide a mechanism to obtain handles to both the input and output of a single command. However, this can be accomplished with the ***IPC::Open2*** and ***IPC::Open3*** modules. Module **IPC::Open2** provides function ***open2*** that allows us to obtain a handles for a command's **STDIN** and **STDOUT**. In addition, we can obtain a handle to the **STDERR** with function ***open3*** in the module **IPC::Open3**.

Function **open2** takes three main arguments. The first two are the filehandles for the standard input and standard output, respectively. These are supplied either as references to typeglobs or as **FileHandle** objects. The third argument is the command to execute. Additional arguments are passed as arguments to the new process without shell processing. Function **open3** takes four main arguments—the standard output filehandle, the standard input filehandle, the standard error filehandle and the command to execute. Note that the first two arguments are reversed with function **open3**.

```perl
1   #!/usr/bin/perl
2   # Fig. 18.8: fig18_08.pl
3   # Demonstrates using backticks.
4
5   use warnings;
6   use strict;
7
8   my $date;
9   my $version;
10
11  if ( $^O =~ /Win/ ) {
12      $version = ( `ver` );
13      $date = ( `date /t` );
14  }
15  else {
16      $version = ( `uname -r -s` );
17      $date = ( `date` );
18  }
19
20  print( "The Operating system version is $version");
21  print( "\n", $date );
```

```
The Operating system version is
Microsoft Windows 2000 [Version 5.00.2195]

Tue 11/28/2000
```

```
The Operating system version is Linux 2.2.14-6.1.1

Tue Nov 28 06:26:43 EST 2000
```

Fig. 18.8 Using backticks.

Common Programming Error 18.2

*Providing the filehandles for reading and writing in the wrong order for an **open2** or **open3** function call can cause hard-to-track errors. Always double check these arguments.*

Both functions return the *pid* for the process which was forked to execute the command. If there is an error creating this process, both processes **die** instead of returning. The first line of the error message starts with either **open2** or **open3** to help you determine the problem. Figure 18.9 shows an example using function **open2**. The program of Fig. 18.10 is executed by line 12 of Fig. 18.9.

Common Programming Error 18.3

*Be careful when controlling the **STDIN** and **STDOUT** from a function—it is easy to make fatal errors. For example, two programs can be waiting for each other's output before continuing their own execution. This is known as deadlock.*

```perl
1   #!/usr/bin/perl
2   # Fig. 18.9: fig18_09.pl
3   # Demonstrating the open2 function.
4
5   use warnings;
6   use strict;
7   use IPC::Open2;
8
9   $| = 1;
10  my $command = 'perl fig18_10.pl';
11
12  open2( \*INPUT, \*OUTPUT, $command ) or
13     die( "Cannot open: $!" );
14
15  for ( 1 .. 20 ) {
16     print( OUTPUT $_, "\n" );
17     my $read = <INPUT>;
18     print( $_, '   ', $read );
19  }
20
21  close( OUTPUT ) or die( "Cannot close OUTPUT: $!" );
22  close( INPUT ) or die( "Cannot close INPUT: $!" );
```

```
1    MyItnkr.UtBnc
2    My6jwfxg7zFGE
3    My3G3DtIRpQEA
4    Myza94uYasdEE
5    MyCBteM4CIuTk
6    MyWRtG.HnvdL2
7    Myb8qLeBJ6TlM
8    MyE6k76L3NeoE
9    MyxpYOghD0TIE
10   MyI8Uhkz4HPjY
11   MyB3G7m.CDII6
12   MyugXM4mJTc1c
13   My9OUTHS6M.jg
```

(continued top of next page)

Fig. 18.9   Using **open2** (part 1 of 2).

```
                                         (continued from previous page)
14   My8UYE/LL8dgU
15   MyYAcz4F1r.to
16   MycPbNadoaNYo
17   MyXdTeyyc1DNY
18   MyTm8RxjwtKO.
19   My2Q98KujB0i6
20   MyecGYzUxpdvk
```

Fig. 18.9 Using **open2** (part 2 of 2).

```perl
1   #!/usr/bin/perl
2   # Fig. 18.10: fig18_10.pl
3   # Helper to fig18_09.pl.
4
5   use warnings;
6   use strict;
7
8   $| = 1;
9
10  while ( <STDIN> ) {
11     print( crypt( $_, "My cats' breath smells like cat food" ) );
12     print( "\n" );
13  }
```

Fig. 18.10 The helper program to **fig18_09.pl**.

18.5 Communicating Between Processes

Perl provides us with ways to communicate between parent and child processes created with **fork** by connecting filehandles using function **pipe**. The first argument to function **pipe** is the name of the filehandle for reading and the second argument is the filehandle for writing. If you use function **pipe** before using **fork** to create separate processes, you can write from one process and read the results in another process. Again you have to be careful to avoid deadlock when doing this. You also might want to set special variable **$|** on the write handle to flush after each output. Figure 18.11 shows an example using **pipe**.

```perl
1   #!/usr/bin/perl
2   # Fig. 18.11: fig18_11.pl
3   # Using pipe to communicate with child processes.
4
5   use warnings;
6   use strict;
7   use IO::Handle;
8
9   pipe( CHILDINPUT, PARENTOUTPUT );
10  pipe( PARENTINPUT, CHILDOUTPUT );
11
12  PARENTOUTPUT->autoflush( 1 );
```

Fig. 18.11 Using function **pipe** to communicate between a parent process and a child process (part 1 of 2).

```
13   CHILDOUTPUT->autoflush( 1 );
14   STDOUT->autoflush( 1 );
15
16   if ( my $pid = fork() ) {
17
18      for ( 1 .. 10 ) {
19         print( PARENTOUTPUT "$_\n" );
20         print( "I said $_, " );
21         chomp( my $response = <PARENTINPUT> );
22         print( "and he said $response!\n" );
23      }
24
25      close( PARENTOUTPUT ) or
26         die( "Cannot close PARENTOUTPUT: $!" );
27      close( PARENTINPUT ) or
28         die( "Cannot close PARENTINPUT: $!" );
29   }
30   elsif ( defined( $pid ) ) {
31      close( PARENTOUTPUT ) or
32         die( "Cannot close PARENTOUTPUT: $!" );
33      close( PARENTINPUT ) or
34         die( "Cannot close PARENTINPUT: $!" );
35
36      while ( <CHILDINPUT> ) {
37         chomp();
38         print( CHILDOUTPUT $_ * 20, "\n" );
39      }
40
41      close( CHILDOUTPUT ) or
42         die( "Cannot close CHILDOUTPUT: $!" );
43      close( CHILDINPUT ) or
44         die( "Cannot close CHILDINPUT: $!" );
45      exit();
46   }
47   else {
48      die( "Fork did not work" );
49   }
50
51   print( "And that is the end of the conversation.\n" );
```

```
I said 1, and he said 20!
I said 2, and he said 40!
I said 3, and he said 60!
I said 4, and he said 80!
I said 5, and he said 100!
I said 6, and he said 120!
I said 7, and he said 140!
I said 8, and he said 160!
I said 9, and he said 180!
I said 10, and he said 200!
And that is the end of the conversation.
```

Fig. 18.11 Using function **pipe** to communicate between a parent process and a child process (part 2 of 2).

We can also create processes that communicate with each other using function **open**. Opening a handle to the filename "**-**" returns a handle that is a duplicate of **STDIN**. Now if we open a pipe to **-**, by opening either **| -** or **- |**, the open command does a fork and returns the *pid* of the new process. If we open to **| -**, it causes the **STDIN** of the new process to be connected to the opened filehandle. If we open to **- |**, the **STDOUT** of the child is connected to the new filehandle. If this filehandle is closed, the parent process waits for the child process to finish, with the return value of the child process stored in **$?**.

This can be useful to filter input or output for a part of your script. In Fig. 18.12 we use **open** to create a filter that adds line numbers to the output of the child process. [*Note:* This program was tested on Linux.]

Portability Tip 18.4

Opening a handle to - | or | - does not work on the Windows platform.

```perl
1   #!/usr/bin/perl
2   # Fig. 18.12: fig18_12.pl
3   # Using open to fork and filter output.
4
5   use warnings;
6   use strict;
7
8   $| = 1;
9
10  if ( my $pid = open( CHILD, "-|" ) ) {
11     my $i;
12
13     while ( <CHILD> ) {
14        print( "Line ", ++$i, ": $_" );
15     }
16
17     close( CHILD ) or die( "Cannot close: $!" );
18  }
19  elsif ( defined( $pid ) ) {
20     print( "I am doing some\n" );
21     print( "processing here\n" );
22     print( "that produces\n" );
23     print( "multiple lines\n" );
24     print( "of output.\n" );
25     exit();
26  }
27  else {
28     print( "Could not fork." );
29  }
```

```
Line 1: I am doing some
Line 2: processing here
Line 3: that produces
Line 4: multiple lines
Line 5: of output.
```

Fig. 18.12 Using **open** to filter output.

18.6 Signal Handling

Processes also can communicate with *signals*, which are messages that are delivered to a program by the operating system, then handled by the program. There are many signals that can be sent and different actions that are taken in handling these signals. The process of receiving signals and performing the necessary actions is known as *signal handling*. Signals can be generated due to errors (e.g., writing to a closed pipe), events (e.g., when a timer finishes) or user input (e.g., *<ctrl>-c*), or they can be generated internally from your program.

Each process has a default handler for each signal. You can either let Perl handle signals for your program or you can set custom handlers to be called when a signal occurs. Figure 18.13 lists some common signals.

We can override the handling for most signals. The only exceptions to this are **SIGKILL** and **SIGSTOP**, which are used as a last resort for unresponsive programs. To set signal handlers, we use the hash **%SIG**. In the hash, we use the end of the signal name as the key (e.g., **INT** for **SIGINT**), and the corresponding value is either a code reference or the name of the subroutine to execute when that signal is received. Figure 18.14 shows an example of setting our own custom handler for **SIGINT**. You can cause a **SIGINT** signal by pressing *<ctrl>-c* on most platforms.

Portability Tip 18.5

The results of programs that use signal handling differ across operating systems.

Name	Default Action	Usual Cause or Use
SIGINT	**die**	When user inputs *<ctrl>-c*
SIGQUIT	core-dump	When user inputs *<ctrl>-*
SIGTERM	**die**	Sent by the shell's **kill** command when no signal name is given
SIGPIPE	**warn**	When a process tries to write to a closed pipe or socket
SIGCHLD	none	When a child stops running
SIGALRM	none	When a timer set by the **alarm** function finishes
SIGHUP	**die**	When a process's controlling terminal is disconnected
SIGFPE	**die**	Mathematical errors like division by zero
SIGKILL	**die**	Used to cause immediate program termination
SIGSTOP	stop the process	Used to stop the process
SIGUSR1	none	Extra signal for use of program
SIGUSR2	none	Extra signal for use of program

Fig. 18.13 Some common signals.

```perl
1   #!/usr/bin/perl
2   # Fig. 18.14: fig18_14.pl
3   # Demonstrates using %SIG to define our own signal handlers.
4
5   use warnings;
6   use strict;
7
8   my $count = 3;
9   $| = 1;
10
11  $SIG{ 'INT' } = \&stop;
12
13  while ( $count ) {
14     print( "Hooray!" );
15     print( "\n" );
16     sleep( 1 );
17  }
18
19  sub stop
20  {
21     $SIG{ 'INT' } = \&stop;
22     $count--;
23     print( "$count\n" );
24
25     unless ( $count ) {
26        print( "Sorry, I did not want to stop...\n" );
27     }
28  }
```

```
Hooray!
Hooray!
2
Hooray!
Hooray!
Hooray!
1
Hooray!
0
Sorry, I did not want to stop...
```

Fig. 18.14 Specifying custom signal handlers.

We overrode the **SIGINT** handler such that the user must type *<ctrl>-c* three times to stop the program. Line 11 specifies that our function **stop** should be called when the signal occurs. Notice that line 20 reassigns the signal handler. On some operating systems, after a signal handler is called its value in **%SIG** reverts back to its default signal handler. For **SIGINT**, this would terminate the program. To avoid this, we have to reassign the signal handler in the handling subroutine.

Portability Tip 18.6

Some operating systems revert to the default signal handler after a signal is caught. To ensure portability, you must reassign the handler when you catch a signal.

There are two more special signals defined by Perl: **__DIE__** and **__WARN__**. (Note that each of these is preceded and followed by two underscore characters.) These handlers are called in response to executing functions **die** or **warn**, respectively. Assigning a signal handler to **$SIG{ __DIE__ }** or **$SIG{ __WARN__ }** allows you to control what Perl does when a program reports an error through these functions. Your signal handlers for **die** and **warn** are disabled when they are invoked the first time. Thus, you can use **die** or **warn** inside your signal handler without causing infinite recursion.

To reestablish the default handler for a signal or to ignore a signal, Perl provides two special values that can be specified for individual signals—**DEFAULT** and **IGNORE**. If a signal's value is set to **DEFAULT**, the default handler is reinstated. If a signal's value is set to **IGNORE**, the program will ignore that signal.

When a signal is received, the executing code is interrupted so the signal can be processed. Normally, this is not a problem because can pick up where it left off after it handles the signal. Such functions are said to be *re-entrant*. Some functions, however, are not re-entrant and cannot be restarted where they left off. For example, few system functions are re-entrant. This can cause problems if Perl is in the middle of allocating memory.

Software Engineering Observation 18.1

To avoid problems with signal handlers and code that is not re-entrant, signal handlers should be as small as possible. You might simply change a variable to reflect that the signal has been called, then return. You can then check in your main program to see if the signal has been thrown, and perform the necessary actions outside your handler. This minimizes the interruption caused by handling the signal.

18.7 Sending Signals

In addition to handling signals, a program can also send signals to other processes. To send a signal to a process, use function **kill**. The first argument is the signal you want to send, and the remaining arguments are the processes to which to send the signal. A negative process argument indicates that the signal should be sent to the parent process and all the child processes of that parent. The signal can be specified either by using the numeric value of the signal, or the string name of the signal (without the **SIG** at the beginning). For signal number 0, **kill** returns true if the process is still alive; otherwise, it returns false. Figure 18.15 shows an example of sending a signal to a child process.

```perl
1   #!/usr/bin/perl
2   # Fig. 18.15: fig18_15.pl
3   # Sending signals to child processes using kill.
4
5   use warnings;
6   use strict;
7   use POSIX qw( :signal_h :errno_h :sys_wait_h );
8
9   $SIG{ USR1 } = \&user1;
10  $SIG{ USR2 } = \&user2;
11  $| = 1;
12
```

Fig. 18.15 Sending signals to child processes using **kill** (part 1 of 2).

```
1   sub user1
2   {
3       $SIG{ USR1 } = \&user1;
4       print( "I have received SIGUSR1.\n" );
5   }
6
7   sub user2
8   {
9       $SIG{ USR2 } = \&user2;
10      print( "I have received SIGUSR2.\n" );
11  }
12
13  if ( my $pid = fork() ) {
14      kill( 'USR1', $pid );
15      kill( 'USR2', $pid );
16      print( "I have just sent two signals.\n" );
17      sleep( 2 );
18      print( "Now I am going to send a few more.\n" );
19      kill( USR2 => $pid );
20      kill( USR1 => $pid );
21      print( "Parent done.\n" );
22  }
23  elsif ( defined( $pid ) ) {
24      sleep( 5 );
25      print( "Kid done.\n" );
26      exit();
27  }
28  else {
29      print( "Forking error...\n" );
30  }
31
32  wait();
```

```
I have just sent two signals.
I have received SIGUSR2.
I have received SIGUSR1.
Now I am going to send a few more.
Parent done.
I have received SIGUSR2.
I have received SIGUSR1.
Kid done.
```

Fig. 18.15 Sending signals to child processes using **kill** (part 2 of 2).

When a child process ends, it stays in the process table, so the parent can determine that the child terminated and whether or not the child terminated normally. If many child processes are created and they are not removed from the process table when they terminate, the process table accumulates dead processes. These are called *zombies*. Eliminating the zombies is call *reaping* and is performed with the **wait** or **waitpid** functions.

To avoid collecting zombies, you can set a handler for the **SIGCHLD** signal, which is sent to the parent when a child exits. In this handler, you can call the **wait** or **waitpid** functions and perform additional operations as necessary. If you do not need to perform tasks when a child process terminates, set **$SIG{ CHLD } = 'IGNORE'** to prevent the child from remaining in the process table.

Software Engineering Observation 18.2

*Be aware that the **SIGCHLD** signal is also thrown when a child is suspended, not just when it exits. Thus, you should use the **WIFEXITED** function from the **POSIX** module to ensure that the process actually terminated.*

18.8 OLE Automation

In this chapter, we have explored Perl's ability to interact with external programs and processes. On the Windows platform, Microsoft has developed a technology known as *Object Linking and Embedding (OLE)*, which goes one step further, enabling programs to manipulate and operate within external programs. OLE provides an interface for Windows applications to work together in a seamless, integrated manner. The OLE interface was originally intended for use with Microsoft Visual Basic, but the Perl **Win32::OLE** module offers the same functionality from in a Perl program. Figure 18.16 shows a simple OLE script that interacts with Microsoft Word. When you run the program, immediately type a line of text and press *Enter*. [*Note:* This program is for Microsoft Windows only.]

Line 9 queries the user for a line of text, which will be used to create a new Microsoft Word document. To interact with Word, line 11 creates an OLE **Word.Application** object. We access properties of this object using the arrow operator as shown in line 14:

```
$word->{ Visible } = 1
```

Variable **$word** functions as a reference to a hash here. In this case, we set the **Visible** property of the Word application object to 1 (or true), causing the Word application window to become active and visible.

```perl
1   #!/usr/bin/perl
2   # Fig. 18.16: fig18_16.pl
3   # Simple OLE example.
4
5   use warnings;
6   use strict;
7   use Win32::OLE;
8
9   chomp( my $line = <STDIN> );
10
11  my $word = CreateObject Win32::OLE( "Word.Application" )
12      or die( "Error opening a document in Word: $!" );
13
14  $word->{ Visible } = 1;
15  $word->Documents->Add();
16  $word->Selection->Font->{ Size } = 100;
17  $word->Selection->Font->{ SmallCaps } = 1;
18  $word->Selection->Font->{ Animation } = 3;    # sparkle text
19  $word->Selection->TypeText( $line );
```

Fig. 18.16 Simple OLE script (part 1 of 2).

Fig. 18.16 Simple OLE script (part 2 of 2).

We then use the **$word** object to **Add** a new document (line 15) and set font characteristics (lines 16–18). Finally, we type the text entered by the user into the new Word document (using the **TypeText** method) and the program ends.

There are hundreds of different properties and methods available in Microsoft Word through OLE, which can make the prospect of writing OLE scripts seem daunting at first. However, the available properties and methods are clearly documented and organized. You can browse this documentation in ActiveState's ActivePerl using an *object browser,* available in the ActivePerl HTML documentation under **ActivePerlComponents**, **Windows Specifics**. (An object browser is also available within the Visual Basic environment. From Microsoft Word, select **Tools**, then **Macro**, then **Visual Basic Editor** and press *F2* to open the object browser.)

For example, if you browse the Microsoft Word Object Library using the **Object Browser**, you can examine the **Font** object and find what sort of settings are available. In the preceding example, we found that the **Animation** property took a value of type **WdAnimation**. Scrolling further down, under the **WdAnimation** type, we find the various animation effects that can be applied to the **Font** object, each of which is associated with a constant integer value. As can be seen in Fig. 18.17, the **Object Browser** indicates that the sparkle text effect has the value 3, which we use in line 18 of Fig. 18.16.

Because OLE is a Visual Basic-related technology, a great way to learn to use OLE is to study Visual Basic scripts and learn how to translate them to Perl. The Perl **Win32::OLE** module interface is designed to be similar. See the ActiveState documentation for further details.

SUMMARY

- Sometimes it is useful to process several tasks concurrently.

- Most programming languages do not enable programmers to specify concurrent activities. Rather, they provide only a simple set of control structures that enable programmers to perform one action at a time, then proceed to the next action after the previous action completes.

- The kind of concurrency that computers perform today is normally implemented as operating systems primitives available only to highly experienced systems programmers.

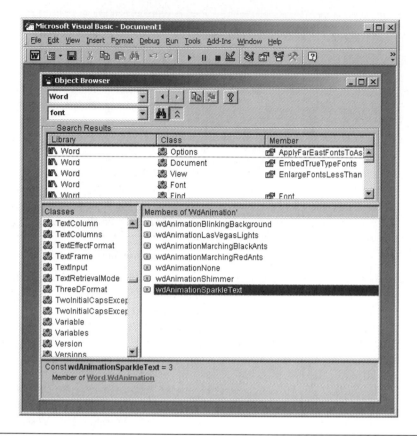

Fig. 18.17 Using the object browser.

- One way to implement concurrency is to have each task operate in completely separate memory spaces. Each of these is known as a process. The other way is to have threads of execution operating in the same memory space. This is known as multithreading.

- Creating a thread is more efficient than creating a process because a new virtual memory space does not need to be created.

- Processes protect us from having one process manipulating shared data without the other process knowing about it. This type of a problem is known as a race condition and is a common problem with multithreading.

- One of the main uses of Perl is as a glue language. Perl can take disparate programs that do not fit together well and bridge the gaps between them so they can work together. Perl allows us to access the shell to run other programs and grab control of their input or output.

- Some operating systems, such as Unix, have the built-in ability to make separate processes. There are system commands that create and manage processes. On systems that directly support processes, Perl uses the basic system commands to implement the process functions. On systems that do not have such system commands, processes are emulated by cloning the interpreter and executing the separate processes in their own instances of the interpreter.

- The simplest way to create a new process is to use function **fork**. When **fork** is called, it either calls the system's **fork** function (if there is one) to create a new process, or emulates it by cloning the interpreter.

- The process that calls **fork** is known as the parent process.

- Any process that is forked from this process is known as a child process.

- Each process has a unique process id number, or *pid*.

- When the **fork** function is called, it creates a new child process which is identical to the parent process. The only difference between the two processes is the return value of the **fork** call. In the **child** process, it returns 0, while in the parent process, the *pid* of the child is returned. If the **fork** call is not successful, it returns **undef**.

- The order in which actions occur in forked processes is not as well defined as if all the actions are performed in one process.

- If the special variable **$|** (also known as **$OUTPUT_AUTOFLUSH**) has a nonzero value, the selected output channel will be flushed automatically when a **print** or **write** statement executes.

- Function **wait** waits for all the children of a particular process to finish before allowing the parent process to continue its execution. This function returns the *pid* of a finished child, or -1 if there are no more children.

- If you want to wait for a specific process to complete, you can use function **waitpid**, which takes a process id as the first argument. It waits for that process to finish then returns the *pid* of that process. If there is no child for that *pid*, or it is already dead, the **waitpid** function returns -1.

- The exit status of the child process is stored in special variable **$?**.

- The **exec** function uses the shell to invoke its argument (a shell command) then replaces the current process with the executing command. Thus when the command finishes, the process ends.

- Shell wild-card processing is performed on the first element passed to **exec**.

- The **system** command can also be used to execute shell commands by using **fork** to create a separate process and setting the original process to **wait** until the child process completes.

- To enhance portability, it is good to check the **$^O** special variable to see what operating system we are using before deciding what command to execute.

- The **open** function lets us emulate the functionality of command-line piping. By placing a pipe at the beginning of the string specifying what command to execute, we can execute that command and have the input of that program be attached to the filehandle opened. Having the pipe at the end of the string attaches the handle to the output of the command. These handles can be treated like any other handles. To write to the input of a program we just print or write to the handle which is piped to the input of the program. To read the output from a program, we read from the piped handle just like we would read from any other file handle. They can be read from using angle brackets or written to using a **print** statement.

- Function **open** lets us emulate the functionality of command-line piping by placing a pipe (|) symbol in the string that specifies the command to execute. If the pipe is placed at the beginning of the string, the input of the program to execute is attached to the specified file handle. If the pipe is at the end of the string, the output of the program to execute is attached to the specified handle. These handles can be treated like any other file handles.

- There is another shorthand way to run a shell command and capture its output. This is the **qx//** operator, also known as the quoted execution operator. Like the other quoting operators, this has special quoting characters—backquotes, or backticks ` `. Variables between the backticks are interpolated, then the resulting string is passed to the shell for execution. In a scalar context, a single string with all the output is returned. In a list context, a list of values in which each line of output is a separate element is returned.

- The **IPC::Open2** and **IPC::Open3** modules allow us to get handles to both the input and output of a command. The **IPC::Open2** module gives us the **open2** function, which allows us to obtain a filehandle for each of **STDIN** and **STDOUT**. If we want to see **STDERR** as well, we use the **open3** function from the **IPC::Open3** module.

- When two programs are waiting for each other's output before continuing their own execution, this is known as deadlock.

- Perl provides us with ways to communicate between parent and child processes created with **fork** by using the **pipe** function to connect two filehandles so the output from one process can be used as the input to another.

- The first argument to **pipe** is the name of the filehandle for reading and the second argument is the filehandle for writing.

- Signals are messages delivered by the operating system to a program, then handled by the program. There are many different signals that can be sent and different actions which are taken in handling these signals.

- The process of receiving signals and performing the necessary actions is known as signal handling.

- Each process has a default handler for each signal. You can either let Perl handle your signals for you, or you can set custom handlers to be called when a signal occurs.

- We can override the handling for most signals. To set signal handlers, we use the hash **%SIG** to specify the signal and its corresponding handler.

- The results of programs that use signal handling differ across operating systems.

- There are two special signals defined by Perl: **__DIE__** and **__WARN__**. Their handlers are called whenever **warn** or **die** is called. By assigning values to **$SIG{ __DIE__ }** or **$SIG{ __WARN__ }**, you can control what Perl does when a program reports an error through **die** or **warn**.

- To reestablish the default handler for a signal or to ignore a signal, Perl provides two special values that can be specified for individual signals—**DEFAULT** and **IGNORE**.

- When a signal is received, the executing code is interrupted so the signal can be processed.

- Programs can send signals to other processes with function **kill**. The first argument is the signal to send. The remaining arguments are the processes to which to send the signal. If a negative process argument is specified, the signal is sent to the parent process and all its children.

- When a process ends, it stays in the process table so the parent can determine if the process terminated and whether or not the process terminated normally.

- Child processes that have terminated execution and still remain in the process table are called zombies. To avoid collecting zombies, set a handler for the **SIGCHLD** signal, which is sent when a child exits. In this handler, call the **wait** or **waitpid** functions.

- On the Windows platform, Microsoft has developed a technology known as Object Linking and Embedding (OLE) which enables programs to manipulate and operate within external programs. OLE provides an interface for Windows applications to work together in a seamless, integrated manner. The OLE interface was originally intended for use with Microsoft Visual Basic, but the Perl **Win32::OLE** module offers the same functionality in a Perl program.

TERMINOLOGY

$$ special variable	child process
$? special variable	clone
$^O special variable	command-line piping
$| special variable	concurrency
$PID special variable	dead process
$PROCESS_ID special variable	deadlock

die handler
dir command
exec function
exit function
FileHandle objects
fork function
glue language
handle
in parallel
IPC::Open2 module
IPC::Open3 module
kill function
LWP module
more command
multithreading
object browser
Object Linking and Embedding (OLE)
OLE interface
open function
open2 function
open3 function
operating system
parent process
pid (process id number)
pipe function
POSIX module
primitives
process
quoted execution operator
qx// operator
race condition

reaping
shell
shell command
shell processing
shell wild card
SIGALRM signal
SIGCHLD signal
SIGFPE signal
SIGHUP signal
SIGINT signal
SIGKILL signal
signal handling
signals
SIGPIPE signal
SIGQUIT signal
SIGSTOP signal
SIGTERM signal
SIGUSR1 signal
SIGUSR2 signal
system call
system function
systems programmers
thread
wait function
waitpid function
warn handler
WIFEXITED function
wildcard expansion
Win32::OLE module
zombies

SELF REVIEW EXERCISES

18.1   Fill in the blanks:

   a)   When two paths of execution run simultaneously but in separate memory spaces, they are
        know as _____. When they share memory, they are known as _____.

   b)   The **fork** function returns the _____ in the parent process and _____ in the
        child process.

   c)   _____ is the output autoflush special variable.

   d)   To wait for a child process we can use the _____ or _____ functions.

   e)   The exit status of a child process is returned in the _____ special variable.

   f)   The _____ function replaces the current process by running a shell command.

   g)   To check what operating system we are using, we can use the _____ special vari-
        able.

   h)   The **qx//** operator is known as the _____ _____ operator.

   i)   To run a command and capture the **STDOUT**, **STDIN** and **STDERR** from it, use module
        _____.

   j)   To create filehandles that can communicate between processes, we can use the
        _____ or _____ functions.

   k)   Messages sent by the OS to a process are known as _____.

l)   The _____ message is sent when *<ctrl>-c* is pressed.

m)   The _____ message is sent when a child exits.

18.2   For each of the following, write a single statement that performs the indicated task. You may assume that any needed modules have been loaded.

a)   From a Perl script, run the Perl interpreter while passing the name of a file and arguments to it without having shell processing performed on that filename. When it is finished running, it should not return to the original script.

b)   Store the results of a **dir** command on DOS systems, or an **ls** command on UNIX systems into the array **@results**.

c)   Make the **HEAD** filehandle write to the **TAIL** filehandle.

d)   Make it so when the user presses *<ctrl>-c*, nothing happens.

e)   Restore the default handler for when a program dies.

f)   Send a process with the process id **$pid** the **SIGINT** signal.

g)   Print the string **running** if a process with the process id **$pid** is still running.

h)   Wait for process **$pid** to finish.

ANSWERS TO SELF-REVIEW EXERCISES

18.1   a) processes, threads. b) process id number or *pid*, 0. c) **$|**. d) **wait**, **waitpid**. e) **$?**. f) **exec**. g) **$^O**. h) quoted execution. i) **IPC::Open3**. j) **pipe**, **open**. k) signals. l) **SIGINT**. m) **SIGCHLD**.

18.2   a) **exec("perl", "filename", "arguments");**
b) **my @results = `dir`;** or **my @results = `ls`;**
c) **pipe(TAIL, HEAD);**
d) **$SIG{ INT } = 'IGNORE';**
e) **$SIG{ __DIE__ } = 'DEFAULT';**
f) **kill(INT => $pid);** or **kill('INT', $pid);**
g) **print("running") if (kill(0, $pid));**
h) **waitpid($pid);**

EXERCISES

18.3   Use the **fork** and **exec** functions to emulate the **system** function. The parent should use the **wait** function to wait until the child finishes before continuing. Have the program run the command **"dir *.*"**.

18.4   Use the **exec** function to make a menu that allows the user to choose which program they would like to run. The user should be given a choice of three programs. You can use whichever three programs you choose.

18.5   Create an output filter that performs word wrapping. If a line is longer than a certain number of characters, it should be split into multiple lines. The number of characters per line should be specified on the command line. Have the program read in keyboard input from the user. It will take that input and format it as specified, putting the result in **file.txt**. Implement this in each of the following two ways:

a)   Using the **open** function to open a pipe to yourself.

b)   Using the **pipe** and **fork** functions to do the same thing.

18.6   Use function **kill** to stop a process. First send it a **SIGINT** signal. Wait three seconds. If it did not respond to the **SIGINT** signal, send it a **SIGKILL** signal. [This question for UNIX/Linux users.]

18.7   Set a signal handler on **SIGINT** to query the user about whether he or she really wants to quit after they type *<ctrl>-c*.

19

Security

Objectives

- To be able to recognize potential CGI security issues.
- To learn how to create more secure programs.
- To use of cryptography to prevent data tampering.
- To understand public-key/private-key cryptography.
- To learn about popular security protocols.
- To understand digital signatures, digital certificates and certification authorities.
- To become aware of various threats to secure systems, such as viruses and denial-of-service attacks.
- To understand emerging security techniques, such as biometrics and steganography.

Three may keep a secret, if two of them are dead.
Benjamin Franklin

Attack—Repeat—Attack.
William Frederick Halsey, Jr.

Private information is practically the source of every large modern fortune.
Oscar Wilde

There must be security for all—or not one is safe.
The Day the Earth Stood Still, screenplay by Edmund H. North

No government can be long secure without formidable opposition.
Benjamin Disraeli

Outline

19.1 Introduction

The explosion of e-business and e-commerce is forcing businesses and consumers to focus on Internet security. Consumers are buying products, trading stocks and banking online. They are providing their credit-card numbers, social-security numbers and other highly confidential information through Web sites. Businesses are sending confidential information to clients and vendors over the Internet. At the same time, we are experiencing increasing numbers of security attacks. Individuals and organizations are vulnerable to data theft and hacker attacks that can corrupt files and even shut down e-businesses. Security is fundamental to e-business. According to a study by International Data Corporation (IDC), organizations spent \$6.2 billion on security consulting in 1999, and IDC expects the market to reach \$14.8 billion by 2003.[1]

Modern computer security addresses various problems and concerns associated with protecting electronic communications and maintaining network security. There are four fundamental requirements of a successful, secure transaction: *privacy*, *integrity*, *authentication* and *nonrepudiation*. *The privacy issue is the following*: How do you ensure that the information you transmit over the Internet has not been captured or passed on to a third party without your knowledge? *The integrity issue is the following*: How do you ensure that the information you send or receive has not been compromised or altered? *The authentication issue is the following*: How do the sender and receiver of a message prove their identities to each other? *The nonrepudiation issue is the following*: How do you legally prove that a message was sent or received?

In addition to these requirements, network security addresses the issue of *availability*: How do we ensure that the network and the computer systems to which it connects will stay in operation continuously?

Web programming gives you lots of power. But it also exposes your computer to attacks. We will show some examples of how poorly written programs can be compromised, then show how to avoid making these mistakes. We will show you the tools at your disposal to help you write secure programs and we will demonstrate approaches that lead to secure programming.

The first part of the chapter focuses on security from a Perl programming standpoint and the remainder of the chapter considers other security issues, from secure electronic transactions to secure networks and the fundamentals of secure business, known as *s-business*. We will discuss how e-commerce security is achieved using current technologies. We encourage you to visit the Web resources provided in Section 19.22 to learn more about the latest developments in e-commerce security. These resources include many demos that you will find to be informative and entertaining.

19.2 What Makes a Program Insecure

Never trust anything coming from the user. Some of the worst security mistakes stem from assuming that users are following certain rules in their submissions. Just because the program you write is asking for data that should come in a certain form does not mean that the people using the program will comply and enter the data in that form. Not checking the data you receive can have serious consequences. Anything the user can modify can also lead to security holes—for example, data passed between programs using hidden fields and some of the environment variables in the **%ENV** hash.

Users who maliciously target systems and try to break them are known as *crackers*. Crackers are usually skilled programmers. Some crackers break into systems just for the thrill of it, without causing any harm to the compromised systems (except, perhaps, humbling and humiliating their owners); others have malicious intent. Either way, crackers are breaking the law by accessing or damaging private information and computers.

The term *hacker* is frequently used to refer to people who program with malicious intent. This term is, in fact, a misnomer. The word *hacker* simply refers to someone who is a skilled programmer. Many of the most prominent Perl programmers refer to themselves as Perl hackers, indicating that they use Perl as their language of choice, not that they use it to break the law.

Developing a defensive programming approach is important. It is a good idea to be aware of the capabilities of crackers and to think of ways to avoid being a target. For example, do not name a program that provides access to a Web site **login.cgi** (or something similar)—some crackers write programs that find programs with obvious names like this and try to break into them. The remaining sections in this chapter discuss potential security holes and how to fix them.

19.3 Using User Data with Shell Commands

The first issue we cover is one of the most dangerous security-related mistakes—allowing user input to interface directly with the shell or operating system. This problem includes passing user input to the **open**, **exec** or **system** functions or enclosing user input in backticks (**` `**). Figure 19.1 uses **open** to open a file. The name of the file is based on a string input by the user. This particular CGI program was executed on the Apache Web server for Windows, but should work on any system, provided that the **#!** line is changed. [*Note:* The file that is read by this program should reside in the same directory as the program.]

```perl
1  #!perl
2  # Figure 19.1: fig19_01.pl
3  # Passing form results directly to the open function
4
5  use warnings;
6  use strict;
7  use CGI qw( :standard );
8
9  print( header(), start_html(
10     "Passing user input directly to function open" ) );
11
12 my $cgi = new CGI();
13
14 unless ( $cgi->param() ) {
15    print( "Type your first name and press the Enter key. " );
16
17    my $form = new CGI();
18
19    print( $form->startform(),
20            $form->textfield( 'name', '', 20 ),
21            $form->endform() );
22 }
23 else {
24    my $name = $cgi->param( 'name' );
25
26    print( "Hello $name.", br(),
27            "Here is what is in $name.log", br() );
28    open( LOGFILE, "$name.log" )
29       or die( "Could not open $name.log" );
30    print( "$_<br>" ) while ( <LOGFILE> );
31 }
32
33 print( end_html() );
```

Fig. 19.1   Passing user input directly to function **open** (part 1 of 2).

Fig. 19.1   Passing user input directly to function **open** (part 2 of 2).

The problem with Fig. 19.1 is in line 28, where we pass **$name**, which contains text input by the user, to function **open**. The program assumes that the user is honest and enters his or her name, not a string intended to compromise the system.

Good Programming Practice 19.1

Always validate user input before allowing that input to interact with the shell or operating system.

What if the user enters a string starting with one of the special symbols that **open** uses to determine the type of filehandle to create? If the string starts with either **>** or **>>**, the file will be opened for writing instead of reading. If the symbol is **>** and the file already exists, the file's contents will be discarded. In either case, the remainder of the program would no longer work correctly. This type of error occurs only when the file-open mode is not stated explicitly in the call to function **open**.

Software Engineering Observation 19.1

*When opening a file for reading only, include the optional **<** before the filename. This prevents accidental modification of the file when it is opened in the default read/write mode.*

The real damage occurs when the string starts with the pipe symbol, **|**. This allows the user to execute any shell command. As an example, Fig. 19.2 shows the results of entering "**| dir *.*,**" as the user input, which opens a pipe to the system call **dir *.* ,.log**, and performs a directory listing on Windows (on UNIX/Linux, replace **dir** with **ls**). As you can see, the command allows the user to view the contents of the **cgi-bin** directory. This is not particularly harmful, but what if the user had entered "**| del *.*,**" on a Windows computer, or "**| rm *.*,**" on a UNIX/Linux computer. Each of these commands deletes the entire contents of a directory, potentially causing serious damage to the Web server.

Function **open** is not the only command that can cause serious security leaks. Functions **exec** and **system** interact directly with the shell. Also, backtick quoting causes commands to be run directly from the shell. Figure 19.3 shows how backtick quotes can compromise security. This example takes user input and intentionally encloses that input in backticks. This causes the user input to be sent directly to the shell for execution.

On line 25, backticks are used to execute the user input. The third screen capture shows the results of typing "**dir**" as input when the program is executing as part of a Windows Web server. Note that any other command could have been used instead of **dir**. As you can see, this feature, too, can be exploited to expose a major security leak.

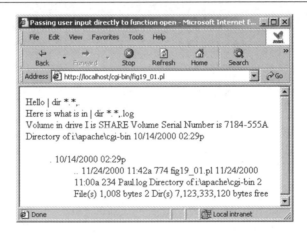

Fig. 19.2   Executing a system command input by the user.

```
1   #!perl
2   # Figure 19.3: fig19_03.pl
3   # Another potential security risk: backticks.
4
5   use warnings;
6   use strict;
7   use CGI qw( :standard );
8
9   print( header(), start_html( "Backtick security issue" ) );
10
11  my $cgi = new CGI();
12
13  unless ( $cgi->param() ) {
14     print( "Type some text, then press Enter",
15             " and I will display it for you." );
```

Fig. 19.3   Potential security issues with backticks (part 1 of 3).

```
16      my $form = new CGI();
17      print( $form->startform(),
18              $form->textfield( 'words', '', 20 ),
19              $form->endform() );
20   }
21   else {
22      my $words = $cgi->param( 'words' );
23      print( "You entered: $words.", br() );
24      print( "Attempting to execute: $words.", br() );
25      my @matches = `$words`;
26
27      if ( @matches ) {
28          print( br(), join( br(), @matches ) );
29      }
30      else {
31          print( "'$words' was not a shell command.", br() );
32      }
33   }
34
35   print( end_html() );
```

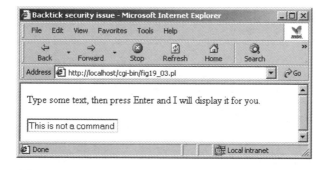

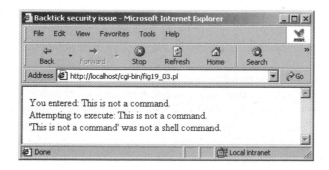

Fig. 19.3   Potential security issues with backticks (part 2 of 3).

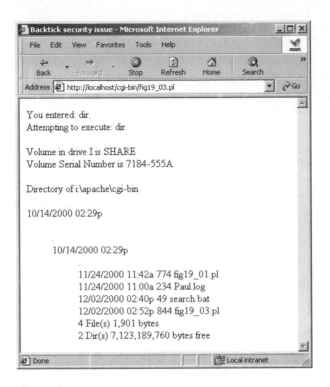

Fig. 19.3   Potential security issues with backticks (part 3 of 3).

19.4 Defensive Programming

How do we avoid such programming pitfalls? Again, never trust data coming from outside your program. Always assume that someone will try to break your program; always program in such a way to make it impossible for such a person to do so. Using such an approach is known as *defensive programming*.

First, think of all the different ways in which the input could cause problems. Many security problems are caused by user-input strings containing *shell metacharacters*, like the pipe symbol (|). These characters have special meanings for the shell. Some other shell metacharacters are |, /, ;, and *. One way to fix this problem is to add a regular expression to see if the string input by the user contains these characters before we pass it to the command line. This method will fix problems with some inputs. The problem with this method, however, is that we are assuming we know all the ways in which a user-input string can break the code. What if we forget a way or do not realize that a particular metacharacter could be bad? The list of shell metacharacters is not complete; any character we missed could lead to a security hole. Also, each operating system may have different shell metacharacters. Thus, the security issues might differ from platform to platform. For example, some Unix platforms use the ^ character to provide the functionality of the pipe (|) character.

Rather than making a list of all harmful characters, one way to ensure that no harmful characters slip through is to make a list of characters that are guaranteed to be safe. By allowing only these safe characters to be passed, we ensure that no harmful characters get by. Applying this method to the backticks example, we might specify that the user is allowed to input only word characters. The program in Fig. 19.3 is rewritten using this method in Fig. 19.4.

```perl
1   #!perl
2   # Figure 19.4: fig19_04.pl
3   # Preventing improper input.
4
5   use warnings;
6   use strict;
7   use CGI qw( :standard );
8
9   print( header(), start_html( "Prevent improper input" ) );
10
11  my $cgi = new CGI();
12
13  unless ( $cgi->param() ) {
14     print( "Type some text, then press Enter",
15             " and I will display it for you." );
16     my $form = new CGI();
17     print( $form->startform(),
18             $form->textfield( 'words', '', 20 ),
19             $form->endform() );
20  }
21  else {
22     my $words = $cgi->param( 'words' );
23     print( "You entered: $words.", br() );
24
25     if ( $words =~ /^\w*$/ ) {
26        print( "Attempting to execute: $words.", br() );
27        my @matches = `$words`;
28
29        if ( @matches ) {
30           print( br(), join( br(), @matches ) );
31        }
32        else {
33           print( "'$words' was not a shell command.", br() );
34        }
35     }
36     else {
37        print( "Invalid input. Re-enter without any symbols." );
38     }
39  }
40
41  print( end_html() );
```

Fig. 19.4   Preventing input that contains symbols (part 1 of 2).

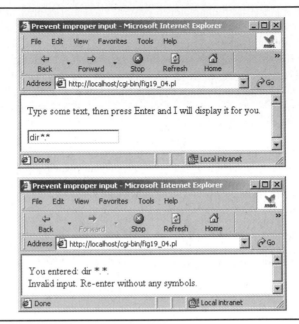

Fig. 19.4   Preventing input that contains symbols (part 2 of 2).

The regular expression we use as part of the **if** condition on line 25 allows the input to be used in line 27 only if it is composed entirely of word characters. This procedure will prevent any special symbols that could be used to damage our system from being passed to the shell.

19.5 Taint Mode

Perl provides a mechanism that forces you to think about security and does not let you use data external to your program in calls to the shell. This feature is called *taint mode*, which is enabled by running Perl with the **-T** flag. On any system on which the shebang notation is recognized, placing the **-T** at the end of the shebang line that starts your program will enable taint mode.

When taint mode is on, all data not originally defined in the program are marked as tainted. If tainted data are used with a function that interacts with the shell, a runtime error occurs and the program terminates. For example, if you pass a tainted variable into a subroutine that would use it in a nonsecure manner, taint mode will catch this problem. This feature allows you to use functions from other modules without having to worry about whether those functions properly test the data for security issues before potentially passing the data to the shell or operating system for execution.

When data are received in a program from an external source (such as the user), they are marked as tainted. Any variable to which tainted data are assigned is also marked as tainted. Thus, in the code

```
my $c = <STDIN>;
$d = $c;
```

both **$c** and **$d** are considered to be tainted.

Tainted data can be "cleaned" with regular expressions. When you use parentheses to extract a portion of the tainted data into one of the $1, $2, …, or $9 variables, that portion of the data is no longer tainted. Figure 19.5 re-implements the program of Fig. 19.4 with taint mode enabled.

The first line of the program (i.e., the shebang line) enables taint mode with the -T option. The data received from the **param** call on line 22 are tainted because they are not defined in the program. To clean the tainted data we use the regular expression in line 25, taking the string only if it contains exclusively word characters. After the regular expression executes **$word** is still tainted. However, the parentheses in the regular expression cause the result to be cleaned and placed in variable $1, which in this case should contain the same value as **$word**. Note that using taint mode in this program forces us to validate the data with a regular expression so that we can clean the data. If you remove the parentheses in the regular expression, the program will terminate prematurely.

Good Programming Practice 19.2

Taint mode is a powerful tool which ensures that data are validated before they can be used in a nonsecure manner. For this reason, you should enable taint mode in all CGI programs.

```perl
1   #!perl -T
2   # Figure 19.5: fig19_05.pl
3   # Using taint mode.
4
5   use warnings;
6   use strict;
7   use CGI qw( :standard );
8
9   print( header(), start_html( "Prevent improper input" ) );
10
11  my $cgi = new CGI();
12
13  unless ( $cgi->param() ) {
14     print( "Type some text, then press Enter",
15            " and I will display it for you." );
16     my $form = new CGI();
17     print( $form->startform(),
18            $form->textfield( 'words', '', 20 ),
19            $form->endform() );
20  }
21  else {
22     my $words = $cgi->param( 'words' );
23     print( "You entered: $words.", br() );
24
25     if ( $words =~ /^(\w*)$/ ) {
26        print( "Attempting to execute: $1.", br() );
27        my @matches = `$1`;
28
29        if ( @matches ) {
30           print( br(), join( br(), @matches ) );
31        }
```

Fig. 19.5   Taint mode (part 1 of 2).

```
32              else {
33                  print( "'$words' was not a shell command.", br() );
34              }
35          }
36          else {
37              print( "Invalid input. Re-enter without any symbols." );
38          }
39      }
40
41      print( end_html() );
```

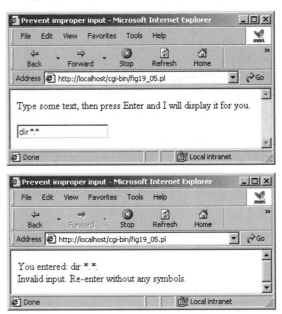

Fig. 19.5   Taint mode (part 2 of 2).

19.6 Printing User Input to a Web Page

Passing user input directly to the shell is just one potential security issue. There are other security issues for which taint mode does not help. For example, problems can also arise in a CGI program that prints the user's input in an HTML page. The user could input HTML tags that would be interpreted as part of the page, causing the page to render improperly. More serious effects can occur when the user input includes scripting code, such as a Java-Script program, that can be executed by the Web browser. Figure 19.6 shows a program that is vulnerable to this sort of attack.

```
1   #!perl
2   # Fig. 19.6: fig19_06.pl
3   # Guestbook program.
4
```

Fig. 19.6   A vulnerable guestbook program (part 1 of 3).

```
5   use warnings;
6   use strict;
7   use CGI qw( :standard );
8
9   print( header(), start_html( "Guestbook" ), h1( "Guestbook" ) );
10
11  if ( param() ) {
12      print h3( "Thank you for signing our guestbook!!!" ),
13
14      my $name = param( "name" );
15      my $email = param( "email" );
16      my $message = param( "message" );
17
18      open( FILE, ">>guestbook.log" ) or
19          die( "Cannot open guestbook" );
20      print( FILE "\n", hr(), "From: ",
21          a( { -href => "mailto:$email" }, $name ), br(), br(),
22          $message );
23      close( FILE );
24  }
25
26  open( FILE, "guestbook.log" ) or die( "Cannot open guestbook" );
27
28  print while ( <FILE> );
29  close( FILE );
30
31  print( h4( "Please sign our guestbook:" ), start_form(),
32      "Name: ", textfield( -name => "name" ), br(),
33      "E-mail: ", textfield( -name => "email" ), br(),
34      "Enter your message:", br(),
35      textarea( -name => "message", -rows => 5, -columns => 50,
36                -wrap => 1 ),
37      br(), submit( -name => "Sign the Guestbook" ), end_form(),
38      end_html() );
```

Fig. 19.6   A vulnerable guestbook program (part 2 of 3).

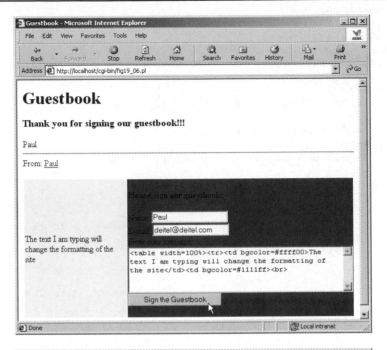

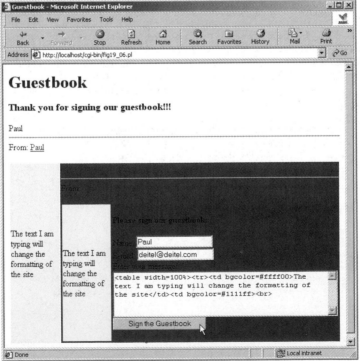

Fig. 19.6   A vulnerable guestbook program (part 3 of 3).

This guestbook program creates a page in which the guestbook contents are displayed followed by a form that allows users to sign the guestbook. The program opens the guestbook file on line 26 and outputs the contents of the file on line 28. Lines 31–38 output the form. If the user signs the guestbook, lines 11–24 take the input from the user (lines 14–16) and write it to the guestbook (lines 18–23).

The problem with this program, as you can see in the sample screen captures, is that the user can type anything in the text area, including HTML, and that input will be added to the guestbook. In the sample screen captures, the user added an open-ended **table** element. When the guestbook was sent back to the client, the user input was interpreted by the browser and used to render the page. In addition, the **table** element was not terminated by the user, so each click of the **Sign the Guestbook** button makes the effect even worse.

We can use regular expressions to filter out harmful HTML tags from user input. Again, in the spirit of defensive programming, it is better to allow input that you know will not cause a problem, rather than to block dangerous input and potentially not catch all cases that can cause security breaches. Figure 19.7 rewrites the guestbook program of Fig. 19.6 to filter out all HTML tags except **
** from the text of the message. If any tags are entered in the **Name** or **E-mail** fields of the guestbook form, the program generates an error message.

Line 16 uses the regular expression **/<.*>/** to search for anything resembling a HTML tag in the **Name** and **E-mail** fields. If HTML tags are found, lines 17–20 print a message asking the user to reenter his or her input without the tags.

```perl
1   #!perl
2   # Fig. 19.7: fig19_07.pl
3   # Guestbook program which filters HTML tags.
4
5   use warnings;
6   use strict;
7   use CGI qw( :standard );
8
9   print( header(), start_html( "Guestbook" ), h1( "Guestbook" ) );
10
11  if ( param() ) {
12     my $name = param( "name" );
13     my $email = param( "email" );
14     my $message = param( "message" );
15
16     if ( $name =~ /<.*>/ || $email =~ /<.*>/ ) {
17        print( h3( "HTML tags not allowed in Name or E-mail" ),
18           br(), "Please correct your entry and re-send", br(),
19           "To include the < or > symbols, use &ampgt or &amplt.",
20           br() );
21     }
22     else {
23        print( h3( "Thank you for signing our guestbook!!!" ) );
24
```

Fig. 19.7 Tag-filtering guestbook program (part 1 of 4).

```
25          # filter to remove HTML tags
26          print( $message =~
27              s/<([^>]*)>/( $1 eq "BR" || $1 eq "br" ) ?
28              "<$1>" : "\&lt$1\&gt"/ge );
29
30          open( FILE, ">>guestbook.log" ) or
31              die( "Cannot open guestbook" );
32          print( FILE "\n", hr(), "From: ",
33              a( { -href => "mailto:$email" }, $name ), br(), br(),
34              $message );
35          close( FILE );
36      }
37  }
38
39  open( FILE, "guestbook.log" ) or die( "Cannot open guestbook" );
40
41  print while ( <FILE> );
42  close( FILE );
43
44  print( hr(), h4( "Please sign our guestbook:" ), start_form(),
45      "Name: ", textfield( -name => "name" ), br(),
46      "E-mail: ", textfield( -name => "email" ), br(),
47      "Enter your message:", br(),
48      textarea( -name => "message", -rows => 5, -columns => 50,
49                  -wrap => 1 ), br(),
50      h4( "Warning: Filtering HTML tags except &ltbr&gt" ),
51      br(), submit( -name => "Sign the Guestbook" ), end_form(),
52      end_html() );
```

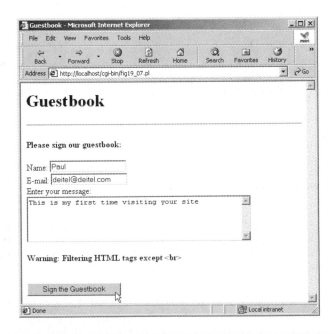

Fig. 19.7   Tag-filtering guestbook program (part 2 of 4).

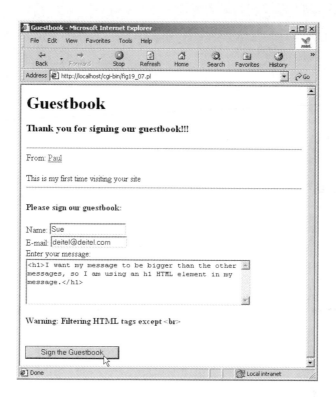

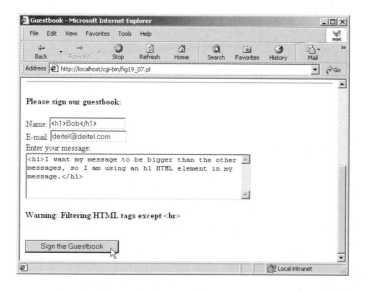

Fig. 19.7   Tag-filtering guestbook program (part 3 of 4).

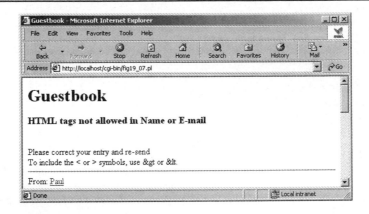

Fig. 19.7   Tag-filtering guestbook program (part 4 of 4).

Lines 26–28 use the substitution operator to filter the HTML tags (except **
) in the user input. This procedure is done by matching a tag with the pattern **/<([^>]*)>/. The text of the tag is captured into **$1** with the parentheses. A conditional operator is used to leave the tag unchanged if **$1** equals **br** or **BR**; otherwise, the surrounding **<** and **>** are replaced with **&lt** and **&gt**, respectively. The **g** and **e** modifiers are used at the end of the regular expression, because the right side of the regular expression needs to be evaluated and the substitution needs to be performed throughout the string.

19.7 Denial-of-Service Attacks

A *denial-of-service attack* occurs when a cracker attempts to use up system resources to deny normal users from being able to make use of a site or network. There are many forms of denial-of-service attacks; these vary by the resource being monopolized and the method being used to do so. Denial-of-service attacks can disrupt service on a Web site and even shut down critical systems such as telecommunications systems or flight-control centers.

Most denial-of-service attacks are not exploitations of poorly programmed pages. Instead, most attacks flood servers with data packets, overwhelming the servers and making it impossible for legitimate users to download information. These denial-of-service attacks usually require the power of a network of computers working simultaneously to generate enough packets to become a problem. When the packet flooding does not come from a single source, but from many separate computers, it is known as a *distributed denial-of-service attack*. In February 2000, distributed denial-of-service attacks shut down several high-traffic Web sites including Yahoo!, eBay, CNN Interactive and Amazon.

Such an attack is rarely a group effort. Instead, it is implemented by an individual who has installed viruses on various computers, designed to gain illegitimate use of the computers to carry out the attack. Distributed denial-of-service attacks can be difficult to stop, because it is not clear which requests on a network are from legitimate users and which are part of the attack. It is particularly difficult to catch the culprit of such an attack, because the attack is not carried out directly from the attacker's computer.

Another type of denial-of-service attack targets the *routing tables* of a network. Routing tables essentially form the road map of a network, providing directions for data to get from one computer to another. This type of attack is accomplished by modifying the routing tables, possibly sending all data to one address in the network.

Although not much can be done from a programming perspective to prevent most of these attacks, some attacks can be prevented. These attacks generally have to do with the size of the input being accepted.

For example, if we go back to our guestbook example, a user is able to input whatever text he or she wants into the form. What if a user posted a huge message with many megabytes of text? The CGI module would attempt to read all the text the user sent and assign it to a variable, potentially causing the server to run out of memory or to run slowly.

A remote user could also force your program to accept a large upload. This can occur even if your program is not explicitly programmed to accept uploads. The CGI module will accept the upload and store it in a temporary directory, perhaps filling all available hard-drive space. The file will be deleted when the program terminates, but the damage could have already been done.

Luckily, the CGI module provides us with two ways to avoid this kind of a problem, through the use of special variables. The **$CGI::POST_MAX** variable can be used to limit the size of a **post** from a form. If the **post** is larger than the specified size in bytes, the program will quit and output an error message. The upper limit applies to uploads as well as ordinary posts. To disable uploads entirely, set **$CGI::DISABLE_UPLOADS** to **1**. This command prevents the program from accepting any file uploads. Other posting functions will still operate normally.

If you want to have the error message print back to the user, so that the user knows what he or she did wrong, you can use the **CGI::Carp** module, as follows:

```
use CGI::Carp 'fatalsToBrowser';
```

Now, even though a malicious user cannot use all your disk space in one large post, he or she can still do so through many individual posts if your program is writing them all to a file (as in the guestbook program). To prevent this problem, you can check the size of the file. If the file exceeds a certain size, you can trim it, or you can prevent the user from writing anything else to it. The guestbook program is rewritten with these concerns in mind in Fig. 19.8.

Line 11 sets the maximum posting size (**$CGI::POST_MAX**) to **512** bytes. Line 12 sets **$CGI::DISABLE_UPLOADS** to **1** (true) to prevent the user from uploading a file. We have also added a check on line 49 to ensure that the guestbook file is not too large before we output a form with which the user can sign the guestbook. Lines 61 and 62 print a message saying that the guestbook is full. The size limit on the guestbook is set at 1024 bytes for demo purposes.

```
1   #!perl
2   # Fig. 19.8: fig19_08.pl
3   # Guestbook program that attempts to limit
4   # denial of service attacks.
5
6   use warnings;
7   use strict;
8   use CGI qw( :standard );
9   use CGI::Carp 'fatalsToBrowser';
10
```

Fig. 19.8   Avoiding denial-of-service attacks (part 1 of 3).

```
11   $CGI::POST_MAX = 512;
12   $CGI::DISABLE_UPLOADS = 1;
13
14   print( header(), start_html( "Guestbook" ), h1( "Guestbook" ) );
15
16   if ( param() ) {
17      my $name = param( "name" );
18      my $email = param( "email" );
19      my $message = param( "message" );
20
21      if ( $name =~ /<.*>/ || $email =~ /<.*>/ ) {
22         print( h3( "HTML tags not allowed in Name or E-mail" ),
23            br(), "Please correct your entry and re-send", br(),
24            "To include the < or > symbols, use &ampgt or &amplt.",
25            br() );
26      }
27      else {
28         print( h3( "Thank you for signing our guestbook!!!" ) );
29
30         # filter to remove HTML tags
31         print( $message =~
32            s/<([^>]*)>/( $1 eq "BR" || $1 eq "br" ) ?
33            "<$1>" : "\&lt$1\&gt"/ge );
34
35         open( FILE, ">>guestbook.log" ) or
36            die( "Cannot open guestbook" );
37         print( FILE "\n", hr(), "From: ",
38            a( { -href => "mailto:$email" }, $name ), br(), br(),
39            $message );
40         close( FILE );
41      }
42   }
43
44   open( FILE, "guestbook.log" ) or die( "Cannot open guestbook" );
45
46   print while ( <FILE> );
47   close( FILE );
48
49   unless ( -s "guestbook.log" > 1024 ) {
50      print( hr(), h4( "Please sign our guestbook:" ),
51         start_form(), "Name: ", textfield( -name => "name" ),
52         br(), "E-mail: ", textfield( -name => "email" ), br(),
53         "Enter your message:", br(),
54         textarea( -name => "message", -rows => 5, -columns => 50,
55                   -wrap => 1 ), br(),
56         h4( "Warning: Filtering HTML tags except &ltbr&gt" ),
57         br(), submit( -name => "Sign the Guestbook" ),
58         end_form() );
59   }
60   else {
61      print( h4( "Sorry, the guestbook is full." ),
62         "Please try again later.\n" );
63   }
```

Fig. 19.8   Avoiding denial-of-service attacks (part 2 of 3).

```
64
65    print( end_html() );
```

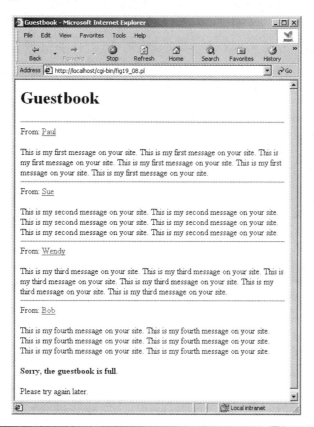

Fig. 19.8   Avoiding denial-of-service attacks (part 3 of 3).

19.8 Other Security Attacks

Other serious security threats are *viruses* and *worms*. Viruses are computer programs—usually sent as an attachment or hidden in audio clips, video clips and games—that attach to or overwrite other programs to replicate themselves. Viruses can corrupt your files or even wipe out your hard drive. Before the Internet became commonly used, viruses spread through files and programs (such as video games) transferred to computers by removable disks. Today, viruses are spread over a network simply by sharing infected files embedded in e-mail attachments, documents or programs. A worm is similar to a virus, except that a worm can spread and infect files on its own over a network; worms do not need to be attached to another program to spread. Once a virus or worm is released, it can spread rapidly, often "infecting" millions of computers worldwide within hours or even minutes.

Viruses, one of the most dangerous threats to network security, are typically malicious programs. There are many classes of computer viruses. A *transient virus* attaches itself to a specific computer program. The virus is activated when the program is run and deactivated when the program is terminated. A more powerful type of virus is a *resident virus*, which, once loaded into the memory of a computer, operates for the duration of the computer's use. Another type of virus is the *logic bomb*, which triggers when a given condition is met, such as a *time bomb* that is triggered when the clock on the computer matches a certain time or date.

A *Trojan horse* virus is a malicious program that hides within a friendly program or simulates the identity of a legitimate program or feature while actually causing damage to the computer or network in the background. The Trojan horse virus gets its name from the story of the Trojan War, in Greek history. In this story, Greek warriors at war with the Trojans hid inside a wooden horse, which the Trojans took within the walls of the city of Troy. When night fell and the Trojans were asleep, the Greek warriors came out of the horse and opened the gates to the city, letting the Greek army enter the gates and destroy the city of Troy. Trojan horse viruses can be particularly difficult to detect, since they appear to be legitimate, useful programs. In June 2000, news spread of a Trojan horse virus disguised as a video clip sent as an e-mail attachment. The Trojan horse virus was designed to give the attacker access to the infected computers, potentially to launch a denial-of-service attack against Web sites.[15]

Two of the most famous viruses to date are *Melissa*, which struck in March 1999, and the *ILOVEYOU virus*, which hit in May 2000. Both viruses cost organizations and individuals billions of dollars. The Melissa virus spread in a Microsoft Word document sent via e-mail. When the document was opened on a computer, the virus was triggered. Melissa accessed the Microsoft Outlook address book on the computer and automatically sent the infected Word attachment by e-mail to the first 50 people in the address book. Each time another person opened the attachment, the virus would send out another 50 messages. Once into a system, the virus infected any subsequently saved files.

The ILOVEYOU virus was sent as an attachment to an e-mail posing as a love letter. The message in the e-mail said, "Kindly check the attached love letter coming from me." Once the attachment was opened on a computer, the virus accessed the Microsoft Outlook address book on the computer and sent out messages to the addresses listed, helping to spread the virus rapidly worldwide. The virus corrupted all types of files, including system files. Networks at companies and government organizations worldwide were shut down for days trying to remedy the problem and contain the virus. Estimates for damage caused by the ILOVEYOU virus were as high as $10 billion to $15 billion, with the majority of the damage done in just a few hours.

Viruses and worms are not just limited to computers. In June 2000, a worm named *Timofonica* that was propagated through e-mail quickly made its way into the cellular phone network in Spain, sending prank calls and leaving text messages on many people's phones. No serious damage was done, nor did the worm infect the cell phones, but experts predict that we will see many more viruses and worms spread to cell phones in the future.[16] Also, viruses spread through handheld devices are starting to appear.

Why do these viruses spread so quickly? One reason is that many people are too willing to open executable files from unknown sources. Have you ever opened an audio clip or video clip from a friend? Have you ever forwarded that clip to other friends? Do you know who created the clip and if any viruses are embedded in it? Did you open the ILOVEYOU file to see what the love letter said?

Most antivirus software is reactive, going after viruses once they are discovered, rather than protecting against unknown viruses. New antivirus software, such as Finjan Software's SurfinGuard® (**www.finjan.com**), looks for executable files attached to e-mail and runs the executables in a secure area to test if they attempt to access and harm files. For more information about antivirus software, see the feature on **McAfee.com** antivirus utilities.

Web defacing is another popular form of attack by hackers, wherein the hackers illegally enter an organization's Web site and change the contents. CNN Interactive has issued a special report titled "Insurgency on the Internet," which contains news stories about hackers and their online attacks. Included is a gallery of hacked sites. One notable case of Web defacing occurred in 1996, when Swedish hackers changed the Central Intelligence Agency's Web site (**www.odci.gov/cia**) to read "Central Stupidity Agency." The hackers put obscenities, messages and links to adult-content sites on the page. Many other popular and large Web sites have been defaced.

Cybercrime can have significant financial implications for an organization.[13] Companies need to protect their data, intellectual property, customer information, etc. Implementing a *security policy* is key to protecting your organization's data and network. When developing a security plan, organizations must assess their vulnerabilities and possible threats to security. What information do they need to protect? Who are the possible attackers, and what is their intent—data theft or damaging the network? How will the organization respond to incidents?[14] For more information about security and security plans, visit **www.cerias.com** and **www.sans.org**. Visit **www.baselinesoft.com** to see a list of books and CD-ROMs on security policies. Baseline Software's book *Information Policies Made Easy: Version 7* includes over 1000 security policies. This book is used by numerous Fortune 200 companies.

McAfee.com Antivirus Utilities

McAfee.com provides a variety of antivirus utilities (and other utilities) for users whose computers are not continuously connected to a network, for users whose computers are continuously connected to a network (such as the Internet) and for users connected to a network via wireless devices, such as personal digital assistants and pagers.

For computers that are not continuously connected to a network, McAfee provides its antivirus software *VirusScan®*. This software is configurable to scan files for viruses on demand or to scan continuously in the background as the user does his or her work.

For computers that are network and Internet accessible, McAfee provides its online **McAfee.com** Clinic. Users with a subscription to McAfee Clinic can use the online virus software from any computer they happen to be using. As with VirusScan software on stand-alone computers, users can scan their files on demand. A major benefit of the Clinic is its *ActiveShield* software. Once installed, ActiveShield can be configured to scan every file that is used on the computer or to scan just the program files. It can also be configured to check automatically for virus definition updates and notify the user when such updates become available. The user simply clicks on the supplied hyperlink in an update notification to connect to the Clinic site and clicks on another hyperlink to download the update. Thus, users can keep their computers protected with the most up-to-date virus definitions at all times. For more information about McAfee, visit **www.mcafee.com**. Also, check out Norton security products from Symantec, at **www.symantec.com**. Symantec is a leading security-software vendor. Its product Norton™ Internet Security 2000 provides protection against hackers, viruses and threats to privacy for both small businesses and individuals.

The rise in cybercrimes has prompted the U.S. government to take action. Under the National Information Infrastructure Protection Act of 1996, denial-of-service attacks and distribution of viruses are federal crimes punishable by fines and jail time. For more information about the U.S. government's efforts against cybercrime or to read about recently prosecuted cases, visit the U.S. Department of Justice's Web site, at **www.usdoj.gov/criminal/cybercrime/compcrime.html**. Also check out **www.cybercrime.gov**, a site maintained by the Criminal Division of the U.S. Department of Justice.

The *CERT®* (*Computer Emergency Response Team*) *Coordination Center* at Carnegie Mellon University's Software Engineering Institute responds to reports of viruses and denial-of-service attacks and provides information on network security, including how to determine if your system has been compromised. The site provides detailed incident reports of viruses and denial-of-service attacks, including descriptions of the incidents, their impact and the solutions. The site also includes reports of vulnerabilities in popular operating systems and software packages. The *CERT Security Improvement Modules* are excellent tutorials on network security. These modules describe the issues and technologies used to solve network security problems. For more information, visit the CERT Web site, at **www.cert.org**.

To learn more about how you can protect yourself or your network from hacker attacks, visit AntiOnline™, at **www.antionline.com**. This site has security-related news and information, a tutorial entitled "Fight-back! Against Hackers," information about hackers and an archive of hacked sites. You can find additional information about denial-of-service attacks and how to protect your site at **www.irchelp.org/irchelp/nuke**.

19.9 Using Hidden Fields

Another potential security issue occurs with values placed in **hidden** HTML **input** elements. Such values are not actually hidden. Even though they are not visible on a Web page when the page is rendered in the browser, it is a relatively simple matter for the user to view the HTML source code to see what a hidden element contains, and it is almost as simple to modify the values.

Figure 19.9 allows the user to "bid" on a product by filling out a form with what he or she thinks a product is worth. When the users submit their bids, the program compares the bids with each product's minimum price and prints a table indicating which bids were accepted and which were too low. A user can then opt to buy the products whose bids were high enough.

```perl
1   #!perl
2   # Fig. 19.9: fig19_09.pl
3   # Using hidden fields in an non-secure manner.
4
5   use warnings;
6   use strict;
7   use CGI::Pretty ":standard";
8
9   print( header(), start_html( 'Bid on Deitel Books' ) );
10
11  # There are two separate sections--one for bidding/reviewing,
12  # one for reporting a purchase.
```

Fig. 19.9   Using hidden fields in a nonsecure manner (part 1 of 4).

```
13   unless ( param( 'Buy It' ) ) {
14      my ( %prices, @rows, $total );
15
16      # Set up the products table and prices hash
17      open( FILE, 'products.txt' ) or die( "Cannot open file" );
18
19      while ( <FILE> ) {
20         my ( $book, $price, @row ) = split( /::/ );
21         $prices{ $book } = $price;
22         unshift( @row, $book );
23         push( @row, '$'.textfield( -name => $book,
24                                    -size => '5' ) );
25         push( @rows, td( \@row ) );
26      }
27
28      # make a table of all the bids made
29      my %bids;
30
31      foreach my $name ( param() ) {
32         $bids{ $name } =
33            param( $name ) if ( param( $name ) > 0 );
34      }
35
36      if ( %bids ) {
37         my @bidRows = ( th( [ 'Product', 'Bid', 'Result' ] ) );
38
39         foreach my $key ( keys( %bids ) ) {
40            my $bidRow =
41               td( [ $key, sprintf( '$%.2f', $bids{ $key } ) ] );
42
43            if ( $bids{ $key } > $prices{ $key } ) {
44               $bidRow .= td( 'OK' );
45               $bidRow .= hidden( -name => $key,
46                                  -value => $bids{ $key } );
47               $bidRow .= hidden( -name => 'bid', -value => $key );
48               $total += $bids{ $key };
49            }
50            else {
51               $bidRow .= td( 'Too low' );
52            }
53
54            push( @bidRows, $bidRow );
55         }
56
57         push( @bidRows, td( [ 'Total', sprintf( '$%.2f', $total ),
58            submit( -name => 'Buy It', -value => 'Buy It' ) ] ) );
59
60         print( start_form(), table( { border => '1' },
61            caption( h3( 'Current Bids' ) ), Tr( [ @bidRows ] ), ),
62            end_form() );
63      }
64
```

Fig. 19.9   Using hidden fields in a nonsecure manner (part 2 of 4).

```
65      # make the products table
66      print( start_form(),
67         table( { border => '3' },
68            caption( h1( 'Product List' ) ),
69            Tr( { -valign => 'top' },
70               [ th( [ 'Product Name', 'Description', 'Bid' ] ),
71                 @rows,
72                 td( [ '', '', submit( -name => 'Review' ) ] )
73               ] ) ), end_form() );
74   }
75   else {
76      my ( $total, @rows );
77
78      foreach ( param( 'bid' ) ) {
79         $total += param( $_ );
80         push( @rows, td( $_ ).td( { align => 'right' },
81            sprintf( '$%.2f', param( $_ ) ) ) ) );
82      }
83
84      if ( @rows ) {
85         print( h1( 'Order Processed' ), table( { border => '3' },
86            caption( h4( 'Products Ordered' ) ),
87            Tr( [ th( [ 'Product', 'Price' ] ), @rows,
88                  th( [ 'Total', sprintf '$%.2f', $total ] )
89               ] ) ) );
90      }
91      else {
92         print( h4( 'You have not ordered anything. Please go ',
93            'back and revise any bids which were too low.' ) );
94      }
95   }
96
97   print( end_html() );
```

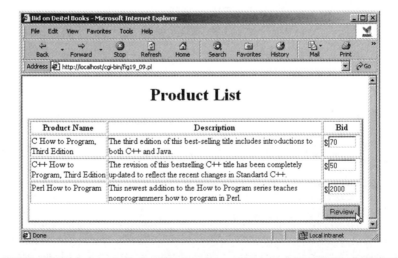

Fig. 19.9   Using hidden fields in a nonsecure manner (part 3 of 4).

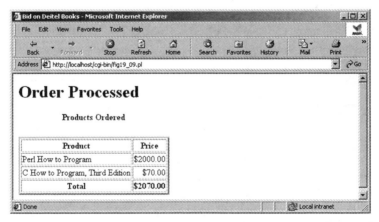

Fig. 19.9   Using hidden fields in a nonsecure manner (part 4 of 4).

This program uses hidden fields to maintain the user's bid information and pass data between different parts of the program. The products' names, descriptions and minimum prices are kept in a separate file (**products.txt**). Each line in this file represents a separate product, with each field separated by two colons.

Lines 17–26 read in the file, create a hash of the items and their prices for bid comparison purposes and prepare the products' names and descriptions so they can be output in an HTML table. Line 20 separates each entry in **products.txt** into parts using function **split**. The first element, the product's name, is assigned to **$book**. The second element, the price, is assigned to **$price**. The third element, the product's description, is assigned as the only element in array **@row**. Line 21 creates an entry in the **%prices** hash for the current book and its minimum price. Line 22 adds the name of the book to the **@row** array. Line 23 adds a text-field form element to **@row**. The name attribute of the text field is set to the product name. The data in this array will be used to form one row of the product-list table in the Web page. Next, line 25 converts the array **@row** to a string that represents cells in an HTML table using function **td**. The result is pushed onto the **@rows** array that holds all the rows for the table.

Lines 29–34 create the hash **%bids** to store the user's bids (if there are any). The name of the product is the key and the bid is the corresponding value. If any bids were made, an HTML table is output to allow the clients to review their bids (lines 36–63). The **submit** button (line 58) allows the user to specify that he or she wishes to buy the products.

Lines 39–55 create the data for an HTML table in which the bids will appear. An array holds each row of the table. The first two elements of each row are the name of the product and the bid, respectively (lines 40 and 41). If the bid is high enough (line 43), the third column will say **OK**. Also, two hidden fields are added (lines 45–47)—one with the same name as the product and the amount of the bid as the value and one containing the name **bid** and the name of the product bid on as the value. The hidden fields allow the program to remember the products on which bids were made and the amount of the bids when the client decides to buy them. If the bid was not high enough, the third column contains **Too low** (line 51) instead and the bid is not saved in a hidden field. To complete the table, lines 57 and 58 add a final row consisting of the total price of all the items.

Now all of the tables are ready to be printed. Lines 57–62 print the table for reviewing the bids, and lines 66–73 print the table listing of all the products. You will notice that each table has a separate form, so the program can perform different tasks if the user has just entered a bid or if the user wants to buy the items on which he or she has bid previously.

Lines 75–95 process the case in which the user decides to buy the products on which he or she has bid previously. In a real Web application, this part of the program would obtain user information that would allow us to charge the customer for the items and ship the items to the customer. In this example, we simply output the items the user would have purchased. To do so, we prepare a table listing all of the products on which the user bid and the prices that were paid. All the information for this table is read from the hidden input elements in a form. The **bid** parameter holds the names of the items on which the user bid. Each item has a parameter in which the name of the product is the name of the parameter and the bid is the corresponding value.

The problem with this page is that the program does not check the validity of the values in hidden fields. Although they are called "hidden" fields and are not displayed in a Web browser, they are not actually hidden; by looking at the HTML, one can easily see the values of the hidden fields. Also, by saving the HTML document to a file and modifying it, we can change the values of the hidden fields. In this case, to take advantage of the lack of data verification, users could modify values in the first table containing the bids they made on the products. The HTML for the current bids table is shown in Fig. 19.10. [*Note:* The HTML was reformatted for inclusion in the book.]

```
1   <form method="post" action="/cgi-bin/fig19_09.pl"
2          enctype="application/x-www-form-urlencoded">
3   <table border="1">
4      <caption><h3>Current Bids</h3></caption>
5      <tr><th>Product</th><th>Bid</th><th>Result</th></tr>
6      <tr><td>Perl How to Program</td><td>$2000.00</td><td>OK</td>
7          <input type="hidden" name="Perl How to Program"
8                  value="2000">
9          <input type="hidden" name="bid"
10                 value="Perl How to Program">
11     </tr>
12     <tr><td>C How to Program, Third Edition</td><td>$70.00</td>
13         <td>OK</td>
14         <input type="hidden"
15                 name="C How to Program, Third Edition"
16                 value="70">
17         <input type="hidden" name="bid"
18                 value="C How to Program, Third Edition">
19     </tr>
20     <tr><td>C++ How to Program, Third Edition<td>$50.00</td>
21         <td>Too low</td>
22     </tr>
23     <tr><td>Total</td><td>$2070.00</td>
24         <td><input type="submit" name="Buy It" value="Buy It" />
25         </td>
26     </tr>
27  </table>
28  </form>
```

Fig. 19.10   HTML for table .

As you can see, the hidden fields are easy to view and modify in the HTML source code (lines 7–10 and 14–18). By changing the values on lines 8 and 16 to absurdly low values, we can trick this program into selling us the books at much lower prices. For example, if we modify lines 7 and 8 as follows:

```
<input type="hidden" name="Perl How to Program"
        value="1">
```

the price of the book becomes 1. If the user saves the HTML in his or her own file, he or she will also need to modify the form's action to specify the server on which the CGI program resides. In this case, the user would modify line 1 of Fig. 19.10 as follows:

```
ACTION="http://localhost/cgi-bin/fig19_09.pl"
```

Then, when the user loads the HTML document from his or her own computer and clicks on the **Buy It** button, the **post** is redirected from the saved (and compromised) HTML file back to our original program. This procedure enables the user to trick the CGI program into selling one of the books for only one dollar when, in fact, the original bid in the sample screen capture of Fig. 19.9 was 2000 dollars. The result of using the compromised Web page is shown in Fig. 19.11. You can see that trusting hidden fields can be dangerous.

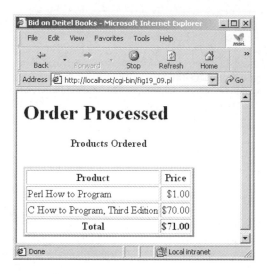

Fig. 19.11 Output of cracked program.

The obvious solution to this problem is to check the data in the hidden fields against the minimum values before allowing the user to buy any products. There are, however, some situations in which you need to be able to have data in hidden fields, but do not have a quick and easy way to verify the data. One way around this problem is to use another field, called a *digest*, that contains the data that you wish to verify in an encrypted form. The next few sections go over the theory behind encryption and how to use it to your benefit.

19.10 Introduction to Cryptography Theory

The channels through which data pass over the Internet are not secure; therefore, any private information that is being passed through the channels must be protected. To secure information, data can be encrypted. *Cryptography* transforms data by using a *key*—a string of digits that acts as a password—to make the data incomprehensible to all but the sender and the intended receivers. Unencrypted data are called *plaintext*; encrypted data are called *ciphertext*. Only the intended receivers should have the corresponding key to decrypt the ciphertext into plaintext. A *cipher*, or *cryptosystem*, is a technique or algorithm for encrypting messages.

Cryptographic ciphers were used as far back as the time of the ancient Egyptians. In ancient cryptography, messages were encrypted by hand, usually with a method based on the alphabetic letters of the message. The two main types of ciphers were *substitution ciphers* and *transposition ciphers*. In a substitution cipher, every occurrence of a given letter is replaced by a different letter; for example, if every "a" is replaced by a "b," every "b" by a "c," etc., the word "security" would encrypt to "tfdvsjuz." In a transposition cipher, the ordering of the letters is shifted; for example, if every other letter, starting with "s," in the word "security" creates the first word in the ciphertext and the remaining letters create the second word in the ciphertext, the word "security" would encrypt to "scrt euiy." Complicated ciphers were created by combining substitution and transposition ciphers. For example, using the substitution cipher first, and then the transposition cipher, the word "security" would encrypt to "tdsu fvjz." The problem with many historical ciphers is that their security relied on the sender and receiver to remember the encryption algorithm and keep it secret. Such algorithms ("algorithm" is a computer science term for "procedure") are called *restricted algorithms*. Restricted algorithms are not feasible to implement among a large group of people. Imagine if the security of U.S. government communications relied on every U.S. government employee to keep a secret; the encryption algorithm would easily be compromised.

Modern cryptosystems are digital. Their algorithms are based on the individual *bits* of a message rather than on the letters of the alphabet. A computer stores data as a *binary string*, which is a sequence of ones and zeros. Each digit in the sequence is called a bit. Encryption and decryption keys are binary strings with a given *key length*. For example, 128-bit encryption systems have a key length of 128 bits. Longer keys have stronger encryption; it takes more time and computing power to "break the code."

Until January 2000, the U.S. government placed restrictions on the strength of cryptosystems that could be exported from the United States, by limiting the key length of the encryption algorithms. Today, the regulations on exporting cryptosystems are less stringent. Any cryptosystem may be exported as long as the end user is not a foreign government or from a country with embargo restrictions on it.[2]

19.11 Using Encryption

Perl provides many modules that can be used to encrypt data. In this section, we use a digest to verify data. A digest is an encrypted version of the data that cannot be decrypted back to the original data. However, if we encrypt the data again with the same key that was used originally and it matches the digest, we know the data have not been compromised.

There are many algorithms that can be used to create digests. Most take two arguments—the data and the key used to encrypt the data—and return the digest. The only way to get the same digest from that data is to use the same key. Without the key, it is extremely difficult to create the same digest from the data.

Figure 19.12 shows an example that uses the *RSA Data Security, Inc., MD5 Message-Digest algorithm* (module **Digest::MD5**) to encrypt data and create a digest. Including both the data and the digest as hidden fields allows the CGI program to detect whether the data has been compromised.

Line 8 includes the module that performs the encryption, the **Digest::MD5** module, and specifies that base-64 encrypting (**md5_base64**) will be used. [*Note:* There are other encryption modules and other encrypting functions. Search CPAN to find the one that is appropriate for your application.]

Line 10 sets the key that we will use to encode the digest. In this case ,we just assign the string in the program, for simplicity, but it is generally a good idea to have it stored outside the program; otherwise, if someone gets a peek at your code, they will know the key string. If you do this, make sure the file that holds the key is not in the **cgi-bin** directory or any other directory that could be accessible to crackers.

```
1   #!perl -T
2   # Fig. 19.12: fig19_12.pl
3   # Uses hidden fields in an insecure manner
4
5   use warnings;
```

Fig. 19.12 Using digests (part 1 of 5).

```
6   use strict;
7   use CGI::Pretty ":standard";
8   use Digest::MD5 qw( md5_base64 );
9
10  my $encodeString = 'An encoder string';
11
12  print( header(), start_html( 'Bid on Deitel Books' ) );
13
14  # There are two separate sections--one for bidding/reviewing,
15  # one for reporting a purchase.
16  unless ( param( 'Buy It' ) ) {
17     my ( %prices, @rows, $total );
18
19     # Set up the products table and prices hash
20     open( FILE, 'products.txt' ) or die( "Cannot open file" );
21
22     while ( <FILE> ) {
23        my ( $book, $price, @row ) = split( /::/ );
24        $prices{ $book } = $price;
25        unshift( @row, $book );
26        push( @row, '$'.textfield( -name => $book,
27                                   -size => '5' ) );
28        push( @rows, td( \@row ) );
29     }
30
31     # make a table of all the bids made
32     my %bids;
33
34     foreach my $name ( param() ) {
35        $bids{ $name } =
36           param( $name ) if ( param( $name ) > 0 );
37     }
38
39     if ( %bids ) {
40        my @bidRows = ( th( [ 'Product', 'Bid', 'Result' ] ) );
41
42        foreach my $key ( keys( %bids ) ) {
43           my $bidRow =
44              td( [ $key, sprintf( '$%.2f', $bids{ $key } ) ] );
45
46           if ( $bids{ $key } > $prices{ $key } ) {
47              $bidRow .= td( 'OK' );
48              $bidRow .= hidden( $key.'digest',
49                 md5_base64( $key, $bids{ $key },
50                    $encodeString ) );
51
52              $bidRow .= hidden( -name => 'bid', -value => $key );
53                 $bidRow .= hidden( -name => $key,
54                                    -value => $bids{ $key } );
55              $total += $bids{ $key };
56           }
57           else {
58              $bidRow .= td( 'Too low' );
```

Fig. 19.12 Using digests (part 2 of 5).

```
59              }
60
61          push( @bidRows, $bidRow );
62      }
63
64      push( @bidRows, td( [ 'Total', sprintf( '$%.2f', $total ),
65          submit( -name => 'Buy It', -value => 'Buy It' ) ] ) );
66
67      print( start_form(), table( { border => '1' },
68          caption( h3( 'Current Bids' ) ), Tr( [ @bidRows ] ), ),
69          end_form() );
70  }
71
72  # make the products table
73  print( start_form(),
74      table( { border => '3' },
75          caption( h1( 'Product List' ) ),
76          Tr( { -valign => 'top' },
77              [ th( [ 'Product Name', 'Description', 'Bid' ] ),
78                @rows,
79                td( [ '', '', submit( -name => 'Review' ) ] )
80              ] ) ), end_form() );
81  }
82  else {
83      my ( $total, @rows );
84
85      foreach my $name ( param( 'bid' ) ) {
86
87          if ( param( $name.'digest' ) ne
88              md5_base64( $name, param( $name ),
89                          $encodeString ) ) {
90              print( h1( "You have tampered with the fields!!!" ),
91                  end_html() );
92              die();
93          }
94
95          $total += param( $name );
96          push( @rows, td( $name ).td( { align => 'right' },
97              sprintf( '$%.2f', param( $name ) ) ) );
98      }
99
100     if ( @rows ) {
101         print( h1( 'Order Processed' ), table( { border => '3' },
102             caption( h4( 'Products Ordered' ) ),
103             Tr( [ th( [ 'Product', 'Price' ] ), @rows,
104                 th( [ 'Total', sprintf '$%.2f', $total ] )
105                 ] ) ) );
106     }
107     else {
108         print( h4( 'You have not ordered anything. Please go ',
109             'back and revise any bids which were too low.' ) );
110     }
111 }
```

Fig. 19.12 Using digests (part 3 of 5).

```
112
113  print( end_html() );
```

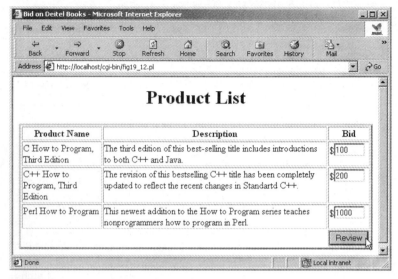

Fig. 19.12   Using digests (part 4 of 5).

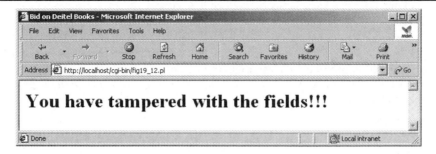

Fig. 19.12   Using digests (part 5 of 5).

Lines 48–50 create the digest with the **md5_base64** function and create a hidden field in which to store the digest. The name attribute of this file is set to the name of the product with the word "**digest**" appended to it, and the corresponding value is the digest itself. Function **md5_base64** returns a string that appears to be nothing more than a meaningless series of letters. For example, a bid of 200 for *Perl How to Program* produces the string **fEkLjAcfHlZZUFr8K4F8/w**.

In lines 87–93, the program confirms that each hidden value received has not been compromised. If the arguments to function **md5_base64** are identical to the original function call that created the digest, the string created by the new call should match the digest. If so, we have verified that the hidden values have not been compromised. The last screen capture in Fig. 19.12 shows the resulting Web page if the user attempts to compromise the data as discussed in Fig. 19.10 and Fig. 19.11.

You can find the **MD5** module on CPAN. CPAN also has numerous other modules that are designed to help you with security. There is a security and encryption section, which can be found at the following URL:

```
www.perl.com/CPAN-local/modules/by-category/
14_Security_and_Encryption/
```

Unfortunately, digests can verify only data that is known in advance. Other methods must be used to transmit data so that if it is intercepted, they cannot be read. Such encryption typically is accomplished by using communications protocols that encrypt the data being sent. The following sections discuss the theory and options for this type of communication.

19.12 Secret-key Cryptography

In the past, organizations wishing to maintain a secure computing environment used *symmetric cryptography*, also known as *secret-key cryptography*. Secret-key cryptography uses the same symmetric secret key to encrypt and decrypt a message (Fig. 19.13). In this case, the sender encrypts a message using the symmetric secret key, and then sends the encrypted message and the symmetric secret key to the intended recipient. A fundamental problem with secret-key cryptography is that before two people can communicate securely, they must find a way to exchange the symmetric secret key securely. One approach is to have the key delivered by a courier, such as a mail service or Federal Express. While this approach may be feasible when two individuals communicate, it is not efficient for securing communication in a large network, nor can it be considered completely secure; the privacy and the integrity of the message could be compromised if the key is intercepted as it is passed between the sender and the receiver over unsecure channels. Also, since both parties in the transaction use the same key to encipher and decipher a message, you cannot authenticate which party created the message. Finally, to keep communications private with each receiver, a different key is required for each receiver, so organizations could have huge numbers of symmetric secret keys to maintain.

An alternative approach to the key-exchange problem is to have a central authority, called a *key distribution center* (*KDC*). The key distribution center shares a (different) symmetric secret key with every user in the network. In this system, the key distribution center generates a *session key* to be used for a transaction (Fig. 19.14). Next, the key distribution center distributes the session key to the sender and receiver, encrypted with the symmetric secret key they each share with the key distribution center. For example, say a merchant and a customer want to conduct a secure transaction. The merchant and the customer each have unique symmetric secret keys that they share with the key distribution center. The key distribution center generates a session key for the merchant and customer to use in the transaction. The key distribution center then sends the session key for the transaction to the merchant, encrypted using the symmetric secret key the merchant already shares with the center. It then sends the same session key for the transaction to the customer, encrypted using the symmetric secret key the customer already shares with the key distribution center. Once the merchant and the customer have the session key for the transaction, they can communicate with each other, encrypting their messages using the shared session key.

Using a key distribution center reduces the number of courier deliveries (again, by means such as mail or Federal Express) of symmetric secret keys to each user in the network. In addition, users can have a new symmetric secret key for each communication with other users in the network, which greatly increases the overall security of the network. However, if the security of the key distribution center is compromised, then the security of the entire network is compromised.

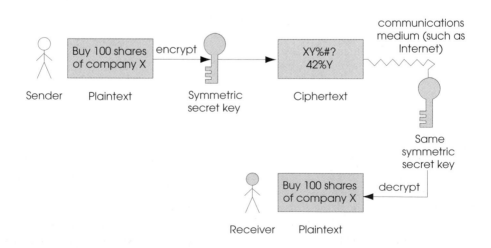

Fig. 19.13 Encrypting and decrypting a message using a symmetric secret key.

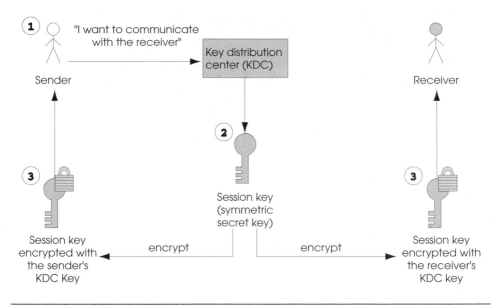

Fig. 19.14 Distributing a session key with a key distribution center.

One of the most commonly used symmetric encryption algorithms is the *Data Encryption Standard* (*DES*), which was developed by the National Security Agency (NSA) and IBM in the 1950s. DES has a key length of 56 bits. For many years, DES has been the standard set by the U.S. government and the American National Standards Institute (ANSI). However, cryptanalysts today believe that DES is not completely secure, because the key length is too short, making it easy to crack. As a result, the current standard of symmetric encryption is *Triple DES*, a variant of DES that is essentially three DES systems in a row, each having its own secret key. The U.S. government is in the process of selecting a new, more secure standard for symmetric encryption. The new standard will be called the *Advanced Encryption Standard* (*AES*). The *National Institute of Standards and Technology* (*NIST*), which sets the cryptographic standards for the U.S. government, is currently evaluating algorithms from five finalists, based on strength, efficiency, speed and a few other characteristics.[3]

19.13 Public-Key Cryptography

In 1976, *Whitfield Diffie* and *Martin Hellman*, researchers at Stanford University, developed *public-key cryptography* to solve the problem of exchanging keys securely. Public-key cryptography is asymmetric. It uses two inversely related keys: a *public key* and a *private key*. The private key is kept secret by its owner. The public key is freely distributed. If the public key is used to encrypt a message, only the corresponding private key can decrypt it, and vice versa (Fig. 19.15). Each party in a transaction has both a public key and a private key. To transmit a message securely, the sender uses the receiver's public key to encrypt the message. The receiver decrypts the message using his or her unique private key. No one else knows the private key, so the message cannot be read by anyone other than the intended receiver; this system ensures the privacy of the message. The defining property of a secure public-key algorithm is that it is computationally infeasible to deduce the private key from the public key. Although the two keys are mathematically related, deriving one from the other would take enormous amounts of computing power and time, enough to discourage attempts to deduce the private key. An outside party cannot participate in communication without the correct keys. Thus, the security of the entire process is based on the secrecy of the private keys. If a third party obtains the decryption key, then the security of the whole system is compromised. If the security of a system is compromised, you can simply change the key, instead of changing the whole encryption or decryption algorithm.

Either the public key or the private key can be used to encrypt or decrypt a message. For example, if a customer uses a merchant's public key to encrypt a message, only the merchant can decrypt the message, using the merchant's private key. Thus, the merchant's identity can be authenticated, since only the merchant knows the private key. However, the merchant has no way of validating the customer's identity, since the encryption key the customer used is publicly available.

If the decryption key is the sender's public key and the encryption key is the sender's private key, the sender of the message can be authenticated. For example, suppose a customer sends a merchant a message encrypted using the customer's private key. The merchant decrypts the message using the customer's public key. Since the customer encrypted the message using his or her private key, the merchant can be confident of the customer's identity. This system works as long as the merchant can be sure that the public key with which the merchant decrypted the message belongs to the customer, not to a third party posing as the customer. The problem of proving ownership of a public key is discussed in Section 19.17.

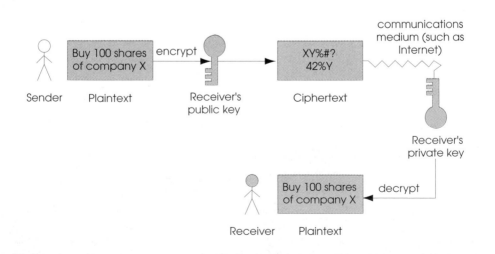

Fig. 19.15 Encrypting and decrypting a message using public-key cryptography.

These two methods of public-key encryption can actually be used together to authenticate both participants in a communication (Fig. 19.16). Suppose that a merchant wants to send a message securely to a customer so that only the customer can read it, and suppose also that the merchant wants to provide proof to the customer that the merchant (not an unknown third party) actually sent the message. First, the merchant encrypts the message using the customer's public key. This step guarantees that only the customer can read the message. Then the merchant encrypts the result using the merchant's private key, which proves the identity of the merchant. The customer decrypts the message in reverse order. First, the customer uses the merchant's public key. Since only the merchant could have encrypted the message with the inversely related private key, this step authenticates the merchant. Then the customer uses the customer's private key to decrypt the next level of encryption. This step ensures that the content of the message was kept private in the transmission, since only the customer has the key to decrypt the message.

The most commonly used public-key algorithm is *RSA*, an encryption system developed by Ron Rivest, Adi Shamir and Leonard Adleman in 1977. These three MIT professors founded *RSA Security, Inc.*, in 1982. Today, their encryption and authentication technologies are used by most Fortune 1000 companies and leading e-commerce businesses. With the emergence of the Internet and the World Wide Web, their security work has become even more significant and plays a crucial role in e-commerce transactions. Their encryption products are built into hundreds of millions of copies of the most popular Internet applications, including Web browsers, commerce servers and e-mail systems. Most secure e-commerce transactions and communications on the Internet use RSA products. For more information about RSA, cryptography and security, visit **www.rsasecurity.com**.

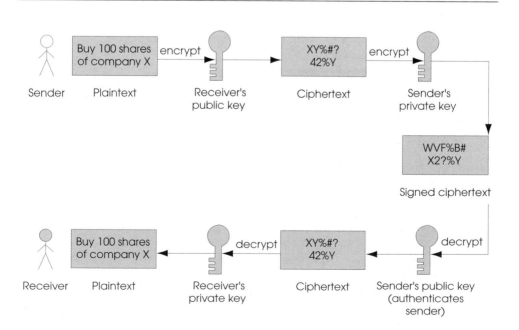

Fig. 19.16 Authentication with a public-key algorithm.

Pretty Good Privacy (PGP) is a public-key encryption system used to encrypt e-mail messages and files. It is freely available for noncommercial use. PGP is based on a "web of trust"; each client in a network can vouch for another client's identity to prove ownership of a public key. The "web of trust" is used to authenticate each client. To learn more about PGP and to download a free copy of the software, go to the MIT Distribution Center for PGP, at **web.mit.edu/network/pgp.html**.

19.14 Key Agreement Protocols

A drawback of public-key algorithms is that they are not efficient for sending large amounts of data. They require significant computer power, which slows down communication. Thus, public-key algorithms should not be thought of as a replacement for symmetric secret-key algorithms. Instead, public-key algorithms can be used to allow two parties to agree upon a key to be used for symmetric secret-key encryption over an unsecure medium. The process by which two parties can exchange keys over an unsecure medium is called a *key agreement protocol*. A *protocol* sets the rules for communication: Exactly what encryption algorithm(s) is (are) going to be used?

The most common key agreement protocol is a *digital envelope* (Fig. 19.17). When using a digital envelope, the message is encrypted using a symmetric secret key, and then the symmetric secret key is encrypted using public-key encryption. For example, a sender encrypts a message using a symmetric secret key. The sender then encrypts that symmetric secret key using the receiver's public key. The sender attaches the encrypted symmetric secret key to the encrypted message and sends the receiver the entire package. The sender could also digitally sign the package before sending it to prove the sender's identity to the receiver (Section 19.16). To decrypt the package, the receiver first decrypts the symmetric secret key using the receiver's private key. Then, the receiver uses the symmetric secret key to decrypt the actual message. Since only the receiver can decrypt the encrypted symmetric secret key, the sender can be sure that only the intended receiver can read the message.

19.15 Key Management

Maintaining the secrecy of private keys is crucial to keeping cryptographic systems secure. Most compromises in security result from poor *key management* (i.e., the mishandling of private keys, resulting in key theft) rather than from attacks that attempt to decipher the keys.[4]

A main component of key management is *key generation*—the process by which keys are created. A malicious third party could try to decrypt a message by using every possible decryption key. Keys are made secure by choosing a key length so large that it is computationally infeasible to try all such combinations.

Key-generation algorithms are sometimes unintentionally constructed to choose only from a small subset of possible keys. If the subset is small enough, then it may be possible for a malicious third party to try every possible key to crack the encryption (see Section 19.18, on cryptanalysis). Therefore, it is important to have a key-generation program that is truly random.

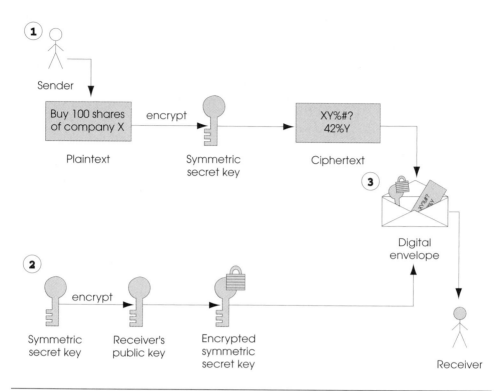

Fig. 19.17 Creating a digital envelope.

19.16 Digital Signatures

Digital signatures, the electronic equivalent of written signatures, were developed to be used in public-key cryptography to solve the problems of authentication and integrity. A digital signature authenticates the sender's identity, and, like a written signature, digital signatures are difficult to forge. To create a digital signature, a sender first takes the original plaintext message and runs it through a *hash function*, which is a mathematical calculation that gives the message a *hash value*. For example, you could take the plaintext message "Buy 100 shares of company X," run it through a hash function and get a hash value of 42. The hash function could be as simple as adding up all the 1s in a message, though it is usually more complex. The hash value is also known as a *message digest*. The chance that two different messages will have the same message digest is statistically insignificant. *Collision* occurs when multiple messages have the same hash value. It is computationally infeasible to compute a message from its hash value or to find two messages with the same hash value.

Next, the sender uses the sender's private key to encrypt the message digest. This step creates a digital signature and authenticates the sender, since only the owner of that private key could encrypt the message. The original message, encrypted with the receiver's public key, the digital signature and the hash function, is sent to the receiver. The receiver uses the sender's public key to decipher the original digital signature and reveal the message digest. The receiver then uses his or her own private key to decipher the original message. Finally, the receiver applies the hash function to the original message. If the hash value of the original message matches the message digest included in the signature, then there is *message integrity*; the message has not been altered in transmission.

There is a fundamental difference between digital signatures and handwritten signatures. A handwritten signature is independent of the document being signed. Thus, if someone can forge a handwritten signature, they can use that signature to forge multiple documents. A digital signature is created using the contents of the document. Therefore, your digital signature is different for each document you sign.

Digital signatures do not provide proof that a message has been sent. Consider the following situation: A contractor sends a company a digitally signed contract, which the contractor later would like to revoke. The contractor could do so by releasing its private key and then claiming that the digitally signed contract came from an intruder who stole the contractor's private key. *Timestamping*, which binds a time and date to a digital document, can help solve this problem, called *nonrepudiation*. For example, suppose the company and the contractor are negotiating a contract. The company requires the contractor to digitally sign the contract and then have the document digitally timestamped by a third party called a *timestamping agency*. The contractor sends the digitally signed contract to the timestamping agency. The privacy of the message is maintained, since the timestamping agency sees only the encrypted, digitally signed message (as opposed to just the original plaintext message). The timestamping agency affixes the time and date of receipt to the encrypted, signed message and digitally signs the whole package with the timestamping agency's private key. The timestamp cannot be altered by anyone except the timestamping agency, since no one else possesses the timestamping agency's private key. Unless the contractor reports its private key to have been compromised before the document was timestamped, the contractor cannot legally prove that the document was signed by a third party. The sender could also require the receiver to digitally sign and timestamp the message as proof of receipt. To learn more about timestamping, visit **AuthentiDate.com** (**www.authentidate.com**).

The U.S. government's digital-authentication standard is called the *Digital Signature Algorithm* (*DSA*). The U.S. government recently passed digital-signature legislation that makes digital signatures as legally binding as handwritten signatures. This legislation will result in an increase in e-business. For the latest news about U.S. government legislation in information security, visit **www.itaa.org/infosec**. For more information about the bills, visit the following government sites:

```
thomas.loc.gov/cgi-bin/bdquery/z?d106:hr.01714:
thomas.loc.gov/cgi-bin/bdquery/z?d106:s.00761:.
```

19.17 Public-Key Infrastructure, Certificates and Certification Authorities

One problem with public-key cryptography is that anyone with a set of keys could potentially assume another party's identity. For example, say a customer wants to place an order with an online merchant. How does the customer know that the Web site being accessed indeed belongs to that merchant and not to a third party that posted the site and is masquerading as the merchant to steal credit-card information? *Public Key Infrastructure* (*PKI*) integrates public-key cryptography with *digital certificates* and *certification authorities* to authenticate parties in a transaction.

A digital certificate is a digital document issued by a *certification authority (CA)*. A digital certificate includes the name of the subject (the company or individual being certified), the subject's public key, a serial number, an expiration date, the signature of the trusted certification authority and any other relevant information (Fig. 19.18). A CA is a financial institution or other trusted third party, such as *VeriSign*. The CA takes responsibility for authentication, so it must carefully check information before issuing a digital certificate. Digital certificates are publicly available and are held by the certification authority in *certificate repositories*.

The CA signs the certificate by encrypting either the subject's public key or a hash value of the public key using the CA's own private key. The CA has to verify every subject's public key. Thus, users must trust the public key of a CA. Usually, each CA is part of a *certificate authority hierarchy*. A certificate authority hierarchy is a chain of certificate authorities, starting with the *root certification authority*, which is the Internet Policy Registration Authority (IPRA). The IPRA signs certificates using the *root key*. The root signs certificates only for *policy creation authorities*, which are organizations that set policies for obtaining digital certificates. In turn, policy creation authorities sign digital certificates for CAs. CAs sign digital certificates for individuals and organizations.

VeriSign, Inc., is a leading certificate authority. For more information about VeriSign, visit **www.verisign.com**. For a listing of other digital-certificate vendors, please see Section 19.22.

Fig. 19.18 A portion of the VeriSign digital certificate. (Courtesy of VeriSign.)

Periodically changing key pairs is helpful in maintaining a secure system in case your private key is compromised without your knowledge. The longer you use a given key pair, the more vulnerable the keys are to attack. As a result, digital certificates are created with an expiration date, to force users to switch key pairs. If your private key is compromised before its expiration date, you can cancel your digital certificate and get a new key pair and digital certificate. Canceled and revoked certificates are placed on a *certificate revocation list* (*CRL*). CRLs are stored with the certification authority that issued the certificates.

Many people still perceive e-commerce to be unsecure. In fact, transactions using PKI and digital certificates are more secure than exchanging private information over phone lines, through the mail or even paying by credit card in person. After all, when you go to a restaurant and the waiter takes your credit card to the back of the restaurant to process your bill, how do you know the waiter did not write down your credit-card information? In contrast, the key algorithms used in most secure online transactions are nearly impossible to compromise. By some estimates, the key algorithms used in public-key cryptography are so secure that even millions of today's computers working in parallel could not possibly break the code in a century. However, as computing power rapidly increases, key algorithms that are considered strong today could be easily breakable in the near future.

To obtain a digital certificate to digitally sign your personal e-mail messages, visit **www.verisign.com** or **www.thawte.com**. VeriSign offers a free 60-day trial, or you can purchase the service for a yearly fee. Thawte offers free digital certificates for personal e-mail. Web-server certificates may also be purchased through Verisign and Thawte; however, they are more expensive than e-mail certificates.

Digital-certificate capabilities are built into many e-mail packages. For example, in Microsoft Outlook, you can go to the **Tools** menu and select **Options**. Then click on the **Security** tab. At the bottom of the dialog box, you will see the option to obtain a digital ID. Selecting the option will take you to a Microsoft Web site with links to several worldwide certification authorities. Once you have a digital certificate, you can digitally sign your e-mail messages.

19.18 Cryptanalysis

Even if keys are kept secret, it still may be possible to compromise the security of a system. Trying to decrypt ciphertext without knowledge of the decryption key is known as *cryptanalysis*. Commercial encryption systems are constantly being researched by cryptologists to ensure that the systems are not vulnerable to a cryptanalytic attack. The most common form of cryptanalytic attacks are those in which the encryption algorithm is analyzed to find relations between bits of the encryption key and bits of the ciphertext. Often, these relations are only statistical in nature and incorporate outside knowledge about the plaintext. The goal of such an attack is to determine the key from the ciphertext.

Weak statistical trends between ciphertext and keys can be exploited to gain knowledge about the key if enough ciphertext is known. Proper key management and expiration dates on keys help prevent cryptanalytic attacks. Also, using public-key cryptography to securely exchange symmetric secret keys allows you to use a new symmetric secret key to encrypt every message.

19.19 Security Protocols

Everyone using the Web for e-business and e-commerce needs to be concerned about the security of their personal information. There are several protocols that provide transaction security, such as *Secure Sockets Layer* (*SSL*) and *Secure Electronic Transaction*™ (*SET*™). We discuss these security protocols in the next two subsections.

19.19.1 Secure Sockets Layer (SSL)

The *Secure Sockets Layer* (*SSL*) *protocol*, developed by Netscape Communications, is a non proprietary protocol commonly used to secure communication on the Internet and the Web.[5, 6] SSL is built into many Web browsers, including Netscape Communicator, Microsoft Internet Explorer and numerous other software products. It operates between the Internet's TCP/IP communications protocol and the application software.

In a standard correspondence over the Internet, a sender's message is passed to a *socket*, which transmits information in a network; the socket interprets the message in Transmission Control Protocol/Internet Protocol (TCP/IP). TCP/IP is the standard set of protocols used for communication between computers on the Internet. Most Internet transmissions are sent as sets of individual message pieces, called *packets*. At the sending side, the packets of a message are numbered sequentially, and error-control information is attached to each packet. TCP/IP routes packets to avoid traffic jams, so each packet might travel a different route over the Internet. At the receiving end, TCP/IP makes sure that all of the packets have arrived, puts them in sequential order and determines if the packets have arrived without alteration. If the packets have been altered, TCP/IP retransmits them. TCP/IP then passes the message to the socket at the receiver's end. The socket translates the message back into a form that can be read by the receiver's application. In a transaction using SSL, the sockets are secured using public-key cryptography.

SSL uses public-key technology and digital certificates to authenticate the server in a transaction and to protect private information as it passes from one party to another over the Internet. SSL transactions do not require client authentication. To begin, a client sends a message to a server. The server responds and sends its digital certificate to the client for authentication. Using public-key cryptography to communicate securely, the client and server negotiate *session keys* to continue the transaction. Session keys are symmetric secret keys that are used for the duration of one transaction. Once the keys are established, the communication proceeds between the client and the server by using the session keys and digital certificates.

Although SSL protects information as it is passed over the Internet, it does not protect private information, such as credit-card numbers, once the information is stored on a merchant's server. When a merchant receives credit-card information with an order, the information is often decrypted and stored on the merchant's server until the order is placed. If the server is not secure and the data are not encrypted, an unauthorized party can access the information. Hardware devices called *peripheral component interconnect* (*PCI*) *cards* designed for SSL transactions can be installed on Web servers to secure data for an entire SSL transaction from the client to the Web server.[7] The PCI card processes the SSL transactions, freeing the Web server to perform other tasks. Visit **www.phobos.com/Products/infamily.htm** for more information about these devices. For more information about the SSL protocol, check out the Netscape SSL tutorial, at **developer.netscape.com/tech/security/ssl/protocol.html**, and the Netscape Security Center site, at **www.netscape.com/security/index.html**.

19.19.2 Secure Electronic Transaction™ (SET™)

The *Secure Electronic Transaction (SET) protocol*, developed by Visa International and MasterCard, was designed specifically to protect e-commerce payment transactions.[8, 9] SET uses digital certificates to authenticate each party in an e-commerce transaction, including the customer, the merchant and the merchant's bank. Public-key cryptography is used to secure information as it is passed over the Web.

Merchants must have a digital certificate and special SET software to process transactions. Customers must have a digital certificate and *digital wallet* software. A digital wallet is similar to a real wallet; it stores credit (or debit) card information for multiple cards, as well as a digital certificate verifying the cardholder's identity. Digital wallets add convenience to online shopping; customers no longer need to reenter their credit-card information at each shopping site.[10]

When a customer is ready to place an order, the merchant's SET software sends the order information and the merchant's digital certificate to the customer's digital wallet, thus activating the wallet software. The customer selects the credit card to be used for the transaction. The credit-card and order information are encrypted by using the public key of the merchant's bank's and sent to the merchant along with the customer's digital certificate. The merchant then forwards the information to its bank to process the payment. Only the merchant's bank can decrypt the message, since the message was encrypted using the bank's public key. The merchant's bank then sends the amount of the purchase and its own digital certificate to the customer's bank to get approval to process the transaction. If the customer's charge is approved, the customer's bank sends an authorization back to the merchant's bank. The merchant's bank then sends a credit-card authorization to the merchant. Finally, the merchant sends a confirmation of the order to the customer.

In the SET protocol, the merchant never sees the client's proprietary information. Therefore, the client's credit-card number is not stored on the merchant's server, considerably reducing the risk of fraud.

Although SET is designed specifically for e-commerce transactions and provides a high level of security, it has yet to become the standard protocol used in the majority of transactions. Part of the problem is that SET requires special software on both the client and server side; that requirement increases transaction costs. Also, the transactions are more time consuming than transactions using other protocols, such as SSL. Both Visa and MasterCard have taken steps to reduce the financial burden on merchants, in an effort to encourage more merchants to use SET. However, with higher transaction fees and little pressure from customers to use SET, many businesses are still reluctant to switch.[12]

SET Secure Electronic Transaction LLC is an organization formed by Visa and MasterCard to manage and promote the SET protocol. For more information about SET, visit **www.setco.org**, **www.visa.com** and **www.mastercard.com**. Visa provides a demonstration of an online shopping transaction using SET at **www.visa.com/nt/ecomm/security/main.html**. GlobeSet, a digital-wallet software vendor, also offers a tutorial of a SET transaction that uses a digital wallet; it may be found at **www.globeset.com**.

Microsoft Authenticode

How do you know that the software you ordered online is safe and has not been altered? How can you be sure that you are not downloading a virus that could wipe out your computer? Do you trust the source of the software? With the emergence of e-commerce, many software companies are offering their products online, so that customers can download software directly onto their computers. Security technology is used to ensure that the downloaded software is trustworthy and has not been altered. *Microsoft Authenticode*, combined with VeriSign digital certificates (or *digital IDs*), authenticates the publisher of software and detects whether the software has been altered. Authenticode is a security feature built into Microsoft Internet Explorer.

To use Microsoft Authenticode technology, each software publisher must obtain a digital certificate specifically designed for the purpose of publishing software; such certificates may be obtained through certification authorities, such as VeriSign (Section 19.17). To obtain a certificate, a software publisher must provide its public key and identification information and sign an agreement that it will not distribute harmful software. This requirement gives customers legal recourse if any downloaded software from certified publishers causes harm.

Microsoft Authenticode uses digital-signature technology to sign software (Section 19.14). The signed software and the publisher's digital certificate provide proof that the software is safe and has not been altered.

When a customer attempts to download a file, a dialog box appears on the screen displaying the digital certificate and the name of the certificate authority. Links to the publisher and the certificate authority are provided so that customers can learn more about each party before they agree to download the software. If Microsoft Authenticode determines that the software has been compromised, the transaction is terminated.

To learn more about Microsoft Authenticode, visit the following sites:

```
msdn.microsoft.com/workshop/security/authcode/signfaq.asp
msdn.microsoft.com/workshop/security/authcode/authwp.asp
```

19.20 Network Security

The goal of network security is to allow authorized users access to information and services, while preventing unauthorized users from gaining access to, and possibly corrupting, the network. There is a trade-off between network security and network performance: Increased security often decreases the efficiency of the network.

19.20.1 Firewalls

A basic tool in network security is the *firewall*. The purpose of a firewall is to protect a *local area network* (*LAN*) from intruders outside the network. For example, most companies have internal networks that allow employees to share files and access company information. Each LAN can be connected to the Internet through a gateway, which usually includes a firewall. For years, one of the biggest threats to security came from employees inside the firewall. Now that businesses rely heavily on access to the Internet, an increasing number of security threats are originating outside the firewall—from the hundreds of millions of people connected to the company network by the Internet.[17] A firewall acts as a safety barrier for data flowing into and out of the LAN. Firewalls can prohibit all data flow not expressly allowed, or they can allow all data flow that is not expressly prohibited. The choice between these two models is up to the network security administrator and should be based on the need for security versus the need for functionality.

There are two main types of firewalls: *packet-filtering firewalls* and *application-level gateways*. A packet-filtering firewall examines all data sent from outside the LAN and automatically rejects any data packets that have local network addresses. For example, if a hacker from outside the network obtains the address of a computer inside the network and tries to sneak a harmful data packet through the firewall, the packet-filtering firewall will reject the data packet, since it has an internal address, but originated from outside the network. A problem with packet-filtering firewalls is that they consider only the source of data packets; they do not examine the actual data. As a result, malicious viruses can be installed on an authorized user's computer, giving the hacker access to the network without the authorized user's knowledge. The goal of an application-level gateway is to screen the actual data. If the message is deemed safe, then the message is sent through to the intended receiver.

Using a firewall is probably the single most effective and easiest way to add security to a small network.[18] Often, small companies or home users who are connected to the Internet through permanent connections, such as DSL lines, do not employ strong security measures. As a result, their computers are prime targets for hackers to use in denial-of-service attacks or to steal information. It is important for all computers connected to the Internet to have some degree of security on their systems. There are numerous firewall software products available. Several products are listed in the Web resources provided in Section 19.22.

19.20.2 Kerberos

Firewalls do not protect you from internal security threats to your local area network. Internal attacks are common and can be extremely damaging. For example, disgruntled employees with network access can wreak havoc on an organization's network or steal valuable, proprietary information. It is estimated that 70 to 90 percent of attacks on corporate networks are internal.[19] *Kerberos* is a freely available, open-source protocol developed at MIT. It employs symmetric secret-key cryptography to authenticate users in a network and to maintain the integrity and privacy of network communications.

Authentication in a Kerberos system is handled by a main Kerberos system and a secondary *ticket-granting service (TGS)*. This system is similar to key distribution centers, which were described in Section 19.12. The main Kerberos system authenticates a client's identity to the TGS; the TGS authenticates the client's rights to access specific network services.

Each client in the network shares a symmetric secret key with the Kerberos system. This symmetric secret key may be used by multiple TGSs in the Kerberos system. The client starts by entering a login name and password into the Kerberos authentication server. The authentication server maintains a database of all clients in the network. The authentication server returns a *ticket-granting ticket (TGT)* encrypted with the symmetric secret key that the client shares with the authentication server. Since the symmetric secret key is known only by the authentication server and the client, only the client can decrypt the TGT, thus authenticating the client's identity. Next, the client sends the decrypted TGT to the TGS to request a *service ticket.* The service ticket authorizes the client's access to specific network services. Service tickets have a set expiration time. Tickets may be renewed by the TGS.

19.20.3 Biometrics

An innovation in security is likely to be *biometrics.* Biometrics uses unique personal information, such as fingerprints, eyeball iris scans or face scans, to identify a user. This system eliminates the need for passwords, which are much easier to steal. Have you ever written down your passwords on a piece of paper and put the paper in your desk drawer or wallet? These days, people have passwords and PIN codes for everything—Web sites, networks, e-mail, ATM machines and even cars. Managing all of those codes can become a burden. Recently, the cost of biometric devices has dropped significantly. Keyboard-mounted fingerprint-scanning devices are being used in place of passwords to log into systems, check e-mail or access secure information over a network. Each user's iris scan, face scan or fingerprint is stored in a secure database. Each time a user logs in, his or her scan is compared with the database. If a match is made, the login is successful. Two companies that specialize in biometric devices are IriScan (**www.iriscan.com**) and Keytronic (**www.keytronic.com**). For additional resources, see Section 19.22.

Currently, passwords are the predominant means of authentication; however, we are beginning to see a shift to smart cards and Biometrics. Microsoft recently announced that it will include the *Biometric Application Programming Interface (BAPI)* in future versions of Windows, which will make it possible for companies to integrate biometrics into their systems.[20] *Two-factor authentication* uses two means to authenticate the user, such as biometrics or a smart card used in combination with a password. Though this system could potentially be compromised, using two methods of authentication is more secure than just using passwords alone.

One of the major concerns with biometrics is the issue of privacy. Implementation of fingerprint scanners means that organizations will be keeping databases with each employee's fingerprint. Do people want to provide their employers with such personal information? What if those data are compromised? To date, most organizations that have implemented biometric systems have received little, if any, resistance from employees.

19.21 Steganography

Steganography is the practice of hiding information within other information. The term literally means "covered writing." Like cryptography, steganography has been used since ancient times. Steganography allows you to take a piece of information, such as a message or image, and hide it within another image, message or even an audio clip. Steganography takes advantage of insignificant space in digital files, in images or on removable disks.[21] Consider a simple example: If you have a message that you want to send secretly, you can hide the information within another message, so that no one but the intended receiver can read it. For example, if you want to tell your stockbroker to buy a stock and your message must be transmitted over an unsecure channel, you could send the message "BURIED UNDER YARD." If you have agreed in advance that your message is hidden in the first letters of each word, the stock broker picks these letters off and sees "BUY."

An increasingly popular application of steganography is *digital watermarks* for protection of intellectual property. An example of a conventional watermark is shown in

Fig. 19.19. A digital watermark can be either visible or invisible. It is usually a company logo, copyright notification or other mark or message that indicates the owner of the document. The owner of a document could show the hidden watermark in a court of law, for example, to prove that the watermarked item was stolen.

Digital watermarking could have a substantial impact on e-commerce. Consider the music industry. Music publishers are concerned that MP3 technology is allowing people to distribute illegal copies of songs and albums. As a result, many publishers are hesitant to put content online, as digital content is easy to copy. Also, since CD-ROMs are digital, people are able to upload their music and share it over the Web. Using digital watermarks, music publishers can make indistinguishable changes to a part of a song at a frequency that is not audible to humans, to show that the song was, in fact, copied.

Blue Spike's Giovanni™ digital watermarking software uses cryptographic keys to generate and embed steganographic digital watermarks into digital music and images (Fig. 19.20). The watermarks can be used as proof of ownership to help digital publishers protect their copyrighted material. The watermarks are undetectable by anyone who is not privy to the embedding scheme, and thus the watermarks cannot be identified and removed. The watermarks are placed randomly.

Giovanni incorporates cryptography and steganography. It generates a symmetric secret key based on an encryption algorithm and the contents of the audio or image file that will carry the watermark. The key is then used to place (and eventually decode) the watermark. The software identifies the perceptually insignificant areas of the image or audio file, enabling a digital watermark to be embedded inaudibly, invisibly and in such a way that if the watermark is removed, the content is likely to be damaged.

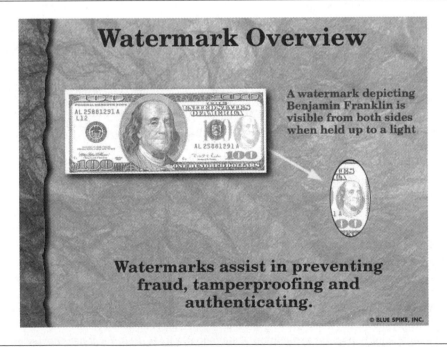

Fig. 19.19 Example of a conventional watermark. (Courtesy of Blue Spike, Inc.)

Fig. 19.20 An example of steganography: Blue Spike's Giovanni digital watermarking process. (Courtesy of Blue Spike, Inc.)

Digital watermarking capabilities are built into some image-editing software applications, such as Adobe PhotoShop 5.5 (**www.adobe.com**). Companies that offer digital watermarking solutions include Digimarc (**www.digimark.com**) and Cognicity (**www.cognicity.com**).

19.22 Internet and World Wide Web Resources

Security Resource Sites

www.securitysearch.net
This is a comprehensive resource for computer security. The site has thousands of links to products, security companies, tools and more. The site also offers a free weekly newsletter with information about vulnerabilities.

www.esecurityonline.com
This site is a great resource for information on online security. The site has links to news, tools, events, training and other valuable information and resources on security.

www.epic.org
The *Electronic Privacy Information Center* deals with protection of privacy and civil liberties. Visit this site to learn more about the organization and its latest initiatives.

theory.lcs.mit.edu/~rivest/crypto-security.html
The *Ronald L. Rivest: Cryptography and Security* site has an extensive list of links to resources on security, including newsgroups, government agencies, FAQs, tutorials and more.

www.w3.org/Security/Overview.html
The *W3C Security Resources* site has FAQs, information about W3C security and e-commerce initiatives and links to other security-related Web sites.

web.mit.edu/network/ietf/sa
The Internet Engineering Task Force (IETF), which is an organization concerned with the architecture of the Internet, has working groups dedicated to Internet security. Visit the *IETF Security Area* to learn about the working groups, join the mailing list or check out the latest drafts of the IETF's work.

dir.yahoo.com/Computers_and_Internet/Security_and_Encryption
The *Yahoo Security and Encryption* page is a great resource for links to Web sites on security and encryption.

www.counterpane.com/hotlist.html
The Counterpane Internet Security, Inc., site includes links to downloads, source code, FAQs, tutorials, alert groups, news and more.

www.rsasecurity.com/rsalabs/faq
This site contains an excellent set of FAQs about cryptography from RSA Laboratories, one of the leading makers of public key cryptosystems.

www.nsi.org/compsec.html
Visit the National Security Institute's *Security Resource Net* for the latest security alerts, government standards and legislation, as well as links to FAQs on security and other helpful resources.

www.itaa.org/infosec
The Information Technology Association of America (ITAA) *InfoSec* site has information about the latest U.S. government legislation related to information security.

staff.washington.edu/dittrich/misc/ddos
The *Distributed Denial of Service Attacks* site has links to news articles, tools, advisory organizations and even a section on security humor.

www.infoworld.com/cgi-bin/displayNew.pl?/security/links/ security_corner.htm
The Security Watch site on **Infoword.com** has loads of links to resources on security.

www.antionline.com
AntiOnline has security-related news and information, a tutorial entitled "Fight-back! Against Hackers," information about hackers and an archive of hacked sites.

www.microsoft.com/security/default.asp
The Microsoft security site has links to downloads, security bulletins and tutorials.

www.grc.com
This site offers a service to test the security of your computer's Internet connection.

Magazines, Newsletters and News Sites

www.networkcomputing.com/consensus
The *Security Alert Consensus* is a free weekly newsletter with information about security threats, holes, solutions and more.

www.infosecuritymag.com
Information Security Magazine has the latest Web security news and vendor information.

www.issl.org/cipher.html
Cipher is an electronic newsletter on security and privacy from the Institute of Electrical and Electronics Engineers (IEEE). You can view current and past issues online.

securityportal.com
The *Security Portal* has news and information about security, cryptography and the latest viruses.

www.scmagazine.com
SC Magazine has news, product reviews and a conference schedule for security events.

www.cnn.com/TECH/specials/hackers
Insurgency on the Internet, from CNN Interactive, has news on hacking and a gallery of hacked sites.

rootshell.com/beta/news.html
Visit Rootshell for security-related news and white papers.

Government Sites for Computer Security

www.cit.nih.gov/security.html
This site has links to security organizations, resources on security and tutorials on PKI, SSL and other protocols.

cs-www.ncsl.nist.gov
The *Computer Security Resource Center* is a resource for network administrators and others concerned with security. This site has links to incident-reporting centers, information about security standards, events, publications and other resources.

www.cdt.org/crypto
Visit the Center for Democracy and Technology for U.S. legislation and policy news regarding cryptography.

www.epm.ornl.gov/~dunigan/security.html
This site has links to loads of security-related sites. The links are organized by subject and include resources on digital signatures, PKI, smart cards, viruses, commercial providers, intrusion detection and several other topics.

www.alw.nih.gov/Security
The *Computer Security Information* page is an excellent resource, providing links to news, newsgroups, organizations, software, FAQs and an extensive number of Web links.

www.fedcirc.gov
The Federal Computer Incident Response Capability deals with the security of government and civilian agencies. This site has information about incident statistics, advisories, tools, patches and more.

axion.physics.ubc.ca/pgp.html
This site has a list of freely available cryptosystems, along with a discussion of each system and links to FAQs and tutorials.

www.ifccfbi.gov
The Internet Fraud Complaint Center, founded by the Department of Justice and the FBI, fields reports of Internet fraud.

www.disa.mil/infosec/iaweb/default.html
The Defense Information Systems Agency's *Information Assurance* page includes links to sites on vulnerability warnings, virus information and incident-reporting instructions, as well as other helpful links.

Internet Security Vendors

www.rsasecurity.com
RSA is one of the leaders in electronic security. Visit its site for more information about its current products and tools, which are used by companies worldwide.

www.ca.com/protection
Computer Associates is a vendor of Internet security software. It has various software packages to help companies set up a firewall, scan files for viruses and protect against viruses.

www.checkpoint.com
Check Point™ Software Technologies Ltd. is a leading provider of Internet security products.

www.mycio.com
MyCIO provides Internet security software and services.

www.opsec.com
The Open Platform for Security (OPSEC) has over 200 partners that use it to develop security products and solutions to allow for interoperability and increased security over a network.

www.baltimore.com
Baltimore is an e-commerce security solutions provider. Its most popular product is UniCERT, a digital-certificate product that is used in PKI. It also offers SET, public-key cryptography and digital-certificate solutions.

www.ncipher.com
nCipher is a vendor of hardware and software security products. Its products include an SSL accelerator that speeds up transaction of SSL Web servers and a secure key-management system.

www.entrust.com
Entrust Technologies provides e-security products and services.

www.tenfour.co.uk
TenFour provides software for secure e-mail.

www.antivirus.com
ScanMail® is an e-mail virus detection program for Microsoft Exchange.

www.contenttechnologies.com/ads
Content Technologies is a security software provider. Its products include firewall and secure e-mail programs.

www.zixmail.com
Zixmail™ is a secure e-mail product that allows you to encrypt and digitally sign your messages using different e-mail programs.

www.pgp.com/scan
PGP Security software protects your site from denial-of-service attacks.

web.mit.edu/network/pgp.html
At this site, you can download *Pretty Good Privacy®* freeware, which allows you to send messages, files, etc., securely.

www.radguard.com
Radguard provides large-scale security solutions for e-businesses.

www.certicom.com
Certicom provides security solutions for the wireless Internet.

www.raytheon.com
Raytheon Corporation's *SilentRunner* monitors activity on a network to find internal threats, such as data theft or fraud.

SSL and SET

developer.netscape.com/tech/security/ssl/protocol.html
This Netscape page has a brief description of SSL, plus links to an SSL tutorial and FAQs.

www.netscape.com/security/index.html
The Netscape Security Center is an extensive resource for Internet and Web security. You will find news, tutorials, products and services on this site.

`psych.psy.uq.oz.au/~ftp/Crypto`
This FAQs page has an extensive list of questions and answers about SSL technology.

`www.setco.org`
The Secure Electronic Transaction LLC was formed through Visa and MasterCard to work on the SET specification. Visit this Web site to learn more about SET and the companies using SET in their products, and check out the brief FAQs list and glossary.

`www.visa.com/nt/ecomm/security/main.html`
Visa International's security page includes information on SSL and SET. The page contains a demonstration of an online shopping transaction, which explains how SET works.

`www.mastercard.com/shoponline/set`
The *MasterCard SET* Web site includes information about the SET protocol, a glossary of SET-related terms, the latest developments regarding SET and a demonstration walking you through the steps of a purchase using SET technology.

`www.openssl.org`
The *Open SSL Project* provides a free, open-source toolkit for SSL.

Public-key Cryptography

`www.entrust.com`
Entrust produces effective security software products using PKI.

`www.cse.dnd.ca`
The Communication Security Establishment has a short tutorial on PKI that defines PKI, public-key cryptography and digital signatures.

`www.magnet.state.ma.us/itd/legal/pki.htm`
The Commonwealth of Massachusetts Information Technology page has loads of links to sites related to PKI that contain information about standards, vendors, trade groups and government organizations.

`www.ftech.net/~monark/crypto/index.htm`
The Beginner's Guide to Cryptography is an online tutorial and includes links to other sites on privacy and cryptography.

`www.faqs.org/faqs/cryptography-faq`
The *Cryptography FAQ's* page has an extensive list of questions and answers.

`www.pkiforum.org`
The PKI Forum promotes the use of PKI.

`www.counterpane.com/pki-risks.html`
Visit the Counterpane Internet Security, Inc.'s site to read the article "Ten Risks of PKI: What You're Not Being Told About Public Key Infrastructure."

Digital Signatures

`www.ietf.org/html.charters/xmldsig-charter.html`
The *XML Digital Signatures* site was created by a group working to develop digital signatures using XML. You can view the group's goals and drafts of its work.

`www.elock.com`
E-Lock Technologies is a vendor of digital-signature products used in PKI. This site has an FAQs list covering cryptography, keys, certificates and signatures.

`www.digsigtrust.com`
The Digital Signature Trust Co. is a vendor of digital-signature and PKI products. The site has a tutorial entitled "Digital Signatures and Public Key Infrastructure (PKI) 101."

Digital Certificates

www.verisign.com
VeriSign creates digital IDs for individuals, small businesses and large corporations. Check out its Web site for product information, news and downloads.

www.thawte.com
Thawte Digital Certificate Services offers SSL, developer and personal certificates.

www.silanis.com/index.htm
Silanis Technology is a vendor of digital-certificate software.

www.belsign.be
Belsign issues digital certificates in Europe. It is the European authority for digital certificates.

www.certco.com
Certco issues digital certificates to financial institutions.

www.openca.org
Set up your own CA using open-source software from The OpenCA Project.

Digital Wallets

www.globeset.com
GlobeSet is a vendor of digital-wallet software. Its site has an animated tutorial demonstrating the use of an electronic wallet in an SET transaction.

www.trintech.com
Trintech digital wallets handle SSL and SET transactions.

wallet.yahoo.com
The *Yahoo! Wallet* is a digital wallet that can be used at thousands of Yahoo! stores worldwide.

Firewalls

www.interhack.net/pubs/fwfaq
This site provides an extensive list of FAQs on firewalls.

www.spirit.com/cgi-bin/report.pl
Visit this site to compare firewall software from a variety of vendors.

www.zeuros.co.uk/generic/resource/firewall
Zeuros is a complete resource for information about firewalls. You will find FAQs, books, articles, training and magazines on this site.

www.thegild.com/firewall
The *Firewall Product Overview* site has an extensive list of firewall products, with links to each vendor's site.

csrc.ncsl.nist.gov/nistpubs/800-10
Check out this firewall tutorial from the U.S. Department of Commerce.

www.watchguard.com
WatchGuard® Technologies, Inc., provides firewalls and other security solutions for medium-sized to large organizations.

www.networkice.com
BlackICE Defender, from Network ICE, combines a firewall with intrusion detection.

Kerberos

www.nrl.navy.mil/CCS/people/kenh/kerberos-faq.html
This site provides an extensive list of FAQs on Kerberos from the Naval Research Laboratory.

web.mit.edu/kerberos/www
The site for *Kerberos: The Network Authentication Protocol* contains a list of FAQs provided by MIT.

www.contrib.andrew.cmu.edu/~shadow/kerberos.html
The Kerberos Reference Page has links to several informational sites, technical sites and other helpful resources.

www.pdc.kth.se/kth-krb
Visit this site to download various Kerberos white papers and documentation.

Biometrics

www.iosoftware.com/products/integration/fiu500/index.htm
This site describes a security device that scans a user's fingerprint to verify identity.

www.identix.com/flash_index.html
Identix specializes in fingerprinting systems for law enforcement, access control and network security. Using its fingerprint scanners, you can log on to your system, encrypt and decrypt files and lock applications.

www.iriscan.com
Iriscan's *PR Iris*™ can be used for e-commerce, network and information security. The scanner takes an image of the user's eye for authentication.

www.keytronic.com
Key Tronic manufactures keyboards with fingerprint-recognition systems.

Steganography and Digital Watermarking

www.bluespike.com/giovanni/giovmain.html
Blue Spike's *Giovanni* watermarks help publishers of digital content protect their copyrighted material and track their content that is distributed electronically.

www.outguess.org
Outguess is a freely available steganographic tool.

www.cl.cam.ac.uk/~fapp2/steganography/index.html
The Information Hiding Homepage has technical information, news and links related to digital watermarking and steganography.

www.demcom.com
DemCom's *Steganos Security Suite* software allows you to encrypt and hide files within audio, video, text or HTML files.

www.digimarc.com
Digimarc is a leading provider of digital-watermarking software solutions.

www.cognicity.com
Cognicity specializes in digital-watermarking solutions for the music and entertainment industries.

Newsgroups

news:comp.security.firewalls

news:comp.security.unix

news:comp.security.misc

news:comp.protocols.kerberos

SUMMARY

- There are four fundamental requirements of a successful, secure transaction: privacy, integrity, authentication and nonrepudiation.

- The privacy issue is as follows: How do you ensure that the information you transmit over the Internet has not be captured or passed on to a third party without your knowledge?

- The integrity issue is as follows: How do you ensure the information you send or receive has not been compromised or altered?

- The authentication issue is as follows: How do the sender and receiver of a message prove their identities to each other?

- The nonrepudiation issue is as follows: How do you legally prove that a message was sent or received?

- The issue of availability is as follows: How can we allow authorized users in a network to access information and services, while keeping unauthorized users out?

- The channels through which data passes over the Internet are not secure; therefore, any private information that is being passed through these channels must be protected.

- Network security addresses the issue of availability: How do we ensure that the network and the computer systems to which it connects will stay in operation continuously?

- Some of the worst security mistakes occur as a result of user input; program that does not handle invalid input correctly can have serious security holes.

- Users who maliciously target systems and try to break them are known as *crackers*. Crackers are usually skilled programmers.

- The word *hacker* refers to someone who is a skilled programmer.

- A major security issue is allowing user input to interface directly with the shell or operating system. Always validate user input before allowing that input to interact with the shell or operating system.

- Always assuming that someone will try to break into your program and thus programming in such a way to make it impossible such a person them to do so is known as defensive programming.

- Many security problems are caused by user-input strings containing shell metacharacters, like the pipe symbol (|). These characters have special meanings for the shell.

- Perl provides a mechanism that forces you to think about security and does not let you use data external to your program in calls to the shell. This feature is called *taint mode*, which is enabled by running Perl with the **-T** flag.

- When taint mode is on, all data that is not originally defined in the program are marked as tainted. If tainted data is used with a function that interacts with the shell, a runtime error occurs and the program terminates.

- Tainted data can be "cleaned" with regular expressions.

- Another security issue occurs when the user inputs HTML tags that can be interpreted as part of the page, causing the page to render improperly. More serious effects can occur when the user input includes scripting code, such as a JavaScript program, that can be executed by the Web browser.

- A denial-of-service attack occurs when a network's resources are taken up by an unauthorized individual, leaving the network unavailable for legitimate users; typically, the attack is performed by flooding servers with data packets.

- When the packet flooding does not come from a single source, but from many separate computers, it is known as a distributed denial-of-service attack.

- Another type of denial-of-service attack targets the routing tables of a network. Routing tables essentially form the road map of a network, providing directions for data to get from one computer to another. This type of attack is accomplished by modifying the routing tables, possibly sending all data to one address in the network.

- A remote user could also force your program to accept a large upload. This situation can occur even if your program is not explicitly programmed to accept uploads. The CGI module will accept the upload regardless of whether it was programmed to do so and store it in a temporary directory, perhaps filling available hard-drive space.

- The **$CGI::POST_MAX** variable can be used to limit the size of a **post** from a form. If the **post** is larger than the specified size in bytes, the program will quit and output an error message.

- To disable uploads entirely, set **$CGI::DISABLE_UPLOADS** to **1**. This step prevents your programs from accepting any file uploads. Other posting functions will still operate normally.

- If you want to have the error message print back to the user so that he or she knows what he or she did wrong, you can use the **CGI::Carp** module as follows:

```
use CGI::Carp 'fatalsToBrowser';
```

- Viruses are computer programs—usually sent as an attachment or hidden in audio clips, video clips and games—that attach to or overwrite other programs to replicate themselves.

- A worm is similar to a virus, except that it can spread and infect files on its own over a network; worms do not need to be attached to another program to spread.

- A transient virus attaches itself to a specific computer program. The virus is activated when the program is run and deactivated when the program is terminated.

- A resident virus, once loaded into the memory of a computer, operates for the duration of the computer's use.

- A type of virus called the *logic bomb* triggers when a given condition is met, such as a time bomb that is triggered when the clock on the computer matches a certain time or date.

- A Trojan horse virus is a malicious program that hides within a friendly program or simulates the identity of a legitimate program or feature, while actually causing damage to the computer or network in the background.

- Web defacing is another popular form of attack by hackers, wherein the hackers illegally enter an organization's Web site and change the contents.

- Implementing a security policy is key to protecting your organization's data and network. When developing a security plan, organizations must assess their vulnerabilities and the possible threats to security.

- Another potential security issue occurs with values placed in **hidden** HTML **input** elements. Such values are not actually hidden. Even though they are not visible on a Web page when the page is rendered in the browser, it is a relatively simple matter for the user to view the HTML source code to see what a hidden element contains, and it is almost as simple to modify the values.

- One way around this problem is to use another field, called a *digest*, which contains the data that you wish to verify in an encrypted form.

- To secure information, data can be encrypted.

- Cryptography transforms data by using a key—a string of digits that acts as a password—to make the data incomprehensible to all but the sender and the intended receivers.

- Unencrypted data are called *plaintext*; encrypted data are called *ciphertext*.

- A cipher, or cryptosystem, is a technique or algorithm for encrypting messages.

- The problem with many historical ciphers is that their security relied on the sender and receiver to remember the encryption algorithm and keep it secret. Such algorithms are called *restricted algorithms*. Restricted algorithms are not feasible to implement among a large group of people.

- Modern cryptosystems are digital. Their algorithms are based on the individual bits of a message, rather than on letters of the alphabet.

- Longer keys have stronger encryption; it takes more time and computing power to break the encryption code.

- A digest is an encrypted version of data that cannot be decrypted back to the original data.

- Unfortunately, digests can verify only data that is known in advance. Other methods must be used to transmit data so that if it is intercepted it cannot be read. Such encryption typically is accomplished by using communications protocols that encrypt the data being sent.

- Secret-key cryptography uses the same symmetric secret key to encrypt and decrypt a message.

- In a network with a key distribution center (KDC), each user shares one symmetric secret key with the key distribution center.

- Session keys are symmetric secret keys that are used for the duration of a transaction.

- One of the most commonly used symmetric encryption algorithms is the Data Encryption Standard (DES), which was developed by the National Security Agency (NSA) and IBM in the 1950s.

- The current standard of symmetric encryption is Triple DES, a variant of DES that is essentially three DES systems in a row, each having its own secret key.

- The U.S. government is in the process of selecting a new, more secure standard for symmetric encryption. The new standard will become the Advanced Encryption Standard (AES).

- In 1976, Whitfield Diffie and Martin Hellman, two researchers at Stanford University, developed public-key cryptography to solve the problem of exchanging keys securely.

- Public-key cryptography is asymmetric. It uses two inversely related keys: a public key and a private key. The private key is kept secret by its owner. The public key is freely distributed.

- If the public key is used to encrypt a message, only the corresponding private key can decrypt it, and vice versa.

- If the user's decryption key is the public key and his or her encryption key is private, the sender of the message can be authenticated.

- The most commonly used public-key algorithm is RSA, an encryption system developed by Ron Rivest, Adi Shamir and Leonard Adleman in 1977.

- Pretty Good Privacy (PGP) is a public-key encryption system used to encrypt e-mail messages and files. It is freely available for noncommercial use. PGP is based on a "web of trust"; each client in a network can vouch for another client's identity to prove ownership of a public key.

- The process by which two parties can exchange keys over an unsecure medium is called a *key agreement protocol*.

- The most common key agreement protocol is a digital envelope.

- Maintaining the secrecy of private keys is crucial to keeping cryptographic systems secure. Most compromises in security result from poor key management, rather than from attacks that attempt to decipher the keys.

- Keys are made secure by choosing a key length so large that it is computationally infeasible to try all combinations of potential keys.

- Digital signatures, the electronic equivalent of written signatures, were developed to be used in public-key cryptography to solve the problems of authentication and integrity.

- To create a digital signature, a sender first takes the original plaintext message and runs it through a hash function, which is a mathematical calculation that gives the message a hash value. The hash value is also known as a *message digest*.

- Collision occurs when multiple messages have the same hash value. It is computationally infeasible to compute a message from its hash value or to find two messages with the same hash value.

- A digital signature authenticates the sender's identity, and, like a written signature, it is difficult to forge.

- If the hash value of the original message matches the message digest included in the signature, then there is message integrity: The message has not been altered in transmission.

- There is a fundamental difference between digital signatures and handwritten signatures. A handwritten signature is independent of the document being signed. Thus, if someone can forge a handwritten signature, they can use that signature to forge multiple documents. A digital signature is created using the contents of the document. Therefore, your digital signature is different for each document you sign.

- A timestamping agency affixes the time and date of receipt to the encrypted, signed message and digitally signs the whole package with the timestamping agency's private key.

- The digital authentication standard of the U.S. government is called the Digital Signature Algorithm (DSA).

- Public-key infrastructure (PKI) adds digital certificates to the process of authentication.

- A certification authority (CA) is a financial institution or other trusted third party, such as VeriSign.

- Digital certificates are publicly available and are held by the certification authority in certificate repositories.

- Digital certificates are created with an expiration date to force users to switch key pairs. If your private key is compromised before its expiration date, you can cancel your digital certificate and get a new key pair and digital certificate. Canceled and revoked certificates are placed on a certificate revocation list (CRL). CRLs are stored with the certification authority that issued the certificates.

- By some estimates, the key algorithms used in public-key cryptography are so secure that even millions of computers working in parallel could not possibly break the code in a century.

- Trying to decrypt ciphertext without knowledge of the decryption key is known as *cryptanalysis*.

- The Secure Sockets Layer (SSL) protocol is a nonproprietary protocol commonly used to secure communication on the Internet and the Web.

- TCP/IP is the standard set of protocols used for communication between computers on the Internet.

- Most Internet transmissions are sent as sets of individual message pieces, called packets.

- SSL uses public-key technology and digital certificates to authenticate the server in a transaction and to protect private information as it passes from one party to another over the Internet.

- Although SSL protects information as it is passed over the Internet, it does not protect private information, such as credit-card numbers, once the information is stored on a merchant's server.

- Hardware devices called *peripheral component interconnect* (*PCI*) *cards* designed for SSL transactions can be installed on Web servers to secure data for an entire SSL transaction from the client to the Web server.

- SET uses digital certificates to authenticate each party in an e-commerce transaction, including the customer, the merchant and the merchant's bank.

- A digital wallet is similar to a real wallet; it stores credit (or debit) card information for multiple cards, as well as a digital certificate verifying the cardholder's identity.

- In the SET protocol, the merchant never actually sees the client's proprietary information. Therefore, the client's credit-card number is not stored on the merchant's server, considerably reducing the risk of fraud.

- Microsoft Authenticode uses digital-signature technology to sign software. The signed software and the publisher's digital certificate provide proof that the software is safe and has not been altered.

- A firewall protects a local area network (LAN) from intruders outside the network.

- A packet-filtering firewall examines all data sent from outside the LAN and automatically rejects any data packets that have local network addresses.

- The goal of an application-level gateway is to screen the actual data. If the message is deemed safe, then the message is sent through to the intended receiver.

- Kerberos is a freely available, open-source protocol developed at MIT. It employs symmetric secret-key cryptography to authenticate users in a network and to maintain the integrity and privacy of network communications.

- Biometrics uses unique personal information, such as fingerprints, eyeball iris scans or face scans, to identify a user. This system eliminates the need for passwords, which are much easier to steal.

- Microsoft recently announced that it will include the Biometric Application Programming Interface (BAPI) in future versions of Windows, which will make it possible for companies to integrate biometrics into their systems.

- Two-factor authentication uses two means to authenticate the user, such as biometrics or a smart card used in combination with a password.

- Steganography is the practice of hiding information. The term literally means "covered writing."

- An increasingly popular application of steganography is digital watermarks for protection of intellectual property. A digital watermark can be either visible or invisible.

TERMINOLOGY

%ENV hash	collision
| (pipe symbol)	computer security
128-bit encryption system	crackers
ActiveShield	cryptanalysis
Advanced Encryption Standard (AES)	cryptanalyst
ANSI (American National Standards Institute)	cryptanalytic attack
antivirus software	cryptographic ciphers
application-level gateway	cryptographic standard
asymmetric algorithm	cryptography
asymmetric key	cryptologists
authentication	cryptosystem
Authenticode (from Microsoft)	Data Encryption Standard (DES)
availability	data packet
binary string	decipher
biometric	decryption
Biometric API (BAPI)	decryption key
bit	defensive programing
CERT (Computer Emergency Response Team)	denial-of-service attack
CERT Security Improvement Modules	Diffie–Hellman key agreement protocol
certificate authority hierarchy	**Digest::MD5** module
certificate repository	digital-authentication standard
certificate revocation list (CRL)	digital certificate
certification authority (CA)	digital envelope
cgi-bin	digital IDs
cipher	digital signature
ciphertext	Digital Signature Algorithm (DSA)

taint mode   Timofonica
tainted   transient virus
TCP/IP (Transmission Control Protocol/   transmitting messages securely
   Internet Protocol)   transposition cipher
td function in **CGI.pm**   Triple DES
ticket granting service (TGS)   Trojan horse virus
ticket granting ticket (TGT)   VeriSign
time bombs   virus
timestamp   Web defacing
timestamping   Web programming
timestamping agency   worm

SELF REVIEW EXERCISES

19.1   Fill in the blanks in each of the following statements:
   a) Malicious users who attempt to compromise systems are known as _____.
   b) Programming with the assumption that someone will try to break into your program is known as _____ _____.
   c) Characters that have special meanings for the shell are known as _____.
   d) The mechanism that does not allow you to use data derived from outside your program in a call to the shell without meaning to is known as _____ and is set by running Perl with the _____ flag set.
   e) You can use _____ to clean tainted data.
   f) A _____ occurs when a cracker attempts to use up system resources to deny normal users from being able to make use of a site or network.
   g) The road map of a network is known as the _____.
   h) The _____ variable will limit the size of a **post** that a program will accept, and the _____ variable can be used to prevent a program from accepting uploads.
   i) A _____ is a malicious program spread by sharing infected files, whereas a _____ does not need to be attached to a program to spread.
   j) A _____ is a malicious program that hides within a friendly program or simulates the identity of a legitimate program or feature.
   k) An attack wherein crackers illegally enter an organization's Web site and change its contents is known as _____.
   l) The string that is used to encrypt data and acts as a password is known as a _____.
   m) An encrypted version of data used for verification purposes is known as a _____.
   n) The encryption method that uses a single key known only to the two parties communicating to encrypt and decrypt the data is known as _____.
   o) The cryptography system wherein each user has a public and private key is known as _____.
   p) The most common key agreement protocol is a _____.
   q) Most compromises in security result from poor _____, rather than from attacks that attempt to decipher keys.
   r) The problem of nonrepudiation can be solved using _____, where a date and a time are bound into a digital document.
   s) Trying to decrypt ciphertext without knowledge of the decryption key is known as _____.
   t) SSL stands for _____.
   u) A _____ acts as a safety barrier for data flowing into and out of a LAN by prohibiting all data flow not expressly allowed.
   v) The practice of hiding information inside other information is known as _____.

      w) A _____ is used to authenticate the sender of a document.

      x) The recent network attacks that have hit companies such as eBay and Yahoo are known as _____.

      y) A digital fingerprint of a document can be created using a _____.

      z) The four main issues addressed by cryptography are _____, _____, _____ and _____.

19.2 State whether each of the following is *true* or *false*. If *false*, explain why.

      a) You have to check data coming from the user only if the data involves a call to the shell.

      b) Taint mode will prevent you from passing tainted data to the shell even if you do not know you are doing so.

      c) Setting **$CGI::POST_MAX** and **$CGI::DISABLE_UPLOADS** will prevent all denial-of-service attacks.

      d) Most denial-of-service attacks are a result of programming errors.

      e) Using hidden fields without first checking their contents can lead to security errors.

      f) A digest can be decrypted to reveal the encrypted data.

      g) Public-key cryptography is when both parties in a transaction have the same key for encryption and decryption.

      h) In a transaction with SSL, the packets are secured using secret-key cryptography.

      i) The Secure Electronic Transaction protocol was specifically designed to protect e-commerce payment transactions.

      j) In a public key algorithm, one key is used for both encryption and decryption.

      k) Digital certificates are intended to be used indefinitely.

      l) The Secure Sockets Layer protects data stored on a merchant's server.

      m) Digital signatures can be used to provide undeniable proof of the author of a document.

      n) In a network of 10 users communicating using public-key cryptography, only 10 keys are needed in total.

      o) The security of modern cryptosystems lies in the secrecy of the algorithm.

      p) Users should avoid changing keys as much as possible, unless they have reason to believe the security of the key they are using has been compromised.

      q) Increasing the security of a network often decreases its functionality and efficiency.

      r) Firewalls are the single most effective way to add security to a small computer network.

      s) Kerberos is an authentication protocol that is used over TCP/IP networks.

ANSWERS TO SELF REVIEW EXERCISES

19.1   a) crackers.   b) defensive programming.   c) shell metacharacters.   d) taint mode, **-T**. e) regular expressions.   f) denial-of-service attack.   g) routing tables.   h) **$CGI::POST_MAX**, **$CGI::DISABLE_UPLOADS**. i) virus, worm. j) Trojan horse virus. k) Web defacing. l) key. m) digest. n) symmetric, or secret-key, cryptography. o) public-key cryptography. p) digital envelope. q) key management. r) timestamping. s) cryptanalysis. t) Secure Sockets Layer. u) firewall. v) steganography. w) digital signature. x) distributed denial-of-service attacks. y) hash function. z) privacy, authentication, integrity, nonrepudiation.

19.2   a) False. There are other situations, such as outputting user-input data to an HTML page, that can cause problems.

      b) True.

      c) False. It cannot prevent packet flooding or other types of attacks.

      d) False. Denial-of-service attacks are a result of limited resources, some of which are beyond the control of the programmer.

      e) True.

      f) False. Digests cannot be decrypted.

g) False. This statement refers to secret-key cryptography.

h) False. Packets are secured using public-key cryptography.

i) True.

j) False. The encryption key is different from the decryption key. One is made public, and the other kept private.

k) False. Digital certificates are created with an expiration date to encourage users to periodically change their public key/private key pair.

l) False. Secure Sockets Layer is an Internet security protocol, which secures the transfer of information in electronic communication. It does not protect data stored on a merchant server.

m) False. A user who digitally signed a document could later intentionally give up his or her private key, then claim that the document was written by an imposter. Thus, timestamping a document is necessary so that users cannot repudiate documents written before the pubic key/private key pair is reported as invalidated.

n) False. Each user needs a public key and a private key. Thus, in a network of 10 users, 20 keys are needed in total.

o) False. The security of modern cryptosystems lies in the secrecy of the encryption and decryption keys.

p) False. Changing keys often is a good way to maintain the security of a communication system.

q) True.

r) True.

s) True.

EXERCISES

19.3   Write a regular expression to clean tainted data. The regular expression should only accept data which can be interpreted as a dollar value. The leading dollar sign is optional and they should be allowed to have zero, one or two digits after the optional decimal point. Test your regular expression on data accepted on **STDIN**.

19.4   Write a program that strips data coming in from a file of all HTML tags. The **
, **<b>, **<i>**, and **<p>** tags (as well as their closing tags) should not be stripped.

19.5   Modify the program in Fig. 19.3 to discourage denial-of-service attacks. The size limit on **post**s should be 10 and uploads should be denied altogether. If this is implemented correctly, when someone enters a string of more than 10 characters or tries to upload, they will only be prompted again.

19.6   Write a program which uses hidden fields to verify data. The program should give the user a form in which to write a message. Their message will be printed back to them, and they will have a form to add onto the message. Hidden fields should be used to ensure the message is not compromised. Show the program as well as the HTML code that someone might use to compromise the security of the system.

19.7   The program below has a security problem. Add a regular expression so that the program checks the validity of the name entered. Note that the command **"/urs/games/fortune"** is a Linux/Unix command, and so this program can only be run on a Linux server.

```
1   #!/usr/bin/perl
2   # Ex. 19.7: Ex19_07Before.pl
3   # Telling the user their fortune.
4
5   use warnings;
```

```
6   use strict;
7   use CGI qw( :standard );
8
9   print( header(), start_html( "Fortune" ) );
10  print( h2( "Fortune" ), startform() );
11  print( "What is your name? " );
12  print( textfield( "name" ), br() );
13
14  if ( my $name = param( "name" ) ) {
15
16     print( "Hello, $name, your quote of the day is: " );
17     print( br() );
18     my @quote = `/usr/games/fortune`;
19     my $quote = join( br, @quote );
20
21     print( $quote );
22
23     open( OUT, ">>/home/httpd/htdocs/fortunes/$name.for" ) or
24        die( "Cannot open file for appending" );
25
26     print( OUT hr(), ( join( br(), @quote ) ) );
27     close( OUT ) or die( "Cannot close file: $!" );
28
29     open( FILE, "</home/httpd/htdocs/fortunes/$name.for" ) or
30        die( "Cannot open $name.for" );
31     print( br(), hr() );
32     print( "Here are all the fortunes you have " );
33     print( "received to date:\n" );
34
35     while ( <FILE> ) {
36        print( $_ );
37     }
38
39     close( FILE ) or die( "Cannot close file: $!" );
40
41  }
42
43  print( end_form(), end_html() );
```

19.8 How can online businesses prevent hacker attacks such as Denial of Service or virus attacks?

19.9 Define the following security terms.
  a) digital signature
  b) hash function
  c) symmetric-key encryption
  d) digital certificate
  e) denial-of-service attack
  f) worm
  g) message digest
  h) collision
  i) Triple DES

19.10 Define each of the following security terms and give an example of how it is used.
  a) secret-key cryptography

b) public-key cryptography
c) digital signature
d) digital certificate
e) hash function
f) SSL
g) Kerberos
h) firewall

19.11 Identify and describe each of the following acronyms.
a) PKI
b) RSA
c) CRL
d) AES
e) SET

19.12 List the four problems dealt with by cryptography and give a real world example of each one.

19.13 Compare symmetric key algorithms with public key algorithms. What are the benefits/drawbacks of each type of algorithm? How are these differences manifested in the real world uses of these two types of algorithms?

19.14 The Visa International Web Site includes an interactive demonstration of the Secure Electronic Transaction (SET) protocol that uses animation to explain this complicated protocol in a way that most people will understand. Visit Visa at **www.visa.com/nt/sec/no_shock/ intro_L.html** to view the demo. Write a short summary of SET. How does SET differ from SSL? Why are digital wallets important? How are they used? If you were asked to choose between the two protocols, which would you choose and why?

19.15 Explain how, in a network using symmetric key encryption, a Key Distribution Center can play the role of an authenticator of parties.

19.16 Go to the VeriSign Web site at **www.verisign.com**. Write an analysis of the features and security of VeriSign's digital certificates. Then go to five other certification authorities and compare the features and security of their digital certificates to VeriSign.

19.17 Research the Secure Digital Music Initiative (**www.sdmi.org**). Describe how security technologies such as digital watermarks can help music publishers protect their copyrighted work.

19.18 Distinguish between packet-filtering firewalls and application-level gateways.

WORKS CITED

The notation <**www.domain-name.com**> indicates that the citation is for information found at the Web site.

1. A. Harrison, "Xerox Unit Farms Out Security in $20M Deal," *Computerworld* 5 June 2000: 24.

2. RSA Laboratories, "RSA Laboratories' Frequently Asked Questions About Today's Cryptography, Version 4.1," <**www.rsasecurity.com/rsalabs/faq**>, RSA Security, Inc., 2000.

3. A. Harrison, "Advanced Encryption Standard," *Computerworld* 29 May 2000: 57.

4. RSA Laboratories, "RSA Laboratories' Frequently Asked Questions About Today's Cryptography, Version 4.1," <**www.rsasecurity.com/rsalabs/faq**>, RSA Security, Inc. 2000.

5. S. Abbot, "The Debate for Secure E-Commerce," *Performance Computing* February 1999" 37-42.

6. T. Wilson, "E-Biz Bucks Lost Under the SSL Train," *Internet Week* 24 May 1999: 1,3.

7. M. Bull, "Ensuring End-to-End Security with SSL," *Network World* 15 May 2000: 63.

8. S. Machlis, "IBM Hedges its Bets on SET," *Computerworld* 20 July 1998: 4.

9. J. McKendrick, "Is Anyone SET for Secure Electronic Transactions," *ENT* 4 March 1998: 44, 46.

10. W. Andrews, "The Digital Wallet: A concept revolutionizing e-commerce," *Internet World* 15 October 1999: 34-35.

11. "Securing B2B," *Global Technology Business* July 200: 50-51.

12. S. Machlis, "MasterCard Makes SET More Attractive," *Computerworld* 12 January 1998: 3.

13. R. Marsland, "Hidden Cost of Technology," *Financial Times* 2 June 2000: 5.

14. F. Avolio, "Best Practices in Network Security," *Network Computing* 20 March 2000: 60-72.

15. H. Bray, "Trojan Horse Attacks Computers, Disguised as a Video Chip," *The Boston Globe* 10 June 2000: C1+.

16. A. Fisenberg, "Viruses Could Have Your Number," *The New York Times* 8 June 2000: E7.

17. R. Marshland, "Hidden Cost of Technology," *Financial Times* 2 June 2000: 5.

18. T. Spangler, "Home Is Where the Hack Is," *Inter@ctive Week* 10 April 2000: 28-34.

19. S. Gaudin, "The Enemy Within," *Network World* 8 May 2000: 122-126.

20. D. Deckmyn, "Companies Push New Approaches to Authentication," *Computerworld*, 15 May 2000: 6.

21. S. Katzenbeisser and F. Petitcolas, Ed., *Information Hiding: Techniques for Steganography and Digital Watermarking* (Norwood, MA: Artech House, Inc., 2000) 1-2.

RECOMMENDED READINGS

Berinato, S. "Feds Sign Off on e-Signatures." *eWeek* 29 May 2000: 20-21.

Deitel, H. *An Introduction to Operating System*s. Second Edition, Reading, MA: Addison Wesley, 1990.

DiDio, L. "Private-key Nets Unlock e-Commerce." *Computerworld* 16 March 1998: 49-50.

Ford, W., and M. Baum. *Secure Electronic Commerce: Building the Infrastructure for Digital Signatures and Encryption.* Upper Saddle River, NJ: Prentice Hall, 1997.

Garfinkel, S. and Spafford, G. *Web Security and Commerce.* Cambridge, MA: O'Reilly, 1997.

Ghosh, A. *E-Commerce Security: Weak Links, Best Defenses.* New York, NY: Wiley Computer Publishing, 1998.

Goncalves, M. *Firewalls: A Complete Guide.*New York, NY: McGraw-Hill, 2000.

Kippenhahn, R. *Code Breaking.* New York, NY: The Overlook Press, 1999.

Kosiur, D. *Understanding Electronic Commerce.* Redmond, WA: Microsoft Press, 1997.

Marsland, R. "Hidden Cost of Technology." *Financial Times* 2 June 2 2000: 5.

Pfleeger, C. *Security in Computing: Second Edition.* Upper Saddle River, NJ: Prentice Hall, 1997.

RSA Laboratories. *"RSA Laboratories' Frequently Asked Questions About Today's Cryptography, Version 4.1."* <**www.rsasecurity.com/rsalabs/faq**> RSA Security Inc., 2000.

Sager, I. "Cyber Crime." *Business Week* 21 February 2000: 37-42.

Schneier, B. *Applied Cryptography: Protocols, Algorithms and Source Code in C.* New York, NY: John Wiley & Sons, Inc., 1996.

Sherif, M. *Protocols for Secure Electronic Commerce.* New York, NY: CRC Press, 2000.

Smith, R. *Internet Cryptography.* Reading, MA: Addison Wesley, 1997.

Spangler, T. "Home Is Where The Hack Is." *Inter@ctive Week* 10 April 2000: 28-34.

Wrixon, F. *Codes, Ciphers & Other Cryptic & Clandestine Communication* New York, NY: Black Dog & Leventhal Publishers, 1998.

20

Data Structures

Objectives

- To understand the concepts behind the creation of custom data structures.
- To be familiar with the basic data structures: linked lists, stacks, queues, doubly linked lists, and trees.
- To understand how the built-in hash data type works.

Much that I bound, I could not free;
Much that I freed returned to me.
Lee Wilson Dodd

'Will you walk a little faster?' said a whiting to a snail,
'There's a porpoise close behind us, and he's treading on my tail.'
Lewis Carroll

There is always room at the top.
Daniel Webster

Push on — keep moving.
Thomas Morton

I think that I shall never see
A poem lovely as a tree.
Joyce Kilmer

Outline

20.1 Introduction

Thus far in the text, we have studied Perl's built-in *data structures*, such as arrays and hashes. While Perl's built-in data structures are frequently all you need to manipulate data, sometimes you need to build customized data structures. This chapter introduces other *dynamic data structures* that grow and shrink at execution time.

Linked lists are collections of data items "lined up in a row;" insertions and deletions can be made anywhere in a linked list. *Stacks* are important in compilers and operating systems; insertions and deletions are made at only one end of a stack—its *top*. *Queues* represent waiting lines; insertions are made at the back (also referred to as the *tail*) of a queue, and deletions are made from the front (also referred to as the *head*) of a queue. *Binary trees* facilitate high-speed searching and sorting of data, efficient elimination of duplicate data items, representing file system directories and compiling expressions into machine language. These data structures have many other interesting applications. We also demonstrate how to build your own hash to provide you with a better understanding of how hashes work.

This chapter discusses each of the major types of data structures and implements programs that create and manipulate them. In several examples, we use Perl's object-oriented capabilities to create and package these data structures for reusability and maintainability.

The examples in this chapter are practical programs that you will be able to use in more advanced courses and in industrial applications. The programs are especially heavy on reference manipulation.

20.2 Self-referential Structures

A *self-referential structure* contains a member that refers to a structure of the same type. We have demonstrated examples of self-referential structures in our discussions of arrays of arrays and hashes of hashes. Using self-references with hashes and arrays, we were able to make data structures that were more powerful than ordinary arrays and hashes. Other dynamic data structures use the same programming principles.

Most data structures are composed of *nodes* that consist of data and references to other nodes (called *links*) in the data structure. The links are used to "tie" one node to another node of the same type. The program can follow the links from node to node to *traverse* the data structure and manipulate the data in each node.

Self-referential structures can be linked together to form useful data structures, such as lists, queues, stacks and trees. Figure 20.1 illustrates two self-referential objects linked together to form a list. A backslash—representing a reference with the value **undef**—is placed in the link member of the second self-referential structure to indicate that the link does not refer to another structure. The slash is for illustration purposes; it does not correspond to the backslash character. An **undef** reference normally indicates the end of a data structure.

Common Programming Error 20.1

*Not setting the link in the last node of a list to **undef** is a common logic error.*

Software Engineering Observation 20.1

A pitfall of self-referential structures is the potential for memory leaks. When using self-referential structures, watch out for circular references, and be sure to break them as soon as they are no longer needed.

20.3 Linked Lists

A *linked list* is a linear collection (i.e., a sequence) of self-referential structures, called nodes, connected by reference links—hence, the term "linked list." A linked list is accessed via a reference to the first node of the list. Each subsequent node is accessed via the link-reference member stored in the previous node. By convention, the link reference in the last node of a list is set to **undef** to mark the end of the list. Data are stored in a linked list dynamically: Each node is created as necessary. A node can contain data of any type. Stacks and queues are also linear data structures and, as we will discuss, are constrained versions of linked lists. Trees are nonlinear data structures.

Normally if you need a list of data, an array is a perfect solution. Lists of data can be stored in arrays, but linked lists can provide additional advantages. In many other programming languages, a linked list is appropriate when the number of data elements to be represented in the data structure is unpredictable. Linked lists are dynamic, so the length of a list can increase or decrease as necessary. Many programming languages use fixed-size arrays—the number of elements does not change after the array is created. Of course, Perl automatically manages memory, so arrays grow and shrink as needed. The only real problem with Perl arrays is inserting data in, or removing data from, the middle of an array. Removing elements from the middle of an array causes all the elements to one side to have to be shifted to fill the hole. With a linked list, however, we can insert data in, or remove data from, the middle of the list without moving any other data elements in memory. This can be important if we are inserting and deleting from a large, sorted set of data.

Performance Tip 20.1

Insertion into and deletion from a sorted array can be time consuming; all the elements following the inserted or deleted element must be shifted appropriately.

Fig. 20.1   Two self-referential class objects linked together.

Performance Tip 20.2

Insertion into a linked list is fast; only two references have to be modified (after you have identified the place in which to do the insertion). All existing nodes remain at their current locations in memory.

Linked lists can be maintained in sorted order simply by inserting each new element at the proper point in the list (it does, of course, take time to identify the proper insertion point). Existing elements in the list do not need to be moved.

Performance Tip 20.3

The elements of an array are stored contiguously in memory. This allows immediate access to any array element because the address of any element can be calculated directly based on its offset from the beginning of the array. Linked lists do not afford such immediate access to their elements; an element can be accessed only by traversing the list from the front.

Linked-list nodes are normally not stored contiguously in memory. Rather, they are logically contiguous. Typically, a linked list is accessed through a reference to the first node—known as the *head* or *head, reference.* Each node has a link to the next node, so we follow the links down the list until we reach the end node. The end node's link has the value **undef**. Figure 20.2 illustrates a linked list with several nodes. In the figure, the variable **$linkedList** is the head reference.

Performance Tip 20.4

Using dynamic memory allocation (instead of arrays) for data structures that grow and shrink at execution time can save memory. Keep in mind, however, that references occupy space and that dynamic memory allocation incurs the overhead of function calls.

The program in Fig. 20.3 shows the code for a simple linked list. In this program, we manipulate the list manually as part of the example. In the program in Fig. 20.6, we will implement an object-oriented version of a linked list.

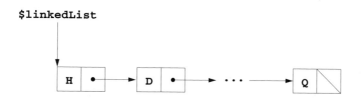

$linkedList

Fig. 20.2   Graphical representation of a linked list.

```
1   #!/usr/bin/perl
2   # Figure 20.3: fig20_03.pl
3   # A simple demonstration of linked lists.
4
```

Fig. 20.3   Implementation of a linked list (part 1 of 3).

```perl
 5  use warnings;
 6  use strict;
 7
 8  my $linkedList = undef;   # defines head reference
 9
10  traverseList( $linkedList );   # output current list contents
11
12  # add an element to $linkedList
13  $linkedList = { data => "haircut", nextLink => $linkedList };
14
15  # add more elements to $linkedList
16  $linkedList = { data => "batteries", nextLink => $linkedList };
17  $linkedList = { data => "groceries", nextLink => $linkedList };
18  $linkedList = { data => "cleaning", nextLink => $linkedList };
19
20  print( "\nAfter adding four elements to the list, ",
21        "the list contains:\n" );
22  traverseList( $linkedList );   # output current list contents
23
24  # swap first two elements
25  my ( $first, $second ) = ( $linkedList, $linkedList->{ nextLink } );
26  $first->{ nextLink } = $second->{ nextLink };
27  $second->{ nextLink } = $first;
28
29  # aim head reference at new first element
30  $linkedList = $second;
31
32  print( "\nAfter swapping the first two elements, ",
33        "the list contains:\n" );
34  traverseList( $linkedList );   # output current list contents
35
36  # delete third element
37  $second = $linkedList->{ nextLink };
38
39  my $third = $linkedList->{ nextLink }->{ nextLink };
40  $second->{ nextLink } = $third->{ nextLink };
41  $third = undef;
42
43  print( "\nAfter deleting the third element, ",
44        "the list contains:\n" );
45  traverseList( $linkedList );   # output current list contents
46
47  # Function to output the contents of the linked list it
48  # receives as an argument.
49  sub traverseList
50  {
51     my $current = shift();
52
53     if ( !defined( $current ) ) {
54        print( "The list is empty.\n" );
55        return;
56     }
57
```

Fig. 20.3   Implementation of a linked list (part 2 of 3).

```
58        while ( defined( $current ) ) {
59           print( "$current->{ data }" );      # print current data
60           $current = $current->{ nextLink };   # move to next node
61
62           if ( defined( $current ) ) {         # if next node exists,
63              print( " --> " );                 # output -->
64           }
65        }
66
67        print( "\n" );
68     }
```

```
The list is empty.

After adding four elements to the list,
the list contains:
cleaning --> groceries --> batteries --> haircut

After swapping the first two elements,
the list contains:
groceries --> cleaning --> batteries --> haircut

After deleting the third element,
the list contains:
groceries --> cleaning --> haircut
```

Fig. 20.3   Implementation of a linked list (part 3 of 3).

In this list implementation, we use anonymous hashes for the nodes. The value associated with the **nextLink** key holds a reference to the next node in the list, and the value associated with the **data** key holds the data associated with the node. Any data representation that enables us to store the data and the link to the next node could have been used here.

Line 8 defines reference **$linkedList**, which will refer to the first element of the list. This reference is initially **undef**, because no list nodes have been created yet. Line 10 calls our function **traverseList** (defined at lines 49–68) to output the current contents of the list. The list is empty, so the function outputs a message stating this fact.

The statements at lines 13–18 each insert an element at the head of the list. To make an insertion, we create a new node as an anonymous hash. For example, in line 13

```
$linkedList = { data => "haircut", nextLink => $linkedList };
```

the new node's **nextLink** member is assigned the current value of the head reference, **$linkedList**; thus, the new node now refers to the previous first node in the list (i.e., nothing, because there were no nodes in the list). The resulting anonymous hash is assigned to **$linkedList**, so the head reference now refers to the new first node. Similarly, line 16

```
$linkedList = { data => "batteries", nextLink => $linkedList };
```

assigns to the new node's **nextLink** member the current value of the **$linkedList**; thus, the new node refers to the node containing the data "**haircut**." Then, the resulting anonymous hash is assigned to the **$linkedList**, so the head reference now refers to the new first node, containing the data "**batteries**." Figure 20.4 illustrates the preceding operation for a list that contains elements. Part a) of the figure shows the list and the new node when the new node is created (i.e., the right side of the assignment on line 16). The dotted arrow in part a) illustrates the creation of the link between the new node and the current first node in the list. The arrow pointing to the new node in part a) represents the temporary reference that will be assigned to **$linkedList** in part b).The dotted arrow in part b) shows the operation in which the new node becomes the new first node of the list. As the insertion statement terminates, the temporary reference that refers to the new node will be destroyed.

Lines 25–30 demonstrate swapping of elements. We begin by creating variables **$first** and **$second** and assigning to them the first two elements in the list (line 25). Next, the first node's **nextLink** is assigned the second node's **nextLink** (line 26). Now, both nodes refer to the same element in the list. Then, the second node's **nextLink** link is assigned the first node (line 27). All that remains is to change the reference that previously referred to the first node (in this case, the head reference) to refer to the new first node, which was previously the second node (line 30).

Lines 37–41 (the result of which is illustrated in Fig. 20.5) remove the third element of the list. Part a) of the illustration shows the linked list and the references **$second** and **$third** after lines 37 and 39 are executed. In part b), the dotted lines indicate the references that are modified to make the second element refer to the fourth element (line 40) and to remove the remaining reference to the third element (line 41). At this point, there are no references to the third element, so it will be garbage collected.

Function **traverseList** (lines 49–68) walks through (or *traverses*) a linked list and outputs its elements. This function starts at the head of the list (which is passed to it) and determines if the **$current** node is undefined (line 53). If the node is not undefined, the **while** structure (line 58) prints the data in that node, proceeds to the next node in the list and repeats the process. Note that if the link in the last node of the list does not contain the value **undef**, the printing algorithm will erroneously attempt to print past the end of the list.

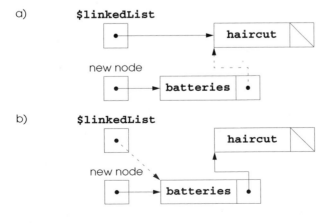

Fig. 20.4   Inserting a new node in a list.

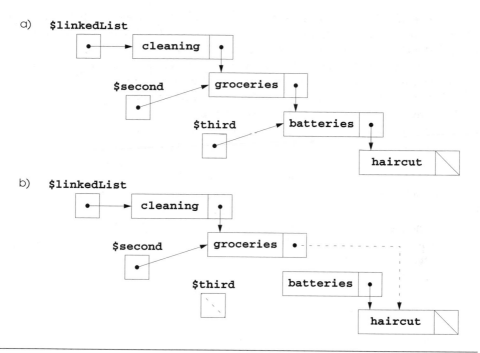

Fig. 20.5   Removing a node from a list.

This example performed all the list manipulations manually. When using these data structures in real-world applications, however, it is preferable to call functions to perform the list manipulations, rather than for the programmer to determine the individual references to manipulate. This is where object-oriented programming is useful. Figure 20.6 shows an implementation of a linked list (**LinkedList.pm**) that uses a hash to store a node and uses object orientation to encapsulate the data. This implementation maintains the data in the list in sorted order. The main program (**fig20_06.pl**) allows you to interact with a list and test its capabilities dynamically.

Note the use of Perl's object-oriented programming capabilities. Lines 7–18 define the package **ListNode** and the constructor for a **ListNode** object. The constructor uses its arguments to initialize the **data** and **nextLink** members of a new node (line 14). Lines 20–127 define the package **LinkedList**, the **LinkedList** constructor and functions **insertNode**, **deleteNode**, **head** and **printList** for manipulating the data in a **LinkedList**.

The **LinkedList** constructor (lines 23–31) creates an empty list (line 27). Function **insertNode** (lines 34–59) determines the location at which a new node should be inserted, and then inserts that node. Lines 38 and 39 create references **$previous** and **$current**. Reference **$previous** will refer to the node that will appear before the node to be inserted. If this reference has the value **undef**, the new node is being inserted as the first node in the list. Reference **$current** will refer to the node in front of which the new node will be placed. The **while** structure in lines 46–49 loops while the data value to insert is greater than the data value in the current node. During each iteration of the loop, **$pre-**

vious is assigned the value of **$current**, and **$current** is assigned the next node in the list. When the loop terminates, lines 53–58 determine if the new node is being inserted as the first node in the list or a later node and perform the insertion.

Function **deleteNode** (lines 62–94) uses techniques similar to those used in **insertNode** to determine the location of the node to delete. Lines 66 and 67 create references **$previous** and **$current**. Reference **$previous** will refer to the node before the node to be deleted. Reference **$current** will refer to the node to be deleted. The **while** structure in lines 73–76 loops while the data value to delete is not equal to the data value in the current node. During each iteration of the loop, **$previous** is assigned the value of **$current**, and **$current** is assigned the next node in the list. When the loop terminates, lines 80–93 determine if the data value to delete is in the list. If so, the function determines if the first node or some other node in the list is being deleted and performs the necessary link manipulations to remove the element from the list. The function returns a value of 1 if the delete operation is successful; otherwise, it returns a value of 0.

Function **head** simply returns the first node in the list. Function **printList** traverses the list and outputs each element. The main program (lines 128–183) allows you to interactively manipulate the list.

There are other ways to implement linked lists. For example, some linked lists keep track of the *tail* of the list, which makes it easier to append an element to the end of a list. Some lists have a dummy node at the head of the list. As a result, every node that contains data automatically has a predecessor node, which eliminates the need for testing the special case of inserting or removing the head node. Another variant of the linked list is the *circular linked list*, which has no end: The last element in the list points to the first element in the list.

```perl
1   # Fig. 20.6: LinkedList.pm
2   # Object-oriented linked-list implementation.
3
4   use warnings;
5   use strict;
6
7   package ListNode;    # start package ListNode
8
9   # ListNode constructor
10  sub new
11  {
12     my $type = shift();
13     my $class = ref( $type ) || $type;
14     my $self = { data => $_[ 0 ], nextLink => $_[ 1 ] };
15
16     bless( $self, $class );
17     return $self;
18  }
19
20  package LinkedList;  # start package LinkedList
21
```

Fig. 20.6   Object-oriented linked list implementation—**LinkedList.pm** (part 1 of 3).

```perl
22   # LinkedList constructor
23   sub new
24   {
25      my $type = shift();
26      my $class = ref( $type ) || $type;
27      my $self = { head => undef };
28
29      bless( $self, $class );
30      return $self;
31   }
32
33   # function to insert a new node in the list in ascending order
34   sub insertNode
35   {
36      my ( $self, $data ) = @_;
37
38      my $previous = undef;
39      my $current = $self->head();
40
41      # This loop determines the nodes between which the new
42      # node will be inserted. When this loop completes, variable
43      # $previous references the node before the one being
44      # inserted and $current references the node after the one
45      # being inserted.
46      while ( defined( $current ) && $data gt $current->{ data } ) {
47         $previous = $current;
48         $current = $current->{ nextLink };
49      }
50
51      # if $previous is still undefined, we are inserting
52      # at the head of the list.
53      unless ( defined( $previous ) ) {
54         $self->{ head } = new ListNode( $data, $current );
55      }
56      else {
57         $previous->{ nextLink } = new ListNode( $data, $current );
58      }
59   }
60
61   # function to remove a node from the list
62   sub deleteNode
63   {
64      my ( $self, $data ) = @_;
65
66      my $previous = undef;
67      my $current = $self->head();
68
69      # This loop locates the node to delete. When this loop
70      # completes, variable $previous references the node before
71      # the one being deleted and $current references the node
72      # being deleted.
73      while ( defined( $current ) && $data ne $current->{ data } ) {
74         $previous = $current;
```

Fig. 20.6   Object-oriented linked list implementation—**LinkedList.pm** (part 2 of 3).

```perl
75            $current = $current->{ nextLink };
76        }
77
78        # if we found the element in the list,
79        # we delete it and return 1
80        if ( defined( $current ) ) {
81
82            unless ( defined( $previous ) ) {
83                $self->{ head } = $self->{ head }{ nextLink };
84            }
85            else {
86                $previous->{ nextLink } = $current->{ nextLink };
87            }
88
89            return 1;   # element was deleted
90        }
91        else {
92            return 0;   # element was not deleted
93        }
94    }
95
96    # function that returns the head reference for the list
97    sub head
98    {
99        return $_[ 0 ]->{ head };
100   }
101
102   # function that traverses the list and outputs each element
103   sub printList
104   {
105       my $self = shift();
106
107       if ( !defined( $self->head() ) ) {
108           print( "List is empty.\n\n" );
109           return;
110       }
111
112       print( "The list is:\n" );
113       my $current = $self->{ head };
114
115       while ( defined( $current ) ) {
116           print( $current->{ data } );          # print current data
117           $current = $current->{ nextLink };    # move to next node
118
119           if ( defined( $current ) ) {          # if next node exists,
120               print( " --> " );                 # output -->
121           }
122       }
123
124       print( "\n" );
125   }
126
127   return 1;
```

Fig. 20.6   Object-oriented linked list implementation—**LinkedList.pm** (part 3 of 3).

```perl
128  #!/usr/bin/perl
129  # Fig. 20.6: fig20_06.pl
130  # Using class LinkedList.
131
132  use warnings;
133  use strict;
134  use LinkedList;
135
136  my $ll = new LinkedList();
137  my $choice;
138
139  instructions();
140
141  do {
142     print( "? " );
143     chomp( $choice = <STDIN> );
144
145     insertIt() if ( $choice eq 'i' );
146
147     deleteIt() if ( $choice eq 'd' );
148
149     instructions() if ( $choice eq '?' );
150
151     print( "\n" );
152  } while ( $choice ne 'q' );
153
154  # inserts a node in the list and outputs the list
155  sub insertIt
156  {
157     print( "Enter a string: " );
158     chomp( my $item = <STDIN> );
159     $ll->insertNode( $item );
160     $ll->printList();
161  }
162
163  # deletes a node from the list and outputs the list
164  sub deleteIt
165  {
166     print( "Enter string to be deleted: " );
167     chomp( my $item = <STDIN> );
168     print( $ll->deleteNode( $item )? "$item deleted.\n" :
169         "$item not found.\n" );
170     $ll->printList();
171  }
172
173  # displays the instructions
174  sub instructions
175  {
176     print << 'DONE';
177  Enter your choice:
178     i to insert an element into the list.
179     d to delete an element from the list.
180     q to end.
```

Fig. 20.6   Object-oriented linked-list implementation—**fig20_04.pl** (part 1 of 2).

```
181     ? to print instructions.
182  DONE
183  }
```

```
Enter your choice:
   i to insert an element into the list.
   d to delete an element from the list.
   q to end.
   ? to print instructions.
? i
Enter a string: C
The list is:
C

? i
Enter a string: A
The list is:
A --> C

? i
Enter a string: E
The list is:
A --> C --> E

? d
Enter string to be deleted: E
E deleted.
The list is:
A --> C

? d
Enter string to be deleted: A
A deleted.
The list is:
C

? d
Enter string to be deleted: C
C deleted.
List is empty.

? q
```

Fig. 20.6   Object-oriented linked-list implementation—**fig20_04.pl** (part 2 of 2).

20.4 Doubly Linked Lists

One of the restrictions of the linked lists we have worked with thus far is that we can traverse the lists in only one direction. If we would like to traverse the list in both the forward and backward directions, we can add a link that connects each node to its preceding node. Such a list is known as a *doubly linked list*.

Performance Tip 20.5

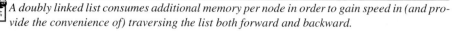

A doubly linked list consumes additional memory per node in order to gain speed in (and provide the convenience of) traversing the list both forward and backward.

Inserting and deleting from doubly linked lists is similar to the operations with singly linked lists; there is just one more reference per node that needs to be updated. Figure 20.7 shows an implementation of a doubly linked list. This implementation uses a dummy head node like we mentioned in Section 20.3 to simplify the list manipulations.

This implementation of a doubly-linked list uses dummy nodes at both the head and the tail of the list so that we do not have to determine whether a particular node has a node before or after it. The implementation uses two classes—**DoublyLinkedListNode** (lines 7–20) and **DoublyLinkedList** (lines 22–147). Class **DoublyLinkedListNode** contains one additional link reference, called **previousLink**, to allow each node to refer to the previous node in the list.

Class **DoublyLinkedList** provides a constructor to set up the list, function **insertNode** to insert a node at the current position in the list, function **deleteNode** to remove the current node in the list, function **nextNode** to move to the next node in the list, function **previousNode** to move to the previous node in the list, function **goToHead** to move to the beginning of the list, function **data** to return the data in the current element of the list and function **printAll** to output the contents of the list. This implementation of the doubly linked list keeps track of the current position with a reference called **cursor**. Functions **insertNode**, **deleteNode**, **nextNode**, **previousNode**, **gotToHead** and **data** all use the **cursor** to determine which node in the list to manipulate. The main program (lines 148–179) demonstrates the functions of class **DoublyLinkedList**.

```
1   # Figure 20.7: DoublyLinkedList.pm
2   # Implementation of a doubly linked list.
3
4   use warnings;
5   use strict;
6
7   package DoublyLinkedListNode;
8
9   # DoublyLinkedListNode constructor
10  sub new
11  {
12     my $type = shift();
13     my $class = ref( $type ) || $type;
14     my $self = { previousLink => $_[ 0 ],
15                  nextLink => $_[ 1 ],
16                  data => $_[ 2 ] };
17
18     bless( $self, $class );
19     return $self;
20  }
21
```

Fig. 20.7   Object-oriented implementation of a doubly-linked list—
DoublyLinkedList.pm (part 1 of 4).

```perl
22   package DoublyLinkedList;
23
24   # DoublyLinkedList constructor
25   sub new
26   {
27      my $type = shift();
28      my $class = ref( $type ) || $type;
29      my $self = { };
30
31      # head and tail dummy nodes
32      $self->{ head } = new DoublyLinkedListNode();
33      $self->{ head }{ nextLink } =
34         new DoublyLinkedListNode( $self->{ head } );
35      $self->{ cursor } = $self->{ head }{ nextLink };
36
37      bless( $self, $class );
38      return $self;
39   }
40
41   # inserts an element before the cursor and
42   # sets the cursor to that element.
43   sub insertNode
44   {
45      my ( $self, $data ) = @_;
46
47      if ( !defined( $data ) ) {
48         return;
49      }
50
51      my $newnode = new DoublyLinkedListNode(
52         $self->{ cursor }->{ previousLink },
53         $self->{ cursor }, $data );
54
55      $self->{ cursor }->{ previousLink }->{ nextLink } = $newnode;
56      $self->{ cursor }->{ previousLink } = $newnode;
57   }
58
59   # deletes the current cursor element and returns the deleted
60   # node's data ( or undefined if no node is selected ).
61   sub deleteNode
62   {
63      my ( $self ) = shift();
64
65      if ( !defined( $self->{ cursor }->{ data } ) ) {
66         print "You don't have an element selected\n";
67         return undef;
68      }
69
70      $self->{ cursor }->{ previousLink }->{ nextLink } =
71         $self->{ cursor }->{ nextLink };
72      $self->{ cursor }->{ nextLink }->{ previousLink } =
73         $self->{ cursor }->{ previousLink };
```

Fig. 20.7   Object-oriented implementation of a doubly-linked list—
DoublyLinkedList.pm (part 2 of 4).

```
74
75      my $deleted = $self->{ cursor }->{ data };
76      $self->{ cursor } = $self->{ cursor }->{ nextLink };
77
78      return $deleted;
79   }
80
81   # moves the cursor to the next node in the list
82   sub nextNode
83   {
84      my $self = shift();
85
86      if ( defined( $self->{ cursor }->{ nextLink } ) &&
87           defined( $self->{ cursor }{ nextLink }{ data } ) ) {
88         $self->{ cursor } = $self->{ cursor }{ nextLink };
89         return $self->{ cursor }{ data };
90      }
91      else {
92         print( "Can not go to the next node.\n" );
93         return undef;
94      }
95   }
96
97   # moves the cursor to the previous node in the list
98   sub previousNode
99   {
100     my $self = shift();
101
102     unless( defined( $self->{ cursor }{ previousLink } ) &&
103        defined( $self->{ cursor }{ previousLink }{ data } ) ) {
104
105        print( "Can not go to the previous node.\n" );
106        return;
107     }
108
109     $self->{ cursor } = $self->{ cursor }->{ previousLink };
110     return $self->{ cursor }->{ data };
111  }
112
113  # moves the cursor to the head of the list
114  sub gotoHead
115  {
116     $_[ 0 ]->{ cursor } = $_[ 0 ]->{ head }{ nextLink };
117     return $_[ 0 ]->{ cursor }->{ data };
118  }
119
120  # returns the data at the current cursor location
121  sub data
122  {
123     return $_[ 0 ]->{ cursor }->{ data };
124  }
125
```

Fig. 20.7   Object-oriented implementation of a doubly-linked list—
            DoublyLinkedList.pm (part 3 of 4).

```perl
126  # prints the list contents
127  sub printAll
128  {
129      my $self = shift();
130      my $current = $self->{ head }{ nextLink };
131
132      if ( !defined( $current->{ data } ) ) {
133          print( "The list is empty.\n\n" );
134          return;
135      }
136
137      print( "HEAD <--> " );
138
139      while ( defined( $current->{ data } ) ) {
140          print( "$current->{ data } <--> " );
141          $current = $current->{ nextLink };
142      }
143
144      print( "TAIL\n" );
145  }
146
147  return 1;
```

Fig. 20.7   Object-oriented implementation of a doubly-linked list—
DoublyLinkedList.pm (part 4 of 4).

```perl
148  #!/usr/bin/perl
149  # Figure 20.7: fig20_07.pl
150  # Using a doubly-linked list.
151
152  use warnings;
153  use strict;
154  use DoublyLinkedList;
155
156  my $dll = new DoublyLinkedList();
157
158  for ( 1 .. 5 ) {
159      $dll->insertNode( $_ );
160  }
161
162  print( "The list contains:\n" );
163  $dll->printAll();    # display list contents
164  print( "\nThe head is ", $dll->gotoHead(), ".\n" );
165
166  $dll->nextNode();        # move to next node
167  $dll->deleteNode();      # delete node at current position
168  $dll->nextNode();        # move to next node
169  $dll->deleteNode();      # delete node at current position
170  print( "\nAfter deleting two elements, ",
171          "The list contains:\n" );
172  $dll->printAll();    # display list contents
```

Fig. 20.7   Object-oriented implementation of a doubly-linked list—**fig20_07.pl**
(part 1 of 2).

```
173
174  print( "\nNow at ", $dll->data(), ".\n" );
175  print( "Now at ", $dll->previousNode(), ".\n" );
176  print( "Now at ", $dll->previousNode(), ".\n" );
177
178  print( "Attempting to go before the first list element:\n" );
179  $dll->previousNode();
```

```
The list contains:
HEAD <--> 1 <--> 2 <--> 3 <--> 4 <--> 5 <--> TAIL

The head is 1.

After deleting two elements, The list contains:
HEAD <--> 1 <--> 3 <--> 5 <--> TAIL

Now at 5.
Now at 3.
Now at 1.
Attempting to go before the first list element:
Can not go to the previous node.
```

Fig. 20.7   Object-oriented implementation of a doubly-linked list—**fig20_07.pl**
(part 2 of 2).

20.5 Stacks and Queues

A *stack* is a constrained version of a linked list; new nodes can be added to a stack and removed from a stack only at the top (i.e., at one end of the list). For this reason, a stack is referred to as a *last-in, first-out* (*LIFO*) data structure. The link member in the bottom (i.e., the last) node of the stack is set to **undef** to indicate that it is at the bottom of the stack.

Common Programming Error 20.2

*Not setting the link in the bottom node of a stack to **undef** is a common logic error.*

The primary functions used to manipulate a stack are normally called *push* and *pop*. Function *push* adds a new node to the top of the stack. Function *pop* removes a node from the top of the stack and returns the data object from the popped node.

Stacks have many interesting applications. For example, when a function call is made, the called function must know how to return to its caller, so the return address is pushed onto the *program execution stack*. If a series of function calls occurs, the value returned by each function is pushed onto the stack in last-in, first-out order so that each function can return a value to its caller. Stacks support recursive function calls in the same manner as they support conventional nonrecursive function calls.

The program execution stack contains the space created for lexical variables on each invocation of a function during a program's execution. When the function returns to its caller, the space for the function's lexical variables is popped off the stack, and those variables are no longer known to the program. Stacks are also used by compilers in the process of evaluating arithmetic expressions and generating machine-language code to process the expressions.

Another common data structure is the *queue*. A queue, which is also a constrained version of a list, is similar to a checkout line in a supermarket: The first person in line is serviced first, and other customers enter the line only at the end and wait to be serviced. Queue nodes are removed only from the *head* of the queue and are inserted only at the *tail* of the queue. For this reason, a queue is referred to as a *first-in, first-out* (*FIFO*) data structure. The insert and remove operations are often known as *enqueue* and *dequeue* operations.

Queues have many applications in computer systems. For example, most computers have only a single processor, so only one user at a time can be serviced. Entries for the other users are placed in a queue. The entry at the front of the queue is the next to receive service. Each entry gradually advances to the front of the queue as users are serviced.

Queues are also used to support print spooling. A multiuser environment may have only a single printer. Many users may be generating outputs to be printed. If the printer is busy, other outputs to it may still be generated. These are "spooled" to disk (much as thread is wound onto a spool) where they wait in a queue until the printer becomes available.

Information packets also wait in queues in computer networks. Each time a packet arrives at a network node, it must be routed to the next node on the network along the path to the packet's final destination. The routing node routes one packet at a time, so additional packets are enqueued until the router can route them.

A file server in a computer network handles file-access requests from many clients throughout the network. However, servers have a limited capacity to service requests from clients. When that capacity is exceeded, client requests wait in queues.

In other languages, stack and queue data structures are implemented with a variation of a linked list. However, Perl already provides the **push**, **pop**, **shift** and **unshift** functions, which can be used to perform stack and queue manipulations with arrays as the underlying data structure. Thus, if you use an array exclusively with either **push** and **pop** or **shift** and **unshift**, you will get the LIFO behavior of a stack. If you use an array exclusively with either **push** and **shift** or **unshift** (*enqueue*) and **pop** (*dequeue*), you will get the FIFO behavior of a queue. Figure 20.8 shows an example of the use of these functions to manipulate an array as a stack and as a queue. Using the results displayed in the output window, compare the order in which elements are inserted and removed to see the LIFO behavior of a stack and the FIFO behavior of a queue.

Performance Tip 20.6

*The **push** and **pop** functions are more efficient than the **shift** and **unshift** function for implementing a stack.*

```
1   #!/usr/bin/perl
2   # Figure 20.8: fig20_08.pl
3   # Demonstrating stacks and queues.
4
```

Fig. 20.8   Stacks and queues (part 1 of 3).

```perl
 5   use warnings;
 6   use strict;
 7
 8   my ( @stack, @queue );
 9
10   print( "Using the stack:\nPush 1 to 20\n" );
11
12   for ( 1 .. 20 ) {
13      push( @stack, $_ );
14   }
15
16   print( "Pop the top 10 elements: " );
17
18   for ( 1 .. 10 ) {
19      print( pop( @stack ), " " );
20   }
21
22   print( "\nPush 21 to 25\n" );
23
24   for ( 21 .. 25 ) {
25      push( @stack, $_ );
26   }
27
28   print( "Pop remaining elements: " );
29
30   while ( @stack ) {
31      print( pop( @stack ), " " );
32   }
33
34   print( "\n\nUsing the queue:\nEnqueue 1 to 20\n" );
35
36   for ( 1 .. 20 ) {
37      push( @queue, $_ );
38   }
39
40   print( "Dequeue first 10 elements: " );
41
42   for ( 1 .. 10 ) {
43      print( shift( @queue ), " " );
44   }
45
46   print( "\nEnqueue 21 to 25...\n" );
47
48   for ( 21 .. 25 ) {
49      push( @queue, $_ );
50   }
51
52   print( "Dequeue remaining elements: " );
53
54   while ( @queue ) {
55      print( shift( @queue ), " " );
56   }
```

Fig. 20.8   Stacks and queues (part 2 of 3).

```
Using the stack:
Push 1 to 20
Pop the top 10 elements: 20 19 18 17 16 15 14 13 12 11
Push 21 to 25
Pop remaining elements: 25 24 23 22 21 10 9 8 7 6 5 4 3 2 1

Using the queue:
Enqueue 1 to 20
Dequeue first 10 elements: 1 2 3 4 5 6 7 8 9 10
Enqueue 21 to 25...
Dequeue remaining elements: 11 12 13 14 15 16 17 18 19 20 21 22 23 24 25
```

Fig. 20.8   Stacks and queues (part 3 of 3).

20.6 Trees

Linked lists, stacks and queues are *linear data structures* (i.e., *sequences*). A tree is a nonlinear, two-dimensional data structure. Tree nodes contain two or more links. This section discusses *binary trees* (see Fig. 20.9)—trees whose nodes all contain two links (none, one or both of which may be **undef**). The *root node* is the first node in a tree. Each link in the root node refers to a *child*. The *left child* is the first node in the *left subtree*, and the *right child* is the first node in the *right subtree*. The children of a node are called *siblings*. A node with no children is called a *leaf node*. Computer scientists normally draw trees from the root node down—exactly the opposite of the way most trees grow in nature.

In this section, a special binary tree called a *binary search tree* is created. A binary search tree (with no duplicate node values), has the characteristic that the values in any left subtree are less than the value in its parent node, and the values in any right subtree are greater than the value in its parent node. Figure 20.10 illustrates a binary search tree with 12 integer values. Note that the shape of the binary search tree that corresponds to a set of data can vary, depending on the order in which the values are inserted into the tree.

The program in Fig. 20.11 creates an object-oriented implementation of a binary search tree of integer values and traverses it three ways—using recursive *inorder*, *preorder* and *postorder traversals*. The program generates 15 random numbers and inserts each in the tree, ignoring duplicate values.

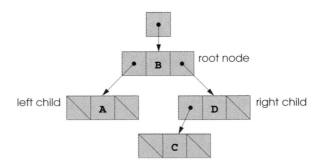

Fig. 20.9   Graphical representation of a binary tree.

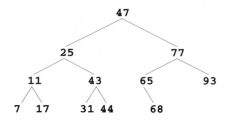

Fig. 20.10 Binary search tree.

The implementation of a binary search tree in Fig. 20.11 has two classes: **TreeNode** and **BinarySearchTree**. Class **TreeNode** provides the primary functionality, and class **BinarySearchTree** acts as the user's interface to the underlying nodes.

```perl
1    # Fig. 20.11: BinarySearchTree.pm
2    # Implementation of a binary search tree.
3
4    use warnings;
5    use strict;
6
7    package TreeNode;
8    my $class;
9
10   # TreeNode constructor
11   sub new
12   {
13      my $type = shift();
14      $class = ref( $type ) || $type;
15      my $self =
16         { left => undef, data => shift(), right => undef };
17
18      bless( $self, $class );
19      return $self;
20   }
21
22   # insert a TreeNode in a tree that contains nodes;
23   # ignore duplicate values
24   sub insert
25   {
26      my ( $self, $data ) = @_;
27
28      if ( $data < $self->{ data } ) {
29         if ( defined( $self->{ left } ) ) {
30            $self->{ left }->insert( $data );
31         }
32         else {
33            $self->{ left } = new TreeNode( $data );
34         }
35      }
```

Fig. 20.11 Binary search tree—**BinarySearchTree.pm** (part 1 of 4).

```
36        elsif ( $data > $self->{ data } ) {
37            if ( defined( $self->{ right } ) ) {
38                $self->{ right }->insert( $data );
39            }
40            else {
41                $self->{ right } = new TreeNode( $data );
42            }
43        }
44    }
45
46    # performs a preorder traversal of a binary search tree
47    sub preOrder
48    {
49        my $self = shift();
50
51        print( "$self->{ data } " );
52
53        $self->{ left }->preOrder()
54            if ( defined( $self->{ left } ) );
55
56        $self->{ right }->preOrder()
57            if ( defined( $self->{ right } ) );
58    }
59
60    # performs an inorder traversal of a binary search tree
61    sub inOrder
62    {
63        my $self = shift();
64
65        $self->{ left }->inOrder()
66            if ( defined( $self->{ left } ) );
67
68        print( "$self->{ data } " );
69
70        $self->{ right }->inOrder()
71            if ( defined( $self->{ right } ) );
72    }
73
74    # performs a postorder traversal of a binary search tree
75    sub postOrder
76    {
77        my $self = shift();
78
79        $self->{ left }->postOrder()
80            if ( defined( $self->{ left } ) );
81
82        $self->{ right }->postOrder()
83            if ( defined( $self->{ right } ) );
84
85        print( "$self->{ data } " );
86    }
87
```

Fig. 20.11   Binary search tree—**BinarySearchTree.pm** (part 2 of 4).

```perl
88   # recursively outputs the binary tree in a tree format turned
89   # on its side with the root node at the left of the output, the
90   # rightmost child at the top of the output and the leftmost
91   # child at the bottom of the output
92   sub outputTree
93   {
94      my ( $self, $depth ) = @_;
95
96      if ( defined( $self->{ right } ) ) {
97         $self->{ right }->outputTree( $depth + 3 );
98      }
99
100     print( ' ' x $depth, "$self->{ data }\n" );
101
102     if ( defined( $self->{ left } ) ) {
103        $self->{ left }->outputTree( $depth + 3 );
104     }
105  }
106
107  package BinarySearchTree;
108
109  # BinarySearchTree constructor
110  sub new
111  {
112     my $type = shift();
113     my $class = ref( $type ) || $type;
114
115     my $self = { root => undef };
116     bless( $self, $class );
117     return $self;
118  }
119
120  # inserts a node in a binary search tree
121  sub insertNode
122  {
123     my ( $self, $data ) = @_;
124
125     unless ( defined( $self->{ root } ) ) {
126        $self->{ root } = new TreeNode( $data );
127     }
128     else {
129        $self->{ root }->insert( $data );
130     }
131  }
132
133  # begins the preorder traversal
134  sub printPreOrder
135  {
136     my ( $self, $node ) = @_;
137     $self->{ root }->preOrder();
138  }
139
```

Fig. 20.11   Binary search tree—**BinarySearchTree.pm** (part 3 of 4).

```
140  # begins the inorder traversal
141  sub printInOrder
142  {
143     my ( $self, $node ) = @_;
144     $self->{ root }->inOrder();
145  }
146
147  # begins the postorder traversal
148  sub printPostOrder
149  {
150     my ( $self ) = shift();
151     $self->{ root }->postOrder();
152  }
153
154  # begin output of tree in tree format
155  sub printTree
156  {
157     my ( $self ) = shift();
158     $self->{ root }->outputTree( 0 );
159  }
160
161  return 1;
```

Fig. 20.11 Binary search tree—**BinarySearchTree.pm** (part 4 of 4).

```
162  #/usr/bin/perl
163  # Fig. 20.11: fig20_11.pl
164  # Using a binary search tree.
165
166  use warnings;
167  use strict;
168  use BinarySearchTree;
169
170  my $tree = new BinarySearchTree();
171
172  print( "The numbers being placed in the tree are:\n" );
173
174  for ( 1 .. 15 ) {
175     my $data = int( rand( 15 ) );
176     print( "$data " );
177     $tree->insertNode( $data );
178  }
179
180  print( "\n\nThe tree looks like:\n" );
181  $tree->printTree();
182
183  print( "\nThe preOrder traversal is: \n" );
184  $tree->printPreOrder();
185
186  print( "\n\nThe inOrder traversal is: \n" );
187  $tree->printInOrder();
188
```

Fig. 20.11 Implementation of a binary search tree: **fig20_11.pl** (part 1 of 2).

```
189  print( "\n\nThe postOrder traversal is: \n" );
190  $tree->printPostOrder();
```

```
The numbers being placed in the tree are:
9 7 12 10 9 13 2 2 8 13 8 12 3 3 14

The tree looks like:
            14
         13
      12
         10
   9
         8
      7
            3
         2

The preOrder traversal is:
9 7 2 3 8 12 10 13 14

The inOrder traversal is:
2 3 7 8 9 10 12 13 14

The postOrder traversal is:
3 2 8 7 10 14 13 12 9
```

Fig. 20.11 Implementation of a binary search tree: `fig20_11.pl` (part 2 of 2).

Class **TreeNode**'s constructor (lines 11–20) initializes a new node. Each new **TreeNode** is a leaf node, so both its **left** and **right** references have the value **undef**.

The **TreeNode** function **insert** (lines 24–44) compares the value to be inserted with the **data** value in the root node. If the value to be inserted is less than the value in the **data** root node, the program determines if the left subtree is empty (line 29). If not, **insert** recursively calls itself (line 30) for the left subtree to insert the value in the left subtree. Otherwise, a new **TreeNode** is allocated and initialized with the integer being inserted, and the **left** reference is set to the new node (line 33). *A node can be inserted only as a leaf node in a binary search tree.* If the value to be inserted is greater than the value in the **data** root node, the program determines if the right subtree is empty (line 37). If not, **insert** recursively calls itself (line 38) for the right subtree to insert the value in the right subtree. Otherwise, a new **TreeNode** is allocated and initialized with the integer being inserted, and the **right** reference is set to the new node (line 41).

Functions **preOrder** (lines 47–58), **inOrder** (lines 61–72) and **postOrder** (lines 75–86) each traverse the tree and print the node values. The **inOrder** traversal steps are:

1. Traverse the left subtree with a recursive call to **inOrder** (line 65).

2. Process the value in the node (i.e., print the value in the node at line 68).

3. Traverse the right subtree with a recursive call to **inOrder** (line 70).

The value in a node is not processed until the values in its left subtree are processed. The **inOrder** traversal of the tree in Fig. 20.10 returns the following sequence:

```
7 11 17 25 31 43 44 47 65 68 77 93
```

Note that the **inOrder** traversal of a binary search tree processes the values in the nodes in ascending order. The process of creating a binary search tree actually sorts the data, and thus this process is called the *binary tree sort*.

The steps for the **preOrder** traversal are as follows:

1. Process the value in the node (line 51).
2. Traverse the left subtree with a recursive call to **preOrder** (line 53).
3. Traverse the right subtree with a recursive call to **preOrder** (line 56).

The value in each node is processed as the node is visited. After the value in a given node is processed, the values in the left subtree are processed, and then the values in the right subtree are processed. The **preOrder** traversal of the tree in Fig. 20.10 returns:

```
47 25 11 7 17 43 31 44 77 65 68 93
```

The steps for the **postOrder** traversal are as follows:

1. Traverse the left subtree with a recursive call to **postOrder** (line 79).
2. Traverse the right subtree with a recursive call to **postOrder** (line 82).
3. Process the value in the node (line 85).

The value in each node is not processes until the values of its children are processes. The **postOrder** traversal of the tree in Fig. 20.10 returns the following sequence:

```
7 17 11 31 44 43 25 68 65 93 77 47
```

Recursive function **outputTree** (lines 92–105) displays the binary tree. The function outputs the tree row by row, with the top of the tree at the left of the screen and the bottom of the tree toward the right of the screen. Each row is output vertically. Note that the rightmost leaf node appears at the top of the output in the rightmost column, and the root node appears at the left of the output. Each column of output starts three spaces to the right of the preceding column. Function **outputTree** should receive an argument **$depth**, which represents the number of spaces preceding the value to be output (this variable should start at zero, so that the root node is output at the left of the screen). The function uses a modified inorder traversal to output the tree: It starts at the rightmost node in the tree and works back to the left.

Class **BinarySearchTree** (lines 107–161) provides the interface that programmers use to interact with **TreeNode**s. The **BinarySearchTree** constructor (lines 110–118) creates an empty binary tree by setting the **root** reference to **undef** (line 115). Function **insertNode** (lines 121–131) determines if the tree is empty (line 125). If so, it inserts a new node; otherwise, it calls **TreeNode**'s **insert** function to locate the insertion point and insert the new node. Functions **printPreOrder** (lines 134–138), **printInOrder** (lines 141–145) and **printPostOrder** (lines 148–152) call **TreeNode**'s **preOrder**, **inOrder** and **postOrder** functions, respectively, to initiate traversals of the binary search tree. Function **printTree** calls **TreeNode**'s **output-Tree** function to begin displaying the tree.

The main program (lines 162–190) creates a tree of 15 random integer values and outputs the tree, followed by the results of the preorder, inorder and postorder traversals.

The binary search tree facilitates *duplicate elimination*. As the tree is created, attempts to insert a duplicate value are recognized, because a duplicate value follows the same "go left" or "go right" decisions on each comparison as the original value did. Thus, the duplicate value eventually is compared with a node containing the same value. The duplicate value may simply be discarded at this point. In Fig. 20.11 this occurs after line 43, because we do not test for the case in which the data we are attempting to insert is equal to the data in a given node.

Searching a binary tree for a value that matches a key value is fast, especially for *tightly packed* trees. In a tightly packed tree, each level contains about twice as many elements as does the previous level. Figure 22.11 contains a tightly packed binary tree. So, a binary search tree with *n* elements has a minimum of $\log_2 n$ levels, and thus at most $\log_2 n$ comparisons would have to be made either to find a match or to determine that no match exists. This means, for example, that when searching a (tightly packed) 1000-element binary search tree, approximately 10 comparisons need to be made, because $2^{10} > 1000$. When searching a (tightly packed) 1,000,000-element binary search tree, at most 20 comparisons need to be made, because $2^{20} > 1,000,000$.

There are a number of variations on trees. For example, some trees have more than two subtrees per node. Some trees have a variable number of subtrees per node. CPAN provides several predefined tree modules (**www.cpan.org**).

20.7 Hashes

Another nonlinear data structure we have been using for some time is the *hash*, or *hash table*. This data structure is one of the built-in data types in Perl, so you have not had to worry about what is going on behind the scenes.

A hash table consists of multiple containers, known as *buckets*, where values are stored. A *hash function* is used to determine in which bucket a particular value will be stored. Hash functions must always map equal values to the same bucket. Good hash functions will cause an even distribution of elements across all the buckets.

Next, we show a basic example in which the buckets of the hash table are the elements of an array. The hash function takes a string as an argument and returns the index of the array element in which the string is to be stored. Multiple values could be stored in the same bucket, so each array element references another array that holds the values in that bucket. Figure 20.12 shows our implementation of a hash table.

```
1   # Fig. 20.12: Hashtable.pm
2   # Simple hash table implementation.
3
4   use warnings;
5   use strict;
6
7   package Hashtable;
8
9   # Hashtable constructor
10  sub new
11  {
12     my $type = shift();
13     my $class = ref( $type ) || $type;
14
```

Fig. 20.12 Hashtable implementation—**Hashtable.pm** (part 1 of 3).

```
15      my $self = { table => [ ]};
16      $self->{ size } = shift() || 23;   # 23 is default size
17      $self->{ function } =
18          shift() || hashFunction( $self->{ size } );
19
20      foreach ( 0 .. $self->{ size } - 1 ) {
21          $self->{ table }->[ $_ ] = [ ];
22      }
23
24      bless( $self, $class );
25      return $self;
26  }
27
28  # inserts an element in the table
29  sub insert
30  {
31      my $self = shift();
32      my $data = shift();
33
34      my $index = $self->{ function }->( $data );
35      push( @{ $self->{ table }[ $index ] }, $data );
36      return $index;
37  }
38
39  # removes an element from the table
40  sub remove {
41      my $self = shift();
42      my $data = shift();
43
44      my $index = $self->{ function }->( $data );
45
46      foreach ( 0 .. $#{ $self->{ table }[ $index ] } ) {
47          if ( $self->{ table }[ $index ][ $_ ] eq $data ) {
48              print "Deleting $data\n";
49              splice( @{ $self->{ table }[ $index ] },
50                      $_, 1, @{ [] } );
51              return 1;
52          }
53      }
54
55      return 0;
56  }
57
58  # outputs the contents of the table
59  sub printTable
60  {
61      my $self = shift();
62
63      for ( my $i = 0; $i < $self->{ size }; $i++ ) {
64          print "Bucket $i: @{ $self->{ table }[ $i ] }\n";
65      }
66  }
67
```

Fig. 20.12   Hashtable implementation—**Hashtable.pm** (part 2 of 3).

```
68   # calculates the location of a key in the table
69   sub hashFunction
70   {
71      my $size = shift();
72
73      return sub
74      {
75         my $string = shift();
76         my $number;
77
78         while ( $string ) {
79            $number += ord( substr( $string, 0, 1, '' ) );
80         }
81
82         return $number % $size;
83      }
84   }
85
86   return 1;
```

Fig. 20.12 Hashtable implementation—**Hashtable.pm** (part 3 of 3).

```
87   #!/usr/bin/perl
88   # Fig. 20.12: fig20_12.pl
89   # Simple hash table implementation.
90
91   use warnings;
92   use strict;
93   use Hashtable;
94
95   my $ht = new Hashtable( 11 );
96   my $choice = '';
97
98   instructions();
99   print( "? " );
100  chomp( $choice = <STDIN> );
101
102  while ( $choice ne 'q' ) {
103
104     if ( $choice eq 'i' ) {
105        print( "Enter several strings on separate lines\n",
106              "('DONE' to terminate input):\n" );
107        chomp( my $data = <STDIN> );
108
109        while ( $data ne 'DONE' ) {
110           print( "Inserted '$data' into slot ",
111                 $ht->insert($data), "\n" );
112           chomp( $data = <STDIN> );
113        }
114
115        print( "\n" );
116     }
```

Fig. 20.12 Hashtable implementation—**fig20_12.pl** (part 1 of 3).

```perl
117     elsif ( $choice eq 'r' ) {
118        print( "What element would you like to remove? " );
119        chomp( my $data = <STDIN> );
120
121        unless ( $ht->remove( $data ) ) {
122           print( "Could not delete $data\n\n" );
123        }
124        else {
125           print( "\n" );
126        }
127     }
128     elsif ( $choice eq 'd' ) {
129        $ht->printTable();
130        print( "\n" );
131     }
132     elsif ( $choice eq '?' ) {
133        instructions();
134     }
135     else {
136        print( "Please enter a valid command. ",
137                "Enter '?' for instructions.\n\n" );
138     }
139
140     print( "? " );
141     chomp( $choice = <STDIN> );
142  }
143
144  sub instructions
145  {
146  print <<DONE
147
148  Enter 'i' to insert numbers.
149  Enter 'r' to remove numbers.
150  Enter 'd' to display hash table.
151  Enter '?' to print these instructions.
152  Enter 'q' to quit.
153  DONE
154  }
```

```
Enter 'i' to insert numbers.
Enter 'r' to remove numbers.
Enter 'd' to display hash table.
Enter '?' to print these instructions.
Enter 'q' to quit.
? i
Enter several strings on separate lines
('DONE' to terminate input):
hello
Inserted 'hello' into slot 4
there
Inserted 'there' into slot 8
```

(continued on next page)

Fig. 20.12 Hashtable implementation—**fig20_12.pl** (part 2 of 3).

```
                                                    (continued from previous page)
happy
Inserted 'happy' into slot 7
birthday
Inserted 'birthday' into slot 8
to
Inserted 'to' into slot 7
you
Inserted 'you' into slot 8
new
Inserted 'new' into slot 0
year
Inserted 'year' into slot 4
DONE

? d
Bucket 0: new
Bucket 1:
Bucket 2:
Bucket 3:
Bucket 4: hello year
Bucket 5:
Bucket 6:
Bucket 7: happy to
Bucket 8: there birthday you
Bucket 9:
Bucket 10:

? r
What element would you like to remove? birthday
Deleting birthday

? d
Bucket 0: new
Bucket 1:
Bucket 2:
Bucket 3:
Bucket 4: hello year
Bucket 5:
Bucket 6:
Bucket 7: happy to
Bucket 8: there you
Bucket 9:
Bucket 10:

? q
```

Fig. 20.12 Hashtable implementation—**fig20_12.pl** (part 3 of 3).

To convert a string to a number, **hashFunction** (lines 69–84) totals the ASCII value of each character in the string. Perl built-in function **ord** returns the ASCII value of the first character in its argument. We then use the modulus operator to return the remainder when the total of the ASCII values is divided by the number of buckets in the table. This function is not an ideal hash function, however, because it maps certain related strings to the same bucket. If the strings are all composed of the same letters, just rearranged, they will all be converted to the same number, and thus be mapped to the same bucket. A better hash function might put a different weight on each character, depending on where it is in the string.

A good hash function is important because the efficiency of a hash is directly related to how evenly distributed the elements are in the buckets. Assume that we have 20 elements stored in ten buckets. If the elements are evenly distributed, with two elements per bucket, then at most two elements must be searched to locate the value. If every element ends up in the same bucket, then all the elements must be searched! In that case, the hash table would have the efficiency of a linear search.

SUMMARY

- Dynamic data structures can grow and shrink at execution time.

- Linked lists are collections of data items "lined up in a row"; insertions and deletions can be made anywhere in a linked list.

- Stacks are important in compilers and operating systems; insertions and deletions are made at only at one end of a stack—its top.

- Queues represent items waiting in a line; insertions are made at the back (also referred to as the tail) of a queue, and deletions are made from the front (also referred to as the head) of a queue.

- Binary trees facilitate high-speed searching and sorting of data, efficient elimination of duplicate data items, representing file system directories and compiling expressions into machine language.

- A self-referential structure contains a member that refers to a structure of the same type. Self-referential structures can be linked together to form useful data structures, such as lists, queues, stacks and trees.

- Creating and maintaining dynamic data structures requires dynamic memory allocation—the ability for a program to obtain more memory space at execution time to hold new nodes and to release space no longer needed.

- A linked list is a linear collection (i.e., a sequence) of self-referential structures, called nodes, connected by reference links.

- A linked list is accessed via a reference to the first node of the list. Each subsequent node is accessed via the link-reference member stored in the previous node.

- By convention, the link reference in the last node of a list is set to **undef** to mark the end of the list.

- A node can contain data of any type, including objects of other classes.

- A linked list is appropriate when the number of data elements to be represented in the data structure is unpredictable. Linked lists are dynamic, so the length of a list can increase or decrease as necessary.

- Linked lists can be maintained in sorted order simply by inserting each new element at the proper point in the list.

- List nodes are normally not stored contiguously in memory. Rather, they are logically contiguous.

- A stack is a constrained version of a linked list; new nodes can be added to a stack and removed from a stack only at the top. A stack is referred to as a last-in, first-out (LIFO) data structure.

- The link member in the bottom node of a stack is set to **undef** to indicate the bottom of the stack.

- The primary functions used to manipulate a stack are **push** and **pop**. Function **push** adds a new node to the top of the stack. Function **pop** removes a node from the top of the stack and returns the **data** object from the popped node.

- Stacks have many interesting applications. For example, when a function call is made, the called function must know how to return to its caller, so the return address is pushed onto the program execution stack. If a series of function calls occurs, the successive return values are pushed onto the stack in last-in, first-out order, so that each function can return a value to its caller.

- The program execution stack contains the space created for local variables on each invocation of a function. When the function returns to its caller, the space for the function's local variables is popped off the stack, and those variables are no longer known to the program.

- Stacks are also used by compilers in the process of evaluating arithmetic expressions and generating machine-language code to process the expressions.

- A queue is a constrained version of a list.

- A queue is similar to a checkout line in a supermarket: The first person in line is serviced first, and other customers enter the line only at the end and wait to be serviced.

- Queue nodes are removed only from the head of the queue and are inserted only at the tail of the queue. For this reason, a queue is referred to as a first-in, first-out (FIFO) data structure.

- The insert and remove operations for a queue are known as *enqueue* and *dequeue*.

- Queues have many applications in computer systems. For example, most computers have only a single processor, so only one user at a time can be serviced. Entries for the other users are placed in a queue. The entry at the front of the queue is the next to receive service. Each entry gradually advances to the front of the queue as users are serviced.

- Queues are also used to support print spooling. A multiuser environment may have only a single printer, however, many users may be generating outputs to be printed. If the printer is busy, other outputs to it may still be generated. These outputs are "spooled" to disk (much as thread is wound onto a spool), where they wait in a queue until the printer becomes available.

- Information packets also wait in queues in computer networks. Each time a packet arrives at a network node, it must be routed to the next node on the network along the path to the packet's final destination. The routing node routes one packet at a time, so additional packets are enqueued until the router can route them.

- A file server in a computer network handles file-access requests from many clients throughout the network. However, servers have a limited capacity to service requests from clients. When that capacity is exceeded, client requests wait in queues.

- A tree is a nonlinear, two-dimensional data structure.

- Tree nodes contain two or more links.

- A binary tree is a tree whose nodes all contain two links. The root node is the first node in a tree.

- Each link in the root node refers to a child. The left child is the first node in the left subtree, and the right child is the first node in the right subtree.

- The children of a given node are called *siblings*. A node with no children is called a *leaf node*.

- Computer scientists normally draw trees from the root node down.

- A binary search tree (with no duplicate node values) has the characteristic that the values in any left subtree are less than the value in its parent node, and the values in any right subtree are greater than the value in its parent node.

- A node can be inserted only as a leaf node in a binary search tree.

- An inorder traversal of a binary search tree processes the values in the nodes in ascending order.

- The process of creating a binary search tree actually sorts the data, and thus this process is called the *binary tree sort*.

- In a preorder traversal, the value in each node is processed as the node is visited. After the value in a given node is processed, the values in the left subtree are processed, and then the values in the right subtree are processed.

- In a postorder traversal, the value in each node is processed after the values of its children.

- The binary search tree facilitates duplicate elimination. As the tree is created, attempts to insert a duplicate value are recognized, because a duplicate follows the same "go left" or "go right" decisions on each comparison as the original value did. Thus, the duplicate eventually is compared with a node containing the same value. The duplicate value may simply be discarded at this point.

- Searching a binary tree for a value that matches a key value is fast, especially for tightly packed trees. In a tightly packed tree, each level contains about twice as many elements as does the previous level. So, a binary search tree with n elements has a minimum of $\log_2 n$ levels, and thus at most $\log_2 n$ comparisons would have to be made either to find a match or to determine that no match exists. This means, for example, that when searching a (tightly packed) 1000-element binary search tree, approximately 10 comparisons need to be made, because $2^{10} > 1000$. When searching a (tightly packed) 1,000,000-element binary search tree, at most 20 comparisons need to be made, because $2^{20} > 1,000,000$.

TERMINOLOGY

binary search tree	linear data structure
binary tree	linked list
binary tree sort	node
bucket	nonlinear data structure
child node	**ord** function
children	parent node
circular linked list	pop
delete a node	postorder traversal of a binary tree
dequeue	preorder traversal of a binary tree
doubly linked list	program execution stack
duplicate elimination	push
dynamic data structures	queue
enqueue	recursive tree-traversal algorithms
FIFO (first in, first out)	right child
hash	right subtree
hash function	root node
hash table	self-referential class
head of a list	stack
head of a queue	subtree
inorder traversal of a binary tree	tail of a queue
insert a node	tightly packed tree
leaf node	top of a stack
left child	traversal
left subtree	tree
LIFO (last in, first out)	visit a node

SELF-REVIEW EXERCISES

20.1 Fill in the blanks in the following statements:
  a) A _____ contains a member that references a structure of the same type.
  b) Moving from one node to another is called _____ a data structure.
  c) The first node of a linked list is known as the _____ of the list.
  d) A _____ is a list where elements are accessed LIFO and a _____ is FIFO.
  e) A linked list that has an extra link in each node to allow forward and backward traversals is known as a _____.
  f) A _____ is a tree with only two subtrees per node.
  g) In a _____ traversal, a node is processed after both of its subtrees are processed.
  h) A _____ is used to determine in which bucket of a hash table an element will be placed.

20.2 State whether each of the following is *true* or *false*. If *false*, explain why.
  a) A linked list is more efficient than an array for inserting an element onto the end of a list.
  b) A stack accesses elements in FIFO order.
  c) Stacks and queues are more constrained versions of lists.
  d) A doubly linked list has four links per node.
  e) All trees have nodes with two subtrees.
  f) A node with no children is known as a leaf node.
  g) An inorder traversal processes a node before processing its subtrees.
  h) A hash table maintains the order in which elements were inserted.
  i) Good hash functions will cause an even distribution of elements across buckets.

ANSWERS TO SELF-REVIEW EXERCISES

20.1 a) self-referential structure. b) traversing. c) head. d) stack, queue. e) doubly linked list. f) binary tree. g) postorder. h) hash function.

20.2 a) False. Linked lists are more efficient only for adding elements in the middle of the list.
  b) False. A queue accesses elements in FIFO.
  c) True.
  d) False. A doubly linked list has two links per node.
  e) False. Binary trees have only two subtrees per node, but other types of trees can have different numbers of subtrees per node.
  f) True.
  g) False. A preorder traversal processes a node before processing its subtrees.
  h) False. A hash table does not maintain insertion order.
  i) True.

EXERCISES

20.3 Modify the program in Fig. 20.6 to create a circular doubly-linked list. The list should have no head or tail. The list should be accessed only through a cursor element that refers to a node in the list. The five functions available to the user are to get the value of the node at the current location of the cursor, to move the cursor forward, to move the cursor backward, to delete the node at the location of the cursor and to insert an element in front of the node at the current location of the cursor. You should use an object-oriented implementation.

20.4 A *stream* is an infinite list. It is, of course, impossible to hold an infinite list in memory. If the list has some sort of pattern or formula that can be used to determine its elements, we can mimic the behavior of an infinite list by calculating elements only when they are going to be used. We can do so using a linked-list-like implementation by having the last calculated element point to a reference to a function that calculates the next value and adds a new node with that value to the end of the linked list. Write an implementation of an infinite list that consists of all the even numbers.

20.5   Create a tree in which each node can have four children. The leftmost child should hold values less than half the value of the parent node. The next child should hold values that are less than the value of the parent node, but more than half the value of the parent node. The third child should hold values greater than the value of the parent node, but less than twice the value of the parent node. The final child should only hold values which are twice the value of the parent node.

20.6   Add a **deleteNode** function that deletes a node from a binary search tree. The function should delete only the node specified—all subtrees of that node should still be in the tree. The function should actually delete the whole node, not just set its value to **undef**. Finally, the tree should still abide by the rules governing the binary search tree—i.e., for each node in the tree, all the nodes in the left subtree should be less than that node, and all the nodes in the right subtree should be greater than that node. [Hint: After deleting the node, replace it with a node from one of its subtrees to maintain the integrity of the tree.]

20.7   We can get an idea of the efficiency of Perl's internal hashing algorithm by looking at the value of a hash in scalar context. When a hash is evaluated in a scalar context it returns a string that is a fraction representing the number of buckets that have elements compared with the total number of buckets. To maintain optimal efficiency, if the hash is starting to fill up (i.e., most of the buckets are full), Perl rehashes the hash by making more buckets and redistributing the elements. The built-in hash function is fairly clever, and the hash expands as you add elements to maintain optimal efficiency for hash-table lookups. Write a program that creates a hash and inserts the numbers from 1 to 100 in the hash. After inserting each element, output a line of text showing the number inserted in the hash and the scalar representation of the hash. What do you notice about how the hash allocated more dynamic memory?

21

Graphics/Tk

Objectives

- To learn about some of Perl's graphical capabilities.
- To explore the **GD** module's graphical object capabilities.
- To use the **GD** module's ability to alter the sizes of images and to copy images.
- To learn how to use Perl's chart modules.
- To understand the basic concepts of graphical user interfaces (GUIs).
- To learn about Perl's **Tk** module and the GUI components associated with it.
- To implement a simple GUI application.

An actor entering through the door, you've got nothing. But if he enters through the window, you've got a situation.
Billy Wilder

Seeing is believing.
Proverb

A picture shows me at a glance what it takes dozens of pages of a book to expound.
Ivan Sergeyevich

I claim not to have controlled events, but confess plainly that events have controlled me.
Abraham Lincoln

Outline

21.1 Introduction

Graphics convey information and make programs visually appealing. Everywhere we look, we see graphics—video games, billboards, movies, etc. Good examplescan be found in World Wide Web pages. The majority of Web pages have graphics. Pictures are one form of graphics commonly found on Web pages. Pictures provide an enormous quantity of information. Graphics are more than just pictures; they are the elements of a picture. Colors, lines, rectangles, patterns, text, etc. are all graphics. Graphics are visual images.

Perl does not have any built-in graphics manipulation functions, yet we can use Perl to generate complex graphics and *graphical user interfaces* (also called *GUIs*). Many modules have been developed to offer these capabilities. We will look at three of the most popular modules in this chapter. We begin to understand basic graphics concepts by discussing the **GD** module. From there, we move on to discuss modules that create more high-end graphics, charts and sophisticated GUIs.

21.2 GD Module: Creating Simple Shapes

The *GD* module is used to create and manipulate images, similar to a basic drawing or painting application. The major difference between the **GD** module and drawing applications is that the programmer must specify in text commands, rather than physically drawing, what it is that he or she wishes to accomplish. Figure 21.1 demonstrates a simple program that creates some shapes.

```
1   #!/usr/bin/perl
2   # Fig 21.1: fig21_01.pl
3   # Using the GD module to create shapes.
4
5   use strict;
6   use warnings;
7   use GD;
8
9   my $image = new GD::Image( 320, 320 );
10
```

Fig. 21.1   Using the **GD** module (part 1 of 2).

```
11    my $white = $image->colorAllocate( 255, 255, 255 );
12    my $red = $image->colorAllocate( 255, 0, 0 );
13    my $green = $image->colorAllocate( 0, 255, 0 );
14    my $blue = $image->colorAllocate( 0, 0, 255 );
15    my $black = $image->colorAllocate( 0, 0, 0 );
16    my $purple = $image->colorAllocate( 255, 0, 255 );
17
18    $image->filledRectangle( 15, 15, 150, 150, $red );
19    $image->arc( 200, 200, 50, 50, 0, 360, $black );
20    $image->fill( 200, 200, $blue );
21    $image->rectangle( 100, 100, 200, 125, $green );
22    $image->fillToBorder( 150, 110, $green, $green );
23
24    my $polygon = new GD::Polygon();
25    $polygon->addPt( 20, 300 );
26    $polygon->addPt( 20, 175 );
27    $polygon->addPt( 100, 175 );
28
29    $image->polygon( $polygon, $blue );
30    $image->fill( 50, 200, $purple );
31
32    $polygon->setPt( 0, 30, 300 );
33    $polygon->setPt( 1, 110, 300 );
34    $polygon->setPt( 2, 110, 175 );
35
36    $image->filledPolygon( $polygon, $black );
37
38    open( PICT, ">fig21_02.png" ) or
39        die( "Can not open picture: $!" );
40
41    binmode( PICT );
42    print( PICT $image->png() );
43    close( PICT ) or die( "Can not close file: $!" );
```

Fig. 21.1   Using the **GD** module (part 2 of 2).

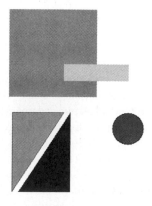

Fig. 21.2   Contents of **fig21_02.png**.

The program uses many of the **GD** module's methods, so let us go through it line by line. Line 7 imports the **GD** module. Line 9 creates a new **GD** image object. We pass to the constructor the *width* and *height* of the image we wish to create (in this case, 320 pixels wide by 320 pixels high). The upper-left corner of this area has an *x coordinate* of 0 and a *y coordinate* of 0. The *x* coordinate increases from left to right across the image and the *y* coordinate increases from top to bottom in the image. Then we define some colors (lines 11–16). The color **$white** becomes the background color for our picture. We define this color using the **colorAllocate** method, passing it the red, green and blue values that compose the color. The **GD** module uses the *RGB (red, green, blue) color scheme*, in which the red, green and blue parts of the color are specified as integers in the range 0–255. We also define colors red, green, blue, black and purple and set them to the corresponding variables. We now have a palette and we can refer to any of those six colors by their variable names.

Next we create some predefined polygons. We use the **$image** object's **filled-Rectangle** method to create a filled rectangle (line 18). The first two arguments define one corner of the rectangle. The third and fourth arguments define the diagonally opposite corner. The fifth argument is the color. In this case, the whole rectangle will be red.

We create a circle using method **arc** (line 19). The first two arguments passed to **arc** are the coordinates of the center of the circle. The next two arguments are the horizontal and vertical radius. The next two arguments provide degree bounds for the sweep of the arc. In this case, the bounds are 0 and 360 so this will sweep out the full circle. The final argument is the color. Notice that this method will not fill in the arc. We are forced to do this manually on line 20 by calling **GD**'s **fill** method. The first two arguments of this method specify a pixel. The paint will spread out from this pixel until a pixel is found that is not the same color as the starting pixel. The third argument is the color of the paint.

On line 21, we use **GD**'s **rectangle** method. This method to creates a hollow rectangle. We would like to fill this rectangle with color manually. We could use our **fill** method to do so, but half of the rectangle we just created is red (it overlaps with the previous rectangle) and the other half is white (blank canvas). The **fill** method fills only until it hits a pixel of a different color than the previous one. If we started filling in the white portion, only that area would get colored. Likewise, if we started filling in the red portion, only that part would be colored. **GD** provides a method to work around this problem called **fillToBorder**. This method takes the same arguments as **fill**, but adds one more argument before the fill color. The third argument in this method is the border-color argument. The method will fill in the designated area until it reaches a pixel that is colored with the specified border color. In this case, we fill in the inside of the rectangle in green until we hit a border of green, the outside of the rectangle.

Next, we explore **GD**'s **Polygon** class. On line 24, we create an instance of the **Polygon** class. The polygon is null—it has no points. Then, we create some points in this polygon using method **addPt**. This method takes two arguments—the *x* coordinate and the *y* coordinate of the point with respect to the upper-left *(0, 0)* coordinate of the image. We add three points to the polygon, then we add the polygon to the image using method **polygon** (line 29). This method takes a polygon object and a border color and adds the polygon to the image. Next, we change the points in our polygon so that we can draw the polygon again in a different position. We use **Polygon**'s **setPt** method to do this. This method takes three arguments. The last two arguments are the *x* and *y* coordinates of the new point. The first argument is the number of the point we wish to change. It is important to note that this numbering starts at zero. Once we have changed our polygon, we add it to our image, this time using method *fillPolygon*. This method is draws a polygon filled with a color.

Finally, we would like to output our picture object to a file for later viewing. So, in line 38, we open a file. Line 41 sets the output mode of the file to binary with function *bin-mode*, so that when the image is stored, the bytes of memory containing the image are written in the image's native format, rather than a platform-specific format. Then, we output the image after converting it to a *.png* (*Portable Network Graphics*) *file* with method *png*. Figure 21.2 contains the image that was created in Fig. 21.1.

21.3 GD Module: Image Manipulation

The **GD** module also provides methods to manipulate images. For example, it allows us to copy images and resize images. Figure 21.3 presents a small program to demonstrate these features, and Fig. 21.4 shows the resulting image that is created.

Line 9 of Fig. 21.3 is a different version of the constructor we saw previously. The name of this constructor is *newFromPng*. It creates an image object from an existing *.png* file—in this case **fig21_02.png**, the picture we created in the previous program. Next we get the size of the picture using method *getBounds*, which returns the width and height of the image. We then use function **map** to multiply each element of **@dimensions** by 2 and store the results in **@newDimensions**. Line 13 creates a new image with these dimensions. Lines 14 and 15 use method *copyResized* to copy the old image and into the new image and change its size. Method **copyResized** takes nine arguments. The first is the image object to copy. The next two arguments are the coordinates of the starting pixel in the destination (new) image, and the two subsequent arguments denote the starting pixel in the source (original) image. The sixth and seventh arguments (from **@newDimensions**) are the size of the new, resized image. The eighth and ninth arguments are the size of the initial image. Thus, this method copies from **$image** a rectangle starting from *(0, 0)* with the dimensions specified in the **@dimensions** array, resizes the rectangle to the dimensions in **@newDimensions** and places the results into **$newImage** starting at point *(0, 0)*. This procedure copies the image and doubles its width and height. Finally, lines 17–21 open an output file, set the **binmode** of that file and output the image as a *.png* file.

```
1   #!/usr/bin/perl
2   # Fig 21.3: fig21_03.pl
3   # A program to enlarge a picture.
4
5   use GD;
6   use strict;
7   use warnings;
8
9   my $image = GD::Image->newFromPng( "fig21_02.png" );
10  my @dimensions = $image->getBounds();
11  my @newDimensions = map( { $_ * 2 } @dimensions );
12
13  my $newImage = new GD::Image ( @newDimensions );
14  $newImage->copyResized( $image, 0, 0, 0, 0, @newDimensions,
15      @dimensions );
```

Fig. 21.3   Doubling the size of an image (part 1 of 2).

```
16
17   open( FILE, ">fig21_04.png" ) or
18      die( "Could not write to file: $!" );
19
20   binmode( FILE );
21   print( FILE $newImage->png() );
22
23   close( FILE ) or die( "Can not close file: $!" );
```

Fig. 21.3   Doubling the size of an image (part 2 of 2).

Fig. 21.4   Contents of `fig21_04.png`.

21.4 Chart Module

Perl provides a module for creating custom charts and graphs. This module is called **Chart**, and it is extended by modules **Chart::Lines**, **Chart::Bars** and **Chart::Points**, among others. Figure 21.5 uses module **Chart::Lines**, and Fig. 21.6 presents the chart image that is created as a result of the program.

```
1   #!/usr/bin/perl
2   # Fig 21.5: fig21_05.pl
3   # Using the Chart module.
4
5   use strict;
6   use warnings;
7   use Chart::Lines;
8
9   my $line = new Chart::Lines();
10  my $file = "fig21_06.png";
11  my @labels = ( "first", "second" );
12  my %colors = ( "dataset0" => [ 100, 100, 255 ],
13      "dataset1" => [ 255, 100, 100 ],
14      "background" => [ 150, 235, 200 ] );
15
16  $line->set( "title" => "Test Chart", "x_label" => "letter" );
17  $line->set( "y_label" => "number", "legend" => "left" );
18  $line->set( "legend_labels" => \@labels, "colors" => \%colors );
19  $line->set( "grey_background" => 0 );
20
21  my @Xlabels = ( 'a', 'b', 'c', 'd' );
22  my @dataset1 = ( 1, 2, 3, 4 );
23  my @dataset2 = ( 2, 3, 5, 9 );
24
25  my @data = ( \@Xlabels, \@dataset1, \@dataset2 );
26
27  $line->png( $file, \@data );
```

Fig. 21.5   Using the **Chart** module.

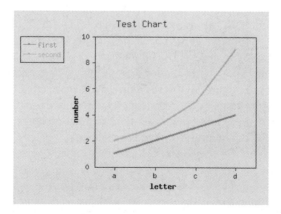

Fig. 21.6   Contents of **fig21_06.png**.

Line 7 of Fig. 21.5 imports module **Chart::Lines** so we can create a line graph. Line 9 creates a line-graph object. All **Chart** objects are initialized with default values that can be changed using method *set*. Most of this program deals with customizing our graph. The variable **$file** (line 10) holds the name of our output file, **@labels** (line 11) holds the names of our data sets and **%colors** (lines 12–14) is a hash that maps a region of our chart (in this case **"background"**, **"dataset0"** and **"dataset1"**) to a color speci-fied by three RGB values. We define these variables here to make the rest of our program easier to update. Method **set** receives as arguments key/value pairs in which the key denotes what we wish to set and the value denotes the new value for that key. For instance, in **"title => "TestChart"** (line 16), **"title"** is the key and **"TestChart"** is the new value. The title of the chart is thus set to **"TestChart"**.

Line 16 changes the title of our chart and the X (horizontal) label. Line 17 changes the Y (vertical) label and alters the placement of the legend, putting it to the left of the image. Line 18 sets the legend labels to the **@labels** array and sets colors to the **%colors** hash. Line 19 sets the **"grey_background"** value to zero. This means that our image will not have a soft-grey background behind it. Each of these lines changes some of the chart's default settings. You can change as many or as few of these values as you wish.

The next part of our program specifies the data to graph. Lines 21–23 create arrays that store values. The **@Xlabels** array holds the horizontal values for our chart. The **@dataset1** and **@dataset2** arrays hold our data. We can specify as many data sets as we want. Once we have created these arrays, we place their references into the **@data** array (line 25). While this step is not absolutely necessary, it does make it easier to modify and maintain the data. Finally, line 27 uses the **Chart::Lines** module's *png* method to convert our **@data** (passed as a reference argument) into a **.png**, which then gets stored with filename **$file** (**fig21_06.png** in this program).

21.5 Introduction to GUI

While modules **GD** and **Chart** can be used to create pretty graphics, it would be difficult to use them to create a full-fledged graphical user interface. For that, Perl offers *Tk*—a GUI *toolkit*. Tk was originally designed to work with the language Tcl, but eventually, Tk was ported to other languages. It can be used with Java, Python and Perl.

To implement Tk in Perl, we use the *Tk* module. This is a complex module that has many subclasses. For simplicity, we will be using only the general **Tk** module, so that we can teach you the basics of creating powerful GUIs.

Why are GUIs such a popular technology? A graphical user interface presents a user-friendly interface to a program. A GUI gives a program a distinctive "look" and "feel." By providing different applications with a consistent set of intuitive user interface components, GUIs allow the user to spend less time trying to remember complex keystroke sequences and more time using the program in a productive manner.

GUIs are built from *GUI components* (sometimes called *controls* or *widgets*—short-hand notation for *window gadgets*). A GUI component is an object with which the user interacts via the mouse or the keyboard. In the remainder of the chapter, we will discuss how to create GUI components (sometimes we will just call them *components*) and use them to put together sophisticated GUI programs.

21.6 Introduction to Tk

Tk is implemented with an *event-handler loop*—a loop in which the program waits for a user interaction (or *event*) to occur. This event could be a mouse click, a keystroke or any of a wide range of other possible events. When an event occurs, the event-handler loop re-ceives the event and invokes a function you specify to handle the event.

In a basic Perl/Tk program, the first step is to create a *main window*. The term *window* refers to a graphical object that appears on the screen and contains GUI components with which the user can interact. A good example of a window is your Web browser's window. The main window is created with the statement

```
$main = new MainWindow();
```

which calls **Tk**'s **MainWindow** constructor to build a new window. After the preceding statement, variable **$main** references a **MainWindow** object. You can also create other main *top-level windows*. A top-level window is a stand-alone window that provides a lot of the same functionality as a main window. The key difference is that when the main window is closed, the program terminates and all other windows in the application close. If a top-level window is closed, it has does not affect the main window; only *child windows* of that top-level window are closed. A child is created by another window, called the *parent window*.

A window is itself a GUI component, but if we do not place other GUI components inside the window, it will not be of much use in the program. Normally, windows contain other GUI components, such as messages to the user (called *labels*), buttons, checkboxes and many other types of GUI components. When we create GUI components, we need to configure them, i.e., specify their type, where they will appear in the window, etc. We will see specific functions for GUI component configuration in the next example. The functions enable us to place GUI components in windows; otherwise, the components will not be displayed.

After we have created a window and GUI components to be displayed in the window, the last step is to start the *main loop* to handle events in the window. The function call

```
MainLoop();
```

opens all of our main windows so the user can interact with them. Function **MainLoop** should be the last statement in your program to ensure that the main window and its GUI components are configured before the window is displayed; otherwise the components may not be displayed properly. Figure 21.7 shows a simple Perl/Tk program. Unlike in the programs presented previously, these images created are not stored in a file so they may be viewed later; they are shown on the screen as the program runs, so the user can interact with them.

```
1   #!/usr/bin/perl
2   # Fig 21.7: fig21_07.pl
3   # A simple Perl/Tk program.
4
5   use warnings;
6   use strict;
7   use Tk;
8
9   my $main = new MainWindow();
10
11  my $label = $main->Label();
12  my $button = $main->Button();
```

Fig. 21.7   Simple Perl/Tk program (part 1 of 2).

```
13
14   $label->configure( -text => 'Look at me!' );
15   $button->configure( -text => 'Exit', -command => \&destroy );
16
17   $label->pack();
18   $button->pack();
19
20   MainLoop();
21
22   sub destroy
23   {
24       $main->destroy();
25   }
```

Fig. 21.7   Simple Perl/Tk program (part 2 of 2).

Figure 21.7 demonstrates the steps for creating a basic windowed application. Line 9 creates the main window. Lines 11 and 12 create a *label component* and a *button component* using the **Label** and **Button** methods, respectively. Then, lines 14 and 15 configure these GUI components appropriately. The label component (**$label**) **-text** attribute's value is set to **'Look at me!'**. This value becomes the text on the label. The button component (**$button**) **-text** attribute's value is set to **'Exit'**. This value becomes the text on the button. Also, the button's **-command** attribute is set to a function reference. This function is used as a *callback*—a function that specifies an action to perform in response to an event. In this case, when the button gets clicked, the callback function in invoked. Lines 17 and 18 then place our GUI components using the **pack** method. This method places the GUI components in appropriate locations in the window. In this case, the default action is that the first component gets placed at the top of the window and the second component just below it. The **pack** method can take arguments that affect the placement of a GUI component, as shown in a later example. Finally, in line 20, we call **MainLoop** to display the window.

There is one function definition (lines 22–25) in this program that comes after the call to function **MainLoop**. This function is the callback function for the button's event. The function can be defined after **MainLoop** gets called because the function definition does not affect the placement of the GUI components. When the user clicks the button, function **destroy** is invoked. Line 24 calls the main window's **destroy** method to close the window and terminate the program.

21.7 Tk: GUI Components

Figure 21.8 demonstrates a Perl/Tk program that explores some more about GUI components. As the program runs, it opens four windows. These windows are shown in the figures following the program (Fig. 21.9, Fig. 21.10, Fig. 21.11 and Fig. 21.12).

```perl
1   #!/usr/bin/perl
2   # Fig 21.8: fig21_08.pl
3   # Perl/Tk program using GUI components.
4
5   use strict;
6   use warnings;
7   use Tk;
8
9   our $main = new MainWindow();
10
11  my @animals =
12     qw( aardvark baboon cheetah dog elephant yak zebu );
13
14  $main->Label( -text => "Select an animal:" )->pack();
15  my $list = $main->Listbox();
16  $list->insert( 'end', @animals );
17  $list->bind( '<Double-1>' => \&choose1 );
18  $list->pack();
19
20  MainLoop();
21
22  sub choose1
23  {
24     my $animal = $list->get( $list->curselection() );
25     my $color;
26     my $window = $main->Toplevel();
27
28     $window->Label( -text => "Select a color:" )->pack();
29     my @colors = qw( grey brown black tan );
30
31     foreach ( @colors ) {
32        $window->Radiobutton( -text => $_,
33           -variable => \$color, -value => $_ )->pack();
34     }
35
36     $window->Button( -text => 'Choose', -command =>
37        [ \&choose2, $animal, \$color, $window ] )->pack();
38  }
39
40  sub choose2
41  {
42     my ( $animal, $color, $parent ) = @_;
43     my $value = 0;
44     $color = $$color;
45     my $window = $parent->Toplevel();
46
47     $window->Scale( '-orient' => 'horizontal',
48        '-from' => 0, '-to' => 100, '-tickinterval' => 20,
49        '-label' =>
50           'Select a size in feet:', '-length' => 200,
51           -showvalue => 1,
52        '-variable' => \$value, )->pack();
53
```

Fig. 21.8   Perl/Tk program using GUI components (part 1 of 2).

```
54      $window->Button( -text => 'Choose',
55          -command =>
56              [ \&choose3, $animal, $color, \$value, $window ], )->
57              pack();
58  }
59
60  sub choose3
61  {
62      my ( $animal, $color, $value, $parent ) = @_;
63      my $window = $parent->Toplevel();
64
65      $window->Label( -text => "Your animal is a $animal." )->
66          pack();
67      $window->Label( -text => "It's color is $color." )->pack();
68      $window->Label( -text =>
69          "It's size is $$value feet tall." )->pack();
70
71      $window->Button( -text => 'Done',
72          -command => \&destroy )->pack();
73  }
74
75  sub destroy
76  {
77      $main->destroy()
78  }
```

Fig. 21.8   Perl/Tk program using GUI components (part 2 of 2).

Lines 11 and 12 define an array of strings that will be placed in a *listbox* GUI component. A listbox displays a list of items from which the user can select. Lines 14–18 create two GUI components—a label and a listbox. Line 14 creates a label component that asks the user to select an animal. Notice that we create and **pack** this component on the same line. If we do not need to reference the component later in the program (which is the case for this label), then we can shorten what was previously a two-line operation into one line. As always, this type of step represents a trade-off between readability and performance. By condensing the operation into one line, we sacrifice some readability, but also eliminate the need to create a variable to reference the GUI component. Line 15 creates a listbox component and line 16 populates it with our **@animals** array—each string in the array is inserted in the listbox. Line 17 uses method *bind* to specify the callback function (**choose1**) for the listbox's *<Double-1>* action, which occurs when the user double clicks an element in the list. Line 18 attaches the listbox to the window and line 20 starts the main loop. This resulting window is shown in Fig. 21.9.

Double clicking one of the animals in the listbox invokes function **choose1** (lines 22–38). A listbox has several different events for which callbacks can be registered with method **bind**. In this example, **Double-1** specifies the primary action—double clicking. Other values we can use to specify the primary action are *Control*, **Shift** and **Lock**, to specify a key that should be pressed when the listbox is clicked; *Double* and *Triple*, to specify the number of clicks; and **Button1**, **Button2**, etc., to specify a particular mouse button to press.

listbox

Fig. 21.9   `Fig21_08.pl`'s main window.

Line 24 uses the *get* and *curselection* methods to store the animal name in variable **$animal**. Method **curselection** returns the currently selected item in the listbox. Method **get** returns the value of that item. Line 26 creates a new top-level window using the function *Toplevel*. Line 28 creates a label that asks the user to choose a color. Lines 31–34 then iterate through the **@colors** array and create a *radiobutton component*, using the method *Radiobutton*, for each color. The **-text** option specifies the name of the radiobutton, **-value** specifies the value of the radiobutton and **-variable** specifies where to store the value when the radiobutton is selected. All of the radiobuttons specify the same variable, so only one radiobutton can be selected at a time. When a new radiobutton is selected, its value replaces the previous contents of **-value**. The last thing we do for this window is create a button that allows the user to choose the color for the animal; to do so, we call function **choose2**, passing it **$animal**, a reference to **$color** and **$window**. Figure 21.10 shows what the second-level window looks like.

Now consider function **choose2** (lines 40–58). First we acquire the arguments that were passed to the function. Then, line 44 does something odd: It takes the reference to the color that we sent to the function and dereferences it. Why did we not just send only the value of the color in the first place? This is a subtle point that is part of the **Tk** module. The problem stems from the fact that we create the radiobutton component before the user has actually selected a radiobutton. We tell the button that when it gets pressed, it is to call the **choose2** function and pass it three arguments (**$animal**, **\$color** and **$window**). But **$color** does not have any value yet; none of the radiobuttons are selected, so **$color** is still equal to **undef**. Because **$color** is a lexical variable, Perl makes it undergo deep binding. This means that our radiobutton component will always send the **choose2** function the value of **$color** when it was originally created—that is **undef**. To prevent this, we are forced to pass a reference to the value and dereference the value later.

Line 45 creates another top-level window (Fig. 21.11) that is a child of the previous top-level window. Lines 47–52 use method *Scale* to create a *scale component* for selecting a value within a given range of values. The scale component has many customizable attributes, including **-orient**, **-from**, **-to**, **-tickinterval**, **-label**, **-length**, **-showvalue** and **-variable**. Attributes **-from** and **-to** declare the range of the scale. Attribute **-tickinterval** determines the distance between ticks on the scale. Attribute **-length** determines the length of the scale on the window. Attribute **-showvalue** tells the component to show its current value. Attribute **-variable** tells the component in which variable it should store its value. Once we have created the scale, we create another button.

When clicked, this button calls function **choose3** (lines 60–73) and passes as arguments **$animal**, **$color**, a reference to the **$value** variable (again, the reference is passed to bypass the normal deep binding encountered in closures) and the current **$window**. This window is shown in Fig. 21.11.

Function **choose3** creates the final window in this example (Fig. 21.12). Line 62 gets the values that were passed to the function, and line 63 creates another top-level window. Lines 65–68 then create three label components, showing each of the user's choices. Finally, lines 71–72 create a button that calls the **destroy** function, which kills the program.

21.8 Tk Case Study: A GUI Application

This section presents an example of a more significant GUI application (Fig 21.13). In this program we develop a calculator using the **Tk** module. It is a simple, four-operation (addition, subtraction, multiplication and division) calculator with a full graphical user interface that was completely implemented with Perl/Tk.

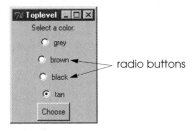

Fig. 21.10 Fig21_08.pl's first top-level window.

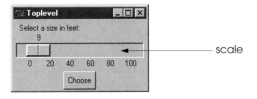

Fig. 21.11 Fig21_08.pl's third window.

Fig. 21.12 Fig21_08.pl's final window.

This program only has one window—the main window created in line 9. Lines 10–49 specify the calculator's GUI components and other variables used by the program.

Line 10 creates the variables **$number1** and **$number2**, which will contain the first and second numbers to be used in the calculator operations. Line 12 creates a label and sets it to the default area in the window, the top. At this point, **$label** is not configured to say anything (and thus cannot be seen yet), but later in the program, this label will show the current number to the user. For instance, if you look at the sample screen captures for this program, the label holds the values **'123'**, **'567'** and **'690'**.

```perl
1   #!/usr/bin/perl
2   # Fig 21.13: fig21_13.pl
3   # GUI Calculator with Tk.
4
5   use strict;
6   use warnings;
7   use Tk;
8
9   my $calculator = new MainWindow();
10  our ( $number1, $number2 );
11  my $oldOperator = '';
12  our $label = $calculator->Label( width => '21' )->pack();
13
14  my @frames;
15
16  for ( 1 .. 3 ) {
17     push( @frames,
18        $calculator->Frame()->pack( -side => 'top' ) );
19  }
20
21  my $frame4 = $calculator->Frame()->pack( -side => 'top' );
22  my $frame5 = $calculator->Frame()->pack( -side => 'top' );
23
24  for ( 1 .. 9 ) {
25     my $frame = $frames[ int( ( $_ - 1 ) / 3 ) ];
26     $frame->Button( text => $_,
27        command => [ \&number, $_ ] )->pack( -side => "left" );
28  }
29
30  $frame4->Button( text => 'Enter',
31     command => [ \&calculate, '=' ] )->pack( -side => "left");
32
33  $frame4->Button( text => '0',
34     command => [ \&number, 0 ] )->pack( -side => "left" );
35
36  $frame4->Button( text => 'Clear',
37     command => [ \&calculate, 'cl' ] )->pack( -side => "left" );
38
39  $frame5->Button( text => '+',
40     command => [ \&calculate, '+' ] )->pack( -side => "left" );
41
```

Fig. 21.13 GUI calculator program (part 1 of 4).

```perl
42   $frame5->Button( text => '-',
43      command => [ \&calculate, '-' ] )->pack( -side => "left" );
44
45   $frame5->Button( text => '*',
46      command => [ \&calculate, '*' ] )->pack( -side => "left" );
47
48   $frame5->Button( text => '/',
49      command => [ \&calculate, '/' ] )->pack( -side => "left" );
50
51   MainLoop();
52
53   sub number
54   {
55      my $digit = shift();
56      $number1 = $number1 ? $number1 . $digit : $digit;
57      $label->configure( text => $number1 );
58
59      if ( $oldOperator eq '=' ) {
60         $number2 = 0;
61      }
62   }
63
64   sub calculate
65   {
66      my $operation = shift();
67
68      if ( $operation eq 'cl' ) {
69         clear();
70         $label->configure( text => $number1 );
71      }
72      elsif ( $operation eq '=' ) {
73
74         if ( $oldOperator ) {
75
76            if ( $oldOperator eq '/' && ( $number1 == 0 ) ) {
77               $label->configure(
78                  text => 'Error: Divide by zero.' );
79               clear();
80            }
81            else {
82
83               if ( $oldOperator eq '+' ) {
84                  $number2 += $number1;
85               }
86               elsif ( $oldOperator eq '-' ) {
87                  $number2 -= $number1;
88               }
89               elsif ( $oldOperator eq '*' ) {
90                  $number2 *= $number1;
91               }
92               elsif ( $oldOperator eq '/' ) {
93                  $number2 /= $number1;
94               }
```

Fig. 21.13 GUI calculator program (part 2 of 4).

```
95
96                    $number1 = 0;
97                    $oldOperator = $operation;
98                    $label->configure( text => $number2 );
99                }
100            }
101        else {
102            $number2 = $number1;
103            $number1 = 0;
104            $oldOperator = $operation;
105        }
106    }
107    elsif ( $oldOperator ) {
108
109        if ( ( $oldOperator eq '/' ) && ( $number1 == 0 ) ) {
110            $label->configure( text => 'Error: Divide by zero' );
111            clear();
112        }
113        else {
114
115            if ( $oldOperator eq '+' ) {
116                $number2 += $number1;
117            }
118            elsif ( $oldOperator eq '-' ) {
119                $number2 -= $number1;
120            }
121            elsif ( $oldOperator eq '*' ) {
122                $number2 *= $number1;
123            }
124            elsif ( $oldOperator eq '/' ) {
125                $number2 /= $number1;
126            }
127            elsif ( $oldOperator eq '=' ) {
128                $number2 = $number1 || $number2;
129            }
130
131            $number1 = 0;
132            $oldOperator = $operation;
133            $label->configure( text => $number2 );
134        }
135    }
136    else {
137        $number2 = $number1;
138        $number1 = 0;
139        $oldOperator = $operation;
140    }
141 }
142
143 sub clear
144 {
145    $number2 = 0;
146    $number1 = 0;
147    $oldOperator = "";
```

Fig. 21.13 GUI calculator program (part 3 of 4).

148 }

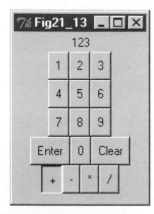 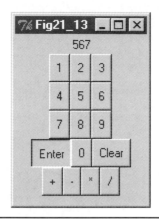 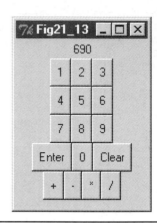

Fig. 21.13 GUI calculator program (part 4 of 4).

The next section of the program introduces a new GUI component—the *frame*. This component is created using method ***Frame*** and enables us to enhance the look and feel of the calculator and to gain more control over the placement of other components. Frames contain other components—what we eventually see is not the frame component itself, but the other components inside it. Notice that in this program we do not specify any arguments to method **Frame**; however, there are many that we can specify, such as the background color (***-background***) and the three-dimensional appearance (***-relief***). Lastly, notice that when we create the frames (lines 18, 21 and 22), we pack them using method **pack**. This step is required to place the components in the window. Although we cannot actually see the frame component itself, it is still a GUI component and therefore must be packed.

Lines 16–22 create the five frames we will be using for this program—one for each row on the calculator. The first frame contains the buttons **1**, **2** and **3**; the second contains the buttons **4**, **5** and **6**; etc. Each frame is **pack**ed toward the top of the window. Because **$label** is already set to be at the top, the first frame ends up directly below the label, the second frame directly below that, and so on.

Lines 24–28 create the buttons to be placed in the first three frames. These buttons are created in order and packed to the left, so that the buttons will be in order from left to right. [*Note:* You can see how **pack** works by changing its arguments. For example, change **'left'** to **'right'** or **'top'** to **'bottom'**, and run the program to see the results.]

All of the buttons in the first three frames (as well as the **0** button in the fourth frame) are set to call the function **number** (lines 53–62) with the value of the number of the button as an argument. This function configures **$label** and resets the second number used in the calculation to 0 if the operation is a new calculation. Line 56 uses the **?:** operator to determine whether or not **$number1** is defined. If it is, the digit entered is appended to the end of **$number1**. This step is for the case when the user enters a number with more than one digit. The last two frames also have three buttons. They all run the function **calculate** with their respective operation as the argument, except for the **'0'** button mentioned previously.

The function **calculate** begins by checking to see if the operation was to clear the calculator (line 68). If it was, we call the function **clear** (lines 143–148) to reset the values. Lines 72–106 handle the case when the operation is **'='** (i.e., when the user clicked the

Enter button). Line 74 determines if **$oldOperator** exists. This variable contains the operator before the **'='** was entered. So, if the user clicked the **3** button, then the **+** button, then the **4** button, then **Enter**, the old operator is **'+'**, because this is the operator that occurred before the **'='**. If **$oldOperator** exists, the calculation is performed (lines 83–94), the variables are reset (lines 96 and 97) and the result is displayed (line 98). If, however, **$oldOperator** does not exist, **$oldOperator** is set to the new operation.

Often when using calculators, people do not click the **Enter** button after only one value. Instead, they perform a series of operations, expecting the values to be calculated as they go. For example, a user might enter the following: **3+4+5+6**, **Enter**. After **3+4+** is entered, **7** should still be calculated and stored, even though the user has not clicked the **Enter** button yet. Lines 107–135 handle this case, performing the calculations as they did in the earlier portions of the program. Lines 136–140 reset variables in the case that **$oldOperator** does not exist.

SUMMARY

- The **GD** module is used to create and manipulate images.
- To define colors in the **GD** module, use method **colorAllocate**.
- To create a filled rectangle, use the **GD** module's **filledRectangle** method.
- To create a circle, use the **GD** module's **arc** method. The first two arguments are the coordinates for the center of the circle. The next two arguments are the horizontal radius and vertical radius. The subsequent arguments provide degree bounds for the sweep of the arc.
- To fill objects with a color, use the **GD** module's **fill** method.
- The **GD** module's **rectangle** method creates a hollow rectangle.
- The **GD** module's **fillToBorder** method is similar to the **fill** method, but it fills until it reaches the color given as the border color.
- To create a polygon, use the **GD** module's **Polygon** class.
- To create points in an instance of class **Polygon**, use method **addPt**.
- Method **polygon** draws a polygon with the specified points (from the **addPt** method) and the specified border color.
- Use **Polygon**'s **setPt** method to change the location of points in a polygon.
- Method **fillPolygon** draws a polygon filled with a color.
- To specify binary mode for a file, use function **binmode**.
- Method **png** converts an image to a **.png** (Portable Network Graphics) file.
- The **GD** constructor **newFromPng** creates an image object from an existing **.png** file.
- The **GD** method **getBounds** returns the width and height of an image.
- **GD**'s **copyResized** method copies an image into a new image and resizes it.
- Perl provides the **Chart** module to create custom charts and graphs. This module is extended by modules **Chart::Lines**, **Chart::Bars** and **Chart::Points**, among others.
- All **Chart** objects are initialized with default attributes that can be changed with method **set**. Method **set** receives as arguments key/value pairs in which the key denotes the attribute to set and the value denotes the new value of that attribute.
- You can create a full-fledged graphical user interfaces with the **Tk** module.
- A graphical user interface presents a user-friendly interface to a program. By providing different applications with a consistent set of intuitive user interface components, GUIs allow the user to

spend less time trying to remember complex keystroke sequences and more time using the program in a productive manner.

- GUIs are built from GUI components (sometimes called controls or widgets). A GUI component is an object with which the user interacts via the mouse or the keyboard.

- An event-handler loop waits for user interactions (events) to occur. When an event occurs, the even-handler loop receives the event and calls an appropriate callback function to handle the event.

- A window contains other GUI components that enable the user to interact with the program.

- A first step in a Perl/Tk program is to create a main window.

- A top-level window is different from a main window in that closing a main window terminates the program and closes all other child windows in the program, while closing a top-level window closes only that window and its children—the main window is not affected.

- A child can be closed without affecting its parent, but when a parent window closes, all of its child windows close as well.

- When we create GUI components, we need to configure them. If we do not configure them, the components will not be displayed.

- After we have created the main window and its GUI, the main event-handler loop can be started with a call to function **MainLoop**. This call should be the last statement in the program, to ensure that all the GUI components are configured properly before the window is displayed.

- **Tk**'s **Label** method creates a label component.

- **Tk**'s **Button** method create a button component.

- A callback is a function that specifies an action to perform in response to an event.

- **Tk**'s **pack** method places a GUI component in an appropriate location in a window. The default is that the first component gets placed at the top, the second component just below it, and so on.

- **Tk**'s **Listbox** method creates a listbox component.

- **Tk**'s **bind** method links callback functions with GUI-component events.

- **Tk**'s **Toplevel** method creates a new top-level window.

- **Tk**'s **Radiobutton** method creates a radiobutton component.

- **Tk**'s **Scale** method creates a scale component. This function has many options with which to customize the features of the component, including the range of the scale, the distance between ticks on the scale and the length of the scale.

- **Tk**'s **Frame** method creates a frame component. This GUI component contains other components and enhances the programmer's control over the layout of the window.

TERMINOLOGY

addPt method in class **Polygon**
arc method in **GD.pm**
-background option for method **Frame**
binary output
bind method in module **Tk**
binmode function
button component
Button method in **Tk.pm**
callback
Chart module
Chart::Bars module

Chart::Lines module
Chart::Points module
children window
colorAllocate method in **GD.pm**
components
Control action
controls
copying and resizing images
copyResized method in **GD.pm**
curselection method in **Tk.pm**
Double action

Double-1 action
Doubling the size of an image
event handler loop
fill method in **GD.pm**
filledRectangle method in **GD.pm**
fillPolygon method in class **Polygon**
fillToBorder method in **GD.pm**
frame component
Frame method in **Tk.pm**
-from option for method **Scale**
full graphical user interface
GD module
get method in **Tk.pm**
getBounds method in **GD.pm**
graphical user interface
GUI
GUI application
GUI components
label component
Label method in **Tk.pm**
-label option for method **Scale**
-length option for method **Scale**
listbox component
main loop
main window
MainLoop method in **Tk.pm**
MainWindow method in **Tk.pm**
newFromPng method in **GD.pm**
-orient option for method **Scale**
pack method in **Tk.pm**

.png file
png method in **GD.pm**
png method in module **Chart::Lines**
Polygon class in **GD.pm**
polygon method in class **Polygon**
radiobutton component
Radiobutton method in module **Tk**
rectangle method in **GD.pm**
-relief option for method **Frame**
scale component
Scale method in **Tk.pm**
set method in **Chart.pm**
setPt method in class **Polygon**
-showvalue option for method **Scale**
Tcl
-text option for method **Radiobutton**
-tickinterval option for method **Scale**
Tk
Tk module
-to option for the **Scale** method
Toolkit
top-level window
Triple action
-value option of method **Radiobutton**
-variable option of method **Radiobutton**
-variable option of method **Scale**
widgets
window
window gadgets

SELF-REVIEW EXERCISES

21.1   Fill in the blanks in each of the following statements:

a) The _____ module allows you to create color images.

b) The _____ color that you allocate becomes the background color for your image.

c) To create a circle in **GD**, use the _____ method.

d) The colors for a chart are passed as a _____ reference and the labels for the chart are passed as an _____ reference.

e) Tk is implemented using an _____ loop.

f) Creating a Tk program involves the creation of _____ and _____.

g) All widgets must be placed in windows to be seen. This is done using the built-in _____ method.

h) The _____ widget provides greater control over Tk's built-in geometry manager.

i) You can specify certain actions, called _____, when events occur.

21.2   Determine whether each of the following statements is *true* or *false*. If *false*, explain why.

a) **GD**'s **fill** and **fillToBorder** methods are identical.

b) You can use the **GD** module to create any geometric image.

c) You should use **Chart**'s **set** function to create the data for the graph.

d) A call to **MainLoop** is required in all Tk applications.

e) **Tk**'s **bind** method will associate a callback with a widget.

f) A parent window closes if any of its child windows close.

g) A **Tk** program can have only one **MainWindow**, but any number of top-level windows.

ANSWERS TO SELF-REVIEW EXERCISES

21.1   a) **GD**. b) first. c) **arc**. d) hash, array. e) event-handler. f) windows, GUI components.
g) **pack**. h) **Frame**. i) callbacks.

21.2   a) False. Function **fill** will fill in the designated area until it reaches a pixel of a different
color. Function **fillToBorder** will fill in the designated area until it reaches a pixel
of the specified color, i.e., the border color of the shape to be filled.

b) True.

c) False. **Chart**'s **set** function is used to change graph data, not create it.

d) True.

e) True.

f) False. When a parent window closes, all of its child windows close, but not vice versa.

g) False. Using Tk we can create many main windows, top-level windows and children windows.

EXERCISES

21.3   Write a program using **GD** that outputs a chess/checkerboard in **.png** format.

21.4   Use the **Chart::Bars** module to create a graph of the functions $y = 3x$ and $y = x^2$.

21.5   Use the **GD** module to create a randomized image. Create 10 totally random colors. Then create a much larger number (around 2000) of triangles and add them to an image using a random color chosen from the 10 that you have created. Output the resulting image to a **.png** file.

21.6   Write a program using the **Tk** module that will create a checkerboard and place one checker on it. Hint: Create a canvas GUI component using the **Canvas** method.

21.7   Create a graphical user interface for the chat program from Chapter 17. Use the **Tk** module.

22

Extensible Markup Language (XML)

Objectives

- To understand what XML is.
- To be able to mark up data using XML.
- To become familiar with the types of markup languages created with XML.
- To understand the relationship between DTDs, Schemas and XML.
- To be able to use the Perl modules for XML document parsing and manipulation.
- To understand the fundamentals of DOM-based parsing.
- To understand the fundamentals of SAX-based parsing.
- To understand the concept of an XML namespace.
- To be able to create simple XSL stylesheets.

Knowing trees, I understand the meaning of patience.
Knowing grass, I can appreciate persistence.
Hal Borland

Like everything metaphysical, the harmony between thought and reality is to be found in the grammar of the language.
Ludwig Wittgenstein

Outline

22.1 Introduction

XML (*Extensible Markup Language*) was developed in 1996 by the *World Wide Web Consortium's (W3C's) XML Working Group* and—like HTML—is related to *Standard Generalized Markup Language (SGML)*. XML is a widely-supported, *open technology* (i.e., nonproprietary technology) for data exchange.

Although XML and HTML are both subsets of SGML, XML provides distinct advantages over HTML. HTML is a markup language for describing how content is rendered.

XML is a markup language for describing structured data—content is separated from presentation. Because an XML document contains only data, applications decide how to display the data. For example, a PDA (personal digital assistant) may render data differently than a cellular phone or desktop computer.

Unlike HTML, XML permits document authors to create their own markup for virtually any type of information. This extensibility enables document authors to create entirely new markup languages to describe specific types of data, including mathematical formulas, chemical molecular structures, music, recipes, etc. Some of the markup languages created with XML include MathML (for mathematics), VoiceXML™ (for speech), SMIL™ (the Synchronous Multimedia Integration Language—for multimedia presentations), CML (for chemistry) and XBRL (Extensible Business Reporting Language—for financial data exchange).

Because XML tags describe the data they contain, it is possible to search, sort, manipulate and render an XML document using related technologies, such as the *Extensible Stylesheet Language (XSL)*—which we discuss later in the chapter.

XML documents are highly portable. Special software is not required to open an XML document—any text editor that supports ASCII/Unicode characters can be used. One important characteristic of XML is that it is both human readable and machine readable.

In order to process an XML document—which typically ends in the **.xml** extension—a software program called an *XML parser* (or an *XML processor*) is required. Most XML parsers are available at no charge and are available for a variety of programming languages (such as Perl, Java™, Python, C, etc.). Parsers check an XML document's syntax and can support the *Document Object Model (DOM)* and/or the *Simple API for XML (SAX)*. DOM-based parsers build a tree structure containing the XML document's data in memory. This allows the data to be programmatically manipulated. SAX-based parsers process the document and generate events when tags, text, comments, etc. are encountered. These events return data from the XML document. Several Independent Software Vendors (ISVs) have developed XML parsers, which can be found at ***www.xml.com/xml/pub/Guide/ XML_Parsers***. In Sections 22.7 and 22.10 we discuss DOM and SAX, respectively.

An XML document can reference an optional *Document Type Definition (DTD)* file, which defines how the XML document is structured. When a DTD is provided, some parsers (called *validating parsers*) are able to read the DTD and check the XML document structure against it. If the XML document conforms to the DTD, then the XML document is valid. Parsers that cannot check for document conformity ignore the DTD and are called *non-validating parsers*. We discuss DTDs in Section 22.5.

If an XML parser is able to successfully process an XML document (that does not have a DTD), the XML document is considered *well formed* (i.e., it is syntactically correct). By definition, a valid XML document is also a well-formed XML document.

In this chapter, we present fundamental XML concepts as well as several Perl XML modules. The chapter concludes with a substantial case study that uses XML and Perl to create a message forum.

22.2 Perl and XML

Because Perl has such powerful text-processing capabilities, it is an ideal language for XML processing. Support for XML is provided through a large collection of XML modules which are freely available. This chapter primarily focuses on the two most mature Perl/

XML modules: **XML::Parser**, and **XML::DOM**. There are many other XML-related modules which we do not cover in this chapter. At the time this chapter was written, a search of CPAN for the keyword **XML** yielded 165 modules.

Portability Tip 22.1

XML is defined by the World Wide Web Consortium (W3C) to be application and vendor neutral—which ensures maximum portability. [Deitel & Associates, Inc. is a W3C member.]

Software Engineering Observation 22.1

Many people in the XML community expect that XML will become the de facto standard for data exchange within a few years.

Software Engineering Observation 22.2

To be usable by an application, an XML document must, as a minimum, be well formed.

22.3 Structuring Data

In this section and throughout this chapter, we will create our own XML markup. With XML, element types can be declared to describe data. This allows programmers an incredible amount of flexibility in using their own tags when describing different types of data. Tags delimit the start and end of each element.

Common Programming Error 22.1

XML is case sensitive. Using the wrong case for an XML tag is a syntax error.

Common Programming Error 22.2

In an XML document, the marked-up data must consist of a start tag and a matching end tag.

Common Programming Error 22.3

Unlike in HTML, attributes must have their value enclosed in double quotes ("") or single quotes (' ').

In Fig. 22.1, we mark up a simple news article using XML tags the same way we would use HTML tags. We begin with the optional *XML declaration* on line 1. Value **version** indicates the XML version to which the document conforms. The current XML standard is version **1.0**. New versions of XML will be released by the World Wide Web Consortium as XML evolves to meet the requirements of many fields, especially e-commerce.

Good Programming Practice 22.1

An XML document should include a XML declaration.

```
1   <?xml version = "1.0"?>
2
3   <!-- Fig. 22.1: article.xml       -->
4   <!-- Article structured with XML -->
5
```

Fig. 22.1 News article formatted with XML (part 1 of 2).

```
6   <article>
7
8       <title>Simple XML</title>
9
10      <date>December 3, 2000</date>
11
12      <author>
13          <FirstName>Tem</FirstName>
14          <LastName>Nieto</LastName>
15      </author>
16
17      <summary>XML is pretty easy.</summary>
18
19      <content>Once you have mastered HTML, XML is easily
20          learned. You must remember that XML is not for
21          displaying information but for managing information.
22      </content>
23
24  </article>
```

Fig. 22.1 News article formatted with XML (part 2 of 2).

Comments (lines 3 and 4) in XML use the same syntax as HTML. Every XML document must contain exactly one element (called a *root element*) that contains every other element. In Fig. 22.1, **article** (line 6) is the root element. Lines preceding the root element are collectively called the *prolog*. XML element and attribute names can be of any length and may contain letters, digits, underscores, hyphens and periods. However, they must begin with either a letter or an underscore.

Common Programming Error 22.4

Using either a space or a tab in an XML element or attribute name is an error.

Good Programming Practice 22.2

XML elements and attributes should be meaningful and human readable. For example, use **<address>** *instead of* **<adr>**.

Common Programming Error 22.5

Attempting to create more than one root element is an error.

Element **title** (line 8) contains text that describes the article's title. Similarly, **date** (line 10), **summary** (line 17) and **content** (line 19) each contain text that describes the date, summary and content, respectively.

Any element (such as **article** and **author**) that contains other elements is called a *container element*. Elements inside a container element are collectively called *children*.

XML is a technology for structuring data. Unlike HTML, an XML document does not contain any formatting information. For example, when an XML document is loaded into Internet Explorer 5 (IE5), it is parsed by IE5's parser msxml and displayed. Figure 22.2 shows **article.xml** (Fig. 22.1) displayed in IE5. Notice that what is displayed by IE5 is virtually identical to Fig. 22.1—because, again, an XML document does not contain formatting information. We will discuss how the data in an XML document can be formatted later in the chapter when we study the Extensible Stylesheet Language (XSL).

Common Programming Error 22.6

Overlapping XML tags is a syntax error. For example, **`<x><y>hello</x><y>`** *is illegal.*

Notice the minus sign (-) and plus sign (+) in Fig. 22.2. These are not part of the XML document, but are placed there by IE5 next to all container elements. A minus sign indicates that all child elements are being displayed. When clicked, a minus sign becomes a plus sign (which collapses the container element and hides all children) and vice versa. This behavior is similar to viewing the directory structure of your machine using Windows Explorer (or other similar programs such as File Manager, etc.). In fact, a directory structure is often modelled as a series of tree structures with each drive letter (e.g., **C:**, etc.) representing the *root* of a tree. Each folder (that contains at least one folder inside it) is a *node* in the tree. XML documents (when they are parsed by a DOM-based XML parser) have their data placed into a tree structure. [*Note:* an XML parser is a piece of software that processes an XML document.]

Now that we have seen a simple XML document, let us examine a slightly more complex XML document that marks up a business letter (Fig. 22.3).

As with the previous example, we begin the document's definition with the XML declaration on line 1. This explicitly states the XML version to which the document conforms.
Line 6

```
<!DOCTYPE letter SYSTEM "letter.dtd">
```

specifies that this XML document has a *document type definition (DTD)* file associated with it. DTD files define the grammatical rules for an XML document and are optional. E-commerce applications frequently use DTDs to ensure that XML documents are structured properly. This markup contains three items: the name of the root element (**letter**) to which the DTD is applied, the keyword **SYSTEM** (which in this case denotes an *external DTD*—a DTD declared in a separate file), and the DTD's name and location (i.e., **letter.dtd** in the current directory). DTD documents typically end with the **.dtd** extension. We discuss DTD files and **letter.dtd** in detail in Section 22.5.

The output of Fig. 22.3 shows the results of validating the document using Microsoft's *XML Validator*. Various tools (many of which are free) exist that check a document's conformity against DTDs and Schema (discussed momentarily). Visit **www.w3.org/XML/ Schema** for a list of validating tools. Microsoft XML Validator is available free of charge from

```
msdn.microsoft.com/downloads/samples/Internet/xml/
xml_validator/sample.asp
```

Root element **letter** contains the child elements **contact**, **salutation**, **paragraph**, **closing** and **signature**. The first **contact** element (line 10) has attribute **type** which is assigned the value **from** (which identifies the letter's sender). The second **contact** element (line 21) has attribute **type** which is assigned value **to** (which identifies the letter's recipient). In a **contact** element, the contact's name, address and phone number are stored. Element **salutation** (line 32) marks up the letter's salutation.

The letter's body is marked up with a **paragraph** element. Elements **closing** (line 39) and **signature** (line 40) mark up the closing sentence and the signature of the letter's author, respectively.

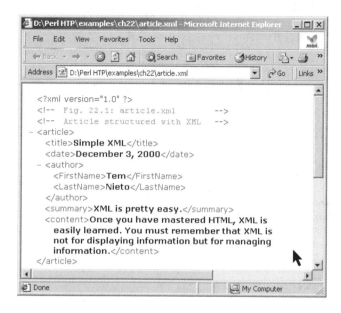

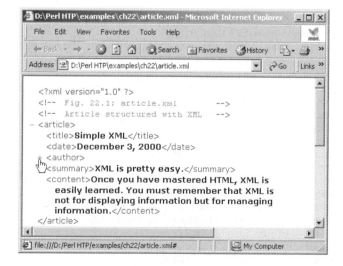

Fig. 22.2 IE5 displaying **article.xml**.

Notice that on line 18, we introduce *empty element* **flag**—which does not mark up any text. Empty element **flag** indicates the gender of the contact. This allows us to correctly address the recipient as Mr. (if **gender** is "**M**") or Ms. (if **gender** is "**F**"). Empty elements must be closed, either by placing a slash at the end of the element (as shown on line 18) or by explicitly writing a closing tag as in

```
<flag gender = "F"></flag>
```

```
 1   <?xml version = "1.0"?>
 2
 3   <!-- Fig. 22.3: letter.xml             -->
 4   <!-- Business letter formatted with XML  -->
 5
 6   <!DOCTYPE letter SYSTEM "letter.dtd">
 7
 8   <letter>
 9
10      <contact type = "from">
11         <name>John Doe</name>
12         <address1>123 Main St.</address1>
13         <address2></address2>
14         <city>Anytown</city>
15         <state>Anystate</state>
16         <zip>12345</zip>
17         <phone>555-1234</phone>
18         <flag gender = "M"/>
19      </contact>
20
21      <contact type = "to">
22         <name>Joe Schmoe</name>
23         <address1>Box 12345</address1>
24         <address2>15 Any Ave.</address2>
25         <city>Othertown</city>
26         <state>Otherstate</state>
27         <zip>67890</zip>
28         <phone>555-4321</phone>
29         <flag gender = "M"/>
30      </contact>
31
32      <salutation>Dear Sir:</salutation>
33
34      <paragraph>It is our privilege to inform you about our new
35         database managed with XML. This new system allows
36         you to reduce the load of your inventory list server by
37         having the client machine perform the work of sorting
38         and filtering the data.</paragraph>
39      <closing>Sincerely</closing>
40      <signature>Mr. Doe</signature>
41
42   </letter>
```

Fig. 22.3   A business letter marked up as XML (part 1 of 2).

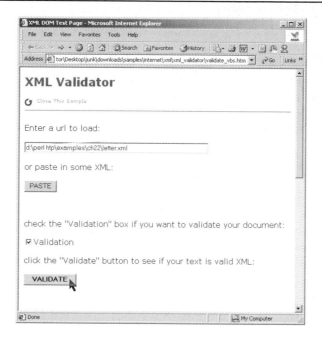

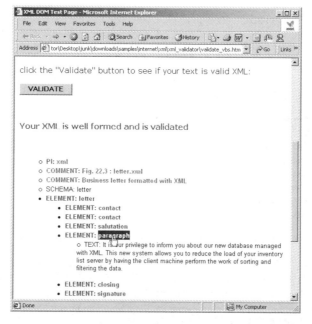

Fig. 22.3   A business letter marked up as XML (part 2 of 2).

Common Programming Error 22.7

Not terminating an empty element with a closing tag or a forward slash (/) is an error.

22.4 XML Namespaces

Because XML allows document authors to create their own tags, *naming collisions* (i.e., two different elements that have the same name) can occur. For example, we may use the element **book** to mark up data about one of our publications. A stamp collector may also create an element **book** to mark up data about a book of stamps. If both of these elements were used in the same document there would be a naming collision and it would be difficult to determine which kind of data each element contained.

Namespaces provide a means for document authors to prevent collisions. For example,

```
<subject>Math</subject>
```

and

```
<subject>Thrombosis</subject>
```

use a **subject** element to mark up a piece of data. However, in the first case the subject is something one studies in school, whereas in the second case the subject is in the field of medicine. These two **subject** elements can be differentiated using namespaces. For example

```
<school:subject>Math</school:subject>
```

and

```
<medical:subject>Thrombosis</medical:subject>
```

Both **school** and **medical** are *namespace prefixes*. Namespace prefixes are prepended to element and attribute names in order to specify the namespace in which the element or attribute can be found. Each namespace prefix is tied to a *uniform resource identifier (URI)* that uniquely identifies the namespace. Document authors can create their own namespace prefixes as shown in Fig. 22.4 (lines 6 and 7). Virtually any name may be used for a namespace, except the reserved namespace *xml*.

Figure 22.4 demonstrates how to create namespaces. In this document, two distinct **file** elements are differentiated using namespaces.

Lines 6 and 7

```
<directory xmlns:text = "urn:deitel:textInfo"
           xmlns:image = "urn:deitel:imageInfo">
```

use the XML namespace keyword *xmlns* to create two namespace prefixes: **text** and **image**. The values assigned to attributes **xmlns:text** and **xmlns:image** are called *Uniform Resource Identifiers (URIs)*. By definition, a URI is a series of characters used to differentiate names.

```
1   <?xml version = "1.0"?>
2
3   <!-- Fig. 22.4 : namespace.xml -->
4   <!-- Namespaces                 -->
5
```

Fig. 22.4   Listing for **namespace.xml** (part 1 of 2).

```
 6   <directory xmlns:text = "urn:deitel:textInfo"
 7                xmlns:image = "urn:deitel:imageInfo">
 8
 9      <text:file filename = "book.xml">
10         <text:description>A book list</text:description>
11      </text:file>
12
13      <image:file filename = "funny.jpg">
14         <image:description>A funny picture</image:description>
15         <image:size width = "200" height = "100"/>
16      </image:file>
17
18   </directory>
```

Fig. 22.4   Listing for **namespace.xml** (part 2 of 2).

In order to ensure that a namespace is unique, the document author must provide a unique URI. Here, we use the text **urn:deitel:textInfo** and **urn:deitel:imageInfo** as URIs. A common practice is to use *Universal Resource Locators (URLs)* for URIs, because the domain names (e.g., **deitel.com**) used in URLs are guaranteed to be unique. For example, lines 6 and 7 could have been written as

```
<directory xmlns:text = "http://www.deitel.com/xmlns-text"
            xmlns:image = "http://www.deitel.com/xmlns-image">
```

where we use URLs related to the Deitel & Associates, Inc. domain name (**www.deitel.com**). These URLs are never visited by the parser—they only represent a series of characters for differentiating names and nothing more. The URLs need not even exist or be properly formed.

Lines 9–11

```
<text:file filename = "book.xml">
   <text:description>A book list</text:description>
</text:file>
```

use the namespace prefix **text** to describe elements **file** and **description**. Notice that end tags have the namespace prefix **text** applied to them as well. Lines 13–16 apply namespace prefix **image** to elements **file**, **description** and **size**.

In order to eliminate the need to place a namespace prefix in each element, authors may specify a *default namespace* for an element and all of its child elements. Fig. 22.5 demonstrates using default namespaces.

We declare a default namespace using the **xmlns** attribute with a URI as its value (line 6). Once this default namespace is in place, child elements that are part of this namespace do not need a namespace prefix. Element **file** (line 9) is in the namespace corresponding to the URI **urn:deitel:textInfo**. Compare this to Fig. 22.4, where we prefixed the **file** and **description** elements with the namespace prefix **text** (lines 9–11).

The default namespace applies to all elements contained in the **directory** element. However, we may use a namespace prefix in order to specify a different namespace for particular elements. For example, the **file** element on line 13 uses the prefix **image** to indicate it is in the namespace corresponding to the URI **urn:deitel:imageInfo**.

```
1   <?xml version = "1.0"?>
2
3   <!-- Fig. 22.5 : defaultnamespace.xml -->
4   <!-- Using Default Namespaces          -->
5
6   <directory xmlns = "urn:deitel:textInfo"
7               xmlns:image = "urn:deitel:imageInfo">
8
9       <file filename = "book.xml">
10          <description>A book list</description>
11      </file>
12
13      <image:file filename = "funny.jpg">
14          <image:description>A funny picture</image:description>
15          <image:size width = "200" height = "100"/>
16      </image:file>
17
18  </directory>
```

Fig. 22.5   Using default namespaces.

22.5 Document Type Definitions (DTD) and Schema

In this section, we discuss two types of documents—Document Type Definitions and Schema—used to describe an XML document's structure.

Software Engineering Observation 22.3

Because XML document content can be structured many different ways, an application cannot tell if the document data it receives is complete, missing data or ordered properly. DTDs and Schema solve this problem by providing an extensible means of describing a document's contents. An application can use a DTD or schema document to perform a validity check on the document's contents.

22.5.1 Document Type Definitions

In Fig. 22.3, we presented a simple business letter marked up with XML. The business letter's list of element types, attributes and their relationships to each other are specified using a document type definition (*DTD*). Although a DTD is optional, it is recommended for document conformity. DTDs provide a method for type checking an XML document, thus verifying its *validity* (e.g., tags contain the proper attributes, elements are in proper sequence, etc.). The set of rules that structure a document is done with *EBNF* (*Extended Backus-Naur Form*) *grammar*—not XML syntax. XML parsers need additional functionality to read a DTD because of the EBNF grammar. We define, in Fig. 22.6, the set of rules (i.e., the grammar) for structuring the business letter document of Fig. 22.3. This DTD file is the one referenced on line 6 of Fig. 22.3.

```
1   <!-- Fig. 22.4: letter.dtd        -->
2   <!-- DTD document for letter.xml   -->
3
```

Fig. 22.6   Business letter DTD (part 1 of 2).

```
4    <!ELEMENT letter (contact+, salutation, paragraph+,
5                      closing, signature )>
6
7    <!ELEMENT contact (name, address1, address2, city, state,
8                       zip, phone, flag)>
9    <!ATTLIST contact type CDATA #IMPLIED>
10
11   <!ELEMENT name (#PCDATA)>
12   <!ELEMENT address1 (#PCDATA)>
13   <!ELEMENT address2 (#PCDATA)>
14   <!ELEMENT city (#PCDATA)>
15   <!ELEMENT state (#PCDATA)>
16   <!ELEMENT zip (#PCDATA)>
17   <!ELEMENT phone (#PCDATA)>
18   <!ELEMENT flag EMPTY>
19   <!ATTLIST flag gender (M | F) "M">
20
21   <!ELEMENT salutation (#PCDATA)>
22   <!ELEMENT closing (#PCDATA)>
23   <!ELEMENT paragraph (#PCDATA)>
24   <!ELEMENT signature (#PCDATA)>
```

Fig. 22.6   Business letter DTD (part 2 of 2).

Line 4's ***ELEMENT*** *element type declaration* defines the rules for element **letter**. In this case, **letter** contains one or more **contact** elements, one **salutation** element, one or more **paragraph** elements, one **closing** element and one **signature** element, in that sequence. The *plus sign* (**+**) *occurrence indicator* indicates one or more occurrences for an element. Other operators include the *asterisk* (*****), which indicates any number of occurrences and the *question mark* (**?**), which indicates either zero occurrences or exactly one occurrence. If an occurrence indicator is omitted, exactly one occurrence is assumed.

The **contact** element definition (line 7) specifies that it contains the **name**, **address1**, **address2**, **city**, **state**, **zip**, **phone** and **flag** elements—in that order. Exactly one occurrence of each is expected.

Line 9

```
<!ATTLIST contact type CDATA #IMPLIED>
```

uses the **!ATTLIST** *element* type declaration to define an attribute (i.e., **type**) for the **contact** element. Keyword ***#IMPLIED*** specifies that if the parser finds a **contact** element without a **type** attribute, it is allowed to choose its own value or ignore it. So the XML document is still valid if a **contact** element does not have a **type** attribute. Other types of default values include ***#REQUIRED*** and ***#FIXED***. Keyword ***#REQUIRED*** specifies that the attribute must be declared in the document, and the keyword ***#FIXED*** specifies that the attribute must be declared with the given fixed value. If it is not declared, then the parser, by default, uses the fixed value that is specified with the declaration. For example,

```
<!ATTLIST address zip #FIXED "02115">
```

indicates that the value **02115** is always used for attribute **zip**. Flag **CDATA** specifies that **type** attribute contains a string that will not be processed by the parser and is passed to the application as is.

Software Engineering Observation 22.4

DTD syntax does not provide any mechanism for describing an element's (or attribute's) data type.

Flag **#PCDATA** (line 11) specifies that the element can store *parsed character data* (i.e., text). Parsable character data should not contain markup. The characters less than (**<**), greater than (**>**) and ampersand (**&**) should be replaced by their entities (i.e., **<**, **>** and **&**). However, the ampersand character can be inserted when used with entities.
    Line 18

```
<!ELEMENT flag EMPTY>
```

creates an empty element named **flag**. Keyword **EMPTY** specifies that the element does not contain any text. Empty elements are commonly used for their attributes.

Portability Tip 22.2

DTDs ensure that XML documents generated by different programs are consistent.

Common Programming Error 22.8

Any element, attribute, tag or relationship not explicitly defined by a DTD is an error.

22.5.2 W3C XML Schema

In this section, we introduce an alternative to DTDs—called *schemas*—for validating XML documents. Many developers in the XML community feel DTDs are not flexible enough to meet today's programming needs. For example, DTDs cannot be manipulated (e.g., searched, transformed into different representation such as HTML, etc.) in the same manner as XML documents can because DTDs are not XML documents. DTDs are inherited from SGML—which limits much of what can be done with them. These types of limitations have led to the development of schema.

    Unlike DTDs, schema do not use the Extended Backus-Naur Form (EBNF) grammar. Instead, schema use XML syntax. Because schema are XML documents, they can be manipulated (e.g., elements added, elements removed, etc.) like any other XML document. We will discuss how to manipulate XML documents programmatically, shortly.

    Like DTDs, schemas must be used with validating parsers. In the near future, schemas are expected to replace DTDs as the primary means of describing document structure.

    Two major schema models exist: *W3C XML Schema* and *Microsoft XML Schema*. In this section, we focus on W3C XML Schema. [*Note*: New schema models (e.g., *RELAX*—**www.xml.gr.jp/relax**) are beginning to emerge.]

    The W3C XML Schema is a *Candidate Recommendation* (i.e., the last step in the recommendation process) at the time of this writing. For the latest specification of W3C XML Schema, visit **www.w3.org/XML/Schema**. [*Note*: Because W3C XML Schema was only a Candidate Recommendation at the time of this writing, the syntax presented here is subject to change.]

Software Engineering Observation 22.5

DTDs are inherited from SGML and are gradually being replaced by schema.

Software Engineering Observation 22.6

Schema documents use XML syntax and are therefore XML documents.

Software Engineering Observation 22.7

Schemas are XML documents that conform to DTDs, which define the structure of a schema. These DTDs are bundled with the parser and are used to validate the schemas that authors create.

Software Engineering Observation 22.8

Many organizations and individuals are creating DTDs and schemas for a broad range of categories (e.g., financial transactions, medical prescriptions, etc.). These collections— called repositories—*are often available free for download from the Web (e.g.,* **www.dtd.com**).

A DTD describes an XML document's structure—not its element content. For example,

    `<quantity>5</quantity>`

contains character data. Element **quantity** can be validated to confirm that it does indeed contain content (e.g., **PCDATA**), but its content cannot be validated to confirm that it is numeric; DTDs do not provide such a capability. So, unfortunately, markup such as

    `<quantity>hello</quantity>`

is also considered valid. The application using the XML document containing this markup would need to test if **quantity** is numeric and take appropriate action if it is not.

With XML Schema, element **quantity**'s data can indeed be described as numeric. When the preceding markup examples are validated against an XML Schema that specifies element **quantity**'s data must be numeric, **5** conforms and **hello** fails. An XML document that conforms to a schema document is *schema valid* and a document that does not conform is invalid.

Software Engineering Observation 22.9

Because schema are XML documents that conform to DTDs, they must be valid.

Figure 22.7 shows a W3C XML Schema (i.e., **xml-schema.xsd**). Although virtually any filename extension may be used, W3C XML Schema commonly use the **.xsd** extension.

W3C XML Schema use the URI **http://www.w3.org/2000/10/XMLSchema** and *namespace prefix* **xsd**. Root element **schema** contains the document definitions.

In W3C XML Schema, element **element** (line 7) defines elements. Attributes **name** and **type** specify the **element**'s name and data type, respectively. Attribute **ref** (line 12) references the existing element definition for **message**. This indicates that **greeting** can have element **message** as a child element.

```
1    <?xml version = "1.0"?>
2
3    <!-- Fig. 22.7 : xml-schema.xsd   -->
4    <!-- Example W3C XML Schema        -->
5
6    <xsd:schema xmlns:xsd = "http://www.w3.org/2000/10/XMLSchema">
7       <xsd:element name = "message" type = "xsd:string"/>
8
9       <xsd:element name = "greeting" type = "greetingType"/>
10
11      <xsd:complexType name = "greetingType" content = "mixed">
12         <xsd:element ref = "message"/>
13      </xsd:complexType>
14
15      <xsd:element name = "myMessage" type = "myMessageType"/>
16
17      <xsd:complexType name = "myMessageType">
18         <xsd:element ref = "greeting" minOccurs = "0"
19            maxOccurs = "1"/>
20         <xsd:element ref = "message" minOccurs = "1"
21            maxOccurs = "unbounded"/>
22      </xsd:complexType>
23   </xsd:schema>
```

Fig. 22.7   W3C XML Schema document.

When an element has a type such as **string**, it is prohibited from containing attributes and child elements. Any element (e.g., **greeting** in line 9) that contains attributes or child elements, must define a type—called a *complex type*—that defines each attribute and child element. Lines 11–13 use element **complexType** to define an element type that has **mixed content** (i.e., the combination of character data and markup). The **element** named **greeting** (line 9) specifies the **name** of this **complexType** in its **type** attribute to indicate element **greeting** contains mixed content.

Lines 17–22 use element **complexType** to create an element that contains an optional **greeting** element followed by one or more **message** elements. Attribute **maxOccurs** with the value **unbounded** (line 21) indicates that there is no limit on the maximum number of **message** elements contained in a **myMessage** element.

Figure 22.8 shows an XML document that conforms to Fig. 22.7's schema. We use Icon Information-Systems' XML development environment (*XML Spy 3.0*) for validation.

```
1    <?xml version = "1.0"?>
2
3    <!-- Fig. 22.8 : intro3.xml          -->
4    <!-- Introduction to W3C XML Schema  -->
5
6    <myMessage
7       xmlns:xsd   = "http://www.w3.org/2000/10/XMLSchema-instance"
8       xsd:noNamespaceSchemaLocation = "xml-schema.xsd">
9
```

Fig. 22.8   Document that conforms to **xml-schema.xsd** (part 1 of 2).

```
10      <greeting>Welcome to W3C XML Schema!</greeting>
11      <message>This is a message.</message>
12      <message>This is another message.</message>
13
14    </myMessage>
```

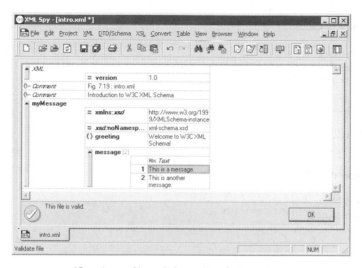

(Courtesy of Icon Information Systems.)

Fig. 22.8   Document that conforms to **xml-schema.xsd** (part 2 of 2).

A 30-day trial version of XML Spy 3.0 is available at no charge from **www.xmlspy.com/download.html**.

Software Engineering Observation 22.10

Independent Software Venders (ISVs) such as Oracle, Apache Foundation Organization, etc. are beginning to provide parsers that support W3C XML Schema.

Good Programming Practice 22.3

*By convention, W3C XML Schema authors use namespace prefix **xsd** when referring to the URI **http://www.w3.org/2000/10/XMLSchema***

22.6 Customized Markup Languages

XML allows authors to create their own tags to precisely describe data. Consequently, many different kinds of XML have been created for structuring data in various fields. Some of these markup languages are: *MathML (Mathematical Markup Language), Scalable Vector Graphics (SVG), Wireless Markup Language (WML), Extensible Business Reporting Language (XBRL), Extensible User Interface Language (XUL)* and *Product Data Markup Language (PDML).* The following subsections describe MathML, XBRL and other custom markup languages.

22.6.1 MathML

Until recently, mathematical expressions have typically been displayed using images or specialized software packages such as TeX and LaTeX. This section introduces MathML, which was developed by the W3C for describing mathematical notations and expressions. One application that can parse and render MathML is the W3C's *Amaya*™ browser, which can be downloaded at no charge from

www.w3.org/Amaya/User/BinDist.html

This Web page contains several download links for Windows 95/98/NT, Linux® and Solaris™. Amaya documentation and installation notes are also available at the W3C Web site. Amaya is also an HTML/XML editor.

We now take a calculus expression and mark it up as MathML. Figure 22.9 marks up the expression which contains an integral symbol and a square-root symbol. We embed the MathML content directly into an HTML file by using the HTML **MATH** *element* (line 9).

```
1   <!DOCTYPE HTML PUBLIC "-//W3C//DTD HTML 4.0 Transitional//EN">
2   <html>
3
4   <!-- Fig. 22.9 mathml.html        -->
5   <!-- Calculus example using MathML -->
6
7   <body>
8
9   <MATH>
10     <mrow>
11        <msubsup>
12           <mo>&Integral;</mo>
13           <mn>0</mn>
14           <mrow>
15              <mn>1</mn>
16              <mo>-</mo>
17              <mi>y</mi>
18           </mrow>
19        </msubsup>
20
21        <msqrt>
22           <mrow>
23              <mn>4</mn>
24              <mo>&InvisibleTimes;</mo>
25              <msup>
26                 <mi>x</mi>
27                 <mn>2</mn>
28              </msup>
29              <mo>+</mo>
30              <mi>y</mi>
31           </mrow>
32        </msqrt>
33
34        <mo>&delta;</mo>
```

Fig. 22.9 A calculus expression marked up with MathML (part 1 of 2).

```
35              <mi>x</mi>
36          </mrow>
37      </MATH>
38      </body>
39      </html>
```

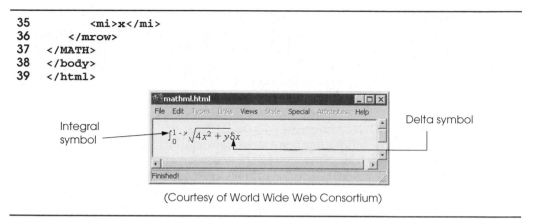

Integral symbol   Delta symbol

(Courtesy of World Wide Web Consortium)

Fig. 22.9   A calculus expression marked up with MathML (part 2 of 2).

Element **mrow** (line 10) is a container element. It allows the document's author to properly group together related elements. In this case we use **mrow** to group our calculus expression.

The integral symbol is represented by the entity **∫** (line 12), while the superscript and subscript markup is specified using **msubsup** (line 11). We use tag **<mo>** to mark up the integral operator. Element **msubsup** requires three child elements: The expression (e.g., the integral entity) to which the subscript and superscript are applied (line 12), the subscript expression (line 13) and the superscript expression (lines 14–18), respectively. Element **msqrt** represents a square root expression. We use element **mrow** (line 22) to group the expression contained in the square root.

Element **mn** (line 13) marks up the number (i.e., 0) that represents the subscript. Element **mrow** marks up the expression (i.e., **1-y**) that specifies the superscript expression used by **msubsup**. To mark up variables in MathML, element **mi** (line 17) is used. Collectively, the three child elements within **mrow** define the expression **1-y**.

Line 24 uses entity **⁢** to specify a multiplication operation without a *symbolic representation* (i.e., a multiplication symbol is not displayed between the **4** and the **x²**). Element **msup** (line 25) marks up an expression containing a base and an exponent. This element contains two child elements: The base and the exponent (i.e., the superscript). Because each argument contains exactly one element, additional **mrow** elements are not needed. Although not used in this example, MathML does provide element **msub** for marking up an expression that contains a subscript.

Line 34 introduces the entity **δ** for representing a delta symbol. Because it is an operator, it is marked up using element **mo**. To see other operations and symbols provided by MathML, visit **www.w3.org/Math**.

22.6.2 WML

The *Wireless Markup Language* (*WML*) is an XML-based language that allows text portions of Web pages to be displayed on wireless devices, such as cellular phones and personal digital assistants (PDA). WML works with the *Wireless Application Protocol* (*WAP*) to deliver this content. WML is similar to HTML but does not require input devices such as a keyboard or mouse for navigation.

Consider a PDA that requests a Web page on the Internet. A WAP gateway receives the request, translates it, and sends it to the appropriate Internet server. The server responds by sending the requested WML document. The WAP gateway parses this document's WML and sends the proper text to the PDA. For additional information on WML and WAP, visit `www.wapforum.org` or `www.xml.com/pub/Guide/WML`.

22.6.3 XBRL

XBRL (Extensible Business Reporting Language)—previously called *XFRML*—is a markup language derived from XML for facilitating the creation, exchange and validation of financial information (e.g., annual budgets, dividends, etc.) between vendors and corporations. XBRL was developed by the *American Institute of Certified Public Accountants (AICPA)* and other organizations. It conforms to the general principles of US *GAAP (General American Accounting Principles)* and complies to standards set by various committees such as *IASC (International Association for Statistical Computing)*. It sets no new standards in financial reporting; instead, it improves their usage and the efficiency of accessing information. XBRL is designed to be compatible with future changes in financial reporting standards.

22.6.4 ebXML

Electronic Business XML (ebXML) is a markup language initiated by the *United Nations body for Trade Facilitation and Electronic Business (UN/CEFACT)* and *OASIS (Organization for the Advancement of Structured Information Standards)* to develop and standardize an XML document structure for exchanging business data. The goal of ebXML is to reduce the cost of electronic trading for small to medium sized businesses. Visit `www.ebxml.org` for more information.

22.6.5 FpML

Financial Products Markup Language (FpML) is an emerging standard for exchanging financial information over the Internet. Information exchanged includes interest rate swaps (a contractual agreement between two parties), forward rate agreements, etc. It is an easy-to-use and license-free protocol developed by a group of corporate bodies which includes banks, software companies and other financial institutions. The main advantage of adopting FpML is for platform independent data exchange. Visit `www.fpml.org` for more details.

22.6.6 Other Markup Languages

Literally hundreds of markup languages are derived from XML. Everyday developers are finding new uses for XML. In Fig. 22.10, we summarize some of these markup languages.

22.7 Document Object Model (DOM)

Although an XML document is a text file, retrieving data from the document using traditional sequential file access techniques is neither practical nor efficient, especially for documents where data needs to be dynamically added or deleted.

As mentioned earlier, when an XML document is successfully parsed, a tree structure containing the document's data is stored in memory. Figure 22.11 shows the tree structure for the document **article.xml** discussed in Fig. 22.1. This hierarchal tree structure is called a *Document Object Model (DOM)*. Each name (e.g., **article**, **date**, **first-Name**, etc.) is called a *node*. A node such as **author** that contains other nodes (called *child nodes*) is called a *parent node*. Nodes that are peers (e.g., **firstName** and **lastName**) are called *sibling nodes*. Child nodes of a given node are called *descendent nodes* and parent nodes of a given node are called *ancestor nodes*.

Markup Language	Description
Chemical Markup Language (CML)	CML was developed by Peter Murray-Rust. It is used by chemists to interchange descriptions of molecules, formulas and other chemical data. CML documents can be parsed and rendered by the Jumbo browser. Visit the CML home page at **www.xml-cml.org**.
VoiceXML™	VoiceXML was developed by the VoiceXML forum founded by AT&T, IBM, Lucent and Motorola. It provides interactive voice communication between humans and computers through a telephone, PDA (Personal Digital Assistant) or desktop computer. VoiceXML documents can be parsed using the VoiceXML SDK developed by IBM. Visit **www.voicexml.org** for more information on VoiceXML.
Synchronous Multimedia Integration Language (SMIL™)	SMIL is used for multimedia presentations. It was primarily developed by the W3C with contributions from other companies. Visit **www.w3.org/AudioVideo** for more on SMIL.
Vector Markup Language (VML)	VML marks up graphics information. It was developed by Microsoft, Hewlett-Packard and other companies. For more information on VML, visit **www.w3.org/TR/NOTE-VML**.
Product Data Markup Language (PDML)	PDML is a markup language developed for product data interchange among businesses and government agencies. For more information on PDML, visit **www.pdml.org**.
Commerce XML (cXML)	cXML is a markup language that provides a protocol for business transactions on the Internet. For more information on cXML, visit **www.cxml.org/home**.
XMI (XML Metadata Interchange)	XMI is used for metadata interchange between modelling applications/tools that are based on UML™ (Unified Modelling Language) and metadata repositories like MOF (Meta Object Facility). XMI is a specification submitted to the OMG™ (Object Management Group) by IBM, Oracle, Unisys and others. Visit **www.omg.org** for more information.
Trading Partner Agreement Markup Language (tpaML)	tpaML is an XML-based markup language developed by IBM that defines an electronic trading partner agreement (TPA) document. A TPA contains information about the organizations involved in the contract, the business protocols (e.g., cXML), etc. For more information on tpaML, visit **www-4.ibm.com/software/developer/library/tpaml.html**.

Fig. 22.10 Various markup languages derived from XML (part 1 of 2).

Markup Language	Description
Small to Medium Business XML (SMBXML)	SMBXML was developed for small to medium sized business transactions. For more information on SMBXML, visit **www.smbxml.org**.
Financial XML (FinXML)	FinXML is an XML based framework developed by the Financial consortium that provides a standard format for exchanging financial data between financial institutions. For more information on FinXML, visit **www.finxml.org**.
Financial Information Exchange Markup Language (FixML)	FixML was developed by a consortium of over 20 financial firms and is a standard for data exchange between financial institutions. For more information on FixML visit **www.fixprotocol.org**.

Fig. 22.10 Various markup languages derived from XML (part 2 of 2).

The DOM has a single *root node* that contains all other nodes in the document. Each node is an object that has properties, methods and events. Properties associated with a node can be used to fetch its name, value, child nodes, etc. Methods allow us to create, delete and append nodes, load XML documents, etc. Events are fired when an XML document finishes loading, a node property changes, etc. These properties, methods and events are exposed by the XML parser as a programmatic library—called an *Application Programming Interface (API)*.

22.8 XML::DOM

The **XML::DOM** module provides an interface to manipulating XML documents in accordance with the Document Object Model approved by the W3C. The **XML::DOM** currently implements the W3C's Level 1 DOM Recommendation (i.e., the Recommendation that specifies the standard interfaces for manipulating HTML and XML documents) and is currently being updated to conform to the Level 2 Recommendation (i.e., the Recommendation that extends the Level 1 Recommendation by providing additional XML interfaces). Module **XML::DOM** also provides a number of extensions to the DOM. We will mention some of these extensions momentarily.

The **XML::DOM** parser creates a tree-like structure for the XML document, with objects for the nodes instead of array references. All of these objects inherit from one of three main classes. The first, the **Node** class, represents an actual XML element, node, comment, etc. in the document and has the properties for an **XMLDOMNode** (i.e., a node object that encapsulates an element, attribute, comment, etc.). The second, a **NodeList**, is like an array of nodes where individual nodes can be accessed by index number. A **NamedNodeMap** is the final class, and corresponds to a hash of nodes where each node can be accessed by name.

The classes that inherit from **Node** represent the different XML entity types. A *Document element* represents the entire XML document. *Element nodes* represent XML elements. *Text nodes* represent non-markup text. *Attr nodes* are created for each attribute in a XML tag, and *Comment nodes* are created for comment sections. **Document** nodes can contain **Element**, **Text** and **Comment** nodes. **Element** nodes can contain other nodes and can have **Attr**, **Element**, **Text** and **Comment** nodes.

The **XML::DOM** module also defines four node types that extend the DOM. These are *ElementDecl* for **<!ELEMENT>** declarations, *AttlistDecl* for **<!ATTLIST>** declarations, *XMLDecl* for **<?xml?>** declarations, and *AttDef* for attribute definitions in an **AttlistDecl**. Although we do not use these extensions in this chapter, we simply wanted to mention a few of the DOM extensions.

Figure 22.12 shows an example that uses the **XML::DOM** module to dynamically manipulate the contents of an XML document (Fig. 22.13).

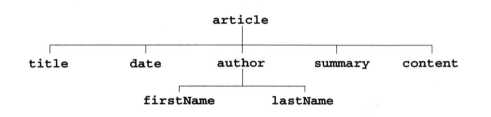

Fig. 22.11 Tree structure for **article.xml**.

```perl
1   #!/usr/bin/perl
2   # Fig. 22.12: contacts.pl
3   # Using the XML::DOM module to manipulate an XML Document.
4
5   use warnings;
6   use strict;
7   use XML::DOM;
8
9   open( CONTACTS, "+<contact.xml" )
10      or die ( "Error opening contact.xml" );
11
12  my $parser = new XML::DOM::Parser;
13  my $document = $parser->parse( \*CONTACTS );
14
15  printlist( $document );
16  instructions();
17  my $choice = 6;
18
19  while ( $choice ne 'q' ) {
20     print( "\n? " );
21     chomp( $choice = <STDIN> );
22
23     if ( $choice eq 'a' ) {
24        addContact( $document );
25     }
26     elsif ( $choice eq 'l' ) {
27         printlist( $document );
28     }
```

Fig. 22.12 Using the **XML::DOM** module to update **contact.xml** (part 1 of 3).

```
29         elsif ( $choice eq 'i' ) {
30             instructions( $document );
31         }
32         elsif ( $choice ne 'q' ) {
33             print( "$choice is not an option." .
34                     " Enter i for instructions.\n");
35         }
36     }
37
38     seek( CONTACTS, 0, 0 );
39     truncate( CONTACTS, 0 );
40     $document->print( \*CONTACTS );
41
42     sub printlist
43     {
44         my $document = shift;
45         my $root =
46             $document->getElementsByTagName( "contacts" )->item( 0 );
47         my $contactList = $root->getChildNodes();
48
49         print( "Your contact list: \n" );
50
51         for my $i ( 1 .. $contactList->getLength - 1 ) {
52             my $contact = $contactList->item( $i );
53             next unless ( $contact->getNodeName eq 'contact' );
54
55             my $first = $contact->getElementsByTagName( "FirstName" );
56             my $text =
57                 $first->item( 0 )->getChildAtIndex( 0 )->getData();
58
59             my $lastN = $contact->getElementsByTagName( "LastName" );
60             my $last =
61                 $lastN->item( 0 )->getChildAtIndex( 0 )->getData();
62
63             print( "$text $last\n" );
64         }
65     }
66
67     sub addContact
68     {
69         my $document = shift;
70         my $root =
71             $document->getElementsByTagName( "contacts" )->item( 0 );
72
73         print( "Enter the name of the person you wish to add: " );
74         chomp( my $name = <STDIN> );
75         my ( $first, $last ) = split( / /, $name );
76
77         my $firstNode = $document->createElement( "FirstName" );
78         $firstNode->addText( $first );
79
80         my $lastNode = $document->createElement( "LastName" );
81         $lastNode->addText( $last );
```

Fig. 22.12   Using the **XML::DOM** module to update **contact.xml** (part 2 of 3).

```
82
83      my $contact = $document->createElement( "contact" );
84      $contact->appendChild( $firstNode );
85      $contact->appendChild( $lastNode );
86
87      $root->appendChild( $contact );
88   }
89
90   sub instructions
91   {
92      print( "\n\n",
93              "Enter 'a' to add a contact.\n",
94              "Enter 'l' to list the contacts.\n",
95              "Enter 'i' for instructions.\n",
96              "Enter 'q' to quit.\n" );
97   }
```

```
Your contact list:
John Black
Sue Green
Bob Red
Mary Blue
Mike White
Jane Brown
Bill Gray


Enter 'a' to add a contact.
Enter 'l' to list the contacts.
Enter 'i' for instructions.
Enter 'q' to quit.
? a
Enter the name of the person you wish to add: Bart Fuscha

? l
Your contact list:
John Black
Sue Green
Bob Red
Mary Blue
Mike White
Jane Brown
Bill Gray
Bart Fuscha

? q
```

Fig. 22.12 Using the **XML::DOM** module to update **contact.xml** (part 3 of 3).

```
1   <?xml version = "1.0"?>
2
```

Fig. 22.13 Contact list used by the program of Fig. 22.12 (part 1 of 2).

```
3    <!-- Fig. 27.13: contact.xml -->
4    <!-- A contact list          -->
5
6    <contacts>
7
8        <contact>
9            <LastName>Black</LastName>
10           <FirstName>John</FirstName>
11       </contact>
12
13       <contact>
14           <LastName>Green</LastName>
15           <FirstName>Sue</FirstName>
16       </contact>
17
18       <contact>
19           <LastName>Red</LastName>
20           <FirstName>Bob</FirstName>
21       </contact>
22
23       <contact>
24           <LastName>Blue</LastName>
25           <FirstName>Mary</FirstName>
26       </contact>
27
28       <contact>
29           <LastName>White</LastName>
30           <FirstName>Mike</FirstName>
31       </contact>
32
33       <contact>
34           <LastName>Brown</LastName>
35           <FirstName>Jane</FirstName>
36       </contact>
37
38       <contact>
39           <LastName>Gray</LastName>
40           <FirstName>Bill</FirstName>
41       </contact>
42
43   </contacts>
```

Fig. 22.13   Contact list used by the program of Fig. 22.12 (part 2 of 2).

This program allows the user to add names to the contact list XML document, **contact.xml**. To do this, we open the **contact.xml** file for reading and writing on line 9. Line 12 creates a new ***XML::DOM::Parser*** *object*, a parser derived from **XML::Parser**. We use this to parse the file (line 13) by passing the filehandle to the **parse** method. This returns a **Document** object which we assign to **$document**. Recall that a **Document** object represents the entire XML document.

On line 15 we use our **printlist** subroutine (defined in lines 42–65) to print the contact list. Line 16 prints out the instructions for using this program. The **while** loop on lines 19–36 get the user's choice and call the appropriate subroutine.

The **printlist** subroutine (lines 42–65) prints the contact list. Line 44 gets the document object and line 46 calls the *getElementsByTagName method* to return a *NodeList* of **contacts** elements. We get the first one using the *item method*. Line 47 gets a **NodeList** of all the **contact** elements in the **contacts** element using the *getChildNodes method*.

Lines 51–64 loop through each of the **contact** elements printing out the names. We use a **foreach** to iterate from 0 to the number of elements, returned by the **getLength** method, minus one. Line 52 gets the current element we are examining with the **item** method. If it is not a **contact** element we skip it (line 53).

Line 55 get the text in the **FirstName** tag. We use the *getElementsByTagName* and **item** methods to retrieve the **FirstName** element. We then use the *getChildAt-Index method* to get the text node in the **FirstName** element which should be the text of the name. We extract the text of this node using the **getData** method (line 57). Lines 59–61 use the same techniques to get the last name. Line 63 prints the name.

The **addContact** (67–88) subroutine allows the user to add a contact to the list. We get the root of the contacts list like we did in the **printlist** subroutine on lines 70 and 71. Lines 73–75 prompt the user for the name they wish to enter and use the **split** function to separate the first and last names. Line 77 creates a new **FirstName** element with the *createElement method*, and line 78 adds a text node to this new element with the **addText** method. Lines 80 and 81 create the **LastName** element in a similar manner. Line 83 creates a **contact** element and lines 84 and 85 add the **FirstName** and **Last-Name** elements to it using the **appendChild** method. Line 87 uses the **appendChild** method again to add the node to the **contacts** element.

When the user has finished adding names, we need to save them to the file. To do this we use the **seek** function to return to the beginning of the file, delete what was in the file using the **truncate** function, and use the **Document** object's **print** method to print the modified XML back to the file.

22.9 DOM Methods

In this section, we provide several tables that list key DOM methods. Figure 22.14 describes some **Node** methods, Fig. 22.15 describes some **NodeList** methods, Fig. 22.16 describes some **NamedNodeMap** methods, Fig. 22.17 describes some **Document** methods, Fig. 22.18 describes some **Element** methods, Fig. 22.19 describes some **Attr** methods and Fig. 22.20 describes some **Text** and **Comment** methods.

Method	Description
getNodeType	Returns an integer representing the node type (see the Module Documentation for this list).
getNodeName	Returns the name of the node. If the node does not have a name, a string consisting of **#** followed by the type of the node is returned.
getNodeValue	Returns a string or undefined depending on the node type.

Fig. 22.14 Some **Node** object methods (part 1 of 2).

Method	Description
getParentNode	Returns the parent node.
getChildNodes	Returns a **NodeList** (Fig. 22.15) with all the children of the node. When called in list context, it returns a regular Perl list of the children.
getFirstChild	Returns the first child in the **NodeList**.
getLastChild	Returns the last child in the **NodeList**.
getPreviousSibling	Returns the node preceding this node, or undefined.
getNextSibling	Returns the node following this node, or undefined.
getAttributes	Returns a **NamedNodeMap** (Fig. 22.16) containing the attributes for this node.
insertBefore	Inserts the node passed as the first argument before the existing node passed as the second argument. If the new node is already in the tree, it is removed before insertion. The same behavior is true for other methods that add nodes.
replaceChild	Replaces the second argument node with the first argument node.
removeChild	Removes the child node passed to it.
appendChild	Appends the node passed to it to the list of child nodes.
getElementsByTagName	Returns a **NodeList** of all nodes in the subtree with the name specified as the first argument ordered as they would be encountered in a preorder traversal. An optional second argument specifies either the direct child nodes (**0**), or any descendant (**1**).
print	Prints the entire subtree to the filehandle object passed to it. Other versions of **print** include **printToFile** and **printToFileHandle**.
getChildAtIndex	Returns the child node at the specified index in the child list.
addText	Appends the string passed to it to the last **Node** if it is a **Text** node, otherwise creates a new **Text** node for the string and adds it to the end of the child list.
isAncestor	Returns true if the node passed is a parent of the node, or is the node itself.

Fig. 22.14 Some **Node** object methods (part 2 of 2).

Method	Description
item	Passed an index number, will return the element at that index. Indices range from 0 to length − 1
getLength	Returns the total number of nodes in the list.

Fig. 22.15 Some **NodeList** methods.

Method	Description
getNamedItem	Returns a node in the **NamedNodeMap** with the specified name or undefined if there were none.
setNamedItem	Stores a node passed to it in the **NamedNodeMap**. Two nodes with the same name cannot be stored in the same **NamedNodeMap**.
removeNamedItem	Removes a specified node from the **NamedNodeMap**.
getLength	Returns the total number of nodes in the **NamedNodeMap**.
getValues	Returns a **NodeList** containing all the nodes in the **NamedNodeMap**.

Fig. 22.16 Some **NamedNodeMap** methods.

Method	Description
getDocumentElement	Returns the root node of the document tree.
createElement	Creates and returns an element with the specified tag name.
createAttribute	Creates and returns an attribute with the specified name and value.
createTextNode	Creates and returns a text node that contains the specified text.
createComment	Creates a comment to hold the specified text.

Fig. 22.17 Some **Document** methods.

Method	Description
getTagName	Returns the name of the element.
setTagName	Changes the name of the element to the specified name.
getAttribute	Returns the value of the specified attribute.
setAttribute	Changes the value of the attribute passed as the first argument the value passed as the second argument.
removeAttribute	Removes the specified attribute.
getAttributeNode	Returns the specified attribute node.
setAttributeNode	Adds a new attribute node with the specified name.

Fig. 22.18 Some **Element** methods.

Method	Description
getValue	Returns the specified attribute's value.

Fig. 22.19 Some **Attr** methods (part 1 of 2).

Method	Description
setValue	Changes the value of the attribute to the specified value.
getName	Returns the name of the attribute.

Fig. 22.19 Some **Attr** methods (part 2 of 2).

Method	Description
getData	Returns the data contained in the node (text or comment).
setData	Sets the node's data.
getLength	Returns the number of characters contained in the node.

Fig. 22.20 Some **Text** and **Comment** methods.

22.10 Simple API for XML (SAX)

SAX was developed by the members of the *XML-DEV mailing list* and was released in May of 1998. SAX is an alternate method for parsing XML documents that uses an *event-based model*—notifications called *events* are raised as the document is parsed.

SAX and DOM are dramatically different APIs for accessing information in XML documents. DOM is a tree-based model that stores the document's data in a hierarchy of nodes. Because all the document's data is in memory, data can be quickly accessed. DOM also provides facilities for adding or removing nodes (i.e., modifying the document).

SAX-based parsers invoke methods when markup (e.g., a start tag, end tag, etc.) is encountered. With this event-based model, no tree structure is created by the SAX-based parser to store the XML document's data—data is passed to the application from the XML document as it is found. This results in greater performance and less memory overhead than with the DOM. In fact, Many DOM parsers use a SAX parser to retrieve data from a document for building the DOM tree. However, many programmers find it easier to traverse and manipulate XML documents using the DOM tree structure. As a result, SAX parsers are typically used for reading XML documents that will not be modified. SAX-based parsers are available for a variety of programming languages (e.g., Perl, Java, Python, etc.).

Performance Tip 22.1

SAX-based parsing is often more efficient than DOM-based parsing when processing large XML documents, because the entire document is not committed to memory.

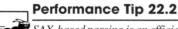

Performance Tip 22.2

SAX-based parsing is an efficient means of parsing documents that need only be parsed once.

Performance Tip 22.3

DOM-based parsing is often more efficient than SAX-based parsing when specific information must be retrieved from the document quickly.

Performance Tip 22.4

SAX-based parsers are commonly used in situations where memory must be conserved.

Software Engineering Observation 22.11

SAX was developed independently of the W3C and has been widely supported by industry. DOM is the official W3C recommendation.

22.11 Parsing XML with `XML::Parser`

In this section, we discuss the module **XML::Parser** which provides an interface to the **expat** *XML parser* written by James Clark. The **XML::Parser** module allows you to choose which model (SAX or DOM) you want to use. SAX-based parsing is the default option for the module. As the file is being read in, the parser reads the input to identify the XML markup. As markup is encountered, *event handlers* (i.e., methods) are called. For example, when a start tag is encountered, the **Start** *handler* is called, and when character data is encountered, the **Char** *handler* is called. Custom implementations for these handlers can be specified to process the XML in different ways.

Figure 22.21 shows an example of SAX-based parsing. This program allows the user to specify an XML document on the command line. The program returns information about each instance of that tag in the document. Figure 22.22 lists the XML document that was parsed to produce the output when **box** is passed as the second argument.

Line 7 **use**s the **XML::Parser** module, and line 11 creates a **new** parser object to perform the parsing. Setting the **ErrorContext** option indicates that we want any errors encountered in the XML document to be reported in *context*, in this case specifying that we want two lines on either side of the error printed. Line 13 sets the event handlers. When character data is encountered, the **charHandler** subroutine is called. If it is a start tag, the **startHandler** subroutine is called, and if it is an end tag, the **endHandler** subroutine is called. More event handlers are included in Fig. 22.23—see the module documentation for a complete listing. Line 18 tells the parser to parse the file specified at the command line.

The subroutines (lines 20–59) which handle the events generated by the XML parser. They are passed different arguments depending on what kind of an event occurs. The first argument to all handlers is an **Expat** instance which contains information about the state of the parser. This object is defined by the **XML::Parser::Expat** *module* which is a low-level interface to the parser, **expat**.

The **startHandler** subroutine (lines 20–36) is called whenever a start tag is encountered. As with every handler, the first argument passed to it is an **Expat** object. The second argument is a string holding the element name, and the remaining arguments are the attributes of the element in a name, value list. Line 22 assigns these arguments to variables.

```
1   #!/usr/bin/perl
2   # Fig. 22.21: taginfo.pl
3   # SAX example.
4
5   use warnings;
```

Fig. 22.21 Using **XML::Parser** to perform event-driven parsing (part 1 of 3).

```perl
 6   use strict;
 7   use XML::Parser;
 8
 9   my ( $file, $tag ) = @ARGV;
10
11   my $parser = new XML::Parser( ErrorContext => 2 );
12
13   $parser->setHandlers( Char => \&charHandler,
14                         Start => \&startHandler,
15                         End   => \&endHandler  );
16
17   my $depth = 0;
18   $parser->parsefile( $file );
19
20   sub startHandler
21   {
22      my ( $expat, $element, @attributes ) = @_;
23      return if ( !$element );
24      if ( $element eq $tag ) {
25         print( "\n", ' ' x $depth,
26            "<$tag> starts on line ", $expat->current_line(), "\n" );
27         $depth += 3;
28
29        print( ' ' x $depth, "Parent tag: ",$expat->current_element(),
30            "\n", ' ' x $depth, "Depth: ", $expat->depth(), "\n",
31            ' ' x $depth, "Attributes: @attributes\n" );
32      }
33      elsif ( $expat->current_element() eq $tag ) {
34         print( ' ' x $depth, "Child: $element\n" );
35      }
36   }
37
38   sub endHandler
39   {
40      my ( $expat, $element ) = @_;
41
42      if ( $element eq $tag ) {
43         $depth -= 3;
44
45         print( ' ' x $depth, "<\\$element> ends on line ",
46            $expat->current_line(), "\n\n" );
47      }
48   }
49
50   sub charHandler
51   {
52      my ( $expat, $data ) = @_;
53
54      if ( $expat->current_element() eq $tag ) {
55         $data =~ s/^\s+//;
56         $data =~ s/\s+$//;
57         print( ' ' x $depth, "Data: $data\n" ) if ( $data );
58      }
59   }
```

Fig. 22.21   Using **XML::Parser** to perform event-driven parsing (part 2 of 3).

```
<box> starts on line 8
   Parent tag: boxlist
   Depth: 1
   Attributes: size big
   Data: This is the big box.

   <box> starts on line 11
      Parent tag: box
      Depth: 2
      Attributes: size medium
      Data: Medium sized box
      Child: item
      Child: thing
   <\box> ends on line 15

   Child: parcel

   <box> starts on line 18
      Parent tag: box
      Depth: 2
      Attributes: type small
      Data: smaller stuff

      <box> starts on line 20
         Parent tag: box
         Depth: 3
         Attributes: type tiny
         Data: tiny stuff
      <\box> ends on line 20

   <\box> ends on line 21

<\box> ends on line 23
```

Fig. 22.21 Using **XML::Parser** to perform event-driven parsing (part 3 of 3).

```
1   <?xml version = "1.0"?>
2
3   <!-- Fig. 22.22: boxes.xml        -->
4   <!-- Article structured with XML -->
5
6   <boxlist>
7
8      <box size = "big">
9         This is the big box.
10
11        <box size = "medium">
12           Medium sized box
13           <item>Some stuff</item>
14           <thing>More stuff</thing>
15        </box>
```

Fig. 22.22 Example XML file used in Fig. 22.21 (part 1 of 2).

```
16
17          <parcel></parcel>
18          <box type = "small">
19              smaller stuff
20              <box type = "tiny">tiny stuff</box>
21          </box>
22
23      </box>
24
25  </boxlist>
```

Fig. 22.22 Example XML file used in Fig. 22.21 (part 2 of 2).

Handler	Arguments	Description
Init	Expat	Called just before the parsing of a document starts.
Final	Expat	Called after parsing has finished.
Start	Expat, Element, Attributes	Called when a starting XML tag is encountered.
End	Expat, Element	Called when a closing XML tag is encountered.
Char	Expat, Data	Called when non-markup is encountered.
Comment	Expat, Data	Called when a comment is encountered.

Fig. 22.23 Some **XML::Parser** events.

If the element is a start tag of the type specified on the command line, we print out information about the tag on lines 24–32. The **Expat** object holds the state information for the parse, which can be accessed using its object methods. Lines 45 and 46 print the line number the tag occurred on using the ***current_line*** *method*. The **$depth** variable is used for indentation. The **depth** method of the **Expat** object can be used to obtain the depth of an element, as on line 29, but because we need to know how many tags enclose the current tag, we have to keep track of it ourselves. Line 30 calls the ***current_element*** *method* to obtain the name of the element enclosing the tag being parsed. Line 33 uses this method to test if the enclosing element is the type of tag for which we are looking. If so, we print out that the element is a child of that element. Additional **Expat** methods are listed in Fig. 22.24.

The **endHandler** subroutine (lines 38–48), called whenever a closing tag is encountered. It is passed an **Expat** object and the name of the closing tag. If this is a closing tag of the type we are looking for, we decrement the **$depth** variable to decrease the indent, and print that this end tag was found. The ***current_line*** *method* is used to print the line number on which the end tag was found.

The **charHandler** subroutine (lines 50–59) is called whenever non-markup text is encountered. If this text is enclosed in tags of the type we are looking for, we remove any leading and trailing whitespace that might have been used to format the XML document (lines 55 and 56) and print the data (line 57). Because the parser does not ignore whitespace, we need to remove it.

22.12 `Data::Dumper` and XML

Module ***Data::Dumper*** "dumps" information. In this section, we use **Data::Dumper** to dump the results of DOM-based parsing. This technique allows us to easily view the tree structure created by the parser with a minimal amount of programming.

We can use the DOM implementation of **XML::Parse**r by adding the ***Style =>*** ***'Tree'*** *option* to the **XML::Parser** constructor call. A parser object created with this option set returns a reference to a tree when the **parse** method is called.

The tree is made up of array references which hold the information for the XML elements and text. Nodes in the tree consist of two elements in an array. There are two types of nodes. A node representing text has a first element of 0 and a second element which is the text. A node representing a XML element has the name of that element as the first element and an array reference which holds information about the attributes and nested data in the element. The first element in these array references is a hash reference which the name-value pairs of the attributes of the element. The rest of the array holds the nodes of any nested data.

To demonstrate the structure of the tree, we parse an XML document and use the **Data::Dumper** module to print out the resulting tree (Fig. 22.25). The **Data::Dumper** produces strings of Perl code which can be **eval**ed to retrieve all of the variable values. In this case, we will be using it to provide a visual representation of the tree.

Lines 10–15 create a string with an excerpt from **letter.xml** (Fig. 22.3) that will be parsed. Because the parser cannot ignore whitespace, we removed as much of the whitespace as possible. Line 17 creates the **XML::Parser** object, setting **Style** to **Tree** for tree based parsing. We use the **parse** method on line 19 to parse the XML. The **parse** method can be called with either a string or a filehandle. The tree returned is assigned to **$tree**. We then use the **Data::Dumpers Dump** function to convert the array reference into a string which is then printed out.

From the output produced by this program, the document's tree structure is evident. For example, for the **<name>John</name>** element, an two array elements were produced. The first was the string **name**, indicating the name of the element, and the second was an array reference with the content of the tag. The first element of this anonymous array is an empty hash reference, indicating there were no attributes for the element, the second element is **0**, indicating that there is text, and the third element is the text, **John**. You will also notice that any whitespace or newlines had nodes created for them.

22.13 Extensible Style Language (XSL)

Extensible Stylesheet Language (*XSL*) defines how an XML document's data is rendered. The relationship between XML and XSL is similar to the relationship between HTML and Cascading Style Sheets (CSS)—although XSL is much more powerful than CSS. An XML document's data does not have to be rendered using an XSL document, CSS can also be used. An *XSL document* provides the rules for displaying (or organizing) an XML document's data. XSL also provides elements that define rules for how one XML document is transformed into another text-based document (e.g., XML, HTML, etc.). The subset of XSL concerned with transformations is called *XSL Transformations (XSLT)*.

Software Engineering Observation 22.12

XSL allows data presentation to be separated from data description.

Figure 22.26 lists an XML document that marks up various sports. The output shows the results of the transformation rendered in Internet Explorer 5. We discuss the specific XSL stylesheet for this in Fig. 22.27.

Method	Used for
current_line	Returns the current line number.
current_column	Returns the current column number of the parse.
current_byte	Returns how many bytes have been parsed.
depth	Returns the size of the context list.
element_index	Returns how many elements have been parsed.
finish	Unsets all handlers. The document is still parsed, but no handlers are called.

Fig. 22.24 Some **Expat** methods.

```perl
1   #!/usr/bin/perl
2   # Fig. 22.25: tree.pl
3   # Using Data::Dumper to print the results of tree-based parsing.
4
5   use warnings;
6   use strict;
7   use Data::Dumper;
8   use XML::Parser;
9
10  my $xml =<<"DONE";
11  <letter><contact type = "from"><name>John</name>
12     <phone>555-1234</phone></contact>
13     <salutation format = "formal">Dear Sir:</salutation>
14  </letter>
15  DONE
16
17  my $parser = new XML::Parser( Style => 'Tree', ErrorContext => 2 );
18
19  my $tree = $parser->parse( $xml );
20
21  print( Data::Dumper->Dump( [ $tree ] ) );
```

Fig. 22.25 Using the **Data::Dumper** module to print the results of tree based parsing (part 1 of 2).

```
$VAR1 = [
          'letter',
          [
            {},
            'contact',
            [
              {
                'type' => 'from'
              },
              'name',
              [
                {},
                0,
                'John'
              ],
              0,
              '
      ',
              'phone',
              [
                {},
                0,
                '555-1234'
              ]
            ],
            0,
            '
      ',
            'salutation',
            [
              {
                'format' => 'formal'
              },
              0,
              'Dear Sir:'
            ],
            0,
            '
      '
    '
          ]
        ];
```

Fig. 22.25 Using the `Data::Dumper` module to print the results of tree based parsing (part 2 of 2).

```
1  <?xml version = "1.0"?>
2  <?xml:stylesheet type = "text/xsl" href = "elements.xsl"?>
3  <!-- Fig. 22.26 : games.xml -->
4  <!-- Sports Database       -->
5
```

Fig. 22.26 XML document containing a list of sports (part 1 of 2).

```
6    <sports>
7
8       <game id = "783">
9          <name>Cricket</name>
10
11          <para>
12             More popular among commonwealth nations.
13          </para>
14       </game>
15
16       <game id = "239">
17          <name>Baseball</name>
18
19          <para>
20             More popular in America.
21          </para>
22       </game>
23
24       <game id = "418">
25          <name>Soccer (Football)</name>
26
27          <para>
28             Most popular sport in the world.
29          </para>
30       </game>
31
32    </sports>
```

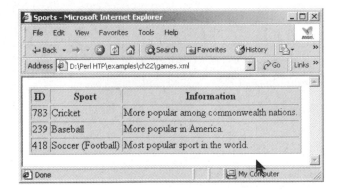

Fig. 22.26   XML document containing a list of sports (part 2 of 2).

Line 2

<?xml:stylesheet type = "text/xsl" href = "elements.xsl"?>

is a processing instruction that specifies a reference to the XSL stylesheet **elements.xsl**. Value **type** specifies that **elements.xsl** is a **text/xsl** file.

Figure 22.27 transforms the XML document shown in Fig. 22.26 into an HTML document.

```
1    <?xml version = "1.0"?>
2
3    <!-- reference XSL stylesheet URI    -->
4    <xsl:stylesheet xmlns:xsl = "http://www.w3.org/TR/WD-xsl">
5
6    <!-- Fig. 22.27 : elements.xsl        -->
7    <!-- A simple XSLT transformation     -->
8
9    <xsl:template match = "/">
10
11      <html>
12
13        <title>Sports</title>
14
15        <body>
16
17           <table border = "1" bgcolor = "cyan">
18
19           <thead>
20             <tr>
21                <th>ID</th>
22                <th>Sport</th>
23                <th>Information</th>
24             </tr>
25           </thead>
26
27            <!-- insert each name and para element value into -->
28            <!-- a table row.                                 -->
29            <xsl:for-each select = "sports/game">
30               <tr>
31                  <td><xsl:value-of select = "@id"/></td>
32                  <td><xsl:value-of select = "name"/></td>
33                  <td><xsl:value-of select = "para"/></td>
34               </tr>
35            </xsl:for-each>
36
37            </table>
38
39        </body>
40
41      </html>
42    </xsl:template>
43
44    </xsl:stylesheet>
```

Fig. 22.27 Using XSLT to create elements and attributes.

Line 4

```
<xsl:stylesheet xmlns:xsl = "http://www.w3.org/TR/WD-xsl">
```

is the ***stylesheet*** start tag—which begins every XSL stylesheet. Namespace prefix **xsl** is bound to the URI **http://www.w3.org/TR/WD-xsl**. [*Note*: This is the URI

Internet Explorer 5 supports—not the most recent URI—***http://www.w3.org/1999/XSL/Transform***.]
  Line 9

```
<xsl:template match = "/">
```

uses the ***match*** attribute to select the document root of an XML document. The **/** *character* selects the root element of an XML document. In Fig. 22.26, the child nodes of the document root are two comment nodes (lines 3 and 4) and the **sports** element node (line 6).
  Lines 11–25 (Fig. 22.27) are used verbatim. Line 29

```
<xsl:for-each select = "sports/game">
```

uses the ***for-each*** element to iterate through the XML document's tree looking for **game** elements. The **for-each** element is similar to Perl's **foreach** repetition structure. Each iteration adds a row to the HTML table.
  Line 31

```
<td><xsl:value-of select = "@id"/></td>
```

retrieves the value of the **game**'s **id** attribute and writes it as table data. Element ***value-of*** retrieves the selected node's data.
  Lines 32–33

```
<td><xsl:value-of select = "name"/></td>
<td><xsl:value-of select = "para"/></td>
```

write the **name** and **para** element values as table data.

22.14 Generating XML in Perl

Generating XML in Perl is similar to generating HTML. For example, to create a CGI script which outputs XML, all we have to do is use **print** or **write** functions to print XML tags to **STDOUT**.
  As an example, we are going to write a CGI script to create XML from data in a text file. The text file will contain the contact list from Fig. 22.13. It will be formatted such that each line of the file holds a name in the form **lastname, firstname**. We will write a CGI script that generates the XML from this data.

```
1   #!/perl/bin/perl
2   # Fig. 22.28: xmlgenerator.pl
3   # Converting a comma separated list data source to XML.
4
5   use warnings;
6   use strict;
7
8   print <<'HEADER';
```

Fig. 22.28 Generating XML in a CGI script (part 1 of 2).

```
 9   Content-Type: text/xml
10
11   <?xml version = "1.0"?>
12   <?xml:stylesheet type = "text/xsl" href = "/contact_list.xsl"?>
13   HEADER
14
15   print( "<contacts>\n\n" );
16
17   open( NAMES, "names.txt" ) or die ( "Error opening names.txt" );
18
19   while ( <NAMES> ) {
20      chomp;
21
22      # escape any characters not allowed in XML content.
23      s/&/&amp;/;
24      s/</&lt;/;
25      s/>/&gt;/;
26      s/"/&quot;/;
27      s/'/&apos;/;
28
29      my ( $last, $first ) = split( /, / );
30
31      print( "    <contact>\n",
32             "        <LastName>$last</LastName>\n",
33             "        <FirstName>$first</FirstName>\n",
34             "    </contact>\n\n" );
35   }
36
37   close( NAMES );
38
39   print( "</contacts>\n" );
```

Fig. 22.28 Generating XML in a CGI script (part 2 of 2).

Lines 8–13 use a heredoc to print out the header information for the XML that is generated. Line 9, **Content-Type: text/xml**, is a header indicating that our script is generating text which is XML. Line 11 prints the type of XML we are using and line 12 prints the processing instruction that references the XSL stylesheet. We are using the same file as we used for the original **contact.xml** file. Finally, the closing tag for the root element is printed on line 39.

After we have printed out the headers, we start printing the XML by printing the opening root element tag on line 15. We then **open** the file where the data is stored on line 17 and use the **while** loop on lines 19–35 to print out the elements for each name in the file.

The **while** loop iterates through the file one line at a time. Because the **<**, **>**, **&**, **'** and **"** symbols cannot occur in XML data without errors, we replace any occurrences of these characters with their escape sequences on lines 23–27. The last and first names are extracted from the line using the **split** function on line 29, and the XML elements for the name are printed on lines 31–34.

22.15 Case Study: Message Forums with Perl and XML

In this section, we use XML and many XML-related technologies to create one of the most popular types of Web sites: a *message forum*. Message forums are "virtual" bulletin boards where various topics are discussed. Common features of message forums include discussion groups, questions and answers, and general comments. Many Web sites host message forums. For example,

> **www.egroups.com**
> **web.eesite.com/forums**
> **www.deja.com**

are popular message forums. [*Note*: The implementation of this message board requires Internet Explorer 5. We have provided an additional section at the end that discusses how other client browsers such as Netscape may be used.]

Figure 22.29 summarizes the files used in the message forum. The main page generated by **default.pl** displays the list of available message forums, which are stored in the XML document **forums.xml**. Hyperlinks are provided to each XML message forum document and to script **addForum.pl**, which adds a forum to **forums.xml** and creates a new XML message forum (e.g., **forum2.xml**) using the message forum template **template.xml**.

File Name	Description
forums.xml	XML document listing all available forums and their filenames.
default.pl	Main page, providing navigational links to the forums.
template.xml	Template for a message forum XML document.
addForum.pl	Adds a forum.
feedback.xml	Sample message forum.
formatting.xsl	Document for transforming message forums into HTML.

Fig. 22.29 Message forum documents (part 1 of 2).

File Name	Description
addPost.pl	Adds a message to a forum.
invalid.html	Used to display an error message.
site.css	Stylesheet for formatting HTML documents.

Fig. 22.29 Message forum documents (part 2 of 2).

Each XML message forum document (e.g., **feedback.xml**) is transformed into an HTML document using XSLT document **formatting.xsl**. The CSS document **site.css** formats the HTML for display. New messages are posted to a forum by **addPost.pl**. If errors occur when the document is processed, **invalid.html** is displayed. Some of the key interactions between documents are illustrated in Fig. 22.30.

22.15.1 Displaying the Forums using XML::Parser

This section introduces the documents used for organizing and displaying the message forums. For this case study, we provide a sample forum named **feedback.xml** (Fig. 22.31) to show the structure of a form document.

Notice on line 4 the reference to the stylesheet **formatting.xsl**. This XSL document, which we discuss later in the chapter, transforms the forum to HTML for display. Every forum document has root element **forum**, which contains one attribute named **file**. This attribute's value is the name of the forum's XML document. Child elements include **name**, for specifying the title of the forum, and **message**, for marking up the of the message. A message contains a user name, a message title and the message text, which are marked up by elements **user**, **title** and **text**, respectively.

Every message forum name and filename is stored in a document named **forums.xml** (Fig. 22.32). As forums are added, this document is modified to add the new forum names and filenames.

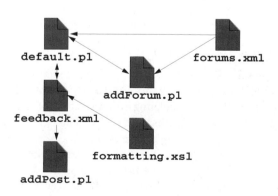

Fig. 22.30 Key interactions between message forum documents.

```
1    <?xml version = "1.0"?>
2    <!-- Fig. 22.31: feedback.xml -->
3
4    <?xml:stylesheet type = "text/xsl" href = "../XML/formatting.xsl"?>
5
6    <forum file = "feedback.xml">
7       <name>Feedback</name>
8
9       <message timestamp = "Mon Nov  27 13:18:15 2000">
10          <user>Emily</user>
11          <title>Nice forums!</title>
12          <text>These forums are great! Well done, all.</text>
13       </message>
14
15   </forum>
```

Fig. 22.31 XML document representing a forum containing one message.

```
1    <?xml version = "1.0"?>
2    <!-- Fig. 22.32: forums.xml -->
3
4    <?xml:stylesheet type = "text/xsl" href = "formatting.xsl"?>
5
6    <forums>
7
8       <forum filename = "feedback.xml">
9          <name>Feedback</name>
10      </forum>
11
12   </forums>
```

Fig. 22.32 XML document containing data for all available forums.

Root element **forums** (line 6) contains one or more **forum** child elements. Initially, one forum (i.e., **Feedback**) is provided. Each forum element has attribute **filename** and child element **name**. This forum corresponds to the XML document presented in Fig. 22.31.

Visitors to the message forum are first greeted by the Web page displayed in Fig. 22.33, which displays links to all forums and provides forum management options. Initially, only two links are active—one to the **Feedback** forum and one to create a new forum. The links for modifying and deleting forums are to be created by the reader in chapter exercises and are therefore disabled here. This Perl CGI script **use**s the **XML::Parser** module (line 8) to parse **forums.xml**.

In order to perform the parsing, we open **forums.xml** (line 13) and obtain a *shared lock* on the file (line 15) using **flock**. The first argument to **flock** is a filehandle. The second argument is one of four different lock types. If the second argument is a **1**, it locks the file with a *shared lock* (i.e., more than one script may read from the file at the same time). We use the **Fcntl** module's **:flock** tag (line 9) so we can use **LOCK_SH** instead of the number **1** (line 15) to specify a shared lock.

Lines 16 and 17

```
$parser = new XML::Parser( Handlers => { Start => \&startTag,
    Char  => \&text       } );
```

instantiate an event-based parser object. A set of handlers, i.e., references to programmer-defined subroutines, are declared and passed to the **Parser** constructor. For example, the assignment of subroutine **startTag** to handler **Start** indicates that every time the parser encounters a start tag, it invokes subroutine **startTag**. Similarly, every time the parser encounters character data, it invokes subroutine **text**.

```
1   #!perl
2   # Fig. 22.33: default.pl
3   # Default page for XML forums
4
5   use warnings;
6   use strict;
7   use CGI qw( :standard );
8   use XML::Parser;
9   use Fcntl qw( :flock );
10
11  my ( $parser, @files, @forums, @items );
12
13  open( XML, "+<../htdocs/XML/forums.xml" ) or
14     die( "Could not open: $!" );
15  flock( XML, LOCK_SH );
16  $parser = new XML::Parser( Handlers => { Start => \&startTag,
17     Char  => \&text       } );
18  $parser->parse( \*XML );
19  close( XML );
20
21  print( header, start_html( -title => "Deitel Message Forums",
22     -style => { -src => "/XML/site.css" } ) );
23
24  print( h1( "Deitel Message Forums" ) );
25
26  @items = map { a( { -href => "/XML/$files[ $_ ]" },
27     $forums[ $_ ] ) } ( 0 .. $#files );
28
29  print( p( strong( "Available Forums" ),
30     ul( li( \@items ) ) ) );
31
32  @items = ( a( { -href => "addforum.pl" }, "Add a Forum" ),
33             "Delete a Forum", "Modify a Forum" );
34
35  print( p( strong( "Forum Management" ), ul( li( \@items ) ) ),
36        end_html );
37
38  sub startTag
39  {
40    my ( $expat, $element, %attributes ) = @_;
41    push( @files, $attributes{ "filename" }) if $element eq "forum";
42  }
```

Fig. 22.33 Opening page for message forums (part 1 of 2).

```
43
44   sub text
45   {
46      my ( $expat, $string ) = @_;
47      push( @forums, $string ) if $expat->in_element( "name" );
48   }
```

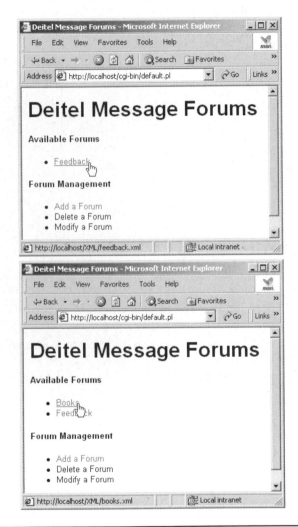

Opening page
after a forum
named **Books**
has been
created

Fig. 22.33   Opening page for message forums (part 2 of 2).

Line 18

```
$parser->parse( \*XML );
```

invokes the parser object's **parse** method to parse **forums.xml**. We pass this method a
reference to a filehandle. Method **parse** creates the arrays of filenames and forum names.
Once the parsing is complete, we close **forums.xml** (line 19).

In lines 21–36, we output the HTML shown in Fig. 22.33. We set the attribute **-style** (line 22) in order to use a Cascading Style Sheet to format the page. Lines 25 and 26

```
@items = map { a( { -href => "/XML/$files[ $_ ]" },
    $forums[ $_ ])} ( 0 .. $#files );
```

use **map** to create an array (**@items**) containing links to the various forums. To create this array, we call function **a** (i.e., an anchor) to create anchors for the filenames and forum names. One link is created for each element in **@files** (line 26).

After array **@items** is created, we create a reference to it (line 30) and use **li**'s distributive property to output an unordered list (i.e., **ul**) to the page.

We reuse array **@items** in lines 32 and 33 to create an array of links to forum-management options. These links are written to the client in lines 35 and 36.

Lines 38–48 are the handler subroutines that the parser calls. The parser passes arguments to these subroutines. The first argument passed to all handlers is an **Expat** object (defined in the **XML::Parser::Expat** *module*) that describes the element encountered. This object is a low-level interface to *expat*, an XML parser written in C by James Clark. We use this **Expat** object in **startTag**, which we discuss momentarily.

The other arguments passed to a handler vary, depending on the handler. A **Start** handler is passed the name of the start tag and an attribute name-value pair list. In line 40, we assign these arguments to the variables **$expat**, **$element** and **%attributes**, respectively. A **Char** handler is passed a string containing the character data, which we assign to variable **$string** in the **text** subroutine in line 46.

In **startTag**, we check if we have encountered the start tag of a **forum** element (line 41). If so, we extract the **filename** attribute from the element and **push** it onto an array of filenames (**@files**). Similarly, in subroutine **text**, we call method **in_element** for the object referenced by **$expat** to determine if the text was found within a **name** element. If so, we **push** the found text (**$string**) onto a list of forum names (**@forums**).

22.15.2 Using **XML::DOM** to Add Forums and Messages

In this section, we discuss the scripts and documents used to add forums and messages. The Perl script that adds a new forum is shown in Fig. 22.34. It uses the **XML::DOM** module to manipulate XML documents in accordance with the W3C DOM recommendation.

When the script is initially executed, it is not passed any parameters. The **if** statement in line 11 directs program flow immediately to line 52. Lines 52–64 output a simple form that prompts the user for a forum name and a filename for the XML document to be created. When the form is submitted, the script is executed again. This time, **param** returns true, and lines 12–50 are executed.

```
1  #!perl
2  # Fig. 22.34: addForum.pl
3  # Adds a forum to the list
4
5  use warnings;
6  use strict;
```

Fig. 22.34   Script that adds a new forum to **forums.xml** (part 1 of 3).

```perl
 7   use CGI qw( :standard );
 8   use XML::DOM;
 9   use Fcntl qw( :flock :DEFAULT );
10
11   if ( param ) {
12      my ( $parser, $document, $forums, $forum, $name );
13
14      my ( $file, $newfile ) = ("forums.xml", param( "filename" ));
15      $newfile =~ /^\w+\.xml$/ or die( "Not a valid file: $!" );
16
17      sysopen( NEW, "../htdocs/XML/$newfile", O_WRONLY|O_EXCL|O_CREAT )
18         or die( "Could not create: $!" );
19      open( FORUMS, "+<../htdocs/XML/$file" ) or
20         die( "Could not open: $!" );
21      flock( FORUMS, LOCK_EX );
22
23      $parser = new XML::DOM::Parser;
24      $document = $parser->parse( \*FORUMS );
25      $forums = $document->getDocumentElement;
26
27      $forum = $document->createElement( "forum" );
28      $forum->setAttribute( "filename", $newfile );
29      $forums->insertBefore( $forum, $forums->getFirstChild );
30
31      $name = $document->createElement( "name" );
32      $name->addText( param( "name" ) );
33      $forum->appendChild( $name );
34
35      seek( FORUMS, 0, 0 );
36      truncate( FORUMS, 0 );
37      $document->print( \*FORUMS );
38      close( FORUMS );
39
40      $document = $parser->parsefile( "../htdocs/XML/template.xml" );
41      $forum = $document->getDocumentElement;
42      $forum->setAttribute( "file", $newfile );
43
44      $name = $document->createElement( "name" );
45      $name->addText( param( "name" ) );
46      $forum->appendChild( $name );
47
48      $document->print( \*NEW );
49      close( NEW );
50      print( redirect( "default.pl" ) );
51   }
52   else {
53      print( header, start_html( -title => "Add a forum",
54         -style => { -src => "/XML/site.css" } ) );
55      print( start_form(),
56         "Forum Name", br(),
57         textfield( -name => "name", -size => 40 ), br(),
58         "Forum File Name", br(),
59         textfield( -name => "filename", -size => 40 ), br(),
```

Fig. 22.34 Script that adds a new forum to `forums.xml` (part 2 of 3).

```
60            submit( -name => "submit", value => "Submit" ),
61            reset(), end_form(),
62         a( { -href => "/cgi-bin/default.pl" }, "Return to Main Page" ),
63            end_html() );
64    }
```

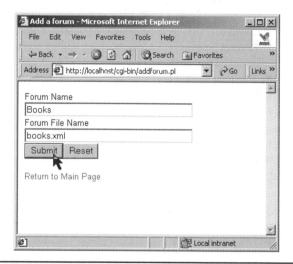

Fig. 22.34 Script that adds a new forum to **forums.xml** (part 3 of 3).

In line 15, we examine the filename posted to the script to make sure it contains only alphanumeric characters and ends with **.xml**; if not, the script terminates. This helps prevent the possibility of someone writing to a system file or otherwise gaining unrestricted access to the server. If the filename is valid, we attempt to create the new file in lines 17 and 18 using function **sysopen**. This file is write only (i.e., **O_WRONLY**). The **sysopen** operation will fail if the file already exists, as specified by **O_EXCL**. Constant **O_CREAT** specifies that the file should be created if it does not exist.

In lines 19 and 20, we open file **forums.xml** for reading and writing (**+<**) and obtain an *exclusive lock* (i.e., only this script can access the file's contents), because we will be altering the file. This lock is released when the script terminates.

The **XML::DOM::Parser** object created in line 23 is a derivation of the **XML::Parser** object discussed in Fig. 22.12. Method **parse** creates a DOM representation of the document (a W3C **Document** object), which we assign to variable **$document**. In line 25, we call **getDocumentElement** to access the root element **forums**.

Because we wish to create a new **forum** element within **forums**, we call the **Document** object's method **createElement** in line 27 with the name of the new element (**forum**). We set the **filename** attribute of the newly created element (an **Element** object) by calling **setAttribute** with the name and value of the attribute. Line 29

```
$forums->insertBefore( $forum, $forums->getFirstChild );
```

inserts the new **$forum** before the first child of **$forums** (found with method **getFirstChild**) by calling method **insertBefore**. This way, the most recently added forums appear first in the forum list.

The **forum** element contains only one piece of information—the forum name—which we add in lines 31–33. We first create another new element (line 31). To add character data between the start and end tags of the new element, we call method **addText** in line 32 with the name entered by the user in the form, i.e., **param("name")**. We then add this child element to **$forum** with the method *appendChild* (line 33).

To rewrite over the old file, we *seek* (line 35) to the beginning and delete any existing data (by truncating the file to size 0). We use method **print** to print the updated XML document to filehandle **FORUMS**, and then we close the filehandle (lines 37 and 38).

Line 40 parses file **template.xml** (Fig. 22.35, which is discussed momentarily) by calling method **parsefile** and assigns the new document to **$document**. We again call **getDocumentElement** to get the empty forum (line 41) and then set its **file** attribute to contain the given filename (line 42). In lines 44–46, we add the **name** element, much as we did earlier in lines 31–33. We output the final result to **NEW** and close the filehandle in lines 48 and 49. The user is returned to the default page in line 50.

After updating **forums.xml** to include the new forum, we must create a new XML document that represents the forum. To simplify things, we provide a template XML document named **template.xml** (Fig. 22.35), which we use for all new forums. The template contains an empty **forums** element, to which we add the forum name and filename.

Figure 22.36 is a program that allows users to add messages. When the documents are rendered using **formatting.xsl** (Fig. 22.37), a link to **addPost.pl** is added to the page, which includes the current forum's filename. This filename is passed as a parameter to **addPost.pl** (e.g., **addPost.pl?file=forum1.xml**) in Fig. 22.36.

If a single parameter (i.e., the filename) is passed, the script execution proceeds to lines 40–56, which outputs a simple form. The form includes fields for the user name, message title and message text and passes the forum filename as a hidden value (line 51). Note that if no parameters are passed to the script, the script has been accessed in an inappropriate way, and the user is redirected to an error document (line 58).

When the form data are submitted, the posted information is processed, starting by the script starting in line 11. As in the previous example (Fig. 22.34), we validate the filename, open the file and obtain an exclusive lock (lines 15–18). We parse the forum file, create a new **message** element, set the **timestamp** attribute and append the **timestamp** attribute as a child to the **forum** element (lines 21–26).

In lines 28–32, we create elements representing the **user**, **title** and **text**, and add text based on the values entered in the form (obtained by **param**). We then **seek** and **truncate** to eliminate the old data, and then we write the new XML markup to **FORUM** in lines 34–36, after which the filehandle is closed and the user is **redirect**ed to the newly created XML document.

22.15.3 Alterations for Non-XSL Browsers

The forum system implemented in this case study uses an XSL stylesheet to display XML documents in the client's browser. This XSL file (**formatting.xsl**) is shown in Fig. 22.37. Lines 18–53 contain the template for the **forum** element, and lines 55–84 describe the template for rendering each message element in the forum file.

This XSL stylesheet consists of a series of HTML tags and *XSL templates*. Each XSL template defines a rule that is applied to a given element. For example, the XSL template on line 18 **match**es the **forum** element. When a **forum** element is found, the HTML contained in the template element is written to the *result tree* (i.e., the transformed document). Other **template**s (i.e., line 36) are applied as they are encountered when element **apply-templates** is processed.

```
1    <?xml version = "1.0"?>
2
3    <!-- Fig. 22.35 : template.xml -->
4
5    <?xml:stylesheet type = "text/xsl" href = "../XML/formatting.xsl"?>
6    <forum>
7    </forum>
```

Fig. 22.35 XML template used to generate new forums.

```
1    #!perl
2    # Fig. 22.36: addPost.pl
3    # Adds a posting to a forum
4
5    use warnings;
6    use strict;
7    use CGI qw( :standard );
8    use XML::DOM;
9    use Fcntl qw( :flock );
10
11   if ( param( "submit" ) ) {
12      my ( $parser, $document, $forum, $message, $element );
13
14      my $file = param( "file" );
15      $file  =~ /^\w+\.xml$/ or die( "Not a valid file: $!" );
16      open( FORUM, "+<../htdocs/XML/$file" )
17         or die( "Could not open: $!" );
18      flock( FORUM, LOCK_EX );
19
20      $parser = new XML::DOM::Parser;
21      $document = $parser->parse( \*FORUM );
22      $forum = $document->getDocumentElement;
23
24      $message = $document->createElement( "message" );
25      $message->setAttribute( "timestamp", scalar( localtime ) );
26      $forum->appendChild( $message );
27
28      foreach ( qw( user title text ) ) {
29         $element = $document->createElement( $_ );
30         $element->addText( param( $_ ) );
31         $message->appendChild( $element );
32      }
33
34      seek( FORUM, 0, 0 );
35      truncate( FORUM, 0 );
36      $document->printToFileHandle( \*FORUM );
37      close( FORUM );
38      print( redirect( "/XML/$file" ) );
39   }
```

Fig. 22.36 Script that adds a new message to a forum (part 1 of 2).

```
40  elsif ( param ) {
41     my $file = param( "file" );
42     print( header, start_html( -title => "Add a posting",
43        -style => { -src => "/XML/site.css" } ) );
44     print( start_form(),
45        "User", br(),
46        textfield( -name => "user", -size => 40 ), br(),
47        "Message Title", br(),
48        textfield( -name => "title", -size => 40 ), br(),
49        "Message Text", br(),
50        textarea( -name => "text", -cols =>  40, -rows => 5 ),
51        br(), hidden( -name => "file", -value => $file ),
52        submit( -name => "submit", -value => "Submit" ),
53        reset(), end_form(),
54        a( { -href => "/XML/$file" }, "Return to Forum" ),
55           end_html() );
56  }
57  else {
58     print( redirect( "error.html" ) );
59  }
```

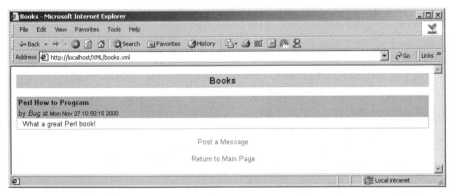

Fig. 22.36   Script that adds a new message to a forum (part 2 of 2).

```
 1   <?xml version = "1.0"?>
 2
 3   <!-- Fig. 22.37 : formatting.xsl -->
 4
 5   <xsl:stylesheet xmlns:xsl = "http://www.w3.org/TR/WD-xsl">
 6
 7      <xsl:template match = "*|@*|text()|cdata()|comment()|pi()">
 8         <xsl:copy><xsl:apply-templates
 9            select = "*|@*|text()|cdata()|comment()|pi()"/></xsl:copy>
10      </xsl:template>
11
12      <xsl:template match = "/">
13         <html>
14         <xsl:apply-templates select = "*"/>
15         </html>
16      </xsl:template>
17
18      <xsl:template match = "forum">
19         <head>
20            <title><xsl:value-of select = "name"/></title>
21            <link rel = "stylesheet" type = "text/css"
22               href = "../XML/site.css"/>
23         </head>
24
25         <body>
26            <table width = "100%" cellspacing = "0"
27               cellpadding = "2">
28               <tr>
29                  <td class = "forumTitle">
30                     <xsl:value-of select = "name"/>
31                  </td>
32               </tr>
33            </table>
34
35            <br/>
36            <xsl:apply-templates select = "message"/>
37            <br/>
38
39            <center>
40               <a>
41                  <xsl:attribute name = "HREF">../cgi-bin/ad-
dPost.pl?file=<xsl:value-of select = "@file"/>
42
43
44                  </xsl:attribute>
45                  Post a Message
46               </a>
47               <br/>
48               <br/>
49              <a href = "../cgi-bin/default.pl">Return to Main Page</a>
50            </center>
51
52         </body>
```

Fig. 22.37 XSL stylesheet used to format and display XML forum files (part 1 of 2).

```
53     </xsl:template>
54
55     <xsl:template match = "message">
56        <table width = "100%" cellspacing = "0"
57           cellpadding = "2">
58           <tr>
59
60              <td class = "msgTitle">
61                 <xsl:value-of select = "title"/>
62              </td>
63
64           </tr>
65
66           <tr>
67              <td class = "msgInfo">
68                 by
69                 <em><xsl:value-of select = "user"/></em>
70                 at
71                 <span class = "date">
72                    <xsl:value-of select = "@timestamp"/>
73                 </span>
74              </td>
75           </tr>
76
77           <tr>
78              <td class = "msgText">
79                 <xsl:apply-templates select = "text"/>
80              </td>
81           </tr>
82
83        </table>
84     </xsl:template>
85
86  </xsl:stylesheet>
```

Fig. 22.37 XSL stylesheet used to format and display XML forum files (part 2 of 2).

However, support for XSL is currently available only for Internet Explorer 5 and higher. This means that our message forum application will send XML documents to some browsers (e.g., Netscape Navigator 4.7) that will not know how to render them. To create a more portable application, we will need to include a server-side XML parser that will translate the forum XML documents into HTML.

There is a module named **XML::XSLT**, written by Geert Josten and Egon Willighagen and available on CPAN, that transforms XML using an XSL stylesheet. However, the module is still in its alpha stages (partly because XSL itself is a W3C Candidate Recommendation). For this example, therefore, we use **XML::Parser** to transform the XML forum files.

We first need to make some minor modifications to the existing code in **default.pl** (Fig. 22.33) and **addPost.pl** (Fig. 22.36). Instead of including links to the XML forum files themselves, we want to direct clients to a CGI script that will parse the XML document and display the appropriate HTML. However, it is more efficient to direct browsers that support XSL straight to the XML. We therefore insert a browser check at line 24 of **default.pl** and line 10 of **addPost.pl**:

```perl
if ( $ENV{ "HTTP_USER_AGENT" } =~ /MSIE/i ) {
    $prefix = "../XML/";
}
else {
    $prefix = "forum.pl?file=";
}
```

The check sets variable **$prefix** according to whether or not MSIE (Microsoft Internet Explorer) appears in the ***HTTP_USER_AGENT*** environment variable. For simplicity, we assume Internet Explorer 5 is the only version of MSIE being used and do not test for older versions. Note that **use strict** requires that we declare **$prefix** using **my** earlier in the program.

Once **$prefix** has been set, we may use it to customize the URLs generated by the scripts. For example, in line 26 of **default.pl**, we change

```perl
a( { -href => "/XML/$files[ $_ ]" }, $forums[ $_ ] )
```

to the more versatile

```perl
a( { -href => "$prefix$files[ $_ ]" }, $forums[ $_ ] )
```

This change directs Internet Explorer users to **../XML/forum.xml**, as before, but sends users of other browsers to **forum.pl?file=forum.xml**, a CGI script (**forum.pl**) that receives a single parameter (i.e., the filename). Similar changes are made in lines 43 and 54 of **addPost.pl**. [*Note*: These modified files are available in the Chapter 22 examples **XSL** directory on the CD-ROM that accompanies this book. The files are named **default_new.pl** and **addPost_new.pl**. Rename the files to **default.pl** and **addPost.pl**, respectively, and place them in the **cgi-bin** directory.]

Figure 22.38 shows **forum.pl**, which transforms the XML documents to HTML. The figure also includes the rendered HTML output. We use Netscape's Communicator to render the HTML.

```perl
1   #!perl
2   # Fig. 22.38: forum.pl
3   # Display forum postings for non-XSL browser
4
5   use warnings;
6   use strict;
7   use CGI qw( :standard *center *table );
8   use XML::Parser;
9   use Fcntl qw( :flock );
10
11  print( redirect( "error.html" ) ) if not param();
12
13  my ( $file, $parser, %info );
14
15  $file = param( "file" );
16  $file =~ /^\w+\.xml$/ or die( "Not a valid file: $!" );
17  open( FORUM, "../htdocs/XML/$file" ) or
18      die( "Could not open: $!" );
```

Fig. 22.38 Script that transforms an XML forum file into HTML (part 1 of 3).

```perl
19   flock( FORUM, LOCK_SH );
20
21   $parser = new XML::Parser( Style    => "Subs",
22                              Handlers => { Char => \&text } );
23   $parser->parse( \*FORUM );
24   close( FORUM );
25
26   sub forum
27   {
28      print( header );
29   }
30
31   sub forum_
32   {
33      print( br, start_center,
34         a( { -href => "/cgi-bin/addPost.pl?file=$file" },
35             "Post a Message" ),
36         br, br,
37         a( { -href => "/cgi-bin/default.pl" },
38             "Return to Main Page" ),
39         end_center, end_html );
40   }
41
42   sub name_
43   {
44      print( start_html( -title => $info{ "name" },
45         -style => { -src => "/XML/site.css" } ),
46         start_table( { -width       => "100%",
47                        -cellspacing => "0",
48                        -cellpadding => "2"    } ),
49
50         Tr( td( { -class => "forumTitle" }, $info{ "name" } ) ),
51         end_table, br );
52   }
53
54   sub message
55   {
56      my ( $expat, $element, %attributes ) = @_;
57      $info{ "date" } = $attributes{ "timestamp" };
58   }
59
60   sub message_
61   {
62      print( start_table( { -width       => "100%",
63         -cellspacing => "0",
64         -cellpadding => "2"    } ),
65         Tr( [ td( { -class   => "msgTitle" }, $info{ "title" } ),
66            td( { -class   => "msgInfo" },
67                " by " . em( $info{ "user" } ) . " at " .
68                span( { -class => "date" }, $info{ "date" } ) ),
69            td( { -class   => "msgText" }, $info{ "text" } ) ] ),
70         end_table );
71   }
```

Fig. 22.38 Script that transforms an XML forum file into HTML (part 2 of 3).

```
72
73  sub text
74  {
75      my ( $expat, $string ) = @_;
76      $info{ $expat->current_element } = $string;
77  }
```

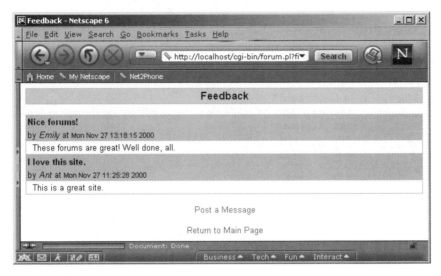

Netscape Communicator browser window ©1999 Netscape Communications
Corporation. Used with permission. Netscape Communications has not authorized,
sponsored, endorsed, or approved this publication and is not responsible for its
content.

Fig. 22.38 Script that transforms an XML forum file into HTML (part 3 of 3).

If no filename is passed to the script, the user is redirected to an error page (line 11).
The basic program procedure (validating the filename, opening, locking, parsing and
closing the XML document) in lines 15–23 is similar to the procedure of the last few examples. In line 7, we add ***center** and ***table** to import tag **:standard**, thus instructing
CGI.pm to create **start_center**, **start_table**, **end_center** and **end_table**
subroutines for us, which generate the corresponding HTML tags.

One notable change appears in line 21, where we set the parser **Style** attribute to the
value **Subs**. The **XML::Parser Subs** style automatically creates handlers set to subroutines with names derived from the corresponding tag names. For example, every time an
opening **<message>** tag is encountered, subroutine **message** is called. Closing-tag handler subroutines are marked by a trailing underscore; a closing **</message>** tag results
in subroutine **message_** being invoked.

Subroutines **forum** and **forum_** (lines 26 and 31) show how the **Subs** style is used.
When the opening **<forum>** tag is found, subroutine **forum** outputs the HTTP header
(line 28). Its companion closing tag is handled by subroutine **forum_**, which prints two
hyperlinks at the bottom of the page, along with the closing HTML tag (lines 33–39).

Note that we declare our own handler for character data (line 21), because the **Subs** style does not automatically create one for us. The handler subroutine **text** is listed in lines 73–77. Because the majority of the data in the XML document we are parsing is represented by character data, we create hash **%info** (line 13) to store these data so they may be used by other handlers. Subroutine **text**, in turn, simply places the encountered string into hash **%info**, using the **current_element** as the key name. For example, text found within **<title>** tags is placed in **$info{ "title" }**.

Because the textual data are placed into **%info** only *after* we encounter the opening tag that contains them, we access the data in the closing-tag handlers (**name_** and **message_**). Thus, in lines 44 and 51 of subroutine **name_**, we can access the forum title, which has been placed into **$info{ "name" }** by subroutine **text**.

Subroutine **message** (lines 54–58) reads the **message** element's value for attribute **timestamp** and (like subroutine **text**) stores the value in hash **%info**. That value, along with the values for **user**, **title** and **text**, are output by subroutine **message_**. Note that in lines 65–70, we use the distributive property of the table-row function **Tr** with an anonymous array (contained in square brackets **[]**) to create three rows, each with one data cell.

22.16 Internet and World Wide Web Resources

www.xml.org
XML.org is a reference for XML, DTDs, schemas and namespaces.

www.w3.org/style/XSL
Provides information on XSL which includes the topics on what is new in XSL, learning XSL, XSL-enabled tools, XSL specification, FAQs, XSL history, etc.

www.w3.org/TR
W3C technical reports and publications page. Contains links to working drafts, proposed recommendations, recommendations, etc.

www.xmlbooks.com
Contains a list of recommended XML books by Charles Goldfarb—one of the original designers of GML (General Markup Language) from which SGML was derived.

www.xmlsoftware.com
Contains links for downloading XML-related software. Download links include XML browsers, conversion tools, database systems, DTD editors, XML editors, etc.

www.xml-zone.com/
The Development Exchange XML Zone is a complete resource for XML information. This site includes a FAQ, news, articles, links to other XML site and newsgroups.

wdvl.internet.com/Authoring/Languages/XML/
Web Developer's Virtual Library XML site includes tutorials, a FAQ, the latest news and extensive links to XML sites and software downloads.

www.xml.com
Visit **XML.com** for the latest news and information about XML, conference listings, links to XML Web resources organized by topic, tools and more.

msdn.microsoft.com/xml/default.asp
The MSDN Online XML Development Center features articles on XML, Ask the Experts chat sessions, samples and demos, newsgroups and other helpful information.

www.w3.org/xml
The W3C (World Wide Web Consortium) works to develop common protocols to ensure interoperability on the Web. Their XML page includes information about upcoming events, publications, software and discussion groups. Visit this site to read about the latest developments in XML.

www.oasis-open.org/cover/xml.html
The SGML/XML Web Page is an extensive resource that includes links to several FAQs, online resources, industry initiatives, demos, conferences and tutorials.

www.gca.org/whats_xml/default.htm
The GCA site has an XML glossary, list of books, brief descriptions of the draft standards for XML and links to online drafts.

www.xmlinfo.com
XMLINFO is a resource site with tutorials, a list of recommended books, documentation, discussion forums and more.

xdev.datachannel.com
The title of this site is xDev: The Definitive Site for Serious XML Developers. This Web site includes several short tutorials with code examples, toolkits downloads and a reference library.

www.ibm.com/developer/xml
The IBM XML Zone site is a great resource for developers. You will find news, tools, a library, case studies, events and information about standards.

developer.netscape.com/tech/metadata/index.html
The XML and Metadata Developer Central site has demos, technical notes and news articles related to XML.

www.projectcool.com/developer/xmlz
The Project Cool Developer Zone site includes several tutorials covering introductory through advanced XML.

www.poet.com/products/cms/xml_library/xml_lib.html
POET XML Resource Library includes links to white papers, tools, news, publications and Web links.

www.ucc.ie/xml
This site is a detailed XML FAQ. Check out responses to some popular questions or submit your own questions through the site.

www.bell-labs.com/project/tts/sable.html
The Sable Markup Language is designed to markup text for input into speech synthesizers.

www.xml-cml.org
This site is a resource for the Chemical Markup Language (CML). It includes a FAQ list, documentation, software and XML links.

www.tcf.nl/3.0/musicml/index.html
MusicML is a DTD for sheet music. Visit this site for examples and the specification.

www.hr-xml.org
The HR-XML Consortium is a nonprofit organization working to set standardized XML tags for use in Human Resources.

www.textuality.com/xml
Contains FAQ and the Lark non-validating XML parser.

www.cpan.org
Modules **XML::Parser** and **XML::DOM** can be downloaded at this site, the official central repository for Perl builds and modules.

www.perl.com
Perl.com is the first place to look for information about Perl. The homepage provides up-to-date news on Perl, answers to common questions about Perl, and an impressive collection of links to Perl resources of all kinds on the Internet. It includes sites for Perl software, tutorials, user groups and demos.

www.zvon.org
Provides an XML tutorial.

SUMMARY

- XML (Extensible Markup Language) was developed in 1996 by the World Wide Web Consortium's (W3C's) XML Working Group and is a widely-supported, open technology for data exchange.

- XML is a markup language for describing structured data—content is separated from presentation.

- Unlike HTML, XML permits document authors to create their own markup for virtually any type of information. This extensibility enables document authors to create entirely new markup languages to describe specific types of data, including mathematical formulas, chemical molecular structures, music, recipes, etc.

- Because XML tags describe the data they contain, it is possible to search, sort, manipulate and render an XML document using related technologies, such as the Extensible Stylesheet Language (XSL).

- XML documents are highly portable. Special software is not required to open an XML document—any text editor that supports ASCII/Unicode characters can be used. One important characteristic of XML is that it is both human readable and machine readable.

- In order to process an XML document a software program called an XML parser (or an XML processor) is required. Most XML parsers are available at no charge and are available for a variety of programming languages (such as Perl, Java™, Python, C, etc.). Parsers check an XML document's syntax and can support the Document Object Model (DOM) and/or the Simple API for XML (SAX). DOM-based parsers build a tree structure containing the XML document's data in memory. SAX-based parsers process the document and generate events when tags, text, comments, etc. are encountered.

- An XML document can reference an optional Document Type Definition (DTD) file, which defines how the XML document is structured. When a DTD is provided, some parsers (called validating parsers) are able to read the DTD and check the XML document structure against it. If the XML document conforms to the DTD, then the XML document is valid. Parsers that cannot check for document conformity ignore the DTD and are called non-validating parsers.

- If an XML parser is able to successfully process an XML document (that does not have a DTD), the XML document is considered well formed (i.e., it is syntactically correct). By definition, a valid XML document is also a well-formed XML document.

- Because Perl has such powerful text-processing capabilities, it is an ideal language for XML processing. Support for XML is provided through a large collection of XML modules which are freely available.

- Because XML allows document authors to create their own tags, naming collisions (i.e., two different elements that have the same name) can occur. Namespaces provide a means for document authors to prevent collisions.

- Namespace prefixes are prepended to element and attribute names in order to specify the namespace in which the element or attribute can be found. Each namespace prefix is tied to a uniform resource identifier (URI) that uniquely identifies the namespace. Document authors can create their own namespace prefixes. Virtually any name may be used for a namespace, except the reserved namespace **xml**.

- In order to eliminate the need to place a namespace prefix in each element, authors may specify a default namespace for an element and all of its child elements.

- DTDs provide a method for type checking an XML document, thus verifying its validity (e.g., tags contain the proper attributes, elements are in proper sequence, etc.). The set of rules that structure a document is done with EBNF (Extended Backus-Naur Form) grammar—not XML syntax. XML parsers need additional functionality to read a DTD because of the EBNF grammar.

- Unlike DTDs, schema do not use the Extended Backus-Naur Form (EBNF) grammar. Instead, schema use XML syntax. Because schema are XML documents, they can be manipulated (e.g., elements added, elements removed, etc.) like any other XML document.

- Like DTDs, schemas must be used with validating parsers. In the near future, schemas are expected to replace DTDs as the primary means of describing document structure.

- Two major schema models exist: W3C XML Schema and Microsoft XML Schema. Alternative schema models (e.g., RELAX) are beginning to emerge.

- W3C XML Schema use the URI **http://www.w3.org/2000/10/XMLSchema** and namespace prefix **xsd**. Root element **schema** contains the document definitions.

- Any element that contains attributes or child elements, must define a type—called a complex type—that defines each attribute and child element.

- XML allows authors to create their own tags to precisely describe data. Consequently, many different kinds of XML have been created for structuring data in various fields. Some of these markup languages are: MathML (Mathematical Markup Language), Scalable Vector Graphics (SVG), Wireless Markup Language (WML), Extensible Business Reporting Language (XBRL), Extensible User Interface Language (XUL) and Product Data Markup Language (PDML).

- The Wireless Markup Language (WML) is an XML-based language that allows text portions of Web pages to be displayed on wireless devices, such as cellular phones and personal digital assistants (PDA). WML works with the Wireless Application Protocol (WAP) to deliver this content. WML is similar to HTML but does not require input devices such as a keyboard or mouse for navigation.

- XBRL (Extensible Business Reporting Language) is a markup language derived from XML for facilitating the creation, exchange and validation of financial information (e.g., annual budgets, dividends, etc.) between vendors and corporations. XBRL was developed by the American Institute of Certified Public Accountants (AICPA) and other organizations.

- Electronic Business XML (ebXML) is a markup language initiated by the United Nations body for Trade Facilitation and Electronic Business (UN/CEFACT) and OASIS (Organization for the Advancement of Structured Information Standards) to develop and standardize an XML document structure for exchanging business data. The goal of ebXML is to reduce the cost of electronic trading for small to medium sized businesses.

- Financial Products Markup Language (FpML) is an emerging standard for exchanging financial information over the Internet. Information exchanged includes interest rate swaps (a contractual agreement between two parties), forward rate agreements, etc.

- The **XML::DOM** module provides an interface to manipulating XML documents in accordance with the Document Object Model approved by the W3C. The **XML::DOM** currently implements the W3C's Level 1 DOM Recommendation and is currently being updated to conform to the Level 2 Recommendation. Module **XML::DOM** also provides a number of extensions to the DOM.

- Module **XML::XSLT**, written by Geert Josten and Egon Willighagen, transforms XML using an XSL stylesheet. This module is still in its alpha stages.

- The **XML::DOM** parser creates a tree-like structure for an XML document, with objects for the nodes instead of array references. Each of these classes inherit from one of three main classes: **Node**, **NodeList** and **NamedNodeMap**.

- A **Document** element represents the entire XML document. **Element** nodes represent XML elements. **Text** nodes represent non-markup text. **Attr** nodes are created for each attribute in a XML tag and **Comment** nodes are created for comment sections. **Document** nodes can contain **Element**, **Text** and **Comment** nodes. **Element** nodes can contain other nodes and can have **Attr**, **Element**, **Text** and **Comment** nodes.

- SAX was developed by the members of the XML-DEV mailing list and was released in May of 1998. SAX is an alternate method for parsing XML documents that uses an event-based model—notifications called events are raised as the document is parsed.

- SAX and DOM are dramatically different APIs for accessing information in XML documents. DOM is a tree-based model that stores the document's data in a hierarchy of nodes. Because all the document's data is in memory, data can be quickly accessed. DOM also provides facilities for adding or removing nodes (i.e., modifying the document).

- SAX-based parsers invoke methods when markup (e.g., a start tag, end tag, etc.) is encountered. With this event-based model, no tree structure is created by the SAX-based parser to store the XML document's data—data is passed to the application from the XML document as it is found. SAX-based parsers are available for a variety of programming languages (e.g., Perl, Java, Python, etc.).

- Module **XML::Parser** provides an interface to the **expat** XML parser written by James Clark. The **XML::Parser** module allows you to choose which model (SAX or DOM) you wish to use. SAX-based parsing is the default option for the module.

- Module **Data::Dumper** "dumps" information. We used this module in the chapter to view the tree structure created by the parser.

- Extensible Stylesheet Language (XSL) defines how an XML document's data is rendered. The relationship between XML and XSL is similar to the relationship between HTML and Cascading Style Sheets (CSS)—although XSL is much more powerful than CSS. An XML document's data does not have to be rendered using an XSL document, CSS can also be used.

- An XSL document provides the rules for displaying (or organizing) an XML document's data. XSL also provides elements that define rules for how one XML document is transformed into another text-based document (e.g., XML, HTML, etc.). The subset of XSL concerned with transformations is called XSL Transformations (XSLT).

TERMINOLOGY

#IMPLIED flag
#PCDATA flag
.dtd file extension
.xml file extension
.xsd extension
addText method
ancestor node
appendChild method
apply-templates element
asterisk (*****) occurrence indicator
Attr node
Cascading Style Sheets (CSS)
CDATA flag

Char handler
child nodes
CML (Chemical Markup Language)
Comment node
complexType element
createAttribute
createComment
createElement
createElement method
createTextNode
current_byte
current_column
current_element method

setTagName
setValue
sibling node
Simple API for XML (SAX)
SMBXML (Small to Medium Business XML)
SMIL (Synchronized Multimedia Integration
Language)
Standard Generalized Markup Language (SGML)
Start handler
-style attribute (**starthtml**)
style attribute (**XML::Parser**)
Style=>'Tree' option
stylesheet
Subs attribute value
SVG (Scalable Vector Graphics)
symbolic representation
Synchronized Multimedia Integration Language
(SMIL)
SYSTEM flag
Text nodes
truncate method
type attribute
URI (Uniform Resource Identifier)
URL (Universal Resource Locator)
valid document
validating XML parser
validity
value-of
VML (Vector Markup Language)
VoiceXML
W3C (World Wide Web Consortium)

W3C XML Schema
WAP (Wireless Application Protocol)
well formed document
WML (Wireless Markup Language)
XBRL (Extensible Business Reporting Language)
xml declaration
XML markup
XML Metadata Interchange (XMI)
xml namespace
XML node
XML parser
XML root
XML Schema
XML **version**
XML::DOM
XML::DOM module
XML::DOM::Parser class
XML::Parser
XML::Parser module
XML::Parser::Expat module
XML::XSLT module
xml:stylesheet
XMLDOMNode
xmlns keyword
XSL (Extensible Stylesheet Language)
XSL document
XSL specification
XSL stylesheet
XSL templates
xsl:template
XSLT (XSL Transformations)

SELF-REVIEW EXERCISES

22.1   What is the purpose of the **startTag** and **text** subroutines in Fig. 22.33? What do they do?

22.2   Why must we use **XML::DOM** instead of **XML::Parser** to add forums and messages?

22.3   In Fig. 22.38, why do we output most of the HTML in the closing tag handlers?

22.4   Which of the following are valid XML element names?
   a) yearBorn
   b) **year.Born**
   c) **year Born**
   d) **year-Born1**
   e) **2_year_born**
   f) **--year/born**
   g) **year*born**
   h) **.year_born**
   i) **_year_born_**
   j) **y_e-a_r-b_o-r_n**

22.5   State whether the following are *true* or *false*. If *false*, explain why.
   a) XML is a technology for creating markup languages.
   b) XML markup text is delimited by forward and backward slashes (**/** and ****).
   c) Unlike HTML, all XML start tags must have corresponding end tags.
   d) Parsers check an XML document's syntax and may support the Document Object Model and/or the Simple API for XML.
   e) URIs are strings that identify resources such as files, images, services, electronic mailboxes and more.
   f) When creating new XML tags, document authors must use the set of XML tags provided by the W3C.
   g) The pound character (**#**), the dollar sign (**$**), ampersand (**&**), greater-than (**>**) and less-than (**<**) are examples of XML reserved characters.

ANSWERS TO SELF-REVIEW EXERCISES

22.1   The **startTag** and **text** subroutines are handlers that are called when the XML parser encounters an opening tag or character data, respectively. Subroutine **startTag** takes the filename attribute of the tag and pushes its value onto array **@files** (if the tag that triggered the handler was a **<forum>** tag). Subroutine **text** pushes the string value encountered onto array **@forums** if the character data is found within a **name** element.

22.2   **XML::DOM** creates a DOM structure representing XML data which we can then modify and save to a file as XML. This allows us to add nodes which represent new forums and messages. **XML::Parser** simply parses XML, and thus cannot be used to modify the underlying XML document.

22.3   Because **XML::Parser** is an event-based parser, when we encounter the start tag of an element which contains a child node of character data, that character data has not yet been seen by the parser. Once we reach the end tag, we know that any character data surrounded by the tags has been handled by subroutine **text**, and the necessary information stored in hash **%info**.

22.4   a, b, d, i, j.

22.5   a) True. b) False. In an XML document, markup text is any text delimited by angle brackets (**<** and **>**) with a forward slash being used in the end tag. c) True. d) True. e) True. f) False. When creating new tags, programmers may use any valid name except the reserved word **xml** (also **XML**, **Xml**, etc.). g) False. XML reserved characters include the ampersand (**&**), the left-angle bracket (**<**) and the right-angle bracket (**>**) but not **#** and **$**.

EXERCISES

22.6   Implement the **Delete a Forum** option in **default.pl**. Selecting this option should display the initial screen, but with each forum name followed by a hyperlink to a script named **delForum.pl**. This script should remove the given forum from **forums.xml**, and delete the underlying XML document. [*Hint*: look at the **getElementsByTagName** and **removeChild** methods described in the **XML::DOM** documentation.]

22.7   Implement the **Modify a Forum** option in **default.pl** such that individual messages can be deleted. Selecting this option should display the initial screen, but with each forum name followed by a hyperlink to a script named **modForum.pl**. Script **modForum.pl** should display the messages as in **forum.pl**, but each message title should be followed by a link to a script named **delPost.pl**, which removes the given message from the current forum. [*Hint*: look at the **getElementsByTagName**, **removeChild**, and **item** methods described in the **XML::DOM** documentation.]

22.8   Create an XML document that marks up the nutrition facts for a package of Grandma Deitel's Cookies. A package of Grandma Deitel's Cookies has a serving size of 1 package and the following nutritional value per serving: 260 calories, 100 fat calories, 11 grams of fat, 2 grams of saturated fat, 5 milligrams of cholesterol, 210 milligrams of sodium, 36 grams of total carbohydrates, 2 grams of fiber, 15 grams of sugars and 5 grams of protein.Render the XML documents in Internet Explorer 5. [*Hint*: Your markup should contain elements describing the product name, serving size/amount, calories, sodium, cholesterol, proteins, etc. Mark up each nutrition fact/ingredient listed above. Use nested elements as necessary.]

22.9   Write an XSL stylesheet for your solution to Exercise 22.8 that displays the nutritional facts in an HTML table.

23

Accessibility

Objectives

- To introduce the World Wide Web Consortium's Web Content Accessibility Guidelines 1.0 (WCAG 1.0).
- To use the **alt** attribute of the **<img>** tag to describe images to blind and vision impaired people, to mobile Web device users, to search engines, etc.
- To make tables more accessible to page readers by using the **headers** attribute in HTML 4.01.
- To verify that HTML tags are used properly and to ensure that Web pages are viewable on any type of display or reader.
- To better understand how VoiceXML™ will change the way people with disabilities access information on the Web.

I once was lost, but now am found,
Was blind, but now I see.
John Newton

'Tis the good reader that makes the good book...
Ralph Waldo Emerson

23.1 Introduction

On April 7, 1997, the World Wide Web Consortium (W3C) launched the *Web Accessibility Initiative* (WAI™). *Accessibility* refers to the level of usability of an application or Web site for people with disabilities. The vast majority of Web sites are considered inaccessible to people with visual, learning or mobility impairments. A high level of accessibility is difficult to achieve because there are many different disabilities, language barriers, hardware and software inconsistencies, etc. As greater numbers of people with disabilities begin to use the Internet, it is imperative that Web site designers increase the accessibility to their sites. The WAI is an attempt to make the Web more accessible; its mission is described at **www.w3.org/WAI**.

As a member of the World Wide Web Consortium, Deitel & Associates, Inc. is committed to supporting the WAI. This chapter discusses some of the techniques for developing accessible Web sites. The Web Content Accessibility Guidelines 1.0 (**www.w3.org/TR/WCAG10**) are divided into a three-tier structure of checkpoints according to their priority. *Priority one checkpoints* are those that must be met in order to ensure accessibility; we focus on these in this chapter. *Priority two checkpoints*, though not essential, are highly recommended. *Priority three checkpoints* slightly improve accessibility. The WAI also presents a supplemental list of *quick tips*, which contains checkpoints aimed at solving priority one problems. More information on the WAI Quick Tips can be found at **www.w3.org/WAI/References/Quicktips**.

23.2 Providing Alternatives for Multimedia Content

One important WAI requirement is to ensure that every image, movie and sound used on a Web page is accompanied by a description that clearly defines its purpose. One way of accomplishing this is to include a description of each item using the **alt** attribute of the **<img>** and **<input>** tags. A text equivalent for **object** elements should also be provided, because they do not have an **alt** attribute in the HTML 4.01 specification. Figure 23.1 demonstrates using the **alt** attribute of the **<img>** tag.

The lack of well-defined **alt** elements increases the difficulty of navigating the Web for visually impaired users. Specialized *user agent*s, such as *screen readers* (programs which allow users to hear what is being displayed on their screen) and *braille displays* (devices that receive data from screen reading software and output the data as braille) allow blind and visually impaired people to access text-based information that is normally displayed on the screen. A user agent is an application that interprets Web page source code and translates it into formatted text and images. Web browsers such as Internet Explorer and Netscape Communicator as well as screen readers are examples of user agents.

Web pages with large amounts of multimedia content are difficult for user agents to interpret, unless they are designed properly. Images, movies and other non-HTML objects cannot be read by screen readers. Providing multimedia-based information in a variety of ways (i.e., using the **alt** attribute or providing inline descriptions of images) helps maximize the content's accessibility.

Lines 15–19 specify a *Cascading Style Sheet (CSS)* that formats the HTML. In this particular case, the **body**'s background is set to green and the foreground **color** is set to **black**. Each paragraph element is formatted one times the size of the font (i.e., **1em**). Line 18 creates a *class* named **center** that specifies a **center** alignment. This class is used in lines 31and 38 to center text for two **p** elements. CSS is discussed in detail in Chapter 26.

Figure 23.2 shows a Perl script which facilitates the inclusion of the **alt** attribute into existing Web pages that are placed in the **htdocs** directory. The script uses the **HTML::Parser** module to extract image information from an HTML document. It then displays the images in an HTML form with a text field for each image where the user may enter descriptive text to be used with the **alt** attribute. [*Note*: For simplicity, we search for lowercase HTML tags and attributes.]

To parse the HTML document we create two specialized subclasses of **HTML::Parser**. The first of these is **ImgFinder** (lines 9 through 31) which finds all images in the document. In lines 13 through 30 we define subroutine **start**, which is called for each start tag found in the document. **HTML::Parser** calls the subroutine with five arguments, but we only need two of them: **$tag**, the tag name, and **$attributes**, a reference to a hash of the tag attribute name-value pairs.

```
1    <!DOCTYPE HTML PUBLIC "-//W3C//DTD HTML 4.0 Transitional//EN">
2    <html lang = "en">
3
4    <!-- Fig. 23.1 alttag.html                                -->
5    <!-- Using the alt tag to make an image accessible -->
6
7    <head>
8    <meta http-equiv = "Content-Type"
9    content = "text/html; charset=iso-8859-1">
10
11   <title>
12   How to use the "ALT" attribute
13   </title>
14
15   <style type = "text/css">
16   body { background: #00ff00; color: black }
17   p { margin-top: 1em }
18   .center { text-align: center }
19   </style>
```

Fig. 23.1   Using the **alt** attribute of the **<img>** tag (part 1 of 3).

```
20   </head>
21
22   <body>
23   <h1>How to use the "ALT" attribute</h1>
24   <p>Below we compare two images, one with the
25   "ALT" attribute present, and one without. The
26   "ALT" appears as a tool tip in the first
27   image, but more importantly, will help users
28   who cannot view information conveyed graphically.
29   </p>
30
31   <p class = "center">
32   This image has the "ALT" attribute<br>
33   <img alt = "This is a picture of the Advanced
34   Java How To Program Text Book" src = "advjhtp1cov.jpg"
35   width = "182" height = "238">
36   </p>
37
38   <p class = "center">
39   This image does not have the "ALT" attribute<br>
40   <!-- This markup should be changed            -->
41   <!-- because there is no alt attribute         -->
42   <img src = "advjhtp1cov.jpg" width = "182" height="238">
43   </p>
44   </body>
45   </html>
```

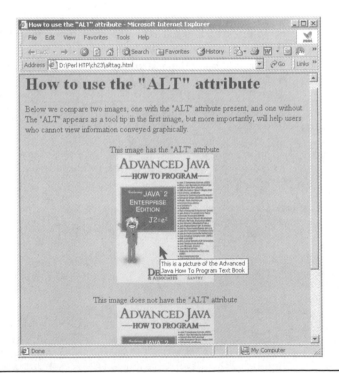

Fig. 23.1   Using the **alt** attribute of the **<img>** tag (part 2 of 3).

Fig. 23.1   Using the **alt** attribute of the **<img>** tag (part 3 of 3).

If **$tag** indicates that the start tag is an **<img>** tag (line 17), we extract the **src** and **alt** attribute values from hash **%$attributes**. In line 21, we check to see if an image with this **src** name has already been found in the document by checking hash **%images** in package **main**, and if so, we skip it. Each new image found is added to this hash (line 28) after processing it.

The image processing simply consists of printing tags which display the image above an HTML form text field where the user may enter **alt** text (lines 22 through 25). Note that any existing **alt** text is retained as the default value for the text field.

The second specialized subclass of **HTML::Parser** we create is **AltMaker** (lines 32 through 71). This parser simply adds the given alt attributes to the appropriate **<img>** tags, leaving the rest of the HTML document unchanged. The entire new document is output to a filehandle opened in package **main** (hence the references to **main::FILE** in lines 57, 63 and 69).

Subroutine **start** in lines 36 through 58 uses two more of the arguments passed to it: **$order** (a reference to an array of the tag attribute names in the order they appear) and **$original** (the original tag found, including the angle brackets **<>**).

As with **ImgFinder**, we skip past all tags which are not **<img>** tags (line 40). If the tag does not contain an **alt** attribute, we add it to the end of array **@$order** (line 44). In line 47, we set the value for the **alt** attribute. We reuse hash **%images** from package **main** for this purpose—this time, it holds the **alt** text for each image using the image **src** attribute value as a key. If no **alt** text is given, we use the empty string (line 47).

Lines 49 through 52 build a new **<img>** tag by adding attribute name-value pairs for each element in **@$order**. This preserves the original order of the attributes in the tag. In line 57, the tag is output to the file. Note that for all non-**<img>** tags, the original tag is output, unchanged. The **end** and **text** subroutines (lines 60 through 70) perform a similar function, simply outputting the end tags or text as they appear in the original HTML document.

Line 72 begins the **main** body of the script, returning us to package main. Hash **%images** (which is used in different ways by each parser) is declared in line 73. If no parameters are passed to the script, lines 76 through 80 output a simple form which queries the user for the file name of the HTML document in which to add **alt** image information. Note that this document must be located within the Web document root (i.e., **htdocs** for Apache) for the script to function properly.

```perl
1    #!/usr/bin/perl
2    # Fig. 23.2: altMaker.pl
3    # Program that inserts ALT attributes into HTML <IMG> tags
4
5    use warnings;
6    use strict;
7    use CGI qw( :standard *center :cgi-lib escapeHTML );
8
9    package HTML::Parser::ImgFinder;
10   require HTML::Parser;
11   our @ISA = "HTML::Parser";
12
13   sub start
14   {
15      my ( undef, $tag, $attributes, undef, undef ) = @_;
16
17      if ( $tag eq 'img' ) {
18         my $alt  = $$attributes{ 'alt' };
19         my $name = $$attributes{ 'src' };
20
21         unless ( $main::images{ $name } ) {
22            print( "<img src = \"../$name\"><br/><br/>\n" );
23            print( "<input type = \"text\" size = \"40\"" );
24            print( "name = \"$name\" value = \"$alt\">" );
25            print( "<br/><br/><hr/>\n" );
26         }
27
28         $main::images{ $name } = 1;
29      }
30   }
31
32   package HTML::Parser::AltMaker;
33   require HTML::Parser;
34   our @ISA = "HTML::Parser";
35
36   sub start
37   {
38      my ( undef, $tag, $attributes, $order, $original ) = @_;
```

Fig. 23.2   Script to add **alt** information to **<img>** tags (part 1 of 5).

```perl
39
40     if ( $tag eq 'img' ) {
41        my $key = $$attributes{ 'src' };
42
43        unless ( exists $$attributes{ 'alt' } ) {
44           push @$order, 'alt';
45        }
46
47        $$attributes{ 'alt' } = $main::images{ $key } || "";
48
49        $original = "<img";
50        foreach $key ( @$order ) {
51           $original .= " $key = \"$$attributes{ $key }\"";
52        }
53
54        $original .= ">";
55     }
56
57     print main::FILE $original;
58  }
59
60  sub end
61  {
62     my $tag = $_[ 1 ];
63     print main::FILE "</$tag>";
64  }
65
66  sub text
67  {
68     my $text = $_[ 1 ];
69     print main::FILE $text;
70  }
71
72  package main;
73  our %images = ();
74
75  unless ( param ) {
76     print( header, start_html( "Enter file name" ),
77        h2( "Enter file name:" ), start_form,
78        filefield( -name => "file" ), br, br,
79        submit( -name => "submit", -value => "Submit file" ),
80        end_form, end_html );
81
82  }
83  elsif ( param( "submit" ) eq "Submit file" ) {
84     my $file = param( "file" );
85     my $parser = new HTML::Parser::ImgFinder;
86
87     print( header, start_html( "Images found" ), start_center,
88        h2( "Enter ALT descriptions for the images below." ),
89        i( "File is $file" ), start_form );
90
91     $parser->parse_file( $file );
```

Fig. 23.2   Script to add **alt** information to **<img>** tags (part 2 of 5).

```perl
92
93      print( br, hidden( -name => "file" ),
94         submit( -name => "submit", -value => "Submit ALT tags" ),
95         submit( -name => "submit", -value => "Do another page" ),
96         end_form, end_html );
97
98   }
99   else {
100     my $file = param( "file" );
101     my $parser = new HTML::Parser::AltMaker;
102
103     %images = Vars;
104     foreach ( keys %images ) {
105        $images{ $_ } = escapeHTML( $images{ $_ } );
106     }
107
108     ( my $newfile = $file ) =~ s/\./_tmp./;
109
110     open( FILE, "> $newfile" ) or die( "Could not open: $!" );
111     $parser->parse_file( $file );
112     close( FILE );
113
114     unlink( $file ) or die ( "Could not delete: $!" );
115     rename( $newfile, $file ) or die( "Could not rename: $!" );
116
117     if ( param( "submit" ) eq "Do another page" ) {
118        print( redirect( "altMaker.pl" ) );
119     }
120     else {
121        my $base = $ENV{ "DOCUMENT_ROOT" };
122
123        $file =~ s#\\#/#g;
124        $file =~ s#^$base##i;
125        print( redirect( "..$file" ) );
126     }
127   }
```

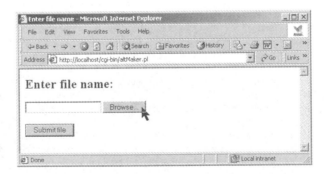

Fig. 23.2   Script to add **alt** information to **<img>** tags (part 3 of 5).

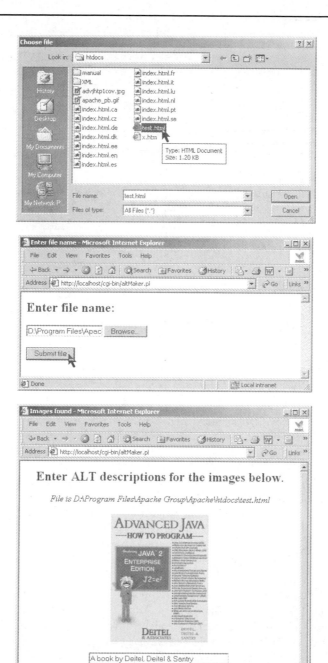

Fig. 23.2   Script to add **alt** information to **<img>** tags (part 4 of 5).

Fig. 23.2   Script to add **alt** information to **<img>** tags (part 5 of 5).

When the user clicks the **Submit File** button, the script is called again and lines 83 through 98 are executed. We begin an HTML form in line 87. In line 91, **$parser** (an instance of **ImgFinder**) parses the given HTML document (using method **parse_file**) and prints out the images and form elements. Note that the **name** of each text field is simply the file **src** name of the associated image (line 24).

When the script is called for the third time, lines 99 through 127 add the new **alt** data to the HTML document. We use the **Vars** function (imported by the **:cgi-lib** import tag in line 7) to put all of the name-value pairs from the posted form into hash **%images** (line 103). As explained above, the hash key is the **src** file name, and its value, the **alt** text. We iterate through each **alt** value in **%images** (lines 104 through 106) to HTML-escape the alt strings so that characters such as ampersands and angle brackets are printed correctly.

In lines 110 through 112 we create a temporary file name, open it, create the new HTML document (using the **AltMaker** parser), and close the temporary file. The old file is deleted (line 114) and the temporary file is given the old file's name (line 115). If the user selected **Do another page**, we redirect to **altMaker.pl** and the process begins again (line 118). Otherwise, we display the newly created document by constructing its URL and redirecting (lines 121 through 125).

Web designers should avoid misuse of the **alt** attribute; it is intended to provide a short description of an HTML object which may not load properly on all user agents. For example, if the **alt** attribute describes a sales growth chart, it should not describe chart data. Instead, it should specify the chart's title. The chart's data should be included in the Web site's text or by using the **longdesc** attribute, which is intended to augment the

ALT's description. The value of the **longdesc** attribute is a text-based URL which is linked to a Web page that describes the image. [*Note:* If an image is used as a hyperlink and the **longdesc** attribute is also used, there is no set standard as to which page is loaded when the image is clicked.]

*Server-side image maps (*images stored on a Web server with areas designated as hyperlinks*)* are another troublesome technology for some Web users—particularly those who cannot use a mouse. Server-side image maps require clicks to initiate their actions.User agent technology is unable to make server-side image maps accessible to blind people or to others who cannot use a mouse. If equivalent text links are not provided when a server-side image map is used, some users will be unable to navigate the site. User agent manufacturers will provide accessibility to server-side image maps, in the future. Until then, if image maps are used, we recommend using *client-side image maps* (image maps whose links are designated in the Web page's source and thus can be understood by non-graphical user agents). For more information regarding the use of image maps, visit **www.w3.org/TR/REC-html40/struct/objects.html#h-13.6**.

Good Programming Practice 23.1

Always provide generous descriptions and corresponding text links to all image maps.

Using a screen reader to navigate a Web site can be time consuming and frustrating as screen readers are unable to interpret pictures and other graphical content. One method of combatting this problem is to include a link at the top of each of Web page that provides easy access to the page's content. Users can use the link to bypass an image map or other inaccessible element, by jumping to another part of the page or to a different page.

23.3 Maximizing Readability by Focusing on Structure

Many Web sites use tags for aesthetic purposes rather than the purpose for which they were intended. For example, one might use the header tag, **<h1>**, to make text large and bold. This may achieve the desired visual effect, but it creates a problem for screen readers. When the screen reader software encounters text tagged as **<h1>**, it may verbally inform the user that they have reached a new section; this can confuse the user. Only use tags such as **<h1>** in accordance with their HTML specification. The **<h1>** tags are intended for use only as headings to introduce important sections of a document. Instead of using **<h1>**, the **<b>** (bold) tag should be used to achieve the same visual effect. Please use the Web Content Accessibility Guidelines 1.0 at **www.w3.org/TR/WCAG** for further examples. [*Note:* the **<strong>** tag may also be used to make text bold, however the inflection in which that text is spoken by screen readers may be affected.]

Another accessibility issue is *readability*. When creating a Web page intended for the general public, it is important to consider the reading level at which it is written. Web site designers can make their site more readable through the use of smaller words, as some users may have difficulty reading large words. Users from other countries may have difficulty understanding slang and other non-traditional language, so these should also be avoided.

The *Web Content Accessibility Guidelines 1.0* suggest using a paragraph's first sentence to convey its subject. Immediately stating the point makes finding crucial information much easier and allows those unable to comprehend large amounts of text to bypass unwanted material.

A good way to evaluate a Web site's readability is by using the *Gunning Fog Index*. The Gunning Fog Index is a formula which produces a readability grade when applied to a text sample. For more information on the Gunning Fog Index see **www.w3.org/TR/ WAI-WEBCONTENT-TECHS**.

23.4 Accessibility in HTML Tables

Complex Web pages often contain tables and screen readers are incapable of translating tables in an understandable manner, unless they are designed properly. For example, the *CAST eReader*, a screen reader developed by the Center for Applied Special Technology (**www.cast.org**), starts at the top-left-hand cell and reads left to right and top to bottom. This is known as reading a table in a *linearized* manner. A screen reader reads the table in Fig. 23.3 as follows:

```
Price of Fruit Fruit Price Apple $0.25 Orange $0.50 Banana
$1.00 Pineapple $2.00
```

HTML does not provide any capabilities for dealing with this problem. The Web Content Accessibility Guidelines 1.0 recommend using Cascading Style Sheets (CSS) instead of tables unless the content, in your table, linearizes in an understandable way.

```
1    <html>
2    <!-- Fig. 23.3 noheaders.html -->
3
4    <head>
5    <title>EXAMPLE WITHOUT HEADERS</title>
6
7    </HEAD>
8
9    <body bgcolor = "#7E0810" text = "#ffffff">
10
11   <center><b> Price of Fruit </b></center>
12   <table width = "47%" border = "1" align = "center">
13      <tr>
14         <td>Fruit</td>
15         <td>Price</td>
16      </tr>
17      <tr>
18         <td>Apple</td>
19         <td>$0.25</td>
20      </tr>
21      <tr>
22         <td>Orange</td>
23         <td>$0.50</td>
24      </tr>
25      <tr>
26         <td>Banana</td>
27         <td>$1.00</td>
28      </tr>
29      <tr>
```

Fig. 23.3   HTML table without accessibility modifications (part 1 of 2).

```
30        <td>Pineapple</td>
31        <td>$2.00</td>
32      </tr>
33    </table>
34    </body>
35    </html>
```

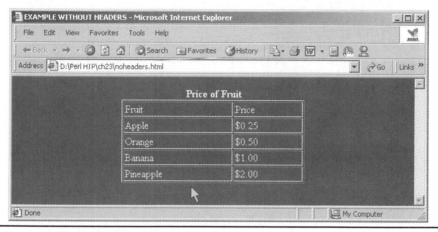

Fig. 23.3   HTML table without accessibility modifications (part 2 of 2).

If this were a large table, the output would be confusing for the person using the screen reader. By modifying the **<td>** tag with the **headers** attribute and modifying *header cells* (cells specified by the **<th>** tag) with the **id** attribute, you can ensure that a table is read as intended. Figure 23.4 demonstrates how these modifications change the way a table is interpreted.

```
1    <html>
2    <!-- Fig. 23.4 headers.html -->
3
4    <head>
5    <title>HEADERS EXAMPLE</title>
6
7    </head>
8
9    <body bgcolor = "#7E0810" text = "#ffffff">
10
11   <!-- This table uses the ID and HEADERS attributes       -->
12   <!-- Using them ensures readability by text-based browsers -->
13   <!-- It also uses a SUMMARY attribute -->
14   <!-- SUMMARY explains the table to a screen reader         -->
15
16   <table summary = "This table uses TH elements and ID and HEADER
17     attributes to make the table readable by screen readers"
18   width = "47%" border = "1" align = "center">
19   <caption><b>Price of Fruit
20   </b></caption>
```

Fig. 23.4   HTML table optimized for screen reading (part 1 of 2).

```
21    <tr>
22      <th id = "fruit">Fruit</th>
23      <th id = "price">Price</th>
24    </tr>
25    <tr>
26      <td headers = "fruit">Apple</td>
27      <td headers = "price">$0.25</td>
28    </tr>
29    <tr>
30      <td headers = "fruit">Orange</td>
31      <td headers = "price">$0.50</td>
32    </tr>
33    <tr>
34      <td headers = "fruit">Banana</td>
35      <td headers = "price">$1.00</td>
36    </tr>
37    <tr>
38      <td headers = "fruit">Pineapple</td>
39      <TD HEADERS = "price">$2.00</td>
40    </tr>
41  </table>
42  </body>
43  </html>
```

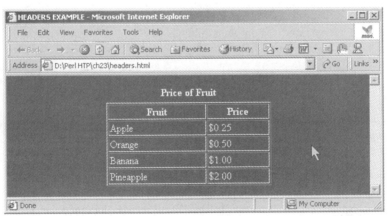

Fig. 23.4   HTML table optimized for screen reading (part 2 of 2).

This table does not appear to be different from a standard HTML table. However, to a person using a screen reader, this table is entirely different. Instead of reading the table from left to right and top to bottom, the table is now read in a more intelligent manner. A screen reader would vocalize the data from the table in Fig. 23.4 as follows:

```
Caption: Price of Fruit
Summary: This table uses TH and the ID and HEADERS attributes
to make the table readable by screen readers.
Fruit: Apple, Price: $0.25
Fruit: Orange, Price: $0.50
Fruit: Banana, Price: $1.00
Fruit: Pineapple, Price: $2.00
```

Every cell in the table is preceded its corresponding header, when read by the screen reader. This helps the listener understand the table. The **headers** attribute is specifically intended for tables which hold large amounts of data. In practice, a table the size of the one in our example would probably not warrant the need for the **headers** attribute. Most small tables linearize fairly well as long as the **<th>** tag. It also helps to use the **summary** and **CAPTION** attributes are used to describe them. For more examples demonstrating how to make tables more accessible, visit **www.w3.org/TR/WCAG**.

23.5 Accessibility in HTML Frames

Frames are a technique Web designers use to display more than one HTML file at a time and are a convenient way to ensure that certain content is always on screen. Unfortunately, frame often lack a proper description. This prevents users with text-based browsers, or users who lack sight, from navigating the Web site.

The most important part of documenting a site with frames is making sure that all of the frames are given a meaningful description within the **<title>** tag. Examples of good titles might be: "*Graphical Navigation Frame*" or "*Main Content Frame.*" Users with text-based browsers such as Lynx, a Web browser, must choose which frame they want to open, and the use of descriptive titles can make this choice much simpler for them. However, giving frames titles does not solve all frame navigation problems.

The **<noframes>** tag allows the designer to offer alternative content to user's whose browsers do not support frames. For an example of how to use the **<noframes>** tag see Chapter 25.

Good Programming Practice 23.2

Always give a text equivalent for frames to ensure that user agents, which do not support frames, are given an alternative.

Good Programming Practice 23.3

*Include a description of the each frame's contents within the **<noframes>** tag.*

The Web Content Accessibility Guidelines 1.0 suggest using Cascading Style Sheets as an alternative to frames because they can provide similar results and are highly customizible. Unfortunately, the ability to display multiple HTML documents at a time requires the second generation of Cascading Style Sheets (CSS2), which is not yet fully supported by many user agents. The advantage of Cascading Style Sheets is that a user who has a text-based user agent can turn off style sheets and still have access to important content.

23.6 Using Voice Synthesis and Recognition with VoiceXML™

A joint effort by AT&T, IBM®, Lucent and Motorola has created an XML application which uses *speech synthesis* to enable the computer to speak to the user. This technology, called *VoiceXML*, has tremendous implications for visually impaired people and for the illiterate. Not only does VoiceXML read Web pages to the user, but it also includes *speech recognition* technology—a technology which enables computers to understand words spoken into the microphone—enabling it to interact with users. An example of a speech recognition tool is IBM's *ViaVoice* (**www-4.ibm.com/software/speech**).

VoiceXML is processed by a VoiceXML interpreter or VoiceXML browser; Web browsers might incorporate these interpreters in the future. Because VoiceXML is derived from XML it is platform independent. When a VoiceXML document is loaded, a *voice server* sends a message to the VoiceXML browser and begins a conversation between the user and the computer.

Voice Server SDK, which was developed by IBM, is a free beta version of a VoiceXML interpreter and can be used for desktop testing of VoiceXML documents. Visit **www.alphaworks.ibm.com** for hardware and software specifications and for more information on Voice Server SDK. Instructions on how to run VoiceXML documents can be obtained along with the software.

Figure 23.5 is an example of a VoiceXML document. The document's text is spoken to the user and the text embedded within the VoiceXML tags will allow for interactivity between the user and their browser. The output included in Fig. 23.5 demonstrates a conversation that might take place between the user and the computer when this document is loaded:

```
1   <?xml version = "1.0"?>
2   <vxml version = "1.0">
3
4   <!-- Fig. 23.5: main.vxml -->
5   <!-- Voice page           -->
6
7   <link next = "#home">
8      <grammar>home</grammar>
9   </link>
10
11  <link next = "#end">
12     <grammar>exit</grammar>
13  </link>
14
15  <var name = "currentOption" expr = "'home'"/>
16
17  <form>
18     <block>
19        <emp>Welcome</emp> to the voice page of Deitel and
20        Associates. To exit any time say exit.
21        To go to home page any time say home.
22     </block>
23     <subdialog src = "#home"/>
24  </form>
25
26  <menu id = "home">
27     <prompt count = "1" timeout = "10s">
28        You have just entered the Deitel home page.
29        Please make a selection by speaking one the
30        following options:
31        <break msecs = "1000 "/>
32        <enumerate/>
33     </prompt>
34
```

Fig. 23.5   A home page written in VoiceXML (part 1 of 3).

```
35         <prompt count = "2">
36            Please say one of the following.
37            <break msecs = "1000 "/>
38            <enumerate/>
39         </prompt>
40
41         <choice next = "#about">About us</choice>
42         <choice next = "#directions">Driving directions</choice>
43         <choice next = "publications.vxml">Publications</choice>
44      </menu>
45
46   <form id = "about">
47      <block>
48         About Deitel and Associates, Inc.
49         Deitel and Associates, Inc. is an internationally
50        recognized corporate training and publishing organization,
51         specializing in programming languages, Internet and World
52         Wide Web technology and object technology education.
53         Deitel and Associates, Inc. is a member of the World Wide
54         Web Consortium. The company provides courses on Java, C++,
55         Visual Basic, C, Internet and World Wide Web programming
56         and Object Technology.
57         <assign name = "currentOption" expr = "'about'"/>
58         <goto next = "#repeat"/>
59      </block>
60   </form>
61
62   <form id = "directions">
63     <block>
64        Directions to Deitel and Associates, Inc.
65        We are located on Route 20 in Sudbury,
66        Massachusetts, equidistant from route
67       <sayas class = "digits">128</sayas> and route
68       <sayas class = "digits">495</sayas>.
69       <assign name = "currentOption" expr = "'directions'"/>
70       <goto next = "#repeat"/>
71     </block>
72   </form>
73
74   <form id = "repeat">
75      <field name = "confirm" type = "boolean">
76         <prompt>
77            To repeat say yes. To go back to home, say no.
78         </prompt>
79
80         <filled>
81            <if cond = "confirm==true">
82               <goto expr = "'#' + currentOption"/>
83            <else/>
84              <goto next = "#home"/>
85            </if>
86         </filled>
87
```

Fig. 23.5   A home page written in VoiceXML (part 2 of 3).

```
88        </field>
89     </form>
90
91     <form id = "end">
92        <block>
93           Thank you for visiting Deitel and Associates voice page.
94           Have a nice day.
95           <exit/>
96        </block>
97     </form>
98  </vxml>
```

Computer:
**Welcome to the voice page of Deitel and Associates. To exit any time
say exit. To go to the home page any time say home.**

User:
Home

Computer:
**You have just entered the Deitel home page. Please make a selection
by speaking one of the following options: About us, Driving directions, Publications.**

User:
Driving directions

Computer:
**Directions to Deitel and Associates, Inc.
We are located on Route 20 in Sudbury,
Massachusetts, equidistant from route 128
and route 495.
To repeat say yes. To go back to home, say no.**

Fig. 23.5   A home page written in VoiceXML (part 3 of 3).

A VoiceXML document is made up of a series of dialogs and sub-dialogs, which result
in speech induced interaction between the user and the computer. The highest-level tags
which implement the dialogs are the **<form>** and **<menu>** tags. A **form** element presents
information and gathers data from the user pertaining to a set of *field* variables. A **menu**
element provides different options to the user and transfers control to other dialogs in the
document based on the user's selections. The **menu** element on line 26 enables the user to
select, verbally, the page to which they would like to link. The **<choice>** tag, which is
always an element of either a **menu** or a **form**, presents these options to the user. Its
attribute, **next**, indicates the page which is loaded after the user makes their selection, by
speaking the words in the **<choice>** tag into a microphone. In this example, the first and
second **choice** elements on lines 41 and 42 transfer control to a *local dialog* (i.e., a location within the same document) when they are selected. The third **choice** element transfers the user to the document **publications.vxml**

Figure 23.6 provides an explanation of each of the VoiceXML tags used in the previous example.

VoiceXML Tag	Explanation
`<assign>`	Assigns a value to a variable.
`<block>`	Presents information to the user without any interaction between user and computer (i.e., the computer does not expect any input from the user).
`<break>`	Instructs the computer to pause its speech output for a specified period of time.
`<choice>`	Specifies an option in a **menu** element.
`<enumerate>`	Lists all the available options to the user.
`<exit>`	Exits the program.
`<filled>`	Contains elements to be executed when the computer receives input for a **form** element from the user.
`<form>`	Gathers information from the user for a set of variables.
`<goto>`	Transfers control from one dialog to another.
`<grammar>`	Specifies grammar for the expected input from the user.
`<if>`, `<else>`, `<elseif>`	Control statements used for making logic decisions.
`<link>`	A transfer of control similar to the **goto** statement, but a **link** can be executed at any time during the program's execution.
`<menu>`	Provides user options and transfers control to other dialogs based on the selected option.
`<prompt>`	Specifies text to be read to the user when a decision must be made.
`<subdialog>`	Calls another dialog. Control is transferred back to the calling dialog after the subdialog is executed.
`<var>`	Declares a variable.
`<vxml>`	The top-level tag which specifies the document should be processed by a VoiceXML interpreter.

Fig. 23.6   Elements in VoiceXML.

23.7 JAWS® for Windows

JAWS (Job Access With Sound) is one of the leading screen readers on the market today. It was created by Henter-Joyce a division of Freedom Scientific™, a company that tries to help visually impaired people to use technology.

To download a demonstration version of JAWS, visit **www.hj.com/JAWS/ JAWS37DemoOp.htm** and click the **JAWS 3.7 FREE Demo** link. This demo will run for 40 minutes, after which it will terminate. The computer must be rebooted before another 40 minute session can be started.

The JAWS demo is fully functional and includes an extensive help menu that is highly customizible. The user can select which voice to utilize, the rate at which text is spoken and create keyboard shortcuts. Although the demo is in English, the full version of JAWS 3.5 allows the user to choose one of several supported languages.

JAWS also includes special key commands for popular programs, such as Microsoft Internet Explorer and Microsoft Word. For example, when browsing in Internet Explorer, JAWS' capabilities extend beyond just reading the content on the screen. If JAWS is enabled, pressing *Insert + F7*, in Internet Explorer, opens a **Links List** dialog, which displays all the Web page links. For more information about JAWS and the other products offered by Henter-Joyce, visit **www.hj.com**.

23.8 Other Accessibility Tools

Most of the accessibility products offered today are aimed at helping hearing and visually impaired people. However, software does exist to help those with other types of disabilities. This section describes some other accessibility products we have not yet discussed.

One such product is the *braille keyboard*. A braille keyboard is similar to a standard keyboard except that in addition to having the letters written on every key it has the equivalent braille symbol. Most often, braille keyboards are combined with a speech synthesizer or a braille display, so the user is able to interact with the computer and verify that their typing is correct.

In fact, speech synthesis is another area of research being done to help people with disabilities. Speech synthesizers are not new to the computer world. They have been used to aid those who are unable to verbally communicate for many years. However, the growing popularity of the Web has prompted a great deal of work in the field of speech synthesis and speech recognition. These technologies are allowing the handicapped to utilize computers more than ever before. The development of speech synthesizers is also enabling other technologies to improve such as VoiceXML and *AuralCSS* (**www.w3.org/TR/REC-CSS2/aural.html**). These tools allow visually impaired people and those who cannot read to access Web sites.

Visually impaired people are not the only beneficiaries of the effort being made to improve *markup languages*—languages such as HTML, designed to layout and link text files. The deaf also have a great number of tools to help them interpret auditory information delivered over the Web. Hearing-impaired Web users will soon benefit from what is called *Synchronized Multimedia Integration Language* (SMIL™). This markup language is designed to add extra *tracks*—layers of content found within a single audio or video file. The additional tracks can contain data such as closed captioning.

Products are also being designed to help severely handicapped persons, such as those with quadriplegia, a form of paralysis which effects the body from the neck down. One such product, *EagleEyes*, developed by researchers at Boston College, (**www.cs.bc.edu/~eagleeye**) is a system that translates eye movements into mouse movements. The user moves the mouse cursor by moving their eyes or head, through the use of electrodes.

These are just a few of the accessibility projects and technologies that currently exist. For more information on Web and general computer accessibility, see the following section entitled Internet and World Wide Web Resources.

23.9 Internet and World Wide Web Resources

There are many accessibility resources on the Internet and World Wide Web and this section lists a variety of them.

www.w3.org/WAI

The World Wide Web Consortium's *Web Accessibility Initiative (WAI)* site promotes design of universally accessible Web sites. This site will help you keep up-to-date with current guidelines and forthcoming standards for Web accessibility.

www.w3.org/TR/WCAG10

This page is a note published by the WCAG working group. It discusses techniques that can be used to comply with the WAI. This is a great resource and can be used to find additional information on many of the topics covered in this chapter.

deafness.about.com/health/deafness/msubmenu6.htm

This is the home page of **deafness.about.com**. It is an excellent resource to find information pertaining to deafness.

www.cast.org

CAST stands for the Center for Applied Special Technology. They offer software intended to help individuals with disabilities use a computer, including a valuable accessibility checker—free of charge. The accessibility checker is a Web-based program that validates accessibility.

www.trainingpost.org/3-2-inst.htm

This site presents a tutorial on the Gunning Fog Index. The Gunning Fog Index is a method of grading text on its readability.

www.w3.org/TR/REC-CSS2/aural.html

This page discusses Aural Style Sheets, outlining the purpose and uses of this new technology.

laurence.canlearn.ca/English/learn/newaccessguide/indie

INDIE is an acronym which stands for "Integrated Network of Disability Information and Education." This site provides a search engine which help users find out information about disabilities.

java.sun.com/products/java-media/speech/forDevelopers/JSML

This site outlines the specifications for JSML, Sun Microsystem's Java Speech Markup Language. This language, like VoiceXML, could drastically improve accessibility for visually impaired people.

www.slcc.edu/webguide/lynxit.html

Lynxit is a development tool that allows users to view any Web site just as a text-only browser would. The site's form allows you to enter a URL and returns the Web site in text-only format.

www.trill-home.com/lynx/public_lynx.html

This site allows you to use browse the Web using a Lynx browser. Doing so will allow you to see how your page will load for users without the most current technologies.

www.wgbh.org/wgbh/pages/ncam/accesslinks.html

This site provides links to other accessibility pages across the Web.

ocfo.ed.gov/coninfo/clibrary/software.htm

This is the U.S. Department of Education's Web site for software accessibility requirements. It is aimed at helping developers produce accessible products.

www.alphaworks.ibm.com

This is the home page for IBM Alphaworks. It provides information on VoiceXML and offers a download of the beta version of Voice Server SDK.

www-3.ibm.com/able/access.html

This is the homepage of IBM's accessibility site. It provides information on IBM products and their accessibility and also discusses hardware, software and Web accessibility.

www.microsoft.com/enable/dev/guidelines/software.htm

This Web site presents Microsoft's guidelines to designing accessible software.

www.w3.org/TR/voice-tts-reqs
This page explains the speech synthesis markup requirements for voice markup languages.

deafness.about.com/health/deafness/msubvib.htm
This site provides information on deafness; it outlines vibrotactile devices. These devices allow deaf people to experience audio in the form of vibrations.

web.ukonline.co.uk/ddmc/software.html
This site provides links to software for people with disabilities.

www.hj.com
Henter-Joyce a division of Freedom Scientific provides software for the blind and visually impaired people. It is the home of JAWS.

www.abledata.com/text2/icg_hear.htm
This page contains a consumer guide that discusses technologies for hearing-impaired people.

www.washington.edu/doit
The University of Washington's DO-IT (Disabilities, Opportunities, Internetworking and Technology) site provides information and Web development resources for creating universally accessible Web sites.

www.webable.com
The WebABLE site contains links to many disability-related Internet resources and is geared towards those looking to develop technologies for people with disabilities.

www.speech.cs.cmu.edu/comp.speech/SpeechLinks.html
The Speech Technology Hyperlinks page has over 500 links to sites related to computer-based speech and speech recognition tools.

www.islandnet.com/~tslemko
The Micro Consulting Limited site contains shareware speech synthesis software.

www.chantinc.com/technology
This is the Chant Web site, which discusses speech technology and how it works. Chant also provides speech synthesis and speech recognition software.

SUMMARY

- Accessibility, the level of usability for people with disabilities, is difficult to maintain because of disabilities, language barriers, hardware and software inconsistencies and other variables.

- One important WAI requirement is to ensure that every image, movie and sound used on a Web page is accompanied by a description that clearly defines its purpose. One way of accomplishing this is to include a description of each item using the **alt** attribute of the **<img>** and **<input>** tags.

- A text equivalent for **object** elements should also be provided, because they do not have an **alt** attribute in the HTML 4.01 specification.

- Specialized user agents, such as screen readers (programs which allow users to hear what is being displayed on their screen) and braille displays (devices that receive data from screen reading software and output the data as braille) allow blind and visually impaired people to access text-based information that is normally displayed on the screen.

- A user agent is an application that interprets Web page source code and translates it into formatted text and images. Web browsers such as Microsoft Internet Explorer and Netscape Communicator and the screen readers mentioned throughout this chapter are examples of user agents.

- Images, movies and other non-HTML objects cannot be read by screen readers. Providing multi-media-based information in a variety of ways (i.e., using the **alt** attribute or providing inline descriptions of images) helps maximize the content's accessibility.

- The **longdesc** attribute is intended to augment the description provided by the **alt** attribute. The value of the **longdesc** attribute hold be a text-based URL, which describes the image.

- If you use image maps, we recommend using client-side image maps (image maps which have links that can be understood by non-graphical user agents), providing generous descriptions and providing corresponding text links to all image maps.

- Many Web sites use tags for aesthetic purposes rather than the purpose for which they were intended. For cxample, one might use the header tag, **<h1>**, to make text in the middle of a paragraph large and bold.

- Another accessibility issue is readability. When creating a Web page intended for the general public, it is important to consider the reading level at which it is written.

- The Web Content Accessibility Guidelines 1.0 suggest using a paragraph's first sentence to convey its subject. Immediately stating the point makes finding crucial information much easier and allows those unable to comprehend large amounts of text to bypass unwanted material.

- A good way to evaluate the readability of your Web site is by using the Gunning Fog Index. The Gunning Fog Index is a formula which produces a readability grade when applied to a Web site.

- Complex Web pages often contain tables and screen readers are incapable of translating tables in an understandable manner, unless they are designed properly.

- Screen readers start at the top-left-hand cell and read left to right and top to bottom. This is known as reading a table in a linearized manner.

- By modifying the **<td>** tag with the **headers** attribute and modifying header cells (cells specified by the **<th>** tag) with the **id** attribute, you can ensure that a table will be read as intended.

- The most important part of documenting a site with frames is making sure that all of the pages in a frameset are given a meaningful description within the **<title>** tag. Users with text-based browsers such as Lynx, a UNIX-based Web browser, must choose which frame they want to open, and the use of descriptive titles can make this choice much simpler for them.

- Always give a text equivalent for a frameset to ensure that user agents that do not support frames are given an alternative. To do so, use the **<noframes>** tag.

- The **<noframes>** tag explains that the user's browser does not support frames and provides the user with a link to another page (which you need to provide) where they can view the material without frames.

- The Web Content Accessibility Guidelines 1.0 suggest using Cascading Style Sheets as an alternative to frames because they provide similar results and are highly customizible.

- VoiceXML reads Web pages to the user using speech synthesis software and also includes speech recognition technology—a technology which enables computers to understand words spoken into the microphone—enabling it to interact with users.

- The text of a VoiceXML document will be spoken to the user and the code embedded within special VoiceXML tags will allow for interactivity between the user and his or her browser.

- A **form** element, in VoiceXML, presents information and gathers data from the user pertaining to a set of field variables.

- A **menu** element, in VoiceXML, provides different options to the user and transfers control to other dialogs in the document based on the user's selections.

- The **<choice>** tag, which is always an element of either a **menu** or a **form**, presents VoiceXML options to the user. Its attribute, **next**, indicates the page which is to be loaded after the user makes his or her selection. A selection is made by repeating the words in the **<choice>** tag into your microphone.

- A timeout either enables or disables a certain action after the computer has idled for a specified amount of time. A common example of a timeout is a screen saver.

- A style sheet formats every Web site you visit according to your own personal preferences.

- Web designers often forget to take accessibility into account when creating Web sites.

- JAWS (Job Access With Sound) is one of the leading screen readers on the market today.

- A braille keyboard is similar to a standard keyboard except that in addition to having the letters written on every key it has the equivalent braille symbol. Most often, braille keyboards are combined with a speech synthesizer (software which enables the computer to speak aloud) or a braille display, so the user is able to interact with the computer and verify that his or her typing is correct.

- Markup languages are languages designed to layout and link text files; HTML is the most common example of a markup language.

- Synchronized Multimedia Integration Language (SMIL™) is a language designed to add extra tracks, which contain data such as closed captioning, to multimedia content.

- EagleEyes, developed by researchers at Boston College is a system that translates eye movements into mouse movements. It allows the user to move the mouse cursor by moving his or her eyes or head, through the use of electrodes.

TERMINOLOGY

<assign> tag in VoiceXML
<b> tag (bold)
<block> tag in VoiceXML
<break> tag in VoiceXML
<caption>
<choice> tag in VoiceXML
<enumerate> tag in VoiceXML
<exit> tag in VoiceXML
<filled> tag in VoiceXML
<form> tag in VoiceXML
<goto> tag in VoiceXML
<grammar> tag in VoiceXML
<h1>
<if>, <else>, <elseif> tags in VoiceXML
<img> tag
<link> tag in VoiceXML
<menu> tag in VoiceXML
<noframes> tag
<prompt> tag in VoiceXML
<strong> tag
<subdialog> tag in VoiceXML
<td> tag
<th> tag
<title> tag
<var> tag in VoiceXML
<vxml> tag in VoiceXML
a division of Freedom Scientific
accessibility

accessibility options in Internet Explorer 5.0
alt attribute
AuralCSS
braille display
braille keyboard
Cascading Style Sheets (CSS)
client-side image map
CSS2
default settings
EagleEyes
field variable
frames
Gunning Fog Index
header cells
headers attribute of **<td>** tag
IBM ViaVoice
id attribute
JAWS (Job Access With Sound) by Henter-Joyce
linearized reading of a table
local dialog
longdesc attribute
Lynx
markup language
priority 1 checkpoint
priority 2 checkpoint
priority 3 checkpoint
quick tips
read typed characters

readability	user agent
screen reader	ViaVoice
server-side image map	Voice Server
speech recognition	Voice Server SDK
speech synthesizer	VoiceXML
style sheet	Web Accessibility Initiative (WAI)
SUMMARY	Web Content Accessibility Guidelines 1.0
Synchronized Multimedia Integration Language	(WCAG 1.0)
(SMIL)	Window Border Size
system caret	World Wide Web Consortium (W3C)
text-to-speech	

SELF-REVIEW EXERCISES

23.1   Expand the following acronyms:
   a) W3C
   b) WAI
   c) JAWS
   d) SMIL
   e) CSS

23.2   Fill in the blanks in each of the following.
   a) The highest priority of the Web Accessibility Initiative is to ensure that each _____, _____ and _____ is accompanied by a description which clearly defines its purpose.
   b) Although they can be used as a great layout tool, _____ are difficult for screen readers to interpret and convey clearly to a user.
   c) In order to make your framesets accessible to the handicapped, it is important to include _____ tags on your page.
   d) Blind people using computers are often assisted by_____ and _____.

23.3   State whether each of the following is *true* or *false*. If the statement is *false*, explain why.
   a) Screen readers have no problem reading and translating images.
   b) Image maps are no problem for screen readers to translate so long as the programmer has made changes to his code to improve accessibility.
   c) When writing pages for the general public, it is important to consider the reading difficulty level of the text you are writing.
   d) Left-handed people have been helped by the improvements made in speech-recognition technology more than any other group.

ANSWERS TO SELF-REVIEW EXERCISES

23.1   a) World Wide Web Consortium. b) Web Accessibility Initiative. c) Job Access With Sound. d) Synchronized Multimedia Integration Language. e) Cascading Style Sheets.

23.2   a) Image, Movie, Sound. b) Tables. c) `<noframes>`. d) Braille displays, braille keyboards.

23.3   a) False. Screen readers have no way of telling a user what is shown in an image. If the programmer includes an `alt` attribute inside the `<img>` tag, the screen reader will read this to the user. b) False. Screen readers have no way of translating image maps, no matter what programming changes are made. The solution to this problem is to include text-based links alongside all image maps. c) True. d) False. Although left-handed people can utilize speech-recognition technology like everyone else, speech-recognition technology has the largest impact on the blind and those who have trouble typing.

EXERCISES

23.4   Insert code into the following examples to make them handicapped accessible. The contents of images and frames should be apparent from the context and filenames:

a) ```
<img src = "dogs.jpg" width = "300" height = "250">
```

b) ```
<table border = "1" width = "75%" align = "center">
<tr><th>language</th><th>version</th></tr>
<tr><td>html</td><td>4.0</td></tr>
<tr><td>perl</td><td>5.0</td></tr>
<tr><td>windows</td><td>2000</td></tr>
</table>
```

c) ```
<html>
<head><title>Antfarms 'R Us</title></head>
<body>
<map name = "links">
<area href = "index.html" shape = "rect" coords = "50, 120,
80, 150">
<area href = "catalog.html" shape = "circle" coords = "220,
30, 20">
</map>
<img src = "antlinks.gif" width = 300 height = 200 usemap =
"#links">
</body>
</html>
```
```

Bonus: Introduction to HyperText Markup Language 4: Part I

Objectives

- To understand the key components of an HTML document.
- To be able to use basic HTML elements to create World Wide Web pages.
- To be able to add images to your Web pages.
- To understand how to create and use hyperlinks to traverse Web pages.
- To be able to create lists of information.

To read between the lines was easier than to follow the text.
Henry James

Mere colour, unspoiled by meaning, and annulled with definite form, can speak to the soul in a thousand different ways.
Oscar Wide

I've gradually risen from lower-class background to lower-class foreground.
Marvin Cohen

Outline

24.1 Introduction

[*Note*: This chapter is provided to support the examples that use HTML. Readers who are not familiar with HTML should read this chapter before studying the examples that use CGI. This chapter is also appropriate for readers wanting a short review of HTML.]

Welcome to the wonderful world of opportunities being created by the World Wide Web. The Internet is now three decades old, but it was not until the World Wide Web became popular in the 1990s that this current explosion of opportunities began. It seems that exciting new developments occur almost daily—a pace of innovation unlike what we have seen with any other technology. In this chapter, you will begin developing your own Web pages.

We begin unlocking the power of the Web in this chapter with *HTML*—the *HyperText Markup Language*. HTML is not a procedural programming language like C, Fortran, Cobol or Pascal. Rather it is a *markup language* for identifying the elements of a page so that a browser, such as Microsoft's Internet Explorer or Netscape's Communicator, can render that page on your computer screen.

In this chapter we introduce the basics of creating Web pages in HTML. We write many simple Web pages. In later chapters we introduce more sophisticated HTML techniques, such as *tables*, which are particularly useful for structuring information from databases. We will also introduce Cascading Style Sheets, which are used to make Web pages more visually appealing.

24.2 Markup Languages

HTML is a *markup language*. It is used to format text and information. This "marking up" of information is different from the intent of traditional programming languages, which is to perform actions in a designated order. In the next several chapters, we discuss HTML markup in detail.

In HTML, text is marked up with *elements*, delineated by *tags* that are keywords contained in pairs of angle brackets. For example, the HTML *element* itself, which indicates that we are writing a Web page to be rendered by a browser, begins with a start tag of **<html>** and terminates with an end tag of **</html>**. These elements format your page in a specified way. Over the course of the next two chapters, we introduce many of the commonly used tags and how to use them.

Good Programming Practice 24.1

HTML tags are not case sensitive. However, keeping all the letters in one case improves program readability. Although the choice of case is up to you, we recommend that you write all of your code in lowercase. Writing in lowercase ensures greater compatibility with future markup languages that are designed to be written with only lowercase tags and elements.

Common Programming Error 24.1

Forgetting to include end tags for elements that require them is a syntax error and can grossly affect the formatting and look of your page. Unlike conventional programming languages, a syntax error in HTML does not usually cause page display in browsers to fail completely.

24.3 Editing HTML

In this chapter we show how to write HTML in its *source-code form*. We create *HTML documents* using a text editor and store them in files with either the **.html** or **.htm** file name extension. A wide variety of text editors exist. We recommend that you initially use a text editor called Notepad, which is built into Windows. Notepad can be found inside the **Accessories** panel of your **Program** list, inside the **Start** menu. You can also download a free HTML source-code editor called HTML-Kit at **www.chami.com/html-kit**. Unix users can use popular text editors like *vi* or *emacs*.

Good Programming Practice 24.2

*Assign names to your files that describe their functionality. This practice can help you identify documents faster. It also helps people who want to link to your page, by giving them an easier-to-remember name for the file. For example, if you are writing an HTML document that will display your products, you might want to call it **products.html**.*

Errors in conventional programming languages like Perl, C, C++ and Java often prevent the program from running. Errors in HTML markup are usually not fatal. The browser will make its best effort at rendering the page, but will probably not display the page as you intended.

The file name of your *home page* (the first of your HTML pages that a user sees when browsing your Web site) should be **index.html**, because when a browser does not request a specific file in a directory, the normal default Web server response is to return **index.html** (this may be different for your server) if it exists in that directory. For example, if you direct your browser to **www.deitel.com**, the server actually sends the file **www.deitel.com/index.html** to your browser.

24.4 Common Elements

Throughout these HTML chapters we will present both HTML source code and a sample screen capture of the rendering of that HTML in Internet Explorer 5. Figure 24.1 shows an HTML file that displays one line of text.

Lines 1 and 2

```
<!DOCTYPE HTML PUBLIC "-//W3C//DTD HTML 4.01//EN"
        "http://www.w3.org/TR/html4/strict.dtd">
```

are required in every HTML document and are used to specify the *document type*. The document type specifies which version of HTML is used in the document and can be used with a validation tool, such as the W3C's **validator.w3.org**, to ensure an HTML document conforms to the HTML recommendation. In these examples we create HTML version 4.01 documents. All of the examples in these chapters have been validated through the Web site **validator.w3.org**.

The HTML document begins with the opening **<html>** tag (line 3) and ends with the closing **</html>** tag (line 17).

Good Programming Practice 24.3

Always include the **<html>**...**</html>** *tags in the beginning and end of your HTML document.*

```
1   <!DOCTYPE HTML PUBLIC "-//W3C//DTD HTML 4.01//EN"
2            "http://www.w3.org/TR/html4/strict.dtd">
3   <html>
4
5   <!-- Fig. 24.1: main.html -->
6   <!-- Our first Web page   -->
7
8   <head>
9      <title>Perl How to Program - Welcome</title>
10  </head>
11
12  <body>
13
14     <p>Welcome to Our Web Site!</p>
15
16  </body>
17  </html>
```

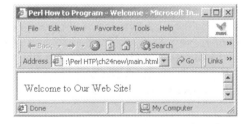

Fig. 24.1   Basic HTML file.

Good Programming Practice 24.4

Place comments throughout your code. Comments in HTML are placed inside the **<!--**...**-->** *tags. Comments help other programmers understand the code, assist in debugging and list other useful information that you do not want the browser to render. Comments also help you understand your own code, especially if you have not looked at it for a while.*

We see our first *comments* (i.e., text that documents or describes the HTML markup) on lines 5 and 6

```
<!-- Fig. 24.1: main.html -->
<!-- Our first Web page   -->
```

Comments in HTML always begin with **<!--** and end with **-->**. The browser ignores any text and/or tags inside a comment. We place comments at the top of each HTML document giving the figure number, the file name and a brief description of the purpose of the example. In subsequent examples, we also include comments in the markup, especially when we introduce new features.

Every HTML document contains a **head** element, which generally contains information about the document, and a **body** element, which contains the page content. Information in the **head** element is not generally rendered in the display window but may be made available to the user through other means.

Lines 8–10

```
<head>
   <title>Perl How to Program - Welcome</title>
</head>
```

show the **head** element section of our Web page. Including a **title** element is required for every HTML document. To include a title in your Web page, enclose your chosen title between the pair of tags **<title>**...**</title>** in the **head** element.

Good Programming Practice 24.5

Use a consistent title naming convention for all pages on your site. For example, if your site is called "Al's Web Site," then the title of your links page might best be "Al's Web Site - Links," etc. This practice presents a clearer picture to those browsing your site.

The **title** element names your Web page. The title usually appears on the colored bar at the top of the browser window, and will also appear as the text identifying your page if a user adds your page to their list of **Favorites** or **Bookmarks**. The title is also used by search engines for cataloging purposes, so picking a meaningful title can help search engines direct a more focused group of people to your site.

Line 12

```
<body>
```

opens the **body** element. The body of an HTML document is the area where you place the content of your document. This includes text, images, links, forms, etc. We discuss many elements that can be inserted in the **body** element later in this chapter. Remember to include the end **</body>** tag before the closing **</html>** tag.

Various elements enable you to place text in your HTML document. We see the *paragraph element* on line 14

```
<p>Welcome to Our Web Site!</p>
```

All text placed between the **<p>**...**</p>** tags forms one paragraph. Most Web browsers render paragraphs as set apart from all other material on the page by a line of vertical space both before and after the paragraph. The HTML in line 12 causes Internet Explorer to render the enclosed text as shown in Fig. 24.1.

Our code example ends on lines 16 and 17 with

```
</body>
</html>
```

These two tags close the body and HTML sections of the document, respectively. As discussed earlier, the last tag in any HTML document should be **</html>**, which tells the browser that all HTML coding is complete. The closing **</body>** tag is placed before the **</html>** tag because the body section of the document is entirely enclosed by the HTML section. Therefore, the body section must be closed before the HTML section.

24.5 Headers

The six *headers* are used to delineate new sections and subsections of a page. Figure 24.2 shows how these elements (**h1** through **h6**) are used. Note that the actual size of the text of each header element is selected by the browser and can vary significantly between browsers. In Chapter 26, we discuss how you can "take control" of specifying these text sizes and other text attributes as well.

```
1   <!DOCTYPE HTML PUBLIC "-//W3C//DTD HTML 4.01//EN"
2             "http://www.w3.org/TR/html4/strict.dtd">
3   <html>
4
5   <!-- Fig. 24.2: header.html -->
6   <!-- HTML headers          -->
7
8   <head>
9      <title>Perl How to Program - Headers</title>
10  </head>
11
12  <body>
13
14     <h1>Level 1 Header</h1>     <!-- Level 1 header -->
15     <h2>Level 2 header</h2>     <!-- Level 2 header -->
16     <h3>Level 3 header</h3>     <!-- Level 3 header -->
17     <h4>Level 4 header</h4>     <!-- Level 4 header -->
18     <h5>Level 5 header</h5>     <!-- Level 5 header -->
19     <h6>Level 6 header</h6>     <!-- Level 6 header -->
20
21  </body>
22  </html>
```

Fig. 24.2   Header elements **h1** through **h6** (part 1 of 2).

Fig. 24.2   Header elements **h1** through **h6** (part 2 of 2).

 Good Programming Practice 24.6

Adding comments to the right of short HTML lines is a clean-looking way to comment code.

Line 14

```
<h1>Level 1 Header</h1>
```

introduces the ***h1*** *header element*, with its start tag ***<h1>*** and its end tag ***</h1>***. Any text to be displayed is placed between the two tags. All six header elements, **h1** through **h6**, follow the same pattern.

Look-and-Feel Observation 24.1

Putting a header at the top of every Web page helps those viewing your pages understand what the purpose of each page is.

24.6 Linking

The most important capability of HTML is its ability to create hyperlinks to other documents, making possible a world-wide network of linked documents and information. In HTML, both text and images can act as *anchors* to *link* to other pages on the Web. We introduce anchors and links in Fig. 24.3.

```
 1    <!DOCTYPE HTML PUBLIC "-//W3C//DTD HTML 4.01//EN"
 2               "http://www.w3.org/TR/html4/strict.dtd">
 3    <html>
 4
 5    <!-- Fig. 24.3: links.html       -->
 6    <!-- Introduction to hyperlinks  -->
 7
 8    <head>
 9       <title>Perl How to Program - Links</title>
10    </head>
11
12    <body>
13
14       <h1>Here are my favorite Internet Search Engines</h1>
15
16       <p><strong>Click the Search Engine address to go to that
17          page.</strong></p>
18
19       <p><a href = "http://www.yahoo.com">Yahoo</a></p>
20
21       <p><a href = "http://www.altavista.com">AltaVista</a></p>
22
23       <p><a href = "http://www.askjeeves.com">Ask Jeeves</a></p>
24
25       <p><a href = "http://www.webcrawler.com">WebCrawler</a></p>
26
27    </body>
28    </html>
```

Fig. 24.3   Linking to other Web pages.

The first link can be found on line 19

```
<p><a href = "http://www.yahoo.com">Yahoo</a></p>
```

Links are inserted using the ***a*** *(anchor) element*. The anchor element is unlike the elements we have seen thus far in that it requires certain *attributes* (i.e., markup that provides information about the element) to specify the hyperlink. Attributes are placed inside an element's start tag and consist of a name and a value. The most important attribute for the **a** element is the location to which you would like the anchoring object to be linked. This location can be any resource on the Web, including pages, files and email addresses. To specify the address to link to, add the ***href*** *attribute* to the anchor element as follows: **<a href = "***address***">**. In this case, the address we are linking to is **http://www.yahoo.com**. The hyperlink (line 19) makes the text **Yahoo** a link to the address specified in **href**.

Anchors can use **mailto** URLs to provide links to email addresses. When someone selects this type of anchored link, most browsers launch the default email program to initiate an email message to the linked address. This type of anchor is demonstrated in Fig. 24.4.

```
1   <!DOCTYPE HTML PUBLIC "-//W3C//DTD HTML 4.01//EN"
2                "http://www.w3.org/TR/html4/strict.dtd">
3   <html>
4
5   <!-- Fig. 24.4: contact.html  -->
6   <!-- Adding email hyperlinks -->
7
8   <head>
9      <title>Perl How to Program - Contact Page</title>
10  </head>
11
12  <body>
13
14     <p>My email address is <a href = "mailto:deitel@deitel.com">
15     deitel@deitel.com</a>. Click the address and your browser
16     will open an email message and address it to me.</p>
17
18  </body>
19  </html>
```

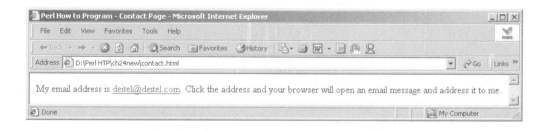

Fig. 24.4   Linking to an email address.

We see an email link on lines 14 and 15

```
<p>My email address is <a href = "mailto:deitel@deitel.com">
deitel@deitel.com</a>. Click the address and your browser
```

The form of an email anchor is **<a href = "mailto:***emailaddress***">...</a>**. It is important that this whole attribute, including the **mailto:**, be placed in quotation marks.

24.7 Images

We have thus far dealt exclusively with text. We now show how to incorporate images into Web pages (Fig. 24.5).

```
1   <!DOCTYPE HTML PUBLIC "-//W3C//DTD HTML 4.01//EN"
2               "http://www.w3.org/TR/html4/strict.dtd">
3   <html>
4
5   <!-- Fig. 24.5: picture.html  -->
6   <!-- Adding images with HTML -->
7
8   <head>
9       <title>Perl How to Program - Welcome</title>
10  </head>
11
12  <body>
13
14      <p><img src = "xmlhtp.jpg" height = "238" width = "183"
15          alt = "Demonstration of the alt attribute"></p>
16
17  </body>
18  </html>
```

Fig. 24.5   Placing images in HTML files.

The image in this code example is inserted in lines 14 and 15

```
<p><img src = "xmlhtp.jpg" height = "238" width = "183"
    alt = "Demonstration of the alt attribute"></p>
```

You specify the location of the image file in the **img** element. This is done by adding the **src** = "*location*" attribute. You can also specify the **height** and **width** of an image, measured in pixels. The term pixel stands for "picture element." Each pixel represents one dot of color on the screen. This image is 183 pixels wide and 238 pixels high.

Good Programming Practice 24.7

*Always include the **height** and the **width** of an image inside the **img** tag. When the browser loads the HTML file, it will know immediately how much screen space to give the image and will therefore lay out the page properly, even before it downloads the image.*

Common Programming Error 24.2

Entering new dimensions for an image that change its inherent width-to-height ratio distorts the appearance of the image. For example, if your image is 200 pixels wide and 100 pixels high, you should always make sure that any new dimensions have a 2:1 width-to-height ratio.

The **alt** attribute is required for every **img** element. In Fig. 24.5, the value of this attribute is

```
alt = "Demonstration of the alt attribute"
```

Attribute **alt** is provided for browsers that have images turned off, or that cannot view images (e.g., text-based browsers). The value of the **alt** attribute will appear on-screen in place of the image, giving the user an idea of what was in the image. The **alt** attribute is especially important for making Web pages *accessible* to users with disabilities, as discussed in Chapter 23, Accessibility.

Good Programming Practice 24.8

*Include a description of the purpose of every image using the **alt** attribute in the **img** tag.*

Now that we have discussed placing images on your Web page, we will show you how to transform images into anchors to provide links to other sites on the Internet (Fig. 24.6).

```
1   <!DOCTYPE HTML PUBLIC "-//W3C//DTD HTML 4.01//EN"
2              "http://www.w3.org/TR/html4/strict.dtd">
3   <html>
4
5   <!-- Fig. 24.6: nav.html          -->
6   <!-- Using images as link anchors -->
7
8   <head>
9      <title>Perl How to Program - Navigation Bar</title>
10  </head>
11
```

Fig. 24.6   Using images as link anchors (part 1 of 2).

```
12   <body>
13
14      <p>
15         <a href = "links.html">
16         <img src = "buttons/links.jpg" width = "65" height = "50"
17            alt = "Links Page"></a><br>
18
19         <a href = "list.html">
20         <img src = "buttons/list.jpg" width = "65" height = "50"
21            alt = "List Example Page"></a><br>
22
23         <a href = "contact.html">
24         <img src = "buttons/contact.jpg" width = "65" height = "50"
25            alt = "Contact Page"></a><br>
26
27         <a href = "header.html">
28         <img src = "buttons/header.jpg" width = "65" height = "50"
29            alt = "Header Page"></a><br>
30      </p>
31
32   </body>
33   </html>
```

Fig. 24.6   Using images as link anchors (part 2 of 2).

We see an image hyperlink in lines 15–17

```
<a href = "links.html">
<img src = "buttons/links.jpg" width = "65" height = "50"
   alt = "Links Page"></a><br>
```

Here we use the **a** element and the **img** element. The anchor works the same way as when it surrounds text; the image becomes an active hyperlink to a location somewhere on the Internet, indicated by the **href** attribute inside the **<a>** tag. Remember to close the anchor element when you want the hyperlink to end.

If you direct your attention to the **src** attribute of the **img** element,

```
src = "buttons/links.jpg"
```

you will see that it is not in the same form as that of the image in the previous example. This is because the image we are using here, **about.jpg**, resides in a subdirectory called **buttons**, which is in the main directory for our site. We have done this so that we can keep all our button graphics in the same place, making them easier to find and edit.

You can always refer to files in different directories simply by putting the directory name in the correct format in the **src** attribute. If, for example, there was a directory inside the **buttons** directory called **images**, and we wanted to put a graphic from that directory onto our page, we would just have to make the source attribute reflect the location of the image: **src = "buttons/images/filename"**.

You can even insert an image from a different Web site into your site (after obtaining permission from the site's owner, of course). Just make the **src** attribute reflect the location and name of the image file. On line 17

```
alt = "Links Page"></a><br>
```

we introduce the **br** *element* in line 17, which causes a *line break* to be rendered in most browsers.

24.8 Special Characters and More Line Breaks

In HTML, the old QWERTY typewriter setup no longer suffices for all our textual needs. HTML 4.01 has a provision for inserting special characters and symbols (Fig. 24.7).

```
1   <!DOCTYPE HTML PUBLIC "-//W3C//DTD HTML 4.01//EN"
2              "http://www.w3.org/TR/html4/strict.dtd">
3   <html>
4
5   <!-- Fig. 24.7: contact2.html        -->
6   <!-- Inserting special characters    -->
7
8   <head>
9      <title>Perl How to Program - Contact Page</title>
10  </head>
11
12  <body>
13
14     <!-- Special characters are entered using the form &code; -->
15     <p>My email address is <a href = "mailto:deitel@deitel.com">
16     deitel@deitel.com</a>. Click the address and your browser
17     will automatically open an email message and address it to my
18     address.</p>
```

Fig. 24.7   Inserting special characters into HTML (part 1 of 2).

```
19
20       <hr> <!-- Inserts a horizontal rule -->
21
22       <p>All information on this site is <strong>&copy;</strong>
23       Deitel <strong>&amp;</strong> Associates, 2001.</p>
24
25       <!-- Text can be struck out with a set of <del>...</del>  -->
26       <!-- tags, it can be set in subscript with <sub>...</sub>, -->
27       <!-- and it can be set into superscript with <sup...</sup> -->
28       <p><del>You may copy up to 3.14 x 10<sup>2</sup> characters
29       worth of information from this site.</del> Just make sure
30       you <sub>do not copy more information</sub> than is allowable.
31       </p>
32
33       <p>No permission is needed if you only need to use <strong>
34       &lt; &frac14;</strong> of the information presented here.</p>
35
36   </body>
37   </html>
```

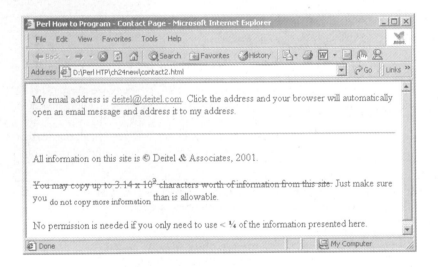

Fig. 24.7   Inserting special characters into HTML (part 2 of 2).

There are some *special characters* inserted into the text of lines 22 and 23

```
<p>All information on this site is <strong>&copy;</strong>
Deitel <strong>&amp;</strong> Associates, 2001.</p>
```

All special characters are inserted in their code form. The format of the code is always **&**code**;**. An example of this is **&**, which inserts an ampersand. Codes are often abbreviated forms of the character (like **amp** for ampersand and **copy** for copyright) and can also be in the form of *hex codes*. (For example, the hex code for an ampersand is 38, so another method of inserting an ampersand is to use `&#38;`.) Please refer to the chart in Appendix A for a listing of special characters and their respective codes.

In lines 28–31, we introduce three new styles.

```
<p><del>You may copy up to 3.14 x 10<sup>2</sup> characters
worth of information from this site.</del> Just make sure
you <sub>do not copy more information</sub> than is allow-
able.
</p>
```

You can indicate text that has been deleted from a document by including it in a **del** element. This could be used as an easy way to communicate revisions of an online document. Many browsers render the **del** element as strike-through text. To turn text into *superscript* (i.e., raised vertically to the top of the line and made smaller) or to turn text into *subscript* (the opposite of superscript, lowers text on a line and makes it smaller), use the **sup** and **sub** elements, respectively.

Line 20

```
<hr> <!-- Inserts a horizontal rule -->
```

inserts a horizontal rule, indicated by the **`<hr>`** tag. A horizontal rule is rendered by most browsers as a straight line going across the screen horizontally. The **hr** element also inserts a line break directly below it.

24.9 Unordered Lists

Figure 24.8 demonstrates displaying text in an *unordered list*. Here we reuse the HTML file from Fig. 24.3, adding an unordered list to enhance the structure of the page. The *unordered list element* **ul** creates a list in which every line begins with a bullet mark in most Web browsers.

```
1   <!DOCTYPE HTML PUBLIC "-//W3C//DTD HTML 4.01//EN"
2              "http://www.w3.org/TR/html4/strict.dtd">
3   <html>
4
5   <!-- Fig. 24.8: links2.html              -->
6   <!-- Unordered list containing hyperlinks   -->
7
8   <head>
9      <title>Perl How to Program - Links</title>
10  </head>
11
12  <body>
13
14     <h1>Here are my favorite Internet Search Engines</h1>
15
16
17     <p><strong>Click the Search Engine address to go to that
18        page.</strong></p>
19
```

Fig. 24.8   Unordered lists in HTML (part 1 of 2).

```
20      <ul>
21         <li><a href = "http://www.yahoo.com">Yahoo</a></li>
22
23         <li><a href = "http://www.altavista.com">AltaVista</a></li>
24
25         <li><a href = "http://www.askjeeves.com">Ask Jeeves</a></li>
26
27         <li><a href = "http://www.webcrawler.com">WebCrawler</a></li>
28      </ul>
29
30   </body>
31   </html>
```

Fig. 24.8   Unordered lists in HTML (part 2 of 2).

The first list item appears on line 21

```
<li><a href = "http://www.yahoo.com">Yahoo</a></li>
```

Each entry in an unordered list is a *li* (*list item*) element. Most Web browsers render these elements with a line break and a bullet mark at the beginning of the line.

24.10 Nested and Ordered Lists

Figure 24.9 demonstrates *nested lists* (i.e., one list inside another list). This feature is useful for displaying information in outline form.

```
 1    <!DOCTYPE HTML PUBLIC "-//W3C//DTD HTML 4.01//EN"
 2              "http://www.w3.org/TR/html4/strict.dtd">
 3    <html>
 4
 5    <!-- Fig. 24.9: list.html              -->
 6    <!-- Advanced Lists: nested and ordered   -->
 7
 8    <head>
 9       <title>Perl How to Program - Lists</title>
10    </head>
11
12    <body>
13
14       <h1>The Best Features of the Internet</h1>
15
16       <ul>
17          <li>You can meet new people from countries around
18             the world.</li>
19          <li>You have access to new media as it becomes public:
20
21             <!-- This starts a nested list, which uses a modified  -->
22             <!-- bullet. The list ends when you close the <ul> tag -->
23             <ul>
24                <li>New games</li>
25                <li>New applications
26
27                   <!-- Another nested list -->
28                   <ul>
29                      <li>For business</li>
30                      <li>For pleasure</li>
31                   </ul> <!-- This ends the double nested list -->
32                </li>
33
34                <li>Around the clock news</li>
35                <li>Search engines</li>
36                <li>Shopping</li>
37                <li>Programming
38
39                   <ul>
40                      <li>XML</li>
41                      <li>Java</li>
42                      <li>HTML</li>
43                      <li>Scripts</li>
44                      <li>New languages</li>
45                   </ul>
46
47                </li>
48
49             </ul> <!-- This ends the first level nested list -->
50          </li>
51
52          <li>Links</li>
53          <li>Keeping in touch with old friends</li>
```

Fig. 24.9   Nested and ordered lists in HTML (part 1 of 2).

```
54            <li>It is the technology of the future!</li>
55
56     </ul>    <!-- This ends the primary unordered list -->
57
58     <h1>My 3 Favorite <em>CEOs</em></h1>
59
60     <!-- Ordered lists are constructed in the same way as    -->
61     <!-- unordered lists, except their starting tag is <ol> -->
62     <ol>
63        <li>Bill Gates</li>
64        <li>Steve Jobs</li>
65        <li>Michael Dell</li>
66     </ol>
67
68  </body>
69  </html>
```

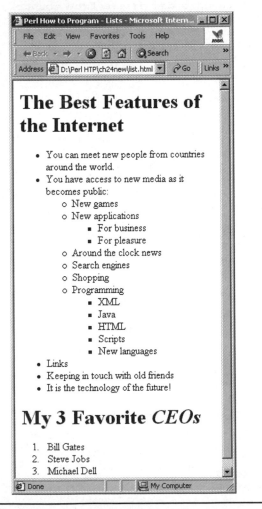

Fig. 24.9   Nested and ordered lists in HTML (part 2 of 2).

Our first nested list begins on line 23, with its first element on 24

```
<ul>
    <li>New games</li>
```

A nested list is created in the same way as the list in Fig. 24.8, except that the nested list is itself contained in a list element. Most Web browsers render nested lists by indenting the list one level and changing the bullet type for the list elements.

Good Programming Practice 24.9

Indenting each level of a nested list in your code makes the code easier to edit and debug.

In Fig. 24.9, lines 16–56 show a list with three levels of nesting. When nesting lists, be sure to insert the closing **</ul>** tags in the appropriate places. Lines 62–66

```
<ol>
    <li>Bill Gates</li>
    <li>Steve Jobs</li>
    <li>Michael Dell</li>
</ol>
```

define an *ordered list* element with the tags **<ol>...</ol>**. Most browsers render ordered lists with a sequence number for each list element instead of a bullet. By default, ordered lists use decimal sequence numbers (1, 2, 3, ...).

24.11 Internet and World Wide Web Resources

There are many resources available on the World Wide Web that go into more depth on the topics we cover. Visit the following sites for additional information on this chapter's topics.

www.w3.org
The *World Wide Web Consortium* (W3C), is the group that makes HTML recommendations. This Web site holds a variety of information about HTML—both its history and its present status.

www.w3.org/TR/html401
The *HTML 4.01 Specification* contains all the nuances and fine points in HTML 4.01.

www.w3schools.com/html
The HTMl School. This site contains a complete guide to HTML, starting with an introduction to the WWW and ending with advanced HTML features. This site also has a good reference for the features of HTML.

www2.utep.edu/~kross/tutorial
This University of Texas at El Paso site contains another guide for simple HTML programming. The site is helpful for beginners, because it focuses on teaching and gives specific examples.

www.astentech.com/tutorials/HTML.html
This site contains links and rates over 40 HTML tutorials located all over the Web.

www.w3scripts.com/html
This site, an offshoot of *W3Schools*, is a repository for code examples exhibiting all of the features of HTML, from beginner to advanced.

SUMMARY

- HTML is not a procedural programming language like C, Fortran, Cobol or Pascal. It is a markup language that identifies the elements of a page so a browser can render that page on the screen.

- HTML is used to format text and information. This "marking up" of information is different from the intent of traditional programming languages, which is to perform actions in a designated order.

- In HTML, text is marked up with elements, delineated by tags that are keywords contained in pairs of angle brackets.

- HTML documents are created using text editors.

- All HTML documents stored in files require either the **.htm** or the **.html** file name extension.

- Making errors while coding in conventional programming languages like C, C++ and Java often produces a fatal error, preventing the program from running. Errors in HTML code are usually not fatal. The browser will make its best effort at rendering the page but will probably not display the page as you intended. In our Common Programming Errors and Testing and Debugging Tips we highlight common HTML errors and how to detect and correct them.

- For most Web servers, the filename of your home page should be **index.html**. When a browser requests a directory, the default Web server response is to return **index.html**, if it exists in that directory.

- The document type specifies which version of HTML is used in the document and can be used with a validation tool, such as the W3C's **validator.w3.org**, to ensure an HTML document conforms to the HTML specification.

- **<html>** tells the browser that everything contained between the opening **<html>** tag and the closing **</html>** tag is HTML.

- Comments in HTML always begin with **<!--** and end with **-->** and can span across several source lines. The browser ignores any text and/or tags placed inside a comment.

- Every HTML file is separated into a header section and a body.

- Including a title is mandatory for every HTML document. Use the **<title>...</title>** tags to do so. They are placed inside the header.

- **<body>** opens the **body** element. The body of an HTML document is the area where you place all content you would like browsers to display.

- All text between the **<p>...</p>** tags forms one paragraph. Most browsers render paragraphs as set apart from all other material on the page by a line of vertical space both before and after the paragraph.

- Headers are a simple form of text formatting that typically increase text size based on the header's "level" (**h1** through **h6**). They are often used to delineate new sections and subsections of a page.

- The purpose of HTML is to mark up text; the question of how it is presented is left to the browser itself.

- People who have difficulty seeing can use special browsers that read the text on the screen aloud. These browsers (which are text based and do not show images, colors or graphics) might read **strong** and **em** with different inflections to convey the impact of the styled text to the user.

- You should close tags in the reverse order from that in which they were started to ensure proper nesting.

- The most important capability of HTML is creating hyperlinks to documents on any server to form a world-wide network of linked documents and information.

- Links are inserted using the **a** (anchor) element. To specify the address you would like to link to, add the **href** attribute to the anchor element, with the address as the value of **href**.

- Anchors can link to email addresses. When someone clicks this type of anchored link, their default email program initiates an email message to the linked address.

- The term pixel stands for "picture element". Each pixel represents one dot of color on the screen.

- You specify the location of the image file with the **src = "***location***"** attribute in the **<img>** tag. You can specify the **height** and **width** of an image, measured in pixels.

- **alt** is provided for browsers that cannot view pictures or that have images turned off (text-based browsers, for example). The value of the **alt** attribute will appear on-screen in place of the image, giving the user an idea of what was in the image.

- You can refer to files in different directories by including the directory name in the correct format in the **src** attribute. You can insert an image from a different Web site onto your site (after obtaining permission from the site's owner). Just make the **src** attribute reflects the location and name of the image file.

- The **br** element forces a line break. If the **br** element is placed inside a text area, the text begins a new line at the place of the **
** tag.

- HTML 4.01 has a provision for inserting special characters and symbols. All special characters are inserted in the format of the code, always **&***code***;**. An example of this is **&**, which inserts an ampersand. Codes are often abbreviated forms of the character (like **amp** for ampersand and **copy** for copyright) and can also be in the form of hex codes. (For example, the hex code for an ampersand is 38, so another method of inserting an ampersand is to use **&**.)

- The **del** element marks text as deleted, which is rendered with a strike through by most browsers. To turn text into superscript or subscript, use the **sup** and **sub** elements respectively.

- Most visual Web browsers place a bullet mark at the beginning of each element in an unordered list. All entries in an unordered list must be enclosed within **<ul>**...**</ul>** tags, which open and close the unordered list element.

- Each entry in an unordered list is contained in an **li** element. You then insert and format any text.

- Nested lists display information in outline form. A nested list is a list that is contained in an **li** element. Most visual Web browsers indent nested lists one level and change the bullet type to reflect the nesting.

- An ordered list (**<ol>**...**</ol>**) is rendered by most browsers with a sequence number instead of a bullet at the beginning of each list element. By default, ordered lists use decimal sequence numbers (1,2,3, …).

TERMINOLOGY

&
.htm
.html
<!--…--> (comment)
<body>...</body>
<hr> element (horizontal rule)
a element (anchor; <a>...</a>)
alt
anchor
attributes of an HTML tag
clear = "all" in
closing tag
color
comments

content of an HTML element
del element
em element (...)
emphasis
h1 element (<h1>...</h1>)
h2 element (<h2>...</h2>)
h3 element (<h3>...</h3>)
h4 element (<h4>...</h4>)
h5 element (<h5>...</h5>)
h6 element (<h6>...</h6>)
head element (<head>...</head>)
height
horizontal rule
href attribute of <a> element

HTML (HyperText Markup Language)
HTML document
html element (**<html>…</html>**)
HTML file
HTML tags
html-kit
hyperlink
hypertext
image
img element
index.html
line break element (**
…</br>**)
link
link attribute of **body** element…
mailto:
Markup Language
opening tag
p element (paragraph; **<p>…</p>**)
presentation of a Web Page

RGB colors
size = in **<font>**
source-code form
special characters
src attribute in **img** element
strong element (**…**)
structure of a Web page
sub (subscript)
sup (superscript)
tags in HTML
text in **body**
text-based browser
title element (**<title>…</title>**)
unordered list (**<ul>…</ul>**)
Web site
width attribute
width by percentage
width by pixel
World Wide Web

SELF-REVIEW EXERCISES

24.1 State whether the following are *true* or *false*. If *false*, explain why.
   a) The document type for an HTML document is optional.
   b) The use of the **em** and **strong** elements is deprecated.
   c) The name of your site's home page should always be **homepage.html**.
   d) It is a good programming practice to insert comments into your HTML document that explain what you are doing.
   e) A hyperlink is inserted around text with the **link** element.

24.2 Fill in the blanks in each of the following:
   a) The _____ element is used to insert a horizontal rule.
   b) Superscript is formatted with the _____ element and subscript is formatted with the _____ element.
   c) The _____ element is located within the **<head>…</head>** tags.
   d) The least important header is the _____ element and the most important text header is _____.
   e) The _____ element is used to create an unordered list.

24.3 Identify each of the following as either an element or attribute:
   a) **html**
   b) **width**
   c) **href**
   d) **br**
   e) **h3**
   f) **a**
   g) **src**

ANSWERS TO SELF-REVIEW EXERCISES

24.1 a) False. The document type is required for HTML documents. b) False. The use of the **i** and **b** elements is deprecated. Elements **em** and **strong** may be used instead. c) False. The name of your home page should always be **index.html**. d) True. e) False. A hyperlink is inserted around text with the **a** (anchor) element.

24.2   a) **hr**. b) **sup**, **sub**. c) **title**. d) **h6**, **h1**. e) **ul**.

24.3   a) Tag. b) Attribute. c) Attribute. d) Tag. e) Tag. f) Tag. g) Attribute.

EXERCISES

24.4   Use HTML to mark up the second paragraph of this chapter (i.e., the one following the Note). Use **h1** for the section header, **p** for text, **strong** for the first word of every sentence, and **em** for all capital letters.

24.5   Why is this code valid? (*Hint*: you can find the W3C specification for the **p** element at **www.w3.org/TR/html4**)

```
<p>Here's some text...
<hr>
<p>And some more text...</p>
```

24.6   Why is this code invalid? [*Hint*: you can find the W3C specification for the **br** element at the same URL given in Exercise 24.5.]

```
<p>Here's some text...<br></br>
And some more text...</p>
```

24.7   We have an image named **deitel.gif** that is 200 pixels wide and 150 pixels high. Use the **width** and **height** attributes of the **img** tag to a) increase image size by 100%; b) increase image size by 50%; c) change the width-to-height ratio to 2:1, keeping the width attained in a).

24.8   Create a link to each of the following: a) **index.html**, located in the **files** directory; b) **index.html**, located in the **text** subdirectory of the **files** directory; c) **index.html**, located in the **other** directory in your *parent directory* [*Hint*: **..** signifies parent directory.]; d) A link to the President of the United States' email address (**president@whitehouse.gov**); e) An **FTP** link to the file named **README** in the **pub** directory of **ftp.cdrom.com** [*Hint*: remember to use **ftp://**].

25

Bonus: Introduction to HyperText Markup Language 4: Part II

Objectives

- To be able to create tables with rows and columns of data.
- To be able to control the display and formatting of tables.
- To be able to create and use forms.
- To be able to create and use image maps to aid hyperlinking.
- To be able to make Web pages accessible to search engines.
- To be able to use the **frameset** element to create more interesting Web pages.

Yea, from the table of my memory
I'll wipe away all trivial fond records.
William Shakespeare

25.1 Introduction

In the previous chapter, we discussed some basic HTML features. We built several complete Web pages featuring text, hyperlinks, images and such formatting tools as horizontal rules and line breaks.

In this bonus chapter, we discuss more substantial HTML elements and features. We will see how to present information in *tables*. We discuss how to use forms to collect information from people browsing a site. We explain how to use *internal linking* and *image maps* to make pages more navigable. We also discuss how to use *frames* to make navigating Web sites easier.

By the end of this chapter, you will be familiar with most commonly used HTML tags and features. You will then be able to create more complex Web sites. In the next bonus chapter, Cascading Style Sheets (CSS), we will show you how to make your Web sites more visually appealing.

25.2 Basic HTML Tables

HTML 4.0 *tables* are used to mark up tabular data, such as data stored in a database. The table in Fig. 25.1 organizes data into rows and columns.

```
1   <!DOCTYPE HTML PUBLIC "-//W3C//DTD HTML 4.01//EN"
2            "http://www.w3.org/TR/html4/strict.dtd">
3   <html>
4
5   <!-- Fig. 25.1: table.html -->
6   <!-- Basic table design   -->
7
```

Fig. 25.1   HTML table (part 1 of 2).

```
 8   <head>
 9       <title>Perl How to Program - Tables</title>
10   </head>
11
12   <body>
13
14       <h1>Table Example Page</h1>
15
16       <!-- The <table> tag opens a new table and lets you put in -->
17       <!-- design options and instructions                       -->
18       <table border = "1" width = "40%">
19
20       <!-- Use the <caption> tag to summarize the table's contents -->
21       <!-- (this helps the visually impaired)                      -->
22       <caption>Here is a small sample table.</caption>
23
24       <!-- The <thead> is the first (non-scrolling) horizontal    -->
25       <!-- section. Use it to format the table header area.       -->
26       <!-- <th> inserts a header cell and displays bold text      -->
27       <thead>
28          <tr><th>This is the head.</th></tr>
29       </thead>
30
31       <!-- All of your important content goes in the <tbody>. -->
32       <!-- Use this tag to format the entire section           -->
33       <!-- <td> inserts a data cell, with regular text         -->
34       <tbody>
35          <tr><td>This is the body.</td></tr>
36       </tbody>
37
38       </table>
39
40   </body>
41   </html>
```

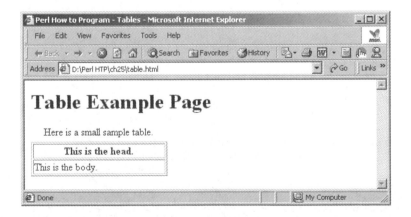

Fig. 25.1   HTML table (part 2 of 2).

All tags and text that apply to the table go inside the **`<table>`** element, which begins on line 18

```
<table border = "1" width = "40%">
```

The ***border*** *attribute* lets you set the width of the table's border in pixels. If you the border to be invisible, you can specify **`border = "0"`**. In the table shown in Fig. 25.1, the value of the border attribute is set to **1**. The ***width*** attribute sets the width of the table as either a number of pixels or a percentage of the screen width.

Line 22

```
<caption>Here is a small sample table.</caption>
```

inserts a ***caption*** element into the table. The text inside the **`caption`** element is inserted directly above the table in most visual browsers. The caption text is also used to help *text-based browsers* interpret the table data.

Tables can be split into distinct horizontal and vertical sections. The first of these sections, the head area, appears in lines 27–29

```
<thead>
   <tr><th>This is the head.</th></tr>
</thead>
```

Put all header information (for example, the titles of the table and column headers) inside the ***thead*** element. The ***tr***, or *table row element*, is used to create rows of table cells. All of the cells in a row belong in the **`<tr>`** element for that row.

The smallest unit of the table is the *data cell*. There are two types of data cells, one type—the **`th`** element—is located in the table header. The other type—the **`td`** element—is located in the table body. The code example in Fig. 25.1 inserts a header cell using the **`th`** element. Header cells, which are placed in the **`<thead>`** element, are suitable for column headings.

The second grouping section, the **`tbody`** element, appears in lines 34–36

```
<tbody>
   <tr><td>This is the body.</td></tr>
</tbody>
```

Like **`thead`**, the ***tbody*** element is used for formatting and grouping purposes. Although there is only one row and one cell (line 35) in the above example, most tables will use **`tbody`** to group the majority of their content in multiple rows and multiple cells.

Look-and-Feel Observation 25.1

Use tables in your HTML pages to mark up tabular data.

Common Programming Error 25.1

Forgetting to close any of the elements inside the ***table*** *element is an error and can distort the table format. Be sure to check that every element is opened and closed in its proper place to make sure that the table is structured as intended.*

25.3 Intermediate HTML Tables and Formatting

In the previous section and code example, we explored the structure of a basic table. In Fig. 25.2, we extend our table example with more structural elements and attributes.

The table begins on line 16. The ***colgroup*** *element*, used for grouping columns, is shown on lines 22–25

```
1   <!DOCTYPE HTML PUBLIC "-//W3C//DTD HTML 4.01//EN"
2             "http://www.w3.org/TR/html4/strict.dtd">
3   <html>
4
5   <!-- Fig. 25.2: table2.html     -->
6   <!-- Intermediate table design  -->
7
8   <head>
9      <title>Perl How to Program - Tables</title>
10  </head>
11
12  <body>
13
14     <h1>Table Example Page</h1>
15
16     <table border = "1">
17        <caption>Here is a more complex sample table.</caption>
18
19     <!-- <colgroup> and <col> are used to format entire   -->
20     <!-- columns at once. SPAN determines how many columns -->
21     <!-- the col tag effects.                              -->
22     <colgroup>
23        <col align = "right">
24        <col span = "4">
25     </colgroup>
26
27     <thead>
28
29        <!-- rowspans and colspans combine the indicated number -->
30        <!-- of cells vertically or horizontally                -->
31        <tr>
32           <th rowspan = "2">
33              <img src = "camel.gif" width = "205" height = "167"
34                 alt = "Picture of a camel">
35           </th>
36           <th colspan = "4" valign = "top">
37              <h1>Camelid comparison</h1><br>
38              <p>Approximate as of 8/99</p>
39           </th>
40        </tr>
41
42        <tr valign = "bottom">
43           <th># of Humps</th>
44           <th>Indigenous region</th>
45           <th>Spits?</th>
```

Fig. 25.2   Complex HTML table (part 1 of 2).

```
46                <th>Produces Wool?</th>
47           </tr>
48
49        </thead>
50
51        <tbody>
52
53           <tr>
54              <th>Camels (bactrian)</th>
55              <td>2</td>
56              <td>Africa/Asia</td>
57              <td rowspan = "2">Llama</td>
58              <td rowspan = "2">Llama</td>
59           </tr>
60
61           <tr>
62              <th>Llamas</th>
63              <td>1</td>
64              <td>Andes Mountains</td>
65           </tr>
66
67        </tbody>
68
69        </table>
70
71  </body>
72  </html>
```

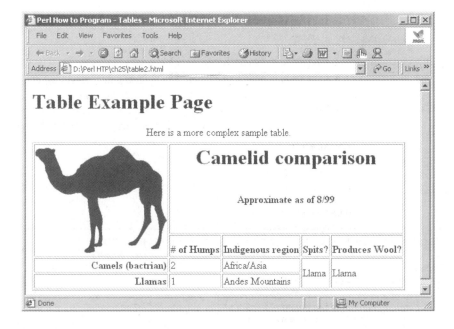

Fig. 25.2   Complex HTML table (part 2 of 2).

```
<colgroup>
   <col align = "right">
   <col span = "4">
</colgroup>
```

The **colgroup** element can be used to group and format columns. Each **col** element in the **<colgroup>**...**</colgroup>** tags can format any number of columns (specified with the **span** attribute). Any formatting to be applied to a column or group of columns can be specified in both the **colgroup** and **col** tags. In this case, we align the text inside the leftmost column to the right. Another useful attribute to use here is **width**, which specifies the width of the column.

Most visual Web browsers automatically format data cells to fit the data they contain. However, it is possible to make some data cells larger than others. This effect is accomplished with the **rowspan** and **colspan** attributes, which can be placed inside any data cell element. The value of the attribute specifies the number of rows or columns to be occupied by the cell, respectively. For example, **rowspan = "2"** tells the browser that this data cell will span the area of two vertically adjacent cells. These cells will be joined vertically (and will thus span over two rows). An example of **colspan** appears in line 36

```
<th colspan = "4" valign = "top">
```

where the header cell is widened to span four cells.

We also see here an example of vertical alignment formatting. The **valign** attribute accepts the following values: **"top"**, **"middle"**, **"bottom"** and **"baseline"**. All cells in a row whose **valign** attribute is set to **"baseline"** will have the first text line occur on a common baseline. The default vertical alignment in all data and header cells is **valign = "middle"**.

The remaining code in Fig. 25.2 demonstrates other uses of the **table** attributes and elements outlined above.

 Common Programming Error 25.2

*When using **colspan** and **rowspan** in table data cells, consider that the modified cells will cover the areas of other cells. Compensate for this in your code by reducing the number of cells in that row or column. If you do not, the formatting of your table will be distorted, and you may inadvertently create more columns and/or rows than you originally intended.*

25.4 Basic HTML Forms

HTML provides several mechanisms to collect information from people viewing your site; one is the *form* (Fig. 25.3).

```
1    <!DOCTYPE HTML PUBLIC "-//W3C//DTD HTML 4.01//EN"
2              "http://www.w3.org/TR/html4/strict.dtd">
3    <html>
4
5    <!-- Fig. 25.3: form.html   -->
6    <!-- Form Design Example 1   -->
7
```

Fig. 25.3   Simple form with hidden fields and a text box (part 1 of 2).

```
 8   <head>
 9      <title>Perl How to Program - Forms</title>
10   </head>
11
12   <body>
13
14      <h1>Feedback Form</h1>
15
16      <p>Please fill out this form to help us improve our site.</p>
17
18      <!-- This tag starts the form, gives the method of sending -->
19      <!-- information and the location of form scripts.          -->
20      <!-- Hidden inputs give the server non-visual information   -->
21      <form method = "post" action = "/cgi-bin/formmail">
22
23      <p>
24         <input type = "hidden" name = "recipient"
25            value = "deitel@deitel.com">
26         <input type = "hidden" name = "subject"
27            value = "Feedback Form">
28         <input type = "hidden" name = "redirect"
29            value = "main.html">
30      </p>
31
32      <!-- <input type = "text"> inserts a text box -->
33      <p><label>Name:
34         <input name = "name" type = "text" size = "25">
35      </label></p>
36
37      <p>
38         <!-- Input types "submit" and "reset" insert buttons -->
39         <!-- for submitting or clearing the form's contents  -->
40         <input type = "submit" value = "Submit Your Entries">
41         <input type = "reset" value = "Clear Your Entries">
42      </p>
43
44      </form>
45
46   </body>
47   </html>
```

Fig. 25.3   Simple form with hidden fields and a text box (part 2 of 2).

The form begins on line 21

```
<form method = "post" action = "/cgi-bin/formmail">
```

with the ***form*** element. The ***method*** attribute indicates the way the information gathered in the form will be sent to the *Web server* for processing. Use ***method = "post"*** in a form that causes changes to server data, for example when updating a database. The form data will be sent to the server as an *environment variable,* which scripts are able to access. The other possible value, **method = "get"**, should be used when your form does not cause any changes in server-side data, for example when making a database request. The form data from **method = "get"** is appended to the end of the URL (for example, **/cgi-bin/formmail?name=bob&order=5**). Also be aware that **method = "get"** is limited to standard characters, and cannot submit any special characters.

A *Web server* is a machine that runs a software package such as Microsoft's PWS (Personal Web Server), Microsoft's IIS (Internet Information Server), Apache, etc. Web servers handle browser requests. When a browser requests a page or file somewhere on a server, the server processes the request and returns an answer to the browser. In this example, the data from the form goes to a CGI (Common Gateway Interface) script, which is a means of interfacing an HTML page with a script (i.e., a program) written in Perl, C, Tcl or other languages. The script then handles the data fed to it by the server and typically returns some information for the user. The **action** attribute in the **form** tag is the URL for this script; in this case, it is a simple script that emails form data to an address. Most Internet Service Providers (ISPs) will have a script like this on their site, so you can ask your system administrator how to set up your HTML to use the script correctly.

For this particular script, there are several pieces of information (not seen by the user) needed in the form. Lines 24–29

```
<input type = "hidden" name = "recipient"
   value = "deitel@deitel.com">
<input type = "hidden" name = "subject"
   value = "Feedback Form">
<input type = "hidden" name = "redirect"
   value = "main.html">
```

specify this information using *hidden input elements.* The **input** element is common in forms and always requires the ***type*** attribute. Two other attributes are ***name***, which provides a unique identifier for the **input** element, and ***value***, which indicates the value that the ***input*** element sends to the server upon submission.

As shown above, hidden inputs always have the attribute ***type = "hidden"***. The three hidden inputs shown are typical for this kind of CGI script: An email address to which the data will be sent, the subject line of the email and a URL to which the user is redirected after submitting the form.

Good Programming Practice 25.1

*Place hidden **input** elements in the beginning of a form, right after the opening **<form>** tag. This makes these elements easier to find and identify.*

The usage of an **input** element is defined by the value of its **type** attribute. We introduce another of these options in lines 33–35

```
<p><label>Name:
   <input name = "name" type = "text" size = "25">
</label></p>
```

The input **type = "text"** inserts a one-line text box into the form (line 34). A good use of the textual input element is for names or other one-line pieces of information. The **label** element on lines 33–35 provide a description for the **input** element on line 34.

We also use the **size** attribute of the **input** element to specify the width of the text input, measured in characters. You can also set a maximum number of characters that the text input will accept using the **maxlength** attribute.

Good Programming Practice 25.2

When using **input** *elements in forms, be sure to leave enough space with the* **maxlength** *attribute for users to input the pertinent information.*

Common Programming Error 25.3

Forgetting to include a **label** *element for each form element is a design error. Without these labels, users will have no way of knowing what the function of individual form elements is.*

There are two types of **input** elements in lines 40 and 41

```
<input type = "submit" value = "Submit Your Entries">
<input type = "reset" value = "Clear Your Entries">
```

that should be inserted into every form. The **type = "submit" input** element allows the user to submit the data entered in the form to the server for processing. Most visual Web browsers place a button in the form that submits the data when clicked. The **value** attribute changes the text displayed on the button (the default value is **"submit"**). The input element **type = "reset"** allows a user to reset all form elements to the default values. This can help the user correct mistakes or simply start over. As with the **submit** input, the **value** attribute of the **reset input** element affects the text of the button on the screen, but does not affect its functionality.

Common Programming Error 25.4

Be sure to close your form code with the **</form>** *tag. Neglecting to do so is an error and can affect the functionality of other forms on the same page.*

25.5 More Complex HTML Forms

We introduce additional form input options in Fig. 25.4.

```
1   <!DOCTYPE HTML PUBLIC "-//W3C//DTD HTML 4.01//EN"
2              "http://www.w3.org/TR/html4/strict.dtd">
3   <html>
4
5   <!-- Fig. 25.4: form2.html   -->
6   <!-- Form Design Example 2   -->
7
```

Fig. 25.4   Form including textareas, password boxes and checkboxes (part 1 of 3).

```
 8   <head>
 9      <title>Perl How to Program - Forms</title>
10   </head>
11
12   <body>
13
14      <h1>Feedback Form</h1>
15
16      <p>Please fill out this form to help us improve our site.</p>
17
18      <form method = "post" action = "/cgi-bin/formmail">
19
20      <p>
21         <input type = "hidden" name = "recipient"
22            value = "deitel@deitel.com">
23         <input type = "hidden" name = "subject"
24            value = "Feedback Form">
25         <input type = "hidden" name = "redirect"
26            value = "main.html">
27      </p>
28
29      <p><label>Name:
30         <input name = "name" type = "text" size = "25">
31      </label></p>
32
33      <!-- <textarea> creates a textbox of the size given -->
34      <p><label>Comments:
35         <textarea name = "comments" rows = "4" cols = "36">
36         </textarea>
37      </label></p>
38
39      <!-- <input type = "password"> inserts a textbox whose    -->
40      <!-- readout will be in *** instead of regular characters -->
41      <p><label>Email Address:
42         <input name = "email" type = "password" size = "25">
43      </label></p>
44
45      <p>
46         <strong>Things you liked:</strong><br>
47
48         <label>Site design
49         <input name = "thingsliked" type = "checkbox"
50            value = "Design"></label>
51
52         <label>Links
53         <input name = "thingsliked" type = "checkbox"
54            value = "Links"></label>
55
56         <label>Ease of use
57         <input name = "thingsliked" type = "checkbox"
58            value = "Ease"></label>
59
60         <label>Images
```

Fig. 25.4   Form including textareas, password boxes and checkboxes (part 2 of 3).

```
61              <input name = "thingsliked" type = "checkbox"
62                 value = "Images"></label>
63
64           <label>Source code
65              <input name = "thingsliked" type = "checkbox"
66                 value = "Code"></label>
67        </p>
68
69        <p>
70           <input type = "submit" value = "Submit Your Entries">
71           <input type = "reset" value = "Clear Your Entries">
72        </p>
73
74        </form>
75
76    </body>
77    </html>
```

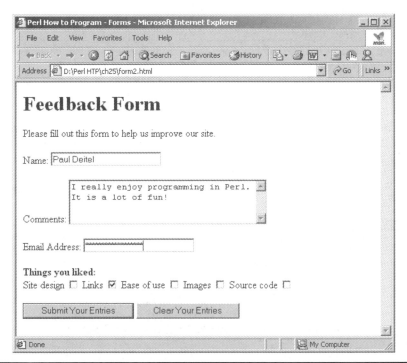

Fig. 25.4   Form including textareas, password boxes and checkboxes (part 3 of 3).

Lines 35 and 36

```
<textarea name = "comments" rows = "4" cols = "36"></textarea>
```

introduces the **_textarea_** element. The **textarea** element inserts a text box into the form. You specify the size of the box with the **_rows_** *attribute*, which sets the number of rows that will appear in the **textarea**. With the **_cols_** *attribute*, you specify how wide the **textarea** should be. This **textarea** is four rows of characters tall and 36 characters wide. Any default text that you want to place inside the **textarea** should be contained in the **textarea** element.

The input **type = "password"** (line 42)

```
<input name = "email" type = "password" size = "25">
```

inserts a text box with the indicated size. The password input field provides a way for users to enter information that the user would not want others to be able to read on the screen. In visual browsers, the data the user types into a password input field is shown as asterisks. However, the actual value the user enters is sent to the server. Non-visual browsers may render this type of input field differently.

Lines 48–66 introduce another type of form element, the checkbox. Every **input** element with **type = "checkbox"** creates a new checkbox item in the form. Checkboxes can be used individually or in groups. Each checkbox in a group should have the same **name** (in this case, **name = "thingsliked"**). This notifies the script handling the form that all of the checkboxes are related to one another.

Common Programming Error 25.5

*When your form has several checkboxes with the same **name**, you must make sure that they have different **value**s, or else the script will have no way of distinguishing between them.*

Additional form elements are introduced in Fig. 25.5. In this form example, we introduce two new types of input options. The first of these is the *radio button*, introduced (lines 71–89). Inserted into forms with the **input** attribute **type = "radio"**, radio buttons are similar in function and usage to checkboxes. Radio buttons are different in that only one element in the group may be selected at any time. All of the **name** attributes of a group of radio inputs must be the same and all of the **value** attributes different. Insert the attribute **checked** to indicate which radio button you would like selected initially. The **checked** attribute can also be applied to checkboxes.

Common Programming Error 25.6

*When you are using a group of radio inputs in a form, forgetting to set the **name** values to the same name will let the user select all the radio buttons at the same time: an undesired result.*

```
1   <!DOCTYPE HTML PUBLIC "-//W3C//DTD HTML 4.01//EN"
2              "http://www.w3.org/TR/html4/strict.dtd">
3   <html>
4
5   <!-- Fig. 25.5: form3.html   -->
6   <!-- Form Design Example 3   -->
7
8   <head>
9      <title>Perl How to Program - Forms</title>
10  </head>
11
12  <body>
13
```

Fig. 25.5   Form including radio buttons and pulldown lists (part 1 of 4).

```
14        <h1>Feedback Form</h1>
15
16        <p>Please fill out this form to help us improve our site.</p>
17
18        <form method = "post" action = "/cgi-bin/formmail">
19
20        <p>
21           <input type = "hidden" name = "recipient"
22              value = "deitel@deitel.com">
23           <input type = "hidden" name = "subject"
24              value = "Feedback Form">
25           <input type = "hidden" name = "redirect"
26              value = "main.html">
27        </p>
28
29        <p><label>Name:
30           <input name = "name" type = "text" size = "25">
31        </label></p>
32
33        <p><label>Comments:
34           <textarea name = "comments" rows = "4" cols = "36"></textarea>
35        </label></p>
36
37        <p><label>Email Address:
38           <input name = "email" type = "password" size = "25">
39        </label></p>
40
41        <p>
42           <strong>Things you liked:</strong><br>
43
44           <label>Site design
45           <input name = "things" type = "checkbox" value = "Design">
46           </label>
47
48           <label>Links
49           <input name = "things" type = "checkbox" value = "Links">
50           </label>
51
52           <label>Ease of use
53           <input name = "things" type = "checkbox" value = "Ease">
54           </label>
55
56           <label>Images
57           <input name = "things" type = "checkbox" value = "Images">
58           </label>
59
60           <label>Source code
61           <input name = "things" type = "checkbox" value = "Code">
62           </label>
63        </p>
64
65        <!-- <input type = "radio"> creates a radio button. The     -->
66        <!-- difference between radio buttons and checkboxes is      -->
```

Fig. 25.5   Form including radio buttons and pulldown lists (part 2 of 4).

```
67      <!-- that only one radio button in a group can be selected  -->
68      <p>
69         <strong>How did you get to our site?:</strong><br>
70
71         <label>Search engine
72         <input name = "how get to site" type = "radio"
73            value = "search engine" checked></label>
74
75         <label>Links from another site
76         <input name = "how get to site" type = "radio"
77            value = "link"></label>
78
79         <label>Deitel.com Web site
80         <input name = "how get to site" type = "radio"
81            value = "deitel.com"></label>
82
83         <label>Reference in a book
84         <input name = "how get to site" type = "radio"
85            value = "book"></label>
86
87         <label>Other
88         <input name = "how get to site" type = "radio"
89            value = "other"></label>
90
91      </p>
92
93      <!-- The <select> tag presents a drop down menu with -->
94      <!-- choices indicated by the <option> tags           -->
95      <p>
96         <label>Rate our site:
97
98         <select name = "rating">
99            <option selected>Amazing:-)</option>
100           <option>10</option>
101           <option>9</option>
102           <option>8</option>
103           <option>7</option>
104           <option>6</option>
105           <option>5</option>
106           <option>4</option>
107           <option>3</option>
108           <option>2</option>
109           <option>1</option>
110           <option>The Pits:-(</option>
111        </select>
112
113        </label>
114     </p>
115
116     <p>
117        <input type = "submit" value = "Submit Your Entries">
118        <input type = "reset" value = "Clear Your Entries">
119     </p>
```

Fig. 25.5   Form including radio buttons and pulldown lists (part 3 of 4).

```
120
121      </form>
122
123  </body>
124  </html>
```

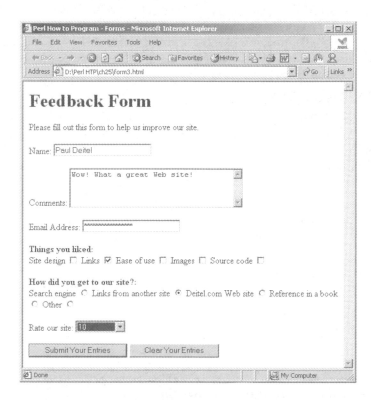

Fig. 25.5   Form including radio buttons and pulldown lists (part 4 of 4).

The last type of form input that we introduce here is the **select** element (lines 98–111). This will place a selectable list of items inside your form.

```
<select name = "rating">
   <option selected>Amazing:-)</option>
   <option>10</option>
   <option>9</option>
   <option>8</option>
   <option>7</option>
   <option>6</option>
   <option>5</option>
   <option>4</option>
   <option>3</option>
   <option>2</option>
   <option>1</option>
   <option>The Pits:-(</option>
</select>
```

This type of form input is created using a **select** element. Inside the opening **<select>** tag, be sure to include the **name** attribute.

To add an item to the list, add to the **select** element an *option* element containing the text to be displayed. The **selected** attribute, like the **checked** attribute for radio buttons and checkboxes, applies a default selection to your list.

The preceding code will generate a pull-down list of options in most visual browsers, as shown in Fig. 25.5. You can change the number of list options visible at one time using the *size* attribute of the **select** element. Use this attribute if you prefer an expanded version of the list to the one-line expandable list.

25.6 Internal Linking

In Chapter 24, we discussed how to link one Web page to another using text and image anchors. Figure 25.6 introduces *internal linking*, which lets you create named anchors for hyperlinks to particular parts of an HTML document.

```
1   <!DOCTYPE HTML PUBLIC "-//W3C//DTD HTML 4.01//EN"
2            "http://www.w3.org/TR/html4/strict.dtd">
3   <html>
4
5   <!-- Fig. 25.6: links.html   -->
6   <!-- Internal Linking        -->
7
8   <head>
9      <title>Perl How to Program - List</title>
10  </head>
11
12  <body>
13
14     <!-- <a name = "..."></a> makes an internal hyperlink -->
15     <p><a name = "features"></a></p>
16     <h1>The Best Features of the Internet</h1>
17
18     <!-- An internal link's address is "xx.html#linkname" -->
19     <p><a href = "#ceos">Go to <em>Favorite CEOs</em></a></p>
20
21     <ul>
22        <li>You can meet people from countries around the world.</li>
23
24        <li>You have access to new media as it becomes public:
25           <ul>
26              <li>New games</li>
27              <li>New applications
28                 <ul>
29                    <li>For Business</li>
30                    <li>For Pleasure</li>
31                 </ul>
32              </li>
33
```

Fig. 25.6   Using internal hyperlinks to make your pages more navigable (part 1 of 3).

```
34              <li>Around the Clock news</li>
35              <li>Search Engines</li>
36              <li>Shopping</li>
37              <li>Programming
38                 <ul>
39                    <li>HTML</li>
40                    <li>Java</li>
41                    <li>Dynamic HTML</li>
42                    <li>Scripts</li>
43                    <li>New languages</li>
44                 </ul>
45              </li>
46           </ul>
47        </li>
48
49        <li>Links</li>
50        <li>Keeping In touch with old friends</li>
51        <li>It is the technology of the future!</li>
52     </ul>
53
54
55     <p><a name = "ceos"></a></p>
56     <h1>My 3 Favorite <em>CEOs</em></h1>
57
58     <p>
59        <a href = "#features">Go to <em>Favorite Features</em></a>
60     </p>
61
62     <ol>
63        <li>Bill Gates</li>
64        <li>Steve Jobs</li>
65        <li>Michael Dell</li>
66     </ol>
67
68  </body>
69  </html>
```

Fig. 25.6   Using internal hyperlinks to make your pages more navigable (part 2 of 3).

Fig. 25.6   Using internal hyperlinks to make your pages more navigable (part 3 of 3).

Line 15

```
<p><a name = "features"></a></p>
```

shows a named anchor for an internal hyperlink. A named anchor is created using an **a** element with a **name** attribute. Line 15 creates an anchor named **features**. Because the name of the page is **list.html**, the URL of this anchor in the Web page is **list.html#features**. Line 59

```
<a href = "#features">Go to <em>Favorite Features</em></a>
```

shows a hyperlink with the anchor **features** as its target. Selecting this hyperlink in a visual browser would scroll the browser window to the **features** anchor (line 15). Examples of this occur in Fig 25.6, which shows two different screen captures from the same page, each at a different anchor. You can also link to an anchor in another page using the URL of that location (using the format **href = "page.html#name"**).

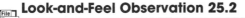

Look-and-Feel Observation 25.2

Internal hyperlinks are most useful in large HTML files with lots of information. You can link to various points on the page to save the user from having to scroll down and find a specific location.

25.7 Creating and Using Image Maps

We have seen that images can be used as links to other places on your site or elsewhere on the Internet. We now discuss how to create *image maps* (Fig. 25.7), which allow you to designate certain sections of the image as *hotspots* and then use these hotspots as links.

All elements of an image map are contained inside the **<map>...</map>** tags. The required attribute for the **map** element is **name** (line 17)

```
<map name = "picture">
```

As we will see, this attribute is needed for referencing purposes. A hotspot on the image is designated with the *area* element. Every *area* element has the following attributes: `href` sets the target for the link on that spot, *shape* and *coords* set the characteristics of the area and `alt` functions just as it does in the `img` element.

```
1   <!DOCTYPE HTML PUBLIC "-//W3C//DTD HTML 4.01//EN"
2              "http://www.w3.org/TR/html4/strict.dtd">
3   <html>
4
5   <!-- Fig. 25.7: picture.html      -->
6   <!-- Creating and Using Imape Maps  -->
7
8   <head>
9      <title>Perl How to Program - Image Map</title>
10  </head>
11
12  <body>
13
14     <p>
15     <!-- <map> opens and names an image map formatting area -->
16     <!-- and to be referenced later -->
17     <map name = "picture">
18
19       <!-- The "shape = rect" indicates a rectangular area, with -->
20       <!-- coordinates of the upper-left and lower-right corners -->
21        <area href = "form.html" shape = "rect"
22           coords = "3, 122, 73, 143" alt = "Go to the feedback form">
23        <area href = "contact.html" shape = "rect"
24          coords = "109, 123, 199, 142" alt = "Go to the contact page">
25        <area href = "main.html" shape = "rect"
26           coords = "1, 2, 72, 17" alt = "Go to the homepage">
27        <area href = "links.html" shape = "rect"
28           coords = "155, 0, 199, 18" alt = "Go to the links page">
29
30       <!-- The "shape = polygon" indicates an area of cusotmizable -->
31       <!-- shape, with the coordinates of every vertex listed    -->
32        <area href = "mailto:deitel@deitel.com" shape = "poly"
33           coords = "28, 22, 24, 68, 46, 114, 84, 111, 99, 56, 86, 13"
34           alt = "Email the Deitels">
35
36       <!-- The "shape = circle" indicates a circular area with -->
37       <!-- center and radius listed                           -->
38        <area href = "mailto:deitel@deitel.com" shape = "circle"
39           coords = "146, 66, 42" alt = "Email the Deitels">
40     </map>
41
42     <!-- <img src=... usemap = "#name"> says that the indicated -->
43     <!-- image map will be used with this image                -->
44     <img src = "deitel.gif" width = "200" height = "144"
45        alt = "Harvey and Paul Deitel" usemap = "#picture">
46     </p>
47
```

Fig. 25.7   Picture with links anchored to an image map (part 1 of 2).

```
48    </body>
49    </html>
```

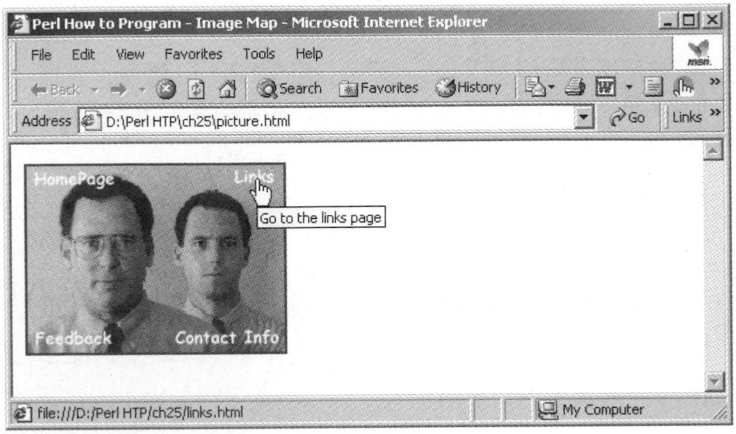

Fig. 25.7   Picture with links anchored to an image map (part 2 of 2).

The markup on lines 21 and 22

```
<area href = "form.html" shape = "rect"
    coords = "3, 122, 73, 143" alt = "Go to the feedback form">
```

causes a *rectangular hotspot* to be drawn around the *coordinates* given in the **coords** attribute. A coordinate pair consists of two numbers, which are the locations of the point on the *x* and *y* axes. The *x* axis extends horizontally from the upper-left corner and the *y* axis vertically. Every point on an image has a unique *x–y* coordinate. In the case of a rectangular hotspot, the required coordinates are those of the upper-left and lower-right corners of the rectangle. In this case, the upper-left corner of the rectangle is located at 3 on the *x* axis and 122 on the *y* axis, annotated as (*3, 122*). The lower-right corner of the rectangle is at (*73, 143*).

Another map area is in lines 32–34

```
<area href = "mailto:deitel@deitel.com" shape = "poly"
    coords = "28, 22, 24, 68, 46, 114, 84, 111, 99, 56, 86, 13
    alt = "Email the Deitels">
```

In this case, we use the value **poly** for the **shape** attribute. This creates a hotspot in the shape of a polygon using the coordinates in the **coords** attribute. These coordinates represent each vertex, or corner, of the polygon. The browser will automatically connect these points with lines to form the area of the hotspot.

shape = "circle" is the last shape attribute that is commonly used in image maps. It creates a *circular hotspot*, and requires both the coordinates of the center of the circle and the radius of the circle, in pixels.

To use the image map with an **img** element, you must insert the **usemap = "#**_name_**"** attribute into the **img** element, where *name* is the value of the **name** attribute in the **map** element. Lines 44 and 45

```
<img src = "deitel.gif" width = "200" height= "144" alt =
"Harvey and Paul Deitel" usemap = "#picture">
```

show how the image map **name = "picture"** is applied to the **img** element.

25.8 <meta> Tags

People use search engines to find interesting Web sites. Search engines usually catalog sites by following links from page to page and saving identification and classification information for each page visited. The main HTML element that search engines use to catalog pages is the *meta* tag (Fig. 25.8).

A **meta** tag contains two attributes that should always be used. The first of these, *name*, identifies the type of **meta** tag you are including. The *content* attribute provides information the search engine will catalog about your site.

```
1   <!DOCTYPE HTML PUBLIC "-//W3C//DTD HTML 4.01//EN"
2              "http://www.w3.org/TR/html4/strict.dtd">
3   <html>
4
5   <!-- Fig. 25.8: main.html        -->
6   <!-- <meta> and <!doctype> tags  -->
7
8   <head>
9      <!-- <meta> tags give search engines information they need -->
10     <!-- to catalog your site                                  -->
11     <meta name = "keywords" content = "Webpage, design, HTML,
12        tutorial, personal, help, index, form, contact, feedback,
13        list, links, frame, deitel">
14
15     <meta name = "description" content = "This Web site will help
16        you learn the basics of HTML and Webpage design through the
17        use of interactive examples and instruction.">
18
19     <title>Perl How to Program - Welcome</title>
20  </head>
21
22  <body>
23
24     <h1>Welcome to Our Web Site!</h1>
25
26     <p>We have designed this site to teach about the wonders of
27     <em>HTML</em>. We have been using <em>HTML</em> since version
28     <strong>2.0</strong>, and we enjoy the features that have been
29     added recently. It seems only a short time ago that we read
30     our first <em>HTML</em> book. Soon you will know about many of
31     the great new features of HTML 4.01.</p>
32
33     <p>Have Fun With the Site!</p>
34
35  </body>
36  </html>
```

Fig. 25.8   Using **meta** to provide keywords and a description.

Lines 11–13 demonstrate the **meta** tag.

```
<meta name = "keywords" content = "Webpage, design, HTML,
    tutorial, personal, help, index, form, contact, feedback,
    list, links, frame, deitel">
```

The **content** of a **meta** tag with *name = "keywords"* provides search engines with a list of words that describe key aspects of your site. These words are used to match with searches—if someone searches for some of the terms in your **keywords meta** tag, they have a better chance of being informed about your site in the search engine output. Thus, including **meta** tags and their **content** information will draw more viewers to your site.

The *description* attribute value (lines 15–17)

```
<meta name = "description" content = "This Web site will help
    you learn the basics of HTML and Webpage design through the
    use of interactive examples and instruction.">
```

is quite similar to the **keywords** value. Instead of giving a list of words describing your page, the **content**s of the keywords **meta** element should be a readable 3-to-4 line description of your site, written in sentence form. This description is also used by search engines to catalog and display your site.

Software Engineering Observation 25.1

meta *elements are not visible to users of the site and must be placed inside the header section of your HTML document.*

25.9 **frameset** Element

All of the Web pages we have designed so far have the ability to link to other pages but can display only one page at a time. Figure 25.9 introduces *frames*, which can help you display more than one HTML file at a time. Frames, when used properly, can make your site more readable and usable for your users.

```
1   <!DOCTYPE HTML PUBLIC "-//W3C//DTD HTML 4.01 Frameset//EN"
2              "http://www.w3.org/TR/html4/frameset.dtd">
3   <html>
4
5   <!-- Fig. 25.9: index.html   -->
6   <!-- HTML Frames I           -->
7
8   <head>
9      <meta name = "keywords" content = "Webpage, design, HTML,
10        tutorial, personal, help, index, form, contact, feedback,
11        list, links, frame, deitel">
12
13     <meta name = "description" content = "This Web site will help
14        you learn the basics of HTML and Webpage design through the
15        use of interactive examples and instruction.">
16
17     <title>Perl How to Program - Main</title>
```

Fig. 25.9   Web site using two frames—navigation and content (part 1 of 2).

```
18   </head>
19
20   <!-- The <frameset> tag gives the dimensions of your frame -->
21   <frameset cols = "110,*">
22
23      <!-- The individual frame elements specify which pages -->
24      <!-- appear in the given frames                        -->
25      <frame name = "nav" src = "nav.html">
26      <frame name = "main" src = "main.html">
27
28      <noframes>
29         <p>This page uses frames, but your browser does not support
30         them.</p>
31
32         <p>Please, <a href = "nav.html">follow this link to browse our
33         site without frames</a>.</p>
34      </noframes>
35
36   </frameset>
37   </html>
```

Fig. 25.9   Web site using two frames—navigation and content (part 2 of 2).

On lines 1 and 2

```
<!DOCTYPE HTML PUBLIC "-//W3C//DTD HTML 4.01 Frameset//EN"
        "http://www.w3.org/TR/html4/frameset.dtd">
```

we encounter a new document type. The document type specified here indicates that this HTML document uses frames. You should use this document type whenever you use frames in your HTML document.

The framed page begins with the opening **frameset** tag, on line 21

```
<frameset cols = "110,*">
```

This tag tells the browser that the page contains frames. The **cols** attribute of the opening **frameset** tag gives the layout of the frameset. The value of **cols** (or **rows**, if you will be writing a frameset with a horizontal layout) gives the width of each frame, either in pixels or as a percentage of the screen. In this case, the attribute **cols = "110,*"** tells the browser that there are two frames. The first one extends 110 pixels from the left edge of the screen, and the second frame fills the remainder of the screen (as indicated by the asterisk).

Now that we have defined the page layout, we have to specify what files will make up the frameset. We do this with the **frame** element in lines 25 and 26

```
<frame name = "nav" src = "nav.html">
<frame name = "main" src = "main.html">
```

In each **frame** element, the **src** attribute gives the URL of the page that will be displayed in the frame. In the preceding example, the first frame (which covers 110 pixels on the left side of the **frameset**) will display the page **nav.html** and has the attribute **name = "nav"**. The second frame will display the page **main.html** and has the attribute **name = "main"**.

The purpose of a **name** attribute in the **frame** element is to identify the frame, enabling hyperlinks in a **frameset** to load in their intended target **frame**. For example,

```
<a href = "links.html" target = "main">
```

would load **links.html** in the frame whose **name** attribute is **"main"**.

A target in an anchor element can also be set to a number of preset values: **target="_blank"** loads the page in a new blank browser window, **target="_self"** loads the page into the same window as the anchor element, **target="_parent"** loads it in the parent **frameset** (i.e., the **frameset** which contains the current frame) and **target="_top"** loads the page into the full browser window (the page loads over the **frameset**).

In lines 28–34 of the code example in Fig. 25.9, the **noframes** element displays HTML in those browsers that do not support frames.

Portability Tip 25.1

*Not everyone uses a browser that supports frames. Use the **noframes** element inside the **frameset** to direct users to a non-framed version of your site.*

Look-and-Feel Observation 25.3

Frames are capable of enhancing your page, but are often misused. Never use frames to accomplish what you could with other, simpler HTML formatting.

25.10 Nested **framesets**

You can use the **frameset** element to create more complex layouts in a framed Web site by nesting **frameset** areas as in Fig. 25.10.

The first level of **frameset** tags is on lines 21 and 22

```
<frameset cols = "110,*">
    <frame name = "nav"src = "nav.html">
```

The **frameset** and **frame** elements here are constructed in the same manner as in Fig. 3.9. We have one frame that extends over the first 110 pixels starting at the left edge.

The second (nested) level of the **frameset** element covers only the remaining **frame** area that was not included in the primary **frameset**. Thus, any frames included in the second **frameset** will not include the left-most 110 pixels of the screen. Lines 26–29 show the second level of **frameset** tags.

```
1   <!DOCTYPE HTML PUBLIC "-//W3C//DTD HTML 4.01 Frameset//EN"
2              "http://www.w3.org/TR/html4/frameset.dtd">
3   <html>
4
5   <!-- Fig. 25.10: index2.html -->
6   <!-- HTML Frames II            -->
7
8   <head>
9
10  <meta name = "keywords" content = "Webpage, design, HTML,
11     tutorial, personal, help, index, form, contact, feedback,
12     list, links, frame, deitel">
13
14  <meta name = "description" content = "This Web site will help
15     you learn the basics of HTML and Webpage design through the
16     use of interactive examples and instruction.">
17
18  <title>Perl How to Program - Main</title>
19  </head>
20
21  <frameset cols = "110,*">
22     <frame name = "nav" src = "nav.html">
23
24     <!-- Nested framesets are used to change the formatting -->
25     <!-- and spacing of the frameset as a whole            -->
26     <frameset rows = "175,*">
27        <frame name = "picture" src = "picture.html">
28        <frame name = "main" src = "main.html">
29     </frameset>
30
31     <noframes>
32        <p>This page uses frames, but your browser does not support
33        them.</p>
34
35        <p>Please, <a href = "nav.html">follow this link to browse our
36        site without frames</a>.</p>
37     </noframes>
38
39  </frameset>
40  </html>
```

Fig. 25.10 Framed Web site with a nested frameset (part 1 of 2).

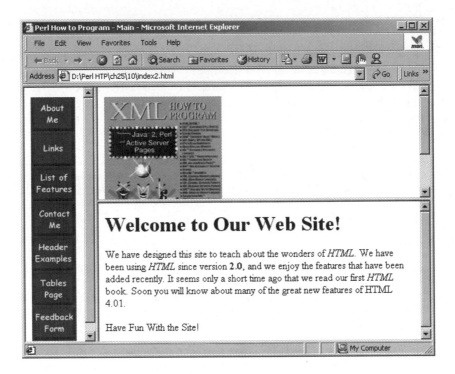

Fig. 25.10   Framed Web site with a nested frameset (part 2 of 2).

```
<frameset rows = "175,*">
   <frame name = "picture" src = "picture.html">
   <frame name = "main" src = "main.html">
</frameset>
```

In this **frameset** area, the first frame extends 175 pixels from the top of the screen, as indicated by the **rows = "175,*"**. Be sure to include the correct number of **frame** elements inside the second **frameset** area. Also, be sure to include a **noframes** element and to close both of the **frameset** areas at the end of the Web page.

 Testing and Debugging Tip 25.1

When using nested **frameset** *elements, indent every level of* **frame** *tag. This makes the page clearer and easier to debug.*

 Look-and-Feel Observation 25.4

Nested **frameset***s can help you create visually pleasing, easy-to-navigate Web sites.*

25.11 Internet and World Wide Web Resources

There are many Web sites that cover the more advanced and difficult features of HTML. Several of these sites are featured here.

www.geocities.com/SiliconValley/Orchard/5212
Adam's Advanced HTML Page is geared to those looking to master the more advanced techniques of HTML. It includes instructions for creating tables, frames and marquees and other advanced topics.

www.w3scripts.com/html
This site, an offshoot of *W3Schools*, is a repository for code examples exhibiting all of the features of HTML, from beginner to advanced.

www.blooberry.com/indexdot/html
Index Dot HTML, The Advance HTML Reference... The name speaks for itself. This site has a great directory and tree-based index of all HTML elements plus more.

www.markradcliffe.co.uk/html/advancedhtml.htm
The *Advanced HTML Guide* gives insights into improving your site using HTML in ways you might not have thought possible.

SUMMARY

- HTML tables organize data into rows and columns. All tags and text that apply to a table go inside the **<table>**...**</table>** tags. The **border** attribute lets you set the width of the table's border in pixels. The **width** attribute sets the width of the table—you specify either a number of pixels or a percentage of the screen width.

- The text inside the **<caption>**...**</caption>** tags is inserted directly above the table in the browser window. The caption text is also used to help text-based browsers interpret the table data.

- Tables can be split into distinct horizontal and vertical sections. Put all header information (such as table titles and column headers) inside the **<thead>**...**</thead>** tags. The **tr** (table row) element is used for formatting the cells of individual rows. All of the cells in a row belong within the **<tr>**...**</tr>** tags of that row.

- The smallest area of the table that we are able to format is the data cell. There are two types of data cells: ones located in the header (**<th>**...**</th>**) and ones located in the table body (**<td>**...**</td>**). Header cells, usually placed in the **<thead>** area, are suitable for titles and column headings.

- Like **thead**, the **tbody** is used for formatting and grouping purposes. Most tables use **tbody** to house the majority of their content.

- **td** table data cells are left aligned by default. **th** cells are centered by default.

- Just as you can use the **thead** and **tbody** elements to format groups of table rows, you can use the **colgroup** element to group and format columns. **colgroup** is used by setting in its opening tag the number of columns it affects and the formatting it imposes on that group of columns.

- Each **col** element contained inside the **<colgroup>**...**</colgroup>** tags can in turn format a specified number of columns.

- You can add a background color or image to any table row or cell with either the **bgcolor** or **background** attributes, which are used in the same way as in the **body** element.

- It is possible to make some table data cells larger than others by using the **rowspan** and **colspan** attributes. The attribute value extends the data cell to span the specified number of cells.

- The **valign** (vertical alignment) attribute of a table data cell accepts the following values: **"top"**, **"middle"**, **"bottom"** and **"baseline"**.

- All cells in a table row whose **valign** attribute is set to **"baseline"** will have the first text line on a common baseline.

- The default vertical alignment in all data and header cells is **valign="middle"**.

- HTML provides several mechanisms—including the **form**—to collect information from people viewing your site.

- Use **method = "post"** in a form that causes changes to server data, for example when updating a database. The form data will be sent to the server as an environment variable, which scripts are able to access. The other possible value, **method = "get"**, should be used when your form does not cause any changes in server-side data, for example when making a database request. The form data from **method = "get"** is appended to the end of the URL. Because of this, the amount of data submitted using this **method** is limited to 4K. Also be aware that **method = "get"** is limited to standard characters, and cannot submit any special characters.

- A Web server is a machine that runs a software package such as Apache or IIS; servers are designed to handle browser requests. When a user uses a browser to request a page or file somewhere on the server, the server processes this request and returns an answer to the browser.

- The **action** attribute in the **form** tag is the path to a script that processes the form data.

- The input element is common in forms, and always requires the **type** attribute. Two other attributes are **name**, which provides a unique identification for the **input**, and **value**, which indicates the value that the **input** element sends to the server upon submission.

- The input **type="text"** inserts a one-line text bar into the form. The value of this **input** element and the information that the server sends to you from this **input** is the text that the user types into the bar. The **size** attribute determines the width of the text input, measured in characters. You can also set a maximum number of characters that the text input will accept by inserting the **maxlength="***length***"** attribute.

- You must make sure to include a **label** element for each form element to indicate the function of the element.

- The **type="submit" input** element places a button in the form that submits data to the server when clicked. The **value** attribute of the **submit** input changes the text displayed on the button.

- The **type="reset"** input element places a button on the form that, when clicked, will clear all entries the user has entered into the form.

- The **textarea** element inserts a box into the form. You specify the size of the box (which is scrollable) inside the opening **<textarea>** tag with the **rows** attribute and the **cols** attribute.

- Data entered in a **type="password"** input appears on the screen as asterisks. The password is used for submitting sensitive information that the user would not want others to be able to read. It is just the browser that displays asterisks—the real form data is still submitted to the server.

- Every **input** element with **type="checkbox"** creates a new checkbox in the form. Checkboxes can be used individually or in groups. Each checkbox in a group should have the same **name** (in this case, **name="things"**).

- Inserted into forms by means of the **input** attribute **type="radio"**, radio buttons are different from checkboxes in that only one in the group may be selected at any time. All of the **name** attributes of a group of radio inputs must be the same and all of the **value** attributes different.

- Insert the attribute **checked** to indicate which radio button you would like selected initially.

- The **select** element places a selectable list of items inside your form. To add an item to the list, insert an **option** element in the **<select>...</select>** area and type what you want the list item to display on the same line. You can change the number of list options visible at one time by including the **size="***size***"** attribute inside the **<select>** tag. Use this attribute if you prefer an expanded version of the list to the one-line expandable list.

- A location on a page is marked by including a **name** attribute in an **a** element. Clicking this hyperlink in a browser would scroll the browser window to that point on the page.

- An image map allows you to designate certain sections of the image as hotspots and then use these hotspots as anchors for linking.
- All elements of an image map are contained inside the **<map>**…**</map>** tags. The required attribute for the **map** element is **name**.
- A hotspot on the image is designated with the ***area*** element. Every **<area>** tag has the following attributes: **href** sets the target for the link on that spot, ***shape*** and ***coords*** set the characteristics of the area and **alt** function just as it does in **<img>** tags.
- **shape="rect"** creates a rectangular hotspot around the coordinates of a **coords** element.
- A coordinate pair consists of two numbers, which are the locations of the point on the *x* and *y* axes. The *x* axis extends horizontally from the upper-left corner and the *y* axis vertically. Every point on an image has a unique *x-y* coordinate, annotated as *(x, y)*.
- In the case of a rectangular hotspot, the required coordinates are those of the upper-left and lower-right corners of the rectangle.
- The **shape="poly"** creates a hotspot of no preset shape—you specify the shape of the hotspot in the **coords** attribute by listing the coordinates of every vertex, or corner of the hotspot.
- **shape="circle"** creates a circular hotspot; it requires both the coordinates of the center of the circle and the length of the radius, in pixels.
- To use an image map with a graphic on your page, you must insert the **usemap="#*name*"** attribute into the **img** element, where "name" is the value of the **name** attribute in the **map** element.
- The main element that interacts with search engines is the **meta** element.
- **meta** tags contain two attributes that should always be used. The first of these, **name**, is an identification of the type of **meta** tag you are including. The **content** attribute gives the information the search engine will be cataloging.
- The **content** of a **meta** tag with **name="keywords"** provides the search engines with a list of words that describe the key aspects of your site. By including **meta** tags and their content information, you can give precise information about your site to search engines. This will help you draw a more focused audience to your site.
- The **description** value of the **name** attribute in the **meta** tag should be a 3-to-4 line description of your site, written in sentence form. This description is used by the search engine to catalog and display your site.
- **meta** elements are not visible to users of the site and should be placed inside the header section of your HTML document.
- The **frameset** tag tells the browser that the page contains frames.
- **cols** or **rows** gives the width of each frame in pixels or as a percentage of the screen.
- In each **frame** element, the **src** attribute gives the URL of the page that will be displayed in the specified frame.
- The purpose of a **name** attribute in the **frame** element is to give an identity to that specific frame, in order to enable hyperlinks in a **frameset** to load their intended **frame**. The **target** attribute in an anchor element is set to the **name** of the **frame** in which the new page should load.
- A target in an anchor element can be set to a number of preset values: **target="_blank"** loads the page in a new blank browser window, **target="self"** loads the page into the same window as the anchor element, **target="_parent"** loads the page into the parent **frameset** and **target="_top"** loads the page into the full browser window.
- Not everyone viewing a page has a browser that can handle frames. You therefore need to include a **noframes** element inside of the **frameset**. You should include regular HTML tags and ele-

ments within the **<noframes>**…**</noframes>** tags. Use this area to direct the user to a non-framed version of the site.

- By nesting **frameset** elements, you can create more complex layouts.

TERMINOLOGY

<!doctype…**>**
<meta> tag
<option>
ACTION attribute in **form** element
area
border property of **table** element
caption element
cell of a table
CGI script
checked
circular hotspot
col element
colgroup element
cols attribute of **table** element
colspan attribute of **td** element
column of a table
coords attribute inside **area** element
data cell
environment variable
form
frame element (**<frame>**…**</frame>**)
frameset element
header cell
hotspot
image map
indenting lists
input element (**<input>**…**</input>**)
input type="button"
input type="checkbox"
input type="password"
input type="radio"
input type="reset"
input type="submit"
input type="text"
input type="textarea"
internal linking
list
map element
maxlength="#"

method="get"
method="post"
name attribute in **input** element
name="recipient" in **input** element
name="redirect" in **input** element
name="subject" in **input** element
nested lists
noframes
noresize attribute in **frame**
ol (ordered list) element (**<ol>**…**</ol>**)
rectangular hotspot
row of a table
rowspan attribute of **td** element
scrolling attribute in **frame**
select element (**<select>**…**</select>**)
shape attribute inside **area** element
size attribute in **select**
src attribute of **frame** element
table
table element (**<table>**…**</table>**)
target="_blank"
target="_blank"
target="_parent"
target="_top"
tbody
td (table data) element (**<td>**…**</td>**)
text-based browser
th (header cell) element (**<th>**…**</th>**)
thead element (**<thead>**…**</thead>**)
tr (table row) element (**<tr>**…**</tr>**)
type=1 attribute of **<ol>**
type=a attribute of **<ol>**
type=A attribute of **<ol>**
type=i attribute of **<ol>**
type=I attribute of **<ol>**
ul (unordered list) element (**<ul>**…**</ul>**)
usemap="name" attribute in **img**
value attribute of **input** element
Web server

SELF-REVIEW EXERCISES

25.1   State whether the following are *true* or *false*. If *false*, explain why.
  a) The width of all data cells in a table must be the same.
  b) The **thead** element is mandatory in a **table**.

c) You are limited to a maximum of 100 internal links per page.

d) All browsers can render **frameset**s.

25.2 Fill in the blanks in each of the following statements.

a) The _____ attribute in an **input** element inserts a button that, when clicked, will clear the contents of the form.

b) The spacing of a **frameset** is set by including the _____ attribute or the _____ attribute inside of the **<frameset>** tag.

c) The _____ element inserts a new item in a list.

d) The _____ element tells the browser what version of HTML is included on the page. Two types of this element are _____ and _____.

e) The common shapes used in image maps are _____, _____ and _____ .

25.3 Write HTML tags to accomplish the following:

a) Insert a framed Web page with the first frame extending 300 pixels across the page from the left side.

b) Insert an ordered list that will have numbering by lowercase Roman numerals.

c) Insert a scrollable list (in a form) that will always display four entries of the list.

d) Insert an image map onto a page using **deitel.gif** as an image and **map** with **name="hello"** as the image map, and have "**hello**" be the **alt** text.

ANSWERS TO SELF-REVIEW EXERCISES

25.1 a) False. You can specify the width of any column either in pixels or as a percentage of the total width of the table. c) False. The **thead** element is used only for formatting purposes and is optional (but it is recommended that you include it). d) False. You can have an unlimited number of hyperlink locations on any page. e) False. Text-based browsers are unable to render a **frameset** and must therefore rely on the information that you include inside the **<noframes>...</noframes>** tag.

25.2 a) **type = "reset"**. b) **cols**, **rows**. c) **li**. d) **<!doctype...>**, **transitional**, **frameset**. e) **poly**, **circle**, **rect**.

25.3 a) **<frameset cols = "300,*">...</frameset>** b) **<ol type = "i">...</ol>** c)**<select size = "4">...</select>** d)**<img src = "deitel.gif" alt = "hello" usemap = "#hello">**

EXERCISES

25.4 Categorize each of the following as an element or an attribute:

a) **width**
b) **td**
c) **th**
d) **frame**
e) **name**
f) **select**
g) **type**

25.5 What will the **frameset** produced by the following code look like? Assume that the pages being imported are blank with white backgrounds and that the dimensions of the screen are 800 by 600. Sketch the layout, approximating the dimensions.

```
<frameset rows = "20%,*">
<frame src = "hello.html" name = "hello">
   <frameset cols = "150,*">
   <frame src = "nav.html" name = "nav">
   <frame src = "deitel.html" name = "deitel">
   </frameset>
</frameset>
```

25.6   Assume that you have a document with many subsections. Write the HTML markup to create a frame with a table of contents on the left side of the window, and have each entry in the table of contents use internal linking to scroll down the document frame to the appropriate subsection.

26

Bonus: Cascading Style Sheets™ (CSS)

Objectives

- To take control of the appearance of a Web site by creating stylesheets.
- To use a stylesheet to give all the pages of a Web site the same look and feel.
- To use the **class** attribute to apply styles.
- To specify the precise font, size, color and other properties of displayed text.
- To specify element backgrounds and colors.
- To understand the box model and be able to control the margins, borders and padding.
- To use stylesheets to separate presentation from content.

Fashions fade, style is eternal.
Yves Saint Laurent

A style does not go out of style as long as it adapts itself to its period. When there is an incompatibility between the style and a certain state of mind, it is never the style that triumphs.
Coco Chanel

How liberating to work in the margins, outside a central perception.
Don DeLillo

Our words have wings, but fly not where we would.
George Eliot

26.1 Introduction

Cascading Style Sheets (*CSS*) allow you to specify the style of your page elements (spacing, margins, etc.) separately from the structure of your document (section headers, body text, links, etc.). This *separation of structure from presentation* allows greater manageability and makes changing the style of your document easier.

26.2 Inline Styles

There are many ways to declare styles for a document. Figure 26.1 presents *inline styles* in which an individual element's style is declared using the ***style*** attribute.

```
1   <!DOCTYPE HTML PUBLIC "-//W3C//DTD HTML 4.01//EN"
2              "http://www.w3.org/TR/html4/strict.dtd">
3   <html>
4
5   <!-- Fig. 26.1: inline.html -->
6   <!-- Using inline styles       -->
7
8   <head>
9      <title>Perl How to Program - Inline Styles</title>
10  </head>
11
12  <body>
13
14     <p>This text does not have any style applied to it.</p>
15
16     <!-- The style attribute allows you to declare inline   -->
17     <!-- styles. Separate multiple styles with a semicolon. -->
```

Fig. 26.1   Inline styles (part 1 of 2).

```
18      <p style = "font-size: 20pt">This text has the <em>font-size</em>
19      style applied to it, making it 20pt.</p>
20
21      <p style = "font-size: 20pt; color: #0000ff">This text has the
22      <em>font-size</em> and <em>color</em> styles applied to it,
23      making it 20pt. and blue.</p>
24
25  </body>
26  </html>
```

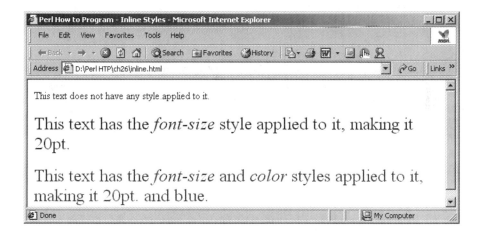

Fig. 26.1   Inline styles (part 2 of 2).

Our first inline style declaration appears on line 18

```
<p style = "font-size: 20pt">This text has the <em>font-size</em>
```

The **style attribute** allows you to specify a style for an element. Each *CSS property* (in this case, **font-size**) is followed by a colon then by the value of the property. On line 18 we declare the **p** element to have 20-point text size.

Line 21

```
<p style = "font-size: 20pt; color: #0000ff">This text has the
```

specifies two properties separated by a semicolon. In this line we also set the **color** of the text to blue using the hex code **#0000ff**. Color names may be used in place of hex codes as we will see in the next example. Note that inline styles override any other styles applied by the methods we cover later in this chapter.

26.3 Creating Style Sheets with the `style` Element

In Fig. 26.2 we declare styles in the **head** of the document. These styles may be applied to the entire document.

The **style** element on line 12

```
<style type = "text/css">
```

begins the *style sheet*. Styles that are placed here apply to matching elements in the entire document, not just a single element as with inline styles. The **type** attribute specifies the *MIME type* of the stylesheet. MIME is a standard for specifying the format of content— some other MIME types are **text/html**, **image/gif**, and **text/javascript**. Regular text style sheets always use the MIME type **text/css**.

```
1   <!DOCTYPE HTML PUBLIC "-//W3C//DTD HTML 4.01//EN"
2             "http://www.w3.org/TR/html4/strict.dtd">
3   <html>
4
5   <!-- Fig. 26.2: declared.html                        -->
6   <!-- Declaring a style sheet in the header section.  -->
7
8   <head>
9      <title>Perl How to Program - Style Sheets</title>
10
11     <!-- This begins the style sheet section. -->
12     <style type = "text/css">
13
14        em        { background-color: #8000ff;
15                    color: white }
16
17        h1        { font-family: arial, sans-serif }
18
19        p         { font-size: 14pt }
20
21        .special { color: blue }
22
23     </style>
24  </head>
25
26  <body>
27
28     <!-- This class attribute applies the .blue style -->
29     <h1 class = "special">Deitel & Associates, Inc.</h1>
30
31     <p>Deitel & Associates, Inc. is an internationally recognized
32     corporate training and publishing organization specializing
33     in programming languages, Internet/World Wide Web technology
34     and object technology education. Deitel & Associates, Inc. is
35     a member of the World Wide Web Consortium. The company
36     provides courses on Java, C++, Visual Basic, C, Internet and
37     World Wide Web programming, and Object Technology.</p>
38
39     <h1>Clients</h1>
40     <p class = "special"> The company's clients include many
41     <em>Fortune 1000 companies</em>, government agencies, branches
42     of the military and business organizations. Through its
43     publishing partnership with Prentice Hall, Deitel & Associates,
44     Inc. publishes leading-edge programming textbooks, professional
45     books, interactive CD-ROM-based multimedia Cyber Classrooms,
46     satellite courses and World Wide Web courses.</p>
```

Fig. 26.2   Declaring styles in the **head** of a document (part 1 of 2).

```
47
48    </body>
49    </html>
```

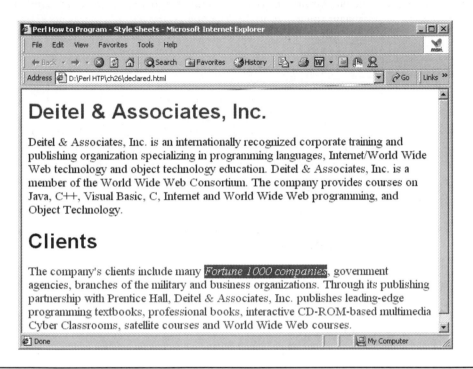

Fig. 26.2   Declaring styles in the **head** of a document (part 2 of 2).

The body of the stylesheet on lines 13–22

```
em      { background-color: #8000ff;
          color: white }

h1      { font-family: arial, sans-serif }

p       { font-size: 14pt }

.special { color: blue }
```

declares the *CSS rules* for this style sheet. We declare rules for the **em**, **h1** and **p** elements. All **em**, **h1** and **p** elements in this document will be modified with the specified properties. Notice that each rule body begins and ends with a curly brace (**{** and **}**). We also declare a *style class* named **special** on line 21. Class declarations are preceded with a period and are applied to elements only of that specific class (as we will see momentarily).

The CSS rules in a style sheet use the same syntax as inline styles—the property is followed by a colon (**:**) and the value of that property. Multiple properties are separated with a semicolon (**;**). The ***color*** property specifies the color of text in an element. Property ***background-color*** specifies the background color of the element.

The **font-family** property (line 17) specifies the name of the font that should be displayed. In this case, we use the **arial** font. The second value, **sans-serif**, is a *generic font family*. Generic font families allow you to specify a general type of font instead of a specific font. This allows much greater flexibility since not every client will have the same specific fonts installed. In this example, if the **arial** font is not found on the system, the browser will instead display another **sans-serif** font (such as **helvetica** or **verdana**). Other generic font families are **serif** (e.g., **times new roman** or **Georgia**), **cursive** (e.g., **script**), **fantasy** (e.g., **critter**) and **monospace** (e.g., **courier** or **fixedsys**).

The **font-size** property specifies the size to use to render the font—in this case we use 14 points. Other possible measurements besides **pt** are covered later in the chapter. You can also use the relative values **xx-small**, **x-small**, **small**, **smaller**, **medium**, **large**, **larger**, **x-large** and **xx-large**. In general, relative values for **font-size** are preferred because, as an author, you do not know the specific measurements of the display for each different client. For example, someone may wish to view your page on a hand-held computer with a small screen. Specifying an 18pt font size in your stylesheet will prevent such a user from seeing more than one or two characters at a time. However, if you specify a relative font size, such as **large** or **larger**, the actual size will be determined by the user's browser and will therefore be displayed properly.

On line 29

```
<h1 class = "special">Deitel & Associates, Inc.</h1>
```

the **class** attribute applies a style class, in this case **special** (this was declared as **.special** in the stylesheet). Note that the text appears on screen with *both* the properties of an **h1** element (i.e., **arial** or **sans-serif** font) and the properties of the **.special** style class applied (i.e., **color** blue).

The **p** element and the **.special** class style are applied to the text on lines 40–46. All styles applied to an element (the *parent*, or *ancestor element*) also apply to elements contained in that element (*descendant elements*). The **em** element *inherits* the style from the **p** element (namely, the 14-point font size on line 19). However, because the **em** element has its own **color** property, this overrides the **color** property of the **special** class. We discuss the rules for resolving these kinds of conflicts in Section 26.4.

26.4 Conflicting Styles

CSS stylesheets are *cascading* because styles may defined by a user, an author and a *user agent* (e.g., a Web browser). Styles defined by authors take precedence over styles defined by the user, and styles defined by the user take precedence over styles defined by the user agent. Styles defined for parent and ancestor elements are also inherited by child and descendant elements. In this section we discuss the rules for resolving conflicts between styles defined for elements and those inherited from parent and ancestor elements.

We showed an example of inheritance in Fig. 26.2, in which a child **em** element inherited the **font-size** property from its parent **p** element. However, in Fig. 26.2 the child **em** element also had a **color** property that conflicted with (i.e., had a different value than) the **color** property of its parent **p** element. Properties defined for child and descendant elements have a greater *specificity* than properties defined for parent and ancestor elements.

According to the CSS specification, conflicts are resolved in favor properties with a higher specificity. Figure 26.3 has more examples of inheritance and specificity.

```
1   <!DOCTYPE HTML PUBLIC "-//W3C//DTD HTML 4.01//EN"
2              "http://www.w3.org/TR/html4/strict.dtd">
3   <html>
4
5   <!-- Fig 26.3: advanced.html    -->
6   <!-- More advanced style sheets  -->
7
8   <head>
9      <title>Perl How to Program - More Styles</title>
10
11     <style type = "text/css">
12
13        a.nodec   { text-decoration: none }
14
15        a:hover   { text-decoration: underline;
16                    color: red;
17                    background-color: #ccffcc }
18
19        li em     { color: red;
20                    font-weight: bold }
21
22        ul        { margin-left: 75px }
23
24        ul ul     { text-decoration: underline;
25                    margin-left: 15px }
26
27     </style>
28  </head>
29
30  <body>
31
32     <h1>Shopping list for <em>Monday</em>:</h1>
33
34     <ul>
35        <li>Milk</li>
36        <li>Bread
37           <ul>
38              <li>White bread</li>
39              <li>Rye bread</li>
40              <li>Whole wheat bread</li>
41           </ul>
42        </li>
43        <li>Rice</li>
44        <li>Potatoes</li>
45        <li>Pizza <em>with mushrooms</em></li>
46     </ul>
47
48     <p><a class = "nodec" href = "http://food.com">Go to the Grocery
49     store</a></p>
50
```

Fig. 26.3   Inheritance in style sheets (part 1 of 2).

```
51    </body>
52    </html>
```

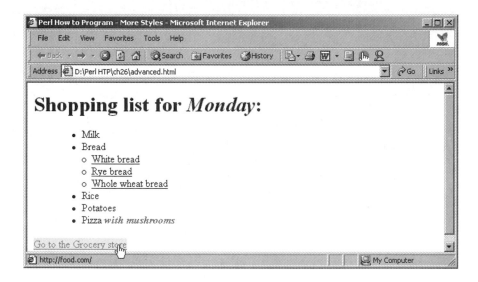

Fig. 26.3   Inheritance in style sheets (part 2 of 2).

Line 13

```
a.nodec   { text-decoration: none }
```

applies the **text-decoration** property to all **a** elements whose **class** attribute is set
to **nodec**. The default browser rendering of an **a** element is to underline, but here we set
it to **none**. The **text-decoration** property applies *decorations* to text within an element. Other possible values are *overline*, *line-through* and *blink*. The *.nodec*
appended to **a** is an extension of class styles—this style will apply only to **a** elements that
specify **nodec** as their class.

Lines 15–17

```
a:hover   { text-decoration: underline;
            color: red;
            background-color: #ccffcc }
```

specify a style for **hover**, which is a *pseudo-class*. Pseudo-classes give the author access
to content not specifically declared in the document. The **hover** pseudo-class is dynamically activated when the user moves the mouse cursor over an **a** element.

Portability Tip 26.1

*Always test stylesheets on all intended client Web browsers to ensure that the display is rea-
sonable.*

Lines 19 and 20

```
li em    { color: red;
           font-weight: bold }
```

declare a style for all **em** elements that are descendants of **li** elements. In the screen output of Fig. 26.3 notice that **Monday** is not made red and bold because it is not contained in an **li** element. However, **with mushrooms** (line 45) is contained in an **li** element and therefore is made red and bold.

The syntax for applying rules to multiple elements is similar. For example, to apply the rule on lines 19 and 20 to both **li** and **em** elements, you would separate the elements with commas, as follows:

```
li, em   { color: red;
           font-weight: bold }
```

Lines 24 and 25

```
ul ul    { text-decoration: underline;
           margin-left: 15px }
```

specify that all nested lists (**ul** elements that are descendants of **ul** elements) will be underlined and have a left-hand margin of 15 pixels (margins and the box model will be covered in Section 26.9).

A pixel is a *relative-length* measurement—it varies in size based on screen resolution. Other relative lengths are **em** (the size of the font), **ex** (the so-called "x-height" of the font, which is usually set to the height of a lowercase x) and percentages (e.g., **margin-left: 10%**). To set an element to display text at 150% of its normal size, you could use the syntax

```
font-size: 1.5em
```

The other units of measurement available in CSS are *absolute-length* measurements, i.e., units that do not vary in size based on the system. These are **in** (inches), **cm** (centimeters), **mm** (millimeters), **pt** (points—1 **pt**=1/72 **in**) and **pc** (picas—1 **pc** = 12 **pt**).

Good Programming Practice 26.1

Whenever possible, use relative length measurements. If you use absolute length measurements, your document may not be readable on some client browsers (e.g, wireless phones).

Software Engineering Observation 26.1

*There are three possible sources for styles sheets—browser defaults, preset user styles and author styles (e.g., in the **style** section). Author styles have a greater precedence than most preset user styles, so most conflicts are resolved in favor of the author styles.*

In Fig. 26.3, the whole list is indented because of the 75-pixel left-hand margin for top-level **ul** elements, but the nested list is indented only 15 pixels (not another 75 pixels) because the child **ul** element's **margin-left** property overrides the parent **ul** element's **margin-left** property.

26.5 Linking External Style Sheets

As we have seen, style sheets are an efficient way to give a document a uniform theme. With *external linking*, you can give your whole Web site a uniform look—separate pages on your site can all use the same style sheet, and you only need to modify only a single file to make changes to styles across your whole Web site. Figure 26.4 shows an external style sheet, and Fig. 26.5 shows the syntax for including an external style sheet in an HTML document (line 11).

```
1   /* Fig. 26.4: styles.css    */
2   /* An external stylesheet    */
3
4   a         { text-decoration: none }
5
6   a:hover { text-decoration: underline;
7               color: red;
8               background-color: #ccffcc }
9
10  li em     { color: red;
11              font-weight: bold}
12
13  ul        { margin-left: 2cm }
14
15  ul ul     { text-decoration: underline;
16              margin-left: .5cm }
```

Fig. 26.4   An external style sheet (**styles.css**).

```
1   <!DOCTYPE HTML PUBLIC "-//W3C//DTD HTML 4.01//EN"
2               "http://www.w3.org/TR/html4/strict.dtd">
3   <html>
4
5
6   <!-- Fig. 26.5: imported.html        -->
7   <!-- Linking external style sheets   -->
8
9   <head>
10     <title>Perl How to Program - Importing Style Sheets</title>
11     <link rel = "stylesheet" type = "text/css" href = "styles.css">
12  </head>
13
14  <body>
15
16     <h1>Shopping list for <em>Monday</em>:</h1>
17     <ul>
18        <li>Milk</li>
19        <li>Bread
20           <ul>
21              <li>White bread</li>
22              <li>Rye bread</li>
23              <li>Whole wheat bread</li>
24           </ul>
25        </li>
26        <li>Rice</li>
27        <li>Potatoes</li>
28        <li>Pizza <em>with mushrooms</em></li>
29     </ul>
```

Fig. 26.5   Linking an external style sheet (part 1 of 2).

```
30
31      <p>
32      <a href = "http://food.com">Go to the Grocery store</a>
33      </p>
34
35   </body>
36   </html>
```

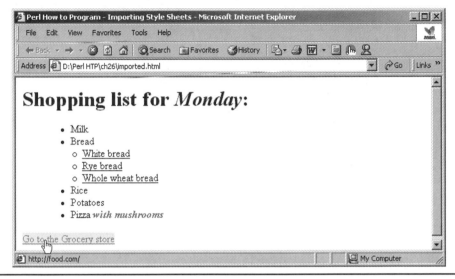

Fig. 26.5   Linking an external style sheet (part 2 of 2).

Line 11 (Fig. 26.5) shows a **link** element, which specifies a *relationship* between the current document and another document using the **rel** attribute. In this case, we declare the linked document to be a **stylesheet** for this document. We use the **type** attribute to specify the MIME type as **text/css** and provide the URL for the stylesheet with the **href** attribute.

Software Engineering Observation 26.2

Stylesheets are reusable. Creating them once and reusing them reduces programming effort.

Software Engineering Observation 26.3

*The **link** element can be placed only in the **head** element. Other relationships you can specify between documents are **next** and **previous**, which would allow you to link a whole series of documents. This could let browsers print a large collection of related documents at once (in Internet Explorer, select **Print all linked documents** in the **Print...** submenu of the **File** menu).*

26.6 Positioning Elements

In the past, controlling the positioning of elements in an HTML document was difficult; positioning was basically up to the browser. CSS introduces the **position** property and a capability called *absolute positioning*, which gives authors greater control over how documents are displayed (Fig. 26.6).

```
1    <!DOCTYPE HTML PUBLIC "-//W3C//DTD HTML 4.01//EN"
2               "http://www.w3.org/TR/html4/strict.dtd">
3    <html>
4
5    <!-- Fig 26.6: positioning.html        -->
6    <!-- Absolute positioning of elements  -->
7
8    <head>
9       <title>Perl How to Program - Absolute Positioning</title>
10   </head>
11
12   <body>
13
14      <p><img src = "i.gif" style = "position: absolute; top: 0px;
15         left: 0px; z-index: 1" alt = "First positioned image"></p>
16      <p style = "position: absolute; top: 50px; left: 50px;
17         z-index: 3; font-size: 20pt;">Positioned Text</p>
18     <p><img src = "circle.gif" style = "position: absolute; top: 25px;
19        left: 100px; z-index: 2" alt = "Second positioned image"></p>
20
21   </body>
22   </html>
```

Fig. 26.6   Positioning elements with CSS.

Lines 14 and 15

```
<p><img src = "i.gif" style = "position: absolute; top: 0px;
   left: 0px; z-index: 1" alt = "First positioned image"></p>
```

position the first **img** element (**i.gif**) on the page. Specifying an element's **position** as *absolute* removes it from the normal flow of elements on the page and instead, positions the element according to distance from the *top*, *left*, *right* or *bottom* margins of its *containing block* (i.e., an element such as **body** or **p**). Here we position the element to be **0** pixels away from both the **top** and **left** margins of the **body** element.

The **z-index** attribute allows you to properly layer overlapping elements. Elements that have higher **z-index** values are displayed in front of elements with lower **z-index** values. In this example, **i.gif**, with a **z-index** of 1, is displayed at the back; **circle.gif**, with a **z-index** of 2, is displayed in front of that; the **h1** element ("Positioned Text"), with a **z-index** of 3, is displayed in front of both of the others. If you do not specify **z-index**, the elements that occur later in the document are displayed in front of those that occur earlier.

Absolute positioning is not the only way to specify page layout—*relative positioning* is shown in Fig. 26.7.

```
1    <!DOCTYPE HTML PUBLIC "-//W3C//DTD HTML 4.01//EN"
2              "http://www.w3.org/TR/html4/strict.dtd">
3    <html>
4
5    <!-- Fig. 26.7: positioning2.html      -->
6    <!-- Relative positioning of elements   -->
7
8    <head>
9       <title>Perl How to Program - Relative Positioning</title>
10
11      <style type = "text/css">
12
13         p            { font-size: 1.3em;
14                        font-family: verdana, arial, sans-serif }
15
16         span         { color: red;
17                        font-size: .6em;
18                        height: 1em }
19
20         .super       { position: relative;
21                        top: -1ex }
22
23         .sub         { position: relative;
24                        bottom: -1ex }
25
26         .shiftleft  { position: relative;
27                        left: -1ex }
28
29         .shiftright { position: relative;
30                        right: -1ex }
31
32      </style>
33   </head>
34
35   <body>
36
37      <p>The text at the end of this sentence
38      <span class = "super">is in superscript</span>.</p>
39
```

Fig. 26.7 Relative positioning of elements (part 1 of 2).

```
40    <p>The text at the end of this sentence
41    <span class = "sub">is in subscript</span>.</p>
42
43    <p>The text at the end of this sentence
44    <span class = "shiftleft">is shifted left</span>.</p>
45
46    <p>The text at the end of this sentence
47    <span class = "shiftright">is shifted right</span>.</p>
48
49    </body>
50    </html>
```

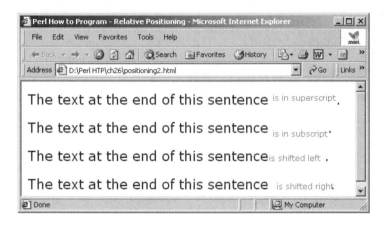

Fig. 26.7   Relative positioning of elements (part 2 of 2).

Setting the **position** property to *relative*, as in lines 20 and 21,

```
.super   { position: relative;
           top: -1ex }
```

will first lay out the element on the page, then offset the element by the specified **top**, **bottom**, **left** or **right** values. Unlike absolute positioning, relative positioning keeps elements in the general flow of elements on the page.

 Common Programming Error 26.1

Because relative positioning keeps elements in the flow of text in your documents, be careful to avoid overlapping text unintentionally.

26.7 Backgrounds

CSS also gives you control over the backgrounds of elements. We have used the **back-ground-color** property in previous examples. You can also add background images to your documents using CSS. In Fig. 26.8, we add a corporate logo to the bottom-right corner of the document—this logo stays fixed in the corner, even when the user scrolls up or down the screen.

The code that adds the background image in the bottom-right corner of the window is on lines 13–16

```
body   { background-image: url(logo.gif);
         background-position: bottom right;
         background-repeat: no-repeat;
         background-attachment: fixed; }
```

The ***background-image*** property (line 13) specifies the URL of the image to use, in the format **url(fileLocation)**. You can also specify ***background-color*** to use in case the image is not found.

The ***background-position*** property (line 14) positions the image on the page. You can use the keywords **top**, **bottom**, **center**, **left** and **right** individually or in combination for vertical and horizontal positioning. You can also position using lengths, specifying the horizontal length followed by the vertical length. For example, to position the image centered vertically (positioned at 50% of the distance across the screen) and 30 pixels from the top, you would use

```
 1  <!DOCTYPE HTML PUBLIC "-//W3C//DTD HTML 4.01//EN"
 2             "http://www.w3.org/TR/html4/strict.dtd">
 3  <html>
 4
 5  <!-- Fig. 26.8: background.html            -->
 6  <!-- Adding background images and indentation  -->
 7
 8  <head>
 9     <title>Perl How to Program - Background Images</title>
10
11     <style type = "text/css">
12
13        body   { background-image: url(logo.gif);
14                 background-position: bottom right;
15                 background-repeat: no-repeat;
16                 background-attachment: fixed; }
17
18        p       { font-size: 18pt;
19                 color: #aa5588;
20                 text-indent: 1em;
21                 font-family: arial, sans-serif; }
22
23        .dark { font-weight: bold; }
24
25     </style>
26  </head>
27
28  <body>
29
30     <p>
31     This example uses the background-image,
```

Fig. 26.8   Adding a background image with CSS (part 1 of 2).

```
32        background-position and background-attachment
33        styles to place the <span class = "dark">Deitel
34        & Associates, Inc.</span> logo in the bottom,
35        right corner of the page. Notice how the logo
36        stays in the proper position when you resize the

37        browser window.
38        </p>
39
40   </body>
41   </html>
```

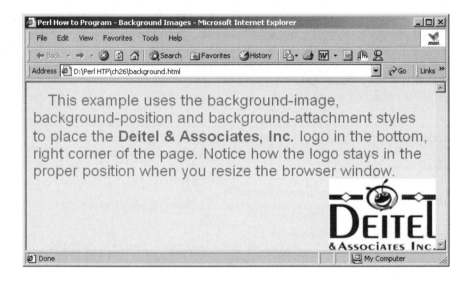

Fig. 26.8 Adding a background image with CSS (part 2 of 2).

```
background-position: 50% 30px;
```

The **background-repeat** *property* (line 15) controls the *tiling* of the background image. Tiling places multiple copies of the image next to each other to fill the background. Here we set the tiling to **no-repeat** so that only one copy of the background image is placed on screen. The **background-repeat** property can be set to **repeat** (the default) to tile the image vertically and horizontally, **repeat-x** to tile the image only horizontally or **repeat-y** to tile the image only vertically.

The final property setting, **background-attachment: fixed** (line 16), fixes the image in the position specified by **background-position**. Scrolling the browser window will not move the image from its set position. The default value, **scroll**, moves the image as the user scrolls the browser window down.

Line 20,

```
text-indent: 1em;
```

indents the first line of text in the element by the specified amount. You might use this to make your Web page read more like a novel, in which the first line of every paragraph is indented.

Line 23,

```
.dark { font-weight: bold }
```

uses the **font-weight** *property* to specify the "boldness" of text. Values besides **bold** and **normal** (the default) are **bolder** (bolder than **bold** text) and **lighter** (lighter than **normal** text). You can also specify the value using multiples of 100 from 100 to 900 (i.e., **100**, **200**, ..., **900**). Text specified as **normal** is equivalent to **400** and **bold** text is equivalent to **700**. Most systems do not have fonts that can be scaled this finely so using the **100**...**900** values might not display the desired effect.

Another CSS property you can use to format text is the **font-style** property, which allows you to set text to **none**, **italic** or **oblique** (**oblique** will default to **italic** if the system does not have a separate font file for oblique text).

We introduce the **span** element on lines 33 and 34

```
<span class = "dark">Deitel & Associates, Inc.</span>
```

Element **span** is a grouping element—it does not apply any inherent formatting to its contents. Its main use is to apply styles or **ID** attributes to a block of text. It is displayed inline (a so-called *inline-level element*) with other text, with no line breaks. A similar element is the **div** element, which also applies no inherent styles, but is displayed on its own line, with margins above and below (a so-called *block-level element*).

26.8 Element Dimensions

The dimensions of each element on the page can be specified using CSS (Fig. 26.9).

```
1  <!DOCTYPE HTML PUBLIC "-//W3C//DTD HTML 4.01//EN"
2             "http://www.w3.org/TR/html4/strict.dtd">
3  <html>
4
5  <!-- Fig. 26.9: width.html                    -->
6  <!-- Setting box dimensions and aligning text  -->
7
8  <head>
9     <title>Perl How to Program - Box Dimensions</title>
10
11    <style type = "text/css">
12
13       div { background-color: #ffccff;
14             margin-bottom: .5em }
15    </style>
16
17 </head>
18
19 <body>
20
```

Fig. 26.9 Setting box dimensions and aligning text (part 1 of 2).

```
21    <div style = "width: 20%">Here is some
22    text that goes in a box which is
23    set to stretch across twenty precent
24    of the width of the screen.</div>
25
26    <div style = "width: 80%; text-align: center">
27    Here is some CENTERED text that goes in a box

28    which is set to stretch across eighty precent of
29    the width of the screen.</div>
30
31    <div style = "width: 20%; height: 30%; overflow: scroll">
32    This box is only twenty percent of
33    the width and thirty percent of the height.
34    What do we do if it overflows? Set the
35    overflow property to scroll!</div>
36
37    </body>
38    </html>
```

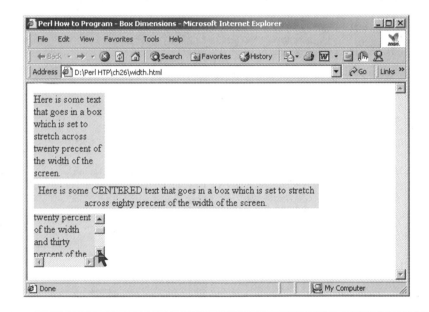

Fig. 26.9   Setting box dimensions and aligning text (part 2 of 2).

The inline style on line 21

```
<div style = "width: 20%">Here is some
```

shows how to set the **width** of an element on screen; here we indicate that this **div** element should occupy 20% of the screen width (which 20% of the screen depends on how the element is aligned, most elements are left-aligned by default). The height of an element can be set similarly, using the **height** property. Relative lengths and absolute lengths may also be used to specify **height** and **width**. For example, you could set the width of an element using

```
width: 10em
```

to have the element's width be equal to 10 times the size of the font.

Line 26

```
<div style = "width: 80%; text-align: center">
```

shows that text within an element can be aligned to the **center**—other values for the **text-align** property are **left**, **right** and justify.

One problem with setting both element dimensions is that content inside might sometimes exceed the set boundaries, in which case the element is simply made large enough for all the content to fit. However, on line 31

```
<div style = "width: 20%; height: 30%; overflow: scroll">
```

we can set the **overflow** property to **scroll**; this adds scrollbars if the text overflows the boundaries.

26.9 Text Flow and the Box Model

A browser normally places text and elements on screen in the order they appear in the HTML document. However, as we saw with absolute positioning, it is possible to remove elements from the normal flow of text. *Floating* allows you to move an element to one side of the screen—other content in the document will then flow around the floated element. In addition, each block-level element has a box drawn around it, known as the *box model*—the properties of this box are easily adjusted (Fig. 26.10).

In addition to text, whole elements can be *floated* to the left or right of a document. This means that any nearby text will wrap around the floated element. For example, in lines 29 and 30

```
<div style = "float: right; margin: .5em; text-align: right">
   Corporate Training and Publishing</div>
```

we float a **div** element to the **right** side of the screen. As you can see, the text from lines 32–38 flows cleanly to the left and underneath this **div** element.

The second property we set in line 29, **margin**, specifies the distance between the edge of the element and any other element on the page. When elements are rendered on the screen using the box model, the content of each element is surrounded by *padding*, a *border* and a *margin* (Fig 26.10).

Margins for individual sides of an element can be specified by using **margin-top**, **margin-right**, **margin-left** and **margin-bottom**.

A related property, **padding**, is set for the **div** element on lines 40 and 41

```
<div style = "float: right; padding: .5em; text-align:
right"> Leading-edge Programming Textbooks</div>
```

The *padding* is the distance between the content inside an element and the edge of the element. Like the margin, the padding can be set for each side of the box with **padding-top**, **padding-right**, **padding-left** and **padding-bottom**.

A portion of lines 49 and 50

```
<span style = "clear: right">Here is some unflowing text.
Here is some unflowing text.</span>
```

shows that you can interrupt the flow of text around a **float**ed element by setting the *clear* property to the same direction the element is **float**ed—**right** or **left**. Setting the **clear** property to *all* interrupts the flow on both sides of the document.

```
1    <!DOCTYPE HTML PUBLIC "-//W3C//DTD HTML 4.01//EN"
2              "http://www.w3.org/TR/html4/strict.dtd">
3    <html>
4
5    <!-- Fig. 26.10: floating.html          -->
6    <!-- Floating elements and element boxes  -->
7
8    <head>
9       <title>Perl How to Program - Flowing Text Around
10        Floating Elements</title>
11
12       <style type = "text/css">
13
14          div { background-color: #ffccff;
15                margin-bottom: .5em;
16                font-size: 1.5em;
17                width: 50% }
18
19          p   { text-align: justify; }
20
21       </style>
22
23    </head>
24
25    <body>
26
27       <div style = "text-align: center">Deitel & Associates, Inc.</div>
28
29       <div style = "float: right; margin: .5em; text-align: right">
30          Corporate Training and Publishing</div>
31
32       <p>Deitel & Associates, Inc. is an internationally recognized
33       corporate training and publishing organization specializing
34       in programming languages, Internet/World Wide Web technology
35       and object technology education. Deitel & Associates,
36       Inc. is a member of the World Wide Web Consortium. The company
37       provides courses on Java, C++, Visual Basic, C, Internet and
38       World Wide Web programming, and Object Technology.</p>
39
40       <div style = "float: right; padding: .5em; text-align: right">
41          Leading-edge Programming Textbooks</div>
```

Fig. 26.10 Floating elements, aligning text and setting box dimensions (part 1 of 2).

```
42
43      <p>The company's clients include many Fortune 1000 companies,
44      government agencies, branches of the military and business
45      organizations. Through its publishing partnership with Prentice
46      Hall, Deitel & Associates, Inc. publishes leading-edge
47      programming textbooks, professional books, interactive
48      CD-ROM-based multimedia Cyber Classrooms, satellite courses
49      and World Wide Web courses.<span style = "clear: right">Here
50      is some unflowing text. Here is some unflowing text.</span></p>
51
52  </body>
53  </html>
```

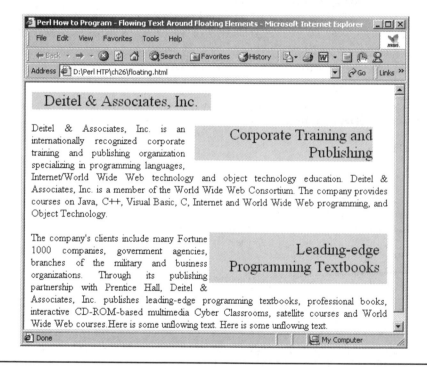

Fig. 26.10 Floating elements, aligning text and setting box dimensions (part 2 of 2).

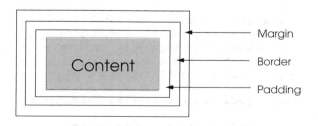

Fig. 26.11 Box model for block-level elements.

Another property of every block-level element on screen is the border. The border lies between the padding space and the margin space, and has numerous properties to adjust its appearance (Fig. 26.12).

In this example, we set three properties: the **border-width**, **border-style** and **border-color**. The **border-width** property may be set to any of the CSS lengths, or the predefined values of **thin**, **medium** or **thick**. The **border-color** sets the color used for the border (this has different meanings for different borders).

As with padding and margins, each of the border properties may be set for individual sides of the box (e.g., **border-top-style** or **border-left-color**). Also, as shown on line 40

```
<div class = "thick groove">This text has a border</div>
```

it is possible to assign more than one class to an HTML element using the **class** attribute.

The **border-style**s are **none**, **hidden**, **dotted**, **dashed**, **solid**, **double**, **groove**, **ridge**, **inset** and **outset**. Figure 26.13 illustrates these border styles.

As you can see, the **groove** and **ridge border-style**s have opposite effects, as do **inset** and **outset**.

```
1   <!DOCTYPE HTML PUBLIC "-//W3C//DTD HTML 4.01//EN"
2            "http://www.w3.org/TR/html4/strict.dtd">
3   <html>
4
5   <!-- Fig. 26.12: borders.html      -->
6   <!-- Setting borders of an element  -->
7
8   <head>
9      <title>Perl How to Program - Borders</title>
10
11     <style type = "text/css">
12
13        body    { background-color: #ccffcc }
14
15        div     { text-align: center;
16                  margin-bottom: 1em;
17                  padding: .5em }
18
19        .thick  { border-width: thick }
20
21        .medium { border-width: medium }
22
23        .thin   { border-width: thin }
24
25        .groove { border-style: groove }
26
27        .inset  { border-style: inset }
28
29        .outset { border-style: outset }
30
31        .red    { border-color: red }
32
```

Fig. 26.12 Applying borders to elements (part 1 of 2).

```
33              .blue     { border-color: blue }
34
35      </style>
36   </head>
37
38   <body>
39
40      <div class = "thick groove">This text has a border</div>
41      <div class = "medium groove">This text has a border</div>
42      <div class = "thin groove">This text has a border</div>
43
44      <p class = "thin red inset">A thin red line...</p>
45      <p class = "medium blue outset">And a thicker blue line</p>
46
47   </body>
48   </html>
```

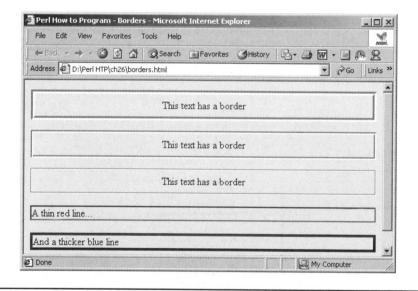

Fig. 26.12 Applying borders to elements (part 2 of 2).

```
1    <!DOCTYPE HTML PUBLIC "-//W3C//DTD HTML 4.01//EN"
2              "http://www.w3.org/TR/html4/strict.dtd">
3    <html>
4
5    <!-- Fig. 26.13: borders2.html    -->
6    <!-- Various border-styles         -->
7
8    <head>
9       <title>Perl How to Program - Borders</title>
10
```

Fig. 26.13 Various **border-style**s (part 1 of 2).

```
11    <style type = "text/css">
12
13        body    { background-color: #ccffcc }
14
15        div     { text-align: center;
16                  margin-bottom: .3em;
17                  width: 50%;
18                  position: relative;
19                  left: 25%;
20                  padding: .3em }
21    </style>
22
23   </head>
24
25   <body>
26
27      <div style = "border-style: solid">Solid border</div>
28      <div style = "border-style: double">Double border</div>
29      <div style = "border-style: groove">Groove border</div>
30      <div style = "border-style: ridge">Ridge border</div>
31      <div style = "border-style: inset">Inset border</div>
32      <div style = "border-style: outset">Outset border</div>
33
34   </body>
35   </html>
```

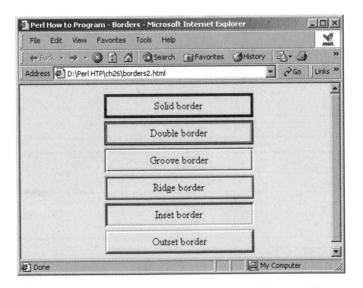

Fig. 26.13 Various **border-style**s (part 2 of 2).

26.10 User Style Sheets

An important issue to keep in mind when adding style sheets to your site is what kind of users will be viewing your site. Users have the option to define their own *user style sheets* to format pages based on their own preferences—for example, visually impaired people might want to increase the text size on all pages they view. As a Web-page author, if you are not careful, you might inadvertently override user preferences with the styles defined on your Web pages. This section explores possible conflicts between *user styles* and *author styles*. Figure 26.14 is a simple example of a Web page using the **em** measurement for the **font-size** property to increase text size on the page.

```
1   <!DOCTYPE HTML PUBLIC "-//W3C//DTD HTML 4.01//EN"
2              "http://www.w3.org/TR/html4/strict.dtd">
3   <html>
4
5   <!-- Fig. 26.14: user.html    -->
6   <!-- User styles             -->
7
8   <head>
9      <title>Perl How to Program - User Styles</title>
10
11     <style type = "text/css">
12
13        .note { font-size: 1.5em }
14
15     </style>
16  </head>
17
18  <body>
19
20     <p>Thanks for visiting my Web site. I hope you enjoy it.</p>
21     <p class = "note">Please Note: This site will be moving soon.
22     Please check periodically for updates.</p>
23
24  </body>
25  </html>
```

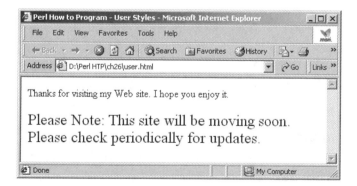

Fig. 26.14 Modifying text size with the **em** measurement .

In line 13

```
.note { font-size: 1.5em }
```

we multiply by 1.5 the font size of all elements with **class = "note"** (see lines 20 and 21). Assuming the default browser font size of 12 points, this same text size increase could also have been accomplished by specifying

```
.note { font-size:  18pt }
```

However, what if the user had defined their own **font-size** in a user style sheet? Because the CSS specification gives precedence to author styles over user styles, this conflict would be resolved with the author style overriding the user style. This can be avoided by using relative measurements (such as **em** or **ex**) instead of absolute measurements (such as **pt**).

Adding a user style sheet (Fig. 26.15) in Internet Explorer 5 is done by selecting **Internet Options...** located in the **Tools** menu. In the dialog box that appears, click **Accessibility...**, check the **Format documents using my style sheet** check box and type in the location of your user style sheet. Note that you also have the option of overriding colors, font styles, and font sizes specified on Web pages with your own user styles.

User style sheets are created in the same format as the linked external style sheet shown in Fig. 26.4. A sample user style sheet is shown in Fig. 26.16.

The Web page shown in Fig. 26.14 is re-rendered in Fig. 26.17, this time with the user style sheet from Fig. 26.16 applied.

Because the code for this page uses a relative **font-size** measurement of **1.5em**, it multiplies the original size of the affected text (**20pt**) by **1.5** times, giving it an effective size of **30pt**.

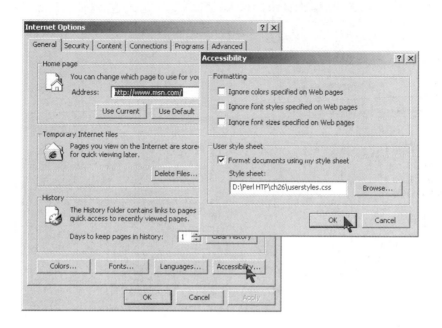

Fig. 26.15 Adding a user style sheet in Internet Explorer 5.

```
1   /* Fig. 26.16: userstyles.css */
2   /* A user stylesheet          */
3
4   body      { font-size: 20pt;
5               background-color: #ccffcc }
6
7   a         { color: red }
```

Fig. 26.16 A sample user style sheet.

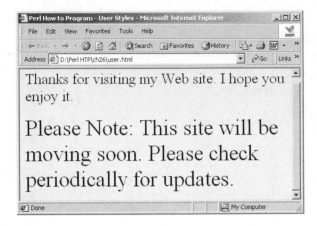

Fig. 26.17 A Web page with user styles enabled.

26.11 Internet and World Wide Web Resources

www.w3.org/Style/CSS
The W3C Cascading Style Sheets Homepage contains the CSS links and resources deemed most important by the people in charge of the Web.

www.w3.org/TR/REC-CSS2
The W3C *Cascading Style Sheets, Level 2* specification contains a list of all the CSS properties. The specification is also filled with helpful examples detailing the use of many of the properties.

www.w3.org/TR/REC-CSS1
This site contains the W3C *Cascading Style Sheets, Level 1* specification.

style.webreview.com
This site has several charts of CSS properties, including a listing of which browsers support which attributes, and to what extent.

www.blooberry.com/indexdot/css/index.html
Index Dot CSS is a good reference source for CSS properties, syntax and more.

www.w3schools.com/css
The *W3Schools CSS site* has a good CSS tutorial and script repository.

SUMMARY

- The inline style allows you to declare a style for an individual element using the **style** attribute in that element's opening HTML tag.
- Each CSS property is followed by a colon, then the value of that attribute.
- The **color** property sets the color of text. Color names and hex codes may be used as the value.
- Styles that are placed in the **<style>** section apply to the whole document.
- **style** element attribute **type** specifies the MIME type (the specific encoding format) of the style sheet. Regular text style sheets always use **text/css**.
- Each rule body begins and ends with a curly brace (**{** and **}**).

- Style class declarations are preceded with a period and are applied to elements of that specific class.
- The CSS rules in a style sheet use the same format as inline styles—the property is followed by a colon (**:**) and the value of that property. Multiple properties are separated with a semicolon (**;**).
- The **background-color** attribute specifies the background color of the element.
- The **font-family** attribute specifies the name of the font that should be displayed. Generic font families allow you to specify a type of font instead of a specific font for greater display flexibility. The **font-size** property specifies the size to use to render the font.
- The **class** attribute applies a style class to an element.
- All styles applied to a parent element also apply to child elements inside that element.
- Pseudo-classes give the author access to content not specifically declared in the document. The **hover** pseudo-class is activated when the user moves the mouse cursor over an **a** element.
- The **text-decoration** property applies decorations to text within an element, such as **underline**, **overline**, **line-through** and **blink**
- To apply rules to multiple elements separate the elements with commas in the stylesheet.
- A pixel is a relative-length measurement—it varies in size based on screen resolution. Other relative lengths are **em** (font size), **ex** ("x-height" of the font—the height of a lowercase x) and percentages.
- The other units of measurement available in CSS are absolute-length measurements, i.e., units that do not vary in size based on the system. These are **in** (inches), **cm** (centimeters), **mm** (millimeters), **pt** (points—1 **pt**=1/72 **in**) and **pc** (picas—1 **pc** = 12 **pt**)
- External linking can help give a Web site a uniform look—separate pages on a site can all use the same styles. Modifying a single file can then make changes to styles across an entire Web site.
- **link**'s **rel** attribute specifies a relationship between a document and another document.
- The CSS **position** property allows absolute positioning, which gives us greater control over how documents are displayed. Specifying an element's **position** as **absolute** removes it from the normal flow of elements on the page, and positions it according to distance from the **top**, **left**, **right** or **bottom** margins of its parent element.
- The **z-index** property allows you to properly layer overlapping elements. Elements that have higher **z-index** values are displayed in front of elements with lower **z-index** values.
- Unlike absolute positioning, relative positioning keeps elements in the general flow of elements on the page, and offsets them by the specified **top**, **left**, **right** or **bottom** values.
- Property **background-image** specifies the URL of the image to use, in the format **url (**_file-Location_**)**. Specify the **background-color** to use if the image is not found. The property **background-position** positions the image on the page using the values **top**, **bottom**, **center**, **left** and **right** individually or in combination for vertical and horizontal positioning.
- The **background-repeat** property controls the tiling of the background image. Setting the tiling to **no-repeat** displays one copy of the background image on screen. The **background-repeat** property can be set to **repeat** (the default) to tile the image vertically and horizontally, to **repeat-x** to tile the image only horizontally or **repeat-y** to tile the image only vertically.
- The property setting **background-attachment: fixed** fixes the image in the position specified by **background-position**. Scrolling the browser window will not move the image from its set position. The default value, **scroll**, moves the image as the user scrolls the window.
- The **text-indent** property indents the first line of text in the element by the specified amount.
- The **font-weight** property specifies the "boldness" of text. Values besides **bold** and **normal** (the default) are **bolder** (bolder than **bold** text) and **lighter** (lighter than **normal** text). You can also specify the value using multiples of 100 from 100 to 900 (i.e., **100**, **200**, ..., **900**). Text specified as **normal** is equivalent to **400** and **bold** text is equivalent to **700**.

- The **font-style** property allows you to set text to **none**, **italic** or **oblique** (**oblique** will default to **italic** if the system does not have a separate font file for oblique text, which is normally the case).

- **span** is a generic grouping element—it does not apply any inherent formatting to its contents. Its main use is to apply styles or **ID** attributes to a block of text. It is displayed inline (a so-called in-line element) with other text, with no line breaks. A similar element is the **div** element, which also applies no inherent styles, but is displayed on a separate line, with margins above and below (a so-called block-level element).

- The dimensions of page elements can be set using CSS using the **height** and **width** properties.

- Text within an element can be **center**ed using **text-align**—other values for the   **text-align** property are **left** and **right**.

- One problem with setting both element dimensions is that content inside might sometimes exceed the set boundaries, in which case the element is simply made large enough for all the content to fit. However, you can set the **overflow** property to **scroll**; this adds scroll bars if the text overflows the boundaries we have set for it.

- Browsers normally place text and elements on screen in the order they appear in the HTML file. Elements can be removed from the normal flow of text. Floating allows you to move an element to one side of the screen—other content in the document will then flow around the floated element.

- Each block-level element has a box drawn around it, known as the box model—the properties of this box are easily adjusted.

- The **margin** property determines the distance between the element's edge and any outside text.

- CSS uses a box model to render elements on screen—the content of each element is surrounded by padding, a border and margins

- Margins for individual sides of an element can be specified by using **margin-top**, **margin-right**, **margin-left** and **margin-bottom**.

- The padding, as opposed to the margin, is the distance between the content inside an element and the edge of the element. Padding can be set for each side of the box with **padding-top**, **padding-right**, **padding-left** and **padding-bottom**.

- You can interrupt the flow of text around a **float**ed element by setting the **clear** property to the same direction the element is **float**ed—**right** or **left**. Setting the **clear** property to **all** interrupts the flow on both sides of the document.

- A property of every block-level element on screen is its border. The border lies between the padding space and the margin space and has numerous properties to adjust its appearance.

- The **border-width** property may be set to any of the CSS lengths, or the predefined values of **thin**, **medium** or **thick**.

- The **border-style**s available are **none**, **hidden**, **dotted**, **dashed**, **solid**, **double**, **groove**, **ridge**, **inset** and **outset**. Keep in mind that the **dotted** and **dashed** styles are available only for Macintosh systems.

- The **border-color** property sets the color used for the border.

- It is possible to assign more than one class to an HTML element using the **class** attribute.

TERMINOLOGY

<link> element	**arial** font
absolute positioning	**background**
absolute-length measurement	**background-attachment**

SELF-REVIEW EXERCISES

26.1 Assume that the size of the base font on a system is 12 points.
   a) How big is 36 point font in ems?
   b) How big is 8 point font in ems?
   c) How big is 24 point font in picas?
   d) How big is 12 point font in inches?
   e) How big is 1 inch font in picas?

26.2 Fill in the blanks in the following questions:
   a) Using the _____ element allows you to use external style sheets in your pages.
   b) To apply a CSS rule to more than one element at a time, separate the element names with a _____.
   c) Pixels are a _____ length measurement unit.
   d) The **hover** _____-_____ is activated when the user moves the mouse cursor over the specified element.
   e) Setting the **overflow** property to _____ provides a mechanism for containing inner content without compromising specified box dimensions.
   f) While _____ is a generic inline element that applies no inherent formatting, the _____ is a generic block-level element that applies no inherent formatting.
   g) Setting the **background-repeat** property to _____ will tile the specified **background-image** only vertically.
   h) If you **float** an element, you can stop the flowing text by using the _____ property.
   i) The _____ property allows you to indent the first line of text in an element.
   j) Three components of the box model are the _____, _____ and _____.

ANSWERS TO SELF-REVIEW EXERCISES

26.1 a) 3 ems. b) .75 ems. c) 2 picas. d) 1/6 inch. e) 6 picas.

26.2 a) **link**. b) comma. c) relative. d) pseudo-element. e) **scroll**. f) **span**, **div**. g) **y-repeat**. h) **clear**. i) **text-indent**. j) content, padding, border or margin.

EXERCISES

26.3 Write a CSS rule that makes all text 1.5 times larger than the base font of the system and colors it red.

26.4 Write a CSS rule that removes the underline from all links inside list items (**li**) and shifts them left by 3 **em**s.

26.5 Write a CSS rule that places a background image halfway down the page, tiling horizontally. The image should remain in place when the user scrolls up or down.

26.6 Write a CSS rule that gives all **h1** and **h2** elements a padding of .5 **em**s, a **groove**d border style and a margin of .5 **em**s.

26.7 Write a CSS rule that changes the color of all elements with attribute **class="green-Move"** to green and shifts them down 25 pixels and right 15 pixels.

27

Bonus: Introduction to Python Programming

Objectives

- To understand basic Python data types.
- To understand string processing and regular expressions in Python.
- To use exception handling.
- To perform basic CGI tasks in Python.
- To construct programs that interact with databases using the Python Database Application Programming Interface (DB-API).
- To learn basic object-oriented programming syntax in Python.
- To develop graphical user interfaces with Python and Tcl/Tk.

Art is the imposing of a pattern on experience, and our aesthetic enjoyment is recognition of the pattern.
Alfred North Whitehead

No rule is so general, which admits not some exception.
Robert Burton

Outline

27.1 Introduction[1]

Python is an interpreted, cross-platform, object-oriented language. Python can be used to write large-scale Internet search engines, small administration scripts, GUI applications, CGI scripts and more. The creator of the language, Guido van Rossum, combined a clean syntax with popular elements from several existing languages to produce Python.

Python is a freely distributed, open-source technology. Python's open-source nature has encouraged a wide base of developers to submit modules that extend the language. Using Python's core modules and those freely available on the Web, programmers can develop applications that accomplish a great variety of tasks. Python's interpreted nature facilitates rapid application development (RAD) of powerful programs. GUI applications, in particular, can be quickly tested and developed using Python's interface to Tcl/Tk (among other GUI toolkits).

Python is often compared with Perl, because the two languages can be used to accomplish similar programming tasks. In fact, Perl is generally considered better than Python for system administration scripting and regular expression processing tasks (i.e., the tasks for which Perl was originally designed). However, Python is becoming increasingly more popular among Perl programmers because Python was designed from the beginning to be structured and object-oriented with a clean, easy-to-read syntax. Thus, many programmers consider Python well-equipped to build large-scale, object-oriented, extensible applications. In this chapter, we present several examples in areas that we hope will substantiate this claim.

---

1. The Perl resources posted at our Web site **www.deitel.com** include step-by-step instructions on installing Python on Windows and Unix/Linux platforms. You can find the resources for all our books by clicking the "Downloads/Resources" link.

27.1.1 A first Python program

In this section, we examine a simple Python program and discuss how to work with the Python programming environment. Python can be executed on a program stored in a file, or Python can be run in *interactive mode*, where users can enter lines of code one at a time. Interactive mode enables program writers to test small blocks of code quickly and leads to a relatively rapid development time for most Python projects.

Figure 27.1 is a simple Python program that prints the words **Welcome to Python!** to the screen. Lines 1 and 2 contain single-line comments that describe the program. Comments in Python begin with the **#** character; Python ignores all text in the current line after this character. Line 4 uses the **print** statement to write the text **Welcome to Python!** to the standard output (in this case, the screen).

Python statements can be executed in one of two ways. The statements can be typed into a file (as in Fig. 27.1). Python files typically end with **.py**, although other extensions (e.g., **.pyw** on Windows) can be used. Python is then invoked on the file by typing

```
python file.py
```

at the command line, where **file.py** is the name of the Python file. [*Note:* To invoke Python, the system path variable must be properly set to include the **python** executable. The Perl resources posted at our Web site **www.deitel.com** include step-by-step instructions on how to set the appropriate variable. You can find the resources for all our books by clicking the "Downloads/Resources" link.] The output box of Fig. 27.1 contains the results of invoking Python on **first.py**.

Python statements can also be interpreted dynamically. Typing

```
python
```

at the command prompt runs Python in *interactive mode*.

 Testing and Debugging Tip 27.1

In interactive mode, Python statements can be entered and interpreted one at a time. This mode is often useful when debugging a program (i.e., discovering and removing errors in programs).

Figure 27.2 shows Python running in interactive mode on Windows. The first two lines display information about the version of Python being used. The third line begins with the *Python prompt* (**>>>**). A Python statement is interpreted by typing a statement at the Python prompt and pressing the *Return* key.

```
1   # Fig. 27.1: fig27_01.py
2   # A first program in Python
3
4   print "Welcome to Python!"
```

```
Welcome to Python!
```

Fig. 27.1　Comments and printing in Python.

```
Python 2.0 (#8, Oct 16 2000, 17:27:58) [MSC 32 bit (Intel)] on win32
Type "copyright", "credits" or "license" for more information.
>>> print "Welcome to Python!"
Welcome to Python!
>>> ^Z
```

Fig. 27.2   Python in interactive mode.

The **print** statement on the third line prints the text **Welcome to Python!** to the standard output (in this case, the screen). After printing the text to the screen, the Python prompt is displayed (line 5) and Python waits for the next statement to be entered by the user. We exit Python by typing *Crtl-Z* (on Microsoft Windows systems) and pressing the *Return* key. [*Note:* On UNIX and Linux systems, *Ctrl-D* exits Python.]

27.1.2 Python keywords

Before we discuss Python programming in more detail, we present a list of Python's *keywords* (Fig. 27.3). These words have special meaning in Python and cannot be used as variable names, function names or other objects.

A list of Python keywords can also be obtained from the ***keyword*** *module*. Figure 27.4 illustrates how to obtain the list of Python keywords in interactive mode.

27.2 Basic Data Types, Control Structures and Functions

This section introduces basic data types, control structures and functions, using a simple program (Fig. 27.5). In this program, we define two functions that use control structures to perform the operations of those functions.

Line 5

```
def greatestCommonDivisor( x, y ):
```

is the function definition header for function **greatestCommonDivisor**. This function computes the *greatest common divisor* of two numbers—the largest integer that divides evenly into both numbers. Keyword **def** marks the beginning of the function definition. The function takes two parameters: **x** and **y**. The list of parameters is placed inside parentheses (**( )**), and the parameter list is followed by a *colon (**:**)*.

Python keywords						
and	continue	else	for	import	not	raise
assert	def	except	from	in	or	return
break	del	exec	global	is	pass	try
class	elif	finally	if	lambda	print	while

Fig. 27.3   Python keywords.

```
Python 2.0 (#8, Oct 16 2000, 17:27:58) [MSC 32 bit (Intel)] on win32
Type "copyright", "credits" or "license" for more information.
>>> import keyword
>>> print keyword.kwlist
['and', 'assert', 'break', 'class', 'continue', 'def', 'del', 'elif',
'else', 'except', 'exec', 'finally', 'for', 'from', 'global', 'if',
'import', 'in', 'is','lambda', 'not', 'or', 'pass', 'print', 'raise',
'return', 'try', 'while']
>>>
```

Fig. 27.4   Printing Python keywords in interactive mode.

```
1   # Fig. 27.5: fig27_05.py
2   # Program to illustrate basic data types, control structures and
3   # functions.
4
5   def greatestCommonDivisor( x, y ):
6      gcd = min( x, y )
7
8      while gcd >= 1:
9
10        if ( x % gcd ) == ( y % gcd ) == 0:
11           return gcd
12        else:
13           gcd -= 1
14
15  def determineIfPythonPerl( name ):
16
17     if name == "Python":
18        print "You entered Python!"
19     elif name == "Perl":
20        print "You entered Perl!"
21     else:
22        print "You did not enter Python or Perl."
23
24  number1 = int( raw_input( "Enter a positive integer: " ) )
25  number2 = int( raw_input( "Enter a positive integer: " ) )
26
27  print "The greatest common divisor is", \
28     greatestCommonDivisor( number1, number2 )
29
30  for entry in range( 5 ):
31     language = raw_input( "\nEnter a programming language: " )
32     determineIfPythonPerl( language )
```

```
Enter a positive integer: 30
Enter a positive integer: 2
The greatest common divisor is 2
```
                                        (continued top of next page)

Fig. 27.5   Program illustrating basic data types, control structures and functions (part 1 of 2).

```
                                                          (continued from previous page)
Enter a programming language: Tcl
You did not enter Python or Perl.

Enter a programming language: Java
You did not enter Python or Perl.

Enter a programming language: C++
You did not enter Python or Perl.

Enter a programming language: Python
You entered Python!

Enter a programming language: Perl
You entered Perl!
```

Fig. 27.5   Program illustrating basic data types, control structures and functions (part 2 of 2).

Common Programming Error 27.1

Forgetting to place a colon after a function definition header or after a control structure is a syntax error.

Line 6

```
gcd = min( x, y )
```

calls Python *function **min*** on parameters **x** and **y**. This function returns the smallest of the two values. We assign the value returned by **min** to local variable **gcd**. Python variables declared in a function "go out of scope" when that function terminates. This means that variable **gcd** can only be accessed from within function **greatestCommonDivisor** and cannot be accessed from the main portion of the program. [*Note:* A variable's scope is related to the namespace to which that variable belongs. For more information about the namespace of a program, see Section 27.11.]

Notice that line 6 is indented. Unlike many other languages, Python determines the beginning and end of a statement based on whitespace. Each new line begins a new statement. Groups of statements that belong to the same block of code are indented by the same amount. The language does not specify how many spaces to indent, only that the indentation must be consistent.

Common Programming Error 27.2

Inconsistent indentation in a Python program causes a syntax error.

Line 8

```
while gcd >= 1:
```

describes the beginning of a Python ***while*** *loop*. The code in the **while** block will execute as long as **gcd** is greater-than or equal-to 1.

Line 10

```
if ( x % gcd ) == ( y % gcd ) == 0:
```

is a Python *if* *statement*. If the specified condition is true (i.e., the condition evaluates to any non-zero number), the code in the **if** block is executed. The statement uses the *modulo operator (%)* to determine if parameters **x** and **y** can be evenly divided by variable **gcd**. Notice that Python expressions can be "chained." This code is identical to

```
if x % gcd == 0 and y % gcd == 0:
```

and to

```
if ( x % gcd == 0 ) and ( y % gcd == 0 ):
```

If the expression in line 10 evaluates to true, we have found the greatest common denominator. Line 11 returns this value from the function. *Keyword* **return** exits the function and returns the specified value.

If the expression in line 10 evaluates to false (i.e., the condition evaluates to zero), the code in the **else** block executes (lines 12 and 13). This code decrements variable **gcd** by 1 using the *-= operator* and has the same effect as the statement

```
gcd = gcd - 1
```

Python defines several such operators, including **+=**, **-=**, ***=**, **/=** (integer division), **%=** (modulo division) and ****=** (exponentiation).

The **determineIfPythonPerl** function (lines 15–22) takes parameter **name** that contains a string. Lines 17–22 use the *if/elif/else control structure* to evaluate expressions based on the value of parameter. If the value of **name** is equal to the string **"Python"** (line 17), the function prints **"You entered Python!"** Otherwise, if the value of **name** is equal to the string **"Perl"** (line 19), the function prints **"You entered Perl!"** If the value of **name** does not match either of these strings (line 21), the function prints **"You did not enter Python or Perl."**. We discuss string manipulation in further detail in Section 27.4.

Line 24

```
number1 = int( raw_input( "Enter a positive integer: " ) )
```

calls Python *function* **raw_input** that retrieves input from the program user. This function may optionally take a string argument that is displayed as a prompt to the user. The **raw_input** function returns a string, but we need an integer for use in our **greatestCommonDivisor** function. The Python *int function* converts non-integer data types to integers. We store the integer returned from function **int** in local variable **number1**. Line 25 retrieves a value for **number2** in a similar fashion.

Common Programming Error 27.3

A numerical value obtained via the **raw_input** *function must be converted from a string to the proper numerical type. Trying to numerically manipulate a string representation of a numerical value may result in a logical or syntax error.*

Lines 27 and 28

```
print "The greatest common divisor is", \
    greatestCommonDivisor( number1, number2 )
```

print the greatest common divisor of the two numbers to the screen. The backslash character (****) at the end of line 27 is a *line-continuation character* that allows us to continue a statement on the next line. The *comma* (**,**) that follows the string tells Python that we want to print additional items after the string. In this case, the additional item is the integer value returned by the call to function **greatestCommonDivisor**. Notice from the output that Python automatically inserts a space between the last character in the string and the integer value.

Common Programming Error 27.4

Forgetting to include a line-continuation character (****) at the end of a statement that continues onto the next line is a syntax error.

Line 30

```
for entry in range( 5 ):
```

begins a Python *for* loop. The call to Python function **range(5)** returns the values **0**, **1**, **2**, **3** and **4**. [*Note:* The function actually returns a *list* that contains these values. We discuss lists in Section 27.3.] The **for** loop iterates through these values and, on each iteration, assigns a value to variable **entry** and then executes the statements in the **for** block (lines 31 and 32). Thus, the statements in the **for** loop are executed five times. These statements retrieve a string from the user and pass that string to function **determineIfPythonPerl**. Notice the "**\n**" *escape sequence* at the beginning of the string in line 31. This is a special Python character that prints a *newline* to the screen. A newline causes the cursor (i.e., the current screen position indicator) to move to the beginning of the next line on the screen. Figure 27.6 lists some common Python escape sequences. After the program calls function **determineIfPythonPerl** on five user-defined strings, the program exits.

Python is a case-sensitive language. This means that Python treats variable **x** (lower case) and variable **X** (upper case) as two different variables. Similarly the statement

```
Def = 3
```

is a valid Python statement, but the statement

```
def = 3
```

Escape sequence	Meaning
\n	Newline (line feed).
\r	Carriage return.
\f	Form feed.
\t	Tab.
\v	Vertical tab.
\'	Single quote.
\"	Double quote.
\b	Backspace.
****	Backslash.

Fig. 27.6   Escape sequences.

causes a syntax error when interpreted, because **def** is a keyword and therefore not a valid variable name.

Good Programming Practice 27.1

*Using variable or function names that resemble keywords (e.g., variable **Def**) may cause confusion to the program writer and readers. Avoid using such variable or function names.*

27.3 Tuples, Lists and Dictionaries

In addition to basic data types that store integers and strings, Python defines three data types for storing more complex data: the *list*—a sequence of related data, the *tuple* (pronounced too-ple)—a list whose elements may not be modified, and a *dictionary*—a list of values that are accessed through their associated keys. These data types are high-level implementations of simple data structures that enable Python programmers to quickly and easily manipulate many types of data. Some Python modules (e.g., **Cookie** and **cgi**) use these data types to provide simple access to their underlying data structures. Figure 27.7 is a program that illustrates tuples, lists and dictionaries.

```
1   # Fig. 27.7: fig27_07.py
2   # A program that illustrates tuples, lists and dictionaries.
3
4   # tuples
5   aTuple = ( 1, 2, 3 )              # create tuple
6   firstItem = aTuple[ 0 ]          # first tuple item
7   secondItem = aTuple[ 1 ]         # second tuple item
8   thirdItem = aTuple[ 2 ]          # third tuple item
9
10  print "The first item in the tuple is", firstItem
11  print "The second item in the tuple is", secondItem
12  print "The third item in the tuple is", thirdItem
13  print
14
15  firstItem, secondItem, thirdItem = aTuple
16  print "The first item in the tuple is", firstItem
17  print "The second item in the tuple is", secondItem
18  print "The third item in the tuple is", thirdItem
19  print
20
21  aTuple += ( 4, )     # add an item to the end of the tuple
22  print "Added an item to the tuple using the += operator"
23  print
24
25  # print each item in tuple
26  print "The raw tuple data is:", aTuple
27  print "The items in the tuple are:"
28
29  for item in aTuple:
30      print item,
31
32  print        # end previous line
33  print        # blank line
```

Fig. 27.7   Program illustrating tuples, lists and dictionaries (part 1 of 3).

```
34
35   # lists
36   aList = [ 1, 2, 3 ]      # create list
37   aList[ 0 ] = 0           # change first element of list
38   aList.append( 5 )        # add item to end of list
39
40   print "The raw list data is:", aList    # print list data
41   print
42
43   aList += [ 4 ]      # add an item to the end of the list
44   print "Added an item to the list using the += operator"
45   print
46
47   # print each item in the list
48   print "The items in the list are:"
49
50   for item in aList:
51       print item,
52
53   print        # end previous line
54   print        # blank line
55
56   # dictionaries
57   aDictionary = { 1 : "January", 2 : "February", 3 : "March",
58                   4 : "April", 5 : "May", 6 : "June", 7 : "July",
59                   8 : "August", 9 : "September", 10 : "October",
60                   11 : "November" }
61   aDictionary[ 12 ] = "December"              # add item to dictionary
62
63   print "The raw dictionary data is:", aDictionary
64   print
65   print "The entries in the dictionary are:"
66
67   for item in aDictionary.keys():
68       print "aDictionary[ ", item, " ] = ", aDictionary[ item ]
```

```
The first item in the tuple is 1
The second item in the tuple is 2
The third item in the tuple is 3

The first item in the tuple is 1
The second item in the tuple is 2
The third item in the tuple is 3

Added an item to the tuple using the += operator

The raw tuple data is: (1, 2, 3, 4)
The items in the tuple are:
1 2 3 4

The raw list data is: [0, 2, 3, 5]
```

(continued top of next page)

Fig. 27.7   Program illustrating tuples, lists and dictionaries (part 2 of 3).

```
                                                    (continued from previous page)
Added an item to the list using the += operator

The items in the list are:
0  2  3  5  4

The raw dictionary data is: {12: 'December', 11: 'November', 10: 'Oc-
tober', 9: 'September', 8: 'August', 7: 'July', 6: 'June', 5: 'May', 4:
'April', 3: 'March', 2: 'February', 1: 'January'}

The entries in the dictionary are:
aDictionary[ 12  ] =  December
aDictionary[ 11  ] =  November
aDictionary[ 10  ] =  October
aDictionary[  9  ] =  September
aDictionary[  8  ] =  August
aDictionary[  7  ] =  July
aDictionary[  6  ] =  June
aDictionary[  5  ] =  May
aDictionary[  4  ] =  April
aDictionary[  3  ] =  March
aDictionary[  2  ] =  February
aDictionary[  1  ] =  January
```

Fig. 27.7   Program illustrating tuples, lists and dictionaries (part 3 of 3).

Line 5

```
aTuple = ( 1, 2, 3 )
```

creates a tuple, with elements **1**, **2** and **3**. Tuples are created as a comma-separated list of values inside parentheses. A tuple can contain any combination of data type (e.g., strings, integers, other tuples, etc.). Lines 6–8 illustrate the use of the *[ ] operator* to access specific elements using an index. The first element in a tuple has index 0.

Tuple element contents are *immutable*—they cannot be modified. So, the statement

```
aTuple[ 0 ] = 0
```

produces a run-time error similar to

```
Traceback (innermost last):
  File "<interactive input>", line 1, in ?
TypeError: object doesn't support item assignment
```

because the value at index 0 has already been set.

Common Programming Error 27.5

Trying to access an element out-of-range (i.e., an element at an index that does not exist) also produces a runtime error.

As an example of the preceding common programming error, the statement

```
print aTuple[10]
```

would produce a run-time error similar to

```
Traceback (innermost last):
  File "<interactive input>", line 1, in ?
IndexError: tuple index out of range
```

because **aTuple** does not have a 10th element. Line 15

```
firstItem, secondItem, thirdItem = aTuple
```

unpacks the items of the tuple into three variables. This statement produces the same results as lines 6–8.

Line 21

```
aTuple += ( 4, )
```

uses the **+=** operator to add an element to the end of variable **aTuple**. The right-hand side of the operator must be a tuple. The value **(4,)** is a *one-element tuple*. The comma after the tuple element value is mandatory, because the value **(4)** is an integer.

The output of line 26 shows how the **print** statement handles a variable that is a tuple. Lines 29 and 30 use a **for** loop to print out each element in variable **aTuple**.

The statement in line 29

```
for item in aTuple:
```

assigns the first element in **aTuple** (i.e., **aTuple[0]**) to variable **item**. Line 30 then prints **item** to the screen. By default, the **print** statement writes a newline character (e.g., a carriage return) at the end of its output; however, the comma in line 30 prevents Python from printing the newline character. In the next iteration of the **for** loop, the **print** statement will write text to the screen on the same line as the previous **print** statement. Lines 32 and 33 **print** a new line and a blank line to the screen, respectively, after all the elements in the tuple have been displayed

Line 36

```
aList = [ 1, 2, 3 ]
```

creates a *list* that contains elements **1**, **2** and **3**. Python lists are similar to tuples, except that lists are *mutable*—an element at an index that has been defined may be altered. Line 37 illustrates this fact by assigning the value **0** to the element in the list at index 0. Line 38 adds an element to the end of a list by calling method **append**. Lists also support several other methods (Fig. 27.8).

Method	Purpose
append(*item* **)**	Inserts *item* at the end of the list.
count(*element* **)**	Returns the number of occurrences of *element* in the list.
extend(*newList* **)**	Inserts *newList* at the end of the list.
index(*element* **)**	Returns the index of the first occurrence of *element* in the list. If element is not in the list, a **ValueError** exception occurs. [*Note:* We discuss exception in Section 26.5]

Fig. 27.8 Python list methods (part 1 of 2).

Method	Purpose
insert(*index*, *item* **)**	Inserts *item* at position *index*.
pop([*index*] **)**	Removes and returns the last element in the list. If parameter *index* is specified, removes and returns the element at position *index*.
remove(*element* **)**	Removes the first occurrence of *element* from the list. If *element* is not in the list, a **ValueError** exception occurs.
reverse()	Reverses the items in the list.
sort([*function*] **)**	Sorts items of the list. Optional parameter *function* is a comparison function that may be user-defined.

Fig. 27.8   Python list methods (part 2 of 2).

The output from the statement in line 40 illustrates how the **print** statement handles a variable that is a list. Line 43 adds the integer 4 to variable **aList** using the **+=** operator. The value on the right side of the operator must be a list. In this case, the list contains one element. The **for** statement (lines 50 and 51) **print**s each element of the list to the screen.

Lines 57–60 create a Python dictionary. Each entry in a dictionary has two parts—a *key* and a *value*—and a dictionary consists of a set of zero or more comma-separated key-value pairs inside braces. A value in a dictionary is manipulating using that value's key. The key must be of an immutable data type (e.g., number, string or tuple that contains only immutable data types); dictionary values may be any data type. Each key-value pair takes the form *key : value*.

Line 61 illustrates how to add a new element to a dictionary using the **[]** operator. Because a value must be accessed using its corresponding key, each key in a dictionary must be unique. Therefore, the statement

```
aDictionary[ 11 ] = "Nov."
```

will change the value associated with key **11** from **November** to the abbreviation **"Nov."**.

Lines 67 and 68 use a **for** loop to print each key-value pair in variable **aDictionary**. Method **keys** returns an unordered list of all the keys in the dictionary. Dictionaries support several other methods (Fig. 27.9). The **for** loop iterates over each key and **print**s the key and its corresponding value to the screen. Each value in the dictionary is accessed using the **[]** operator (line 68).

Method	Description
clear()	Deletes all items from the dictionary.
copy()	Creates a copy of the dictionary.
get(*key* [, *falseValue*] **)**	Returns the value associated with *key*. If *key* is not in the dictionary and if *falseValue* is specified, returns the specified value.

Fig. 27.9   Dictionary methods (part 1 of 2).

Method	Description
has_key(*key*)	Returns **1** if *key* is in the dictionary; returns **0** if *key* is not in the dictionary.
items()	Returns a list of tuples that are key-value pairs.
keys()	Returns a list of keys in the dictionary.
setdefault(*key* [, *falseValue*])	Behaves similarly to method **get**. If key is not in the dictionary and *falseValue* is specified, inserts the key and the specified value into dictionary.
update(*newDictionary*)	Adds all key-value pairs from *newDictionary* to the current dictionary.
values()	Returns a list of values in the dictionary.

Fig. 27.9   Dictionary methods (part 2 of 2).

27.4 String Processing and Regular Expressions

Programmers use string processing to accomplish a variety of tasks. System administration scripts can use Python modules and strings to rapidly process text files. Web programmers can use Python CGI scripts to validate user-entered data from an HTML form or to aggregate and display data from a variety of sources. This section discusses simple string processing in Python, including the use of *regular expressions*. Regular expressions are patterns of characters used to search through text files, databases, etc. A regular expression string defines a pattern with which text data can be compared. Unlike Perl, regular expressions are not part of the core Python language, but regular expression processing capability is available in the standard *Python **re** module*.

Figure 27.10 illustrates the use of strings in Python. Let us first discuss simple string assignments. Lines 5 and 6

```
string1 = "This is a string."
print string1
```

assign the value **"This is a string."** to variable **string1** and **print**s that value to the screen. In lines 8 and 9, we assign a similar value to variable **string2** and print that string.

```
1   # Fig. 27.10: fig27_10.py
2   # Program to illustrate use of strings
3
4   # simple string assignments
5   string1 = "This is a string."
6   print string1
7
8   string2 = "This is a second string."
9   print string2
10
```

Fig. 27.10   Using strings (part 1 of 2).

```
11   # string concatenation
12   string3 = string1 + " " + string2
13   print string3
14
15   # using operators
16   string4 = '*'
17   print "String with an asterisk: " + string4
18   string4 *= 50
19   print "String with 50 asterisks: " + string4
20
21   # using quotes
22   print "This is a string with \"double quotes.\""
23   print 'This is another string with "double quotes."'
24   print 'This is a string with \'single quotes.\''
25   print "This is another string with 'single quotes.'"
26   print """This string has "double quotes" and 'single quotes.'"""
27
28   # string formatting
29   name = raw_input( "Enter your name: " )
30   age = raw_input( "Enter your age: " )
31   print "Hello, %s, you are %s years old." % ( name, age )
```

```
This is a string.
This is a second string.
This is a string. This is a second string.
String with an asterisk: *
String with 50 asterisks:
**************************************************
This is a string with "double quotes."
This is another string with "double quotes."
This is a string with 'single quotes.'
This is another string with 'single quotes.'
This string has "double quotes" and 'single quotes.'
Enter your name: Brian
Enter your age: 33
Hello, Brian, you are 33 years old.
```

Fig. 27.10 Using strings (part 2 of 2).

In line 12, three strings: **string1**, **" "** and **string2** are concatenated using the operator **+**. We then print this string (**string3**) to the screen.

Lines 16 and 17 create and print a string with a single character—an asterisk. Line 18

```
string4 *= 50
```

uses the ***=** operator to multiply **string4** 50 times and store the result back in **string4**. We print the resulting string in line 19. Python also defines the **+=** operator for strings, which effectively concatenates a new string to the end an existing string.

Lines 22–26 illustrate the use of quotes in a string. Line 22

```
print "This is a string with \"double quotes.\""
```

illustrates one method of displaying double quotes inside a string. The double quotes are displayed using the *escape character* (****). If we omit the escape character, then Python will interpret the double quote character as marking the end of the string, rather than as a simple character within the string itself. Line 23

```
print 'This is another string with "double quotes."'
```

illustrates another method of displaying quotes inside a string. Notice that the string is contained within single quotes (`'`). Python strings may be contained within either double quotes or single quotes. As line 23 illustrates, if a string is contained within single quotes, then double quotes within the string do not need to be "escaped" with the backslash character. Similarly, if a string is contained within double quotes (line 25), then single quotes within the string do not need to be escaped.

If we do not want to use such escape characters in a string, we can place the entire string within pairs of three consecutive double quote characters (line 26). This is called a *triple-quoted string*—triple-quoted strings may alternatively be surrounded by sets of three consecutive single quote characters (`'''`). Python ignore whitespace (including newlines) that occurs in a triple-quoted string. We use this feature later in this chapter to output large blocks of HTML from CGI scripts.

In lines 29 and 30, we use Python function **raw_input** to input the user's name and age. In line 31, we format a string to incorporate the input data. The **%** *format character* acts as a place holder in the string. The *format character* **s** indicates that we want to place another string within the current string at the specified point. Figure 27.11 lists several *format characters* for use in string formatting. [*Note:* See Appendix E on Number systems for a discussion of numeric terminology in Fig. 27.11.] In line 31

```
% ( name, age )
```

we use the **%** *operator* to indicate that the formatting characters in the string are to be replaced with the values listed between the parentheses. Python constructs the string from left to right by matching a placeholder with the next value specified between parentheses and replacing the formatting character with that value.

Symbol	Meaning
c	Single character (i.e., a string of length one).
s	String.
d	Signed decimal integer.
u	Unsigned decimal integer.
o	Unsigned octal integer.
x	Unsigned hexadecimal integer (using format **abcdef**).
X	Unsigned hexadecimal integer (using format **ABCDEF**).
f	Floating-point number.
e, E	Floating-point number (using scientific notation).
g, G	Floating-point number (using least-significant digits).

Fig. 27.11 String-format characters.

Figure 27.12 uses some of Python's regular expression operations. Line 4

```
import re
```

imports the *re (regular expression) module.* A *module* contains data and functions that a program can use to accomplish a specific task. After a program imports a module, the program can make use of these data and functions. In our example, importing the **re** module enables us to access data and functions that facilitate regular-expression processing.

Line 8

```
expression1 = re.compile( r"Test" )
```

compiles the regular expression **Test**, using the **re** module's **compile** *method*. This method returns an instance of a **RegexObject** *object*, and we store this instance in **expression1**.

```
1   # Fig. 27.12: fig27_12.py
2   # Program searches a string using the regular expression module.
3
4   import re
5
6   searchString = "Testing pattern matches"
7
8   expression1 = re.compile( r"Test" )
9   expression2 = re.compile( r"^Test" )
10  expression3 = re.compile( r"Test$" )
11  expression4 = re.compile( r"\b\w*es\b" )
12
13  if expression1.match( searchString ):
14      print '"Test" was found.'
15
16  if expression2.match( searchString ):
17      print '"Test" was found at the beginning of the line.'
18
19  if expression3.match( searchString ):
20      print '"Test" was found at the end of the line.'
21
22  result = re.findall( expression4, searchString )
23
24  if result:
25      print 'There are %d words(s) ending in "es":' % \
26      ( len( result ) ),
27
28      for item in result:
29          print " " + item,
30
31  print
```

```
"Test" was found.
"Test" was found at the beginning of the line.
There are 1 words(s) ending in "es":  matches
```

Fig. 27.12 Using regular expressions to search a string.

Common Programming Error 27.6

Compiling a regular expression string speeds up a regular expression comparison that uses that string.

Figure 27.13 lists the regular expression symbols recognized by the **re** module. Unless otherwise specified, a regular expression character matches as many occurrences of a pattern as possible. For example, the regular expression **hel*o** matches strings that have the letters **he**, followed by any number of **l**'s, followed by an **o** (e.g., **"heo"**, **"helo"**, **"hello"**, **"helllo"**, etc.). Lines 8–11 use a few of these symbols to compile four regular expression patterns.

The **r** character before the string indicates that the string is a *raw string*. Python handles backslash characters in raw strings differently than "normal" strings, and treating all regular expressions as raw strings protects us from writing strings that may be interpreted in a way we did not intend. For example, without the raw-string character, the regular-expression string in line 11 would have to be compiled as **\\b\\w*es\\b**, because the backslash characters must be escaped. Using the raw string form prevents the regular-expression parser from interpreting the backslash as an escape character.

Line 13 uses the **RegexObject**'s *match method* to test **searchString** using the regular expression **expression1**. The **match** method returns a **MatchObject**. If match does not find any matching substrings, the method returns **None**; therefore, we only need to test the return value to determine whether any matches were found. [*Note:* **None** is a Python type whose value indicates that no value exists. In a Python **if** statement, **None** evaluates to false.] If a match is found, we print an appropriate message to the screen.

Character	Matches
^	Beginning of string.
$	End of string.
.	Any character, except a newline.
*	Zero or more occurrences of the pattern.
+	One or more occurrences of the preceding pattern.
?	Zero or one occurrences of the preceding pattern.
{m, n}	Between **m** and **n** occurrences of the preceding pattern.
\b	Word boundary (i.e., the beginning or end of a word).
\B	Non-word boundary.
\d	Digit ([**0–9**]).
\D	Non-digit.
\w	Any alpha-numeric character.
[...]	Any character defined by the set.
[^...]	Any character not defined by the set.

Fig. 27.13 Some of **re** module's regular expression characters.

Line 22

```
result = re.findall( expression4, searchString )
```

uses **re** module's ***findall*** *method* to store in variable **result** a list of all substrings in **searchString** that match the regular expression **expression4**. If **findall** returns any matches, we print a message to the screen that indicates how many words were found (lines 24–26). When run on a list, Python *function **len*** returns the number of elements in that list. Lines 28 and 29 **print** each item in the list, followed by a space. We end the program by printing a new line.

27.5 Exception handling

In an interpreted language like Python, errors pose a unique problem, because many errors caught at compilation time for a compiled language are not caught until run time in an interpreted language. These errors often cause Python programs to display cryptic messages to users and produce undesirable results. Additionally, some errors are more serious than others. For example, an error might occur that causes a program to crash before writing its data to a database. The user may lose hours of work due to an error over which the user has no control.

Exception handling enables programs and programmers to identify an error when it occurs and to take appropriate action. Exception handling is geared to situations in which a block code that detects an error is unable to deal with that error. Such a block of code will *raise an exception*. The programmer can write code that then *catches the exception* and handles the error in a "graceful" manner.

Python accomplishes exception handling through the use of ***try/except*** *blocks*. Any code contained in a **try** block that causes an error raises an exception. The **except** block then catches the exception (i.e., handles the error). The core Python language defines a hierarchy of exceptions. A Python **except** block can catch one of these exceptions, a subset of these exceptions or it can not specify any exceptions, in which case the code block will catch all exception. Figure 27.14 shows how dividing a number by zero raises a **ZeroDivisionError** exception.

Figure 27.15 presents a simple program that illustrates exception handling in Python. The program requests two numbers from the user, then attempts to divide the first number by the second.

Lines 4–11 define a function that prompts the user for a number and returns the number that the user enters. The function is a **while** loop that prompts the user for a number until the user enters a valid value (i.e., a number).

```
Python 2.0 (#8, Oct 16 2000, 17:27:58) [MSC 32 bit (Intel)] on win32
Type "copyright", "credits" or "license" for more information.
>>> 1 / 0
Traceback (most recent call last):
  File "<stdin>", line 1, in ?
ZeroDivisionError: integer division or modulo
>>>
```

Fig. 27.14 Interactive session illustrating a **ZeroDivisionError** exception.

```
1   # Fig. 27.15: fig27_15.py
2   # A simple program that illustrates exceptions.
3
4   def getNumber():
5
6       while 1:    # creates infinite loop
7           try:
8               theNumber = float( raw_input( "Enter a number: " ) )
9               return theNumber
10          except ValueError:
11              print "Value entered was not a number."
12
13  def divideNumbersString( x, y ):
14      try:
15          result = x / y
16      except ZeroDivisionError:
17          return "Cannot divide by zero!"
18      else:
19          return "The result of division is: %f" % result
20
21  number1 = getNumber()
22  number2 = getNumber()
23
24  print divideNumbersString( number1, number2 )
```

```
Enter a number: 4
Enter a number: 2
The result of division is: 2.000000
```

```
Enter a number: 4
Enter a number: 0
Cannot divide by zero!
```

```
Enter a number: a
Value entered was not a number.
Enter a number: 1
Enter a number: 9
The result of division is: 0.111111
```

Fig. 27.15 Demonstrating exception handling.

Lines 7–9 define a ***try*** *block*. Any code in the **try** block that causes an exception to be raised will be "caught" and handled in the corresponding ***except*** *block* (lines 11 and 12). The **try** block calls Python function **raw_input** to get the user input, then converts the user-entered value to a floating-point number via Python *function **float***. If the user enters a numerical value at the prompt, the function **return**s that value (line 9). If the user does not enter a numerical value at the prompt, the **float** function raises a ***ValueError*** *exception*, which is caught by the **except** block (lines 10 and 11). This block prints out an appropriate message before program control returns to the top of the **while** loop.

Lines 13–19 define function **divideNumbersString**, which attempts to divide two parameters and returns a string that contains the results. In the **try** block (lines 15 and 16), the function attempts to divide the two parameters. If the division raises exception *ZeroDivisionError*, the function explicitly catches the exception in lines 16 and 17. In this case, the function returns an appropriate error message.

A **try** block may optionally specify a corresponding *else block* (lines 18 and 19). If the code in the **try** block does not raise an exception, then the program executes the code in the **else** block. If an exception is raised in the **try** block, the **else** block is skipped. In general, we want to minimize the amount of code contained in a **try** block. Usually, we only place code in a **try** block that could raise an exception that we are capable of handling. In the **else** block, we place code (that should not raise any exceptions) that we want to run if no exception is raised in the **try** block. In our example, the **else** block **return**s a string that contains the result of the division.

The remainder of the program calls function **getNumber** twice (lines 21 and 22), to get two numbers from the user. The program then calls function **divideNumberString** (line 24), passing the user-entered numbers as parameters. The return value of this function call is printed to the screen.

27.6 Introduction to CGI programming

Like Perl, Python has many uses on the Web. Modules **cgi** (to access to HTML forms), **Cookie** (to read and write cookies), **smtplib** (to work with SMTP messages), **urllib** (to work with Web data), **ftplib** (to perform client-side ftp tasks), **HTMLgen** (to generate HTML pages) and others provide powerful extensions that Web programmers can use to write CGI scripts quickly for almost any task. This section introduces Python CGI programming. Sections 27.7–27.9 present more detailed CGI applications. We assume the reader has installed and configured the Apache Web server. Apache does not need any special configuration to run a Python script; a script need merely be placed in the specified **cgi-bin** directory.

Figure 27.16 gathers all CGI environment variables and values and organizes them in an HTML table that is then displayed in a Web browser. Line 1

```
#!c:\Python\python.exe
```

is a *directive* (sometimes called the *pound-bang* or *sh-bang*) that provides to the server the location of the Python executable. This directive must be the first line in a CGI script. For UNIX-based machines, this value might be

```
#!/usr/bin/python  or  #!/usr/local/bin/python
```

depending on the actual location of the Python executable).

```
1   #!c:\Python\python.exe
2   # Fig. 27.16: fig27_16.py
3   # Program to display CGI environment variables
4
5   import os
```

Fig. 27.16 Displaying environment variables (part 1 of 2).

```
6
7   print "Content-type: text/html"
8   print
9
10  print """<html><head><title>Environment Variables</title>
11  </head><table border = "0" celmargin = "5">"""
12
13  rowNumber = 0
14  backgroundColor = "#FFFFFF"
15
16  for item in os.environ.keys():
17     rowNumber += 1
18
19     if rowNumber % 2 == 0:
20        backgroundColor = "#FFFFFF"
21     else:
22        backgroundColor = "#DDDDDD"
23
24     print """<tr bgcolor = %s><td>%s</td><td>%s</td></tr>""" \
25        % ( backgroundColor, item, os.environ[ item ] )
26
27  print """</table></body></html>"""
```

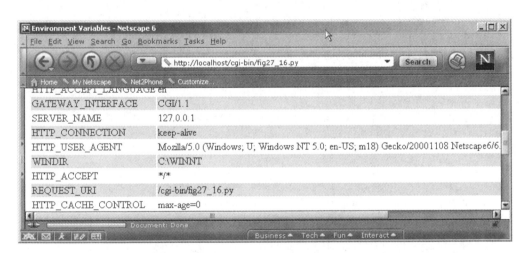

Netscape Communicator browser window ©1999 Netscape Communications Corporation. Used with permission. Netscape Communications has not authorized, sponsored, endorsed, or approved this publication and is not responsible for its content.

Fig. 27.16 Displaying environment variables (part 2 of 2).

Lines 7 and 8

```
print "Content-type: text/html"
print
```

print a valid HTTP header. Browsers use HTTP headers to determine how to handle the incoming data, and a valid header must be sent to ensure that the browser displays the information correctly. The blank line below the header is required; without this line, the content will not be delivered properly to the client.

The **environ** *data member* (line 16) of module **os** holds all the environment variables. This data member acts like a dictionary; therefore, we can access its values via *function* **keys**. In lines 16–22, we print a new row in the table for each item returned by method **os.environment.keys**. This row contains the key and the key's value.

27.7 Form Processing and Business Logic

HTML **FORM**s allow users to enter data to be sent to a Web server for processing. Once the server receives the form, a server program processes the data. Such a program could help people purchase products, send and receive Web-based e-mail, take a political poll, etc. These types of Web applications allow users to interact with the server.

Figure 27.17 uses an HTML **FORM** to allow users to input personal information for a mailing list. This type of registration might be used to store user information in a database.

The **form** element (line 17) specifies how the information enclosed by tags **<form>** and **</form>** should be handled. The first attribute, **method = "post"**, directs the browser to send the form's information to the server. The second attribute, **action = "cgi-bin/fig27_18.py"**, directs the server to execute the **fig27_18.py** Python script, located in the **cgi-bin** directory. The names given to the input items (e.g., **firstname**) in the Web page are important when the Python script is executed on the server. These names allow the script to refer to the individual pieces of data the user submits. When the user clicks the button labeled **Register**, both the input items and the names given to the items are sent to the **fig27_18.py** Python script.

```
1   <!DOCTYPE html PUBLIC "-//W3C//DTD HTML 4.0 Transitional//EN">
2   <!-- Fig. 27.17: fig27_17.html -->
3
4   <html>
5   <head>
6   <title>Sample FORM to take user input in HTML</title>
7   </head>
8
9   <body background = "images/back.gif">
10  <basefont face = "arial,sans-serif" size = "2">
11
12      <font size = "+2">
13         <strong>This is a sample registation form.</strong>
14      </font><br>
15      Please fill in all fields and click Register.
16
```

Fig. 27.17   HTML form to collect user information (part 1 of 3).

```
17      <form method = "post" action = "/cgi-bin/fig27_18.py">
18         <img src = "images/user.gif"><br>
19         <font color = "blue">
20            Please fill out the fields below.<br>
21         </font>
22
23         <img src = "images/fname.gif">
24         <input type = "text" name = "firstname"><br>
25         <img src = "images/lname.gif">
26         <input type = "text" name = "lastname"><br>
27         <img src = "images/email.gif">
28         <input type = "text" name = "email"><br>
29         <img src = "images/phone.gif">
30         <input type = "text" name = "phone"><br>
31
32         <font size = "-2">
33            Must be in the form (555)555-5555<br><br>
34         </font>
35
36         <img src = "images/downloads.gif"><br>
37         <font color = "blue">
38            Which book would you like information about?<br>
39         </font>
40
41         <select name = "book">
42            <option>Perl How to Program
43            <option>Python How to Program
44            <option>E-business and E-commerce How to Program
45            <option>Internet and WWW How to Program
46            <option>C++ How to Program 3e
47            <option>Java How to Program 3e
48            <option>Visual Basic How to Program
49         </select>
50         <br><br>
51
52         <img src = "images/os.gif"><br>
53         <font color = "blue">
54            Which operating system are you
55            currently using?<br>
56         </font>
57
58         <input type = "radio" name = "os" value = "Windows NT"
59         checked>
60         Windows NT
61         <input type = "radio" name = "os" value = "Windows 2000">
62         Windows 2000
63         <input type = "radio" name = "os" value = "Windows 95_98">
64         Windows 95/98<br>
65         <input type = "radio" name = "os" value = "Linux">
66         Linux
67         <input type = "radio" name = "os" value = "Other">
68         Other<br>
69         <input type = "submit" value = "Register">
```

Fig. 27.17   HTML form to collect user information (part 2 of 3).

```
70
71        </form>
72    </body>
73    </html>
```

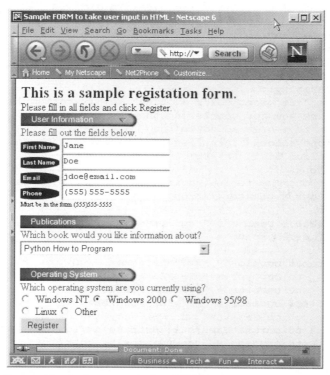

Netscape Communicator browser window ©1999 Netscape Communications Corporation. Used with permission. Netscape Communications has not authorized, sponsored, endorsed, or approved this publication and is not responsible for its content.

Fig. 27.17   HTML form to collect user information (part 3 of 3).

Figure 27.18 takes user information from **fig27_17.html** and sends a Web page to the client indicating that the information was received. Line 6 **import**s the **cgi** module. This module provides functionality for writing CGI scripts in Python, including access to HTML form values.

```
1    #!c:\Python\python.exe
2    # Fig. 27.18: fig27_18.py
3    # Program to read information sent to the server from the
4    # form in fig27_17.html.
5
```

Fig. 27.18   Script to process user data from **fig27_17.html** (part 1 of 4).

```
6   import cgi
7   import re
8
9   # the regular expression for matching most American phone numbers.
10  telephoneExpression = \
11      re.compile( r'\(\d\d\d\)\d\d\d-\d\d\d\d' )
12
13  def printContent():
14      print "Content-type: text/html"
15      print
16
17  def printReply():
18      print """"Hi <font color = "blue"><b>%(firstName)s</b></font>.
19          Thank you for completing the survey.<BR>
20          You have been added to the
21          <font color = "blue"><strong>%(book)s </strong></font>
22          mailing list.<br><br>
23
24          <strong>The following information has been saved
25          in our database:</strong><br>
26
27          <table border = "0" cellpadding = "0"
28              cellspacing = "10">
29
30          <tr><td bgcolor = "#FFFFAA">Name </td>
31              <td bgcolor = "#FFFFAA">Email</td>
32              <td bgcolor = "#FFFFAA">Phone</td>
33              <td bgcolor = "#FFFFAA">OS</td></tr>
34
35          <tr><td>%(firstName)s %(lastName)s</td><td>%(email)s</td>
36              <td>%(phone)s</td><td>%(os)s</td></tr>
37          </table>
38
39          <br><br><br>
40
41          <center><font size = "-3">
42          This is only a sample form.
43          You have not been added to a mailing list.
44          </font></center>
45          """ % personInfo
46
47  def printPhoneError():
48
49      print """<font color = "red" size = "+2">
50          INVALID PHONE NUMBER</font><br>
51          A valid phone number must be in the form
52          <strong>(555)555-5555</strong>
53          <font color = "blue"> Click the Back button,
54          enter a valid phone number and resubmit.<br><br>
55          Thank You."""
56
57  def printFormError():
58
```

Fig. 27.18 Script to process user data from `fig27_17.html` (part 2 of 4).

```
59      print """"<font color = "red" size = "+2">
60         FORM ERROR</font><br>
61         You have not filled in all fields.
62
63         <font color = "blue"> Click the Back button,
64         fill out the form and resubmit.<br><br>
65         Thank You.</font>"""
66
67   printContent()
68
69   form = cgi.FieldStorage()
70
71   try:
72      personInfo = { 'firstName' : form[ "firstname" ].value,
73                     'lastName' : form[ "lastname" ].value,
74                     'email' : form[ "email" ].value,
75                     'phone' : form[ "phone" ].value,
76                     'book' : form[ "book" ].value,
77                     'os' : form[ "os" ].value }
78   except:
79      printFormError()
80
81   if telephoneExpression.match( personInfo[ 'phone' ] ):
82      printReply()
83   else:
84      printPhoneError()
85      printPhoneError()
```

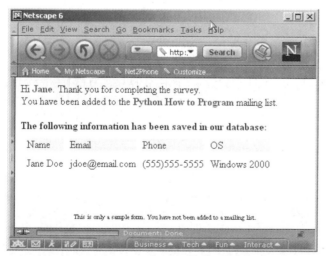

Netscape Communicator browser window ©1999 Netscape Communications Corporation. Used with permission. Netscape Communications has not authorized, sponsored, endorsed, or approved this publication and is not responsible for its content.

Fig. 27.18 Script to process user data from **fig27_17.html** (part 3 of 4).

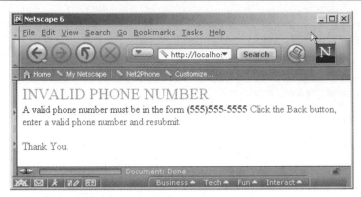

Netscape Communicator browser window ©1999 Netscape Communications
Corporation. Used with permission. Netscape Communications has not authorized,
sponsored, endorsed, or approved this publication and is not responsible for its
content.

Fig. 27.18   Script to process user data from `fig27_17.html` (part 4 of 4).

Line 67 begins the main portion of the script and calls function **printContent** that
prints the proper HTTP header. Line 69 creates an instance of class *FieldStorage* and
assigns the instance to reference **form**. This class contains information about any forms in
the posting page. The **try** block (lines 71 through 77) creates a dictionary that contains the
appropriate values from each defined element in **form**. Each value is accessed via the
value data member of a particular **form** element. For example, line 73

```
'lastName' : form[ "lastname" ].value,
```

assigns the **value** of the **lastname** field of **form** to the dictionary key **'lastName'**.

If the value of any element in **form** is **None**, the **try** block throws and exception, and
we call function **printFormError**. This function (lines 57–65) prints a message in the
browser that informs the user the form has not been properly completed and instructs the
user to click the **Back** button to fill out the form and resubmit it.

Line 81 tests the user-submitted phone number against the specified format. We compile the regular expression **telephoneExpression** in lines 10 and 11. If the expression's **match** method returns a value, we call the **printReply** function (discussed
momentarily). If the **match** method does not return a value (i.e., the phone number is not
in the proper format), we call function **printPhoneError**. This function (lines 47–55)
displays a message in the browser that informs the user that the phone number is in
improper format and instructs the user to click the **Back** button to change the phone
number and resubmit the form.

If the user has correctly filled out the form, we call function **printReply** (lines 17–
45). This function thanks the user and displays an HTML table with the information gathered from the form. Notice that we format the output with values from the **personInfo**
dictionary. Line 21

```
<font color = "blue"><strong>%(book)s </strong></font>
```

inserts the value of the string variable **book** into the string after the percent sign (**%**). Line 45 tells Python that the string variable **book** is a key in the dictionary **personInfo**. Thus, the text

```
%(book)s
```

is replaced with the value stored in **personInfo['book']**.

27.8 Cookies

When a client visits a Web site, the server for that Web site may *write a cookie* to the client's machine. This cookie can be accessed by servers within the Web site's domain at a later time. Cookies are usually small text files used to maintain *state information* for a particular client. State information may contain a username, password or specific information that might be helpful when a user returns to a Web site. Many Web sites use cookies to store a client's postal zip code. The zip code is used when the client requests a Web page from the server. The server may send the current weather information or news updates for the client's region. The scripts in this section write cookie values to the client and retrieve the values for display in the browser.

Figure 27.19 is an HTML form that asks the user to enter three values. These values are passed to the **fig27_20.py** script, which writes the values in a client-side cookie.

```
1   <!DOCTYPE html PUBLIC "-//W3C//DTD HTML 4.0 Transitional//EN">
2   <!-- Fig. 27.19: fig27_19.html -->
3
4   <html>
5      <head>
6         <title>Writing a cookie to the client computer</title>
7      </head>
8
9   <body background = "images/back.gif">
10  <basefont face = "arial,sans-serif" size = "2">
11
12     <font size = "+2">
13        <b>Click Write Cookie to save your cookie data.</b>
14     </font><br>
15
16     <form method = "post" action = "cgi-bin/fig27_20.py">
17        <strong>Name:</strong><br>
18        <input type = "text" name = "name"><br>
19
20        <strong>Height:</strong><br>
21        <input type = "text" name = "height"><br>
22
23        <strong>Favorite Color</strong><br>
24        <input type = "text" name = "color"><br>
25
26        <input type = "submit" value = "Write Cookie">
27     </form>
28
```

Fig. 27.19   HTML form to get cookie values from user (part 1 of 2).

```
29   </body>
30   </html>
```

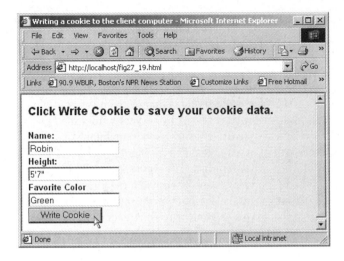

Fig. 27.19 HTML form to get cookie values from user (part 2 of 2).

Figure 27.20 is the script that retrieves the form values from **fig27_19.html** and stores those values in a client-side cookie. Line 6 **import**s the **Cookie** module.

```
1    #!C:\Python\python.exe
2    # Fig. 27.20: fig27_20.py
3    # Writing a cookie to a client's machine
4
5    import cgi
6    import Cookie
7    import time
8
9    form = cgi.FieldStorage()   # get form information
10
11   try:  # extract form values
12      name = form[ "name" ].value
13      height = form[ "height" ].value
14      color = form[ "color" ].value
15   except:
16      print "Content-type: text/html"
17      print
18      print """<h3>You have not filled in all fields.
19      <font color = "blue"> Click the Back button,
20      fill out the form and resubmit.<br><br>
21      Thank You. </font></h3>"""
22   else:
23      # construct cookie expiration date and path
24      expirationFormat = "%A, %d-%b-%y %X %Z"
```

Fig. 27.20 Writing a cookie to a client's machine (part 1 of 2).

```
25      expirationTime = time.localtime( time.time() + 300 )
26      expirationDate = time.strftime( expirationFormat,
27         expirationTime )
28      path = "/"
29
30      # construct cookie contents
31      cookie = Cookie.Cookie()
32
33      cookie[ "Name" ] = name
34      cookie[ "Name" ][ "expires" ] = expirationDate
35      cookie[ "Name" ][ "path" ] = path
36
37      cookie[ "Height" ] = height
38      cookie[ "Height" ][ "expires" ] = expirationDate
39      cookie[ "Height" ][ "path" ] = path
40
41      cookie[ "Color" ] = color
42      cookie[ "Color" ][ "expires" ] = expirationDate
43      cookie[ "Color" ][ "path" ] = path
44
45      # print cookie to user and page to browser
46      print cookie
47
48      print "Content-type: text/html"
49      print
50
51      print """<body background = "/images/back.gif">
52      <basefont face = "arial,sans-serif" size = "3">
53      The cookie has been set with the folowing data: <br><br>
54
55      <font color = "blue">Name:</font> %s<br>
56      <font color = "blue">Height:</font> %s<br>
57      <font color = "blue">Favorite Color:</font>
58      <font color = "%s"> %s<br>""" % (name, height, color, color)
59
60      print """<br><a href= "fig27_21.py">
61      Read cookie values</a>"""
```

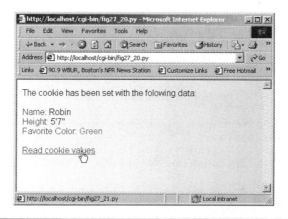

Fig. 27.20 Writing a cookie to a client's machine (part 2 of 2).

Line 9 retrieves the form values via **cgi** method **FieldStorage**. We handle the form values using a **try/except/else** block. The **try** block (lines 11–14) attempts to retrieve the form values. If the user has not completed one or more of the form fields, the code in this block raises an exception. The exception is caught in the **except** block (lines 15–21), and the program outputs an appropriate message to the browser.

The code in the **else** block executes after the program successfully retrieves all the form values. Line 24

```
expirationFormat = "%A, %d-%b-%y %X %Z"
```

specifies the format for the expiration value of the cookie. The format characters in this string are defined by the *time* module. For a complete list of **time** tokens and their meanings, see

```
www.python.org/doc/current/lib/module-time.html
```

The *time* function (line 25) of module **time** returns a floating-point value that is the number of seconds since the "*epoch*" (i.e., the first day of 1970). We add 300 seconds to this value to set the **expirationTime** for the cookie. We then format the time using the *localtime* function. This function converts the time in seconds to a nine-element tuple that represents the time in local terms (i.e., according to the time zone of the machine on which the script is running). Lines 26 and 27 call the *strftime* function to format a time tuple into a string. This line effectively formats tuple **expirationTime** as a string that follows the format specified in **expirationFormat**.

Line 31

```
cookie = Cookie.Cookie()
```

creates an instance of *class* ***Cookie***. An object of class **Cookie** acts like a dictionary, so values can be set and retrieved using familiar dictionary syntax. Lines 33–43 set the values for the cookie, based on the user-entered values retrieved from the HMTL form.

Line 46 writes the cookie (assuming the user's browser has enabled cookies). The cookie must be written before we write the content-type (lines 48 and 49) to the browser. Lines 51–58 display the cookie's values in the browser.

Figure 27.21 is the CGI script that retrieves cookie values from the client and displays the values in the browser. Line 16

```
cookie.load( os.environ[ "HTTP_COOKIE" ] )
```

retrieves the cookie values from the client. Cookies are stored in the environment variable **HTTP_COOKIE**. The *load* method of class **Cookie** extracts cookie values from a string. If no cookie value exists, then the program raises a **KeyError** exception. We catch the exception in lines 17–18 and print an appropriate message in the browser.

```
1   #!C:\Python\python.exe
2   # Fig. 27.21: fig27_21.py
3   # Program that retrieves and displays client-side cookie values
4
5   import Cookie
6   import os
```

Fig. 27.21 CGI script that retrieves and displays client-side cookie values (part 1 of 2).

```
7
8   print "Content-type: text/html"
9   print
10
11  print """<body background = "images/back.gif">
12  <basefont face = "arial, sans-serif" size = "3">"""
13
14  try:
15     cookie = Cookie.Cookie()
16     cookie.load( os.environ[ "HTTP_COOKIE" ] )
17  except KeyError:
18     print """<strong>Error reading cookies</strong>"""
19  else:
20     print """<strong>The following data is saved in a cookie
21     on your computer.</strong><br><br>"""
22
23     print """<table border = "5" cellspacing = "0"
24         cellpadding = "10">"""
25
26     for item in cookie.keys():
27        print """<TR>
28           <td bgcolor = "#AAAAFF">%s</td>
29           <td bgcolor = "#AAAAAA">%s</td>
30        </tr>""" % ( item, cookie[ item ].value )
31
32     print """</TABLE>"""
```

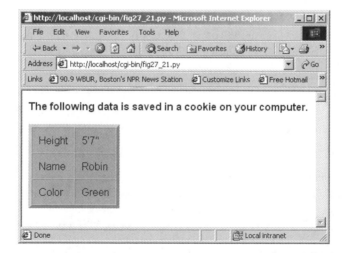

Fig. 27.21 CGI script that retrieves and displays client-side cookie values (part 2 of 2).

If the program successfully retrieves the cookie values, the code in lines 19–32 displays the values in the browser. Because cookies act like dictionaries, we can use the **keys** method (line 26) to retrieve the names of all the values in the cookie. Lines 26–30 print these names and their corresponding values in a table.

27.9 Database Application Programming Interface (DB-API)

Python's open-source nature encourages independent developers to contribute additions to the language. In earlier versions of Python, many developers contributed modules that provided interfaces to several databases. Unfortunately, these interfaces rarely resembled one another; if an application developer wanted to change the application's database, the whole program had to be rewritten.

The *Python Database Special Interest Group (SIG)* was formed to develop a specification for *Python database application programming interface (DB-API)*. The specification is now in version 2.0, and modules that conform to this specification exist for many databases. In this section we illustrate the Python interface to MySQL (*module **MySQLdb***) and to Microsoft Access (*module **odbc***). The following two sections discuss manipulating databases in Python. Because of Python's standard database interface, we can reuse much of the code used to manipulate data in these two databases.

27.9.1 Setup

The next programming example assumes the user has installed either MySQL or Microsoft Access (or both). The **odbc** module is included in Mark Hammond's ***win32all*** *extensions for Windows*, and the **MySQLdb** module must be downloaded and installed. [*Note:* The Perl resources posted at our Web site **www.deitel.com** include step-by-step instructions on installing **win32all** and **MySQLdb**. You can find the resources for all our books by clicking on the "Downloads/Resources" link.]

27.9.2 Simple DB-API program

Figure 27.22 is an HTML form that allows the user to select a database to query and to execute a query string on that database. The form calls the **fig27_23.py** script that displays the results of the query in the browser.

```
1    <!DOCTYPE html PUBLIC "-//W3C//DTD HTML 4.0 Transitional//EN">
2    <!-- Fig. 27.22: fig27_22.html -->
3
4    <html>
5       <head>
6          <title>Database query</title>
7       </head>
8
9    <body background = "images/back.gif">
10   <basefont face = "arial,sans-serif" size = "2">
11
12      <font size = "+2">
13         <strong>Enter a search string and click Find.</strong>
14      </font><br>
15
16      <form method = "post" action = "cgi-bin/fig27_23.py">
17         <input type = "text" name = "search"><br>
18         <input type = "submit" value = "Find"><br>
```

Fig. 27.22   Form to input an SQL statement from the user (part 1 of 2).

```
19           <input type = "radio" name = "database"
20              value = "MySQL" checked>
21           MySQL
22           <input type = "radio" name = "database"
23              value = "Access">
24           Microsoft Access
25        </form>
26     </body>
27     </html>
```

Netscape Communicator browser window ©1999 Netscape Communications Corporation. Used with permission. Netscape Communications has not authorized, sponsored, endorsed, or approved this publication and is not responsible for its content.

Fig. 27.22   Form to input an SQL statement from the user (part 2 of 2).

Figure 27.23 is the CGI script that executes the user-entered query from **fig27_22.html** on the database specified by the user. Lines 11–21 define function **getConnection**, which returns a ***connection*** *object* to the appropriate database. If parameter **databaseType** has value **"MySQL"** then the function **import**s the **MySQLdb** module (line 15) and creates an appropriate **connection** object. If parameter **databaseType** has value **"Access"**, then the function **import**s the **odbc** module and creates the appropriate **connection** object.

```
1    #!c:\Python\python.exe
2    # Fig. 27.23: fig27_23.py
3    # A program to illustrate Python's database connectivity.
4
5    import cgi
6
7    def printContent():
8        print "Content-type: text/html"
9        print
10
11   def getConnection( databaseType, databaseName ):
12       connection = None
13
```

Fig. 27.23   CGI script that queries a database and writes results to a browser (part 1 of 3).

```
14        if databaseType == 'MySQL':
15            import MySQLdb
16            connection = MySQLdb.connect( db = databaseName )
17        elif databaseType == 'Access':
18            import odbc
19            connection = odbc.odbc( databaseName )
20
21        return connection
22
23  # get results from form
24  form = cgi.FieldStorage()
25
26  printContent()                              # print HTML header
27
28  try:
29        queryString = form[ "SEARCH" ].value
30        database = form[ "DATABASE" ].value
31  except:
32        print """<font color = "red" size = "+2">
33          FORM ERROR</font><br>
34          You did not enter a query string.<br>
35          <font color = "blue"> Click the Back button,
36          fill out the form and resubmit.<br><br>
37          Thank You.</font>"""
38  else:
39
40        # connect to database and get cursor
41        connection = getConnection( database, "Deitel" )
42        cursor = connection.cursor()
43
44        try:
45            cursor.execute( queryString )    # execute user's query
46        except:
47            print """An error occurred in your query statement."""
48        else:
49            results = cursor.fetchall()      # store results in list
50
51            # display results
52            print """Database used: <font color = "blue">
53            %s</font><br>""" % database
54            print """<table border = "1" cellpadding = "3">"""
55
56            for row in results:
57                print "<tr>"
58
59                for entry in row:
60                    print "<td>%s</td>" % entry
61
62            print """</table>"""
63
64        cursor.close()                       # close cursor
65        connection.close()                   # close connection
```

Fig. 27.23 CGI script that queries a database and writes results to a browser (part 2 of 3).

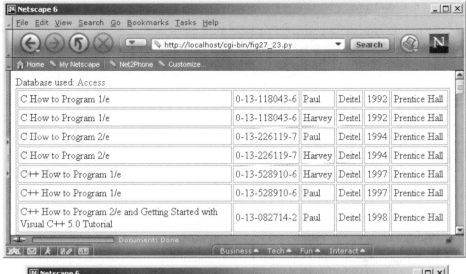

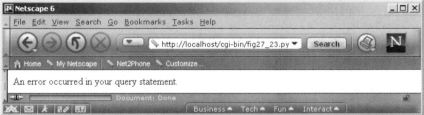

Netscape Communicator browser window ©1999 Netscape Communications Corporation. Used with permission. Netscape Communications has not authorized, sponsored, endorsed, or approved this publication and is not responsible for its content.

Fig. 27.23 CGI script that queries a database and writes results to a browser (part 3 of 3).

Line 26 retrieves the form using the **FieldStorage** class from module **cgi**. In lines 29 and 30, we extract the values from the form. If the user did not fill in the query string, line 29 raises an exception. We catch this exception in line 31–37, where we print an appropriate message in the browser.

If the script successfully retrieves the values from the form, the code in lines 38–65 executes. Line 41 calls function **getConnection** to get a **connection** to the specified database. Line 42

```
cursor = connection.cursor()
```

creates a ***cursor*** *object* using the ***cursor*** *method* of the appropriate DB-API implementation. The **cursor** enables us to execute queries on the database. Line 45 uses **cursor**'s *method **execute*** to execute a query on the database. If **queryString** contains an SQL syntax error, the **execute** method raises an exception. We catch this exception in lines 46 and 47 and print an appropriate message in the browser.

If the script successfully executes the **queryString** on the database, the code in lines 48–62 executes. The **cursor**'s **fetchall** method retrieves all the records that match the query. This method returns a list of tuples. Each tuple in the list is one row of the results, and each value in the tuple corresponds to a column in that row.

Lines 51–62 display the query results in the browser. We first display a line that indicates from which database the results were retrieved (lines 52–54). Lines 56–60 print a row in an HTML table for each row in the query results.

After the script completes its output (e.g., error messages or results), we **close** the **cursor** and the **connection** and set both variables to **None**.

Good Programming Practice 27.2

The Python DB-API implementation automatically closes a connection to a database when the program exits, still, we include this code as a matter of good practice.

27.10 Object-Oriented Programming

This section presents a brief overview of Python object-oriented constructs; we assume the reader has basic knowledge of object-oriented programming (OOP) concepts, including inheritance. Our examples present a simple class **Employee** that contains information about a company employee and a class **Hourly** that inherits from class **Employee**.

Figure 27.24 defines class **Employee**. Line 4

```
class Employee:
```

begins the **class** definition. All methods and data arc placed within this **class** block. Line 5

```
def __init__( self, first, last ):
```

declares *method **__init__***. Method **__init__** is a special method defined by Python; this method is called when an object of class **Employee** is created. Python classes may define any of several special methods. For a complete list of these special methods and their purposes, see the official Python documentation at **www.python.org/doc/current/ref/customization.html**.

The first parameter of method **__init__** is called *self*. Unlike some programming languages (e.g., C++), methods of a Python class need an object with which to reference data and methods of that class. This object is passed in as the first parameter of every Python method. By convention, this parameter is named **self**.

```
1   # Fig: 27.24: Employee.py
2   # An employee class
3
4   class Employee:
5      def __init__( self, first, last ):
6         self.firstName = first
7         self.lastName = last
8
9      def __str__( self ):
10        return "%s, %s" % ( self.lastName, self.firstName )
```

Fig. 27.24 Python base class **Employee**.

The remaining two parameters in the constructor correspond to the employee's first and last name, respectively. Lines 6 and 7

```
self.firstName = first
self.lastName = last
```

initialize data members **firstName** and **lastName** using the corresponding parameter values. To add a data member to a class, the data member must be assigned a value. Data members may be assigned a value anywhere within the **class** block. Once the data member has been assigned a value, it may be accessed by any method, via the **self** parameter. Line 9

```
def __str__( self ):
```

begins the definition of the special Python *method __str__*. This method is called whenever a **print** statement is executed on the class. This method returns a string that contains the **Employee**'s last name, followed by a comma, followed by the **Employee**'s first name.

Figure 27.25 contains the definition for class **Hourly**, which inherits from class **Employee**. The output from an interactive session is displayed after the class definition.

```
1   # Fig. 27.25: Hourly.py
2   # An hourly employee class
3
4   import Employee
5
6   class Hourly( Employee.Employee ):
7
8       def __init__( self, first, last, initHours, initWage ):
9           Employee.Employee.__init__( self, first, last )
10          self.hours = initHours
11          self.wage = initWage
12
13      def __str__( self ):
14          return "%s, %s is an hourly worker with pay of $%.2f." \
15              % ( self.lastName, self.firstName, self.getPay())
16
17      def getPay( self ):
18          return self.hours * self.wage
```

```
Python 2.0 (#8, Oct 16 2000, 17:27:58) [MSC 32 bit (Intel)] on win32
Type "copyright", "credits" or "license" for more information.
>>> import Employee
>>> employee = Employee.Employee( "Jane", "Doe" )
>>> import Hourly
>>> hourly = Hourly.Hourly( "John", "Doe", 20, 20.00 )
>>> workerList = [ employee, hourly ]
>>> for item in workerList:
...     print item
...
Doe, Jane
Doe, John is an hourly worker with pay of $400.00.
>>>
```

Fig. 27.25 Python class **Hourly**; inherits from **Employee**.

In line 4, we **import** the module that defines class **Employee**. If a class inherits from a class that is defined in a different module, that module must be **import**ed. Line 6

```
class Hourly( Employee.Employee ):
```

begins the definition for class **Hourly**. The *parentheses indicate inheritance*, and the parent class name is placed inside the parentheses. The text **Employee.Employee** indicates that class **Hourly** inherits from class **Employee**, which is defined in the **Employee** module. We must use the **.** operator to access the class. For example, if the **Employee** module also defined a **Wage** class, we could inherit from the **Wage** class by placing the text **Employee.Wage** inside parentheses.

The class constructor (lines 8–11) takes parameters that specify the first name, last name initial hours and initial wage. Line 9

```
Employee.Employee.__init__( self, first, last )
```

calls the **__init__** method of class **Employee** and passes the parameters first and last to initialize the first name and last name. Even though these data members are initialized in the base class, they can still be accessed in the derived class via **self**. Lines 10 and 11 initialize the **initHours** and **initWage** data members of class **Hourly**.

Lines 17 and 18 define the simple method **getPay**. This method calculates and returns the person's pay based on data members **hours** and **wage**. Lines 13–15 define special method **__str__**, which returns a string that contains the workers' first name, last name and pay.

27.11 Case Study: GUI Database Application

This section contains a program that provides a graphical user interface (GUI) for a local database. This case study illustrates Python's rapid-application development capabilities. This section assumes a certain level of knowledge on the part of the reader: the topics covered include database access (Chapter 15), object-based programming (Chapter 14 and Section 27.10) and familiarity with Tk/Tcl Graphical User Interface (GUI) development (Chapter 21).

The GUI is composed of three main subsections (see Fig. 27.26). The top subsection enables the user to select a database from a list of available databases, open that database and close that database. The middle subsection displays information about the currently opened database. The left side of this subsection displays a list of tables in the database. When the user clicks a table in this list, the columns from this table are displayed in the text widget on the right side of the subsection. The bottom subsection of the GUI enables the user to enter a query string to execute on the currently opened database. When the user clicks the **Execute Query** button or presses the *Return* key, the statement is executed on the database. The results of this statement are displayed in a pop-up text dialog.

27.11.1 Gadfly

Our program displays information stored in a *Gadfly* database—a relational database written completely in Python. This database is a freely available, open-source application that supports a significant subset of the Structured Query Language (SQL). The Python interface to Gadfly conforms to the Python Database interface specification (Section 27.9), so users familiar with this interface can quickly implement applications that use Gadfly.

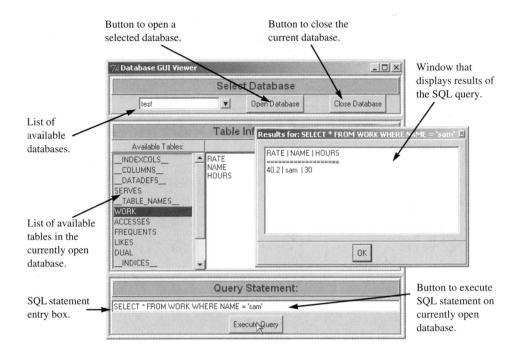

Fig. 27.26 Database GUI viewer. (Courtesy of Tcl/Tk.)

27.11.2 `Tkinter`

Tk is a GUI extension to the scripting language Tcl. Python uses *module* **`Tkinter`** to talk to Tcl/Tk in a logical manner. Each Tk widget is a Python object; for example, the Tk Text widget is implemented as class **`Text`** in module **`Tkinter`**. All **`Tkinter`** objects inherit from *class* **`Widget`**. Tk initialization values are passed as keyword parameters to an object's constructor. Operations such as geometry managers are implemented as methods, and widget options can be accessed via calls to appropriate methods.

Our application takes advantage of Python *module* **Pmw**, which defines several *Python Mega Widgets*. Python Mega Widgets are widgets that combine several common Tk widgets into a single useful "mega-widget." For example, the Python Mega Widget **`ScrolledText`** combines a Tk text widget with Tk scrollbar widgets to create a convenient widget in which to display large amounts of text.

27.11.3 Setup

This example requires several components to be downloaded and installed. The Perl resources posted at our Web site **www.deitel.com** include step-by-step instructions on installing Gadfly, Tcl/Tk, the **`Tkinter`** module and Python Mega Widgets (**Pmw**). You can find the resources for all our books by clicking the "Downloads/Resources" link.

27.11.4 GUI Database Viewer Implementation

This section presents the Python implementation for our application. The application consists of only one file: **DatabaseViewer.py**. We discuss this file in detail in the remainder of the section. To run the program, type

> python DatabaseViewer.py

at the command prompt. [*Note:* **Tkinter** can crash under *Pywin* (the Windows Python IDE). To run this program properly under Windows, be sure to use the command shell. To access the command shell (on Windows 2000), click the **Start** button, select **Run**, type **cmd** and click **OK**.]

The file **DatabaseViewer.py** (Fig. 27.27) defines class **DatabaseViewer**, which contains all the code for our application. Lines 2–9 **import** all the necessary Python modules. Line 6

> from Tkinter import *

imports all submodules from the **Tkinter** module. The *from/import* *statement* enables us to access **Tkinter** components without using the **.** operator. The *glob module* (line 5) is used to retrieve filenames from a directory. Module **tkMessageBox** (line 7) defines several types of dialog boxes.

Line 11 begins the class **DatabaseViewer** definition; this class inherits from the *Tkinter class* *Frame*. Special method **__init__** is defined in lines 13–33. To initialize this class, we must first call the **__init__** method of base class **Frame** (line 14), passing parameter **self**.

```
1    # Fig. 27.27: DatabaseViewer.py
2    # A GUI Database Viewer
3
4    import os, string
5    import glob
6    from Tkinter import *
7    import tkMessageBox
8    import Pmw
9    from gadfly import gadfly
10
11   class DatabaseViewer( Frame ):
12
13      def __init__( self ):
14         Frame.__init__( self )
15
16         self.gadflyPath = "C:\\Python\\Gadfly"   # path to database
17         self.databaseDirectories = {} # database locations
18         self.databaseNames = []        # list of available databases
19         self.connection = None         # connection to database
20         self.currentQuery = StringVar()  # current query string
21         self.queryDisplay = None         # query results text dialog
22
23         # populate databaseNames list
24         os.path.walk( self.gadflyPath, self.getDatabase, 0 )
```

Fig. 27.27 GUI database interface (part 1 of 6).

```
25
26            # configure master
27            self.master.title( 'Database GUI Viewer' )
28            self.master.columnconfigure( 0, weight = 1 )
29            self.master.rowconfigure( 0 , weight = 1 )
30            self.master.grid()
31
32            # build GUI components
33            self.buildGUI()
34
35        def destroy( self ):
36            self.closeDatabase()
37            Frame.destroy( self )
38
39        def getDatabase( self, path, dirname, names ):
40            """Get names of all databases in specified directory."""
41            os.chdir( dirname )        # change directories
42
43            # get list of all database files in gadfly directory
44            databaseFiles = glob.glob( "*.gfd" )
45
46            for database in databaseFiles:
47                databaseName = database[ :-4 ]
48                self.databaseNames.append( databaseName )
49                self.databaseDirectories[ databaseName ] = dirname
50
51        def createSection( self, parent, labelText, numberOfColumns ):
52            """Creates a subsection of a frame."""
53
54            # create enclosing frame
55            frame = Frame( parent, relief = 'groove', borderwidth = 5 )
56            frame.columnconfigure( tuple( range( numberOfColumns ) ),
57                weight = 1 )
58
59            # create label for frame
60            label = Label( frame, text = labelText,
61                font = ( 'Arial', 12, 'bold' ),  background =
62                'dark gray', foreground = 'dark blue', relief = 'ridge',
63                borderwidth = 3 )
64            label.grid( row = 0, columnspan = numberOfColumns,
65                sticky = 'new' )
66
67            return frame
68
69        def createButton( self, parent, name, action, gridRow,
70            gridColumn ):
71            """Creates a button."""
72            return Button( parent, text = name, command = action ) \
73                .grid( row = gridRow, column = gridColumn )
74
75        def buildGUI( self ):
76            """Build database viewer display."""
77
```

Fig. 27.27   GUI database interface (part 2 of 6).

```
78              #-------------------Configure self----------------------#
79              Pmw.initialise()
80              self.grid( row = 0, column = 0, sticky = 'nesw' )
81              #------------------------------------------------------------#
82
83              #-------------Build 'Select Database' Section-----------#
84              databaseFrame = self.createSection( self,
85                 "Select Database", 3 )
86              databaseFrame.grid( row = 0, column = 0, sticky = 'nesw',
87                 columnspan = 2 )
88
89              # allows users to select from databases
90              self.databaseComboBox = Pmw.ComboBox( databaseFrame,
91                 scrolledlist_items = self.databaseNames, dropdown = 1 )
92              self.databaseComboBox.grid( row = 1, column = 0, padx = 3,
93                 sticky = 'e' )
94
95              # button to open selected database
96              openDatabaseButton = self.createButton( databaseFrame,
97                 "Open Database", self.openDatabase, 1, 1 )
98
99              # button to close current database
100             closeDatabaseButton = self.createButton( databaseFrame,
101                "Close Database", self.closeDatabase, 1, 2 )
102             #------------------------------------------------------------#
103
104             #------------Build 'Table Information' Section----------#
105             tableFrame = self.createSection( self,
106                "Table Information", 2 )
107             tableFrame.grid( row = 1, column = 0, columnspan = 2,
108                sticky = 'nesw', pady = 5 )
109
110             # List of available tables
111             Label( tableFrame, text = "Available Tables:", relief =
112                'raised' ).grid( row = 1, column = 0, sticky = 'nesw' )
113             self.tableList = Pmw.ScrolledListBox( tableFrame,
114                selectioncommand = self.displayColumnInfo )
115             self.tableList.configure( listbox_height = 11 )
116             self.tableList.grid( row = 2, column = 0, sticky = 'nesw' )
117
118             # Information about selected table
119             Label( tableFrame, text = "Column Names:", relief =
120                'raised' ).grid( row = 1, column = 1, sticky = 'nesw' )
121             self.tableDisplay = Pmw.ScrolledText( tableFrame,
122                text_wrap = 'none' )
123             self.tableDisplay.configure( text_height = 13 )
124             self.tableDisplay.configure( text_width = 50 )
125             self.tableDisplay.grid( row = 2, column = 1,
126                sticky = 'nesw' )
127             #------------------------------------------------------------#
128
129             #-----------Build 'Query Statement' Section--------------#
130             queryFrame = self.createSection( self,
```

Fig. 27.27   GUI database interface (part 3 of 6).

```
131                "Query Statement:", 1 )
132            queryFrame.grid( row = 2, column = 0, sticky = 'nesw',
133                columnspan = 2 )
134
135            # Entry field for query statement
136            self.queryEntry = Pmw.EntryField( queryFrame,
137                command = self.executeQuery, entry_textvariable =
138                self.currentQuery )
139            self.queryEntry.grid( row = 1, column = 0, sticky = 'ew',
140                pady = 5 )
141
142            # Button to execute statement
143            queryExecuteButton = self.createButton( queryFrame,
144                "Execute Query", self.executeQuery, 2, 0 )
145            #-----------------------------------------------------------#
146
147        def openDatabase( self ):
148            """Open selected database."""
149
150            if self.connection:
151                tkMessageBox.showerror( "Database already open",
152                    "You must close the current database before "
153                    + "opening a new one." )
154                return
155
156            # open database
157            try:
158
159                # get path to specified database
160                databaseName = self.databaseComboBox.get()
161                databasePathname = os.path.join( self.gadflyPath,
162                    self.databaseDirectories[ databaseName ] )
163                self.connection = gadfly( databaseName,
164                    databasePathname )
165            except KeyError:
166                tkMessageBox.showerror( "Select Database",
167                    "You must first select a database to open." )
168                return
169            except:
170                tkMessageBox.showerror( "Database Error",
171                    "Error opening database." )
172                return
173
174            # get table info
175            cursor = self.connection.cursor()
176            cursor.execute( "select * from __table_names__" )
177            results = cursor.fetchall()
178
179            # display list of tables
180            for item in results:
181                self.tableList.insert( 0, item[ 1 ] )
182
183            cursor.close()
```

Fig. 27.27 GUI database interface (part 4 of 6).

```
184
185    def displayColumnInfo( self ):
186       """Display columns from selected table."""
187
188       if self.connection == None:
189          return
190
191       # get a record from this table
192       tableName = self.tableList.getcurselection()
193       cursor = self.connection.cursor()
194       cursor.execute( "select * from %s" % tableName )
195       results = cursor.description
196
197       # display column information
198       self.tableDisplay.clear()
199
200       for row in results:
201          self.tableDisplay.insert( END, row[ 0 ] + '\n' )
202
203       cursor.close()
204
205    def executeQuery( self ):
206       """Execute user-entered query statement."""
207
208       # user must open database to execute query
209       if self.connection == None:
210          tkMessageBox.showerror( "Open Database",
211             "You must first select and open a database." )
212          return
213
214       cursor = self.connection.cursor()
215
216       # execute query, raise exception on error
217       try:
218          queryString = self.currentQuery.get() # retrieve string
219          queryString = queryString.replace( '"', "'" )
220          cursor.execute( queryString )
221          results = cursor.pp()
222       except Exception, errorMessage:
223          results = "The SQL statement cannot be executed.\n" \
224             + "The full SQL error message is:\n\n%s" \
225             % errorMessage
226
227       # display results in new window
228       if self.queryDisplay:
229          self.queryDisplay.destroy()
230
231       self.queryDisplay = Pmw.TextDialog( title =
232          "Results for: %s" % queryString, defaultbutton = 0 )
233       self.queryDisplay.configure( text_height = 10 )
234       self.queryDisplay.configure( text_width = 50 )
235       self.queryDisplay.insert( END, results )
236       self.queryDisplay.configure( text_state = "disabled" )
```

Fig. 27.27   GUI database interface (part 5 of 6).

```
237          self.queryDisplay.activate( globalMode = 'nograb' )
238
239          cursor.close()
240
241      def closeDatabase( self ):
242          """Close current database."""
243
244          if self.connection == None:
245              return
246
247          # close connection and clear display fields
248          self.connection.close()
249          self.connection = None
250          self.databaseComboBox._entryfield.clear()
251          self.tableList.clear()
252          self.tableDisplay.clear()
253
254  if __name__ == "__main__":
255      DatabaseViewer().mainloop()
```

Fig. 27.27   GUI database interface (part 6 of 6).

Lines 16–19 initialize data members that contain the information needed to locate and connect to Gadfly databases. To open a database, the **gadfly** module needs to know the name of the database and its location. *Data member **gadflyPath*** (line 16) stores the location of the main Gadfly directory. To run this example on another computer, this value may need to be changed, to reflect the proper Gadfly location. Data member **database-Directories** (line 17) is a list of directories under the Gadfly path that contain Gadfly databases. Method **getDatabase** fills in values for this list. Data member **database-Names** (line 18) is a list of names of Gadfly databases located under the Gadfly directory. The values of this data member are also set in method **getDatabase**. Data member **connection** stores a Gadfly database object; this value is initialized to **None**.

Lines 20 and 21 declare GUI-related class data members. Data member **currentQuery** (line 20) contains a user-entered query string that will be executed against an open Gadfly database. This data member is bound to a **Tkinter** entry field in our display. Method **StringVar** creates an instance of a **Tkinter** string variable. Entry field values cannot be manipulated directly by a program, but must be accessed via an object (e.g., a **StringVar**). We will discuss how to access a **StringVar** value when we discuss method **executeQuery**.

Line 21 declares and initializes data member **queryDisplay**. This data member corresponds to a **Tkinter** dialog that displays the results of a user-entered query. The dialog "pops up" when the user clicks the **Execute Query** button, or if the user presses the *Return* key after entering a query. We discuss this data member in more detail when we discuss method **executeQuery**.

Line 24

```
os.path.walk( self.gadflyPath, self.getDatabase, 0 )
```

calls *function **walk*** of *module **os.path***. This method walks through the contents and subdirectories of the directory path specified by the first argument. The method specified by the second argument is called on each directory or subdirectory from the first argument. This method takes as parameters the list specified by the third argument. In this case, method **getDatabase** (that takes no parameters) is called on each directory or subdirectory in the **gadflyPath**. Method **getDatabase** creates a list of all database names in a particular directory and the location of those databases.

Lines 27–30 configure the parent of the **DatabaseViewer** frame. Line 27 sets the title of the master. Lines 28–30 configure **Tkinter** geometry manager values. Methods **columnconfigure** and **rowconfigure** specify the columns and rows that expand when the window is resized.

These method calls illustrate the use of *keyword arguments* in Python function calls. Keyword arguments are named parameters defined in a function or method header. When calling a function or method, values are passed to keyword arguments by assigning a value to the name of the parameter. For example, argument **weight** is the name of a keyword parameter for methods **columnconfigure** and **rowconfigure** whose value can be passed to the method with the syntax

```
weight = value
```

For more information on keyword arguments, see the standard Python tutorial at **www.python.org/doc**. Method **grid** calls the **Tkinter** grid manager for the master. Line 33 calls method **buildGUI** to construct and display the GUI components of our application.

Method **destroy** (lines 35–37) is called when the user exits the program and the application's GUI is destroyed. We first call method **closeDatabase** to close the connection to a potentially open database. We then call method **destroy** of the base class **Frame**.

Lines 39–49 define method **getDatabase**. This method compiles a list of all Gadfly database files and their locations in a specified directory. Line 40 contains the documentation string for this method. This string can be accessed via an object of class **DatabaseViewer**, with the line

```
databaseViewerObject.getDatabase.__doc__
```

that returns a string with the value

```
"Get names of all databases in specified directory."
```

Line 41 calls *function* **chdir** of module **os** to change to the directory specified by parameter **dirname**. All Gadfly database files end with the *file extension* **.gfd**. Line 44

```
databaseFiles = glob.glob( "*.gfd" )
```

calls *function* **glob** and passes the string **"*.gfd"** as a parameter. Function **glob** returns all files in the current directory that match the pattern specified by the parameter. We store this list in the local variable **databaseFiles**, so that this local variable now contains a list of all database files in the current directory.

Line 46 begins a **for** loop that iterates through each Gadfly database file in local variable **databaseFiles**. Line 47

```
databaseName = database[ :-4 ]
```

uses the *slice operator (:)* to retrieve all but the last four letters (i.e., the period and **gfd**) from the database filename and stores the remaining string in local variable **database-Name**. This local variable now contains the name of the database. Line 48 adds the **databaseName** to the list of databases stored in data member **databaseNames**. Line 49 adds an entry to data member **databaseDirectories** that corresponds to the location of this database.

The next three methods handle the creation and display of the application's GUI. Our GUI is subdivided into several "sections," composed of a **Tkinter Frame** with a **Label**. Method **createSection** constructs one of these sections. This method takes four parameters. The first parameter is the required **self** parameter. Parameter **parent** is the parent of the section to be created. Parameter **labelText** contains the value of the text to be displayed by the label. Parameter **numberOfColumns** specifies the number of columns in the section. The label created by this method will span all the columns in the section.

Lines 55 and 56 construct the section's frame, with the specified **parent**. The code

```
tuple( range( numberOfColumns ) )
```

in line 56 creates a tuple that contains values in the range *0 to numberOfColumns - 1*, inclusive. All the columns specified in this tuple will expand if the frame is resized.

Lines 60–65 create the label for this section. This label has a dark gray background with a dark blue foreground (i.e., text color). The *grid method* causes the label to span the number of columns specified by parameter **numberOfColumns**. Line 67 returns the **Frame** created by this method. Notice that we do not call the **grid** method for the **Frame** within this function. Instead, the grid method is called at a later time, on the object that the function returns.

Method **createButton** (lines 69–73) constructs a **Tkinter** button for our application. This method takes six parameters. Parameter **name** specifies the text to be displayed on the button. Parameter **action** specifies the command that is executed when the button is clicked. Parameters **gridRow** and **gridColumn** specify the row and column within the parent, where the button will be placed.

Method **buildGUI** is the largest method in this class. This method constructs and displays the GUI for our database-viewer application. Recall that the GUI is composed of three main subsections. These subsections are created in order, as indicated by the corresponding comments.

Lines 78–81 initialize the **DatabaseViewer** frame. Line 79 calls the Python Mega Widget method **initialise**, which must be called before using any **Pmw** components. Line 80 calls the **Tkinter** geometry manager method **grid**.

Lines 83–102 build the top subsection of the GUI. This section contains a *Pmw ComboBox* widget (lines 90–93). The drop-down portion of the combo box contains all the available Gadfly databases. *Initialization option scrolledlist_items* specifies this list. This subsection also contains the **Open Database** and **Close Database** buttons (lines 95–101) that call the **openDatabase** and **closeDatabase** methods, respectively.

Lines 104–127 build the middle subsection of our GUI. We create the list of available tables for the currently opened database in lines 110–116. We first create an appropriate label in lines 111 and 112. We then create a **Pmw ScrolledListBox** widget that contains the list of tables. The values in this list are set by method **openDatabase**, which is called when the user clicks the **Open Database** button. This widget is stored in data member **self.tableList** (created and initialized in this method), so that method **openDatabase** may access the widget, when necessary. The *initialization option* **selectioncommand** indicates that when the user selects a tables from the list, method **displayColumnInfo** executes. This method displays column information from the current table.

Line 115

```
self.tableList.configure( listbox_height = 11 )
```

uses the **Pmw configure** *method* to set the height of the listbox component of the **ScrolledListBox** to 11.

Lines 118–126 create the components necessary to display information about a specific table. Column information for a table is inserted in this widget by the **displayColumn-Info** method, when the user selects that table. Line 121 and 122 create and initialize class data member **tableDisplay**—a **Pmw ScrolledText** widget. In lines 123 and 124, we set the **height** and **width** attributes, respectively, of the widget's **textbox** component.

Lines 129–145 build the bottom section of the GUI. Lines 135–140 create the data member **queryEntry**—a **Pmw EntryField** widget. The user enters a query string in this widget that can be executed on the database that is currently opened. Selection option **command** (line 137) specifies that method **executeQuery** is called when the user presses the *Return* key while the widget has *focus*. A widget has focus if the user has selected that widget, causing all keyboard events to be sent to that widget. The initialization option **entry_textvariable** binds class data member **currentQuery** to the widget. This data member holds the value of the user-entered query string. We discuss access to this variable when we discuss method **executeQuery**.

Method **openDatabase** (lines 147–183) opens the database selected in the database drop-down list and displays table information from that database in a scrolled list box. Lines 150–154 check whether a database is currently open. If a database is not currently open, data member **connection** has value **None**. If a database is currently open, then the line

```
if self.connection
```

evaluates to **1** (true). In this case, we display a **tkMessageBox** error dialog that tells the user to close the current database before opening a new one.

Lines 156–168 attempt to open a selected database. Line 160 retrieves the item currently selected in data member **dataComboBox** by calling function **get**. If no item is currently selected, this function raises a **KeyError** exception. We catch this exception in lines 165–168, where we display an error dialog with an appropriate message and then exit the method.

Local variable **databasePathname** (line 161) uses *function **join*** of module **os.path** to create the full path to the selected Gadfly database. Lines 163 and 164 open a connection to the database, using the name of the database and its full location. If an exception is raised, we display an error dialog and exit the method (lines 169–172).

If no exceptions have been raised thus far—i.e., the user has selected a database, and the application has successfully connected to that database—we can now display information about the database. Line 176

```
cursor.execute( "select * fom __table_names__" )
```

demonstrates Gadfly's introspection capabilities (i.e., a Gadfly database's ability to provide data about itself). The *table* **__table_names__** contains a list of all the tables in the database. We store the list of these tables in local variable **results** (line 177). Lines 179–181 display the list of tables by **insert**ing each table name into the **tableList** *PMW ScrolledListBox* widget. As a good practice, we close the **cursor** object in line 203.

Method **executeQuery** (lines 205–239) is called when the user presses the *Enter* key in the application's **queryEntry** widget, or if the user clicks the **Execute Query** button. We first check that a database is currently open (lines 209–212). If no database is currently open, we display an error dialog and exit the method.

If a database is currently open, we create a **cursor** object for that database. Line 218 retrieves the value of the user-entered query string, stored in data member **queryString**. Recall that the constructor initialized this data member to a **StringVar** and that we bound the data member to the **queryEntry** widget. Method **get** enables us to retrieve the value of a **StringVar** data member bound to a widget.

Line 219 uses Python string method **replace** to replace all double quotes (**"**) in the query string with single quotes (**'**). Without this line, the query

```
select * from table where column = "columnName"
```

raises an error when we tried to execute it, because double quotes mark the end of a string. By replacing double quotes with single quotes, we avoid this problem.

Line 220 executes the query on the database. *Method* **pp** formats the results of the query into an easily readable string that we store in private data member **results**. If the query string contains an SQL syntax error, the program raises an exception. We catch this exception in line 222, along with the error message returned by the exception. We then store an appropriate string in local variable **results** that tells the user an error has occurred.

Next, we display the results of the query in a pop-up text dialog. Line 231 creates a *Pmw TextDialog* widget whose **title** contains the SQL query. We store this widget in data member **queryDisplay**. *Initialization option* **defaultbutton** specifies the button that will be pressed if the user presses the *Return* key; a value of 0 in this case indicates that the first button (the **OK** button) is the default button. Lines 233 and 234 set the height and width, respectively, of the widget's textbox component.

Line 235

```
self.queryDisplay.insert( END, results )
```

inserts the results (either database records or an error message) into the text dialog. Line 236

```
self.queryDisplay.configure( text_state = "disabled" )
```

disables text-editing in the text dialog. Line 237

```
self.queryDisplay.activate( globalMode = 'nograb' )
```

activates (shows) the dialog and configures it so the user can work in the main application window without closing the text dialog. If we did not include this line, the user would have to close the query results dialog, for example, before entering a new query string. Because the text dialog may already be visible when the user executes a query, we include lines 227–229. These lines **destroy** the text dialog, if it already exists, so we can then configure the dialog to display the new results. After we have displayed the results, we close the cursor in line 239, as a good programming practice.

Method **closeDatabase** closes the current database and cleans up the display. We first determine whether a database is currently open (line 244). If no database is currently open, we simply return from the method. If a database is open, we close the **connection** (line 248) and set the value of the data member to **None**. We then clear the database name from the **databaseComboBox** and clear the **tableList** and **tableDisplay** widgets (lines 250–252).

The remainder of the program takes advantage of the potential of each Python file to be used as a module. If a Python file is run on its own (e.g., by invoking Python on the file), then all data members in the file are placed in the *namespace* **__main__**. A module's name can be accessed using the variable **__name__**. Line 254

        if __name__ == "__main__":

determines if the current namespace is **__main__**. If this condition is true (i.e., the file is run as a script, rather than **import**ed by another file), line 255 creates a nameless **Database-Viewer** object and invokes its **mainloop** *function*, effectively running the application.

It also is possible that another program may **import DatabaseViewer** for use in another GUI application. If this is the case, line 254 will not be true, and the **mainloop** function will not be invoked. The **import**ing program is then free to manipulate objects of class **DatabaseViewer** as it chooses.

27.12 Operator Precedence Chart

This section contains the operator precedence chart for Python (Fig. 27.28). The operators are shown in decreasing order of precedence from top to bottom.

Operator	Type	Associativity
` `	string conversion	left to right
{ }	dictionary creation	left to right
[ ]	list creation	left to right
( )	tuple creation	left to right
[:]	slicing	left to right
[ ]	subscript access	left to right
.	member access	left to right
~	bitwise not	left to right
+ –	unary plus unary minus	right to left
**	exponentiation	left to right
* / %	multiplication division modulus (remainder)	left to right

Fig. 27.28 Python operator precedence chart (part 1 of 2).

Operator	Type	Associativity
+ -	addition subtraction	left to right
<< >>	left shift right shift	left to right
&	bitwise AND	left to right
^	bitwise XOR	left to right
|	bitwise OR	left to right
< <= > >= <>, != ==	less than less than or equal greater than greater than or equal not equal equal	right to left
is, **is not**	identity	left to right
in, **not in**	membership tests	left to right
not	boolean NOT	left to right
and	boolean AND	left to right
or	boolean OR	left to right
lambda	lambda expressions (anonymous functions)	left to right

Fig. 27.28 Python operator precedence chart (part 2 of 2).

27.13 Internet and World Wide Web Resources

www.python.org
This is the Python home page. From this site, you can download the latest version of Python for all platforms. The site also posts all the Python documentation and provides links to other resources, such as additional modules, tutorials, search engines and special-interest groups.

starship.python.net
This Web site provides resources for Python developers. Members of Python Software Activity (PSA) post Python modules and utilities on this site.

www.python.org/download/download_mac.html
This site provides information on and links to a MacOS version of Python.   www.python.org/sigs
A list of Special Interest Groups (SIGs—for topics such as databases, creating a Python compiler, XML processing and Python in education—is available at this site).

www.vex.net/parnassus
This site contains many third-party Python modules which are freely available for download.

www.biopython.org
This is the home page for an association that provides resources for Python developers working in the field of molecular biology. Developers can download the BioPython software package and collaborate with other developers to complete projects.

starship.python.net/crew/mhammond
Mark Hammond, a leading Python/Windows developer maintains the home page for Python for Windows Extensions.

www.pythonware.com
Secret Labs AB is a company that offers application development tools for Python. The Pythonware Web site provides links to Secret Labs AB products and other Python resources.

grail.sourceforge.net
Grail is an extensible Web browser written in Python. Information and source code for Grail can be found at this site.

www.corrt.com/info/pyisp-list.html
This site posts a list of Internet Service Providers (ISPs) that provide Python support.

www.python.org/doc/FAQ.html
Python.org maintains the official list of Frequently Asked Questions about Python at this site.

ftp://ftp.python.org/pub/python/binaries-1.4/pythonwin/html/ Windows_Faq.htp
A small FAQ file on Python; Windows topics can be found at this site.

starship.python.net/crew/davem/cgifaq
This site posts a Python/CGI FAQ.

www.devshed.com/Server_Side/Python/CGI
This site posts an article/tutorial on writing CGI programs in Python.

www.webtechniques.com/archives/1998/02/kuchling
This site contains an article that discusses creating a CGI framework in Python.

www.linuxgazette.com/issue19/python.html
This site contains an article that discusses generating HTML pages in Python.

starship.python.net/crew/jrush/Webbot
This site contains a demonstration of a Webbot written in Python.

starship.python.net/crew/aaron_watters/pws.html
This site provides instructions for configuring IIS/PWS for Python / CGI scripts.

members.nbci.com/alan_gauld/tutor/tutindex.htm
This site contains a Python tutorial geared towards novice programmers. The tutorial's goal is to teach programming fundamentals using Python.

www.python.org/doc/howto/regex/regex.html
This site contains a tutorial on using Python regular expressions.

www.python.org/topics/xml
This is the **python.org** starting point for Python/XML development.

www.digicool.com
This is the home page for Digital Creations, the developers of Zope—a Web application server written in Python.

www.devshed.com/Server_Side/Zope/Intro
This article presents an introduction to Zope, a Web application server written in Python.

www.python.org/windows/win32com
This site contains resources for Python/COM development.

www.pythonware.com/library/tkinter/tkclass/index.htm
This site contains an introduction to **Tkinter**, a Python GUI development library.

www.python.org/topics/tkinter/doc.html
This site contains links to **Tkinter** documentation.

www.chordate.com/gadfly.html
This is the home page for Gadfly, a relational database written in Python.

www.python.org/windows/OdbcHints.html
This site contains a few notes on using Python and ODBC.

www.python.org/windows/win32/odbc.html
An introduction to Python's **odbc** module can be found at this site.

starship.python.net/crew/bwilk/access.html
This site contains a few notes on using Python and Microsoft Access.

www.python.org/doc/essays/comparisons.html
Guido van Rossum has posted an essay on this page that compares Python with other popular languages, like Java, C++ and Perl.

www.vic.auug.org.au/auugvic/av_paper_python.html
This article contains an overview of Python and lists many uses and features of the language.

www.networkcomputing.com/unixworld/tutorial/005/005.html
This site contains an introduction to Python, as well as a tutorial.

SUMMARY

- Python is an interpreted, cross-platform, object-oriented language. It is a freely distributed, open-source technology.

- Using Python's core modules and those freely available on the Web, programmers can develop applications that accomplish a great variety of tasks.

- Python's interpreted nature facilitates Rapid Application Development (RAD).

- Comments in Python begin with the **#** character; Python ignores all text in the current line after this character.

- Python statements can be executed in one of two ways. The statements can be typed into a file and then invoking Python on that file. Python statements can also be interpreted dynamically by typing them in at the Python interactive prompt.

- Python keywords words have special meaning in Python and cannot be used as variable names, function names and other objects. A list of Python keywords can also be obtained from the **keyword** module.

- The keyword **def** marks the beginning of the function definition. The function's parameter list is followed by a colon (**:**).

- Python is a case-sensitive language.

- Python determines the beginning and end of a statement based on whitespace. Each new line begins a new statement, and groups of statements that belong to the same block of code are indented by the same amount.

- Keyword **return** causes the program to exit and to return the specified value.

- Python function **raw_input** retrieves input from the program user. This function may optionally take a string argument that is a prompt to the user.

- The Python **int** function converts non-integer data types to integers.

- The backslash character (****) is the line-continuation character.

- The "**\n**" escape code is a special Python character that prints a newline to the screen.
- Tuples are created as a comma-separated list of values in parentheses (**( )**). A tuple can contain any data type (e.g., strings, integers, other tuples, etc.) and may contain elements of different types.
- Tuples are immutable—after a tuple is created, an element at a defined index cannot be modified.
- The **+=** operator adds an element to the end of a tuple.
- By default, the **print** statement writes a newline character (e.g., a carriage return) at the end of its output; however, a comma placed at the end of a **print** statement tells Python to leave out the newline.
- Python lists consist of a sequence of zero or more elements inside brackets (**[ ]**)
- Python lists are mutable—an element at an index that has been defined may be altered.
- Method **append** adds an element to the end of a list.
- Each entry in a dictionary has two parts: the key and the value, and a dictionary consists of a set of zero or more comma-separated key-value pairs inside braces (**{ }**).
- A value in a dictionary is accessed using that value's key. The key must be unique and of an immutable data type (e.g., number, string or tuple that contains only immutable data types); values may be any data type.
- A regular expression string defines a pattern against which text data can be compared. Regular expression processing capability is available in the standard Python module **re**.
- Unless otherwise specified, a regular-expression character matches as many occurrences of a regular expression as possible.
- Compiling a regular expression string (using **re** method **compile**) speeds up a regular expression comparison that uses that string.
- Strings can be contained in single quotes (**' '**), double quotes (**" "**), or a set of three single or double quotes (**''' '''** or **""" """**)
- The **%** format character acts like a place holder in the string. Python defines several format characters for use in string formatting
- Importing a module enables programmers to use functions defined by that module.
- The **r** before a string indicates that the string is a raw string. Python handles backslash characters in raw strings differently than "normal" strings.
- **re** module's **findall** method returns a list of all substrings in a particular string that match a specified regular expression.
- Exception handling enables programs and programmers to identify an error when the error occurs and to take appropriate action. Python accomplishes exception handling through the use of **try/except** blocks.
- Any code contained in a **try** block that causes an error raises an exception. The **except** block then catches the exception (i.e., handles the error).
- An **except** block can specify a particular exception to catch.
- A **try** block may optionally specify a corresponding **else** block. If the code in the **try** block does not raise an exception, then the program executes the code in the **else** block. If an exception is raised in the **try** block, then the **else** block is skipped.
- The pound-bang (**#!**) directive—the directive that specifies the location of the Python executable— must be the first line in a CGI script.

- Browsers use HTTP headers to determine how to handle the incoming data, and a valid header must be sent to ensure that the browser displays the information correctly.

- HTML **FORM**s allow users to enter data to be sent to a Web server for processing. Once the server receives the form, a server program processes the data.

- The **cgi** module provides functionality for writing CGI scripts in Python, including access to HTML form values.

- **cgi** method **FieldStorage** provides access to HTML form values.

- When a client visits a Web site, the server for that Web site may write a cookie to the client's machine. This cookie can be accessed by servers within the Web site's domain at a later time.

- The **Cookie** module provides access to cookies.

- An object of class **Cookie** acts like a dictionary, so values can be set and retrieved using familiar dictionary syntax.

- The **time** function of module **time** returns a floating-point value that is the number of seconds since the "epoch" (i.e., the first day of 1970).

- An object of class **Cookie** acts like a dictionary, so values can be set and retrieved using familiar dictionary syntax.

- Cookies are stored in the environment variable **HTTP_COOKIE**.

- The **load** method of module **Cookie** extracts cookie values from a string. If no cookie value exists, then the program raises the **KeyError** exception.

- The Python Database Special Interest Group (SIG) was formed to develop a specification for Python database application-programming interface (DB-API).

- The keyword class begins a Python class definition. All methods and data are placed within this **class** block.

- Method **__init__** is a special method defined by Python; the method is called when an object of a particular class is created.

- Methods of a Python class need an object with which to reference data and methods of that class. This object is passed in as the first parameter of every Python method. By convention, this parameter is named **self**.

- Data members may be assigned a value anywhere within the **class** block. Once the data member has been assigned a value, it may be accessed by any method, via the **self** parameter.

- Special Python method **__str__** is called whenever a **print** statement is executed on the class. This method returns a string that represents the class in some logical manner.

- Parentheses after a **class** definition line indicate inheritance, and the parent class name is placed inside the parentheses.

- Gadfly is a freely-available open-source database that supports a significant subset of the Structured Query Language (SQL). The Python interface to Gadfly follows the Python Database interface specification.

- Python uses module **Tkinter** to talk to the Tcl/Tk GUI package in a logical manner. Each Tk widget is a Python object and widget options can be accessed by calling the appropriate methods.

- Python Mega Widgets (PMW) are widgets that combine several common Tk widgets into a single useful "mega-widget."

- Entry field values cannot be directly accessed by a program, but must be accessed via an object (e.g., a **StringVar**).

- Class method **destroy** is called when the user exits the program and the application's GUI is destroyed.
- Class documentation strings provide descriptions of a class.
- If a Python file is run on its own (e.g., by invoking Python on the file), then all data members in the file are placed in the namespace **__main__**. A module's name can be accessed via the variable **__name__**.

TERMINOLOGY

' (single quote) character
" (double quote) character
""" (triple quote) characters
comment character
#! (pound-bang) directive
% formatting character
% modulo operator
% operator
%= operator
(DB-API)
**= operator
*= operator
, (comma) character
. (dot) operator
. operator
/= operator
: (colon) character
: (slice) operator
[] operator
\ (backslash) character
\n escape character
__doc__
__init__ method
__main__
__name__
__str__ method
__table_names__
{} characters
"chained" expressions
"no-op" instruction
+ operator
+= operator
-= operator
and
Apache Web server
append method
catch an exception
cgi module
CGI scripts
chdir function of module os
class

columnconfigure method
compiling a regular expression
concatenated strings
configure method
connection object
constructor
Cookie class
Cookie module
Ctrl-Z/Ctrl-D character
cursor object
Database Application Programming Interface
Database Special Interest Group (SIG)
debugging
def
destroy method
dictionary
documentation string
else
EntryField widget
environ data member of module os
epoch
escape character
exception handling
expiration value of a cookie
fetchall method of class cursor
FieldStorage class
findall method of module re
float function
focus
for
formatting character
Frame class
Gadfly
gadfly module
get method
glob module
graphical user interface (GUI)
greatest common divisor
grid method
HTML FORM
HTTP header

`HTTP_COOKIE` environment variable

`if`

`if/elif`

`if/else`

immutable data type

`import`

importing a module

indentation of statements

inheritance

`int` function

interactive mode

`join` function of module `os.path`

key/value pair

`KeyError` exception

`keys`

`keyword` module

`lib` directory of Python path

list

`load` method of class `Cookie`

`localtime` function of module `time`

`mainloop`

`match` method

`MatchObject`

`min` function

module

mutable data type

`MySQLdb` module

newline

`None`

object-based programming

Object-Oriented Programming (OOP)

`odbc` module

open-source technology

`os` module

out-of-range element

packing a tuple

`pass`

`Pmw` module

pound-pang directive

`pp` method

`print` statement

Python Mega Widgets

Python prompt

Python Search Path

query

raise an exception

`range`

rapid-application development (RAD)

raw string

`raw_input`

`re` module

`RegexObject`

regular expressions

`replace` method

`return`

`rowconfigure` method

`ScrolledListBox` widget

`ScrolledTest` widget

`self` parameter

`strftime` function of module `time`

string formatting

string manipulation

string processing

`StringVar` class

Structured Query Language (SQL)

Tcl/Tk

`time` function

`time` module

`time` tokens

`Tkinter` module

`tkMessageBox` module

triple-quoted string

`try/except`

`try/except/else`

tuple

unpacking a tuple

van Rossum, Guido

`walk` function of module `os.path`

`while`

Widget class

`win32all` extensions

writing a cookie

`ZeroDivisionError` exception

SELF-REVIEW EXERCISES

27.1 Fill in the blanks in each of the following statements:

a) Comments in Python begin with the _____ character.

b) Python statements can be executed in one of two ways. The statements can be typed into a file and then _____ or statements can be _____.

c) The keyword _____ marks the beginning of a Python function definition.

d) Function `raw_input` returns a _____.

e) Python defines three data types for storing complex data: _____, _____ and _____. Programmers can also define a _____ that can hold data and define methods for manipulating that data.

f) Tuples are _____ (element values at defined indices may not be changed); whereas lists are _____ (element values at defined indices may be changed).

g) Python accomplishes _____ through the use of **try/except** blocks.

h) Python classes may define the special method _____, which acts as that class's constructor.

i) By convention, the method argument that refers to an object of the class itself is called _____.

j) Python uses module _____ to talk to Tcl/Tk in a logical manner.

27.2 State whether each of the following is *true* or *false*. If *false*, explain why.

a) Python is an interpreted language.

b) To exit Python, type **exit** at the Python prompt.

c) Forgetting to indent after a colon is a style error.

d) The underscore character (_) marks the continuation of a Python statement onto the next line.

e) Elements must be added to a list by calling list method **append**.

f) A tuple is a valid data type for use as a dictionary key.

g) The pound-bang (**#!**) directive—which tells a server where to find the Python executable—must be the first line in a CGI script.

h) An object of class **Cookie** acts like a dictionary, so values can be set and retrieved using familiar dictionary syntax.

i) Each method of a Python class must take at least one parameter that refers to an object of the class itself.

j) Gadfly is a relational database written completely in Python.

27.3 How can a Python CGI script determine a client's IP address?

27.4 For each of the following code examples, identify and correct the error(s):

a) ```print hello```

b) ```
aTuple = (1, 2)
aTuple[0] = 2
```

c) ```
if 0  <   3
    print "0 is less than 3."
```

d) ```
for counter in range(10):
    print counter
```

**27.5** Write a one- to three-line block of code for each of the following tasks:

a) Create a string with 50 exclamation points (**!**) using the **\*** operator.

b) Print out even numbers from 0 to 100.

c) Convert a user-entered number from a string to an integer.

d) Determine if a user-entered integer is odd.

e) Add a one-element item to the end of an empty tuple.

## ANSWERS TO SELF-REVIEW EXERCISES

**27.1**    a) pound (**#**).  b) Python is invoked on the file, dynamically interpreted in an interactive session.  c) **def**.  d) string.  e) tuples, lists, dictionaries, class.  f) immutable, mutable.  g) exception handling.  h)__**init**__.  i) **self**.  j) **Tkinter**.
```

27.2   a) True. b) False. Type *Crtl-Z* in Microsoft Windows or *Ctrl-D* in Linux/UNIX. c) False. Forgetting to indent after a colon is a syntax error. d) False. The backslash character (****) marks the continuation of a Python statement onto the next line. e) False. Lists can also be augmented by calling the **extend** method or the **+=** operator, for example. f) True. g) True. h) True. i) True. j) True.

27.3   A client's IP address is contained in the **REMOTE_ADDR** environment variable of the **os** module.

27.4   a) Logical or syntax error. If the desired result is to output the word "hello," the proper code is **print "hello"** The code in the problem will print the value of variable **hello**, if a variable by that name exists; the code raises an error if the variable does not exist. b) Syntax error. Tuple values cannot be modified in this way. c) Syntax error. A colon (**:**) must follow the **if** statement. d) Syntax error. The line after the **for** statement must be indented.

27.5   a) `theString = '!' * 50`

b)
```
for item in range( 101 ):
    if item % 2 == 0:
        print item
```

c)
```
number = raw_input( "Enter a number" )
integer = int( number )
```

d)
```
number = int( raw_input( "Enter an integer" ) )
if number % 2 == 1:
    print "The number is odd."
```

e)
```
emptyTuple = ( )
emptyTuple += ( 1, )
```

EXERCISES

27.6   Describe how input from an HTML **FORM** is retrieved in a Python program.

27.7   Figure 27.5 defines function **greatestCommonDivisor** that computes the greatest common divisor of two positive integers. Euclid's algorithm is another method of computing the greatest common divisor. The following steps define Euclid's algorithm for computing the greatest common divisor of two positive integers **x** and **y**:

1. *while y > 0*
    a) *z = y*
    b) *y = x modulo z*
    c) *x = z*
2. *return x*

Write a function **Euclid** that takes two positive integers and computes their greatest common divisor using Euclid's algorithm.

27.8   Modify functions **greatestCommonDivisor** and **Euclid** from Exercise 27.7, so that each function counts the number of modular divisions performed (i.e., the number of times the function uses the **%** operator). Each function should return a tuple that contains the calculated greatest common divisor and the number of modular divisions performed. Run each function on the pairs of integers in Fig. 27.28, and fill in the rest of the table. Which function takes fewer modular divisions, on average?

27.9   Write a Python program named **states.py** that declares a variable **states** with value **"Mississippi Alabama Texas Massachusetts Kansas"**. Using only the techniques discussed in this chapter, write a program that does the following:

Integer pairs	Number of modular divisions for `greatestCommonDivisor`	Number of modular divisions for Euclid
1, 101	_____	_____
3, 30	_____	_____
45, 1000	_____	_____
13, 91	_____	_____
100, 1000	_____	_____
2,2	_____	_____
777,77	_____	_____
73,12	_____	_____
26,4	_____	_____
99,27	_____	_____
Average:	_____	_____

Fig. 27.29 Comparing functions `greatestCommonDivisor` and `Euclid`.

a) Search for a word in variable **states** that ends in **xas**. Store this word in element 0 of an array named **statesList**.

b) Search for a word in **states** that begins with **k** and ends in **s**. Perform a case-insensitive comparison. [*Note:* passing **re.I** as a second parameter to method compile performs a case-insensitive comparison.] Store this word in element 1 of **statesList**.

c) Search for a word in **states** that begins with **M** and ends in **s**. Store this word in element 2 of the array.

d) Search for a word in **states** that ends in **a**. Store this word in element 3 of the array.

e) Search for a word in **states** at the beginning of the string that begins with **M**. Store this word at element 4 of the array.

f) Output the array **statesList** to the screen.

27.10 In Section 27.6, we discussed CGI environment variables. Write a CGI script that displays a user's IP address in the user's browser.

27.11 Write a CGI script that logs a user into a Web site. The user should be presented with a Web page that contains a form into which users enter their login name and password. The form sends the the user-entered information to a Python script. This script checks a database for the user's login name and validates their password. If the login name and password are valid, the Python script writes a **"Login successful"** message to the browser; if the login name and/or password are invalid, the Python script writes a **"Login unsuccessful"** message to the browser.

HTML Special Characters

The table of A.1 shows many commonly used HTML special characters—called *character entity references* by the World Wide Web Consortium. For a complete list of character entity references, see the site

`http://www.w3.org/TR/REC-html40/sgml/entities.html`

Character	HTML encoding	Character	HTML encoding
non-breaking space	` `	ê	`&#234;`
§	`&#167;`	ì	`&#236;`
©	`&#169;`	í	`&#237;`
®	`&#174;`	î	`&#238;`
π	`&#188;`	ñ	`&#241;`
∫	`&#189;`	ò	`&#242;`
Ω	`&#190;`	ó	`&#243;`
à	`&#224;`	ô	`&#244;`
á	`&#225;`	õ	`&#245;`
â	`&#226;`	÷	`&#247;`
ã	`&#227;`	ù	`&#249;`
å	`&#229;`	ú	`&#250;`
ç	`&#231;`	û	`&#251;`
è	`&#232;`	•	`&#8226;`
é	`&#233;`	™	`&#8482;`

Fig. A.1 HTML special characters.

HTML Colors

Colors may be specified by using a standard name (such as **aqua**) or a hexadecimal RGB value (such as **#00FFFF** for aqua). Of the six hexadecimal digits in an RGB value, the first two represent the amount of red in the color, the middle two represent the amount of green in the color, and the last two represent the amount of blue in the color. For example, **black** is the absence of color and is defined by **#000000**, whereas **white** is the maximum amount of red, green and blue and is defined by **#FFFFFF**. Pure **red** is **#FF0000**, pure green (which the standard calls **lime**) is **#00FF00** and pure **blue** is **#00FFFF**. Note that **green** in the standard is defined as **#008000**. Figure B.1 contains the HTML standard color set. Figure B.2 contains the HTML extended color set.

Color name	Value	Color name	Value
aqua	#00FFFF	navy	#000080
black	#000000	olive	#808000
blue	#0000FF	purple	#800080
fuchsia	#FF00FF	red	#FF0000
gray	#808080	silver	#C0C0C0
green	#008000	teal	#008080
lime	#00FF00	yellow	#FFFF00
maroon	#800000	white	#FFFFFF

Fig. B.1   HTML standard colors and hexadecimal RGB values.

Color name	Value	Color name	Value
aliceblue	#F0F8FF	dodgerblue	#1E90FF
antiquewhite	#FAEBD7	firebrick	#B22222
aquamarine	#7FFFD4	floralwhite	#FFFAF0
azure	#F0FFFF	forestgreen	#228B22
beige	#F5F5DC	gainsboro	#DCDCDC
bisque	#FFE4C4	ghostwhite	#F8F8FF
blanchedalmond	#FFEBCD	gold	#FFD700
blueviolet	#8A2BE2	goldenrod	#DAA520
brown	#A52A2A	greenyellow	#ADFF2F
burlywood	#DEB887	honeydew	#F0FFF0
cadetblue	#5F9EA0	hotpink	#FF69B4
chartreuse	#7FFF00	indianred	#CD5C5C
chocolate	#D2691E	indigo	#4B0082
coral	#FF7F50	ivory	#FFFFF0
cornflowerblue	#6495ED	khaki	#F0E68C
cornsilk	#FFF8DC	lavender	#E6E6FA
crimson	#DC1436	lavenderblush	#FFF0F5
cyan	#00FFFF	lawngreen	#7CFC00
darkblue	#00008B	lemonchiffon	#FFFACD
darkcyan	#008B8B	lightblue	#ADD8E6
darkgoldenrod	#B8860B	lightcoral	#F08080
darkgray	#A9A9A9	lightcyan	#E0FFFF
darkgreen	#006400	lightgoldenrodyellow	#FAFAD2
darkkhaki	#BDB76B	lightgreen	#90EE90
darkmagenta	#8B008B	lightgrey	#D3D3D3
darkolivegreen	#556B2F	lightpink	#FFB6C1
darkorange	#FF8C00	lightsalmon	#FFA07A
darkorchid	#9932CC	lightseagreen	#20B2AA
darkred	#8B0000	lightskyblue	#87CEFA
darksalmon	#E9967A	lightslategray	#778899
darkseagreen	#8FBC8F	lightsteelblue	#B0C4DE
darkslateblue	#483D8B	lightyellow	#FFFFE0
darkslategray	#2F4F4F	limegreen	#32CD32
darkturquoise	#00CED1	linen	#FAF0E6
darkviolet	#9400D3	magenta	#FF00FF

Fig. B.2   HTML extended colors and hexadecimal RGB values (part 1 of 2).

Color name	Value	Color name	Value
deeppink	#FF1493	mediumaquamarine	#66CDAA
deepskyblue	#00BFFF	mediumblue	#0000CD
dimgray	#696969	mediumorchid	#BA55D3
mediumpurple	#9370DB	plum	#DDA0DD
mediumseagreen	#3CB371	powderblue	#B0E0E6
mediumslateblue	#7B68EE	rosybrown	#BC8F8F
mediumspringgreen	#00FA9A	royalblue	#4169E1
mediumturquoise	#48D1CC	saddlebrown	#8B4513
mediumvioletred	#C71585	salmon	#FA8072
midnightblue	#191970	sandybrown	#F4A460
mintcream	#F5FFFA	seagreen	#2E8B57
mistyrose	#FFE4E1	seashell	#FFF5EE
moccasin	#FFE4B5	sienna	#A0522D
navajowhite	#FFDEAD	skyblue	#87CEEB
oldlace	#FDF5E6	slateblue	#6A5ACD
olivedrab	#6B8E23	slategray	#708090
orange	#FFA500	snow	#FFFAFA
orangered	#FF4500	springgreen	#00FF7F
orchid	#DA70D6	steelblue	#4682B4
palegoldenrod	#EEE8AA	tan	#D2B48C
palegreen	#98FB98	thistle	#D8BFD8
paleturquoise	#AFEEEE	tomato	#FF6347
palevioletred	#DB7093	turquoise	#40E0D0
papayawhip	#FFEFD5	violet	#EE82EE
peachpuff	#FFDAB9	wheat	#F5DEB3
peru	#CD853F	whitesmoke	#F5F5F5
pink	#FFC0CB	yellowgreen	#9ACD32

Fig. B.2   HTML extended colors and hexadecimal RGB values (part 2 of 2).

ASCII Character Set

	0	1	2	3	4	5	6	7	8	9
ASCII character set										

	0	1	2	3	4	5	6	7	8	9
0	nul	soh	stx	etx	eot	enq	ack	bel	bs	ht
1	nl	vt	ff	cr	so	si	dle	dc1	dc2	dc3
2	dc4	nak	syn	etb	can	em	sub	esc	fs	gs
3	rs	us	sp	!	"	#	$	%	&	`
4	(	)	*	+	,	-	.	/	0	1
5	2	3	4	5	6	7	8	9	:	;
6	<	=	>	?	@	A	B	C	D	E
7	F	G	H	I	J	K	L	M	N	O
8	P	Q	R	S	T	U	V	W	X	Y
9	Z	[	\	]	^	_	'	a	b	c
10	d	e	f	g	h	i	j	k	l	m
11	n	o	p	q	r	s	t	u	v	w
12	x	y	z	{	|	}	~	del		

Fig. C.1   ASCII Character Set.

The digits at the left of the table are the left digits of the decimal equivalent (0-127) of the character code, and the digits at the top of the table are the right digits of the character code. For example, the character code for "**F**" is 70, and the character code for "**&**" is 38. *Note:* Most users of this book are interested in the ASCII character set used to represent English characters on many computers. The ASCII character set is a subset of the Unicode character set used by Java to represent characters from most of the world's languages. For more information on the Unicode character set, visit the World Wide Web site **http://unicode.org/**.

Operator Precedence Chart

This appendix contains the operator precedence chart for Perl (Fig. D.1) . The operators are shown in decreasing order of precedence from top to bottom.

Operator	Type	Associativity
terms and list operators	**print @array** or **sort (4, 2, 7)**	left to right
->	member access	left to right
++ --	increment decrement	none
**	exponentiation	right to left
! ~ \ + -	logical NOT bitwise one's complement reference unary plus unary minus	right to left
=~ !~	matching negated match	left to right
* / % x	multiplication division modulus repetition	left to right
+ - .	addition subtraction string concatenation	left to right

Fig. D.1   Perl operator precedence chart (part 1 of 3).

Operator	Type	Associativity
`<<` `>>`	left shift right shift	left to right
named unary operators	unary operators, e.g. `-e` (filetest)	none

`<`
`>`
`<=`
`>=`
`lt`
`gt`
`le`
`ge`
	numerical less than
	numerical greater than
	numerical less than or equal
	numerical greater than or equal
	string less than
	string greater than
	string less than or equal
	string greater than or equal
		none

`==`
`!=`
`<=>`
`eq`
`ne`
`cmp`
	numerical equality
	numerical inequality
	numerical comparison (returns -1, 0 or 1)
	string equality
	string inequality
	string comparison (returns -1, 0 or 1)
		none

`&`	bitwise AND	left to right
`|` `^`	bitwise inclusive OR bitwise exclusive OR	left to right
`&&`	logical AND	left to right
`||`	logical OR	left to right
`..`	range operator	none
`?:`	conditional operator	right to left

`=`
`+=`
`-=`
`*=`
`/=`
`%=`
`**=`
`.=`
`x=`
`&=`
`|=`
`^=`
`<<=`
`>>=`
`&&=`
`||=`
	assignment
	addition assignment
	subtraction assignment
	multiplication assignment
	division assignment
	modulus assignment
	exponentiation assignment
	string concatenation assignment
	repetition assignment
	bitwise AND assignment
	bitwise inclusive OR assignment
	bitwise exclusive OR assignment
	left shift assignment
	right shift assignment
	logical AND assignment
	logical OR assignment
		right to left

Fig. D.1   Perl operator precedence chart (part 2 of 3).

Operator	Type	Associativity
`,` `=>`	expression separator; returns value of last expression expression separator; groups two expressions	left to right
`not`	logical NOT	right to left
`and`	logical AND	left to right
`or` `xor`	logical OR logical exclusive OR	left to right

Fig. D.1   Perl operator precedence chart (part 3 of 3).

Number Systems

Objectives

- To understand basic number systems concepts such as base, positional value, and symbol value.
- To understand how to work with numbers represented in the binary, octal, and hexadecimal number systems
- To be able to abbreviate binary numbers as octal numbers or hexadecimal numbers.
- To be able to convert octal numbers and hexadecimal numbers to binary numbers.
- To be able to covert back and forth between decimal numbers and their binary, octal, and hexadecimal equivalents.
- To understand binary arithmetic, and how negative binary numbers are represented using two's complement notation.

Here are only numbers ratified.
William Shakespeare

Nature has some sort of arithmetic-geometrical coordinate system, because nature has all kinds of models. What we experience of nature is in models, and all of nature's models are so beautiful.
It struck me that nature's system must be a real beauty, because in chemistry we find that the associations are always in beautiful whole numbers—there are no fractions.
Richard Buckminster Fuller

Outline

E.1 Introduction

In this appendix, we introduce the key number systems that programmers use, especially when they are working on software projects that require close interaction with "machine-level" hardware. Projects like this include operating systems, computer networking software, compilers, database systems, and applications requiring high performance.

When we write an integer such as 227 or -63 in a program, the number is assumed to be in the *decimal (base 10) number system.* The *digits* in the decimal number system are 0, 1, 2, 3, 4, 5, 6, 7, 8 and 9. The lowest digit is 0 and the highest digit is 9—one less than the *base* of 10. Internally, computers use the *binary (base 2) number system.* The binary number system has only two digits, namely 0 and 1. Its lowest digit is 0 and its highest digit is 1—one less than the base of 2. Figure E.1 summarizes the digits used in the binary, octal, decimal and hexadecimal number systems.

As we will see, binary numbers tend to be much longer than their decimal equivalents. Programmers who work in assembly languages and in high-level languages that enable programmers to reach down to the "machine level," find it cumbersome to work with binary numbers. So two other number systems the *octal number system (base 8)* and the *hexadecimal number system (base 16)*—are popular primarily because they make it convenient to abbreviate binary numbers.

In the octal number system, the digits range from 0 to 7. Because both the binary number system and the octal number system have fewer digits than the decimal number system, their digits are the same as the corresponding digits in decimal.

The hexadecimal number system poses a problem because it requires sixteen digits—a lowest digit of 0 and a highest digit with a value equivalent to decimal 15 (one less than the base of 16). By convention, we use the letters A through F to represent the hexadecimal digits corresponding to decimal values 10 through 15. Thus in hexadecimal we can have numbers like 876 consisting solely of decimal-like digits, numbers like 8A55F consisting of digits and letters, and numbers like FFE consisting solely of letters. Occasionally, a hexadecimal number spells a common word such as FACE or FEED—this can appear strange to programmers accustomed to working with numbers. Figure E.2 summarizes each of the number systems.

Each of these number systems uses *positional notation*—each position in which a digit is written has a different *positional value.* For example, in the decimal number 937 (the 9, the 3, and the 7 are referred to as *symbol values*), we say that the 7 is written in the *ones position*, the 3 is written in the *tens position*, and the 9 is written in the *hundreds position.* Notice that each of these positions is a power of the base (base 10), and that these powers begin at 0 and increase by 1 as we move left in the number (Fig. E.3).

Binary digit	Octal digit	Decimal digit	Hexadecimal digit
0	0	0	0
1	1	1	1
	2	2	2
	3	3	3
	4	4	4
	5	5	5
	6	6	6
	7	7	7
		8	8
		9	9
			A (decimal value of 10)
			B (decimal value of 11)
			C (decimal value of 12)
			D (decimal value of 13)
			E (decimal value of 14)
			F (decimal value of 15)

Fig. E.1 Digits of the binary, octal, decimal and hexadecimal number systems.

Attribute	Binary	Octal	Decimal	Hexadecimal
Base	2	8	10	16
Lowest digit	0	0	0	0
Highest digit	1	7	9	**F**

Fig. E.2   Comparison of the binary, octal, decimal and hexadecimal number systems.

Positional values in the decimal number system			
Decimal digit	9	3	7
Position name	Hundreds	Tens	Ones
Positional value	100	10	1
Positional value as a power of the base (10)	10^2	10^1	10^0

Fig. E.3   Positional values in the decimal number system.

For longer decimal numbers, the next positions to the left would be the *thousands position* (10 to the 3rd power), the *ten-thousands position* (10 to the 4th power), the *hundred-thousands position* (10 to the 5th power), the *millions position* (10 to the 6th power), the *ten-millions position* (10 to the 7th power), and so on.

In the binary number 101, we say that the rightmost 1 is written in the *ones position*, the 0 is written in the *twos position*, and the leftmost 1 is written in the *fours position*. Notice that each of these positions is a power of the base (base 2), and that these powers begin at 0 and increase by 1 as we move left in the number (Fig. E.4).

For longer binary numbers, the next positions to the left would be the *eights position* (2 to the 3rd power), the *sixteens position* (2 to the 4th power), the *thirty-twos position* (2 to the 5th power), the *sixty-fours position* (2 to the 6th power), and so on.

In the octal number 425, we say that the 5 is written in the *ones position*, the 2 is written in the *eights position*, and the 4 is written in the *sixty-fours position*. Notice that each of these positions is a power of the base (base 8), and that these powers begin at 0 and increase by 1 as we move left in the number (Fig. E.5).

For longer octal numbers, the next positions to the left would be the *five-hundred-and-twelves position* (8 to the 3rd power), the *four-thousand-and-ninety-sixes position* (8 to the 4th power), the *thirty-two-thousand-seven-hundred-and-sixty eights position* (8 to the 5th power), and so on.

In the hexadecimal number 3DA, we say that the A is written in the *ones position*, the D is written in the *sixteens position*, and the 3 is written in the *two-hundred-and-fifty-sixes position*. Notice that each of these positions is a power of the base (base 16), and that powers begin at 0 and increase by 1 as we move left in the number (Fig. E.6).

For longer hexadecimal numbers, the next positions to the left would be the *four-thousand-and-ninety-sixes position* (16 to the 3rd power), the *sixty-five-thousand-five-hundred-and-thirty-six position* (16 to the 4th power), and so on.

Positional values in the binary number system			
Binary digit	1	0	1
Position name	Fours	Twos	Ones
Positional value	4	2	1
Positional value as a power of the base (2)	2^2	2^1	2^0

Fig. E.4   Positional values in the binary number system.

Positional values in the octal number system			
Decimal digit	4	2	5
Position name	Sixty-fours	Eights	Ones
Positional value	64	8	1
Positional value as a power of the base (8)	8^2	8^1	8^0

Fig. E.5   Positional values in the octal number system.

Positional values in the hexadecimal number system			
Decimal digit	3	D	A
Position name	Two-hundred-and-fifty-sixes	Sixteens	Ones
Positional value	256	16	1
Positional value as a power of the base (16)	16^2	16^1	16^0

Fig. E.6   Positional values in the hexadecimal number system.

E.2 Abbreviating Binary Numbers as Octal Numbers and Hexadecimal Numbers

The main use for octal and hexadecimal numbers in computing is for abbreviating lengthy binary representations. Figure E.7 highlights the fact that lengthy binary numbers can be expressed concisely in number systems with higher bases than the binary number system.

Decimal number	Binary representation	Octal representation	Hexadecimal representation
0	0	0	0
1	1	1	1
2	10	2	2
3	11	3	3
4	100	4	4
5	101	5	5
6	110	6	6
7	111	7	7
8	1000	10	8
9	1001	11	9
10	1010	12	A
11	1011	13	B
12	1100	14	C
13	1101	15	D
14	1110	16	E
15	1111	17	F
16	10000	20	10

Fig. E.7   Decimal, binary, octal and hexadecimal equivalents.

A particularly important relationship that both the octal number system and the hexadecimal number system have to the binary system is that the bases of octal and hexadecimal (8 and 16 respectively) are powers of the base of the binary number system (base 2). Consider the following 12-digit binary number and its octal and hexadecimal equivalents. See if you can determine how this relationship makes it convenient to abbreviate binary numbers in octal or hexadecimal. The answer follows the numbers.

Binary Number	Octal equivalent	Hexadecimal equivalent
`100011010001`	`4321`	`8D1`

To see how the binary number converts easily to octal, simply break the 12-digit binary number into groups of three consecutive bits each, and write those groups over the corresponding digits of the octal number as follows

`100`	`011`	`010`	`001`
4	**3**	**2**	**1**

Notice that the octal digit you have written under each group of thee bits corresponds precisely to the octal equivalent of that 3-digit binary number as shown in Fig. E.7.

The same kind of relationship may be observed in converting numbers from binary to hexadecimal. In particular, break the 12-digit binary number into groups of four consecutive bits each and write those groups over the corresponding digits of the hexadecimal number as follows

`1000`	`1101`	`0001`
8	**D**	**1**

Notice that the hexadecimal digit you wrote under each group of four bits corresponds precisely to the hexadecimal equivalent of that 4-digit binary number as shown in Fig. E.7.

E.3 Converting Octal Numbers and Hexadecimal Numbers to Binary Numbers

In the previous section, we saw how to convert binary numbers to their octal and hexadecimal equivalents by forming groups of binary digits and simply rewriting these groups as their equivalent octal digit values or hexadecimal digit values. This process may be used in reverse to produce the binary equivalent of a given octal or hexadecimal number.

For example, the octal number 653 is converted to binary simply by writing the 6 as its 3-digit binary equivalent 110, the 5 as its 3-digit binary equivalent 101, and the 3 as its 3-digit binary equivalent 011 to form the 9-digit binary number 110101011.

The hexadecimal number FAD5 is converted to binary simply by writing the F as its 4-digit binary equivalent 1111, the A as its 4-digit binary equivalent 1010, the D as its 4-digit binary equivalent 1101, and the 5 as its 4-digit binary equivalent 0101 to form the 16-digit 1111101011010101.

E.4 Converting from Binary, Octal, or Hexadecimal to Decimal

Because we are accustomed to working in decimal, it is often convenient to convert a binary, octal, or hexadecimal number to decimal to get a sense of what the number is "really" worth. Our diagrams in Section E.1 express the positional values in decimal. To convert a number to decimal from another base, multiply the decimal equivalent of each digit by its positional value, and sum these products. For example, the binary number 110101 is converted to decimal 53 as shown in Fig. E.8.

To convert octal 7614 to decimal 3980, we use the same technique, this time using appropriate octal positional values as shown in Fig. E.9.

To convert hexadecimal AD3B to decimal 44347, we use the same technique, this time using appropriate hexadecimal positional values as shown in Fig. E.10.

Converting a binary number to decimal					
Positional values:	32	16	8	4	2	1
Symbol values:	1	1	0	1	0	1
Products:	1*32=32	1*16=16	0*8=0	1*4=4	0*2=0	1*1=1
Sum:	= 32 + 16 + 0 + 4 + 0 + 1 = 53					

Fig. E.8   Converting a binary number to decimal.

Converting an octal number to decimal			
Positional values:	512	64	8	1
Symbol values:	7	6	1	4
Products	7*512=3584	6*64=384	1*8=8	4*1=4
Sum:	= 3584 + 384 + 8 + 4 = 3980			

Fig. E.9   Converting an octal number to decimal.

Converting a hexadecimal number to decimal			
Positional values:	4096	256	16	1
Symbol values:	A	D	3	B
Products	A*4096=40960	D*256=3328	3*16=48	B*1=11
Sum:	= 40960 + 3328 + 48 + 11 = 44347			

Fig. E.10   Converting a hexadecimal number to decimal.

E.5 Converting from Decimal to Binary, Octal, or Hexadecimal

The conversions of the previous section follow naturally from the positional notation conventions. Converting from decimal to binary, octal, or hexadecimal also follows these conventions.

Suppose we wish to convert decimal 57 to binary. We begin by writing the positional values of the columns right to left until we reach a column whose positional value is greater than the decimal number. We do not need that column, so we discard it. Thus, we first write:

Positional values: 64   32   16   8   4   2   1

Then we discard the column with positional value 64 leaving:

Positional values: 32   16   8   4   2   1

Next we work from the leftmost column to the right. We divide 32 into 57 and observe that there is one 32 in 57 with a remainder of 25, so we write 1 in the 32 column. We divide 16 into 25 and observe that there is one 16 in 25 with a remainder of 9 and write 1 in the 16 column. We divide 8 into 9 and observe that there is one 8 in 9 with a remainder of 1. The next two columns each produce quotients of zero when their positional values are divided into 1 so we write 0s in the 4 and 2 columns. Finally, 1 into 1 is 1 so we write 1 in the 1 column. This yields:

Positional values:	32	16	8	4	2	1
Symbol values:	1	1	1	0	0	1

and thus decimal 57 is equivalent to binary 111001.

To convert decimal 103 to octal, we begin by writing the positional values of the columns until we reach a column whose positional value is greater than the decimal number. We do not need that column, so we discard it. Thus, we first write:

Positional values:	512	64	8	1

Then we discard the column with positional value 512, yielding:

Positional values:	64	8	1

Next we work from the leftmost column to the right. We divide 64 into 103 and observe that there is one 64 in 103 with a remainder of 39, so we write 1 in the 64 column. We divide 8 into 39 and observe that there are four 8s in 39 with a remainder of 7 and write 4 in the 8 column. Finally, we divide 1 into 7 and observe that there are seven 1s in 7 with no remainder so we write 7 in the 1 column. This yields:

Positional values:	64	8	1
Symbol values:	1	4	7

and thus decimal 103 is equivalent to octal 147.

To convert decimal 375 to hexadecimal, we begin by writing the positional values of the columns until we reach a column whose positional value is greater than the decimal number. We do not need that column, so we discard it. Thus, we first write

Positional values:	4096	256	16	1

Then we discard the column with positional value 4096, yielding:

Positional values:	256	16	1

Next we work from the leftmost column to the right. We divide 256 into 375 and observe that there is one 256 in 375 with a remainder of 119, so we write 1 in the 256 column. We divide 16 into 119 and observe that there are seven 16s in 119 with a remainder of 7 and write 7 in the 16 column. Finally, we divide 1 into 7 and observe that there are seven 1s in 7 with no remainder so we write 7 in the 1 column. This yields:

Positional values:	256	16	1
Symbol values:	1	7	7

and thus decimal 375 is equivalent to hexadecimal 177.

E.6 Negative Binary Numbers: Two's Complement Notation

The discussion in this appendix has been focussed on positive numbers. In this section, we explain how computers represent negative numbers using *two's complement notation*. First we explain how the two's complement of a binary number is formed, and then we show why it represents the negative value of the given binary number.

Consider a machine with 32-bit integers. Suppose

```
$value = 13;
```

The 32-bit representation of **$value** is

```
00000000 00000000 00000000 00001101
```

To form the negative of **$value** we first form its *one's complement* by applying Perl's bitwise not operator (**~**):

```
$onesComplementOfValue = ~$value;
```

Internally, **~$value** is now **$value** with each of its bits reversed—ones become zeros and zeros become ones as follows:

```
$value:
00000000 00000000 00000000 00001101

~$value  (i.e., $value's ones complement):
11111111 11111111 11111111 11110010
```

To form the two's complement of **$value** we simply add one to **$value**'s one's complement. Thus

```
Two's complement of $value:
11111111 11111111 11111111 11110011
```

Now if this is in fact equal to -13, we should be able to add it to binary 13 and obtain a result of 0. Let us try this:

```
  00000000 00000000 00000000 00001101
+11111111 11111111 11111111 11110011
-------------------------------------
  00000000 00000000 00000000 00000000
```

The carry bit coming out of the leftmost column is discarded and we indeed get zero as a result. If we add the one's complement of a number to the number, the result would be all 1s. The key to getting a result of all zeros is that the twos complement is 1 more than the one's complement. The addition of 1 causes each column to add to 0 with a carry of 1. The carry keeps moving leftward until it is discarded from the leftmost bit, and hence the resulting number is all zeros.

Computers actually perform a subtraction such as

```
$x = $a - $value;
```

by adding the two's complement of **$value** to **$a** as follows:

```
$x = $a + ( ~$value + 1 );
```

Suppose **$a** is 27 and **$value** is 13 as before. If the two's complement of **$value** is actually the negative of **$value**, then adding the two's complement of value to a should produce the result 14. Let us try this:

```
$a (i.e., 27)          00000000 00000000 00000000 00011011
+(~$value + 1) +11111111 11111111 11111111 11110011
                       -------------------------------------
                        00000000 00000000 00000000 00001110
```

which is indeed equal to 14.

SUMMARY

- When we write an integer such as 19 or 227 or -63 in a program, the number is automatically assumed to be in the decimal (base 10) number system. The digits in the decimal number system are 0, 1, 2, 3, 4, 5, 6, 7, 8, and 9. The lowest digit is 0 and the highest digit is 9—one less than the base of 10.

- Internally, computers use the binary (base 2) number system. The binary number system has only two digits, namely 0 and 1. Its lowest digit is 0 and its highest digit is 1—one less than the base of 2.

- The octal number system (base 8) and the hexadecimal number system (base 16) are popular primarily because they make it convenient to abbreviate binary numbers.

- The digits of the octal number system range from 0 to 7.

- The hexadecimal number system poses a problem because it requires sixteen digits—a lowest digit of 0 and a highest digit with a value equivalent to decimal 15 (one less than the base of 16). By convention, we use the letters A through F to represent the hexadecimal digits corresponding to decimal values 10 through 15.

- Each number system uses positional notation—each position in which a digit is written has a different positional value.

- A particularly important relationship that both the octal number system and the hexadecimal number system have to the binary system is that the bases of octal and hexadecimal (8 and 16 respectively) are powers of the base of the binary number system (base 2).

- To convert an octal number to a binary number, simply replace each octal digit with its three-digit binary equivalent.

- To convert a hexadecimal number to a binary number, simply replace each hexadecimal digit with its four-digit binary equivalent.

- Because we are accustomed to working in decimal, it is convenient to convert a binary, octal or hexadecimal number to decimal to get a sense of the number's "real" worth.

- To convert a number to decimal from another base, multiply the decimal equivalent of each digit by its positional value, and sum these products.

- Computers represent negative numbers using two's complement notation.

- To form the negative of a value in binary, first form its one's complement by applying JavaScript's bitwise complement operator (~). This reverses the bits of the value. To form the two's complement of a value, simply add one to the value's one's complement.

TERMINOLOGY

base	digit
base 2 number system	hexadecimal number system
base 8 number system	negative value
base 10 number system	octal number system
base 16 number system	one's complement notation
binary number system	positional notation
bitwise complement operator (~)	positional value
conversions	symbol value
decimal number system	two's complement notation

SELF-REVIEW EXERCISES

E.1   The bases of the decimal, binary, octal, and hexadecimal number systems are _____, _____, _____, and _____ respectively.

E.2   In general, the decimal, octal, and hexadecimal representations of a given binary number contain (more/fewer) digits than the binary number contains.

E.3   (True/False) A popular reason for using the decimal number system is that it forms a convenient notation for abbreviating binary numbers simply by substituting one decimal digit per group of four binary bits.

E.4   The (octal / hexadecimal / decimal) representation of a large binary value is the most concise (of the given alternatives).

E.5   (True/False) The highest digit in any base is one more than the base.

E.6   (True/False) The lowest digit in any base is one less than the base.

E.7   The positional value of the rightmost digit of any number in either binary, octal, decimal, or hexadecimal is always _____.

E.8   The positional value of the digit to the left of the rightmost digit of any number in binary, octal, decimal, or hexadecimal is always equal to _____.

E.9   Fill in the missing values in this chart of positional values for the rightmost four positions in each of the indicated number systems:

decimal	1000	100	10	1
hexadecimal	...	256	...	...
binary	...	...	...	...
octal	512	64	8	1

E.10   Convert binary **110101011000** to octal and to hexadecimal.

E.11   Convert hexadecimal **FACE** to binary.

E.12   Convert octal **7316** to binary.

E.13   Convert hexadecimal **4FEC** to octal. [*Hint*: First convert 4FEC to binary then convert that binary number to octal.]

E.14   Convert binary **1101110** to decimal.

E.15   Convert octal **317** to decimal.

E.16   Convert hexadecimal **EFD4** to decimal.

E.17   Convert decimal **177** to binary, to octal, and to hexadecimal.

E.18   Show the binary representation of decimal **417**. Then show the one's complement of **417**, and the two's complement of **417**.

E.19   What is the result when the one's complement of a number is added to itself?

SELF-REVIEW ANSWERS

E.1   **10, 2, 8, 16**.

E.2   Fewer.

E.3   False.

E.4   Hexadecimal.

E.5   False. The highest digit in any base is one less than the base.

E.6   False. The lowest digit in any base is zero.

E.7   **1** (the base raised to the zero power).

E.8   The base of the number system.

E.9   Fill in the missing values in this chart of positional values for the rightmost four positions in each of the indicated number systems:

decimal	**1000**	**100**	**10**	**1**
hexadecimal	**4096**	**256**	**16**	**1**
binary	**8**	**4**	**2**	**1**
octal	**512**	**64**	**8**	**1**

E.10   Octal **6530**; Hexadecimal **D58**.

E.11   Binary **1111 1010 1100 1110**.

E.12   Binary **111 011 001 110**.

E.13   Binary **0 100 111 111 101 100**; Octal **47754**.

E.14   Decimal **2+4+8+32+64=110**.

E.15   Decimal **7+1*8+3*64=7+8+192=207**.

E.16   Decimal **4+13*16+15*256+14*4096=61396**.

E.17   Decimal **177**
to binary:

```
256 128 64 32 16 8 4 2 1
128 64 32 16 8 4 2 1
(1*128)+(0*64)+(1*32)+(1*16)+(0*8)+(0*4)+(0*2)+(1*1)
10110001
```

to octal:

```
512 64 8 1
64 8 1
(2*64)+(6*8)+(1*1)
261
```

to hexadecimal:

```
256 16 1
16 1
(11*16)+(1*1)
(B*16)+(1*1)
B1
```

E.18   Binary:

```
512 256 128 64 32 16 8 4 2 1
256 128 64 32 16 8 4 2 1
(1*256)+(1*128)+(0*64)+(1*32)+(0*16)+(0*8)+(0*4)+(0*2)+
(1*1)
110100001
```

One's complement: **001011110**
Two's complement: **001011111**
Check: Original binary number **+** its two's complement

```
110100001
001011111
---------
000000000
```

E.19   Zero.

EXERCISES

E.20   Some people argue that many of our calculations would be easier in the base **12** number system because **12** is divisible by so many more numbers than **10** (for base **10**). What is the lowest digit in base **12**? What might the highest symbol for the digit in base **12** be? What are the positional values of the rightmost four positions of any number in the base **12** number system?

E.21   How is the highest symbol value in the number systems we discussed related to the positional value of the first digit to the left of the rightmost digit of any number in these number systems?

E.22   Complete the following chart of positional values for the rightmost four positions in each of the indicated number systems:

decimal	**1000**	**100**	**10**	**1**
base 6	**. . .**	**. . .**	**6**	**. . .**
base 13	**. . .**	**169**	**. . .**	**. . .**
base 3	**27**	**. . .**	**. . .**	**. . .**

E.23   Convert binary **100101111010** to octal and to hexadecimal.

E.24   Convert hexadecimal **3A7D** to binary.

E.25   Convert hexadecimal **765F** to octal. (Hint: First convert **765F** to binary, then convert that binary number to octal.)

E.26   Convert binary **1011110** to decimal.

E.27   Convert octal **426** to decimal.

E.28   Convert hexadecimal **FFFF** to decimal.

E.29   Convert decimal **299** to binary, to octal, and to hexadecimal.

E.30   Show the binary representation of decimal **779**. Then show the one's complement of **779**, and the two's complement of **779**.

E.31   What is the result when the two's complement of a number is added to itself?

E.32   Show the two's complement of integer value **−1** on a machine with 32-bit integers.

Career Resources

Objectives

- To explore the various online career services.
- To examine the advantages and disadvantages of posting and finding jobs online.
- To review the major online career services Web sites available to the job seeker.
- To explore the various online services available to employers seeking to build their workforce.

I found Rome a city of bricks and left it a city of marble.
Augustus Caesar

People don't choose their careers; they are engulfed by them.
John Dos Passos

What is the city but the people?
William Shakespeare

A great city is that which has the greatest men and women, If it be a few ragged huts it is still the greatest city in the whole world.
Walt Whitman

Outline

F.1 Introduction

The Internet provides worldwide access to a vast number of job opportunities. *Entry-level positions*, or positions commonly sought by individuals who are entering a specific field or the job market for the first time; contracting positions; executive-level positions and middle-management-level positions are all available on the Web. Job seekers can learn how to write a resume and cover letter, post them online and search through job listings to find the jobs that best suit their needs. Employers can post jobs that can be searched by an enormous pool of applicants. Online interviews, testing services and other resources also expedite the recruiting process. [*Note*: The unemployment rate in the United States is at its lowest point in 30 years.[1]]

Applying for a position online is a relatively new method of exploring career opportunities. By allowing the majority of the job search to be conducted from the desktop, online recruiting services streamline the process and allow job seekers to concentrate their energies in careers that are of interest to them. Job seekers can explore opportunities according to geographic location, position, salary or benefits package.

Storing and distributing resumes digitally, e-mail notification of possible positions, salary and relocation calculators, job coaches and self-assessment tools are among the resources job seekers can find online to help them in their career searches. These sites also provide information on continuing education.

Perl is one of the hottest technologies in industry today and many Perl-related job opportunities exist. In this appendix, we examine some of the career services and related resources available on the Web. Web sites such as **www.bstar.net/perljobs** and `perl.apache.org/jobs.html` list many Perl-related employment opportunities. Many of the other Web sites we discuss in this appendix provide similar resources.

F.2 Online Career Services

There are approximately 40,000 career-advancement services on the Internet today.[2] These services include large, comprehensive job sites, such as **monster.com** (see the upcoming feature), as well as interest-specific job sites such as **justPerljobs.com**. In this section, we will explore some of the resources available to employers and job seekers and address some of the advantages and disadvantages of online career services.

Finding a job online can greatly reduce the amount of time spent applying for a position. Instead of searching through newspapers and mailing resumes, job seekers can request a specific position in a specific industry through a search engine. Resumes can be stored digitally, customized quickly to meet job requirements and e-mailed instantaneously. Potential candidates can also learn more about a company by visiting its Web site. Most sites are free to job seekers. These sites typically generate their revenues by charging employers for posting job opportunities and by selling advertising space on their Web pages.

Career services, such as **FlipDog.com**, search a list of employer job sites to find positions. By searching links to employer Web sites, FlipDog is able to identify positions from companies of all sizes. This feature enables job seekers to find jobs that employers may not have posted outside the corporation's Web site.

Job seekers can visit **FlipDog.com** and choose, by state, the area in which they are looking for a position. Applicants can also conduct worldwide searches. After a user selects a region, FlipDog requests the user to specify a job category containing several specific positions. The user's choice causes a list of local employers to appear. The user can choose a specific employer or request that FlipDog search the employment databases for jobs offered by all employers. This is similar to another site, **ComputerJobs.com**. Like FlipDog, the user searches by area first and then job category, with several options including C++ jobs, graphics positions and Perl jobs.

Other services, such as employment networks, also help job seekers in their search. Sites such as **Vault.com** (see the upcoming feature) and **WetFeet.com** allow job seekers to post questions about employers and positions in designated chat rooms and bulletin boards.

The large number of applicants presents a challenge to both job seekers and employers. On many recruitment sites, matching resumes to positions is conducted by *resume-filtering software*. The software scans a pool of resumes for keywords that match the job description. While this software increases the number of resumes that receive some attention, it is not a foolproof system. For example, the resume-filtering software might overlook someone with similar skills to those listed in the job description, or someone whose current abilities would enable them to learn the skills required for the position. Other shortcomings include digital transmission and including catchy keywords.

Confidentiality is another disadvantage of online career services. In many cases, a job candidate will want to search for job opportunities anonymously. This reduces the possibility of offending the candidate's current employer. Posting a resume on the Web increases the likelihood that the candidate's employer might come across it when recruiting new employees. The traditional method of mailing resumes and cover letters to potential employers does not impose the same risk.

Monster.com

Super Bowl ads and effective marketing have made **Monster.com** one of the most recognizable online brands. In fact, in the 24 hours following Super Bowl XXXIV, 5 million job searches occurred on **Monster.com**.[3] The site allows people looking for jobs to post their resumes, search job listings, read advice and information about the job-search process and take proactive steps to improve their careers. These services are free to job seekers. Employers can post job listings, search resume databases and become featured employers.

Posting your resume at **Monster.com** is simple and free. **Monster.com** has a resume builder that allows you to post a resume to its site in 15–30 minutes. You can store up to 5 resumes and cover letters on the **Monster.com** server. Some companies offer their employment applications directly through the **Monster.com** site. **Monster.com** has job postings in every state and all major categories. You can limit access to your personal identification information. As one of the leading recruiting sites on the Web, **Monster.com** is a good place to start your job search or to find out more about the search process.

Vault.com[4]

Vault.com allows potential employees to seek out additional, third-party information for over 3000 companies. By visiting the *Insider Research* page, Web users have access to a profile on the company of their choice, as long as it exists in **Vault.com**'s database. In addition to **Vault.com**'s profile, there is also a link to additional commentary by company employees. Most often anonymous, these messages can provide prospective employees with potentially valuable, decision-making information. However, users must also consider the integrity of the source. For example, a disgruntled employee may leave a posting that is not a good representation of the corporate culture of his or her company.

The **Vault.com** *Electronic Watercooler*™ is a message board that allows visitors to post stories, questions and concerns and to advise employees and job seekers. In addition, the site provides e-newsletters and feature stories designed to help job seekers in their search. Individuals seeking information on the best business, law and graduate schools can also find information on **Vault.com**.

Job-posting and career-advancement services for the job seeker are also featured on **Vault.com**. These services include *VaultMatch*, a career service that e-mails job postings as requested, and *Salary Wizard*™, which helps job seekers determine what they are worth. Online guides to with advice for fulfilling your career ambitions are also available.

Employers can also use the site. *HR Vault*, a feature of **Vault.com**, provides employers with a free job-posting site. It also features career-management advice, employer-to-employee relationship management and recruiting resources. HR Vault can be visited directly at **vault.com/hr_channel/index.cfm?object-group_id=302**.

According to recent studies, the number of individuals researching employment positions through other means, such as referrals, newspapers and temporary agencies, far outweighs the number of job seekers researching positions through the Internet.[5] Optimists feel, however, that this disparity is largely due to the early stages of e-business development. Given time, online career services will become more refined in their posting and searching capabilities, decreasing the amount of time it takes for a job seeker to find jobs and employers to fill positions.

F.3 Career Opportunities for Employees

In this section, we will explore a variety of career services Web sites. We will include sites that provide opportunities for technically trained individuals, independent contractors, students and young professionals and executives.

F.3.1 Comprehensive Career Sites

As mentioned previously, there are many sites on the Web that provide job seekers with career opportunities in multiple fields. **monster.com** is the largest of these sites, attracting the largest number of unique visitors per month. Other popular online recruiting sites include **JobsOnline.com**, **HotJobs.com** and **Headhunter.net**.

Searching for a job online can be a conducted in a few steps. For example, during an initial visit to **JobsOnline.com**, a user is required to fill out a registration form. The form requests basic information, such as name, address and area of interest. After registering, members can search through job postings according to such criteria as the number of days posted, category and location. Contact information is provided for additional communication. Registered members are offered access to XDrive™ (**www.xdrive.com**), which provides 25 MB of storage space for resumes, cover letters and additional communication. Stored files can be shared through any Web browser or Wireless Application Protocol (WAP) enabled device.[6] **Driveway.com** offers a similar service, allowing individuals to store, share and organize files online. An online demonstration of the service can be found at **www.driveway.com**. The animated demo walks the user through the features offered by the service. **Driveway.com** offers 100 MB of space, and the service is free.[7]

Other sites, such as Cruel World (see the upcoming feature), allow you to store and send your resume directly.

F.3.2 Technical Positions

The amount of time for an employer to fill a technical position can be greatly reduced by using an industry-specific site. Career sites designed for individuals seeking technical positions are among the most popular online career sites. In this section, we review several sites that offer recruiting and hiring opportunities for technical positions.

Dice.com (**www.dice.com**) is a recruiting Web site that focuses on technical fields. Fees to companies are based on the number of jobs they post and the frequency with which the postings are updated. Job seekers can post their resumes and search the job database for free.

JustComputerJobs.com directs job seekers toward 39 specific computer technologies for their job search. Language-specific sites include **JustJavaJobs.com**,

`JustCJobs.com` and `JustPerlJobs.com`. Hardware, software and communications technology sites are also available.

Other technology recruiting sites include `Bid4Geeks.com`, `HotDispatch.com` and `www.cmpnet.com/careerdirect`.

F.3.3 Contracting Online

The Internet also serves as a forum for job seekers to find employment on a project-by-project basis. Online contracting services allow businesses to post positions for which they want to hire outside resources, and individuals can identify projects that best suit their interests, schedules and skills. [*Note*: Approximately six percent of America's workforce falls into the category of independent contractor.[9]]

`Guru.com` (`www.guru.com`) is a recruiting site for contract employees. Independent contractors, private consultants and trainers use `guru.com` to find short-term and long-term contract assignments. Tips, articles and advice are available for contractors who wish to learn more about their industry. Other sections of the site teach you how to manage your business, buy the best equipment and deal with legal issues. `Guru.com` includes an online store where you can buy products associated with small-business management, such as printing services and office supplies. Companies wishing to hire contractors need to register, but individuals seeking contract assignments do not.

`Monster.com`'s Talent Market™ offers online auction-style career services to free agents. Interested users design a profile, listing their qualifications. After establishing a profile, free agents "Go Live" to start the bidding on their services. The bidding lasts for five days during which users can view the incoming bids. At the close of five days, the user can choose the job of their choice. The service is free for users, bidding employers pay a commission on completed transactions.

Cruel World[8]

Cruel World is a free, online career advancement service for job seekers. After becoming a registered member, your information is matched with available positions in the Cruel World database. When an available job matches your criteria, *JobCast*®, a feature of Cruel World, sends an e-mail alerting you of the available position. If you are interested, you can send your resume to the employer that posted the position, customized to the job's requirements. If you do not wish to continue your search, you can simply send a negative response via e-mail.

The client list, or the list of companies seeking new employees through Cruel World, can be viewed at `www.cruelworld.com/corporate/aboutus.asp` Additional features on the site include hints for salary negotiation; a self-assessment link to `CareerLeader.com`, where, for a small fee, members can reassess their career goals under the advisement of career counselors, and a relocation calculator, for job seekers who are considering changing location.

Employers seeking to hire new talent can post opportunities through Cruel World. posting positions requires a fee. A demonstration of the service can be viewed at `www.cruelworld.com/clients/quicktour1.asp`. The demonstration is a three-step slide of JobCast.

---

eLance.com is another site where individuals can find contracting work. Interested applicants can search eLance's database by category, including business, finance and marketing. These projects, or *requests for proposals* (RFPs), are posted by companies worldwide. When you find a project for which you feel you are qualified, you submit a bid on the project. Your bid will contain your required payment, a statement detailing your skills and a feedback rating drawn from other projects on which you have worked. If your bid is accepted, you are given the project, and the work is conducted over eLance's file-sharing system, enabling both the contractor and the employer to contact one another quickly and easily. For an online demonstration, visit **www.elance.com** and click on the **demonstration** icon.

FreeAgent (**www.freeagent.com**) is another site designed for contracting projects. Candidates create an *e.portfolio* that provides an introductory "snapshot" of their skills, a biography, a list of their experience and references. An interview section of the portfolio lists questions and the applicant's answers. Examples of e.portfolios can be found at **www.freeagent.com/splash/models.asp**. Free Agent's *e.office* offers a benefits package to outside contractors, including health insurance, a retirement plan and reimbursement for business-related expenses, among other features.

Other Web sites that provide contractors with projects and information include eWork® Exchange (**www.ework.com**), **MBAFreeAgent.com**, **Aquent.com** and **WorkingSolo.com**.

F.3.4 Executive Positions

The Internet provides career opportunities ranging from entry-level positions to senior level positions. Executive career advancement sites usually include many of the features that you might find on a comprehensive job-search site. In this section, we discuss the challenges of and opportunities for finding an executive position online.

Searching for an executive position online differs from finding an entry-level position online. The Internet allows individuals to continually survey the job market. However, candidates for executive-level positions must exercise a higher level of confidentiality when determining who is able to view their resume. Applying for an executive position online is an extensive process. Because of the high level of scrutiny passed on a candidate during the hiring process, the initial criteria presented by an executive level candidate are often more specific than the criteria presented by the first-time job seeker. Executive positions are often difficult to fill, due to the high demands and large amount of experience required for the jobs.

SixFigureJobs (**www.sixfigurejobs.com**) is a recruitment site designed for experienced executives. Resume posting and job searching is free to job seekers. Other sites designed for helping executives find positions include **www.execunet.com** and **www.nationjob.com**.

F.3.5 Students and Young Professionals

The Internet provides students and young professionals with many tools to get them started in the job market. Individuals still in school and seeking internships, individuals who are just graduating and individuals who have been in the workforce for a few years make up the target market. Additional tools specifically designed for this *demographic*, or a population defined by a specific characteristic, are also available. For example, journals kept by previous interns provide prospective interns with information regarding what to look for in an internship, what to expect and what to avoid. Many of these sites will provide information to start young professionals in the right direction, such as matching positions to college or university major.

Experience.com is a career services Web site geared toward the younger population. Members can search for positions according to specific criteria, such as geographic location, job category, keywords, commitment (i.e. full time, part time, internship), amount of vacation and amount of travel time. After applicants register, they can send their resumes directly to the companies posting on the site. In addition to the resume, candidates also provide a personal statement, a list of applicable skills and their language proficiency. Registered members also receive access to the site's *Job Agent*. Members can set up to three Job Agents. The agents search for available positions, based on the criteria posted by the member. If a match is made, the site contacts the candidate via e-mail.[10,11]

Internshipprograms.com helps students find internships. In addition to posting a resume and searching for an internship, students can also use the relocation calculator and read through information and tips on building resumes and writing essays. The *City Intern* program provides travel, housing, entertainment and guides to interns interviewing or accepting a position in an unfamiliar city, making them feel more at home in a new location.

In addition to its internship locators, undergraduate, graduate, law school, medical school and business school services, the Princeton Review's Web site (**www.review.com**) offers career services to graduating students. While searching for a job, students and young professionals can also read through the site's news reports or even increase their vocabulary by visiting the "word for the day."

Other Web sites geared toward the younger population include **campuscareer-center.com**, **brassringcampus.com** and **collegegrads.com**.

F.3.6 Other Online Career Services

In addition to Web sites that help you find and post jobs online, there are a number of Web sites that offer features that will enhance your search, prepare you for searching online, help you design your resume or help you calculate the cost of relocating.

Salary.com helps job seekers gauge their expected income, based on position, level of responsibility and years of experience. The search requires job category, ZIP code and specific job title. Based on this information, the site will return an estimated salary for an individual living in the specified area, and employed in the position described. Estimates are returned based on the average level of income for that position.

In addition to being a resource for finding employment, **www.careerpower.com** also provides individuals with tests that will help them realize their strengths, weaknesses, values, skills and personality traits. Based on the results, which can be up to 10–12 pages per test, users can best decide what job category they are best qualified for and what career choice will be best suited to their personal ambitions. The service is available for a fee.

InterviewSmart™ is another service offered through CareerPower that prepares job seekers of all levels for the interviewing process. The service can be downloaded for a minimal fee or can be used on the Web for free. Both versions are available at **www.career-power.com/CareerPerfect/interviewing.htm#is.start.anchor**.

Additional services will help you find a position that meets your unique needs, or design your resume to attract the attention of employers. **Dogfriendly.com**, organized by geographic location, helps job seekers find opportunities that allow them to bring their pets to work, and **cooljobs.com** is a searchable database of unique job opportunities.

F.4 Online Opportunities for Employers

Recruiting on the Internet provides several benefits over traditional recruiting. For example, Web recruiting reaches a much larger audience than posting an advertisement in a local newspaper. Given the breadth of the services provided on most online career services Web sites, the cost of posting online can be considerably less expensive than posting positions through traditional means. Generally, jobs posted online are viewed by a larger number of job seekers than jobs posted through traditional means. However, it is important not to overlook the benefits of combining these efforts with human-to-human interaction. There are many job seekers who are not yet comfortable with the process of finding a job online. Often, online recruiting is used as a means of freeing up a recruiter's time for the interviewing process and final selection.

F.4.1 Posting Jobs Online

When searching for job candidates online, there are many things employers need to consider. The Internet is a valuable tool for recruiting, but one that takes careful planning to get the best results. It provides a good supplementary tool, but should not be considered the complete solution for filling positions. Online services, such as WebHire (**www.webhire.com**), enhance a company's online employment search (see the upcoming feature).

WebHire™ [12]

Designed specifically for recruiters and employers, WebHire is a multifaceted service that provides employers with end-to-end recruiting solutions. The service offers job-posting services as well as candidate searches. The most comprehensive of the services, *WebHire™ Enterprise*, locates and ranks candidates found through resume-scanning mechanisms. Clients will also receive a report indicating the best resources for their search. Other services, available through the *WebHire™ Employment Services Network*, include preemployment screening, tools for assessing employees' skill levels and information on compensation packages. An employment law advisor helps organizations design interview questions.

WebHire™ Agent is an intelligent agent that searches for qualified applicants, based on your job specifications. When WebHire Agent identifies a potential candidate, an e-mail is automatically sent to that candidate to generate interest. WebHire Agent then ranks applicants according to the skills information it gains from the Web search; the information is stored, so that new applicants are distinguished from those who have already received an e-mail from the site.

Yahoo!® Resumes, a feature of WebHire, allows recruiters to find potential employees by typing in keywords to the Yahoo! Resumes search engine. Employers can purchase a year's membership to the recruiting solution for a flat fee; there are no per-use charges.

There are a variety of sites that allow employers to post jobs online. Some of these sites require a fee, which generally runs between $100–$200. Postings typically remain on the Web site for 30–60 days. Employers should be careful to post to sites that are most likely to be visited by eligible candidates. As we discovered in the previous section, there are a variety of online career services focused on specific industries, and many of the larger, more comprehensive sites have categorized their database by job category.

When designing a posting, the recruiter should also consider the vast number of postings already on the Web. Defining what makes your position unique, including information such as benefits and salary, might convince a qualified candidate to further investigate the position.[13]

Boston Herald *Job Find* (**www.jobfind.com**) also charges employers to post on its site. The initial fee entitles the employer to post up to three listings. Employers have no limitations on the length of their postings.

HotJobs.com career postings are cross-listed on a variety of other sites, thus increasing the number of potential employees that see the job listings. Like **monster.com** and **jobfind.com**, **hotjobs.com** requires a fee per listing. Employers also have the option of becoming **HotJobs.com** members. Employers also receive access to HotJobs' *Private Label Job Board*s (private corporate employment sites), online recruiting technology and online career fairs.

Other Web sites providing employers with employee recruitment services include **CareerPath.com**, America's Job Bank (**www.ajb.dni.us/employer**), CareerWeb (**www.cweb.com**), **Jobs.com** and **Career.com**..

F.4.2 Diversity in the Workplace

Every workplace inevitably develops its own culture. Responsibilities, schedules, deadlines and projects all contribute to a working environment. However, perhaps the most defining elements of a *corporate culture* are the employees. For example, if all employees were to have the same skills and the same ideas, then the workplace would lack diversity. It might also lack creativity and enthusiasm. One way to increase the dynamics of an organization is to employ people of all backgrounds and cultures.

The Internet hosts demographic-specific sites for employers seeking to increase diversity in the workplace. Increasing diversity enhances organizations in many ways. By recruiting people from different backgrounds, new ideas and perspectives are brought forth, helping businesses meet the needs of a larger, more diverse target audience.[14]

Blackvoices.com and **hirediversity.com** are demographic-specific Web sites. BlackVoices™, which functions primarily as a portal, features job searching capabilities and the ability for prospective employees to post resumes. HireDiversity is divided into several categories, including African American, Hispanic and opportunities for women. Other online recruiting services place banner advertisements on ethnic Web sites for companies seeking diverse workforces.

The Diversity Directory (**www.mindexchange.com**) offers international career-searching capabilities. Users selecting the **Diversity** site can find job opportunities, information and additional resources to help them in their career search. The site can be searched according to demographics (African American, Hispanic, alternative lifestyle, etc.) or by subject (employer, position, etc.) through hundreds of links. Featured sites include **BilingualJobs.com**, *Latin World* and *American Society for Female Entrepreneurs*.

The Internet also provides people with disabilities opportunities for career advancement. Many sites have sections dedicated to job seekers with disabilities. In addition to providing job-searching capabilities, these sites include additional resources, such as equal opportunity documents and message boards. The *National Business and Disability Council* (*NBDC*) provides employers with information on employing people with disabilities, such as integration and accessibility, as well as opportunities for job seekers.

F.4.3 Recruiting Services

There are many services on the Internet that help employers match individuals to positions. The time saved by conducting preliminary searches on the Internet can then be dedicated to interviewing qualified candidates and making the best matches possible.

Advantage Hiring, Inc. (**www.advantagehiring.com**) provides employers with a resume-screening service. When a prospective employee submits a resume for a particular position, Advantage Hiring, Inc., presents *Net-Interview*™, a small questionnaire to supplement the information presented on the resume. The site also offers *SiteBuilder*, a service that helps employers build an employee recruitment site. An online demonstration can be found at **www.advantagehiring.com**. The demonstration walks the user through the Net-Interview software, as well as a number of the other services offered by Advantage Hiring.

Recruitsoft.com is an application service provider (ASP) that offers companies recruiting software on a *pay-per-hire* basis; that is, Recruitsoft receives a commission on hires made via its service. *Recruiter WebTop*™ is the company's online recruiting software. It includes a host of features, such as Web-site hosting, an employee-referral program, skill-based resume screening, applicant-tracking capabilities and job-board posting capabilities. A demonstration of Recruiter WebTop's *Corporate Recruiting Solutions* can be found at **www.recruitsoft.com/process**. The demonstration shows how recruiting solutions find and rank potential candidates. More information about Recruitsoft's solution can be viewed in a *QuickTime* media player demonstration, found at **www.recruitsoft.com/corpoVideo**.[15]

RecruitingSolutions (**www.recruitingsoftware.com**) provides Web-based solutions for the online recruiting process. *RecruitingCenter*™ allows companies to integrate career services on their Web sites.

Peoplescape.com is an online service that help employers recruit employees and maintain a positive work environment once the employee has been hired. In addition to searches for potential candidates, Peoplescape also offers *PayCheck*™, *LegalCheck*™ and *PeopleCheck*™. These services help to ensure that compensation offers are adequate, legal guidelines are met during the hiring process and in the workplace and candidates have provided accurate information both on their resume and during the hiring process.

For job seekers, Peoplescape offers searching capabilities, insights to career transitions, a job compensation calculator that takes benefits and bonuses into consideration when exploring a new job possibility and a series of regularly posted articles relevant to the job search.[16]

To further assist companies in their recruiting process, Web sites such as **Refer.com** reward visitors for successful job referrals. Highly sought-after positions can earn thousands of dollars. If you refer a friend or a family member and they are hired, you receive a commission.

Other online recruiting services include **Hire.com**, **MorganWorks.com** and **Futurestep.com**™.

F.4.4 Testing Potential Employees Online

The Internet has also provided employers with a cost-effective means of testing their prospective employees in such categories as decision making, problem solving and personality. Services such *eTest* help to reduce the cost of in-house testing and to make the interview process more effectively. Test results, given in paragraph form, present the interested individual's strengths and weaknesses. Based on these results, the report suggests interview methods, such as asking open-ended questions, or questions that require more than a "yes" or "no" response. Sample reports and a free-trial test can be found at **www.etest.net**.

Employers and Job seekers can also find career placement exercises at **www.advisorteam.net/AT/User/kcs.asp**. Some of these services require a fee. The tests ask several questions regarding the individual's interests and working style. Results help candidates to determine the best career for their skills and interests.

F.5 Internet and World Wide Web Resources

Information Technology (IT) Career Sites

www.dice.com
Dice.com is a recruiting Web site that focuses on the computer industry.

www.peoplescape.com
This site provides career advancement services for both employers and job seekers. Its services include PayCheck™, LegalCheck™ and PeopleCheck™, to assist employers in the hiring process.
www.guru.com
This is a recruiting site for contract employees. Independent contractors, private consultants and trainers can use **guru.com** to find short-term and long-term work.

www.hallkinion.com
This is a Web recruiting service for individuals seeking IT positions.

www.techrepublic.com
This site provides employers and job seekers with recruiting capabilities and information regarding developing technology.

www.justcomputerjobs.com
This site serves as a portal with access to language-specific sites, including Java, Perl, C and C++.

www.bid4geeks.com
This career services site is geared toward the technical professional.

www.hotdispatch.com
This forum provides software developers with an opportunity to share projects, discuss code and ask questions.

Career Sites

www.careerbuilder.com
A network of career sites, including IT Careers, *USA Today* and MSN, CareerBuilder attracts 3 million unique job seekers per month. This site also provides resume-builder and job-searching agents.

www.recruitek.com
This free site caters to jobs seekers, employers and contractors.

www.monster.com
This site, the largest of the online career sites, allows people looking for jobs to post their resumes, search job listings and read advice and information about the job-search process. It also provides a variety of recruitment services for employers.

www.jobsonline.com
Similar to **monster.com**, this site provides opportunities for job seekers and employers.

www.hotjobs.com
This online recruiting site offers cross-listing possibilities on additional sites.

www.jobfind.com
This job site is an example of locally targeted job-search resources. **JobFind.com** targets the Boston area.

www.flipdog.com
This site allows online job candidates to search for career opportunities. It employs intelligent agents to scour the Web and return jobs matching the candidate's request.

www.cooljobs.com
This site highlights unique job opportunities.

www.computerjobs.com
This site allows the user to find specific jobs based on area and technology as well as level of experience.

www.webprogrammingjobs.com
This site provides job listings for several IT professions, as well as specific sites for C++, Visual Basic and Web programming.

www.tech-engine.com
This recruiting site offers job listings and links to various career guides within the site.

Other Career Web Sites
The following sites provide job opportunities and information and employer services:

www.careerpath.com

www.cweb.com

www.career.com

www.jobs.com

www.careerpower.com

www.careermag.com

Executive Positions

www.sixfigurejobs.com
This is a recruitment site designed for experienced executives.

www.leadersonline.com
This career services Web site offers confidential job searches for mid-level professionals. Potential job matches are e-mailed to job candidates.

Diversity

www.latpro.com
This site is designed for Spanish- and Portuguese-speaking job seekers. In addition to provide resume-posting services, the site enables job seekers to receive matching positions via e-mail. Advice and information services are also available.

www.blackvoices.com

This site hosts a career center designed to match African American job seekers with job opportunities.

www.hirediversity.com

This site targets a variety of demographics. In addition to services for searching for and posting positions, resume-building and up-dating services are also available. Specialized groups include African Americans, Asian Americans, people with disabilities, women and Latin Americans.

People with Disabilities

www.halftheplanet.com

This site represents people with disabilities. The site is large and includes many different resources and information services. A special section is dedicated to job seekers and employers.

www.wemedia.com

This site is designed to meet the needs of people with disabilities. It also includes a section for job seekers and employers.

www.disabilities.com

This site provides users with a host of links to information resources on career opportunities.

www.rileyguide.com

This site includes a section with opportunities for people with disabilities, which can be viewed at **www.dbm.com/jobguide/vets.html#abled**.

www.mindexchange.com

The diversity section of this site provides users with several links to additional resources regarding people with disabilities and employment.

www.usdoj.gov/crt/ada/adahom1.htm

This is the Americans with Disabilities Act home page.

www.abanet.org/disability/home.html

This is the Web site for The Commission on Mental and Physical Disability Law.

janweb.icdi.wvu.edu

The Job Accommodation Web site offers consulting services to employers regarding the integration of people with disabilities in the workplace.

General Resources

www.vault.com

This site provides potential employees with inside information on over 3000 companies. In addition, job seekers can search through available positions and post and answer questions on the message board.

www.wetfeet.com

Similar to **vault.com**, this site allows visitors to ask questions and receive "insider information" on companies that are hiring.

Free Services

www.sleuth.com

On this site job seekers can fill out a form that indicates their desired field of employment. Job Sleuth™ searches the Internet and returns potential matches to the user's inbox. The service is free.

www.refer.com

This site rewards visitors for successful job referrals. If you refer a friend or family member and they are hired, you receive a commission.

`www.ajb.org`
America's Job Bank is an online recruiting service provided through the Department of Labor and the state employment service. Searching and for posting positions on the site are free.

`www.xdrive.com`
This free site provides members with 25 MB of storage space for housing documents. XDrive is able to communicate with all browser types and has wireless capabilities.

`www.driveway.com`
Similar to **XDrive.com**, this Web site provides users with 100 MB of storage space. Users can back up, share and organize the information. **Driveway.com** works on all platforms.

Special Interest

`www.eharvest.com/careers/index.cfm`
This site provides job seekers interested in agricultural positions with online career services capabilities.

`www.opportunitynocs.org`
This career services Web site is for both employers and job seekers interested in nonprofit opportunitites.

`www.experience.com`
This Web site is designed specifically for young professionals and students seeking full-time, part-time and internship positions.

`www.internshipprograms.com`
Students seeking internships can search job listings on this site. It also features City Intern, to help new interns become acquainted with a new location.

`www.brassringcampus.com`
This site provides college graduates and young professionals with less than five years of experience with job opportunities. Additional features help users buy a car or find an apartment.

Online Contracting

`www.ework.com`
This online recruiting site matches outside contractors with companies needing project specialists. Other services provided through eWork include links to online training sites, benefits packages and payment services and online meeting and management resources.

`www.elance.com`
Similar to **eWork.com**, eLance matches outside contractors with projects.

`www.freeagent.com`
Similar to other sites in this category, Freeagent matches contractors with projects.

`MBAFreeAgent.com`
This site is designed to match MBAs with contracting opportunities.

`Aquent.com`
This site provides access to technical contracting positions.

`WorkingSolo.com`
This site helps contractors start working for themselves.

Recruiting Services

`www.advantagehiring.com`
This site helps employers screen resumes.

www.morganworks.com

MorganWorks.com is an online recruiting-services provider.Its services include outsourced recruiting, searchable candidate databases, career-site-building services, career-searching capabilities and international executive searches.

www.etest.net

This site provides employers with testing services to assess the strengths and weaknesses of prospective employees. Acquired information can be used for better hiring strategies.

www.hire.com

Hire.com's eRecruiter is an application service provider that helps organizations streamline their Web-recruiting process.

www.futurestep.com

Executives can register confidentially at **Futurestep.com** to be considered for senior executive positions. The site connects registered individuals to positions. It also offers career management services.

www.webhire.com

This site provides employers with end-to-end recruiting solutions.

Perl-Specific Job Resources

perl.apache.org/jobs.html

This page provides a straightforward listing of various **mod_perl** jobs around the world.

www.justperljobs.com

This fun and user-friendly site provides listings of Perl-related jobs as well as the option to post jobs and resumes.

www.1perlstreet.com

This unique and innovative site provides numerous Perl resources, including tutorials, code examples and a search engine to facilitate finding Perl jobs.

SUMMARY

- The Internet can improve your ability to recruit employees and find career opportunities from around the world.

- Job seekers can learn how to write a resume and cover letter, post them online and search through job listings to find the jobs that best suit their needs.

- Employers can post jobs that can be searched by an enormous pool of applicants.

- Storing and distributing resumes digitally, e-mail notification of possible positions, salary and relocation calculators, job coaches and self-assessment tools are among the resources that job seekers can find online to help them in their career searches.

- There are approximately 40,000 career-advancement services on the Internet today.

- Finding a job online can greatly reduce the amount of time spent applying for a position. Potential candidates can also learn more about a company by visiting its Web site.

- Most sites are free to job seekers. These sites typically generate their revenues by charging employers to post their job opportunities and by selling advertising space on their Web pages.

- Sites such as **Vault.com** and **WetFeet.com** allow job seekers to post questions about employers and positions in designated chat rooms and bulletin boards.

- On many recruitment sites, the match of a resume to a position is conducted by *resume filtering software*.

- Confidentiality is disadvantage of online career services.

- According to recent studies, the number of individuals researching employment positions through means other than the Internet, such as referrals, newspapers and temporary agencies, far outweighs the number of Internet job seekers.

- Career sites designed for individuals seeking a technical position are among the most popular on-line career sites.

- Online contracting services allow businesses to post positions for which they want to hire outside resources, and individuals can identify projects that best suit their interests, schedules and skills.

- The Internet provides students and young professionals with some of the necessary tools to get them started in the job market. The target market is made up of individuals still in school and seeking internships, individuals that are just graduating and individuals who have been in the workforce for a few years.

- There are a number of Web sites that offer features that will enhance your job search, prepare you for searching online, help design your resume or help you calculate the cost of relocating.

- Web recruiting reaches a larger audience than posting an advertisement in the local newspaper.

- Given the breadth of the services provided on most online career services Web sites, the cost of posting online is considerably less expensive than posting positions through traditional means.

- There are a variety of sites that allow employers to post jobs online. Some of these sites require a fee, which generally runs between $100–$200. Postings remain on the Web site for approximately 30–60 days.

- Employers should try to post to sites that are most likely to be visited by eligible candidates.

- When designing a job posting, defining what makes your position unique and including information such as benefits and salary might convince a qualified candidate to further investigate the position.

- The Internet hosts demographic-specific sites for employers seeking to increase diversity in the workplace.

- The Internet has also provided employers with a cost-effective means of testing their prospective employees in such categories as decision making, problem solving and personality.

WORKS CITED

1.   C. Wilde, "Recruiters Discover Diverse Value In Web Sites," *Information Week* 7 February 2000: 144.

2.   J. Gaskin, "Web Job Sites Face Tough Job," *Inter@ctive Week* 14 August 2000: 50.

3.   J. Gaskin, "Web Job Sites Face Tough Job," *Inter@ctive Week* 14 August 2000: 50.

4.   `www.vault.com`

5.   J. Gaskin, "Web Job Sites Face Tough Job," *Inter@ctive Week* 14 August 2000: 50.

6.   `<www.jobsonline.com>`

7.   `<www.driveway.com>`

8.   `www.cruelworld.com`

9.   D. Lewis, "Hired! By the Highest Bidder," *The Boston Globe* 9 July 2000: G1.

10.   `<www.experience.com>`

11.   M. French, "Experience, Inc., e-recruiting for jobs for college students," *Mass High Tech* 7 February - 13 February 2000: 29.

12. *www.webhire.com*

13.   M. Feffer, "Posting Jobs on the Internet," <**www.webhire.com/hr/spotlight.asp**> 18 August 2000.

14.   C. Wilde, "Recruiters Discover Diverse Value in Web Sites," *Information Week* 7 February 2000: 144.

15.   <**www.recruitsoft.com**>

16.   <**www.peoplescape.com**>

Perl 6 Web Resources

G.1 Introduction

In this appendix, we discuss Perl 6 (the next major version of Perl) which is still in the early stages of development. We overview the current status of the project and provide a list of Web resources that will allow the reader to follow Perl 6 as it develops. [*Note*: Although support for Perl 5 will continue, future versions of Perl 5 will primarily contain bug fixes, not language enhancements.]

G.2 Future of Perl

At the *O'Reilly Open Source Conference* in the summer of 2000, Larry Wall, the creator of the Perl programming language, announced that the development of Perl 6 had begun. In his speech, Wall outlined his vision for the next version of Perl.

Perl 6 is a complete rewrite of the language which will result in a more powerful version of Perl that has a simpler syntax. Wall says Perl 6 will be better, faster and more robust; and that he will take ideas from other programming languages (such as Java™) and incorporate them into Perl 6.

Chip Salzenberg, a member of the Perl community, has been working on a project for a couple of years called *Topaz*. Topaz was started as a plan to rewrite the internals of Perl 5 using C++[1] that would eventually evolve into Perl 6. Although the actual code developed by Salzenberg for Topaz will not be used for Perl 6, the knowledge he gained from working on Topaz will be valuable to the developers of Perl 6.

The initial Perl 6 specification will be drafted by Wall and a core group of Perl developers, then released to the Perl community for feedback. Wall wants Perl 6 to be designed by the Perl community. Each piece of the language will be written by a small group of developers, rather than the entire Perl community. This approach will allow each piece to receive more attention from its developers and allow developers to be matched with their area of expertise.

The Perl 5 environment uses the *XS macro-language*, which Wall feels complicates the use of the Perl 5. In Perl 6, XS will be replaced by a technology that is simpler and more straightforward. At the time of this writing, this replacement technology had yet to be publicly announced.

One primary goal is to create a smooth migration from Perl 5 to Perl 6. Because Perl 6 will not be backwards compatible with Perl 5, Perl 6 is likely to include a translator that will translate Perl 5 source code to Perl 6. Wall feels that the vast majority of Perl 5 code will translate easily into Perl 6.

Another primary goal of the Perl 6 project is to restructure the Perl community. Rather than having one large mailing list where every topic related to Perl is discussed, the plan is to divide the mailing list into multiple mailing lists corresponding to specific topics. Members interested in a particular aspect of Perl will register for the appropriate mailing list.

An alpha version of Perl 6 is likely to be available in early 2001. Before the final release, at least one beta version and a vendor liaison version will be released. At the time of this writing, release dates had not yet been announced.

G.3 Internet and World Wide Web Resources

www.perl.org/perl6/pr/initial.txt
This is a copy of the Perl 6 press release from July 18, 2000.

www.perl.org/perl6/pr/initial_meeting.html
This site offers documentation on the Perl 5 Porters meeting regarding Perl 6 held in July 2000. This document discusses the need for Perl 6 ranging from technical reasons to social reasons.

www.infoworld.com/articles/ec/xml/00/03/24/000324ecperl.xml
This article by David Legard discusses the debut of Perl 6. The article also discusses some topics related to Perl 6 such as the current version of Perl and the features of the new version.

www.zdnet.com/devhead/stories/articles/0,4413,2609879,00.html
This ZDNet article, *Developers to Polish Perl*, discusses the differences between Perl 5 and Perl 6.

www.oreillynet.com/pub/a/linux/rt/07282000/transcript.html
This is a transcript of a round table discussion between members of the Perl community related to the development and planning of Perl 6.

theoryx5.uwinnipeg.ca/CPAN/perl/pod/perlfaq1/What_is_perl6_.html
This is an overview of Perl 6 and what lies in its future.

slashdot.org/articles/00/07/19/203221.shtml
This article talks about the meeting between Larry Wall and some of his colleagues that initiated the development of Perl 6.

topaz.sourceforge.net
This site is the home page for the *Topaz* project. It explains what the project is, its status and other relevant information.

dev.perl.org/~ask/als
This document is a bulleted list of the key items Larry Wall discussed regarding Perl 6 in his keynote speech at the Atlanta Linux Showcase. The items in this list are features that may be included in Perl 6.

www.perl.com/pub/2000/09/perl6mail.html
The document, *Guide to the Perl 6 Working Groups*, includes announcements about Perl 6 and discusses some of the key issues related to the Perl 6 language.

www.perl.com/pub/2000/07/perl6.html

This page discusses Perl 5 and why Larry Wall decided to develop Perl 6. It also provides a question-and-answer section related to Perl 6.

infotrope.net/opensource/software/perl6/plan.pdf

This PDF document is a roadmap of the Perl 6 development process. Included in the document is a time line presenting specific goals of the project and tentative dates of completion.

dev.perl.org/rfc

This site includes an extensive list of the Perl 6 Request for Comments (RFC). Each item in the list is a link to the actual RFC document.

dev.perl.org/lists

Because of the nature of the Perl 6 project, there are many different mailing lists relating to each individual topic. This site contains a list of those mailing lists. Each list provides an e-mail address to which you can send e-mail subscribing to that list.

WORKS CITED

1.   *"Perl 6 To Be Complete Rewrite (But Not What You Think)."* <**slashdot.org/articles/00/07/19/203221.shtml**>.

Bibliography

Castro, E. *Perl and CGI for the World Wide Web*. Berkeley, CA: Peachpit Press, 1999.

Christiansen, T., and Torkington, N. *Perl Cookbook*. Sebastopol, CA: O'Reilly & Associates, 1998.

Descartes, Alligator, and Bunce, Tim. *Programming the Perl DBI*. Sebastopol, CA: O'Reilly & Associates, 2000.

Friedl, J.E.F. *Mastering Regular Expressions*. Sebastopol, CA: O'Reilly & Associates, 1997.

Guelich, S., Gundavaram, S., and Birznieks, G. *CGI Programming with Perl*. Sebastopol, CA: O'Reilly & Associates, 2000.

Hall, J.N., and Schwartz, R.L. *Effective Perl Programming*. Reading, MA: Addison-Wesley Longman, 1998.

Harlan, David, et al. *Special Edition Using Perl 5 for Web Programming*. Indianapolis, IN: Que® Corporation, 1996.

Hoffman, P.E. *Perl 5 for Dummies*. Foster City, CA: IDG Books Worldwide, 1997.

Holzner, S. *Perl Core Language Little Black Book*. Scottsdale, AZ: The Coriolis Group, 1999.

Laurie, Ben, and Laurie, Peter. *Apache: The Definitive Guide*. Sebastopol, CA: O'Reilly & Associates, 1999.

Lemay, Laura. *Sams Teach Yourself Perl in 21 Days*. Indianapolis, IN: Sams Publishing, 1999.

Medinets, David. *Perl 5 by Example*. Indianapolis, IN: Que® Corporation, 1996.

Peschko, E.S., and DeWolfe, M. *Perl Developer's Guide*. USA: McGraw-Hill, 2000.

Pierce, Clinton. *Sams Teach Yourself Perl in 24 Hours*. Indianapolis, IN: Sams Publishing, 2000.

Schilli, M. *Perl Power!*. Reading, MA: Addison-Wesley Longman, 1999.

Schwartz, R.L. *Learning Perl: Second Edition*. Sebastopol, CA: O'Reilly & Associates, 1999.

Sebesta, R.W. *A Little Book on Perl*. Upper Saddle River, NJ: Prentice Hall, 2000.

Siever, E., et al. *Perl in a Nutshell*. Sebastopol, CA: O'Reilly & Associates, 1999.

Srinivasan, S. *Advanced Perl Programming*. Sebastopol, CA: O'Reilly & Associates, 1999.

Stein, Lincoln. *Official Guide to Programming with CGI.pm*. New York: John Wiley & Sons, 1998.

Wall, Larry, et al. *Programming Perl: Third Edition.* Sebastopol, CA: O'Reilly & Associates, 2000.

Walsh, Nancy. *Learning Perl/Tk.* Sebastopol, CA: O'Reilly & Associates, 1999.

Wyke, R.A., and Duncan, Luke. *The Perl 5 Programmer's Reference.* Research Triangle Park, NC: Ventana Communications Group, 1997.

Index

License Agreement and Limited Warranty

agreement. You may not copy the Documentation or the SOFTWARE, except that you may make a single copy of the SOFTWARE for backup or archival purposes only. You may be held legally responsible for any copying or copyright infringement which is caused or encouraged by your failure to abide by the terms of this restriction.

4. USE RESTRICTIONS: You may not network the SOFTWARE or otherwise use it on more than one computer or computer terminal at the same time. You may physically transfer the SOFTWARE from one computer to another provided that the SOFTWARE is used on only one computer at a time. You may not distribute copies of the SOFTWARE or Documentation to others. You may not reverse engineer, disassemble, decompile, modify, adapt, translate, or create derivative works based on the SOFTWARE or the Documentation without the prior written consent of the Company.

5. TRANSFER RESTRICTIONS: The enclosed SOFTWARE is licensed only to you and may not be transferred to any one else without the prior written consent of the Company. Any unauthorized transfer of the SOFTWARE shall result in the immediate termination of this Agreement.

6. TERMINATION: This license is effective until terminated. This license will terminate automatically without notice from the Company and become null and void if you fail to comply with any provisions or limitations of this license. Upon termination, you shall destroy the Documentation and all copies of the SOFTWARE. All provisions of this Agreement as to warranties, limitation of liability, remedies or damages, and our ownership rights shall survive termination.

7. MISCELLANEOUS: This Agreement shall be construed in accordance with the laws of the United States of America and the State of New York and shall benefit the Company, its affiliates, and assignees.

8. LIMITED WARRANTY AND DISCLAIMER OF WARRANTY: The Company warrants that the SOFTWARE, when properly used in accordance with the Documentation, will operate in substantial conformity with the description of the SOFTWARE set forth in the Documentation. The Company does not warrant that the SOFTWARE will meet your requirements or that the operation of the SOFTWARE will be uninterrupted or error-free. The Company warrants that the media on which the SOFTWARE is delivered shall be free from defects in materials and workmanship under normal use for a period of thirty (30) days from the date of your purchase. Your only remedy and the Company's only obligation under these limited warranties is, at the Company's option, return of the warranted item for a refund of any amounts paid by you or replacement of the item. Any replacement of SOFTWARE or media under the warranties shall not extend the original warranty period. The limited warranty set forth above shall not apply to any SOFTWARE which the Company determines in good faith has been subject to misuse, neglect, improper installation, repair, alteration, or damage by you. EXCEPT FOR THE EXPRESSED WARRANTIES SET FORTH ABOVE, THE COMPANY DISCLAIMS ALL WARRANTIES, EXPRESS OR IMPLIED, INCLUDING WITHOUT LIMITATION, THE IMPLIED WARRANTIES OF MERCHANTABILITY AND FITNESS FOR A PARTICULAR PURPOSE. EXCEPT FOR THE EXPRESS WARRANTY SET

FORTH ABOVE, THE COMPANY DOES NOT WARRANT, GUARANTEE, OR MAKE ANY REPRESENTATION REGARDING THE USE OR THE RESULTS OF THE USE OF THE SOFTWARE IN TERMS OF ITS CORRECTNESS, ACCURACY, RELIABILITY, CURRENTNESS, OR OTHERWISE.

IN NO EVENT, SHALL THE COMPANY OR ITS EMPLOYEES, AGENTS, SUPPLIERS, OR CONTRACTORS BE LIABLE FOR ANY INCIDENTAL, INDIRECT, SPECIAL, OR CONSEQUENTIAL DAMAGES ARISING OUT OF OR IN CONNECTION WITH THE LICENSE GRANTED UNDER THIS AGREEMENT, OR FOR LOSS OF USE, LOSS OF DATA, LOSS OF INCOME OR PROFIT, OR OTHER LOSSES, SUSTAINED AS A RESULT OF INJURY TO ANY PERSON, OR LOSS OF OR DAMAGE TO PROPERTY, OR CLAIMS OF THIRD PARTIES, EVEN IF THE COMPANY OR AN AUTHORIZED REPRESENTATIVE OF THE COMPANY HAS BEEN ADVISED OF THE POSSIBILITY OF SUCH DAMAGES. IN NO EVENT SHALL LIABILITY OF THE COMPANY FOR DAMAGES WITH RESPECT TO THE SOFTWARE EXCEED THE AMOUNTS ACTUALLY PAID BY YOU, IF ANY, FOR THE SOFTWARE.

SOME JURISDICTIONS DO NOT ALLOW THE LIMITATION OF IMPLIED WARRANTIES OR LIABILITY FOR INCIDENTAL, INDIRECT, SPECIAL, OR CONSEQUENTIAL DAMAGES, SO THE ABOVE LIMITATIONS MAY NOT ALWAYS APPLY. THE WARRANTIES IN THIS AGREEMENT GIVE YOU SPECIFIC LEGAL RIGHTS AND YOU MAY ALSO HAVE OTHER RIGHTS WHICH VARY IN ACCORDANCE WITH LOCAL LAW.

ACKNOWLEDGMENT

YOU ACKNOWLEDGE THAT YOU HAVE READ THIS AGREEMENT, UNDERSTAND IT, AND AGREE TO BE BOUND BY ITS TERMS AND CONDITIONS. YOU ALSO AGREE THAT THIS AGREEMENT IS THE COMPLETE AND EXCLUSIVE STATEMENT OF THE AGREEMENT BETWEEN YOU AND THE COMPANY AND SUPERSEDES ALL PROPOSALS OR PRIOR AGREEMENTS, ORAL, OR WRITTEN, AND ANY OTHER COMMUNICATIONS BETWEEN YOU AND THE COMPANY OR ANY REPRESENTATIVE OF THE COMPANY RELATING TO THE SUBJECT MATTER OF THIS AGREEMENT.

Should you have any questions concerning this Agreement or if you wish to contact the Company for any reason, please contact in writing at the address below.

Robin Short
Prentice Hall PTR
One Lake Street
Upper Saddle River, New Jersey 07458

The DEITEL & DEITEL Suite of Products...

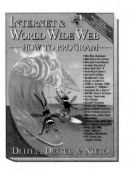

XML How to Program

BOOK / CD-ROM

©2001, 1000 pp., paper
(0-13-028417-3)

This new book in
the Deitels' *How to
Program* series is a
comprehensive guide
to programming
in XML. It explains how to use XML to create
customized tags and includes several chapters
that address standard custom markup languages
for science and technology, multimedia, commerce
and other fields. The authors include concise
introductions to Java, VBScript, Active Server
Pages and Perl/CGI, providing readers with the
essentials of these programming languages and
server-side development technologies to enable
them to work effectively with XML. The book also
includes cutting-edge topics such as XQL, SMIL
and VoiceXML as well as a real-world e-commerce
case study. A complete chapter on Web accessibility
that addresses Voice XML is also included. It also
includes tips such as valuable insights into Common
Programming Errors, Software Engineering
Observations, Portability Tips and Debugging Hints.

Perl How to Program

BOOK / CD-ROM

©2001, 1000 pp., paper
(0-13-028418-1)

This comprehensive
new guide to pro-
gramming with Perl
emphasizes the use
of the Common
Gateway Interface (CGI) with Perl to create
powerful dynamic Web content for e-commerce
applications. The book begins with a clear and
careful introduction to the concepts of structured
programming at a level suitable for beginners,
and proceeds through advanced topics such as
references and complex data structures. Key Perl
topics such as regular expressions and string
manipulation are covered in detail. The authors
address important and topical issues such as
object-oriented programming, the Perl database
interface (DBI), graphics and security. Also
included is a treatment of XML, a bonus chapter
introducing the Python programming language,
and a complete chapter on Web accessibility
that addresses programming and technologies
relevant to accessibility for people with disabilities.
The text also includes tips such as valuable
insights into Common Programming Errors,
Software Engineering Observations, Portability
Tips and Debugging Hints.

e-Business &
e-Commerce
for Managers

©2001, 900 pp., paper
(0-13-032364-0)

This innovative new
text is a comprehensive
overview of building
and managing an
e-business. It explores
topics such as the
decision to bring a business online, choosing a
business model, accepting payment, marketing
strategies and security, as well as many other
important issues. Features, Web resources and
online demonstrations supplement the text and
direct readers to additional materials. The book
also includes an appendix that develops a complete
Web-based shopping cart application using HTML,
VBScript, Active Server Pages and an Access
database. Plus, company-specific sections provide
"real-world" examples of the concepts presented
in the book.

Advanced
Java How to
Program

BOOK / CD-ROM

©2001, 1100 pp., paper
(0-13-089560-1)

Expanding on the
world's best-selling
Java text, *Advanced
Java How to Program*
includes an in-depth discussion of advanced
topics, aiding developers in producing significant,
scalable Java applications and distributed systems.
The book integrates such technologies as Swing,
multithreading, RMI, JDBC, servlets, Java XML
and Enterprise JavaBeans into a complete,
rigorous, production-quality system, thus allowing
developers to take better advantage of the
leverage and platform-independence provided
by the Java 2 platform.

Java How to Program
Third Edition

©2000, 1360 pp., paper bound w/CD-ROM (0-13-012507-5)

This edition of the world's best-selling Java textbook incorporates Sun Microsystems' latest version of Java, the Java 2 Software Development Kit (J2SDK). The introduction of new functionality in this upgrade has made Java a friendlier and more accessible programming language. Reviewers of the book were unanimous in praising the Deitels for making the best use of these enhancements and writing the introductory chapters in an engaging and accessible style. Designed for beginning through intermediate readers, it uses the Deitels' proven "live-code" approach with hundreds of complete working programs, valuable programming tips, more than 16,000 lines of code and over 1400 interesting and challenging exercises. The graphical user interface examples use Sun's new Swing GUI components. The authors have added significant coverage of JDBC, JavaBeans, RMI, Servlets, Java 2D, Java Media Framework, Collections, Serialization, Inner Classes and other topics. Includes several examples and projects on multi-tier, client/server systems development. The CD-ROM contains a complete Java Integrated Development Environment, source code for all examples in the text, and hyperlinks to valuable Java demos and resources on the Internet.

C++ How to Program
Third Edition

© 2001, 1168 pp., paper (0-13-089571-7)

The world's best-selling C++ text teaches programming by emphasizing structured and object-oriented programming, software reuse and component-oriented software construction. This comprehensive book uses the Deitels' signature "live-code" approach, presenting every concept in the context of a complete, working C++ program followed by a screen capture showing the program's output. It also includes a rich collection of exercises and valuable insights into Common Programming Errors, Software Engineering Observations, Portability Tips and Debugging Hints. The Third Edition includes a new case study that focuses on object-oriented design with the UML and illustrates the entire process of object-oriented design from conception to implementation. In addition, it adheres to the latest ANSI/ISO C++ standards. The accompanying CD-ROM contains Microsoft® Visual C++ 6.0 Introductory Edition software, source code for all examples in the text and hyperlinks to C++ demos and Internet resources.

C How to Program
Third Edition

BOOK / CD-ROM

© 2001, 1253 pp., paper (0-13-089572-5)

Highly practical in approach, the Third Edition of the world's best-selling C text introduces the fundamentals of structured programming and software engineering and gets up to speed quickly. This comprehensive book not only covers the full C language, but also reviews library functions and introduces object-based and object-oriented programming in C++ and Java, as well as event-driven GUI programming in Java. The Third Edition includes a new 346-page introduction to Java 2 and the basics of GUIs, and the introduction to C++ has been condensed to 298 pages and updated to be consistent with the most current ANSI/ISO C++ standards. Plus, icons throughout the book point out valuable programming tips such as Common Programming Errors, Portability Tips and Testing and Debugging Tips.

Getting Started with Microsoft® Visual C++™ 6 with an Introduction to MFC

BOOK / CD-ROM

© 2000, 163 pp., paper (0-13-016147-0)

This exciting book is intended to be a companion to the ANSI/ISO standard C++ best-selling book, *C++ How to Program, Second Edition.* Learn how to use Microsoft's Visual Studio 6 integrated development environment (IDE) and Visual C++ 6 to create Windows programs using the Microsoft Foundation Classes (MFC). The book includes 17 "live-code" Visual C++/MFC programs with screen captures, dozens of tips, recommended practices and cautions and exercises accompanying every chapter. It includes coverage of Win32 and console applications, online documentation and Web resources, GUI controls, dialog boxes, graphics, message handling, the resource definition language and the debugger.

Visual Basic® 6 How to Program

BOOK / CD-ROM

© 1999, 1015 pp., paper bound w/CD-ROM (0-13-456955-5)

Visual Basic 6 is revolutionizing software development for conventional and Internet/Intranet-based applications. This text explains Visual Basic 6's extraordinary capabilities. Part of the Deitels' *Visual Studio* series, this book uses the Deitels' "live-code" approach to cover Internet/Intranet, World Wide Web, VBScript, ActiveX, ADO, multimedia, animation, audio, video, files, database, networking, graphics, strings, data structures, collections, GUI and control creation. The accompanying CD-ROM contains Microsoft's *Visual Basic 6 Working Model Edition* software, source code and hyperlinks to valuable Visual Basic resources.

ORDER INFORMATION

SINGLE COPY SALES:
Visa, Master Card, American Express, Checks, or Money Orders only
Toll-Free: 800-643-5506; Fax: 800-835-5327

GOVERNMENT AGENCIES:
Prentice Hall Customer Service (#GS-02F-8023A)
Phone: 201-767-5994; Fax: 800-445-6991

COLLEGE PROFESSORS:
For desk or review copies, please visit us on the World Wide Web at www.prenhall.com

CORPORATE ACCOUNTS:
Quantity, Bulk Orders totaling 10 or more books. Purchase orders only — No credit cards.
Tel: 201-236-7156; Fax: 201-236-7141
Toll-Free: 800-382-3419

CANADA:
Pearson Education Canada
26 Prince Andrew Place
Don Mills, ON M3C 2T8 Canada
Tel: 416 447 5101; Fax: 416 443 0948
E-mail: phcinfo.pubcanada@pearsoned.com

UK/IRELAND:
Pearson Education
Edinburgh Gate
Harlow, Essex CM20 2JE UK
Tel: 01279 623928; Fax: 01279 414130
E-mail: enq.orders@pearsoned-ema.com

EUROPE, MIDDLE EAST & AFRICA:
Pearson Education
P.O. Box 75598
1070 AN Amsterdam, The Netherlands
Tel: 31 20 5755 800; Fax: 31 20 664 5334
E-mail: amsterdam@pearsoned-ema.com

ASIA:
Pearson Education Asia
317 Alexandra Road #04-01
IKEA Building
Singapore 159965
Tel: 65 476 4688; Fax: 65 378 0370

JAPAN:
Pearson Education
Nishi-Shinjuku, KF Building 101
8-14-24 Nishi-Shinjuku, Shinjuku-ku
Tokyo, Japan 160-0023
Tel: 81 3 3365 9001; Fax: 81 3 3365 9009

INDIA:
Pearson Education Indian Liaison Office
90 New Raidhani Enclave, Ground Floor
Delhi 110 092, India
Tel: 91 11 2059850 & 2059851
Fax: 91 11 2059852

AUSTRALIA:
Pearson Education Australia
Unit 4, Level 2
14 Aquatic Drive
Frenchs Forest, NSW 2086, Australia
Tel: 61 2 9454 2200; Fax: 61 2 9453 0089
E-mail: marketing@pearsoned.com.au

NEW ZEALAND/FIJI:
Pearson Education
46 Hillside Road
Auckland 10, New Zealand
Tel: 649 444 4968; Fax: 649 444 4957
E-mail: sales@pearsoned.co.nz

SOUTH AFRICA:
Pearson Education
P.O. Box 12122
Mill Street
Cape Town 8010 South Africa
Tel: 27 21 686 6356; Fax: 27 21 686 4590

LATIN AMERICA:
Pearson Education Latinoamerica
815 NW 57th Street Suite 484
Miami, FL 33158
Tel: 305 264 8344; Fax: 305 264 7933

Coming Soon

The Complete Advanced Java Training Course

ISBN 0-13-091275-1

The Complete Perl Training Course

ISBN 0-13-089554-7

The Complete XML Training Course

ISBN 0-13-089556-3

- Fully searchable, electronic version of the textbook, complete with hyperlinks
- Hours of detailed audio descriptions for the fully tested "live" program code
- Complete programs that students can run with the click of a mouse and copy onto their own computers
- Many programming exercises, half with answers
- Practice exams with hundreds of test questions
- Hundreds of self-review questions, all with answers
- Hundreds of tips, marked with icons, that show how to write code that is portable, reusable and optimized for performance
- Intuitive browser-based interface with full-text searching and hyperlinking

Runs on Windows 95, 98, NT and Windows 2000

The Complete Java 2 Training Course Third Edition

BOXED SET

©2000, boxed set (0-13-085247-3)

This set includes the book *Java How to Program, Third Edition*, a complete Java integrated development environment, and the fully interactive *Java 2 Multimedia Cyber Classroom* CD-ROM that features:

- Fully searchable, electronic version of the textbook, complete with hyperlinks
- 200+ complete Java 2 programs with approximately 16,000 lines of fully tested "live code"
- 1100+ questions and exercises, over half of them with answers
- 400+ helpful hints and tips, marked with icons
- Over 10 hours of audio describing key Java concepts and programming techniques
- A browser-based display engine

Runs on Windows 95, 98, NT and Windows 2000

The Complete Visual Basic 6 Training Course

BOXED SET

©1999, boxed set (0-13-082929-3)

You get the world's number-one VB6 interactive *Multimedia Cyber Classroom* CD-ROM plus a worldwide best-selling VB6 book and Microsoft's *VB6 Working Model Software*—ideal for experienced VB5, C/C++ and Java programmers as well as for new programmers interested in VB6's latest features.

- Fully searchable, electronic version of the textbook, complete with hyperlinks
- Over six hours of audio explaining key VB6 concepts
- Hundreds of VB6 programs with thousands of lines of fully tested code
- Hundreds of interactive programming exercises
- Master ActiveX, objects, TCP/IP networking, VBScript, multimedia, GUIs, data structures, control creation and more!

Runs on Windows 95, 98, NT and Windows 2000

Coming Fall 2000, the award-winning Deitel & Deitel Cyber Classroom Series will be available from Prentice Hall over the World Wide Web. This is an ideal solution for students and programming professionals who prefer the convenience of Internet delivery to CD-ROM delivery, or who work on platforms not supported by the CD-ROM version of the Cyber Classrooms.

The Web-based Cyber Classrooms will run on any computer that supports version 4 of either Netscape Navigator or Internet Explorer and the free Real Networks RealPlayer version 7 or higher. The Web-based version will require a 56K modem or higher connection to the Internet.

The Web-based Cyber Classrooms will contain all of the features of the CD-ROM versions, including the Deitels' signature "live code" approach to teaching programming languages. All of the audio will be available through the Web, as will the sample program code, programming tips, exercises and so forth.

We are excited to announce enhanced Web-based versions of the Deitel & Deitel Cyber Classroom Series coming in 2001. The enhanced versions will attempt to recreate the experience of being in a live programming seminar. They will contain substantially more media than the current Cyber Classrooms, including extensive use of both audio and video. The enhanced versions will also include synchronous and asynchronous communications tools to support sophisticated instructor-to-student and student-to-student communication.

For more information, please visit **www.phptr.com/phptrinteractive**.

Turn back one page for details on the Cyber Classroom CD-ROMs and Complete Training Courses!

For those interested in
C++

Advanced C++ How to Program: This book builds on the pedagogy of *C++ How to Program, Third Edition*, and features more advanced discussions of templates, multiple inheritance, and other key topics. We are co-authoring this book with Don Kostuch, one of the world's most experienced C++ educators.

For those interested in
Microsoft® Visual C++

Visual C++ 7 How to Program: This book combines the pedagogy and extensive coverage of *C++ How to Program, Third Edition* with a more in-depth treatment of Windows programming in Visual Studio 7. We have carefully culled the best material from each of these areas to produce a solid, two-semester, introductory/intermediate level treatment.

Getting Started with Microsoft® Visual C++™ 7 with an Introduction to MFC, Second Edition: This book builds on the first edition introduced for Visual Studio 6. It features a much enhanced, yet still introductory, treatment of MFC.

For those interested in
C#

C# How to Program: This book discusses Microsoft's brand new C# language being introduced in Visual Studio 7.

For those interested in
Python

Python How to Program: This book introduces the increasingly popular Python language which makes many application development tasks much easier to accomplish than with traditional, recent object-oriented languages.

For those interested in
Flash

Flash 5 How to Program: Hundreds of millions of people browse Flash-enabled Web sites daily. This first book in our Multimedia series introduces the powerful features of Flash 5 and includes a detailed introduction to programming with the completely revamped Flash 5 scripting language.

For those interested in
Java

Java How to Program, Fourth Edition, Volume I and ***Java How to Program, Fourth Edition, Volume II:*** These books build on the pedagogy of *Java How to Program, Third Edition,* expanding our intermediate-level treatment of Java to two 1000-page volumes. The volumes include extensive treatments of XML and object-oriented design with UML.

For those interested in
Microsoft® Visual Basic

Visual Basic 7 How to Program, Second Edition: This book builds on the pedagogy of the first edition, which was developed for Visual Studio 6. It has a much enhanced treatment of developing Web-based e-business and e-commerce applications. The book includes an extensive treatment of XML.

New & Improved Deitel Web Site!

Deitel & Associates, Inc. is in the process of upgrading www.deitel.com. The new site will feature Macromedia Flash® enhancements and additional content to create a valuable resource for students, professors and professionals. Features will include FAQs, Web resources, e-publications and online chat sessions with the authors. We will include streaming audio clips where the authors discuss their publications. Web-based training demos will also be available at the site.

Turn the page to find out more about Deitel & Associates!

License Agreement and Limited Warranty

Using the CD-ROM

Microsoft Windows users may access the contents of this CD through the interface provided in the file **AUTORUN.EXE**. If a startup screen does not pop up automatically when you insert the CD into your computer, double click on the icon for **AUTORUN.EXE** to launch the program or launch the file **WELCOME.HTM** in your browser. Linux users should launch **WELCOME.HTM** in a browser to get started.

Contents of the CD-ROM

- ActiveState ActivePerl 5.6
- Perl 5.6.0
- MySQL 3.223.x
- The following software developed by the Apache Software Foundation (www.apache.org):
  - Apache 1.3.2
- Live links to websites mentioned in the book *Perl How to Program*
- Live code examples from the book *Perl How to Program*

Software and Hardware System Requirements

- Intel Pentium 133 MHz or faster processor (200 MHz recommended)
- Microsoft Windows 95 or later, or
- Microsoft Windows NT 4.0 (or later) or
- Red Hat Linux 6.0 (or later)
- 32 Mb (48 MB recommended)
- CD-ROM drive
- Internet connection